Howell

COLLIER'S
NEW
ENCYCLOPEDIA

A SELF-REVISING REFERENCE WORK
WITH LOOSE-LEAF FEATURES

IN TEN BOUND VOLUMES, SUPPLEMENTED BY A LOOSE-
LEAF VOLUME. PROFUSELY ILLUSTRATED, COLOR
FRONTISPIECES, NINETY-SIX MAPS

VOLUME NINE

ANNIVERSARY EDITION

P. F. COLLIER & SON COMPANY
NEW YORK

List of Maps

"SOW—TRILOGY"

SPAIN AND PORTUGAL

SCALE OF STATUTE MILES
0 10 20 40 60 80 100 120 140

SCALE OF KILOMETERS
0 20 40 60 80 100 120 140 160 180 200 220 240

Important towns are shown in heavy face type
Railways shown thus

AZORES ISLANDS
(PORTUGUESE)

SCALE OF MILES
0 20 40 60 80 100

MADEIRA IS.
(PORTUGUESE)

MILES
0 10 20 40

CANARY ISLANDS
(SPANISH)

SCALE OF MILES
0 20 40 60 80

Long. C West 4° from D Greenw. 2°

SOW THISTLE, the popular name given to a species of a genus of composite plants, *Sonchus.* There are about 50 species, mostly herbaceous, but some forming shrubs or small trees. Some of the first may be considered cosmopolitan, while the woody sorts are almost restricted to the Canaries and to the island of Madeira. The most common species in Great Britain is the common sow thistle, *Sonchus oleraceus.* It is very abundant as a weed, is greedily fed upon by many animals, and is sometimes used on the European continent as a pot-herb. It grows to a height of two or three feet, with a branching stem and small yellow flowers. The *S. alpinus* forms a tall and fine plant, with fresh and sharply defined foliage and large heads of beautiful blue flowers. The *S. arvensis* is found in Massachusetts and southern New York.

SPA, or **SPAA,** a town of Belgium, and a watering place of world-wide celebrity; in a romantic valley amid hills which form part of the Ardennes chain, 27 miles S. E. of Liege, and 22 miles S. W. of Aix-la-Chapelle. The prettily-built town consists almost entirely of inns and lodging houses. The mineral springs are efficacious in complaints of the liver, nervous diseases, dyspepsia, etc. Spa water is exported to all quarters of the globe. Spa is also famed for the manufacture of wooden toys, which are stained brown by being steeped in the mineral waters. It was frequented as a watering place as early as the 14th century, and has given its name to many mineral springs. Here the German Great Headquarters were established in 1918, where consultations were held concerning the armistice and from whence the German delegates set out for the French lines to meet Marshal Foch and sue for peace.

SPACE, in geometry, the room in which an object, actual or imaginary, exists. All material objects possess length, breadth, and thickness; in other words, they exist in space of three dimensions. Plane surfaces have only two dimensions —length and breadth, and straight lines but one dimension—length. Hence we have notions of space of one dimension and of two dimensions, as distinguished from the three dimensional space in which we live. The question has arisen, and has been warmly discussed, as to whether space of four, and perhaps of higher dimensions exists. Zöllner believes that it does, and that some persons have some of the power of beings living in space of four dimensions, and thus accounts for many of the phenomena of Spiritualism. For example, while a being living in space of two dimensions could only get in or out of a square by passing through one of its sides, a human being could enter the square from above; so, he argues, a person having the properties of a four-dimensional being could enter or leave a closed box or room on its fourth-dimensional side. In metaphysics, a conjugate of material existence. Empirical philosophers maintain that notions of space are derived from our knowledge of existence; transcendentalists that these notions are innate.

In music, one of the four intervals between the five lines of a staff. They take their names from the notes which occupy them; thus, the spaces of the treble staff, counting upward, are F, A, C, and E, and of the bass, A, C, E, and G.

In physics, the room in which the Cosmos or universe exists.

In printing, the interval between words in printed matter; also pieces of type-metal shorter than type, used to produce such spaces or to separate letters in words, of varying thickness, so as to justify the line.

SPAIN, a kingdom in the S. W. of Europe, forming with Portugal the great S. W. peninsula of Europe. It is separated from France on the N. E. by the chain of the Pyrenees, and is otherwise bounded by Portugal and the Atlantic and Mediterranean. In greatest breadth N. and S. it measures 540 miles; greatest length E. and W., 620 miles. Continental area, 190,055 square miles. Including the Canary and Balearic islands and north and west African possessions, 194,-783 square miles. Pop., about 20,400,000. The war with the United States deprived her of Cuba, Porto Rico, the Philippine and Sulu islands, and Guam; and a treaty with Germany, Feb. 8, 1899, of the Marianne (or Ladrone), Caroline, and Pelew islands. On Nov. 8, 1900, Spain sold the islands of Cagayan and Sibutu to the United States for $100,000. Her last remaining colonies are in Africa with pop. 292,000. Spain formerly comprised the ancient kingdoms and provinces of New and Old Castile, Leon, Asturias, Galicia, Estremadura, Andalusia, Aragon, Murcia, Valencia, Catalonia, Navarre, and in the Basque Provinces. These since 1854, for administrative purposes, have been divided into 49 provinces, including the Balearic and Canary islands. The capital is Madrid; next in population are Barcelona, Valencia, Seville, and Malaga.

Physical Features.—The coast line is not much broken, but sweeps round in gentle curves, presenting few remarkable headlands or indentations. The interior is considerably diversified, but its characteristic feature is its central table-land, which has an elevation of from 2,200 to 2,800 feet, and a superficial extent of not less than 90,000 square miles. It descends gradually on the W. toward Portugal; but on the E., toward the provinces of Catalonia and Valencia, it presents an abrupt steep or line of cliffs, with the character of an ancient sea margin. It is bounded on the N. by the Asturian and Cantabrian mountains, reaching an elevation of about 8,500 feet; on the S. by the Sierra Morena; and is crossed from E. to W. by the Douro, Tagus, and Guadiana rivers. Between these limits it is intersected by two important ranges of mountains running nearly E. and W., the N. being the Guadarrama with its continuations, separating the valleys of the Douro and Tagus, and attaining in one of its peaks a height of 8,200 feet; and the S., the Sierra de Toledo and its continuation between the Tagus and the Guadiana. S. of the Sierra Morena is the valley of the Guadalquivir river. Besides these ranges there is the chain of the Pyrenees, which, though partly belonging to France, presents its boldest front to Spain and has its loftiest summits within it. The highest peak in the ranges is La Maladetta or Pic de Nethou (11,165 feet); but the highest peak in Spain is Mulhacen (11,420 feet), belonging to the Sierra Nevada in the S. The latter chain possesses some of the wildest scenery in Europe. The chief rivers enter the Atlantic, but in the N. E. is the Ebro, a tributary of the Mediterranean. The Douro, Tagus, and Guadiana belong partly to Portugal. The lakes are few and unimportant.

Minerals.—The whole country teems with mineral wealth, the minerals including in greater or less quantities gold, silver, quicksilver, lead, copper, iron, zinc, calamine, antimony, tin, coal, etc. The exploitation of the minerals has, however, in recent times been mostly accomplished by foreign capital, while most of the ore is exported to foreign countries in its raw state. The quantity and value of the principal minerals produced in 1918 was as follows: Anthracite coal, 377,216 metric tons, valued at 21,226,434 pesetas; copper, 1,007,668 metric tons, valued at 19,121,-407 pesetas; iron, 4,692,651 metric tons, valued at 52,889,055 pesetas; bituminous coal, 6,134,986 metric tons, valued at 341,251,718 pesetas; lignite coal, 726,848 metric tons, valued at 26,581,717 pesetas; lead, 216,133 metric tons, valued at 60,751,403 pesetas. Other mineral products are asphalt, mercury, sulphur, zinc, phosphate, manganese, silver, salt,

and wolfram. There are about 135,000 persons engaged in the mineral industry. The total value of the output of 1918 was 545,916,704 pesetas.

Climate.—The climate varies much in different localities. On the elevated table-land it is both colder in winter and hotter in summer than usual under the same latitude. In the plains and on the coasts the hot summer is followed by a cold rainy season, terminating in April in a beautiful spring. The mean temperature at Malaga in summer is 77° F., in winter 57°; at Barcelona 77° and 50°; and at Madrid 75° and 44.6°. The rainfall is small; in the interior between 8 and 12 inches per annum. In some parts of the S. the climate is almost tropical. The hot S. wind of Andalusia, known as the solano, and the cold N. wind called the gallego, are peculiar to Spain.

Vegetable Products and Agriculture.—About one-sixth of the acreage is under wood; the more remarkable trees being the Spanish chestnut and several varieties of oak, and in particular the cork oak. Fruits are extremely abundant, and include, in addition to apples, pears, cherries, plums, peaches, and apricots, the almond, date, fig, orange, citron, olive, and pomegranate; and in the lower districts of the S. the pineapple and banana. The culture of the vine is general, and great quantities of wine are made, both for home consumption and exportation. The more important farm crops are wheat, rice, maize, barley and legumes. In the S. cotton and the sugar cane are grown. Hemp and flax, esparto, the mulberry for rearing silk worms, saffron, licorice, are also to be mentioned. The only large animals in a wild state are the wolf, common in all the mountainous districts, and the bear and chamois, found chiefly in the Pyrenees. Domestic animals include the merino sheep in great numbers, horses, mules, asses, horned cattle, and pigs. The chief agricultural products in 1919 were as follows: Wheat, 77,-660,040 cwt.; barley, 33,946,488 cwt.; oats, 9,597,534 cwt.; rye, 12,295,808 cwt.; maize, 14,920,464 cwt. Other important products are rice, beans, kidney beans, peas, lentils, and tares. In 1919 3,300,-965 acres were employed in grape cultivation. The production was 7,914,252,-192 pounds of grapes, yielding 543,-904,788 gallons of wine. There are about 4,000,000 acres devoted to olive culture. The other important products are esparto, flax, hemp, and pulse. There are important industries connected with the preparation of wine and fruits. Silk culture is carried on in Valencia, Murcia, and other provinces. There are about 30 sugar cane factories and about 40 beet root sugar factories.

Manufactures and Commerce.—The manufactures of Spain are not as a whole important, but considerable advances have been made in recent times. The most important industries are the manufacture of cotton, woolens and linens, cutlery and metal goods, paper, silk, leather, tobacco, and cigars, besides wine, flour, and oil. There are about 750 concerns engaged in the manufacture of cotton. These employ about 70,000 looms with about 2,700,000 spindles. In woolen manufacture there are about 9,000 looms with about 665,000 spindles. The paper-making industry is of importance. There are about 150 paper mills engaged in the making of writing, printing, packing, and cigarette paper. Other important industries are glass making and the manufacture of corks. The total imports in 1918 were valued at £24,394,077. The exports were valued at £37,917,084. The chief articles of import were cotton and its manufactures, food stuffs, machinery, tobacco, gold, animals, wool, hair and silk. The chief articles of export are food stuffs and wine, metals and their manufactures, drug and chemical products, cotton and its manufactures, wool and its manufactures timber and its manufactures, and animals and their products. The total value of wine exported in 1918 was £3,725,137. The larger number of imports are received from the United States, the United Kingdom, and France. The chief exports are to France, United Kingdom, and the United States.

Transportation.—There are about 10,000 miles of railway, of which about 7,000 are of normal gauge and about 4,000 of varying gauges. In October, 1919, the first underground electric railway service in Spain was inaugurated in Madrid, which covers a distance of about 5 miles. The railway systems belong to private companies but are nearly all subsidized by the government. There are about 70,000 miles of telegraph line and there is wireless connection with all important countries. The merchant navy consisted in 1919 of 475 steamers of 691,328 tons net, and 448 sailing vessels of 74,970 tons net. The chief shipping centers are Bilbao and Barcelona.

Finances.—The total revenue in 1919 was 1,648,800,000 pesetas, and the expenditure 2,065,065,000 pesetas. The estimated revenue in 1920-21 was 1,962,830,000 pesetas, and the estimated expenditure 2,373,155,000 pesetas. The national debt on January 1, 1920, amounted to 12,026,280,212 pesetas.

Education.—A very large proportion of the population is illiterate. In 1910, the last date for which authoritative statistics are available, nearly 60 per cent. could neither read nor write. Education is nominally obligatory, but the law is not strictly enforced. There are about 27,000 public schools and about 6,000 private schools. The total number of pupils is about 2,700,000. Public and primary schools are supported by the government, which spent in 1918 43,726,597 pesetas for educational purposes. Secondary education is carried on in institutions or middle class schools, of which there must be at least one in every province. There are about 60 of these institutions, with about 55,000 pupils. There are 11 universities, which were attended by about 25,000 students. These universities are at Barcelona, Granada, Madrid, Murcia, Ovido, Salamanca, Santiago, Seville, Valencia, Valladolid, and Saragossa. In addition there is a medical school at Cadiz and one in the Canary Islands.

Army and Navy.—Military service is compulsory for a total period of 18 years. A general staff was established in 1916. The country is divided into 8 territorial districts, each under a captain-general. The peace strength of the army in 1920 was fixed at 216,649 men of all ranks. Of these, about 65,000 were in Morocco. The army is organized into 16 divisions, each including two brigades of infantry and one of artillery. There is a corps of aviators and the service in military aviation has been reorganized on a large scale. The navy consists of three dreadnoughts, one pre-dreadnought, and seven cruisers. There were in 1920, in addition to 13 destroyers, 26 modern torpedo boats, and 12 gun boats. A number of cruisers, destroyers, submarines, and other similar vessels were under construction in 1921. The total strength of the navy is about 10,500 sailors and about 4,500 marines.

Government.—By the constitution of 1876 Spain is declared a constitutional monarchy, with executive power vested in the king, and the legislative power in the Cortes with the king. The Cortes consists of a Senate and Congress. The Senate is composed of three classes: Those who sit by right of birth or official position, members nominated by the crown (these two classes not numbering more than 180 together), and 180 elected by the largest taxpayers of the kingdom and certain corporate bodies. The Congress contains 417 deputies, elected by citizens of 25 years of age who have enjoyed full civil rights in any muncipality for two years. Voting is compulsory for males of 25 or over. Each province has its own parliament, and each commune its own elected ayuntamiento presided over by the alcalde, for municipal and provincial administration.

People and Religion.—The people of Spain are of very mixed origin, the most ancient inhabitants, the Iberians (now represented probably by the Basques or Biscayans of the N. E.), being afterward mingled with Celts, Phœnicians, and Carthaginians, Roman colonists, Goths, Jews, and Arabs or Moors. They are generally of medium height and of spare habit, with black hair, dark eyes, and sallow complexion. Under the constitution the state binds itself to maintain the Roman Catholic religion, but a restricted liberty of worship is permitted to Protestants, of whom, however, there are very few. There are nine archbishops, the Archbishop of Toledo being primate. Houses for monks no longer exist, having been abolished by law in 1841.

History.—Spain was first known to the Phœnicians, subsequently to the Carthaginians, and, in the 3d century B. C., to the Romans. It was completely subdued under Augustus, after which it enjoyed tranquillity for nearly 400 years. This state of peace was disturbed by the irruption of the Northern barbarians, the Suevi, the Vandals, and the Alani. Christianity was introduced about the end of the 6th century; the invasion of the Moors took place in the beginning of the 8th; and they overran the whole country except the Asturias. They were finally expelled in 1492. Under Charles V., Spain made a great figure in the general affairs of Europe. He reigned 40 years, and in 1556 abdicated in favor of his son, Philip II., who died in 1598 and bequeathed to his successor, Philip III., Belgium, Naples, Sicily, and Portugal. Charles II., the last prince of the Austrian branch, reigned from 1668 to 1700; after which began the well-known war for the succession to the Spanish dominions, in which the claim of Austria was supported by the grand alliance against Louis XIV. Notwithstanding the opposition of the Allies, however, the grandson of Louis XIV. reigned in Spain, relinquishing the Belgic provinces to the house of Austria. Philip V., the first king of the French line, had a long and turbulent reign. After him Ferdinand VI., a prudent prince, introduced various reforms and maintained peace, but dying in 1759 his son, Charles III., went to war with Great Britain. Peace ensued in 1763 and continued till 1778, when Spain, at first neutral in the American War of Independence, was pre-

vailed on to take up arms against England, and obtained, at the peace of 1783, the Floridas and the island of Minorca. Charles IV. succeeded to the crown in 1788, became soon after a party to the coalition against Republican France; but was, after Prussia, the first of the Great Powers to conclude a treaty of peace, in 1795. In little more than a year afterward, the cabinet of Spain joined its late opponent and declared war against England. The abdication of the royal family of Spain took place at Bayonne in May, 1808. It was followed by the general resistance of the inhabitants, by the invasion of their country by Napoleon I., and by the subsequent expulsion of the French by the troops of Great Britain combined with those of Portugal and Spain. The dissatisfaction and indignation excited by the tyrannical proceedings of Ferdinand led, in the beginning of 1820, to a revolution of great importance, by which the constitution of the Cortes, as established in 1812, was restored, and such salutary restraints established on the power of the crown as seemed best calculated for securing the rights of the people. In 1823 Spain was again invaded by French troops under the Duke d'Angoulême, whose object was to put down the new government and to restore Ferdinand to absolute power. They penetrated the country without resistance; and having laid siege to Cadiz, the king was given up to them, and afterward the town. In 1833, on the death of Ferdinand VII., the queen-mother, Christina, was appointed queen-regent during the minority of her daughter Isabella, to whom, by his will, he bequeathed his throne. On this, Don Carlos, the late king's brother, laid claim to the crown, when a civil war which lasted till 1840 ensued. In that year the partisans of Don Carlos were finally defeated. The next event of importance was the contest between Espartero, the regent, and the Queen-Dowager Christina, for the supreme power during the minority of the queen. Espartero was successful from 1840 to 1843, but was compelled to flee before O'Donnell and Narvaez, and was not restored till 1847. Espartero's success obliged Christina to retire to France, whence she returned after his fall, Narvaez and the Moderados having control of the government. Isabella was now declared of age, married her cousin, Francis d'Assisi, and succeeded to the throne as Isabella II. During her reign the Liberals and Conservatives successively gained control of the government. The disputes finally ended in a successful revolt of the Liberals, the queen being obliged to fly to

© E. M. Newman

TOWERS OF THE ALHAMBRA, AS THEY ARE SEEN FROM GRANADA, SPAIN

See Spain, p. 1

See Spain, p. 1

CASKET IN THE CATHEDRAL AT SEVILLE, SPAIN, ONCE SUPPOSED TO HOLD THE BONES OF COLUMBUS

France, and the throne being offered in 1870 to Amadeus, a son of Victor Emanuel. Finding his task too difficult, he resigned in 1873. A republic was now formed, with Castelar as its leading spirit, but it was soon brought to an end, and the throne was offered in 1874 to Alfonso, the young son of the exiled Queen Isabella. Alfonso XII. died in 1885; and on the birth of a posthumous son, May 17, 1886, the regency was intrusted to his widow, Christina. In 1902 this son came to the throne under the title of Alfonso XIII.

Long-disturbed conditions in Cuba resulted in 1898 in war with the United States. (See SPANISH-AMERICAN WAR; CUBA.) Alfonso became of age in 1902 and the regency was terminated. During the years following, changes in the cabinet occurred with great frequency. In 1904 closer relations were established with France, in regard to the common policy in Morocco. On May 31, 1906, King Alfonso married Princess Ena of Battenberg, a granddaughter of Queen Victoria of England. During 1908-09 there was an outbreak of anarchistic activities and an attempt at revolution occurred at Barcelona. This led to the trial and execution of the anarchist Ferrer. Several reforms in the religious system were undertaken and put into effect in 1910-11. At the outbreak of the World War, in 1914, Spain at once declared its neutrality and this was continued throughout the conflict. There was strong pressure brought to bear at various times to induce the government to take side with either of the belligerents, and several changes in the cabinet were the result of these endeavors. When the war broke out a Conservative cabinet was in power. This was forced to resign in June, 1915, and was succeeded by a Liberal cabinet led by Count Romanones. The Liberals and their supporters demanded improvement in the economic conditions of the country, which resulted in 1915-16 in industrial disturbances throughout the country. There were strikes in Madrid, Valencia, and other industrial centers. These reached a crisis in 1916 when a general strike was declared. This was met promptly by the government with the declaration of martial law throughout the country.

Reliance of the government on military force in dealing with the strike greatly strengthened the influence of organizations of army officers, the so-called Defence Juntas, which opposed the conduct of public affairs as carried on by the Cortes and the continual succession of ministries. The effort to establish Spanish authority in the Riff, the Mediterranean coast slope of Morocco, a region accorded to Spain in 1907, was prolonged and rendered costly by the resistance of the Riff tribesmen. In July, 1921, Spanish forces under Silvestre, attacked near Anual in Morocco, suffered a disastrous defeat and were driven back with heavy loss in the region of Melilla. The Defence Juntas attacked the government as responsible for the disorganization that had led to the defeat of the Silvestre forces. The Liberal party, while opposed to military interference in government, were not united. A decree of November, 1922, abolished the Juntas, and rendered those maintaining them subject to trial.

The Captain-General of Catalonia, Primo de Rivera, Marquis of Estella, Sept. 13, 1923, declared revolt against the ministry of Señor Alhucemas. He had the backing of troops in the northeast of Spain, and the sympathy of military commanders elsewhere. King Alfonso refused to authorize military measures against him, whereupon the ministry resigned, and the King called upon Primo de Rivera to form a government. There thus began, Sept. 15, with suspension of the constitutional régime of 1875, a virtual dictatorship, which was destined to outlast the numerous constitutional ministries that had preceded it. Primo de Rivera became sole minister, and set up a military directorate, a group of department heads responsible to him, but not directly to the crown. He established martial law, created a strict censorship, warned the working class in a manifesto that agitations would not be tolerated, refused a demand that the King call the Cortes as provided by the constitution, and replaced municipal government in many places with his own appointees, chiefly officers. The dictatorship reduced the budget deficits occasioned by the war expenditure in Morocco. Spanish forces there were withdrawn in 1924 to a restricted area. Subventions to the railroads were stopped.

The costly war in Morocco was ended in 1926 by French and Spanish coöperation. It left Spanish government finances somewhat oppressed. Primo de Rivera undertook in 1928 to check fluctuation in the exchange value of the peseta, by borrowing $25,000,000 in the United States and creating a stabilization committee to buy and sell exchange. He also created a government oil monopoly which in 1928 took over the properties of foreign oil merchants. A modified National assembly called in 1927 undertook in 1928 to shape a new constitution.

SPALATO, or SPALATRO, a town of Dalmatia, Jugo-Slavia; on a promontory on the E. side of the Adriatic; 160 miles S. E. of Fiume. Here in a most beautiful situation the Emperor Diocletian built for himself a colossal palace, to which he retired when he abdicated the throne in 305. The palace faced the sea, looking S.; its walls were from 570 to 700 feet long and 50 to 70 feet high, and inclosed an area of 9½ acres. It stood square, like a Roman camp, and had a gate in the middle of each side, and was of the most solid construction. Architecturally it is of the highest interest in that it contains several features that presage the architectural styles and devices of modern times.

Within the palace area is a building supposed to be the mausoleum of the emperor. Since the year 650 this edifice has been a Christian cathedral; it contains a magnificent marble pulpit. All the interior buildings and nearly all the exterior walls of this gigantic palace are still standing in a fairly good state of preservation. But the interior was converted into a town in 639 by the citizens of Savona who escaped the destruction of their town by the Avars, and it has been occupied ever since. The existing city of Spalato lies, more than half of it, outside the palace walls. It has a lively trade in grain, cattle, oil, horses, etc., the Lasva railway (1895-1897) connecting it with Bosnia and the Danubian lands. Its industries embrace the manufacture of liquors (rosoglio and maraschino). Pop. about 31,500.

SPALDING, ALBERT, an American violinist, born in Chicago, in 1888. He was educated in music in New York, Florence, and Paris, and made his first appearance in the latter city in 1905. Following this, he made a tour of the chief cities of Europe. He appeared with the Damrosch Orchestra in New York City in 1908 and followed this by a concert tour in the United States, and by tours in all of the principal cities of Europe, in Egypt, Cuba, and the West Indies. He was a composer of music for the violin. During the World War he served in the Signal Service as interpreter in Italy.

SPAN, a measure of length, being the distance between the tips of the thumb and little finger when the fingers are expanded to their fullest extent. This space averages about 9 inches, which accordingly is the fixed measure given to the span.

SPANDAU, a town and first-class fortress of Prussia; situated at the confluence of the Havel and the Spree; 8 miles W. by N. of Berlin. The principal defense of the capital on that side, it has very strong modern fortifications, including a citadel. In the "Julius tower"

of this structure is preserved in gold the "Reichskriegsschatz" $30,000,000 that the government, according to a law of 1871, keeps in reserve for a great war. Spandau before the World War was the seat of large government cannon foundries, factories for making gunpowder and other munitions of war, and has an arsenal. The town, one of the oldest of Brandenburg, was a favorite residence of the electors. It surrendered to the Swedes in 1634, to the French in 1806, and in 1813 to the Prussians. Pop. about 90,000.

SPANIEL, the name given to several varieties or breeds of dogs. Their distinguishing characteristics are a rather broad muzzle, remarkably long and full ears, hair plentiful and beautifully waved, particularly that of the ears, tail, and hinder parts of the thighs and legs. The prevailing color is liver and white, sometimes red and white or black and white, and sometimes deep brown, or black on the face and breast, with a tan spot over each eye. The English spaniel is a superior and very pure breed. The King Charles' dog is a small variety of the spaniel used as a lapdog. The Maltese dog is also a small species of spaniel. The water spaniels, large and small, differ from the common spaniel only in the roughness of their coats, and in uniting the aquatic propensities of the Newfoundland dog with the fine hunting qualities of their own race. Spaniels possess a great share of intelligence, affection, and obedience, which qualities, combined with much beauty, make them highly prized as companions.

SPANISH-AMERICAN WAR, a war between Spain and the United States, which took place in 1898. It arose in large part out of the condition of affairs in Cuba, where Spanish oppression had led to outbreaks for several generations, in some of which American citizens had been involved. The Cubans had revolted in 1895 and the revolt had been suppressed by the Spanish authorities with much ruthlessness. The severity merely drove discontent under cover and sporadic acts of violence continued with an accompaniment of hardship to the civil population to which the people of the United States could not remain indifferent. As a result of a decision in the direction of intervention come to by the United States Government, Secretary of State Richard Olney offered on April 6, 1896, the friendly offices of the United States for the purpose of saving Cuba from impoverishment and of ameliorating the condition of foreigners in the country. The offer was rejected by the Spanish Government and President

Cleveland, in his annual message to Congress in December, 1896, referred to the obligations which might devolve on the United States if Spain should show itself incapable of coping with conditions. Shortly after President McKinley was inaugurated things began to come to a head and Congress appropriated $50,000 for Cuban relief. As the relations between the two countries had begun to assume a critical aspect General Weyler, whose severity had earned for him the hatred of the Cuban population, was recalled by the Spanish Government and General Blanco commissioned to take his place. A period of plain speaking on the part of the United States succeeded and in response to a declaration that the United States could not view with indifference the indefinite prolongation of existing conditions the Spanish Government promised that on the restoration of order it would establish local autonomy in the island. In the meantime an influential element in the United States promoted the feeling in favor of war, and fuel was added to the flame by the publication of a letter written by the Spanish Minister criticizing President McKinley, which had been stolen from the mails. Early in 1898, however, the tragic event occurred which had the result of precipitating the conflict, for on the evening of Feb. 15 the United States battleship "Maine" was blown up in Havana harbor, with a loss of 266 men. The responsibility for the act was never fully demonstrated, though investigations were made by boards appointed both by the United States and Spain. The American board reported that a submarine mine was the cause of the explosion, and the general sentiment laid the culpability at the door of the Spanish authorities. As a result of the warlike feeling engendered in the United States, Congress, on March 8, appropriated $50,000,000 for national defense, and on March 11 mobilization of the regular army was begun. President McKinley had entered into pourparlers with the Spanish Government, but not satisfied by its representations decided to lay the matter before Congress. Meanwhile the Cuban Junta demanded recognition as the lawful government, and on April 19 Congress declared the people of Cuba free and independent, demanded the surrender of Spanish authority over the island, and empowered and directed the President to enforce this resolution by the army and navy. An ultimatum embodying these demands was signed and despatched by the President on April 20, and Spain was given until the 23d to make a satisfactory reply. The Spanish Minister in reply demanded his passports and the American Minister in Madrid was handed his passports. Spain declared war on April 24 and the United States followed suit on April 25.

Naval action followed almost at once, Captain W. T. Sampson bombarding Matanzas on April 27. Meanwhile Commodore Dewey, stationed at Hongkong, received orders to proceed to the Philippine Islands and commence operations at once against the Spanish fleet, capturing or destroying the vessels. The order had been sent on the day of the declaration of war and five days later he approached under cover of darkness Manila harbor, having under his command 9 vessels and 131 guns. The fight that followed in the early morning after his entry was an unequal one. It lasted four hours and resulted in the destruction of the Spanish fleet, consisting of 10 vessels, 120 guns, and 1,796 men, as it lay at anchor in Cavite Bay, and the local fortifications. The loss on the American side included only six wounded. Meanwhile the portion of the Spanish fleet located in Cuban waters was locked up in Santiago Bay by the fleet under Captain Sampson, and worldwide interest was aroused by the attempt of Lieut. R. P. Hobson to make escape impossible by the sinking of the collier "Merrimac" at the harbor mouth. Finally the Spanish fleet under Admiral Cervera put out to sea on July 3. In the conflict that followed, the Spanish ships were either destroyed or driven ashore, with a loss of 350 men killed and 1,700 captured. The loss on the American side was 1 killed and 10 wounded.

The battles on land were less unequal. On June 20 Gen. W. R. Shafter landed at Daiguiri with 815 officers and 16,072 men, the Spaniards withdrawing to their intrenchments near Santiago. At Las Guasimas American troops under General Wheeler dislodged the Spanish troops with a loss of 68 men, killed and wounded, the Spanish losing 28. In July United States troops aided by Cubans attacked the Spanish front at El Caney and San Juan. On July 16, following a siege, Santiago capitulated, under an agreement by which Spanish soldiers were to be taken to Spain. Meanwhile a brief campaign of over two weeks (July 25-Aug. 13), under Gen. Nelson A. Miles in Porto Rico, ended with an armistice. On Aug. 13 the city of Manila surrendered to Admiral Dewey and General Merritt, and 13,000 soldiers surrendered. Then after less than four months of fighting peace preliminaries were begun through the French Ambassador and on Aug. 12 the peace protocol was concluded. The subsequent pourparlers endured till Dec. 10, when the treaty was signed in Paris, under which

Spain withdrew from Cuba, Porto Rico, Guam and the Philippines, the United States paying $20,000,000. The political status of the inhabitants of the ceded countries were left to be determined between them and the United States Government.

SPANISH MAIN (*i. e.*, main land), a name given to the N. coast of South American from the Orinoco to Darien, and to the shores of the former Central American provinces of Spain contiguous to the Caribbean Sea. The name, however, is often popularly applied to the Caribbean Sea itself, and in this sense occurs frequently in connection with the buccaneers. See BUCCANEER.

SPAR, in mineralogy, a term employed to include a great number of crystallized, earthy, and some metallic substances, which easily break into rhomboidal, cubical, or laminated fragments with polished surfaces, but without regard to the ingredients of which they are composed. Among miners the term spar is frequently used alone to express any bright crystalline substance.

SPARGO, JOHN, an American author, born at Stithians, Cornwall, England, in 1876. He was educated in the public schools and then took extension courses at Oxford and Cambridge. Early in his

JOHN SPARGO

life he bcame interested in socialism and was one of the comparatively few Englishmen who publicly opposed the Boer War. He came to the United States in 1901 and from then on was active as a socialistic worker, lecturer and writer.

After having served as a member of the National Executive Committee of the Socialist Party and as a delegate to most

EDWIN ERLE SPARKS

of the important conventions, he resigned from the Socialist Party in May, 1917, being opposed to the Socialist opposition to the entrance of the United States into the World War, as well as to the Socialist support of the Russian Communists. He was one of the founders of the National Party, of the American Alliance for Labor and Democracy, and of the Prospect House Social Settlement, Yonkers, N. Y. In 1919 he was appointed a member of the Industrial Conference. Besides numerous pamphlets and magazine articles on art, and on social and economic questions, he wrote: "Socialism" (1906); "Capitalist and Laborer" (1907); "The Spiritual Significance of Modern Socialism" (1908); "Karl Marx, His Life and Work" (1909); "Elements of Socialism" (with Professor Arner, 1911); "Applied Socialism" (1912); "Syndicalism, Industrialism, Unionism, and Socialism" (1913); "Americanism and Social Democracy" (1918); "Bolshevism" (1919); "The Psychology of Bolshevism" (1920), etc.

SPARKS, EDWIN ERLE, an American educator, born in Licking co., Ohio, in 1860. He was educated at Ohio State University, Harvard, and the University of Chicago, receiving from the latter institution the degree of Ph.D. in 1900. He also holds honorary degrees from Lehigh University and Allegheny College. From 1884-1885 he was an assistant in history at Ohio State University, from 1885-1890 he taught school in Ohio, and from 1890-1895 he was principal of the preparatory department and teacher of history at Pennsylvania State College. From 1895-1907 he was connected with the University of Chicago successively as lecturer, instructor, assistant professor, associate professor, and professor of American History, curator of the historical museum, and dean of the University College. In 1908 he became president of Pennsylvania State College. He was a member of various historical and patriotic societies and committees. He wrote "Expansion of the American People" (1899); "Formative Incidents in American Diplomacy" (1902); "The United States of America" (2 vols., 1904); "Foundations of National Development" (1907); etc. He also contributed many essays and articles on historical and educational topics to periodicals and journals.

SPARKS, JARED, an American historian; born in Willington, Conn., May 10, 1789; was graduated at Harvard College in 1815; studied theology; and was ordained in the Unitarian Church in Baltimore in 1819. He took part in the doctrinal controversy with orthodox theologians; was chosen chaplain of the National House of Representatives in 1821; edited the "Unitarian Miscellany and Christian Monitor" in 1821-1823; conducted the "North American Review" in 1824-1831; and was the originator and first editor of the "American Almanac and Repository of Useful Knowledge." He was Professor of Ancient and Modern History at Harvard in 1839-1849; president of the college in 1849-1863; and the author of a large number of sermons, biographical and historical works, theological papers, etc., most notably "The Library of American Biography" and "Correspondence of the American Revolution." He died in Cambridge, Mass., March 14, 1866.

SPARROW, in ornithology, *Passer domesticus*, the house sparrow, a well known bird, the constant follower of civilized man. It ranges over Europe, into the N. of Africa and Asia, and has been introduced into America and Australia. Sparrows are found in crowded cities and in manufacturing towns. Mantle of male brown striped with black; head bluish-gray; two narrow bands, one white and the other rusty-yellow, on wings; cheeks grayish-white, front of neck black, underparts light gray. From a high antiquity, their great fecundity, their attachment to their young, their extreme pugnacity, and the large tolls they levy on the farmer and market gardener have been commented on by writers on ornithology. In many places a small sum is paid for the destruction of these birds, the legislatures of some of the States having made appropriations for this fund. The name sparrow is also loosely applied to several of the *Fringillidæ*.

SPARROW HAWK, in ornithology, the *Accipiter nisus*, extending across Europe, through Asia to Japan. The adult male is about 12 inches long, dark-brown on the upper surface, softening into gray as the bird grows old; the entire under surface is rusty-brown, with bands of a darker shade. The female is about 15 inches long, the upper surface nearly resembling that of the male bird in ground-color, but having many of the feathers white at the base; under surface grayish-white, with dark transverse bars. The sparrow hawk is very destructive to small quadrupeds and young birds. The hen lays four or five eggs irregularly blotched with brownish-crimson on a bluish-white ground. The name is also applied to the American falcon, the Australian collared sparrow hawk, the European kestrel, and the New Zealand quail hawk.

SPARTA, or LACEDÆMON, a celebrated city of ancient Greece; capital of Laconia and of the Spartan state, and the chief city in the Peloponnesus; on the W. bank of the Eurotas river, and embraced a circuit of 6 miles. Sparta was a scattered city consisting of five separate quarters. Unlike Athens it was plainly built, and had few notable public buildings; consequently there are no imposing ruins to be seen here as in Athens, and the modern Sparta is only a village of some 4,000 inhabitants. Laconia, the district in which Sparta was situated, was the S. E. division of the Peloponnesus, bounded on the W. by Messenia, from which it was separated by the chain of Taygetus, on the N. by Arcadia and Argolis, and on the E. and S. by the sea. The Eurotas (Vasilopotamo, "king of rivers") here flows through a picturesque valley and empties into the Gulf of Laconia.

The Spartan state was founded, according to tradition, by Lacedæmon, son of Zeus. The most celebrated of its legendary kings was Menelaus. It is said to have been conquered by the Heraclidæ from N. Greece about 1080, who established a dyarchy or double dynasty of two kings in Sparta. Apart from this legend it is accepted as a historical fact that the Spartans were the descendants of the Dorians who invaded the Peloponnesus about that period, and that from an early period they followed a set of rigorous laws which they ascribed to Lycurgus. Shortly after their settlement in the Peloponnesus it is probable that the Spartans extended their sway over all the territory of Laconia, a portion of the inhabitants of which they reduced to the condition of slaves. They also waged war with the Messenians, the Arcadians, and the Argives, against whom they were so successful that before the close of the 6th century B. C. they were recognized as the leading people in all Greece.

Early in the following century began the Persian wars, in which a rivalry grew up between Athens and Sparta. This rivalry led to the Peloponnesian war, in which Athens was humiliated and the old ascendency of Sparta regained. (See GREECE.) Soon after this the Spartans became involved in a war with Persia, and Athens, Thebes, Corinth, and some of the Peloponnesian states took this opportunity to declare war against them. This war, known as the Bœotian or Corinthian war, lasted eight years and increased the reputation and power of Athens. To break the alliance of Athens with Persia, Sparta, in 387 B. C., concluded with the latter power the peace known by the name of Antalcidas; and the designs of Sparta became apparent when she occupied, without provocation, the city of Thebes, and introduced an aristocratical constitution there. Pelopidas delivered Thebes, and the celebrated Theban war (378-363) followed, in which Sparta was much enfeebled. During the following century Sparta steadily declined, though one or two isolated attempts were made to restore its former greatness. The principal of these was made by Cleomenes (236-222), but his endeavors failed, because there were then scarcely 700 of Spartan descent, and the majority of these were in a state of beggary. With the rest of Greece Sparta latterly passed under the dominion of the Romans in 146 B. C.

The Spartans differed from the other Greeks in manners, customs, and constitution. Their kings (two of whom always reigned at once) ruled only through the popular will, acting as umpires in disputes, and commanding the army. The Spartans proper, that is, the descendants of the Dorians, occupying themselves with war and the chase, left all ordinary labor to the Helots (slaves), while the class known as Periœci (descendants of the ancient inhabitants of the country) engaged in commerce, navigation, and manufactures. The distinguishing traits of the Spartans were severity, resolution, and perseverance, but they were also accounted faithless and crafty. When a child was born, if it proved vigorous and sound the state received it into the number of citizens, otherwise it was thrown into a cave on Mount Taygetus. They wore no outer garment except in bad weather, no shoes at any time, and they were obliged to make their beds of rushes from the Eurotas. The principal object of attention during the periods of boyhood and youth was physical education, which consisted in running, leaping, throwing the discus, wrestling, boxing, the chase, etc. The Spartans were the only people of Greece who avowedly despised learning and excluded it from the education of youth. The education of the Spartan females was also different from that of the Greeks elsewhere. Instead of remaining at home, as in Athens, spinning, they danced in public, wrestled with each other, ran on the course, threw the discus, etc.

SPARTACUS, the leader of the Roman slaves in the great revolt which broke out about 73 B. C.; a Thracian by birth, who from a shepherd became a leader of a band of robbers when he was captured and sold to a trainer of gladiators at Capua. On the murder of his father by the Romans he had made an oath to wage war against Rome; and he formed a conspiracy to escape, and, when it was discovered, broke out with some 70 followers, with whom he made for the crater of Vesuvius, where hordes of runaway slaves soon joined him. He first overpowered and seized the arms of a force sent against him from Capua, next routed an army of 3,000 men under C. Clodius, and so passed from victory to victory, overrunning southern Italy and sacking many of the cities of Campania, his numbers growing to 100,000 men. Spartacus, who failed to get support from the Italian communities, and from the first knew the real weakness of his position, strove to persuade his victorious bands to march N. to the Alps and disperse to their native regions; but they were intoxicated with victory, and saw glittering before their eyes all the plunder of Italy. Against his better judgment he continued the war, showing himself a consummate captain in the strategy and valor with which he routed one Roman consular army after another, and the policy by which for long he assuaged the jealousies and dissensions among his followers. At length in 71 M. Licinius Crassus received the command, and after

I—1

some time of cautious delay forced Spartacus into the narrow peninsula of Rhegium, from which, however, he burst out through the Roman lines with a portion of his force. Crassus urged the Senate to recall Lucullus from Asia and Pompey from Spain, but meantime he himself pursued active hostilities against the dreaded enemy. Spartacus finding all hope at an end made a dash on Brundusium, hoping to seize the shipping and get across the Adriatic, but was foiled by the presence of Lucullus, whereupon he fell back on the river Silarus, and there made a heroic stand against Crassus till he was cut down.

SPARTANBURG, a city and county-seat of Spartanburg co., S. C.; on the Glenn Springs, the Carolina, Clinchfield and Ohio and South Carolina, the Charleston and Western Carolina, and the Southern railroads; 98 miles N. of Columbia. Here are Wofford College (M. E., S.), Converse College for Women, Converse College, State Deaf, Dumb and Blind Institute, Kennedy Public Library, street railroad and electric light plants, National and State banks, and daily and weekly newspapers. It has cotton mills, ironworks, lumber mills, limestone quarries, and iron mines. When the United States entered the World War in 1917 one of the 16 divisional cantonments, Camp Wadsworth, for the training of National Guard troops, was established near the town. Most of the New York State troops were trained there. Pop. (1910) 17,517; (1920) 22,638.

SPARTEL, CAPE, a promontory at the entrance to the Straits of Gibraltar, and about 1,000 feet above the sea.

SPAULDING, FRANK ELLSWORTH, an American educator, born at Dublin, N. H., in 1866. He was educated at Amherst College, the University of Berlin, the University of Leipzig, and the Sorbonne. Beginning with 1895 he was successively superintendent of schools at Ware, Mass., Passaic, N. J., Newton, Mass., Minneapolis, Minn., and Cleveland, Ohio. In 1920 he became professor of school administration and head of the department of education at the Graduate School, at Yale University. He was a member of the General Education Board, of the Army Educational Commission, and of the American Academy of Political and Social Science. Besides contributing many articles on educational subjects to magazines he wrote "The Individual Child and His Education" (1904); "Learning to Read,
I—2

a Manual for Teachers" (1907); and compiled several graded readers.

SPAULDING, OLIVER LYMAN, JR., an American military officer, born at St. Johns, Mich., in 1875. He was educated at the University of Michigan and was commissioned a second lieutenant of artillery in 1898, rising successively through the ranks until he became a brigadier-general in 1918. He was a graduate of the Artillery School, the Army Staff College, the Army War College, and the Graduate School of Fire for Field Artillery. He saw service at various times in Alaska, China, the Philippine Islands, Panama, the Mexican Border, France, and Germany. During the World War he commanded the 55th and 165th F. A. Brigades and acted as Chief of the Historical Section, General Staff, A. E. F., February to June, 1919.

SPAVIN, a disease of horses which occurs under two different forms, both interfering with soundness. In young, weakly, or overworked subjects the hock-joint is sometimes distended with dark-colored thickened synovia or joint oil. This is bog spavin. The second variety of spavin is the more common. Toward the inside of the hock, at the head of the shank bones, or between some of the small bones of the hock, a bony enlargement may be seen and felt. This is bone spavin. At first there is tenderness, heat, swelling, and considerable lameness; but as the inflammation in the bone and its investing membrane abates the lameness may entirely disappear, or a slight stiffness may remain.

SPAWN, the eggs or ova of fishes, frogs, etc., from which, when fertilized by the males, a new progeny arises that continues the species. In the oviparous fishes with distinct sexes the eggs are impregnated externally, and arrive at maturity without the aid of the mother. The spawn being deposited by the female, the male then pours on it the impregnating fluid. In the ovoviviparous fishes sexual intercourse takes place, and the eggs are hatched in the uterus. Fishes exhibit a great variety in regard to the number of their eggs. In the spawn of a codfish, for example, no fewer than 3,500,000 eggs have been found. In general, before spawning, fish forsake the deep water and approach the shore, and some fish leave the salt water and ascend the rivers before spawning, and then return again. See FISH CULTURE.

SPEAR, a weapon of offense, consisting of a wooden shaft or pole varying in length up to eight or nine feet, and provided with a sharp piercing point. The spear may be regarded as the prototype of the various forms of piercing weapons, such as the arrow, bolt, and dart, which are projected from bows, catapults, or other engines, and the javelin, assegai, and lance, held in or thrown by the hand.

In its earliest form the spear would

with fish and other bones, and their fighting spears have sometimes poisoned tips.

SPEARMAN, FRANK HAMILTON, an American author, born in Buffalo, N. Y., in 1859. He was educated in public and private schools and at Lawrence University, Appleton, Wis. He wrote, besides many short stories in magazines

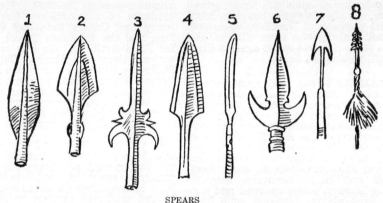

SPEARS

1—Prehistoric bronze	3—Mediæval type	5—Japanese	7—West African
2—Prehistoric bronze	4—Old British	6—German, 15th Century	8—Philippine

naturally consist of a simple pole of tough wood sharpened to a point at one extremity, which point might be both formed and hardened by charring in fire. From this an improvement would consist in fitting to the shaft a separate spear head of bone, or flint. To flint heads succeeded heads of bronze, but these came only late in the bronze period, and were still in use when the Homeric poems were composed. The bronze spear heads found in Great Britain and in Northern Europe generally were cast with sockets, into which the end of the shaft was inserted, but on the eastern Mediterranean coasts tanged spear heads were used. These spear heads were various in form and size, some being three-edged like the old bayonets, others were expanded leaf-shaped blades, some barbed, and some having loopholes either in socket or blade by which they were lashed to the shaft.

The war lance of the mediæval knights was 16 feet long; the weapon of modern cavalry regiments known as lancers may be from 8½ to 11 feet long, usually adorned with a small flag near the head. The Persians at the present day forge spear heads, for ornamental purposes only, with two and sometimes three prongs. The modern spears of savage tribes, used equally for hunting and for warlike purposes, are frequently barbed

and numerous economic articles in reviews: "The Nerve of Foley" (1900); "Held for Orders" (1901); "Doctor Bryson" (1902); "The Daughter of a Magnate" (1902); "The Close of the Day" (1904); "Whispering Smith" (1906); "Robert Kimberly" (1911); "The Mountain Divide" (1912); "Merrilie Dawes" (1913); "Nan of Music Mountain" (1917).

SPEARMINT, or **SPIREMINT,** in botany, a mint, *Mentha viridis,* with oblong, lanceolate, sub-acute, serrate leaves, and slender spikes of flowers. Found in watery places. It is used in cookery as a sauce, and yields an aromatic and carminative oil, oil of spearmint.

SPEARS, JOHN RANDOLPH, an American author; born in Ohio in 1850. He published "The Gold Diggings of Cape Horn"; "The Port of Missing Ships, and Other Stories"; "The History of Our Navy"; "Our Navy in the War With Spain"; "History of the American Slave Trade"; "History of New England Whalers" (1908); "History of the American Navy" (1909); "Story of the American Merchant Marine" (1909); "Master Mariner" (1911).

SPEARS, RAYMOND SMILEY, an American author, born at Bellevue, Ohio, in 1876. He was educated in public schools and became a reporter on the New York "Sun." He contributed many short stories and articles on travel to magazines, securing his material by extensive tours on foot, in boats, automobiles, etc. He was a member of the editorial staff of the "Adventure Magazine" and published "Camping on the Great Rivers" (1912); "Camping on the Great Lakes" (1913); "The Cabin Boat Primer" (1913), etc.

SPECIE PAYMENTS, SUSPENSION OF, AND RESUMPTION OF, terms signifying the regulation of currency during times of stress, as during a war. Suspension of specie payments means that the Government and the banks suspend payments in metal coin, silver or gold, and issue instead "credit money," in paper. This was done in the United States in 1862, when the Government found itself compelled to borrow more money than could be raised by the banks of the country. In other words, the need of money by the Government, suddenly expended, found the money in circulation inadequate to meet that need. So paper money must be issued to fill the gap. When this is done recklessly and without restriction, as it was in 1862, this paper currency depreciates in value. The resumption of specie payments after such a period of financial dislocation must necessarily be very gradual. In the above instance resumption was not begun till 1879, and then it was several years more before normal conditions were restored. During the Civil War the Government was again compelled to suspend specie payments because of the vast quantity of metal currency which was being hoarded by the people. A large volume of Treasury notes were, therefore, issued and made to take the place of metal money. It was 1879 before the resumption of specie payments in this case could be begun. During the World War the United States was practically the only belligerent country which was not compelled to suspend specie payments, the result being that its currency is now at a premium in all other countries.

SPECIES, in biology, a somewhat ambiguous term used to denote a limited group of organisms, resembling each other, and capable of reproducing similar organisms, animal or vegetable, as the case may be. A species is defined by Haeckel as "the sum of all cycles of reproduction which, under similar conditions of existence, exhibit similar forms." Linnæus held that all species were the direct descendants from and had the characters of primevally created forms, and in this he was followed by those who accepted the first chapter of Genesis in a strictly literal sense. Buffon and Cuvier, leaving the question of origin on one side, held the distinguishing marks of a species to be similarity and capability of reproduction. But besides varieties and races in various species of animals and plants, dimorphism, and in others trimorphism, exists so that close similarity cannot be taken as a criterion, and the value attached to external resemblances varies in the case of different observers. At a later date was added the physiological definition that all the individuals of every species were capable of producing fertile offspring by intercrossing, whereas sexual intercourse between different species produced only sterile offspring or was actually infertile; and, though subject to exceptions, this definition is generally true. The descent of any given series of individuals from a single pair, or from pairs exactly similar to each other, is in no case capable of proof.

Darwin in his "Origin of Species" says: "I look at the term species as one arbitrarily given for the sake of convenience to a set of individuals closely resembling each other, and that it does not essentially differ from the term variety, which is given to less distinct and more fluctuating forms" (see DARWINIAN THEORY.) That book popularized the idea of the mutability of species, the chief factor in which Darwin believed to be Natural Selection, though he afterward modified his views to some extent as to its importance. A later theory of the origin of species is that of Physiological Selection, propounded by W. G. J. Romanes, F. R. S., who holds that many species have arisen on account of variations in the reproductive system, leading to some infertility with parent forms—mutual sterility being thus regarded as one of the conditions, and not as one of the consequences of specific differentiation.

In logic, a predicable that expresses the whole essence of its subject in so far as any common term can express it. The names species and genus are merely relative, and the same common term may in one case be the species which is predicated of an individual, and in another case the individual of which a species is predicated. Thus the individual, George, belongs to the logical species man, while man is an individual of the logical species animal.

SPECIFIC GRAVITY. See GRAVITY, SPECIFIC.

SPECK VON STERNBURG, HER-MANN, BARON, a German diplomat, born at Leeds, England, in 1852. He studied military and naval science and international law, and served in the German army in the Franco-Prussian War. He was from 1885 to 1890 military attaché at Washington. In 1891 he became Secretary to the Legation in China. In the year following he served at Buenos Aires and at Belgrade, Serbia. He was appointed First Secretary to the German Embassy at Washington in 1898, and this was followed in 1900 by his appointment as Consul General for British India and Ceylon. He became German Ambassador to the United States in 1903. Largely through his efforts tariff arrangements were perfected between Germany and the United States, in 1906-1907. He died in 1908.

SPECTROSCOPE, an instrument for observing spectra, or for spectrum analysis. With a single glass prism, the few most prominent lines in a solar spectrum may be seen by using a narrow slit to admit the light, which was the first great improvement made upon Newton's experiment, since a hole or wide slit gives confusion of effect. The second great improvement was to place a collimating lens behind the slit at its focal distance, whereby all the rays from the slit became a parallel bundle before passing through the prism. Finally a small telescope was mounted behind the prism to magnify and define the image thus obtained. The whole arranged on a table, with means of adjusting the collimating and eye tubes at the proper angles with the prism, forms the ordinary single-prism spectroscope. Further prisms may be added to increase the dispersion. Arrangements are often added for throwing the image of a micrometer scale upon the spectrum, or a reflecting prism may be placed over half of the slit to reflect the solar spectrum into the instrument for comparison with the one under observation. It is in this way that spectra are compared with the solar lines, which are carefully mapped and form the standard of reference. By combining prisms of the different refractive and dispersive powers, a strong spectrum may be obtained without deflection. Such prisms may be contained in quite a small tube with slit and lens, and are called direct-vision spectroscopes, which are much used for microscopic observation. Instruments specially fitted for the purpose are called star spectroscopes, and there are also special sun spectroscopes, such being necessarily different in practical details from ordinary or chemical spectroscopes. It has become very usual to employ the spectra from diffraction gratings instead of prisms. The higher order spectra thus produced are very pure, and have the advantage of giving the lines in the true position due to their relative wave lengths alone, while prisms compress some groups of lines and extend others, according to the peculiar dispersion of the glass. Spectroscopes thus constructed are called grating spectroscopes.

One of the largest spectroscopes in the world was completed in 1899 by Prof. John A. Brashear, an astronomer of Allegheny, Pa., for Dr. Hans Hauswaldt, a scientist of Magdeburg, Germany. This powerful concave grating instrument is 21 feet long and requires a room about 25 feet square in which to operate it. The grating used on the spectroscope has a six-inch aperture and is ruled with 110,000 lines. So accurately are these lines ruled that none of them varies more than $\frac{3}{1000000}$ of an inch from the correct position; and so powerful is the instrument that whereas an ordinary spectroscope would show from 100 to 200 lines belonging to the spectrum of iron, this apparatus will reveal more than 2,000.

SPECTRUM, in optics, the colored image or images produced when the rays from any source of light are decomposed or dispersed by refraction through a prism. It has been proved that whiteness is simply a totality of effect produced by the simultaneous effects of many colors falling at once upon the retina. It has been shown (see RE-FRACTION) how a beam of light is deflected on meeting at any inclination the surface of a denser medium, and it is obvious that by using a prism with two inclined surfaces, the beam may be permanently deflected. It is found that each different color, representing a different length of wave, is differently refracted by the prism, or has its own special index of refraction; hence the prism separates or spreads out, in order, according to their refrangibility, all the different colors of which the beam is composed. This appearance is the spectrum of that particular light. Solids or liquids heated to incandescence—as the particles of soot in a candle flame—always yield an unbroken band of colors shading into one another; this is called a continuance spectrum. Incandescent gases generally yield lines or bands only, and this is a line or banded spectrum. When portions of what would have been a continuous spectrum are intercepted or cut out by an intervening medium this is called an absorption spectrum. Besides the waves of such a length as cause visual effects, there are many more beyond the red at one end of the spectrum and the violet at the other, which produce powerful chemical and heating effects. This portion is sometimes called the invisible spectrum, sometimes described as the ultra-red or ultra-violet spectrum. Its length greatly exceeds that of the visible spectrum, and it is found to comprise lines and bands precisely analogous to those occurring in the luminous portion.

SPECTRUM ANALYSIS, in physics and chemistry, the determination of the chemical composition, the physical condition, or both, of any body by the spectrum of the light which it emits or suffers to pass through it, under certain conditions. (See SPECTROSCOPE.)

SPEDDING, JAMES, an English historian, born near Bassenthwaite, Cumberland, England, June, 1808. The labors of his whole life were concerned with the works of Lord Bacon; and his first work, "Evenings with a Reviewer" (2 vols., privately printed in 1848, published 1881), was an elaborate review of Macaulay's essay on the great philosopher. He published "The Works of Francis Bacon" (7 vols. 1857-1859); "Life and Letters of Francis Bacon" (7 vols. 1870-1876); "Life and Times of Francis Bacon" (2 vols. 1878); and a volume of miscellaneous "Reviews and Discussions" (1869). He died in London, March 9, 1881.

SPEECH, spoken language; uttered sounds intended to convey meaning, and produced by the organs of voice, namely, the larynx, and the mouth and its parts, including the tongue and teeth. In speech two great classes of sounds are produced, these being usually known as vowels and consonants. Vowels are pronounced by sounds coming primarily from the larynx and passing with comparative freedom through the mouth cavity, though modified in certain ways; while consonants are formed by sounds caused by the greater or less interruption of the current of air from the larynx in the mouth. Vowels can be uttered alone and independently of consonants, and their sounds can be prolonged at will; consonants have no importance in speech as apart from vowels, and are named consonants from being used along with vowels. Both vowel and consonant sounds are very numerous if we investigate the different languages of the world, but any one language only has a fraction of those that may be used. A single sound may convey an idea of itself and thus form a word, or several may be combined to form a word, and if the word is uttered by several distinct successive changes in position of the vocal organs it is a word of so many syllables. Words, again, are combined to form sentences or complete statements, and the aggregate of words used by any people or community in mutual intercourse forms its language. See PHILOLOGY; VOICE: VOWEL.

SPEED, JAMES, an American lawyer; born in Jefferson co., Ky., March 11, 1812; was graduated at St. Joseph's College in that State; commenced the practice of law in Louisville, and in 1847 was elected to the lower house of the Legislature, and in 1861 to the Senate. The outbreak of the Civil War found Judge Speed an uncompromising Union man, and he took charge of the recruiting stations in Kentucky. He was a brother of JOSHUA F. SPEED, the friend of Abraham Lincoln, and it was probably through this acquaintance with his brother that Lincoln came to select Speed for a place in his cabinet, though he had previously gained distinction as a lawyer and professor in the Law School of Transylvania University at Lexington. Speed was appointed Attorney-General in November, 1864, and was retained in the office by President Johnson after the assassination of Mr. Lincoln till July, 1866, when he resigned. He died June 25, 1887.

SPEEDWELL, the common name of plants of the genus *Veronica*, natural order *Scrophulariaceae*, natives of tem-

COMMON SPEEDWELL

perate climates all over the world. The species consist of herbs, undershrubs, or shrubs. The flowers are of a blue, white, or red color, having two stamens. *V. Virginica* has a white corolla. *V. officinalis*, or common speedwell, was once extensively used as a substitute for tea, and also as a tonic and diuretic. *V. Teucrium*, or germander-leaved speedwell, has much the same properties as common speedwell, and *V. Chamaedrys*, or germander speedwell, is a very general favorite, on account of its being among the very first that opens its flowers in the early spring.

SPEER, ROBERT ELLIOTT, an American missionary secretary, born in Huntingdon, Pa., in 1867. He graduated from Princeton University in 1889, and from the Princeton Theological Seminary in the following year. In 1891 he was appointed secretary of the Presbyterian Board of Foreign Missions, and made tours in connection with this work in China, Persia, Korea, and Japan in 1896-1897. In 1909 he visited South America, and in 1915 Japan, China, the Philippine Islands, and Siam. During the World War he was a member of the advisory committee on the religious and moral activities of the Army and Navy. He wrote "Missions and Politics in Asia" (1898); "Missionary Principles and Practice" (1902); "Christianity and the Nations" (1910); "South American Problems" (1912); "Studies in the Gospel of John" (1915).

SPEKE, JOHN HANNING, an African explorer; born near Bideford, England, in May, 1827. He entered the Indian army at the age of 17, served in Sir Colin Campbell's division through the campaign in the Punjab, and during his annual leave of absence made exploring expeditions in the Himalayas and in Tibet, especially studying the botany, geology, and natural history of the region, and collecting specimens. He subsequently accompanied Captain Burton in his exploration of Eastern Africa, and in 1858 reached the head of the great lake Nyanza, under the Mountains of the Moon, and since called Victoria Nyanza. Desirous of ascertaining whether the Nile has its source in that lake, he set out from Zanzibar in 1860, accompanied by Captain Grant, to find the S. end of the lake; and after heroic struggles against extraordinary difficulties succeeded in his object, spent some time on the shores of the Nyanza, and striking the Nile at Urondogoni retraced its course to the lake. His "Journal of the Discovery of the Source of the Nile" appeared in 1863, and a pamphlet, entitled "What Led to the Discovery of the Source of the Nile," in 1864. He died Sept. 15, 1864.

SPELLING REFORM, the purpose of which is to simplify spelling by the elimination of meaningless letters. In 1898 the American National Education Association adopted twelve words for simplification in spelling: program, tho, altho, thoro, thorofare, thru, thruout, catalog, prolog, decalog, demagog, and pedagog. In 1906 there was organized in New York the Simplified Spelling Board, headed by Prof. Brander Matthews and amply subsidized by Andrew Carnegie. This body drew up a plan for a revision of English spelling of a far more sweeping nature. The following are the chief changes recommended:

(a) The use of e instead of the diagraph æ, except at the end of a word; as in medieval, for mediæval.

(b) The elimination of the silent b before t, as dout for doubt.

(c) The use of e instead of ea in words having the short e sound; hed for head, welth for wealth.

(d) The elimination of the final gh when it is silent, as in thru for through, or tho for though; and the substitution of f in such words as laf for laugh.

(e) The substitution of er for re in such words as theatre and centre.

(f) The omission of the silent g and the silent k before n, as in nome for gnome, or naw for gnaw; and nife for knife.

(g) The substitution of f for ph when the latter is pronounced like f, as in fenomena for phenomena; or sfere for sphere.

A strong campaign was begun after the above plan was agreed upon to persuade newspaper editors throughout the country to lead the way in educating the people in the new idea. Special field agents were maintained, who spent their whole time traveling to interview local editors and school boards and to lecture before civic bodies. Some important publications have supported the movement, in part if not entirely, notably "The Outlook" and "The Literary Digest." Thousands of local newspapers also indicate in their columns their conversion to the idea. Undoubtedly there is sound logic on the side of the advocates of spelling reform, but the sentiment of the people for old forms seems inclined to give way before reason very slowly. This was well illustrated in the effort of Theodore Roosevelt to popularize simplified spelling in 1906. Being then President, Mr. Roosevelt issued an order instructing the public printer to adopt the simplified spelling in all documents prepared in the executive departments. In spite of his personal popularity, President Roosevelt was compelled, shortly afterward, to rescind this order, so strong and persistent was the popular protest against the innovation. In Great Britain and her colonies there has also been a movement for simplified spelling. In 1911 an official conference of all the educational departments of the Empire met in London, the delegates to which were appointed by their respective governments. This conference passed a resolution declaring simplified spelling "a matter of urgent importance." After this authoritative declaration, Nova Scotia, Australia and New Zealand instituted first steps in spelling reform in their departments of education.

SPELT, in botany, an inferior kind of wheat, *Triticum spleta;* called also German wheat. It has a stout, almost solid straw, with strong spikes of grain. It is more hardy than common wheat, and grows in Bavaria and other parts of Germany, in the south of France, and in elevated situations in Switzerland where common wheat would not ripen.

SPELTER, a commercial name for zinc; also a technical abbreviation of spelter-solder, an impure zinc of a yellowish color used in soldering brass joints. It is known in Germany as *gelbliches englischer zinte*, and possibly owes its color to the presence of a small amount of copper. The word is also applied to an alloy sometimes used in the composition of bell metal. See ZINC.

SPENCER, a town in Worcester co., Mass.; on the Boston and Albany railroad; 11 miles S. W. of Worcester. It contains the Richard Sugden Public Library, the David Prouty High School, a National bank, street railroad and electric light plants, and a number of weekly newspapers. It has manufactories of wire, boots, brass goods, shoes, and woolen goods. Pop. (1910) 6,740; (1920) 5,930.

SPENCER, HERBERT, an English philosopher; born in Derby, England, April 27, 1820. His father was a schoolmaster in that town. At the age of 17 he entered on the profession of a railway engineer, in London; but about eight years afterward he gave up this profession, which lacked interest for him. He had already contributed various papers to the "Civil Engineers' and Architects' Journal"; and in the later half of 1842 he wrote a series of letters to the "Nonconformist" newspaper on "The Proper

Sphere of Government," which were republished in pamphlet form in 1843. These letters imply a belief in human progress based on the modifiability of human nature through adaptation to its

HERBERT SPENCER

social surroundings, and maintain the tendency of these social arrangements "of themselves to assume a condition of stable equilibrium."

From 1848 to 1853 he was sub-editor of the "Economist" newspaper; and at this time he developed the ethical and political consequences of the ideas he had already enunciated, and sought an independent basis for them. Hence his first important work, "Social Statics" (1850; abridged and revised, 1892). It is thus noticeable that Spencer's philosophical activity began with ethical and social questions. The conception of the evolution of man and society as determined by circumstances, and the idea that organic and social evolutions are under the same law, preceded the elaboration of those scientific ideas which in the complete "System of Philosophy" are made to serve as their basis. It was gradually developed and applied by him in a series of articles contributed in the following years to reviews.

In these essays the doctrine of evolution began to take definite form, and to be applied to various departments of inquiry. The publication of Darwin's "Origin of Species," in 1859, gave a wide basis of scientific proof for what had hitherto been matter of speculation, and first showed the important part played by natural selection in the development of organisms.

As early as 1860 he had announced the issue of a "System of Synthetic Philosophy," already in course of preparation, which, beginning with the first principles of all knowledge, proposed to trace how the law of evolution was gradually realized in life, mind, society, and morality. In pursuance of this comprehensive design Spencer published "First Principles" (1862); "Principles of Biology" (2 vols. 1864-1867); "Principles of Psychology" (2d ed. 2 vols. 1870-1872); "Principles of Sociology" (3 vols. 1876-1896); "Principles of Ethics" (2 vols. 1879).

The method of his "System" is deductive; though the deductions, large and small, are always accompanied by inductive verifications.

Metaphysically Spencer's system is founded on the doctrine of relativity deduced by Hamilton and Mansel from Kant, but carried by him, as he says, a step further. Along with the definite consciousness of things known in relation to one another there is implied an indefinite consciousness of an absolute existence, in the recognition of which as inscrutable science and religion find their reconciliation.

The principles of morality are looked on by Spencer as the copestone of his system, all his other investigations being only preliminary to them. Ethics, he holds, has its root in physical, biological, psychological, and social phenomena, for by them the conditions of human activity are prescribed and supplied. The best conduct is that which most fully realizes evolution—which promotes the greatest totality of life in self, offspring, and the race—the balance of egoism and altruism being attained by a compromise between these contending principles. The measure of life is said to be pleasure, but the Utilitarian school is at fault in assuming that the end (greatest happiness) is better known than the means to it (morality); and in ignoring the fact that accumulated experiences of utility have become consolidated in the superior races into a moral sense.

Modern scientists are generally disposed to regard Spencer as out-of-date, but it should be remembered that he deeply influenced contemporary speculation and was one of the few modern thinkers who carried out the attempt to give a systematic account of the universe in its totality. He died December 8, 1903.

SPENCER, SELDEN PALMER, a United States Senator from Missouri, born in Erie, Pa., in 1862. He graduated from Yale in 1884, and from the law department of Washington University in 1886. He engaged in the practice of law in St. Louis in the same year. He served as a member of the State House of Representatives in 1895-1896, and as judge of the 8th Judicial Circuit of Missouri, from 1897 to 1903. He was a successful candidate for the United States Senate in 1905, and was elected in 1918 to fill the unexpired term of William J. Stone.

SPENCER GULF, an extensive inlet of South Australia; length about 200 miles, breadth at widest about 90 miles, and at inner extremity about 3 miles.

SPENDER, E. HAROLD, a British author and journalist, born at Bath, England, in 1864. He was educated at Bath College and was Exhibitioner at University College, Oxford. He went on the staff of the "Echo" in 1887, and in 1889 became lecturer for the Oxford University Extension Delegacy. He was on the staff of the "Pall Mall Gazette," 1891-1893; "Westminster Gazette," 1893-1895; "Daily Chronicle," 1895-1899; "Manchester Guardian," 1899-1900, and "Daily News," 1900-1914. He devoted himself to propaganda during the World War. His works include: "Story of the Home Rule Session"; "At the Sign of the Guillotine"; "Through the High Pyrenees"; "The Arena"; "Home Rule"; "General Botha"; "David Lloyd George."

SPENSER, EDMUND, one of the major English poets, born in London in 1552; educated at the Merchant Taylors' School and at Pembroke College, Cambridge. His parents were in moderate circumstances, and he owed his education to certain charitable foundations.

EDMUND SPENSER

His preparation for college was directed by Richard Mulcaster, one of the most famous schoolmasters of his time, who believed in educating not the mind alone, or the body alone, but "the whole man." Spenser's knowledge of the classics was extensive. and he had thorough command of French and Italian. In his time learning was regarded as a supreme test of a poet, and Spenser's mind was unusually sensitive to all intellectual influences: education, statecraft, theories of poetry, religious ideas, the Platonism that was at the foundation of Renaissance thought, mediæval romance and allegory, history and antiquities, to say nothing of the adventurous and colorful life about him. His friends were men like Raleigh and Sidney; his sympathies were with the progressive party, headed by Leicester and later by Essex, who urged that England's destinies were bound up in curbing the power of Spain, in establishing an English dominion in America, and in gaining the mastery of the sea.

All these interests, literary, philosophical, and political, are reflected in his poetry. He left Cambridge in 1576. For some time he was secretary to the Bishop of Rochester, and became interested in the political aspects of Puritanism. By 1579 he was in London, intimate with Sidney, planning to enter the service of the Earl of Leicester, with a considerable body of poetry ready for publication, and with plans already made for the writing of his great epic. In this year he published his first important poetical work, the "Shepheard's Calender," a collection of twelve pastoral eclogues, one for each month of the year. Some of the eclogues deal with the abuses in the church and constitute a defense of political Puritanism; others tell a poetical love story; there are also examples of the singing-match, of the dirge, of the panegyric, and other forms familiar to the pastoral *genre*. The learning, the variety of theme, the exquisite melody of his verse, proved that in the "new poet" England was hearing the first authentic voice of a muse that had been silent since the death of Chaucer.

At about the same time, Spenser wrote a satire in the form of a beast epic, "Mother Hubberd's Tale." This is a rogues progress of Fox and Ape. He satirizes the ignorance of the clergy, the folly of the upstart courtier, the new-fangleness of court life. He praises the brave courtier in lines that constitute a famous portrait of Sidney. He also introduces an episode in which the rogues steal the crown of the lion and bring the realm to destruction, identifying the fox-ape conspiracy with the plan of Burghley and Simier to bring about a marriage between Elizabeth and the Duke of Anjou. The Puritans looked with horror upon the proposed alliance. Sidney wrote in denunciation of it and

was excluded from court; Spenser, seeking to aid Leicester, "overshot himself" and was exiled to Ireland, in 1580, as secretary to Lord Grey.

Of Spenser's life in Ireland during the next few years we know little. He took with him some part of the "Faerie Queene," his greatest poem, and in 1589 he came in contact with Raleigh, read to him part of his poem, and was persuaded by him to go to London and present it to the Queen. In 1590 the first three books, one fourth the poem as he had planned it, were published, and immediately won fame. The poem was planned as the epic of the new England, celebrating the return of the old British line through the Welsh house of Tudor; interpreting certain cardinal events of the time; and pointing out England's destiny. This part of Spenser's design comes out in the chronicle passages, in the love of Arthur (the spirit of England, at times identified with Leicester) for Gloriana, the Faerie Queen (Elizabeth); and in such passages as the defense of Elizabeth's policy in the fifth book, the legend of Justice. Some of the great knights are to be identified with famous Englishmen, as Artegal for Lord Grey, Calidore for Sidney, and the like. Besides this historical and contemporary matter, the poem was to be a treatise on "the brave courtier," the Renaissance ideal of education. Arthur typifies Magnificence, or greatness of mind; Redcross stands for Holiness; Guyon for Temperance; Calidore for Courtesy, and the like. By this means all the virtues and qualities of the ideal man were to be represented. Finally, the poem is a treasury of romance. England is fairyland, as in the old romance of Malory, and men and their deeds, and the policies of imperial England are seen through the glass of enchantment. The poem might, therefore, be read as a moral allegory, as a political allegory, or simply as a treasury of romance. The long stanza lent itself to every variety of pictorial effect and of mood. Spenser can be dramatic, languorous, lyrical. He can be stern with moral fervor or sensuous and seductive. He has been called the painter of the English poets. The extraordinary richness and variety of his epic is seen not only in its poetical qualities, which have never been surpassed, but also in the way in which it sums up the thought and ideals of an epoch. Love of travel, of conquest, of science, of every form of philosophy; theories of the state and of conduct; the learning of a time when learning was held to be one of the highest ideals of the man of affairs as well as of the recluse—all these are found in combinations of the utmost subtlety and variation. At times the allegory is confusing to the lay reader, and the narrative seems inconsequent. It is not a poem that can be read continuously, but is rather for times and seasons. So read, one realizes the influence it has had on every great English poet since its publication.

After his great success, Spenser collected some earlier poems in a small anthology, wrote a charming pastoral called "Colin Clout's Come Home Againe," in which he told of his London experiences and paid tribute to Raleigh, and continued his epic. The second section of the poem, containing books IV-VI appeared in 1596. A fragment consisting of two cantos of Mutability was not printed until after his death; the design was only half finished. Besides the works already named there are many shorter poems, chief among them two marriage hymns of enduring beauty, a sonnet sequence addressed to the lady whom he married in 1595, and four hymns in which he expressed in perfect verse the mystical and Platonic philosophy with which his name is inseparably linked. He died in London in 1599.

SPERMACETI, a neutral, inodorous, and nearly tasteless, fatty substance, extracted from the oily matter of the head of the sperm whale by filtration and treatment with potash-ley. It is white, brittle, soft to the touch, sp. gr., 0.943 at 15°, melts from 38° to 47°, and is chiefly used in ointments and cerates. Spermaceti was formerly given as a medicine; now it is chiefly employed externally as an emollient and in the preparation of a blistering paper.

SPERM OIL, the oil of the spermaceti whale, which is separated from the spermaceti and the blubber (see SPERMACETI). This kind of oil is much purer than train oil, and burns away without leaving any charcoal on the wicks of lamps. In composition it differs but slightly from common whale oil.

SPERM WHALE, or CACHALOT, the *Physeter macrocephalus*, a species of cetacea belonging to the section of the whale order denominated "toothed" whales, generally met with in the Pacific, but occasionally also on the coast of Greenland. The large blunt head in an old male is sometimes thirty feet long, and forms about a third of the total length of the body; while the "blowholes" or S-shaped nostrils are situated in the front part of the head. The weight of an adult animal is estimated

at about 200 tons, and in a male 66 feet long the flipper measured 5 feet 3 inches, and the two-lobed tail fin has a breadth of nearly 20 feet. The top of the back is continued almost in a straight line from the upper part of the head; the belly is enormous, but the body thins off toward the wide tail. The color is a blackish-gray, which may exhibit greenish or bluish hues on the upper parts. The teeth of the lower jaw average each about three inches in length. This whale is of considerable commercial value. See SPERMACETI.

SPERRY, CHARLES STILLMAN, an American naval officer, born in Brooklyn, N. Y., in 1847. He graduated from the United States Naval Academy in 1866, and rising through the various grades, became a commander in 1894, captain in 1900, and rear-admiral in 1906. During the Spanish-American War he was on ordnance duty at the Brooklyn Navy Yard. He served in the Philippines, in command of the "Yorktown," in 1899, and took an active part in the campaign for the pacification of the islands. In 1903 he was appointed president of the Naval War College, and in 1907 was one of the American representatives at the Second Hague Conference. He was in command of the Second Squadron on the cruise of the American battleships around the world in 1908, was retired in 1909 and died in 1911.

SPERRY, ELMER AMBROSE, an American electrical engineer, born at Cortland, N. Y., in 1860. He was educated at the State Normal and Training School, Cortland, N. Y., and at Cornell University. He was the founder of the Sperry Electric Co., of Chicago; of the Sperry Electric Railway Co., Cleveland, Ohio, and of the Sperry Gyroscope Co., Brooklyn, N. Y. An inventor of great originality, he held over 400 patents in the United States and in Europe. His inventions included the gyro-compass, aeroplane and ship stabilizers, fire-control apparatus, electric chain mining machinery, arc lamps, etc. He was a member of the Naval Consulting Board and of many scientific societies. His inventions brought numerous awards. He was made president of the American Society of Mechanical Engineers in 1928.

SPEY, a river in Scotland, issues from a lake of the same name in Invernessshire, between Loch Laggan and Loch Lochy, flows N. E. through the beautiful valley of Strathspey, forming in part of its course part of the boundary between the counties of Elgin and Banff, and falls into the Moray Firth a little below

Garmouth, after a course of about 96 miles. It has a very rapid course, is used for floating down timber, and is noted for its salmon fisheries.

SPEYER, or **SPEIER** (French, Spires), the capital of the Bavarian Palatinate and the seat of a bishop; on the Rhine, 14 miles S. W. of Heidelberg. The most important buildings are the cathedral, the Hall of Antiquities, the Altpörtel, and the remains of the Retscher or imperial palace. The cathedral, reckoned the finest specimen of Romanesque architecture in Europe, was founded in 1030 by Konrad II. as a burial place for himself and his successors, and completed in 1061 by his grandson, Heinrich IV., the opponent of Pope Gregory the Great. On several occasions it suffered severely at the hands of the French, especially in 1794, when it was turned into a barn; but in 1822 it was reconstructed, and in 1858 the work of restoration was completed. Its length is 485 feet, breadth of nave nearly 50 feet, height of the four towers 237 feet. The interior is richly decorated with some of the finest specimens of modern German art. Speyer has cigar and vinegar works, and does a little transit trade on the Rhine. Under the Romans, Speyer was known as Augusto Nemetum, and during the Middle Ages it was a place of considerable importance, 29 imperial diets having been held within its walls, at one of which (1529) the Reformers offered the protest which procured for them the name of Protestants. During the wars of Louis XIV. in the Palatinate, Speyer was several times sacked by the French, and in 1689 the whole town was committed to the flames. Pop. about 25,000.

SPEZIA, the principal naval port of Italy; near the head of a deep and commodious bay on the W. side of the peninsula; 56 miles S. E. of Genoa. It was Napoleon I. who first recognized the suitability of this bay for the purposes to which the Italians, instigated thereto by Cavour, have now put it. An artificial breakwater (built in 1860), 2,400 feet long, covers the entrance; while formidable batteries of the heaviest artillery (supplemented by torpedo appliances) bristle on the hills that overlook the bay and on the island of Palmeria that guards its entrance. Here the Italians have constructed the great national arsenal, and build their large warships, and have their ship repairing yards and docks, and their naval victualling yards, store houses, etc. There are also in the town large barracks, a military hospital, as well as schools of

navigation, an iron foundry, and manufactures of cables, sail-cloth, and white lead. During the World War, Spezia was a naval port of great importance. The adjacent country produces excellent olive oil. The beauty of the bay and the lovely climate cause Spezia to be much frequented as a seaside resort. It was on the shores of this bay that Shelley spent the last few months of his life, while at the town of Spezia Charles Lever lived and wrote for some years. Pop. about 73,500.

SPEYER, SIR EDGAR, a British capitalist, born at Frankfort-on-Main, in 1862. He was educated at the Real Gymnasium, Frankfort-on-Main, Germany. He became a partner in his father's three firms—Speyer Bros., London; Speyer & Co., New York, and L. Speyer, Ellissen, Frankfort-on-Main. He was resident partner in the Frankfort

SIR EDGAR SPEYER

firm till 1887, when he took direction of the London house, and retired from the New York and Frankfort firms in 1914. He is one of the founders of the Whitechapel Art Gallery, and was in 1905 a member of the Company Law Amendment Committee. He was made a Baronet in 1906 and a Privy Councillor in 1909.

SPEYER, JAMES, an American banker, born in New York City, in 1861. He was educated in Germany, and in 1883 entered the banking house of his father, at Frankfort-on-the-Main. After service in the Paris and London branches, he was given charge of the New York branch, becoming finally head of the firm. He was one of the most prominent financiers in New York and was trustee and director in various financial and industrial organizations. He presented to the Teachers College of the Columbia University the Speyer School in 1902, and was trustee of Columbia and a director of several other educational and philanthropic institutions.

SPEZZIA, a Greek island at the entrance to the Gulf of Nauplia; area, 6½ square miles; pop. 6,899, engaged chiefly in commercial pursuits. The town of Spezzia has a good harbor.

SPHALERITE, or **ZINC BLENDE**, Native Zinc Sulphide. Also known as Blende and Black Jack, the iron which it usually contains giving it a black color. It is an important ore of zinc, containing approximately 67 per cent. of the metal. It is very widely distributed.

SPHERE, in astronomy, a term formerly applied to any one of the concentric and eccentric revolving transparent shells in which the heavenly bodies were supposed to be fixed, and by which they were carried so as to produce their apparent motions. The word now signifies the vault of heaven, which to the eye seems the concave side of a hollow sphere, and on which the imaginary circles marking the positions of the equator, the ecliptic, etc., are supposed to be drawn. It is that portion of limitless space which the eye is powerful enough to penetrate, and appears a hollow sphere because the capacity of the eye for distant vision is equal in every direction.

In geometry, a solid or volume bounded by a surface, every point of which is equally distant from a point within, called the center. Or it is a volume that may be generated by revolving a semicircle about its diameter as an axis. The distance from any part of the surface to the center is called a radius of the sphere. Every section of a sphere made by a plane is a circle, and all sections made by planes equally distant from the center are equal. A circle of the sphere whose plane passes through the center is a great circle; all other circles are small circles. All great circles are equal, and their radii are equal to the radii of the sphere. The surface of a sphere is equal to the product of the diameter by the circumference of a great circle; or it is equivalent to the area of four great circles. Denoting the radius of the sphere by r, and its diameter by d, we have the following formula for the surface:

$$s = 4pr^2 = pd^2 = 3.14159 \quad . \quad . \quad d^2.$$

The volume of a sphere is equal to the product of its surface by one-third of its radius. It is also equivalent to two-thirds of the volume of its circumscribing cylinder. The following formula gives the value of the volume of any sphere, whose radius is r and diameter is d: $v = \frac{4}{3} pr^6$. Spheres are to one another as the cubes of their diameters.

In logic, the extension of a general conception; the individuals and species comprised in any general conception. The doctrine of the sphere is the application of geometrical principles to geography and astronomy. An oblique sphere, or spherical projection, is the projection made on the plane of the horizon of any place not on the equator or at the poles.

SPHERICAL TRIGONOMETRY. See Trigonometry.

SPHEROID, in geometry, a solid, resembling a sphere in form, and generated by the revolution of an ellipse about one of its axes. If an ellipse be revolved about its transverse axis, the spheroid generated is called a prolate spheroid; if it be revolved about its conjugate axis, the spheroid generated is called an oblate spheroid. The earth is an oblate spheroid—that is, flattened at the poles so that its polar is less than its equatorial diameter.

SPHEX, a genus of hymenopterous insects of the family *Sphegidæ*, closely allied to the true wasps. The sphex wasps are solitary in habit, and there are no workers as in the social forms. The female hollows out, at the end of a long passage, three or four chambers, in each of which she deposits an egg and a store of food for the larva she will never see. The food consists of grasshoppers or other insects, and Fabre gives a minute account of the way in which the sphex attacks her victim, and, after a long and violent struggle, throws it on its back and stings it in the neck and between the thorax and abdomen, each time piercing a ganglion. The insect, completely paralyzed, but alive, and therefore not liable to putrefaction, is then dragged to the mouth of the nest, where it is relinquished for a short time while the wasp enters alone to see that all is right. So automatic is this habit of reconnoitering that if the grasshopper be removed a little distance the wasp drags it back to the same spot and again enters alone. This was tested by the observer 40 times in succession, and each time the wasp paid her preliminary visit of inspection. Four paralyzed insects are placed in each chamber, which is sealed up as it is finished. When all are full the mouth of the passage is also closed, and the nest is abandoned.

SPHINX, a Greek word signifying the "strangler," applied to certain symbolical forms of Egyptian origin, having the body of a lion, a human or an animal head, and two wings. Various other

EGYPTIAN SPHINX

combinations of animal forms have been called by this name, though they are rather griffins or chimæras. Human-headed sphinxes have been called androsphinxes; that with the head of a ram, a criosphinx; and that with a hawk's head, a hieracosphinx. The form when complete had the wings added at the sides; but these are of a later period and seem to have originated with the Babylonians or Assyrians. In the Egyptian hieroglyphics the wingless sphinx bears the name of *Neb,* or lord, and *Akar,* or intelligence, corresponding to the account of Clement that this emblematic figure depicted intellect and force. Others see in it the idea of resurrection, symbolized by the triumph of the dawn over the darkness of night. The idea that it allegorized the overflow of the Nile when the sun was in the constellations Leo and Virgo appears to be unfounded. In Egypt the sphinx also occurs as the symbolical form of the monarch considered as a conqueror, the head of the reigning king being placed on a lion's body, the face bearded, and the usual head dress. Thus used, the sphinx was generally male; but in the case of female rulers that figure has a female head and the body of a lioness.

The most remarkable sphinx is the Great Sphinx at Gizeh (Gîza), a colossal form hewn out of the natural rock, and lying about a quarter of a mile S. E. of the Great Pyramid. It is sculptured out of a spur of the rock itself, to which masonry has been added in certain places to complete the shape, and it measures 172 feet 6 inches long by 56 feet high (Vyse, "Pyramids" iii: 107). Immediately in front of the breast Caviglia found in 1816 a small naos or chapel, formed of three hieroglyphic tablets,

dedicated by Thothmes III. and Rameses II. to the sphinx, whom they adore under the name of Haremkhu, or Harmachis, as the Greek inscriptions found at the same place call it—*i. e.,* the Sun on the Horizon. These tablets formed three walls of the chapel; the fourth, in front, had a door in the center and two couchant lions over it. A small lion was found on the pavement, and an altar between its fore paws, apparently for sacrifices offered to it in the time of the Romans. Before the altar was a paved causeway or dromos leading to a walled staircase of 30 steps repaired in the reign of M. Aurelius and L. Verus on May 10, 166, A. D. In the reigns of Severus and his sons, A. D. 199-200, another dromos, in the same line as the first, and a diverging staircase were constructed., while some additions had been made to the parts between the two staircases in the reign of Nero. Votive inscriptions of the Roman period, some as late as the 3d century, were discovered in the walls and constructions; and on the second digit of the left claw of the sphinx an inscription in pentameter Greek verses, by one Arrian, probably of the time of Severus, was discovered. In addition to these walls of unburnt brick, galleries and shafts were found in the rear of the sphinx extending toward the N.

To the S. of the sphinx Mariette in 1852 found a dromos which led to a temple of the time of the 4th dynasty, built of huge blocks of alabaster and red granite. In the midst of the great chamber of this temple were found seven diorite statues, five mutilated and two entire, of the

GREEK SPHINX

monarch Chafra or Chephren, which are fine examples of the oldest Egyptian sculpture. Later discoveries prove it to have been a monument of at least the age of the 4th dynasty, or contemporary with the pyramids.

Besides the Great Sphinx, avenues of sphinxes have been discovered at Sakkara, forming an approach to the Serapeum of Memphis, and elsewhere.

SPHINX

Sphinxes of the time of the Shepherd dynasty have been found at Tanis, and another of the same age is in the Louvre; while a granite sphinx, found behind the "vocal Memnon," and inscribed with the name of Amenophis III., is at Petrograd. An avenue of criosphinxes, each about 17 feet long, is still seen at Karnak, and belongs to the time of Horus, one of the last monarchs of the 18th dynasty. Various small sphinxes are in the different collections of Europe, but seldom are of any very great antiquity.

The Theban sphinx of Greek legend, whose myth first appears in Hesiod, is described as having a lion's body, female head, bird's wings, and serpent's tail, ideas probably derived from Phœnician sources. She was said to be the issue of Orthros, the two-headed dog of Geryon, by Chimæra, or of Typhon and Echidna, and was sent from Ethiopa to Thebes by Hera to punish the transgression of Laius, or according to other accounts, by Dionysus or Ares. The sphinx was a favorite subject of ancient art, and appears in reliefs, on coins of Chios and others towns, and often as a decoration of arms and furniture. In Assyria and Babylonia representations of sphinxes have been found, and the same are not uncommon on Phœnician works of art.

SPHINX BABOON, the *Cynocephalus sphinx*, a large species from the west of Africa. They are good-tempered and playful when young, but become morose and fierce as they grow older. They bear confinement well, and are common in menageries.

SPHINX MOTH (*Sphinx Convolvuli*), a species of moth belonging to the family *Sphingidae*, and deriving its popular name from a supposed resemblance which its caterpillars present when they

raise the fore part of their bodies to the "sphinx" of Egyptian celebrity. The sphinx moth is common in some parts of the United States.

SPICE ISLANDS. See MOLUCCAS.

SPICES, aromatic and pungent vegetable substances used as condiments and for flavoring food. They are almost exclusively the productions of tropical countries. In ancient times and throughout the Middle Ages all the spices known in Europe were brought from the East; and Arabia was regarded as the land of spices, but rather because they came through it or were brought by its merchants than because they were produced in it, for they were really derived from farther E. They owe their aroma and pungency chiefly to essential oils which they contain. They are yielded by different parts of plants; some, as pepper, cayenne pepper, pimento, nutmeg, mace, and vanilla, being the fruit or particular parts of the fruit; while some, as ginger, are the root stock; and others, as cinnamon and cassia, are the bark. Tropical America produces some of the spices, being the native region of cayenne pepper, pimento, and vanilla; but the greater number are from the East.

SPIDER, in zoölogy, the popular name of any individual of Huxley's *Araneina*. The species are very numerous and universally distributed, the largest being found in the tropics. The abdomen is

BIRD SPIDER

without distinct divisions, and is generally soft and tumid; the legs are eight in number, seven-jointed, the last joint armed with two hooks usually toothed like a comb. The distal joint of the falces is folded down on the next, like the blade of a pocket knife on the handle, and the duct of a poison gland in the cephalothorax opens at the summit of the terminal joint. There are two or four pulmonary sacs and a tracheal system; eyes generally eight in number; no auditory organs have been discovered. Their most characteristic organ is the arachnidium, the apparatus by which fine silky threads—in the majority of the species utilized for spinning a web—are produced. In *Epeira diadema*, the common garden spider, more than 1,000 glands, with separate excretory ducts, secrete the viscid material of the web. These ducts ultimately enter the six prominent arachnidial mammillæ, projecting from the hinder end of the ab-

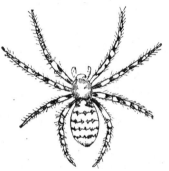

ORB SPIDER

domen, and having their terminal faces beset with minute arachnidial papillæ, by which the secretion of the gland is poured out.

By means of these silky threads, spiders form their dwellings and construct ingenious nets for the capture of their prey; these threads serve also as a safeguard against falling, and as a means of support from one elevated object to another, being thrown out as a sort of flying bridge. The webs are in high repute for stanching blood; the threads are employed for the cross lines in astronomical telescopes, and have been made into textile fabrics as articles of curiosity. Spiders are essentially predaceous. The fate of the victim is always the same—the claw joints of the falces are buried in the body, inflicting a poisonous wound, and the juices are then sucked out by the muscular apparatus appended to the œsophagus of the spider. The bite of none of the species is dangerous to man. (See TARANTULA.) They are extremely pugnacious, and in their combats often sustain the loss of a limb, which, like the Crustaceans, they have the power of reproducing. The eggs are numerous, and usually enveloped in a cocoon or egg case; the young undergo no metamorphosis.

SPIDER FLY (*Ornithomyia*), a genus of dipterous insects, chiefly allied to the forest fly. The genus are parasitical on

birds, never on quadrupeds. *O. avicularia* frequently infests the common fowl, the

SPIDER FLY

blackcock, and other birds. It is greenish-yellow, with smoke-colored wings.

SPIDER MONKEY, a general name applied to many species of platyrhine or New World monkeys, but more especially to the members of the genus *Ateles*, which are distinguished by the great relative length, slenderness, and flexibility of their limbs, and by the prehensile power of their tails. A familiar

SPIDER MONKEY

species is the chameck (*A. Chameck*), which occurs abundantly in Brazil. The body is about 20 inches, the tail 2 feet long, and the color is a general black. The coaita (*A. panicus*), another typical species, has an average length of 12 inches; the tail measures over 2 feet long, and the fur is of a glossy black hue.

SPIDERWORT, the common name of plants of the genus *Tradescantia*, one species of which, *T. virginica*, is cultivated in gardens.

SPIEGELEISEN, a name applied to a variety of cast iron which is coarsely crystalline, the large crystal planes having bright reflections. It contains about 5 per cent. carbon and considerable manganese. See IRON and STEEL.

SPIELHAGEN, FRIEDRICH, a German novelist; born in Magdeburg, Feb. 24, 1829, but passed all his youth at Stralsund. From the gymnasium there he proceeded in 1847 to the universities successively of Bonn, Berlin, and Greifswald, afterward settling at Leipsic in 1854 as a docent, at Hanover in 1859, and at Berlin in 1862, in the last two places till 1884 as a newspaper editor. His works, of which eight have been translated into English, are some 30 in number, in over 50 volumes, and include: "Klara Vere" (1857) ; "On the Dunes" (1858) ; "Enigmatical Natures" (1860) ; "The Von Hohensteins" (1863) ;

FRIEDRICH SPIELHAGEN

"Little Rose of the Court" (1864) ; "In Rank and File" (1866) ; "The Village Coquette" (1868) ; "Hammer and Anvil" (1868) ; "Ever Onward" (1872) ; "Ultimo" (1873) ; "The Freshet" (1876) ; "Quisisana" (1879-1880) ; "Angela" (1881) ; "Uhlenhans" (1884) ; "Noblesse Oblige" (1888) ; "A New Pharaoh" (1889) ; "Susi" (1895) ; and many dramatic works and much miscellany. He died in 1911.

SPIKE, in botany, that kind of inflorescence in which sessile flowers, or flowers having very short stocks, are arranged around an axis, as in the greater plantain, common vervain, common lavender, and some species of sedge. In rye, wheat, barley, darnel, and many other grasses there is a sort of compound spike—i. e., the flowers or fruits are arranged together in spikelets on short stalks, which again surround the top of the culm in the form of a spike. The catkin, the spadix, and the cone may be regarded as varieties of the spike.

SPIKENARD, in botany: (1) Nardostachys jatamansi, called in Hindustan jatamansi and balckhar. The root, which is from 3 to 12 inches long, sends up many stems, with little spikes of purple flowers, which have four stamens. It grows in the Himalayas at an elevation of from 11,000 to 15,000, or in Sikkim to 17,000 feet. (2) Valeriana celtica, and in various countries other plants.

In perfumes, an aromatic substance derived from the root of Nardostachys jatamansi. It was highly prized by the ancients, and used by them both in baths and at feasts as an unguent. The "ointment of spikenard" with which our Lord was anointed as He sat at meat in the house of Simon of Bethany was prepared from it.

SPINACH, or SPINAGE, a wholesome though somewhat insipid vegetable, consisting of the leaves of Spinacia oleracea, a diœcious annual belonging to the natural order Chenopodiaceæ. It is a native of Siberia, whence it passed W., reaching England more than three centuries ago. Three varieties are in cultivation—the round-seeded, the Flanders, and the prickly-seeded, which unitedly yield a continued supply from April to November, and to a moderate extent through winter and spring. The plant is of rapid growth, but that the leaves may be succulent and properly flavored the soil should be rich and the situation open and airy. S. tetrandra, from the Caucasus, an annual and unisexual herb, is of equal value to the preceding, though less known. The name has also been given to several plants not belonging to Spinacia. New Zealand spinach is Tetragonia expansa, a trailing plant with thick succulent leaves, natives of Australasia, South America, and Japan. Patience spinach (Rumex patientia) was formerly common in gardens. The beet spinach (Beta cicla), a native of the seashores in southern Europe, has long been grown for its leaves, which are dressed in the same manner as spinach.

SPINAL ANÆSTHESIA, insensibility to pain produced by injecting an anæsthetic into the spinal fluid. It was first used by Dr. Leonard Corning, of New York, in the year 1885, and in Europe by August Bier, of Berlin. It is chiefly of value where the health of the patient renders general anæsthesia inadvisable, as, for instance, in diseases of the respiratory organs, in alcoholism or diabetes. It is generally employed for operations on the lower part of the body, the injection being made through the fourth lumbar interspace while the patient is sitting in an upright position. Jonnesco, of Bucharest, however, injected the anæsthetic into the dorsal region of the spinal canal, and was thus able to anæsthetize and operate on the upper part of the body. Cocaine was used in the earlier experiments, but eucaine, novocaine and stovaine were later substituted as being less toxic. Jonnesco used a mixture of stovaine and strychnine. When only the lower part of the body is to be operated on, it is possible to anæsthetize that part only, the patient retaining consciousness throughout the operation. Generally speaking, spinal anæsthesia is more common on the European continent than in the United States or in England. In the latter countries it is looked upon only as a substitute for general anæsthesia. It frequently produces undesirable after effects, including general weakness, nausea, and even partial temporary paralysis. Jonnesco's method of application is looked upon as dangerous, although it is claimed in Europe that it is no more dangerous than general anæsthesia and that the percentage of deaths is even less. It is possible that its use may develop as improvements in methods of application are worked out.

SPINAL CORD, the name given in anatomy to the great cord or rod of nervous matter which is inclosed within the backbone or spine of vertebrates. The spinal cord in man, which is from 15 to 18 inches long, has direct connection with the brain by means of the medula oblongata, and passes down the back till it terminates in a fine thread at the level of the first lumbar vertebra. Lodged in the bony vertebræ it varies in thickness throughout, and like the brain is invested by membranes called respectively *pia mater* and *dura mater*. Situated between these two are the delicate layers of the *arachnoid* membrane, inclosing a space which contains the cerebrospinal fluid. Besides these protective coverings there is also a packing of fatty tissue which further tends to diminish all shocks and jars. The spinal nerves, to the number of 31 on each side, pass out from the cord at regular intervals, pierce the *dura mater*, escape from the backbone, and ramify thence through the soft parts of the body. Eight pairs pass off in the region of the neck called the cervical nerves, 12 pairs are dorsal, 5 are lumbar, and 5 sacral, while the last pair comes off behind the coccyx. In its structure the spinal cord consists of gray and white matter. The gray matter, which is characterized by large cells, is gathered in the center into two crescent-shaped masses connected at the central part of the cord. The white matter, consisting mainly of fibers, is outside of and surrounds these gray crescents. In its functions the spinal cord forms a tract along which sensory

1—3

impressions may pass to the brain, and along which motor impulses may travel to the muscles. It is besides a great reflex center. See BRAIN: NERVE: SPINE.

SPINAL MENINGITIS, an inflamma-tion of the meninges, the membranes covering the spinal cord. The membranes are three in number: the *pia mater*, which is in contact with the substance of the cord; the *dura mater*, which serves as a lining to the spinal canal; and the *arachnoid*, a webbed structure between the *pia mater* and the *dura mater*. An inflammation affecting the meninges of both the brain and the cord is called cerebrospinal meningitis. In spinal meningitis all three membranes are usually involved. Acute spinal meningitis is often caused by sunstroke, exposure to cold, and injury to the spine, and is occasionally a complication in cases of scarlatina, typhoid fever and pneumonia. The preliminary symptoms include pain, chill, fever, vomiting and a general sense of disarrangement. The shooting pains in the region of the cord are rendered more acute when the back is touched or moved, and the pain is transmitted to those parts of the body with which the cold is immediately connected, and in extreme cases the paroxysms may lead to a chronic bending of the spinal column. After a period of fever lasting some days a condition of paralysis supervenes which may result in death from exhaustion. Where the patient recovers convalescence is usually protracted over several months, but where the illness is long drawn out complications in the renal and vesical regions may lead to a fatal issue. The *pia mater* in these cases becomes congested and reddish with the accompaniment of hemorrhages. There is an issue of matter varying in color from gray to green on the surface of the *pia*, with congestion of the spinal fluid. Inflammation may pass from one membrane to another, as well as to the substance of the spinal cord, and free action may be prevented to such an extent that the membranes may be held together. The malady may be acute or chronic, and the chronic differs from the acute chiefly in the fact that the processes are prolonged, and there is an absence of fever. In acute cases, complete rest in bed is the first requisite, care being taken that there is no pressure on the affected parts. The bowels should be kept clean, the spine should be cupped, and ice afterward applied. Where the pain is great suitable drugs may be administered to give relief. Recourse may be added to external counter-irritants to assuage the pain in the spine. In chronic and prolonged cases cold douches and such treatment as will relieve the inflammation will greatly help the patient.

SPINAL NERVES, the name applied to the paired nerves which arise from the spinal cord, and which are distributed to the various parts of the body. The spinal nerves are so named in contradistinction to the cranial nerves, or those which originate from the brain itself. Thirty-one pairs of spinal nerves arise from the spinal cord of man. They pass from the spinal cord and spine through the intervertebral foramina, or openings between the bodies of the vertebræ. Eight pairs are cervical; 12 are dorsal nerves, also named thoracic; 5 are lumbar, 5 sacral, and 1 coccygeal. Each spinal nerve arises by two roots, an anterior and posterior, from the spinal column. The posterior root has a nerve mass or ganglion, which is wanting in the anterior. The fibers of the anterior roots are motor in nature, *i. e.*, impulses travel by these roots outward from the cord or brain to the body. The fibers of the posterior roots are sensory, *i. e.*, impulses are conveyed by these fibers to the cord or brain. The anterior and posterior fibers unite just beyond the nervous ganglion to form a single nerve trunk, in which the two sets of fibers are indistinguishable. See NERVE.

SPINDLE, in spinning, a pendent piece of wood for twisting and winding the fibers drawn from the distaff, or the pin used in spinning wheels for twisting the thread, and on which the thread, when twisted, is wound. It is applied also to a measure of yarn: in cotton a spindle of 18 hanks is 15,120 yards; in linen a spindle of 24 heers is 14,400 yards.

SPINE, the term applied to the backbone of a vertebrated animal, and so called from the thorn-like processes of the vertebræ. The human vertebral column is composed, in the child, of 33 separate pieces, but in the adult the number is only 26, several pieces having become blended together. These separate bones are arranged one on the top of the other, with a layer of gristle between each which helps to unite them, while this union is completed by partially movable joints and strong fibrous ligaments. The first 7 vertebræ, which are called cervical, occupy the region of the neck; 12 form the supports from which spring the ribs, and constitute the main portion of the back, being accordingly called dorsal; 5 in "the small of the back" are denominated lumbar; 5 pieces follow which, in the adult, unite to form

the sacrum; and 4 which unite to form the coccyx. The vertebral column so arranged presents two forward curves, the first in the neck, the second at the lower part of the back; and two corresponding backward curves. The vertebræ differ in form according as they belong to the cervical, dorsal, or lumbar region, but they have all certain characteristics in common. Each possesses what is called a body, an arch which incloses a ring, and various projections and notches by means of which the bones are articulated. When the vertebræ are in position the rings are all situated one above the other, and so form a cavity or canal in which lies the protected spinal cord. The disease to which this bony structure is most liable is called angular curvature of the spine. Beginning with inflammation it goes on to ulceration (caries), till one or more of the vertebræ becomes soft and breaks down. The result of this is that the vertebræ are crushed together, the backbone bent, and a projection or hump gradually formed behind. The modern method of treatment is to apply to the patient's body, from the hips to the arm pits, a continuous bandage of plaster of Paris. Lateral curvature of the spine is not so much due to disease of the column as to a relaxed condition of the body. Strengthening food, regular, moderate exercise, and cold bathing may prove sufficient to effect a cure.

SPINE, in botany, a sharp process from the woody part of a plant. It differs from a prickle, which proceeds from the bark. A spine sometimes terminates a branch, and sometimes is axillary, growing at an angle formed by the branch or leaf with the stem. The wild apple and pear are armed with spines; the rose, bramble, gooseberry, etc., are armed with prickles. The term is applied in zoölogy to a stout, rigid, and pointed process of the integument of an animal, formed externally by the epidermis and internally of a portion of the cutis or corresponding structure.

SPINEL, in mineralogy: (1) The type species of a group of minerals called the spinel group, crystallizing in the isometric system, and being compounds of protoxides and sesquioxides with the typical formula ROR_2O_3. (2) A mineral ocurring in crystals of octahedral habit, and very rarely massive. Hardness, 8.0; sp. gr., 3.5-4.1; luster, vitreous to splendent, sometimes dull; color, many shades of red, also blue, green, yellow, brown, and black; sometimes nearly white, or colorless; transparent to opaque; fracture, conchoidal. Composition: When pure, alumina, 72.0; magnesia, 28.0=100, corresponding with the formula, $MgOAl_2O_3$; but the magnesia is often partly replaced by other protoxides, and the alumina by sesquioxides, giving rise to many varieties. Dana thus distinguishes them:

(1) Ruby or magnesia-spinel; with sp. gr. 3.52-3.58; (a) spinel-ruby, deep red: (b) balas-ruby, rose-red; (c) rubicelle, yellow or orange-red; (d) almandine, violet.

(2) Ceylonite, or iron-magnesia spinel =pleonaste, containing much iron; color, dark green to black.

(3) Magnesia-lime-spinel; color, green.

(4) Chlorospinel; color, grass-green, with the iron constituent as sesquioxide.

(5) Picotite, containing over 7 per cent of oxide of chromium.

SPINET, in music, a musical stringed instrument resembling the harpsichord, and, like that instrument, now superseded by the pianoforte. Each note had but one string, which was struck by a quilled jack acted on by one of the finger keys. The strings were placed horizontally, and nearly at right angles to the keys; and the general outline of the instrument resembled that of a harp laid in a horizontal position, on which account the spinet, when first introduced, was called the couched harp.

SPINGARN, JOEL ELIAS, an American educator and author, born in New York in 1875. He was educated at Columbia and Harvard and from 1899 to 1911 was successively tutor, adjunct-professor, and professor of comparative literature at Columbia University. He took an active interest in politics as a Progressive Republican, was chairman of the board of directors of the National Association for the Advancement of Colored People, and in 1919 became a member of the board of directors of a New York publishing house. During the World War he was a major of infantry. He wrote: "A History of Literary Criticism in the Renaissance" (1899); "The New Criticism" (1911); "The New Hesperides and Other Poems" (1911); "Creative Criticism" (1917). He also edited "Critical Essays of the Seventeenth Century" (3 vols. 1908-1909); "Temple's Essays" (1909), etc.

SPINOZA, BARUCH, or BENEDICT DE SPINOZA, a Dutch philosopher; born in Amsterdam, Holland, November 24, 1632. He was trained in Talmudic and other Hebrew lore by Rabbi Morteira; acquired a knowledge of Latin from the freethinking physician Van den Ende; came under the influence of the new philosophic teaching of Descartes; ceased to attend the synagogue; refused a pension offered by the rabbis for his conformity, and was expelled from the Israelitish community; fled from Amsterdam to the suburbs to escape the enmity of the fanatical Jews; removed from thence, after five years' seclusion, to Rynsburg, where he lived till 1663; subsequently went to Voorburg; and ultimately (1671) settled in The Hague. By his craft as a grinder of optical lenses he maintained a frugal position in the households of the friends with whom he lived. He refused a pension from the French king and a professorship in Heidelberg because their acceptance might hazard freedom of thought and conduct; but he accepted a legacy from his friend De Vries. The first result of his labor was published anonymously in 1670 under the title of "Theological-Political Tract," and because it put forth a strong plea for liberty of speech in philosophy it was placed on the "Index" by the Catholics and condemned by the authorities in Holland. Such, indeed, was the storm which this treatise occasioned that the author himself published nothing further. After his death all his unpublished writings were conveyed to Amsterdam, and there the "Posthumous Works" was published (1677). In the "Ethics," therein included, his system of philosophy was developed; each of its five books being dignified by a series of axioms and definitions after the method of Euclid in his geometry. In all there are 27 definitions, 20 axioms, and 8 postulates; and the central conception of the whole system is that God, who is the inherent cause of the universe, is one absolutely infinite substance, of which all the several parts which we recognize are but finite expressions; that man, being but a part of this greater whole, has neither a separate existence nor a self-determining will; but that he can, by means of knowledge and love, so far control his passions as to enter into the joy which springs from this idea of an all-embracing God. He died February 21, 1677.

SPIRAL, in geometry, a curve which may be generated by a point moving along a straight line, in the same direction, according to any law, while the straight line revolves uniformly about a fixed point, always continuing in the same plane. The portion generated during one revolution is called a spire. The moving point is the generatrix of the curve, the fixed point is the pole of the spiral, and the distance from the pole to any position of the generatrix is the radius vector of that point. The law according to which the generatrix moves along the revolving line is the law of the spiral, and determines the nature of the curve. Any position of the revolving line, assumed at pleasure, is called the initial line. Spirals are known by the names of their inventors, or by terms derived from the properties by which they are characterized; as, the spiral of Archimedes, hyperbolic spirals, logarithmic spirals, parabolic spirals, etc. Also a helix or curve wound screw-wise round a cylinder.

SPIRAL NEBULÆ, luminous heavenly areas occupied according to a prevalent theory by aggregations of stars and other matter such as compose the Galaxy or Milky Way. They are supposedly millions of light years distant, and in most known cases are receding. Observations of the spiral nebulæ were conducted by Dr. Edwin Hubble (1923-28) at the Mount Wilson Observatory, with the aid of the 100-inch telescope and of photographic apparatus. According to the results of these studies, there were evidences of some 2,000,000 spiral nebulæ existing in space, beyond the limits of the Milky Way, which has been supposed to be itself a spiral nebula, or analogous body. Photographs of some 400 spiral nebulæ were studied by Dr. Hubble and these nebulæ were found to be distributed in space with a certain apparent uniformity as to intervening distances. Dr. Walter S. Adams of the Mt. Wilson observatory reported in December, 1928, that the 100-inch telescope had revealed a spiral nebula, the most distant object of which measurement had yet been attempted, receding at the phenomenal rate of 2,500 miles a second. This motion was attributed to a distortion effect due to the curvature of space.

SPIRES. See SPEYER.

SPIRIT, an immaterial intelligent substance or being; vital or active principle, essence, force, or energy, as distinct from matter; life or living substance considered apart from material or corporeal existence; as the soul of man, as distinguished from the body wherein it dwells. Hence, a ghost; a specter; a supernatural apparition or manifestation; also, sometimes, an elf; a fay; a sprite. Also, real meaning; intent; in contradistinction to the letter or to formal statement; and characteristic quality, particularly such as is derived from the individual genius or the personal character; as, the spirit of the law.

In chemistry, a name generally applied to fluids, mostly of a lighter specific character than water, and obtained by distillation. Thus, the essential oil of turpentine is called spirit of turpentine. Essential oils dissolved in alcohol are called spirits, as spirit of aniseed, peppermint, etc., because formerly prepared by distilling the herbs with alcohol. The volatile alkali ammonia, distilled and condensed in cold alcohol, is called spirit of ammonia; even hydrochloric acid is often called spirit of salts. But in a stricter sense the term spirit is understood to mean alcohol in its potable condition, of which there are very numerous varieties deriving their special characters from the substances used in their production, as brandy, rum, whisky, gin, arrack, etc.

In theology, the Spirit, or Holy Spirit, the Holy Ghost; the Spirit of God, or the third person of the Trinity. The spirit also denotes the human spirit as animated by the Divine Spirit. Rectified spirit, proof spirit made pure by distillation.

SPIRIT LEVEL, an instrument used for determining a line or plane parallel to the horizon, and also the relative heights of two or more stations. It consists of a glass tube nearly filled with alcohol, preferably colored. The remaining space in the tube is a bubble of air, and this occupies a position exactly in the middle of the tube when the latter is perfectly horizontal. The tube is mounted on a wooden bar, which is laid on a beam or other object to be tested; or it is mounted on a telescope or theodolite, and forms the means of bringing these instruments to a level, the slightest deviation from the horizontal position being indicated by the bubble rising toward the higher end of the tube. Spirit level quadrant, an instrument furnished with a spirit level and used for taking altitudes.

SPIRITUALISM, the term used in philosophy to indicate the opposite of materialism, and the belief in the existence and life of the spirit apart from, and independent of, the material organism, and in the reality and value of intelligent intercourse between spirits embodied and spirits disembodied. The belief in spirit manifestations has long obtained, but in its limited and modern form spiritualism dates from the Fox sisters in 1848. In this year a Mr. and Mrs. Fox, who lived with their two daughters, Margaret and Leah, at Hydeville, N. Y., were disturbed by repeated and inexplicable rappings throughout the house. At length it was accidentally discovered by one of the daughters that the unseen "rapper" was so intelligent as to be able to reply to various pertinent questions, and so communicative as to declare that he was the spirit of a murdered peddler. When this discovery was noised abroad a be-

lief that intercourse could be obtained with the spirit world became epidemic, and numerous "spirit circles" were formed in various parts of America. The manifestations thus said to be received from the spirit were rappings, table turnings, musical sounds, writings, the unseen raising of heavy bodies, and the like. The first professional medium who visited Europe was a Mrs. Hayden, and she was followed in 1855 by Daniel D. Home, who visited nearly all the courts of Europe. He claimed to possess unusual powers, and was said to be able to float up to the ceiling or out of the window into the next room. Such claims not only attracted the curious and converted the unthinking, but also received the attention of legal and scientific men. In America, Judge Edmonds and Professor Hare undertook to expose their fallacy, but both had to admit the genuineness of some of the evidence; while in England such eminent converts as A. R. Wallace, W. Crookes, F. R. S., and Professor De Morgan were inclined to put their credence in the truth of the phenomena. The London Dialectical Society appointed a committee to investigate the phenomena, and the report (1871) admits the genuineness of the phenomena, but does not seek to explain their origin. In the United States, the believers in spiritualism are very numerous, and have many newspapers, magazines, and books to explain and enforce their belief. In 1884 the London Spiritualist Alliance was founded, and was incorporated in 1896. The chief work of the society has been to maintain and expound the principles of spiritualism. In the United States a National Spiritualist Association was organized at Washington, D. C., in 1893. There were in 1920 about 1,000 working societies throughout the country; 22 state associations; 32 camp meeting organizations and perhaps 1,000 local associations in various cities and towns. There were 200 churches; 500 ordained ministers, and 600,000 members. It is estimated that there are about 1500 public mediums throughout the United States. See PSYCHICAL RESEARCH.

The Belief.—The popular belief seems to be that the phenomena of spiritualism are the result either of self-delusion on the part of believers, unconscious deception on the part of the medium, or clever conjuring. The more recent investigations of the Psychical Society seem to show that there are forces connected with hypnotism and its kindred phenomena which may explain the occult occurrences of spiritualism on natural, though hitherto little known, laws. The belief of spiritualism is that our exist-

ence in this world is but one stage in an endless career; that the whole material world exists simply for the development of spiritual beings, death being but a transition from this existence to the first grade of spirit life; that our thoughts and deeds here will affect our conditions later; and that our happiness and progress depend wholly on the use we make of our opportunities and faculties on this plane.

SPITHEAD, a roadstead on the S. coast of England, and a favorite rendezvous of the British navy; is the E. division—the SOLENT (*q. v.*) being the W.—of the strait that separates the Isle of Wight from the mainland. It is protected from all winds, except those from the S. E., and its noted security warranted the name which has been applied to it by sailors of the "King's bed-chamber." It receives its name from the "Spit," a sandbank stretching S. from the Hampshire shore for 3 miles; and it is 14 miles long by about 4 miles in average breadth. Spithead has been strongly defended since 1864 by fortifications completing those of Portsmouth.

SPITZBERGEN, or **SVALBARD ISLANDS,** a group of islands in the Arctic Ocean; between lat. 76° 30′ and 80° 40′ N.; lon. 9° and 22° E. The archipelago was annexed by Norway in 1925. The largest islands are West Spitzbergen and Northeast Land. Total area about 27,000 square miles. The coasts present immense glaciers and mountain chains, some of which exceed 4,000 feet in height. The climate is intensely cold; and vegetation is confined to a few plants of rapid growth. For four months in winter the sun is below the horizon, and for an equal period in summer the sun is always above the horizon. The larger forms of animal life are foxes, bears, and reindeer, while sea fowl are numerous. The islands are rich in coal. In 1918 more than 100,000 tons were shipped to Scandinavian ports alone. The group appears to have been discovered as early as 1194 by Norwegian navigators, and was again visited in 1596 by the Dutch navigator Barentz in endeavoring to effect a N. E. passage to India. Among the later explorers are Leigh Smith, Nordenskjöld, Andreasen, Johannesen, Nansen, and Sverdrup. Until the World War ended in 1918 the political status of Spitzbergen was undefined. The treaty of Brest-Litovsk (1917) between Germans and Bolshevists disclosed that Germany proposed to control the islands. Great Britain therefore in the summer of 1918 despatched an expedition under Sir Ernest Shackleton to seize the German coal fields, which were thenceforth worked in the interests of Great Britain. In 1919 the Supreme Council in Paris granted Norway suzerainty over the archipelago. American holdings were sold to Europeans.

SPITZKA, EDWARD ANTHONY, an American physician, born in New York, in 1876. He was educated in the College of the City of New York and at the College of Physicians and Surgeons. From 1904 to 1906 he was demonstrator of anatomy; from 1906 to 1914 professor of general anatomy at Jefferson Medical College, Philadelphia; acting also from 1911 to 1914 as director of the Daniel Baugh Institute of Anatomy, Philadelphia. In the latter year he began the private practice of medicine in New York, specializing in nervous and mental diseases. He has made exhaustive studies of the brains of eminent men, as well as those of criminals. He was a member of several scientific societies, and during the World War served with the Medical Reserve Corps, becoming lieutenant-colonel. Died Sept. 5, 1922.

SPLEEN, one of the abdominal glands at the left side of the body, close to the stomach and pancreas. It is somewhat oval-shaped and concave internally, where it is divided by a fissure named the ilium. Here blood vessels enter and leave the organ, and the nerves also enter. The upper extremity of the spleen is thick; the lower which is in contact with the colon, is more pointed. The average length of the spleen is 5 inches, its breadth 3 or 4 inches, and its thickness 1 or 1½ inches Its weight is about seven ounces. The spleen is a meshwork of fibers or trabeculæ, supporting a soft matter named the spleen pulp. Microscopically examined, the latter is found to consists of blood corpuscles in a a state of disintegration. The spleen substance also includes certain small round bodies, attached to the sheaths of the blood-vessels of the spleen, and named Malpighian or splenic corpuscles. During digestion the spleen increases in size, but under starvation it decreases, and the Malpighian bodies disappear. The spleen is supplied with blood by the splenic artery; its nerves are derived from the right pneumogastric nerve, and from the left semilunar ganglia. This organ may be excised from man and other animals without impairing the health. Most of the diseases of the spleen occur as secondary affections in connection with other diseases, such as ague and leucocythæmia. Amyloid degeneration of the spleen is frequently associated with a similar disease in the

liver or kidneys. The spleen is enlarged and increased in density, and it feels to the touch like wax. Splenitis or inflammation of the spleen is rare in this country, but is common in tropical malarial districts and is usually associated with ague. The symptoms are pain in the left side, in the hypochondriac region, and considerable tumefaction. The hypertrophied spleen may encroach on the stomach, and by upward pressure disturb the heart's action, or it may extend downward into the pelvic region. The diffuse inflammation may terminate by resolution, but pus may form or the spleen may become gangrenous. Tumefaction generally subsides rapidly; but more or less hypertrophy may remain. Atrophy of the spleen is a much less frequent affection.

SPLICE. See KNOTS.

SPLÜGEN, an Alpine pass in the Grisons, Switzerland; at an altitude of 6,946 feet; connects the valley of the Farther Rhine with that of a tributary of the Adda; and has been used for crossing the Alps since the time of the Romans. The existing road, 24 miles long and 14½ feet wide, was made by the Austrian Government in 1812-1822. It is protected against avalanches by several galleries and refuges.

SPOFFORD, AINSWORTH RAND, an American librarian; born in Gilmanton, N. H., Sept. 12, 1825. He was a journalist to 1861, when appointed chief assistant librarian of the Congressional Library, and was librarian in 1864-1897, when he became again chief assistant. He was famed for a comprehensive and accurate knowledge of books and their contents, and besides many essays and articles on historical, literary, and scientific subjects for the current journals published: "The American Almanac," for several years; and, with others, edited "Library of Choice Literature" (10 vols. Philadelphia, 1881-1888); "Library of Wit and Humor" (1884); and "A Practical Manual of Parliamentary Rules" (1884); and wrote "A Book for All Readers" (1900). He died Aug. 11, 1908.

SPOFFORD, HARRIET PRESCOTT, an American author; born in Calais, Me., April 3, 1835; was graduated at the Putnam Free School, Newburyport, Mass., in 1852. In 1859 she published "In a Cellar" in the "Atlantic Monthly." This story made her reputation, and thereafter she became a regular contributor to the chief periodicals of the country. Among her publications are:

A CORRIDOR IN THE ESCORIAL, BUILT BY PHILIP II OF SPAIN

See **Spain**, p. 1

© E. M. Newman

INTERIOR OF THE MOSQUE AT CORDOVA, SPAIN

See Spain, p. 1

"Sir Rohan's Ghost"; "The Amber Gods, and Other Stories"; "New England Legends"; "Hester Stanley and St. Marks"; "A Master Spirit"; "Old Washington" (1906), etc. She died on Aug. 15, 1921.

SPOKANE, a city of Washington, the country seat of Spokane co. It is on the Northern Pacific, the Great Northern, the Oregon-Washington Railroad and Navigation Company, the Spokane International, the Chicago, Milwaukee and St. Paul, the Chicago, Burlington and Quincy, and other railroads. It has in all 6 trans-continental lines and 12 branches. Situated at the foot of a valley, midway between the rise and mouth of the Spokane river, it is 350 miles E. of Seattle and 375 miles N. E. of Portland. It is the commercial center of the eastern part of the State of Washington, and of the northern part of Idaho, and the distributing point for a great agricultural, lumbering, horticultural, and stock raising region. The climate is unusually healthful. The annual normal temperature is 48° and there is seldom excessive heat or cold. The city rises from the banks of the Spokane river on the N. and S., to an elevation of 1,900 feet above sea-level. The streets are on the level portions while the houses are chiefly on the slopes. Latah creek, a tributary of the Spokane river, is spanned by a concrete bridge 1,070 feet long. The Monroe Street bridge is also of concrete, with an arch of 281 feet long.

The Spokane river provides water power from which 172,000 horse power has been developed. This is used for street lighting, street car and interurban trolley service, and manufacturing. There is an excellent park system which includes about 2,000 acres of land. There are 43 park places and 8 playgrounds. The educational advantages are exceptional. In addition to public and private schools there are several institutions of higher learning, some located within the city and others in adjacent towns. There are 35 grade schools, a parental school, two high schools, a school for defectives, 5 parochial schools, and 7 colleges and technical institutions. Gonzaga University is the largest Roman Catholic institution of its kind in the N. W. The city has over 300 manufacturing establishments, with an annual output valued at $75,000,000 and employing 12,000 people. Among the leading products are lumber, flour, breakfast foods, paper, brick, meats, iron, agricultural machinery, dairy products, cement, clothing, crackers, candy, extracts, and soap.

There is also a large jobbing and wholesale business. The city is the center of an important mining district. In 1919 there were 14 banks with a total capital of $4,325,000 and deposits of $53,220,725. There are many newspapers, over 140 churches, and a public library with 75,000 volumes. The fire and police departments are of the latest municipal models. There are hospitals and other public institutions. The growth of the city dates from 1881, when the Northern Pacific Railway was completed at this point. Pop. (1900) 36,848; (1910) 104,402; (1920) 104,437.

SPOLETO, an archiepiscopal city of ancient Umbria in the middle of Italy; on a rocky hill, 75 miles N. E. of Rome. It is commanded by a citadel which dates from the days of the Goths, and has a fine cathedral, built in the time of the Lombard dukes, and containing fine frescoes by Lippo Lippi. The churches of St. Domenico, St. Peter, St. Gregory, and St. Nicholas present interesting architectural features. Water is brought to the city by a 7th century aqueduct, 270 feet high and 680 long. The ancient Spoletium had its origin in a Roman colony planted here about 240 B. C.; Hannibal was repulsed in an assault he made on the town (217 B. C.) after the battle of Lake Trasimene. Under the Lombards it became the capital of an independent duchy, and its dukes ruled over great part of Central Italy. Having been united to Tuscany, it was bequeathed by the Countess Matilda to the Pope (1115). Pop. commune, about 26,000; town, about 10,000.

SPONGE, *Spongida*, a horny substance valued for its ready imbibition of water, and consisting of the keratode skeleton of certain Protozoa or lowest animals. A sponge is thus a colony of living animals. Such a colony communicates with the outer world by means of certain openings (capable of being closed at will), traceable in an ordinary sponge, and of which the larger are named oscula and the smaller pores. By the latter, currents of water are continually drawn into the sponge, while through the oscula currents are as continually discharged. These currents are kept up through the action of the minute vibratile processes named cilia, which are limited usually to certain spaces of the canals named ciliated chambers. The main use of this circulation in the sponge is evidently nutritive. Particles of food are thereby swept into the organisms, while oxygen is also inhaled and effete matters exhaled.

Sponge reproduction is effected by means of specially developed masses of protoplasm named spores, which are formed in autumn, and which on liberation in spring are found to contain small reproductive particles, which after a free existence develop into sponges. Sexual reproduction is represented by the union of certain cells representing ova or eggs, and other cells representing spermatozoa. After fecundation a sponge-egg undergoes the stages of segmentation common to the developing eggs of all animals, till the morula or mulberry stage is reached. Thereafter the egg becomes elongated and swims freely about in the water. An internal cavity is next formed, this cavity communicating by a mouth externally, and being bounded by two layers (ectoderm and endoderm). In this stage the young sponge is a gastrula. Latterly the outer cilia disappear, internal cilia are developed, and the sponge ultimately fixes itself, and circulation is established. Sponges are classified either as the keratosa (horny), silicea (flinty, *e. g.*, "Venus's flower basket," or euplectella), and calcarea (*e. g.*, sycon). A more philosophical arrangement divides the sponge class into families: (1) *Fibrospongiæ* (fibrous, including silicea); (2) *Myxospongiæ* (*Halisarca*); *Calcispongiæ* (*e. g.*, sycon and calcareous generally). Fossil sponges are of frequent occurrence.

The sponges of commerce come from the Eastern Mediterranean Sea, the West Indies, and the coast of Florida. In the Archipelago, Crete, Cyprus, on the coasts of Asia Minor, Syria, Barbary, and the Bahama Islands, sponge fisheries constitute a very important industry. The finest sponges are obtained in Turkish waters.

Sponges of a coarse texture and large honey-combing are found all along the coast of Tripoli and Tunis. The West Indian trade is of importance. The Bahamas and the coast of Florida are the best fishing grounds. The qualities most in commercial demand are "wool," "reef," and "velvet"; the other kinds go by the names of "boat," "silk" or "glove," "grass," "hardhead," "mixed," "yellow," and "refuse." West Indian sponge is harsher, coarser, and less durable than its Mediterranean congener.

The Mediterranean sponge fisheries are the oldest and have long produced the greatest sponge output of any region. The Florida fisheries have grown in importance of recent years with great rapidity, owing to the development since 1905 of the method of gathering sponges by the use of divers. This process was developed by sponge fishers of Greek origin. By its use they are able to gather as far as sixty feet below the surface. The divers work in pairs, relieving each other in shifts. They wear diving helmets, breast plates, rubber suits and weighted shoes. The fishery is carried on in schooners of Greek type, of a size up to twenty tons, and its chief port is Tarpon Springs, Fla. The fishing grounds lie chiefly in the Gulf of Mexico between St. John's Pass and St. Marks. Florida prohibits the pursuit of the fishery in waters within the State limits. An older type of fishery, known in Florida as hooking, consists of drawing the sponge from the bottom by the aid of a three-pronged hook at the end of a long pole. The hook fishermen work in pairs, using dories. A sponge glass, a sort of bucket with a glass bottom, enables the fisherman to see the bottom. This type of fishing has its centre at Key West, and is practiced among the Florida Keys, at depths up to forty feet, but chiefly at depths not greater than fifteen feet.

The quantity of sponges sold at the Tarpon Springs Sponge Exchange in Florida, in 1925, was 434,672 pounds, valued at $715,097. This total included 242,020 pounds of large wool, 29,968 pounds of small wool, 120,748 of yellow, 28,622 of grass, and 13,314 pounds of wire sponges.

The process of curing the sponge, carried on by the fishermen, is laborious. The gelatinous matter within the living sponge must be allowed partly to decompose, and must then be forced out, before it can dry within the fibres, by an alternation of washing and pressing or beating.

SPONTANEOUS COMBUSTION. See Combustion.

SPONTINI, GASPARO, an Italian composer; born in Majolatti, near Jesi, in the Roman States, Nov. 14, 1774. He was educated at the Conservatorio de la Pietà of Naples, and began his career when 17 years of age as the composer of an opera, "The Punctilio of Women." This was followed by some 16 operas, produced within six years, for the theatres of Italy and Sicily, but not a note of which has survived. In 1803 Spontini went to Paris; in 1807 he was appointed music director to the Empress Josephine; and in 1808 he produced his most famous work, "The Vestal," with brilliant and decisive success. His "Fernando Cortez" appeared in 1809; and the next year witnessed his appointment to the directorship of the Italian Opera in Paris, which he held for 10 years. In 1820 the magnificent appointments offered by the court of Prussia tempted him to leave Paris for Berlin, in which capital his three grand operas. "Nourmahal," (founded on "Lalla Rookh"), "Alcidor," and "Agnes of Hohenstauffen," were produced with great splendor. Spontini continued to reside as first chapel master in Berlin till the death of the king in 1840. The latter period of his sojourn at Berlin was embittered by professional disputes; and in 1842 he repaired to Paris, where in 1839 he had been elected one of the five members of th Académie des Beaux Arts. He died in Majolatti, Jan. 14, 1851.

SPOONBILL, in ichthyology, the genus *Polyodon*. In ornithology, any individual of the genus *Platalea;* specifically *P. leucorodia,* the white spoonbill, found over the greater part of Europe and Asia and the N. of Africa. The adult male is about 32 inches long; plumage white with pale pink tinge; at the junction of the neck with the breast there is a band of buffy yellow; the naked skin on the

SPOONBILL

throat is yellow; legs and feet black; bill about eight inches long, very much flattened and grooved at the base, the expanded portion yellow, the rest black. There is a white occipital crest in both sexes. The spoonbill possesses no power of modulating its voice. The windpipe is bent on itself, like the figure 8, the coils applied to each other and held in place by a thin membrane. This peculiarity does not exist in young birds. The roseate spoonbill (*P. ajaja*), a native of the United States, has rose-colored plumage.

SPOONER, CHARLES HORACE, an American educator, born in Charleston, N. H., in 1858. He was educated at Norwich University. From 1879 to 1889 he was instructor in various preparatory schools. From 1889 to 1891 he was principal of schools in Fitchburg, Mass., and from 1891 to 1904, instructor of mathematics at the Manual Training School of Washington University. In 1904 he became president of Norwich University, Northfield, Vt., retiring in 1915, being made president emeritus in the following year.

SPOONER, JOHN COIT, a United States Senator from Wisconsin, born in Lawrenceburg, Ind., in 1843. He graduated from the University of Wisconsin in 1864. He fought in the Civil War, and rose to the rank of major. In 1867 he was admitted to the bar and for many years practised in Wisconsin. He served as a member of the State Assembly in 1872, and in 1885 was elected to the United States Senate, serving until 1891. He was re-elected in 1897 and retained his seat until 1907, when he resigned to take up the practice of law in New York City. He was greatly distinguished as a lawyer and as an authority on international law. During his service in the Senate, he was recognized as one of its strongest members. In 1898 he was a member of the British-American Joint High Commission. He died in 1919.

SPORADES, the general name for a group of small islands in the Grecian Archipelago, lying to the E. of the Cyclades. They belonged formerly partly to Greece and partly to Turkey. The principal are Scio, or Chios, Samos, Cos, Rhodes, Lesbos, and Patmos. By the Treaty of Peace with Turkey the islands were allotted to Italy, but they had to be ceded to Greece, with the exception of Rhodes, in the signing of the Treaty.

SPORE, the reproductive body in a cryptogam, which differs from a seed in being composed simply of cells and not containing an embryo. Called also sporules. Applied also to the reproductive bodies produced either singly or at the tips of the fruit-bearing threads in fungi. Plants reproduce themselves in two different ways, "vegetatively" or "truly." The vegetative mode of reproduction is merely a continuous growth of parts already formed. It is quite common in nature. Sometimes entire buds separate from the parent plant and produce independent plants. This happens, for example, with some of the buds in the axils of the leaves of *Lilium bulbiferum.* Sometimes entire pieces of a creeping stem separate from the main stem and begin an independent life. This happens in the case of the strawberry plant. Artificially also a vegetative mode of reproduction is easily brought about. Every one knows how gardeners propagate many species of plants by means of cuttings. As a rule the more lowly the plant the more easy is it to make a successful cutting, and the smaller may the cutting be. Thus, a single leaf or even a small part of leaf of a moss plant, will often, if cut off and placed in a suitable soil, grow into a complete moss plant. In the true mode of reproduction the growth is not continuous. Certain cells of a plant are set apart for this function. These cells are called spores. In plants higher than the *Thallophytes*, such cells do not grow directly into a plant like that from which they have come, but they give rise to a plant which in its turn, when it reaches maturity, produces cells of two sorts, male and female, which unite with one another, and then form the new cell of dual origin there grows a plant like that from which the spore originally came. Thus, on the under surface of the fronds of ferns there may often be seen many small spore cases. The spores fall to the ground, and produce a little green plant called the prothallium of the fern. The prothallium produces the sex elements. These unite, and from their union grows a new "fern." This indirect mode of reproduction is spoken of as the alternation of generations.

In the *Thallophytes* (algæ, fungi, etc.), the cells which function as spores receive a variety of names, such as telentospores, aredospores, sporidia, stylospores, tetraspores, zoöspores (which are motile), conidia. These names are meant to emphasize some point in their mode of origin and development. In the *Bryophytes* (liverworts and mosses) and in the *Pteridophytes* (ferns, horsetails, etc.), they are always called simply spores. But some of the *Pteridophytes* (vascular cryptogams), for instance salvinia, produce two kinds of spores, male and female, and hence they are called heterasphorus ferns, horsetails, or lycopods as the case may be. In the *Spermophytes* also (seed plants or phanerogams) the spores are of two kinds. The pollen grains represent the male spores, microspores; and the female spores are contained within the ovule.

The sexual generation, the prothallium, which is formed from the spore, loses its character as an independent plant as we ascend the scale of plants from the vascular cryptogams to the phanerogams. In homosporous ferns it lives for a long time; in the heterosporous ferns they, the male and female prothallia, never become entirely separate from the spores, though they burst through the spore cases; in the *coniferæ* they remain entirely within the spore case. In the phanerogams

they are still further reduced; the ovule is the macrosporangium.

SPOTTED FEVER, the name given to a form of malignant typhus fever, which is accompanied by a rash or eruption of red spots. See TYPHUS.

SPOTTISWOODE, WILLIAM, an English mathematician; born in London, Jan. 11, 1825; was educated at Harrow and Balliol College, Oxford. For some time he lectured at Balliol, and in 1846 he succeeded his father as the head of the great printing house of Eyre & Spottiswoode. Though throughout life an energetic man of business, he found time for much original work as well as for travels in Eastern Russia, Croatia, and Hungary. His contributions to the "Proceedings" of the Royal Society and of the London Mathematical Society and his admirable lectures on the "Polarization of Light" (1874), are known to all students. Spottiswoode was treasurer of the British Association (1861-1874), of the Royal Institution (1865-1873), and of the Royal Society (1871-1878); president of Section A (1865) and of the British Association itself (1878), of the London Mathematical Society (1870-1872), and of the Royal Society from 1879 till his death in London, June 27, 1883.

SPOTTSYLVANIA COURT-HOUSE, a small village in Virginia, 55 miles N. by W. of Richmond, the scene of one of the most desperate battles of the American Civil War. On May 10, 1864, during the Wilderness campaign, Grant attacked Lee in his earthworks, and was repulsed with dreadful slaughter; yet on the next day he wrote to the Secretary of War, "I propose to fight it out on this line if it takes all summer," and on the 12th repeated the assault, when Hancock's corps carried and held the "bloody angle." The next morning Lee, unable to bear his share of the heavy losses, withdrew within an inner line of intrenchments, and on the 20th Grant, having failed to dislodge him, moved round his flank toward Richmond.

SPRAGUE, LEVI L., an American educator, born in Beekman, N. Y., in 1844. He was educated at the Wyoming Seminary and Allegheny College, Pa. His entire educational career was spent at Wyoming Seminary, Kingston, Pa., where he began teaching in 1868, and of which he became president in 1882. He took a prominent part in Methodist Episcopal affairs and was trustee of Wyoming Seminary, Syracuse University, the Wyoming Conference, as well as a delegate to three General conferences, in 1892, 1896 and 1904. He wrote "Practical Bookkeeping" (1873); "Practical Grammar" (1894).

SPRAGUE, FRANK JULIAN, an American engineer and inventor, born in Milford, Conn., in 1857. He graduated from the United States Naval Academy, in 1878, and served as engineer in the navy until 1883, when he resigned to devote his attention to electrical work. He founded, in 1884, the Sprague Electric Railway & Motor Co., which, using his constant speed electric motor, was the first to engage in general manufacture and the introduction of industrial electric motors. He was a pioneer in the electrification of railways, and in 1887 equipped the first modern trolley railway in the United States, in Richmond, Va. He invented and perfected many applications used in the electrical systems of railways. During the World War he was engaged in the development of fuses in air and depth bombs. He was a member and official of many scientific societies and was awarded many prizes and medals for his inventions. He was the author of many scientific papers on electricity.

SPRAT, the *Clupea sprattus*, a well-known fish, common on all Atlantic coasts of Europe, extending to the Baltic and the W. half of the Mediterranean. Scales smooth and easily shed; lower jaw prominent, oval patch of small teeth on tongue.

SPRECKELS, RUDOLPH, an American banker and civic reformer, born in San Francisco, Cal., in 1872, the son of Claus Spreckels. He was educated in the public schools of San Francisco and at an early age began work in his father's sugar refinery. He was soon appointed president of the Hawaiian Commercial & Sugar Co., which he developed from a losing to a profitable venture. He became identified with the gas company which furnished San Francisco with gas and reorganized that company, freeing it from many abuses. At the time of the San Francisco fire, in 1906, he was a member of the committee of 50, and was also a member of the committee of 5 of the San Francisco Relief and Red Cross Funds. In the same year he organized and financed the San Francisco graft prosecution, and took an active part in the political uprising against corporation control of State and city governments. He was an official and director in many important financial institutions.

SPREE, a river of Prussia, rises in the E. of Saxony, on the borders of Bohemia, and after a winding course of 227 miles, but bearing generally N. and N. W., falls into the Havel at Spandau; area of drainage basin, 3,655 square miles. The principal towns on its banks are Bautzen, Kottbus, and Berlin. By the Frederick William or Müllrose canal it is connected with the Oder. It has been reopened below Berlin to admit vessels of large tonnage.

SPRENGER, JACOB, of the Order of Preachers, and Professor of Theology in Cologne, and HENRICUS INSTITOR (Latinized form of Krämer), two names of enduring infamy as the authors of the famous "Malleus Maleficarum" or "Hexenhammer" (1489), which first formulated in detail the doctrine of witchcraft, and formed a text-book of procedure for witch trials. They were appointed inquisitors under the bull "Summis desiderantes affectibus" of Innocent VIII. in 1484, and their work is arranged in three parts—"Things that pertain to Witchcraft"; "The Effects of Witchcraft"; and "The Remedies for Witchcraft." It discusses the question of the nature of demons; the causes why they seduce men and particularly women; transformations into beasts, as wolves and cats; and the various charms and exorcisms to be employed against witches. They tell with complete composure of mind how in one place 40, in another 50, persons were burned by their means. The book contains no distinct allusion to the proceedings at the Witches' Sabbath any more than did the "Formicarium" (1440) of John Nider, whose fifth book is devoted to the subject of sorcery. See WITCHCRAFT.

SPRING, an elastic substance of any kind, having the power of recovering, by its elasticity, its natural state, after being bent or otherwise forced, interposed between two objects in order to impart or check motion or permit them to yield relatively to each other. Also, one of the four seasons of the year; that season in which plants begin to spring and vegetate; the vernal season. In the Northern Hemisphere the spring season begins about March 21, when the sun enters the sign of Aries and ends about June 22, at the time of the summer solstice. Popularly, however, spring is considered to begin in February or March, and end in April or May.

As a nautical term: (1) A crack in a mast or yard, running obliquely or transversely. (2) A rope or hawser passed from the stern of a ship and made fast to the cable on the anchor from the bow, by which she is riding. The object is to bring the broadside to bear in any direction. (3) A check on a cable while unshackling it. (4) A rope extending diagonally from the stern of one ship to the head of another, to make one ship sheer off to a greater distance.

In physical geography and geology, an overflow of water or other liquid. When rain falls on a porous soil it is rapidly absorbed, the surface of the soil being soon dry again. Meanwhile the water has percolated downward till it has, at a greater or less depth, been intercepted by an impervious stratum, where it gradually forms a reservoir. It then presses with great force laterally, and a system of subterranean drainage is established. If the reservoir be on an elevation and a boring be made on a lower level to any of the branches leading from it, the water will rise in the bore to the surface and shoot up into the air to a height proportional to the pressure from the reservoir, as an artesian well, which is akin to a spring. Springs are of two kinds, land and perennial springs, the former existing where there is a porous soil with an impervious subsoil, the latter deriving their waters from deeper sources. Perennial springs include thermal springs and geysers. Sometimes springs contain much earthy material; thus there are calcareous, sulphurous and gypseous, siliceous, ferruginous, saline, carbonated and petroleum springs. They are then called mineral springs.

SPRINGBOK, in zoölogy, the *Antilope euchore*, an antelope exceedingly common in South Africa. It is about 30 inches high, the horns lyrate, very small in the female; color yellowish dun, white beneath. Two curious folds of skin ascend from the root of the tail, and terminate near the middle of the back; they are usually closed, but open out when the animal is in rapid motion, and disclose a large triangular white space, which is otherwise concealed.

SPRINGFIELD, a city, capital of the State of Illinois, and county-seat of Sangamon co.; on the Wabash, the Baltimore and Ohio Southwestern, the Chicago, Peoria, and St. Louis, the Chicago and Alton, the Illinois Central, the Cincinnati, Hamilton and Dayton, and the Illinois Traction railroads; 190 miles S. of Chicago. It contains the State capitol; court house; United States Government building; the governor's mansion; the former residence of President Lincoln; the Lincoln National Monument in Oak Ridge Cemetery; State fair grounds; State Military Park, etc. Here also are Concordia College (Luth.), Bettie Stuart Institute, St. Agatha's School (P. E.), State and other libraries, State

arsenal, the Wabash railroad and St. John's hospitals, street railroad and electric light plants, waterworks, National and other banks, and numerous daily, weekly, and monthly periodicals. The trade and industry of the city are greatly promoted by rich coal mines in the vicinity. Springfield is especially noted for the extensive manufactory of the Illinois Watch Company. It also has many large printing and publishing houses, textile works, planing mills, machine shops, boiler works, manufactories of soap, automobile tires, electric meters, brick, clothing, etc. The city was founded in 1819; became the county-seat in 1823; and received its city charter in 1840. It was made the capital of Illinois in 1837, and the Legislature convened here for the first time in 1839. Pop. (1910) 51,-678; (1920) 59,183.

SPRINGFIELD, a city and county-seat of Hampden co., Mass.; on the Connecticut river, and on the New York, New Haven, and Hartford, the Boston and Albany, and the Central of New England railroads; 99 miles W. of Boston. The city is noted for its beauty, being laid out with wide streets, and having many magnificent churches and residences. Here are a School for Christian Workers, public library, handsome court house, a fine group of municipal buildings, museums, International Y. M. C. A. College, hospitals, a United States armory and arsenal, United States Government building, street railroad and electric light plants, National and other banks, and numerous daily, weekly, and monthly periodicals. The industries include the manufacture of firearms, railway cars, knit goods, clothing, paper, envelopes, watches, boilers, engines, machinery, silverware, jewelry, skates, carriages, buttons, needles, toys, printed books, motor cycles, brass goods, woolen goods, chemicals, etc. Springfield was founded by William Pynchon with colonists from Roxbury in 1636. The Indians burned the town during King Philip's War in 1675. In Shay's rebellion in 1787 the United States arsenal was attacked. The city was incorporated in 1852. Pop. (1910) 88,926; (1920) 129,614.

SPRINGFIELD, a city and county-seat of Green co., Mo.; on the St. Louis, Iron Mountain and Southern, and the St. Louis and San Francisco railroads; 130 miles S. of Jefferson City. It is on the summit of the Ozark Mountains in a rich lead and zinc section, and has a healthful climate. There are Drury College (Cong.), a normal school, high school, United States Government building, street railroad and electric light plants, St. John's Hospital, National and Confederate cemeteries, National and State banks, and daily and weekly newspapers. It has two extensive railroad shops, wagon and carriage factories, a foundry and iron works, and other industrial plants. In the early part of the Civil War several battles occurred in the city and vicinity, in one of which (known as the battle of Wilson's Creek, Aug. 10, 1861), the Federal general, Nathaniel Lyon, was defeated and killed. Pop. (1910) 35,201; (1920) 39,631.

SPRINGFIELD, a village in Union co., N. J.; on the Rahway river and on the Lackawanna railroad; 8 miles S. W. of Newark. It has several churches and manufactories of paper, shoes, and hats. Springfield is celebrated as the scene of a battle between the American and British forces, June 23, 1780. The British, under General Knyphausen, advanced from Elizabethtown about 5 o'clock in the morning. They were opposed by General Greene, but owing to the superior number of the enemy he was compelled to evacuate Springfield, which was then burned by the British. During the action the Rev. James Caldwell, chaplain in the New Jersey brigade, is said to have distributed the hymn books from the neighboring Presbyterian Church among the soldiers for wadding, saying at the same time, "Now put Watts into them, boys." This battle prevented further advance on the part of the British. The American loss was about 72 and that of the British about 150. Pop. (1920) 1,715.

SPRINGFIELD, a city and county-seat of Clarke co., O.; on the Mad river and on the Detroit, Toledo, and Ironton, the Ohio Electric, the Erie, and the Cleveland, Cincinnati, and St. Louis railroads; 45 miles W. of Columbus. It is in a rich agricultural section. Here are a United States Government building, public library, Wittenberg College (Luth.), waterworks, a sewer system, street railroad and electric light plants, numerous churches, hospitals, homes, several National and other banks, and daily, weekly, and monthly periodicals. The city is noted for its extensive manufacture of agricultural implements. The other manufactures include electric motors, motor trucks, emery wheels, gas and gasoline engines, automobile tires and tubes, etc. Pop. (1910) 46,921; (1920) 60,840.

SPRING HILL COLLEGE, an educational institution in Mobile, Ala.; founded in 1836 under the auspices of the Roman Catholic Church; reported at the close of 1919: Professors and instructors, 24; students, 239; president, Rev. J. C. Kearns.

SPRING-RICE, SIR CECIL ARTHUR, an English diplomat; born in 1859. He was educated at Oxford University and entered the diplomatic service. He served as secretary of legation at Brussels, Washington, Tokyo, Berlin, and Constantinople. From 1906 to 1908 he was minister and consul general to Persia, and from 1908 to 1912 minister to Sweden. He succeeded James Bryce as ambassador to the United States in the latter year. At the outbreak of the World War he filled his difficult post in Washington with great tact. He died in 1918.

SPRING VALLEY, a city of Illinois, in Bureau co., on the Illinois river and on the Chicago, Rock Island, and Pacific, the Chicago and Northwestern, and the Chicago, Burlington, and Quincy railroads. It has a public library, high schools, and a hospital. Pop. (1910) 7,035; (1920) 6,493.

SPROUL, WILLIAM CAMERON, an American manufacturer and public official, born in Octoraro, Lancaster co., Pa., in 1870. He was educated at Swarthmore College. He received honorary degrees from Franklin and Marshall College, Pennsylvania College, Lafayette College, Pennsylvania Military College, the University of Pennsylvania, and the University of Pittsburgh. He was the organizer and president of various manufacturing concerns in Chester Pa., also organized and developed numerous railroads, mining, traction, and power enterprises in West Virginia, held an active interest in many banks, and owned the Chester, Pa., "Daily Times" and "Morning Republican." Beginning with 1896, he was a member of the Pennsylvania State Senate for a period of 22 years, serving as president *pro tem.* from 1903 to 1905. In 1919 he was elected to a four-year term as governor of Pennsylvania. He was a member of the Historical Society of Pennsylvania, and of numerous patriotic and social societies and clubs.

SPRUCE FIR, in botany, a popular name for many species of the genus *Abies*, specifically *A. excelsa*, a fine evergreen which sometimes reaches a height of 150 feet, with a straight, though not very thick trunk and a regular pyramidal form. Leaves scattered equally round the twigs; four-cornered, mucronate, dull green; cones cylindrical, pendulous, with blunt, sinuate, slightly toothed scales. It is a native of the N. of Germany and Norway, whence it is often called the Norway spruce. It is commonly planted in Southern Europe, and affords an excellent shelter for game. Its timber is the white deal of commerce. It is not so durable as the Scotch pine, but is prized for masts, spars, scaffolding poles, etc. In Norway it takes 70 or 80 years to arrive at maturity. By incision it yields a resin whence turpentine and Burgundy pitch are manufactured.

The white spruce fir (*A. alba*) has the leaves somewhat graucous, rather pungent; the cones narrow, oval, tapering, with even, undivided scales. It is found in North America, where it reaches the height of 40 to 50 feet. The black spruce is *A. nigra*, from the very cold parts of North America. The leaves are short, the cones ovate oblong, obtuse, with ragged, round scales. It grows to 70 or 80 feet high. The timber is very valuable. The black spruce of British Columbia is *A. menziesii*. The red spruce (*A. rubra*) is also North American. It is about 50 feet high, and its timber is used for sail yards.

SPRY, WILLIAM, an American public official, born in Windsor, Berkshire, England, in 1864. He came to America in 1875 and was educated in the public schools of Utah. After a short business career in Salt Lake City, he devoted himself to farming and stock raising, and also became president of a bank in Salt Lake City, as well as director of various other institutions. Beginning with 1894, he has held public office continuously, serving successively as county collector, city councilman, president of the State Board of Land Commissioners, United States marshal for Utah, and from 1909 to 1917 was governor of Utah.

SPUR, a metal instrument composed of a shank, neck, and prick or rowel, fastened to the heel of a horseman to goad his horse to greater speed. Its use cannot with certainty be traced further back than Roman times. Early spurs had no neck, a prick being riveted to the shank. Prick spurs had straight necks in the 11th century and bent ones in the 12th. Rowels first appeared early in the 14th. The spurs of mediæval knights were gilt and those of esquires silvered. "To win his spurs" meant to gain knighthood.

SPURGE, a vast genus (upward of 700 species) of herbs, shrubs, or soft-wooded trees with fleshy branches, abounding in milky juice. An extensive group, abounding in South Africa, have suc-

culent, spiny or unarmed, often melon-shaped or cactus-like stems. The flower heads resemble single flowers, consisting of a calyx-like cap-shaped involucre, with 4-5 teeth, alternating with as many large horizontal glands, which enclose 10-15 male and 1 central female flower; the capsule separating when ripe into its three 2-valved constituent carpels. The genus is represented in all climates excepting the Arctic. Eleven non-important species are natives of Great Britain, and three others are more or less naturalized. Of the latter the caper spurge (*E. Lathyris*) has seeds containing a powerfully purgative oil. The most noteworthy medicinal species are *E. resinifera*, furnishing the intensely acrid gum-resin known in commerce as euphorbium, used principally as a vesicant in veterinary practice; *E. ipecacuanha* of North America — called wild ipecac — the root bark of which possesses emetic, expectorant, and cathartic properties; *E. corollata*, of which the root is officinal in the United States pharmacopœia as an emetic; and *E. neriifolia* of India, yielding a juice employed externally in native medicine, while the root is used as a remedy in snake bites. Various species with brilliant scarlet bracts are grown for ornament.

SPURGE LAUREL, the *Daphne Laureola*, a shrub possessing acrid properties, flowering in March and April.

SPURGEON, CHARLES HADDON, an English preacher; born in Kelvedon, England, June 19, 1834. In 1850 his sympathies drew him toward the Baptists, and, removing to Cambridge in 1851, he began to deliver cottage sermons in the neighborhood. At the age of 18 he had charge of a small Baptist congregation in the village of Waterbeach. In 1854 he entered on the pastorate of the New Park Street Chapel, London, where his preaching proved so attractive that in two years' time the building had to be greatly enlarged. His hearers continuing to increase, the Surrey Music Hall was for some time engaged for his use; and finally his followers built for him his well-known "Tabernacle" in Newington Butts, opened in 1861. The evangelistic and philanthropic agencies in connection with this immense chapel comprise the Stockwell Orphanage, a pastor's college, where hundreds of young men are trained for the ministry; the Golden Lane Mission, etc. Spurgeon preached in the Tabernacle every Sunday to thousands of hearers. His sermons were published weekly from 1854, and yearly volumes were issued from 1856. They had an enormous circulation, many of them being translated into various languages. He wrote: "John Plowman's Talk," "Morning by Morning," "Evening by Evening," "The Treasury of David," "Lectures to My Students," "The Saint and his Saviour," etc.; and from 1865 edited a monthly magazine, "The Sword and the Trowel." He died in Mentone, France, Jan. 31, 1892.

SPY, a secret emissary sent into the enemy's camp or territory to inspect their works, ascertain their strength and their intentions, to watch their movements, and report thereon to the proper officer. By the laws of war among all civilized nations a spy is subjected to capital punishment. To be treated as a spy one must first be caught in the enemy's territory, and in dress other than the adopted military uniform of his country. It must also be clearly shown that the object of the accused person is to gain information for the enemy which it would be to their advantage to know. If, when captured, the prisoner can show that his errand in getting through was of a personal nature, or that he was trading with the enemy, he can only be held as a prisoner of war. In trying a spy his military rank counts for much. An officer of high rank receives a more thorough trial than a private, though both are tried by court-martial. In the United States the verdict is sent to the President or the Secretary of War or Navy, for approval before execution. When a spy is caught in the act all these formalities are omitted. He is tried by a drum-head court-martial; allowed to make an explanation and a verdict is rendered without much deliberation. If he is found guilty the verdict is sent to the highest commanding officer in camp, and on his approval is carried out, after which a full report is made to the President. The two most famous spies in American history are Nathan Hale and Maj. John Andre.

SPY WEDNESDAY, an old name given to the Wednesday immediately preceding Easter, in allusion to the betrayal of Christ by Judas Iscariot.

SQUAD, a small body of troops assembled for drill, inspection, or other purposes. The awkward squad is composed of those recruits who have not received sufficient training to take part in regimental drill.

SQUADRON, in military language, a force of cavalry commanded by a captain, and averaging 100 to 150 men. Each squadron is composed of two

I—4

troops, each commanded by a captain for purposes of administration, but united under the senior for service in the field. Three to six form a regiment. The squadron is frequently considered the tactical unit of cavalry. As a naval term, a division of a fleet; a detachment of ships of war employed on a particular service or station, and under the command of a junior flag officer. In the United States Navy 11 ships or less constitute a squadron. The fleet is usually divided into van, center and rear squadrons.

SQUARE, in geometry, a quadrilateral figure, both equilateral and equiangular, or, in other words, a figure with four equal sides and equal angles. In measuring superficial areas it is only necessary to multiply one side by itself to have the area of the square, because each of the sides may be considered as the basis or as the perpendicular height. Thus a square the sides of which measure 4 feet is equal to 16 square feet, that is, 16 squares each 1 foot high and 1 foot long. To square a figure (for example, a polygon) is to reduce the surface to a square of equivalent area by mathematical means. It has often been attempted to square the circle, but this has been proven impossible. In arithmetic and algebra the square of a number is the number or quantity produced by multiplying a number or quantity by itself. Thus 64 is the square of 8, for $8 \times 8 = 64$.

SQUARE, in military tactics, a body of infantry formed into a rectangular figure with several ranks or rows of men facing on each side, with officers, horses, colors, etc., in the center. The front rank kneels, the second and third stoop, and the remaining ranks (generally two) stand. This formation is usually employed to resist a cavalry charge. Hollow squares are frequently formed with the faces fronting inward when orders and instructions, etc., are to be read, and the like.

SQUARE ROOT, in mathematics, a quantity which, being taken twice as a factor, will produce the given quantity. Thus, the square root of 25 is 5, because $5 \times 5 = 25$; so also 2-3 is the square root of $\frac{4}{9}$, since $\frac{2}{3} \times \frac{2}{3} = \frac{4}{9}$; x^2 is the square root of x^4, since $x^2 \times x^2 = x^4$; $a+x$ is the square root of $a^2 + 2ax + x^2$, and so on. When the square root of a number can be expressed in exact parts of 1, that number is a perfect square, and the indicated square root is said to be commensurable. All other indicated square roots are incommensurable.

SQUARES, METHOD OF LEAST, an arithmetical process of great importance for combining observations, or sets of observations, so as to obtain the most probable value of a quantity which depends on these observations. It is in fact the scientific method of taking certain averages, and it finds its most constant use in astronomy and other physical sciences. The necessity for applying the method arises from the fact that when the greatest precision of measurement is sought, repeated measurements of the same quanity do not agree. Thus, the altitude of a star at culmination, if carefully measured night after night by the same observer through the same instrument, will in general come out a little different in the different observations. All the measurements will, however, lie within a certain range of variation; and if all are equally trustworthy, the arithmetical mean will give the most probable value of the real altitude. The differences between this mean and the individual measurements on which it is founded are called the residuals. The important mathematical property of these residuals is that the sum of their squares is less than the sum of the squares of the differences between the individual measurements and any other single quantity that might be taken. Now, this principle of "least squares" holds not only for the simple case just described, but also for more complicated cases in which one observed quantity (y) is to be expressed as an algebraical function of another or of several independently observed quantities (x). Here the object is to find the most probable values of the assumed constants or parameters which enter into the formula. When these values are calculated we can calculate in terms of them and the observed x's a value of y corresponding to each set of observations. Comparing the calculated y's with the observed y's, we get a set of residuals the sum of whose squares is a minimum if the parameters have been calculated according to a particular process. It is this process which is described as the method of least squares. Its basis is found in the mathematical principles of probability.

SQUASH, in botany and horticulture, a popular name for any species of the genus *Cucurbita;* specifically, *C. melopepo.* Leaves cordate, obtuse, somewhat five-lobed; tendrils denticulated, or converted into small leaves; calyx with the throat much dilated; fruit flattened at both ends with white, dry, spongy fruit which keeps fresh for many months. It is boiled and eaten with meat.

SQUASH, a ball game of which tennis is believed to be a development. It is played in a court at one end of which rises a wall and the contest revolves on the ability of the players, who are provided with rackets, to strike the ball and send it against the wall above a certain line, keeping it all the time within certain enclosed spaces indicated by a central line on the floor and cross lines which divide it usually into four spaces. The players wait till the ball bounces on the floor and meet it before it touches the floor a second time. Skill is shown both in measuring the amount of energy expended in striking the ball and so placing it within the enclosed spaces as to make it difficult for the opponent to meet it. Points are recorded against the player who fails to meet the ball on the bounce, or who sends it against the wall below the line indicated or who so places the ball that in rebounding from the wall it falls outside the indicated space on the floor. The game is exhilarating and players often acquire such skill in hitting that the ball is kept on the bounce for a considerable time. The game is more simple than tennis, and the racket and ball are usually of a heavier make, owing to the greater wear and tear.

SQUID, a popular name of certain cuttle fishes belonging to the dibranchiate group of the class *Cephalopoda,* and included in several genera, of which the most familiar is that of the calamaries.

SQUIER, GEORGE OWEN, an American army officer, born at Dryden, Mich., in 1865. He graduated from the United States Military Academy in 1887 and received the degree of Ph.D. from Johns Hopkins University in 1903. In 1887 he was appointed second lieutenant of artillery and gradually rose to the rank of major general, which he received in 1917. Much of his service in the army was devoted to the Signal Corps, of which branch he was placed in command in 1913. In February, 1917, he was made chief signal officer of the United States Army, and from May 20, 1918, he was in charge of the army air service. His other assignments included service as United States military attaché in London in 1912. He did important research work in electricity, especially in connection with the telephone and telegraph. He was a member of the National Academy of Sciences, received the D.S.M., and was made a Knight Commander of the British Order of St. Michael and St. George. His seientific work was rewarded by the award of the Elliott Cresson gold medal, and of the Franklin medal.

SQUILL (*Scilla*), a genus of *Liliaceæ* numbering about 72 known species of bulbous plants with radical linear leaves; usually blue flowers (rarely purple or white), in racemes on leafless scapes; perianth segments six, free or nearly so; capsule three-angled, loculicidally three-valved, seeds small, swollen. The genus is confined to the Old World. Three are British. *S. autumnalis*, in which the leaves are autumnal, succeeding the flowers, is confined to a few counties in Southern England; while *S. verna*, with leaves appearing in spring in anticipation of the light-blue fragrant flowers, is met with in localities near the coast between Cornwall and Shetland. The third is the familiar wild hyacinth often called "bluebell" in England, the "English Iacint" of old writers, the *Hyacinthus nonscriptus* of Linnæus, now named *S. nutans*. It is common from Ross S., often occurring in such profusion as to render large tracts of woodland a sheet of blue from April to June.

The medicinal squill belongs to an allied genus of the tribe *Scilleæ*, named *Urginea*, comprising 24 species spread through the whole of Africa, and reaching Hindustan and Southern Europe. It is the species known as *U. scilla* or *maritima* (formerly *S. maritima*), a native of the coast district from Syria to the Canaries, appearing also in the Cape flora. From a bulb of four to six inches in diameter leaves are produced in spring, followed in autumn by a raceme of whitish flowers borne by a round scape of one to three feet high. Medicinally, squill is used as a diuretic in certain forms of dropsy, and as an expectorant.

SQUIRE, an attendant on a knight; a knight's shield or armor-bearer. (2) An attendant on a person of noble or royal rank; hence, colloquially, an attendant on a lady; a beau, a gallant; a male companion, a close attendant or follower. (3) The title of a gentleman next in rank to a knight. (4) A title popularly given to a country gentleman. (5) A title given to magistrates and lawyers in some parts of the United States. In New England it is given especially to justices of the peace and judges; in Pennsylvania to justices of the peace only.

SQUIRES, VERNON PURINTON, an American educator, born at Cortland, N. Y., in 1866. He was educated at the State Normal School, Cortland, N. Y., Brown University, and the University of Chicago. After some years of teaching at preparatory schools, he became professor of English at the University of North Dakota in 1897, serving until 1901, and returning in the same capacity to this institution in 1902. In 1914 he was made dean of the College of Liberal Arts of the University of North Dakota. He was a member of several educational societies and lectured frequently at chautauquas and educational gatherings.

SQUIRREL, in zoölogy, a popular name for any of the *Sciuridæ;* widely distributed in America, Europe, the Caucasus, Southern Siberia, and probably in Persia. It is a little animal with bright black eyes; from 8 to 10 inches in length, with a bushy tail nearly as long; color gray or reddish-brown,

CALIFORNIA GROUND SQUIRREL

white beneath, but the hue varies with the seasons, in Lapland and Siberia the upper surface becomes gray, and in Central Europe is sprinkled with gray in the winter. Squirrels haunt woods and forests, nesting in trees. They feed on nuts, acorns, beech mast, which they store up, birds' eggs, and the young bark and shoots. They pass the winter in a state of partial hibernation, waking up in fine, warm weather. They are monogamous, and the female produces three or four young, usually in June. In Lapland and Siberia they are killed in great numbers for the sake of their winter coat. This is inferior to the fur of the North American gray squirrel (*S. carolinensis*).

SQUIRREL FLYING-PHALANGER, in zoölogy, the *Petaurus sciureus;* from South Australia, about eight or nine inches long, with a tail as long as the body. Color, ash-gray with a black stripe from the nose to the root of the tail, cheeks white with a black patch, under surface white.

SQUIRREL MONKEY, the *Callithrix sciureus*, from South America. It is about 10 inches long, with a tail half as

KAIBAB SQUIRREL

much again; fur olive-gray on the body, limbs red, muzzle dark. They are affectionate and playful in disposition.

SRINAGAR, a city and capital of the State of Kashmir, in the Western Himalyas, situated in the valley of Kashmir, on both banks of the Jehlum. The city extends along the river for about 2 miles, and is exceedingly picturesque, though on nearer approach the streets are found to be narrow and dirty. The Jama Masjid, a large mosque said to be capable of containing 60,000 persons, is situated in the city, and in the environs are beautiful gardens and the lake mentioned in Moore's "Lalla Rookh." Srinagar has manufactures of shawls, paper, leather, firearms, otto of roses, etc. Pop. about 130,000.

STAAL, MARGUERITE JEANNE, BARONESS DE, a French author; born in Paris, May 30, 1684, the daughter of a poor painter named Cordier, whose name she dropped for that of her mother, Delaunay. She had a sound education at the convent of Saint Louis at Rouen, and at 27 was attached to the person of the imperious and intriguing Duchesse de Maine at the little court of Sceaux. Her devotion to the interests of the duchess brought her two years in the Bastille, where she had a love affair with the Chevalier de Menil. In 1735 she married Baron de Staal, an officer of the Guard. Her "Mémoires" (4 vols. 1755), show intellect and observation, as well as remarkable mastery of subtle irony, and are written in a style clear, firm, and individual. Her "Complete Works" appeared at Paris in two volumes in 1821. She died in Paris, June 16, 1750.

STACPOOLE, HENRY DE VERE STACPOOLE, a British writer and publicist. He was educated at Malvern College, and studied medicine at St. George's and St. Mary's hospitals. He practiced for some time as a doctor and was first drawn towards literature by the works of Carlyle and the German metaphysicians and poets. His works include: "Social Comedy"; "The Bourgeois"; "Fanny Lambert"; "The Doctor"; "The Pearl Fishers"; "The North Sea and Other Poems"; "The Beach of Dreams." His works have been translated into other languages and he has written much for the magazines.

STADIUM, in Greek antiquities, a measure of 125 geometrical paces or 625 Roman feet, 606 feet 9 inches of English measure, and thus somewhat less than an English furlong. It was the principal Greek measure of length. Also the course for foot races at Olympia in Greece, and elsewhere. It was exactly a stadium in length. The name is also applied to amphitheaters, and college athletic fields, as the Harvard Stadium, and the Palmer Stadium at Princeton.

STADTHOLDER, a title given in the Netherlands to a governor of a province who was also commander-in-chief of the forces. This title, however, received its special significance in 1580, when the provinces of Holland and Zealand revolted against the authority of Spain, and unitedly accepted William, Prince of Orange, as their stadtholder. The prince was assassinated before he was formally invested with his office, but the title was conferred on his son, Prince Maurice, and remained as the hereditary title of the chief of the state till Holland was annexed by France in 1802. This title was finally dropped in 1814, when the Prince of Orange was recalled from England and declared King of the Netherlands by an assembly of notables. See NETHERLANDS.

STAËL-HOLSTEIN, ANNE LOUISE GERMAINE, BARONESS DE, a French author; born in Paris, April 22, 1766, where her father, M. Necker, afterward the celebrated minister of France, was then a banker's clerk. At the age of 20 she became the wife of Baron De Staël-Holstein, the Swedish ambassador at Paris. At first sanguine in the cause of the Revolution, she soon became warmly interested in the sufferings of its victims, especially the queen, whom she had the courage to defend in print. In 1800 she began the series of her works on speculative philosophy, by publishing her essay "Literature Considered in its

Connection with Society"; and her very equivocal novel "Delphine" appeared in 1802. In that year her husband died. Madame de Staël was much too independent to be acceptable to Napoleon, who banished her from Paris, and afterward ordered her to confine herself to her château at Coppet, on the Lake of Geneva. From 1803 till 1815 she traveled much in Germany, Italy, and England, and visited Sweden and Russia. Her "Corinne," in form a novel, an eloquent tribute to the antiquities and scenery of Italy, appeared in 1807. Her most ambitious work, "On Germany," printed at Paris in 1810, was seized by the police. After the second restoration she lived chiefly in Switzerland, where she contracted a secret marriage with M. de Rocca. "Thoughts on the French Revolution" and her "Ten Years of Exile," appeared after her death, which occurred July 14, 1817.

STAFF, a kind of artificial stone used for covering and ornamenting buildings. It is made chiefly of powdered gypsum or plaster of Paris, with a little cement, glycerin, and dextrine, mixed with water until it is about as thick as molasses, when it may be cast in molds into any shape. To strengthen it coarse cloth or bagging, or fibers of hemp or jute, are put into the molds before casting. It becomes hard enough in about a half hour to be removed and fastened on the building in construction. Staff may easily be bent, sawed, bored, or nailed. Its natural color is murky white, but it may be made of any tint to resemble any kind of stone.

Staff was invented in France about 1876 and was used in the construction and ornamentation of the buildings of the Paris Expositions of 1878 and of 1890. It was also largely used in the construction of the buildings of Columbian Exhibition at Chicago in 1893, at the Omaha and Buffalo Expositions in 1898 and 1900, and at later expositions and on temporary buildings of other kinds.

STAFF, GENERAL. See MILITARY ORGANIZATION, UNITED STATES.

STAFFA, a celebrated island on the W. of Scotland, 4 miles S. W. of Ulva, 6 N. by E. of Iona, and 54 W. of Oban. It forms an oval uneven table-land, rising at its highest to 144 feet above the water, 1½ miles in circumference, and 71 acres in area. In the N. E., in the lee of the prevailing winds, is a tract of low shore, stretching out in beaches and forming a landing place; but elsewhere the coast is girt with cliffs from 84 to 112 feet high. Regarded in section, the rocks show themselves to be of three kinds—conglomerated tufa, forming the basement; columnar basalt, arranged in colonnades, which form the façades and the walls of the chief caves; and amorphous basalt, overlying the columnar basalt, but pierced here and there by the ends of columns and by angular blocks. The most remarkable feature of the island is Fingal's, or the Great Cave, the entrance to which is formed by columnar ranges on each side, supporting a lofty arch. The entrance is 42 feet wide and 66 feet high, and the length of the cave is 227 feet. The floor of this marvelous chamber is the sea, which throws up flashing and many-colored lights against the pendent columns, whitened with calcareous stalagmite, that form the roof, and against the pillared walls of the cave.

STAFFORDSHIRE, an inland county of England. Area, 1,128 square miles. Pop. about 300,000. The capital of the county is Stafford (pop. about 30,000). In the north and in the south the county is hilly, with wild moorlands in the north. In the midland regions the surface is low and undulating. Throughout the entire county there are vast and important coal fields. In the southern part there are also rich iron ore deposits. The so-called Black Country, between Birmingham and Wolverhamton, about 15 miles in length, is one of the principal iron and steel manufacturing districts of England. The largest river is the Trent. The soil is chiefly clay and agriculture is not highly developed. The manufacturing interests, however, are of great importance and diversity, and besides the above mentioned steel and iron industries they include the manufacture of bricks, chemicals, cotton goods, glass, leather goods, pottery, shoes, silk, and of many other articles. The pottery industry is centered around Stoke-on-Trent and the brewing industry around Burton-on-Trent.

STAG, or RED DEER (*Cervus elaphus*), a typical species of *Cervidæ* or deer, occurring in the N. of Europe and Asia. It was once found throughout the whole of Great Britain, but is now confined to the Scotch Highlands. The horns or antlers are round and have a basal snag in front. The females are hornless and are named hinds. The horns of the first year are mere bony projections; they advance in development during the second year, when the stag is named a brocket. In each succeeding year the horns grow more and more branched, the stag being named a hart in its sixth year, when the horns may be said to reach their maximum size. As in all deer, the horns are shed annually. The average height of a full-grown stag is about four feet at the

STAG

shoulders; the winter coat is grayish-brown; in summer, brown is the prevailing tint. The food of the stag consists of grasses and the young shoots of trees, lichens forming the greater part of its food in winter. The pairing season occurs in August, and the males then engage in combats for the females and become peculiarly fierce. The flesh is somewhat coarse.

STAG BEETLE, in entomology, any individual of the family *Lucanidæ;* specifically *L. cervus*, one of the larger

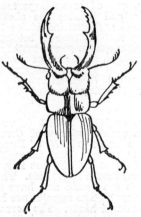

STAG BEETLE

insects, the male being about 2 inches long. Their projecting mandibles are denticulated, and somewhat resemble stag's horns; with these they can inflict

a pretty severe wound. The stag beetle is common in forests, and flies about in the evening in summer. The larva feeds on the wood of the oak and the willow, into the trunks of which it eats its way, and lives for a considerable time before undergoing a metamorphosis. Some of the tropical stage beetles are very brilliantly colored.

STAGG, AMOS ALONZO, an American physical director, born in West Orange, N. J., in 1862. He graduated from Yale in 1888, and from the International Y. M. C. A. College, Springfield, Mass., in 1892. From 1892 to 1900 he was associate professor and director of the department of physical culture and athletics of the University of Chicago, and in 1900 became full professor. He became a member of the football rules committee in 1904, and was a member of various American committees on Olympic Games, as well as, in 1911 and 1912, president of the Society of Directors of Physical Education in Colleges. The athletic field of the University of Chicago was named in his honor "Stagg Field."

STAGGERS, a popular term applied to several diseases of horses. Mad or sleepy staggers is inflammation of the brain, a rare but fatal complaint, marked by high fever, a staggering gait, violent convulsive struggling, usually terminating in stupor. Grass or stomach staggers is acute indigestion. It is most common in summer and autumn, is indicated by impaired appetite, distended abdomen, dull aspect, unsteady gait, and is remedied by full doses of purgative medicine.

STAGHOUND, the Scotch deerhound, called also the wolf dog, a breed that is rapidly dying out. These dogs hunt chiefly by sight and are used for stalking deer, for which purpose a cross between the rough Scotch greyhound and collie or the foxhound is also often employed. True staghounds are wiry-coated, shaggy, generally yellowish-gray, but the most valuable are dark iron-gray, with white breast.

STAHL, ROSE, an American actress; born in Montreal, Canada. She played for many years in stock companies, and in 1897 made her first important appearance in "A Soldier of the Empire." She later was seen in "An American Gentleman"; "A Man of the World"; and "The Chorus Lady." The latter play was produced steadily from 1904 to 1911, and was successful both in the United States and in London.

STAINER, SIR JOHN, an English composer; born in London, June 6, 1840; was a chorister at St. Paul's from his 7th

A SPONGE WHARF AT KEY WEST, FLA.

See **Sponge**, p. 33

© Publishers' Photo Service   See **Stalactite** and **Stalagmite**, p. opposite

STALACTITES AND STALAGMITES IN THE BELLAMAS NATURAL CAVES, MATANZAS, CUBA

to his 16th year; appointed organist first at St. Michael's College, Tenbury, then in 1859 to Magdalen College, Oxford, and ultimately in 1872 to St. Paul's. While at Oxford he graduated both in arts and music. He was inspector of music to the Educational Department and the author of the oratorio "Gideon" (1875); the cantatas, "The Daughter of Jairus," "Mary Magdalene," "The Crucifixion"; a treatise on the "Theory of Harmony" (1871); "Music of the Bible" (1879); "Organ Playing"; etc.; joint author with W. A. Barrett of "Dictionary of Musical Terms" (1876), and editor of "Music Primers." He died in 1901.

STAIRS, a succession of steps raised one above the other, affording means of communication between two points at different heights in a building, etc. Originally the stairs were placed from story to story in straight flights, like ladders, and were often external, being sheltered by a projection from the roof, but to save space the spiral form was adopted, the stair being contained in a cylindrical building projecting from the outside of the edifice. In this construction a central axis or newel reaching from the ground to the roof serves to support the inner ends of the steps, and the outer ends are let into the walls. The spiral form is still used in certain circumstances, but the finest stairs are now constructed in straight sections separated from each other by a wide step or platform called a landing.

STAKE NET, a form of net for catching salmon, consisting of a sheet of network stretched on stakes fixed into the ground, generally in rivers or where the sea ebbs and flows, with contrivances for entangling and catching the fish.

STALACTITE and **STALAGMITE,** formations of carbonate of lime. Stalactitic formations occur chiefly in long and more or less fantastic-shaped masses suspended from the roofs of caverns in limestone rocks. The flatter deposits, called stalagmites, are formed on the floor of the cavern by the water there depositing that portion of the carbonate of lime which is not separated during the formation of the stalactite. The most remarkable instances of their occurrence in Great Britain are in the cavern at Castleton in Derbyshire, and Macallaster Cave in the Isle of Skye. The grotto of Antiparos in the Archipelago, the Woodman's Cave in the Harz in Germany, that of Auxelle in France, and Luray (Virginia) and Mammoth (Kentucky) Caves in the United States are striking instances of their formation in other countries.

STALYBRIDGE, a cotton town of Cheshire and Lancashire, England, 7½ miles E. by N. of Manchester. Dating only from 1776, it has huge factories for the spinning of cotton yarns and calico-weaving, iron foundries, and machine shops, a town hall, market buildings, a mechanics' institute, an Odd Fellows' hall, and, between it and Ashton-under-Lyne to the W., the Stamford Park. Pop. (1918) 27,500.

STAMEN, in botany, the male organ of a flower, called by the old botanists an apex and a chive. Morphologically it is a transformed leaf. It consists of a filament, an anther, and pollen. The last two are essential, the first is not. When anther and pollen are wanting, the stamen is called a sterile or abortive. If the stamens are equal in number to the petals then normally they alternate with them. They always originate from the space between the base of the petals and the base of the ovary, but they may cohere with other organs, whence the terms epigynous, hypogynous, and perigynous. Cohesion among themselves may make them monadelphous, diadelphous, or polyadelphous. They may be on different flowers, or even different plants, from the pistils, whence the terms monœcious or diœcious. Other terms used of stamens are exserted, included, declinate, didynamous, and tetradynamous. The stamens taken collectively form the androœceum or male apparatus of the flower.

STAMFORD, a city in Fairfield co., Conn.; on Long Island Sound, and on the New York, New Haven, and Hartford railroad; 34 miles E. of New York. Here are the Ferguson Library, high school, hospital, town hall, parks, waterworks, street railroad and electric light plants, several National and savings banks, and a number of daily and weekly newspapers. It is the residence place of many New York business men. The industries include woolen mills, lumber mills, and manufactories of carriages, chemicals, wire, pianos, paints, chocolate, hardware, stoves, straw hats, machinery, shoes, locks, dye-stuffs, pottery, etc. Pop. (1910) 25,138; (1920) 35,096.

STAMFORD, a municipal borough of England, chiefly in Lincolnshire, but partly also in Northamptonshire; on the Welland, 12 miles W. N. W. of Peterborough. Hengist is said to have here defeated the Picts and Scots in 449, and Stamford thereafter is notable as one of the Danish "five burghs," for the persecution of its Jews (1190), for its colony of Flemish Protestants (1572), as the birthplace of the earliest provincial newspaper, the Stamford "Mercury" (1695), and for its famous bull-running on Nov.

13, from King John's time till 1839. Among its many interesting buildings should be mentioned St. Mary's, with a fine spire, All Saints, with a fine tower and steeple, St. Martin's, with Lord Burghley's grave, a town hall, corn exchange, literary institute, a bridge, Brown's Hospital (15th century), and boys' and girls' high schools. "Burghley House, by Stamford town," is a magnificent Renaissance pile, dating from 1575, with a noble park, carvings by Grinling Gibbons, and a great collection of pictures. The trade and industries are mainly agricultural. Pop. about 10,000.

STAMMERING, or STUTTERING, an infirmity of speech, the result of failure in co-ordinate action of certain muscles and their appropriate nerves. It is analogous to some kinds of lameness, to cramp or spasm, or partial paralysis of the arms, wrists, hands, and fingers, occasionally suffered by violinists, pianists, and swordsmen; to the scrivener's palsy, or writer's cramp, of men who write much.

Stammering may be hereditary, and it may be acquired by imitation. It may be the result of mental strain or shock. Fever may bring it on, epilepsy, hysteria, and nervous affection, temporary failure of health, any excitement, soreness of the mouth. It rarely shows itself earlier than at 4 or 5 years of age. It usually begins in youth, but may be produced at any later age.

Stammering occurs in the mouth, the organ of articulation. Its proximate cause is always in the larynx, the organ of voice. Sometimes the lungs, the organ of breathing, complicate the uncertainty and unsteadiness of the vocal cords and the vocal chink in the larynx.

Stammering can be cured. It often disappears gradually without effort at cure. Improvement generally takes place as age advances. In some cases resolute endeavor is demanded. A waving motion of the arms, time kept to a baton, were favored as cures at one time. They were on the lines of the musical methods of cure—intoning, chanting, singing—which were based on the fact that most stammerers can sing. These brief instructions should be tried. Regulate the breath. Work for a habitual use of the chest voice—*i. e.* for deeper, steadier vibration of the vocal chords—because people generally stammer in a head voice. Take exercise, in a chest voice, on the sound (seldom vowels) at which a stumble is apt to be made. Special attention should be paid to possible eye-strain, difficult nasal-breathing, adenoid growths, and diseased tonsils.

STAMP, a term specifically applied to the public mark or seal made by a government or its officers upon paper or parchment whereon private deeds or other legal agreements are written, and for which certain charges are made for purposes of revenue. The name is also applied to a small piece of stamped paper issued by government, to be attached to a paper, letter, or document liable to duty. See STAMP DUTY.

STAMP ACT, an act for regulating the stamp duties to be imposed on various documents, specifically an act passed by the British Parliament in 1765, imposing a stamp duty on all paper, parchment, and vellum used in the American colonies, and declaring all writings on unstamped paper, etc., to be null and void. The indignation roused by this act was one of the causes of the Revolutionary War.

STAMP DUTY, a tax or duty imposed on pieces of parchment or paper, on which many species of legal instruments are written. In Great Britain stamp duties on legal instruments used to be chiefly secured by prohibiting the reception of them in evidence unless they bore the stamp required by the law. By the Customs and Inland Revenue Act (1888), however, the not stamping of bonds, conveyances, leases, mortgages, or settlements, is held to be an offense punishable by a fine of $50. The internal revenue acts of the United States of 1862, and subsequent years, required stamps for a great variety of subjects, under severe penalties in the way of fines and invalidating of written instruments; stamps for tobacco are still in use. See TAX.

STAMP MILL, a contrivance of great utility in reducing hard mineral ores to a pulverized condition. It consists of an engine containing a series of heavy iron shod pestles.

STANCHFIELD, JOHN BARRY, an American lawyer and public official, born in Elmira, N. Y., in 1855. He graduated from Amherst College in 1876 and from Harvard Law School in the following year. In 1878 he was admitted to the bar and practiced at Elmira from 1878 to 1900. During a part of the time he was a partner of David Bennett Hill. From 1885 to 1905 he was a member of the firm of Reynolds, Stanchfield & Collin, New York. His political career included service as mayor of Elmira from 1886 to 1888, and as assemblyman in 1895-1896. In 1900 he was Democratic candidate for governor of New York and in 1901 was Democratic nominee for United States senator. He was one of the best known lawyers who practiced in New York City, and took part in many important cases. Died June 25, 1921.

STANDARD, a flag or ensign round which men rally, or under which they unite for a common purpose; a flag or carved symbolical figure, etc., erected on a long pole or staff, serving as a rallying point or the like. The ancient military standard consisted of a symbol carried on a pole like the Roman eagle, which may be considered as their national standard. Each cohort had its own standard surmounted with a figure of Victory, an open hand, etc., the pole being decorated with circular medalions, crescents, etc. The labarum was the peculiar standard adopted by Constantine. In mediæval times the standard was not square, like the banner, but elongated, like the guidon and pennon, but much larger, becoming narrow and rounded at the end, which was slit, unless the standard belonged to a prince of the blood-royal. The size of the standard was regulated by the rank of the person whose arms it bore. It was generally divided into three portions— one containing the arms of the knight, then came his cognizance or badge, and then his crest; these being divided by bands, on which was inscribed his war cry or motto, the whole being fringed with his livery or family colors. Cavalry standards are properly banners of a small size. The corresponding flags used by infantry regiments are called colors. In the United States Army the standards are the national and regimental silk flags, which are carried by cavalry and field artillery regiments.

STANDARD OIL COMPANY, a union of business interests that have held since 1880 a predominant position in the petroleum industry. Its rise goes back to 1867, when the firm of Rockefeller, Andrews & Flagler was formed. The next important step in its progress occurred three years later, when the firm was reorganized under the name of the Standard Oil Company of Ohio, then controlling something like 10 per cent. of the industry. During the years that followed, the interests of the company developed to such an extent that in 1880 it, in company with other firms in which the same men were interested, attained to the control of something like 90 per cent. of the industry. The business genius of the founders played no small part in the phenomenal growth of the company, but methods that were not wholly legitimate were charged against it, recourse having been had to the securing of discriminating rates of transportation that gave the company an

unfair advantage over its competitors. In 1882 the company was reorganized as the Standard Oil Trust, and all the stock holdings of 14 companies, together with the majority holdings in 26 other companies, were put in the hands of 9 trustees having irrevocable powers of attorney. By this arrangement the stockholders of the several companies so brought together received trust certificates on which dividends were declared, amounting to $70,000,000, the 9 trustees being the owners of $46,000,000 of the total amount. Litigation then marked the progress of the group and a decision in the courts of Ohio in 1892 pronouncing the trust form of organization illegal, led to its dissolution, the stocks of the companies being distributed to the holders of trust certificates on a pro rata plan, which ruse altered the form and not the substance of the trust. Seven years later the plan of a holding company was evolved and the Standard Oil Company of New Jersey was organized. The company issued securities in exchange for the stocks in the hands of the trustees and other individuals, having an authorized capital of $110,000,000. This was made the basis of extensive developments, particularly in the foreign field. By 1904 the refineries of the company, despite independent developments of petroleum fields that had taken place, consumed 84.2 per cent. of the crude oil of the entire country, and produced 86.5 per cent. of the refined oil. As a result of the Sherman Anti-Trust Law the dissolution of the company was ordered in 1909, the decision of the United States District Court of St. Louis being confirmed by the Supreme Court in 1911. The stock was redistributed, but the combination of interests still worked in a manner that continued to keep control of the industry in the same hands. The earnings of the group between 1899 and 1905 grew from $34,420,314 to $57,459,356.

STANDARDS, UNITED STATES NATIONAL BUREAU OF, a bureau of the Department of Commerce of the United States Government, charged by law with the custody of the national standards of weights and measures; the comparison with them of the standards used in scientific investigations, engineering, commerce, and educational institutions; the construction or reproduction of such standards, their multiples and subdivision; the testing and calibration of standard measuring apparatus; the solution of problems arising in connection with standards; and the determination of physical constants and the properties of materials, when such data are of great importance to scientific or manufacturing interests and are not to be obtained with sufficient accuracy elsewhere. The Bureau of Standards, which took the place of the former Office of Standard Weights and Measures, was organized by Act of Congress approved March 3, 1901, with Dr. S. W. Stratton as its first director, who continued in that position in 1920. The scientific work of the bureau is carried on by the divisions of Weights and Measures, Heat and Thermometry, Electricity, Optics, Chemistry, Structural Engineering and Miscellaneous Materials, Engineering Research, and Metallurgy. The bureau publishes an annual report of the director, and from time to time various bulletins.

STANDARD TIME, a system of time-reckoning, chiefly for the convenience of railroads in the United States, established by mutual agreement in 1883 on principles first suggested by Charles F. Dowd, of Saratoga Springs, N. Y. The United States, beginning at its extreme E. limit and extending to the Pacific coast, is divided into four time-sections: E., central, mountain, and Pacific. The E. section, the time of which is that of the 75th meridian, lies between the Atlantic Ocean and an irregular line drawn from Detroit, Mich., to Charleston, S. C. The central, the time of which is that of the 90th meridian, includes all between the last-named line and an irregular line from Bismarck, N. D., to the mouth of the Rio Grande. The mountain, the time of which is that of the 105th meridian, includes all between the last-named line and the W. boundary of Montana, Idaho, Utah, and Arizona. The Pacific, the time of which is that of the 120th meridian, includes all between the last-named line and the Pacific coast. The difference in time between adjoining sections is one hour. Thus, when it is 12 o'clock noon in New York City (E. time) it is 11 o'clock A. M. (central time) at Chicago, and 10 o'clock A. M. at Denver (mountain time), and at San Francisco, 9 o'clock A. M. (Pacific time). The true local time of any place is slower or faster than the standard time as the place is E. or W. of the time meridian; thus, the true local time at Boston, Mass., is 16 minutes faster than E. standard time, while at Buffalo, N. Y., it is 16 minutes slower, the 75th time meridian being half way between Boston and Buffalo. Local time and standard time agree at Denver, Col., as Denver is on the 105th meridian of the mountain section. In Europe, Spain and Holland first adopted standard time.

STANDISH, MYLES, an American soldier; born in Duxbury, Lancashire, about 1584; served in the Netherlands; and, though not a member of the Leyden congregation, sailed with the "Mayflower" colony to Massachusetts in 1620, and became the champion of the Pilgrims against the Indians. During the first winter his wife died, and the traditional account of his first effort to secure another partner has been made familiar by Longfellow. In 1622, warned of a plot to exterminate the English, he enticed three of the Indian leaders into a room at Weymouth, where his party, after a desperate fight, killed them, and a battle that followed ended in the flight of the natives. Standish was the military head of the colony, and long its treasurer. A monument, 100 feet high and surmounted by a statue, has been erected to him on Captain's Hill at Duxbury. In 1632 he settled at Duxbury, Mass., where he died, Oct. 3, 1656.

STANFORD, LELAND, an American philanthropist; born in Watervliet, Albany co., N. Y., March 9, 1824; studied law; was admitted to the bar in 1849, and the same year began to practice at Port Washington, Wis. In 1852 he went to California, where he engaged in mining, but in 1856 removed to San Francisco, and there engaged in business, laying the foundation of a fortune estimated at more than $50,000,000. In 1860 he made his entrance into public life as a delegate to the Chicago convention that nominated Abraham Lincoln for the presidency. Subsequently he was elected president of the Central Pacific railroad in 1861; was governor of California in 1861-1863; and in 1885 was elected to the United States Senate. In memory of a deceased son, Leland Stanford, Jr., he gave $20,000,000 for the founding of Leland Stanford University at Palo Alto, Cal. He died in Palo Alto, June 21, 1893.

STANHOPE, the name of a noble English family. JAMES, 1st Earl Stanhope; born in Paris, France, in 1673. He entered the army, served as Brigadier-General under the Earl of Peterborough at the capture of Barcelona in 1705, was appointed Commander-in-Chief of the British forces in Spain, and in 1708 took Port Mahon. After the accession of George I. he devoted himself to politics, and became the favorite minister of that monarch. He died in London, Feb. 5, 1721. CHARLES, the 3d earl; grandson of the preceding; born in London, England, Aug. 3, 1753; was celebrated chiefly as an inventor, a patron of science, and the avowed advocate of republicanism. His chief inventions were an arithmetical machine and a new printing press, which bears his name. He died in London, Dec. 15, 1816. PHILIP HENRY, 5th earl, grandson of the preceding; born in Walmer, Kent, Jan. 31, 1805. He filled various official positions in the ministry of Sir Robert Peel, but he was best known under his title of Lord Mahon, as the author of a "History of the Succession War in Spain" (1832), a "Life of Belisarius," a "History of England from the Peace of Utrecht to the Peace of Versailles, 1713-1783" (1854), a "Life of Pitt" (1861), and a "History of the Reign of Queen Anne" (1870). He was the founder of the Stanhope prize for a historical essay in connection with Oxford University. He died in Bournemouth, Hampshire, Dec. 24, 1875. LADY HESTER LUCY, an English traveler; daughter of the 3d Earl Stanhope, born in Chevening, England, March 12, 1776. For many years she resided with her uncle, William Pitt, and when he died in 1806 she received a government pension of $6,000. In 1810 she left England, visited various places in the East, and finally settled in Syria. She established herself in the deserted convent of Mar Elias in the Lebanon, adopted the style and dress of an Arab chief, and by her kindness and masculine energy exercised great influence over the Bedouins. Her "Memoirs" were published in 1845-1846. She died in Mar Elias, Syria, June 23, 1839.

STANISLAUS AUGUSTUS, STANISLAUS II., the last King of Poland, son of Count Stanislaus Poniatowski; born in

STANISLAUS II.

Wolczyn, Lithuania, Jan. 17, 1732. Sent by Augustus III. of Poland on a mission to St. Petersburg, he became a favorite with the grand-princess (afterward the Empress Catherine), by whose influence he was crowned King of Poland at Warsaw in 1764. The nobility, however, were discontented with this interference on the part of Russia, and forcibly compelled the king to abdicate (1771). He protested against the various partitions of Poland, formally resigned his sovereignty in 1795, and finally died in St. Petersburg, Feb. 12, 1798, as a pensioner of the Emperor Paul I.

STANISLAUS LESZCZYNSKI, STANISLAUS I., King of Poland, afterward Duke of Lorraine and Bar; born in Lemberg, Galicia, Oct. 20, 1677. His father was grand treasurer to the Polish crown, and he himself was voivode of Posen, when he was recommended to the Warsaw assembly by Charles XII. of Sweden as a candidate for the vacant throne of Poland. He was accordingly elected and crowned (1705), but after the disastrous battle of Poltava (1709), when his patron Charles XII. was defeated, he had to flee from Poland. He found refuge in France ultimately, where his daughter Maria became wife to Louis XV. Assisted by the French king he sought to establish his claim to the throne of Poland in 1733, but, opposed by the united powers of Saxony and Russia, he had again to retire into France, where he held possession of the duchies of Lorraine and Bar until his death. His writings were published under the title of "Works of the Beneficent Philosopher" (1765). He died Feb. 23, 1766.

STANLAWS, PENRHYN (PENRYHN STANLEY ADAMSON), an American portrait painter, born in Dundee, Scotland, in 1877. He came to the United States in 1891 and studied art at Paris and London. He exhibited at the Paris Salon in 1904, and in 1908 opened a studio in New York. He built the Hoted des Artistes in New York City, the largest studio building in the United States, and was president of the Hotel des Artistes, Inc. He wrote two plays, "Instinct" (1912) and "The End of the Hunting" (1915). Besides his portrait work, he was especially well known for his frequent cover designs for many of the most prominent magazines.

STANLEY, SIR ALBERT (HENRY), a British public official, born at Derby, England, in 1875. He was educated at an American college and technical schools, and was general manager of the American electric railways for 12 years, chiefly the Detroit United Railways and the Public Service Railways of New Jersey. He became conservative Unionist Member of Parliament for Ashton-under-Lyme in 1916, and in that year was also made president of the Board of Trade.

STANLEY, ARTHUR PENRHYN, an English clergyman; son of the Bishop of Norwich, born in Alderley, Cheshire, Dec. 13, 1815; was educated at Rugby under Dr. Arnold (1829-1834). As a scholar of Balliol, he gained the New-digate, Ireland, and other university dis-tinctions; took a first class in classics (1837); and was elected fellow of Uni-versity College (1840). Taking orders, he was for 12 years tutor of his college; Select Preacher (1845-1846); secretary to the Oxford University Commission (1850-1852); canon of Canterbury (1851-1858); Regius Professor of Ecclesiastical History and canon of Christ Church (1858-1864); in 1863 de-clined the archbishopric of Dublin; and became next year the Dean of Westmin-ster. St. Andrews University conferred on him the degree of LL.D (1871), and he was installed its rector (1875). He made a tour in the East (1852-1853), and again as chaplain to the Prince of Wales (1862), performed the Protestant marriage of the Duke of Edinburgh at St. Petersburg (1874), and visited the United States (1878). The leader after Maurice's death of the "Broad Church" party, he showed sympathies with free thought by his action in the "Essays and Reviews" and Colenso controver-sies; by his presence at the second "Old Catholic" Congress; by invitations to Dissenters and Max Müller to preach or lecture in the Abbey. Among his numerous publications are the "Life of Arnold" (1844, 9th ed. 1875); "Sermons and Essays on the Apostolic Age" (1846, 3d ed. 1874); "Memoir of Bishop Stan-ley" (1850); "Epistles to the Corin-thians, with Notes and Dissertations" (1854, 4th ed. 1876); "Historical Memorials of Canterbury Cathedral" (1854, 6th ed. 1872); "Sinai and Palestine" (1855, 20th ed. 1874); "Lectures on the Eastern Church" (1861, 4th ed. 1869); "Lectures on the Jewish Church" (3 series, 1862-1875, 7th ed. 1877); "Historical Memorials of Westminster Abbey" (1867, 4th ed. 1874); "Essays on Questions of Church and State from 1850 to 1870" (1870); "The Athanasian Creed" (1871); "Lec-tures on the Church of Scotland" (1872); and "Addresses and Sermons at St. Andrews" (1877). He married in 1863 Lady Augusta Bruce, daughter of the 7th Earl of Elgin. He died in his deanery, July 18, 1881, and was buried in the chapel of Henry VIII., Westmin-ster Abbey.

STANLEY, AUGUSTUS OWSLEY, an American public official, born in Shelby-ville, Ky., in 1867. He graduated from Centre College in 1889. In 1894 he was admitted to the bar and began the prac-tice of law at Henderson, Ky. He was elected to the 58th Congress, and was successively re-elected until 1915, in which year he was elected governor of Kentucky. He was elected United States Senator in 1918, for the term ending 1925.

STANLEY, SIR HENRY MORTON, an English explorer; born near Denbigh, Wales, in 1840; name originally John Rowlands. When three years old he be-came an inmate of the poorhouse at St. Asaph, where he made such progress in the school that he was employed as a teacher of other children at Mold, Flint-shire, when he went away at the age of 13. Two years later he sailed as cabin boy on board a vessel bound for New Orleans, and in that city he found a friend in a merchant, who adopted him and gave him his own name, but died

HENRY M. STANLEY

leaving no will. Young Stanley, left to his own resources, went to California, where he sought his fortune in the gold mines. When the Civil War broke out he became a soldier in the Confederate army. He was made prisoner, and sub-sequently took service in the United States navy, becoming acting ensign on the ironclad "Ticonderoga." After the close of the war he became a newspaper correspondent, writing a series of letters from Crete and Asia Minor. When the English expedition was sent against King Theodore of Abyssinia in 1867 he accompanied it as commissioner of the New York "Herald." He made his reputation as a correspondent by sending an account of Lord Napier's victory to London before the official dispatches arrived. In 1868 he went to Spain to report the Carlist War for the same paper. He was called away from there in October, 1869, to go in search of Dr. David Livingstone in Africa, from whom no news had been received for more than two years, and who was reported to have been killed, but whom James G. Bennett, proprietor of the "Herald," believed to be still alive. He arrived at Zanzibar in January, 1871, where he organized a large expedition of 192 men, which he sent off in five parties. His objctive point was Ujiji, which he reached, and found Livingstone, Nov. 10, 1871. After remaining with the veteran Scotch missionary and explorer four months he returned, Livingstone refusing to give up his enterprise till he had completed his work. In 1874 he set out on a second African expedition for the "Herald" and London "Daily Telegraph." At Zanzibar he learned that Livingstone had died in the autumn on the shore of Lake Bangweolo. He reached Victoria Nyanza in February, 1875. He was the first to circumnavigate Victoria Lake, and discovered the Shimeeyu river. He reached England again in February, 1878. Then came the Belgian enterprise, out of which was developed the Free State of Kongo, with Stanley as its conductor, with large means at his disposal. Near the close of 1886 Stanley, under the auspices of the Egyptian Government and of English societies and individuals, undertook an expedition for the relief of Emin Pasha. For this purpose he left England in January, 1887, and returned in 1890, after escorting Emin Bey and a large troop of followers from the interior to the coast. He wrote "How I Found Livingstone," "Through the Dark Continent," "Congo and the Founding of its Free State," "Slavery and the Slave Trade," "In Darkest Africa," "Through South Africa," etc. He was made a D. C. L. of Oxford University in 1890, and the same year was married to Miss Dorothy Tennent in Westminster Abbey. In 1890-1891 he made a lecturing tour of the United States, and in 1895 was elected to Parliament. He died May 10, 1904.

STANLEY FALLS, a cataract, and also a trading station, on the Kongo, 1,413 miles from the mouth of the river. Stanley Falls Station is at the head of navigation for good-sized vessels, and is in the heart of equatorial Africa. Here is an important entrêpot of the African International Association.

STANLEY POOL, a lake-like expansion of the Kongo, 250 square miles in extent, dotted with islands, 325 miles from the sea. Kallina Point marks its lower extremity, and Inga Peak dominates the entrance to the united river above the pool. Stanley Pool is an important station of the African International Association, and several bodies of missionaries are laboring there.

STANNARD, MRS. (HENRIETTA ELIZA VAUGHAN PALMER), an English novelist, writing under the pseudonyms JOHN STRANGE WINTER and VIOLET WHYTE; born in York, England, Jan. 13, 1856. She wrote among others: "Cavalry Life" (1881); "Regimental Legends" (1883); "Bootles's Baby" (1885), very popular; "Houp-la" (1885); "A Siege Baby" (1887); "Only Human"; "Grip"; "Heart and Sword"; and over 40 other novels. She died in 1911.

STANOVOI, or **YABLONOI,** a mountain chain in the N. E. of Asia, which forms the boundary between Siberia and Manchuria, skirts the Sea of Okhotsk, and is continued, though with gradually diminishing height, to the shores of Bering Strait. The whole length of the chain has been estimated at 3,000 miles. The E. part is often distinctively called Yablonoi. This mountain range gives rise to the rivers Amur and Anadir on its S. and E. side, and to the Yenisei, Lena, Indighirka, and Kolyma on the N. and W. side.

STANTON, EDWIN McMASTERS, an American statesman; born in Steubenville, O., Dec. 19, 1814; was admitted to the bar in 1836; and began to practice in Cadiz, O. He soon rose to eminence and in December, 1860, was appointed Attorney-General of the United States. In 1862 he succeeded Simon Cameron as Secretary of War and held that office for six years. His opposition to President Johnson's plan of reconstruction led the latter to request his resignation in 1867. He refused to resign, but on Aug. 12 surrendered his office under protest to General Grant as secretary ad interim. On Jan. 13, 1868, the United States Senate reinstated him, but the President appointed Adjt.-Gen. Lorenzo Thomas to fill his place. Stanton refused to vacate the office, however, and the impeachment of the President followed. On the President's acquittal, Stanton resigned and resumed law practice. On Dec. 20, 1869, he was nominated by President Grant as an associate justice of the Supreme Court of the United States, but died before taking his seat, in Washington, Dec. 24.

STANTON, ELIZABETH CADY, an American reformer; born in Johnstown,

N. Y., Nov. 12, 1815; was graduated at Emma Willard's Seminary, in Troy, N. Y., in 1832; called the first Woman's Rights Convention in Seneca Falls, N. Y., in 1848; addressed the New York Legislature on the rights of married women in 1854, and in advocacy of divorce for drunkenness in 1860; and was an unsuccessful candidate for Congress in 1868. She was a member of numerous Woman's Suffrage societies, editor of "The Revolution," and the author of "The History of Woman Suffrage"; "Eighty Years and More"; "The Woman's Bible"; and other works. She died in 1902.

STANTON, FRANK LEBBY, an American poet and journalist, born at Charleston, S. C., in 1857. After being connected with various newspapers in Atlanta, Ga., he joined the staff of the Atlanta "Constitution," where for several years he contributed daily verse and prose. He published "Songs of the Soil" (1894); "Comes One With a Song" (1898), and "Little Folks Down South" (1904). Died January 7, 1927.

STANTON, OSCAR FITZALAN, an American naval officer, born in Sag Harbor, N. Y., in 1834. He was appointed a midshipman in the United States Navy in 1849, and gradually rose through the various grades of the service, becoming a rear admiral in July, 1894, just before he was retired. He served in various posts throughout the Civil War, and saw service in Chinese and Japanese waters from 1872 to 1874. Besides holding commands on various vessels of the United States Navy, his assignments included service at the New York Navy Yard (1864-1865), Norfolk Navy Yard (1874-1877), Newport Torpedo Station (1878), Naval Station, New London, Conn. (1885-1889), Newport Training Station (1890-1891), and the Philadelphia Naval Home (1891-1893). He was a member of various patriotic and naval societies.

STANTON, THEODORE, an American journalist, son of Henry B. and Elizabeth Cady; born in Seneca Falls, N. Y., Feb. 10, 1851. He was a correspondent for the New York "Tribune" at Berlin from 1880, and later engaged as a journalist in Paris. He translated Goff's "Life of Thiers" (1879), and wrote: "The Woman Question in Europe" (1884) and "Life of Rosa Bonheur" (1910). He edited several volumes of letters relating to the World War.

STANWOOD, EDWARD, an American editor, born in Augusta, Me., in 1841.

He was educated at Bowdoin College, from which he also received an honorary degree in 1894. From 1867 to 1882 he was assistant editor, and from 1882 to 1883 editor of the Boston "Daily Advertiser." From 1887 to 1911 he was managing editor of the "Youth's Companion." He acted as special agent on several of the United States manufacturing censuses, was a trustee of Bowdoin College, and a member and recording secretary of the Massachusetts Historical Society. He wrote, besides many articles for domestic and foreign reviews and for many other periodicals: "History of Presidential Elections" (1884); "History of the Presidency" (1898 and 1912); "American Tariff Controversies" (1903); "James Gillespie Blaine" (1905). Died Oct. 11, 1923.

STANZA, a number of lines or verses regularly adjusted to each other, and properly ending in a full point or pause; a part of a poem ordinarily containing every variety of measure in that poem; a combination or arrangement of lines usually recurring, whether like or unlike in measure. A stanza is variously termed terzina, quartetto, sestina, ottava, etc., according as it consists of three, four, six, eight, etc., lines.

STAPLE, the modern form of the Anglo-Saxon word *stapel*, meaning a heap, or regularly piled up accumulation, of goods; hence a place where goods are stored up for sale. In the Middle Ages, when the term was in common use, a staple meant both the trading town for particular commodities and the commodities that were wont to be exposed for sale there.

STAR, one of the self-luminous bodies which surrounds our solar system on all sides. They are distinguished from the planets by their flickering light, by the comparative constancy of their relative positions in space, and by their inappreciable diameter even when viewed by the most powerful optical instruments. The number of stars visible to the naked eye is estimated at about 5,000; and these have from an early age been grouped in constellations and classified according to their brightness or magnitude. Those belonging to the first six magnitudes are visible to the naked eye; but the telescope reveals myriads which are distinguished down to the 16th magnitude. The earliest catalogue which has come down to us is that in Ptolemy's "Almagest," supposed to have been compiled by Hipparchus (150 B. C.). Ptolemy gives 1,030 stars, of which several cannot now be certainly identified. The last important catalogue before the invention of the telescope was that of Tycho Brahe, who redetermined with still greater accuracy the positions of 1,005 stars. Of telescope surveys, catalogues, Argelander's was till lately the largest, enumerating more than 300,000 down to the 9th magnitude, all between the North pole and 2° S.

The photographic mapping of stars, after some 40 years of labor, was completed in 1927. Nineteen observatories in divers parts of the world coöperated in taking the photographs that compose the chart. This consists of some 30,000 photographs, on which are shown 15,000,000 stars. By no means all the stars visible through the telescope were photographed, no effort being made to show those beyond the 14th magnitude. One of the chief purposes in the photographing of the stars thus is to record their exact positions. The record is designed to afford means for comparison with observations in future times. By means of such changes of position as may be observed, astronomers may learn more of the nature and extent of heavenly motions outside the solar system.

The large majority of stars are of constant magnitude, but there are variable stars, which vary in brightness periodically. Algol, in the constellation Perseus, fluctuates between the 2d and 4th magnitudes in about three days. Mira in the constellation Cetus is such another star, bursting out at intervals of 11 months as a 2d or 3d magnitude star. At times, stars have suddenly appeared where none were known before. The most remarkable of these are the ones described by Tycho Brahe (1572), that observed by Kepler (1604-1606), and the star of 1866, which blazed out suddenly in Corona Borealis. Near the place of the first a small telescopic star now exists, and the last was entered as a 9th-magnitude star in Argelander's catalogue. The spectrum of the 1866 star as examined by Huggins consisted of a continuous spectrum crossed not only by the usual dark absorption lines, but also by bright lines which corresponded in part with the spectrum lines of hydrogen. The general similarity of the stellar spectra to the solar spectrum is a convincing proof, if any further were needed, that our sun is a star.

According to the nature of their spectra, stars have been grouped under four types: Type I., of which Sirius, the brightest known star, is one, has a continuous spectrum with a very few absorption lines; in Type II. the spectrum is crossed by numerous fine lines, as in the sun's spectrum; in Type III., to which a Orionis and a Herculis belong, fluted spaces begin to appear; and in Type IV., which

includes the red stars, fluted spaces only exist. According to the accepted theory of spectrum analysis, the continuous spectrum indicates a higher temperature than the broken one. As a star is cooling, its spectrum passes through all these types, and thus our sun is at a later stage in its life history than Sirius, though it may not be really any older, since it is probably much smaller than Sirius, whose development will therefore be slower. Our sun cannot be compared in size or splendor to some of its distant compeers. The telescope reveals many stars to be really double.

One of the most interesting of these is Sirius, from the irregularity of whose movements Peters and Auwers had concluded that it was accompanied by an attendant star or at least a large planet; and in 1862 such a companion was discovered by the younger Clark in the very direction in which theory had predicted it to be at that time. Its great minuteness renders detection hopeless except in very favorable circumstances. The motions of Procyon indicate a similar doubleness, but its companion has not yet been seen. Triple and multiple stars forming one system are also not uncommon. For instance, u Herculis, recognized as a double star by Herschel, is really a triple star, the small Herschelian companion having been resolved into two in 1856 by Alvan Clark. An interesting optical property of these binary systems is that the color of the one component is frequently the complement of that of the other. A very remarkable double star is 61 Cygni, famous as the first star whose distance from the sun was calculated directly from its parallax, i. e., from the angular distance between its positions as viewed from opposite extremities of the earth's orbit.

This, however, is not the nearest star; it is nearly twice as far away as a Centauri, which according to Henderson has a parallax of $0''.91$, corresponding to a distance of 226,000 times the radius of the earth's orbit, or more than twenty millions of millions of miles (20×10^{12}). In other words, light, which travels at the rate of 236,000 miles per second, takes nearly three years to pass from the nearest fixed star to us. The parallax of at least half the stars of the 1st magnitude is probably less than one-tenth of a second, so that their average distance is greater than two million radii of the earth's orbit. Though, to the naked eye, stars have probably occupied the same relative positions from the earliest of historic times, the telescope reveals that they are not strictly fixed. Many have appreciable proper motions, among others 61 Cygni, as was before noticed.

1-5

Its annual motion is 5″ .2, which is exceeded, however, by that of Groombridge, 1830, a star of the 7th magnitude, whose proper motion is 7″. As a general rule, the brightest stars have the greatest proper motion, and stars below the 3d magnitude move only a few seconds in 100 years.

This motion in the heavens cannot be taken even as an approximate estimate of the velocity with which any star is moving, since only the portion of the real velocity which is resolved perpendicular to the line of sight is measurable. Spectrum analysis has, however, given us a means of measuring the velocity along the line of sight. The physical meaning of the dark absorption lines which cross the spectra of the sun and stars has been pointed out under SPECTRUM ANALYSIS. They indicate the absence of certain rays of definite refrangibility and wave length from the solar or stellar light which reaches us. Since each star spectrum has its own peculiar lines, these must be due to absorption by the star's own outer envelope or atmosphere. Now, exactly as ocean waves will appear shorter or longer than they really are according as the observer is sailing against or with them, so will the wave length of each individual ray be shortened or lengthened according as we approach or recede from the source of light, and each absorption line in the spectrum, corresponding as it does to a ray of definite wave length, will be displaced toward the violet or red respectively. By comparison with the spectrum of the substance to which a determined portion of these lines corresponds, this displacement may be measured, and from its relation to the particular wave length the ratio of the relative velocity of approach or recession of the star to the velocity of light can be easily calculated. Stars which show periodic variations of magnitude are called variable stars. Among these are Mira and Algal. Up to 1920 about 750 of these stars were known. Their average period of variation is about 300 days and some are 1,000 times brighter at maximum than at minimum. It is believed that these are the giants among the stars. At their maximum some are 150 times brighter than the sun.

STARBOARD, the right side of a ship when the eye is directed toward the head, stem, or prow.

STAR CATALOGUES, lists of catalogues of the stars arranged according to their positions, generally their right ascensions and declinations, though some of the early catalogues were arranged according to the positions in latitude and longitude. The early catalogues, and those accompanying uranometries, are arranged in constellations, and then in the order of position under each constellation. This system was, of course, fit only for the few stars visible with the naked eye. Modern catalogues resulting from accurate determinations of position give the places to hundredths of a second of time and tenths of a second of arc. Such catalogues also give the precession of each star in right ascension and declination, in order to reduce the position to any desired epoch, for the places of the stars are always changing, or rather the coordinate plane to which they are referred is always shifting its position on account of precession of the equinoxes.

STARCH, one of the commonest organic compounds ($C_6H_{10}O_5$), is produced by chlorophyll-bearing plants, and forms the chief solid constituent of many seeds and tubers, e. g., rice and potatoes. It is white, amorphous, pulverizes, and is insoluble in cold water. In hot water it expands and gelatinizes. Iodine alters its color to a deep blue. Heated with certain dilute acids, and with chemical substances employed in the assimilative systems of animals, starch produces dextrin, glucose, maltose, and other derivatives. It affords the chief carbohydrate supply in nutrition of higher animals.

STAR CHAMBER, a British tribunal which met in the old council chamber of the palace of Westminster, and is said to have received its name from the roof of that apartment being decorated with gilt stars, or because in it "starres" or Jewish bonds had been kept. It is supposed to have originated in acts of the king's council, whose powers in this respect had greatly declined when in 1487 Henry VII. revived them. A statute conferred on the chancellor, the treasurer, and the keeper of the privy seal, with the assistance of a bishop and a temporal lord of the council, and chief justices, or two other justices in their absence, a jurisdiction to punish without a jury misdeeds of sheriffs and juries, riots and unlawful assemblies. Privy councillors later were members.

The civil jurisdiction of the Star Chamber comprised controversies between English and foreign merchants, testamentary causes, disputes between the heads and commonalty of corporations, lay and ecclesiastical, and claims to deodands. As a criminal court it could inflict any punishment short of death, and had cognizance of forgery, perjury, riots, maintenance, fraud, libels, conspiracy, etc. Treason, murder, and felony could be brought under the jurisdiction of the Star Chamber, where the king chose to remit the capital sentence. The form of proceeding was by written information and interrogatories, except when the accused person confessed.

Regardless of the existing rule that the confession must be free and unconstrained, pressure of every kind, including torture, was used to procure acknowledgments of guilt; admissions of the most immaterial facts were construed into confessions; and fine, imprisonment, and mutilation inflicted on a mere oral proceeding, without hearing the accused, by a court consisting of the immediate representatives of prerogative. In 1641 a bill was carried in both Houses which decreed the abolition of the Star Chamber and the equally unpopular High Commission Court.

STARFISH, in zoölogy, a popular name for any individual of the family *Asteriadæ* or *Asteridæ;* applied specifically to the common starfish, *A.* (*Uraster*) *rubens,* a familiar object on the Atlantic coasts. The body is more or less star shaped, and consists of a central portion, or disk, surrounded by five or more lobes, or arms, radiating from the body and containing prolongations of the vis-

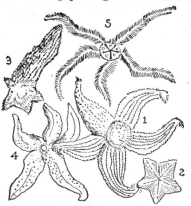

STARFISHES AND BRITTLE STARS

1—Common Starfish (Asterias rubens);
2—Gibbous Starlet (Asterina gibbosa);
3—Common Starfish, reproducing rays;
4—Eyed Cribella (Cribella oculata);
5—Lesser Sand-star (Ophiura albida).

cera; but in some forms the central disk extends so as to include the rays, rendering the animal pentagonal in shape. The integument is of a leathery texture, and is often strengthened by calcareous plates or spines. The mouth is situated in the center of the lower surface of the body, and the anus is either absent or on the upper surface. Locomotion is

effected by means of peculiar tube-like processes, which are protruded from the under surface of the arms. The nervous system consists of a gangliated cord surrounding the mouth, and sending filaments to each of the arms. The young generally pass through a free larval stage, and parthenogenesis seems to occur in Asterias. Starfish are extremely voracious, and are very annoying to fishermen by devouring their bait. They possess in a high degree the power of reproducing lost members and abound in all seas.

STARGARD, a town of East Pomerania, Prussia; on the navigable Ilna, 25 miles E. S. E. of Stettin. Its well-preserved walls are surmounted by handsome towers, and its chief buildings are the Gothic Marienkirche of the 16th century, with richly adorned interior, a Rathhaus of the 11th century, the quaint Protzensche Haus, and a higher Bürgerschule of 1860. It manufactures woolens, linens, leather, etc., and trades in grain and cattle. Stargard, destroyed by the Poles in 1120, was raised to the rank of a town in 1229, joined the Hanseatic League, and was strongly fortified. It was important during the Thirty Years' War. Pop. about 27,500.

STARK, JOHN, an American military officer; born in Londonderry, N. H., Aug. 28, 1728; joined the troops under Major Rogers in the war against the French and Indians in 1754; rendered efficient service at Ticonderoga in 1758, and was actively employed in the subsequent campaign. In 1775, after the battle of Lexington, he received a colonel's commission, and recruited a regiment which formed the left of the American line at Bunker Hill. In December, 1776, he marched with his regiment under General Gates to re-enforce Washington and was with him at the battles of Princeton and Trenton. In 1777 he resigned his commission, feeling slighted by Congress in its list of promotions. When, however, information was received that Ticonderoga had been taken, he set out at the head of a small force, met and defeated Baum's forces at Bennington, and likewise defeated the British re-enforcements of 500 men which Burgoyne had sent to Baum's aid. For this victory he was promoted Brigadier-General and later joined General Gates at Bemis Heights; but the term of his militia having expired, he returned to New Hampshire and recruited a new force. With these he cut off Burgoyne's retreat from Saratoga, and in 1778 was placed in command of the Northern Department. Later he served in Rhode Island, New

Jersey, and at West Point in 1779-1780; and was one of the court which condemned Major André. After the war he returned to his farm. He died in Manchester, N. H., May 8, 1822.

STARLING, in ornithology, a popular name for any individual of the genus *Sturnus,* sometimes extended to the whole family but specifically applied to *S. vulgaris,* the common starling, abundant in most parts of the continent of Europe, frequently visiting Northern Africa in its winter migrations. The male is about eight inches long, general color of the plumage black, glossed with blue and purple, the feathers, except those of the head and fore neck, having a triangular white spot on the tip. The female is very similar, but has the feathers tipped with broader spots, those on the upper parts being light brown. The eggs are from 4 to 6 in number, light blue in color and are deposited in some hole or crevice. Starlings feed on snails, worms, and insects; they are gregarious, uniting in large flocks. They become exceedingly familiar in confinement, and display great imitative powers.

STAR OF BETHLEHEM, the celestial phenomenon described in the New Testament as accompanying the birth of Christ. Some astronomers have attempted to account for this on the hypothesis of the conjunction of two or more bright planets in about the same part of the sky at that time, but with little success. At various times since the appearance of Tycho Brahe's star in the constellation Cassiopeia in 1572, the celebrated Nova of that year, it has been suggested that this might be a variable star of long period, though there is nothing now in the vicinity of the place of this star brighter than the 12th or 13th magnitude. Astronomers, since the invention of the telescope, have kept a pretty close watch of the few faint stars in the immediate vicinity of the place indicated by Tycho Brahe's measures to see if any of them changed in brightness, but without any evidence of such change. There is no good reason for supposing any such periodicity in the star, or any other star now known.

STAR OF BETHLEHEM, in botany, *Ornithogalum umbellatum;* natural order *Liliaceæ;* a bulbous-rooted plant with white star-like flowers. It is common in many parts of Europe and is naturalized in some of the United States.

STAROSTS, in Poland, those noblemen who were reckoned among the dignitaries of the land, and who received a castle or landed estate from the crown domains. Some of the starosts had civil and criminal jurisdiction over a certain district, others merely enjoyed the revenues of the starosty.

STARR, FRANCES (GRANT), an American actress, born at Oneonta, N. Y., in 1886. She was educated in the public schools of Albany and made her first appearance on the stage in that city in 1901. She joined the Murray Hill Stock Co. of New York City and while playing there attracted the attention of David Belasco, who undertook her theatrical training. Under his direction she appeared as leading lady in "The Music Master"; "The Easiest Way," "The Secret." "Little Lady in Blue," and "Tiger, Tiger," the latter in 1919-1920.

STAR ROUTES, a term used in connection with the United States postal service. Prior to 1845 it was the custom in letting the contracts for the transportation of inland mails, other than by railroad or steamboat routes, to give the preference to bidders who offered stage or coach service. This was abolished by act of Congress, March 3, 1845, which provided that the postmaster-general should let all such contracts to the lowest bidder tendering sufficient guarantee for faithful performance, without any condition except to provide for due celerity, certainty and security of transportation. These bids for such service became classified as "celerity, certainty and security bids," and for brevity were designated on the route registers by three stars (***) and known as star routes.

Early in 1881 rumors were in circulation of extensive frauds in this branch of the mail service. It was charged that there was a "ring" to defraud the government in which were included some of the large contractors, the Second Assistant Postmaster-General, some of the subordinates in the department, a United States Senator, and others. Proceedings were begun, but no conviction was secured either on these charges or on others which were made in 1883.

STARS AND BARS, the flag of the Confederate States of America. It was merely an adaptation of the stars and stripes, having 3 "alternate stripes red and white," instead of 13 such stripes, and a circle of white stars on a blue field, corresponding to the number of States of the confederacy.

STAR-SPANGLED BANNER, THE, the national anthem of the United States. It was written by Francis Scott

Key on board the frigate "Surprise" in the course of the bombardment of Fort McHenry, Md., by the British fleet in 1814. The words on Key's suggestion were sung to the tune of "Anacreon in Heaven," which is supposed to have been composed by John Stafford Smith about 1773. The anthem, as soon as it became known, attained great popularity and the first public singing is said to have taken place in a tavern near the Holiday Street Theater, Baltimore, the singer being Ferdinand Durang. The moving character, both of the sentiments and the melody, has placed it among the most thrilling of the national hymns of any country. "The Star-Spangled Banner" (Washington, 1914), by O. G. T. Sonneck describes the evolution of the anthem, and contains different versions of the text and music.

STARVATION or INANITION, the physical effect produced by the total want of food and water. The symptoms of starvation in man are: an increasing loss of weight, severe pain in the stomach, loss of strength, sleeplessness, great thirst, in some cases stupor, and in other cases nervous excitement with convulsions. Death occurs in about eight days. With a good supply of water, however, life may be prolonged, in the absence of solid food, for a period of two or three weeks, and cases have been known of persons surviving for two months and more. Gradual starvation may result from continued low percentage of nutritive elements in the daily diet.

STATE, a whole people united into a body politic; a civil and self-governing community. Also, any body of men constituting a community of a particular character in virtue of certain political privileges, who partake either directly or by representation in the government of their country; an estate; as, The Lords spiritual and temporal and the Commons are the states (or estates) of the realm in Great Britain.

In the plural, the legislative body in the island of Jersey, England. It consists of 55 persons, including the bailiff of the island, who is *ex officio* president. The lieutenant-governor has a power of veto, and the States may not be convened without his consent. Guernsey has an analogous body, the Deliberative States, and a more popular assembly, the Elective States. In both islands the States deal only with questions of internal administration.

Also, one of the commonwealths or bodies politic which together go to compose a Federal republic, and which stand in certain specified relations with the central or national government, and, as regards internal affairs, are more or less independent; as, the State of Pennsylvania.

STATE BANKS, financial institutions doing a banking business under the supervision of the State, which guarantees its integrity to a greater or lesser extent, according to the individual State's laws, the relation between the bank and the State being similar to the relation between a National bank and the Federal Government. The State bank had its origin in New York, in the Free Banking Law of 1838, which terminated an evil system, or lack of system, under which banking corporations and private individuals were granted charters through special privileges, often by bribery and subterfuge. The law of 1838 extended banking privileges to all corporations willing to conform to its provisions, and so laid the groundwork on which the national banking system was based by Federal legislation. Since it is impossible to describe even superficially the characteristic features of the State banking systems in all the States, an outline of the National banking system, which is based on the original laws of New York and Massachusetts, will give a more concrete idea of underlying principles, more especially since the banking legislation of the younger States has been in turn taken from Federal legislation.

The first of the various acts of Congress constituting the legislation on which rests our National banking system was passed in February, 1863, which authorized certain banks to issue notes on bonds deposited in the United States Treasurey. In June, 1864, this law was revised and amended and a bureau was established in the Treasury Department, in charge of the Comptroller of the Currency, which was to supervise the newly created National banking system. In cities of six thousand population or over banks must have at least $100,000 capital. In smaller communities $50,000 was the limit, though this has since been reduced to $25,000. No bank could begin business before half of its capital stock had been paid in, and then the balance must be paid in within 5 months, in monthly installments. At least 30 per cent. of the paid in capital must be converted into United States bonds and deposited in the United States Treasury, 90 per cent. of whose market value could be represented in notes issued by the bank. The entire amount of these notes, however, was then limited to $300,000,000, but this limitation was later removed. Banks in rural communities were required to keep on reserve funds equal to 15 per cent. of their outstanding notes and deposits of which three-fifths might be re-deposited with other National banks in 17 specified large cities, known as reserve cities. Banks in these reserve cities must maintain reserves equal to 25 per cent. of their deposits and outstanding notes, but half of these reserves might be deposited in the National banks in New York City, the central reserve city. Later Chicago and St. Louis were also ranked as central reserve cities. The rural banks were compelled to provide for redemption of their notes at par by National banks in reserve cities. These latter must make similar arrangements with National banks in the central reserve cities. Added to these various restrictions was the semi-annual inspection of the books of all National banks by inspectors representing the Comptroller of the Currency, which was supposed to protect depositors against dishonesty or bad business judgment on the part of the bank officials.

It is on more or less the same principles as the above system that the State banking systems are founded. Some slight differences and modifications there are. As an instance, Massachusetts has no State banks of discount and deposit. New York, California and Texas and several other States authorize corporations to transact discount and deposit banking, savings bank and trust company business under one charter. This kind of banking, known as "department store banking," is now also largely permitted the National banks under the Federal Reserve Law of 1913, making it difficult for the State banks in those States which have not made similar provisions to compete with the National banks. State banks, on the other hand, are more likely to be closely adapted to the needs of the local communities, especially in the agricultural districts, where rural credit is a problem.

State banks outnumber National banks two to one. On June 30, 1927, there were 15,690 State banks, representing a decrease of 2,958 from the 1923 total. The total resources of all the State banks in the country amounted to over $16,564,-000,000. Individual deposits amounted to $12,936,590,000. Loans, discounts, and investments in bonds and securities totaled $12,926,127,000.

STATE, DEPARTMENT OF, an executive department of the United States Government, established by Act of Congress, July 27, 1789. At its head is the Secretary of State, who is appointed by the President and confirmed by the Senate and who is a member of the Cabinet. Through him communication is made between the United States Government and any of the States or any foreign country. He has charge of the great seal of the United States; directs ambassadors and consuls, and is custodian of the laws and treaties.

STATEN ISLAND, an island comprising Richmond co., N. Y.; bounded on the N. by the Kill van Kull, on the E. by New York Bay and the Narrows, on the S. S. E. by Raritan Bay and the Lower Bay, and on the W. by Staten Island Bay; is about 13 miles long with an extreme width of 8 miles; area, 58½ square miles. It forms Richmond Borough of New York City; within it are Tottenville, Port Richmond, Linoleumville, Edgewater, Stapleton, Tompkinsville and New Brighton. At the Narrows on the E. shore are Fort Wadsworth and a line of water batteries; on the Lower Bay are Midland Beach and South Beach, waterside resorts; and on the N. shore are Sailors' Snug Harbor, a home for infirm and aged seamen.

The island, long accessible only by water, was connected with New Jersey by two great vehicular bridges, opened June 20, 1928; the one, between Howland Hook and Elizabeth, being 8,000 feet long, and the other, between Tottenville and Perth-Amboy, more than 10,000 feet. Both were constructed by the two abutting States through the Port of New York Authority. Pop. (1910) 85,969; (1920) 116,531.

STATEN ISLAND, an island off the S. E. coast of Tierra del Fuego, separated from the mainland by the Strait of Le Maire.

STATER, in numismatics, the name of certain coins current in ancient Greece and Macedonia. The gold stater of Athens was worth about $3.89; the silver stater about 86 cents, and the Macedonian gold stater $5.11.

STATES-GENERAL, so called in contradistinction to the local *états provinciaux;* National representative assembly of France up to the Revolution. Under the Karolings there was an annual assembly of clergy and nobles, called either the *Champ de Mars* or the *Champ de Mai,* according to the time of meeting, but it had little of a representative character. The States-General properly so called was first assembled by Philippe le Bel in 1302, on the occasion of his disagreements with the Pope. It was composed of representatives of the three estates, nobles, clergy, and *tiers-état* or *bourgeoisie*. It assembled at pretty frequent intervals during the 14th century and not so regularly in the 15th and 16th centuries, being principally occupied with financial matters, though its functions in the imposition of taxation, etc., were very undefined, and its powers were encroached on from time to time by the royal authority. It had no legislative power whatever. The last States-General before the famous one which heralded the Revolution was that held under Louis XIII. in 1614. From that date till May 5, 1789, the crown absorbed the whole functions of taxation as well as of government. The States-General of 1789, almost immediately on its constitution, was resolved by the secession of the representatives of the *tiers-état* into the Assemblée Nationale.

The name States-General is also applied to the legislative body of Holland, lineally descended from the Estates-General of the United Province, which took such a prominent and honorable part in the revolt of the Netherlands.

STATESVILLE, a city of North Carolina, the county seat of Iredell co. It is on the Southern railway. Its industries include furniture factories, cotton mills, flour mills, tanneries, foundries, tobacco factories, and ironworks. It is the seat of the Statesville Female College and Long's Sanitarium. Pop. (1910) 4,599; (1920) 7,895.

STATICE, in botany, sea-lavender; the typical genus of *Staticeæ*. Perennial herbs, with radical leaves, and unilateral spikes on a panicled scape; calyx funnel-shaped, plaited, dry, and membranous; petals united at the base, bearing the stamens. Known species 50 or 60, including *S. caroliniana* the marsh rosemary of this country.

STATIC, or **STRAYS**, erratic electrical disturbances in wireless communication, whose origin is not yet fully known. Some strays appear to be due to distant lightning discharges. Others, according to present theory, are caused by electrical disturbances in the upper atmosphere.

STATICS, briefly, the dynamics of equilibrium, as kinetics is the dynamics of motion. In modern phraseology they are said to make up together the science of dynamics, since both deal with the effects of forces. According to Newton's first and second laws of motion, change of motion in a given mass indicates the existence of a force which is in the direction in which the change of motion occurs, and is measured by the product of the mass into the rate of this change, or what is called the acceleration. Thus, a falling stone of mass M suffers a constant acceleration g per second; hence the force pulling it down, *i. e.*, its weight, is measured by the product Mg. While the stone is descending, the problem is one of kinetics; but when it reaches the surface of the earth its motion relatively to the earth ceases, there is no accleration, and the problem becomes statical. Every kinetical problem may be reduced to a statical problem by introducing into the material system forces whose effects will balance the various accelerations to which the different parts of the system are subject.

STATIONERS' HALL, the hall of the "Master and Keepers or Wardens and Commonalty of the Mystery or Art of the Stationers of the City of London." The Company was incorporated in 1557, and had till the passing of the Copyright Act in 1842 an absolute monopoly, as all printers were obliged to serve an apprenticeship to a member of the Company, and every publication, from a Bible to a ballad, was required to be "Entered at Stationers' Hall." This registration is no longer compulsory, but the practice of registering is still useful in making good claims of copyright. The series of registers of books entered for publication, commencing in 1554, is of enormous value in the history of English literature. A transcript of these from 1554 to 1640 was published by Professor Arber in five volumes. See COPYRIGHT.

STATISTICS, a collection of facts, arranged and classified, respecting the condition of a people in a state or community, or of a class of people, their health, longevity, domestic economy, their social, moral, intellectual, physical and economical condition, resources, etc., especially those facts which can be stated in numbers or tables of numbers, or in any tabular and classified arrangement. Also, that department of political science which classifies, arranges, and discusses statistical facts. The Italians were the first to recognize the importance of statistics. The earliest English work on the subject was Graunt's "Observations on the Bills of Mortality," published in 1661. The first International Statistical Congress was held at Brussels in 1853. In every civilized country the science of statistics now forms the basis of most inquiries regarding the condition of the people, and no important legislation is attempted without reference, direct or indirect, to the facts which it tabulates.

STATUTE, a law proceeding from the government of a State; the written will of the legislature solemnly expressed according to the forms necessary to constitute it the law of the State. A statute which contravenes a provision of the constitution of a State by whose legislature it was enacted, or of the United States Constitution, is void. Statutes are either public or private (in the latter case affecting an individual or a company); but the term is usually restricted to public acts of a general and permanent character. Statutes are said to be declaratory of the law as it stood before their passing; remedial, to correct defects in the common law; and penal, imposing prohibitions and penalties. The term statute is commonly applied to the acts of a legislative body consisting of representatives. In monarchies not having representative bodies, the laws of the sovereign are called edicts, decrees, ordinances, rescripts, etc.

STAUNTON, a city of Illinois, in Macoupin co. It is on the Wabash, the Litchfield and Madison, and the Illinois Traction railroads. In the neighborhood are coal mines, and oil and gas wells. Among its public buildings is the Labor Temple. Pop. (1910) 5,048; (1920) 6,-027.

STAUNTON, a city and county-seat of Augusta co., Va.; on the Chesapeake and Ohio and the Baltimore and Ohio railroads; 136 miles W. N. W. of Richmond. It is situated in the fertile and beautiful Shenandoah valley. Here are the State Institution for the Deaf, Dumb, and Blind, the Mary Baldwin Seminary, the Staunton Military Academy, the Staunton Female Seminary, the Wesleyan Female Institute, the Western State Hospital, Masonic Temple, City Hall, park, street railroad and electric light plants, waterworks, National and State banks, and several daily and weekly newspapers. It has manufactories of ice, sash and blinds, cigars, flour, organs, machinery, building material, agricultural implements, carriages, etc. Pop. (1910) 10,604; (1920) 10,623.

STAUNTON, a river of Virginia which rises in Montgomery co., and flows E. across Roanoke co., reaching the Blue Ridge, through which it breaks, so forming picturesque scenery and marvels in rapid descent. It is said to fall 1,000 feet in 20 miles. It has devious windings after it emerges from the mountain depths. It unites with the Dan river at Clarksville, Mecklenburg co., to form the Roanoke; length, 200 miles.

STAUROLITE or **FAIRY STONE,** a mineral found in various parts of the United States, in the Tyrol, in Cornwall (England) and in other parts. Chemically, it is a hydrated silicate of iron, aluminum and magnesium and occurs as brown rhombic crystals, having a cruciform arrangement, and a sub-vitreous lustre. Its specific gravity is 3.5 and hardness 7.5.

STAVANGER, the most important town in the S. W. of Norway; on the S. side of Bukken Fjord; 100 miles S. of Bergen. It has two harbors and derives its importance from its connection with the fisheries of the adjacent coast. The town dates back to the 9th century, but has been frequently destroyed by fire, and is now quite a modern place. The cathedral, a Gothic structure, was founded by an English bishop (Reinald) in the 11th century, but was restored in 1866. Of late years it has become a favorite rendezvous of tourists. Pop. (1918) 46,100.

STAVROPOL, formerly a Russian province in the Caucasus and recently part of the Kuban Republic. It has an area of 23,398 square miles, comprising largely untimbered prairies and extensively cultivated for grain. The country was colonized a century ago by Cossacks, but the inhabitants include Poles, Armenians, Greeks and Slavic Russians. Pop. about 1,300,000. The city of Stavropol, capital of the province, is situated on the Atchla, 307 miles southwest of Astrakan. Soap, flour, and leather goods are the products of the chief industries. Pop. about 80,000.

STEAD, WILLIAM THOMAS, an English journalist; born in Embleton, Northumberland, July 5, 1849. He is widely known as editor of the "Review of Reviews," which he founded in January, 1890. He published "The Maiden Tribute of Modern Babylon" (1885). In 1893 he established "Borderland," a periodical devoted to spiritualism. Among his published books are "The United States of Europe" (1899); "Peers or People" (1907). He died in 1912.

STEAM, in physics, water in its gaseous form. It is a colorless, invisible gas, quite distinct from the visible cloud which issues from a kettle, etc., which is composed of minute drops of water produced by the condensation of the steam as it issues into the colder air.

© Keystone View Company

A STEAM-DRIVEN PUNCH CUTTING HOLES THROUGH ¾-INCH STEEL SHIP PLATES

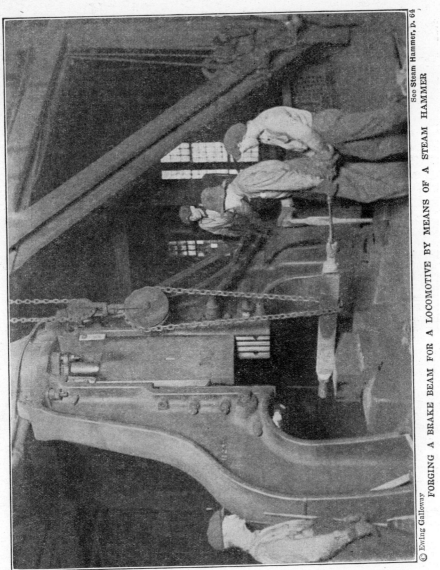

See Steam Hammer, p. 64

FORGING A BRAKE BEAM FOR A LOCOMOTIVE BY MEANS OF A STEAM HAMMER

Under ordinary atmospheric pressure, water boils in an open vessel at a temperature of 212°, and the steam always has this temperature, no matter how fast

or on a screw. The term especially belongs to steam river craft; ocean-going craft being called steamers, steamships, etc. The first steamboat was built

MODERN STEAMSHIP

the water is made to boil. The heat which is supplied simply suffices to do the work of converting the liquid water at 212° into gaseous steam at 212°, without raising the temperature of the steam at all. If the temperature of steam at 212° is lowered by only a very small amount, part of the steam is condensed; hence steam at this temperature is termed moist or saturated steam. At high temperatures and pressures, steam behaves like a perfect gas; but at lower pressures and at temperatures near the boiling point of water, its behavior differs markedly from that of perfect gases; and this change of properties has to be taken into account in all calculations connected with the expansion of steam in steam engines. The terms high pressure and low pressure are applied to steam without any sharply defined limit between them. If the steam is superheated by passing it through hot pipes, it is converted into dry steam, which, within certain limits, behaves like a perfect gas. If, instead of allowing the steam to escape freely, the water is boiled in a closed vessel, the steam accumulates, and both pressure and temperature rapidly increase, till the former becomes several times greater than that of the atmosphere. If now the steam is allowed to escape, it rapidly expands, and if it escapes into the cylinder of a steam engine the expansion can be utilized and converted into work. As the steam expands, its pressure of course becomes less and less till it is not greater than that of the atmosphere; and at the same time its temperature is reduced, the reduction depending on the rapidity with which expansion takes place.

STEAMBOAT, a boat or vessel propelled by steam acting either on paddles

by Denis Papin, who navigated it safely down the Fulda as long ago as 1707. Unfortunately this pioneer craft was destroyed by jealous sailors, and even the very memory of it was lost for three-quarters of a century. In 1775 Perrier, another Frenchman, built an experimental steam vessel at Paris. Eight years later, in 1783, Jouffroy took up the idea that had been evolved by Papin and Perrier and built a steamboat which did good service for some time on the Saone.

The first American to attempt to apply steam to navigation was John Fitch, a Connecticut mechanic, who made his in-

STEAMBOAT OF 1736

itial experiments in the year 1785. To what extent Fitch was indebted to the three illustrious French inventors named above we are not informed, but that his models were original there is not the least doubt. In the first he employed a large pipe kettle for generating the steam, the motive power being side paddles working after the fashion of oars on a common rowboat. In the second Fitch craft the same mode of propulsion was adopted with the exception that the paddles were made to imitate a revolving wheel and were fixed to the stern—clearly foreshadowing the present stern-wheeler.

This last mentioned boat was the first American steam vessel that can be pronounced a success. It made its first trip to Burlington in July, 1788. But, after

The oldest and simplest consists of a bent tube partially filled with mercury, one end of which springs from the boiler, so that the steam rising in the

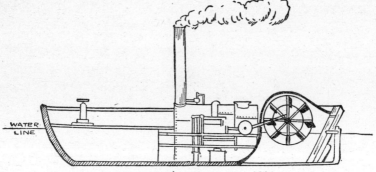

SYMINGTON'S STEAMBOAT, 1801

all, it was not till after the opening of the 19th century that steam navigation started into actual life. In 1801 Symington designed a boat for towing, which attained a speed of 3½ miles an hour. In 1807 Robert Fulton, an American, in conjunction with one Robert R. Living-

THE GREAT EASTERN

ston, built the "Clermont" and established a regular packet service between New York and Albany.

STEAM NAVIGATION. See SHIP and SHIPPING.
See STEAM TURBINE and STEAM.

STEAMER, or RACE-HORSE DUCK (*Micropterus brachypterus*), a species of marine duck from 35 to 40 inches in length, distinguished by its small, short wings, and the swiftness with which it paddles over the surface of the water. It is found in Patagonia and the Falkland Islands.

STEAM GAUGE, an instrument attached to a boiler to indicate the pressure of steam. There are many varieties.

tube forces up the mercury in proportion to the amount of pressure.

STEAM HAMMER, a hammer worked by means of steam. The idea of a steam hammer seems to have occurred first to James Watt, who patented it in 1784. William Deverell also took out a patent for a steam hammer in 1806; but it does not appear that in either case the idea was carried into operation. In 1839 James Nasmyth invented the steam hammer called after him, and patented it in 1842. In the older forms of steam hammer, the hammer head, attached to one end of a lever, was raised by the action of a cog wheel or cam acting on the other end of the lever, and was then allowed to fall by its own weight. Hammers of this description are often called steam tilts. In Nasmyth's hammer the head is attached to the piston rod of an inverted cylinder supported vertically, and the piston is raised by the action of the steam admitted into the cylinder below the piston. The hammer is allowed to fall by its own weight, or is driven downward with still greater velocity by the action of steam admitted into the cylinder above the piston. The admission of steam into the cylinder is regulated by a side valve worked by a lever, and the force of the stroke can be controlled to such an extent by regulating the admission of steam, that the largest hammer can be made to crack a nut, or to come down on a mass of iron with a momentum of many hundred foot tons. The weight of the hammer ranges from about 200 pounds to 25 tons; and the object to be struck is placed on an anvil consisting of a slab of iron resting on a huge mass of piles and concrete, which frequently descends a great depth

STEEL MILLS AND ORE VESSEL AT CLEVELAND, OHIO

See **Steel**, p. 67

 See **Steel,** p. 67

A BESSEMER CONVERTER IN OPERATION IN THE PENNSYLVANIA STEEL INDUSTRY

into the ground. There are numerous other forms.

STEAM NAVIGATION. In 1815 a steamboat made a passage from Glasgow to London, and in 1818 one plied from New York to New Orleans. In 1819 the "Savannah," an American vessel of 380 tons burden, with side wheels, built at Corlear's Hook, N. Y., by Crocker and Fickitt, made the first trip by steam across the Atlantic, sailing from the United States to England and thence to St. Petersburg. At Liverpool she made a great sensation, being mistaken at one time for a vessel on fire. Canvas was used during the last part of the voyage, because after about 12 days out the engine had consumed all the coal which could be carried. There was no room for cargo when she was stored with coal. It was not till 1820 that steam packets were established between Holyhead and Dublin. The year 1838 is memorable in the history of steam navigation. The steamer "Sirius" sailed from Cork on April 4, the "Great Western" from Bristol on the 8th of the same month, both arrived in New York on the 23d, the "Sirius" being only 12 or 14 hours ahead of the "Great Western," the latter having made the trip in about 14 days. The passage is now often made from Queenstown to New York in less than five days. The opening of the Suez Canal greatly promoted swift steam communication with India, China, and the East, and Australia. Steam vessels are now to be found on all seas and lakes and navigable streams. See STEAMBOAT; SHIP AND SHIPPING.

STEAM TURBINE. The principles underlying the steam turbine are very simple, much more so, indeed, than those of the reciprocating engine. It is, therefore, not surprising that turbines of a single and crude type were invented very early in history. The first steam turbine is believed to have been constructed by Hero of Alexandria, in the year 120 B. C. He boiled water in a cauldron, caused the steam to pass through pipes to two jets, fixed at opposite edges of a disc, the jets being turned at right angles to the plane of the disc and in opposite directions. The force of the escaping steam caused the disc to revolve. Nearly eighteen hundred years later, in 1629 A. D., Branca turned a wheel by impinging a jet of steam on to paddles fixed to the circumference. These two simple turbines illustrate the two types now in use—the reaction turbine and the impulse turbine, motion being produced in the former by the reaction of steam escaping from an orifice, and in the latter by the impact of particles of steam upon a movable vane.

The next invention on these lines, after Branca's, was that of Wolfgang de Kempelen, who produced a reaction turbine in the year 1784, James Watt constructing a similar machine almost simultaneously. It was not, however, until the comparatively recent date of 1883 that the steam turbine received practical application. In that year De Laval designed a turbine which he used to turn an early model of the cream separator which is still associated with his name. In his machine, which is of the impulse type, a specially constructed nozzle causes a jet of steam to impinge on to buckets arranged on the rim of a revolving cylinder. The velocity of the steam is very high, as much as 2,500 feet per second, and the cylinder revolves at from 10,000 to 30,000 revolutions per minute, the higher speed being used in machines of smaller size. Owing to this high velocity, this type of turbine is not used for marine engines, but finds a common application for driving dynamos.

C. A. Parsons, of England, built the first large turbine in 1884. This was capable of producing about 10 horse power and made use of both the impulse and the reaction principle. It consisted of a cylindrical case, containing a shaft or spindle, the diameter of this spindle being less than the internal diameter of the cylinder. An annular space was thus left between the two. On the inside of the cylindrical case were numerous rings of inwardly projecting blades, while, on the shaft, were mounted corresponding outwardly projecting blades. These two sets of blades occupied the space between the cylinder and the spindle. When steam was admitted it met a ring of fixed blades on the wall of the cylinder. These blades deflected it in such a manner that it impinged upon the corresponding blades of the spindle, and imparted to them a rotary motion. The diameter of the cylinder increased in successive stages toward the exhaust. The blades in the first few rows are of copper, the others of a special brass alloy.

The Curtis turbine is similar to the Parsons, but depends upon the impulse principle, steam being admitted through a series of nozzles. The steam is expanded almost to exhaust pressure in the nozzles, so that there is no appreciable difference of pressure between the front and back end. It follows that the end thrust, which has to be taken care of in the Parsons turbine, is almost entirely avoided in this engine. Moreover, owing to the expansion of steam in the nozzles, the front blades are not subjected to the action of superheated steam and so do not require to be constructed of special metal for resisting high temperatures. Regulation of speed is obtained by closing one or more nozzles.

Other types of turbine are the Riedler-Stumpf, the Rateau, the Melins and Pfenniger, the Schulz, and the Zölly. While each one has its special features, they all follow the general principles outlined above. As an indication of the speed at which the shafts run in different engines, the following figures may be taken as representative. The velocity of the tips of the rotating blades in the Parsons turbine is 100-150 feet per second at the front end, and at the back end, where the diameter of the shaft increases, 300-350 feet per second. In the Rateau, the speed is 350-400 feet per second, and in the Curtis a little higher. On the other hand, the buckets in the De Laval and the Riedler-Stumpf turbines reach a velocity of 1,000 feet per second.

STEAM TURBINES, MARINE. The first vessel to be fitted with turbines was the "Turbinia." In 1897 she was equipped with turbines of the Parsons type, three engines being used, high pressure, intermediate and low. Each shaft was fitted with three propellers. She attained the remarkable speed of 34½ knots per hour, and the results obtained in her trials were considered so successful that the adoption of turbines in other vessels very quickly followed. In 1900 the British destroyer "Viper," turbine driven, made 36½ knots per hour. Passenger vessels, being built for convenience rather than speed, naturally did not make such a remarkable showing, but nevertheless, greater speeds were attained than had been found possible with the ordinary reciprocating engine. The first turbine driven passenger vessel was the "King Edward," which reached 20½ knots in 1901. The first transatlantic liners fitted with turbines were the "Victorian" and "Virginian," whose maximum speed reached only 17 knots per hour. In 1907, however, the Cunard line built the "Lusitania" and the "Mauretania." These were quadruple screw turbines of 67,-000 indicated horse power, equipped with two high pressure, two low pressure, and two reversing turbines. These vessels were capable of maintaining an average speed of 26 knots per hour. In 1906, the British battleship "Dreadnought" was built and fitted with turbines, this being the first battleship to be so equipped. During her trials a

speed of 21.25 knots was attained. Of recent years the number of vessels which have been equipped with turbines of improved pattern has been very great, the advantage of the turbine for marine work being now generally recognized. The superiority of turbines over reciprocating engines is not solely due to the extra speed which can be attained. A turbine is lighter, of simpler construction, and more compact than a reciprocating engine. There is also much less vibration. At high speed there is a marked economy of fuel, but at low or moderate speed, the turbine consumes more coal than the reciprocating engine.

For general purposes, the turbine is proving more satisfactory than the reciprocating engine in nearly all cases where high speed is required. It is, however, of little use for low speeds, or in those cases where a heavy resistance has to be overcome when starting from rest. It is peculiarly adapted for driving dynamos. Its simpler construction is a strong point in its favor, its moving parts being much fewer than in the reciprocating engine. Moreover, the fact that the steam acts directly on the moving shaft without the intervention of pistons, connecting rods, etc., leads to greater efficiency. The comparatively late date at which it was developed for practical purposes is explained by the need for special steels and other alloys possessing the unusual strength and other properties required in engines of this type. In this connection, Kempe's "Engineer's Year Book" states, "A very important fact in the evolution of the steam turbine has been the introduction of the high grade steels now available, which alone have made the highest peripheral speeds now to be met with possible, and further developments may be expected to follow any reduction in the cost of finest steels."

STEAM WHISTLE, a sounding device connected with the boiler of a steam engine, either stationary, locomotive, or marine, for the purpose of announcing the hours of work, signaling, etc. In the ordinary locomotive steam whistle the foot is bolted onto the fire box, has an opening for the admission of steam, and is provided with a cock, by turning which steam is permitted to rush into the hollow piece, which is provided with holes around its lower and narrower portion, through which the steam rushes into the cavity of the cup, and, passing out through the narrow annular opening, impinges against the rim of the bell, causing a shrill, piercing sound. The calliope is a series of such whistles tuned to a scale and operated by keys.

STEAM WINCH, a form of hoisting apparatus in which rotary motion is imparted to the winding axle from the piston rod of a steam engine, directly or intermediately, through bevel gearing. The former is more rapid; the latter affords greater power. Specially used for loading and unloading ships.

STEARATES, compounds of stearic acid with the alkalies and metals. They have the consistence of hard soaps and plasters, and are mostly insoluble in water. Stearate of potassium, $C_{18}H_{35}KO_2$, separates on cooling from a solution of one part stearic acid and one part potassic hydrate in 10 parts of water. It forms shining delicate needles, having a faint alkaline taste, and dissolves in 6.7 parts boiling alcohol and 25 parts boiling water. Acid stearate of potassium, $C_{18}H_{35}KO_2 \cdot C_{18}H_{36}O_2$, obtained by decomposing the neutral salt with 1,000 parts of water. When dried and dissolved in alcohol it separates in silvery scales, inodorous and soft to the touch. It dissolves in four parts of boiling absolute alcohol.

STEARIC ACID, in chemistry, $C_{18}H_{35}O \cdot OH$, an acid discovered by Chevreul, and found as a frequent constituent of fats derived from the animal and vegetable kingdoms, and especially abundant as a tristearin in beef and mutton suet. It may be obtained by saponifying the fat with soda lye, decomposing with sulphuric acid, dissolving the fatty acids in alcohol, and repeatedly crystallizing, the first portions of the fatty acid only being taken. When pure it crystallizes from alcohol in nacreous laminæ or needles, is tasteless and inodorous, and has a distinct acid reaction. Its specific gravity is nearly that of water, it melts at 69-69.2°, distills in a vacuum without alteration, and is sparingly soluble in alcohol, more so in ether and benzene.

STEARINE, or **STEARIN,** in chemistry, $C_{57}H_{110}O_6$, the chief ingredient of suet and tallow, or the harder ingredient of animal fats, oleine being the softer one. It is obtained from mutton suet by repeated solution in ether and crystallization. It may also be obtained by pressing tallow between hot plates, and afterward dissolving in hot ether, which on cooling deposits the stearine. It has a pearly luster, is soft to the touch, but not greasy. It is insoluble in water, but soluble in hot alcohol and ether. When treated with superheated steam it is separated into stearic acid and glycerin, and when boiled with alkalies is saponified, that is, the stearic acid combines with the alkali, forming soap, and glycerin

I—6

is separated. When melted it resembles wax.

STEDMAN, EDMUND CLARENCE, an American poet and banker; born in Hartford, Conn., Oct. 8, 1833; was a student at Yale, but did not graduate. In 1852 he became editor of the Norwich "Tribune," and later of the Winsted "Herald." He was a war correspondent of the New York "World" during the American Civil War. In 1884 he became a stock broker in New York City. He wrote: "Poems Lyric and Idyllic" (1860); "Alice of Monmouth, and Other Poems" (1864); "The Blameless Prince, and Other Poems" (1869); "Hawthorne, and Other Poems" (1877); "Lyrics and Idylls" (1879); "Poems Now First Collected" (1897); and poems for special occasions, the "Dartmouth Ode"; "Gettysburg"; etc. The best known of his critical works are: "Victorian Poets" (1875; revised and supplemented, 1887 and 1891); "Edgar Allan Poe" (1880); and "Poets of America" (1885). He edited in collaboration with Ellen M. Hutchinson "A Library of American Literature" (1888-1890). He died Jan. 18, 1908.

STEED, H. WICKHAM, an English journalist and writer, born in 1871. He was educated at the universities of Jena, Berlin, and Paris. For many years he was acting correspondent of the London "Times" at Berlin, and following this he served in the same capacity in Rome and Vienna. In 1913 he was appointed special editor of the "Times." He made a specialty of Austrian and Balkan affairs and was considered an authority on the subject. He took an active part in the deliberations at the Paris Peace Conference and was consulted on questions relating to Austria-Hungary and the Balkan States. In 1920 he was appointed editor of the London "Times." He wrote "The Socialist and Labour Movement in England, Germany, and France" (1894); "The Hapsburg Monarchy" (1914); "England in the War" (1915); "The English Effort" (1916); "Democratic Britain" (1918).

STEEL. Steel may in a general way be defined as a variety or condition of iron capable of being melted and cast, hammered and welded, and of being tempered, or hardened and softened. It is thus in its properties intermediate between malleable and cast iron, and in its composition it also occupies a middle place between these two varieties. The proportion of carbon contained in the metal is the chief element in determining its character, cast iron containing generally from 2.5 to about 5 per cent. of carbon, steel having from .05 to 1.80, and the proportion in malleable iron varying from .016 up to about .34; but there are other circumstances which also go to determine the nature and quality of any of the kinds.

The methods by which steel of various qualities are now produced are numerous, but they may all be included under these heads: (1) The partial decarbonization of cast iron; (2) the addition of carbon to malleable iron; and (3) the complete decarbonization of pig iron, and the addition of the necessary carbon by means of pig iron or other kinds rich in carbon to the molten mass. By the first of these processes what are known as natural steel and puddled steel are produced. Natural steel is made from pure varieties of pig iron (white or fusible gray pig, from spathic or magnetic ores) by melting it with charcoal on the hearth of a refining furnace, as in the corresponding operation in the manufacture of malleable iron; the operation being so controlled that it can be stopped when the desired amount of decarbonization has been effected. Natural steel, known also as Corinthian steel, from having been largely made in that province, was formerly in great request on the Continent for tool making. Puddled steel is a similar but less pure product, made also direct from cast iron on the bed of a puddling furnace, the puddling being stopped before the complete oxidation of the carbon. In this process, also, the only difference from the analogous stage in malleable iron manufacture consists in stopping the operation at an earlier stage. The steel of the famous works of Krupp at Essen is made by this process, and it is largely used for machine castings, railway wheel tires, and other large works.

The kinds of steel produced by the imparting of carbon to malleable iron are known as cementation steel, and the varieties included under this head embrace the most valuable classes of steel. The production of cementation steel depends on the fact that when malleable iron is heated to a high temperature in contact with carbonaceous matter without access of air, it absorbs carbon, and thus becomes converted into steel. Bar iron of the highest quality only is used for making cementation steel, and the bars are embedded in powdered charcoal and packed in a chamber heated by a furnace. The temperature is gradually raised, and kept uniformly at a full red heat (about 2,000° F.) for about a week, at the end of which time the furnace is allowed to cool slowly down, which requires another fortnight.

To make it homogeneous, the bars are faggoted, heated to welding heat, and hammered or rolled, the resulting material being "shear steel." When, instead of being hammered, the blister steel is melted in crucibles and cast in molds, it forms "crucible cast steel," the purest of all varieties of steel, and that which is principally used for files, cutlery, and fine tools generally.

Siemens-Martin steel is produced by what may be regarded as a modification of the cementation process, since in it malleable iron is carburetted by means of pig iron or other compound rich in carbon. On the hearth of an open furnace heated by gas on the regenerative system a quantity of pig iron is melted, and to that scrap iron, old rails, etc., heated to redness, are gradually added. When by the examination of test pieces it is found that the quantity of carbon is sufficiently reduced, by the addition of malleable iron, for the kind of steel required, the charge is run off. The Siemens-Martin process is also conducted in a manner modified as follows: The pig iron and malleable scrap are melted together, an operation which occupies from two and one-half to three hours, and thereupon a quantity of iron ore (hæmatite) is added to the furnace, which in giving off its combined oxygen decarbonizes the entire charge. When the decarbonization is found to be complete, from 8 to 10 per cent. of spiegeleisen (or about 2 per cent. of ferromanganese), previously raised to a red heat, is thrown into the furnace. After about 10 minutes this will be thoroughly dissolved, the carbon disseminated through the mass, and the charge ready for being tapped off. Steel so made is now largely used for rails, wagon wheels and axles, and it is being introduced for boilers, ships' plates, and other similar purposes.

Bessemer steel forms the subject of a separate article. Steel presents physical characteristics so distinct from those of malleable iron that it may be for practicable purposes regarded as a distinct metal. Its most remarkable physical characteristic is its power of becoming exceedingly hard by sudden cooling from a high heat, and of passing through many grades of hardness downward from that point by the process of tempering. The tempering is accomplished by reheating the metal to a certain degree and allowing it gradually to cool, and according to the heat to which it is raised is the resulting temper, the higher the heat the softer being the steel. Sir Joseph Whitworth introduced a method of compressing with enormous force cast steel in its fluid state, and demonstrated that thereby the tensile strength and homogeneity of the metal are increased in a remarkable manner. See IRON AND STEEL; BESSEMER STEEL.

STEEL ENGRAVING, the art of engraving on steel plates for the purpose of producing prints or impressions in ink on paper and other substances. The process of decarbonizing steel so that it could be engraved was invented by Jacob Perkins, of Newburyport, Mass., in 1814.

STEEL, MRS. FLORA ANNIE (WEBSTER), an English novelist; born in Harrow-on-the-Hill, England, April 2, 1847. At 21 she married an Indian civilian and went to Bengal, where she became prominent in educational affairs, and was appointed inspectress of female schools. On the expiration of her husband's term of service, she returned with him to England and devoted herself to literary work. Her published works include: "From the Five Rivers" (1893); "Miss Stuart's Legacy" (1893); "The Potter's Thumb" (1894); "Flower of Forgiveness" (1894); "Red Rowans" (1895); "On the Face of the Waters" (1895); "In the Tideway" (1896); and "In the Permanent Way" (1897); "The Host of the Lord" (1900); "Voices of the Night," etc.

STEEL, FREDERIC DORR, an American illustrator, born at Marquette, Mich., in 1873. He studied art at the National Academy of Design and at the Art Students' League, New York. Beginning with 1897 he contributed illustrations to many of the leading periodicals, specializing in drawings for "direct process" reproduction. He was awarded the bronze medal at the St. Louis Exposition, in 1904, and was a member of the Society of Illustrators.

STEELE, SIR RICHARD, a British author; born in Dublin, Ireland, in March, 1672; was educated at Charter House School and Oxford; entered the army and was promoted captain. He commenced his literary career in 1702 by writing for the stage. In 1709 he began the "Tatler," and four years later assisted with the "Spectator" and "Guardian"; soon after he entered the House of Commons as a member for Stockport, but was expelled for writing a satire, supposed to be a breach of privilege. On the accession of George I., he was knighted, given several lucrative posts and returned to Parliament. Steele is best known as an essayist. He wrote a religious treatise, "The Christian Hero" (1790). Among his plays are: "The Funeral, or Grief à la Mode," "The Tender Husband," "The Lying Lover,"

and "The Conscious Lovers." He died near Camarthen, Wales, Sept. 1, 1729.

STEELE, WILBUR DANIEL, an American author, born at Greensboro, N. C., in 1886. He was educated at the University of Denver and studied art at the Museum of Fine Arts, Boston, the Académie Julien, Paris, and the Art Students' League, New York. He wrote "Storm" (1914); "Land's End" (1918); and many short stories in numerous monthly and weekly magazines.

STEEL SKELETON CONSTRUCTION, a form of building construction by which the loads and stresses are transmitted to the foundation by a framework of metal or re-enforced concrete, with girders at each story supporting the walls enclosed. It represents one of the greatest developments in building from the earliest days of architecture. It proves the solution to the problem that arose from the concentration of population in a confined area and it was only natural that the idea should first take shape in what was destined to become the most congested area, in respect to volume of business interests and number of people, in the whole world. The height of buildings had always been determined by consideration of security, utility and cost, and until the advent of the steel skeleton six or seven stories were regarded as nearly as far as the builder could go. In the seventies the rising value of real estate set property owners seeking for a plan of raising more revenue from their investments, and gradually buildings rose until a height of 10 and sometimes 12 stories. The huge quantities of masonry called for in these lofty buildings set property owners and builders under the necessity of seeking out devices that would enable them to economize in material and in the ground occupied. Piers were made thinner and columns were put up to receive the ends of the beams and girders and so relieve the piers of the weight of floor. Finally, in 1889, it was found that the thickness of the piers could be reduced still further by taking from the piers the weight of the walls and placing the four walls on girders set between the wall columns at every floor level. It was thus that the principle underneath Steel Skeleton Construction was revealed. It relegated stone to a subsidiary relation in construction. The essential part of the building became a firmly bound framework of steel able to support not merely the floors and roof, but the walls, interior and external, together with every other part of the building, and constructed on lines sufficient to withstand every condition of wind and weather. In the new type of building the ancient thick supporting walls are known no more. The walls no longer carry loads; they serve merely as a clothing or curtain to the powerful frame of steel which carries the building upward.

The first iron girders and beams used in the United States came from Europe about 1840 and their value in the construction of buildings began to become apparent from that time on. Iron beams were used in the floor construction of Cooper Union in New York City in 1860, and steel beams began to be manufactured in 1885. As soon as the principle of steel skeleton construction was perceived steel came to be used throughout the entire building, though cast iron continued to be used in some buildings for columns and bases. As steel grew continually stronger and cheaper a great impetus was given to building construction all over the country, and buildings of great width and height now rose in the course of as many months as formerly it would have taken years for their construction. The height of buildings is now only limited by its relation to the foundation and the service capable of being rendered by a proper system of elevators proportionate to the area of floor space. The amount of space saved by the thinning of the walls has been large. Many buildings are now built in which the amount of stone used is negligible. Even in the central business quarters of large cities the buildings are not a few which are apparently made up of steel and glass. Where formerly a building of 10 stories was regarded as risky, now buildings of over 40 stories are regarded as a moderate development. A building can now be erected at the rate of one story every three or four days, and as the frame directly supports the walls at each story it is not an uncommon sight to see the upper part of a building inclosed by walls while the lower part continues to reveal only the steel frame.

The members of the steel skeleton are completed in their construction at the mill and are assembled and riveted together on the site of the proposed building. Angles, plates, channels and other rolled sections are built up into girders and columns. As much as is possible of the riveting is done at the mill, the rest being attended to at the site of the building. In order to distribute the weight of load columns, bases or bearing plates are placed between the column and its foundation. The columns may be of steel or cast iron, hollow circles or hollow squares or H shapes being in use where the strength is sufficient as being the most economical. Slabs or arches of terracotta or concrete laid between steel I-beams make up the floor construction. The floor area is determined by its division into units of from 15 to 20 or more feet, according to the size of the rooms required. Single or double girders, built up or riveted, placed between the columns, hold up the ends of the floor beams. In high and narrow skeleton buildings cantilever girders are sometimes called for to distribute the weight evenly over the footings. The great height of steel buildings in relation to the area of their site has likewise made methods of wind-bracing necessary, the systems employed being sway-bracing, knee-bracing, and portal-arch bracing, the aim in each case being to hold the steel frame in its several parts more securely to its foundation. While the advantages derived from steel skeleton construction are many and obvious, there are some disadvantages. There is always the liability to corrosion in the metal frame, while the danger to life and limb from their great height and the concentration of population made possible has been often illustrated. While they represent a tremendous development in the art of building, they are erected for convenience rather than for endurance or beauty, though in this latter respect numerous improvements have been made in late years. This disadvantage may be lessened by new rules and devices, but steel skeleton construction has become a necessary adjunct to our material civilization, and greater development may be looked for in the near future.

STEELTON, a borough in Dauphin co., Pa., on the Susquehanna river, the Pennsylvania canal, and the Philadelphia and Reading, and the Pennsylvania railroads; 3 miles E. of Harrisburg. It contains electric railroads, a National bank, and daily and weekly newspapers. Here are the extensive plant of the Pennsylvania Steel Company, a flour mill, shirt factory, planing mill, and brick works. Pop. (1910) 14,246; (1920) 13,428.

STEELYARD, a balance or weighing machine consisting of a lever with unequal arms. It is of two kinds. The common steelyard, or Roman balance, is formed by suspending the article to be weighed from the end of the shorter arm, or placing it in a scale depending therefrom and sliding a determinate weight along the longer one till an equilibrium is obtained. The longer arm is so graduated that the figure opposite to which the weight rests indicates the weight of the article at the extremity of the shorter arm. The second form is the

Danish balance, which differs from the Roman in having the counterpoise fixed at one end and the fulcrum slid along the graduated beam.

STEEN, JAN, a Dutch painter; born in Leyden, Netherlands, in 1626; studied under Adrian van Ostade; joined the Leyden Guild of Painters in 1648, and for some time carried on the trade of a brewer at Delft. A sympathetic observer of human life, he painted genre pictures from every plane of life, the lowest as well as the highest. The grave humor of his style is best seen in such pictures as the "Doctor Visiting His Patient," a "Cavalier Giving Lessons on the Guitar to a Lady," "Domestic Life," "Tavern Company," "The Oyster Girl," "Work and Idleness," "Bad Company," "Old Age," and particularly the pieces of childhood; e. g., the pictures called "St. Nicholas" and "Twelfth Night." He died in Leyden in 1679.

STEEPLECHASE, a horserace run not on a course of smooth, flat turf, but across the open country, over hedges, ditches, walls, and whatever other obstacles lie in the way. This variety of sport seems to have had its origin (traditionally) in the frolic of a merry party of fox hunters, who agreed to race in a straight line toward a steeple visible in the distance, an event which is recorded to have happened in Ireland in 1803; further particulars of it, however, are not known. Nevertheless this was not the earliest race of the kind. One took place in Ireland in 1752 from the church of Buttevant (Cork co.) to the church of St. Leger, a distance of 4½ miles. In the year 1816 a ride in England of 20 miles across country against time (under one hour and nine minutes) was regarded as something extraordinary, though about that time steeplechase matches were coming into fashion with the young fox hunters of the day. The sport began to assume its existing shape about the year 1831. In 1866 the Grand National Hunt Committee was formed for the purpose of laying down rules and regulations for the proper conducting of steeplechase meetings. The principal race in this class of sport in the United Kingdom is the Grand National, which was instituted at Liverpool the headquarters of steeplechasing in 1839; it is now run on different courses in different years. The Meadowbrook Club is the pioneer of steeplechasing in the United States.

STEEVENS, GEORGE WARRINGTON, an English journalist and writer, born at Sydenham, in 1869. He was educated at Balliol College, Oxford. After serving on the editorial staff of the "Pall Mall Gazette" for several years, he became, in 1897, special correspondent of the "Daily Mail." In this capacity he visited the United States, Egypt, Greece, India, and other countries. His letters to the "Daily Mail" were republished under the titles "The Land of the Dollar" (1897); "With the Conquering Turk" (1897); "With Kitchener to Khartum" (1898); "The Tragedy of Dreyfus" (1899); "From Cape Town to Ladysmith" (1900). He served as correspondent in the Boer War and the hardships which he endured there led to his death at Ladysmith, while it was besieged by the Boers, in 1900. He was considered the most eminent war correspondent of his time.

STEFFENS, (JOSEPH) LINCOLN, an American writer and lecturer, born in San Francisco, Cal., in 1866. He graduated from the University of California in 1889 and studied philosophy at the universities of Berlin, Heidelberg, Leipzig, and Paris. He was a newspaper editor in New York City from 1892 to 1902, when he became managing editor of "McClure's Magazine." From 1906 to 1911 he was an associate editor of the "American" and "Everybody's" magazines. His researches into the mismanagement and corruption of municipal politics, published in various newspapers and magazines, resulted in great improvement in these conditions. He wrote "The Shame of the Cities" (1904); "The Struggle for Self-Government" (1906); "Upbuilders" (1909); "The Least of These" (1910). He was a frequent contributor of articles and short stories to magazines.

STEGOSAURIDÆ, a family of *Stegosauria*; vertebræ biconcave; ischia directed backward, with the sides meeting in the median line; astragalus coalesced with tibia, metatarsals short. Genera: *Stegosaurus*, some 30 feet long, well armed with enormous bucklers, some of which were spinous, from the Jurassic beds of the Rocky Mountains; *Diracedon* and *Amosaurus*.

STEIN (stīn), **CHARLOTTE VON**, the intimate friend of Goethe; born in Weimar, Germany, Dec. 25, 1742; married in 1764 to the duke's master of the horse. Her friendship with Goethe was broken suddenly after the poet's return from Italy (1788). They were, however, in some measure reconciled before Frau von Stein died. Goethe's "Letters" to her were first published in 1848-1851, and again, with additions, in 1883-1885;

and another final collection was issued by the German Goethe Society in 1886. The lady's letters to Goethe were destroyed by her shortly before her death. She wrote a tragedy, "Dido." She died in Weimar, Jan. 6, 1827.

STEIN, HEINRICH FRIEDRICH KARL, BARON VON, a Prussian statesman; born in Nassau, Germany, Oct. 26, 1757. After being educated at Göttingen and studying public law at Wetzlar, he entered the Prussian civil service, and after filling several important offices, was, in 1786, appointed president of the Westphalian Chambers, which post he held till 1804, in which year he became Minister of Finance and Trade. In this capacity he laid the foundation of important social reforms; but, exciting the jealousy of Napoleon, he was exiled to Prague. In 1812 he went to St. Petersburg, where he rendered great services to the Russian Government during the French invasion. Subsequently returning to his own country, he was placed at the head of administrative affairs; retired in 1827. He died June 29, 1831.

STEINBOK, or **STEENBOK,** in zoölogy, the *Antilope tragulus,* from the stony plains and mountains of South Africa; rather more than 3 feet long, and about 20 inches high at the shoulder; red brown above, white below; tail rudimentary; ears large; horns straight, about 4 inches long in the male, absent in female; no false hoofs. Also, the ibex.

STEINMETZ, CHARLES PROTEUS, electrician. Born April 9, 1865, at Breslau in Germany; studied in the universities of Breslau, of Berlin and of Zurich. In spite of a frail and imperfect physique, he developed an unusual power of intellectual application. While still a student, he became a convert to Socialism, and for a time devoted much of his energy to political writing. He thus fell into disfavor with the German authorities. Unable to remain at home, he visited Austria and Switzerland, endeavoring to support himself by articles for the press. At last, in 1889, he emigrated to the U. S., virtually without money means. Employed for a time in a factory at Yonkers, he gained note by producing inventions for the improvement of electrical motors and generators. This led to a connection with the General Electric Company, of which he eventually became chief consulting engineer. He organized extensive laboratories for the company at Schenectady, where he carried on research work in electrical science. The subjects of his investigations included "cold light," or illumination with a minimum of heat generation, and transportation by means of electric power. He remained constant to his Communistic ideas, refusing to accept a salary beyond his needs, running for State Engineer of New York in 1922 on a Socialist ticket, and offering his technical services to Soviet Russia, which declined them. He wrote numerous works on electricity, including "Theory and Calculation of Alternating-Current Phenomena" (1897); "Theoretical Elements of Electrical Engineering"; "General Lectures on Electrical Engineering"; and "Engineering Mathematics." Also, "America and the New Epoch." He was long the president of the American Institute of Electrical Engineers, and in 1902 became professor of electrophysics at Union University. He died Oct. 26, 1923.

STEIWER, FREDERICK. United States Senator from Oregon: born October 13, 1883, at Jefferson, Ore., he studied at Oregon Agricultural College and at the University of Oregon. Entering the law, he served as district attorney and as State senator. He served in the National army from August, 1917, to March, 1919. As candidate of the Republican party, he was elected to the United States Senate in 1926.

STELA, or **STELE,** in architecture, a small column without base or capital, serving as a monument, milestone, or the like. In archæology, a sepulchral slab or column, which in ancient times answered the purpose of a gravestone.

STELVIO, PASS OF THE, the highest carriage road across the Alps (9,042 feet), leads from Bormio near the head of the Italian Valtelline to Sponding in the Vintschgau valley of the Austrian Tyrol. It forms part of the great road between Milan and Innsbruck, and was completed by the Austrian Government in 1825. It has a length of 33 miles, and is remarkable for its magnificent scenery.

STEM, in botany, the ascending axis of a plant. It seeks the light, strives to expose itself to the air, and expands itself to the utmost extent of its nature to the solar rays. With regard to direction, it may be erect, pendulous, nodding, recumbent, flexuous, creeping, or climbing. It is generally cylindrical; but may be triangular, as in *Carex;* square, as in the *Labiatæ;* two-edged, as in some *Cacti;* filiform, as in flax; or leaf-like, as in *Ruscus.* It consists of bundles of vascular and woody tissue embedded in various ways in cellular substance, the whole being inclosed with an epidermis. Stems may be aërial or underground. The most highly developed form of the former is the trunk of a tree, the next is that of a shrub. There are also herbaceous stems. Sometimes a plant appears stemless; only, however, because the stem is short enough to be overlooked. In duration a stem may be annual, biennial, or perennial. In structure is may be exogenous, endogenous, or acrogenous. Aërial stems generally branch and bear leaves, flowers, and fruit. An underground stem, such as the rhizome or the tuber, is frequently mistaken for a root. The potato plant has a subterranean stem.

In mechanics, the projecting-rod which guides a valve in its reciprocations. In mining, a day's work. In music, the line attached to the head of a note. All notes used in modern music but the semibreve, or whole note, have stems; quavers and their sub-divisions have stems and hooks. In writing a "single part" for a voice or instrument, it is usual to turn the stems of notes lying below the middle line of the stave upward, of notes lying above the middle line downward. Notes on the middle line have their stems up or down as seems best. In a "short score," as for four parts the stems of the higher part in each stave are turned up, those of the lower part down. In ornithology, the main stalk of the feather bearing all the other external parts, and usually resembling a greatly elongated cone. At the lower part which is inserted in the skin, it is cylindrical, hollow, and transparent; higher up it is filled with a cellular pith. The parenchymatous portion of the stem is called the shaft, and it is from the flattened sides of this that the barbs issue. In shipbuilding, the upright piece of timber or bar of iron at the fore end of a vessel, to which the forward ends of the stakes are united. With wooden stems the lower end is scarfed into the keel. The upper end supports the bowsprit, and in the obtuse angle is the figure head. The advanced edge of the stem is the cut-water. It is usually marked with a scale of feet, showing the perpendicular height above the keel, so as to mark the draught of water at the forepart. Called also stem post. In vehicles, the bar to which the bow of a falling hood is hinged.

STENCIL, a thin plate of metal, cardboard, leather or other material (brass generally), out of which patterns, numbers, or letters have been cut. The plate is laid on the surface to be painted or marked, and a brush dipped in ink or color is then rubbed over it, the surface receiving the color only through the parts cut out of the plate.

STENDAL, a town of Prussian Saxony; 36 miles N. by E. of Magdeburg; was the former capital of the Altmark and has a Gothic cathedral (1420-1424), a Roland pillar, two old gateways, and a statue of Winckelmann, a native of the place. There are here large railway workshops and important textile industries. Pop. about 27,500.

STENDHAL. See BEYLE, MARIE HENRI.

STENNESS, or **STENNIS,** a loch in the Orkney Islands, a few miles N. E. of Stromness, 14 miles in circumference. It is remarkable for the two groups of standing stones, somewhat similar to those of Stonehenge, which are found on its shores. The smaller group, of which only two remain erect, belong to an area 100 feet in diameter with an outside ditch 50 feet in width. The larger group known as the Ring of Brogar, consists now of 15 stones in an inclosure 340 feet in diameter.

STENOGRAPHY. See SHORTHAND.

STENTOR, the name of a Greek herald in the Trojan war, famous for the loudness of his voice, which was said to equal that of 50 other men together; hence, a person having a very loud strong voice.

STEPHANITE (after the Archduke Stephan of Austria), an ore of silver occurring both in crystals and massive; crystallization, orthorhombic; hardness, 2-2.5; sp. gr. 6.269; luster, metallic; color and streak, iron-black. Composition: Sulphur, 16.2; antimony, 15.3; silver, $68.5 = 100$, corresponding with the formula $5AgS + Sb_2S_3$. Occurs with other silver ores in lodes in various localities.

STEPHEN, the name of several popes; some authorities reckon 9, and others 10, the discrepancy arising from the omission of a pontiff who died between election and consecration (752). (The table under POPE (*q. v.*) includes him, hence the numeration there is different.)

STEPHEN I., ascended the pontifical chair after Lucius, in 253. He had a difference with St. Cyprian and Firmilian about rebaptizing repentant heretics, which practice this Pope condemned. He died in 257.

STEPHEN II., a native of Rome; elected Pope in 752. Astolphus, King of the Lombards, having menaced the city of Rome, Stephen implored the aid of Constantine Copronymus, Emperor of the East; but he being engaged in a war recommended his cause to Pepin, King of the Franks, who marched into Italy and deprived Astolphus of the exarchate of Ravenna and several cities, which he gave to the Pope, thus laying the foundation of the temporal sovereignty of the Church of Rome. He died in 757.

STEPHEN III., succeeded Paul I. in 768. Throughout his career he was at variance with the Lombards and threatened to excommunicate Charles (afterward Charlemagne) and Carloman, sons of Pepin, if they entered into an alliance with them, or intermarried with the daughters of the Lombard king. Charles, however, married Hermengarda, daughter of Desiderius, King of the Lombards, but put her away a year afterward. Stephen was succeeded by Adrian I. He died in 772.

STEPHEN IV., succeeded Leo III. in 816, but died in the same year.

STEPHEN V., elected in succession to Adrian III., in 885. He was a learned pontiff and greatly contributed to relieve the people of Rome from the effects of a terrible famine which had desolated the country shortly before his accession. He died in 891.

STEPHEN VI., became Pope in succession to Boniface VI. in 896. He caused the body of Pope Formosus to be disinterred and cast into an ordinary grave, on the plea that the Pope had been excommunicated by John VIII. anterior to his elevation to the tiara. In 898 the partisans of Formosus burst into an insurrection, and having seized Stephen strangled him.

STEPHEN VII., the successor of Leo VI., was elected to the papacy in 929. There are no reliable records of his pontificate. He died in 931.

STEPHEN VIII., the successor of Leo VII. At the time of his election, 939, Rome was governed by Alberic, son of Marozia, who styled himself "Prince and Senator of all the Romans." The records of his papacy are extremely untrustworthy; but it is stated by one authority that Stephen VIII. was, during a revolt of the Roman populace, rendered a cripple for life. He died in 942.

STEPHEN IX., elected to the papacy in succession to Victor II. in 1057. He had previously filled the office of papal legate at the court of Constantinople. After his elevation, he dispatched legates to Milan to enforce celibacy among the clergy of that church; the disputes on which decree lasted during a quarter of a century. He was a learned and energetic pontiff, but too ambitious of worldly influence. He died in 1058.

STEPHEN, the name of several kings of Hungary, viz.:

STEPHEN I., succeeded his father Geisa in 997. He reformed the manners of his subjects, enacted excellent laws and introduced Christianty into his kingdom. He died in 1038. Stephen was canonized and his memory is held in great veneration throughout Southern Germany, where churches are met everywhere dedicated to his name.

STEPHEN II., succeeded his father Koloman in 1114. He invaded Poland and Austria, and marched into Russia, but was unsuccessful everywhere. He abdicated, retired to a monastery, and died in 1131.

STEPHEN III., crowned king in 1161; was almost immediately deposed by the nobles. He regained the crown, however, in 1165, and reigned till 1174.

STEPHEN IV., ascended the throne in 1161, but was defeated by the preceding in 1163, soon after which he died at Semlin.

STEPHEN V., reigned two years only, but gained an illustrious name by his victories over Ottocar, King of Bohemia, 1270-1272.

STEPHEN, King of England; son of the Count of Blois by his wife Adela, daughter of William the Conqueror; born in Blois, France, in 1105. Being in England on the death of Henry I., he seized on the crown and royal coffers, to the prejudice of Henry's daughter, Matilda, the empress, and was crowned in 1135. Four years elapsed before Matilda was able to land with forces to dispute Stephen's possession of the throne, and after a long civil war that lasted nearly the whole reign and in which Stephen was once taken prisoner but released for Matilda's brother, the Earl of Gloucester, it was finally decided that Stephen should retain the crown for his own life, on condition that Prince Henry, Matilda's son by her first husband, should succeed. These terms were concluded in 1154. He died in Dover, England, Oct. 25, 1154.

STEPHEN, King of Poland, surnamed BATHORI; a noble Hungarian; born in 1532, elected Prince of Transylvania, 1571, and succeeded to Henry of Valois as King of Poland, 1575. He died in Grodno, Poland, Dec. 12, 1586.

STEPHEN, SIR LESLIE, English author; born in London, Nov. 28, 1832. He was educated at Cambridge, and subsequently edited leading London periodicals. His greatest undertaking was the "Dictionary of National Biography" in about 60 volumes, of which he edited the first 26. He published: "Hours in a Library" (1871-1879); "Essays on Free Thinking and Plain Speaking" (1873); "History of English Thought in the Eighteenth Century" (1876); "Science of

Ethics" (1882); "Life of Henry Fawcett" (1885); "An Agnostic's Apology" (1893); "Life of Sir James Fitzjames Stephen" (1896); "Social Rights and Duties" (1896); and "Studies of a Biographer" (1898). He died in 1904.

STEPHENS, ALEXANDER HAMILTON, an American statesman; born near Crawfordsville, Ga., Feb. 11, 1812; was graduated at Franklin College in 1832 and admitted to the bar in 1834. He was chosen a member of the lower branch of the legislature of Georgia in 1836; elected to Congress in 1843; and in 1847 submitted a series of resolutions in relation to the Mexican War, which afterward formed the platform of the Whig party. Shortly after the outbreak of the Civil War he was elected vice-president

ALEXANDER H. STEPHENS

of the Confederate States of America, and on March 21, 1861, delivered a speech in Savannah, in which he declared slavery to be the cornerstone of the new government. In February, 1865, he was at the head of the Peace Commission of the Confederate government in the Hampton Roads conference. After the war he turned his attention to literary pursuits, and published "The War Between the States" and edited the Atlanta "Sun." He was again elected to Congress in 1874, and re-elected in 1876, serving till 1882, when he resigned to become governor of Georgia. He died in Atlanta, Ga., March 4, 1883.

STEPHENS, ALICE BARBER, an American illustrator, born near Salem, N. J., in 1858. She was educated in the public schools of Philadelphia and studied art at the Philadelphia School of Design for Women, the Pennsylvania Academy of Fine Arts, the Académie Julien, Paris, France. Besides illustrating many stories and articles for the most prominent magazines, she became well-known as a wood-engraver and also taught portrait and life classes at the Philadelphia School of Design for Women.

STEPHENS, DAVID STUBERT, an American educator, born in Springfield, O., in 1847. He was educated at Wittenberg College (Ohio), Adrian College (Mich.), the University of Edinburgh, and Harvard University, and received honorary degrees from several American colleges. He saw service in the Civil War and was ordained to the Methodist Protestant ministry in 1880. In 1874 he became professor of logic and philosophy at Adrian College, serving as the president of this institution from 1881 to 1888. From 1888 to 1896 he was editor of the "Methodist Recorder." In 1896 he was made chancellor of the Kansas City (Kan.) University. From 1900 to 1904 he was president of the General Conference of the Methodist Protestant Church, serving in 1901 as a representative from this church to the Ecumenical Conference at London, England. He was active in the movement for the union of the Congregational United Brethren and the Methodist Protestant churches, becoming the permanent chairman of their general council in 1906. He wrote "Wesley and Episcopacy" (1892), and numerous pamphlets on religious subjects.

STEPHENS, JAMES, an Irish poet and novelist. His childhood and youth were spent in wandering about Belfast and Ireland, enduring great hardships. He finally became a clerk in a solicitor's office in Dublin. He published his first volume of verse, entitled "Insurrections," in 1900. This attracted wide attention. It was followed by a second volume of verse, "The Hill of Vision," in 1912. In the same year he published two novels, "Mary, Mary," and "The Crock of Gold." His writings contain evidence of undoubted genius. His later books include "Here Are Ladies" (1913); "The Demi-Gods" (1914); "The Rocky Road to Dublin" (1915); "Songs from the Clay" (1915).

STEPHENS, JAMES, a noted Fenian; born in Kilkenny, 1824; son of an auctioneer's clerk with more of Saxon than of Celtic blood. He had a good education, took early to mathematics, and at 20 obtained an appointment during the making of the Limerick and Waterford railway. He next went to Dublin, and soon became one of the most active agents of the Young Ireland party. He was slightly wounded at the scuffle of Ballingarry (June 29, 1848), lived for three months thereafter among the mountains from Tipperary to Kerry, and then sailed from Cork to France disguised as a lady's servant. For some years he lived mainly at Paris, where he obtained an insight into the working of continental secret societies, and in 1853 journeyed over Ireland making himself acquainted with its conditions and preparing the soil for the Fenian conspiracy. As its "Head Center" he exercised an enormous and despotic influence. He visited the United States early in 1864 to attempt to overthrow the rival schemes formed there by patriots, and was arrested in Dublin on November 10, of the same year. Fourteen days later he made his escape from Richmond Bridewell and made his way to New York, where he was formally deposed by the Fenians. He was allowed to return to Ireland in 1891. He died in Dublin March 29, 1901.

STEPHENS, WILLIAM DENNISON, an American public official, born at Eaton, O., in 1859. He was educated in the public schools of his native city and then taught school and read law. From 1880 to 1887 he did engineering work in connection with railway construction in Ohio, Indiana, Iowa, and Louisiana. In 1887 he removed to Los Angeles, Cal., where he engaged in business. From 1906 to 1907 he was a member of the Los Angeles Board of Education, in 1909 mayor of Los Angeles, and in 1910 president of the board of water commissioners. He was elected to Congress in 1911, serving until 1916, when he resigned upon being appointed lieutenant-governor of California by Governor Johnson. Upon the latter's resignation in 1917, he became governor and was elected for another term in 1919, in which year he was also admitted to the bar. From 1903 to 1917 he was a commissioned officer in the California National Guard.

STEPHENSON, GEORGE, an English engineer; born in Wylam, England, June 9, 1781. At the age of 14 he joined his father in his work as fireman in a colliery. In 1812 he was appointed engineer to the colliery. Soon after this he built his first traveling engine to draw the wagons along the tramway. Improvement followed on improvement in rapid succession, in every department to which steam was applicable. In 1822 he opened the first railway, 8 miles long. The whole system of railway locomotion with all its complications of stations, signals, tenders, and carriages, was completed by the opening of the Liverpool and Manchester railway in 1830. In 1845 he retired from all railway undertakings, after having been instrumental in estab-

GEORGE STEPHENSON

lishing all the foreign and home lines. He died near Chesterfield, England, Aug. 12, 1848.

STEPHENSON, ROBERT, a British civil engineer, only son of George Stephenson; born near Newcastle-upon-Tyne, Oct. 16, 1803; joined his father in

ROBERT STEPHENSON

his operations on the Liverpool line; became the permanent engineer of that company; surveyed several new lines, visited South America to inspect the gold and silver mines of that country; and established a name as the first civil engineer in Europe. Among the works with which Robert Stephenson's name is associated, are the High Level Bridge over the Tyne, the Tweed Viaduct, the Britannia Bridge over the Menai Straits, the Victoria Bridge at Montreal across the St. Lawrence, one of the grandest of engineering achievements, and the Alexandria and Cairo railway. In 1847 he entered Parliament for Whitby; he was a Fellow of the Royal Society, and a member of nearly all the scientific societies of Europe. He published two valuable works, "The Locomotive Steam Engine," and "The Atmospheric Railway System." He died in London Oct. 12, 1859, and was buried in Westminster Abbey, where there is a memorial window in his honor.

STEPNIAK (stĕp'nyak), **SERGIUS MICHAEL DRAGOMANOV,** a Russian revolutionist; born in Gadjatch, Poltava, Russia, in 1841. Exiled in 1876 on account of his criticisms on the system followed by Count Tolstoy, minister of justice, he settled in Geneva in 1887. Among his works are "The Turks Within and Without" (1876); "Underground Russia" (1881); "Tyrannicide in Russia" (1881); "The Russian Peasantry"; "Historical Poland and the Muscovite Democracy" (1881); "Little Russian Internationalism"; "The Propaganda of Socialism"; "Russia under the Czars"; and "The Career of a Nihilist," a novel (1889). He assisted in editing the folk songs of Little Russia. In 1891 he visited the United States. He died in London, England, Dec. 23, 1895.

STEPPE, a term applied to one of those extensive plains which, with the occasional interpolation of low ranges of hills, stretch from the Dnieper across the S. E. of European Russia, round the shores of the Caspian and Aral seas, between the Altai and Ural chains, and occupy the low lands of Siberia. In spring they are covered with verdure, but for the greater part of the year they are dry and barren. There are three different kinds of steppe, viz., grass, salt, and sand steppes, each maintaining peculiar forms of vegetation.

STERE (stār), the French unit for solid measure, equal to a cubic meter, or 35.3156 cubic feet.

STEREO-CHEMISTRY, that branch of chemistry which studies the arrangement of the atoms of a molecule in space. It concerns itself especially with compounds of carbon. Many examples are known where two compounds are found to consist not only of the same atoms but of the same groups of atoms, and yet they differ in their properties, both chemical and physical. For instance, both fumaric acid and maleic acid have the chemical formula $C_4H_4O_4$, and the atoms are grouped in this manner: COOH.CH:CH.COOH. The two compounds are known as *isomers,* and the fact that two substances could exist with the same structural formula, and yet be entirely different and distinct compounds for a long time remained unexplained. The solution to the problem was offered by stereo-chemistry. Following the theories of Van't Hoff, the carbon atom is conceived as being situated at the center of a regular tetrahedron, the groups combined with it being located at the angles. The differing properties of isomers is explained by the theory that the arrangement of the groups at the corners, relative to one another, differs in the two compounds. For instance, if a projection were made of the "solid formula" of the two compounds given above, they would appear as:

$$\begin{array}{cc} \text{H-C-COOH} & \text{H-C-COOH} \\ \| & \| \\ \text{H-C-COOH} & \text{COOH-C-H} \\ \text{Maleic Acid} & \text{Fumaric Acid} \end{array}$$

STEREOCHROMY, a process of mural painting in which water glass is employed to fix or consolidate the colors. It has not proved successful.

STEREOPTICON, a magic lantern having two objective tubes that can be focused on the same part of a screen, and by the alternate projection of pictures from the separate tubes produce the well-known phenomena of "dissolving views."

STEREOSCOPE, a simple and once popular optical contrivance, by which two flat slightly dissimilar pictures of an object are fused into one image, having the actual appearance of relief. A reflecting form of the stereoscope was invented by Professor Wheatstone in 1838. Subsequently Sir David Brewster invented the refracting or lenticular stereoscope, based on the refractive properties of semidouble convex lenses; and this instrument, of which there are numerous forms came into general use. Convex lenses magnify the pictures besides producing a stereoscopic effect. Photography greatly assists the stereoscope in providing perfectly accurate right-and-left monocular views, which are taken simultaneously on a plate in a twin camera. Several modifications of the reflecting stereoscope are distinguished by the names pseudoscope, iconoscope, tele-stereoscope, and polistereoscope, the last being an apparatus which serves the purposes of all the others.

STEREOTYPE, fixed type; hence a plate cast from a plaster, papier-mâché, or composition mold, on which is a fac-simile of the page of type as set up by the compositor, and which, when fitted to a block, may be used under the press, exactly as movable type.

STERNE, LAURENCE, a British author, was the son of Lieutenant Roger Sterne of the British Army, and Agnes Nuttle, an Irishwoman, widow of a Captain Hebert. He was born in Clonmel, Ireland, on Nov. 24, 1713, and went to school in Halifax from the age of 10 till his father's death in 1731. Two years later he was sent at the expense of a cousin to Jesus College, Cambridge, where he graduated B. A. in 1736 and M. A. in 1740. Though quite unfitted for the church, he took orders and after a period as curate at Buckden, became vicar of Sutton-in-the-Forest in Yorkshire. He engaged a curate to attend to the parish, while he spent most of his time in York, where he was a prebendary in the Cathedral. In 1741 he married Eliza Lumley, the orphan daughter of a clergyman, who brought him £40 a year, and in correspondence with whom he invented the term "sentimental" which his writings established in the language to describe a certain phase of tender emotion. In 1743 he added to his other offices the living of Stillington, adjoining Sutton, but continued till 1759 to live at Sutton, preaching there in the morning and at Stillington in the afternoon. He was a "sporting parson," experimented unsuccessfully with farming, and did not get along with his parishioners. Within doors he dabbled in music and painting, read widely, and enjoyed a quite unclerical society, a leader in which was his old college friend, John Hall-Stevenson, at whose house at Skelton met a club called the "Demoniacks." His health was poor and was not improved by his debauches, and his married life was far from calm, as he was always engaged in sentimental love affairs. For his only child, Lydia, he seems to have had a genuine affection.

In 1759, while his wife was suffering from an attack of insanity, partly brought on by her husband's misbehavior, he began to write "Tristram Shandy." He had previously published a couple of sermons and had amused his friends with a satirical skit on a local ecclesiastical quarrel. The first two volumes of "Tristram Shandy," having been refused by a London publisher, were printed at York, and its style and wit, in spite of its rambling digressions, gave it an immediate and sensational success. He went up to London where he was lionized and engaged in innumerable flirtations, while his book was attacked in Yorkshire for its caricatures of local personages and in London by severer critics for its impropriety. On his return he added to his livings the curacy of Coxwold, where he went to live, and spent lavishly the considerable sums he now received from his publishers. The third and fourth volumes of "Tristram" took him to London again in 1760, where he renewed his social triumphs, leaving his wife, now recovered, but hardly happier, at Coxwold. The fifth and sixth volumes followed in 1761, and in the following year, to recover from a severe illness, he went to Paris. There he was received with great distinction, but suffered another attack of hæmorrhage of the lungs and went to the south with his wife and daughter. In the end of 1764 he returned to England alone, bringing the seventh and eighth volumes; and in the next year he made a tour of France and Italy, which formed the basis of his "Sentimental Journey." The ninth and last volume of "Tristram Shandy" appeared in 1767, and the two volumes of "A Sentimental Journey" in 1768.

Meantime Sterne had made the acquaintance of Elizabeth Draper, the wife of an Indian official, with whom he formed a sentimental relation and to whom he wrote his "Journal to Eliza." He never saw her after her return to India in 1767.

"A Sentimental Journey" enhanced his reputation, but Sterne's health was getting worse and worse, and he died in London on March 18, 1768, and was buried in St. George's burial ground. Many of his sermons and letters were published after his death by his wife and daughter, who had been left only debts and manuscripts as a legacy.

Of Sterne's character very little good can be said. His emotional sensibility was unregulated by moral principles, and both the humor and indecency of his writings were genuine expressions of his temperament. But he was master of an easy and graceful English style, a subtle humorist, and an acute observer of human nature. He set agoing a sentimental craze that spread all over Europe and evoked imitations in many languages. He lives now, not by his sentimentality, which has become repellent to modern taste, but by his humor and his style, in regard to which he has few equals.

 See **Steel**, p. 67

IN A PITTSBURGH STEEL MILL. AN INGOT IS IN THE PROCESS OF
BEING ROLLED INTO A STEEL RAIL

 See **Steel**, p. 67

POURING MOLTEN IRON INTO THE LADLES THAT CARRY IT TO THE
OPEN-HEARTH FURNACES

STERNER, ALBERT EDWARD, an American portrait painter, born in London, in 1863, of American parents. He was educated at King Edward's School, Birmingham, and studied art in Paris. In 1879 he removed to the United States. Settling in Chicago, he worked as an artist, scene painter, and lithographer. In 1885 he opened a studio in New York. He illustrated many well-known books and received medals at several expositions. He was an associate member of the National Academy, and was president of the Painter-Gravers of America in 1918.

STERNUM, the breast bone; in man, the flat bone, occupying the front of the chest, and formed by the meeting of the visceral arches. It is flattened from before backward, and presents a slight vertical curve with the convexity in front. It is divided into the manubrium or presternum, the mesosternum, and the ensiform or xiphoid process of metasternum. All mammals and birds possess a sternum, and the presence or absence of a keel on that bone in birds is used as a means of classification. Fishes, amphibians, and ophidians have no sternum, and in saurians the broad portion is generally expanded. Some suppose that the plastron of the *Chelonia* is a highly-developed sternum; others hold that it is a mere integumentary ossification. The name sternum is also given to the plate on each segment of the breat of a crustacean and an arachnidan, but these are integumentary, and have no relation to a true sternum.

STERILITY, the quality or state of being sterile; barrenness. According to Darwin, sterility in animals and plants may be constitutional or accidental and often arises from changed conditions of life. Thus most raptorial birds from the tropics do not lay fertile eggs in captivity in temperate climates, and many exotic plants brought to England have worthless pollen. Sometimes a little more or less water will decide whether or not a plant will seed.

STERILIZED MILK, milk which has been subjected to a process that destroys the bacteria causing lactic or butyric acid fermentation and the germs of disease. Experiments have been made with chemical sterilizers, but these must be used in quantities so large as to be injurious. A freezing temperature checks the development of bacteria, but cannot be relied on, in every instance, to destroy them. Superheated steam is preferable to boiling water, in sterilization. Sterilization is now largely carried on under the supervision of state and county boards of health.

STERLING, originally a substantive, "a coin of true weight," as applied at first to the English penny, then to all current coin. The adjective is now used of all the money of the United Kingdom, and has long been a synonym for pure and genuine.

STERLING, a city in Illinois, in Whiteside co. It is on the Rock river, the Hennepin canal, and the Chicago and Northwestern and the Chicago, Burlington, and Quincy railroads. Its industries include the manufacture of hardware, agricultural implements, gasoline engines, canned goods, paper, machineshop products, etc. There is a public hospital and a library. Pop. (1910) 7,467; (1920) 8,182.

STERLING, GEORGE, an American author, born in Sag Harbor, N. Y., in 1869. He was educated in the private and public schools and at St. Charles College, Ellicott City, Md. He wrote "The Testimony of the Suns and Other Poems" (1903); "A Wine of Wizardry and Other Poems" (1908); "The House of Orchids and Other Poems" (1911); "Beyond the Breakers and Other Poems" (1914); "Exposition Ode" (1915); "Yosemite" (1915); "The Caged Eagle and Other Poems" (1916); "The Binding of the Beast and Other Poems" (1917); "Lilith," a dramatic poem (1919).

STERLING, THOMAS, a United States Senator from South Dakota; born in Fairfield, Ohio, in 1851. He graduated from the Illinois Wesleyan University in 1875. In 1878 he was admitted to the bar and removed to South Dakota in 1882. From 1901 to 1911 he was dean of the College of Law at the University of South Dakota. He was district attorney of Spink co. from 1887 to 1889; a member of the South Dakota Constitution Convention, and a member of the first State Senate in 1890. He was twice elected to the United States Senate, the last time for the term ending 1925.

STERLING, YATES, an American naval officer, born in Baltimore, Md., in 1843. He graduated from the United States Naval Academy in 1863, became an ensign in the same year, and rose through the various grades to the rank of rear-admiral in 1902. During the Civil War he served with the North Atlantic blockading squadron, and participated in both attacks on Fort Fisher.

Besides being at various times in command of various ships in the United States Navy, he saw service with the Hydrographic Office, at the Washington Navy Yard, with the Lighthouse Board, at the naval station at San Juan, P. R., at the navy yard, Puget Sound, and with the Asiastic Fleet, of which he was commander-in-chief from 1904 to 1905. In the latter year, upon reaching the legal age limit, he was retired.

STERLING GOLD, gold having the value or fineness of the standard established by the British Government. It consists of 22 parts (called carats) of pure gold and two parts of alloy, either silver or copper. But fancy gold articles may be manufactured with only 15, 12, or even 9 carats of gold and the rest alloy. One pound Troy of standard gold is coined into 46 sovereigns. There remains a small fraction over; but 46 sovereigns will do for a pound Troy weight. A sovereign weighs 5 dwts. 3.27447 grains; but 5 dwts. 2½ grains is a legal tender. The Bank of England gives £46 14s. 6d. a pound for gold.

STERLING SILVER, silver having the value or fineness of the standard established by the British Government. It consists of 37 parts of silver and 3 of copper. One pound Troy of silver is coined in 66 shillings. A shilling from the mint weighs 15.27272 grains. The standard value of silver is very variable. In 1870 it was worth at the Bank of England 5s. an ounce. In 1890 it varied from 4s. to 4s. 2d. In December, 1919, it was 6s. 7½d. See BIMETALLISM.

STERN, DANIEL, pseudonym of MARIE CATHERINE SOPHIE DE FLAVIGNY, COMTESSE D'AGOULT (dä-gö'), a famous French writer; born in Frankfort-on-the-Main, Germany, Dec. 31, 1805. One of her three daughters, that by Franz Liszt, married Von Bülow, and subsequently Richard Wagner. Her works include: "Moral and Political Essays" (1849); "History of the Revolution of 1848" (1851); and "Nélida," an autobiographical romance. She died in Paris March 5, 1876.

STERNBERG, GEORGE MILLER, an American surgeon; born in Otsego co., N. Y., June 8, 1838; was graduated at the College of Physicians and Surgeons in New York City in 1860. He was appointed an assistant surgeon in the army in 1861; promoted captain and assistant surgeon May 28, 1866; major, Dec. 1, 1875; lieutenant-colonel Jan. 2, 1891; and brigadier-general and surgeon-general May 30, 1893. During the Civil War he served in the Army of the Potomac and in the Department of the Gulf. Afterward he served through several cholera and yellow fever epidemics, and in 1898 at the outbreak of the Spanish-American War he planned the army hospital train, and had charge of the medical service of the army. He was secretary of the Havana Yellow Fever Commission in 1879; president of the American Medical Association in 1898; and the author of "Photo-Micrographs, and How to Make Them"; "Manual of Bacteriology"; "Immunity, Protective Inoculations, and Serum-Therapy"; etc. He died in 1915.

STESICHORUS, one of the nine great lyric poets of antiquity; is said to have been born in 632 B. C., either in Himera in Sicily, or Metaurus in Magna Græcia, and to have died about 556, but nothing certain is known concerning him. His own name, Tisias, he changed to Stesichorus ("leader of choirs") as the inventor of strophe, antistrophe, and epode, and with his predecessor Alcman he stands at the head of Dorian choral poets. His fragments include erotic, pastoral, and mythological pieces, fables and elegies, hymns, pæans, and epithalmia, and are collected in Bergk's "Poeta Lyrici Græci."

STETHOSCOPE, an instrument employed in auscultation. It was invented by Lænnec, who at first used a roll of blotting paper for the purpose of concentrating and conveying sound to the ear; but, according to Tyndall, the philosophy of the stethoscope was enunciated by Dr. Robert Hooke (1635-1702). The common stethoscope consists of a hard rubber funnel to which two flexible rubber ear-tubes are attached. The funnel is applied to the chest, and the tubes to the ear of the physician who perceives the condition of the lungs by the sounds produced when the patient draws long breaths. The phoneidoscope is an improvement which conveys the most minute sounds to the ear.

STETSON, FRANCIS LYNDE, an American lawyer, born at Keeseville, N. Y., in 1846. He graduated from Williams College in 1867 and from the Columbia Law School in 1869. In the same year he was admitted to the bar and engaged in practice in New York as a member of the firm of Stetson, Jennings & Russell, and became one of the best-known lawyers in the United States, appearing as counsel in many important litigations. He was also well known in political life and took a leading part in many reform movements in New York. He was a director of several railways and financial institutions. He died in 1920.

STETSON, HERBERT LEE, an American educator, born at Greene, Me., in 1847. He was educated at the Baptist Union Theological Seminary, and Franklin College, Ind. In 1871 he was ordained to the Baptist ministry, and from then until 1890 was pastor of various churches in Illinois, Indiana, and Iowa. From 1889 to 1900 he was president of Des Moines College, from 1900 to 1913 professor of psychology and pedagogy at Kalamazoo (Mich.) College, of which institution he was acting president from 1911 to 1913, and president after 1913. He also lectured at various times on psychology and religion at the University of Chicago and at Rochester Theological Seminary.

STETTIN, the capital of Pomerania and one of the chief seaports of Germany; on the Oder, 17 miles from its entrance into the Stettiner Haff, 30 miles from the Baltic Sea, and about 83 miles from Berlin. The principal part is built on the left bank of the river, while on the right bank are the suburbs of Lastadie and Silberwiese, connection being maintained by several bridges, one of which is a large railway swing bridge. The town has greatly expanded since the removal of the extensive fortifications by which it was surrounded. Among its more notable features are the old royal palace, now occupied as government buildings, the new town hall, two monumental gateways, several Gothic churches, exchange, theater, etc. Its industries, which are numerous and important, include iron founding, ship building, machine making (one ship building and engineering work employs 4,000 or 5,000 hands), the manufacture of chemicals, cement, sugar, soap, candles, chocolate, etc. It has been a port of some importance since the 12th century. Pop. about 250,000.

STETTINIUS, EDWARD R., an American banker, born at St. Louis, Mo., in 1865. He was educated at St. Louis University. In 1892 he removed to Chicago, where he became an officer in various manufacturing concerns, becoming eventually president of the Diamond Match Co. in 1909. In 1915 he organized for J. P. Morgan & Co. a department for the purchase of munitions and other war materials for the British and French governments, becoming in 1916 a member of this firm. In January, 1918, he was appointed surveyor-general of supplies for the United States War Department; in March, 1918, a member of

the War Council; in April, 1918, second assistant secretary of war; in July, 1918, United States representative on the Inter-Allied Munitions Council, Paris, France; and in August, 1918, special representative of the United States War Department in Europe. In January, 1919, he resigned from Government service and resumed his membership in J. P. Morgan & Co. Died Sept. 3, 1925.

STEUBEN, FREDERIC WILLIAM AUGUSTUS, BARON, an American military officer; born in Magdeburg, Prussia, Nov. 15, 1730. He came to America in 1777 and his offer of service was readily accepted. Having received the appointment of inspector-general, with the rank of major-general, he proved of efficient service to the American army in establishing a system of discipline and

BARON VON STEUBEN

tactics acquired as an officer under Frederick the Great. He spent his whole fortune in clothing his men and gave his last dollar to the soldiers. Congress made tardy reparation, and in 1790 voted him an annuity of $2,500 and a township of land in the State of New York, both of which he divided with his fellow officers. He died on his estate near Utica, N. Y., Nov. 28, 1794. In 1870 the corner stone of a monument to his memory was laid at the Schützen Park.

STEUBENVILLE, a city and county-seat of Jefferson co., O.; on the Wheeling and Lake Erie, the Pittsburg, Cincinnati, Chicago, and St. Louis, and the Pennsylvania railroads; 43 miles W. of Pittsburgh, Pa. It is near a rich bituminous coal region, and is in the heart of an agricultural section. Here are public libraries, parks, waterworks, electric lights, high school, National and private banks, and daily and weekly newspapers. The city has a large coal industry, and manufactories of glass, steel, machinery, pottery, paper, flour, boilers, fire and paving brick, sewer pipe, etc. Pop. (1910) 22,391; (1920) 28,508.

STEVENS, JAMES STACY, an American educator, born in Lima, N. Y., in 1864. He was educated at the University of Rochester and at Syracuse University. From 1885 to 1891 he was instructor of science at Cook Academy, Montour Falls, N. Y. In 1891 he became professor of physics at the University of Maine; in 1915, dean of its College of Arts and Sciences; and from 1917 to 1919, acting head of its department of English. He was a member of several American and foreign scientific societies. Besides frequent contributions to scientific, educational, and literary periodicals, he wrote "Outlines of General Physics" (1900); "Outlines of Laboratory Physics" (1901); "Theory of Measurements" (1915); "A Dramatization of Job" (1917); and "Corollaries of Infinity" (1919).

STEVENS, JOHN CALVIN, an American architect, born at Boston, Mass., in 1855. After graduating from the Portland High School in 1873, he entered an architectural office, later becoming successively a member of various firms. He was a member of many philanthropic and art societies and designed many public buildings and private residences in Maine and in other parts of the United States. He wrote, together with A. W. Cobb, "Examples of Domestic Architecture" (1891).

STEVENS, THADDEUS, an American statesman; born in Danville, Vt., April 4, 1792; was graduated at Dartmouth College in 1814; studied law and was admitted to the Maryland bar. He kept aloof from politics till the election of Jackson in 1828, when he became an active member of the Whig party. In 1833 and for several succeeding years, he was a member of the Pennsylvania Legislature and became distinguished by his opposition to slavery. He was appointed a canal commissioner in 1838, and rendered important services to the state in the promotion of its system of internal improvements. Subsequently he removed to Lancaster, and for six years practiced law. But in 1848 and again in 1850 he was elected to Congress, where he maintained strong opposition to the Fugitive-Slave Law, the Kansas-Nebraska bill, and all measures favoring the independence of the South. In 1858 he was again elected to Congress and retained his seat till his death, in Washington, D. C., Aug. 11, 1868.

STEVENS INSTITUTE OF TECHNOLOGY, an educational non-sectarian institution in Hoboken, N. J.; founded in 1870; reported at the close of 1919: Professors and instructors, 46; students, 522; president, A. C. Humphreys, LL.D.

STEVENSON, ADLAI EWING, an American statesman; born in Christian co., Ky., Oct. 23, 1835; early took an active part in politics as a Democrat, and in 1875-1877 and 1879-1881 represented Illinois in the National House of Representatives. In 1885 was appointed first assistant postmaster-general, and after the renomination of Grover Cleveland in 1892 was chosen the candidate for the vice-presidency. The Democratic candidates were elected, and after the expiration of his term he was appointed a member of the American commission to visit Europe and endeavor to secure the adoption of international bimetallism. In 1908 he was the Democratic candidate for governor of Illinois. He died in 1914.

STEVENSON, BURTON EGBERT, born at Chillicothe, Ohio, in 1872. He was educated at Princeton University, and became city editor of the Chillicothe "Daily News" in 1894; of the Chillicothe "Daily Advertiser" in 1898; and librarian of the Chillicothe public library in 1899. He wrote "At Odds With the Regent" (1900); "A Soldier of Virginia" (1901); "The Heritage" (1902); "The Holladay Case" (1903); "The Marathon Mystery (1904); "The Young Section Hand" (1905); "Affairs of State" (1906); "That Affair at Elizabeth" (1907); "The Quest for the Rose of Sharon" (1909); "The Path of Honor" (1910); "The Spell of Holland" (1911); "The Young Apprentice" (1912); "The Gloved Hand" (1913); "The Charm of Ireland" (1914); "Little Comrade" (1915); "A King in Babylon" (1917). He also edited and compiled several books, among which should be mentioned "Poems of American History" (1908); "A Child's Guide to American Biography" (1909); "Home Book of Verse" (1912); "Home Book of Verse for Young Folks" (1915); and "European Directory, Library War Service, A.L.A." (1918-19).

STEVENSON, EDWARD IRENÆUS (PRIME), an American author and editor, born in 1868. He was admitted to the bar, but never practiced, and was a member of the literary staff of "The Independent," "Harper's Weekly," and other magazines. He became specially well known as a musical, dramatic, and literary critic, and traveled and lectured extensively. He has written many novels and short stories, as well as a large number of articles on literary, musical, and historical topics.

STEVENSON, EDWARD LUTHER, an American educator, born at Rozetta, Illinois, in 1860. He was educated at Franklin (Ind.) College, Johns Hopkins University, and the universities of Jena, Halle, and Heidelberg. From 1881 to 1887 he was principal of high schools and superintendent of schools in Illinois; from 1891 to 1911, professor of history, Rutgers College, New Brunswick, N. J.; from 1910 to 1917 secretary of the Hispanic Society of America, of which society he became acting director in 1915. He also lectured on historical geography, history, and cartographical subjects at Johns Hopkins, Columbia, University of California, and numerous other scientific and educational institutions. He was a member of several domestic and foreign historical and geographical societies, and published: "Maps Illustrating Discovery and Early Exploration in America, 1502-1530" (1903-1906); "Charter of Queens College (now Rutgers) of 1772" (1907); "Hondius World Map of 1611" (1907); "The Marine World Chart of Nicolo de Canerio" (1908); "Early Spanish Cartography of the New World" (1909); "Atlas of Portolan Charts" (1911); "Portolan Charts, Their Origin and Characteristics" (1911); "The Genoese World Map, 1457" (1912); "Christopher Columbus and His Enterprise" (1913); "Willem Janszoon Blaeu, His Life and Work with Facsimile of His Large World Map of 1605" (1914); "Portolan Atlas 'Conte de Ottoma Freducci, 1537'" (1915); "Facsimiles of Portolan Charts" (1917); "Terrestrial and Celestial Globes" (1917).

STEVENSON, (JOSEPH) ROSS, an American theologian, born at Ligonier, Pa., in 1866. He graduated from Washington and Jefferson College in 1886 and from McCormick Theological Seminary in 1889. After taking post-graduate studies in Berlin, he was ordained to the Presbyterian ministry in 1890, and served as pastor for several years in Sedalia, Mo. From 1894 to 1897 he was adjutant professor of ecclesiastical history at McCormick Theological Seminary, and full professor from 1897 to 1902. In the latter year he became pastor of the Fifth Avenue Church, New York City, serving until 1909. From that year till 1914 he was pastor of the Brown Memorial Church, in Baltimore. In 1914 he was elected president of the Princeton Theological Seminary. During the World War he was a member of the International Committee of the Y. M. C. A., and of the War Work Council. He served in France with the Y. M. C. A. and with the Army Educational Commission in 1918-19.

STEVENSON, ROBERT, a Scotch engineer; born in Glasgow, Scotland, June 8, 1772. His father died during his infancy; and his mother having (1786) married Thomas Smith, the first engineer of the Lighthouse Board, young Stevenson was led to the study of engineering. In 1796 he succeeded his stepfather as engineer and inspector of lighthouses; and during his 47 years' tenure of that office he planned and constructed 23 lighthouses round the Scotch coasts, employing the catoptric system of illumination, and his valuable invention of "intermittent" and "flashing" lights. The most remarkable of these erections was that on the Bell Rock. Stevenson was also in great request as a consulting engineer in the matter of roads, bridges, harbors, canals, and railways. He wrote four volumes of professional printed reports, a large work on the Bell Rock lighthouse, some articles in the "Encyclopædia Britannica" and in the "Edinburgh Encyclopædia." He died in Edinburgh July 12, 1850.

STEVENSON, ROBERT LOUIS BALFOUR, a British author; son of Thomas Stevenson; born in Edinburgh, Scotland, Nov. 13, 1850; educated at the University of Edinburgh, was intended for his father's profession, but studied

ROBERT LOUIS STEVENSON

law; in 1873 went abroad for his health; wrote for periodicals till 1878, when his first book appeared; visited California in 1879; spent the winter of 1887-1888 in the Adirondacks; cruised in the Pacific; bought a tract of land ("Vailima" or "Five Streams") in Samoa, where he made his home. He published: "An Inland Voyage" (1878); "Edinburgh: Picturesque Notes" (1878); "Travels With a Donkey in the Cévennes" (1879); "Virginibus Puerisque, and Other Papers" (1881); "Familiar Studies of Men and Books" (1882); "New Arabian Nights" (1882); "Treasure Island" (1883); "The Silverado Squatters" (1883); "The Dynamiter: More New Arabian Nights" (1885), with Mrs. Stevenson; "A Child's Garden of Verse" (1885); "Prince Otto" (1885); "The Strange Case of Dr. Jekyll and Mr. Hyde" (1886); "Kidnapped" (1886); "Underwoods" (1887); "The Merry Men and Other Tales" (1887); "Memoirs and Portraits" (1887); "The Black Arrow" (1888); "The Master of Ballantrae" (1889); "Ballads" (1891); "The Wrecker" (1891-1892); "A Foot-Note to History: Eight Years of Trouble in Samoa" (1892); "David Balfour" (1893); "Island Nights' Entertainments" (1893); "The Ebb Tide" (1894); "Weir of Hermiston" and "St. Ives" (1895-1896), the last two left not quite complete. He died in Vailima, near Apia, Samoa, Dec. 3, 1894.

STEVENSON, SARA YORKE, (Mrs. Cornelius Stevenson), an American archæologist, born at Paris, France, in 1847. She was educated in Paris until 1862, and later lived in Mexico, marrying Cornelius Stevenson of Philadelphia, in 1870. The University of Pennsylvania bestowed upon her the honorary degree of Sc. D., the first honorary degree ever conferred by this institution on a woman. In 1897 she was secretary of the American Exploration Society, and in 1904 president of the department of archæology, University of Pennsylvania. From 1894 to 1901 she was a trustee, and since 1908 curator, of the Philadelphia Museums; and from 1899 to 1903 president of the Pennsylvania branch of the Archæological Institute of America. She took an active part in the civic affairs of Philadelphia, being at various times an officer of the Civic Club, and since 1914 its honorary president. In 1909 she was president of the Pennsylvania Equal Suffrage Society. In 1897 she went to Rome on a special mission for the department of archæology of the University of Pennsylvania, and in 1898 to Egypt for the American Exploration Society. During the World War she was the chairman of various relief committees in Philadelphia, and was made by the French Government Officier d'Instruction Publique. She wrote, besides many articles on Egyptian archæology and other topics: "Maximilian in Mexico." In 1908 she became literary editor of the Philadelphia "Public Ledger."

STEVENS POINT, a city and county-seat of Portage co., Wis.; on the Wisconsin river, and on the Wisconsin Central, the Minneapolis, St. Paul and Sault Ste. Marie, and the Green Bay and Western railroads; 63 miles W. of Appleton. It contains gas and electric lights, National and State banks, State Normal School, and daily and weekly newspapers. It has a large lumbering trade, especially in pine. Here are shops of the Wisconsin Central railroad, and numerous foundries, flour, planing, saw, and shingle mills.

STEWARD, in the original sense, one who looked after the domestic animals and gave them their food; hence, one who provides for his master's table, and, generally, one who superintends household affairs for another. A person employed on a large estate or establishment, or in a family of consequence and wealth, to manage the domestic affairs, superintend the other servants, collect rents, keep the accounts, etc. An officer in a college who provides food for the students and superintends the affairs of the kitchen. An official on a vessel, whose duty it is to distribute provisions to the officers and men. In passenger ships, a man who superintends the distribution of provisions and liquors, waits at table, etc. A fiscal agent of certain bodies; as, the recording steward of a congregation of Methodists.

STEWART, ALEXANDER TURNEY, an American merchant; born near Belfast, Ireland, Oct. 12, 1803; came to the United States in 1823 and engaged in teaching. In 1825 he began, in New York City, a dry-goods business which gradually expanded into one of the largest mercantile concerns in the world. He was a donor of large sums of money to various charitable institutions, and was active in many philanthropic undertakings. He died in New York, April 10, 1876, and was buried in St. Mark's churchyard, from which his remains were stolen on Nov. 7, 1878. It was afterward stated that the remains had been recovered and deposited in the mausoleum of the Cathedral of the Incarnation, erected by Mrs. Stewart in memory of her husband at Garden City, Long Island.

STEWART, CHARLES, an American naval officer; born in Philadelphia, Pa., July 28, 1778; entered the navy in 1789 as lieutenant of the frigate "United States," in which capacity he was employed in the West Indies against French privateers. As commander of the brig "Siren" he participated in the naval operations of 1804 against Tripoli and aided in the destruction of the "Philadelphia." In 1813 he took command of the "Constitution," and in December sailed from Boston on a cruise to the coast of Guiana and the Windward Islands, which resulted in the capture of the British schooner "Picton" and several merchant vessels. A year later he sailed in the same ship on a second cruise, and on Feb. 20, 1815, captured the British ship "Cyane," mounting 34 guns, and the sloop of war "Levant," mounting 21 guns. He commanded a squadron in the Mediterranean in 1816-1820, and in the Pacific in 1821-1823; served on the board of navy commissioners; commanded the home squadron; and had charge of the naval station at Philadelphia. In 1857 he was placed on the retired list, but resumed service in 1859 as commander of the Philadelphia navy yard, and on July 16, 1862, was made rear-admiral on the retired list. He died in Bordentown, N. J., Nov. 7, 1869.

STEWART, DUGALD, a Scotch philosopher; born in Edinburgh, Scotland, Nov. 22, 1753; was educated in Edinburgh and attended the lectures of Dr. Reid in Glasgow. In 1772 he began to assist his father who was Professor of Mathematics in Edinburgh University, being appointed joint-professor three years afterward. In 1778 he agreed to lecture also as a substitute for Adam Ferguson in the chair of moral philosophy, and in 1785 when the latter resigned, Dugald Stewart received the appointment. Besides holding this position for a quarter of a century, from which he spread a fine intellectual and moral influence, Stewart was the author of "Elements of the Philosophy of the Human Mind" (1792-1827), "Outlines of Moral Philosophy" (1793), and accounts of the "Life and Writings of Adam Smith," of Dr. Robertson, and of Dr. Reid. He died in 1828.

STEWART ISLAND, an island of New Zealand, S. of South Island; area, 655 square miles.

STEWART, CHARLES D.. an American writer, born at Zanesville, Ohio, in 1868. He was educated in the public schools of Milwaukee and at Wayland Academy (Wis.). From 1915 to 1916 he was executive secretary to the governor of Wisconsin. Besides contributing many short stories, poems, etc., to magazines, he also wrote "The Fugitive Blacksmith" (1905); "Partners of Providence" (1907); "Essays on the Spot" (1910); "The Wrong Woman" (1912); "Finerty of the Sand-house" (1913);

"Prussianizing   Wisconsin"   (1919); "Buck" (1919).

STEWART, SAMUEL VERNON, an American public official, born in Monroe co., Ohio, in 1872. He was educated at the Kansas State Normal School and at the University of Kansas, and began the practice of law at Virginia City, Montana, in 1898. He was city attorney of the town for 5 years, county attorney of Madison co. for 4 years, chairman of the Democratic State Central Committee from 1910 to 1912, and governor of Montana for two terms (1913-1921).

STEWART, WILLIAM RHINELANDER, an American philanthropist, born in New York City, in 1852. He was educated in private schools and at the Columbia University Law School. After practicing law for some years, he retired and devoted his attention entirely to the administration of his family's estates and to works of philanthropy. Appointed State commissioner of charities in 1882, he served continuously with the exception of 4 years, being president of the board since 1904. He organized in 1900 the State Conference of Charities and Corrections and in 1910 the New York City Conference of Charities and Corrections. He was also prominent in the establishment of Letchworth Village, a farm colony for epileptics, of the State Agricultural and Industrial School for Boys, and of various similar institutions. He was chiefly instrumental in securing the funds for the erection of the Washington Arch, Washington Square, New York. He was a member of the 7th Regiment, warden of Grace Church, and a member of numerous scientific and other societies.

STEYN, MARTINUS THEUNIS, a Boer statesman; born in Winburg, Orange Free State, Oct. 2, 1857; worked on his father's farm till 1876, when he went to England to study. He returned to Africa in 1882 and practised law in Bloemfontein till 1889, when he was made second puisne judge and state attorney. Later he became first puisne judge, and in 1896 was chosen president of Orange Free State. For a number of years before his election to the presidency he had been in communication with President Krüger and their close relations finally resulted in the union of the interests of the Orange Free State and the Transvaal in their struggle against Great Britain. When the Boer War broke out he took the field in person with the Free State troops. When Great Britain in 1910 federated the Orange Free State and Transvaal as the Union of South Africa, Steyn subscribed to the constitution, but he was believed to favor the rebellion of 1915. He died in 1916.

STIBNITE, trisulphide of antimony, an ore consisting of 72.88 antimony and 27.12 sulphur. In color it is lead-gray and is very brittle. It is the source of most of the antimony of commerce. Called also antimony glance. Specific gravity 4.5; crystals orthorhombic.

STICKLEBACK, a popular name for any of the species *Gasterosteus*. The 15-spined stickleback lives in salt or brackish water; the others are fresh-water fish; and all, though small in size, are active, greedy, and extremely destructive to the fry of other fishes. In the breeding season the male stickleback constructs a nest, about three inches wide and six inches deep, of stalks of grass

STIGMA (plural, **STIGMAS**, or **STIGMATA**), a mark made with a red-hot iron, formerly impressed on slaves and malefactors; also a small red speck on the human skin; figuratively, any mark of infamy, disgrace, or reproach which attaches to a person on account of bad conduct; a slur. In anatomy, the projecting part of a Graafian follicle at which rupture occurs. In biology, stigmata are the external openings of the tracheal apparatus in the Insecta and Arachnida. Applied also to the pores of the segmental organs of leeches, and to the openings by which the pneumatocyst communicates with the exterior in some of the Physophoridæ.

In botany, the part of the pistil to which the pollen is applied. It is generally situated at the upper extremity of the style. It is a glandular body, destitute of epidermis, and secretes a vis-

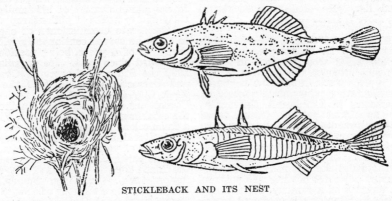

STICKLEBACK AND ITS NEST

and other fibres, cemented together with mucus which exudes from his skin. The 15-spined stickleback (*G. spinachia*) is entirely confined to salt and brackish water; the three-spined stickleback (*G. aculeatus*), the commonest, is found in both fresh and salt water; the short-spined stickleback (*G. brachycentrus*), the 4-spined stickleback (*G. spinulosus*), and the 9-spined or 10-spined stickleback (*G. pungitius*) are confined to fresh water.

STIEGLITZ, JULIUS (OSCAR), an American chemist, born at Hoboken, N. J., in 1867. He was educated in Germany, and from 1892 to 1915 was connected with the chemical department of the University of Chicago. He was a member of many scientific societies, and in 1917 was a member of the division of chemistry of the National Research Council. He was vice-chairman of the division of chemistry from 1919, and was special expert of the Public Health Service in the same year.

cous material, which is most abundant at the period of fecundation. It is sometimes smooth; at others it may be covered with papillæ or with plumose hairs, or it may have around it an indusium. Morphologically viewed, the stigma is the apex of the carpellary leaf. When there is more than one style, each has a stigma; when there are several, they may coalesce so as to have various lobes or divisions. In most cases the stigma is thicker than the style. It varies greatly in form, and may be capitate, penicillate, plumose, or feathery, petaloid, peltate, filiform, or papillose. In some cases the stigma extends down the inner face of the style; it is then called unilateral. In ecclesiology, stigmata is a term borrowed from Gal. vi: 17, "I bear in my body the marks (Greek and Vulgate, *stigmata*) of the Lord Jesus," and applied by ecclesiastical writers to the marks of **STIGMATIZATION** (*q. v.*) St. Paul probably took his metaphor from the fact that pagan soldiers sometimes branded the name of their general on some part of their body. No writer of authority has ever maintained that the stigmata of St. Paul were anything more than the actual marks of suffering inflicted by his persecutors (2d Cor. ii: 23-27).

STIGMARIA, in palæobotany, a pseudo-genus of coal plants, now proved by actual union to be the roots chiefly of *Sigillaria,* but in some cases of *Lepidodendron.* Cylindrical, trunk-like bodies, often more or less compressed, the external surface of which is covered with shallow pits, sometimes with a rootlet projecting. Very abundant in the fireclay of the carboniferous rocks, the old soil in which the *Sigillariæ* grew. The common species is *S. ficoides.*

STIGMATIZATION, the appearance or impression of counterparts of all or some of the wounds received by Jesus in His Passion, in their appropriate positions on the human body. The first case on record, and the most important, is that of St. Francis of Assisi, the founder of the Franciscans. It is said that while the saint was engaged in a fast of 40 days on Mount Alvernus, in the year 1224, a crucified seraph with six wings appeared and discoursed to him of heavenly things. Francis fainted, and on recovering consciousness found himself marked with the wounds of crucifixion in his hands, his feet, and right side. Thomas à Celana and St. Buonaventura attested the case, and Pope Alexander IV. (1254-1261) claimed to have seen the stigmata during the lifetime of St. Francis and after his death. A feast of the Stigmata of St. Francis is celebrated in the Roman Church on September 17. The Dominicans claimed a similar distinction for a saint of their order (St. Catherine of Siena, 1347-1380), and the fact of her stigmatization is recorded in the fifth lection of the office of her feast (April 30) in the Roman Breviary. She is honored with a special feast in her own order, though she is never represented in painting or sculpture with the stigmata. Since then many persons have claimed to have received these marks of divine favor.

STILBITE, a mineral of a shining pearly luster, of a white color, or white shaded with gray, yellow, or red. It has been associated with zeolite, and called foliated zeolite and radiated zeolite.

STIKINE RIVER, the largest and most important stream of southeastern Alaska. Its course is primarily in British Columbia and forms the principal route between the interior of British Columbia and the Pacific Ocean. In the summer steamer service is provided as far as Telegraph Creek, about 175 miles from the mouth of the river.

STILES, CHARLES WARDELL, an American zoologist, born at Spring Valley, N. Y., in 1867. He attended the Wesleyan University in 1885-6, and later studied in Germany and in France. In 1891 he became connected with the Bureau of Animal Industry of the United States Department of Agriculture, and from 1902 was consulting zoologist. He was professor of zoology for the United States Public Health Service, from 1902, and was assistant surgeon-general of this service, from 1919. He also occupied chairs of zoology in several universities, including Georgetown, and Johns Hopkins. He was a member of many international commissions on chemical subjects, and was a member of many scientific societies. He was the author of many books on diseases of cattle and kindred subjects, and was an authority on hookworm and other obscure diseases.

STILICHO, FLAVIUS, a Vandal of great genius and bravery, who distinguished himself at the declining period of the Roman empire, was advanced to the highest dignities of the state by Theodosius the Great, and married Serena, the emperor's adopted daughter, besides being intrusted in 394 with the guardianship of his two sons, Arcadius and Honorius. On the division of the empire, Stilicho became virtual governor of the West, in the character of first minister to Honorius, while the same power in the East was exercised by Rufinus, under Arcadius, the other emperor. The military genius of Stilicho, after this period, was exhibited in the reduction of Africa which had been led into a revolt by Eutropius the successor of Rufinus at the Eastern court, and subsequently in the great contests with Alaric and Radagaisus. In the year 403 he routed the former near Verona, and in 406 put the hosts of the latter to flight and killed their commander. While Stilicho lived he sustained the fortunes of the Roman name, but he was accused of having a secret understanding with Alaric, and was treacherously put to death in 408. The wives and children of 30,000 Germans who were in his service were massacred at the same time.

STILLINGEA, a genus of *Hippomaneæ.* Milky trees or shrubs with alternate leaves, on petioles which have two glands at the apex; flowers monœcious, the males usually in crowded terminal spikes, with a bi-glandular bract at the base; calyx cup-shaped; stamens two, with their filaments united at the base; female solitary; calyx tridentate or trifid; stigmas three, simple; ovary three-celled; fruit capsular, globose, with three cells, each one-seeded. From the warmer areas of Asia and America. *S. sebifera* is the Chinese tallow tree.

STILLMAN, WILLIAM JAMES, an American artist, journalist, author, and traveler; born in Schenectady, N. Y., June 1, 1828; was graduated at Union College in 1848; founded and edited the "Crayon," an art journal in New York. As correspondent of the London "Times" and the New York "Evening Post," and was especially conversant with the affairs of Greece; he was consul-general to Crete, 1865-1869. His published works are: "The Acropolis of Athens" (1870); "The Cretan Insurrection" (1874); "Herzegovina and the Late Uprising" (1877); "On the Track of Ulysses" (1887); "Reminiscences of a Journalist." He died July 8, 1901.

STILLWATER, a city and county seat of Washington co., Minn.; on St. Croix lake and river, and on the Chicago and Northwestern, Northern Pacific, and the Chicago, Milwaukee and St. Paul railroads; 18 miles N. E. of St. Paul. Stillwater contains the State penitentiary, public library, a high school, two convents, hospital, and waterworks. It has flour mills, machine shops, elevators, foundries, etc. Pop. (1910) 10,198; (1920) 7,735.

STIMSON, FREDERIC JESUP, an American lawyer; born in Dedham, Mass., July 20, 1855; was graduated at Harvard University in 1876, and at Harvard Law School in 1878; became assistant attorney-general of Massachusetts in 1884, and later was chosen general counsel to the United States Industrial Commission. He was the author of several law books, novels, essays, mostly under the pseudonym of "J. S. of Dale," including: "Rollo's Journey to Cambridge"; "First Harvests"; "King Noanett"; "Jethro Bacon of Sandwich"; "The American Constitution" (1906); "Popular Law Making" (1910); "The Light of Provence," a play in verse; "My Story," an imagined autobiography of Benedict Arnold (1917).

STIMSON, HENRY LEWIS, an American lawyer and public official, born in New York City, in 1867. He graduated from Yale and from the Harvard Law School. He entered the law firm of Root & Clarke, in 1893, and was a member of the firm of Winthrop & Stimson, from 1901. He served as United States attorney for the Southern District of New York, and was a Republican candidate for governor of New York in 1910. He was Secretary of War in the cabinet of President Taft, from May, 1911, to March, 1913. During the World War he was lieutenant-colonel of the 305th Field Artillery and, later, colonel of the 31st Field Artillery. He served in France 1917-18.

After some years' absence from official life, he was sent to Nicaragua in 1927 as President Coolidge's personal representative to settle the civil war there. Partly by persuasion and partly by representing the likelihood of American military intervention, he induced most of the Liberals to accept the proposal of an election under American supervision. In December, 1927, he was appointed Governor General of the Philippines. In 1928 he did much to win Filipino confidence and to terminate strife between the native and American authorities, by appointing advisers acceptable to the Insular Congress and by opposing the Timberlake resolution for restricting shipment of duty-free sugar from the Philippines to the United States.

STIMULANTS, in pharmacy, agents which increase vital action, first in the organ to which they are applied, and next in the system generally. Stimulants are of three kinds, stomachic, vascular, and spinal. The name is popularly restricted to the first of these, which act on the stomach, expelling flatulence, besides allaying pain and spasm of the intestines. They are also called carminatives. Examples, ginger, capsicum and chillies, cardamoms, mustard, pepper, nutmeg, etc. Some vascular stimulants act on the heart and the larger vessels, others on the smaller ones. Of the first are free ammonia, alcohol in the form of brandy or wine, camphor, aromatics, etc. Of the latter are acetate of ammonia, guaiacum, sassafras, etc. Spinal stimulants increase the function of the spinal cord. Examples, nux vomica, strychnia, cantharides, phosphorus, etc.

STING, in botany, a stinging hair. Stinging hairs are sharp, stiff hairs, containing an acrid fluid which is injected into the wound which they produce; stimuli. Example, the nettle, in which the apex is expanded into a little bulb which is broken off when the sting is slightly touched.

In entomology, a weapon of defense, concealed within the abdomen of bees, wasps, etc., and capable of exsertion, or forming part of the last joint of the tail in scorpions. The sting of the bee appears to the naked eye a simple needle-shaped organ; but the microscope shows that it is formed of three pieces: A short, stout, cylindrico-conical sheath containing two setæ, or lancets, one edge thickened and furnished with teeth directed backward, the other sharp and cutting. The poison apparatus consists of two glandular elongated sacs, and terminates by one or two excretory ducts. Morphologically viewed, a sting is an altered oviduct. The term sting is sometimes inaccurately used for the bite of a venomous serpent, and of the forked tongue of snakes. See SCORPION.

STINGRAY, a fish belonging to the genus *Trygon*, natural order *Elasmobranchii*, family *Trygonidæ*, which is allied to that of the rays proper. It is remarkable for its long, flexible, whiplike tail, which is armed with a protecting bony spine, very sharp at the point, and furnished along both edges with sharp cutting teeth. Only one species (*T. pastinaca*) occurs in the British seas, and is popularly known as the fire flaire. Another species (*Trygon centrura*) is common on the E. coasts of North America. These fishes sometimes inflict serious wounds with their tail.

STINKWOOD, the *Oreodaphne foetida*, a tree of the natural order *Lauraceæ*, a native of the Cape of Good Hope, remarkable for the strong disagreeable smell of its wood, which, however, is hard, very durable, takes an excellent polish, and resembles walnut. It has been used in shipbuilding.

STINT (*Tringa*), a gallatorial bird, a species of sandpiper. Temminck's stint (*T. Temminckii*) is the smallest species of the British sandpipers, length 5½ inches. It inhabits the edges of lakes and inland rivers, and is said to breed in North Europe.

STIPA, feather grass; the typical genus of *Stipeæ*. Inflorescence an erect, somewhat contracted panicle; spikelets one-flowered; glumes two, membranaceous, larger than the floret, outer one involute, with a very long, twisted awn, which finally separates at a joint near its base. Steudel describes 104 species. They are widely distributed, but are most abundant in warm countries. *S. pennata* is the common feather grass. It has rigid, setaceous, grooved leaves, and exceedingly long awns, feathery at the point. It is very ornamental in gardens in summer, and if gathered before the seeds are ripe it retains its long feathery awns, and is sometimes dyed of various colors and used for decorative purposes.

STIPPLE, in engraving, a mode of producing the desired effect by means of dots; also called the "dotted style," in contradistinction to "engraving in lines." See ENGRAVING.

STIPULE, or **STIPULA** (plural, STIPULÆ), in botany, one of two small appendages, generally tapering at the end, situated at the base of a petiole on each side, and generally of a less firm texture than the petiole itself. They either adhere to the base of the petiole or are separate; they may last as long as the leaf, or fall off before it. In texture they may be membranous, leathery, or spiny; in margin entire or laciniated. Stipules are absent in exogens with opposite leaves, in some with alternate leaves, and in the great majority of endogens. They are probably transformed leaves. Also appendages at the base of leaves in *Jungermanniaceæ* and *Hepaticæ*.

STIRES, ERNEST MILMORE, an American Protestant Episcopal clergyman, born in Norfolk, Va., in 1866. He was educated at the University of Virginia and at the Episcopal Theological Seminary of Virginia, becoming a deacon in 1891 and a priest in 1892. After being pastor of churches at West Point, Va., Augusta, Ga., and Chicago, Ill., he became pastor of St. Thomas' Church, New York City. He was at various times chaplain of National Guard units, a member of the Board of Visitors of the United States Military Academy, member of the General Board of Commissions, a trustee of the Cathedral of St. John the Divine, a director in many charitable organizations, and one of the candidates for the P. E. bishopric of New York, after the death of Bishop Greer. Became Bishop of Long Island in 1925.

STIRLINGSHIRE, a fertile county of Scotland, on the isthmus between the Firths of Forth and Clyde, and forming part of the border land between the Highlands and Lowlands; area, 298,579 acres. It is bounded N. by Perth and Clackmannan, from which it is separated by the Forth, E. by the Firth of Forth and Linlithgow, S. by Lanark and Dumbarton, and W. by Dumbarton and Loch Lomond. The parish of Alva forms a detached portion of Stirlingshire, and there is another small portion toward the W. extremity of the Ochils. The district of the "Carse," 36,000 acres in extent, stretching along the Forth, is only a few feet above sea level, but in the W. and S. the surface is varied by tracts of heath, moss, and pasture. In the N. W. is Ben Lomond, in the N. E.

part of the Ochils and in the S. the lower Campsie Fells. Besides the Forth, the streams of Stirlingshire are the Avon, Allander, Kelvin, Endrick, Bannock, Carron, Allan (for about a mile), etc. The county includes rich coal and iron districts. There are some 40,000 acres of oak coppice, yielding a large supply of bark. The soil is varied, and agriculture is in a highly proficient state. Wheat and beans are abundantly produced in the Carse, and potatoes and turnips in the higher "dryfield" farms. The manufacture of carpets, tartans, plaidings, shawls, and other woolens is carried on at Bannockburn, Cambusbarron, etc. There are large ironworks at Carron; cotton mills at Fintry, Balfron, and Milngavie; print-fields at Denny, Milngavie, Lennoxtown, etc.; tanworks at Stirling and Falkirk; and shipping yards at Grangemouth. Pop. about 175,000.

STITCHWORT, the *Stellaria,* a genus of *Caryophyllaceæ,* of which there are about 70 species (7 British)—all slender herbs, widely distributed through the temperate and cold regions of the globe. The best-known members are the great stitchwort (*S. Holostea*), which from its large white flowers in early summer is an ornament of hedgerows and pastures; wood stitchwort (*S. nemorum*), frequent in the N. of England and Scotland in shady places, but not so striking as the above; and the chickweed (*S. media*), native through Arctic and N. temperate regions, and now a cosmopolitan naturalized weed. The great stitchwort was supposed to cure "stitch" in the side, hence the name.

STITT, EDWARD RHODES, an American physician and naval officer, born at Charlotte, N. C., in 1867. He was educated at the University of South Carolina (A. B. 1885, LL. D. 1917); University of Pennsylvania (M. D. 1899), and studied at the London School of Tropical Medicine in 1905. He was appointed a United States naval assistant surgeon in 1889 and became medical director, United States Navy, with the rank of rear-admiral in 1917. He specialized in tropical diseases and for many years served in the Philippine Islands. He was a professor of tropical medicine at Georgetown University, George Washington University, and Jefferson Medical College; a member of the National Board of Medical Examiners; a member of several medical societies; and a teacher, and since 1916 commanding officer, at the United States Naval Medical School. He wrote "Practical Bacteriology—Blood Work and Animal Parisitology" (1908);

"Diagnostics and Treatment of Tropical Diseases" (1914).

STOCK, a name originally applied to a cruciferous garden plant, *Matthiola incana* (called more fully stock gillyflower), but now extended to the various species of *Matthiola,* and to certain allied plants of the same order. They are herbaceous or shrubby, biennial or sometimes perennial, and have single or double fragrant flowers. *M. incana* is probably the parent of the greater number of the hoary-leaved varieties cultivated in Great Britain, and known as Brompton stock, queen stock, etc. *M. annua* is the source of the common or 10 weeks' stocks, and *M. graeca* of the smooth-leaved annual stocks. The Virginia stock (*Malcolmia maritima*) has been introduced from the Mediterranean, and like the species already mentioned is a great favorite in the flower garden on account of its beauty and fragrance.

STOCKADE, an inclosure or pen made with posts and stakes. In civil engineering, a row of piles, or a series of rows with brushwood in the intervals, driven into a sea or river shore, to prevent the erosion of the banks. In fortification, stout timbers planted in the ground so as to touch each other, and loopholed for musketry.

STOCKBRIDGE, FRANK PARKER, an American author and journalist, born at Gardiner, Maine, in 1870. He was educated in the public schools of Washington, D. C., and at the George Washington University, but learned the printer's trade in 1894 and became reporter and editorial writer on the Buffalo "Express." He was the founder and editor of the "American Home Magazine" and later served in various capacities on the "New York American," "Globe," "Herald," "Mail," and the Cincinnati "Times-Star." He was prominently identified with the publicity campaign of President Wilson in 1911 and at various times was editor of the "Town Development Magazine," "Popular Mechanics," and "Old Colony Magazine." He was a member of the A. L. A. and of the Author's League of America, and besides frequently contributing to magazines wrote "Yankee Ingenuity in the War" (1919); and (with M. R. Tabue) "Measure Your Mind" (1920).

STOCKBRIDGE, HORACE EDWARD, an American agricultural chemist, born at Hadley, Mass., in 1857. He was educated at the Massachusetts Agricultural College, Boston University, and at the University of Göttingen. From 1884 to

1885 he was associate professor of chemistry at the Massachusetts Agricultural College; from 1885 to 1889 professor of chemistry and geology at the Imperial College of Agriculture and Engineering, Japan; from 1887 to 1889 chief chemist of the Japanese Government; from 1890 to 1894 president of the N. D. Agricultural College and director of the N. D. Experiment Station; from 1897 to 1906 professor of agriculture at the Florida Agricultural College and director of State agricultural institutions; and from 1906 on, editor of the "Southern Ruralist," Atlanta, Ga. He was a member of many domestic and foreign chemical, agricultural, educational and scientific societies, and from 1916 to 1917 president of the Farmers' National Congress. Besides writing reports and magazine articles on agricultural and scientific topics, he published "Rocks and Soils" (1888); and "Land Teaching" (1910).

STOCK DOVE (*Columba aenas*), the common wild pigeon, 14 inches in length, and with a general bluish gray plumage, the breast being purplish. It raises two or three broods in a season and builds its nest in a tree stump or in a rabbit burrow.

STOCK EXCHANGE, a place and institution where securities are sold and purchased. In its origin it was, as the name implies, merely a place to buy and sell, and as such has had its place in the history of every town and city since men began to barter with each other. In its early history it merely represented an agreed on locality where people could conveniently meet, but the desirability of an enclosed space soon became apparent and in some places, Paris among them, buildings for the convenience of those who desired to use them were erected at the public expense. In course of time the management became organized and rules were made for the enforcing of agreements. The more well-to-do negotiators formed organizations which admitted new members only on the fulfilling of certain conditions. The opportunities afforded of making money made admittance to the organization highly profitable.

Modern trading, national and international, has elevated the Stock Exchange as an institution to an importance such as it never held before, and in the capitals of the larger countries transactions of enormous value are now put through each day. The Paris Bourse long held the position of importance in Europe, but later the Stock Exchange in London, located in the capital city of a great empire, which the facility of intercourse made possible by modern invention has made communicable despite the barrier of great distances, began to occupy the paramount position. Dealing almost entirely in home securities at first the London Stock Exchange began a little more than a century ago to operate in the shares and certificates of other countries. These dealings increased as it became a practice to seek loans in London, and in course of time private securities, such as those belonging to railways, began to be handled along with government stock. Towards the end of the nineteenth century industrial stocks made their appearance in the trading and methods for transferring the stock of mining and similar companies from the promoters to the public began to be developed along lines that did not always prove legitimate. In the New York Stock Exchange the principal part of the trading was from the beginning in railway stock, for the institution rose to importance in an era of great expansion in the railway systems of the country. In recent years following the practice in European countries industrial stocks have figured largely in the New York Stock Exchange, and their introduction signalized a tremendous development in the amount of business conducted. Foreign securities did not assume proportions of importance in the New York Stock Exchange till the opening of the recent great war. American industrial expansion was so great as to be quite enough to attract the attention of brokers, but the early years of the European War and the requirements of European countries could not but have its influence in the United States, and the dealings on the New York Stock Exchange reflected the importance of the transactions that were being made in the United States and other countries at the instance of the belligerent powers. On the other hand government bonds have never figured conspicuously in the dealings of the New York Stock Exchange, agreements relating to them being managed in the main outside of the exchange. This applies also to the foreign government loans that have been negotiated from time to time in the country before the war and during it. The exchanges of the various large cities in the United States have built up traditions of their own which have arisen from the distinctive requirements of their local business interests. Boston has had an important hand in the control of copper-mining companies. The Philadelphia Stock Exchange has all along held importance as the trading center for street-railway securities, and other exchanges throughout the country are regarded as the convenient market for certain well-defined securities in which the local capitalists for one reason or another have interested themselves and their communities.

The stock exchange, as the institution is viewed in the modern sense, may be said to have had its origin at the period of the creation of public debts in the seventeenth century under the system which has since continued to be employed. The incorporation of the East India Company in London is an early example of the raising of public money for corporate purposes through the medium of the Stock Exchanges. In the first quarter of the eighteenth century speculation in the South Sea Company in London habituated the public to investing in such enterprises. In that period in London trading was conducted through independent brokers who resorted to certain well-defined localities but who were not formed in a corporate union. Concentration of business caused the erection of the London Stock Exchange Building in 1801. The members of the New York Stock Exchange had to wait till 1865, before a building was erected to house them independently. The Civil War added greatly to the development of the New York Stock Exchange, and operations largely in that period centered round the competition of capitalists interested in the New York Central railroad and the Erie railroad. Since that time to the present the business on the exchange has been an accurate reflection of the business trend throughout the country. From 1869, the date of the completion of the two transcontinental railways, speculation in the shares of these railway companies grew. James Fisk, Jay Gould, Daniel Drew, Cornelius Vanderbilt and their associates began to attract national attention by the importance of their trading through representatives on the exchange. The crises, the booms, the panics, the tides of prosperity and their reactions have had their reverberations in the exchange which has served as a mirror indicating the steps in the business progress of the country. The great undertakings in the direction of railway building led to frequent issues of securities on the New York Stock Exchange, though the increase of business was not always uniform. The panic of 1893 and the panics that preceded and followed it led to curtailment of business in New York. The year 1898 was marked by a financial recovery that was reflected in a considerable development in the New York Stock Exchange. In that year the rich harvests of the United States coinciding with a period of great scarcity in Europe, the increase in exports and in manufacturing threw into relief the great volume of America's available wealth and fostered confidence in the potentiality of the country such as had never before been known. Capital began to pour into enterprises of all kinds and industrial shares began to multiply on the exchange. In 1901 the renewed confidence added greatly to the volume of speculation, and records of every kind in Stock Exchange history began to be surpassed. Purchase of stock companies by other companies which pledged their credit to raise funds began to be the rule. The movement ended in the Northern Pacific corner of 1901 when rival speculation forced its shares to the price of $1,000, the stock only a little previously having never exceeded the $100 figure. The unstable figures could not last and a tremendous collapse of prices followed. Recovery was speedy, however, and prices rose rapidly. The events leading up to the corner educated speculators to the possibilities which the rivalries of purchasing companies might bring about. In recent years the volume of business done on the New York Stock Exchange has greatly exceeded that of other exchanges.

The membership and methods of business in stock exchanges are now limited by strict rules. Minimum commissions in New York are one-eighth of one per cent on the face value of securities bought for outside customers. Only securities listed by the committee can be dealt in. The prices of seats have ranged from $9,000 to more than $100,000. Penalties for breaches of discipline involve expulsion or suspension for stated periods from the privileges of the Exchange. Fraud, fictitious sales, and acceptance of smaller commissions than those indicated in the rules, are among the offenses most guarded against. A plan of clearing Stock Exchange transactions on the system of a bank clearing house is a modern development in America, though used in Europe, and particularly in Germany, since the middle of the last century.

STOCKHOLM, the capital of the kingdom of Sweden; on several islands and the adjacent mainland, between a bay of the Baltic and Lake Mälar; in a situation that is accounted one of the most picturesque in Europe. The nucleus of Stockholm is an island in mid-channel called "The Town"; on it stand the imposing royal palace (1697-1754); the principal church (St. Nicholas), in which the kings are crowned; the House of the

Nobles (1648-1670), in which that class hold their periodical meetings; the town house; the ministries of the kingdom; and the principal wharf, a magnificent granite quay, fronting E. Immediately W. of the central island lies the Knights' Island (*Riddarholm*); it is almost entirely occupied with public buildings, as the Houses of Parliament; the old Franciscan Church, in which all the later sovereigns of Sweden have been buried; the royal archives and the chief law courts of the kingdom. To the N. of these two islands lie the handsomely built districts of Norrmalm, separated from them by a narrow channel, in which is an islet covered with the royal stables. The principal buildings and institutions in Norrmalm are the National Museum (1850-1865), with extremely valuable collections of prehistoric antiquities, coins, paintings, sculptures; the principal theaters; the Academy of the Fine Arts (1735); the barracks; the Hop Garden, with the Royal Library (1870-1876), and with the statue (1885) of Linnæus; the Academy of Sciences (1739), with natural history collections; the Museum of Northern Antiquities (1873); the Observatory; and technological, medical, sloyd, and other schools.

Ship Island (*Skeppsholm*), immediately E. of "The Town" island, is the headquarters of the Swedish navy, and is built over with marine workshops, shipbuilding yards, etc., and is connected with a smaller island on the S. E., that is crowned with a citadel. Beyond these again, and farther to the E., lies the beautiful island of the Zoölogical Gardens (*Djurgard*). Immediately S. of "The Town" island is the extensive district of Södermalm, the houses of which climb up the steep slopes that rise from the water's edge. Handsome bridges connect the central islands with the N. and S. districts; besides buses and tramways, the principal means of communication are quick little steamboats, some of which extend their journeys to the beautiful islands in Lake Mälar on the W., and E. toward the Baltic Sea (40 miles distant). Besides the institutions already mentioned, Stockholm is the home of the Swedish Academy (1786), Academies of Agriculture (1811), Music (1771), and Military Sciences (1771), a naval school, a school of navigation, of pharmacy, etc. There is considerable industry in the making of sugar, tobacco, silks and ribbons, candles, linen, cotton, and leather, and there are large iron foundries and machine shops. Stockholm does a large shipping business. Its exports consist chiefly of iron and steel, grain, tar, etc.

Though Stockholm was founded by Birger Jarl in 1255, it was not made the capital of Sweden until comparatively modern times. Since then, however, it has grown rapidly. Pop. (1890) 246,151; (1919) 408,456. The principal events in the history of the city have been the sieges of Queen Margaret of Denmark (1389), the battles in the vicinity against the Danes toward the end of the 15th century, the capture of the place by Christian II. of Denmark in 1520, and the Blood Bath he executed among the principal men of the country in what was then the Great Market.

STOCKPORT, a parliamentary and municipal borough of England, partly in Cheshire and partly in Lancashire, 5 miles S. E. of Manchester, on the Mersey. It occupies an elevated site, on which the houses rise in irregular tiers, giving it a picturesque appearance. Its chief structures are St. Mary's Church, Christ Church, the free grammar school, the Sunday-school, the free library, the museum situated in Vernon Park, and the immense railway viaduct which here crosses the Mersey. The cotton trade, connected with which are spinning, weaving, dyeing, etc., is the staple, and there are also foundries, machine shops, breweries, etc. Pop. (1919) 125,629.

STOCKS, an apparatus formerly used for the punishment of petty offenders, such as vagrants, trespassers, and the like. It consisted of a frame of timber, with holes, in which the ankles, and sometimes the ankles and wrists, of the offenders were confined. In farriery, etc., a frame in which refractory animals are held for shoeing or veterinary purposes. In shipbuilding, a frame of blocks and shores on which a vessel is built. In finance, a stock is a fund employed in the carrying on of some business or enterprise, and divided into shares held by individuals who collectively form a corporation. Also a fund in England consisting of a capital debt due by the government to individual holders, who receive a fixed rate of interest on their shares; money funded in government securities; as, the 3 per cent stocks.

STOCKTON, a city and county-seat of San Joaquin co., Calif.; at the head of Stockton Channel, an arm of San Joaquin river, and on the Southern Pacific, the Atchison, Topeka and Santa Fe, the Stockton Terminal and Eastern, the Tidewater Southern, and the Western Pacific railroads; 63 miles E. by N. of San Francisco. Here are the State Insane Asylum, a high school, the Hazleton Public Library, a private sanitarium, St.

Mary's College, opera house, Masonic Temple, hospitals, St. Agnes's Convent, waterworks, street railroad and electric light plants, National, State, and private banks, and daily, weekly, and monthly periodicals. Stockton is an important point for the shipment of wool and wheat. The business of the city includes the furnishing of supplies to the farmers of the San Joaquin valley. Stockton has iron foundries, tanneries, lumber and paper mills, flour mills, machine shops, a terra-cotta plant, car works, warehouses, agricultural implement works, etc. It was established in 1849, and named after Robert Field Stockton, of the United States Navy, who seized California for the Union. Pop. (1910) 23,-253; (1920) 40,296.

STOCKTON, a river-port of England, in the county of Durham, 11 miles E. N. E. of Darlington; on the left bank of the Tees; 4 miles above its mouth. Its Anglican churches include St. Thomas's (1712; restored 1859), with a tower 80 feet high, St. James's (1868), in French First Pointed style, with a spire of 130 feet, and St. John's (1872), a brick edifice of the basilica type; and of numerous non-established places of worship; the finest are the Roman Catholic St. Mary's (1842-1870), designed by the elder Pugin in Early English style, and the United Presbyterian St. Andrew's (1861). Other buildings are the town hall and assembly rooms (1735), the borough hall (1852), exchange (1874), postoffice (1878), free-masons' hall (1872), surgical hospital (1875), and a cattle market constructed (1876). Stockton is now an important railway center. Its harbor, also, improved by a cutting below the town (1808), carries on an extensive trade. A former residence of the Bishop of Durham, Stockton was taken by the Scotch in 1645, and seven years later its castle was demolished by Parliament. Pop. about 60,000.

STOCKTON, FRANCIS RICHARD, an American author; born in Philadelphia, Pa., April 5, 1834; became an engraver and draughtsman; was connected with the Philadelphia "Post," and with "Hearth and Home," New York; joined the editorial staff of "Scribner's Monthly," and became assistant editor of "St. Nicholas"; his earliest writings were odd tales for children, but he attained a high reputation as a writer of short stories, marked by quaintness of subject and treatment and by dry humor. The first of these were the "Rudder Grange Stories," followed by very many others, of which, perhaps, the best known are:

"The Lady or the Tiger?" "The Late Mrs. Null," "The Casting Away of Mrs. Lecks and Mrs. Aleshine," and its sequel, "The

F. R. STOCKTON

Dusantes," "The Hundredth Man," "A Tale of Negative Gravity," etc. He died in Washington, D. C., April 20, 1902.

STOCKTON, ROBERT FIELD, an American naval officer; born in Princeton, N. J., Aug. 20, 1795; entered the navy in 1810; was promoted lieutenant in 1814; engaged in the war with Tripoli in 1814-1815; went to Africa in 1821 in command of the "Erie," where he secured the territory forming the present republic of Liberia; was sent against the pirates and slavers in the West Indies in the fall of the same year; and served as flag-officer in the Mediterranean under Preble in 1838-1839. He was one of the earliest advocates of a steam navy; drew the plans for the steam sloop of war "Princeton," the explosion of one of whose guns at Washington in 1844 caused the death of the secretaries of war and the navy; was actively interested in the construction of the Delaware and Raritan canal; and during the Mexican War, as commander of the naval forces on the Pacific, took possession of California in the name of the United States. On his return in 1850 he resigned his commission; entered politics; and in 1851 was elected to the United States Senate, where he introduced and put through a bill for the abolition of flogging in the navy, and also urged the adoption of measures for coast defense. In 1853, however, he retired from the Senate, and devoted himself to the development of the Delaware and Raritan canal. He died in Princeton, N. J., Oct. 7, 1866.

STODDARD, CHARLES WARREN, an American author; born in Rochester, N. Y., Aug. 7, 1843; studied (without graduating) at the University of California; was for some time an actor; for seven years special traveling correspondent of the San Francisco "Chronicle," visiting nearly every quarter of the globe, including five years in the South Seas; from 1885 to 1887 Professor of English Literature at Notre Dame College, Indiana; and from 1889 at the Catholic University of America. Among his publications are: "South Sea Idylls" (1873); "Summer Cruising in the South Seas" (1874); "Mashallah" (1880); "The Lepers of Molokai" (1885); "Lazy Letters from Low Latitudes" (1894); "Over the Rocky Mountains to Alaska" (1899); "Hither and Yon"; "The Dream Lady"; etc. He died April 24, 1909.

STODDARD, ELIZABETH DREW (BARSTOW), an American novelist and poet; born in Mattapoisett, Mass., May 6, 1823. She was the wife of Richard H. Stoddard, and the author of three distinguished novels, "The Morgesons" (1862); "Two Men" (1865); "Temple House," illustrative of English character and scenery (1867); and "Lolly Dink's Doings," a story for young readers (1874); "Poems." She died Aug. 1, 1902.

STODDARD, RICHARD HENRY, an American poet; born in Hingham, Mass., July 2, 1825; attended schools in New York, and then worked in an iron foun-

RICHARD HENRY STODDARD

dry for some years, meanwhile reading widely, especially in poetry. In 1849 he produced a small volume of poems only to suppress it afterward; but 1852 saw the birth of a sturdier collection. From 1853 to 1870 he served in the New York custom house, in 1870-1873 was clerk to General McClellan and for a year city librarian; he did also much reviewing and writing for the publishers. His poems include "Songs in Summer" (1857); "The King's Bell" (1862); "The Book of the East" (1867); "Lion's Cub" (1891; "Under the Evening Lamp," etc.; he wrote also "Life of Humboldt"; "Abraham Lincoln"; "Life of Washington Irving." He died in New York, May 12, 1903.

STODDARD, WILLIAM OSBORN, an American author; born in Homer, N. Y., Sept. 24, 1835; was graduated at the University of Rochester in 1857, and after serving for a short time in the Civil War was made secretary to President Lincoln, which office he held till 1864 when he became United States marshal of Arkansas. Subsequently he engaged in business and journalism in New York City, where he also held several public offices under the municipal government. He was the author of numerous stories, sketches and poems, including "Life of Abraham Lincoln"; "Chuck Purdy"; "The Sword-Makers' Inn"; "Ulric the Jarl"; "The Boy Lincoln" (1905); "Two Cadets With Washington" (1906); "In the Open" (1908); "Dab Kinzer" (1909); "The Captain of the Cat's Paw" (1914), etc. Died Aug. 29, 1925.

STOESSEL, ANATOLY MIKHAILO-VITCH, a Russian soldier, born in St. Petersburg, in 1848. During the Russo-Japanese War, he was placed, in 1904, in command of the Russian garrison at Port Arthur, and in May of that year, he was defeated by General Oku at Nan-shan. After a siege lasting until Jan. 1, 1905, he surrendered Port Arthur to General Nogi. In 1906 he was tried by court-martial and condemned to death for surrendering the fortress. His sentence, however, was commuted to 10 years' imprisonment in 1908, and a year later he was pardoned and allowed to resign from the service. He died in 1915.

STOICS, the name applied to a body of philosophers who flourished first in Greece about the 4th century, but whose influence finally spread over the whole classical world. Their place in the history of philosophy is immediately after Plato and Aristotle. They divided philosophy into three parts—logic, physics, and ethics. "Logic supplies the method for attaining to true knowledge; physics teach the nature and order of the universe; and ethics draw thence the inferences for practical life."

The only means we have of knowing about a thing is by the impression it makes on us: but we have many impressions which are certainly false: how are we to discriminate between the false and true? The Stoics answered this by asserting that a true impression would come home to us by a sort of "striking evidence." The irresistible force of truth would influence our minds in a way that false impressions were utterly unable to do. Being true, they would force us to believe they were true. In their physics (which were really metaphysics) the stoics enunciated a theory of pantheism.

Material goods are of no importance to the individual, save in so far as they aid him in the pursuit of virtue. The ideal of virtue is painted in the stoic picture of the "Wise Man." Living absolutely in accord with the central principle of the universe, he possesses all knowledge and all aptitudes. He alone is the true statesman, king, educator, critic and physician. In social life none but he can be a true friend. Absolutely independent of earthly things, he leads a life undisturbed by their ceaseless mutations.

The founder of stoicism was Zeno (340-260 B. C.), who opened his school in the "many colored portico" (*Stoa poecile*); hence the name of the sect. After him came Cleanthes, surnamed the Ass from his stubborn patience. Then Chrysippus of Soli in Cilicia who died about 208 B. C. He wrote, it is said, 705 different works, and to him is due the regular exposition of stoicism as a system of philosophy. After him we have a new period. When Greece was brought under subjection to Rome, her systems of philosophy became known to her conquerors, and no system had more adherents than stoicism. Panætius and Posidonius, later rulers of the Porch, were friends of the younger Scipio, Cicero, and Pompey. It is essentially the philosophy of Cicero; its influence is felt in Tacitus, and many references in Horace, Juvenal, and Persius as to the external and internal characteristics of the school show its place in the Roman world.

Among its later adherents were Seneca the tutor and victim of Nero; the slave Epictetus and Marcus Aurelius, the Roman emperor. Its influence was felt in the composition of the Roman law. Specially stoical, though not stoical alone, was the conception of the Law of Nature, "which Nature teaches all animals." Though stoicism as a system fell to pieces with the ancient world, it essentially reappeared in the ascetic forms of Christianity and other religions. But the reason is, not that they were descended from stoicism, but that both came from a common source.

STOKE-POGES, a village of Buckinghamshire, England; 2 miles N. of Slough station. Gray's mother settled here in 1742; the beautiful churchyard is the scene of his "Elegy," and in that churchyard he is buried.

STOKE-UPON-TRENT, a manufacturing town of Staffordshire, England; capital of the "Potteries," on the Trent and the Trent and Mersey canal; 15 miles S. E. of Crewe. It is a modern place dating only from the last quarter of the 18th century, and has a parish church with Wedgwood's grave, a town hall (1835), a market hall (1883), a free library (1878), the Minton memorial building (1858), the Hartshill Infirmary (1868), public baths, and statues of Wedgwood, Minton and Colin Minton Campbell. Its factories of porcelain, earthenware, encaustic tiles, and tessellated pavements are among the largest in the world; and the industries also include coal mining, brickmaking, and the manufacture of iron, engines, machinery, etc. Mrs. Craik was a native. Pop. (1919) 239,316.

STOKES, ANSON PHELPS, an American banker and publicist, born in New York City, in 1838. He became a partner of the firm of Phelps, Dodge & Co., merchants, and later of Phelps, Stokes & Co., bankers. Both companies were successful and he acquired a large fortune. He took an active part in political and social matters in New York, and was the first president of the Reform Club. He was also for a time vice-president of the Civil Service Reform Association, and in 1900 was president of the National Association of Anti-Imperialists Clubs. He gave largely to charity and was prominent in the movement for tariff reform. He wrote "Cruising in the West Indies" (1902); "Cruising in the Caribbean with a Camera" (1903). He died in 1913.

STOKES, CHARLES FRANCIS, an American physician and naval officer, born in New York City, in 1863. He was educated at Adelphi Academy and Polytechnic Institute, Brooklyn, and at the College of Physicians and Surgeons, Columbia University. In 1889 he entered the navy as an assistant surgeon and after being promoted surgeon, medical inspector, and medical director, he became surgeon-general, U. S. N., and chief of the Bureau of Medicine and Surgery with the rank of rear-admiral in 1910. He was retired in 1917.

STOKHOD, a small river in eastern Galicia, along whose banks desperate fighting took place during the World

War, between Austrian and German troops and the Russians. It was in this region, during July, 1916, when the Russian armies were driving the Teutons before them, that the Germans made a determined stand. Victorious along all other parts of the Eastern front, the Russians made futile attacks with very strong forces at several points against the German line along the Stokhod river, notably near Czereviscze, Janmaka and on both sides of the railway running from Kovel to Rovno. Here, during the middle of July, 1916, the Germans received strong re-enforcements and powerful artillery. It was the German resistance here which saved the whole front of the Central Empires from a crushing defeat.

STOLA, a loose garment worn by Roman matrons over the tunic. To the bottom of it a border or flounce was sewed, the whole reaching down so low as to conceal the ankles and part of the feet. It was the characteristic dress of the Roman matrons, as the toga was of the men; divorced women or courtesans were not allowed to wear it. It was usually gathered and confined at the waist by a girdle, and frequently ornamented at the throat by a colored border. It has either short or long sleeves, and was fastened over the shoulder by a fibula.

STOLE, a long, loose garment extending to the feet; also the sucker or shoot of a plant. In the Roman Catholic Church, a narrow band of silk or stuff, sometimes enriched with embroidery and jewels, worn on the left shoulder of deacons, and across both shoulders of bishops and priests, pendent on each side nearly to the ground;—used in the administration of the sacraments and all other sacred functions.

STOLP, a town in the Prussian province of Pomerania; on the river Stolp, 85 miles W. by N. of Danzig; has a castle, some old churches (the castle chapel dating from the 13th century), iron foundries, machinery, and amber manufactures, and an active trade in agricultural products, timber, fish, etc. Pop. about 35,000.

STOMACH, in comparative anatomy, a membranous sac, formed by a dilatation of the alimentary canal, in which food is received and subjected to the processes of digestion among the Vertebrata. The human stomach is an elongated, curved pouch, from 10 to 12 inches long, and 4 or 5 inches in diameter at its widest part, lying almost immediately below the diaphragm, nearly transversely across the upper and left portion of the abdominal cavity, and having the form of a bagpipe. It is very dilatable and contractile, and its average capacity is about 5 pints. The left and larger extremity is called the cardiac, great, or splenic extremity; the right and smaller, is known as the pyloric, from its proximity to the pylorus. The food enters the stomach through the œsophagus by the cardia or cardiac orifice, and after having been acted on by the gastric juice, is passed on in a semi-fluid or pulpy state through the pylorus into the small intestines. The stomach has 4 coats, named from without inward: (1) the serous, (2) the muscular, (3) the areola or sub-mucous, and (4) the mucous coat. The last is a smooth, soft, rather thick and pulpy membrane, generally reddish in color from the blood in its capillary vessels; often ash-gray in old age. After death it becomes a dirty brown, and in acute inflammation, or from the action of strong acrid poisons, it becomes of a bright red, either continuously or in patches. Corrosive poisons also affect its coloration. The surface of the mucous membrane is beset with secreting glands. The stomach is supplied with blood from the cœliac artery, which gives off arterial branches that ramify freely, and the veins return the residual blood into the splenic and superior mesenteric veins, and directly into the portal vein. The lymphatics of the stomach are very numerous, and arise in the mucous membrane. The nerves are large, and consist of the terminal branches of the two pneumogastric nerves belonging to the cerebro-spinal system, and of offsets from the sympathetic system derived from the solar plexus. Their ending has not been traced.

Medical electricians have devised a plan by which the interior of the human stomach may be illuminated for examination. The interior of the stomach is plainly lighted and all its parts are brought into view by a small movable mirror at the end of the tube. In the lower mammals three forms of stomach have been distinguished: (1) Simple, consisting of a single cavity, as in man; (2) Complex, in which there are two or more compartments communicating with each other, as in the kangaroo, the porcupine, and the squirrel; (3) Compound, in which the stomach is separated into a reservoir and a digestive portion. (See RUMINATION.) The family *Camelidæ* have a stomach divided into two compartments by a muscular band—one of the points of difference between them and the other ruminants. The lining of the second stomach, or honeycomb bag, and of a portion of the first stomach, or paunch, is provided with a great number

I—8

of cells in which water is stored up and long retained for use in time of drought and of long journeys over the desert. (See CAMEL.)

In birds there are three small, but distinct dilatations of the alimentary canal, called the crop, gizzard, and proventriculus, and in most reptiles the simplicity of the œsophagus extends to the stomach. In fishes, two forms are found, the siphonal stomach and the cæcal, in which the upper portion gives off a long blind sac. In the higher invertebrata there is a digestive tract with functions analogous to those of the stomach of Vertebrates; in the lower there may (Hydra) or may not (Amœba) be a gastric cavity in which food is ingested and absorbed. In the latter case the living protoplasm closes over its prey, and after a time by a reversing process, the indigestible remains are ejected. To those tracts or cavities, the name stomach is often applied. See DIGESTION.

STOMACH PUMP, in surgery, a suction and force pump for withdrawing the contents of the stomach in cases of poisoning, etc., and also used as an injector. It resembles the ordinary syringe, except that it has two apertures near the end, in which the valve opens different ways, so as to constitute a sucking and forcing passage.

STOMAPODA, an order of crustaceans, having six to eight pairs of legs, mostly near the mouth (hence the name). They are found chiefly in intertropical climates, and are almost without exception marine. The order includes the locust shrimps (*Squilla*), the glass shrimps (*Erichthys*), and the opossum shrimps (*Mysis*).

STONE, the material obtained from rocks; the kind of substance they produce. Also a gem; a precious stone. Something made of stone; as a monument erected to preserve the memory of the dead; a gravestone. Something which resembles a stone; as (a) a calcareous concretion in the kidneys or bladder; hence, the disease arising from a calculus (see CALCULUS); (b) the nut of a drupe or stone fruit; the hard covering inclosing the kernel, and itself inclosed by the pericarp; the hard and bony endocarp of a drupaceous fruit. The word is also applied to a measure of weight in use throughout the northwest and central countries of Europe, but varying much in different places. The English imperial standard stone is a weight of 14 pounds avoirdupois, but there are stones of other weights for particular commodities; thus the stone

of butcher's meat or fish is 8 pounds, of cheese 16 pounds, of hemp 32 pounds, of glass 5 pounds, etc.

Stone is not used as a technical term in either petrology or geology, though it enters into the composition of words in those sciences, as Portland stone.

STONE, ARTIFICIAL. Most varieties of artificial stone (using the term in a restricted sense, excluding brick and terra-cotta) have a base of hydraulic mortar, with which sand and pulverized stone of different kinds are mixed. Mr. Ransome of Ipswich, England, introduced a kind of artificial stone in which siliceous instead of calcareous matter was employed as the cementing material. The process at present followed in the manufacture of this artificial stone consists in carefully mixing well-dried sand and dust of chalk with silicate of soda, obtained by digesting flints under pressure in a boiling solution of caustic soda. After molding, the blocks are exposed to the action *in vacuo* of chloride of calcium in a solution, where, by chemical reaction, the block is transformed into a silicate of lime, a body of unusual strength and durability. The other compound formed is chloride of sodium, or common salt, and is removed with water. The artificial stone of Sorel, a French chemist, is made by mixing a cement formed of the basic oxychloride of magnesium with sand, chalk, or powdered marble. The cement, which may be molded of itself into a hard stone, is procured by acting on protoxide of magnesium (calcined and ground carbonate of magnesia or magnesite) with a concentrated solution of chloride of magnesium.

STONE, ELLEN M., an American missionary; born in Roxbury, Mass., July 24, 1846; received a public school education; settled in Chelsea, Mass., in 1860; became a teacher; and for 11 years was on the staff of the "Congregationalist." She went to Bulgaria as a missionary in 1878. About Sept. 1, 1901, with a companion, Mme. Tsilka, a native Bulgarian teacher, she was kidnaped by brigands who a few days later demanded an indemnity of $110,000, the money to be paid within 30 days. On Sept. 5, the news of Miss Stone's detention reached the United States, and her friends immediately notified the State Department at Washington and began a popular subscription to raise the required amount. The United States Government communicated with the Bulgarian and Turkish authorities, who ordered troops to search for the retreat of the brigands for the purpose of releasing the captives. On

Feb. 6, $72,500 of the ransom demanded was paid, and on Feb. 23 Miss Stone was released. She related her experiences in a book. Died Dec. 14, 1927.

STONE, FRED ANDREW, an American actor, born in Longmont, Colo., 1873. He first appeared on the stage at the age of 11 at Topeka, Kan., began traveling with the Sells-Renfrew Circus in 1886, played "Topsy" in "Uncle Tom's Cabin," and in 1894 formed a partnership with the late David Montgomery, with whom he appeared for many years with great success. Among the plays in which he was most successful were: "Wizard of Oz," "The Red Mill," "The Old Town," and "Tip Top."

STONE, HARLAN FISKE. American lawyer; born at Chesterfield, N. H., in 1872. After graduation at Amherst College in 1894, he went through the Columbia University Law School. In that school he served as lecturer and professor from 1899 to 1905, when he withdrew to practice law in New York. Recalled to the Law School in 1910, he directed it as its dean until 1924. President Coolidge, in April, 1924, appointed him Attorney-General of the United States. As Attorney-General he brought suits against a number of alleged monopolistic combinations notably the group of companies controlling radio patents and the oil-refining interests holding patents for the obtaining of gasoline by the cracking process. He was nominated an Associate Justice of the United States Supreme Court by President Coolidge, Jan. 5, 1925, to succeed Associate Justice Joseph McKenna.

STONE, JOHN STONE, an American electrical engineer, born at Dover, Va., in 1869. He was educated at the School of Mines, Columbia University, and at Johns Hopkins University. From 1890 to 1899 he was an experimentalist with the American Bell Telephone Company, and from 1902 to 1910 successively director, vice-president, chief engineer, and president of the Stone Telegraph and Telephone Company. He was granted over 120 patents on inventions in connection with improvements in telephoning and telegraphy.

STONE, LUCY (BLACKWELL), an American reformer; born in West Brookfield, Mass., Aug. 13, 1818. She was graduated at Oberlin College in 1847. In 1855 she married Dr. Henry B. Blackwell, retaining her own name. She published a protest, "Taxation Without Representation." In 1869 she helped organize the American Woman's Suffrage Association; became connected with the "Woman's Journal" in 1872, and was editor after 1888. Her lectures on woman suffrage made her known throughout the country. She died in Boston, Mass., Oct. 18, 1893.

STONE, MELVILLE ELIJAH, an American journalist; born in Hudson, Ill., Aug. 22, 1848; settled in Chicago, Ill., and was there educated; began his newspaper career in 1864 when he reported for the Chicago "Tribune"; later with a partner he founded the Chicago "Daily News," of which he afterward became sole owner. In 1881 with Victor F. Lawson he founded the Chicago "Morning News" which subsequently became the Chicago "Record." He was made general manager of the Associated Press in 1898. He published a series of reminiscent articles in 1920.

STONE, WILLIAM LEETE, an American author; born in New Paltz, N. Y., April 20, 1792; became a printer in the office of the Cooperstown "Federalist" at the age of 17, and in 1813 began to edit the Herkimer "American." Subsequently he edited the "Hudson Whig," "The Lounger," Albany "Daily Advertiser," Hartford "Mirror," "The Knights of the Round Table" and the New York "Advertiser." His works include: "History of the Great Albany Convention of 1821"; "Tales and Sketches"; "Essays on Social and Literary Topics"; "Life of Joseph Brant"; "Life of Red Jacket— Sa-go-ye-wat-he"; etc. He died in Saratoga Springs, N. Y., Aug. 15, 1844.

STONE, WILLIAM LEETE, an American historian, son of the preceding; born in New York City, April 4, 1835; was graduated at Brown University in 1858 and admitted to the bar in 1859. He was Centennial historian for the State of New York; wrote "The Life and Times of Sir William Johnson, Bart.;" "Revolutionary Letters;" "History of New York City;" "Ballads of the Burgoyne Campaign;" "The Life of George Clinton," etc. He died June 11, 1908.

STONE AGE, or AGE OF STONE, is a term used in archæology to denote the condition of a people using stone as the material for the cutting tools and weapons which, in a higher condition of culture, were made of metals. The expression "age," when used thus, denotes the stage, ancient or recent of stone culture. The duration of such a condition must necessarily have varied from various causes in different areas, and chiefly in consequence of contact with higher degrees of culture. Populations placed in remote situations, and on that account remaining uninfluenced by such contact—like the islanders of the South Pacific and the Eskimos of the extreme North for instance—have remained in their stone age to the 20th century. On the other hand, the populations of the European area, in portions of which there were successive centers of high culture and civilization from a very early period, had all emerged from their stone age, through the use of bronze, many centuries before the Christian era.

The progress of early culture in Europe seems to have been from the South and East, N. and W., so that the emergence of the different populations from their age of stone was accomplished

shores of the Mediterranean, they were contemporary with animals which are now either wholly or locally extinct, such as the mammoth, wooly rhinoceros, cave lion, cave bear, and hyæna, the reindeer, musk ox, and urus. It is an open question to what extent this change of fauna implies a change of climate, but from the geological conditions in which the flint implements of the earliest types are found it is evident that, though extensive changes must have taken place since they were deposited in the river basins,

PALÆOLITHIC

NEOLITHIC

IMPLEMENTS OF THE STONE AGE

much earlier in Southern and Eastern Europe than in the North and West. But while the stone age of different areas is thus not necessarily synchronous, it seems to be true of all European areas that this is the earliest condition in which man has appeared upon them.

There are no data by which the period of the early stone-using populations of Europe can be defined, even approximately. But in England, Belgium, and France, and across the Continent to the

they belong exclusively to the later deposits of the Quaternary period.

The stone age implements of Europe have been divided into two classes—the palæolithic or older stone implements and the neolithic or newer stone implements. This is equivalent to dividing the stone age of Europe into two periods, earlier and later, as the palæolithic implements are found associated with the extinct and locally extinct fauna, while the neolithic implements are found as-

See Steel, p. 67

OPEN-HEARTH FURNACES IN A PITTSBURGH STEEL MILL

© Keystone View Company

See Stromboli, p. 123

AN ERUPTION OF STROMBOLI VOLCANO

sociated with the existing fauna. The palæolithic stone implements are distinguished as a class from the neolithic by their greater rudeness of form, and by the facts that they are exclusively of flint and have been manufactured by chipping only. The neolithic stone implements on the other hand are of finer forms, often highly polished, and made of many varieties of stone besides flint.

The palæolithic implements of flint are mostly so rude that it is impossible to apply to them names indicative of specific use. Those from the river gravels are chiefly flakes, trimmed and untrimmed, for cutting and scraping; pointed implements, some almond-shaped or tongue-shaped; and more obtusely pointed implements, with rounded and often undressed butts. There is also a series of scraper-like implements, and another of oval sharp-rimmed implements, which are more carefully finished than most of the other varieties. The flint implements from the caves present a greater variety of form. They are generally characterized by secondary working, and are therefore much more carefully finished, often in many respects approaching closely to neolithic types.

From the caves also come a series of implements of bone and of carvings on bone which have excited much astonishment on account of the extraordinary contrast between their artistic character and the extreme rudeness of many of the implements of stone with which they are associated. These bone implements consist of well-made needles, borers, javelin or harpoon points barbed on one or both sides, and implements of reindeer horn of unknown use, which are usually carved in relief or ornamented with incised representations of animals, and occasionally of human figures. The animals, as for instance a group of reindeer from the cave of La Madelaine, Dordogne, are drawn with wonderful faithfulness, freedom, and spirit.

The neolithic stone implements consist of axes and axe hammers, knives, daggers, spear and arrow heads, saws, chisels, borers, and scrapers. The axes and axe hammers are made of many varieties of stone besides flint. Some of the finer polished axes are of jade and fibrolite. Most of the other implements were made only of flint and generally finished by chipping, without being ground or polished. Some of the long Danish knives and daggers are marvels of dexterous workmanship, on account of the thinness of the blade and the straightness and keenness of the edge.

The burial customs of the stone age included both inhumation and cremation, the former being, however, the earlier method. No burials of the river drift period have yet been discovered. The cave dwellers of the stone age buried their dead in cavities of the rocks. From a comparison of the remains from such cave cemeteries in different localities it has been concluded that even at this early period Europe was already occupied by more than one race of men. The populations of the neolithic time deposited their dead, with or without previous cremation, in or on the floors of the chambers of dolmens, or great-chambered cairns. The sepulchral pottery accompanying these burials, in Britain at least, is generally of a hard-baked dark-colored paste, and the ornamentation entirely composed of straight lines placed at various angles to each other. The implements found with these interments are mostly of the commoner kind, such as flint knives, scrapers, or strikelights (used with a nodule of pyrites of iron), arrowheads, and more rarely axes and axe hammers of flint or polished stone. The neolithic inhabitants of North and Central Europe were not merely nomadic tribes subsisting on the products of the chase; they practiced agriculture, and possessed the common domestic animals we now possess. The presence in the refuse heaps of their sea coast settlements of the remains of deep-sea fishes shows that they must have possessed boats and fishing lines, as was also the case with the stone age inhabitants of the lake dwellings. The estimates that have been made of the antiquity of the stone age in Europe are necessarily various, but it has been considered that the close of the neolithic period or the time when the use of stone began to be superseded by that of bronze in North Europe cannot have been much later than from 1000 to 1500 B. C. See LAKE DWELLING: STONEHENGE. ARCHÆOLOGY.

STONE FLY, the *Perla*, a genus of insects typical of the order *Plecoptera*. The hind wings are broader than the

STONE FLY

fore wings, and folded at the inner edge. The body is elongated, narrow, and flattened; the wings fold close to the body, which generally bears two terminal bristles. The larvæ are aquatic and much resemble the perfect insect, except in the absence of wings. A number of species—*e. g., P. bicaudata*—are common in Great Britain, and are well known to anglers as an attractive lure for fishes.

STONEHAM, a town in Middlesex co., Mass.; on the Boston and Maine railroad; 12 miles N. by W. of Boston. It contains a high school, a National bank, State armory, sanitarium, parks, public library, and several weekly newspapers. It is celebrated for its shoe and leather industries. It also has a box factory, machine shop, etc. Pop. (1910) 7,090; (1920) 7,873.

STONEHENGE, a very remarkable structure composed of large artificially raised monoliths, situated on Salisbury Plain, in Wiltshire, England. The ancient Britons called it Main Ambers, or "sacred stones." The spot is surrounded by a ditch 50 feet wide; the outer circle consisted of 60 stones, 30 perpendicular, 20 feet high and nearly 4 feet apart. On the tops of these were 30 imposts, regularly united; within this was a second circle of 40 stones, smaller and void of imposts. There are indications of two ovals of stones intervening. Within the second circle was a cell, or adytum, in which was the altar, a huge slab of blue marble. The whole structure consisted of 140 stones. There are three entrances from the plain. The whole is surrounded by a bank of earth 15 feet high and 1,010 feet in circumference. Out of the stones composing the outer circle, 17 remain; in the inner circle 8 are entire, and fragments of 12 others are on the spot. The average elevation of the stones is 14 feet, the breadth 7 feet, and the thickness 3 feet. The inner oval consisted of about 20 smaller stones, of which 11 are standing. Scattered over the plain are about 300 tumuli, or barrows. These, when opened, have been found to contain charred human bones. Accompanying weapons and implements show that they have been utilized both by Britons and Romans for interment.

In 1901, one of the great monoliths fell and was set up again. Excavations then made at the base brought to light the stone implements originally used in cutting the monoliths. This seems to place the erection of Stonehenge before the bronze age, and the inference is that the structure is about 3,400 years old. The edifice was sold at auction in 1915 for $15,000.

STONEMAN, GEORGE, an American military officer; born in Busti, N. Y., Aug. 8, 1822; was graduated at the United States Military Academy in 1846; in Texas in 1861, while in command of Fort Brown he refused to surrender the government property to the Confederates. He was, however, compelled to evacuate the fort. In August, 1861, he became brigadier-general of volunteers and chief of cavalry in the Army of the Potomac. He commanded the cavalry in the Peninsular campaign of 1862, and distinguished himself at Williamsburg; was promoted major-general of volunteers in the following November. He participated in the raid toward Richmond in April-May, 1863, and in the Atlanta campaign in May-July, 1864. He was taken prisoner in Clinton, Ga., in July of that year and held till October. Afterward he served in southwestern Virginia, Tennessee, and North Carolina. He was promoted colonel of the 21st Infantry in July, 1866, and was brevetted brigadier-general and major-general U. S. A. In August, 1871, he resigned from the army and settled in California, of which State he was Democratic governor in 1883-1887. He died Sept. 5, 1894.

STONE MOUNTAIN, a steep, dome-like elevation near Atlanta, Georgia, composed of a mass of granite. It is the site of a colossal memorial cut in the native rock in sculptural relief, to the leaders of the Confederacy, partly completed in 1928 by Augustus Lukeman. The chief figure, an equestrian representation of Robert E. Lee, was unveiled April 8, 1928.

STONES, PRECIOUS, numerous mineral substances, and one of two products of organic origin, used in jewelry and for other ornamental purposes on account of their rarity and beauty. The list of stones which may be regarded as precious cannot be definitely limited, as certain substances appear and disappear with the fluctuations of fashion. There are a few, however, which from all times have occupied a foremost place and have been universally prized as precious stones. In such a rank and position may be placed the diamond, the ruby, the sapphire, the Oriental amethyst, and the emerald, as well as, in a lesser degree, the tourmaline, the aquamarine or pale emerald, the chrysoberyl or cat's eye, the zircon or jargoon, the opal, and the varieties of quartz, such as rock-crystal, agate, amethyst, cairngorm or Scotch topaz, chalcedony, jasper, onyx, sardonyx, etc. Among other beautiful and valuable stones much appreciated for ornamental purposes, but scarcely to be classed as precious stones, there may be included lapis lazuli, crocidolite, labradorite, moonstone, avanturine, and malachite. To the list of precious stones there should be added two substances of animal origin—pearls and red coral—and perhaps also amber, a comparatively rare and valuable fossil resin.

When luster and sparkle are the principal qualities to be revealed, as in the case of the diamond, the surface is most favorably cut into numerous plane facets as either brilliant or rose cut stones. When color is the more important quality of the stone it may, if plane surfaces are wanted, be step or table cut. Such stones also, and translucent and opaque stones, may be cut *en cabochon*—*i. e.*, with curved or rounded surfaces.

One of the most important qualities of a precious stone is its hardness, as on that property depends its power of resisting wear and of keeping the brilliance of its polished surface. It is a property of great constancy, moreover, and in many cases affords a ready means of determining the nature of a stone under examination. Of all known substances diamond is the hardest, and representing it, according to Mohs's scale, by 10, the following is the relative hardness of several of the more important of the precious stones: diamond, 10.0; sapphire, 9.0; ruby, 8.8; chrysoberyl, 8.5; spinel, 8.0; topaz, 8.0; acquamarine, 8.0; emerald, 7.8; zircon, 7.8; tourmaline, 7.5; amethyst, 7.0; moonstone, 6.3; turquoise, 6.0; opal, 6.0. The value of the precious stones produced in the United States in 1919 was $123,046. The largest in value was corundum, $40,304, followed by turquoise, $30,537; quartz, $19,078, and tourmaline, $18,642. See DIAMOND; GEM.

Artificial Precious Stones.—Numerous attempts have been made by eminent investigators to produce artificial precious stones by means of intense heat and pressure and by electrical action; but hitherto these efforts have failed of practical success. In an important memoir published by Sainte Claire Deville and Caron in 1858, they describe various processes by which they obtained small crystals of corundum, ruby, sapphire, etc. By the action of the vapors of fluoride of aluminum and boracic acid on one another, they obtained crystals which, in hardness and in optical properties, resembled natural corundum. When a little fluoride of chromium was added a similar process yielded violet-red rubies; with rather more fluoride of chromium blue sapphires were yielded; and with still more green corundum was obtained. A mixture of equal equivalents of the fluorides of aluminum and glucinum, when similarly acted on by boracic acid, yielded minute crystals of chrysoberyl. The action of fluoride of silicon on zirconia yields small crystals of zircon, and by the action of silica on a mixture of the fluorides of aluminum and glucinum hexagonal plates of extreme hardness were obtained, which in some respects resembled emerald.

In subsequent researches Becquerel, by the use of electric currents of high tension succeeded in obtaining opals, etc., from solutions of silicates. Among the most successful of experimenters in this direction was Ch. Feil, of Paris, who successfully crystallized alumina, and by the introduction of coloring matter produced sapphires and rubies identical in hardness and composition, but not in brilliance, with the natural stones. M. Feil also succeeded in preparing true crystals of spinel, and a blue lime spinel of great hardness, but which were glassy rather than crystalline in structure.

Imitations of precious stones consist of a soft, heavy flint-glass called strass, or paste, appropriately colored, and they may readily be distinguished, among other peculiarities, by their great softness. Fraudulent combinations are made by cementing thin plates of precious materials over, and sometimes under, a body of valueless glass.

STONEWALL JACKSON, a name given to Gen. T. J. Jackson during the Civil War. See JACKSON, THOMAS J.

STONEWARE, a very hard kind of pottery, with which are made jars, drain pipes, and a variety of chemical utensils. It is constituted of plastic clay, united in various proportions with some felspathic mineral sands of different kinds, and in some cases with cement, stone, or chalk. These mixtures are then subjected to a heat sufficiently great to cause a partial fusion of the mass. This condition of semi-fusion is the distinguishing character of stoneware. The finer varieties of stoneware are made from carefully selected clays, which when burnt will not have much color. These are united with some fluxing substance, by which the particular state of semi-fusion above mentioned, is brought about. Formerly the glaze of stoneware was always a salt glaze; recently, however, it has been customary to glaze with a mixture of Cornish stone, flint, etc., as in the manufacture of earthenware. See POTTERY.

STONINGTON, a town in New London co., Conn.; on the Long Island Sound, and on the New York, New Haven, and Hartford railroad; 43 miles S. W of Providence, R. I. It comprises the borough of Stonington and the villages of

Pawcatuck, Mystic, and Old Mystic. There is an excellent harbor, and regular steamboat connection with New York and Boston. Here are a public library, an English and Classical Institute, high schools, a National bank, and a semi-weekly newspaper. The town has important manufactories, including silk, cotton, and woolen goods, printing presses, spools, boilers, iron and brass goods, etc. In August, 1814, the inhabitants successfully defended the town against a British attack. Pop. (1910) 9,154; (1920) 10,236.

STONY POINT, a small rocky promontory on the W. bank of the Hudson river, opposite Verplanck's Point, 42 miles N. of New York City, at the entrance to the Highlands. A fortification of some importance in the Revolutionary War, it was captured and strengthened by the British, but was recovered in a night attack by Wayne. It is connected by a marsh with the shore, and supports a lighthouse and fog-bell tower. In the village here is the house where Benedict Arnold held his treasonable interviews.

STORAGE BATTERY, a battery which when charged can be used for some time as a source of electric current. Gautherot, in 1801, first conceived the idea of such a battery. Faraday, in his "Researches," mentions its practicality. However, it was left to Gaston Planté, in 1860, to construct a practical storage battery.

Storage batteries are of two types—those using lead plates in an acid medium and those using iron-nickel plates in an alkaline medium. The former are subdivided into the Planté cells and the Faure, or "pasted" cells. The reaction which occurs in both the Planté and Faure cells is indicated by the following equation:

$$PbO_2 + 2H_2SO_4 + Pb =$$
Lead Oxide Sulphuric Lead
Acid

$$PbSO_4 + 2H_2O + PbSO_4$$
Lead Water Lead
Sulphate Sulphate

When the battery is being charged the reaction takes place from right to left; that is to say, the lead sulphate on the plates is decomposed, producing lead peroxide on one plate and spongy lead on the other, while sulphuric acid is added to the electrolyte, its specific gravity being thereby increased. When the battery is being discharged, the reaction is reversed and takes place from left to right. In other words, sulphuric acid is taken from the electrolyte to form lead sulphate on both plates, so that the specific gravity falls. In the Planté cell, the active material on the

plates is formed by passage of an electric current through the cell. In order to speed up this process, the lead plates are covered with grooves, so as to present as much surface to the acid as possible. At best, however, this is a slow process, and in order to bring about the same result in less time, the Faure or "pasted" cells were invented. In these, a paste of lead oxide is spread on to a supporting grid of lead. On charging, the material on the positive plate is converted to lead peroxide, while on the negative plate it is reduced to spongy lead.

The Edison battery uses plates of iron and nickel in a bath of caustic potash. The plates consist of shallow perforated tubes of nickel-plated steel, fixed in a sheet-steel grid. In the positive plate, the tubes are filled with alternate layers of nickel hydroxide and flaked metallic nickel. The negative plate contains powdered iron oxide. The reactions which take place are represented by: $2NiO_2 + Fe = Ni_2O_3 + FeO$. During discharge, the reaction proceeds from left to right; that is, oxygen is transferred from the nickel oxide to the iron. On charging, the action is reversed, the higher nickel oxide being produced, while the iron oxide is reduced to iron. In other words, charge and discharge result in a transfer of oxygen from one plate to another, so that no change in the specific gravity of the electrolyte occurs. The chief advantages of the battery are its lightness and the fact that it can remain charged or discharged for any length of time without injury. Its disadvantages are its high cost and its comparatively low efficiency.

The best advice to give as to the treatment of a storage battery is to follow the manufacturers' instructions. Although all makes of storage battery are built on the principles outlined above, each one has its own special features, and no one is so familiar with its peculiar requirements as the manufacturers. The following instructions apply, however, to all makes.

Cells should never be over discharged, because, in the lead cell, when the terminal voltage drops below 1.8 there is a tendency for the plates to buckle and for an insoluble sulphate to be produced. This process is known as "sulphation." For similar reasons, the cell should not be allowed to stand discharged for any length of time. If a battery is not in use for several weeks, it should be charged at least once a month, and, better, once every two weeks. As the electrolyte evaporates, the cell should be re-filled with pure, distilled water. The electrolyte should never be permitted to sink below the level of the top of the plate. The acid does not evaporate and should not need renewing. But if some is accidentally spilled, it should be replaced with chemically pure sulphuric acid of the specific gravity recommended by the makers of the cell. In the case of the Edison cell, a 21 per cent. solution of caustic potash is used instead of sulphuric acid.

STORER, BELLAMY, an American lawyer and diplomatist, born in Cincinnati, Ohio, in 1847. He graduated from Harvard in 1867, and began the practice of law in Cincinnati. He was elected to Congress in 1891, serving until 1895. From 1897 to 1899 he was Minister to Belgium, and from the latter year until 1902 filled the same office in Spain. He was appointed Ambassador to Austria-Hungary in 1902. His alleged activities toward the elevation of Archbishop Ireland to be Cardinal led to his dismissal from his post in 1906. Died Nov. 13, 1922.

STOREY, MOORFIELD, an American lawyer and publicist, born at Roxbury, Mass., in 1845. He graduated from Harvard in 1866, and after studying at the Harvard Law School, was admitted to the bar in 1869. He had previously served as private secretary to Charles Sumner. He took an active part in politics and was prominent in the "Mugwump" movement of 1884. He was a candidate for Congress in 1900, but was defeated. He was president of the Anti-Imperialist League, and of the National Association for the Advancement of the Colored People. He was a member and official in many societies, and was a fellow of the American Academy of Arts and Sciences. He wrote "Life of Charles Sumner" (1900); "Ebenezer Rockwood Hoar" (1911); "The Democratic Party and Philippine Independence" (1915). He also contributed many articles to magazines.

STORK, in ornithology, any individual of the genus *Ciconia*, or of the sub-family *Ciconiinæ*. In form the storks resemble the herons, but are more robust, and have larger bills, shorter toes, with a non-serrated claw on the middle toe. They inhabit the vicinity of marshes and rivers, where they find an abundant supply of food, consisting of frogs, lizards, fishes, and even young birds. Storks are migratory, arriving from the S. at their breeding haunts in the early spring, and departing again in the autumn. The white or house stork, *C. alba*, which is common in many countries of Central Europe, constructs a large nest, most frequently on the chimney of a cottage. The plumage is dirty white, the quills and the longest feathers on the wing

covers black; beak and feet red. The male is about 42 inches long, the female somewhat less. The black stork, *C. nigra*, from the center and E. of Europe, Asia, and Africa, has the upper surface black, the lower parts white. Storks are pro-

INDIAN WOOD STORK

tected by laws in some countries for their services in destroying small mammals and reptiles, and in consuming offal. The wood-ibis, a sub-genus, is found in waters of our Southern States. Heralds have adopted the stork as an emblem of piety and gratitude.

SHOE-BILLED STORK

STORM, a violent commotion or disturbance of the atmosphere, producing or attended by wind, rain, snow, hail, or thunder and lightning; a tempest; often applied to a heavy fall of rain, snow, etc., without a high wind. There is, perhaps, no question in science in which there was long so large an admixture of speculation with fact as in the attempts made to reduce the phenomena of storms under general laws; the reason being that meteorological observatories were too few in number and too wide apart to represent the barometer pressure, the general course of the winds, and the rainfall, without drawing largely on conjecture.

The extent over which storms spread is very variable, being seldom less than 600 miles in diameter, but often two or three times greater, and more rarely even five times that amount. More than the whole of Europe is sometimes overspread by a single storm at one time. The prime difference between storms or cyclones and tornados is that the breadth of the space traversed by the latter is, as compared with that of storms, always quite insignificant. The area of storms is not constant from day to day, but varies in size, sometimes expanding and sometimes contracting; and it is worthy of remark that when a storm contracts in area the central depression gives signs of filling up, and the storm of dying out. On the other hand, when it increases in extent the central depression becomes deeper, the storm increases in violence, and occasionally is broken up into two or even more depressions, which become separate storms, with the wind circling round each. This occurs frequently with summer thunderstorms.

Direction in Which Storms Advance. The direction in which their progressive motion takes place differs in different parts of the world—being perhaps determined by the prevailing winds. Thus, about half the storms of middle and northern Europe travel from the S. W. toward the N. E., and about 19 out of every 20 travel toward some point in the quadrant lying between the N. E. and the S. E. Storms rarely travel toward a W. point; in some of the instances which have been noted the W. course has been arrested at Norway, Denmark, the North Sea, or the British Islands, but such W. course is temporary, the E. course being afterward resumed. Some of the most violent E. storms fall under this head. Storms do not always proceed in the same uniform direction from day to day, and, though the change which occurs in the direction of their progressive motion is generally small, yet occasionally it is very great.

The storms of the Mediterranean follow a different course. While a number take the general E. course of European storms, a larger number originate in the gulfs of Lyons and Genoa, and pursue devious courses over this N. extension of the Mediterranean, till they die out; several advance from Turkey and Greece toward the Alps; and others, comparatively few, advance in an E. course toward the Levant. By far the greater number of the storms of North America take their rise in the vast plain which lies to the E. of the Rocky Mountains, and thence advance in an E. direction over the United States, their course being largely determined by the Great Lakes; some of them cross the Atlantic, and burst on the W. shores of Europe. But the connection of the American with the European storms is not even yet well established. The storms of the West Indies generally take their rise somewhere N. of the region of calms, and, tracing out a parabolic course, proceed first toward the W. N. W., and then turn to the N. E. about lat. 30° N., not a few traversing the E. coasts of North America as far as Nova Scotia. South of the equator they follow an opposite course. Thus, in the Indian Ocean they first proceed toward the S. W., and then gradually curve round to the S. E. The hurricanes of India usually pursue a parabolic path, first traversing the E. coast toward Calcutta, and then turning to the N. W. up the valley of the Ganges. The typhoons of the Chinese Sea resemble, in the course they take, the hurricanes of the West Indies.

Rate at Which Storms Travel.—The average rate of the progressive movement of European storms is about $16\frac{1}{2}$ miles per hour. From an examination of extensive series of storms Professor Loomis has shown that the average rates of progress of storm centers are in miles per hour 28 for the United States, 18 for the middle latitudes of the Atlantic Ocean, 17 for Europe, 15 for the West Indies, and 9 for the Bay of Bengal and China Sea. On Jan. 7-8, 1877, a storm traveled in 24 hours from Indianola, Tex., to Eastport, Me.—1,782 miles, or 78 miles an hour. On the other hand, the rate of progress is, particularly in the tropics, sometimes so slow as to be virtually stationary; and, as already stated, they occasionally recurve on their paths.

Relations of Temperature, Rain, and Cloud to Storms.—Temperature increases at places toward which and over which the front part of the storm is advancing, and falls at those places over which the front part of the storm has already passed. In other words, the temperature rises as the barometer falls, and falls as the barometer rises. When the barometer has been falling for some time clouds begin to overspread the sky, and rain to fall at intervals; as the central depression approaches the rain becomes more general, heavy, and continuous. After the center of the storm approaches, or shortly before the barometer begins to rise, the rain becomes less heavy, falling more in showers than continuously; the clouds break up when the center has passed, and fine weather, ushered in with cold breezes, ultimately prevails. If the temperature begins to rise soon and markedly after the storm has passed, a second storm may be shortly expected.

Direction of the Wind.—If the winds are examined, they will be observed whirling round the area of low barometer in a circular manner, and in a direction contrary to the motion of the hands of a watch, with a constant tendency to turn inward toward the center of lowest pressure, in the manner formulated in Buys-Ballot's law. The wind in storms neither blows round the center of lowest pressure in circles, nor does it blow directly toward that center, but takes a direction nearly intermediate, approaching, however, nearer to the direction and course of the circular curves than of the radii to the center. In the front of the storm the winds blow more toward the center, but in the rear they blow more closely approximate to the circular isobaric lines. Where the direction of the wind differs to any material degree from the above it is light, and consequently more under local influences, which turn it from its true course. In the Southern Hemisphere a rotary motion is also observed round the center of storms, but it takes place in a contrary direction, or in the direction of the motion of the hands of a watch, instead of contrary to that direction, as prevails N. of the equator.

Force of the Wind.—The rule is simple, and without exception—viz., the wind blows from a high to a low barometer with a force proportioned to the barometric gradient or to the difference of the barometric pressures reduced to sea-level. Hence where the isobaric lines crowd together the violence of the storm is most felt, and where they are far asunder the winds are moderate, light, or nil. We thus see the importance of observations from a distance in forecasting the weather. The progressive motion of storms, which may vary from zero to 78 miles an hour, measures the time taken in passing from one place to another, but it gives no indication of the violence of the storm. This is determined by the velocity of the wind round and inward on the center of the storm, which in Europe and the United States frequently amounts to 60 or 80 miles an hour continuously for some time. In intermittent gusts a speed of 120 miles an hour has been several times observed in Great Britain—a velocity which is perhaps sometimes surpassed by storms within the tropics. On the top of Ben Nevis higher velocities, rising to upward of 150 miles, are of not infrequent occurrence.

Causes of Cyclones.—Dove, who did so much in this department of meteorology, held the view that cyclones are formed when two great atmospheric currents, called polar and equatorial, flow side by side, storms being the eddies, as it were, formed along the line of junction. It is to be kept in mind that the qualities of the atmosphere in the front portion of a cyclone are quite different from those in the rear—the former being warm and moist, while the latter are cold and dry. The conclusion is inevitable that the apparent rotation of winds in storms is simply a circulatory movement maintained between two currents, and that no mass of the same air makes the complete circuit of the cyclone.

Forecasting.—Valuable aid in forecasting storms and weather is derived from two important deductions from past observations: (1) A cyclone tends toward a path near to the anticyclone which lies immediately to the right of the progressive motion of the storm at the time. (2) When the rates of fall of the barometer at stations in the W. of Europe are noted, it is found that the path taken by the coming storm is indicated by those stations at which the rates of fall of the barometer are greatest. See METEOROLOGY.

Relations of Storms to the Character of the Season.—This is vital and all-important. Thus, as regards the British Islands, when the general path pursued by storms in their E. course over Europe lies to the S. the winter is severe, inasmuch as the British Islands are then on the N. side of the center of low pressure, and consequently in the stream of the N. and E. winds which there prevail. On the other hand, when the paths of storms lies to the N. the British Islands are on the S. side of the low pressure, and therefore in the stream of the warm, moist, S. and S. W. winds which there prevail.

It is plain that the character of the weather of any particular day or season is wholly determined by the way in which areas of high and of low atmospheric pressure are distributed over the region during that day or season. Further, the weather of the coming season could certainly be predicted for say the British Islands, if only the general path was known which the centers of the Atlantic cyclones will taken in their E. course over Europe; for if the paths of the winter storms be to the N. of Great Britain the winter will be an open one, but if to the S. a severe winter is the certain result. Toward the solution of this highly practical problem we look to seamen to put us in possession of a fuller and, above all, an earlier knowledge of the fluctuations of the surface temperature of the Atlantic, and to high-level observatories for the data required in obtaining a clearer insight into the history and theory of storms. See METEOROLOGY; WEATHER BUREAU; WIND; CYCLONE.

STORM, THEODOR (WOLDSEN) (störm), a German author; born in Husum, Germany, Sept. 14, 1817. He first attracted attention in literature with "The Song-Book of Three Friends" (1843), the work of Tycho and Theodor Mommsen and himself; "Immensee" (43d ed. 1896), a short tale, and a volume of "Poems" (11th ed. 1897). Among his other works are: "Aquis Submersus" (1877); "The Senator's Sons" (1881); "Knight of the White Horse" (1888); etc. He died in Hadamarschen, Germany, July 4, 1888.

STORM SIGNAL, a signal for indicating to mariners, fishermen, etc., the probable approach of a storm.

STORMY PETREL, in ornithology, the *Procellaria pelagica*, common in the North Atlantic. In general appearance it is not unlike a swift, of a sooty black color, with a little white on the wings, and some near the tail. It is popularly believed to be a harbinger of bad weather, and is called by sailors Mother Carey's Chicken, a name which is also applied to other species.

STORNOWAY, the chief town and seaport of Lewis, the largest of the Outer Hebrides, in the N. E. of the island, at the head of the deep inlet of Loch Stornoway, which is sheltered to the N. by a long, irregular peninsula. It has several good public buildings, and on an eminence overlooking the town stands Stornoway Castle, a castellated Tudor edifice, long the residence of Sir James Matheson. A Free Church (for services in English) was opened in 1878. Stornoway is an important fishing station, and it has several saw, carding, and corn mills, etc., and is the seat of an important cattle fair held in July.

Steamers ply regularly between Stornoway and Glasgow, and via Poolewe to Dingwall.

STORRS, EMORY ALEXANDER, an American lawyer; born in Hinsdale, N. Y., August 12, 1835. He read law with his father and Marshall R. Chaplin; was admitted to the bar in Buffalo in 1855, and practiced there for a short time; removed to Chicago in 1859. He became prominent as a criminal lawyer, and for several years figured as counsel in almost every important criminal case in the Chicago courts. He became well known as a presidential campaign orator, and was a delegate-at-large to the National Republican Conventions of 1868, 1872, and 1880, where he was influential in shaping the platform of the party. He died in Ottawa, Ill., Sept. 12, 1885.

STORRS, RICHARD SALTER, an American clergyman; born in Braintree, Mass., Aug. 21, 1821; was graduated at Amherst College in 1839 and at the Andover Theological Seminary in 1845. His first pastorate was in Harvard Congregational Church, Brookline, Mass., where he was ordained Oct. 22, 1845. In 1846 he was called to the Church of the Pilgrims in Brooklyn, N. Y., where he was pastor emeritus at the time of his death. He was one of the founders of the "Independent" in 1848 and remained on its editorial staff till 1861; served on the Brooklyn Park Commission in 1871-1873; was president of the Long Island Historical Society, and of the American Board of Commissioners for Foreign Missions; and the author of numerous books, sermons, orations, discourses, etc. He died in Brooklyn, N. Y., June 5, 1900.

STORTHING (stor'ting), the parliament or supreme legislative assembly of Norway; the great court or representative of the sovereign people. It is elected triennially, and holds annual sessions. When in session it divides itself into two houses, one-fourth of the members constituting the lagthing, and the remaining three-fourths the odelsthing.

STORY, JOSEPH, an American jurist; born in Marblehead, Mass., Sept. 18, 1779. In 1811 he was appointed an associate justice of the United States Supreme Court, and held the office till his death. His works include: "Commentaries on the Constitution of the United States" (1833); "Commentaries on the Conflict of Laws," considered his ablest effort (1834); and "Miscellaneous Writings" (1835). In 1851 his "Life and Letters" was edited by his son, W. W. Story. He died in Cambridge, Mass., Sept. 10, 1845.

STORY, WILLIAM WETMORE, an American sculptor, son of Judge Joseph; born in Salem, Mass., Feb. 19, 1819; was graduated at Harvard in 1838; was admitted to the bar and practiced five years; went to Rome to study art and made Italy his home. Among his sculptures are: a statue of Edward Everett (in the Boston Public Garden); and one of Prescott at Bunker Hill; "Cleopatra"; "Semiramis"; "Judith"; "Jerusalem"; "Medea"; "The Sybil"; etc.; and busts of Judge Story, Lowell, Bryant, etc. He published: "Nature and Art: A Poem"

WILLIAM WETMORE STORY

(1844); "Poems" (1847); "Life and Letters of Joseph Story" (1851); "Poems" (1856); "The American Question" (1862); "Roba di Roma" (1862); "Graffiti d'Italia" (1868); "A Roman Lawyer in Jerusalem" (1870); "Nero: An Historical Play" (1875); "Stephania: A Tragedy" (1875); "Vallombrosa" (1881); "He and She" (1883); "Poems" (1885-1886); "Fiametta" (1886); "Conversations in a Studio" (1890); "Excursions in Art and Letters" (1891); "A Poet's Portfolio" (1894). He died in Vallombrosa, near Florence, Italy, Oct. 7, 1895.

STOTESBURY, EDWARD TOWNSEND, an American financier, born in Philadelphia, Pa., in 1849. He was educated at Friends' Central School, Philadelphia, and after having acquired some mercantile experience, he became connected with the Philadelphia banking house of Drexel and Company, becoming a partner in 1882 and later the head of the concern as well as a member of the firm of J. P. Morgan and Company. He was the chairman of the board of directors of the Philadelphia and Reading Railway Company and an officer or director of many railroad companies and corporations. He was greatly interested in the breeding of thoroughbred horses, was a patron of arts and an owner of an extensive and valuable collection of paintings, sculptures, etc. He also supported for many years grand opera enterprises in Philadelphia. In 1904 he was treasurer of the Republican National Campaign Fund for Roosevelt and 1908 for Taft.

STOUR, a river of England 47 miles long, flowing E. along the Suffolk and Essex boundary to the North Sea at Harwich.

STOURBRIDGE (stur'brij), a market town of Worcestershire, England, on the Stour, at the border of Staffordshire and the Black Country; 4½ miles S. by W. of Dudley and 12 W. by S. of Birmingham. The famous fireclay named for this town is said to have been discovered about 1555 by wandering glassmakers from Lorraine. Stourbridge has glass, earthenware, and firebrick works, besides manufactories of iron nails, chains, leather, etc. It has a grammar school (at which Samuel Johnson passed a year), a corn exchange, county court, mechanics' institute, etc.

STOVAINE, trade name for the hydrochloride of dimethylamino-amyl benzoate. It is a synthetic drug used as a substitute for cocaine as a local anæsthetic. It is claimed that it is less toxic than cocaine.

STOVE, in former times, a room or place artificially heated, such as a bath, a hot-house, etc.
In modern usage, an apparatus in which a fire is made for the purpose of warming a room or house, or for cooking, or for other purposes. They are generally made of iron, sometimes of brick or tiles, or slabs of stone, and are of various forms, according to the heating medium used. On the continent of Europe stoves are generally of earthenware, and are frequently constructed mainly of tiles.

STOVALL, PLEASANT ALEXANDER, an American editor and diplomat, born at Augusta, Ga., in 1857. He was educated at the University of Georgia and became editor of the Athens "Georgian," the Augusta "Chronicle," and the Savannah "Press," of which latter paper he was also proprietor. From 1902 to 1906 and again from 1912 to 1913 he was a member of the Georgia House of

Representatives. From 1913 to 1920 he was United States minister to Switzerland. He wrote "Life of Robert Toombs" (1891).

STOW, JOHN, an English historian; born in London about 1525. He learned his father's business, tailoring, but his bent was toward antiquarian research. His chief publications were "A Summary of Englische Chronicles" (1561); "Annales, or a Generale Chronicle of England from Brute until the present Yeare of Christe" (1580); and "A Survey of London" (1598). He also printed the "Flores Historiarum of Matthew of Westminster" (1567), the "Chronicle of Matthew of Paris" (1571), and the "Historia Brevis of Thomas Walsingham" (1574). He died in London April 6, 1605.

STOWE, CALVIN ELLIS, an American educator; born in Natick, Mass., April 6, 1802; was graduated at Bowdoin College in 1824, at Andover Seminary in 1828; and edited the Boston "Recorder" in 1829-1830. He was Professor of Greek at Dartmouth College in 1830-1832, and of Sacred Literature in Lane Theological Seminary, Cincinnati, O., in 1833-1835. He married Harriet Elizabeth Beecher in January, 1836, and went to Europe to examine the public school systems. He was professor at Bowdoin in 1850; and at Andover in 1852-1864. His publications include a translation of Jahn's "Hebrew Commonwealth" (1829); "Lectures on the Poetry of the Hebrews" (1829); "Report on Elementary Education in Europe"; "Introduction to the Criticism and Interpretation of the Bible" (1835); and "Origin and History of the Books of the Bible" (1867); also addresses and pamphlets. He died in Hartford, Conn., Aug. 22, 1886.

STOWE, CHARLES EDWARD, an American lecturer and writer, born at Brunswick, Maine, in 1850. He was a son of Harriet Beecher Stowe (q. v.) and was educated at Harvard and the Universities of Bonn, Berlin, and Heidelberg. After following the sea for four years, he studied abroad and upon his return was ordained a Congregational minister. He devoted his time to lecturing and wrote "Life of Harriet Beecher Stowe" (1889); "Lives of Distinguished Americans" (1889); "Harriet Beecher Stowe—The Story of Her Life" (with L. B. Stowe, 1912).

STOWE, HARRIET ELIZABETH BEECHER, an American novelist, daughter of Lyman Beecher and sister of

Henry Ward Beecher; born in Litchfield, Conn., June 14, 1811; was educated at Litchfield Academy and at the school of her sister Catherine in Hartford; at the age of 14 she began teaching; in 1832 removed to Cincinnati, O. In 1836 she was married to Prof. Calvin Ellis Stowe; in 1850 she removed to Brunswick, Me., and later to Andover, Mass.; in 1864 she settled in Hartford, Conn., where she spent the remainder of her life. She published: "The Mayflower; or Sketches of Scenes and Characters among the Descendants of the Pilgrims" (1843); "Uncle Tom's Cabin; or, Life among the Lowly" (1852); "Key to Uncle Tom's Cabin" (1853); "Uncle Tom's Emancipation" (1853); "Sunny Memories of Foreign Lands" (1854); "The Mayflower, and Miscellaneous Writings" (1855); "Dred: A Tale of the Great Dismal Swamp" (1856); "Our Charley and What to Do with Him" (1858); "The Minister's Wooing" (1859); "The Pearl of Orr's Island" (1862); "Agnes of Sorrento" (1862); "House and Home Papers" (1864); "Stories about our Boys" (1865); "Religious Poems" (1867); "Queer Litle People" (1867); "The Chimney Corner" (1868); "Oldtown Folks" (1869); with Catherine E. Beecher; "Lady Byron Vindicated" (1870); "Little Pussy Willow" (1870); "Pink and White Tyranny" (1871); "Sam Lawson's Fireside Stories" (1871); "My Wife and I" (1871); "Palmetto Leaves" (1873); "Woman in Sacred History" (1873); "We and our Neighbors" (1875); "Deacon Pitkin's Farm, and Christ's Christmas Presents" (1875); "Footsteps of the Master" (1876); "Captain Kidd's Money, and Other Stories" (1876); "The Ghost in the Mill, and Other Stories" (1876); "Poganuc People" (1878); "A Dog's Mission" (1881); etc. Her best known work, "Uncle Tom's Cabin" (suggested by the life of Josiah Henson) has been translated into many languages, its sale exceeding that of any previous work of English fiction. She died in Hartford, Conn., July 1, 1896.

STOWE, LYMAN BEECHER, an American writer, born at Saco, Maine, in 1880. He was educated at Harvard. From 1909 to 1910 he was assistant editor of the "Circle Magazine"; from 1910 to 1913 secretary and vice-chairman of the Public Service Commission of New York; from 1913 to 1915 secretary of the National Association of Junior Republics; from 1915 to 1918 secretary of the Department of Public Charities, New York City. Besides contributing articles to many magazines and lecturing on social, political, and educational subjects, he was the co-author of "Har-

riet Beecher Stowe—Story of Her Life"
(1912); "Citizens Made and Remade"
(1912); "Booker T. Washington" (1916);
"The Inside Story of Austro-German
Intrigue" (1919).

STRABISMUS, squinting arising from
the optic axes of the eyes in certain individuals not being as in normal cases,

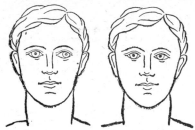

POSITION OF THE EYES IN STRABISMUS

parallel. Strabismus may affect one or
both eyes, and may be upward, downward, inward, outward, or in the intermediate direction.

STRABO, a noted geographer; born
in Amasea, Pontus, about 63 B. C. On
the mother's side he was descended from
a Greek family closely connected with
the kings of Pontus. Of his father we
know nothing. The dates of his visits
to most of the countries through which
he traveled are very doubtful.

The name Strabo, "squint-eyed," is
originally Greek, and its origin is obvious, but whether any of his ancestors
bore it is uncertain. His preceptors were
Tyrannio of Amisus, Aristodemus of
Nysa, and Xenarchus of Seleucia. He
seems to have been possessed of ample
means which he expended on travel, the
results of which, after a lifetime's toil,
he has bequeathed to us in his "Geography." But he also devoted himself to
philosophy, and is cited by Plutarch
(Lucullus 28, Sulla 26) as Strabo, the
philosopher. His work entitled "Histo-
rica Hypomnémata" in 43 books is supposed to have contained a narrative of
the events from the close of the "History" of Polybius to the battle of Actium.

The facts recorded in the "Geography"
of Strabo are in great measure the result of his own observation. The range
of his travels is a wide one, embracing
the territories from Armenia to Tyrrhe-
nia W., and from the Euxine to Ethiopa
S. In his work he is largely indebted
to the geographers who preceded him—
Eratosthenes, Artemidorus, Polybius,
Posidonius, Aristotle, Theopompus, Thucydides, Aristobulus, and others. Of
Greece he seems to have seen less than
of almost any country. He appears,
I—9

however, to have obtained in Rome much
information regarding the Transalpine
regions. Strangely, he disparages the
discoveries of Herodotus, and under-
values the works of Roman writers,
quoting almost none save Fabius Pictor,
Asinius Pollio, and Julius Cæsar.

The principal value of his works lies
in his method. The number of historical facts recorded by him is enormous.
The date of his death is unknown, but
it must be placed between A. D. 21 and 25.
As a writer, Strabo is always clear, simple, and unaffected. His "Geography"
comprises 17 books; 2 introductory, 8
devoted to Europe, 6 to Asia, and 1 to
Africa. The *editio princeps* is the "Aldine" (1516). In 1875 a MS. of the
"Geography" was discovered in the abbey of Grotta Ferrata near Frascati,
older than any of the 28 previously
known MSS., and supplying many lucu-
næ. The best translations are those in
German by C. J. Groskurd (3 vols. 8
vo. 1831-1834). A fair English version
with copious notes and a complete index was published in Bohn's "Classical
Library" (1854, 3 vols. post. 8vo.). An
excellent edition of the text is that of
Aug. Meineke (1852-1853, 3 vols. 8vo.,
2d ed. 1866).

**STRADIVARI, ANTONIO (STRADI-
VARIUS),** an Italian violin maker; born
in Cremona, Italy, about 1649. He was
a pupil of Nicolo Amati, in whose employment he remained till 1700, when
he began making on his own account. It
was he who settled the typical pattern
of the Cremona violin, and his instruments, for tone and finish, have never
yet been excelled. He died in Cremona
Dec. 17, 1737.

**STRAFFORD, THOMAS WENT-
WORTH, EARL OF,** an English statesman, the eldest son of Sir William
Wentworth; born in London, April 13,
1593; educated at Cambridge. After
leaving the university he received the
honor of knighthood. He sat in Parliament for Yorkshire for a number of
years, and when Charles I. asserted that
the Commons enjoyed no rights but by
royal permission, he was strongly opposed by Sir Thomas Wentworth. In
this struggle his abilities were recognized and high terms offered him by the
court, which he accepted, and in 1628
was successively created Baron Wentworth, privy-councillor, and President of
the North. Archbishop Laud selected
him to proceed to Ireland as lord deputy
in 1632. Here he greatly improved the
state of the country, both as regarded
law, revenue, and trade; but to accomplish his ends he did not scruple to use

the strongest and most arbitrary measures. For these services he was created Earl of Strafford. When the Long Parliament met, the very first movement of the party opposed to arbitrary power was to impeach Strafford of high treason, with which charge Pym appeared at the bar of the House of Lords in 1640. His defense, however, was so strong that the original impeachment was deserted for a bill of attainder. The bill passed the Commons by a great majority, and was feebly supported by the House of Lords. The king endeavored to secure his safety, but yielded to the advice of his counselors, backed by a letter from Strafford himself, who urged him, for his own safety, to ratify the bill. Strafford was accordingly beheaded on Tower Hill, May 12, 1641.

STRAIGHT, WILLIAM DICKERMAN, an American financier and public official; born in Oswego, N. Y., in 1880. He was educated at Bordentown (N. J.) Military Institute and at Cornell University, and in 1911 married Dorothy Payne Whitney, the daughter of the late W. C. WHITNEY (*q. v.*). From 1902 to 1904 he was in the Chinese Imperial Maritime Customs Service; from 1904 to 1905 a newspaper correspondent in Korea, Japan, and Manchuria; in 1905 consul-general at Seoul; in 1906 private secretary of the American Minister to Cuba; from 1906 to 1908 consul-general at Mukden; and from November, 1908, to June, 1909, acting chief of the Division of Far Eastern Affairs in the Department of State, Washington, D. C. In 1909 he went to China as the representative of a group of American bankers, and remained there until 1914. Upon his return he was connected for a short time with J. P. Morgan & Company, then studied international law at Columbia and became a vice-president of the American International Corporation. He was a Fellow of the Royal Geographical Society, president of the Asiatic Association, and a trustee of Cornell University. During the World War he served in the Adjutant-General's Department. He died in 1918.

STRAIGHT COLLEGE, an institution for the higher education of negroes, founded in 1869, at New Orleans. It is coeducational. It has an endowment of about $25,000. It is supported chiefly through voluntary contributions. In 1919 there were 474 students and 26 members of the faculty. President, Rev. H. A. M. Briggs.

STRAIN, in mechanics, the force which acts on the material and which tends to disarrange its component parts or destroy their cohesion, or the change resulting from application of such force. See STRESS: STRENGTH OF MATERIALS.

STRAITS SETTLEMENTS, a British crown colony in the Malay Peninsula, deriving its name from the Straits of Malacca, which separate the Malay Peninsula from Sumatra, and form the great trade route between India and China. The capital of the colony and seat of government is Singapore. The governor is assisted by executive and legislative councils. The constituent parts are as follows: SINGAPORE, an island off the S. extremity of the Malay Peninsula; area, 217 square miles. Pop. (1918) estimated, males 274,238; females 113,098. PENANG (including Province Wellesley and Dingings), area 661 square miles. Pop. (1918) estimated, males 188,720; females 117,019. MALACCA is a town and territory 240 miles S. of Penang. Its coast, rocky and barren, extends 42 miles; area, 659 square miles. It is ruled by a resident councilor, subject to the governor of the colony. Pop. (1918) estimated, males 92,340; females 60,668. Total population of Straits Settlements, males 555,298; females 296,785. Included in the administration of the Straits Settlements are the Cocos (or KEELING ISLANDS), a small coral group lying some 700 miles S. W. of Java, and CHRISTMAS ISLAND, which lies 200 miles S. W. of Java. Since 1907 the boundaries of the colony have included the colony of Labuan. The governor is also high commissioner for the Federated Malay States.

STRALSUND (sträl-sönd), a seaport of Prussia; on a narrow strait called the Strela Sound, which divides the mainland from the island of Rügen; 67 miles N. W. from Stettin. It forms an island, connected with the mainland by bridges. Down to 1873 the place was a fortress of the first class. Many of the houses are finely gabled, which gives the town a quaint and ancient look. The most interesting building is the town house (1306), with a museum of antiquities from the island of Rügen. Stralsund carries on a large export trade in malt, corn, fish, wool, coal, groceries, etc., and manufactures leather, gloves, mirrors, earthenware, sugar, starch, oil, and playing cards. Pop. about 35,000. It was founded in 1209, and became one of the most important members of the Hansa. During the Thirty Years' War it successfully withstood a terrible siege (1628) by Wallenstein; but in 1678 it capitulated to the Great Elector after a furious bombardment. It again opened its gates to Prussia and her allies in 1715, to the French in 1807, and to the Danes and others in 1809. The town was held by the Swedes from 1628 to 1814; in the year following (1815) Denmark gave it up to Prussia.

STRANGULATION, an act of violence in which constriction is applied directly to the neck, either around it or in the forepart, in such a way as to destroy life. This definition obviously includes hanging which differs from other forms of strangulation, only in that the body is suspended. The direct cause of death in the great majority of cases is arrest of the respiration owing to pressure on the windpipe—i. e., asphyxia. If much violence is used, death may be produced by direct injury to the upper part of the spinal cord from fracture or dislocation of the cervical vertebræ (as is now the rule in execution by hanging), or by syncope from shock, and in such cases must be almost instantaneous; on the other hand, if the constriction is so applied as to compress the great vessels in the neck and not the windpipe, as may happen in "garotting," it is due to coma, and is somewhat slower than in cases of asphyxia. Or if both vessels and windpipe are compressed, coma and asphyxia may both contribute to cause death.

When suspension of the body has not continued for much more than five minutes, and the parts about the neck have not suffered violence, there is a probability that resuscitation may be established; though many cases are recorded when after only a few minutes' suspension it has been found impossible to restore life. Moreover, if a person who has hanged himself has been cut down sufficiently soon to allow of the respiratory process being restored, he is by no means safe: death often taking place from secondary effects at various periods after the accident.

The treatment to be adopted after the patient has been cut down may be briefly summed up as follows: Exposure to a free current of air, cold affusion if the skin is warm, the application of ammonia to the nostrils, of mustard poultices to the chest and legs, and of hot water to the feet, and the subsequent abstraction of blood if there should be much cerebral congestion; above all, artificial respiration should be used if natural breathing do not at once commence. In manual strangulation the external marks of injury will be in front of the neck, about and below the larynx; and if death has been caused by a ligature the mark round the neck will be circular, whereas in hanging it is usually oblique. The

internal appearances are much the same as in the case of hanging. See ASPHYXIA.

STRANGURY, a symptom of various affections of the urinary organs. It consists in a frequent and irresistible desire to pass water, the urine being discharged in small quantity and accompanied with scalding, cutting pains in the urethra, which sometimes extend to the bladder, the kidneys, and the rectum. Strangury may be caused by idiopathic urethritis, by gonorrhœa, or by such irritating substances as cantharides and oil of turpentine, or by gravel or calculus in the bladder.

STRANSKY, JOSEF, an orchestral conductor, born in Czecho-Slovakia, in 1872. He was educated in the universities of Prague and Leipzig, and studied music at the later city and at Vienna. From 1898 to 1903 he was conductor at the Opera in Prague. From 1903 to 1910 he was conductor of the Opera at Hamburg. He followed this with service in orchestras in Berlin and Dresden. In 1911 he was appointed conductor of the Philharmonic Society of New York. He composed songs, many operas, and much orchestra music.

STRASSBURG, a town and fortress of France, in Alsace; capital of the territory of Alsace-Lorraine; on the Ill; about 2 miles W. of the Rhine, to which its glacis extends; 250 miles E. by S. of Paris, and about 370 miles S. W. of Berlin. By means of canals which unite the Ill with the Rhine, Rhone, and Marne, it is brought into communication with the Atlantic and the Mediterranean. It has always been regarded as a place of strategical importance, and strong fortifications and a pentagonal citadel were erected by Vauban in 1682-1684. Since the siege of 1870 by the Germans these have been considerably altered and strengthened, the new system of defense adopted including 14 detached forts situated from 3 to 5 miles from the center of the town. The streets in the older parts are irregular and quaint of aspect, but since the removal of part of the old fortifications the modern partions have greatly expanded. The chief building is the cathedral, a structure which presents the architectural styles of the centuries from the 11th to the 15th, in which it was built, but whose main element is Gothic. It is surmounted by towers 466 feet high, has a splendid W. façade, with statues and great rose window, fine painted glass windows, and a famous astronomical clock, made in 1547-1580. The other notable buildings are the Church of St. Thomas, the Temple-Neuf or Neukirche, the old Episcopal palace, the town hall, the new university building, opened in 1884, and the new imperial palace. The old Episcopal palace contains the university and town library, numbering 600,000 volumes. There are statues to Gutenberg and General Kléber, in squares correspondingly named, besides others. Its industries are very varied, and include tanning, brewing, machine making, woolen and cotton goods, cutlery, musical instruments, artificial flowers, gloves, chemicals, and the preparation of its celebrated *pâtés de foie gras*. Strassburg, under the name of Argentoratum, is supposed to have been founded by the Romans, who erected it as a barrier against the incursions of the Germans, who ultimately possessed it. In the 6th century the name was changed to Strassburg, and in the beginning of the 10th century it became subject to the emperors of Germany. United to France in 1681, it was ceded with the territories of Alsace and Lorraine to Germany in 1871. By the Treaty of Versailles in 1919, Alsace and Lorraine were restored to France. Pop. about 198,000.

STRASSBURG, UNIVERSITY OF, a university of Alsace-Lorraine. The institution was first founded as a German university, in 1621, maintaining much of its German character, after Strassburg became French territory in 1681. During the French Revolution it disappeared, but was reopened in 1802 as a Protestant academy, and, in 1808, under the university reforms instituted by Napoleon the First, became part of the University of France. After the Franco-Prussian War it once more became a German university and was reopened in 1872. While the Germans were in possession of Alsace-Lorraine, the imperial government expended large sums of money on the university and it soon became a center of German influence and one of the most flourishing universities. Previous to the outbreak of the World War, it had about 2,100 students and an annual budget of $400,000. Its library contains more than 6,000,000 volumes. As a result of the Peace Treaty of Versailles the institution again became a French university.

STRATEGY, the science, as distinguished from the art of war; the direction of a campaign; the combination and employment of his available forces, by a commander-in-chief, to bring a campaign to an end, as distinct from the minor operations by which it is sought to effect that result, and which are subsidiary to the general plan (See TAC-

TICS). Also the use of artifice, stratagem, or finesse in carrying out any project.

STRATFORD, a city of Connecticut, in Fairfield co. It is on the New York, New Haven and Hartford railroad. It has important manufactures, including silverware, paint, brass goods, and wireforming machinery. Pop. (1910) 5,712; (1920) 12,347.

STRATFORD-ON-AVON, a town of Warwickshire, England; 8 miles S. W. of Warwick; on the right bank of the Avon river. The river is here crossed by a fine bridge of 14 pointed arches, now nearly 400 years old, still known as Clopton Bridge, after its builder, Sir Hugh Clopton, an alderman of London, but born in the neighborhood of Stratford, who is also interesting as the builder of the house called The New Place, which was the property of Shakespeare in his later years and the house in which he died, but was destroyed by the owner in 1759. The grounds are now open free. "Shakespeare's House," that is, the house in which he was born, having been purchased by subscription and dedicated to the public in 1847, was restored in 1859, and now contains the Shakespeare library and museum, the Stratford portrait, etc. In the cruciform parish church are his grave and portrait bust, also the font in which he was baptized. The old parish register with the entry of Shakespeare's baptism and burial, is shown near the N. door of the church. The central tower of the church dates from the 13th century. Other monuments are the Shakespeare Memorial Theater, built in 1879 at a cost of over $200,000, intended for occasional Shakespearean celebrations, and possibly as a dramatic college, and having attached to it, a Shakespeare library and museum; the Shakespeare fountain, built by an American, and the Shakespeare monument. Anne Hathaway's cottage, in the neighboring hamlet of Shottery, in the parish of Stratford, was acquired in the public interest in 1892. Among other interesting remains of Shakespeare's time or memorials of Shakespeare are the grammar school in which he was educated (originally endowed in 1482, refounded under Edward VI.), the adjoining Guildhall, in which strolling players used to perform in Shakespeare's time (both buildings restored since 1891), the town hall (rebuilt in 1768 on the site of an older structure of 1633), containing in a niche on its N. side the statue of Shakespeare presented by David Garrick. Apart from Shakespeare, the town is interesting as containing the early home of the mother of John Harvard, founder of America's oldest university. There are several interesting places besides those in and about Stratford, among these the cottage of Mary Arden (the poet's mother), at Wilmcote. The town owes its name to the old ford of the Avon parallel to the bridge on the road from London to the N. W. Shakespeare's tercentenary was celebrated here in 1916, with elaborate ceremonies. Here in August, 1914, the sword of Shakespeare's father was drawn from its scabbard in token that England was at war. The tradition runs that it must not be sheathed until victory crowns British arms. Pop. about 8,500.

STRATFORD, a city of Ontario, Canada, on the River Avon and on several railroads. It is the seat of a collegiate institute, the Provincial Normal School, several other educational institutes, a public library, etc. There are numerous churches, several parks, and the industrial establishments are of considerable importance, including locomotive repair shops, furniture factories, knitting mills, etc. Hydro-electric power is used extensively. Pop. 18,000.

STRATHCLYDE, a former independent kingdom in Scotland. In the 8th century the ancient confederacy of the Britons was broken up into the separate divisions of Wales and English and Scotch Cumbria. Scotch Cumbria, otherwise called Strathclyde, thenceforth formed a little kingdom, comprising the country between Clyde and Solway, governed by princes of its own, and having the fortress town of Alclyde or Dumbarton for its capital. Becoming gradually more and more dependent on Scotland, it was annexed to the Scottish crown at the death of Malcolm I. On the death of Alexander I., without issue in 1124, it was permanently united to the Scotch kingdom under David I.

STRATHCONA AND MOUNT ROYAL, DONALD ALEXANDER SMITH, 1st BARON, a Canadian statesman; born in Scotland in 1820; entered the service of the Hudson Bay Company at an early age, and was the last resident governor of that corporation as a governing body. He was special commissioner during the first Riel rebellion in the Red River settlements in 1869-1870; a member of the first executive council of the Northwest Territory; represented Winnipeg and St. John's in the Manitoba Legislature in 1871-1874; and was a member of the Canadian House of Commons for Selkirk in 1871-1872, 1874, and 1878, and for Montreal West in 1877-1896. He was a director of the St. Paul, Minneapolis, and Manitoba railway; the Great Northern Railway of Minnesota; and the Canadian Pacific Railway Company; and intimately connected with many other corporations and organizations. He was made High Commissioner for Canada in 1896. In 1898 he was Governor of Frazer Institute and Chancellor of McGill University and also of Aberdeen University, Lord Rector in 1903. He gave over $1,000,000 to McGill and Royal Victoria Hospital, Montreal, also $1,000,000 to the King Edward Hospital Fund. He endowed chairs in many colleges and contributed generously to various educational funds. He died in 1914.

STRATHMORE, the general name given to the extensive valley of Scotland which stretches N. E. from Dumbartonshire to Kincardineshire, having on one side the Grampians and on the other the Campsie, Ochil, and Sidlaw Hills; but it is popularly limited to the district which stretches from Methven in Perthshire to Brechin in Forfarshire.

STRATIGRAPHY, that department of geology which deals with the disposition or arrangement of strata, or the order in which they succeed each other.

STRATUM, a bed or mass of matter spread out over a certain surface, in most cases by the action of water, but sometimes also by that of wind. The method in which stratification by the agency of water has been effected in bygone times may be understood by a study of the manner in which successive layers of gravel, sand, mud, etc., are deposited in a river or running brook. The same process has been at work through untold periods of time. The greater part of the earth's crust, in nearly every land, is found to be thus stratified. Strata may be CONFORMABLE (*q. v.*), or UNCONFORMABLE (*q. v.*). In the former case there generally is a considerable approach to parallelism among them. It is, however, inferior in exactness to that of cleavage planes. Strata laid down by water, as a rule, retain fossil remains of the animals and plants imbedded in them when they were soft and plastic. Metamorphism generally destroys these organic remains, but leaves the stratification undisturbed; thus there are two kinds of strata—sedimentary and metamorphic—nearly synonymous with fossiliferous and non-fossiliferous stratified rocks. Most strata have a dip and a strike. The fossils will in most cases show whether strata are lacustrine, fluviatile, or marine. They prove that deposit was very slow. One stratum may overlap another, or a stratum may thin out, or an outcrop of it may exist. As a rule, the lowest are the oldest, but some great convulsion may have tilted over strata in limited areas, so that the oldest have been thrown uppermost. A study of the same beds over a wide expanse of country prevents error in estimating the relative age of strata thus reversed. The thickness of the stratified rocks is believed to be about 20 miles, or 100,000 feet. They are not all present at one place, or even in one country. Though a surprisingly large number are to be found in America, yet some foreign beds require to be inserted in the series, and even then great gaps remain, each representing a lapse of time. For the order of superposition, see FOSSIL: GEOLOGY.

STRAUS, NATHAN, an American merchant and philanthropist, born in Rhenish Bavaria in 1848. At the age of six he came to the United States with his family. He was educated in the public schools of Talbotton, Ga., and at Packard's Business College. In 1866 he became a member of his father's firm,

NATHAN STRAUS

engaged in the import of pottery and glassware. From 1888 to 1914 he was a partner in R. H. Macy & Co. and from 1892 to 1914 a partner in Abraham & Straus, two of the largest New York City department stores. From 1889 to 1893 he was park commissioner of New York City; in 1898 president of the Board of Health, New York City; in 1911 United States delegate to the International Congress for the Protection of Infants at Berlin, and in 1912 to the Tuberculosis Congress at Rome. After his retirement from active business in 1914, he devoted his time exclusively to the many charitable enterprises in which he had been interested for many years. The charity with which his name is especially associated, was the laboratory and distribution system for pasteurized milk to the poor of New York City, resulting in the saving of many thousands of infants annually. After carrying on this work for many years at his own expense he turned the entire plant over to the City of New York as a gift. He also installed similar systems in many other cities of the United States and abroad. His gifts for other charitable purposes were large. Amongst them should be mentioned the installation and maintenance of depots for the distribution of coal to the poor in New York City, the establishment in 1912 of soup kitchens in Jerusalem, the establishment of a health bureau in Palestine, etc. Besides making many addresses on the pasteurization of milk and on other public topics, he wrote "Disease in Milk—the Remedy, Pasteurization" (1917).

STRAUS, OSCAR SOLOMON, an American diplomatist; born in Ottenberg, Rhenish Bavaria, Dec. 25, 1850; came to the United States in 1854 and was graduated at Columbia University in 1871. Subsequently he entered mercantile life. In 1887 he was appointed United States minister to Turkey. He was president of the New York Board of Trade and Transportation; a member of several historical and sociological societies, and the author of a number of books dealing with religion and history. In 1898 he was again appointed minister to Turkey, which office he held till 1900; and on Jan. 14, 1902, President Roosevelt appointed him a permanent member of the Committee of Arbitration at The Hague, to succeed the late ex-president Benjamin Harrison. In 1906 he was appointed Secretary of Commerce and Labor in the Roosevelt cabinet; ambassador to Turkey 1909-1910 and Progressive candidate for governor of New York; arbitrator in the dispute between engineers and managers of Eastern railroads in 1914; chairman of the New York Public Service Commission in 1915; author of "The United States Doctrine of Citizenship." Died May 3, 1926.

STRAUSS, ALBERT, an American banker and public official, born in New York City in 1864. He was educated

at New York City College and from
1882 to 1918 was a member of the banking firm of J. & W. Seligman & Company.
He was also a director of several banks
and industrial corporations. During the
World War he acted in an advisory
capacity on international affairs to the
United States Treasury. In September,
1919, he was appointed a member of the
Federal Reserve Board for the term ex-
piring October, 1928, and was designated as vice-governor of the Federal
Reserve banks. He resigned in March,
1920.

STRAUSS, JOHANN, an Austrian
musician; born in Vienna, Oct. 25, 1825;
began the composition of waltzes at the
age of six, and before he was 18 organized and conducted an orchestra and
captivated the Vienna public with waltzes
and polkas of his own composition. After
composing dance music for many years,
he undertook an operetta, "Indigo," which
was produced in 1871, and met with instantaneous success. Subsequently he
produced "The Forty Thieves," "Cagli-
ostro," "A Night in Venice," "The Gipsy
Baron" (operettas) and numerous waltzes,
the best known being "The Beautiful
Blue Danube." He died in Vienna, June
3, 1899.

STRAUSS, RICHARD, German musical composer; born in 1864 at Munich,
where he studied under E. W. Meyer,
and later became conductor of the Royal
Orchestra. He began composing as a
boy, and early attained rank as a creator of music of high tonal and dramatic
quality, written with thorough understanding of the methods of Wagner. His
orchestral pieces include the tone poems
"Tod und Verklärung," "Tyll Eulen-
spiegel," "Zarathustra," and "Helden-
leben," and his operas "Feuersnot,"
"Salome," "Elektra," and "Rosenkava-
lier." Three of his operas and all his
best known orchestral works were presented at various times in the United
States. By many he has been ranked
as the foremost German composer of the
early 20th century.

**STRAVINSKY, IGOR FEDORO-
VITCH,** a Russian composer, born at
Oranienbaum in 1882. He began the
study of the piano at an early age,
and first attracted attention in 1908 with
his "Scherzo Symphonique." which was
at once proclaimed a striking example
of the new school of music. This was
followed by other pieces with rapid succession. He came to be regarded as the
leader of Futurist music. His works
include a symphonic fantasy, ballets, and
an opera.

STRAW. Apart from the importance
of the straw of various cereal plants as
a feeding and bedding material in agriculture, such substances also possess no
inconsiderable value for packing merchandise, for thatching, for making mattresses, and for door mats. Straw is
also a paper-making material of some
importance, and split, flattened, and colored it is employed for making fancy
articles. But it is in the form of plaits
that straw finds its most outstanding
industrial application, these being used
to an enormous extent for making hats
and bonnets, and for small baskets, etc.
Wheaten straw is the principal material
used in the plait trade, the present great
centers of which are Bedfordshire in
England, Tuscany in Italy, and Canton
in China. At first the plait was what
is called whole straw; that is, straw was
cut into suitable lengths without knots,
and merely pressed flat during the operation of plaiting; and so continued till
the reign of George I., when it was in
great demand for ladies' hats, and some
plait was made of split straw. Since
that time split straw has been chiefly
used.

The English straw used in plaiting is
obtained principally from the varieties
of wheat known as the White Chittin
and the Red Lammas, which succeed
best on the light rich soils of Bedfordshire and the neighboring counties. The
finest and most costly plaits anywhere
made—the Tuscan and Leghorn plaits—
are made in Tuscan villages around Florence, and are not split. The straw there
used—very fine in the pipe and bright
in color—is produced from a variety of
wheat thickly sown and grown in a light
thin soil. Panama hats are not made
of straw, but of the leaves of a variety
of palm (*Carludovica palmata*). An enormous amount of straw plait, of a common but useful quality, has been sent
into the European market from China.
The exports of straw manufactures from
the United States in the fiscal year ending June, 1901, were valued at $412,668;
imports at $335,669.

STRAW BAIL, worthless security furnished by an offender against the law
for his appearance for trial, the bonds
given being fraudulent statements of
property owned by the person offering it.

STRAWBERRY, a well-known fruit
and plant of the genus *Fragaria*, natural
order *Rosaceæ*. It is remarkable for the
manner in which the receptacle, commonly called the fruit, increases and becomes succulent; but the true fruit is
the small seeds or achenes on the surface
of the receptacle. The species are per-

ennial plants throwing out runners which take root and produce new plants; they are natives of temperate and cold climates in Europe, America, and Asia. The following species afford the varieties of cultivated strawberries: (1) Wood strawberry (*F. vesca*), found wild 'in the woods and on hillsides throughout Europe, and now cultivated in gardens, as the red, the white, the American, and Danish Alpine strawberries. (2) The Alpine strawberry (*F. collina*), a native of Switzerland and Germany. The varieties of strawberries called green are the produce of this species. (3) Hautbois strawberry (*F. elatior*), a native of North America. (4) Virginian strawberry (*F. virginiana* or *caroliniana*), a native of Virginia. To this species belongs a great list of sorts cultivated in gardens, and known by the name of scarlet and black strawberries. (5) Large-flowered strawberry (*F. grandiflora*) is supposed to be a native of Surinam, and to have furnished our gardens with the sorts called pine strawberries. (6) Chile strawberry (*F. chilensis*), a native of Chile and Peru, and the parent of a number of mostly inferior strawberries. The strawberry is propagated by seeds, by division of the plant, and by runners. Most of the strawberry plants in the United States are grown by runners.

STREATOR, a city in Lasalle co., Ill.; on the Vermillion river, and on the Burlington Route, the Chicago and Alton, the Wabash, the New York Central, the Chicago, Ottawa and Peoria, and the Atchison, Topeka, and Santa Fé railroads; 93 miles S. W. of Chicago. It is the trade center of a large agricultural and coal district. There are also valuable clay deposits in the city. Here are a high school, public library, park, waterworks, street railroad and electric light plants, several National banks, and a number of daily and weekly newspapers. The city has extensive glass works, foundries, machine shops, flour mills, planing mills, brick works, etc. Pop. (1910) 14,253; (1920) 14,779.

STREET, JULIAN (LEONARD), an American writer, born at Chicago, Ill., in 1879. He was educated in the public schools of Chicago and at Ridley College, St. Catharines, Ontario, Canada. From 1899 to 1901 he was on the reportorial and editorial staff of the New York "Mail and Express." Besides contributing articles and stories to many magazines he wrote: "My Enemy the Motor" (1908); "The Need of Change" (1909); "Paris à la Carte" (1911); "Ship-Bored" (1911); "The Goldfish" (1912); "Welcome to Our City" (1913); "Abroad at Home" (1914); "The Most Interesting American" (1915); "American Adventures" (1917); "After Thirty" (1919).

STREET RAILWAYS, an institution of American origin, though first suggested by the tramways used for carrying coal in the British collieries. Interest in street railways first developed in 1829, when the agitation for steam railways was going on in this country. Finally action was taken, in 1832, and a company was organized in New York City, which began laying a street railway along the Bowery and Fourth Avenue, extending from the Battery to Harlem, which was then the upper limits of the city. The line began to operate in the following year. The cars were built like the stage coaches of those days; they were, in fact, nothing more than stage coaches running on flat iron rails laid on blocks of granite. This venture proved a financial failure, yet four years later, in 1836, another street railway company was formed in Boston and the second street railway was soon after in operation in that city. It was not till over twenty years later that street railways were tried out in England, through the influence of George Francis Train.

Between 1860 and 1880 there was a rapid development of street railways in American cities, and practically every community provided itself with one. Hitherto horses and mules had been the sole means of motive power. Experiments were made with small steam locomotives, but the smoke and soot they created made it impossible to use them within city limits, while their noise also made them objectionable.

In 1873 the first cable car system was put into operation in San Francisco. An underground cable, running along a conduit with an open slot in the top, down which the grip of the car extended from the street above, drew the car along at an even rate, up hill and down, regardless of grade. Huge spools driven by steam wound and unwound the cable in a central power house. The cable system was especially suited to San Francisco, many of whose chief streets were extremely steep, and the cable car became a universal institution in that city. Other cities also began adopting it, including New York. But the cost of laying a cable system was over $100,-000 a mile, and considerable capital was required to establish and operate it. The search for another means of locomotion still continued.

The names of Edison, Field and Thompson will always be associated with the development of the electric railway in this country. It was their inventions and experiments which were to make street railways as universal as they are in American cities to-day. The first electrically driven tramway was exhibited at the Chicago Industrial Exposition, in 1882, but it was not till six years later, in 1888, that the first electric railway system was put into operation, in Richmond, Va., where a line twelve miles in length was laid by Frank J. Sprague, the "father of American street railways." The enterprise in Richmond proved both mechanically and financially successful, and henceforward electricity became more and more the universal motive power for American street railways. Ninety-nine and one-half per cent. of street railways in this country are operated by electricity.

Another side development of street railways in this country, such as was the cable-car, has been the elevated railway. As far back as 1860 the difficulty of operating a tram service along the congested thoroughfares of New York City was brought up for solution. Two alternatives only presented themselves: the tracks must either be laid along an underground tunnel, or raised above the streets on a superstructure. Both schemes were discussed, but the subway proposition seemed too expensive to justify itself. In 1866 construction was begun on the first elevated railway in New York City, running from the Battery to Thirtieth Street, along Greenwich Street and Ninth Avenue. For a while the cable system was used as motive power, but very soon after steam locomotives were installed. Steam remained the motive power until 1902.

The enterprise proved a commercial failure, but elevated railways were obviously a solution to the problem of congested streets in big cities. Boston, Chicago and a number of other large cities followed the example of New York and reared elevated superstructures along their streets.

In 1920 there remained only nine local street railway systems in American cities which operated their lines by means of animal power. There was, in the beginning of the year, over 50,000 miles of street railway tracks, carrying on an average of 150,000 passengers per mile each year. Annually the number of passengers carried amounted to fifteen billions.

During recent years there has been a tendency in the larger cities away from private to municipal ownership in the operation of street railways. In 1911 Seattle took over 203 miles of street railway track, at a cost of $15,000,000.

In 1920 San Francisco owned 64 miles of track and 195 passenger cars, as compared to 286 miles of track and 700 cars operated under private management.

Whether electric street railways, operated along permanently laid tracks, will develop in the future as they have in the past few years, seems to depend in no small measure on the extent of the National sources of supply of gasoline. In many cities, and especially in the suburban districts, gasoline driven motors buses are competing with the street railways so successfully that in many instances the electric lines have been abandoned. In New York City several old street railways have been abandoned in the downtown section of the city and bus lines established to take their places.

STREHLENAU, NICOLAUS NIEMBSCH VON, a German poet, born in 1802.

STRENGTH OF MATERIALS, in mechanics, an important part of the theory of structures, and includes the consideration of all questions relating to the straining of solids. A solid is said to suffer strain when it is in any way altered in volume or figure, and to effect such an alteration external force must be applied. If the strain is not carried so far as to cause disintegration of the solid — that is, if no fracture results — the force or resultant of the forces which produce the strain must be balanced by an internal force conditioned by the molecular structure of the solid. This internal force called into existence by the strain is the one aspect of the stress, of which the original force producing the strain is the other. To every strain, then, there corresponds a stress, which is regarded as the resultant of the stresses which act between the elementary portions into which the solid may be supposed to be divided. When the strain is proportional to the stress — in other words, when Hooke's law holds — the body strained is said to be perfectly elastic; and the elasticity of every solid, even for such cases as moistened clay, is sensibly perfect when the strain does not exceed a certain limit. For every solid, however, there are limits of strain which, if exceeded, give to the body a set or permanent alteration of volume or figure. Hodgkinson has proved that these limits depend on the duration of the strain, so that in all probability any strain if sufficiently long-continued would give a set to any body.

STREPSIPTERA, a small and very peculiar and anomalous order of insects. The females are wingless, and live as parasites in the abdomen of bees, wasps, and other hymenopterous insects. The males have the front pair of wings in the form of twisted filaments, the posterior pair are fan-shaped and membranous. The jaws are rudimentary.

STRESEMANN, GUSTAV, born, Berlin, 1878. Chancellor of Germany following the fall of Cuno in August, 1923. He held office for only a few months and was succeeded in October by Chancellor Marx. Representing the German People's Party, he became minister of foreign affairs Jan. 15, 1925, in the Luther cabinet. He and Luther negotiated for Germany at Locarno in October, 1925, the SECURITY PACT.

STRESS, a convenient term used to express the mutual action between any two portions of matter. Thus the pressure between a table and a book resting on it is of the nature of a stress, which has two aspects, according as we fix our attention on the table or the book. With reference to the former the pressure is downward, with reference to the latter upward, and these two forces, which according to Newton's third law are equal and opposite, form when regarded as a whole the stress. Similarly the attraction of the earth for the sun and the attraction of the sun for the earth are opposite aspects of the same stress, and the same can be said of all forces which obey Newton's third law, i. e., of all known forces which invariably exist in pairs. The so-called centrifugal force is merely the one aspect of the stress whose other aspect is the force which acts upon the body normally to the path. See STRAIN: STRENGTH OF MATERIALS.

STRIATED ROCKS, or STRIATED BOWLDERS, rocks or bowlders with striæ along their surface, the result of the passage over them of masses of ice with projecting stones imbedded in the lower part. Such striated rocks exist along the sides and at the foot of mountain ranges wherever glaciers have descended. They are found also in the Arctic and temperate zones wherever ice has passed from the N. during the glacial period.

STRICKLAND, AGNES, an English historian; born in Reydon Hall, Suffolk, England, Aug. 19, 1806. Her first work, aided by her sister Susannah, was a volume of "Patriotic Songs," followed by "Worcester Field," a historical poem. She wrote: "Queen Victoria from Her Birth to Her Bridal" (1840); "Historic Scenes and Poetic Fancies" (1850); "Lives of the Bachelor Kings of Eng-

land" (1861); "Lives of the Seven Bishops" (1866); "Lives of the Tudor Princesses" (1868). Her best works are "Lives of the Queens of England" (12 vols. 1840-1848), and "Lives of the Queens of Scotland" (8 vols. 1850-1859). She died in Reydon Hall July 8, 1874.

STRICTURE, a term employed in surgery to denote an unnatural contraction, either congenital or acquired, of a mucous canal, such as the urethra, œsophagus, or intestine. When, however, the affected part is not mentioned, and a person is stated to suffer from stricture, it is always the urethral canal that is referred to. Contraction of this canal may be either permanent or transitory; the former is due to a thickening of the walls of the urethra in consequence of organic deposits and is hence termed organic stricture; while the latter may be due either to local inflammation or congestion or to abnormal muscular action; the first of these varieties may be termed inflammatory or congestive stricture, and the second spasmodic stricture. The last named form seldom exists except as a complication of the other kinds of stricture. There are two principal causes of organic stricture—the first being inflammation of the canal, and the second injury by violence. Inflammation is by far the most common cause, and gonorrhœa is the common agent by which it is excited. Not unfrequently stimulating injections thrown into the urethra with the view of checking the gonorrhœal discharge excite an inflammatory action which gives rise to stricture.

The earlier symtoms of stricture are a slight urethral discharge and pain in the canal behind the seat of the stricture at the time of micturition. The stream of urine does not pass in its ordinary form, but is flattened or twisted; and as the disease advances it becomes smaller, and ultimately the fluid may only be discharged in drops. The treatment of organic stricture is too purely surgical to be discussed in these pages.

Spasmodic stricture usually occurs as a complication of organic stricture or of inflammation of the mucous membrane, but may arise from an acrid condition of the urine, from the administration of cantharides, turpentine, etc., and from the voluntary retention of urine for too long a time. The treatment consists in the removal of the causes as far as possible and the hot bath.

STRIKES AND LOCKOUTS. The strike is a feature of industrial life entirely unknown before the development of the factory system of production, which in turn was made possible by the invention of the steam engine and steam-driven machinery. Previously manufacturing had been in the hands of individual artisans, each independent of the other, each producing only for his immediate neighborhood.

The use of machinery made large scale manufacturing possible. It necessitated, however, the assembling of large bodies of workers under one roof, where the machines were installed. Of still more significance, it made the workers dependent on the owners of the machines for their means of livelihood. Industry was becoming complicated. But out of the new arrangement the master employer rose triumphant, supreme in power.

That the masters, or manufacturers, realized their power became evident when they gradually began to cut wages and lengthen working hours, and to displace adult males with women and children. Before this economic oppression the workers stood helpless. No legislation had as yet been passed for their protection, for the conditions were new. There remained only one means of defense, and that was organization. Through united action they might possess enough strength to bring the employers to terms. Their natural weapon of offense and defense would be unanimous action in refusing to work which, if widespread enough, would absolutely paralyze the industry. Under such conditions was the strike originated.

That the employers feared this weapon in the hands of their working people was obvious from the fact that they had quickly used their powerful influence in having legislation passed in the British Parliament making it illegal for workingmen to combine in trade organization. This Act of Parliament compelled the workers' organizations to assume a secret character, and sabotage (q. v.) rather than the strike, became their weapon. To this they in many cases added personal violence against employers and factory foremen and other forms of terrorism.

Fortunately the injustice of the law forbidding organization among workingmen while allowing it among employers, was recognized by men of the influential classes, and in 1824 the law was repealed. In France, where a similar law had been enacted, it was not repealed until 1864.

From the date of the repeal of these laws begins the organized labor movement, whose chief weapon, potentially, if not actually, has always been the strike.

In the United States no laws were ever enacted restricting the rights of the workers to organize, but as far back as the last decade of the 18th century strikes took place among the bakers and shoemakers of New York City and Philadelphia, in which the employers attempted to indict the leaders under the conspiracy laws; without success, however.

Strikes, however, were of comparatively rare occurrence in the United States in the early part of last century before the Civil War. The American workingman was a strong individualist, and he had many vocations into which he might turn if the conditions in one trade did not suit him. There was a scarcity of labor and a great many fields of activity.

The first notable strike in this country was the railway strike of 1877, which began on the Baltimore and Ohio railway, and spread throughout the East. A considerable amount of violence attended it and finally the Federal troops were called out. In 1883 there was a widespread strike of telegraph operators. One of the most memorable strikes of the early period was that of the steel workers at the Carnegie steel mills in Homestead, Pa., in 1892, during which scenes resembling those of the worst days of the French Revolution were enacted. The employers had called into the field large numbers of private detectives, and between them and the strikers armed conflicts took place which at times assumed the dimensions of pitched battles. In 1894 the American Railway Union, the president of which was Eugene V. Debs, the present Socialist leader, called a general strike of railway employees in sympathy with the employees of the Pullman Company. The strikers sought to prevent the railway companies from using the cars of the Pullman Company, and refused to work trains which often carried the United States mail. Grover Cleveland, at that time President, made this the pretext for calling out the Federal troops, and the strike was thus forcibly suppressed, against the protests of the governors of Illinois and several other states.

An illustration of a strike in which the workers triumphed was that of 1906, when the printers of the whole country, through the International Typographical Union, demanded higher wages and shorter hours. The employers contested this effort bitterly, and it was three years before peace again prevailed in the industry, but the printers nevertheless achieved their purpose. The result is that the printers are to-day one of the most solidly organized crafts in the country, and are probably the best paid hand workers in the country. During the fall of 1920, when the high war prices were dropping almost to pre-war levels, and the high cost of living was no longer a pretext for demands for higher wages, the printers in New York City were able to obtain an eleven per cent. raise in wages, already averaging higher than the incomes of most of the professional classes.

After the signing of the armistice, which terminated the World War, in 1918, a world-wide period of labor unrest and disorder set in, accompanied by strikes of wide dimensions. In February, 1919, 45,000 union men went out on a sympathetic strike in Seattle, to aid 25,000 shipyard workers, who had walked out for higher wages a month previously. Within a few days the strike had spread to almost all the other crafts in the city and for over a week the theaters were closed, the street railways ceased running and the majority of the stores were closed. This was the nearest approach to a general strike which had as yet taken place in the United States. So completely was the situation in the hands of the strikers that representatives of hospitals and other charitable institutions waited on the strike committee at union headquarters to beg the right of being supplied with milk for their patients. It was said that municipal authority had been shifted from the City Hall to labor headquarters. This became so intolerable to the general public that a Vigilance Committee was formed, which took the situation in hand, and with public support behind it, managed to persuade a majority of the strikers to return to their jobs, and the strike was broken.

Of a peculiar nature was the police strike which occurred in Boston, in September, 1919, when the police force of the city went out on strike to enforce their demand that they be recognized as a labor organization, and be granted the right to join the American Federation of Labor. Here again public opinion turned strongly against the strikers and caused it to be lost. Eventually all the strikers attempted to return to their jobs, but new men had been employed and a completely new police force was organized. In this case public sentiment had been turned against the striking policemen by the fact that they permitted the criminal elements to carry on a mad orgy of looting and robbery, without offering at least to maintain order.

Ever since the Homestead strike in Pennsylvania, the steel workers in the steel mills had not been organized. In 1919 representatives of the American Federation of Labor determined to attempt to create a solid organization of these workers, whose working conditions were reputed to be very bad, in that they worked long hours and received comparatively poor pay. In September the union leaders requested an interview with Judge Gary, president of the United States Steel Corporation, which employed the large majority of the steel workers. Their object was to discuss with him the question of a steel workers' labor union. Judge Gary refused to meet the leaders, contending that they were not representatives of the men working in his mills. As a result a strike was called, and 268,000 men went out on strike. The United States Senate sent a committee into the field of disturbance to investigate, which reported that the strikers were anxious to negotiate with a view to settling the trouble by means of arbitration. Judge Gary, however, refused to consider negotiations, contending that a moral principle could not be compromised. The strike, therefore, continued. A peculiar feature of the methods employed by the strike committee was the establishment of commissary stations, where the strikers and their families were supplied with food from the co-operative stores, this being the first time that these institutions had become a factor in labor troubles in this country, as they had been for many years back in European countries. The strike continued on into the early part of 1920, but was finally called off, the men returning to their work unconditionally. In the fall of 1920 what remained of the strike fund was taken over by representatives of the American Federation of Labor and efforts were renewed to organize the steel workers.

That strikes are not only the weapons of hand workers was demonstrated in the strike of the actors in the early part of 1919. Rallying about the American Actors Equity Association, the actors demanded a revision of the form of contract which the theatrical managers' association compelled members of their companies to sign. Higher wages and pay for rehearsals were involved. At the call of the strike leaders high priced stars abandoned their plays an hour before the curtain went up and practically every theater in New York City was closed the first night. Later the strike spread to Boston and Chicago. Finally the managers agreed to compromise; the Equity contract was adopted and the result was a complete triumph for the actors.

Of lockouts there have been comparatively few instances in American industrial life. Employers, however, have been more active in a slightly different form of the lockout, known as the blacklist. Men known to be members of labor organizations are listed and these lists are circulated among all the employers of a certain industry. Thus the blacklisted men find themselves unable to obtain employment, wherever they may present themselves.

STRINDBERG, AUGUST, a Swedish author; born in Stockholm Jan. 22, 1849; became successively schoolmaster, physician, telegraph employee, civil servant, painter, private tutor, and librarian of the State. The first book of his that made its mark was "The Red Room" (1879), a bitter satire on conventional (Swedish) society. This made its author enemies, and to their attacks he replied in another stinging satire, "The New Kingdom" (1882); but after its publication he had to go into voluntary banishment, and lived abroad. Two years later he published a collection of short stories ("Married Life"), in which he describes all sorts and conditions of nuptial alliances with cynical frankness. Accused of outraging Christianity in this book, Strindberg repaired to Stockholm, stood his trial, and after making an eloquent defense, was acquitted. His next important work was a plea for the socialistic conception of society in "Utopias in the Real World" (1885). Two books descriptive of the life and manners of the inhabitants of the Stockholm skerries —"The People of Hemsö" (1887) and "Life of the Skerry Men" (1888)—are among the best things he has written; though the plays "The Father" (1887) and "Miss Julia" are powerful and moving dramas. His works of fiction include "Tschandala" (1889), "On the Open Sea" (1890), "In the Offing" (1891), "By the Sea" (1892), "Inferno" (1897), "Alone" (1907), etc. Besides the books mentioned, Strindberg produced—for he was a most prolific worker—a host of others, and in nearly all departments of literature. He died May 14, 1912.

STRINGER, ARTHUR (JOHN ARBUTHNOTT), a Canadian-American author, born at London, Ontario, in 1874. He was educated at Toronto University and the University of Oxford. From 1898 to 1901 he was an editorial writer for the American Press Association and from 1903 to 1904 literary editor of "Success." Besides contributing many short stories to magazines he wrote: "Watchers of Twilight" (1894); "Pauline and Other Poems" (1895); "Epigrams" (1896); "A Study in King Lear" (1897); "The Loom of Destiny" (1898); "The Silver Poppy" (1899); "Lonely O'Malley" (1901); "Hephæstus and Other Poems" (1902); "The Wire Tappers" (1906); "Phantom Wires" (1907); "The Occasional Offender" (1907); "The Woman in the Rain" (1907); "Under Groove" (1909); "Irish Poems" (1911); "Open Water" (1912); "Gun Runner" (1912); "Shadow" (1913); "Prairie Wife" (1915); "Hand of Peril" (1916); "Door of Dread" (1917); "House of Intrigue" (1918); "Man Who Couldn't Sleep" (1919); "Prairie Mother" (1920).

STROBEL, EDWARD HENRY, an American educator; born in Charleston, S. C., Dec. 7, 1855; was graduated at Harvard University in 1877 and at its Law Department in 1882; and was admitted to the bar in 1883. He was secretary of the United States legation in Madrid, Spain, in 1885-1890; a special United States agent to Morocco in 1888 and 1889; and United States minister to Chile in 1894-1897. He was counsel for the latter country before the United States and Chilean Claims Commission in 1899. His publications include: "The Spanish Revolution" (1898); "Specie Payment in Chile" (1896); etc. He died Jan. 15, 1908.

STROBILUS, in botany, a catkin the carpels of which are scale-like, spread open, and bear naked seeds, as in the fruit of the pine; a cone.

STROMBOLI, one of the Lipari Islands; off the N. coast of Sicily; 12 miles in circuit. Its cone, 3,022 feet high, is one of the few volcanoes that are constantly active. At regular intervals showers of stones are ejected, and these almost all fall again within the crater. The ancients regarded Stromboli as the seat of Æolus, and in the Middle Ages it was held to be the entrance to purgatory. The island yields, besides sulphur and pumice-stone, cotton, fruits, and wine.

STRONG, BENJAMIN, an American banker and public official, born at Fishkill-on-Hudson, N. Y., in 1872. He was educated in the public schools of Montclair, N. J., after which he entered the banking business in New York City, becoming later secretary of the Atlantic Trust Co. and of the Metropolitan Trust Co. and president of the Bankers Trust Co. In 1914 he was appointed governor of the Federal Reserve Bank, New York City. He was a member of various scientific, economic, and commercial associations.

STRONG, FRANK, an American educator, born at Venice, N. Y., in 1859. He was educated at Yale University and received honorary degrees from Baker University, Kansas State Agricultural College, and the University of Oregon.

From 1886 to 1888 he practiced law at Kansas City, Mo.; from 1888 to 1892 he was principal of St. Joseph (Mo.) High School; from 1892 to 1895 superintendent of schools at Lincoln, Neb.; from 1897 to 1899 lecturer on history at Yale University; from 1899 to 1902 president of the University of Oregon; and beginning with August, 1902, chancellor of the University of Kansas. He was a member and officer of various educational associations and during the World War served on the Kansas State Council of Defense, on the executive committee of the Kansas Food Administration and on the War Council of the National Association of State Universities. Besides contributing to magazines he wrote "The Life of Benjamin Franklin" and "Government of the American People" (1901).

STRONG, JOSIAH, an American clergyman; born in Naperville, Ill., Jan. 19, 1847; settled with his parents in Hudson, O., in 1852; was graduated at the Western Reserve College in 1869 and received a theological training at Lane Theological Seminary; was ordained in the Congregational Church, and held pastorates in Wyoming and Ohio; was secretary of the Evangelical Alliance for the United States in 1886-1898. In the latter year he was made president of the League for Social Service. His publications include: "Our Country" (1885); "The New Era" (1893); "The Twentieth Century City" (1898); "Religious Movements for Social Betterment" (1900); "Expansion" (1900); "The Challenge of the City" (1907); "My Religion and Everyday Life' (1913); "Our World: and the New World Life" (1915). He died in 1916.

STRONG, RICHARD PEARSON, an American scientist, born at Fortress Monroe, Va., in 1872. He was educated at Yale University and in 1897 received the degree of M.D. from Johns Hopkins University. He also studied at the University of Berlin, and received honorary degrees from Yale and Harvard. After having served as resident house physician at Johns Hopkins Hospital, he was appointed a first lieutenant and assistant surgeon, U. S. A., in July, 1898, and, in the following year, president of the board for investigating tropical diseases in the Philippine Islands. He established and directed the work of the Army Pathological Laboratory and from 1901 to 1913 was director of the government biological laboratory at Manila. From 1907 to 1913 he was professor of tropical medicine at the University of the Philippine Islands, and in 1913 became professor of tropical medicine at Harvard

University. In 1915 he served as medical director of the International and American Red Cross Sanitary Commission to Serbia. During the World War he served in the Medical Reserve Corps, first with the British and French armies and later at A. E. F. Headquarters, being promoted eventually colonel, M. R. C. He was a member of the Headquarters Investigating Committee and of the Inter-Allied Sanitary Commission in charge of the Division of Infectious Diseases. From December, 1918, to April, 1919, he was the director of the Department of Medical Research, American Red Cross, and in August, 1919, became general medical director of the League of Red Cross Societies. He was decorated with the D. S. M. and also received British, French, Chinese and Serbian decorations. He was a delegate to many international congresses and a member and officer of many domestic and foreign medical and scientific societies.

STUART, HENRY CARTER, an American public official, born at Wytheville, Va., in 1855. He was educated at Emory and Henry College and at the University of Virginia. In 1875 he entered business. After serving as a delegate to several Democratic National Conventions, he was from 1903 to 1908 corporation commissioner, and from 1914 to 1918 Governor of Virginia. During the World War he served as chairman of the National Agricultural Advisory Committee. In 1918 he was appointed by President Wilson a member of the commission investigating the packing industry. He also was a member of the Price Fixing Committee of the War Industries Board and in December, 1919, served as a member of the President's Industrial Conference.

STUBBS, WALTER ROSCOE, an American public official, born in Richmond, Ind., in 1858. He studied at the University of Kansas and began his business career as a railroad contractor. Later he became the owner and operator of large cattle ranches in Kansas, Texas, New Mexico, and Colorado. From 1903 to 1907 he was a member of the Kansas House of Representatives, from 1904 to 1908 chairman of the Republican State Committee of Kansas, and from 1909 to 1913 (2 terms) Governor of Kansas. In 1917 he was appointed a member of the United States Live Stock Industry Committee.

STRONG, WILLIAM, a Scotch painter, born at Dumbarton in 1859. He was educated at Dumbarton Academy, Slade School, and University College, London, and has studied and worked in London since 1875. He received the Silver Medal for Etching in the Paris International Exhibition in 1889, and the First Class Gold Medal for Painting in the Dresden International Exhibition in 1897. In 1906 he became an associate in the Royal Academy; and an LL.D., Glasgow, in 1909. He has been president of the International Society of Sculptors, Painters and Gravers since 1918. He wrote "The Earth Fiend," a ballad; and "Death and the Ploughman's Wife."

STRONGYLUS, a genus of nematoid worms belonging to the family *Strongylidæ,* of which this genus is the type. The *S. bronchialis* is a species infesting the bronchial tubes of man, the female attaining the length of an inch. The family characters of this group are a round thread-like body (hence the name), a round or oval mouth, and two terminal spicules provided for the male. The *S. bronchialis* is not of frequent occurrence as a human parasite. It was first discovered in 1790. Allied species (*S. paradoxus*) occur in the lungs of the pig, and (*S. micrurus*) in those of the calf. The *S. gigas* (otherwise known as *Eustrongylus gigas*) is notable as being the largest nematoid parasite found in man or other animals. It attains a length of over 3 feet (female), the male measuring 1 foot. Rare in man, *S. gigas* is found in almost all Carnivora.

STRONSAY, one of the Orkney Islands, 12 miles N. E. of Kirkwall; about 7 miles long and 4½ miles broad. It is of moderate elevation, and its coasts are deeply indented. The soil is mostly good, and is now well cultivated.

STRONTIUM (Sr = 87.5), one of the metals of the alkaline earths, occupying an intermediate position as regards many of its properties to calcium and barium, the other members of the group. It is less abundant in nature than barium, and occurs as a constituent in the minerals strontianite and celestine, which are respectively the carbonate ($SrCO_3$) and sulphate ($SrSO_4$). In the metallic state it is usually white, heavy, oxidizable in air, and decomposing water at ordinary temperatures. The most important compound is strontia (SrO), from which Davy first obtained the metal in 1808 by electrolysis. It resembles baryta, forming a white soluble hydrate (SrO,H_2O), which is the compound formed when the metal decomposes water. Strontia is best prepared by decomposition of the nitrate by heat; while the nitrate ($Sr(NO_3)_2$) and chloride ($SrCl_2$) are easily obtained by treating the mineral carbonate with nitric and hydrochloric acid respectively. It also forms a dioxide (SrO_2), which is prepared as the corresponding barium compound is by exposing the monoxide to a strongly-heated current of oxygen. Strontium and its compounds burn with a very characteristic crimson flame, which gives a well-marked line or banded spectrum.

STROPHANTHUS, a genus of plants belonging to the natural order *Apocynaceæ,* and natives of tropical Africa and Asia. The flowers are in terminal heads; the corolla is funnel-shaped, with its limb divided into five long cord-like segments; the fruit is a double follicle. Each follicle contains a large number of seeds having beautiful comose awns. There are several species, but the best known is the *S. hispidus,* variety *Kombé,* the seeds of which are now largely used in medicine. This species is widely distributed in tropical Africa, and climbs up the highest trees, hanging from one to the other in festoons. An extract of the seeds is used as an arrow poison (Kombé or inee) in districts widely apart, as at Kombé, in the Manganja country, in the Zambesi district, in the Somali country, in the Gaboon district, in Guinea, and in Senegambia.

In the British "Pharmacopœia" strophanthus is defined as the mature ripe seeds of *S. hispidus,* variety *Kombé,* freed from the awns. The seeds contain an active principle, *strophanthin,* which is extremely poisonous, the medicinal dose of it being $\frac{1}{120}$ to $\frac{1}{60}$ grain. Its action and uses are very similar to those of digitalis.

STROPHE, in the Greek drama, the turning of the chorus from the right to the left of the orchestra, the return being the antistrophe; the part of a choral ode sung during the act of so turning; hence, in ancient lyric poetry, a term for the former of two corresponding stanzas, the latter being the antistrophe. The term is sometimes used in relation to modern poetry. In botany, the spirals formed in the development of leaves.

STROPHULUS, in pathology, the red-gum, or tooth-rash; an eruption of minute hard, slightly-red pimples, clustered and scattered, affecting infants or young children. The largest number of pimples are on the face and the neck. It arises from irritation of the stomach. The irritation is slight, and the disease not dangerous. Unimportant variations have led to the establishment of the species *S. intertinctus, S. confertus, S. candidus,* and *S. volaticus.*

STROZZI, the name of a wealthy and illustrious Florentine family. Palla, Filippo, and Piero were the three most renowned members of this princely house, between 1432 and 1537, and who were either exiled or lost their lives in the struggle for liberty against the power of the Medici family.

STRUENSEE, JOHANN FRIEDRICH, COUNT, a Danish statesman; born in Halle-on-the-Saale, Prussian Saxony, Aug. 5, 1737; studied medicine, and in 1768 was appointed physician to the King of Denmark. He soon became a favorite with both the king and queen, and effected the dismissal of all those who were obstacles to his own ambitious plans. In 1770 he advised the king (who was little better than an imbecile) to abolish the council of state, a measure which roused the indignation of the Danish nobility, since it threw all authority into the hands of the queen and the favorite. Struensee by various means gradually usurped the administration of all affairs in the name of the king, and caused himself to be created count. His arrogance now caused a conspiracy against him, and on Jan. 16, 1772, the queen, Struensee, and their partisans were seized. The favorite was brought before a special commission, was found guilty of criminal relations with the queen (on insufficient evidence), convicted, and executed on April 28, 1772.

STRUMA, a river which has its rise in the mountains of Western Bulgaria, flows S. through Macedonia, through Lake Tachyno, and empties into the Ægean Sea 50 miles E. of Salonika. It is identical with the Strymon of antiquity. During the two Balkan wars, in 1912-1913, and again during the World War, after the Bulgarians had joined the Central Empires, it was the scene of heavy fighting. Until September, 1918, it was largely within the Bulgarian lines, but after the final attack by the Allies at that time the Bulgarians were driven back and the Allied troops advanced up both banks of the river.

STRUMA PASS, a cleft in the mountain chain which formerly constituted the frontier between Turkish Macedonia and Bulgaria, through which runs the River Struma, and which constituted one of the gateways into Bulgaria by which the Allied troops advanced into Bulgaria during their successful offensive, in September, 1918.

STRUMNITZA, a town and fortress in Macedonia, held by the Bulgarians against the British contingent of the Allied armies in the Balkans, during the World War. It was at this point that the Allies invaded Bulgaria proper, on September 25, 1918, as part of the general advance, begun a week before, which terminated in the complete collapse of the Bulgarian resistance, and proved the beginning of the end of the war as a whole.

STRUT, a bar in a frame having equal and opposite forces applied to its ends, acting inward and producing upon it a state of compression. Specifically: (1) A diagonal timber which acts as a post or brace to support a principal rafter or purlin. Its lower end is stepped into a tie beam, or on a shoulder of a king or queen post. (2) A brace between joists.

STRUNSKY, SIMEON, an American journalist and writer; born at Vitebsk, Russia, in 1879. While still a boy he removed to the United States and graduated from Columbia University in 1900. In 1906 he became an editorial writer for the New York "Evening Post," and was also literary editor of that paper. His essays were published in several volumes, including "The Patient Observer" (1911); "Post - Impressions" (1914). Other books are: "Belshazzar Court" (1914); a novel, "Professor Latimer's Progress" (1918); and "Little Journeys to Paris" (1918).

STRUVE, FRIEDRICH GEORG WILHELM, a German astronomer; born in Altona, Holstein, April 15, 1793. His whole life was devoted to astronomy in the service of the Russian Government; from 1813 to 1820 observer and Professor Extraordinary of Astronomy in the University of Dorpat; from 1820 to 1838 Professor of Astronomy and director of the same observatory; and from 1839 to 1864 director of the new Imperial Observatory at Pulkova, near Petrograd. His great work in astronomy was the observation and publication of the great Dorpat catalogue of double-stars, generally known as the "Mensuræ Micrometricæ," and denoted by the letter Σ and the "Positiones Mediæ," or results of the meridian observations of the same stars, this catalogue being generally denoted by the letters Σ [PM]. These catalogues have served as the model for all similar work since. The rest of his life was given to the foundation and organization of the great observatory at Pulkova. He died Nov. 23, 1864.

STRY, or STRYI, a town of Austria, in Galicia; on a river of the same name;

was the scene of a great conflagration in April, 1886, which destroyed over 600 houses and most of the public buildings. The chief manufactures are leather goods and matches. Pop. 33,400.

STRYCHNINE, in chemistry, formula, $C_{21}H_{22}N_2O_2$, strychnia, a highly poisonous alkaloid, discovered in 1818 by Pelletier and Caventou in St. Ignatius' beans, and shortly afterward in *Nux vomica* seeds. It is obtained, together with brucine, by boiling *Nux vomica* seeds in dilute sulphuric acid till they become soft, crushing the seeds, and adding to the expressed liquid an excess of calcium hydrate, which throws down the two alkaloids. On washing with cold alcohol, brucine is dissolved, leaving strychnine in an impure state. When pure, it crystallizes in colorless, tetragonal prisms, having a very bitter, and somewhat metallic taste, is almost insoluble in water, absolute alcohol, and ether, but soluble in spirit of wine and chloroform. The symptoms are very marked, and comprise violent tetanic convulsions, laborious respiration, from the tightening of the chest muscles, spasmodic contraction of the heart, and rigidity of the spinal column. These are succeeded by a short calm, after which they are again repeated till death or progress toward recovery ensues, the time being about two hours after taking the poison.

STRYCHNOS, in botany, the typical genus of *Strychneæ*. Calyx, five-parted; corolla tubular, funnel-shaped, limb spreading; stamens five, inserted into the throat of the corolla; ovary two-celled; style one; fruit, a berry with a hard rind and a pulpy sarcocarp; seeds many. Natives of Asia, America, and Australia. *S. Nux Vomica*, the snake wood, strychnine tree, or nux vomica tree, is a moderate-sized evergreen, with dark gray bark and no spines; the leaves entire, strongly three to five nerved; the flowers small, greenish-white; the fruit round, like an orange in color, but smaller, with a brittle rind, a white, gelatinous pulp, and many seeds. It is found on hills and in forests in India and Burma. The seeds, which are about the size and shape of a 25-cent piece, constitute nux vomica and contain strychnine, and it is said, a brown dye. The wood is very bitter, especially the root, which has been given in intermittent fevers and as an antidote to the bites of venomous serpents. *S. potatorum*, a tree about 40 feet high, with only one seed, is the clearingnut tree of India; so called because the seeds render muddy water clear. They are used also in diseases of the eye. The fruit, which is like a black cherry, is eaten by the
I—10

natives; the wood is used for carts, agricultural implements, and building. *S. toxifera*, the Guiana poison plant, is a climber, with a stem covered with long, spreading, red hairs, and five-nerved acuminate leaves. It furnishes the chief ingredient of the poison called woorali, or oorali. *S. tieute*, from Java, has elliptical, acuminate, three-nerved, glabrous leaves, with simple tendrils opposite to them. It yields another deadly poison. *S. ligustrina* is said by Blume to furnish the genuine *Lignum colubrinum*. It is given in Java in paralysis of the lower extremities and as an anthelmintic. *S. pseudoquina*, a Brazilian tree about 12 feet high, has a corky bark (said to be equal to cinchona as a febrifuge), and short-stalked, ovate, quintuple-nerved leaves; all parts of it are intensely bitter except the fruit, which is eaten by children. The fruit of *S. colubrina*, a large Indian climbing shrub, is esteemed by the Telegus as an antidote to the bite of the cobra. The fruit of *S. innocua* is eaten in Egypt.

STRYKER, MELANCTHON WOOLSEY, an American educator; born in Vernon, N. Y., Jan. 7, 1851; was graduated at Hamilton College in 1872 and at the Auburn Theological Seminary in 1876. Subsequently he held pastorates in Auburn, N. Y.; Ithaca, N. Y.; Holyoke, Mass.; and Chicago, Ill.; and in 1892 became president of Hamilton College, serving until 1917. He was the author of numerous hymns and poems, including: "Song of Miriam"; "Lattermath"; "Letter of James"; "English Bible Versions and Origins" (1915); "Three Addresses on Lincoln" (1917).

STRYPA RIVER, a stream in Eastern Galicia, joining the Dniester near Stanislaw, along whose banks severe fighting took place between the Germans and Russians during the World War. During the summer of 1915 the German-Austrian armies had made a sweeping advance and compelled the whole Russian front to fall back. Toward the end of their retreat the Russians suddenly developed unexpected resistance along the Strypa, having been reinforced in this region. While the troops in other sectors of the Eastern front settled down into trench life as the winter months came on, the Russians along the Strypa continued their activities during the cold months, inflicting heavy and continuous losses on the Germans, and prepared the way for the general Russian offensive, which began the following summer.

STUART FAMILY, THE. This house derives it name from the important office of steward of the royal household of Scotland. The name is often written Stewart and occasionally Steuart. The form of Stuart was first assumed when Queen Mary went to France, and was adopted by all her descendants. The founder of the house seems to have been a Norman baron named ALAN, whose second son WALTER entered the service of David I. of Scotland, and became *dapifer* or steward of the royal household. Walter obtained large grants of land from David, and died in 1246. ALEXANDER, the fourth steward, had two sons: JAMES, who succeeded him in 1283, and JOHN, known in history as the Sir John Stewart of Bonkyl, who was killed at Falkirk (July 22, 1298). James was chosen one of the regents on the death of Alexander III., and died in the service of Bruce in 1309. His son, WALTER, the sixth steward, married Marjory, daughter of King Robert I., a union which secured to his family the crown of Scotland in the event of the extinction of the royal line. He died in 1326, and was succeeded by his son, ROBERT, the seventh steward, who, on the death of David II. without issue, succeeded to the crown as Robert II. in 1371.

Succeeding monarchs of this house, with dates of their accession, were: Robert III. (1390); James I. (1424); James II. (1437); James III. (1460); James IV. (1488); James V. (1513); Mary Stuart (1542); James VI. of Scotland (1568); and of England, James I. (1603); Charles I. (1625); Charles II. (1649); and James II. of England (1685).

Mary of Modena, second wife of James II. of England gave birth to James Edward Francis, Prince of Wales, commonly called the Old Pretender, or the Chevalier St. George. In 1715 an unsuccessful attempt was made by the Jacobites, or Stuart party, to set this prince on the throne of his ancestors by force of arms. He married a granddaughter of John Sobieski, King of Poland, by whom he had two sons, Charles Edward, the Young Pretender, and Henry Benedict Maria Clement, who became a cardinal in 1747. The last male representative of the branch of the Stuart line descended from Henrietta Maria, daughter of Charles I., was Francis V., ex-Duke of Modena, who died childless Nov. 20, 1875. Many of the noble families of Scotland are descended from other branches of the Stuart line.

STUART, GILBERT CHARLES, an American painter; born in Narragansett, R. I., Dec. 3, 1755. In his boyhood he went to Edinburgh with a Scotch painter named Alexander, with whom he studied his art; but his master dying, he worked his passage home, and began to paint portraits at Newport. In 1775 he made his way to London, where he led for two years a Bohemian life; but his talent was recognized by his countryman, Benjamin West, who took him into his family, and soon he became a fashionable portrait painter. In 1792, in the fullness of his power and fame, he returned to the United States and painted portraits of Washington, Jefferson, Madison, John Adams, and many of the distinguished men of the period, and was at work on a portrait of John Quincy Adams (afterward finished by Sully), when he died in Boston July 27, 1828.

STUART, JAMES EWELL BROWN, an American military officer; born in Patrick co., Va., in 1833; was graduated at the United States Military Academy in 1854; rose to 1st lieutenant the next year; distinguished himself in the campaign against the Indians in 1857 and became captain in 1860. In 1861 he resigned his commission in the United States Army and entered the Confederate service. He was in charge of the Confederate cavalry at the first battle of Bull Run; and in the following September made a daring attack on the Federal forces at Lewinville, for which he was made a brigadier-general. Soon after this he was promoted major-general and subsequently was engaged in skirmishes and commanded troops at Chancellorsville and at Gettysburg. In 1864 he opposed Sheridan's cavalry, but was mortally wounded in a fight at Yellow Tavern. He died in Richmond, Va., May 11, 1864.

STUART, RUTH McENERY, an American author; born in Avoyelles parish, La., in 1856. Her published writings include: "A Golden Wedding, and Other Tales"; "Carlotta's Intended, and Other Stories"; "The Story of Babette"; "Solomon Crow's Christmas Pockets"; "Pockets, and Other Tales"; "Sonny"; "Napoleon Jackson" (1902); "Aunt Amity's Silver Wedding" (1908); "Sonny's Father" (1910); "The Haunted Photograph" (1911); "The Cocoon" (1915). She died in 1917.

STUBBS, WILLIAM, an English historian; was born in Knaresborough, England, June 21, 1825; was educated at Ripon Grammar School, whence he proceeded to Oxford University and latterly became a fellow of Trinity College. In 1848 he was ordained, and became vicar of Navestock, Essex, in 1850. In 1862 he was appointed librarian of Lambeth Palace, in 1866 Professor of Modern History at Oxford, in 1869 curator of the

Bodleian Library, in 1875 rector of Cholderton, Wilts, in 1879 canon residentiary of St. Paul's, in 1884 bishop of Chester, and in 1888 bishop of Oxford. He edited many valuable historical works in the Rolls Series, including "Chronicles and Memorials of the reign of Richard I." (1864-1865); "Gesta Regis Henrici II." (1867); "Chronicle of Roger Hoveden" (1872-1873); "Memorials of St. Dunstan" (1874); and "Opera Radulphi de Diceto" (1876); his chief work the Constitutional History of England (1874-1878), and many others. He was a member of various English and foreign learned societies. He died April 22, 1901.

STUCCO, a fine plaster used for coating walls. It is usually made of pure lime slaked and settled, mixed with clean sand. Stucco varies in quality and composition with the purpose for which it is intended. For internal decoration gypsum and pounded marble enter into its composition, as well as gelatin or glue in solution. For external work the stucco employed is of a coarser kind, and is variously prepared, the different sorts being generally distinguished by the name of cements. Also the third coat of plastering when prepared for painting, and a popular name for plaster of Paris or gypsum.

STUCK, HUDSON, an American clergyman and explorer; born in England, in 1863. In 1885 he removed to the United States, and in 1892 graduated from the theological department of the University of the South. He was appointed a priest of the Protestant Episcopal Church in 1892, and served as rector of several churches in Texas. In 1904 he was appointed archdeacon of the Yukon. He was interested in mountain climbing and exploration, and on June 7, 1913, with three companions, reached the summit of Mount McKinley, being the first to perform this feat. This was followed by other explorations in Alaska. He was elected a fellow of the Royal Geographical Society of London, and was a member of other scientific societies. He wrote "Ascent of Denali (Mount McKinley)" (1914); "Ten Thousand Miles with a Dog-Sled" (1914); "Voyages on the Yukon and its Tributaries" (1917); "A Winter Circuit of Our Arctic Coast" (1920). He died in 1920.

STUHLWEISSENBURG, a town of Hungary; near the marshes of Sár-Rát, 42½ miles S. W. of Budapest. The chief buildings are the cathedral and the Church of St. Maria, built by Stephen I., the place of crowning and burial. Stuhlweissenburg was the residence of the Hungarian kings from 1027 to 1527, when Bela IV. removed to Ofen. The town manufactures cloth, flannel, cordovan, and knives, and has an important traffic in wool, corn, wine, and live stock. Stuhlweissenburg is believed to be the site of the Roman Floriana. It was held by the Turks at intervals from 1545 to 1688. Pop. about 37,000.

STUKELEY, WILLIAM, an English antiquary; born in Holbeach, Lincolnshire, Nov. 7, 1687, and from the grammar school there passed in 1703 to Corpus Christi College, Cambridge. Having studied medicine he practiced successively at Boston, London, and Grantham; but in 1729 he took orders, and, after holding two Lincolnshire livings, in 1747 was presented to the rectory of St. George the Martyr in Queens Square, London. His 20 works, published between 1720 and 1726, and dealing with Stonehenge, Avebury, and antiquities generally, are marred by a credulity and fancifulness which won for him the title of the "Arch-Druid." He died in London March 3, 1765.

STURDEE, ADMIRAL SIR (FREDERICK CHARLES) DOVETON, 1st bt. cr. 1916, of the Falkland Isles; K. C. B., entered navy in 1871; captain, 1899; rear-admiral, 1908. Chief of staff,

ADMIRAL STURDEE

Mediterranean Fleet, 1905. Commander-in-chief, H. M. S. "Invincible" in action off the Falkland Isles, 1914, when the British Fleet destroyed the German Raiding Squadron. Died May 7, 1925.

STURGEON (*Acipenser*), a genus of ganoid fishes of the family *Acipenseridæ*, order *Chondrostei*. The *Chondrostei* are ganoids without ganoid scales, the skin being either naked or with bony plates, as in the sturgeon. The skull is cartilaginous, but covered externally with bony plates belonging to the skin. The tail is asymmetrical or heterocercal, and the gelatinous notochord persists in the center of the vertebral column throughout life. Spiracles like those of sharks and skates are present in some genera. The distinguishing features of acipenser are these: the body is long and narrow, and the skin is provided with five longitudinal rows of bony shields, each bearing a projecting keel. One row of these bony plates is along each side of the body, one along the back, and one on each side of the ventral surface. The skin between these rows of plates is naked, but contains minute scales which give it a rough surface. The head pro-

there is no copulation, the ova being laid and fertilized on the bottom of the upper parts of rivers, like those of the salmon. The food of sturgeons consists of worms, crustacea, and mollusks, which they seek by routing in the sea bottom with their snouts.

STURGIS, RUSSELL, an American architect; born in Baltimore co., Md., 1836, was graduated at the College of the City of New York in 1856; studied architecture in Europe, and practiced till 1880, when he went to Europe to reside, because of failing health. In 1885, however, he became active in writing and lecturing on art subjects and later edited the art sections in the "Century" and "International" dictionaries, and "Johnson's Universal Cyclopædia," and conducted the "Dictionary of Architecture" in 1901. He was the author of "Manual of Jarves Collection of Early

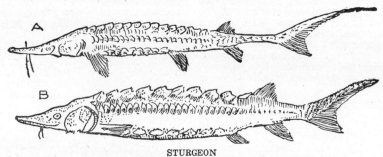

STURGEON

A—Shovel Nosed Sturgeon   B—Common Sturgeon

jects into a flat, pointed snout, provided with fleshy tentacles or barbels; and on the under surface of this snout, some distance behind its extremity, is the mouth, which is without teeth, and capable of protrusion. The gill opening is wide. There are two pairs of fins, the pelvic being situated a long way back, close to the anus. There are two median fins, one dorsal and one ventral, both near the tail. The fin-rays are jointed and flexible. Spiracles are present behind the eyes. The air bladder communicates with the gullet.

There are many species of sturgeon, all confined to the Northern Hemisphere. They live in the sea and great lakes, and ascend the great rivers. All are of considerable size, and supply valuable commodities, for which they are regularly captured on a large scale. These commodities are their flesh, which is palatable and wholesome, their roe (caviare), and their air bladders, from which isinglass is made. The eggs are small and numerous, like those of bony fishes;

Italian Pictures," "Classical Architecture on the Shores of the Mediterranean" and numerous critical monographs on American architects. He died Feb. 11, 1909.

STURM, JOHANNES, a German educational reformer; born in Sleiden, Luxemburg, Oct. 1, 1507. In his 15th year he was sent to school at Liege and continued his studies at the College of Louvain. He devoted himself to acquiring a Latin style and studied Cicero assiduously.

In 1529 he went to Paris, and at first gave himself to medicine, but returned to the study of Cicero, on whom he gave courses of lectures in the College Royal. Besides lecturing on Cicero he also taught dialectics, and had for one of his students Petrus Ramus. When a request was made to him (1536) by the authorities of Strassburg to come to their assistance in reorganizing the education of their town, Sturm accepted their offer. Both in the religion and politics of his time Sturm took a prominent part, and on different occasions was sent on missions to France, England, and Denmark. In religion he took sides with Zwingli against Luther, with whose followers in Strassburg he was in constant controversy, which embittered all the later years of his life.

Guided and inspired by Sturm, the town became one of the most important educational centers in Europe.

Elementary and secondary education were provided for; but it was the ambition of Sturm that the higher studies should also be within reach of every youth of Strassburg. The divided councils of the town, however, and the outlay the organization of such studies would imply delayed Sturm's scheme till as late as 1564. In that year was founded the Strassburg Academy, which, together with the gymnasium, supplied a complete course of instruction in all the learning of the time. It is his chief praise that beyond all his contemporaries he succeeded in corelating public instruction to the moral and intellectual development of his time. He died in Strassburg March 3, 1589.

STÜRMER, BORIS VLADIMIRO-VITCH, a Russian statesman. He studied law at the University of Petrograd, and began his political career as a member of the Russian Senate in 1872. Following the coronation of Nicholas II., he was recalled from the governorship of Novgorod and was made Master of Ceremonies at the Palace. He was again appointed governor of Novgorod in 1894, and in 1896 became governor of Yaroslav. He was appointed president of the Council of Ministers in 1918, and in the same year succeeded Goremykin as minister of foreign affairs. He conspired with Rasputin and Protopopov, former minister of the interior, to poison the minds of the Czar and his wife. This was one of the chief causes of the revolt of 1917. In June, 1917, following the revolution, he was indicted for abuse of his power, and was imprisoned in the fortress of St. Peter and St. Paul, where he died on September 3d. Disclosures made following his death proved that he had betrayed Rumania to the Germans and in other ways taken the part of Germany against the interests of his own country.

STURT, CHARLES, an Australian explorer; born in England; entered the army; and in 1825 was stationed at Sydney, New South Wales, with the rank of captain. In 1828 he led an expedition to explore the interior of Australia, and discovered the Macquarie, Castlereagh,

and Darling rivers. He also explored the Murrumbidgee, and in 1830 discovered the Murray. In 1844 he penetrated to the great barren region nearly in the center of the continent. Subsequently he was made colonial secretary of South Australia, and the exposure to which he was subjected having undermined his health, he received a pension from the colony. He returned to England totally blind. He wrote "Two Expeditions Into the Interior of South Australia in 1828-1831" (London, 1833), and "Narrative of an Expedition Into Central Australia in 1844-1846" (London, 1849). He died in Cheltenham, England, June 16, 1869.

STUTTGART, capital of the Republic of Württemberg, Southern Germany, beautifully situated near the left bank of the Neckar, and closely surrounded by vineyard slopes, 816 feet above the sea. With the exception of part of the lower and older town, it consists of spacious streets and squares lined with fine buildings, among the latter being the new palace, finished in 1807; the old palace (1570); the Stiftskirche, a Gothic structure of the 15th century; the Gothic hospital church, containing a statue of our Saviour by Dannecker; and several other churches; the royal library (400,000 vols.); the museum and picture gallery; the polytechnic school; a great building containing the exchange and concert rooms, etc.; the theater, the town hall, and many other buildings. There are several high-class educational establishments, the polytechnic being the chief. Before the World War Stuttgart was the chief center in south Germany for the book trade, connected with which were paper mills, type foundries, printing presses, and lithographic establishments. The other leading manufactures included dyes, chemicals, woolen and cotton goods, various fancy articles, jewelry, musical instruments, mathematical and scientific instruments, liquors, confectionery, and beer. Stuttgart dates from 1229, and in 1320 became the residence of the counts of Würtemberg. From 1436 to 1482 it was much improved and enlarged, and has since, with only a short interval, been the capital. E. from Stuttgart, and almost connected with it by the royal palace grounds, is the town of Cannstatt. Pop. about 286,000.

STUYVESANT, PETER, a Dutch military governor; born in Holland in 1602; served in the West Indies, was director of the Dutch colony of Curaçoa, and lost a leg in an attack on the Spanish island of St. Martin. In 1647 he was made director-general of the New Netherlands, and reached New Amsterdam (now

New York), in May of that year. Under his direction boundary lines were established between the Dutch and English possessions in America; but the British

PETER STUYVESANT

encroachments persisted till in **August,** 1664, an English fleet appeared in the bay and compelled the surrender of New Amsterdam, after which its name was changed to New York. Stuveysant went to Holland in 1665, but afterward returned and spent the remainder of his life on his farm, called the *Bomerij,* from which the name Bowery was given to a well-known thoroughfare in New York City. He died in August, 1682.

STYE, a little boil on the margin of the eyelid, which commences in the follicle of one eyelash. The tumor generally bursts in a few days, and it is very seldom necessary to puncture it. Warm-water dressings with lint and oil should be applied.

STYLITE, one of a class of anchorites in the early Church who took up their abode on lofty pillars. Their position was an attempt to realize the two fundamental ideas of Christian asceticism— separation from the things of earth, and aspiration after those of heaven. The first Stylite was Simeon, the Syrian (A. D. 390-459), who commenced this mode of life near Antioch, about A. D. 420. His life was one of great austerity. After his death the Stylites became numerous, and peculiar privileges were accorded to them.

STYLOBATE, in architecture, the substructure of a Greek temple below the columns, sometimes formed of three steps which were continued round the peri-

style, and sometimes of walls raised to a considerable height, in which case it was approached by a flight of steps at one end.

STYR, a river of eastern Galicia, emptying into the Pripet Marshes, along which heavy fighting took place between German and Russian forces during the World War, in the fall of 1915. Here, and along the Strypa river, further S., the Russians developed a sudden strength after, for several months, during the summer, being driven back along their whole front by the Teutons. The battle in this region, which began in the first week of October, 1915, continued with unceasing severity into the winter months, and proved the turning point in favor of the Russians, who, in the following spring began an offensive which proved all but disastrous to the armies of the Central Empires along the Eastern front.

STYRAX, in botany, the storax; the typical genus of *Styracaceæ.* Elegant trees and shrubs, mostly with stellate hairs, entire leaves, and racemes of white or cream-colored flowers. Found in the warmer parts of America and Asia; one is European and one African. *S. officinale,* a tree from 15 to 20 feet high, has ovate leaves, shining above, downy beneath, longer than the racemes, which consist of five or six flowers. It is a native of Syria, Greece, and Italy. It furnishes storax, which exudes and hardens in the air when the bark is wounded. *S. benzoin* is the benjamin storax, or gum-benjamin tree. It is found in Sumatra, Java, and the Malay Archipelago generally, and produces benzoin. *S. reticulata, S. ferruginea,* and *S. aurea* yield a gum used as incense. Among other American species are *S. grandiflorus, S. loevigatus,* and *S. pulverulentus, S. serratulum,* and *S. virgatum,* small trees, natives of Bengal, yield gum, but of inferior quality.

STYRIA, a former duchy, now a state in the Austrian Republic, bounded by Upper and Lower Austria, Hungary, Croatia, Carniola, Carinthia, and Salzburg; area, 8,662 square miles. Pop. about 1,400,000. Capital Gratz, 156,000. The duchy, with the exception of the S. part, is mountainous. The Noric Alps traverse the district between the Enns and the Mur; the Styrian Alps between the Mur and the Drave; and the Carnic Alps between the Drave and the Save. These mountains rise to the height of between 7,000 and 8,000 feet, and are rich in minerals. Styria belongs to the basin of the Danube, which drains it by means of the four rivers mentioned above. On the S. plains and in the valleys the land is fertile, and wheat, maize, hemp, flax, and the poppy are raised. The vine thrives well in many districts. The chief sources of wealth are the forests and minerals, dairy farming, mining, and manufactures. Gratz is the capital.

STYX, in mythology, one of the rivers of Hades—the 10th part of the waters of Oceanus—flowing round it seven times with dark and sluggish stream, across which Charon ferries the shades of the departed. The nymph of this stream was the daughter of Oceanus and Tethys, and she first, together with her children, came to the help of Zeus against the Titans. For this service they were taken to Olympus, and she herself became the goddess by whom the most solemn oaths of the immortals were sworn. When such an oath was taken Iris brought some of her sacred water in a golden cup, and whoever swore falsely by it lay speechless and breathless for a year, and was banished nine years from the councils of the gods. A rocky stream falling into the Crathis in the N. E. of Arcadia bore this name, the scenery around it being fittingly weird and desolate.

SUABIA, an ancient German duchy. After bearing the name of Alemannia, its original inhabitants the Alemanni, changed it to Suevia or Schwaben-land, in consequence of the incursion of the Suevi. On the division of the kingdom of the Franks in 843, Suabia, along with Bavaria, became as it were the nucleus of Germany, and its rulers continued for many centuries to hold a prominent place in its history. In 1376 was formed, chiefly by the union of its towns, the celebrated Suabian League. From 1512 to 1806 Suabia formed one of the 10 circles into which the German empire was divided. The name of Suabia is also given to a division of Bavaria. Augsburg is its capital.

SUAKIN or **SUAKIM**, a seaport of the Red Sea, stands on a small rocky island in a bay on its W. side, and is the principal outlet for the commerce of Nubia and of the countries of the Sudan beyond. The island town is connected with the settlement of El-Keff on the adjacent mainland by a causeway. There is some trade in silver ornaments, knives and spear heads, and leather work. The more important exports are silver ornaments, ivory, gums, millet, cattle, hides, and gold; the imports, durra, cottons, flour, sugar, rice, ghi, dates, and coal. Here some 6,000 or 7,000 pilgrims embark every year for Mecca. The Egyptians occupied this port when they extended their power over the Sudan; and in its vicinity several battles were fought between the allied Egyptians and English against the fanatical followers of the Mahdi. Pop. about 10,500.

SUB-DEACON, the lowest step in holy orders in the Roman Catholic Church, the highest of the minor orders among the Greeks. In the Roman Catholic Church, sub-deacons prepare the sacred vessels and the bread and wine for mass, pour the water into the chalice at the offertory, and sing the Epistle; in the Greek Church they prepare the sacred vessels, and guard the gates of the sanctuary. There are no sub-deacons in the Anglican Communion.

SUBJECT, that which is placed under the authority, jurisdiction, dominion, or influence of something else. One who is under the authority, rule, or dominion of another. That on which any mental operation is exercised; that which is treated or handled as an object of examination, thought or discussion; that concerning which anything is affirmed or denied; as, a subject for inquiry or consideration. That on which any physical operation or experiment is performed; as, a subject for medical treatment. The hero of a piece; the person treated of; as, Byron is the subject of one of Macaulay's finest essays. In logic, the term of which the other is affirmed or denied; as, the subject of a proposition. In grammar, the nominative case of a verb. In fine arts, that which it is the desire and aim of the artist to express; as, the subject of a picture. In anatomy, a dead body serving as an object for anatomical dissection. In music, the chief melody or theme of a movement.

SUBLACO, (ancient Sublaqueum), a city of Italy; in hills beside the Teverone; 32 miles E. by N. from Rome. It was the cradle of the Benedictine Order and the place where the printing press was first set up in Italy (1464). There are two monasteries dating from the 6th century, one of which (Santa Scolastica) contains a small but valuable library, while the other was built near the cave in which St. Benedictine lived. The city was greatly favored by Pope Pius VI.; he enlarged its castle (built 1068), erected a church, etc.

SUBLIMATION THEORY, in geology, the hypothesis that mineral veins, or many of them, have been filled by sublimation. Volatile substances occur both in the hot springs and in the gaseous emanations of volcanoes, and might furnish certain constituents for ores and other minerals occurring in veins.

SUBLIME PORTE. See PORTE.

SUBMARINE BOAT, a boat capable of being propelled under the water. The first was probably that constructed by Drebbel, a Dutchman, for James I, and Robert Fulton made an effort in the same direction in 1801. Among recent submarine boats the most noteworthy is the Holland submarine torpedo boat. See SUBMARINE MINES AND NAVIGATION.

SUBMARINE CABLE, a wire, or combination of wires, protected by flexible non-conducting waterproof material, designed to rest on the bottom of a body of water, and serve as a conductor for the currents transmitted by an electro-magnetic telegraphic apparatus.

SUBMARINE MINES AND NAVI-GATION. Submarine mines consist of spherical or cylindrical containers, usually made of steel, and sometimes lined with concrete, filled with a charge of ex-plosives. They are generally anchored in such a manner that they are concealed beneath the surface of the sea, but they are also sometimes allowed to float and drift. They were first used during the American Civil War, 28 vessels being destroyed by them. Their use was developed to a very marked degree in the European War, during which they were employed in enormous numbers by all the belligerents. The North Sea was completely inclosed by two mine barrages, the first being laid early in the war by the British navy across the Straits of Dover, and the second by the combined actions of the American and British navies. This was an immense barrage, stretching from the Orkney Islands off the north coast of Scotland, to the coast of Norway, a distance of 240 miles. It contained more than 70,000 mines, and covered an area of 6,000 square miles. It is claimed that its completion sealed the fate of the German submarine. Previous to the war, the charge employed was usually wet gun-cotton, and the explosion was brought about by successive detonations of ful-minate of mercury and a small secondary charge of dry guncotton. Frequently

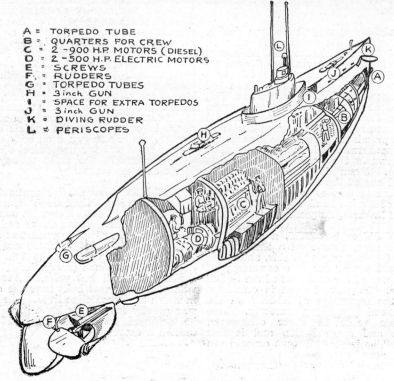

A = TORPEDO TUBE
B = QUARTERS FOR CREW
C = 2-900 H.P. MOTORS (DIESEL)
D = 2-500 H.P. ELECTRIC MOTORS
E = SCREWS
F = RUDDERS
G = TORPEDO TUBES
H = 3 inch GUN
I = SPACE FOR EXTRA TORPEDOS
J = 3 inch GUN
K = DIVING RUDDER
L = PERISCOPES

CROSS SECTION OF A MODERN SUBMARINE

 See **Submarine Mines and Navigation**, p. opposite

A BRITISH VESSEL TORPEDOED AND SET ON FIRE BY A GERMAN SUBMARINE

© International Film Service   A GERMAN SUBMARINE SURRENDERING TO THE AMERICAN DESTROYER "FANNING"

See Submarine Mines and Navigation, p. 134

electrical firing was used, the mines being connected to a station on shore by cable. In recent years, however, guncotton has been replaced by trinitrotoluene." This consisted of two "otters" towed by wire ropes from the side of a vessel. The otters were fitted with saw-like jaws, and a mine would glide along

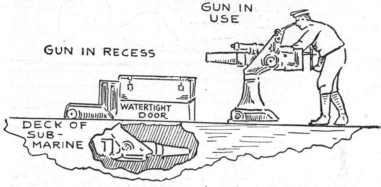

SUBMARINE'S GUNS

luene (T. N. T.) and the North Sea barrage referred to above is said to have contained more than 21 million pounds of this explosive. Much of the wartime development was concerned with rendering explosion more certain and more easily brought about. The American navy was especially successful along these lines. The details of manufacture are necessarily kept a close secret, but it is known that both British and German mines were of the so-called "horn type," being fitted with leaden horns, which projected from the mine. When these horns were struck and broken by a passing ship, or any other body, the explosion of the mine was brought about. The American mine was invented shortly after the United States entered the war. It was fitted with a long antenna which stretched above the mine. When this antenna was struck by a ship the explosion of the mine followed. It is obvious that the radius of action of a mine fitted with such a device is very much greater than that of the horn type. Moreover, the explosion depended upon electrical action, and it was only necessary for a piece of metal to make contact with the antenna for an explosion to follow. Mines are destroyed by "sweepers." A heavy wire is attached to the stern of two vessels, and the wire is kept at a sufficient depth by means of a pipe. The vessels sail through a suspected mine field, and when a mine is caught in the sweep wire, it is dragged along until the wire which holds it to its anchor breaks. The mine then rises to the surface, and can be destroyed by gunfire. Another protective device against mines invented by the British navy during the war was the "para-

the length of the wires until it reached the otter, when the wire would be cut and the mine destroyed.

Submarine Navigation.—Under-water vessels had never been used in warfare to any appreciable extent until the European War of 1914-1918. Many attempts at submarine navigation have been made, however, during the last 300 years. One of the earliest inventors to meet with anything approaching success was Cornelius Drebbell, a Dutchman, who built a boat manned by twelve rowers, and navigated it on the River Thames. This was at the beginning of the 17th century. In 1744 another inventor, named Day, built a boat which he claimed could remain under water for twelve hours. He lost his life, however, in an attempt to prove the truth of his assertion, being drowned in his own boat in Plymouth Sound. In the following year Bushnell, an American, invented a submarine vessel which met with considerable success. Some of the principles employed by him are still used in modern vessels. His boat was fitted with "oars on the principle of a screw," and submerged by admitting water through a valve, the water being pumped out when it was wished to rise to the surface. The next inventor was Robert Fulton, who, in 1800, remained under water for four hours, at a depth of 25 feet, in an egg-shaped vessel of his own devising. He indicated future possibilities in this line by attaching a charge of explosives to an old hulk off the coast of France and blowing her up. In 1830 a German named Bauer made some unsuccessful experiments with a boat which sank, but was later recovered and preserved in the Berlin Naval Academy. The same inventor experimented for the Russians during the Crimean War. In 1851, an American of the name of Phil-

the surface or awash. The vessel was armed with a spar torpedo, but it achieved no great success. The other "David" carried out a successful attack

ARMORED CONNING TOWER WITH 12 inch GUN

BRITISH SUBMARINE

lips demonstrated the possibility of remaining beneath the water by spending a day with his wife and family at the bottom of Lake Michigan, and Delaney, another American inventor, experimented in 1859 with a boat similar to that of Robert Fulton's. During the American Civil War attempts to use submarine boats were made by both Federals and Confederates. Two boats, both known as "The David," were built by the latter. The first was a steam vessel driven by a screw propeller, the funnel protruding above the surface of the water, but the boat proper being below

upon the *Housatonic*, which she sank, but she herself was swamped and sank with her crew. In 1876, G. W. Garrett, an English clergyman invented a submarine which gave promisingly successful results, but a larger model, built on similar lines, was lost off the Welsh coast. He entered into partnership, however, with a Swedish inventor named Nordenfeldt, and they built two submarines, and sold one to Turkey and the other to Greece. A third was built for Russia, but was wrecked and sunk while attempting to sail to Petrograd. All these boats were driven by vertical propellers, and were

SUBMARINE FIRING TORPEDO

propelled by steam. The French navy in 1896-97, built four submarines, driven by electricity, and fitted with compressed air reservoirs. From that time onward the submarine grew rapidly in importance. Inventors were many, among them being the Frenchmen, Goubet, Zédé, and Peral, and the Americans, Simon Lake, J. P. Holland and others.

Modern submarines are of four types, coast defense, cruising, fleet and mine-laying. While generally similar, they necessarily differ in details according to the work they are called upon to perform. Those used for *coast defense* require only a small cruising radius, since they can readily return to their base for fresh supplies of fuel, food and ammunition. For a similar reason, quarters for officers and crew need be only of the simplest

necessarily be larger than the coastal type, and even before the war boats of 800 to 1,200 tons had been built. During the war, both the United States and Great Britain built several of 1,500 to 2,000 tons, and similar large boats were owned by Germany. On the average, the submarine cruiser is 250 to 300 feet long, with a beam of 18 to 25 feet or more. They are swifter than the coastal type, and can attain a speed of 20 knots on the surface, and 14 to 15 knots submerged. More recent vessels have a cruising radius of 10,000 miles. Their armament has steadily increased, and some of the larger boats are equipped with two 5-inch or even 6-inch guns. In the earlier years of the war the German boats were fitted with one or two 3-inch guns, to which very soon was added an

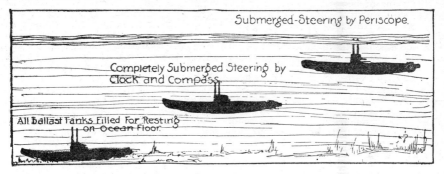

SUBMARINE

kind. Compared with the cruising type they are small, varying from 250 to 600 tons, being 150 to 200 feet long with a beam of 15 to 20 feet. They can attain a speed of as much as 16 knots on the surface, but when submerged this is reduced to 8-11 knots. They have a cruising radius of 1,000 to 2,000 miles, and are usually armed with one 3-inch gun, and sometimes with an anti-aircraft gun in addition. They carry also from four to eight torpedo tubes.

The Submarine Cruiser was the type which showed probably the greatest development during the war. These formed the most active branch of the German navy, and the enormous destruction of Allied and neutral shipping was carried out by them. Because they are away from their base for several days, or even weeks, they must contain sleeping and living quarters for officers and crew, with space for the preparation and cooking of food. In addition, they have to carry a comparatively large number of torpedoes and other needed supplies. It follows that they must

anti-aircraft gun. These were, of course, in addition to the torpedo tubes, which numbered as many as eight. They carried a crew of from 40 to 50 men.

The Fleet Submarine, as its name implies, is intended to accompany the fleet in action. Its radius of action need not necessarily be high, as it can be accompanied by a mother ship carrying supplies of fuel, extra ammunition, food for the crew and other necessities. This type can therefore be smaller than the cruiser, but it must be speedy and also possess seaworthiness. The *submarine mine-layer* was a type evolved by Germany during the war, and proved of great value to her in laying mines off the coast of Great Britain. They carried 16 mines in inclined tubes, which were open at the lower end. The tubes were loaded from the deck, the mines being liberated by a special device under water at the open end.

All types of submarines are now driven by Diesel or gasoline engines when traveling on the surface, but rely on electric motors when submerged. The current for the motors is supplied by storage batteries. An arrangement is made similar to that on the ordinary automobile (see "Electric Battery"), by which the storage batteries can be recharged from a generator driven by the Diesel or gasoline engine when the boat is traveling on the surface. The newer types of cruising submarines can travel upward of 100 miles on a single charge of the batteries. It will be seen, therefore, that even they can remain beneath the surface for comparatively short periods of time, even if other considerations permitted them to keep submerged for any greater period. One of the most difficult problems which confronted early inventors was that of keeping the boat on an even keel. This is now accomplished by means of ballast tanks and horizontal runners, or by means of the gyroscope. But the matter still remains one which requires constant watchfulness. It will be clearly seen that under the conditions existing in a submarine, where the vessel is so to speak in a state of delicate balance, the moving of equipment or of torpedoes, and especially the discharge of torpedoes, presents problems of peculiar difficulty. As indicated above, the problems have to a large extent been solved, but the stability of the submarine still leaves room for improvement. Submerging is effected by admitting water into tanks specially designed for the purpose. Conversely, the boat is brought to the surface by expelling the water from these tanks either by means of compressed air or with the aid of pumps. The speed with which a boat can submerge or rise has increased considerably in recent years, but even now it varies somewhat with conditions. On the average, from one and one-half to three minutes are required for a boat to emerge sufficiently far from the water to use her guns. The periscope, by means of which the observing officer can watch what is taking place on the suface of the water while the boat remains almost completely submerged, is an essential part of submarine equipment, and the principle of reflecting mirrors, on which it depends, is familiar to all. Submarines are costly to build; ton for ton they cost more than twice as much as surface battleships or cruisers. The pre-war cost was estimated at, approximately, $1,000 per ton, but it is certain that the cost of those built under war-time conditions was much higher than this.

Submarine Merchantmen.—The first (and possibly the last) submarine merchantman was the "Deutschland," which crossed the Atlantic with a valuable cargo of dyestuffs from Germany and reached the United States in July, 1916.

The utility of the submarine for carrying cargo is obviously small. Its comparatively slow speed, its high cost of construction, its small capacity and its general inconvenience render it not worth consideration as a cargo carrier. It is improbable that it will ever be used as such in the future, except by a country at war, its mercantile vessels swept from the seas.

Previous to the European War there were many to be found, even among the highest authorities, who prophesied that the submarine had rendered the surface war vessel useless and impotent. In the early months of the war, German submarines scored heavily against British and French cruisers. In the later years of the war the submarine's chief success was against merchantmen. Deadly though it may be, the submarine, by its very nature, is vulnerable. Many methods of destroying it were devised. One of the earliest schemes was the construction of huge nets, two lines of which were placed across the Straits of Dover. The construction of the vast mine fields in the North Sea has already been dealt with in the early part of this article. Another device that was perhaps more dreaded by the submarine than any other was the "depth charge." This was a huge bomb, weighing 600 pounds or more. One or more of these bombs would be dropped from the stern of a destroyer where a submarine was last seen to submerge. They would explode at or near the bottom, and the enormous concussion would bring about the complete destruction of the submarine. The hydrophone was another useful device invented during the war. This was a special type of telephone, by means of which the position of submarines could be detected by noises transmitted through water. These, and other devices, have greatly lessened the deadliness of submarines in legitimate warfare. None the less, they are still recognized as a powerful weapon of both defense and offense, and form an important adjunct to all modern navies.

The French Navy developed in 1927 plans to equip submarine vessels with hydro-airplanes of a special and minute type. The limitation of the submarine naval forces of nations was discussed at the Geneva Naval Conference. The frequency of submarine accidents led to the bestowal of much inventive effort for preventive and rescue appliances. On December 17, 1927, the U. S. Navy Submarine S-4 was sent to the bottom in a collision with the destroyer Paulding, off Provincetown, and all on board, forty in all, were lost, in spite of rescue efforts. Raised in 1928, the S-4 was used to test rescue devices.

SUBMARINE TELEGRAPHY, the transmission of messages by electricity under the sea. The sending of messages by telegraph from one country to another, through wires buried many thousand feet beneath the water has come into general use since 1851, though the conception of its possibility dated back many years prior to that time.

In 1838 it was demonstrated that subaqueous telegraphy was a matter which could be practically handled. This was done in actual experiments by Colonel Pasley of the Royal Engineers at Chatterton in England. Just one year after Pasley's work in England Dr. O'Shaughnessy, the director of the East India Company's telegraph system, transmitted telegraphic signals through insulated wires under the Hugli river in India. About this time numerous inventors in many parts of the world thought of new experiments, and the art of submarine telegraphy began to grow.

Prof. Charles Wheatstone of England suggested in 1840 the practicability of connecting Dover, England, with Calais, France, by a submarine telegraph. In the United States Samuel F. B. Morse, in 1842, transmitted electric signals along a copper wire between Castle Garden and Governor's Island in New York harbor. In 1843 Professor Morse suggested the possibility of connecting Europe and the United States by a submarine cable line. Meanwhile Samuel Colt was operating submarine cables between New York City, Coney Island and Fire Island.

In 1845 Ezra Cornell laid 12 miles of copper wire in the Hudson river between New York and Fort Lee. The wires were insulated and inclosed in a lead pipe and were successfully operated till they were destroyed by ice. In 1846 Charles West obtained permission from the British Government to connect Dover and Calais by copper wire.

In 1851, across the British channel was opened the first important submarine telegraph line. It was laid by English and French capitalists. The cable consisted of four copper wires, insulated with gutta-percha, surrounded by tarred hemp and protected by 10 galvanized iron wires wound spirally around it. The weight of this cable was seven tons to the mile; it was 25 miles long, and was sunk in 120 feet of water. In 1853 six submarine cables were laid connecting various parts of England, Ireland and Scotland. In the following year five more cables were laid in Europe, the longest of which was 64 miles. In 1856 several cables were laid in waters much deeper than formerly. One of these, running from Spezia, Italy, to Corsica, weighed eight tons to the mile, and was sunk to a depth of 600 feet. By 1906 there were sixteen transatlantic serviceable cables. In 1914, before the World War, there were seventeen cables between the United States and Europe.

Post-war Cable Distribution.—By the treaty of Versailles, Germany renounced in behalf of herself and her nationals all rights and titles to former German cables, most of which had been seized or cut during the World War. A total of 20,000 miles of these cables was afterward divided among the principal Allied and Associated Powers, their value being credited to the Reparations account. Two German-American cables, cut and diverted by France and England in the war, continued to be held by these countries. The former Emden-New York cable was diverted by England to Halifax. In the Pacific a controversy arose over the cable from Guam to Shanghai, constituting part of an important line between the United States and China, which passed through the small Pacific island of Yap, assigned to Japan as a mandatory power. The controversy was settled at the Washington conference by a treaty between the U. S. and Japan, granting to the former free access to Yap in all that related to the operation of the Guam-Yap cable or any other cable which the United States might lay to Yap.

It was estimated at the end of 1922 that there were in operation 530 submarine cables with a total length of 242,-195 miles. About 135,000 miles were owned by Great Britain and 71,000 miles by the United States.

SUBMAXILLARY GLAND, in anatomy one of the three salivary glands. It is situated immediately below the base and the inner surface of the inferior maxilla.

SUBORDINARY, in heraldry, a figure borne in charges in coat armor, not considered to be so honorable as an ordinary, to which it gives place and cedes the principal points of the shield. According to some writers, an ordinary when it comprises less than one-fifth of the whole shield is termed a subordinary.

SUBORNATION OF PERJURY, the crime of inducing a person to commit perjury, punishable similarly to perjury.

SUBPŒNA, or SUBPENA, in law, a writ or process commanding the attendance in a court of justice of the witness on whom it is served under a penalty. If the witness refuses or neglects to attend, and has no legal excuse, such as a serious illness, he may be sued in an action of damages, or imprisoned for contempt of court; but his traveling expenses must have been paid beforehand. Also, the process by which a defendant in equity is commanded to appear and answer the plaintiff's bill. Subpœna duces tecum, a writ commanding the attendance of a witness at a trial, and ordering him to bring with him all books, writings, or the like, bearing on the case.

SUB ROSA ("under the rose," *i. e.*, under the obligation of secrecy), a term which possibly had its origin, as Sir Thomas Brown suggests, in the closeness with which the rosebud folds its petals, or in the rose with which Harpocrates, god of silence, was bribed by Cupid not to divulge his mother Venus's amours. A rose is often found sculptured on the ceilings of mediæval banqueting halls and on confessionals.

SUBSIDENCE AND UPHEAVAL, terms applied to movements of the earth's crust.

SUBSIDY, a sum paid, often under a treaty, by one government to another, sometimes to secure its neutrality, but more frequently to meet the expenses of carrying on a war. Specifically, a grant from the government, from a municipal corporation, or the like, to a private person or company to assist in the establishment or support of an enterprise deemed advantageous to the public; a subvention; as, a subsidy to the owners of a line of steamships.

SUBSTANCE, in philosophy, that which is and abides as distinguished from accident, which has no existence of itself, and is essentially mutable. The derivation of the word in this sense is, according to Augustine, from the Latin *subsistere,* and so = that which subsists of or by itself; Locke prefers to connect it with the Latin *substo* = to stand under, to support, to uphold.

The first idea of substance is probably derived from the consciousness of self—the conviction gained by experience that, while sensations, thoughts, and purposes are continually changing, the Ego constantly remains the same. Observation teaches us that bodies external to us remain the same as to quantity or extension, though their color and figure, their state of motion or of rest may be changed. Locke, without departing from the knowable, placed the substance of an object in some essential or fundamental quality, the presence of which maintained, while its removal destroyed, the identity of the object, and Fichte made it consist in a synthesis of attributes; holding that these, synthetically united, gave substance, while substance analyzed gave attributes.

In theology, essence, nature, being. Used specially of the Three Persons in the Godhead, who are said to be the same substance, *i. e.*, to possess one common essence. The principle of substance in philosophy is the law of the human mind by which every quality or mode of being is referred to a substance. In algebra, the operation of putting one quantity in place of another, to which it is equal, but differently expressed.

In theology, the doctrine that in the crucifixion Christ was divinely substituted for, took the place, of, the elect, or of all mankind obeying the law in their stead, suffering the penalty expiating their sins, and procuring for them salvation. Used also of the principle involved in the bloody sacrifices of the Jewish economy (in which the animals were types of Christ). and in a still wider sense of the offering of the lower animals in the place of men, and of unbloody in the place of bloody sacrifices in ethnic religions. See ARMINIANISM: CALVINISM: SACRIFICE.

SUBSTITUTION, the act of substituting or putting one person or thing in the place of another to serve the same purpose.

In chemistry, a term denoting the replacing of one element or group of elements for another. It is the great agent, and covers nearly the whole field of chemical change, and is always attended with some alteration of properties in the compound, the alteration increasing with the amount of substitution. (1) When chlorine replaces hydrogen in marsh gas, forming hydrochloric acid and methyl chloride, $CH_4 + Cl_2 = HCL + CH_3Cl$. (2) When an alcohol radical replaces chlorine, as in trichloride of phosphorus, $3Zn(C_2H_5)_2 + 2PCl_3 = 3ZnCl_2 + 2P(C_2H_5)_3$ (3) A basylous or chlorous radical is replaced one for the other, as when nitrate or silver is decomposed by chloride of sodium, $AgNo_3 + NaCl = NaNo_3 + AgCl$. (4) When hydrogen is replaced by an alcohol radical, as in the case of acting on ammonia with iodide of ethyl, $H_3N + C_2H_5I = HI + \left.\begin{matrix}C_2H_5\\H_2\end{matrix}\right\}N$. (See SALT).

SUBTRACTION, in arithmetic, the operation of finding the difference between one number and another, the less being subtracted from the greater. In algebra the operation is included under addition, the rule for subtraction being change the sign and add. Here there is no convention as to which quantity must be the greater; the algebraic sign of the remainder removes any possible ambiguity.

SUBSTRATUM, in geology, a stratum lying under another. The term subsoil is generally applied to the matters which intervene between the surface soils and the rocks on which they rest; thus, clay is the common substratum or subsoil of gravel.

SUBULARIA, a genus of plants, natural order *Cruciferæ*, found in the gravelly bottoms of lakes, usually in shallow water, in North and Central Europe, North Asia, and the Northern United States. *S. aquatica*, or awlwort, the only species, consists merely of a tuft of white fibrous roots, narrow awl-shaped leaves, and a leafless stalk, bearing a few small white flowers. It is indigenous to Scotland and the N. of England and Ireland.

SUBULICORNIA, or **SUBULICOR-NES**, in entomology, a tribe of *Neuroptera*, or, if that order be divided, of *Pseudo-neuroptera*. It contains two families, *Ephemeridæ* and *Libellulidæ*, having a common character in the form of the antennæ which are short, awl-shaped, and composed of few joints. The wings are membranous, generally much reticulated; the eyes especially in the males, of comparatively large size; and the preparatory states, as in the Perlidæ, are passed in the water. The group which was founded by Latreille, is by no means a natural one, but is retained for the sake of convenience.

SUBUNGULATA, in zoölogy, a group or section of *Ungulata*, distinguished from true Ungulates (*Ungulata Vera*), by the structure of the carpus. The group embraces three sub-orders, *Hyracoidea*, *Proboscidea*, and *Amblypoda*, all of which are in many classifications treated as orders.

SUCCESSION, in music, the order in which the notes of a melody proceed. There are two sorts of succession, regular, or conjoint, and disjunct. A regular or conjoint succession is that in which the notes succeed each other in the order of the scale to which they belong, either ascending or descending. In a disjunct succession the melody is formed of intervals greater than a second. A sequence is sometimes spoken of as a succession, and passages of similar chords or progressions are described as a succession of thirds, fourths, fifths, sixths, sevenths, or octaves, as the case may be.

Acts of succession: In English history, the name given to several acts of Parliament, by which the succession to the crown was limited or modified. The first is an act of Henry IV., declaring Prince Henry heir-apparent to the thrones of

England and France, with remainders to the other children of Henry IV. Other instances occurred in the case of Henry VII., and in regard to the successors of Henry VIII., and the rights of James I., Charles I., and Charles II. The most important is the act of settlement. (See SETTLEMENT, ACT OF).

Apostolic, or Apostolical succession: (See APOSTOLIC).

Geological succession of organic beings: The gradual disappearance of species, genera, families, etc., throughout the world as geological time goes forward, or the more rapid succession of one group of organisms to another within a limited area, as the adaptation of that area to particular forms of life changes, by water giving place to land, salt water to fresh, or the reverse. Within limited areas, however, the same type often persists from the later Tertiary to the present day; as in South America, where the sloth and armadillo have succeeded gigantic Edentates like the megatherium and glyptodon.

Law of succession: The law or rule according to which the succession to the property of deceased persons is regulated. In general this law obtains only in cases in which the deceased person has died intestate, or in which the power of bequeathing property by will is limited by the legislature. In the United States each State has its own law of succession. Usually succession is by stirpes or root.

SUCCESSION WARS, the general name given to contests which took place in Europe during the 18th century on the extinction of certain dynasties or ruling houses. Four such wars are usually enumerated — that of the Spanish succession (1701-1713), of the Polish succession (1733-1738), of the Austrian succession (1740-1748), and of the Bavarian succession (1777-1779). The first and third alone are of sufficient general historical interest to be noticed here.

(1) *War of the Spanish Succession.*— Charles II., king of Spain, having died without direct descendants in November, 1700, claims were raised to the vacant throne by the husbands of his two sisters, Louis XIV., of France, who had married the elder, and the Emperor Leopold I., who had married the younger. Both these monarchs were also themselves grandsons of Philip III., of Spain; but neither desired the Spanish crown for his own head. Louis put forward his grandson Philip of Anjou; while Leopold advocated the claims of his second son, the Archduke Charles. The electoral prince Joseph of Bavaria, grandson of the Emperor Leopold, was

the heir originally designated in King Charles's will, but he died in the beginning of 1699. Both Louis XIV. and his wife had nine years before solemnly renounced the crown of Spain for themselves and their heirs; nevertheless, after Joseph of Bavaria died the agent of Louis XIV. induced Charles of Spain to nominate Philip of Anjou as his successor. Three months after the Spanish monarch's death the French prince entered Madrid, and was crowned as Philip V.; and his accession was at first recognized by all of the European powers except the emperor. Louis, however, soon provoked the United Netherlands and England, and they joined Austria for the purpose of armed opposition to France.

Hostilities were begun by Prince Eugene in Italy in 1701; and in the following year the conflict raged not only in Italy but also in the Netherlands and in Swabia. At first the allies were victorious all along the line: Marlborough took the fortresses on the Meuse and overran the electorate of Cologne; and the Landgrave of Baden had the good fortune to drive back the most redoubtable of the French commanders, Villars, who had crossed the Rhine from Alsace. But the aspect of things was altered in 1703 by Villars, who in conjunction with the Elector of Bavaria, penetrated as far as Tyrol and captured Passau, while the imperialists in Italy were more than held in check by Vendôme. But in the campaign of 1704 Marlborough and Eugene, acting in concert, inflicted a crushing defeat on their opponents at Blenheim and drove them back to France. Two years later the forces of Louis were compelled to withdraw from the Netherlands owing to Marlborough's great victory of Ramillies and his capture of the principal Flemish towns. At the same time Eugene and his relative the Duke of Savoy routed the French near Turin and swept them out of North Italy. Meanwhile the war had extended to the Iberian peninsula. The King of Portugal declared for the allies, and Archduke Charles made himself master of Catalonia, and even for a time held possession of Madrid. The English captured Gibraltar in 1704; but they and the Portuguese sustained a severe defeat from the Duke of Berwick (commanding the French forces) at Almanza in 1707. In this latter year Louis, feeling the severity of the strain, opened negotiations for a settlement. But the allies, having the upper hand, thought to humble him yet more, and the war went on.

An attempt of Vendôme and the Duke of Burgundy to reconquer the Spanish Netherlands in 1708 was frustrated by Marlborough and Eugene, who routed them at Oudenarde; and in the next year they defeated at Malplaquet the hitherto invincible Villars. Yet just when the fortunes of Louis seemed to be at their worst, circumstances intervened in his favor. In England the Whigs were supplanted by the Tories, who voted for peace; and in Austria the Emperor Leopold died and was succeeded by the Archduke Charles. Accordingly the war languished, and, Philip V. having pledged himself that the crowns of Spain and France should not be united, all the allies, except the emperor, signed the treaty of Utrecht on April 11, 1713. The emperor, too, was brought to terms after Villars had overrun the Palatinate and Baden, and he signed peace at Rastatt (March 7, 1714), whereby he acknowledged Philip as king of Spain, and became himself the ruler of the Spanish Netherlands, Naples, Milan, and Sardinia.

(2) *War of the Austrian Succession.* —The Emperor Charles VI. died in 1740, leaving his hereditary dominions — Bohemia, Hungary, and the archduchy of Austria — to his daughter Maria Theresa. She was at once beset by enemies eager to profit from the presumed weakness of a feminine ruler. The Elector Charles Albert of Bavaria, who had refused his signature to the PRAGMATIC SANCTION (*q. v.*), demanded the imperial crown as the descendant of the Emperor Ferdinand I., and he was backed up by France and Spain. Augustus of Saxony and Poland advanced his claim as being the husband of the eldest daughter of the Emperor Joseph I. Frederick the Great of Prussia seized the opportunity to wrest Silesia, which he greatly coveted, from the crown of Austria. The Bavarians and French (under Belleisle) invaded Bohemia, and crowned the elector king of that country at Prague on Dec. 19, 1741. About two months later he assumed the imperial crown at Frankfort-on-Main; yet on the very next day his own capital (Munich) was occupied by the Austrian general Khevenhüller, who, assisted by the high-spirited Hungarians, had advanced up the Danube, and now speedily overran Bavaria. A few months later the empress-queen bought off her most dangerous antagonist, Frederick, by giving up to him Silesia. At this time too, Augustus of Saxony, who had at first made common cause with the French and the Bavarians, withdrew from the contest and made peace with Maria Theresa. In the end of 1742 the Austrians were forced out of Bavaria and the French evacuated Bohemia. The Eng-

lish, who from the first paid a substantial subsidy to Austria, took up arms on her behalf in this same year, and in 1743 defeated the French at Dettingen in Bavaria. In the same year the Austrians repossessed themselves of the Elector Charles Albert's dominions. Saxony now joined the allies and took the field against his former associates. On the other hand, Frederick renewed hostilities and invaded Bohemia; but after a short interval he was once more willing to make peace. About this juncture Charles Albert died, and his son and successor abandoned his father's pretensions to Maria Theresa's dominions. This left France to carry on the struggle alone. But while Austria had the better of the war in Italy, Marshal Saxe captured several of the Flemish fortresses, won the victories of Fontenoy (1745), Rocoux (1746), and Lawfeldt (1747), and reduced the Austrian (formerly Spanish) Netherlands. Peace was at length concluded at Aix-la-Chapelle, Oct. 18, 1748, Prussia retaining Silesia.

SUCCINIC ACID, in chemistry, $C_4H_6O_4$, or $(CH_2COOH)_2$ originally extracted, by distillation in iron retorts, from amber, and later prepared from other substances by chemical reaction and from its elements by synthesis. It is a dibasic acid belonging to the oxalic series, first recognized by Agricola in 1657. It occurs ready formed in amber, in certain plants, and in many animal fluids, and is a product of the oxidation of fatty acids of high molecular weight, and of the alcoholic fermentation of sugar. It is prepared by bringing calcium malate in contact with one-twelfth of its weight of decayed cheese, suspended in three parts of water, and kept for some days at a temperature of 30° to 40°. Succinate of lime is formed, which is collected on a filter, decomposed with sulphuric acid, purified by recrystallization. It crystallizes in monoclinic prisms, is readily soluble in water, less easily in alcohol, and insoluble in ether. It melts at 180° and boils at 235°. It forms neutral and acid salts, those of the alkalies being very soluble in water. A characteristic reaction of succinic acid and soluble succinates is the formation of a red-brown precipitate with ferric salts.

SUCHAU, SUCHOW, previous to the Taiping rebellion, one of the largest cities in China; on the Imperial canal, 56 miles W. N. W. of Shanghai, in the province of Kiangsu. It stands on numerous islands separated by canals, and since 1896 has been accessible as a treaty port. The city walls have a circuit of 10 miles. Suchau has for generations been a noted center of the silk manufacture and of the printing of cheap Chinese classics. It was captured by the Taipings, but recovered by "Chinese" Gordon in 1863, on which occasion the city with its many handsome buildings was almost wholly destroyed. Pop. about 500,000.

SUCHET (sü-shā'), LOUIS GABRIEL, DUKE OF ALBUFERA, a French military officer; born in Lyons, France, March 2, 1770; entered the military service at an early age (1790), and served with distinction under Napoleon, Masséna, Joubert, and Moreau in the Italian and Swiss campaigns. He attained the rank of lieutenant-general before he was 30, and in 1808 received the command of a division in Spain, and was almost constantly victorious till after the battle of Vittoria. His brilliant services in that country obtained him the marshal's staff and the title of duke. After the restoration Suchet was created peer of France. He lost his peerage after the battle of Waterloo, but recovered it in 1819. He died in Marseilles, France, Jan. 3, 1826.

SUCKER, a name applied popularly to the *Remora*, to the lumpsuckers (*Cyclopteridæ*) and to fishes belonging to the teleostean genus *Lipáris*, which is nearly allied to the lumpsuckers. The best-known forms are Montague's sucker, *L. Montagui*, and the common sucker, or sea snail, *L. vulgaris*, which adheres to stones by the united ventral fins. The American fresh-water suckers (*Cetostomidæ*) have fleshy protractile lips for sucking in plants and small animals.

SUCKLING, SIR JOHN, an English author; born in Whitton, Middlesex, England, in 1609, and educated at Trinity College, Cambridge. In 1631-1632 he served as a volunteer under Gustavus Adolphus. In 1639 he equipped a troop of horse for the service of Charles I. against the Scotch. Being implicated in a plot to rescue the Earl of Strafford from the Tower, he was obliged to flee to France in 1640. His writings consist of letters, miscellaneous poems (including ballads and songs), a prose treatise entitled "An Account of Religion by Reason," and several plays—"Aglaura," "The Goblins," and "Brennoralt." He died in Paris in 1642.

SUCTORIA, a name given by different authors to various groups of animals, from the fact that the mouth is more or less developed into a suctorial rather than a masticatory organ; especially the *Aphaniptera* and a group of *Annelida*, containing the leeches.

SUDAMINA, minute transparent vesicles arising on the skin toward the favorable termination of various diseases which have been attended by perspiration, as acute rheumatism, typhus, scarlatina, enteric fever, etc.; developed chiefly on the front of the abdomen and the chest. They are placed under the order *Vesiculæ*.

SUDAN, the Arab name given to the vast extent of country in Central Africa which lies between the Sahara on the N., Abyssinia and the Red Sea on the E., the countries draining to the Kongo basin on the S., and Senegambia on the W. Its area is estimated at 2,000,000 square miles. Egyptian rule was first extended to the Eastern Sudan in the early part of the 19th century by Mohammed Ali, under whom Ibrahim Pasha carried it as far S. as Kordofan and Senaar. An Egyptian expedition under Sir Samuel Baker in 1870 led to the conquest of the equatorial regions on the Nile farther S. than the Sudan proper, of which General Gordon was appointed Governor-General in 1874. On the fall of Ismail Pasha of Egypt, Gordon was recalled, and hordes of Turks, Circassians, and Bashi-Bazouks were let loose to plunder the Sudanese. Egyptian misrule then became intolerable, and in this crisis appeared Mohammed Ahmed of Dongola, who gave himself out to be the Mahdi, the long-expected redeemer of Islam.

The revolt of the Mahdi broke up the Egyptian Sudan into various districts. After the Mahdi's death the insurrection was continued by one of his lieutenants called the Kalifa. In 1897 the Anglo-Egyptian army commenced operations for the recovery of the lost provinces. In 1898 the territory was practically regained, and the last resistance disappeared when the Kalifa was slain, and his followers made prisoners in 1899.

In 1898, there were strained relations between the Egyptian and the French governments, owing to the presence in the Egyptian Sudan of a French force under Major Marchand. The difficulty was settled by Marchand's evacuation of Fashoda, and by the delimitation of the respective "spheres of influence" of the two governments, with a mutual agreement not to acquire territory or political influence beyond the designated boundary. See SUDAN, ANGLO-EGYPTIAN.

SUDAN, ANGLO-EGYPTIAN, the territory lying south of the 27th parallel of latitude, in northeast Africa, under Anglo-Egyptian control. It has an area of 1,014,400 square miles, and the distance from Lake Albert to Egypt is about 1,400 miles. The northern part includes the Nubian Desert, but mountains are found in the central and extreme southern parts. The flat part of the southern region is composed chiefly of swamps. This section has an enormous rainfall, with only two dry months, November and December. The Nile and its tributaries flow through the entire country, from Lake Albert to Egypt.

Anglo-Egyptian Sudan is divided into 13 provinces. The governors are British officers of the Egyptian Army employed under the Sudan Government, or British civil officials of the government. The administration is carried on through British inspectors in charge of districts.

In 1910 a governor's council was created to assist the governor-general in the discharge of his duties. The chief towns are Khartum, pop. about 17,000, the capital; Omdurman, pop. about 85,000; Khartum North, pop. about 12,000.

The chief products are gum arabic, ivory, cotton, ostrich feathers, dates, hides and skins, and gold. The value of the imports in 1918 amounted to £4,024,582, and the exports to £3,923,771. There is a railroad from Wadi Halfa to Khartum, with a connection with the Red Sea at Port Sudan. The total length of the line is approximately 1,500 miles.

The Sennar Dam, a vast structure on the Blue Nile, south of Khartum, was constructed in 1924 and 1925. It is designed to irrigate, by a system of thousands of canals, 300,000 acres at first, and ultimately a possible million acres. Its chief purpose is to supply cotton land, to raise cotton for English mills. The dam is 3,300 meters in length, nearly half as long again as that at Assuan; 120 feet from foundation to top at its greatest depth; 90 feet wide at base, maximum measurement; and is estimated to contain 15,000,000 cubic feet of masonry.

Joint possession of the Sudan by Britain and Egypt ceased in 1924. Following the assassination of Sir Lee Stack, the English Sirdar in Egypt, Lord Allenby demanded that Egyptian troops be removed from the Sudan immediately. The Egyptian Government failing to agree, the Eleventh Sudanese Regiment offered resistance at Khartum, but were subdued after losing fifteen of their number, and Egyptian units and many officials were removed from the Sudan to Egypt.

SUDAN, FRENCH. See FRENCH WEST AFRICA.

SUDERMANN (sö'der-man), HERMANN, a German author; born in Matziken, East Prussia, Sept. 30, 1857. He published: "In the Twilight" (1885); "Dame Care" (1886); "Brothers and Sisters" (1887); "Honor," better known as "Magda" (1888); "The Cat Bridge" (1889); "The Destruction of Sodom" (1890); "Home"; "Battle of the Butterflies"; "Iolanthe's Wedding" (1892); "Once on a Time" (1893); "Luck in the Corner" (1895); "About to Die" (1896); "The Three Heron Feathers" (1897); "Fires of St. John" (1901); "The Joy of Living" (1902); "Roses" (1907); "Beggar of Syracuse" (1911); "Dramatic Cycle"; "The World Made Godless" (1916); "The Song of Songs" (1908). He died November 21, 1928.

SUDETIC MOUNTAINS, an extensive mountain system in the S. E. of Germany, dividing Prussian Silesia and Lusatia from Bohemia and Moravia, and connecting the Carpathians with the mountains of Franconia. It does not form a continuous chain except in the middle, where it is known under the names of Riesengebirge and Isergebirge. The subsidiary chains range on an average from 2,500 to 3,300 feet in altitude.

SUE (sü), **MARIE JOSEPH EUGENE,** a French novelist; born in Paris Dec. 10, 1804. He adopted his father's profession of medicine, became a surgeon in the army, and served in Spain in 1823. In 1825 he joined the naval service, and in the capacity of surgeon was present at the battle of Navarino in 1827. On his father's death in 1829, he inherited a fortune, and having abandoned his profession, he devoted himself to literary composition. His first work was a sea novel entitled "Kernock the Pirate," which was quickly followed by "Plick and Plock," "Atar-Gull," "The Salamander" and the "Lookout of Koatven." Among his first historical novels were "Latreaumont," "Jean Cavalier," and "The Commander." His most famous works are: "The Mysteries of Paris," and "The Wandering Jew." He wrote also: "Arthur"; "Hotel Lambert"; "Mathilde, or the Recollections of a Young Woman"; "The Foundling"; "The Seven Capital Sins"; and "The Mysteries of the People." In 1850 he was elected to the Constituent Assembly, and sat as an advanced radical. After the coup d'état by Napoleon III. in 1851 he left France and retired to Savoy. He died in Annecy, Savoy, July 3, 1857.

SUETONIUS TRANQUILLUS, CAIUS, a Roman author; lived and wrote between A. D. 75 and 160. His father was Suetonius Lenis, a tribune of the 13th legion under Otho. The son

mainly known to us as a biographer and miscellaneous writer was educated for the Roman bar. He seems never to have sought public employment. Pliny speaks in high terms of his writings; his integrity and learning. Suetonius was married, but, so far as is known, had no children. He obtained, through Pliny's interest from the Emperor Trajan the *jus trium liberorum,* a distinguished privilege. Suetonius filled the office of Magister Epistolarum to Hadrian, a position which gave him vast opportunities for seeing and utilizing many important imperial documents. The date of his death is unknown. He was a voluminous writer. His works, in part enumerated by Suidas, consisted of grammatical treatises and works antiquarian, legal, moral, and biographical, most of which have been lost. His "Lives of the Twelve Cæsars," "Lives of Eminent Grammarians," and a portion of "Lives of Eminent Rhetoricians," survive. His "Lives of the Cæsars" still maintains the reputation in which it has been held for centuries. Editions of Suetonius are very numerous. The two earliest were published at Rome, 1470, a third at Venice, 1471. The editions of Burmann (1736, quarto, 2 vols.), of J. A. Ernesti (1748), and of Fr. Oudendorp (1751), are well known.

SUEVI, an appellation of various Germanic tribes in classic authors; used somewhat loosely, as we find it employed to designate peoples widely removed from each other. On six different occasions tribes, probably Germanic, though possibly mixed with Celtic and Slavonic elements, appear in history under this name. (1) Cæsar mentions Suevi living on the E. bank of the Rhine, and possessing 100 villages. (2) Tacitus places them N. and S. of this, on both sides of the Upper and Middle Elbe. (3) In the 2d and 3d centuries they appear along with the Quadi and Marcomanni in Moravia and Bohemia. (4) In 406 Suevi crossed the Rhine along with the Vandals and Alans, and broke into Spain, settling more especially in Leon and Castile, whence they were driven by the Visigoths in 584. (5) In 420 another tribe called Suevi are spoken of in Upper Germany, who left their name to the modern Swabia. (6) In the 6th century we hear of Nordsuevi, with a village Swevon on the Upper Elbe.

SUEZ, a town, on an angle of land near the N. extremity of the Gulf of Suez, and near the S. terminus of the Suez canal. It is walled on all sides but that toward the sea, has an indifferent harbor, but a tolerably good quay. It is divided into an Arab quarter and a European quarter, the latter containing the buildings of the Peninsular and Oriental Steamship Co. Since the opening of the Suez canal, the town has greatly improved, and a railroad connects it with Cairo.

The Gulf of Suez is the W. and larger of the two branches into which the Red Sea divides toward its N. extremity, and washes the E. coasts of Egypt on the W. of the Sinaitic peninsula. Extreme length 200 miles, average width about 20 miles.

The Isthmus of Suez is a neck of land 72 miles wide at its narrowest part, extending from the Gulf of Suez on the S. to the Mediterranean on the N., and connecting the continents of Asia and Africa. The main interest attached to this region, in recent times, has been in the ship canal through the isthmus. Pop. (1897) 17,457.

SUEZ CANAL. It is certain that in ancient times a canal connecting, indirectly, the Mediterranean and Red seas did exist. At what period it was constructed is not so certain. Herodotus ascribes its projection and partial execution to Pharaoh Necho (about 600 B. C.); Aristotle, Strabo, and Pliny fix on the half mythical Sesostris as its originator. The honor of its completion is assigned by some to Darius, King of Persia; by others to the Ptolemies. It began about a mile and a half from Suez, and was carried in a N. W. direction, through a remarkable series of natural depressions, to Bubastis, on the Pelusiac or E. branch of the Nile. Its entire length was 92 miles (of which upward of 60 were cut by human labor), its width from 108 to 165 feet, and its depth 15 (Pliny says 30) feet. How long it continued to be used we cannot tell, but at length it became choked up with sand, was restored by Trajan early in the 2d century A. D., but again became unusable from the same cause, and so remained till the conquest of Egypt by Amrou, the Arab general of the Caliph Omar, who caused it to be re-opened, and named it the "Canal of the Prince of the Faithful," under which designation it continued to be employed for upward of a century, but was finally blocked up by the unconquerable sands, A. D. 767. In this condition it has ever since remained.

The attention of Europe was first turned to a canal here during the invasion of Egypt by Bonaparte, who caused the isthmus to be surveyed by a body of engineers, who arrived at the opinion that the level of the Mediterranean is 30 feet below that of the Red Sea at Suez—an opinion which a subsequent survey proved to be erroneous. In 1847 France, England and Austria sent out a commission to measure accurately the levels of the two seas. The commissioners, M. Talabot, Robert Stephenson, and Signor Nigrelli, ascertained that instead of a difference of 30 feet the two seas have exactly the same mean level. Another examination leading to similar results was made in 1853. Mr. Stephenson expressed himself very strongly against the feasibility of a canal and planned instead a railway from Cairo to Suez, which was opened (1858) and which now conveys overland the Indian and Australian mails. In 1854 a new experimenter appeared in the person of M. de Lesseps, a member of the French diplomatic service in Egypt, who (1856) obtained from the pasha the concession of building a ship canal from Tyneh (near the ruins of ancient Pelusium) to Suez. The peculiarity of M. de Lesseps's plan lay in this, that instead of following an oblique course and uniting his canal with the Nile, as the ancients had done, and as all modern engineers had thought of doing, he proposed to cut a canal right through the isthmus in a straight line to Suez. The colossal feature of M. de Lesseps's plan was the artificial harbors which he proposed to execute at the two ends. In 1855 a new European commission was appointed, which reported that M. de Lesseps's scheme was practicable. The result of the report was the formation of a joint-stock company, and the work was accordingly begun in 1860. Starting from Port Said, the canal crosses about 20 miles of Menzaleh Lake. Through this lagoon it is 112 yards wide at the surface, 26 yards at the bottom, and 26 feet deep. An artificial bank rises 15 feet on each side of this canal. Beyond Menzaleh Lake heavier work begins. The distance thence to Abu Ballah Lake is 11 miles, with a height of ground above the level of the sea varying from 15 to 30 feet. Crossing the last named lake, there is another land distance of 11 miles to Temsah Lake cutting through ground to a depth varying from 30 to 70 or 80 feet, and then 3 miles further across this little lake itself. At El Guisr, or Girsch, occurs the deepest cutting in the whole line, 85 feet below the surface. Ismailia, on Timsah Lake, is regarded as the central point of the canal. The freshwater canal extends from the Nile to Timsah Lake, and was constructed purposely to supply with water the population accumulating at various points on the line of the canal; but it is also used by sailing vessels. On Nov. 16, 1869, the Suez canal was opened in form, with a procession of English and foreign steam-

© Publishers' Photo Service

A VESSEL PASSING THROUGH THE SUEZ CANAL, AS SEEN FROM THE DESERT

See **Suez Canal**, p opposite

STEAMERS PASSING THROUGH THE SUEZ CANAL

See Suez Canal, p. 146

ers, in presence of the Khedive, the Empress of the French, the Emperor of Austria, the Crown Prince of Prussia, and others. An attempt was made by the Turks during the World War (1914-1918) to capture the canal by attacks at Ismailia and other points but they were defeated by the British forces. See EGYPT.

SUFFOLK, a city of Virginia, the county seat of Nansemond co. It is on the Nansemond river, and on the Norfolk and Western, the Seaboard Air Line, the Southern, the Atlantic Coast Line, the Norfolk Southern, and the Virginian railroads. Its industries include car works, stove factories, woodworking and lumber mills. It is also an important railroad center. Pop. (1910), 7,008; (1920) 9,123.

SUFFOLK, a maritime county of southeast England. Area, 1,489 square miles. Pop. about 350,000. The county is divided into East and West Suffolk, the capital of the former being Ipswich (pop. about 75,000), and the capital of the latter Bury St. Edmunds (pop. about 17,500). The largest part of the county is flat, with marshes on its northwestern and northeastern borders. The Lark, the Gipping, and the tributaries of the Waveney and of the Stour are the chief streams. The soil is diversified and in many parts very productive for the ordinary crops.

SUFFRAGE, the right to vote for any purpose, but more especially the right of a person to vote in the election of his political representative. Many writers advocate the universal extension of this right, but in Great Britain and most European countries it is limited by a household or other qualification. In the United States it is practically universal for all male and female citizens and naturalized persons of 21 years and upward.

The history of suffrage has been a record of progress and extension. The most limited form is observed in the first election of the Virginia colony in 1607, and the most extensive today is in Wyoming. By the charter granted to the Virginia Company the members of a council of settlers, chosen by a higher council resident in England, were privileged to choose annually a president from their own number. In accordance with this the first right of suffrage that existed in any permanent American colony was exercised by six members of the council, who, in May, 1607, chose Edward Maria Wingfield as the first president. In 1619 the different towns of Virginia elected by general suffrage, 22 burgesses,

who, assembling at Jamestown, constituted the first legislative body convened in America. In the following year, a few hundred miles N. the Plymouth fathers gathered on the deck of the *Mayflower* and exercised a still more extended right of suffrage in the choice of John Carver as the first governor of the colony. These privileges continued, with only a few changes in Virginia, till the Revolutionary War, excepting that 18 years after the election of Carver in Massachusetts, their mass assemblies were deemed too large and a representative government was established.

Though democratic in principle, a few laws passed by the New England colonists restricted the privilege of suffrage. No person who had not become a freeman by taking the oath of allegiance was permitted to vote. No man, according to a law of 1631, was admitted to the freedom of the body politic who was not a member of some of the churches within the limits of the same. No Quaker was permitted to become a freeman. The two latter restrictions, however, were soon removed. The power of the people was greatly increased through the results of the Revolution, yet in several of the original 13 States the right of suffrage was restricted to property holders or rate payers, and otherwise limited for periods extending in some cases through one or more decades of the past century. The tendency was constantly to the wide limits of manhood suffrage, which was then the prevailing rule, but only as regards white citizens, till the 15th Amendment to the National Constitution in March, 1870, extended the same right to colored citizens. The movement toward the extension of the right to woman carried on for many years finally resulted in a Constitutional Amendment providing for it. See WOMAN SUFFRAGE.

SUFFREN SAINT-TROPES, PIERRE ANDRÉ DE, a French naval hero; born a younger son of a good Provence family, July 17, 1726. At 14 he entered the navy, and first saw fire in the indecisive action with the English off Toulon in 1744. He took part in the unsuccessful attempt to recapture Cape Breton (1746); was captured by Hawke in the Bay of Biscay the next year; but soon exchanged; and after the peace went to Malta and served for six years among the Knights Hospitallers. Again in the French service, he took part in the action off Minorca (May, 1756), was again captured in Boscawen's destruction of the Toulon fleet (1759). He took part in the bombardment of Sallee in 1765. Commander in 1767, he served four years in the service of Malta, and returned to

France with the rank of captain in 1772. Early in 1777 he sailed to America, and his ship began the indecisive battle of Grenada on July 6, 1779. He next served with the allied fleet blockading Gibraltar, and early in 1781 was placed in command of a squadron of five ships for service in the East Indies. After an action at the Cape Verde Islands, he outsailed Commodore Johnstone to the Cape, and so saved the colony for the time. Sailing to Madras, he fought a hard but indecisive battle off Madras, and soon after, in a bloody two days' battle off Providien on the coast of Ceylon, proved himself a consummate master of naval tactics. Having captured Trincomalee, he two days later stood out of the harbor with 15 ships against the English 12, and fought a hard but irregular battle. His last fight (June, 1783) was also indecisive. Suffren arrived in Paris early in 1784, and was received with the greatest honors, and created Vice-Admiral of France. He died in Paris Dec. 8, 1788.

SUFISM, the pantheistic mysticism of the Mohammedan East, which strives for the highest illumination of the mind, the most perfect calmness of the soul, and the union of it with God by an ascetic life and the subjugation of the appetites. This pantheism, clothed in a mysticoreligious garb, has been professed since the 9th and 10th centuries by a sect which is gaining adherents continually among the more cultivated Mohammedans, particularly in Persia and India. The name is from *sufi*, a religious ascetic, an eastern term applied to all members of religious monastic bodies leading an ascetic life. The Sufis were originally devout persons who, perplexed by the discord prevailing among the various systems of Mohammedan philosophy in the 2d century of the Hejira, found consolation in pious mysticism. Their teachings, though at first consonant with orthodox Mohammedanism, gradually led to a mode of thought totally irreconcilable with the Koran. About the beginning of the 10th century the Sufis divided into two branches, one of which followed Bostanie, who openly embraced pantheism, and the other Juneid, who sought to reconcile Sufism with Mohammedanism. Among eminent Persian poets belonging to the Sufis we may mention Hafiz, a distinguished Sufî; Ferîd-eddîn, and Jami. The celebrated philosopher and jurist, Alghazzâlî was also a Sufi.

SUGAR, a sweet, crystallized substance manufactured from the expressed juice of various plants, especially from the sugar cane; also, any substance, more or less resembling sugar in any of its properties; as sugar of lead; figuratively, sweet, honeyed, or soothing words or flattery, used to disguise or hide something distasteful.

In chemistry, $Cn(OH_2)m$, the generic name for a large number of bodies occurring naturally in the animal or vegetable kingdom, or produced from glucosides by the action of ferments or dilute acids. They are all more or less soluble in water, and their solutions exert a rotatory action on polarized light. Some reduce alkaline solutions of copper while others either do not, or do so only to a limited extent. They may all be classed under two heads, viz., unfermentable sugars, as mannite, dulcite, sorbite, etc., and fermentable sugars, as cane sugar, glucose, maltose, etc. Cane sugar, $C_{12}H_{22}O_{11}$, called also saccharose, sucrose, and canose, is found in the juice of many grasses, in the sap of several trees, and in beet and several other roots. It is extracted most easily from sugar cane but on the Continent of Europe and also in the United States it is manufactured on a large scale from beet root. The expressed juice is heated nearly to the boiling point, and a small quantity of slaked lime added. The clear liquid which separates from the coagulum is evaporated as rapidly as possible, and transferred into shallow vessels to crystallize. Drained from the syrup or molasses, it yields the raw sugar of commerce. When further refined by treatment with animal charcoal, poured into molds, and then dried in a stove, the product is loaf sugar. When the crystallization is allowed to proceed very slowly, sugar candy results. Moderately heated it melts, and solidifies on cooling to an amorphous mass, familiar as barley sugar. Pure sugar separates from its solution in transparent colorless crystals, having the figure of a modified monoclinic prism. Its crystals have a sp. gr. of 1.6. Heated above 210°, water is given off and a brown substance known as caramel remains. Cane sugar is transformed into invert sugar by boiling in presence of dilute acids, mineral acting more rapidly than organic acids. Strong sulphuric acid completely decomposes cane sugar, and nitric acid converts it into saccharic acid. It turns a ray of polarized light to the right, $Aj = 73.8$.

SUGAR BEET, a hardy, biennial plant, grown in France, Germany, Austria, Russia, Holland, Belgium, Norway, Sweden, Denmark, Italy, Spain, and, more recently, in the United States, Canada, Australia, New Zealand, and Great Britain. The number of varieties now grown is considerable, but they are all

SUGAR CANE GROWING ON A PLANTATION IN LOUISIANA

See Sugar Cane, p. 149

See **Sugar Cane**, p. opposite

PLANTING SUGAR CANE ON IRRIGATED LAND IN PERU

derived from the Silesian white beet, which was, in turn, a descendant of the sea beet, a common perennial on muddy seashores. In shape, a good sugar beet is long, conical and regular. In weight, after the leaves have been removed, it varies from one to two pounds, and its color may be white, pale pink or grayish. The amount of sugar which it contained was originally only about 10 per cent. of its weight, but this has now been raised, by cultivation, from 16 to 18 per cent. The percentage varies in different zones of the root, being smallest at the root and greatest at the thick part just under the crown. Before extracting the roots are washed free from mud, cut into fine, long shreds, and then extracted with hot water. The juice thus obtained is clarified, concentrated and allowed to crystallize. The exhausted molasses obtained as a by-product is frequently mixed with the extracted beet pulp and sold as cattle-food.

SUGAR CANE, *Saccharum officinarum,* a strong, cane-stemmed grass, from 8 to 12 feet high, producing a large, feathery plume of flowers. It is wild or cultivated in the Southern United States, India, China, the South Sea Islands, the West Indies, and South America, flourishing in the zone or belt from the equator to 35° or 40° N. and S. The land chosen for its cultivation is usually a good loam or light clay well manured. The leafy ends of the canes of the preceding season are cut off, or the whole cane is cut up, each piece being made to contain two nodes or joints. Twenty thousand of these are planted on each acre in January and February, the harvest begins early in December, and the cutting and crushing of the canes are carried on till January or February. There are several varieties of the sugar cane.

SUGARS. Sugar is the generic name for a class of substances belonging to the carbohydrate group. They either occur naturally in the animal or vegetable kingdom, or are produced by the action of dilute acids or ferments on another class of bodies known as glucosides. As a class, they possess a sweet taste, although the degree of sweetness varies greatly with sugars of different kinds. They are readily soluble in water, less soluble and sometimes wholly insoluble in alcohol, and insoluble in ether and similar solvents which will not mix with water. Some sugars undergo alcoholic fermentation with yeast, others change from one sugar to another under the action of dilute acids. Many of them are of great value as foodstuffs. Chemically, they consist of carbon, hydrogen and oxygen, the ratio of hydrogen to oxygen being always the same as in water, namely two atoms of hydrogen to one of oxygen. They are divided into three large groups: (1) The mono-saccharides, having the formula $C_6H_{12}O_6$. (2) The di-saccharides, having the formula $C_{12}H_{22}O_{11}$. (3) The tri-saccharides, having the formula $C_{18}H_{32}O_{16}$. It will be noticed that the formula for the di-saccharides is exactly twice that of the mono-saccharides less one molecule of water, H_2O; while the tri-saccharides are three times the mono-saccharides, less two molecules of water. All the common sugars belong to one of the first two groups.

1. *Mono-saccharides.* The best known sugar among the mono-saccharides is *Dextrose*, commonly known as *Glucose*, although this latter name is also applied to other sugars of a similar character. It occurs in large quantities in grapes and hence is sometimes called grape sugar. Hard nodules of this sugar are frequently found in dried grapes or raisins, and it is a common constituent of sweet fruits, roots and leaves, and also occurs in honey. It is prepared artificially by boiling a solution of cane sugar with dilute acids, and also from starch by similar means, this process being known as "inversion." So-called corn syrup is inverted corn starch. Dextrose crystallizes in warty masses, but is most familiar in the form of syrup. It is less sweet than cane sugar. *Fructose* or *Levulose*, is closely allied to dextrose and occurs with it in many sweet fruits and in honey. When cane sugar is inverted by dilute acids, equal parts of dextrose and levulose are produced, the mixture being known as *"invert sugar."* The other mono-saccharides are of academic interest only.

2. *Di-saccharides.* The commonest di-saccharide is *Sucrose* or *Cane sugar.* The two chief sources from which it is obtained are the sugar cane and the sugar beet. The former contains 15-20 per cent., the latter seldom more than 16 per cent. It also occurs in many sweet fruits, such as the pineapple, the strawberry, etc. Sucrose crystallizes from water in four-sided prisms. It melts at 160° C., and on cooling solidifies to a glassy mass known as barley-sugar. Heated to higher temperatures, it loses water and becomes converted to caramel. It is very soluble in water, at ordinary temperatures dissolving in one-third of its weight of water. Sucrose is the chief constituent of maple sugar.

Maltose or *malt sugar* is formed from

starch by the enzyme *diastase*. Malt is the grain of barley which has been caused to sprout by wetting it, in heaps, with water and then keeping in a warm moist atmosphere. This sprouting brings about the formation of the diastase. On drying the malt and stirring with water, the diastase acts upon the starch, converting it to maltose. Since the passing of the Prohibition Act, large quantities of malt syrup have been placed on the market as a table syrup, a basis for soft drinks, for candy manufacture and other purposes. *Lactose* or *Milk-sugar* is an important constituent of the milk of all mammals, in which it occurs to the extent of about 4 per cent., although the percentage varies somewhat. It can be prepared from milk by treating with rennet, when the curd separates, leaving the sugar in solution in the whey. On evaporation the crude lactose is obtained. The solution may be purified by filtration through charcoal, and the sugar obtained by crystallization. Lactose is far less sweet than cane sugar.

The tri-saccharides are of academic interest only, the most important being *raffinose*.

The action of dilute acids on sugars is of interest and importance. As already stated, sucrose undergoes inversion when its solution is boiled with dilute acids, invert sugar, a mixture of dextrose and levulose, being produced. Similar changes take place in all the disaccharides, under similar conditions, in every case one or more mono-saccharides being formed. Milk sugar gives dextrose and galactose, maltose gives dextrose only. The process is one of splitting the sugar molecule in two with the addition of a molecule of water, thus:

$$C_{12}H_{22}O_{11} + H_2O = 2C_6H_{12}O_6$$

The fermentation of cane sugar, maltose and lactose by yeast can only take place after inversion. This can be brought about either by dilute acids, as described above, or by an organism known as an enzyme. Ordinary yeast contains the enzyme, which inverts cane sugar and maltose, and hence can ferment both these sugars. Dextrose, fructose and invert sugar are fermentable by all yeasts.

Synthetic Sugar.—Creation of sugar from a simpler carbohydrate, formaldehyde, in the laboratory by E. C. C. Baly of the University of Liverpool was reported in 1924. The product, analyzed by J. C. Irvine of St. Andrew's University, was found to contain sugars of the glucose type.

SUGGESTION, in psychology, may be defined as including all proposals to action or belief put into the mind of one person by another and which overcome resistance, not by argument or reason, but by submission or subordination, whether conscious or unconscious, on the part of the recipient. Every human being is to some extent subject to the influence of others' suggestions, which may be communicated in numberless ways, as by spoken words or by indirection. The tendency to yield to suggestion resembles the instinct of imitation. It varies widely in different persons as well as under different conditions. Emotion, fatigue or illness increases suggestibility. The suggestibility of crowds is notorious, as is that of children and of persons on the witness stand. Suggestion plays an important part in almost every field of life. Hypnotism is the extreme case of artificial suggestibility.

SUICIDE, the act of designedly destroying one's own life. To constitute suicide, in a legal sense, the person must be of the years of discretion and of a sound mind. The law of England treats suicide as a felony involving the forfeiture to the crown of all the personal property which the party has at the time he committed the act, including debts due to him; but it is not attended with forfeiture of freehold or corruption of blood. The body of the suicide was formerly required to be buried without Christian rites in the open highway or cross roads, and a stake was thrust through it to mark the public detestation. Suicide was tolerated by the Romans, and was esteemed a virtue in certain cases, by the Stoic and Epicurean philosophers. Valerius Maximus, who wrote in the 1st century, states that a poisonous liquor was kept publicly at Massilia, and that it was given to such as presented themselves before the Senate and procured its approval of their reasons to get rid of life.

Suicide, however, is a very frequent result of insanity, more especially in Christian countries, and the verdict generally given by coroners' juries is that the person destroyed himself while in a state of unsound mind; not so much, however, from the fact of insanity being thereby established, as that any other verdict would distress the surviving relations and friends of the deceased. Suicidal mania or insanity may be defined as a perversion or reversal of the natural instinct of love of life, leading to its destruction. Suicides are more numerous in cities than in town and country life. The chief causes for suicide are vice and crime, madness, delirium, alcoholism, poverty, and moral suffering. In the United States insanity is the leading cause.

SUIDÆ, or SUIDA, in zoölogy, a family of artiodactyle mammals, of the Bunodont group (in which the crowns of the molars are tuberculated). The feet have only two functional toes, the other two being much shorter, and hardly touching the ground. Molars, incisors, and canines are present, the last very large, and, in the males, usually constituting formidable tusks projecting from the side of the mouth. The stomach is generally slightly divided, but is by no means so complex as in the *Ruminantia*. Snout truncated and cylindrical, capable of considerable movement, and adapted for rooting up the ground. The skin is covered with hair to a greater or less extent; tail very short, in some cases rudimentary. The family is divided into three well-marked groups or sub-families: *Suinæ*, true swine (*Sus, Potomachœrus, Babirusa,* and *Porcula*); *Dicotylinæ* (*Peccaries,* with the single genus *Dicotyles,* often classed as a family); and *Phacochœrinæ* (wart hogs, with one genus, *Phacochœrus*). The family probably commenced in the Eocene Tertiary.

SUIR, a river of Ireland, flowing 85 miles S. and E., chiefly along the boundary of the counties of Tipperary, Waterford, Kilkenny, and Wexford, past Clonmel, Carrick, and Waterford, till it meets the Barrow, and immediately afterward falls into Waterford Haven. It is navigable by barges as far as Clonmel.

SUKKUR, a town on the right bank of the Indus, 28 miles S. E. of Shikarpur; it is connected by rail also with Karachi (Kurrachee), and is the terminus of the Bolan Pass railway to Afghanistan. The river is crossed by a magnificent cantilever bridge (1889), or rather by two bridges (one with a span of 820 feet), resting on the fortified island of Bukkur in the middle of the channel. New Sukkur, which grew up after the British occupied (1839) the fort on Bukkur, has considerable trade in silk, cloth, cotton, wool, opium, saltpeter, sugar, brass utensils, piece goods, metals, wines and spirits. Old Sukkur, about a mile away, has a good many old tombs in its vicinity. Pop. about 25,000.

SUKKUR BARRAGE, a dam across the Indus River at Sukkur, India, under construction in 1928; intended to provide water for the irrigation of nearly 6,000,-000 acres of land in northwestern India. The area ultimately to be watered was estimated to equal or exceed the whole agricultural acreage of Egypt. The barrage, 4,725 feet long, with regulators at either end, will maintain a level of the Indus sufficiently high to fill irrigation canals that previously functioned only in seasons of high water. It is expected to increase the Indian cotton crop.

SUKHOMLINOV, VLADIMIR ALEXANDROVITCH, a Russian soldier, born in 1852. He took part in the Russo-Japanese War on the western frontier, and afterward held important military posts in Russian Poland and on the Prussian frontier. He became Minister of War in 1909, resigning in 1915, during the World War. He was an excellent organizer and did much to develop aviation and other branches in the Russian army.

SULEIMAN PASHA, a Turkish military officer; born in Rumelia in 1840. He entered the Turkish army in 1854, fought in Montenegro, Crete, and Yemen between that date and 1875, and in the intervals of peace taught in the Military Academy at Constantinople, and finally presided over it as director. He greatly distinguished himself as a corps commander against the Serbians in 1876, and was in 1877 nominated governor of Bosnia and Herzegovina. When the Russians declared war (1877) against Turkey, Suleiman checked them at Eski Zagra, and destroyed his army in heroic but vain attempts to force them from the Shipka Pass. In October he was appointed commander-in-chief of the Army of the Danube, but failed to accomplish anything, retreated behind the Balkans, and suffered defeat near Philippopolis (January, 1878). Brought before a court-martial, he was condemned to be degraded and kept in a fortress prison for 15 years. The sultan, however, pardoned him, and he died in Constantinople Aug. 11, 1892.

SULIMAN MOUNTAINS, a range on the borders of Afghanistan and British India. The highest summit, Takht-i-Suliman, or "Suliman's Seat," attains an elevation of more than 6,000 feet (according to some estimates 11,000 or 12,000 feet). These mountains are covered with dense forests, and are generally considered the peculiar seat of the aboriginal Afghans.

SULINA, the middlemost of the three chief mouths of the Danube; it quits the Khedrile or most S. branch, and opens into the Black Sea after an E. course of over 50 miles (see DANUBE). It is used for transporting immense quantities of corn, chiefly for the British market.

SULIOTS, or SULIOTES, a people of mixed Albanian and Greek descent, who formerly dwelt in the S. corner of the pashalik of Janina (Epirus), in European Turkey. After having for about 15 years heroically resisted the encroachments of the pasha of Janina on their independence, they were vanquished by Ali Pasha in 1801. In 1820 they fought desperately against the Turks for their old oppressor; and, ultimately, they took a glorious part in the War of Greek Independence, but their country was not included by the treaty of 1829 within the Greek boundary. See JANINA and BOZZARIS.

SULLA, LUCIUS CORNELIUS, a Roman dictator; born in 138 B. C. He received a good education, but was notorious from his youth upward for his excessive dissipation and debauchery. He served with distinction under Marius in the Jugurthine (107 B. C.) and Cimbrian (104-102) wars, and in 93 was chosen prætor. For his services in the Social War (90-88) he was appointed consul (88 B. C.), and the province of

SULLA

Asia, with the conduct of the war against Mithridates, fell to his lot. Marius was also ambitious of this command, and resorted to acts of violence to carry his point, by which Sulla was compelled to escape from Rome. But Sulla re-entered the city at the head of his army, drove Marius to Africa, and then sailed for Greece at the beginning of 87 B. C. He expelled the armies of Mithridates from Europe (86), crossed into Asia (84), and was everywhere victorious, forcing Mithridates to conclude a peace. Marius had died in 86 B. C., but the party of Marius was still strong. Sulla now hastened to Italy, and landed at Brundusium with 40,000 men, 83 B. C. He was joined by many of his friends who had been banished from Rome. He gained four bat-

tles over the Roman forces in person, and defeated a Samnite army under Telesinus. He entered the city victorious in 82, and immediately put to death between 6,000 and 7,000 prisoners of war in the circus. He caused himself to be named dictator for an indefinite period (81 B. C.). In 79 B. C. he laid down his dictatorship, and retiring to Puteoli abandoned himself to debauchery. He died in 78 B. C. See ROME.

SULLIVAN, SIR ARTHUR SEYMOUR, an English composer; born in London, England, May 13, 1842; became a member of the boy choir in the Chapel Royal at St. James's, and at the age of 13 published his first composition. In the following year he won the Mendelssohn scholarship at the Royal Academy of Music, and in 1858, while at Leipsic, he composed his "Feast of Roses" and the music to Shakespeare's "Tempest." Subsequently he produced numerous songs, operas, oratorios, etc. He was knighted in 1883 and made chevalier of the Legion of Honor of France in the same year. He died in London, Nov. 21, 1900.

SULLIVAN, BARRY, an English tragedian; born in Birmingham in 1824; first appeared at Cork in 1840; played at Edinburgh and elsewhere; and at the Haymarket in London as Hamlet in February, 1852. He visited the United States in 1857-1860, and Australia in 1861-1866. He died in Brighton, England, May 3, 1891.

SULLIVAN, JOHN, an American military officer; born in Berwick, Me., Feb. 17, 1740; studied law and obtained a lucrative practice in Durham, N. H. He was commissioned a major of militia in 1772; represented New Hampshire at the Continental Congress held in Philadelphia, Pa., in 1774; was appointed a brigadier-general of the American Army in 1775; and given command of the left wing of the forces then laying siege to Boston. In June, 1776, he was placed in command of the army on the Canadian boundary. After an unsuccessful engagement with the British at THREE RIVERS (q. v.) he retreated to New York, and for a time was chief in command on Long Island; subsequently was promoted major-general. During Washington's campaign, which resulted in the capture of the Hessians at Trenton, Sullivan had command of the right wing of the army. He also participated in the battle of Princeton, and later descended rapidly on Staten Island and took 100 prisoners. He was at the battles of the Brandywine and Germantown, and during the latter action defeated the British left. On Aug. 29, 1778, he attacked the British at Butt's Hill, near Newport, R. I., and after a 12-hours' severe battle, in which about 6,000 men fought on each side, the Americans drove the British from the field at the point of the bayonet. Lafayette pronounced this engagement the best contested one of the whole war. In 1779 Sullivan led 4,000 troops into New York State to put a stop to Indian outrages. During the campaign he drove thousands of Indians out of the State and destroyed their crops and villages. He resigned from the army in 1780 owing to ill health, and was a second time a delegate to the Continental Congress. He later resumed the practice of law in New Hampshire; and was United States judge of that State from 1789 till his death, in Durham, N. H., Jan. 23, 1795.

SULLIVAN, MARK, an American editor and writer; born at Avondale, Pa., in 1874. He was educated at the Normal School, West Chester, Pa., and at Harvard University. From 1893 to 1900 he was part owner of the "Daily Republican," Phœnixville, Pa.; from 1903 to 1904 writer on the Boston "Transcript"; from 1904 to 1906 a member of the New York City bar, and from 1906 to 1917 a member of the editorial staff of "Collier's Weekly," serving as editor from 1912 to 1917. After this he became Washington correspondent of the New York "Evening Post."

SULLIVAN, THOMAS RUSSELL, an American fiction writer and dramatist; born in Boston, Mass., Nov. 21, 1849. His novels include "Tom Sylvester," "Roses of Shadow," "Day and Night Stories," "Ars et Vita" (1893); "Boston, Old and New" (1912), and "Hand of Petrarch" (1913). His plays include "The Catspaw" (1881), "Merely Players" (1886), a dramatization of Stevenson's "Dr. Jekyll and Mr. Hyde," and "Nero," a tragedy. He was joint author with W. W. Chamberlin of "Hearts Are Trumps" produced 1878, and "Midsummer Madness," produced 1880. He died in 1916.

SULLIVAN'S ISLAND, an island at the N. side of the entrance to Charleston harbor, S. C.; 6 miles from Charleston. It is 6 miles long, but very narrow, and is a favorite sea-bathing resort. On it is situated Fort Moultrie, a position of importance during the Civil War.

SULLY, ALFRED, an American military officer; born in Philadelphia, Pa., in 1821; was graduated at the United States Military Academy in 1841, and

assigned to the 2d Infantry, with which he took part in the Seminole War; served in the war with Mexico in 1846-1847; and was then assigned to duty on recruiting service in the North. In 1861-1862 he served in Washington and in the latter year was made colonel of the 3d Minnesota Volunteers; won distinction in the battles of Fair Oaks and Malvern Hill; was promoted brigadier-general of volunteers in October, 1862, and later participated in the battle of Chancellorsville. In 1863 he was given command of the Department of Dakota, and greatly distinguished himself in his campaigns against hostile Indians. At the close of the war he was brevetted major-general of volunteers, and brigadier-general, U. S. A., for gallantry during the war; and was promoted colonel of the 10th Infantry in 1872. He died in Fort Vancouver, Wash., April 17, 1879.

SULLY, MAXIMILIEN DE BETHUNE, DUC DE, Marshal of France and first minister of Henry IV.; born in the château of Rosny, France, Dec. 13, 1559; was educated in the Protestant faith. He distinguished himself at the battle of Ivri in 1590, where he was severely wounded, and was afterward of great assistance to the king in resisting the intrigues of the League. In 1597 he was appointed controller of finance, and by his excellent administration

DUC DE SULLY

largely reduced taxation, and eventually paid off a state debt of 300,000,000 livres. He also received many other offices and dignities, and became adviser of the king in all his councils. His industry was unwearied, and he did all he could to encourage agriculture, which he regarded as the mainstay of the state. In 1606 the territory of Sully-sur-Loire was erected into a duchy in his favor. After the murder of Henry IV. (1610) he retired from court and resigned most of his charges. He now occupied himself chiefly with agriculture, and rarely took part in political affairs. He was created marshal by Richelieu in 1634, and died in Villebon Castle, France, Dec. 22, 1641. He left memoirs which have been published in English.

SULLY - PRUDHOMME, RENÉ FRANCOIS ARMAND (sü-lē'prüd-um'), a French poet; born in Paris, France, May 16, 1839. He wrote: "Stanzas and Poems" (1865); "The Broken Vase"; "The Stables of Augeas"; "The Wildernesses"; "Impressions of War" (collected 1872); "Revolt of the Flowers" (1874); "Reflections on the Art of Versification" (1892). He was elected a member of the Academy in 1881, and in 1901 received one of the Nobel prizes amounting to about $40,000. He died September, 1907.

SULLY, THOMAS, an American artist; born in Horncastle, Lincolnshire, England, in 1783; emigrated to the United States with his parents in 1792; studied painting in Charleston; established himself in Richmond, Va., as a portrait painter in 1803; removed afterward to New York; and in 1809 settled in Philadelphia, where he afterward lived. His reputation as one of the leading American portrait painters is founded on numerous works, the best known of which are the full-length portraits of Dr. Benjamin Rush, Commodore Decatur, Thomas Jefferson, and Lafayette. The Boston Museum possesses his celebrated picture of "Washington Crossing the Delaware." He died in Philadelphia Nov. 5, 1872.

SULPHATES, salts of sulphuric acid. Sulphuric acid is dibasic, forming two classes of sulphates, viz., neutral sulphates, in which the two hydrogen atoms of the acid are replaced by metal, and acid sulphates, in which one hydrogen atom only is so replaced. The general formula of the former class is M_2SO_4, and of the latter $MHSO_4$. (M represents a monovalent metal.) Of the sulphates, some are found native; some are very soluble, some sparingly soluble, and some insoluble. The most important sulphates are: Sulphate of aluminum and potassium, or alum; sulphate of ammonium, employed for making carbonate of ammonia; sulphate of copper, or blue vitriol, much used as an escharotic in surgery, and also used in dyeing and for preparing certain green pigments; sulphate of iron, or green vitriol, used in making ink, and very extensively in dyeing and calico printing; it is also much used in medicine; sulphate of calcium, or gypsum; sulphate of magnesium, or Epsom salts; sulphate of manganese, used in calico printing; sulphate of mercury, used in the preparation of corrosive sublimate and of calomel; bi-sulphate of potash, much used as a flux in mineral analysis; sulphate of sodium, or Glauber's salts; sulphate of quinine, much used in medicine; sulphate of zinc, or white vitriol, used in surgery, also in the preparation of drying oils for varnishes, and in the reserve or resist pastes of the calico printer. Many double sulphates are known.

SULPHOCYANIC ACID, HCNS; hydrogen sulphocyanate; a monobasic acid obtained by decomposing lead sulphocyanate suspended in water, with sulphuretted hydrogen. It is a colorless, very acid liquid, with a pungent acetous odor, and solidifies at —12.5° to hexagonal plates. Heated to 100° it boils, but the greater part suffers decomposition. It colors ferric salts an intense blood-red, and on this account is used, in the form of any of its soluble salts, to detect traces of iron.

SULPHUR. Sulphur, or brimstone, has been known and used from the earliest times. It is found native in mechanical combination with various earthy impurities in most volcanic districts, more particularly in Sicily and the countries bordering on the Mediterranean, and in Louisiana and Texas. The native sulphur of commerce was formerly derived chiefly from Sicily, where it occurs in beds of blue-clayey formation. It is found native in two forms—in transparent amber crystals, as virgin sulphur; or in opaque, lemon-yellow crystalline masses, as volcanic sulphur. It is found in combination with the different metals, forming metallic sulphides, in nearly every portion of the earth. Zinc blende, iron, and copper pyrites, galena, cinnabar, gray antimony, and realgar, are a few instances of the valuable ores containing sulphur. In its oxidized condition, as sulphuric acid, it is also very largely distributed over the mineral kingdom. Sulphur exists in many organic bodies; for example, it is always contained in albumen and the various protein compounds. Native sulphur is purified from the foreign substances mixed with it by distillation in, first, long brick furnaces containing earthen retorts communicating with chambers of the same material; and afterward in iron retorts communicating with chambers of brickwork, in which the sulphur condenses in light flocks, known as flowers of sulphur. When melted and cast, these form the roll brimstone of commerce. Sulphur can also be easily extracted from iron and copper pyrites. At ordinary temperatures, sulphur is a brittle, insoluble, inodorous solid, of a lemon-yellow color, a bad conductor of heat, and a non-conductor of electricity. By friction with silk or wool, it becomes negatively electrified. It is a highly inflammable substance, burning readily in the air at about 450° or 500° F., and giving off suffocating fumes of sulphurous acid gas. At 239° F. it melts, forming a yellow liquid, and slightly increasing in bulk. Provided the above temperature is not exceeded, it remains nearly transparent on cooling, but becomes gradually opaque from interior molecular changes. In close vessels, it may be distilled by raising the heat to about 834° F. Sulphur is very remarkable as affording a striking instance of the occurrence of the allotropic condition of matter. Hydrogen and sulphur vapor, when burnt, from sulphuretted hydrogen. Burnt in oxygen, heated with chlorine, bromine, and iodine, it unites with them, forming well-known compounds. The vapor of sulphur passed over red-hot charcoal forms bisulphide of carbon. Nearly all the metals combine with it at ordinary or increased temperatures. With oxygen, sulphur forms seven different compounds:

Sulphurous acid	H_2SO_3
Sulphuric acid	H_2SO_4
Dithionous acid	$H_2S_2O_3$
Dithionic acid	$H_2S_2O_6$
Trithionic acid	$H_2S_3O_6$
Tetrathionic acid	$H_2S_4O_6$
Pentathionic acid	$H_2S_5O_6$

Sulphur unites with chlorine in two proportions, forming a dichloride and a chloride. The dichloride, SCl_2, is prepared by transmitting a current of chlorine over melted sulphur, the resulting dichloride being collected in a perfectly dry receiver. It is a dark yellow liquid, very volatile, and possesses a peculiar penetrating disagreeable odor. It emits fumes when exposed to moist air, and when dropped into water gradually decomposes into hydrochloric and sulphurous acids and free sulphur. It has a sp. gr. of 1.658, and boils at 280° F. It is used for vulcanizing india-rubber goods. By saturating dichloride of sulphur with chlorine, a dark red liquid chloride is formed. There is reason to suppose that a bichloride exists but it has not yet been isolated. The corresponding bromides are liquids analogous to the chlorides. The iodide is a crystalline brittle gray solid. With nitrogen, sulphur forms a bisulphide which crystallizes in beautiful golden-yellow rhombic crystals. It detonates powerfully by percussion, or when heated to 314° F. Bisulphide of carbon dissolves it readily, alcohol, ether, and oil of turpentine sparingly, and water not at all. Symbol S; at. wt. 32. Prior to 1902 the chief source of sulphur was Sicily. In that year, however, by a remarkable series of inventions, following years of research, Herman Frasch, a chemist, succeeded in extracting sulphur from vast deposits in Louisiana and Texas. The process, in brief, consists in melting the sulphur, which lies underground, by superheated water. It is then driven to the surface by compressed air. The production in the U. S. in 1926, amounting to 1,890,057 long tons, came chiefly from Texas, and was obtained almost wholly by the Frasch process. The U. S. exported in 1926 576,966 tons valued at $10,918,580.

SULPHURETTED WATERS, hot or cold mineral waters holding in solution sulphides or free sulphuretted hydrogen. They are stimulant, diaphoretic, and alterative. The sulphuretted hydrogen imparts to them a nauseous odor like that of rotten eggs. The chief thermal sulphuretted waters are those of Aix-la-Chapelle, Baden, near Vienna, Aix-les-bains, etc.; the chief cold ones are Harrogate and Bocklet. Such baths are recommended in cutaneous, hepatic, uterine, rheumatic, gouty, neuralgic, and other diseases.

SULPHURIC ACID, a very important acid which occurs in nature in large quantities, both in the vegetable and mineral kingdoms, in combination with the various bases, more particularly the alkalies, alkaline earths, and the oxides of iron, copper, lead, zinc, alumina, etc. Its mineral combinations are generally known as vitriols, a name which, in the case of the sulphates of iron, copper, and zinc, has been transferred to the manufactured products. Sulphuric acid is formed by the oxidation of sulphurous acid, or some other oxide of sulphur. In its perfectly anhydrous condition, it occurs as a white crystalline fibrous mass, somewhat resembling asbestos in appearance. It can be molded in the fingers like wax without charring the skin; it fumes in the air, and is very deliquescent, hissing violently when thrown into water; thereby becoming sulphuric acid. It chars wood, paper, sugar, and other similar substances, by abstracting water from them. It melts at 65° F., and boils at 110° F., forming a colorless vapor. It possesses no acid properties whatever, and is not regarded as such by the followers of Gerhardt, by whom it is called sulphuric anhydride. The vapor, when passed through a red-hot tube, is resolved into a mixture of one volume of oxygen with two volumes of sulphurous acid. With sulphur it forms several more or less definite compounds, of a brown, green, and blue color respectively, which have not as yet received sufficient investigation. There are two varieties of sulphuric acid in commerce. The first of these, fuming or Nordhausen sulphuric acid, is obtained by the distillation of the basic sulphate of iron formed by heating crystals of common green vitriol. It is a somewhat viscid liquid, generally of a light-brown color, from containing traces of organic matter, and has a sp. gr. of 1.896. It is believed to be a combination of equal parts of the anhydrous and monohydrated sulphuric acid, and may be represented by the formula $H_2SO_4SO_3$. It solidifies at 32° F. into a mass of transparent colorless crystals. It is chiefly used in the arts for dissolving indigo. The second variety is the ordinary sulphuric acid, or oil of vitriol, of commerce. It is prepared in immense quantities by burning sulphur or roasting pyrites, and oxidizing the resulting sulphurous acid by means of aqueous vapor and certain oxides of nitrogen. When pure, sulphuric acid is a heavy, oily, colorless, inodorous liquid, and having a sp. gr. of 1.842. It is intensely caustic, and chars almost all organic substances, by abstracting water from them. Sulphuric acid is the starting point of nearly every important chemical manufacture. Acetic, nitric, and hydrochloric acids are made by its means; and it will be only necessary to allude to the important part it plays in the manufacture of soda from common salt, to appreciate the saying of Liebig, "that the amount of sulphuric acid made in a country is a sure index of its wealth and prosperity." In the hands of the chemist it has numerous and important uses. Its salts, the sulphates, are among the most important chemical agents in the laboratory. In its concentrated form, it is in daily use by the scientific chemist to promote the crystallization of deliquescent substances in vacuo, from its intense avidity for water. Besides the monohydrate above described, sulphuric acid forms several other well-marked hydrates; among which may be noticed the bihydrate, a colorless liquid, having a sp. gr. of 1.78, and solidifying in transparent colorless prisms at about 40° F.; hence it is often called glacial sulphuric acid. It may be easily formed by mixing the monohydrate with water, till the proper specific gravity is reached. The sulphates arc a numerous and important class of salts. They are mostly composed of an equivalent of acid and an equivalent of the metallic oxide. They vary somewhat in the numbers of atoms of water of crystallization, some being anhydrous, others containing as many as 12 equivalents. Sulphuric acid also forms acid bisalts, of which bisulphate of potash may be taken as an example, $KO.H_2 O.2SO_3$. In a few instances, basic salts are formed; as for instance, the basic sulphate of copper, $CuSO_45H_2O$. Sulphuric acid and its salts are recognized by giving a white precipitate with a soluble salt of barium, insoluble in nitric acid. Formula, H_2SO_4.

SULPHONAL, or SULFONE METHANE, $(CH_3)_2C(SO_2C_2H_5)_2$, a colorless crystalline powder, m. p. 125-126° C, soluble in alcohol, slightly soluble in water and ether. Prepared by combining anhydrous acetone and anhydrous ethlymercaptan by means of a stream of anhydrous hydrochloric acid. It is employed in medicine as a hypnotic, being less dangerous than most drugs of its class, and intermediate in its action between chloral and paraldehyde.

SULPHUROUS ACID, an acid formed by the union of an equivalent of sulphur with two of oxygen in a variety of ways, the most familiar being its production during the combustion of sulphur in the open air or in oxygen. The gas produced is endowed with the properties of a weak acid, and is the sole product of the combustion, provided the air or oxygen be perfectly dry. It has a pungent, suffocating odor, and when in a concentrated form cannot be breathed with impunity. It is not inflammable, and extinguishes burning bodies. It dissolves freely in water, which takes up between 40 and 50 times its bulk of the gas. The solution has the smell and taste of the gas itself, and becomes gradually converted into sulphuric acid from absorbing oxygen from the air. It is widely used in the manufacture of disinfectants and in fumigation.

SULPICIANS, a Roman Catholic congregation of missionary priests founded in 1642 at Paris by the Abbé Ollier. They have a number of houses in Europe and America, and are chiefly engaged in training young men for the priesthood. They are called Sulpicians from the parish of St. Sulpice, where the congregation was first organized.

SULTAN, in Arabic, signifies "mighty one, lord." It is the ordinary title of

Mohammedan rulers. The rulers of Turkey assumed the title of Sultan-es-selatin, "Sultan of sultans." The title sultan was also applied to the sultan's daughters, and his mother, if living, was styled Sultan Valide.

SULU, archipelago, the extreme southern group of the Philippine Islands separating the Sulu and Celebes seas and extending beyond the western extreme of Mindanao, westward to the north end of Borneo. Area, 1,361 square miles. Small islands form groups around a large one. Of these the largest are Sulu (Jolo), 326 square miles; Tawi Tawi, 232 square miles; and Brislain, 478 square miles. Pop. about 90,000. The islands are volcanic and Sulu Island has 12 important summits, the highest being 2,894 feet. The people are Moro and are divided into two classes, the hillmen or agriculturists and the coast men or fishers. Rice and cacao are cultivated, and horses, cattle, and water buffalo are raised. There are no roads, but only mule tracks. Teak and ebony grow in the islands in abundance, besides several other valuable forest products. The mangosteen, breadfruit, orange, and banana grow luxuriantly, cultivated and wild. The islands were long under Spanish suzerainty, but were transferred to the United States, Dec. 10, 1898. The capital was garrisoned May 19, 1899, and an agreement signed by the Sultan on Aug. 20, 1899. The Sultan is acknowledged as the nominal ruler, and the Moros are permitted to practice their religion.

SUMAC (*Rhus*), a genus of shrubs of the natural order *Anacardiaceæ*, with pinnate leaves and small flowers. They all have a lactescent acrid juice, and most of them possess valuable tanning properties. More than 70 species are known. *R. coriaria* is found in the countries about the Mediterranean. Its roots contain a brown, and its bark a yellow dye. The leaves and seeds are used in medicine as astringent and styptic, and the leaves are exported for use in tanning, dyeing, and calico printing. *R. typhina* is an American species with hairy branches, hence its common name of stag's-horn sumac. It produces small red berries, and is cultivated in European gardens for ornament. *R. glabra*, another American species, is also grown for ornament, and its berries and branches are used for dyeing purposes. *R. venenata*, commonly called dogwood or poison sumac, is a shrub of the American swamps. It grows from 12 to 20 feet high, and produces greenish-white flowers.

SUMATRA, an island in the Indian seas immediately under the equator; separated from the peninsula of Malacca by the Straits of Malacca and from Java by the Straits of Sunda; greatest length about 1,000 miles; breadth, about 240 miles; area, 161,600 square miles; pop. about 4,500,000. Banca and other islands adjoin the coast. The W. side of the island is mountainous, with peaks ranging in height from 2,000 feet in the S. to 5,000 feet further N.; and culminating in Indrapura, a volcano 12,572 feet high. The E. side spreads out into interminable plains. There are several volcanoes in the island. Copper, tin, and iron are found in abundance and deposits of coal exist. The chief rivers are the Rokan, Musi, Jambi, and Indragiri, which all form extensive deltas at their mouths. Sumatra enjoys great equability of climate, but in many low-lying parts is unhealthy; rain falls almost incessantly in the S. Mangroves grow near the coast, and at higher elevations myrtles, palms, figs, and oaks of various species are met with. The camphor tree prevails in the N., and among vegetable curiosities are the upas tree and the gigantic rafflesia. Pepper, rice, sugar, tobacco, indigo, cotton, coffee, are cultivated for export, and camphor, benzoin, catechu, gutta-percha and caoutchouc, teak, ebony, and sandalwood are also exported. Rubber and oil have in recent years become valuable products. In 1919, 340,000 acres were planted with rubber. The fauna includes the elephant, the tapir, the rhinoceros, the tiger, the ourang-outang and other apes, some species of deer and antelope, and numerous birds and reptiles. Of the domestic animals the chief is the pig, next to which rank the cow and the horse.

The island is for the most part under the authority of the Dutch, and their possessions are divided into eight provinces. The governor resides at Padang. Sumatra has a very mixed population consisting of Malays, Chinese, Arabs, and many native tribes. The Battas are a peculiar and interesting race approaching the Caucasian type. Writing has been known among them from a very early period, and their ancient books are written in a brilliant ink on paper made of bark. The native tribes of Sumatra have no temples and no priests, but a form of Mohammedanism prevails among the Malays on the coast. Chief towns, Palembang and Padang.

The Dutch acquired their territories in Sumatra in the 16th and 17th centuries. The British formed a settlement at Benkulen in 1685, and in 1811 seized the Dutch possessions on the island. These were restored in 1815, and by treaties in

1834 and 1871 the Dutch were allowed the right to enlarge their territories by treaty, or by conquest and annexation. The tidal wave accompanying the volcanic eruption of Krakatoa in 1883 caused great destruction on the S. coast of Sumatra.

SUMBAWA, one of the chain of the Sunda Islands to the E. of Java; between Lombok (on the W.) and Flores (on the E.); area, 5,192 square miles; pop. about 75,000, all Malays and Mohammedans. They are divided between four native rulers, who owe allegiance to the Dutch governor of Celebes. The islands are mountainous but fertile, and yield rice, tobacco, cotton, sandalwood, etc. In 1815 an eruption of Tambora, the loftiest peak on the island, whereby the altitude was decreased from 14,000 to 7,670 feet, depopulated the kingdoms of Tambora and Papekat, 12,000 lives being lost and great damage done to the whole island by the ashes. Another eruption took place in 1836, and one of another peak, Gunong Api, in 1860, though with little loss.

SUMMER, that season of the year when the sun shines most directly on any region; the warmest season of the year. N. of the equator it is commonly taken to include the months of June, July, and August; though some substitute May, June, and July. The former view conforms better to fact. July, which by this arrangement is midsummer month, is the hottest in the year, for though the maximum of heat is obtained on June 21, the longest day, the amount received for many subsequent days is greater than that lost by radiation, and the temperature continues to increase. Summer is the appropriate season for the hay harvest and for the ripening of the earlier fruits. Astronomically considered, summer begins in the Northern Hemisphere when the sun enters the sign of Cancer about June 21, and continues till September 23, during which time he passes through Cancer, Leo, and Virgo. In the Southern Hemisphere the opposite is the case, it being winter there when it is summer here, and vice versa. During the astronomical summer of the Southern Hemisphere the sun passes through Capricorn, Aquarius, and Pisces.

SUMMIT, a city of New Jersey, in Union co. It is on the Delaware, Lackawanna and Western and the Rahway Valley railroads. It is a favorite residential place on account of its elevation and the beauty of its surrounding scenery. Its public buildings include a public library and a hospital. The chief industry is the manufacture of silk. Pop. (1910) 7,500; (1920) 10,174.

SUMMONS, in law, a writ commanding the sheriff, or other authorized officer, to notify a party to appear in court, to answer a complaint made against him, and in the same writ specify some day therein mentioned.

SUMNER, CHARLES, an American statesman; born in Boston, Mass., Jan. 6, 1811; was educated at Harvard University. In 1834 he was called to the bar, and shortly afterward became reporter of the United States Circuit Court. In 1836 he published three volumes of Judge Story's decisions, subsequently known as "Sumner's Reports," and edited a periodical called the "American Jurist." He visited Europe in 1837, and returned to Boston in 1840, where he resumed his

CHARLES SUMNER

legal practice. Between 1844 and 1846 he edited and published "Vesey's Reports" in 20 volumes. In 1851 he was elected to the Senate of the United States and distinguished himself by his strong antipathy to slavery. In May, 1856, after delivering a speech vigorously attacking the slaveholders, he was violently assaulted by Preston S. Brooks, member from South Carolina. His injuries compelled him to absent himself from public duties for nearly four years. He was a supporter of Lincoln and Hamlin, and in 1861 he became chairman of the Senate Committee on Foreign Relations. He was an enemy to the policy of President Johnson and opposed the home and foreign policy of President Grant. After the latter's re-election in 1872 Sumner seldom appeared in debate. He died in Washington, D. C., March 11, 1874.

SUMNER, EDWIN VOSE, an American military officer; born in Boston, Mass., Jan. 30, 1797. He was a captain in the Black Hawk War; served with distinction in the Mexican War in 1846-1847, especially at the battles of Cerro Gordo and Molino del Rey; was made major in 1846; governor of New Mexico in 1851-1853; in 1855 was made colonel and was one of the escort of Abraham Lincoln from Springfield, Ill., to Washington, D. C., in February, 1861; in March, 1861, promoted brigadier-general U. S. A. During the Civil War he commanded a corps at the battle of Fair Oaks, May 31-June 1, 1862; at Malvern Hill, July 1, and at the battle of Antietam, September 17 of that year; he also commanded one of the three great divisions of Burnside's army at the battle of Fredericksburg, Dec. 13, 1862; was given command of the Department of the Missouri in 1863. He died in Syracuse, N. Y., March 21, 1863.

SUMNER, WILLIAM GRAHAM, an American political economist; born in Paterson, N. J., Oct. 30, 1840; was graduated at Yale in 1863; studied at Geneva, Göttingen, and Oxford; was tutor at Yale in 1866-1869; in 1867 took orders in the Protestant-Episcopal Church; was assistant at Calvary Church, New York, and rector of Church of the Redeemer, Morristown, N. J.; appointed Professor of Political Economy and Social Science at Yale College in 1872. His writings include a translation of Lange's "Commentary on Second Kings" (1872); "History of American Currency" (1874); "Life of Andrew Jackson" (1882); "What Social Classes Owe to Each Other" (1883); "Problems in Political Economy" (1884); "Protectionism" (1885); "History of Banking in the United States" (1896); etc. He died April 12, 1910.

SUMMERALL, CHARLES PELOT, an American army officer, born at Lake City, Fla., in 1867. He was graduated from the United States Military Academy, in 1892, and commissioned a 2d lieutenant of infantry in the same year. In 1893 he was transferred to the artillery service, rising through the various grades to that of colonel, May, 1917. In August, 1917, he was promoted brigadier-general, N. A.; in January, 1918, brigadier-general, U. S. A.; in July, 1918, major-general, N. A., and in April, 1920, major-general, U. S. A. He saw service in the Philippine Islands from 1899 to 1900, and with the China Relief Expedition from 1900 to 1901. In 1902 he located and initiated the construction of Fort William H. Seward, Alaska. He was at various times an instructor at the United States Military Academy, a lecturer at the Army War College and assistant to the chief of the Militia Bureau.

During the World War he was successively a member of the Military Commission to England and France, commander of the 67th Field Artillery Brigade and later of the 1st Field Artillery Brigade, commander of the 1st Division, A. E. F., the 5th Army Corps, the 9th Army Corps and the 4th Army Corps. His service with the A. E. F. in France covered the period from October, 1917, to September, 1919, and included, during 1919, various special missions, membership in the Inter-Allied Military Commission at Fiume and service with the American Mission to Negotiate Peace. Upon his return to the United States he was assigned to the command of the 1st Division at Camp Taylor, Ky.

SUMNER, GEORGE WATSON, an American naval officer, born at Constantine, Mich., in 1841. He was graduated from the United States Naval Academy in 1861, becoming a lieutenant in 1862, and rising through the various grades to the rank of rear-admiral in March, 1899. He saw extensive service in the Civil War. His other assignments included, besides the command of various ships of the United States Navy, service with the Hydrographic Office, the Bureau of Ordnance, the Naval War College and the Navy Yards at New York and Philadelphia. From 1902 to 1903, he was commander-in-chief of the South Atlantic Squadron, retiring at the end of 1903, upon having reached the age limit.

SUMNER, WALTER TAYLOR, an American Protestant Episcopal clergyman, born at Manchester, N. H., in 1873. He was educated at Dartmouth College, and at the Western Theological Seminary, and received honorary degrees from these two universities, and from Northwestern University. He was made a deacon in 1903 and a priest in 1904. From 1903 to 1906, while serving as pastor of St. George's Church, Chicago, he was secretary to the Bishop of Chicago; from 1906 to 1915 he was dean of the Cathedral of St. Peter and St. Paul, and superintendent of the City Missions of the Episcopal Church, Chicago; and in 1915 he was consecrated Bishop of Oregon. He also served as a member of the Chicago Board of Education (1909-1915) and was a member or officer of many religious and charitable associations, commissions, congresses, institutions, etc. Until 1915 he was also chaplain of the 1st Illinois Cavalry, I. N. G.

SUMPTUARY LAWS, laws intended to repress extravagance, especially in eating and drinking, and in dress. They were common in ancient times, and also

appear in the old statute books of most
modern nations. They were more frequently enacted in ancient Rome than in
Greece. After the Twelve Tables, the
first Roman sumptuary law was the Lex
Oppia (215 B. C.), directed exclusively
against female extravagance in dress,
jewelry, etc. The other Roman laws of
this kind were nearly all designed to
suppress extravagance in entertainment.
The Lex Julia (Julian Law), the last
sumptuary law, was passed in the reign
of Augustus. Sumptuary laws were revived by Charlemagne, and in France various laws and decrees of a similar nature were passed down to the reign of
Louis XV. In England these laws were
passed from the reign of Edward III.
down to the time of the Reformation.
Most of them were repealed by an act of
James I., but they were not all expunged
from the statute book till 1856. Sumptuary laws were also passed by the ancient
Scotch legislature, but they were all repealed, evaded, or neglected. As late as
1883, in Montenegro, strong laws were
passed against gloves, umbrellas, and non-
national costumes. Neither in England,
Scotland, nor France do sumptuary laws
appear to have been practically observed
to any great extent. During the World
War nearly all the countries engaged enacted sumptuary laws of some description. The most drastic of these were
aimed at the liquor traffic. Russia put
absolute prohibition into effect, and other
countries greatly restricted the manufacture and consumption of liquors. The
most remarkable sumptuary legislation
put into effect was the 18th Amendment
to the Constitution of the United States,
forbidding the manufacture and sale of
intoxicating liquors. See PROHIBITION.

SUMTER, a city of South Carolina,
the county seat of Sumter co. It is on
the Atlantic Coast Line, the Carolina,
Atlantic and Western, and the Southern
railroads. Its industries include a cotton compress, cotton and cottonseed-oil
mills, magneto works, wagon factories,
etc. The public buildings include St.
Joseph's Academy for Girls and a Y. M.
C. A. building. Pop. (1910) 8,109;
(1920) 9,508.

SUMTER, THOMAS, an American
military officer; born in Virginia in 1734.
He was distinguished for his skill and
success as a partisan leader and was
known among his followers as the "Carolina gamecock." In the early part of the
Revolutionary War he was lieutenant-
colonel of a regiment of South Carolina
riflemen, but after the capture of
Charleston in 1780, he was made a brigadier-general of light cavalry. He gained

several victories over the British troops,
but in September, 1780, was defeated by
General Tarleton. Ten days later he defeated the British general in turn, being
himself dangerously wounded. In the
spring of 1781 he again began active service and took a distinguished part in the

GENERAL THOMAS SUMTER

battle of Eutaw Springs. The thanks
of Congress were tendered him in 1791,
and he was afterward sent to that body
as a representative of South Carolina.
In 1809 he was appointed United States
minister to Brazil and two years later
was elected United States Senator from
his native State. At the close of his
term he retired to private life and died
near Camden, S. C., June 1, 1832.

SUMTER, FORT, (named after Gen.
Thomas Sumter, 1734-1832), an American fort associated with both the beginning and the end of the Civil War;
built of brick, in the form of a truncated
pentagon 38 feet high, on a shoal, partly
artificial, in Charleston Harbor, 3½
miles from the city. On the withdrawal
of South Carolina from the Union in December, 1860, Major Anderson, in command of the defenses of the harbor,
abandoned the other forts and occupied
Fort Sumter, mounting 62 guns, with a
garrison of some 80 men. The attack
on the fort was opened by General Beau-
regard, April 12, 1861, and it surrendered
on the 14th; this event marked the beginning of the war. The Confederates
strengthened it, and added 10 guns and 4
mortars. In April, 1863, an attack by a
fleet of monitors failed. In July batteries were erected on Morris Island,
about 4,000 yards off, from which in a
week 5,000 projectiles, weighing from
100 to 300 pounds, were hurled against

the fort; at the end of that time it was silenced and in part demolished. Yet the garrison held on amid the ruins and in September beat off a naval attack; and in spite of a 40 days' bombardment in October-December, 1863, and for still longer in July and August, 1864, it was not till after the evacuation of Charleston itself, owing to the operations of General Sherman, that the garrison retired, and the United States flag was again raised April 14, 1865; an event soon followed by the evacuation of Richmond and the Confederate surrender.

SUN, the center of our solar and planetary system, and one of the stars in the boundless sidereal universe. It is a hot self-luminous globe of enormous dimensions as compared with any of its planets, and the source from which they derive their heat and whatever life they bear; but considered as a star it is probably only of moderate dimensions and brilliancy.

Distance and Dimensions.—Its mean distance from the earth is about 93,000,-000 miles, probably a little less, a distance which a fast railroad train would traverse in about 250 years, sound (with its terrestrial atmospheric velocity) in about 14 years, a cannon-ball at 1,700 feet per second in about nine years, and which light flies over in about 500 seconds. Its diameter is about 866,500 miles, nearly 110 times that of the earth. With the earth at its center it would take in the whole moon's orbit and have plenty of room for another moon one and three-quarter times as far out as ours and still far inside its surface. Reducing the scale so as to represent the sun by a globe 2 feet in diameter, the earth would be less than ¼ inch in diameter and about 220 feet away, while the distance of the nearest fixed star on this scale would be about 8,000 miles or the actual diameter of the earth. The surface of the sun is about 12,000 times that of the earth, and its volume about 1,300,-000 times.

CORONA OF THE SUN

Mass, Gravity, etc.—The mass of the sun is only about 332,000 times that of the earth, so that its density is only a little over a quarter of the earth's, or about 1.41 times as heavy as water. It is well to keep this in mind in thinking of the probable physical condition of the sun, when we remember that it is largely composed of iron. The attraction of the sun at its surface is about 27.6 times that of the earth at its exterior, so that a 200-pound man would weigh about 5,520 pounds on the sun, a body would fall about 444 feet in a second, instead of 16, as here, and a pendulum which marks

seconds here would vibrate more than five times per second there.

Rotation and Axis.—The motion of the spots across the sun from E. to W. shows that the huge globe rotates regularly on an axis in a period of about 25.3 days, or rather this is the velocity at the solar equator. On each side the speed is slower, till in latitude 40° the period is more than 27 days. Much beyond this the rotation time is unknown, for the spots seldom extend beyond latitudes of 45° N. or S. The cause of this equatorial acceleration is as yet unexplained. The path of the spots also shows that the sun's equator is inclined to the plane of the ecliptic at an angle of about 7° 15′, and that its axis points very nearly to a point half-way between the stars α Lyræ and Polaris.

Photosphere.—The luminous surface of the sun directly visible in telescopes is called the photosphere (Greek *phos*, "bright"). It is probably a sheet of luminous clouds formed by the condensation of substances which exist as gases in the hotter central mass of the sun. Under a moderate magnifying power it looks like rough drawing paper. With higher powers it looks something like snow flakes scattered over gray cloth. These flakes or grains are from 400 to 600 miles across, and are probably bright clouds floating in an atmosphere not so luminous. Near the edge of the sun the photosphere is much less brilliant than at the center, due to absorption of the solar atmosphere.

IDEAL SECTION OF THE SUN

A back disk represents the inner nucleus; a white ring surrounding it is the photosphere, rising at points into faculæ, and depressed at others in spots; immediately above lies the so-called "reversing stratum," in which the lines (called "Fraunhofer," after the discoverer) originate; above this is the scarlet chromosphere, with prominences of various forms and dimensions; and over, and embracing all, is the coronal atmosphere fading gradually away into darkness. In its study with reference to magnitude, imagine the earth as a mere dot placed in the middle of the bottom line and at the center of the moon's orbit.

Spots and Faculæ.—The most prominent feature of the sun's surface is the spots, some of which can almost always be seen except near the time of a sunspot minimum. They are dark depressions in the photosphere, and consist of a central umbra with surrounding penumbra which is not so dark. This penumbra consists of radial filaments, and appears like the sloping sides of the sunspot cavity, as if the photosphere were drawn down into the spot by inward currents. In the central umbra there are also sometimes smaller, darker spots, called "Dawes's holes," from the name of their discoverer. The preceding is the description of what may be called a normal spot before it begins to break up; but they are seldom of so regular a character. Frequently there are several umbræ with a common penumbra, and there are sometimes streaks or "bridges" of the bright photosphere extending clear across the whole spot. The umbra is not always central, and the filaments of the penumbra are frequently twisted and curled into the most fantastic shapes, reminding one of swirling tongues of flame or smoke. The diameter of the umbra of a spot ranges all the way from 500 to 50,000 or 60,000 miles. The whole earth could be dropped into many of them without disturbing the edges. The penumbra surrounding some of the larger groups of spots has sometimes measured as much as 150,000 miles in diameter. The depth of the umbra below the general surface of the photosphere is difficult to determine, but according to the best authorities may range from 500 to 2,500 miles. Surrounding the spots there are generally streaks of the photosphere which are much brighter than its general surface, sometimes extending nearly radially from the spot, and these are called the faculæ (Latin fax, "a torch"). They are elevated ridges of the photosphere, and are much more prominent when near the edge of the sun, where they project up through a part of the atmosphere which dims the general photospheric level. The faculæ are not confined to the spot surroundings, but they are much more abundant there. They probably make surgings or upheavals, which are the surrounding accompaniment of sunspot action.

Life and Distribution of Spots.—They begin from insensible points, rapidly growing larger, but generally do not develop the penumbra till after the umbra is well formed. The projection of a bright streak, or facula, across the nucleus of a spot often precedes its segmentation or breaking up into two or more. When a spot disappears it comes about by the encroachment of the photosphere, which seems to fall into and fill the cavity, leaving its place covered by a group of bright faculæ. In the vicinity of a spot the motion of phospheric and other matter is generally inward, toward and down into the center, and occasionally the latter is enough to be detected by the spectroscope. The duration of a spot ranges from a few days to occasionally more than a year, but is generally a month or two. It is a remarkable fact that their distribution is confined to two zones between 5° and 40°.

Theories of Sun Spots.—The cause of spots is not yet satisfactorily made out, and among the many theories offered we can only note that of Faye, who considers them to be cyclonic, like our terrestrial storms, caused by the forward drift of the equatorial photosphere, and the more probable suggestion of Young that they are depressions or sinks in the photosphere brought about by the diminution of pressure below, which would accompany eruptions in the surroundings of the spot, the cooler, darker gases flowing down into the cavity thus formed. Certain it is that they are intimately associated with eruptions and explosions on the surface or from below, but which is cause and effect, or whether both spot and eruption are caused by some outside influence (like the fall of meteoric matter) is as yet undetermined.

Periodicity of Spots.—The spots have, roughly speaking, a period of about 11 years, but it is very irregular and has not as yet received any satisfactory explanation. At the time of maximum the surface is never free from them, while at minimum none may be in sight for weeks at a time.

Effect on the Earth.—The only certain connection between the spots and terrestrial phenomena is that with the earth's magnetism. The range of magnetic disturbance, or storminess, follows the sunspot curve very closely, and individual outbursts on the sun are frequently accompanied by simultaneous "magnetic storm" and brilliant exhibitions of the Aurora Borealis on the earth. The exact mechanical connection between the two is not yet known, but of its reality there is not the slightest doubt. Endless attempts have been made to connect almost every other phenomenon of terrestrial meteorology with the sun-spot period, but with the single exception above mentioned, none has been satisfactorily established.

Young's Reversing Layer.—Next above the photosphere comes a stratum of unknown thickness, discovered by Professor Young, containing the vapors of many of our terrestrial elements. At the time of a total eclipse, if the slit of a spectroscope is kept just tangent to the disappearing limb of the sun, at the instant of the disappearance of the bright light from the photospheric background the light from this layer flashes out in the spectrum in the shape of bright lines, probably where the dark lines had before been. The point as yet unsettled is whether all the dark lines are thus reversed, and with their relative intensity. Lockyer claims that this so-called layer is of a considerable height, and that at different heights in it, different lines, or the same lines with different intensity, will appear, in accordance with his theory that in the sun our chemical elements are dissociated and float at different levels in the solar atmosphere. This is one of the points to be settled by observation at future eclipses.

Chromosphere and Prominences or Protuberances. — Above the reversing layer and interpenetrating it, or possibly identical with it, if Lockyer's theory should prove true, is an atmosphere of permanent gases called the chromosphere. Hydrogen is the most abundant of these gases, and out of this chromosphere rise the wonderful prominences or protuberances which form so prominent a feature of the sun's surroundings at the time of a total eclipse, and which can be investigated by the spectroscope at any time as they consist almost wholly of hydrogen. They are of all imaginable fantastic shapes, and frequently rise, and are sometimes seen to be rapidly projected to the height of several hundred thousand miles, and at enormous velocities. In such case they are almost always seen to be connected with some active sunspot, and they are unquestionably the results of the upheavals, eruptions, or explosions accompanying the surroundings of the spots. The chromosphere itself all along the limb of the sun, as seen in the hydrogen lines in the spectrum, is not a smooth, flat layer, but consists of filaments like upward tongues of flames, and has been compared to the appearance of a "prairie fire," though there is no actual combustion going on.

Spectrum and Constitution. — Almost all our knowledge of the constitution of the sun has been revealed to us by the spectroscope. It has shown us that not only do many of our so-called chemical elements exist in the sun, but that its temperature is so high that they exist there in the form of gases. Among the elements identified are hydrogen, iron, titanium, calcium, manganese, nickel, cobalt, chromium, barium, sodium, magnesium, and platinum, with a strong probability in favor of copper, palladium, vanadium, molybdenum, uranium, aluminum, cadmium, carbon, and lead. With the exception of carbon all the above are metals. (Hydrogen in its chemical relations ranks as a metal.) A few years ago it was considered that the late Dr. Henry Draper had shown the strong probability of the existence of oxygen in the sun, but the later investigations, while not decisive, tend to negative this conclusion. In this connection

Mr. Lockyer's views must be mentioned. He considers that none of our so-called chemical elements are truly elementary, but that they may all be decomposed into simpler constituents, and that many of them are so dissociated in the sun and the stars. The matter is still one of the most important unsettled questions in the domain of astro-physics. A full exposition of his views may be found in his "Chemistry of the Sun." The revelations of the spectroscope in regard to the chromosphere, prominences, and so-called reversing layer have already been briefly mentioned. It has also been instrumental in revealing the enormous velocities accompanying explosions, and eruptions on the sun. At the limb of the sun we see these revealed by the telescope directly in the huge hydrogen prominences, but the spectroscope shows another component of this velocity in the direction to or from us in the line of sight. In the spectrum of a spot, and of the faculæ round it, the lines are frequently broken and twisted into remarkable shapes, indicating motion to or from us of the gases in question at enormous velocities. In some cases hydrogen has been shown to be rushing toward us with a velocity of 300 miles per second. Occasionally the spectrum of the nucleus of a spot has shown a down-rush of matter into the cavity.

The Solar Corona. — Surrounding all other parts of the solar surface rises the halo of light called the corona, which is only visible at the time of a total eclipse. Though known from the remotest times, little is yet known of its cause or physical condition, and it is the principal object of attack now at the time of every eclipse of the sun. Down near the surface it is very bright and of a pearly or greenish color. Above this it rises, especially at the poles, in short, finely clustered filaments. Over the sunspot zones it generally rises higher in broad streaks, and at times extends out nearly in the direction of the ecliptic in faint streaks looking like gauze wings on the sun. These fade out gradually, and their limit to the eye or the photographic plate is fixed by the brightness of the sky background. Up in the clear air of Pike's Peak, Col., in 1878, these streamers were seen extending at least 9,000,000 miles from the sun. It varies much at different eclipses and is never twice alike, though certain typical forms seem to follow somewhat the maxima and minima of the sunspot period. The total light of the corona is at least two of three times that of the full moon. As its light appears to be relatively rich in the ultra violet part of its spectrum, Dr. Huggins has attempted to photograph it in full sunshine, but thus far it is somewhat doubtful if he has succeeded in this. The spectrum of the corona consists principally of a bright line in the green which has not been identified with that of any terrestrial element, and for which the name coronium has been proposed. The lines of hydrogen are also visible, but not so bright by far as the line in the green. There is also a faint continuous spectrum, and some observers have claimed to see on this the faint absorption lines of the solar spectrum. The nature of the corona is one of the most puzzling things to explain. It cannot be an atmosphere in any sense of the word, as the gaseous pressure there must be less than that of the most perfect vacuum we can make. Comets sweep through it without hindrance. It is a product of some sort of the enormous forces at play in the vicinity of the sun. Meteoric matter, cometic matter, matter ejected from the sun, are probably all concerned in it, and possibly electricity may play some part in the display. It is possible, and indeed perhaps probable, that the zodiacal light which reaches far out toward and perhaps beyond the earth's orbit, is a faint extension of the equatorial coronal streamers.

Radiation.—Compared with other familiar sources of light we find that the amount of it received from the sun is about 600,000 times that from the full moon, 7,000,000,000 times that from Sirius, 40,000,000,000 times that from Vega or Arcturus, and 1,575,000,000,000,-000,000,000,000,000 times as much as a standard candle would give at the distance of the sun. The intrinsic brightness of its disk is about 90,000 times that of a candle flame, 150 times that of the lime in a calcium light, and from two to four times as bright as the brightest spot in the crater of an electric arc light. The darkest part of a sun spot is brighter than the lime light. If the sun were stripped of its atmosphere it would probably shine from two to five times as brightly as at present, and would be of a decidedly blue color. Considering solar radiation in its heating effect and measuring it in terms of its power to melt ice, we find that the total amount of heat received annually would melt a sheet of ice 174 feet thick at the equator, or 136 feet thick over the whole surface of the earth if the radiation were equally distributed in all latitudes. Converted by means of the mechanical equivalent of heat and expressed as energy, we find that, neglecting the absorption of our atmosphere, each square meter of the earth's surface would receive from an overhead sun about two and one-third horse power continuously. Atmospheric absorption cuts this down to about one and a half horse power. Every square meter of the sun's surface is continuously radiating more than 100,000 horse power. A shell of ice 50 feet thick would there be melted in one minute. To keep up such a development of heat by combustion would require that a layer of the best anthracite coal over the whole surface from 16 to 20 feet thick should be burned each hour, a ton an hour for every square foot of surface, at least nine times as much as the consumption of the most powerful blast furnace per foot of grate surface. At this rate the sun, if made of solid coal, would not last 6,000 years. Of this enormous amount of energy, so far as we know, only about .000,000,001 is intercepted and utilized by all the bodies of the solar system, and to the best of our knowledge, and according to human ideas, the rest of it goes to waste.

The intensity of the sun's radiation varies considerably. Observers of the Smithsonian Institution, by a long series of simultaneous observations in Arizona, Chile and South Africa, have reached the conclusion that the intensity of radiation rises and falls in cycles of 25 2-3 months. Variation has been thought connected with sun spots and is believed to affect weather.

Temperature.—While we can measure with a fair degree of accuracy the amount of solar radiation, the determination of the actual temperature of its surface is a very different matter. All that can with certainty be said is that it is much higher than any temperature that can be produced by terrestrial means. The various estimates have taken the widest possible range, depending on the assumed law connecting radiation with temperature. The most reliable estimates place the probable effective temperature as something like 10,000° C., or 18,000° F. There must also be a considerable range of temperature at different depths below its surface.

Sources of Energy.—We have noted the tremendous expenditure of energy by the sun in the form of radiation. A natural question is, How does it keep it up? We have mentioned the insufficiency of any combustion hypothesis. The only others worth mentioning are the meteoric and the contraction theories, as it can easily be shown that the theory of a cooling sun will not suffice, since, if this were the source of its radiant energy, it must have cooled enough within historic times to have affected very decidedly its radiating power. The meteoric theory attempts to account for the keeping up of its supply of energy by the fall of meteoric matter into the sun. A body falling into the sun from any considerable distance will generate by the sudden arrest of its energy of translation an enormous amount of heat, 6,000 times as much as would be generated by its complete combustion if it were a mass of pure carbon. From the fact that meteors are constantly striking the earth we know that they must be all the time falling into the sun, but nevertheless the greater part of the meteoric matter in the vicinity of the sun must circulate round it as the comets do. The most careful estimates seem to indicate that only a very small fraction of the sun's radiant energy can come from the fall of meteors into it. Another theory formerly favored was that of Helmholtz—the contraction hypothesis. Without going fully into the explanation of this it may be briefly stated that, supposing the bulk of the sun to be mainly gaseous, a contraction of about 250 feet per year in its diameter would supply all its present rate of radiation. At this rate it would take nearly 10,000 years to diminish its apparent diameter by a single second of arc, and it is doubtful if this amount could be certainly determined with our present means of measurement of this diameter.

Age and Duration.—Everything points to the conclusion that the present condition of the sun is mainly gaseous, and its future supply of heat depends on that condition. The contraction can only keep up its temperature so long as it is principally in a gaseous state. As soon as any large part of its bulk liquefies (only the thin shell of photospheric clouds is now supposed to be in a liquid condition), it will begin to cool off and its temperature will fall. This means the beginning of the end for life on this earth. Estimates until lately placed this time as not more than 5,000,000 to 10,000,000 years off. But now they are extending to billions of years by reckoning the added energy of solar radio-activity among the sources of the energy emitted.

The history of the sun is involved in obscurity. Knowing the mass of the sun, we can compute how much heat has been generated in its condensation from infinite space or from any assigned dimensions; but as to the rate at which this heat has been radiated in the past ages, and the rate at which contraction has taken place, nothing definite can be stated. It may be considered that the age of the solar system is entirely unknown.

SUN, CITY OF THE, Baalbec, formerly center of sun worship.

SUN, ECLIPSES OF THE, caused by the moon coming between the earth and the sun, may be either partial, total, or annular. In a partial eclipse the observer is situated in the penumbra of the moon's shadow, and only a part of the sun's light is cut off on one side. In a total eclipse the observer is in the umbra of the moon's shadow, and all the light of the sun is cut off except that from the prominences and corona surrounding the sun. In an annular eclipse the disk of the moon is wholly projected on that of the sun, but is not large enough to cover it completely, so that a ring of sunlight is left all around the moon. The apparent diameters of the sun and moon are so nearly equal that their variations with their varying distances make a central eclipse sometimes total and sometimes annular. In fact, the same eclipse may be total for some parts of the earth where the sun and moon are near the meridian at the time, and annular for other parts where they are low down in the E. or the W. at the time of central phase. In the annular eclipse the observer, instead of being in the cone of the moon's shadow, is in the prolongation of that cone, beyond its apex, in the other nap of the cone. At present the only scientific importance of partial and annular eclipses is the use that may be made of them for determining the relative positions of the sun and moon, and thus correcting the elements of the terrestrial and lunar orbits. But the fleeting minutes of every total eclipse are now utilized so far as possible to study the sun's surroundings, especially the mysterious corona (see SUN), and to study the supposed deflection by gravity of the light of stars passing close to the sun disc. Geometrically considered, a solar eclipse is only an occultation of the sun by the moon. Perhaps the most widely observed solar eclipse, that of Jan. 24, 1925, was visible to millions in North America.

SUN, PARALLAX OF THE, or **SOLAR PARALLAX,** the angle subtended by the radius of the earth at a distance equal to that of the earth from the sun. More exactly, it is the angle subtended by the equatorial radius of the earth at the mean distance of the sun, though this would be called, when speaking exactly, the mean equatorial horizontal parallax of the sun. It is, as nearly as we know it to-day, almost 8.8", with an uncertainty of probably not more than 0.01" or 0.02" different from this in either direction. This corresponds to a distance of the sun a little less than

93,000,000 miles. More time, labor, and money have been expended in the determination of the polar parallax than of any other astronomical constant, on account of its importance in giving us an accurate base line with which to gauge the solar system and then strike out into the depths of stellar space. Before the last transit of Venus it was thought that careful observation would give an exceedingly accurate value of this constant; but these hopes were disappointed, and it is known that we have at hand at any time more accurate methods of determining the distance of the sun than from any possible observation of a transit of Venus. The most accurate direct method is likely to be the direct measurement of the parallax of the nearer and brighter asteroids by the heliometer.

SUN YAT-SEN, a Chinese revolutionary leader, born in 1866, near Canton. When still young, he was taken by his parents to Hawaii, where he attended Iolani College. He later graduated from the Hongkong School of Medicine, and for a year practiced at Macao. Soon, however, he gave himself up to the project of driving the Manchu dynasty from China. He attempted a revolt in 1895, which failed, and he fled to Japan and later to Honolulu and San Francisco. He organized the Chinese living abroad in all countries into a reform association to aid the coming revolution. Although large rewards were offered by the government for his death, he escaped without harm. The revolution of 1911 was chiefly successful through the preparations made by him, and he was elected provisional president of the Chinese Republic. He resigned in 1912 in favor of Yuan Shih-kai, in order to induce the latter to join the Republican cause. He later incurred the hostility of Yuan and was obliged to retire to Japan. He continued to agitate for reforms in China and was largely responsible for the rebellions of 1913, 1915, and 1916.

SUNART, LOCH, an inlet in Scotland, in the W. of Argyleshire, opening into the Sound of Mull. It is about 20 miles long, and varies in breadth from less than ½ mile to 3 miles.

SUN BITTERN, in ornithology, the *Eurypya helias,* from the N. parts of South America. It is about 16 inches long; body small and thin, neck long and slender, head like that of a heron, with a long, powerful beak compressed at the sides and slightly arched at the culmen; the plumage is minutely variegated with bars and spots of many colors. It is often made a pet by the Brazilians, who call it pavao (=peacock), whence it is sometimes called the peacock heron.

SUNBURY, a borough and county-seat of Northumberland co., Pa., on the Susquehanna river, and on the Pennsylvania and the Philadelphia and Reading railroads; 56 miles N. of Harrisburg. It is an important shipping point for coal. It contains a court house, high school, and electric railroad, numerous churches, a National bank, and daily and weekly newspapers. It has door and sash mills, coffin and casket factory, hosiery mill, several large railroad shops, nail works, and silk, saw, and rolling mills. Pop. (1910) 13,770; (1920) 15,721.

SUNDA ISLANDS, the name by which all the islands of the Malay Archipelago west of the Molucca and Banda Seas are known. The four large Sundas are Sumatra, Java, Borneo, and Celebes, and the lesser Sundas are Barli, Lombok, Sumbawa, Flores, Timor, etc.; the name is derived from the Sundanese Malayan people of West Java.

SUNDAY, WILLIAM ASHLEY, an American evangelist, born at Ames, Ia., in 1863. He was educated at the High School of Nevada, Ia., and at Northwestern University. From 1883 to 1890 he was a professional baseball player with the Chicago, Pittsburgh, and Philadelphia teams of the National League; from 1891 to 1895 assistant secretary at the Y. M. C. A., Chicago; and since 1896 he has been continuously engaged in evangelistic services. Although his methods were extremely spectacular and found opposition in many quarters, he met with remarkable success and held meetings in most of the important cities of the United States. In 1903 he was ordained a presbyterian minister by the Chicago Presbytery, which body made him a delegate to the General Assembly of the Presbyterian Church, U. S. A., at Columbus, Ohio, May, 1918.

SUNDAY - SCHOOL, according to Schaff, "an assembly of persons on the Lord's day for the study of the Bible, moral and religious instruction, and the worship of the true God. It is a method of training the young and ignorant in the duties we owe to God and to our neighbor." Sunday-schools may be said to have passed through three distinct phases:
(1) Early Christian catechetical schools, for the preparation of converts for church-membership, and the instruction of the young and ignorant in the knowledge of God and of salvation. The scholars committed passages of Scripture

to memory, and their books comprised parts of the Bible in verse, Jewish antiquities, sacred poems, and dialogues.

(2) Schools of the Reformation Period: Luther founded schools for catechetical instruction in 1529, and this custom spread wherever the Reformation gained a foothold. In the Roman Church St. Charles Borromeo, Archbishop of Milan, about 1560 introduced into his diocese a system of schools which continues to the present day; and in 1699 the Venerable de la Salle opened a Sunday-school (*êcole dominicale*) at St. Sulpice. Sunday-schools were opened in Scotland about 1560 by Knox; at Bath, in 1650 by Joseph Alleine; in Roxbury, Mass., in 1674, and at many other places in Great Britain and America between that date and 1778.

(3) Modern Sunday-schools: These date from 1780 or 1781, when Robert Raikes, of Gloucester, England, began to collect a few children from the streets of that city on Sundays, and paid teachers to instruct them in religious knowledge. The improvement in the conduct and morals of the children was so marked that, when Raikes published an account of his success, his example was followed in several other places, and in 1785 a society was formed for the establishment and maintenance of Sunday-schools in all parts of the kingdom, a large sum being expended in the payment of teachers. In 1803 the Sunday-School Union was formed to secure continuous instruction by unpaid teachers, and to publish books and tracts for the benefit of the cause. The first Sunday-schools united secular with religious instruction, as did those of Borromeo and La Salle; but the spread of elementary education has to a large extent removed the necessity of teaching reading and writing on Sundays. The Society of Friends has, however, retained the practice in its large Sunday-morning schools, with great benefit as regards influence over the working classes above the age of childhood, and in some of the Wesleyan Sunday-schools, classes for elementary instruction are held early in the morning. Sunday-schools were introduced into Scotland, Ireland, and America in the years immediately following their establishment in England; the Scotch Society for Promoting Religious Instruction among the Poor was formed in 1796, and the Irish Sunday-School Society was founded in 1809, though a system of Sunday teaching had prevailed in Ireland for some years previously. In later times Sunday-schools have rapidly increased in connection with all Protestant Churches throughout the world. In 1920 there were in the Sunday-schools of all Protestant denominations over 200,000 Sunday-schools, over 2,000,000 teachers, and over 20,000,000 pupils.

SUNDERBUNDS, or SUNDARBANS, a vast tract of forest and swamp forming the most S. portion of the Gangetic delta, at the head of the Bay of Bengal; extreme length along the coast, about 165 miles; greatest breadth, 81 miles; and area, 7,532 square miles. The country is one vast alluvial plain where the continual process of landmaking has not yet ceased. It abounds in morasses and swamps, now gradually filling up, and is intersected by large rivers and estuaries running from N. to S. There is a reclaimed tract along the N. border devoted to the cultivation of rice. The unreclaimed portion near the sea consists of impenetrable jungle and thick underwood traversed by gloomy-looking water courses. The Sunderbunds abound in wild animals, including numerous tigers, leopards, rhinoceros, buffaloes, deer, monkeys, etc., Fish are plentiful, and the python, cobra, and other snakes, together with every description of birds and water fowls, are found.

SUNDERLAND, a seaport and municipal and parliamentary borough of England, at the mouth of the Wear, county of Durham, 13 miles N. E. of Durham, and 12 miles S. E. of Newcastle. It is the largest town of Durham, and includes nearly the whole of three parishes —Sunderland, Bishopwearmouth, and Monkwearmouth. The town is for the most part new and well built. It has parks, a museum, a free library, a school of art, etc. The principal buildings include St. Peter's, an ancient parish church on the site of the monastery in which the Venerable Bede was educated, many other churches and chapels, two theaters, etc. The river is crossed by the famous cast-iron bridge of one arch (236 feet span), built in 1793 and since reconstructed and strengthened. The harbor with its docks covers 78 acres, and its entrance is formed by two stone piers with lighthouses. The staple trade interests of the place are shipping, the coal trade, and ship building, and there are also large factories for the making of marine engines, iron work, bottles, glass, earthenware, rope, etc. Coal is the chief export; the imports are chiefly timber and grain, with various raw materials and provisions, from the Baltic ports and Holland. Pop. (1919) 149,263.

SUNDEW, the genus *Drosera*, of which about 100 species are known; often applied specifically to *D. rotundifolia*, the common sundew, a very remarkable insectivorous plant. The edges of the leaves curve inward, and insects captured are absorbed by the species. The glands, surrounded by drops of a viscid secretion, shine in the sun: hence the name—sundew.

SUNDIAL. See DIAL.

SUNFISH, the *Lampris luna*, called also opah, and kingfish. Also any individual of the genera *Centrarchus, Bryttus,* and *Pomotis,* from the fresh waters of this country. They are small fishes, about six inches long, and are not used for food. Also any individual of the genus *Orthagoriscus.* The common or broad sunfish (*O. mola*), though a native of warmer seas, is often taken in the summer months round the coasts of Northern Europe, and is usually captured when floating on the surface, as if basking in the sun. The largest specimen on record measured about eight feet long, and rather more in depth from the dorsal to the ventral fins. The oblong sunfish, called also oblong tetradon and truncated sunfish, has the height of body less than one-half its total length. It feeds on worms, crabs, and other marine animals, and does not float on the surface like the common sunfish.

SUNFLOWER (*Helianthus*), a genus of coarse, tall, herbaceous plants, with large, rough leaves and yellow flowers, belonging to *Compositæ,* and natives of America. *H. annuus,* an introduction from Peru, which has long been grown as a showy and large-flowered annual in gardens, has recently been found to possess high economic value. In Germany, Russia, India, and other countries it is now grown on a large scale. The seeds in a natural state are excellent food for poultry and pigs; roasted they are said to be a good substitute for coffee; crushed and pressed, they yield a limpid bland oil second in value only to olive oil, while the residuum can be used as an oil cake to fatten cattle; the stalks furnish a good fiber; the blossoms yield a brilliant lasting yellow dye, and the leaves serve as manure. The tubers of the sunflower artichoke (*H. tuberosum*) are saccharine, and serve culinary purposes. As fodder they increase the milk of cows. The foliage is also a good fodder.

SUNN (*Crotalaria juncea*), a large leguminous annual, rising under favorable circumstances to a height of 10 feet, in appearance resembling somewhat the allied Spanish broom. It is indigenous to Southern Asia, and also widely distributed through tropical Australia. In the former country sunn has been cultivated from remote times for its fiber, which is manufactured into rope, sackcloth, nets, twine, and paper. Sunn is also grown as a fodder plant for cattle. The subspecies, *C. tenuifolia,* furnishes Jubbulpore hemp; *C. retusa* yields a fiber for ropes and canvas, and *C. Burhia* for ropes.

SUNNITES, the name commonly given to orthodox Muslims, because in their rule of faith and manners the Sunna, or traditional teaching of the Prophet, is added to the Koran. According to Islam the human mind is incapable of attaining light in law or religion but through the Prophet, and all expressions of God's will are equally important. Reason and conscience are here of no value; memory is all. Hell fire is the award due alike to him that prays without being properly washed and to him that denies the word of the Prophet. Accordingly during the Prophet's life his counsel was eagerly and continually sought; and after his death his example and sayings were collected as of infinite value. After the death of the four rightly guided caliphs, Abu Bekr, Omar, Othman, and Ali, intimate friends of the Prophet, fearful uncertainty arose and gradually occasioned the four schools of the four orthodox imâms. The first of these was Abu Hanîfa, born in Basra of a noble Persian family. He taught in Kufa on the Euphrates. He logically deduced from the Koran all religion and law; for the Koran says (Sura 16: 91) "to thee we have sent down the book which clears up everything." Consequently, when the Koran says (S. 2: 20) "for you have I created the whole earth," it follows that to Muslims belongs all the property of unbelievers. Hence the propriety of piracy and aggressive war against them. In his school arose the famous legists of Irâk, and his system, the most widely spread of the four, is now professed by the Turkish empire. He would never hold any office under government, fearing the doom due according to prophetic tradition to every giver of a wrong decision, namely, to be plunged into hell from a height of 40 days' journey. He died in 767 in prison, where the caliph had confined him for refusing to be cadi over the new capital Bagdad.

In 795 died Mâlik ibn Anas in his 84th year in Medina, where he was born and had lived all his days. There, surrounded by traditions of the Prophet, he had taught after the custom of Medina. Mâlik gathered from the Koran and from local traditions of Mohammed his "Muwâttaa," or "Beaten Path," a complete body of law and religion. His system was established in North Africa by

African students, who found Medina the most convenient school, and in Spain by his Berber pupil Yahya 'bn Yahya. The third orthodox imâm was Ash-Shâfiî of the Koraish tribe, and descended from the Prophet's grandfather, Abdul-Mût-talib. He was born, it is said, on the day of Abu Hanîfa's death. He taught in Cairo, and there he died in 820. He was an eclectic, but leaned more to the traditionary precedents of his teachei Mâlik than to the deductive method of Abu Hanîfa. His system prevailed in Egypt, and was not uncommon E. It still flourishes in the Asiatic islands.

The use of reason and Greek philosophy had by this time wrought such laxity in faith and in public and private conduct that rigid puritanism was a natural concomitant. Its exponent was Ibn Hanbal, the fourth orthodox imâm, who died in 855 in his native city Bagdad, beyond which his system never had much power. He was a pupil of Ash-Shâfiî, whose lectures, however, he would never allow his own pupils to attend. Tradition and Sunna had now immensely increased, and by these alone the Hanbalites were guided. They are now almost extinct. The bulk of tradition had now made editing indispensable, and those huge masses of it began to appear under which the Muslim mind has been crushed to death. Abu Hanîfa had used only 18 traditions, Mâlik 300. Ibn Hanbal used 30,000. These were mainly collected by his friends and pupils. One of these, the excellent Abu Daûd Suleimân, traveling in many Muslim lands, collected 500,000, which he sifted down to 4,800. But of the six accepted collections the standard one was made by Al Bukhârî, a friend and pupil of Ibn Main. He taught in Bagdad, and like the best Muslim theologians was a Persian. He died in 870. Of the 600,000 traditions heard by him he admitted only 7,275, whereof the half are probably genuine. An edition by Krehl appeared at Leyden in 1862-1872, in three volumes. The collection by his Muslim pupil is better arranged, and is more used. The sources of tradition were Ayesha, the first four caliphs, and the six companions of the Prophet, of whom Abu Horaira, a manifest liar, was more prolific than any other. Through one of these channels to Mohammed the isnâd or pedigree of every tradition had to be traceable. The matter is called Hadîth, events, tradition, and is much more entertaining than the Koran. Besides the legal and religious utterances of Mohammed, which are generally in one or two sentences, it embodies endless nonsense about his life and miracles. Whatever in the Hadith can be imitated or obeyed is Sunna, method; compulsory for guidance if connected with religion. Its object is to make needless all appeals to reason and conscience. In legislation it is much less used than formerly; but, like the Koran, it is infallible and unalterable, and its only independent expounders are the four orthodox imâms. Legislation merely means a declaration by the Sheikh-ul-Islâm and his council of ulemâ or doctors that this or that agrees with the Koran or tradition. Reformation of law or religion from within is impossible.

SUNSTROKE (otherwise called HEAT-STROKE, HEAT APOPLEXY, HEAT ASPHYXIA, COUP DE SOLIEL), a very fatal affection of the nervous system, which is very common in India and tropical countries, and also in more favored regions in extremely hot weather. The symptoms of the disease are liable to be greatly modified in different cases. Two contrasted forms are recognized. In the cardiac the heart is chiefly affected, and the symptoms are weakness, faintness, dimness of sight, giddiness, etc. Death may take place either suddenly or more gradually from failure of the circulation. If recovery occur it is complete. This form is said to occur only from direct exposure to the sun's rays. In the cerebrospinal form, the commoner of the two, the symptoms usually come on more gradually; nausea and giddiness may be present at first; but the most striking feature of the disease is either wild delirium or coma, with a pungently hot skin and extremely high temperature— 106° F. or upward. Even those who recover from this form of the disease are apt to suffer for a long period, or it may be permanently, from severe headache, epilepsy, enfeebled mental power, or other nervous disorders. Intermediate varieties are also met with, forming links between these two extremes.

The predisposing causes of sunstroke are (1) an unusually elevated degree of temperature; (2) heavy or unduly tight clothing, particularly if it interfere with the free expansion of the chest; (3) a contaminated atmosphere from overcrowding; (4) all debilitating causes, such as prolonged marches, previous disease, intemperate habits, etc. Death sometimes occurs so suddenly that there is little opportunity for treatment, but the general indications in these cases are the cold douche, from a height of three or four feet, keeping the surface wet and exposed to a current of air, the exclusion of light as far as possible, and the free employment of stimulants. In less rapidly fatal cases the outer clothing should be removed, and the douche applied, as before, over the head and along the spine.

I—13

SUN WORSHIP, a form of nature worship widely, though by no means universally, diffused at the present day among races of low culture. Traces of sun worship appear in the earliest records of the human race. They are present in the old theology of Egypt. Putting aside the later sun gods of Greece and Rome, horses were sacrificed on Mount Taygetus to that Helios to whom Socrates did not think it wrong to pray; and Cicero exclaims at the number of suns set forth by Roman theologians. The worship of Mithra spread from the East into the Roman empire, and that Vedic divinity was at last identified with the sun. In the Old Testament there are solemn denunciations of sun worship (Deut. iv: 19, xvii: 3; Jer. xliii: 13; Ezek. viii: 16-18); for the Israelites were surrounded by sun worshipers, and it is clear from II Kings xxiii: 5, 19, that the rulers of Judah had adopted the cult.

SUN YAT SEN, or **SUN WEN,** Chiese revolutionary leader. Born in Kwangtung province in 1866, he studied at an American mission, later studied medicine at Honkong, and practiced at Macao. He took part in a revolutionary plot in Canton, fled in 1895, and traveled to America and Europe. He conducted revolutionary activities from Japan and England, returned to China in the revolution of 1911, was declared President of China by the Nanking Council, and resigned in favor of Yuan Shih-kai. He opposed the latter's elevation to Emperor in 1915, and was declared President by the Canton parliament in 1921. At Canton he maintained a separate government. Not a military leader, he was an able politician of radical ideals, and wide influence, working for Chinese national elevation. Died March 12, 1925.

SUPEREROGATION, the performance of more than duty requires. The doctrine of supererogation in Church history is the doctrine founded on that of the communion of saints, that the merit of good works done by one Christian belong to the whole body of the faithful. The principle was affirmed in the "Institution of a Christian Man" published by authority of Convocation (A. D. 1537). At the time of the Reformation the sale of indulgences had brought discredit on the doctrine of supererogation, or "as it might more properly be called, the communion of saints in good works," and Article XIV. was directed against the popular belief.

Works of supererogation as defined in Article XIV. of the Church of England, are "voluntary works besides, over, and above God's Commandments."

SUPERIOR, a city, port of entry, and county-seat of Douglas co., Wis.; on Lake Superior, and on the Northern Pacific, the Great Northern, the Chicago, Milwaukee and St. Paul, the Minneapolis, St. Paul and Sault Ste. Marie, the Chicago and Northwestern and the Duluth, South Shore, and Atlantic railroads; opposite Duluth, Minn. It shares with Duluth the commercial advantage of being the extreme W. port of the Great Lake system of the United States. It has three connecting harbors, well sheltered, and deep, making a combined length of 13 miles, with an extreme width of 3 miles. The city comprises the ports known as East, West, South, and Old Superior. Here are the Finnish University, high schools, street railroads, electric lights, a State Normal school, several hospitals, numerous churches, waterworks, National and State banks, and several newspapers. The industries include the manufacture of flour, lumber, lath, shingles, wagons, chairs, barrels, woolen goods, cement, furniture, bags, iron, steel, etc. There are also shipyards, sawmills, coal docks, many grain elevators, and dry docks. Pop. (1910) 40,384; (1920) 39,671.

SUPERIOR, LAKE, the extreme W. and most extensive of the great lakes of the St. Lawrence basin, in North America, being the largest existing body of fresh water. It is of a triangular form, extending between lat. 40° 30' and 49° N., and lon. 80° and 92° 20' W. Its length, E. to W., is about 360 miles, with a mean breadth of about 80 miles, so that its area may be taken at about 28,600 square miles. The mean depth is estimated at 900 feet, and the height of its surface at about 640 feet above the Atlantic. It receives upward of 50 rivers; the chief are the St. Louis, which enters at its S. W. extremity, and the Riviere au Grand Portage. It discharges itself at its E. extremity into Lakes Huron and Michigan, by the river and falls of St. Mary. This lake embosoms many large and well-wooded islands, the chief of which is Isle Royal. The country of the N. and E. is a mountainous embankment of rock, from 200 to 1,500 feet in height; the climate unfavorable, and the vegetation slow and scanty. On the S. the land is also high, generally sandy, sterile, and the coast dangerous, subject to storms, and sudden transitions of temperature, and to fogs and mists. The mean heat in June and July is about 65° F., but an extremely cold winter prevails.

The boundary line between Canada and the United States passes from Lake

Huron up the river St. Mary, the outlet of Lake Superior, through the center of the lower half of this lake, to the mouth of Pigeon river on the N. shore, between Isle Royal and the Canadian coast. The S. coast of the lake from the outlet to Montreal river belongs to the upper peninsula of Michigan. From this river to the St. Louis river at Fond du Lac the coast belongs to Wisconsin, and thence around to Pigeon river to Minnesota. Toward each extremity the lake contracts in width, and at the lower end terminates in a bay which falls into the outlet, the St. Mary's river, at the two opposite headlands of Gros Cape on the N. and Point Iroquois on the S. Thence to the mouth of the St. Mary's at Lake Huron is about 60 miles. The navigation of this river is interrupted 20 miles below its source at the Falls of St. Mary, or, as the place is commonly called, Sault Ste. Marie. Here the river descends in a succession of rapids extending ¾ of a mile, from 18 to 21 feet, the fall varying with the stage of the water in Lake Superior.

A ship canal has been constructed past the falls by the United States Government, so that now the lake is accessible to vessels from the Atlantic Ocean. The rocks around the lake are very ancient, belonging principally to the Laurentian and Huronian systems of the Azoic series, overlaid in some places, especially on the S. side, with patches of the Lower Silurian. The prevalent Laurentian rock is orthoclase gneiss. Among the Huronian rocks are greenstones, slates, conglomerates, quartzites, and limestones. The Lower Silurian rocks are soft sandstones. There is everywhere much evidence of glacial action. The Huronian rocks are well stored with useful minerals. The copper and iron mines of the S. side are celebrated for their extent and richness. The richest copper mines are situated near Kee-wee-naw Point. The metal occurs principally native, and sometimes in single masses of great size. Native silver is found associated with the native copper, and sometimes intimately mixed with it. Gold has been found in small specks at Namainse on the British side. Lead ore occurs in some places. The beds of hæmatite, or red iron ore, at Marquette, on the American side, are of wonderful extent. The water of Lake Superior, remarkable for its coldness, purity, and transparency, is inhabited by many kinds of fish, among which are the delicious white fish and the gray trout.

SUPERPHOSPHATE OF LIME, P_2O_2 $(HO)_4CaO_2$; a compound of phosphoric acid and lime in which only one-third of its acid equivalents is saturated with lime. Technically, it is used to describe an important kind of manure, made by treating ground bones with from one-third to two-thirds of their equivalent of sulphuric acid, whereby acid phosphate of lime is formed, together with a quantity of sulphate of lime corresponding to the sulphuric acid used. By substituting coprolites for bones, a manure of nearly identical composition is obtained. This kind of manure is of the highest value, from its stimulating effects.

SUPERSTITION, credulity regarding the supernatural, or matters beyond human powers; belief in the direct agency of superior powers in certain events; as a belief in witchcraft, apparitions, magic, omens, charms and the like, a belief that the fortunes of individuals are or can be affected by things deemed lucky or unlucky, or that diseases can be cured by charms, incantations or the like. Superstitions concerning various articles of food, animals, days of the week, and even the most ordinary events of life are common, not only among the ignorant and lower classes of mankind, but among the highly educated and cultured.

The origin and influence of these superstitions is an interesting study. Salt, for instance, is probably the only article of food which has been used by every nation and in every age since the beginning of civilization. In ancient times it was very scarce, and very costly. From this grew the Eastern custom that whoever should eat salt together—the most precious possession — must be friends for life. An Oriental will not kill or harm a man with whom he has eaten salt. The belief that it is unlucky to spill salt at the table originated in the legend that at the "Last Supper" Judas Iscariot, who went thence to betray his Lord and Master, upset the salt cellar while reaching out his hand.

Many ancient superstitions were connected with the Sabbath, and especially with the punishment meted out to those who desecrated the holy day. At one place in England a carpenter, who made a peg, and a weaver, who remained at his loom after 12 o'clock on Saturday night, were each smitten with palsy. In France there is a saying that "if you meet a funeral while driving you will have an accident before your drive is over, unless you turn back." Many gamblers will not play on a day in which they meet a funeral and others will bet only on the black in rouge et noir.

Among common superstitions are those which regard as unlucky the seeing of the new moon over the left shoulder; the beginning of a journey or any enterprise on Friday; the passing under a raised ladder, etc.

SUPPURATION, a morbid process which gives rise to the formation of pus, one of the destructive terminations of the inflammatory action. The phenomena of suppuration are thus described: The inflammatory leucocytes, instead of developing into fiber cells and forming tissue, become developed into pus globules, and the exudation breaks down more or less completely into a creamy fluid called pus, which consists of these globules floating in serum, the liquor puris. Suppuration in the interior of the body usually termintes in the formation of an abscess; but in some cases the matter is diffused through the interstices of the part, and is termed diffuse inflammation.

SUPREMACY, PAPAL, the authority, partly spiritual and partly temporal, which the Pope, as Bishop of Rome and successor of St. Peter, claims to exercise over the clergy, and, through them, over the laity, of the whole world. The development of this supremacy dates from the time when Christianity became the State religion of the Roman empire under Constantine. Its influence was great in England under the Norman kings, and reached its highest point in the reign of John (1199-1216), from which period it began to decline, and received its death blow from the Act of Supremacy, in the reign of Henry VIII.

SUPREMACY, ROYAL, the supremacy in the Church of England, as by law established, of the temporal power in all causes purely temporal, and in the temporal accidents of spiritual things. By an act of Henry VIII., the king was declared to be the "only supreme head on earth of the Church of England," though it was expressly declared that he did not "pretend to take any power from the successors of the apostles that was given them by God." In the same year (1535) Fisher, Bishop of Rochester, and Sir Thomas More were beheaded for denying the royal claim. On the accession of Elizabeth the title was kept in the background; but the supremacy of the sovereign in all causes, as well ecclesiastical as civil, was asserted. The royal supremacy was one of the main causes of the Civil War in the 17th century; it received a check at the Revolution of 1688, which enforced toleration of Nonconformity, but in the latter half of the 19th century more than one clergyman was committed to prison for disobeying the ruling of the law courts in ecclesiastical matters.

SUPREME COUNCIL OF THE PARIS PEACE CONFERENCE. In January, 1919, when the representatives of the Allied Powers and those nations which had been associated with them in the war against the Central Empires, assembled in Paris to draft the terms of peace, the delegates of the four powers, England, the United States, France and Italy, assumed the function of a committee to arrange preliminaries. Later, the delegates of Japan were allowed to join this conclave. This supreme council became known as the Big Five, or, more officially, as the Council of Ten. It at once began its task of arranging preliminaries; decisions and communiques were issued in its name, and it drafted the rules which were later to guide the main conference. It also assumed the power to fix the representation of the various states which were to participate. Its sessions were held in secret and its proceedings carefully withheld from the public. The members of the Council were:

Representing the United States: President Woodrow Wilson; Robert Lansing, Secretary of State; Henry White, ex-Ambassador to Rome and Paris; Colonel Edward M. House, and General Tasker K. Bliss.

Representing Great Britain: David Lloyd George British Premier; Andrew Bonar Law, Arthur James Balfour, Viscount Milner, and George Nicoll Barnes.

Representing France: Georges Clemenceau, French Premier; Stephen Pichon, Lucius-Lucien Klotz, Andre Tardieu, and Jules Cambon.

Representing Italy: Villorio Orlando, Italian Premier; Baron Sonnino, and Antonio Salandra.

Representing Japan: Marquis Suiouji, Baron Makino, Viscount Chinda, K. Matsui, and H. Ijuin.

The decisions of the Council regarding representation at the conference caused considerable dissatisfaction among the smaller nations. As an instance, Belgium, which had borne the brunt of the German attack, was allowed only two delegates, whereas Brazil, which had not actively participated in hostilities, was allowed three delegates. Because of the protest of the Belgian representatives Belgium was finally allowed the same number of delegates as Brazil. Other smaller nations likewise found cause for protest, but the Council showed itself disposed to yield in their favor and concessions were made, whereby the smaller nations were allowed joint and separate representation.

After the withdrawal of President Wilson and his party from the peace negotiations, the Supreme Council continued to function, largely through the premiers of the four remaining big powers.

SUPREME COURT OF THE UNITED STATES. In accordance with the provisions of the United States Constitution there was organized in 1789 a Supreme Court, John Jay receiving the first appointment as chief justice. With him were joined as associate justices John Rutledge, of South Carolina; James Wilson, of Pennsylvania; William Cushing, of Massachusetts; John Blair, of Virginia; and James Iredell, of North Carolina. John Jay held the office till 1795, and in 1796 Oliver Ellsworth became chief justice: The latter presided over the court till in 1800 the infirmities of age compelled his resignation. Then came the long and honorable incumbency of Chief-Justice John Marshall, who held the office from his appointment in 1801 to his death in 1835. This was a very notable period in the history of this court, and Judge Marshall's decisions have always been ranked as of pre-eminent ability. In 1836 the appointment of Roger B. Taney to the chief justiceship by President Jackson was confirmed by the Senate, and he took his seat on the bench in January, 1837, entering on his long term of 27 years. It was his celebrated decision in the case of the negro, Dred Scott, relative to the status of the slave race in America that applied the torch to that immense heap of combustibles whose explosion was the Civil War. At the death of Chief-Justice Taney in 1864, President Lincoln appointed as his successor Salmon P. Chase, previously Secretary of the Treasury and author of most of the great financial measures and expedients by which the national credit had been preserved during the war. His official term extended to his death in 1873, and covered the period when the important issues arising from the Civil War were under adjudication. To Chief-Justice Chase fell also by virtue of his office, the duty of presiding at the impeachment trial of President Andrew Johnson. In 1874 the appointment of Morrison R. Waite as chief justice was made by President Grant, and on the death of this able jurist in 1888 devolved on President Cleveland and the Senate the duty of selecting his successor, Melville W. Fuller, who served until his death in 1910. Edward Douglass White, of Louisiana, associate justice, and a Democrat, was appointed his successor as chief justice.

In the formation of the Constitution of the United States it was intended that the three general departments of the government should be of correlative rank and influence. And the decisions of the Supreme Court, especially those rendered since the Civil War, in the construction of the constitutional amendments which were made as a result of that war, have been of such fundamental and far reaching consequences that the value and importance of this tribunal in the United States system of government have been made more strikingly conspicuous than ever before. Its judgments, for example, in regard to civil rights, interstate commerce, prohibition liquor laws, the Mormon question, the right of Congress to authorize the use of paper money in time of peace, the legislation of Congress in regard to the Southern States by so-called "force bills," the relations of the States to the Federal Government, etc., have been of the highest importance, and their influence in the future will be almost incalculable.

A majority of the members suffices to render a valid decision of the court, contrary minority view notwithstanding. This system of procedure has at times been attacked in Congress as rendering it too readily possible to declare unconstitutional the acts of that body. Senator Borah in 1923 proposed that it be required that the court vote at least seven to two when finding a measure unconstitutional. This and another more radical proposal of Senator La Follette were extensively opposed as tending to subordinate the Judiciary. The President fills vacancies in the court by nomination.

The Supreme Court, at its first session in 1790, as already noted, consisted of a chief justice and 5 associates. By successive acts of Congress the number of associate justices was increased to 6 in 1807, to 8 in 1837, and the statute now in force passed in 1869 fixes the number at 9. The retirement of the justices at the age of 70 is not compulsory, but a mere personal privilege. This provision was originally enacted April 10, 1869. Sec. 1, Art. III., of the United States Constitution expressly provides that the judges "shall hold their offices during good behavior," so that if they do not voluntarily take advantage of the foregoing provision and are not removed they are entitled to exercise the duties of their office till death.

The Supreme Court is the judicial court of last resort in the Federal system of courts. The sessions are held in Washington, D. C., and any 6 justices constitute a quorum. Each judge of the court, moreover, must, at least once in every 2 years, attend a term in one of the 9 circuit courts in those parts of the country where those courts are held. The judicial power of the Supreme Court and of the inferior Federal courts extends to all cases in law and equity arising under the Constitution, the laws of the United States, and treaties made under their authority; to all cases affecting ambassadors, other public ministers, and consuls; to all cases of admiralty and maritime jurisdiction; to controversies to which the United States is a party, and to controversies between two or more States or between citizens of different States, etc.; but not to suits against one of the States by citizens of another State, or by citizens or subjects of any foreign state. The Supreme Court has original jurisdiction in cases affecting ambassadors, public ministers and consuls, and when a State is a party; but its chief jurisdiction is appellate. Thus it hears appeals from the circuit courts and from certain district courts having circuit court powers; in civil actions; where the matter in dispute exceeds $5,000, or in equity and maritime cases, $2,000. But there are some cases, as, for example, in regard to patents and copyrights, revenue laws, and civil rights, where an appeal is allowed without regard to the value in dispute. Moreover, if decisions in the highest courts of the various States are in conflict with the Constitution, treaties, or laws of the United States, they may be appealed to the Supreme Court. The Supreme Court in 1927 was composed of William Howard Taft of Connecticut, chief justice, and associate justices Oliver Wendell Holmes (Mass.), Willis Van Devanter (Wyo.), James Clark McReynolds (Tenn.), Louis D. Brandeis (Mass.), George Sutherland (Utah), Pierce Butler (Minn.), Edward Terry Sanford (Tenn.), and Harlan Fiske Stone (New York).

SURABAYA, or SOERABAYA, a large seaport town of Java; on the N. E. coast, and capital of one of the three provinces into which the island is divided by the Dutch; lat. 7° 12′ 30″ S.; lon. 112° 44′ 7″ E.; it is at the mouth of a navigable river, 1½ mile from the seashore. The river separates the European part of the town from the Chinese and the native quarter. The houses are very good, and some are elegant, particularly the country seats of private individuals. Surabaya is situated within that narrow strait which is formed by the islands of Java and Madura, and is defended by batteries. The mouth of the river is also defended. Pop. of town about 120,000. Province area 2,327 square miles. Pop. 2,115,000.

SURAJAH DOWLAH, the last independent nawab of Bengal, under whom was perpetrated the massacre of the Black Hole. He succeeded his grandfather, Ali Verdy Khan, in 1756, and within two months of his accession found a pretext for marching on Calcutta. On the arrival of Clive and Admiral Watson he retreated to Moorshedabad, but was routed at the battle of Plassey (June 23, 1757). He then fled up the Ganges, but was betrayed by a *fakir*, and was put to death by order of the son of Meer Jaffier, the new nawab. Surajah Dowlah's reign lasted 15 months, his age at the time of his death being barely 20.

SURAT, a town of India, Bombay presidency, capital of a district of the same name, on the left bank of the Tapti, about 20 miles above its mouth in the Gulf of Cambay. The town possesses few attractions, and consists of narrow winding streets lined with lofty houses. It contains several public buildings, including two hospitals, and an old castle or fortress now containing public offices. Surat was first heard of in 1512 as sacked by the Portuguese. The first English factory was established here in 1612, and 40 years later all the other possessions of the company were placed in subordination to it. In 1692 the seat of government was transferred to Bombay. Henceforth Surat became a bone of contention between the Mogul deputy and Mahratta invaders. In 1759 the English seized the castle; and in 1799, on the death of the last real nawab, themselves assumed the administration. In 1842 the titular dignity of Nawab of Surat also became extinct. Surat is still a considerable center of trade and minor manufactures. The organization of trade guilds is here highly developed. The chief exports are agricultural produce and cotton. Pop. about 115,000.

SURAKARTA, a trading town on the N. E. coast of Java; near the mouth of the Solo river, opposite the island of Madura; 150 miles W. S. W. of Samarang. It is the chief town of the feudatory State of Surakarta and the residence of the emperor and of many of the native princes and nobles. The emperor's palace is a building of great extent and grandeur. The European town, defended by a strong fort, has a trade in rice, sugar, coffee, pepper, tobacco, etc., and a pop. of about 125,000. State, area 2,191 square miles. Pop. 1,100,000.

SURETY, SURETYSHIP, in law one who is bound with and for another who is primarily liable, and who is called the principal; one who enters into a bond or recognizance to answer for his payment of a debt, or for the performance of some act, and who, in case of the

© Ewing Galloway   See **Sugar Cane**, p. 149

SUGAR CANE READY FOR HARVEST IN THE ISLAND OF JAMAICA, WEST INDIES

THE INTERIOR OF A SUGAR MILL IN CUBA. AT THE LEFT ARE VACUUM VATS IN WHICH THE JUICE IS BOILED
BEFORE ENTERING THE CENTRIFUGAL MACHINE

See Sugar Cane, p. 149

failure of the principal, is liable to pay the debt and damages; a bondsman, a bail. A surety of good behavior is a recognizance or obligation to the commonwealth entered into by a person with one or more sureties before some competent judge of record, whereby the parties acknowledge themselves to be indebted to the commonwealth in a specified amount, with condition to be void if the defendant shall demean and behave himself well, either generally or specially, for the time therein limited. It includes surety for the peace and something more. A justice may bind over all night-walkers, such as keep suspicious company, or are reported to be pilferers or robbers, common drunkards, cheats, idle vagabonds, and other persons whose misbehavior may reasonably bring them within the general words of the statute as persons not of good fame. A surety of the peace is the acknowledgement of a bond to the commonwealth, taken by a competent judge of record, for keeping the peace.

SURFACE, in mathematics, the boundary of a solid, having two dimensions, length and breadth. It may be conceived to be generated by the motion of a straight or curved line, just as a curve is generated by the motion of a point. Of all surfaces, the most important are those of the second order, which are intersected by a straight line in at most two points, and whose curve of section by a plane is a curve of the second order. Hyperboloids, ellipsoids, paraboloids, spheres, cones, and cylinders, and also the limiting case of two planes, are included among the so-called quadric surfaces.

SURFACE TENSION, in liquids, that property in virtue of which a liquid surface behaves as if it were a stretched elastic membrane—say a sheet of india-rubber. The idea is due to Segner (1751); but it was Young who in 1805 first applied it successfully to the explanation of various physical phenomena, such as those of capillarity. The whole subject was subsequently developed in its complete mathematical form by Laplace and Gauss. Pure water has the highest surface tension of any ordinary liquid except mercury. If a little alcohol be dropped on the water, the surface tension will be diminished there. The more powerful surface tension over the pure water will show its superiority by pulling the alcohol over the whole surface till the surface is reduced to uniformity, and equilibrium produced. Drops of liquid, free from all but their own molecular forces, assume spherical forms,

this being the only shape consistent with equilibrium under the influence of equal surface tension at all parts of the curved surface. Ripples on the surface of any liquid progress because of the action of surface tension, which gives rise to an inward pressure on any convex surface. In cohesion figures we have some very exquisite phenomena. These are produced by dropping a dark-colored liquid into a transparent liquid of slightly smaller density. Ordinary ink dropped into water will serve the purpose very well, though better effects are obtained with a solution of permanganate of potash. As the drop meets the water surface, the action of the surface tension pulls the under surface of the drop outward, and transforms the drop into a vortex ring which slowly sinks through the clear fluid. As it so sinks it breaks up into smaller rings and shoots out fantastic ramifications of rare beauty. Ultimately, of course, under the influence of diffusion, the vortex motion decays and the dark liquid mixes with the clear liquid.

SURF DUCK, or SURF SCOTER, a species of duck (*Oidemia perspicillata*), about the size of a mallard, rarely seen on the British coasts, but frequently on the coasts of Labrador, Hudson Bay, and other parts of North America.

SURGEON, one who practises surgery; in a more limited sense, one who cures diseases or injuries of the body by operating manually upon the patient. In a more general sense, one whose occupation is to treat diseases or injuries by medical appliances, whether internal or external.

In ichthyology, a popular name for any species of the genus *Acanthurus*, from the sharp, erectile, lancet-shaped spine with which each side of the tail is armed. In the early stages of their growth these fish are so different from the fully-developed individuals, that for some time the young fish were placed in a separate genus, *Acronurus*.

Surgeon-general, in the United States Army the chief of the medical department. In the British Army a surgeon ranking next below the chief of the medical department.

SURGERY, manual intervention, mediate and immediate, in all lesions or malformations of the human body. It was already an art when medicine proper was but a phase of superstition. The earliest notices of it occur among the Egyptians, who, as we find represented on obelisk and in temple, practiced incisions, scarifications, probably even amputation, long before the date of the Ebers papyrus (3500 B. C.). Castration (to supply eunuchs for the royal harem) was also a frequent operation. Preserved in museums may be seen surgical instruments contemporary with votive offerings of the remotest Egyptian epoch—lancets, tweezers, catheters, uterine specula, iron rods for the actual cautery, etc. Among other indications of early proficiency in ophthalmic surgery, couching cataract must have been known to them.

Jewish surgery, like Jewish medicine, was an importation from the Egyptians. The sexual regulations characteristic of the Jews affected their surgery, from simple circumcision up to the Cæsarean section, which very early in their history was practiced on pregnant women in death as in life.

Without entering into the controversy as to the Greek origin of the Indian healing art, we find surgery enjoying high esteem among the Indians in very remote times. Surgical instruments skillfully made of steel, to the number of 127, still attest their proficiency in cutting and cauterizing. Their surgeons were trained to operate by practicing not on animals or on the dead human subject, but on wax-covered boards, on beasts' skins, or on succulent plants and fruits. Hemorrhage they checked by cold, by compression, and by styptics. The ligature they seem not to have known. Amputation was confined to the hand in cases of intractable hemorrhage. Lips or surfaces of wounds they smeared with an arsenical salve. For intus-susception, volvulus, and such abdominal lesions they practiced laparotomy, while fistula in ano (diagnosed by the speculum) they treated with the knife and corrosives.

As to the surgery of the other Orientals we possess but obscure notices. Among the Persians we find Greeks in general practice under King Cambyses. The Chinese 6 centuries B. C. performed surgical operations.

In Greece surgery had attained high development before Hippocrates put medicine on a rational basis, and in the Hippocratic books we find a rich collection of surgical doctrine and practice drawn from centuries of experience. Even modern appliances were in great part anticipated by him—splints, for example, and bandages of various kinds. The gem of the Hippocratic surgery (according to Häser) is the treatise on injuries of the cranium—fractures, fissures, and contusions with or without depression. For such cases trepanning is the sovereign operation, to be performed as early as possible, less to get rid of effused blood, pus, etc., than, by

removal of the injured osseous structure, to prevent inflammation of the scalp. The removal of extremities which had become gangrenous shows again the Hippocratic surgery in a wonderfully favorable light.

The post-Hippocratic school (its greatest surgeon being Praxagoras of Cos, noted for his cure of volvulus) has little to detain us; but the Alexandrians left a distinct mark on every branch of the healing art—surgery included. Our best knowledge of them comes from Celsus, who names as the most celebrated surgeon of Alexandria Philoxenus, a voluminous writer on the subject.

Roman surgery can hardly claim M. Porcius Cato (234-149 B. C.) as more than a shrewd amateur who left some handy rules for the treatment of fractures, ulcers, nasal polypi, fistulæ, strangury, etc. Archagathus (218 B. C.) was a regular practitioner, known for his skillful handling of dislocations, fractures, and particularly wounds, as the "Vulnerarius." But when from such practice he proceeded to operate with the knife his popularity fled, he was nicknamed the "Carnifex," and had to leave the city. Celsus, the patrician dilettante in medicine, is really the highest name in Roman surgery, though it is doubtful whether he ever operated. Of the eight books of his admirably written work the last two treat of surgery, including plastic replacement of defects in the outer ear, the nose, and the lips; lithotomy as practiced on boys (a celebrated chapter); amputation, previously described by no other author; diseases of the bones, with the operation of trepanning, fractures simple and compound, and dislocations.

Galen, though a master of surgery, and, before his settling in Rome under M. Aurelius, a practitioner of it, seems to have contributed nothing of his own to its doctrine of practice. As he found it (with some notable additions) it remained to the close of the Byzantine period. An intimate knowledge of its modus operandi during these centuries may be inferred from the collection of surgical instruments dug up at Pompeii and now on view at Naples. These are about 300 in number, consisting of some 60 different kinds. The treatment of fractures and dislocations was practically the same from Hippocrates to Paulus Ægineta (A. D. 650). Trepanning received several modifications in practice up to Galen's time, while tracheotomy (introduced by Asclepiades, 1st century) was by Paulus restricted to cases of choking, when the deeper air passages were free. The operation for hernia, perfunctorily dealt with by Hippocrates, had by the epoch of Celsus assumed the practical development in which it is found during the later empire, Heliodorus, under Trajan, being noted for his radical cure of the scrotal form. In Paulus we find a well-nigh exhaustive list of operations for disease or malformation of the genitals, even including syphilis (Häser), while rectal and anal affections (hemorrhoids, fistula, etc.) were skillfully treated by Leonides (A. D. 200), who seems to have used the écraseur as well as the knife and the cautery. Large tumors in the neighborhood of great vessels were untouched by Hippocrates or Celsus, though the latter makes mention of the surgical cure of goîter. Amputation after Celsus is described by Archigenes, hemorrhage being obviated by ligature of the great vessels or constriction of the limb. Flap-amputations were performed by Heliodorus and Leonides. Resection of the humerus, the femur, and the lower jaw proves (according to Häser) the high development to which surgery under the empire had attained, as also do the plastic operations which Antyllus describes with a fullness and freedom unknown to Celsus. A word may be added here for the medico-military service of that time, afloat and ashore, apparently quite as well organized as the combatant arm. Under the Byzantine Emperor Maurice (582-602) the cavalry had an ambulance company whose business it was to bring the severely wounded out of action, and who were provided with water flasks and cordials to relieve the fainting.

The Arabs borrowed their surgery from the Greeks, chiefly from Paulus Ægineta, even more slavishly than their medicine. Their neglect of anatomy and their Oriental repugnance to operations involving the effusion of blood serve to explain the fact that except Abulcasim (died 1122) they contribute no memorable name to this branch of the healing art.

Surgery continued to be looked down on by physicians, all the more that the recently founded universities gave the latter the prestige of a culture denied to the adventurers who healed wounds, reduced dislocations, and set fractured limbs. Throughout the Middle Ages surgical literature seems to have shared the fortunes of medical literature—first the Greeks were in the ascendant then their servile imitators the Arabs. The earliest mediæval writers in surgery were Italians, superseded in the 14th century by the French, while the same period witnessed the first English, Dutch, and German books on the subject. Guy de Chauliac, the highest name in that century, labored to bridge the chasm between surgery and other branches of medicine. For all that, the mediæval surgeon in Eastern Europe remained far behind his predecessors of the Roman and Byzantine empires.

With the 16th century we find surgery sharing the advance communicated to every art by the Renaissance, while its practitioners improved their social standing. In this the way had been led by Paris with her College of Surgeons (Collége de St. Côme, 1279), which in the teeth of the university "faculty" conquered the right to create licentiates in surgery. Other qualifying corporations (in London, for example, and Edinburgh) arose gradually on similar lines. But what crowned the recognition of surgery as a liberal profession was its steady progress as a beneficent public agent in peace as in war. The powerful if eccentric genius of Paracelsus was signally instrumental in this direction; still more so the sound sagacity and nobly philanthropic inspiration of Ambrose Paré (1517-1590). Galileo, Bacon, and Descartes revolutionized scientific method, among the fruits of which was Harvey's discovery of the circulation of the blood. With the diffusion of juster and more comprehensive notions of structure and function surgery took bolder and more effective flights, reaching her highest point in the 17th century under Richard Wiseman, the father of English surgery, from whose "Seven Chirurgical Treatises" may be gathered the great accession he made to sound practice, particularly in tumors, wounds, fractures, and dislocations. In the 18th century Paris improved on her Collége de St. Côme by her Académie de Chirurgie, long the headquarters of the highest professional and literary culture. England contributed Chelseden and Pott; Scotland, James Douglas, the three Monros, Benjamin Bell, and above all John Hunter, to the promotion of a more enlightened practice, based on anatomical and physiological research. London, Edinburgh, and Dublin became centers of surgical education, which, by the admission of Häser, no continental school, not even Paris, could equal in the sovereign qualities of sagacity in diagnosis and assured boldness in operation. Prussia came far behind with her Collegium Medico-Chirurgicum in Berlin, and Austria only in 1780 and 1785 obtained the means of training surgeons of the higher grade, civil and military; while the United States by her school, under Dr. Shippen in Philadelphia, laid the foundation of its subsequent and nobly sustained proficiency.

To the distinguished anatomists Mascagni and Scarpa in Italy, Breschet and

Geoffrey St. Hilaire in France, the brothers John and Charles Bell in Great Britain, the Meckels, Berres, Tiedemann, C. M. Langenback in Germany, seconded by physiologists like the Italian Panizzo, the Scotch Charles Bell, the English Marshall Hall, the French Magendie, Flourens, Duchenne, and Bernard, the German Prochaska, Purkinje, the brothers Weber, and Joannes Müller, surgery owes the mighty advance she made in the first decades of the 19th century. Of these pioneers some were themselves surgeons of the first rank, such as Scarpa and the brothers Bell; while among those who were equally great as teachers or writers and operators must be noticed Desault, Dupuytren, Roux, Delpech, and Lallemand in France; Lizars, Allan Burns, Liston, and Syme in Scotland; Abernethy, Astley Cooper, Brodie, and Lawrence in England; Warren, Mott, and Gross in the United States; Wattman, Siebold, Walther, Chelius, Langenbeck (already mentioned), Stromeyer, Graefe, and Dieffenbach in Germany; Kern, Pitha, and Linhart in Austria; Pirogoff and Szymanovsky in Russia. Anatomico-pathological museums and clinical instruction, displaying a wealth of object lessons impossible before, are among the chief causes of the perfection to which the surgical profession is rapidly attaining. Add to these the introduction of anæsthetics, of the antiseptic ligature and dressing, of the galvano-cautery, of the transfusion of blood, and of the engrafting on patients of tissue taken from the healthy subject, and we can realize the revolution that has so altered the surgeon's art as to make its present position one of the greatest triumphs of human intellect, energy, and resource. The science of surgery received great impetus during the World War. Under the greatest difficulties surgeons in all the armies performed operations of marvelous skill and ingenuity.

SURINAM TOAD, in zoölogy, the *Pipa americana,* a large flat toad found on the edges of swamps in Surinam and the neighboring country. It is about a foot long, with a short, broad, pointed head, the nostrils produced into a leathery tube; large hind limbs with webbed feet; fore feet small, with four slender webbed fingers, terminating in four small projections. It is brownish-olive above, whitish below; the skin is covered with a number of tiny hard granules, interspersed with horny, tubercular projections. It has no tongue, and the jaws and palate are toothless. The species is propagated in an extremely curious manner. When the eggs are laid, the male impregnates them, takes them in his paws, and places them on the back of the female, where they adhere by means of a glutinous secretion, and become by degrees embedded in a series of cells which then form in the skin. When the process is completed a membrane closes over the cells, and the back of the female bears a strong resemblance to a piece of dark honeycomb. In these cells the eggs are hatched and the young undergo their metamorphosis, bursting through the protecting membrane as perfect frogs.

SURMOUNTED, in architecture, denoting an arch or dome which rises higher than a semicircle. In heraldry, a term denoting the position of a charge over which another charge of different color or metal is laid. The annexed figures, which may respectively be blazoned: "Sable," a pile argent surmounted by a chevron gules; and "argent," a cross gules surmounted by another "or."

SURPLICE, the outer garment of an officiating priest, deacon, or chorister in the Church of England and the Roman Catholic Church, worn over their other dress during the performance of religious services. It is a loose, flowing vestment of white linen, generally reaching almost to the feet, with broad, full sleeves. It differs from the alb in being fuller, and in having no girdle, nor embroidery at the foot.

SURREY, HENRY HOWARD, EARL OF, an English poet; born about 1516, was the grandson of the Earl of Surrey who was the victor at Flodden, and who, as a reward for his services, was created Duke of Norfolk. He succeeded to the courtesy title of Earl of Surrey when his father became 2d Duke of Norfolk in 1524. The Howards held an eminent position at the court of Henry VIII., and Surrey's cousin, Catherine Howard, became the king's fifth wife. Surrey was one of the leaders of the early poetic movement under Henry VIII. Most of his poems were translations or adaptations of Italian originals. His translations of the second and fourth books of the Æneid are the first attempt at blank verse in the English language. Shortly before Henry's death Surrey and his father were suspected of aiming at the throne, and were arrested and lodged in the Tower, and Surrey was tried, condemned, and executed on Tower Hill Jan. 19, 1547.

SURREY, an inland county of southeast England. Area, 758 square miles. Pop. about 900,000. The county capital is Guildford (pop. about 25,000). The surface is hilly with a slope toward the Thames. The Mole and Wey are the principal streams. The northern half of the county is fertile, hops and wheat being the chief crops. Market gardening is carried on extensively. The western and southwestern part is covered to a great extent with heath. The manufacturing enterprises are of importance and include beer, cloth, leather, paper, pottery, and silk. As a result of its picturesque scenery the county is one of the most favored residential districts of London business men.

SURROGATE, generally a deputy, a substitute, a delegate, a person appointed to act for another; specifically, the deputy of an ecclesiastical judge, most commonly of a bishop or his chancellor, who grants marriage licenses and probates. Also an officer who presides over the probate of wills and testaments and the settlement of estates.

SURTEES, ROBERT, an English historian; born in Durham, April 1, 1779; was graduated at Oxford (1800), and studied law at the Middle Temple till by his father's death in 1802 he came into the Mainsforth property. Thenceforth he devoted himself to writing his "History and Antiquities of the County Palatine of Durham" (3 vols. 1816-1823), to the fourth volume (1840) of which, completed by the Rev. J. Baine, a "Memoir" by G. Taylor is prefixed. Surtees died Feb. 11, 1834, and in the same year was founded the Surtees Society for editing unpublished MSS. chiefly relating to the Northern Counties.

SURVEYING, the act or art of determining the boundaries, form, area, position, contour, etc., of any portion of the earth's surface, tract of country, coast, etc., by means of measurements taken on the spot; the art of determining the form, area, surface, contour, etc., of any portion of the earth's surface, and delineating it accurately on a map or plan. Land surveying is the art of applying the principles of geometry and trigonometry to the measurement of land. The principal operations are laying down or driving base lines and triangles on either side of the base. In large surveys it is desirable to lay down these triangles by measuring each angle with an instrument called the THEODOLITE (*q. v.*)., by which the accuracy of the measurement of the sides may be checked. Geodesic surveying comprises all the operations of surveying carried on under the supposition that earth is spheroidal. It embraces marine surveying.

Marine or hydrographical surveying ascertains the forms of coast lines, harbors, etc., and of objects on the shore, the entrances to harbors, channels, their depth, width, etc., the position of shoals, the depth of water thereon. Mining surveying may be either for the purpose of determining the situation and position of the shafts, galleries, and other underground excavations of a mine already in existence; or it may be for determining the proper positions for the shafts, galleries, etc., of a mine not yet opened. Railway surveying is a comprehensive term, embracing surveys intended to ascertain the best line of communication between two given points; it also includes all surveys for the construction of aqueducts for the supply of water to towns, etc. Topographical surveying embraces all the operations incident to finding the contour of a portion of the earth's surface, and the various methods of representing it upon a plane surface. When only a general topographical map of a country is wanted, it is, in general, sufficient to survey the country with reference to its fields, roads, rivers, etc.

SURYA, the sun god of Hindu mythology.

SUSA, one of the capitals of ancient Persia; was situated on the Choaspes, and has now been identified with the extensive ruins on the left bank of the Kerkha, about 250 miles S. E. of Bagdad. It had a circumference of 120 stadia, and like Babylon was built of burnt bricks cemented with asphalt. It was without walls, but its citadel, containing the treasury and mausoleum of the Persian kings, was strongly fortified. The founder of Susa is not known with certainty, but it was at least much enlarged by Darius Hystaspes, the ruins of whose palace, repaired by Artaxerxes Longimanus, have been excavated by Loftus and Williams. From the time of Cambyses Susa was a favorite residence of the Persian kings. After Alexander and his successors had fixed their court at Babylon Susa declined in importance, though when besieged by Antigonus in 315 B. C. it was still one of the chief cities of Persia, and even as late as the middle of the 7th century A. D. it offered under Hormuzan an obstinate resistance to the Saracens; but in the 13th century it had become a heap of ruins. The most important of these ruins are those of the palace of Darius, the colonnade of which has a frontage of 343 feet and a depth of 244. In general construction it exactly resembles the Hall of Xerxes at Persepolis. References to Susa abounds in the ancient authors, especially Herodotus. Xenophon, and Arrian.

SUSA, a town of Northern Italy, on a tributary of the Po, at the foot of the Cottian Alps, 32 miles W. of Turin. It has a cathedral (1029), and a triumphal arch erected by the Romanized Sugusian chief to Augustus in 8 B. C. The people grow fruit and grapes, and carry on iron, leather, and silk industries.

SUSANNAH, in Jewish history, the wife of Joakim, and the tribe of Judah. She followed her husband to Babylon as a captive. Two elders or judges of Israel endeavored to seduce her, and, failing in their object, they accused her of adultery. She was condemned to death; but Daniel obtained a reversal of the sentence and succeeded in establishing her innocence. This is stated to have occurred in Babylon about 600 B. C.

SUSITNA VALLEY, the principal watershed of the river of the same name, an affluent of Cook Inlet, Alaska. Area, about 8,000 square miles. The timber resources of the region are of importance and certain sections of it are also well suited for agriculture and stock raising. Part of the government railway between Cook Inlet and Fairbanks traverses the region.

SUSPECTA, in zoölogy, a sub-section of colubrine snakes, having the fangs situated at the back of the jaw behind the common teeth. Head usually covered with shield-like plates. Some are known to be harmless, others are reputed poisonous, though it is doubtful if they really are so. Families *Homalopsidæ*, *Dipsadidæ*, and *Dendrophidæ*.

SUSPENDED ANIMATION, the temporary cessation of the outward signs and of some of the functions of life.

SUSPENSION BRIDGE, a bridge sustained by flexible supports secured at each extremity. The points of support are the tops of strong pillars or small towers, erected for the purpose at each extremity of the bridge. Over these pillars the chains pass, and are attached behind them to rocks or massive frames of iron firmly secured underground. These masses of masonry are named anchorages. The flooring is connected with the chains by means of strong, upright iron rods. See BRIDGE.

SUSPENSION RAILWAY, a railway in which the carriage is suspended from

an elevated track, one carriage on each side of a single track, so as to balance, or suspended between two tracks.

SUSPENSOR, in anatomy, the longitudinal ligament of the liver. In botany, a very delicate thread descending from the foramen of an ovule into the quintine, and bearing at its extremity a globule which is the nascent embryo. It develops from the upper of two cells in a fertilized ovule, of which the lower one becomes the embryo. The suspensor is sometimes long, as in *Boraginaceæ*, *Cruciferæ*, etc., or short as in *Gramineæ*, *Polygonaceæ*, etc. Called also the suspensory cord, the pro-embryo, and by Dutrochet the hypostasis. In surgery, a suspensory bandage.

SUSQUEHANNA, a river of the United States, formed by two branches, an E. or N. branch, 250 miles long from Lake Otsego in New York, and a W. branch, 200 miles from the W. slope of the Alleghanies, which unite at Northumberland in Pennsylvania. The united stream flows S. and S. E., and after a course of 150 miles reaches the head of Chesapeake Bay at Port Deposit, Md. It is a wide but shallow stream, nowhere navigable to any extent, except in the spring.

SUTHERLAND, HOWARD, a United States Senator from West Virginia, born near Kirkwood, Mo., in 1865. He graduated from Westminster College in 1889, and studied law at George Washington University. After serving as editor for several papers, he became connected with the Davis-Elkins coal and railroad interests in West Virginia. He later went into business on his own account, and became president of several important industrial concerns. He served as a member of the West Virginia State Senate, from 1908 to 1912, and was in the United States Congress from 1913 to 1917. In 1916 he was elected to the United States Senate.

SUSSEX, a maritime county, of southeast England. Area, 1,458 sq. miles; pop. about 700,000. The Downs supply pasturage for a famous breed of sheep. Agriculture and cattle raising are the principal industries of the county. The chief rivers are the Arum, Adur, and Ouse. The South Downs, stretching across the county from west to east, end about 20 miles east of Brighton in the lofty cliff of Beachy Head. The district of the Weald is very fertile and richly wooded. West of Brighton, along the coast to the Hampshire border, and in the southeast of the county rich marsh provide superb pasturage. There are gypsum beds near Netherfield, large railway works at Brighton, and important fisheries in many of the coast towns. Capital, Chichester.

SUTHERLAND, a county of north Scotland. Area, 2,028 sq. miles; pop. about 20,000. The majority of the inhabitants speak Gaelic. The county has a coast line of some 60 miles with rugged shores in the northwest and flat shores in the east. Although extensive moors are to be found throughout the county and although the southern and central portions are mountainous, the eastern parts are very fertile. The principal elevations are Ben More (3,273 ft.) and Ben Clibrigg (3,154 ft.); the chief rivers are the Oikel and the Shin. Coal, marble, limestone, granite, etc., are found, and there are important salmon and herring fisheries. Capital, Dornoch.

SUTHERLAND, GEORGE, Associate Justice of the United States Supreme Court; was born in Buckinghamshire, England, March 25, 1862. He graduated from the law school of the University of Michigan in 1883, and was admitted to the bar in Utah. He was a member of the first Utah Senate in 1896. In 1901 he was elected to the House of Representatives, running on the Republican party ticket, declined renomination and was chosen senator the following year, 1904; served two terms in the Senate. In 1922 he represented the United States in the Norwegian war shipping contracts case before the Hague Court of Arbitration. He was appointed to the Supreme Court by President Harding, Sept. 6, 1922. Former president of the American Bar Association (1916). Author of "Constitutionality and World Affairs" (1919).

SUTLEJ, one of the five rivers of the Punjab, in northwestern India; identified both with the Zaradras and the Hypanis of the Greeks. It rises in the lake of Manasarowar, amid the central Himalayas, nearly 20,000 feet above the sea-level, and first flows N. W. for about 200 miles through stupendous mountain gorges; it is then joined by the Spiti, a tributary larger than the main stream, and turns S. E. In this part it is occasionally crossed by suspension bridges of rope and iron. Passing Rampur and Bilaspur, it enters the plains of the Punjab at Rupur, where it is 30 feet deep and more than 500 yards wide in the rainy season. It receives the Beas a little above Sobraon, after a total course of 550 miles. Thenceforth the united stream is known as the Gharra, taking the new name of the Punjab after its junction with the Chenaub, up to the

point where it finally empties itself into the Indus opposite Mīthankote. The principal town on its bank is Ferozpur. Its waters are largely used for irrigation. It is celebrated in history as forming the E. frontier of the Punjab, within which Runjeet Sing was confined. The crossing of the Sutlej after his death by the Sikh army occasioned the first Sikh War of 1843, and on its banks many bloody battles were fought. The Upper Sutlej canals have a total length of 213 miles, and irrigate 135,439 acres in the district of Lahore and Montgomery. The Lower Sutlej and Chenaub canals, in the Multan district, are 632 miles long, and water 242,504 acres.

SUTLER, a person who follows an army and sells to the troops provisions, liquors, or the like. The sutlers attached to regiments in the French army are called *vivandiers.*

SUTRO, ADOLPH HEINDRICH JOSEPH, an American mining engineer; born in Aix-la-Chapelle, Prussia, April 29, 1830; came to the United States in 1850 and settled in San Francisco, Cal. There he engaged in business till 1860, when he conceived the plan of the great "Sutro tunnel," as a means of developing the Comstock mine in Nevada. He interested capitalists in the project and work was begun on the tunnel in 1869. His contract with the mine-owners called for $2.00 royalty on every ton of ore taken from the mines. When the work was completed in 1879 he sold out his interest in the tunnel; went to San Francisco, invested in real estate, and soon became one of the wealthiest men on the Pacific slope. He was a donor of large sums of money to public institutions; founder of the Sutro Library, of San Francisco, and mayor of that city in 1894. After his death there, Aug 8, 1898, his will, in which he bequeathed nearly his whole fortune to the city, was contested and broken.

SUTRO, ALFRED, a British dramatist, born in 1863. He was educated in the City of London School and at Brussels, and afterward devoted himself to the writing of plays and other forms of literature. His works include: "The Cave of Illusion," a play in four acts; "Women in Love, Eight Studies in Sentiment"; "The Foolish Virgins"; "Five Little Plays"; "Freedom," a play in three acts; Maeterlinck's "Wisdom and Destiny," "Life of the Bee," etc. (translations), "Arethusa"; "A Marriage Has Been Arranged"; "The Walls of Jericho"; "The Perfect Lover"; "The Fascinating Mr. Vanderveldt"; "John Glayde's Honor"; "The Barrier"; "The Builder of

Bridges"; "Uncle Anyhow"; "The Choice."

SUTRO, FLORENCE CLINTON, an American musician; born in England; was graduated at the Grand Conservatory of Music in New York with the degree of Mus. D., being the first woman in the United States to receive that degree, and at the Law School of the University of New York. She was a member of numerous literary, musical, and social societies; honorary president of the Grand Conservatory Alumnæ; president of the Hospital for Crippled Children, and prominent as a writer for the advancement of women as composers and musicians. She founded the National Federation of Musical Societies in 1898. She died in 1906.

SUTTEE, a form of widow sacrifice (itself a form of funeral sacrifice), formerly common in Brahmanic India, in which the widow was burnt with her dead husband on the funeral pyre. Many went willingly and gaily to their doom, but others were driven by fear of disgrace, by family influence, by priestly threats, and, in not a few cases, by sheer violence. Suttee was abolished by law in British India Dec. 4, 1829, but it was carried out in some principalities for many years afterward.

SUTTER, JOHN AUGUSTUS, an American pioneer; born in Kandern, Germany, Feb. 15, 1803; was graduated at the Berne Military Academy in 1823; settled in St. Louis, Mo., in 1834, but soon removed to Santa Fé, where he engaged in a lucrative trade with trappers and Indians. Receiving favorable accounts of California he crossed the Rocky Mountains in 1838; sailed down the Columbia river and thence to Hawaii. After going to Sitka, Alaska, he cruised along the Pacific coast and was stranded at the site of San Francisco in July, 1839. During that year he established the first white settlement on the site of Sacramento. In 1841 after receiving a large tract of land from Mexico, he built a fort which he named New Helvetia; was made governor of the frontier country by Mexico, but was held in suspicion by the Mexicans owing to his friendly feelings toward the United States. In 1848 when California was ceded to the United States, he owned many thousand head of cattle, much land, and other property, but owing to the discovery of gold on his estates was overrun by miners, and his workmen left him, and not being able to secure others he was financially ruined. He appealed to the Supreme Court, but was not sustained. Later the Legislature of California granted him a pension of $250 a month. He moved to Lititz, Pa., in 1873. He died in Washington, D. C., June 17, 1880.

SUTTON, RHOADES STANSBURY, an American physician; born in Indiana, Pa., July 8, 1841; was graduated at Washington and Jefferson College in 1862, and at the Medical Department of the University of Pennsylvania in 1865. He was major of volunteers and surgeon in the army during the American-Spanish War. His publications include many contributions on surgery and medicine. He died in 1906.

SUTURE, in ordinary language, the act of sewing; the line along which two things are joined, united, or sewed together, so as to form a seam, or something resembling a seam. Technically, in anatomy, the immovable junction of two parts by their margins; as, the sutures of the skull, *i. e.*, the lines of junction of the bones of which the skull is composed. Various types of suture exist, as the serrated or dentated suture, the squamous or scaly suture, and the harmonic suture or harmonia. Arranged according to their situation, there are coronal, frontal, fronto-parietal, occipito-parietal, and many other sutures. In botany, the line formed by the cohesion of two parts. If the suture formed by the carpellary leaves in a pistil face the center of a flower, it is called the ventral suture; if it face the perianth, the dorsal suture. The former corresponds to the margin, and the latter to the midrib of the carpellary leaf. In entomology, the line formed by the meeting of the elytra of a beetle when they are confluent. In surgery, the uniting of the lips or edges of a wound by stitching. In zoölogy, the outlines of the septa in the Tetrabranchiata, from their resemblance to the sutures of the skull. When these outlines are folded, the elevations are called saddles, and the intervening depressions lobes.

SUVLA BAY, a wide, shallow cove, or bay, on the Ægean coast of the Gallipoli Peninsula, at which point large forces of Allied troops were landed on August 6, 1915, to attack the Turks, who were holding the Gallipoli Peninsula against a force which had already been landed some time previously. The battle preceding and following the landing of these re-enforcements proved disastrous to the Allied forces, under command of Sir Ian Hamilton, and has since been reckoned as one of the most serious blunders committed by the Allies during the World

War. The object had been to take the
Turkish forces by surprise, but this the
nature of the country made impossible,
as became obvious. After several days
of heavy fighting the Allies were compelled to retire from the Suvla Bay
region.

**SUVOROF - RYMNIKSKI, P E T E R
ALEXIS VASSILIVICH, COUNT OF,
PRINCE ITALISKI**, a Russian military
officer; born in Finland, Nov. 25, 1729;
and in his 17th year entered the service
as a common soldier. He served in the
war against Sweden, in the Seven Years'
War, in Poland, and against the Turks,
and rose to be a General of Division in
1773. In 1783 he reduced the Kuban
Tartars under the Russian yoke. In
1787, as chief in command, he conducted
the defense of Kinburn to a successful
issue; and in 1789 he gained the dignity
of count by his great victory on the
banks of the Rymnik, where the Austrian
troops under the Prince of Saxe-Coburg
were surrounded by 100,000 Turks. By
his timely arrival with 10,000 Russians
he not only rescued the Austrians, but
occasioned the utter overthrow of the
enemy. The next, and perhaps the most
sanguinary of his actions, was the storming of Ismail in 1790, which was followed
by the indiscriminate massacre of 40,000
of the inhabitants of every age and both
sexes. He was next employed against
the kingdom of Poland, and conducted a
campaign of which the partition of the
country was the result, receiving a field-
marshal's baton, and an estate. The last
and most celebrated of his services was
his campaign in Italy in 1799. He gained
several brilliant victories at Piacenza,
Novi, etc., drove the French from all the
towns and fortresses of Upper Italy, and
was rewarded with the title of Prince
Italiski. But in consequence of a change
in the plan of operations he passed the
Alps; and the defeat of Korsakof at
Zürich, together with the failure of the
expected assistance from the Austrians,
obliged him to retreat from Switzerland.
On his recall to Russia preparations were
made for his triumphal entry into St.
Petersburg; but having incurred the dis-
pleasure of the Emperor Paul, the preparations were suspended. He died May
18, 1800.

SUWANEE RIVER, a river in southern Georgia, in the Okefinokee Swamp,
which flows in a winding, generally S.
S. W. course through Florida into the
Gulf of Mexico.

SUWALKI, a province of Lithuania,
bounded W. by Eastern Prussia, S. by
Grodno, and separated by the Niemen on
I—14

the N. from Kovno, on the E. from
Wilna; area, 4,844 square miles; pop.
about 718,000. The surface is mountainous in the W. and S., and one-eighth is in
swamp. Timber and grain are produced.
Suwalki, the capital, is situated on the
Hancza, 65 miles S. W. of Kovno. It was
captured by the Germans in 1915. Pop.
about 31,000.

SUWARROW ISLANDS, a group of
three low wooded islands in the Pacific,
about 450 miles N. N. W. of Cook or
Hervey Islands, and about the same distance E. of Samoa. Annexed to Great
Britain in 1889. Pop. about 120.

SUZERAIN, in feudalism, a lord paramount; either the king, as original
holder of the realm, or his immediate
vassals, as grantors in turn to sub-
vassals.

SUZZALLO, HENRY, an American
educator, born at San José, Cal., in 1875.
He was educated at Leland Stanford University and at Columbia. From 1902 to
1907 he was an instructor and assistant
professor of education at Leland Stanford University; from 1907 to 1909 adjunct professor of elementary education,
and from 1909 to 1915 professor of philosophy of education at Columbia University; since May, 1915, president of the
University of Washington. During the
World War he served as chairman of the
Washington State Council of Defense,
Wage Umpire of the National War
Labor Board, and adviser of the War
Labor Policy Board. He was a member
of many educational societies, lectured
extensively, contributed many articles to
educational magazines and in 1919 became editor of the "Riverside Educational Monographs."

SVASTIKA, a religious symbol used
by early races of Aryan stock from
Scandinavia to Persia and India. It consists of a Greek cross, either inclosed in
a circle the circumference of which passes
through its extremities or with its arms
bent back, and was intended to represent
the sun, being found invariably associated with the worship of Aryan sun gods
(Apollo, Odin). Similar devices occur in
the monumental remains of the ancient
Mexicans and Peruvians, and on objects
exhumed from the prehistoric burial
mounds of the United States.

SVEABORG, a fortress in Finland;
sometimes called "the Gibraltar of the
North," protects the harbor and town of
Helsingfors, from which it is 3 miles distant. The fortifications were planned
and first prepared by Count Ehrensvärd

in 1849, and there are an arsenal, docks, slips, and a monument to the "father" of the fortress. The fortifications were betrayed into the hands of the Russians by the Swedish commandant in 1808. It was captured by Finnish forces after the Russian revolution of 1917. Pop. about 1,000.

SVENDSEN, JOHAN SEVERIN, a Swedish composer; born in Christiania, Norway, Sept. 30, 1840. He studied at Leipsic, Paris, and in Italy, conducted concerts in his native town and in 1883 became master of the Chapel Royal, Copenhagen. His works comprise symphonies, an overture, and quartets, quintets, and concertos for strings.

SVERDRUP, OTTO, a Norwegian explorer, born in the District of Helgeland, in 1855. At the age of 17 he began his career at sea, and for a time commanded a merchant vessel. In 1888 he joined Nansen's expedition to Greenland, and in 1893 started with that explorer to the North Pole as commander of the *Fram*. He remained with this ship when it was abandoned by Nansen in 1895, and reached Norway by drifting through the ice in the years following. From 1898 to 1902 he led another expedition in the *Fram* in an attempt to circumnavigate Greenland. This he found impossible, but continued his explorations, and made discoveries of great value. These included Heiberg and Ringnes Land. In 1914 and 1915 he commanded an expedition for the relief of missing Arctic explorers. He wrote "New Land: Four Years in the Arctic Regions" (1904).

SWAHILI, the name given to the people of Zanzibar and the opposite coast belonging to the Bantu stock, with an Arab infusion, and speaking a Bantu tongue modified by Arabic. The Swahili are intelligent and enterprising, and are in demand as porters by travelers into Central Africa. There is a collection of Swahili folk tales (1869) and a handbook by Bishop Steere (1871); and a dictionary by Krapf (1882).

SWAIN, JOSEPH, an American educator; born in Pendleton, Ind., June 16, 1857; was graduated at the Indiana University in 1883, and taught there first as instructor in biology, then as assistant Professor of Mathematics in 1883-1886, and finally as full professor in 1886-1891. He was called to fill a chair in the Leland Stanford University in 1891, and continued there till 1893, when he was made president of the Indiana University. He is the author of numerous scientific papers and has been prominent in connection with various educational organizations. He has been president of Swarthmore since 1902. President of the National Educational Association 1913-1914.

SWALLOW, in ornithology, any one of the numerous passerine birds of the family *Hirundinadæ*. In the United States the best known species are the barn swallow; the cliff, eaves, or chimney swallow; the white bellied or tree swallow, and the bank swallow. The species usually described by naturalists as the type of the family is *Hirundo rustica*, a well-known European visitor, whose arrival from Africa (usually about the middle of April) is eagerly looked for as a sign of approaching summer. Swallows usually arrive in pairs —a male and a female—though several pairs often form a small flight. They return with unfailing regularity to their old haunts, and in May commence building their nests. The eggs, from four to six in number, are white, spotted with a purple-red. The food of the swallow consists entirely of winged insects. These are captured as the birds fly with open mouth, the bristles with which the gap is supplied and the viscid saliva assisting to retain the prey. Like owls, swallows reject the undigested portions of their food in small pellets or castings. The male is about 8 inches long, beak black, forehead, chin, and throat, chestnut; head, neck, back, rump, and upper tail coverts steel-blue; tail very much forked; under surface buffy-white, legs and toes slender and black, claws black and sharp. In the female the tail feathers are not so long.

SWALLOW SHRIKE, in ornithology, a popular name for any individual of the family *Artamidæ*. They resemble swallows in their actions and general mode of life, while in the shape of their bills they exhibit great affinities to some of the shrikes and crow shrikes.

SWAMP DEER, in zoölogy, the *Rucervus duvaucelli*, from India and Assam. It is about 4 feet in height, rich light yellow in color, and congregates in large herds in moist situations. The antlers are large, with a long beam, which branches into an anterior continuation of the main portion, and a smaller posterior tyne which is bifurcated.

SWAMPSCOTT, a town of Massachusetts, in Essex co. It is on the Boston and Maine railroad. From its attractive situation it is a favorite summer resort. Fishing is an important industry. There are parks, and a public library. It is the seat of the Phillips School. Pop. (1910) 6,204; (1920) 8,101.

SWAN, in ornithology, any individual of the genus *Cygnus.* The swans form a sharply-defined group; the body is elon-

BLACK SWAN

gated, the neck very long, head moderate; beak about as long as head; legs short, and placed far back. On the under surface the plumage is thick and fur like; on the upper side the feathers are broad, but both above and below the body is thickly covered with down. Their short legs render the movements on land awkward and ungainly, but in the water these birds are graceful to a proverb. Their food consists of vegetable substances and weeds, their long necks enabling them to dip below the surface and to reach their food at considerable depths. Swans breed in high latitudes, but the domesticated species, *Cygnus olor,* the mute swan, breeds on eyots and the shores of lakes, making a very large nest on land, in which five or six greenish eggs are deposited. The young generally are covered with a gray down till the age of two years, when they assume the characteristic white plumage of the older birds. Three other species visit temperate Europe: the elk, hooper, whooper, or whistling swan (*C. musicus*); Bewick's swan (*C. bewicki*), and the Polish swan (*C. immutabilis*), which owes its specific name to the fact that the cygnets are pure white like the parent birds. The mute swan is the largest and most ma-

WHISTLING SWAN

jestic of the four, and is easily recognized by the black knob at the base on the bill. There are some other species, chiefly from North America, but the most beautiful of the whole genus is the black-necked swan (*C. nigricollis*), from South America; while the most remarkable is the black swan (*C. atratus*), from Australia, first taken to other countries early in the 17th century. So convinced were the ancients that white plumage was of the essence of a swan, that a "black swan" was a proverbial expression for something extremely rare. The stories about the musical voice of the swan appear to have some foundation in fact so far as regards the whooper (*C. musicus*). In astronomy, the constellation CYGNUS (*q. v.*). Figuratively applied to a famous poet; thus Shakespeare is called the Swan of Avon, Vergil the Swan of Mantua.

SWAN RIVER, a river in Western Australia, which colony was originally known as the "Swan River Settlement." Perth, the capital of the colony, is on the Swan river, and Freemantle is at its mouth.

SWANSDOWN, the name for a fine, soft, thick, woolen cloth; or more commonly for a thick cotton cloth with a soft nap on one side.

SWANSEA (Welsh, Abertawe), a seaport of Glamorganshire, South Wales, on the banks and at the mouth of the Tawe river, 45 miles W. N. W. of Cardiff and 216 W. of London. A municipal, parliamentary, and also (since 1888) county borough, it is the most important town in South Wales. Its rapid progress depends on the manufacture of tin plate here and in the neighborhood; on its harbor and docks which afford every convenience for the largest vessels and steamships afloat; and on its geographical position, on a bay affording a spacious, sheltered, and safe anchorage, several hours nearer the open sea than any other port of comparable size in the Bristol Channel. The Harbor Trust of Swansea, with a capital of $7,500,000 and an income of upward of $500,000 per annum, possesses docks constructed since 1847 covering an area of over 60 acres. There is annually manufactured in Swansea and the immediate neighborhood upward of two-thirds of the tin plates manufactured in Great Britain, representing a value of upward of $25,-000,000. There is still a large direct export trade to the United States in tin and (the inferior) terne plates, though this branch of trade was much injured by the tariff legislation of 1890. The chief imports are copper, silver, lead, tin, and nickel, with their ores and alloys, iron and steel in various forms, iron ore, zinc, sulphur, phosphates, flour, grain, esparto, timber bricks, etc. The chief exports are tin, terne, and black plates, coal and coke, copper, zinc, and their ores, iron and steel, alkali, superphosphate, arsenic, etc. The charter dates from the days of King John and Henry III., renewed by subsequent sovereigns. The castle, of which a tower still remains, was founded in 1099 by the Earl of Warwick, but in the reign of Edward IV. passed by marriage from the Herberts to the Somerset family, and is still the property of the Dukes of Beaufort. The grammar school dates from 1682. Pop. (1919) 160,810.

SWARTHMORE COLLEGE, a co-educational institution for higher education, founded in 1864, by the Society of Friends of Swarthmore, Pa. In 1919 there were 487 students and 45 instructors. President, Joseph Swain.

SWARTZ, MIFFLIN WYATT, an American educator, born at Winchester, Va., in 1874. He was educated at the University of Chicago and began teaching at Fort Worth, Texas, in 1900, becoming president of the Woman's College of Alabama in 1915. He was a member of the Southern Association of Schools and Colleges and wrote "Personal and Dramatic Characteristics of the Old in the Drama of Euripides" (1910).

SWAT, or **SUWAT,** a region in Central Asia, W. of the upper Indus river. It is but little known. Its ruler is a chief, called the Akhoond.

SWATAU, a seaport of China which has been opened to foreign trade since 1869; at the mouth of the Han river, 225 miles E. of Canton, in the province of Kwang-tung. It is the seat of great sugar refineries, and bean cake and grass cloth manufactures. Imports (1919) $30,000,000; exports, $11,000,000. The imports consist principally of bean cake and beans, cottons, opium, rice, metals, hemp, silks and woolens, and wheat. Sugar forms the chief item among the exports; besides it tobacco, cloth and nankeens, joss paper, grass cloth (made from a kind of hemp fiber), and tea are sent abroad. Pop. 110,000.

SWAZILAND, a South African native state; on the W. side of the Libomba mountains, and forming geographically an intrusion into the E. side of the Transvaal Colony. It has an area of 6,678 square miles; a pop. of 99,959 natives and 1,700 Europeans. Tobacco, maize, millet, and ground nuts are raised. Considerable tin is exported. The territory is rich in minerals that await development. Revenues (1919) £70,842. Expenditure £82,006. In 1906 the administration of the state was given to the High Commissioner of South Africa. The independence of this little state was recognized by its powerful neighbors, the South African republic (now the Orange River Colony) and the British Government, in 1884; in 1890 the white settlers, mainly gold miners, were put under joint "government committee," appointed by Great Britain and the Boers.

SWEARING, the habit of using the name or attributes of God in a light and familiar manner by way of asseveration or emphasis. It was specially condemned by the Mosaic law, was long punished by severe penalties, and is still an actionable offense in England. By oaths are loosely understood many terms and phrases of a gross and obscene character, as well as those words the use of which specially implies profanity proper. Again, there is a legitimate use of imprecations and curses when intense hatred is to be expressed, and when it is justifiable. It is only taking the sacred name in vain that need be condemned.

To call God to witness is a thing natural enough on occasions of grave asseveration, as in giving witness in courts of law and the like, and it has been from the beginning a custom to take oaths on things sacred or august, as the head of the emperor, the beard of the prophet, the sword blade or hilt, and the Gospels.

"Swift's "Swearer's Bank" (Scott's "Swift," vol. vii.) is a characteristic satire on the profanity of his day. It is computed by geographers, he begins, that there are 2,000,000 in this kingdom (Ireland), of which number there may be said to be 1,000,000 of swearing souls. It is thought that there may be 5,000 gentlemen, each with one oath a day at a shilling each, yielding an annual revenue of $456,250. All classes of citizens contribute to this revenue, the farmers, the commonality, the hundred pretty fellows in Dublin alone at 50 oaths a head daily, the oaths of a little Connaught fair themselves computed at 3,000. Militia under arms are to be exempted, etc.

The Church ever denounced profane swearing, but was powerless to check the practice. St. Chrysostom spent 20 homilies on it, and St. Augustine's judgment is summed up with unnecessary severity in the solemn passage, "Not less do they sin who blaspheme Christ reigning in heaven, than did they who crucified Him walking about on earth." For much of our popular swearing is little more than the mere habit of vocabulary, a sin only from the lips outward, as Bishop Lightfoot said of the habitual profanity of the colliers of his diocese.

In England the growth of Puritanism was marked by a series of attempts to stamp out swearing. In 1601 a measure for this end was introduced into the House of Commons and one was carried in 1623. "Not a man swears but pays his 12 pence," says Cromwell proudly of his Ironsides. As early as 1606 swearing in plays had been forbidden, and even Ben Jonson himself narrowly escaped the $50 penalty. An act of 1645 in Scotland details the penalties to be inflicted, even on ministers of religion. St. Paul's Cathedral is supposed to have been built without an oath, the regulations of Sir Christopher Wren being so stringent, and this may be allowed to remain its most remarkable distinction.

SWEAT, the name given to the perspiration or skin secretions separated from the blood by the sudoriparous glands or sweat glands. The ordinary perspiration is named insensible on account of its being continually given off from the skin by evaporation; the increased secretion of sweat, dependent on exertion and which appears in the form of drops of fluid collected on the surface of the skin, being named sensible sweat. This secretion consists of water, carbonic acid, urea, mineral matters, and sebaceous matter—the latter obtained from the glands of that name existing in the skin. The principal salts in sweat are the chlorides of sodium and potassium, with alkaline phosphates, and sulphates. Traces of oxide of iron also occur in the secretion. The quantity of watery vapor daily excreted by the skin under ordinary circumstances amounts to between 1½ and 2 pounds. Occasionally in some diseases (e. g., jaundice) the sweat may be colored by other secretions, while sanguineous or bloody sweat is not unknown; the cause of its production being, however, obscure. See SKIN.

SWEATING SICKNESS, an extremely fatal epidemical disorder which ravaged Europe, and especially England in the 15th and 16th centuries. It derives its name "because it did most stand in sweating from the beginning till the endyng," and, "because it first beganne in Englande, it was named in other countries the Englishe sweat." It first appeared in London in September, 1485, shortly after the entry of Henry VII. with the army which had won the battle of Bosworth Field on Aug. 22. It was a violent inflammatory fever which after a short rigor, prostrated the powers as with a blow, and, amid painful oppression at the stomach, headache, and lethargic stupor, suffused the whole body with a fetid perspiration. All this took place in the course of a few hours and the crisis was always over within the space of a day and night. The internal heat which the patient suffered was intolerable, yet every refrigerant was certain death. It lasted in London from Sept. 21 to the end of October, during which short period "many thousands" died from it. The physicians could do little or nothing to combat the disease, which at length was swept away from England by a violent tempest on New Year's Day.

In the summer of 1508 it reappeared in London, and in July, 1517, it again broke out in London in a most virulent form, carrying off some of those who were seized by it within four hours. On this occasion the epidemic lasted about four months. In May, 1528—the year in which the French army before Naples was destroyed by pestilence, and in which the putrid fever known as *Trousse-galant* decimated the youth in France—the sweating sickness again broke out in London, and spread rapidly over the whole kingdom.

The following summer, having apparently died out in England, it appeared in Germany, first at Hamburg, where it is recorded that 8,000 persons died of it, and shortly after at Lübeck, Stettin, Augsburg, Cologne, Strassburg, Hanover, etc. In September it broke out in the Netherlands, Denmark, Sweden, and Norway, whence it penetrated into Lithuania, Poland, and Livonia; but after three months it had entirely disappeared from all these countries. For 23 years the sweating sickness totally disappeared, when for the last time (March or April, 1551) it burst forth in Shrewsbury, spread rapidly over the whole of England, but disappeared by the end of September. Since 1551 the disease has never appeared as it did then and at earlier periods. Its nearest ally is sudamina or military eruption, which has appeared in frequent, but usually limited, epidemics in France, Italy, and Germany (still called there "the English sweat"), during the 18th and 19th centuries, sometimes, as in the department of Vienna in 1887, in so severe and even fatal a form as to suggest the older epidemic in miniature. It was epidemic in France in 1906. The disease is allied to the influenza which broke out among the French troops in Picardy in 1917 and thence spread over the world.

SWEATING SYSTEM, the system by which sub-contractors undertake to do work in their own houses or small work-shops, and employ others to do it, making a profit for themselves by the difference between the contract prices and the wages they pay their assistants. Laws have been enacted both in England and the United States to regulate the system, and providing penalties for the employ-ment of children and others in over-crowded and ill-ventilated "sweat shops."

SWEDEN (Swedish, Sverige), a king-dom of northern Europe comprising with Norway and Lapland the whole of the Scandinavian peninsula, of which it forms the E., S., and most important por-tion; having N. E. Russian Finland; E. and S. the Gulf of Bothnia and the Baltic; S. W. the Sound, Cattegat, and Skagerrack; and W. and N. Norway, from which it is for the most part di-vided by the great mountain chain of Scandinavia. Length N. to S. 950 miles; average breadth about 190 miles; area 173,035 square miles; pop. (1920) 5,-904,489. Capital, Stockholm; pop. 419,-440.

Topography—Sweden is divided into three principal regions: Gœthland (Gothia) in the S.; Sweden proper, oc-cupying the center; and Norland (by far the largest part), comprising the re-mainder. These three regions are again subdivided into 24 *lans*, or districts. Sweden is mountainous in the W., but, in general, flat; and it is remarkable that along the whole road from Gotten-burg in the W., to Stockholm in the E., there is not a single acclivity of conse-quence till within a few miles of the latter.

Climate—The climate is less severe than might be expected in so high a lati-tude. In Stockholm the average temper-ature throughout the year is 4 degrees higher than at St. Petersburg. The sum-mers are hot, and spring is almost un-known. In the N., snow covers the ground for 5 or 6 months in the year; and the W. coasts are milder and more humid than the E.

Rivers—The rivers are numerous. The principal are the Dal and the Klar rising in the mountains bordering on Norway, and flowing into the Gulf of Bothnia and the lake of Wener. The Angerman, the Umea, the Skeleftea, the Pitea, the Lulea, and the Tornea, are in Lapland.

Lakes—Nearly one-eighth of the coun-try is covered with lakes. The largest are the Wener, Wetter, and the Malar, all in the S. provinces. In point of size Wener is the third lake in Europe.

Forests.—There are extensive forests. More than 3 parts of the country are under timber. The principal trees are fir, birch, with oak, elm, and beech in the more S. parts.

Zoölogy.—The domestic animals are the same as those of Great Britain. The others are hares and foxes, beavers, wolves and, in the cold provinces of the N., bears, the lemming and the reindeer. Water fowl are abundant and the mos-quitoes are as troublesome as they are in tropical countries.

Agriculture.—Sweden is essentially an agricultural country. About 50 per cent. of the people are engaged in agricultural pursuits. There are about 450,000 farms under cultivation. The area and yield of the principal crops in 1919 was as fol-lows: Wheat, 140,913 hectares, produc-tion 258,972 tons; rye, 372,068 hectares, production 586,689 tons; barley, 166,672 hectares, production 280,678 tons; oats, 712,372 hectares, production 1,111,730 tons; mixed corn, 260,782 hectares, pro-duction 475,749 tons; peas, beans, etc., 44,748 hectares, production 67,756 tons; potatoes, 168,689 hectares, production 2,111,213 tons; sugar beet and fodder roots, 127,650 hectares, production 3,838,-372 tons; hay, 1,342,878 hectares, pro-duction 4,300,969 tons. There were in 1920 about 720,000 horses and about 2,-600,000 head of cattle.

Industries.—The chief industries are related to the mining and production of minerals and metals, and to lumbering and dairying. In the north are found the chief iron ore mines and important saw-mills. The production of iron and steel is found chiefly in central Sweden. Among specialized products are the man-ufacture of cream separators, lighthouse apparatus, motors and electrical machin-ery. The manufacture of porcelain and glass is also important, as are timber and woodworking industries. Among the principal industries are the following, with the value of output in kroners: Bar iron and steel works, 500,850,759; me-chanical workshops, 496,073,165; iron and steel goods factories, 191,488,782; flour and grain mills, 131,924,056; shoe factories, 112,340,571. There are about 300,000 men, about 60,000 women, about 40,000 boys, and about 15,000 girls em-ployed in the factories of the country.

Commerce. — The imports for 1917 were £41,773,733 and the exports £76,-465,387. The chief articles of import were minerals, chiefly coal, metal goods and machinery, animals, textile manu-factures, and hair, hides and other ani-mal products. The principal exports were wood, pulp, paper, and paper man-ufactures, metals, timber, metal goods, and minerals. Prior to the World War Germany took the greater part of the exported goods. The second place was occupied by Great Britain, the third by Norway, and the fourth by Denmark. The imports were chiefly from Germany, Denmark, the United States, Great Britain, Norway and the Netherlands.

Transportation.—There are about 10,-000 miles of railway in the country, of which about 3,400 belong to the state. There are about 50,000 miles of telegraph wire and about 400,000 miles of telephone wire. There are over 1,000 sailing vessels in the merchant marine and nearly 20,000 steam and motor vessels.

Education.—There are about 20,000 elementary schools, with about 25,000 teachers and 715,000 pupils. In 1918 there were 77 public secondary schools, with 26,313 pupils; 49 people's high schools, with 2,976 pupils; 15 normal schools for elementary teachers; and elementary technical schools, navigation schools, military schools, agricultural schools, and other special schools. An elementary education is compulsory and free. The universities are at Upsila and at Lund. There are also private universities at Stockholm and at other cities.

Finance.—The revenues and expenditures in 1920 balanced at £38,981,167. The public debt amounted to £59,811,509.

Army and Navy.—Military service is universal but is aided by a voluntary enlisted personnel. Liability to service begins at the age of 20 and lasts till the end of the 42d year. The field army consists of 6 divisions, with a total peace strength in 1920 of 86,507. The total number of military age is about 650,000.

The navy is entirely a coast defense force. It includes 13 vessels, varying from 3,700 to 7,180 tons. In addition there were, in 1920, 10 destroyers, about 50 torpedo boats, and about 14 submarines.

Government.—A constitutional monarchy. The King of Sweden, formerly also King of Norway, must be a member of the Lutheran Church. His person is inviolable. He has the right to declare war and make peace, and grant pardon to condemned criminals. He nominates to all appointments, both military and civil; concludes foreign treaties, and has a right to preside in the supreme court of justice. The king has an absolute veto against any decrees of the Diet, and possesses legislative power in matters of provincial administration and police. In all other respects, the fountain of law is the Diet. This Diet, or Congress of the realm, consists of two chambers, or estates, both elected by the people, but representing different interests.

History.—The two kingdoms, **Gothland** and Svealand, of which Sweden once consisted, were united in the 13th century by the failure of the royal line in the former. In 1397 by the treaty of Calmar, Sweden became subject to Margaret of Denmark, who has been styled the Semiramis of the North, and who joined the three kingdoms in one. Gustavus Vasa asserted the independence of Sweden and ascended the throne in 1521. He bequeathed the crown to his posterity, who continued to reign, and in general with distinction; but most of them, and in particular, Gustavus Adolphus, his daughter Christina, Charles XII., and Gustavus III., discovered a romantic spirit approaching, in the case of Charles XII., to a degree of infatuation. This dynasty ended in a prince (Gustavus IV.) who had all the eccentricity and hardly any of the talents of his predecessors. In 1809 this last monarch engaging in undertakings totally beyond the resources of his people, was deposed; and next year Marshal Bernadotte of France was elected crown prince, and in 1818 as Charles John XIV., ascended the throne. In 1814 Norway was annexed to Sweden (see NORWAY). In 1857 Charles XV. succeeded his father, Oscar I., and died in 1872, leaving the crown to his son, Oscar II., who reigned thirty-five years.

During the reign of Oscar II. many important measures of economic and social reform were adopted. These included accident insurance for workingmen, limitation of working hours for women and children, and factory legislation. In 1905 the union between Norway and Sweden was peaceably dissolved. (See NORWAY.) King Oscar died in 1907 and was succeeded by his son, Gustavus V. In 1909 a bill establishing manhood suffrage for elections to the Lower House, and effecting changes in the qualifications for the members of the Upper House, was passed. At the outbreak of the World War, in 1914, Sweden declared her neutrality. On Dec. 18, 1914, a conference was held at Malmö, in which the kings of Sweden, Norway, and Denmark took part. As a result of this meeting, on agreement to defend the neutrality of these countries and to protect their economic interests was made. During the early part of 1915 the Swedish Government complained to Great Britain against the arbitrary detention and interference with neutral vessels bound for Sweden. Great Britain based its action on the claim that contraband in large quantities had been imported into Germany by way of Sweden. In order to avoid complications, the Swedish Government published a decree prohibiting exportation to any belligerent country of war munitions or of any material which might be used in their manufacture. A second conference between the rulers of the Scandinavian countries was held in February, 1915. A protest was published against the creation of a war zone by Germany. Throughout the progress of the war there were complaints against both sides on the part of Sweden for alleged violation of her neutrality. In January, 1916, the king urged the strengthening of the Swedish military establishment in order that the country might be prepared against any possible violation of its neutrality. As a result of the Russian revolution in 1917, new problems were faced by Sweden. Chief of these were the recognition of the new republic of Finland. The internal disturbances in that country, which was strongly related to Sweden by national and political ties, were reflected in Sweden. It was finally decided, however, to maintain strict neutrality between the Soviet Government and Finland. Following the close of the war Sweden was greatly affected by the German revolution. Encouraged by its results the Independent Socialist Party made attempts for the abolishment of the monarchial form of government and the establishment of a republic. This agitation quickly subsided, however, on the promise of reforms by the government. These included a new election law and the granting of the franchise to men and women on equal terms. In February, 1918, a controversy arose between Sweden and Finland for the possession of the Aland Islands. These had been occupied by Germany after the collapse of Russia, and therefore their disposition remained in the hands of the Peace Conference. Their population, which was purely Swedish, had appealed after the separation of Finland from Russia to the King of Sweden for annexation. In 1922 Sweden acquiesced in Finland's retaining the islands. In May, 1919, full national suffrage was granted to women, who since 1909 had enjoyed municipal suffrage. In March, 1920, a cabinet composed entirely of Socialists was selected by Hjalmar Branting, prime minister. A trade treaty with Russia was concluded in 1924. Princess Astrid of Sweden, daughter of Prince Carl, King Gustaf's brother, was married to the Crown Prince of Belgium in November, 1926.

A strong anti-military spirit in Sweden inspired the execution of treaties in 1927 with Norway and Belgium, as earlier with Denmark and Finland, in which the parties mutually renounced recourse to war and undertook to settle disputes by arbitration. Owing to extensive electric development, 45 per cent of Swedish farms were served with electricity in 1927. Legislation for the prevention of strikes and for the adjustment of labor disputes was passed in 1928. Elections to the Swedish Parliament were held in September, 1928. These resulted in a loss of seats to the Socialist group and a corresponding gain for the Conservatives; neither the Conservatives nor the Radical and Socialist groups commanded a majority.

SWEDENBORG, EMANUEL, founder of the Church of the New Jerusalem, and one of the most distinguished men of science of the 18th century; born in Stockholm, Sweden, Jan. 29, 1688. He was carefully educated under the care of his father, Bishop of Skara, in W. Gothland, in the principles of the Lutheran Church. After pursuing his studies and taking the degree of Ph. D. at Upsala he went on his travels in 1710, and visited the universities of England, Holland, France, and Germany. On his return, he was appointed assessor extraordinary to the College of Mines, and in 1719 was ennobled, on which occasion his name was changed from Swedberg to Swedenborg. He had in the previous year achieved a great engineering feat, in the transport, over a mountain district, of several galleys and boats for service at the siege of Frederikshald. In 1721, he again traveled to examine mines, etc. He continued his scientific studies till the year 1743, when, as he himself affirms, a new era of his life commenced, and he was permitted to hold intercourse with the inhabitants of the invisible world. In 1747 he resigned his office in the mining college, retired from public life, and spending his time alternately in Sweden and in England, devoted himself to the publication of his theological works. They are filled with illustrations from the scientific and metaphysical lore of their author, and present a remarkable combination of science and theology. Though it is frequently affirmed that Swedenborg labored under a delusion, his writings showed no symptoms of aberration. He was always regarded as a learned and pious man; and it would appear that the story of his insanity rests for its support on the word of a single enemy. He was never married. The believers in his doctrines are now become a numerous body (see SWEDENBORGIANS). Of his very numerous works, only a few of the most important can be named: The "Dædaperboreus" (1716-1718); "Philosophical and Mineralogical Works" (1734); "Œconomia Regni Animalis" (Economy of the Animal Kingdom) and "Regnum Animale" (The Animal Kingdom); in theology, the "Arcana Cœlestia" (The Secrets of Heaven), "Apocalypsis Revelata" (The A p o c a l y p s e Revealed), "De Cultu et Amore Dei" (On the Worship and Love of God), "On Heaven and Hell," "On Conjugal Love," and the "True Christian Religion." He died in London, England, March 29, 1772.

SWEDENBORGIANS. See NEW JERUSALEM, CHURCH OF THE.

SWEDISH BEAMTREE, in botany, the *Pyrus intermedia*, a sub-species of *P. aria.* It has oblong, rather distinctly-lobed leaves, ashy-white below, with 5 to 8 nerves on each side.

SWEENY, THOMAS WILLIAM, an American military officer; born in Cork, Ireland, Dec. 25, 1820; settled in the United States in 1832 and learned the printer's trade. In 1846 he was made 2d lieutenant in the 1st New York Volunteers; took part in the bombardment of Vera Cruz, and in the assault on Churubusco, where he greatly distinguished himself, and lost his right arm. After the Mexican War he was commissioned 2d lieutenant in the 2d United States Infantry, and was often engaged against hostile Indians. In January, 1861, he was promoted captain and assigned to the command of the arsenal in St. Louis. In his command were only 40 recruits, while there were nearly 3,000 hostile minute men in St. Louis. He kept all enemies at bay by the threat that if any violence were attempted he would blow the place to atoms. He became a brigadier-general of volunteers in May, 1861, and later colonel of the 52d Illinois Volunteers, with which regiment he took part in the capture of Fort Donelson. During the first day of the action at Shiloh he held the key of the Union position. He was promoted major of the 16th United States Infantry in October, 1863. During the Atlanta campaign his command captured Snake Creek gap. He also took part in the action at Dallas and Kenesaw mountain; but won his greatest distinction on July 22, 1864, in the engagement before Atlanta. He was retired in May, 1870, with the rank of Brigadier-General U. S. A. He died in Astoria, L. I., April 10, 1892.

SWEEPSTAKES, a gaming transaction in which a number of persons join in contributing a certain stake, which becomes the property of one or several of the contributors on certain conditions. Thus, in a sweepstakes for horses starting in a race, the owner of the winner receives the whole stakes, or a portion of it, the remainder being divided between the second and third. Also, the prize in a horse race, etc., made up of contributions from several persons.

SWEET, BENJAMIN JEFFREY, an American military officer; born in Kirkland, N. Y., April 24, 1832; settled with his parents in Stockbridge, Wis., in 1838; attended Appleton College for a year, and later spent his leisure in the study of law. In 1848 he became a member of the Wisconsin Legislature. At the outbreak of the Civil War he recruited the 21st and 22d Wisconsin regiments, becoming colonel of the former. During the battle of Perryville his regiment formed a part of a corps that through an entire day sustained an attack from the whole army of General Bragg. During the engagement he received a wound which permanently broke his health. Early in 1864 he was placed in command of Camp Douglas, Chicago, where about 10,000 Confederates were imprisoned. In June he learned of a scheme by which the prisoners expected to effect their escape on July 4, and afterward to burn the city. He immediately reinforced the garrison and thus killed the plot. In the following November he discovered another plot to arm the prisoners and burn Chicago. He had only 796 men in the garrison and it was too late to secure reinforcements. He thereupon summoned to his aid John T. Shanks, a Texas ranger, who was a prisoner and knew the Confederate officers, and arranged with him to discover the guilty parties. So well did Shanks perform his task that the leaders of the plot were all apprehended. In recognition of this service Sweet was promoted brigadier-general of volunteers. In January, 1872, he was made 1st Deputy Commissioner of Internal Revenue and removed to Washington, D. C., where he died Jan. 1, 1874.

SWEET BRIAR, or **SWEET BRIER** (*Rosa rubiginosa*), naturalized in the United States, and grows wild, but is often planted in hedges and gardens on account of the sweet balsamic smell of its small leaves and flowers. It is also called the eglantine.

SWEETFLAG (*Acorus Calàmus*), a plant, also called sweetrush, found in marshy places throughout the Northern Hemisphere. The leaves are sword-shaped; the stem bears a lateral, dense, greenish spike of flowers. The root has been employed in medicine since the time of Hippocrates. It is also used by confectioners as a candy, and by perfumers in the preparation of aromatic vinegar, hair powder, etc.

SWEET GUM, the *Liquidambar styraciflua,* a North American tree about 60 feet high with apetalous flowers, in appearance like *Acer campestre.* The wood is fine-grained, and well adapted for furniture; the fragrant gum exuding from it when incisions are made in its bark constitutes liquid-ambar.

SWEET PEA (*Lathyrus odoratus*), a familiar garden annual plant belonging to the natural order *Leguminosæ.* It is a native of Sicily and other parts of the S. of Europe, and has been cultivated for its beautiful and fragrant flowers in American gardens for about 100 years.

The varieties are very numerous, distinguished chiefly by the different shades of color of the flowers. It is so hardy that it may be sown in autumn and will not only withstand the cold of winter, but will bloom earlier and better than when sown in spring. Other species of *Lathyrus* are of interest either as ornamental plants or for food for man or cattle which they yield. The everlasting pea (*L. latifolius*) is an old favorite in flower gardens on account of its handsome but scentless flowers. The roots of *L. tuberosus* are eaten in Holland and other countries where it grows plentifully. The chickling vetch (*L. sativus*) is much used in Switzerland as fodder for cattle. The seeds ground into meal make palatable bread.

SWEET POTATO (*Batatas*), a genus of plants belonging to the natural order *Convolvulacæ. B. edulis,* the true sweet potato, is a twining or climbing plant, with stems 5 or 6 feet long trailing on

SWEET POTATO

the ground or clambering over neighboring shrubs. The leaves are 5 or 6 inches long, heart-shaped at the base; the flowers pale purple, closely resembling those of the common convolvulus. The native country of the plant is a mat-

ter of conjecture. An author of the 16th century found the root much used by the Indians as an article of food. It was introduced into Spain about 1519, and the roots were known in England some time before the introduction of the potato. English supplies in those times were obtained from Spain and the Canary Islands, and the roots, when steeped in wine or made into sweetmeats, were regarded as restorative of failing vigor. The plant is cultivated in India, China, Japan, the Malayan Archipelago, throughout tropical America, and in the southern United States, in southern Europe, the Canary Islands, Madeira, and North Africa. In favorable conditions in the United States the yield per acre is from 200 to 300 bushels. *B. jalapa,* a species of Mexico, though purgative, is so called on account of its being very common in the vicinity of the Mexican town of Jalapa. *B. paniculata,* which has a very wide geographical distribution, is commonly cultivated for food in W. tropical Africa. From the seeds of another species of Batatas the textile material named Natal cotton is obtained.

SWEET SOP, the *Anona squamosa,* a large shrub or tree of stunted irregular growth with spreading branches, indigenous in the West Indies and much cultivated in other tropical countries. It is completely domesticated over a great part of India. The fruit is about the size of an orange, of a glaucous yellowish-green color, covered with projecting scales; pulp white with a tinge of yellow, very sweet. The acrid seeds and the leaves are insecticide.

SWEET WILLIAM, in botany and horticulture, *Dianthus barbatus.* The leaves are lanceolate and nerved; the flowers are aggregated in bundles; petals bearded, whence the book name of bearded pink. It may be single or double; the petals dark purple, red, speckled, or white. Also the *Silene armeria,* common, or Lobel's campion, a very common garden plant, with viscid stems; panicles of pink flowers. It flowers in July and August.

SWETT, SOPHIA MIRIAM, an American writer; born in Brewer, Me., in 186—. She published: "The Lollipops' Vacation"; "Captain Polly"; "Flying Hill Farm"; "The Mate of the Mary Ann"; "Cap'n Thistletop"; "The Ponkarty Branch Road"; "The Boy from Beaver Hollow" (1900) ; etc.

SWEYN, a king of Denmark, father of Canute the Great. He died in 1014, **after**

having established himself in England, though without being crowned there. See DENMARK and ETHELRED II.

SWIFT, the *Hirundo apus* of Linnæus and *Cypselus apus* or *murarius* of modern ornithologists. Though swifts are like swallows in many respects, their structure is almost entirely different, and some naturalists rather class them with the humming birds or the goat suckers. The swift has all four toes directed forward; it is larger than the swallow; its flight is more rapid and steady; and its scream is very different from the twittering of the swallow. It has the greatest powers of flight of any bird that visits Great Britain. Its weight is most disproportionately small to its extent of wing, the former being scarcely an ounce, the latter 18 inches, the length of the body being about 8 inches. Its color is a somber or sooty black, a whitish patch appearing beneath the chin. It builds in holes in the roofs of houses, in towers, or in hollow trees. It leaves Great Britain in August, having arrived from Africa early in May. The *C. melba* or *alpinus,* a larger species with the lower parts dusky white, has its home in the mountainous parts of Central and Southern Europe. A common North American swift is the co-called chimney swallow (*Chaætura pelagica*), which builds its nest in chimneys (see SWALLOW). The swifts or swiftlets of the genus *Collocalia,* which inhabit chiefly the islands of the Indian Ocean from the N. of Madagascar E., construct the edible birds'-nests which are used by Chinese epicures in the making of soup.

SWIFT, EBEN, an American military officer, born at Fort Chadbourne, Tex., in 1854. He was educated at Racine (Wis.) College, Washington University and Dickinson College, and graduated from the United States Military Academy in 1876. In the same year he was commissioned a 2d lieutenant, and rising through the various grades became brigadier-general in 1916 and major-general in 1917. He saw service in the Indian campaigns in Wyoming, Montana, Nebraska, Idaho and Colorado; in Cuba, Porto Rico and the Philippine Islands and at the Mexican border. His other assignments included service with the infantry and cavalry schools, the General Service and Staff College, the Army War College and the Army service schools, of which latter he was commandant. Upon the entrance of the United States in the World War, he became commanding officer of Camp Gordon, Atlanta, Ga., and later of the 82d Division, with which he served in France

until February, 1918. From February to August, 1918, he was chief of the American Military Mission and commander of the United States Forces in Italy, retiring upon reaching the age limit in September, 1918.

SWIFT, JONATHAN (1667-1745), Dean of St. Patrick's, was born in Dublin on Nov. 30, 1667, the posthumous son of Jonathan Swift, an Irish lawyer of English parentage, by Abigail Erick of Leicester. He was educated at Kilkenny and Trinity College, Dublin, from which he graduated with difficulty. During this period he was supported by his uncles, but their generosity was either so limited or so ungracious that Swift felt little gratitude and developed a fierce desire for independence. For his mother he seems to have always had a genuine affection.

On account of the disturbances attendant on the abdication of James II., Swift left Ireland, and after a period with his mother at Leicester, was taken into the family of Sir William Temple,

JONATHAN SWIFT

the statesman and essayist, as a kind of secretary, and proved himself extremely useful. In 1694 he took orders and received a living at Kilroot near Belfast, but after two years was recalled by Temple to prepare his letters and memoirs for publication. He employed his abundant leisure in hard reading, and wrote in 1697 his first important work, "The Battle of the Books," published in 1704. This was a satirical contribution to the famous quarrel of the ancients and moderns, which Temple had brought to England from France. Along with it appeared "The Tale of a Tub," a powerful satire upon the divisions of Christianity, full of effective ridicule of shams and pedantry. Temple died in 1699, and a year or more later, Swift received the livings of Laracor, Agher, and Rathbeggan in Ireland. These he held till 1713, when he was made Dean of St. Patrick's, Dublin. He had not, however, lived in Ireland continuously during these years, but had spent much of his time in London, where he was intimate with Addison, Steel, Congreve, and others of the wits of the time of Queen Anne. He became involved in politics, first on the Whig, after 1708 on the Tory side. It was the great period of political pamphleteering. Swift's pen was much in demand, and he was deep in the intrigues of the time. He worked hard on behalf of the Irish clergy, and did much to relieve the poverty of fellow authors. Among his most important partisan writings during this period were the papers in the "Examiner," between Nov. 2, 1710, and June 14, 1711, directed against the continuation of the war with France, and a pamphlet on "The Conduct of the Allies" (1711). He was closely associated with Harley, Earl of Oxford, and on his fall and the death of Queen Anne in 1714, Swift retired to Dublin.

During his residence with Sir William Temple, Swift had become intimate with Esther Johnson ("Stella"), also a member of the household. After the death of her mother, Stella and her friend, Mrs. Dingley, went to live in Ireland, often occupying Swift's houses at Dublin and Laracor, and for her Swift wrote while he was in London the famous "Journal to Stella." The actual nature of their relation has never been definitely ascertained, many authorities believing that they were married. If there was a marriage it was merely formal, though Stella was passionately devoted to Swift, and he had for her great admiration and affection. But it is probable that his knowledge of his own temperament and his love of independence kept him single. During his sojourn in London he formed a close friendship with Esther Vanhomrigh, who also came to love him devotedly, and who was the inspiration of his poem, "Cadenus and Vanessa." She also followed him to Ireland and in 1723 wrote asking if he were married to Stella. He rode to her house, threw down the letter, and went out without speaking. Esther died from the shock.

Some time after his return to Ireland Swift became interested in the political grievances of that country, and in 1724 he published the series of "Drapier's Letters," which was effective in breaking up a scheme by which, through a bribe to the king's mistress, a certain Wood was to have a patent for copper coinage at the expense of the Irish people. This success made Swift very popular, and inclined him to take up politics again. In 1726 he went to London, visited Gay and Pope, and published "Gulliver's Travels," which became instantly famous. This political allegory has the curious characteristic of being a children's classic and at the same time a pitiless satire on human nature in general and on the politics of his own day in particular. On this visit Swift attempted in vain to get Walpole, now Prime Minister, to share his view of the wrongs of the English in Ireland. He was again in England in the next year, hoping for preferment under the new King, George II., but he was disappointed and returned to Ireland for the last time, tortured by the prospect of the death of Stella, which occurred in January, 1728.

For some years he continued to write political pamphlets, the tone of which showed, if possible, increasing bitterness and ferocity. He quarrelled with most of the people of high station with whom he came in contact, but constantly exerted himself to aid his inferiors. Toward the end of his life his mind began to give way, and during the last three years he lay paralyzed and apathetic. He died on Oct. 19, 1745, and was buried in St. Patrick's Cathedral by the side of Stella. On his grave was carved an inscription by himself, saying that he had gone *"ubi saeva indignatio ulterius cor lacerare nequit."*

Swift is the greatest of English satirists. He wielded a pen of extraordinary power, and expressed by it a temperament of great intensity. He was a pessimist and misanthropist, and the injustices and shams of men stirred him to rage. In his personal relations he was extremely masterful, but to those who submitted he could be tender and affectionate. He left over £10,000 to found a hospital in Dublin, and he spent a large part of his income on charity. Yet he met few people whom he did not insult, and he was early embittered by disappointed ambition. From his friendships and affections he seems to have suffered more than he enjoyed, and the life of no Englishman of letters is so unhappy and so terrible.

SWIFT, LEWIS, an American astronomer; born in Clarkson, N. Y., Feb. 29, 1820; was graduated at Clarkson Academy in 1838, and spent the early part of his life in lecturing. Later he became interested in astronomy, built and set up his own telescope in Rochester, N. Y., and began to make observa-

See **Spring**, p. 37

A GIANT SPRING: A GEYSER IN ERUPTION

ST. MORITZ, FAMOUS FOR WINTER SPORTS

See **Switzerland**, p. 198

tions. For years he searched the heavens for comets, and discovered the notable one of 1862. In 1869 he observed a total solar eclipse and secured valuable results. Two years later he found another comet, and in 1877-1879 discovered other comets, for which he was three times awarded the court prize and received a gold medal from the Imperial Academy of Sciences in Vienna. In 1882 he assumed the directorship of the Warner Observatory, and later took charge of the Lowe Observatory. He was the author of "Simple Lessons in Astronomy" (1888). He died in 1913.

SWILLY, LOUGH, a long narrow inlet of the Atlantic on the N. coast of Donegal, Ireland; enters between Dunaff Head on the E. and Fanad Point, on which there is a lighthouse (fixed light visible 14 miles), on the W. A second lighthouse, on Dunree Head, has a fixed light visible for 13 miles. The entrance is protected by forts. Lough Swilly penetrates about 25 miles inland, and has a width of 3 to 4 miles. On the E. shore is the small town of Buncrana, much resorted to for sea-bathing. On its waters a French fleet under Bompart was destroyed in 1798, and not many years later the British ship "Saldanha" foundered at the entrance in a storm.

SWIFT, LINDSAY, an American educator, born at Boston, in 1856. He was educated at Harvard University and was editor of the Boston Public Library. Besides contributing to many journals and editing several works in American history, he wrote: "Massachusetts Election Sermons" (1897); "The Great Debate Between Hayne and Webster" (1898); "Literary Landmarks of Boston" (1903); "Benjamin Franklin" (1910); "William Lloyd Garrison" (1911).

SWIMMING, the art of propelling one's self through water by motions of the arms and legs; is a highly useful art and a gymnastic exercise of the first order. It has been introduced as a feature of physical training in some public schools. There are numerous mechanical aids to the teaching of swimming, in the form of cork floats, cork jackets, and many inflated india-rubber contrivances. In midsummer, 1875, Captain Boyton paddled himself, clad in a dress of the latter description, across the English Channel from Cape Grisnez to South Foreland; but the most wonderful swimming feat on record is that of Captain Webb, British Mercantile Marine, who in August, 1876, swam from Dover to Calais without artificial floats. The distance as the crow flies is 22½ miles,

but owing to tides and currents the course traversed by Webb was at least 15 miles longer, and the time occupied was 21¾ hours. Two years later a similar feat was accomplished by Mr. Cavill in 12 hours, Cape Grisnez and South Foreland being the points of departure and landing.

Till April 7, 1886, a much-disputed question was the length of time a person could remain under water. On the date given J. Finney, in a tank at the Canterbury Theater of Varieties, London, remained below the surface 4 minutes 29¼ seconds, which time will probably never be equaled, the nearest approach to it being 3 minutes 18¼ seconds on Sept. 27, 1889, by Miss Annie Johnson. The best plunge or standing dive, the body which has to be kept face downward having no progressive action imparted to it other than the impetus of the dive, stands to the credit of G. A. Blake, who on Oct. 10, 1888, at Lambeth Baths, did 75 feet 7 inches. Among other remarkable performances those of T. Burns who dived from Runcorn Bridge (85 feet) in October, 1889, and then swam to Liverpool, from whence he walked to London and dived off London Bridge.

SWIMMING BLADDER, the swim bladder or air bladder of fishes; a hollow sac, formed of several tunics, containing gas, situated in the abdominal cavity, but outside the peritoneal sac, entirely closed or communicating by a duct with intestinal tract. The special function of the swimming bladder is to alter the specific gravity of the fish, or to change the center of gravity. It is absent in the *Leptocardii, Cyclostomata, Chondropterygii,* and *Holocephala,* but occurs in all the *Ganoidei,* in one suborder of which (*Dipnoi*) it possesses anatomical characters, and assumes, to some extent, the functions of a lung; in the genus *Ceratodus,* the swimming bladder, though a single cavity, has symmetrically arranged internal pouches, while in the other genera of the sub-order (*Lepidosiren* and *Protopterus*) it is laterally halved, is supplied with venous blood by a true pulmonary artery, and by its cellular structure closely approaches the lungs of a reptile.

SWINBURNE, ALGERNON CHARLES, an English poet and essayist son of Admiral Charles Henry Swinburne; born in London, England, 1837; was educated at Balliol College, Oxford. His first productions were "Queen Mother" and "Rosamund" (1861). They were followed by two tragedies: "Atalanta in Calvdon" (1864), and "Chastelard" (1865), and by "Poems and Ballads"

(1866), reprinted as "Laus Veneris"; "A Song of Italy" (1867); "William Blake," a critical essay (1867); "Ode on the Proclamation of the French Republic, Sept. 4, 1870"; "Songs Before Sunrise" (1871); "Bothwell," a tragedy (1874);

ALGERNON CHARLES SWINBURNE

"Notes on Charlotte Brontë" (1877); "Mary Stuart: a Tragedy" (1881); "Tristram of Lyonesse" (1882); "A Century of Roundels" (1883); "Marino Faliero: a Tragedy" (1885); "A Study of Victor Hugo" (1886); a collection of essays and criticisms under the title of "Miscellanies" (1886); a poem on the "Armada" (1888); "A Study of Ben Jonson" (1890); "Astrophel, and Other Poems" (1894); "Studies in Prose and Poetry" (1894); "The Tale of Balen" (1896); and "Rosamund" (1899). He died April 10, 1909.

SWINBURNE, WILLIAM THOMAS, an American naval officer, born at Newport, R. I., in 1847. He graduated from the United States Naval Academy in 1866, and in the same year was appointed ensign. He served on various vessels and stations, and from 1886 to 1890 was on duty at the Naval Academy. He became lieutenant-commander in 1887, and was executive officer on the "Boston" from 1890 to 1893. In the latter year he commanded the battalion landed in Honolulu. After four years further service at the Naval Academy, he became commander in 1896. He served in the North Atlantic Fleet during the Spanish-American War, and took part in several engagements. In 1899 he joined the fleet at Manila under Admiral Dewey. He commanded warships, convoys, and troops to the Philippines in the year following. He was promoted to be captain in 1901, and rear-admiral in 1906. From 1906 to 1909 he was commander-in-chief of the Pacific Squadron. In the latter year he was commander of the Naval War College. He retired from active service in 1909.

SWINDON, a municipal borough of England, in Wiltshire, about 75 miles west of London. The town is mentioned as Swindone in the Doomesday Book and is built on an elevation giving a fine view of the surrounding country. There are important locomotive and carriage works of the Great Western railway. Corn and cattle markets, the charter for which dates back to the times of Charles I., are still maintained.

SWINNERTON, FRANK ARTHUR, a British novelist and critic; born at Wood Green, England, in 1884. He began work at 14 in the London office of Hay Nisbet & Co., Glasgow publishers, and was subsequently on the staff of J. M. Dent & Co. Later he became reader to Chatto & Windus, publishers. His works include: "The Merry Heart"; "The Young Idea"; "The Casement"; "The Happy Family"; "George Gissing: a Critical Study"; "On the Staircase"; "R. L. Stevenson: a Critical Study"; "The Chaste Wife"; "Nocturne"; "Shops and Houses"; "September."

SWINTON, JOHN, an American journalist; born in Salton, Scotland, Dec. 12, 1830; early learned the printer's trade; came to Canada about 1853 and afterward to New York City; took part in the Kansas "free State" contest; studied medicine; was chief of editorial staff of the "Times" from 1860 through the war; resigned post of managing editor, but continued his connection with the paper till 1869; then with Horace Greely on the "Tribune" till about 1874; then chief of staff of the "Sun" till 1883, when he resigned to start "John Swinton's Paper," conducting it till 1887. In the spring of 1874 he became the active champion of workingmen; was nominated by them for mayor of New York, but polled only 200 votes; took active part as public speaker, writer, and worker in all the movements of labor in New York after 1874. He wrote "The New Issue" (1870); "Eulogy on Henry J. Raymond" (1870); "John Swinton's Travels" (1880); and an "Oration on John Brown" (1881). He died in Brooklyn, N. Y., Dec. 15, 1901.

SWINTON, WILLIAM, an American educator, brother of John; born in Salton, Scotland, April 23, 1833. During the

Civil War he was war correspondent of the New York "Times"; from 1869 to 1872 he was Professor of English Language and Literature in the University of California. His writings include: "Rambles Among Words"; "Twelve Decisive Battles of the War"; "Campaigns of the Army of the Potomac"; "Word Analysis"; "Studies in English Literature"; and "Outlines of the World's History." He died in New York City Oct. 25, 1892.

SWISS GUARDS, a celebrated corps or regiment of Swiss mercenaries in the French army of the old régime, constituted as "Gardes" by royal decree in 1616. They were ever unswerving in their fidelity to the Bourbon kings, and their courage never blazed more brightly than on the steps of the Tuileries Aug. 10, 1792. They had been ordered to leave Paris by a decree of the Assembly on July 17, but had not yet been sent further than their barracks, when on Aug. 8, in anticipation of insurrection, they were ordered to march to the Tuileries. Michelet gives their number as 1,330; Louis Blanc as 950. But the number may now be taken definitely as nearly 800, including the ordinary guard of the king. In anticipation of a storm Mandat had made admirable arrangements to defend the palace, but the National Guards fraternized with the insurgents, and Mandat was murdered on the steps of the Hôtel de Ville. Meanwhile a growing mob under Santerre, with the famous 500 men of Marseilles at their head, marched on the Tuileries. But before they reached the palace Roederer had persuaded the king to leave the Tuileries and place himself under the protection of the National Assembly. He was accompanied thither by 150 Swiss, besides 200 gentlemen and about 100 National Guards. The remainder were left without orders, uncertain what to do, and when Westermann with his Marseilles and a raging mob made their way through the gates of the Tuileries and across the court the 650 Swiss under Captain Durler faced them on the great staircase. Westermann, an Alsatian, tried to win them over by speaking to them in German. Some one fired a shot and the struggle began. The Swiss had already driven back Westermann with about 100 dead, when the king hearing the firing sent them orders to leave the palace. They fought their retreat across the gardens, while the mob swarmed into the palace and murdered a few wounded men they found there. Those under Durler made their way to the Assembly, were disarmed and placed in the neighboring church of the Feuillants; but those who were posted in the

I—15

corridors and rooms of the palace did not hear the order to retreat, and were speedily attacked and hunted to death. A few fought their way out to the Place Louis XV., where they formed a square under the statue of the king, and were cut to pieces where they stood. Few of those who found refuge in the church of the Feuillants survived that fatal day. Fifty-four were sent to the Abbaye and were among the first to perish in the atrocious September massacres. The heroism of the Swiss Guards was fittingly commemorated in 1821 by the great lion outside one of the gates of Lucerne, cut out of the rock after a model by Thorwaldsen.

SWITCHBACK, a term applied to a zigzagging, alternate back and forward mode of progression up a slope. A "switchback" railway originally meant one where the ascent is up a steep incline simplified by curving the track backwards and forward (and upward) on the face of the slope. Afterward the term came to be applied to a railway where (as at Mauch Chunk, Pa.) the movement of the cars is largely effected by their own weight alone, the descents by gravity and the ascents by a stationary engine. Hence the application to the well-known apparatus for amusing the public at watering places, fairs, and exhibitions: a short length of elevated railway with a series of rounded inclines, so that the car gains enough momentum descending the first steep incline to ascend one or more smaller inclines till it gradually and more slowly works it way to the original level at the far end of the course. Thence it returns in the same way. Sometimes these switchbacks are made circular, called "Russian Mountains." They were introduced into Paris as a popular amusement about 1815. The latest forms of this kind of amusement in the United States are known as the "toboggan," the "steeple-chase" and "loop-the-loop."

SWITHIN, or SWITHUN, St., Bishop of Winchester from 852 to 862. He was tutor to Egbert's son, Ethelwulf, under whom he was made bishop. He was a devoted builder of churches and a man of unusual piety and humility. He built a bridge at the E. side of the city. He died in 862 and was buried in the churchyard of Winchester. A century later he was canonized, and the monks exhumed his body to deposit it in the cathedral. Although the account cannot be found in contemporary chroniclers, the transference of the body is supposed to have taken place on July 15, and to have been delayed by violent rains. Hence the still current belief that if rain falls on

July 15 it will continue to rain for 40 days.

SWITZERLAND, a federal republic of Central Europe; bounded N. by Alsace-Lorraine and Baden, from which it is separated for the most part by the Rhine; N. E. by Würtemberg and Bavaria, from which it is separated by the Lake of Constance; E. by Austria and the principality of Lichenstein, from which it is separated by the Rhine and the Grisons Alps; S. by Italy and France, from which it is separated by the Alps and the Lake of Geneva; and W. and N. W. by France, from which it is separated in part by the Jura Mountains, the Doubs river and Lake Geneva; greatest length, 210 miles; greatest breadth 126 miles. It is composed of 25 cantons and demi-cantons, represented in the government by 189 deputies. The constitution of 1848, revised May 29, 1874, transformed the federation of States into a federal State. The largest cities are Geneva, Zürich, Basel, and Berne, the last being the capital (pop. 112,200); total area, 15,976 square miles; pop. about 3,940,000; revenues (1920) 281,400,000 francs.

Physical Features.—The characteristic physical features of Switzerland are its lofty mountain ranges, enormous glaciers, magnificent lakes, and romantic valleys. The loftiest mountain chains belong to the Alps, and are situated chiefly in the S. The central nucleus is Mount St. Gothard, which unites the principal watersheds of Europe, and sends its waters into four large basins, N. by the Rhine to the German Ocean, S. W. by the Rhone to the Mediterranean, S. E. by the Po to the Adriatic, and E. by the Danube to the Black Sea. In like manner it forms a kind of starting point for the loftiest ranges of the Alps—the Helvetian or Lepontine Alps to which it belongs itself; the Pennine Alps which include Mount Blanc, the culminating point of Europe, beyond the Swiss frontiers in Savoy; and the Rhætian Alps which stretch E. and N. E. across the canton of Grisons into Tyrol. Besides the Alps, properly so called, the only range deserving of notice is that of the Jura, which is linked to the Alps by the small range, the Jorat.

Owing to the mountainous nature and the inland position of the country none of the rivers acquire such a size within its limits as to become of much navigable importance. The Rhine, formed by two head streams in the canton of Grisons, flows N. into the Lake of Constance, and thence W. to Schaffhausen, where it forms the celebrated falls of that name.

Below these falls its navigation properly begins. Its principal affluent in Switzerland is the Aar. The Rhone, rising in the Rhone glacier (Valais), flows N. W. into the Lake of Geneva. Immediately after issuing from the lake at the town of Geneva it receives the Arve, and about 10 miles below leaves the Swiss frontier. The waters which the Po receives from Switzerland are carried to it by the Ticino; those which the Danube receives are carried to it by the Inn. The largest lakes, that of Geneva in the S. W. and of Constance in the N. E., as well as that of Maggiore on the S. side of the Alps, belong partly to other countries; but within the limits of Switzerland, and not far from its center, are Lake Neuchâtel, with Morat and Bienne in its vicinity, Thun, with its feeder, Brienz, Lucerne or Vierwaldstätter see, Sempach, Baldegg, Zug, Zürich, and Wallenstätter see. All these internal lakes belong to the basin of the Rhine.

Geology and Minerals.—All the loftiest Alpine ranges have a nucleus of granite, on which gneiss and mica-slate recline generally at a high angle. Coal-bearing strata are found in the cantons of Valais, Vaud, Freiburg, Bern, and Thurgau, and brown coal is obtained in St. Gall and Zürich. Iron is worked to advantage in several quarters, particularly among the strata connected with the Jura limestone. Rock and common salt are produced to some extent in the cantons of Vaud, Basel, and Aargau. The only other minerals deserving of notice are alabaster and marble, widely diffused, and asphalt, in the Val-de-Travers, in the canton of Valais. Mineral springs occur in many quarters.

Climate and Agriculture.—Owing to differences of elevation the climate is extremely variable even in the same localities. Owing to the same cause, few countries in Europe even of larger extent can boast of a more varied vegetation than Switzerland. In regard to vegetation it has been divided into seven regions. The characteristic product of the first is the vine, which grows up to 1,700 or 1,800 feet above the sea-level. The next is the hilly or lower mountain region, rising to the height of 2,800 feet, and characterized by the luxuriance of its walnut trees, with good crops of spelt and excellent meadows. The third or upper mountain region which has its limit at 4,000 feet, produces forest timber, more especially beech, and has good crops of barley and oats, and excellent pastures. Above this, and up to the height of 5,500 feet, is the fourth or subalpine region, distinguished by its pine forests and maples; here no regular

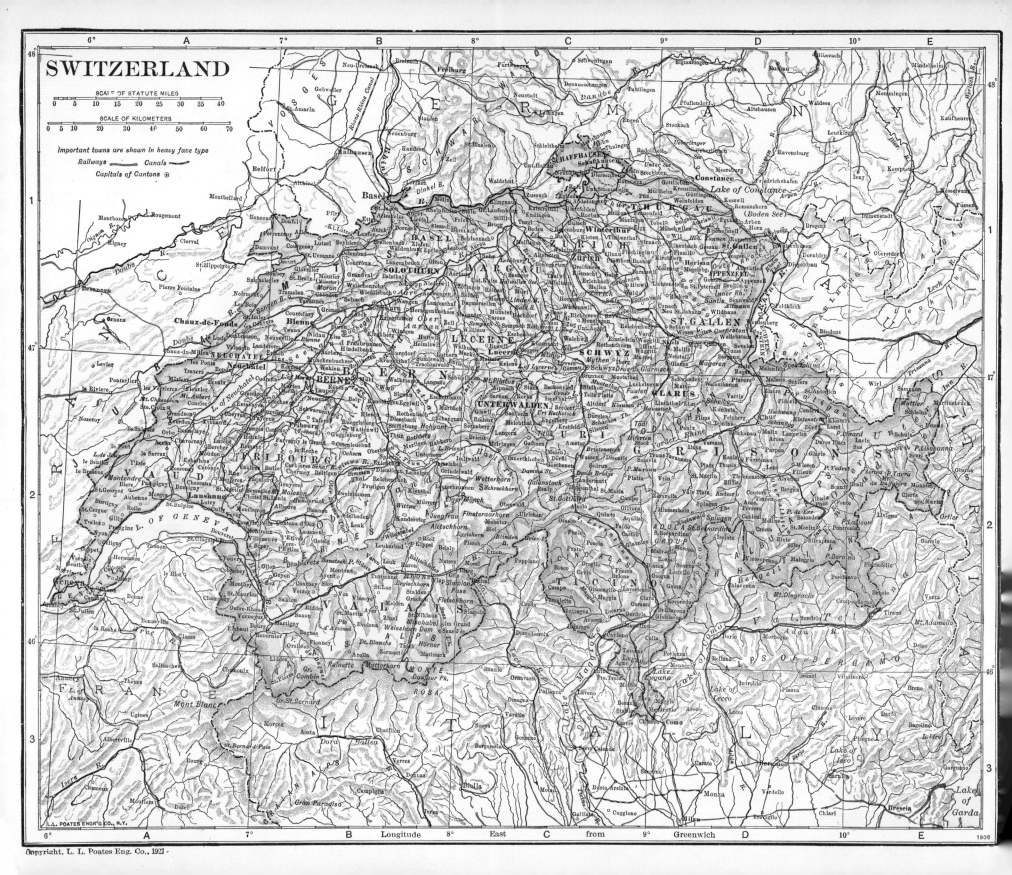

SWITZERLAND

SCALE OF STATUTE MILES
0 5 10 15 20 25 30 35 40

SCALE OF KILOMETERS
0 5 10 20 30 40 50 60 70

Important towns are shown in heavy face type
Railways ——— Canals ∿
Capitals of Cantons ⊙

Longitude   East   from   Greenwich

1908

crops are grown. The fifth or lower alpine region, terminating at 6,500 feet, is the proper region of alpine pastures. In the sixth or upper alpine region the vegetation becomes more and more stunted, and the variation of the seasons is lost. The seventh or last region is that of perpetual snow. Many parts even of the lower regions of Switzerland are of a stony, sterile nature, but on every side the effects of persevering industry are apparent, and no spot that can be turned to good account is left unoccupied. The area of the country is very equally divided among the population. There are nearly 300,000 peasant proprietors. Nearly 30 per cent. of the soil is unproductive, and of the productive area about 36 per cent. is grass and meadows, 29 per cent. forests, 19 per cent. fruit, and 16 per cent. crops and gardens. The wheat production in 1919 was 105,900 tons from 130,233 acres; rye, 41,500 tons from 54,513 acres; oats, 42,000 tons from 57,014 acres; potatoes, 828,000 tons. These are the principal crops. They are not sufficient, however, for the demands of the country and the greater part of the food crops are imported. The principal agricultural industries are the manufacture of cheese and condensed milk. Wine is produced in considerable quantity and tobacco is grown in some of the cantons. The forest area is about 3,300 square miles. It is carefully preserved and is under the jurisdiction of the Federal government.

Manufactures.—Although Switzerland is chiefly an agricultural country, the manufactures are important. There were, in 1918, 9,137 factories. The manufacture of watches and clocks is one of the most important industries. There were exported, in 1918, 15,396,542 clocks. The making of lace has long been one of the most extensive industries of the country. There are nearly 2,000 embroidery establishments, employing nearly 10,000 embroidery machines. The brewing of beer is carried on on a considerable scale. There are over 100 breweries, producing nearly 20,000,000 gallons of beer annually.

Commerce.—The imports in 1919 amounted to £134,821,000 and the exports to £118,718,080. The chief articles of import were cereals, cotton goods, silk goods, mineral substances. The chief articles of export were cotton goods, linen goods, woolen goods, machinery and clocks. The largest portion of imports were obtained from Germany, followed by France, Italy and the United Kingdom. France took the larger portion of exports, but was followed closely by Germany. The imports from the United States for the fiscal year 1920 amounted to $49,215,680, and the exports to the United States for the same period were valued at $46,394,211.

Transportation.—There were in 1919 about 3,700 miles of railway. The cost of construction up to the end of 1918 was about £100,000,000. The state railways are being electrified. There are about 1,800 miles of telegraph line and about 12,294 miles of telephone line.

Education.—There is no central educational administration. Each of the cantons has its own system and regulations. Primary instruction is free. In the northeastern cantons where the inhabitants are chiefly Protestant the proportion attending school to the whole population is as 1 to 5. In the half Protestant and half Roman Catholic cantons the proportion is as 1 to 7, and in the entirely Roman Catholic cantons it is as 1 to 9. There are primary schools in every district and secondary schools from the ages of 12 to 15. There are about 5,000 primary schools with about 15,000 teachers and about 600,000 pupils. The secondary schools number about 535, with about 50,000 pupils. In addition there are commercial schools, technical schools, agricultural schools, and schools for the blind, deaf, and feeble minded. There are 7 universities, those of Basel, Zurich, Bern, Geneva, Lausanne, Fribourg, and Neuchatel.

Finance. The estimated revenue for the year 1920 was £11,256,000, and the estimated expenditure £13,653,861. The chief sources of revenue are finance and customs, posts and railways, and invested capital. The chief expenditures are for posts and railways, interest on the debt, and the army. The public debt on January 1, 1920, was £55,261,460, and the floating debt was £14,400,000, or a total of £69,661,460.

Army.—The army of Switzerland is a national militia, service in which is compulsory and universal. Liability extends from the 20th to the end of the 48th year. The country is divided into 6 divisional districts and the field army consists of 6 divisions and 4 cavalry brigades. There is a staff organization for 3 army corps. The total peace strength is about 140,000. In addition there is a separate force for manning, and fortification, which guards the St. Gothard pass and the Rhone valley. This amounts to about 21,000 men. Landwehr comprises 56 battalions and 36 squadrons. In all about 200,000 men are available for mobilization.

Government and Finance.—The cantons of Switzerland are united together as a Federal republic for mutual defense, but retain their ididvidual independence in regard to all matters of internal administration. The legislative power of the Confederation belongs to a Federal assembly, and the executive power to a Federal council. The Federal Assembly is composed of two divisions, the National Council and the Council of States. The National Council is elected every three years by the cantons—one member to each 20,000. Every lay Swiss citizen is eligible. The Council of States consists of two members from each canton. In addition to its legislative functions the Federal Assembly possesses the exclusive right of concluding treaties of alliance with other countries, declaring war and signing peace, sanctioning the cantonal constitutions, and taking measures regarding neutrality and intervention. The Federal Council consists of seven members elected for three years by the Federal Assembly, every citizen who has a vote for the National Council being eligible for becoming a member of the Federal Council. The seven members of the Federal Council act as chiefs of the seven administrative departments of the republic. The president and vice-president of the Federal Council are the chief magistrates of the republic. They are elected by the Federal Assembly for one year, and are not eligible for re-election till after the expiration of another year. The Federal Tribunal, consisting of 16 members and 9 substitutes elected for six years by the Federal Assembly, decides in the last instance in all matters in dispute between the cantons or between the cantons and the confederation, and acts in general as a high court of appeal. It is divided into a civil and criminal court.

People.—The Swiss are a mixed people in race and language. German, French, Italian, and a corrupt kind of Latin called Rhætian or Roumansch, are spoken in different parts. German is spoken by the majority of inhabitants in 15 cantons, French in 5, Italian in 1 (Ticino), and Roumansch in 1 (the Grisons).

History.—After the conquest of Helvetia by Julius Cæser, the Romans founded in it several flourishing cities which were afterward destroyed by the barbarians. On the decline of the Roman empire it successively formed a part of the kingdom of Burgundy and the dominions of the Merovingian and Carlovingian kings; while the E. part of Switzerland became first subject to the Allemanni, and subsequently it was wholly included in the German Empire under Conrad II. in 1037. The house of Hapsburg had,

from an early period, the supremacy over all the E. part of Switzerland, and it preserved its ascendency till about 1307, when Uri, Schwyz, and Unterwalden entered into a confederacy for mutual aid against Austria, which compact was confirmed after the defeat of Leopold, Duke of Austria, at the battle of Morgarten in 1315. From 1332 to 1353, Lucerne, Zurich, Glarus, Zug, and Berne joined the confederation. Aargau was conquered from Austria in 1415; the abbey and town of St. Gall joined the other cantons in 1451-1454; Thurgau was annexed in 1460; Freiburg and Solothurn admitted in 1481; the Grisons in 1497; Basel and Schaffhausen in 1501; and Appenzell in 1513. About this time Ticino was conquered from the Milanese, and Vaud taken from Savoy by the Bernese in 1560. The remaining cantons were not finally united to the confederation till the time of Napoleon; and the compact, by which all were placed on a perfect equality, only dates from the peace of 1814. Following the political and religious troubles which culminated in the adoption of the liberal constitution of 1848, Neuchatel declared itself independent of the King of Prussia in his title of Prince Neuchatel. The canton was declared a republic, with a constitution similar to that of the other Swiss states. The king protested, but in vain, and in 1857 he finally relinquished his claim. In May, 1874, another revision of the constitution was adopted. It makes civil marriages compulsory, establishes complete liberty of creed, prohibits the appointment of new bishoprics except under Federal approval, excludes Jesuits, forbids new convents, and authorizes the government to expel dangerous foreigners, etc. In 1891 the 600th anniversary of Swiss nationality was celebrated. In 1898 the government began the purchase of the national railways and all the five great railway systems of the country had become state property by 1909. In 1911 the National Assembly passed a measure providing for workingmen's insurance against accident and sickness. This was ratified by a referendum in the following year.

Switzerland during the World War occupied an extremely difficult position in that it was altogether surrounded by belligerent states and also because the sympathies of the people were divided in accordance with their racial characteristics. French Switzerland sympathized strongly with France and German Switzerland with Germany. Following the mobilization of the Swiss army the French-speaking Swiss were called upon to defend the German border and the German-speaking, the French. The

THE GOTTHARD EXPRESS, SWITZERLAND

See Switzerland, p. 198

© Publishers' Photo Service

See Syria, p. 216

BOOTH OF SYRIAN DEALER IN HERDERS' SUPPLIES, WHERE MEMBERS OF SYRIA'S MANY RACES CONGREGATE

Swiss government had taken complete measures to protect her neutrality, and every foot of her frontier was protected by mines or by barbed wire.

Switzerland has always been a haven for political refugees and in the first weeks of the war she was called upon to shelter thousands from all nationalities from the belligerent countries, and throughout the war her territory was thronged with those who had escaped from the countries at war. Her utmost efforts were directed toward alleviating the sufferings of those refugees who were in need. During the progress of the war the country was under great expense for the mobilization of her army. It was at the same time necessary to raise large amounts to assist the destitute and to exercise supervision over the agents of the belligerent countries who used the Swiss cities as headquarters for intrigue and propaganda. In addition to these difficulties the tourist trade on which Switzerland was largely dependent upon for prosperity, was entirely cut off. The great hotels in the latter years of the war became the rest homes for the wounded of the different armies, but the income derived from this source was small compared with what it would have been in times of peace. The necessity of keeping the army mobilized and other extraordinary expenditures resulted in economic disturbances throughout the country. Special taxes were levied and in the middle of 1915 the war had already cost Switzerland over $50,000,000.

Early in 1917 rumors that Germany contemplated the invasion of Switzerland resulted in an increase in the mobilized forces of the country. During the war Switzerland acted as a clearing house for the exchange of disabled prisoners. Thousands of these were sent from the various prison camps to be interned in Switzerland for various periods of time, after which they were in most cases repatriated. By a plebiscite held on May 16, 1920, the Swiss people declared their adherence to the League of Nations by a majority of almost 90,000 votes. Geneva was chosen to be the meeting place of the League, and the first regular session was held in November and December, 1920.

SWOPE, HERBERT BAYARD, an American journalist, born at St. Louis, Mo., in 1882. He was educated in the United States and in Europe. After serving as a reporter on the St. Louis "Post-Dispatch," the Chicago "Tribune," the New York "Herald" and the New York "World," he was war correspondent for the New York "World" with the German armies from 1914 to 1916, and from then on one of the editors of this newspaper. In July, 1918, he was appointed associate member and assistant chairman of the United War Industries Board. During the Paris peace conference he acted as chief correspondent for the "World" and associated papers, and was appointed by the Paris peace conference, chairman of the American Committee on Publicity. In 1917 he was awarded the Pulitzer prize for the most meritorious newspaper work by the College of Journalism, Columbia University. He was a member of the Authors' League of America and of the Academy of Political Science and wrote "Inside the German Empire" (1916).

SWORD, a weapon of offense consisting of a blade fitted into a hilt or handle, with a guard, the blade being formed to cut or to pierce, generally to do both. It

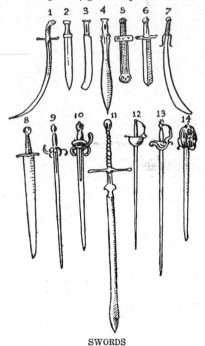

SWORDS

1—Turkish
2—Mycean
3—Egyptian
4—Bronze Age
5—Greek (Ancient)
6—Roman
7—Persian

8—15th Century
9—16th Century
10—Old Scotch
11—Two handed Sword, 15th Century
12—Rapier
13—Rapier
14—Scotch Claymore

is the most highly honored of all weapons, a symbol of military dignity and authority; and it is the instrument with which the monarch confers knightly honors. Its forms and modifications, and the names under which, in different shapes, it has been known in different lands and in successive ages, are beyond computation. It is sufficient to say that the general term includes weapons so diverse as the short cutting and piercing daggers and poignards and the ponderous two-handed swords of the 15th century. The blade may thus vary in length from a few inches to four feet and upward. It may be furnished with a cutting edge on one side only, or on both sides. It may be uniform in breadth throughout with a truncated end, or it may taper from the hilt to a fine point. The blade, moreover, may have a piercing point alone, as in the rapier, and it may be curved throughout its entire length, as in the Oriental scimitar. The hilt, with its many forms of guard, grip, and pommel, similarly adds to the variations of the weapon.

The sword, of course, could not be a weapon of primitive man; but it is easy to trace its development from the forms of weapon in use in the stone and early bronze ages. The sword came into use only when men had attained considerable skill in casting and working bronze, and the ancient bronze swords, many of which have been found throughout Europe with two-edged blades measuring 2 feet in length, are well finished weapons. The early Greek sword was merely a strong two-edged knife; but about 400 B. C. its form was improved and its size doubled by Iphicrates. The *gladius* of the Romans was still of the same form—a straight two-edged blade, heavier and longer, however, than the Greek weapon.

During the early Middle Ages there does not appear to have been much development in the form of the sword in Europe. As shown by the Bayeux Tapestry and other contemporary illustrations, it continued to be a short cutting weapon, with a blade of uniform breadth bluntly pointed, and to give it balance it was channeled from the hilt for about two-thirds of its length. The cross guard, subsequently called the quillons, was short, projecting at right angles from the blade, but sometimes bent forward in the direction of the point.

With the introduction of the two-handed sword, the use of a shield being no longer possible, the guard gradually became more complicated, so as to give greater protection to the hands of the swordsman, and from the use of shell guards and ring guards, etc., the basket hilt, as applied to lighter swords, by degrees developed. The ordinary basket hilt sword, such as is worn by officers of Highland regiments at the present day, is of Italian origin, and grew out

of the Venetian *schiavone*. The rapier— a piercing weapon only, with a blade tapering to a fine point—came into use in the early part of the 16th century, and in the 17th century it became the weapon of fencing and dueling.

From very early times, Toledo, Seville, and some other Spanish towns had a high reputation for the excellence of the swords made by their armorers, and when to their own skill was added the perfect craftsmanship of their Moorish conquerors the renown of Spanish blades became supreme. In the North Italian towns also, as well as at Solingen and Passau in Germany, swords of famous quality were fabricated. Who the original maker of Ferrara blades was is not known, but in the 16th century there was a family of armorers named Ferrara in North Italy, one member of which, called Andrea, was born in 1555.

In modern warfare the sword possesses little more than an honorary military significance.

SWORDBILL, a popular name for any individual of the humming bird genus, *Docimastes*. The bill, which exceeds in length the body of the bird, is a character

SWORDBILL

by which this humming bird may be distinguished at the first glance. One species is known, *D. ensiferus*, an inhabitant of Colombia, Ecuador, and Peru.

SWORDFISH, in astronomy, the constellation, *Dorado*. In ichthyology, a popular name for any individual of the *Xiphiidæ*. They are pelagic fishes, widely distributed in tropical and sub-tropical seas. Their popular name is derived from their formidable sword-like weapon, formed by the coalescence and prolongation of the maxillary and intermaxillary bones beyond the lower jaw; it is very hard and strong, and capable of inflicting terrible wounds. Swordfishes seem to have a mortal antipathy to whales and other large *Cetacea*, attacking them whenever occasion offers, and, so far as is known, always coming off victorious. In their fury swordfishes often attack boats and vessels, evidently mistaking them for cetaceans; and sometimes the sword has been driven through the bot-

SWORDFISH

tom of a ship, and broken off by the fish in vain struggles to withdraw it. Swordfishes are the largest of the *Acanthopterygii*; specimens of the genus *Histiophorus* (the sailorfish), from the Indian and Pacific oceans, reaching a length of from 12 to 15 feet, of which the sword occupies rather more than 3. The common or Mediterranean swordfish sometimes reaches a length of 10 feet, with a proportionately shorter sword; it is bluish-black above, merging into silver below. The flesh is of excellent flavor, and in recent years has become popular in the United States.

SYBARIS, an ancient Greek city of Lower Italy, on the Gulf of Tarentum, supposed to have been built by a colony of Achæans and Trœzenians about 720 B. C. It rapidly rose to an extraordinary degree of prosperity, and the inhabitants were proverbial for their luxury and voluptuousness. It was totally destroyed by the Crotonians, who turned the waters of the river Crathis against it (510 B. C.).

SYBEL (sē'bl), **HEINRICH, VON**, a German historian; born in Düsseldorf, Germany, Dec. 2, 1817; studied at Berlin under Ranke, and became professor at Bonn in 1844 and at Marburg in 1845. In 1861 he was elected by the university to the Prussian Landtag, and in 1874 was returned to the imperial Parliament. In 1878 he was nominated director of the state archives. Of his works the best known in England is his "History of the

French Revolution." He died in Marburg, Germany, Aug. 1, 1895.

SYCAMORE, the *Acer pseudo-platanus*, an umbrageous tree, 40 to 60 feet high; with spreading branches; large, five-lobed, coarsely and unequally serrate leaves, glaucous and downy on the veins beneath; pendulous racemes of greenish flowers, and glabrous fruit furnished with two long, membranous wings. It flowers in May and June. The wood is used for bowls, trenchers, and other turnery. The sap is sacchariferous. It grows wild in Switzerland, Germany, Austria, Italy, and Western Asia. It is a hardy tree, flourishing in spite of high winds or sea spray. When the leaves first appear (in April) they are covered with a clammy juice containing about one part in 11 of sugar, attractive to insects, by which they are perforated and disfigured. The name is also applied to the PLANE TREE (*q. v.*) or buttonwood of America, the *Platanus occidentalis* of scientific nomenclature, and to allied species. In entomology, a European night moth, *Acronycta aceris*, so called because the caterpillar—which, when alarmed, rolls itself up like a millepede—feeds chiefly on the sycamore, though also on the horse chestnut and the oak.

SYCOMORE, or **SYCAMORE**, a tree of the genus *Ficus*, the *F. Sycomorus*, sycamore of Scripture, a kind of fig tree, common in Palestine, Arabia, and Egypt, growing thick and to a great height, and though the grain is coarse, much used in building and very durable. Its fruit is sweet and of a delicate flavor.

SYDENHAM, THOMAS, the "sommo Ippocratista inglese" (supreme English Hippocratist), as Puccinotti styles him; born in Winford Eagle in Dorsetshire in 1624. That he belonged to one of the county families; that at 18 he was entered at Magdalen Hall, Oxford; that his studies were, after two years, interrupted by his having to serve as an officer in the parliamentarian army; that his Oxford curriculum ended in 1648 when he graduated M. B., and shortly after became a Fellow of All Souls—is the sum of our knowledge as to his youth and early manhood. For the next 15 years we lose sight of him. We find him in London in 1663 as a licentiate of the College of Physicians, publishing his "Method of Curing Fevers" in 1666; and 10 years thereafter taking his M. D. at Pembroke Hall, Cambridge. The "Iatrophysical" and "Chemiatric" theories in fashion at the time he treated with scant consideration, and looked on chemistry itself as a mere branch of the apothecary's business. In 1668 he published a second edition of his book on fevers, adding to it a chapter on plague, with a fine poem in Latin elegiacs addressed to him by Locke. A third and enlarged edition, entitled "Medical Observations," appeared in 1676. In 1680 he published two "Letters in Response," the one "On Epidemics," and the other on the "Lues Venera." His "Epistolary Dissertation" on confluent smallpox and hysteria (1682) was followed next year by his yet more famous "Treatise on Podagra," in 1686 appeared his "On the New Fever," and in 1692 his last work, an outline of pathology and therapeutics. An acute attack of gout carried him off Dec. 29, 1689, and he was interred in St. James's Church, Piccadilly, where in 1810 the College of Physicians erected a mural tablet to his memory.

Sydenham's place in the history of medicine has already been given. Seemingly behind his age in science he was really ahead of it in practice. In acute disease he read the forthputting of that activity by which nature sought to right herself—an activity to be watched and, when possible, to be assisted. Chronic diseases he also viewed with the eye of Hippocrates, as due to habits or errors for which we ourselves are mainly responsible, and these he met by appropriate changes in diet and mode of life. Among special contributions to nosology he may be said to have first diagnosed scarlatina and classified chorea. Gout was another ailment on which he left a memorable mark.

SYDNEY, the capital of New South Wales and the parent city of Australia, picturesquely situated on the S. shore of Port Jackson, the shore line being deeply indented by capacious bays or inlets which form harbors in themselves, and are lined with wharves, quays, and warehouses. Some of the older streets are narrow and crooked, bearing a striking resemblance to those of an English town; but the more modern streets, such as George street, Pitt street, Market street, King street, and Hunter street, rank high in order of architectural merit. The steam tramway system is extended to all parts of the suburbs, and water communication between the city and its transmarine suburbs, Balmain, North Shore, Manly Beach, etc., is maintained by numerous steam ferries. Among the most important public buildings are the new government offices, magnificent white freestone structures in the Italian style; the town hall, with a tower 200 feet high, and a very capacious great hall; the postoffice, an Italian building with a tower 250 feet

high; the government house; the university, a Gothic building with a frontage of nearly 400 feet, situated in a fine park; the free public library; school of art; public museum; grammar school; St. Andrew's (Episcopal) Cathedral; St. Mary's (R. C.) Cathedral; the Jewish synagogue; exchange; custom house; mint, parliament houses; hospitals, asylums, and numerous other ecclesiastical, scholastic, and business buildings.

The city is well lighted with gas and electricity. It has a number of extensive and handsome municipal public parks. The places of open-air recreation include the Domain, a beautiful park covering about 140 acres; Hyde Park, 40 acres, near the center of the city; the Botanical Gardens, the finest in the colonies, 38 acres; Moore Park, 600 acres; the Centennial Park, designed to commemorate the colony's centenary (1888), 768 acres; and the race course, 202 acres. The entrance from the Pacific Ocean to Port Jackson, about 4 miles N. E. of Sydney, is 1 mile in width, and is strongly fortified; the bay itself is about 10 miles in length and 3 in average breadth; it is well sheltered, and has a depth of water sufficient to float the largest vessels. Besides wharves and quays there are dry docks and other accommodation for shipping, and the trade of the port is very large. The principal exports are wool, tallow, hides, preserved meat, tin, copper, etc.; the imports, grain, tea, coffee, sugar, wine and spirits, ironware and machinery, cotton and woolen goods, wearing apparel, furniture, etc. Sydney was founded in 1788, and was named in honor of Viscount Sydney, the colonial secretary. It was incorporated in 1842. The discovery of gold in the colony in 1851 gave an immense impetus to its progress. Pop. (1918) 792,300.

SYDNEY, a city of Nova Scotia, Canada, and capital of Cape Breton co., on Sydney Harbor and the Inter-Colonial and the Sydney and Louisbourg railways, about 257 miles N. E. of Halifax. Steamship connections are maintained with Montreal, Quebec, Halifax and Newfoundland. The manufacturing enterprises of the city are of importance, especially the steel works. Population about 20,000.

SYENITE, or **SIENITE,** a name originally applied to the granite of Syene, which contains hornblende, but now generally restricted to a rock which consists of orthoclase, felspar and hornblende only; or where quartz is present only in sufficient quantity to be regarded as an accessory and not as an essential constituent. By the increase in the amount of quartz, and the presence of mica, syenite graduates into a hornblendic granite. Petrologists recognize as a typical syenite the rock of Meissen, near Dresden.

SYKES, GEORGE, an American military officer; born in Dover, Del., Oct. 9, 1822; was graduated at the United States Military Academy in 1842; was promoted 1st lieutenant Sept. 21, 1846; and during the war with Mexico took part at the actions of Monterey, Vera Cruz, Cerro Gordo, Contreras, Churubusco, and the siege and surrender of the City of Mexico. In May, 1861, he was promoted major of the 14th Infantry, and in September of the same year appointed Brigadier-General of volunteers. Later he won distinction at Gaines' Mills, and in the several subsequent operations of the Army of the Potomac; was promoted Major-General of volunteers in November, 1862; took part in the battles of Chancellorsville and commanded the 5th Army Corps during the battle of Gettysburg. At the close of the war he was brevetted Major-General U. S. A. for gallantry in service during the war. He was promoted colonel of the 20th United States Infantry in January, 1868. He died in Brownsville, Tex., Feb. 9, 1880, while in command of Fort Brown. His remains were removed to the West Point cemetery at the expense of Congress and a fine monument was erected to his memory.

SYLHET, or SILHET (Srihatta), a district in the extreme S. of Assam, British India; partly a rich alluvial tract, but to the extent of 32 per cent. uncultivated waste; has an area of 5,413 square miles and a pop. of 2,200,000. The chief town, Sylhet, on the Surmá river, has a pop. of about 15,000, and some trade and manufactures.

SYLLABUS, in Church history, a list embracing the "chief errors and false doctrines of our most unhappy age," compiled by order of Pope Pius IX., and sent, with an encyclical letter, dated Dec. 8, 1864, "to all the bishops of the Catholic world, in order that these bishops may have before their eyes all the errors and pernicious doctrines which he had reprobated and condemned," the number of which amounts to 80, probably in imitation of the 80 heresies mentioned by Epiphanius as existing in the first three centuries. The syllabus is divided into 10 sections, and attacks rationalism, pantheism, latitudinarianism, socialism, errors concerning the Church,

society, natural and Christian ethics, marriage, the power of the Pope, and modern liberalism.

SYLLOGISM, in logic, the regular form of reasoning in which two premises lead necessarily to a conclusion.
Example:
Major Premise. All ruminants are quadrupeds.
Minor Premise. All deer are ruminants.
Conclusion ∴ All deer are quadrupeds.
This syllogism is valid, because the conclusion logically follows from the premises. The conclusion is, moreover, true, because the premises from which it logically follows are true.
A syllogism is said to be valid when the conclusion logically follows from the premises; if the conclusion does not so follow, the syllogism is invalid and constitutes a fallacy, if the error deceives the reasoner himself; but if it is advanced with the intention of deceiving others, it constitutes a sophism.

SYLPHS, in the fantastic system of the Paracelsists, the elemental spirits of the air, just as the salamanders are of fire and the gnomes of earth. They hold an intermediate place between immaterial and material beings. They eat, drink, speak, move about, beget children, and are subject to infirmities like men; but, on the other hand, they resemble spirits in being more nimble and swift in their motions, while their bodies are more diaphanous than those of the human race. They also surpass the latter in their knowledge, both of the present and the future, but have no soul, and when they die nothing is left. They marry with our race, like the Undines and the Gnomes, and the children of such a union have souls and belong to the human race. In common usage the term sylph is applied to a graceful maiden.

SYLVA, CARMEN, pseudonym of Elizabeth, Queen of Rumania, a poet and author; born in Castle Monrepos near Neuwied, Germany, Dec. 29, 1843. In 1869 she was married to Charles, then Prince, now King of Rumania. Among her works (all in German) are: "Rumanic Poems" (1881); "Tempests"; "Songs from the Dimbovitza Valley" (1889). Her tragedy "Master Manole" (1892) had a brilliant success in the Burgh Theater, Vienna. In collaboration with Mite Kremnitz, she wrote some novels: "Astra"; "From Two Worlds"; etc. She died in 1920.

SYLVANITE, an ore of tellurium; crystallization, monoclinic, rarely occurring in distinct crystals, but in an aggregation resembling writing characters; hardness, 1.5-2; sp. gr. 7.9-8.33; luster, metallic; color and streak, steel-gray, sometimes brass-yellow. Composition: Tellurium, 55.8; gold 28.5; silver, 15.7 = 100, which corresponds to the formula (AgAu)3Te. Occurs usually associated with gold.

SYLVANUS, in mythology, a rural Latin deity, who is generally represented as half a man and half a goat. He was sometimes represented as holding a cypress in his hand.

SYLVESTER I., a Pope who governed the Church during the reign of Constantine I. He was famous for the number of churches completed during his reign, among them the basilicas St. Peter's and St. Paul's, for his various Church laws and his influence over the emperor. He held office in 314-335.

SYLVESTER II., a Pope, a native of Auvergne, was of an obscure family, but received a superior education, studying first in the monastery of Aurillac and afterward in Spain. He was made abbot of Bobbio by the Emperor Otho II., and became very distinguished as a teacher. His attainments in science procured him the reputation of a magician. Among the numerous useful inventions attributed to Sylvester II. is the balance clock, which was in use till the adoption of the pendulum in 1650. Sylvester II. was tutor to Otho III., and subsequently head of the school of Rheims, which he made one of the first in Europe, Robert, afterward King of France, was among his pupils. He was called to the papal chair on the death of Gregory V., and administered the affairs of the church with much prudence and moderation. He was the first French pope. He died at a great age in 1003.

SYLVESTER III., for three months the anti-Pope of Benedict IX. and Gregory VI., but deposed by the Synod of Sutri in 1046.

SYLVESTER, JAMES JOSEPH, an English mathematician; born in London Sept. 3, 1814, studied at St. John's College, Cambridge, and was successively professor in University College, London, in the University of Virginia, in the Johns Hopkins University, Baltimore, and at Oxford (Savilian professor, 1883). He published many memoirs in the scientific journals, and received many medals and honors. He died March 15, 1897.

SYLVESTER, JOSHUA, an English author; born in England in 1563. His life was divided between merchandise and poetry, but in neither did he achieve success. Of his original works we have no trace, except the title of the poem published about 1620, entitled "Tobacco Battered and the Pipes Shattered by a Volley of Holy Shot Thundered from Mount Helicon"; but in virtue of the great though short-lived popularity obtained by his English version of the "Divine Weeks and Works" of Du Bartas he lives in literary history a kind of shadowy life. It was especially popular with the Puritans and was one of the sources of inspiration for Milton's "Paradise Lost." He led a somewhat wandering existence and died in Middleburg, Holland, Sept. 28, 1618.

SYMBIOSIS, a biological term introduced by De Bary to denote certain kinds of physiological partnership between organisms of different kinds. Consortism is synonymous. As there are many kinds of organic association, it is convenient to restrict the term symbiosis to such intimate and complementary partnerships as exist between algoid and fungoid elements in lichens, or between unicellular algæ and radiolarians. In organic nature there is no isolation; no organism lives or dies to itself; there are countless vital associations, some very indirect and external—e. g., the mutual dependence of some flowers and insects—others very direct and intimate, as in the symbiosis of algæ and radiolarians. It often happens that two organisms live together without there being any apparent vital bonds between them; thus diatoms may be "epiphytic" on algæ; algæ, lichens, mosses, ferns, orchids, etc., are often epiphytic on trees; many algæ are "epizoic" on animals—e. g., those which live among the hairs of sloths; and one animal may be epizoic on another, as sponges often are on zoöphytes. Again, there may be external partnerships, such as those between pilot fish and shark, or between beef-eater birds and wild cattle. These suggest cases of mutualism or commensalism, such as the partnership between certain hermit crabs and sea anemones. Probably the constant occurrence of colonies of the algæ anabæna in the leaves of the aquatic plant azolla is a similar partnership. Alike in symbiosis and in commensalism the partnerships are advantageous to both of the associated organisms, and are therefore to be distinguished from parasitism, in which the benefit is all on one side. It is useful to distinguish these different grades of association, but it cannot be pretended that the distinctions are rigid.

Apart from lichens, the partnership of unicellular algæ with raidiolarians is the best-known case of symbiosis. The partner algæ—known for a long time as "yellow cells"—used to be variously interpreted as reproductive cells, secretory cells, reserve stores, parasites, and so on; but the researches of Geddes, Brandt, and others demonstrate their algoid and truly symbiotic nature. They have a cellulose wall (except in the *Acanthometridæ* among radiolarians), a nucleus, two pigments, of which one is at least closely analogous to the ordinary chlorophyll of plants; they are able to live and multiply after removal from their host or after its death; in sunlight they evolve oxygen and form starch; they multiply as do free unicellular algæ. From his experiments Geddes inferred that the starch formed by the algæ may be absorbed by the radiolarians; that when they die the algæ are digested by their partners; that during life they absorb carbonic acid and nitrogenous waste from the radiolarians and in turn liberate oxygen which may accelerate the vital functions of their bearers. It seems that the partnership is distinctly advantageous, for the algæ flourish and multiply, and those radiolarians which are without algæ are few and much less common than the vast majority which exhibit symbiosis. Brandt's results are for the most part in agreement with those of Geddes, though divergent on some points of details. The algæ may belong to a distinct genus (*Zooxanthella* of Brandt, *Philozoon* of Geddes), or may be simply the swarmspores of various olive-green seaweeds.

Similar symbiotic algæ occur in some *Foraminifers*, in several *Cœlenterates*, especially otherwise colorless sea anemones, and, according to Geddes, in some species of the *Turbellarian Convoluta*. Brandt maintains that in the fresh-water sponge and in the fresh-water hydra there are symbiotic algæ of the genus *Zoochlorella*, but Ray Lankester has shown to the satisfaction of most naturalists that the pigmented bodies in those animals are no more symbiotic algæ than are green corpuscles in the leaf of a buttercup. Many marine sponges are infested by various kinds of algæ, but we do not know that they exhibit any real symbiosis.

In regard to some green protoza there is much dispute whether the green color is due to chlorophyll bodies or to symbiotic algæ. Some forms—*e. g., Stentor polymorphus, Coleps viridis, Ophrydium viride,* and *Vorticella chlorostigma*—also occur in a colorless state. Geza Entz regards the bodies as algæ, Miss Salitt as chlorophyll corpuscles. Famintzin finds *Zoochlorellæ* in species of *Paramæcium,*

Stentor, and *Stylonichia,* which he regards as symbiotic forms of the Protococcus-like *Chlorella* which he and Beyerinck have discovered living freely. Thus it appears that, while many cases of symbiosis are indubitable, there are other cases in regard to which judgment must be for a time suspended.

SYMBOL, that which specially distinguishes one regarded in a particular character, or as occupying a particular office, and fulfilling its duties; a figure marking the individuality of some being or thing; as, a trident is the symbol of Neptune. In chemistry, an abbreviation of the name of an elementary body: thus C for carbon, H, hydrodgen, P, phosphorous, etc. When two or more of the names begin with the same letter, a second letter is added to the symbol of one of these elements for the sake of distinction: thus Cl=chlorine, Hg=hydrargyrum (mercury), Pb=plumbum (lead), etc. The symbol also represents a definite quantity of the element: thus H always=one part by weight of hydroden, Hg=200 parts of mercury. In theology, a primitive name for the Creed, often occurring in the works of the early fathers. Also sometimes applied to the elements in the Sacrament of the Eucharist.

Mathematical symbols are of four kinds: (1) Those which stand for quantities; such as letters standing for numbers, time, space, or any of the geometrical magnitudes. (2) Those of relation, as the signs, $=$, $>$, $:$ $::$, etc., which indicate, respectively, the relations of equality, inequality, proportion, etc. (3) Those of abbreviation, as $\therefore$, for "hence," $\because$, for "because"; exponents and coefficients are likewise symbols of abbreviation, the symbol consisting in the manner of writing these numbers. (4) Symbols of operation, or those employed to denote an operation to be performed, or a process to be followed; such are the symbols of algebra and the differential and integral calculus, etc., which do not come under the preceding heads. Those of the third class are generally regarded as symbols of operation. Symbols of operation are of two kinds: (1) Those which indicate invariable processes, and are, in all cases, susceptible of uniform interpretations. This kind includes most of what are usually called the signs of algebra, as $+$, $-$, $\times$, $\div$, $\sqrt{}$. (2) Those which indicate general methods of proceeding without reference to the nature of the quantity to be operated on.

SYMBOLICS, a theological term for the study of creeds and confessions of faith, etc., from the ancient meaning of the word symbolon, a brief compendium, a creed.

SYME, JAMES, a Scotch surgeon; born in Fifeshire, Scotland, Nov. 7, 1799; was educated at the High School and University of Edinburgh, and studied anatomy under Barclay and Liston, visiting also Paris and Germany. In 1829 he opened Minto House Hospital, which he carried on for four years with great success as a surgical charity and school of clinical instruction; and in 1833 he was appointed Professor of Clinical Surgery in Edinburgh University. In 1847, on Liston's death, he accepted the same professorship in University College, London; he soon, however, returned to his former chair in Edinburgh and continued to hold it till his death. Among his numerous writings are a "Treatise on the Excision of Diseased Joints," and "Principles of Surgery." He died in Edinburgh June 26, 1870.

SYMMACHUS, QUINTUS AURELIUS, a Roman statesman of the 4th century, A. D., and one of the last great advocates of paganism; was educated in Gaul; and after serving as quæstor and prætor became Corrector of Lucania and the Brutii (365) and Proconsul of Africa (373), and member of the pontifical college. His petition to Gratian, urged on the senate's behalf, for the restoration of the altar of Victory, proved unavailing (382), as did the extant letter addressed by him when præfect of the city (384) to Valentinian. The failure led him to side with the pretender Maximus (387), and for so doing he was impeached of treason, but pardoned and raised to the consulship (391). His death must have taken place after 404, and we have by him 10 books of letters (1653), and fragments of 9 orations, the latter discovered and edited by Mai (1815). "Even saints," says Gibbons, "and polemic saints, treat Symmachus with respect," though Prudentius likened the use to which he applied his talents "to one digging in mud with an instrument of gold and ivory."

SYMMETRICAL, in botany (of the parts of a flower), related to each other in number, the same in number, or one a multiple of the other, as in *Saxifraga*, which has five divisions of the calyx, five petals, and five stamens; or *Epilobium*, which has a four-parted calyx, four petals, and eight stamens.

In mathematics, possessing the attribute of symmetry; having corresponding parts or relations. In geometry, two points are symmetrically disposed with respect to a straight line, when they are on opposite sides of the line and equally distant from it, so that a straight line joining them intersects the given line, and is at right angles to it. A curve is symmetrical with respect to a straight line, when for each point on one side of the line there is a corresponding point on the other side, and equally distant from it. The line is called an axis of symmetry. In conic sections, the axes are the only true axes of symmetry. Two plane figures are symmetrically situated with respect to a straight line, when each point of one has a corresponding point in the other on the opposite side of the axis, and equally distant from it. A line or surface is symmetrical with respect to a plane, when for each point on one side of the plane there is a second point on the other side, equally distant from it. The plane is called the plane of symmetry, and is, in conical sections, a principal plane. Symmetrical lines and surfaces in space cannot, in general, be made to coincide with each other. Spherical triangles are symmetrical when their sides and angles are equal each to each, but not similarly situated. In analysis, an expression is symmetrical with respect to two letters, when the places of these letters may be changed without changing the expression. Thus the expression $x^2 + a^2x + ab + b^2x$ is symmetrical with respect to a and b; for, if we change the place of a and b, we have $x^2 + b^2x + ba + a^2x$, the same expression. An expression is symmetrical with respect to several letters, when any two of them may change places without affecting the expression; thus, the expression $ab + ba^2 + a^2c + c^2a + b^2c + bc^2$ is symmetrical with respect to the three letters, a, b, c.

SYMONDS, JOHN ADDINGTON, an English author; born in Bristol, England, Oct. 5, 1840; was educated at Harrow and at Balliol College, Oxford. His great work is the "Renaissance in Italy" (1875-1886). Among his other works are: "Study of Dante"; "Studies of the Greek Poets"; "Sketches in Italy and Greece"; "Sketches and Studies in Italy"; translation of the "Sonnets of Michael Angelo and Campanella"; "Animi Figura," a collection of sonnets; "Vagabunduli Libellus"; "In Nights and Days"; "Essays Speculative and Suggestive." He died in Rome, Italy, April 19, 1893.

SYMONS, ARTHUR, a British writer of verse and prose, born in Wales, 1865. He was educated at various private schools and began to write early. His works include: "An Introduction to the Study of Browning"; "Days and

Nights"; "Silhouettes"; ''London Nights"; "Amoris Victima"; "Studies in Two Literatures"; "The Symbolist Movement in Literature"; "Images of Good and Evil"; "Collected Poems"; "Plays, Acting and Music"; "Cities"; "Studies in Prose and Verse"; "Spiritual Adventures"; "A Book of Twenty Songs"; "The Fool of the World and Other Poems"; "Studies in the Seven Arts"; "William Blake"; "Cities of Italy"; "The Romantic Movement in English Poetry"; "Knave of Hearts"; "Figures of Several Centuries"; "Tragedies"; "Tristan and Iseult"; "Cities and Sea Coasts and Islands"; "Colour Studies in Paris"; "The Toy Cart."

SYMPATHY, a feeling corresponding to that felt by another; the quality or state of being affected by the affections of another, with feelings corresponding in kind if not in degree; compassion, fellow feeling, commiseration. Sympathy is first evoked in small societies, such as a single family or a small tribe, and gradually extends beyond these limits. One of its moral acquisitions is to go forth toward the lower animals, as shown, for example, by the efforts to prevent their being cruelly and thoughtlessly treated. Also, an agreement of affections or inclinations; a conformity of natural temperament, which makes two persons pleased or in accord with each other; mutual or reciprocal affection or passion; community of inclination or disposition.

In physiology and pathology, reciprocal action of the different parts of the body on each other; an affection of one part of the body in consequence of something taking place in another. Thus, when there is a local injury the whole frame after a time suffers with it. Also the influence exerted over the susceptible organization of one person, as of a hysteric female, by the sight of paroxysms of some nervous disease in another or in others.

SYMPHONY, in music, a form of orchestral composition. The name was originally applied to the purely instrumental portions of works primarily vocal, under it being included overtures to operas and oratorios as well as ritornelli and the introduction to choruses and arias. It received its first restrictive meaning toward the end of the 17th century when, under Lulli and Alessandro Scarlatti, the various instrumental pieces in the operas began to grow in importance: it was then reserved for the opening section or overture which consisted of a series of contrasted movements without definite rule as to their number or arrangement. Subsequently a plan, attributed to Lulli and known as the "ouver-

ture à la manère française," prescribed three movements, the first and third slow and the middle one quick and bright. Its place was eventually taken by the "Italian overture," in which the three movements were retained but in inverse order, the first and last being quick and the second slow.

This form was identical with that of the clavier sonata, to which, however, the overture long remained inferior in respect of the internal structure of its movements, few composers caring to show themselves at their best in pieces to which talkative audiences paid little heed. As a further result of such inattention it seemed to be forgotten that the overture should fitly foreshadow the work which it preceded: its material, consequently, became distinct and independent, so that it was only natural that the best examples should in course of time find their way into the concert room where they met with a more courteous reception.

It was not, however, till 1788, the year in which Mozart wrote his great examples, that the symphony attained the rank of an important work of art. In these three works, the E flat, G minor, and C major symphonies, an extraordinary advance is visible both in expression and in richness of instrumental effect. Haydn, though born nearly 20 years before Mozart, wrote his most important symphonies during the 18 years he survived his younger contemporary. But the symphony was brought to its most perfect stage of development by Beethoven.

The Eroica, C minor, and A major stand as the most perfect examples of the classical symphony, and also mark the close of the classical period. For, as the perfection of the symphony was due to the increased value of the subject matter, it was natural when the emotional domain of music became still more extended that composers should find themselves somewhat circumscribed by the limitations of the old form. Beethoven himself is an instance of this, for the 9th Symphony he substitutes for the usual finale an elaborate choral setting of one of Schiller's odes. Succeeding writers have mostly aimed at a compromise between their poetical instincts and their regard for conventional rule. Among such may be mentioned Schubert, Spohr, Berlioz, Raff, and Schumann, the work of the last being the most important. Mendelssohn was content with the true classical form, and the same in a general way might be said of Brahms.

SYMPHYTISM, in philology, a term applied by Earle to a tendency, in that class of words called by him symbolic, to attach themselves to other words, so that the resulting compound is either really one word, or presents the appearance of being one word.

SYNAGOGUE, a congregation or assembly of Jews for the purpose of worship or the performance of religious rites. Also, a building set apart for Jewish as a church or chapel is for Christian worship. Under the Mosaic law worship of the highest type could take place only at one chosen spot (Deut. xii: 5, 21; xvi: 6), that divinely chosen early in the monarchy being Jerusalem (II Chron. vi: 5, 6), though gatherings took place in various other localities (II Kings, iv: 23). Meetings at stated times for worship do not seem to have arisen till the time of the Exile, when the services of the Temple were perforce in abeyance. They constituted the germ of the subsequent synagogues, which are believed to have begun among the Jews resident out of Palestine. In Psalm lxxiv: 8, the persecutors are represented as burning up all the synagogues of God in the land. Jesus taught or preached and wrought miracles in the synagogues of Capernaum (Matt. xii: 9, Mark i: 21, Luke vii: 5, John vi: 59), in that of Nazareth (Matt xiii: 54, Mark vi: 2, Luke iv: 16), and elsewhere (Luke iv: 15). Many Jewish synagogues are said to have existed in Jerusalem, besides one or more for foreigners (Acts vi:9). Out of Palestine the Apostles found synagogues in Damascus, Antioch in Pisidia, Iconium, Thessalonica, Berea, Athens, Corinth, Ephesus and doubtless also in other places. Synagogues were usually built on elevated sites, suggested by Prov. i: 21, and Ezra ix: 9, often outside cities and towns, by the side of a river or small stream (Acts xvi: 13). The edifice was shaped like a theater, with the door on the W. side, entering which one was conventionally supposed to look E. to Jerusalem. The wooden chest or ark containing the scrolls of the law and vestments was on the E. side, with a canopy above, or in a recess or sanctuary. In front of it were the desk of the reader or preacher and a platform, with arm-chairs for the elders, who faced the ordinary worshipers. The men sat on one side of the synagogue and the women on the other; they were moreover separated by a partition about 6 feet high. A light was kept perpetually burning. The governing body was the elders (Acts xxv: 15), presided over by a ruler of the synagogue (Mark v: 22, Luke xiii: 14), with two judicial colleagues, three almoners or deacons, a leader of the worship (Luke iv: 20), a servant like a care-taker, and the 10 men of leisure pledged to attend and constitute a congregation if no others came. The Law and the Prophets were read, with liturgical prayers, chanting of the psalms, and recitals of the 10 commandments, the whole concluding with a benediction. The synagogues were used not only as places of worship, but as law courts, taking cognizance of petty offenses, the decisions of which were carried out within the sacred edifice.

SYNCOPATION, in grammar, the contraction of a word by the omission of one or more letters or syllables from the middle. In music, suspension or alteration of rhythm by driving the accent to that part of a bar not usually accented. Syncopation may be completed in a bar, or it may be carried by sequence through several bars, or it may be so that more than one bar is involved in the syncopation. Syncopated counterpoint is the fourth species of counterpoint.

SYNCOPE, the name given to that form of death characterized by failure and cessation of the heart's action as its primary feature. The term is also applied to the state of fainting produced by a diminution or interruption of the action of the heart, and of respiration, accompanied with a suspension of the action of the brain and a temporary loss of sensation, volition, and other faculties. Fatal syncope is usually the result of some nervous "shock," resulting from some severe lesion of organs, or from a want of blood, or an altered and abnormal state of blood pressure. Ordinary syncope is caused chiefly by weakness, mental emotion, etc. The fainting patient should be placed on a couch and the head kept low; while great caution must be observed in stimulating the action of the heart.

SYNCRETISM, or **SYNCRATISM,** attempt to establish a comprehensive scheme intended to unite or blend harmoniously one with the other principles or parties in irreconcilable antagonism. Specifically, in philosophy, the blending of the tenets of different schools into a universal system. A party among the Platonists, at the revival of letters, to which belonged Ammonius, Picadella Mirandola, Bessarion, and other eminent men, have received the name of Syncretists.

SYNCRETISTIC CONTROVERSY, the name given to a series of controversies which arose in the Lutheran Church in the 17th century, from the subject of the discussion—the promotion of fellowship and union between the Protestant churches of Germany. These controversies may be grouped into three periods:

(1) From the Colloquy of Thorn (1645), in which it was sought to force a new confession of faith on the Lutheran Church, to the death of Calixtus (1656). George Calixtus was a Professor of Theology at Helmstadt, and his scheme of union was founded on the following propositions: (a) That the fundamental principles of Christianity were maintained pure in the Roman, Lutheran and Reformed Churches. (b) That the tenets and opinions which had been constantly received by the ancient doctors during the first five centuries were to be considered as of equal truth and authority with the express declarations and doctrines of Scripture. (c) That the Churches which received these points, and held the additional tenets of the particular churches as non-essential, should come into peaceful relations, and thus pave the way for a future union. After the death of Calixtus, there was a period of peace for about five years.

(2) From 1661-1669. The conflict was renewed by the wish of the Landgrave of Hesse-Cassel, William VI., to secure a religious constitution broad enough to embrace both the Lutheran and Reformed Churches. The second attempt to have the Consensus adopted, which implicitly condemned Calixtus and his adherents as non-Lutheran and heretical, was a failure, and the subject was abandoned for a time.

(3) In 1675, Calovius, Professor of Divinity at Wittenberg, reopened the controversy, and compelled the University of Jena to disavow all sympathy with the views of Calixtus. The death of Calovius in 1686 put an end to the dispute.

SYNDIC, an officer of government invested with varying powers in different places; a kind of magistrate intrusted with the management of the affairs of a city or community; also one chosen to transact business for others. In the University of Cambridge, England, syndics are chosen from the senate to transact special business, as the regulation of fees, the operations of the Clarendon Press, etc. Mayors of Italian towns are so called.

SYNDICALISM, broadly speaking, is a branch of the general socialist movement which has as its object a complete reorganization of society on a co-operative basis. The first concept of Socialism was that the workers should own and control the industries through a pro-

I—16

letarian state, or government, now known as State Socialism. This idea, well illustrated in Bellamy's famous book, "Looking Backward," presented unpleasant features to many persons otherwise inclined in favor of radicalism and even revolutionary methods. As a reaction against this ideal, which suggested the dangers of a gigantic state bureaucracy, the Syndicalist movement appeared, first in France, in the early 80s of last century, taking its name from the French syndicates, or trade unions. Its chief exponent has been the French writer Georges Sorel, who again has been strongly inspired by the philosophy of Henri Bergson.

The central idea of the Syndicalist is that, not the state, or government, but the workers, organized in bodies following the lines of the big industries, shall assume control of production. It is an enlargement of the old concept of the Early English Christian Socialists, who were obsessed of the idea that the workers should own their own tools, regardless of the fact that under a moderate system of production industrial organization is much more complicated than it was in the days of handicrafts, when hand tools were employed in the manufacture of commodities. Concretely illustrated, the idea is that the railway workers should own and control the railroads, the coal miners should own and control the coal mines, the postal employees should have charge of the post-office service, and the teachers should be in control of the schools. The fallacy in the idea is the assumption that the purpose of industry is to supply jobs to the workers, whereas the only legitimate aim of industry is to supply the necessities and pleasures of life to society at large, to the people, as consumers.

Outside of France, Syndicalism has made comparatively little headway, and even there it went completely to pieces as a movement during the World War, because of the split among the members as to whether they should support the government against Germany or not. Syndicalism holds that government may be almost completely eliminated.

In the United States the Syndicalist idea is represented by the Industrial Workers of the World, an organization which has had relatively little influence. In England, Syndicalism has left its mark in the idea of shop committees, giving the workers a voice in management of the undertakings for which they work.

British guild socialism would place control of the industries in the hands of the labor organizations, but would vest the government with the power of veto, as representing the general body of consumers.

SYNDICATES, originally, councils or bodies of syndics; afterward, associations of persons formed with a view of promoting some particular enterprise, discharging some trust, or the like; now, combinations of capitalists for the purpose of controlling production and raising prices; popularly known in the United States as "trusts."

SYNECDOCHE, in rhetoric, a figure in which the whole is put for a part, or a part for the whole, as the species for the genus, the genus for the species, etc., as, a fleet of 10 sail.

SYNERGISM, in Church history, a type of Semipelagianism which came into prominence in Germany in the 16th century, and which had for its chief representatives Erasmus and Melanchthon. Luther taught that the Fall rendered man incapable of all good, and powerless to contribute anything to his conversion. Synergism, on the other hand, taught that "God does not deal with man as with a block, but draws him so that his will co-operates"; and this view was adopted in the Leipsic Interim (1548). A controversy arose on the subject, caused by the publication of a book in 1558 on the "Liberty of the Will," by Pfeffinger, a professor at Leipsic, which university together with Wittenberg represented the Synergist view. Flacius, Professor of Theology at Jena, took the strictly Lutheran view which was adopted in the Formula of Concord.

SYNESIUS, Bishop of Ptolemais in the Libyan Pentapolis, acted also the various parts of soldier, diplomatist, orator, philosopher and poet; born in Cyrene about A. D. 375. The contemporary of Augustine, he took pride in tracing his descent from the Heraclidæ, the royal family of Sparta, who first colonized the Pentapolis, and inherited wealth and estates in the interior. He studied at Alexandria under Hypatia, whose influence over him proved a dominant and lifelong one. He also studied in Athens, and returned to the Pentapolis, resolved to spend his life in study and in the pursuits of a country gentleman. About 399 he was appointed by his fellow citizens a delegate from Cyrene to bring certain grievances before the Emperor Arcadius at Constantinople. He remained in that city for three years. In his speech "On Kingship" Synesius warns Arcadius sternly of the perilous nature of the times and points out the duties of a good king. During his stay

at Constantinople a revolution took place, Arcadius was driven out by the Scythian general Gainas, and Aurelian, leader of the national party, banished.

While waiting for an audience Synesius wrote a curious book entitled "Concerning Providence." In the form of an allegory he describes the contest between Aurelian and Gainas, under the veil of a conflict between Osiris and Typhon, who personify Good and Evil; and deals with the question why God permits evil and delays so long to interfere. In a few weeks Gainas fell, Synesius attained the end of his mission, and sailed for home. The next eight years were a time of peace and happiness for Synesius; "books and the chase," he writes, "make up my life." About 403 he married a wife belonging to Alexandria. During these years he wrote his treatise "Concerning Dreams," a half-burlesque essay, "The Praise of Baldness" (he was bald himself), his "Dion, or on Self-discipline," the second part of his book on "Providence," several "Hymns," and a great many letters. This peaceful period was interrupted by war. The Libyan nomads made raids on the fertile Pentapolis; there were no soldiers at Cyrene, but Synesius raised a troop of volunteers. The helpless governor Cerealius fled; Cyrene was besieged and Synesius had to organize and direct the defense of the city.

In 411 the people of Ptolemais, fearing the appointment of a corrupt governor, fixed on Synesius as their bishop. Synesius was most unwilling; but at last he yielded and was consecrated at Alexandria in 410. On his return to Ptolemais, finding the new governor Androncus playing the tyrant he boldly excommunicated him, and secured his recall.

The Ausurians invaded the country, and Synesius had again to spend his nights on the ramparts and direct the defense. His only surviving child died. Synesius was broken with troubles, and both his philosophy and his religion appeared to fail him in his need. The city was relieved, but he fell ill and about 413 he died. His last letter was written to Hypatia who retained all his old affection and reverence.

SYNGE, JOHN MILLINGTON, an Irish dramatist and poet, born in 1871. He was educated at Trinity College, Dublin, in 1892, and for 10 years following studied languages and music in Germany, France, and Italy. He finally settled in Paris and devoted himself to the study of French literature. During the period of his stay on the continent, he annually made trips to the **Arran**

Islands, in order to write of the primitive life of its inhabitants. In 1893 he settled in Ireland and devoted himself to writing for the Abbey Theater, in Dublin. He was considered to be the most talented of the dramatists of the Irish Literary Revival. His plays, which were produced in the United States with considerable success, included "The Shadow of the Glen" (1903); "Riders to the Sea" (1904); "The Will of the Saints" (1905); "The Tinker's Wedding" (1909); and "Playboy of the Western World" (1907). He died in 1909.

SYNOD, a meeting or assembly of ecclesiastical persons for mutual deliberation on matters of difficulty or of general interest affecting the churches over which they rule and designed for their guidance. In the early Church there were four kinds of synod. First, an Œcumenical, that is, a General or Universal Synod, commonly called a General Council; second, a National Synod, attended by the clergy of one nation only; third, a Provincial Synod, attended by the clergy of a province; and fourth a Diocesan Synod, attended by the clergy of a single diocese. Among the Presbyterians a synod is a court of review consisting of ministers and elders of contiguous congregations. The supreme council of the church is the General Assembly.

SYNOD OF DORT, a synod held at Dort, Dordt, or Dordrecht, in Southern Holland, in 1618 and 1619, to discuss the views of Arminius, which it condemned.

SYNODICAL PERIOD, in astronomy, the period between two successive conjunctions or oppositions of two heavenly bodies. A synodical month is a lunation, being the period from one full moon to the next full moon or from new moon to next new moon. It is 29 days, 12 hours, 44 minutes, 2.37 seconds.

SYNONYMS, or words having the same signification, strictly speaking, do not exist in any language; and in the popular use of the term synonyms are words sufficiently alike in general signification to be liable to be confounded, but yet so different in special definition as to require to be distinguished. The opposite of synonyms are antonyms.

SYNOPTIC GOSPELS, the first three Gospels, Matthew, Mark, and Luke, which regard events from the same point of view, and present close resemblances to each other. Four hypotheses have been framed to account for the correspondences: (1) That the Synoptic Gospels were derived from a common written source or sources. (2) That the earlier Gospels were consulted in the composition of the later ones. (3) That all the three were derived from oral tradition. (4) That they were all derived partly from oral tradition, but that the second was also copied from the first, and the third from the first and second. The Synoptic Gospels treat of the humanity rather than the divinity of Jesus, though not in any way ignoring the latter.

SYNOVIA and **SYNOVIAL MEMBRANE.** Synovia is a glutinous fluid secreted by synovial membranes. Synovial membranes are simply modifications of serous membranes, and they invest the tendons and sinews that play over joints and otherwise assist articulations. The synovial fluid is therefore merely a secretion from a serous membrane. It appears, however, to differ in certain particulars from ordinary serous secretions, and is more dense and viscid than ordinary serum. Hence synovia is often popularly named "joint oil." In synovia an abundance of albumen is present. Synovial membranes also invest the bursæ, or little pads which underlie such tendons as those of the extensor muscles of the thigh, in which tendon the patella or knee cap is developed. Synovial membranes are liable to inflammation, known as synovitis.

SYNTAX, that part of grammar which treats of the manner of connecting words into regular sentences, constructing sentences by the due arrangement of words or members in their mutual relations according to established usage. In every language there is some fundamental principle which pervades and regulates its whole construction, though it may occasionally admit of particular variations. In some languages the principle of juxtaposition prevails, and little diversity of arrangement is possible, as is the case in English, in which inflections are so few. The relations of the subject, the action, and the object are indicated by their respective positions. In other languages—inflected languages like Latin or Greek—these relations are indicated by the changes in the forms of the words, and the modes of arrangement are various. Still, in the structure and disposition of sentences and parts of sentences the logical relations of the thoughts must regulate the construction, even where it appears to be most arbitrary.

SYNTHESIS, in chemistry, the building up of more or less complex bodies by the direct union of their elements, or of groups of elements. Thus, water can be produced synthetically by the union of two atoms of hydrogen with one atom of oxygen. In logic, the method by composition, in opposition to the method of resolution or analysis. In synthesis, we reason from axioms, definitions, and already known principles, till we arrive at a desired conclusion. Of this nature are most of the processes of geometrical reasoning. In synthesis, we ascend from particular cases to general ones; in analysis, we descend from general cases to particulars.

SYPHILIS, according to Dr. Farr, a disease belonging to the enthetic order of zymotic diseases. It may be defined as a specific disease produced by the contagion of the same disease in another person, and characterized (1) in its primary form by the appearance on the part inoculated of one of two different kinds of a sore or chancre, and (2) in its secondary or constitutional form by various eruptions on the skin, by sore throat, affections of the eye, the glands, the bones, and almost every other tissue of the body. The contagion may be conveyed by direct inoculation during sexual intercourse; accidentally, in other forms of personal contact, and purposely, by inoculation for medical or experimental purposes. There are two kinds of chancre, and in one the disease is merely local, never affecting the constitution; but in the other the constitution is affected, and the disease may break out after long intervals of health, and may be transmitted from one generation to another through the blood of the mother or the semen of the father.

The local form of syphilis appears in three principal varieties—(1) The common soft chancre unaccompanied by bubo; or suppurative syphilitic inflammation. Three or four days after inoculation the sore appears and begins to suppurate at once. The sore has a punched-out appearance, its edges are slightly undermined, and its base is thickened by inflammation of the parts underneath it. The sore heals with no remaining induration in three or four weeks. (2) The sore with suppurating bubo; or ulcerative syphilitic inflammation. The sore is ragged and has a worm-eaten appearance, the glands and the absorbents are affected, and specific abscesses may form in the course of the latter, but no part of the body beyond the gland is affected. In these two forms the treatments consist in keeping the part clean, applying a mercurial wash, poulticing the bubo and opening it as soon as it suppurates. (3) Sloughing and gangrenous sores. In this form the sore may slough and be-

come gangrenous as soon as it is formed, or a previously formed sore may take on a sloughing action. The absorbents are not affected, nor is it followed by secondary symptoms, but the sloughing may proceed with great rapidity, and may prove fatal from exhaustion or hæmorrhage.

The constitutional form of syphilis is distinguished by the appearance on the part affected of a sore called the hard or Hunterian chancre, and by a chronic engorgement of the lymphatic glands forming a bunch of hard knobs under the skin. The sore may appear in from three to five days after exposure to contagion, and it may vary as the disease is derived from a primary or a secondary sore.

The general opinion of the medical profession is that the constitutional form of syphilis can be treated efficiently by mercury only, and that the treatment should commence as soon as the disease declares itself. Much has been written in praise of salvarsan "606," as a cure in the earlier stages, but it has been demonstrated that relapses were more frequent than when mercury was used.

The secondary symptoms of constitutional syphilis do not usually appear till after the primary sore has healed; but the period is quite uncertain, though, in the majority of cases, it is under half a year. The secondary symptoms are sometimes ushered in by what is termed the syphilitic fever; but they are generally in the throat, the sore throat being due to an eruption on the mucous membrane of the mouth or fauces; or in the skin, being usually either roseola, lichen, acne, mucous tubercle, pityriasis, psoriasis or lepra. These eruptions are distinguished from other eruptions which are not specific, partly by their coppery color and by their circular or horseshoe form, and by their tendency to disappear at the center and spread from their edges. The eye and the larynx are affected in the latter secondary stage. Periostitis or nodes are also seen at this period. Other secondary symptoms are the development of mucous tubercles—flat, raised, oval patches, generally situated at or near the junction of the skin and mucous membrane and yielding a contagious secretion, probably a fertile source of inoculation. The mucous tubercle generally disappears rapidly under the local application of calomel. Syphilitic vegetations and condylomata are also contagious.

In the treatment of secondary syphilis it is now generally admitted that the administration of mercury is necessary for the complete eradication of the syphilitic diathesis.

The tertiary stage of syphilis is distinguished from the secondary by the occurrence of an interval of health of longer or shorter duration—days, months or even years—and is characterized by a reproductive process. The affections of the skin are of the suppurative and ulcerative type, such as rupia and ecthyma. The tissues of the bones rapidly soften, and become carious or necrosed. The glands are also deeply affected, even the great secreting and blood glands—the liver, spleen, thyroid, etc. The nervous system is also affected by tertiary deposits in the nerve-structures or their membranes leading to irritation or paralysis. The treatment of the tertiary stage must be conducted on the same principles as that of the secondary stage.

Infantile or congenital syphilis is transmitted to the fœtus in utero, either through the blood of the mother or the semen of the father, or both, and is a form of secondary syphilis, differing from it only in that the primary sore has occurred on the body of the parent instead of the infant itself. The disease is characterized by a persistent coryza, a reddish or copper eruption—roseola or lichen—especially on the genitals and on the palms and soles. Crescentic patches of mucous tubercle are common on the interior of the mouth, the lips, and anus, and there is a peculiar yellowish complexion.

SYRA, the most important, though not the largest of that group of islands in the Ægean Sea known as the Cyclades. It is about 10 miles long by 5 broad, has an area of 32 square miles and is bare, rocky and not very fertile. Its prosperity is of quite modern growth. During the War of Independence Syra remained neutral, hence many fugitives of commercial enterprise flocked thither from Chios and other parts of Greece. Pop. of island about 27,000. The capital Syra or Hermoupolis, is situated on a bay on the E. side of the island. Pop. about 20,000. It rises in terraces from the shore, is well built, and is the seat of government for the Cyclades, and the seat of a Roman Catholic bishop. This port is the chief commercial entrepôt of the Ægean. Exports tobacco, emery stone, valona and sponges.

SYRACUSE, anciently a famous city of Sicily; on the S. E. coast of the island; 80 miles S. S. W. of Messina; was founded by Corinthian settlers about 733 B. C. The colonists seem to have occupied the little isle of Ortygia, which stretches S. E. from the shore. The settlement rapidly rose to prosperity, and toward the end of the 6th century B. C. sent out colonies of its own. Little is known of the early political state of Syracuse; but about 485 the ruling families, probably descendants of the original colonists, were expelled by the lower classes of citizens. Gelon, despot of Gela, restored the exiles and at the same time made himself master of Syracuse. He increased both the population and the power of his new state, and won the highest prestige by a great victory over the Carthaginians at Himera. In his time Achradina, a triangular tableland N. of Ortygia and on the adjoining mainland, was built on. This ultimately became the most extensive and populous quarter; it contained the Agora, a temple of Zeus Olympius, the Prytaneum, with a splendid statue of Sappho and fine monuments to Timoleon and the elder Dionysius, etc. At a later date, and possibly thus early, there were two other quarters in the city—Tyche, occupying a plateau to the W. of Achradina; and Neapolis (New City), stretching along the S. slopes of the plateau, and overlooking the marshes of Anapus and the Great Harbor, a spacious and well-sheltered bay to the S. W. of Ortygia. This islet, however, contained the citadel, which overlooked the docks in the Lesser Harbor on the N.

Hiero, the successor of Gelon, was celebrated throughout the Greek world as a patron of the fine arts and of men of genius, as Æschylus, Pindar, etc. In 467 B. C. the democracy again got the upper hand — Thrasybulus, Hiero's brother and successor, a "tyrant" of the baser sort, being expelled; and for 60 years a free and democratic government was enjoyed, under which Syracuse flourished more than it had ever done. During this period occurred the great struggle with Athens (415-414 B. C.), and the celebrated siege by the Athenian armament, a contest in which the Sicilian city came off victorious. Nine years later Dionysius restored the "tyranny" of Gelon, and during a reign of nearly 40 years greatly increased the strength and importance of the city. It was he who constructed the docks in the Greater and Lesser Harbors, and surrounded the city with fortifications. His fierce war with Carthage (397 B. C.) raised the renown of Syracuse still higher. The reigns of the younger Dionysius and of Dion, the friend of Plato, were unsettled; but after the restoration of public liberty by Timoleon (343 B. C.) a brief season of tranquillity ensued. In 317 B. C., 20 years after the death of the noble Timoleon, Agathocles, a rude soldier of fortune, once more restored the despotic form of government, which continued with scarcely an interruption through the reign (50 years) of the enlightened Hiero II., the friend and ally of Rome, down to the conquest of the city by the Romans after a siege of two years, in which Archimedes perished (212 B. C.). This event was occasioned during the Hannibalic war by Hieronymus, a rash and vain young man, abandoning the prudent policy of his grandfather, Hiero, breaking the alliance with Rome, and joining his and their foes, the Carthaginians. Under the Romans Syracuse slowly declined, though with its handsome public buildings and its artistic and intellectual culture, it always continued to be the first city of Sicily. It was captured, pillaged, and burned by the Saracens in A. D. 878, and after that sank into complete decay.

The modern city, Siracusa, is confined to the original limits, Ortygia, which, however, is no longer an island, but a peninsula. The streets, which are defended by walls and a citadel, are, with few exceptions, narrow and dirty. Syracuse has a cathedral (the ancient temple of Minerva), a museum of classical antiquities, a public library with some curious MSS., numerous churches, monasteries, and nunneries, the ancient fountain of Arethusa (its waters mingled with sea water since the earthquake of 1170), and remains of ancient Greek and Roman temples, aqueducts, the citadel Euryalus, a theater, an amphitheater, and quarries, besides ancient Christian catacombs. The people manufacture chemicals and pottery, and trade in fruits, olive oil, wine (exports), wheat, timber, and petroleum. Pop. about 27,-500.

SYRACUSE, a city of New York, the county seat of Onondaga co. It is on the Onondaga Lake, the New York State Barge Canal, the Delaware, Lackawanna and Western, and the Ontario and Western railroads. There are six interurban lines radiating from the city which give excellent passenger and freight service. The present city includes the former villages of Danford, Geddes, Syracuse, and Salina. Syracuse is an important industrial city. In the manufacture of tool steel and automobile gears, it ranks first. Other industries include the manufacture of agricultural implements, china ware, shoes, typewriters, automobiles, etc. There are within the city limits over 1,000 manufacturing establishments, with a total of over 40,000 employees. Syracuse is situated in the midst of the beautiful lake region of New York State and is surrounded by attractive and diversified scenery. There

are over 60 parks within the city limits, including children's playgrounds, public golf courts, tennis courts, swimming pools, skating rinks, etc. The total area of the park system is 361 acres. The city has an excellent system of public schools, of which there are 40, attended by about 25,000 pupils, with over 700 teachers. In addition there are 25 parochial and private schools. It is the seat of Syracuse University. Among the notable public buildings are the Central High School, a court house, a public library, a city hall, and a museum of fine arts. Its institutions include the State Asylum for Feeble Minded Children, the House of Providence Orphan Asylum, county orphan asylum, an old ladies' home, and five hospitals. The city has over 100 churches and over 50 theaters. There are about 125 miles of paved streets and over 200 miles of sewers. There were in 1920 three national banks, three trust companies, and two savings banks, with total deposits of $132,909,273. The assessed value in 1920 was $181,770,758, and the tax rate $23.18 per thousand. On the State Fair Grounds one of the greatest annual fairs in the United States is held annually. Syracuse was settled about 1805, and became important after the completion of the Erie Canal. It was incorporated as a village in 1825. In the earlier years it had great importance from the deposits of salt and the State purchased a large tract of land containing salt springs, part of which was afterward sold to individuals. The manufacture of salt from the brine pumped out of these springs was formerly the main industry of the city, but is now of minor importance. Pop. (1910) 137,229; (1920) 171,-647.

SYRACUSE UNIVERSITY, a co-educational institution in Syracuse, N. Y.; founded in 1871 under the auspices of the Methodist Episcopal Church; reported at the close of 1919: Professors and instructors, 368; students, 4,033; volumes in the library, 103,222; Chancellor, Rev. J. R. Day, LL.D.

SYRIA, Asiatic Turkey, bounded by Euphrates and Syrian Desert on the east, by the Mediterranean on the west, by Alma Dagh mountains, north, and Egypt, south. Area, 114,530. Pop. before the World War about 3,500,000. The physical conformation of Syria is throughout simple and uniform. A range of mountains, split in the N. into two parallel chains—Libanus and Anti-Libanus—fronts the Mediterranean, ranging in height from 6,000 feet in the N. up to 10,000 feet in the central parts, but falling again in the S. to 3,500 feet. Behind these mountains lies a table-land, that gradually falls away E. to the desert. The prevailing winds being W., the slopes of the mountains next the Mediterranean and the valleys ensconced among them, together with the immediate seaboard, get a tolerably plentiful supply of moisture during the rainy half of the year (October to May); snow even falls on the highest summits of the mountain ranges. The climate on the plateau is generally dry, and in certain localities hot. The valley of the Jordan is remarkably hot. The soil is in many parts possessed of good fertility, and in ancient times, when irrigation was more extensively practiced, yielded a much greater return than it does at the present time. Damascus is noted for its gardens and orchards.

Hauran produces an excellent grade of wheat. Northern Syria is the home of the olive. The vine grows in nearly all parts of the country. Fruit (oranges, figs, etc.) is cultivated on the coast plains. Sheep and goats are the most important of the domestic animals. The principal exports are silk, cereals, wool, olive oil, lemons and oranges, soap, sponges, sesame, licorice, cottons, and tobacco. Manchester (England) goods constitute the chief item in the imports. Besides these there are woolens, rice, copper and iron, sacking, timber, and hides. The chief port is Beyrout, and to it must be added Acre, Caiffa (Haifa), Tyre, and Tripoli. The pop. is estimated at 3,675,000. The bulk of the inhabitants are Mohammedans, but do not all profess the orthodox Sunnite creed: there are the Druses, certain sects of Shiites, and others. The Christians make up about one-fifth of the total. The principal ethnic elements are descendants of the ancient Syrians and Arabs, these last both settled and nomad; there are Jews and Turks also.

The earliest historical records that treat of Syria are those that relate the histories of the Hittites, the Phœnicians, and the Hebrews. The first named were for several centuries supreme in northern Syria, and at times stretched their authority S. as far as the hills of southern Palestine. Yet they had most formidable rivals on both sides of them in Assyria and Egypt, from both of which they acquired skill in manufacturing, industry and the arts and manners of life. The other two peoples mentioned occupied the most prominent place in southern Syria. Southern, as well as most of northern Syria was conquered in the 8th century B. C. by the kings of Assyria; the Jewish kingdoms experienced the same fate at the hands of the Babylonian kings in the 7th and 6th centuries. As previous

to the 9th century B. C. Syria had been the battle ground of the Egyptian and Hittite armies, so after that period it was, as a province of Assyria (Babylonia), involved in the struggle between that great empire and Egypt. Toward the end of the 6th century B. C. Syria fell under the dominion of the Persian empire; and two centuries later it was conquered by Alexander of Macedon. When his empire broke to pieces the Seleucidæ made Antioch the capital of their empire of Syria. From the Seleucidæ it passed, through the hands of Tigranes of Armenia, to the Romans, for whom it was won by Pompey in 64 B. C. Under these new masters the country flourished and became celebrated for its thriving industries, its commercial prosperity, and its architectural magnificence (see BAALBEK: NABATÆANS: PALMYRA). On the division of the Roman world Syria became part of the Byzantine empire, and of it remained a province till its conquest by the Mohammedan Arabs in 636.

The first severe blow it suffered thereafter came from the Mongols in 1260; in 1516 it passed from the Egyptians to the Ottoman Turks. Conquered from Turkey in 1918, Syria, north of Palestine, was placed under French rule as a mandated territory. The northern boundary was fixed by treaty with Turkey in 1921. An uprising of Druses and of other nationalists drove the French from part of the country in 1925; the insurgents attacked Damascus, and the garrison during the action subjected the part of the city in hostile hands to a bombardment for 48 hours (Oct. 18-20). The French High Commissioner, Sarrail, was thereupon replaced by Jouvenel, under whom in 1926 the Druses were driven back to their own territory, but continued guerrilla warfare into 1927. Under the administration of High Commissioner Ponsot the French authorities in 1928 called for the election of a Constituent Assembly of delegates to be elected by the natives and to determine the form of government that Syria should adopt. This assembly was convoked in June, 1928, but failed to make progress, owing to differences between the Nationalist or independence party and their opponents, and was temporarily suspended to provide time for the upgrowth of harmony. The chief question before this body was that as to the adoption of a monarchic or of a democratic government.

SYRIAC, a dialect of Aramaic, and thus one of the Semitic family of languages. It was a vernacular dialect in Syria in the early centuries of our era, but ceased to be spoken generally about the 10th century. A very corrupt form still spoken by a few scattered tribes, and principally by the Nestorians of Kurdistan and Persia. Syriac literature had its rise in the 1st century of our era. At first it was chiefly connected with theological and ecclesiastical subjects, Biblical translations and commentaries, hymns, martyrologies, liturgies, etc., but in course of time it embraced history, philosophy, grammar, medicine, and the natural sciences. The oldest work in the language still extant is the incomplete translation of the Bible called the Peshito. In addition to the Peshito Version, which was recognized as the authorized version by all the various sects of the Syrian Church, there is one made in the beginning of the 7th century by Paul of Tela, a Monophysite; this is based on the Hexaplar Greek Text, that is, the Septuagint with the corrections of Origen, and is of very great value for the criticism of the Septuagint, supplying as far as a version can the lost work of Origen. Another version, the Syro-Philoxenian, translated by Polycarp under the auspices of Philoxenus, Bishop of Hierapolis (488-518), and revised by Thomas of Heraclea in 616, is very inferior to the Peshito. Among the MSS. brought by him from Syria in 1842 Dr. Cureton discovered an imperfect copy of the Gospels, differing widely from the common text, and which he supposed to belong to the 5th century. The most learned representative of the orthodox Syrian Church is undoubtedly Ephræm Syrus, who flourished in the 4th century. The Syriac literature, like the language, was superseded by that of the Arabians. The latest Syriac classic writer is Bar-Hebræus, Bishop of Maraga, who died in 1286. The greater part of this literature has been lost, but much valuable material still remains unedited.

SYRIAN CATHOLICS, a term which should properly include all Christians using a Syriac liturgy, but confined by ecclesiastical writers to converts from the Jacobite or Monophysite Church in Syria.

SYRIAN JACOBITES, the members of the church that once pervaded Syria. The great body of them now reside near Mosul and Mardi, in Mesopotamia, others are in or near Aleppo. A large colony, now however much reduced by conversions to Roman Catholicism, exists in Malabar and Travancore in India. They call themselves Jacobites, nominally from the patriarch Jacob, really from Jacob Bardæus, Bishop of Orfa (Edessa), who died in 558, and who was successful in reuniting the Monophysites. They use the Syriac language in their liturgy.

SYRIAN PROTESTANT COLLEGE, an institution for higher education, founded at Beirut, Syria, in 1863, and opened in 1866. It includes a college of medicine, a college of commerce, a nurses' training school, and a teachers' training course. During the World War the institution was used as a hospital. Before the war it had an enrollment of about 1,000 students. President, Rev. Howard S. Bliss.

SYRIAN RITE, CHURCH OF THE, a portion of the Oriental church which had its seat in Syria, and comprised those Christians who used the Syriac liturgy of St. James. This liturgy was originally composed for the patriarchate of Antioch, which included the churches of Palestine and Mesopotamia, and according to tradition by the Apostle James. There is no Greek MS. of it in existence of an earlier date than the 10th century, but the Syriac liturgy of the same name almost exactly answers the description given of it in various writers. After the Mohammedan conquest (638) the orthodox Syrians were drawn into closer association with the patriarchate of Constantinople, and then adopted the liturgy of St. Chrysostom, which was used by the rest of the Eastern Church. By the orthodox Greek Church of Jerusalem, then, the liturgy of St. James is used in the Greek form only once a year, namely, on the Festival of St. James. But it is still used in its Syriac form by the Monophysites or Jacobites, as well as by the Maronites. The latter renounced the Monothelite heresy (1182), and entered into communion with the Church of Rome, to which they were formally reunited at the Council of Florence (1445); but notwithstanding this union they have always retained a kind of independence, and especially their own liturgical customs. A Maronite college was founded at Rome, 1584, for the education of their clergy, where worship is conducted according to the Syrian rite.

SYRINGA, in botany, the lilac; a genus of Fraxineæ. Deciduous scrubs, with simple leaves, and very fragrant flowers in terminal thyrsoid panicles. Known species about six. Natives apparently of southeastern Europe and central and eastern Asia. Syringa vulgarts is the lilac. S. persica is a smaller species or variety, with pinnatifid leaves, supposed to have come from Persia. There are three common varieties of it in nurseries, the white, the cut-leaved, and the sage-leaved Persian lilac. S. josikæa, a Transylvanian shrub, has scentless flowers. The leaves of S. emodi, a large Himalayan shrub, are eaten by goats.

SYRINGE, a small portable hydraulic instrument of the pump kind, used to draw in a quantity of water or other liquid and eject the same with force. In its simplest form it consists of a small cylindrical tube having an air-tight piston fitted with a rod and handle at the upper end. The lower end terminates in a small tapering tube. This being immersed in the fluid, the piston is drawn back and the liquid is forced into the cylinder by atmospheric pressure. On pushing the piston back again to the lower end of the cylinder the liquid is ejected in a jet. The syringe is used by surgeons, etc., for washing wounds, injecting liquids into animal bodies and similar purposes. Larger forms are used for watering plants, trees, etc.

SYRINX, a nymph beloved by Pan, and, according to the legends, turned into reeds when flying from him. The god is said to have constructed his pipe from those reeds.

SYRPHIDÆ, in entomology, a family of *Diptera*, tribe *Athericera* (having the antennæ of three joints, the apical one with a bristle). The *Syrphidæ* has the antennal bristle finely feathered; the eyes are large, meeting in the males; the ocelli three; proboscis generally short, the terminal lobes fleshy, inclosing three bristles; palpi small, with one joint; abdomen flattened, with five segments; tarsi with two pulvilli. Smooth or hairy insects often seen hovering almost without motion over the flowers of Composites or other plants. The species are numerous, and the larvæ diverse in habits. Most of the latter feed on the roots or bulbs of plants, or live in decaying wood, mud, or sewers, or in the water, or as parasites in the nests of wasps and bumble bees. Genera more than forty, and among them *Syrphus, Volucella, Eristalis, Helophilus*, etc.

SYRPHUS, the typical genus of *Syrphidæ*. The larvæ feed on aphides. One of the most common is S. *pyrastri*, a blue-black fly, with whitish or yellowish transverse bands on the abdomen, black thighs, and yellowish legs. It is sometimes mistaken for a wasp. The larvæ is a footless grub, living on plants infested by aphides.

SYRRHAPTES, in ornithology, a genus of *Pteroclidæ*, with two species. Bill small, conical; nostrils concealed by feathers, tarsi hirsute; toes short, concrete, hirsute above, hallux absent; the two middle tail feathers and first two quills of wings produced into pointed se-

taceous filaments. They normally range from Tartary, Tibet, and Mongolia, to the country round Peking, and occasionally visit eastern Europe; but in 1863 great numbers of them appeared in Europe and reached W. to the shore of the Atlantic.

SYRTIS, the ancient name of two gulfs of the Mediterranean Sea, on the N. coast of Africa. The Syrtis Major, now called the Gulf of Sidra, lies between Tripoli and the tableland of Barca, and forms the most S. part of the Mediterranean. The Syrtis Minor, now called the Gulf of Cabes, lies between Tunis and Tripoli. The shores of both are inhospitable and abound in quicksands.

SYRUP, in popular language, the uncrystallizable fluid finally separated from crystallized sugar in the process of refining. By sugar manufacturers the term syrup is applied to all strong saccharine solutions which contain sugar in a condition capable of being crystallized out, the ultimate uncrystallizable fluid being distinguished as molasses or treacle. In chemistry, a saturated or nearly saturated solution of sugar in water. In pharmacy, syrups; a preparation in which sugar forms an important ingredient and gives a peculiar consistence to the liquid. Its general use is to disguise the flavor of drugs; but in some cases, as in that of the iron iodide, the sugar preserves the active ingredient from undergoing chemical change. About 17 syrups are used in pharmacy. Among them are S. *aurantii,* S. *limonis,* S. *papaveris,* S. *sennæ,* etc.

SYRUS, PUBLIUS, or **PUBLILIUS**, a Roman writer of mimes who flourished about 43 B. C., and was most probably a Syrian slave brought to Rome in early youth, educated and freed by some indulgent master. After Laberius he reigned supreme on the stage, and his mimes, being as full of shrewd epigrammatic wit as broad humor, did not perish with him. About 200 apothegms are still extant under the title "Witticisms of Publius Syrus."

SYZRAN, a town of central Russia, a few miles from the right bank of the Volga and 90 miles S. of Simbirsk. Laid out in 1685, it has tanneries and noted market gardens, and a large trade in grain, timber, salt, and manufactured goods. Pop. about 48,000.

SYZYGIUM, or **SIZYGIUM** (named from the way in which the branches and leaves are united by pairs), a genus of

Myrteæ; trees or shrubs with the flowers in cymes or corymbs, the calyx with its limb undivided; the petals, four or five. *S. jambolanum,* called also *Eugenia jambolana,* is a moderate-sized tree, wild or cultivated all over India. The bark is astringent and is used, as are the leaves, in dysentery. The decoction of the bark constitutes a wash for the teeth; its fresh juice with goat's milk, a medicine for the diarrhœa of children. A vinegar prepared from the unripe fruit is a stomachic; carminative; and diuretic. The fruit is astringent, but is eaten by the natives who in time of famine consume also the kernels. The leaves of *S. terebinthaceum* are used in Madagascar to impart an aroma to baths. *S. guineensis* is worshiped in Gambia and the fruit is eaten.

SZABADKA, a town of Hungary; on the plain that lies between the Danube and the Theiss; 106 miles S. by E. of Budapest. It is the center of a rich agricultural district, with a trade in cattle, skins, wool, corn, fruit, tobacco, etc. Pop. about 94,000.

SZABOITE after Prof. J. Szabó, of Budapest), a mineral occurring in minute crystals in cavities of an andesite, Transylvania; crystallization, triclinic; hardness, 6-7; sp. gr., 3.505; luster, vitreous; color, hair brown to hyacinth-red. Composition: Essentially a silicate of iron and lime. Now shown to be related to hypersthene.

SZAIBELYITE (after Herr Szaibelyi), a mineral occurring in small nodules bristling with acicular crystals in a limestone at Werksthal, Hungary; color, externally white, internally yellow. Essentially a hydrousborate of magnesia.

SZALAY, LASZLO, a Hungarian historian; born in Buda, Hungary, April 18, 1813. He succeeded Kossuth as editor-in-chief of the "Pesti Hirlap" in 1844. Among his works are "History of Hungary" (6 vols. 1850-1863); "Nicolas Eszterúzy" (1862-1866); and "The Book of Statesmen," a collection of political biographies. He died in Salzburg July 17, 1864.

SZARVAS, a town of Hungary, on the Körös river, 80 miles S. E. of Budapest. A famous breed of horses is cultivated here. Pop. about 28,000. Mostly Slovaks, who, however, speak Hungarian.

SZASKAITE (after Szaska, Hungary, where found), an earthy variety of cal-

amine (zinc carbonate), stated to contain cadmium.

SZATMAR-NEMET, a town of Hungary; on both sides of the Szamos; 68 miles E. N. E. of Debreczin; formed in 1715 by the union of Szatmar and Nemet. It manufactures earthenware, canvas, and slibowiz, a kind of brandy distilled from plums. Pop. about 35,000.

SZECHUAN, the largest province of China, in the W.; has Tibet on the N. W. and Yunnan on the S. W.; the remaining boundaries are conterminous with various provinces of China; area 218,500 square miles; pop. about 68,725,-000. It is traversed and watered by the Yang-tsze-Kiang and its affluents, is hilly throughout, mountainous in the W., and rich in natural products, including coal, iron, and other minerals. Opium, silk, salt, sugar, medicines, tobacco, hides, musk, rhubarb, and white wax (produced by an insect) are exported to the annual value of $25,000,000; and European cottons and woolens are imported to the value of $15,000,000 annually. The capital is Ching-tu, the chief commercial town Chung-king, on the Great River, which was opened to foreign trade at the end of 1889. Ichang was thrown open in 1877.

SZEGEDIN, a town of Hungary; at the confluence of the Maros with the Theiss, 118 miles S. E. of Budapest. This town was almost completely destroyed by a terrible flood in March, 1879, out of 6,566 houses, 6,235 being overwhelmed. Since then it has been rebuilt, and now possesses very handsome public buildings, including a town hall, postoffice, law courts, theater, barracks, etc., and is protected against inundations by a double ring of embankments. The Theiss is spanned by a couple of railway bridges and a fine suspension bridge (1,940 feet long), designed by Eiffel. Szegedin manufactures soap, spirits, matches, soda, tobacco, coarse cloth, etc., and carries on an extensive river trade in wood, corn, and wool. A specialty of the place is paprika, a kind of capsicum. From 1526 to 1686 it was occupied by the Turks. Close by Haynau defeated the Hungarians Aug. 3, 1849. Pop. about 118,000.

SZE-MA, or **SUMA KWANG,** one of the most eminent statesmen and writers of China, and as a historian second only to Sze-ma Ts'ien; born in 1009. He is renowned as the author of "The Comprehensive Mirror of History," in 294 books, the labor of 19 years. It covers a period from the beginning of the 4th century B. C. to A. D. 960. He died in 1086.

T

T, t, the 20th letter and the 16th consonant of the English alphabet, is a sharp mute consonant, and closely allied to d, both being dentals. It is formed by pressing the tip of the tongue closely against the root of the upper teeth, and differs from d only in being non-vocal, while d is uttered with the voice. T followed by h in the same syllable has two distinct sounds; the one surd or breathed, as in think, thank, thought; the other sonant, or vocal, as in this, that, though. Ti before ia, ie, io, and unaccented, usually passes into sh, as in nation, portion, partial, which are pronounced nashon, porshon, parshal. When s or x precedes ti, the t retains its proper sound, as in question; before u it is often softened into ch (as in church), as also is such words as mixture, posture, etc. In accordance with Grimm's law, t in English (as also in Dutch, Icelandic, Gothic, etc.) is represented in Latin, Greek and Sanskrit by d, and in German by s or z. Thus English tooth (for tonth) = Latin *dens* (genitive *dentis*), Greek *odous* (genitive *odontos*), Sanskrit *dant*, German *zahn*; English heart = Latin *cor* (genitive *cordis*), Greek *kardia*, Sanskrit *kridaya*, German *herza*; English eat = Latin *edo*, Greek *edō*, Sanskrit *ad*, Old High German *ëzan*, German *essen*. If the t is preceded by s, this rule does not apply, as in English stand = Latin *sto*, Greek *histēmi*, German *stehen*. Th in English, etc., is represented in Latin, Greek and Sanskrit by t, and in German by d; thus, English thou = Latin *tu*, Greek *tu*, Sanskrit *tvam*, German *du*; English three = Latin *tres*, Greek *treis*, Sanskrit *tri*, Old High German *dri*, German *drei*. In a few instances t in English represents an l in Latin, as in tear (s.) = Latin *lacrima*. T has crept in (1) after s, as in behest, amongst, against, amidst, whilst, betwixt; (2) in tyrant = Old French *tiran*, Latin *tyrannus*; parchment = Old French *parchemin*; cormorant = French *cormoran*; ancient = French *ancien*; pheasant = Old French *phaisan*. Th represents an original d in hither, thither, whether, faith = Old French *feid*, Latin *fides*. T is often doubled in the middle of words, occasionally at the end, as in butt, mitt. T is often used to denote things of the shape of the capital letter; T-bandage, T-square, etc.

T, as a symbol, in Roman mediæval numerals, denoted 160, and with a stroke over it, 160,000; in formulas, t = time.

Marked with a t; a thief, an expression equivalent to the *trim literarum homo* of Plautus. The English phrase derives its force from the fact that thieves were formerly branded in the hand with the letter T.

To a t: Exactly; to a nicety; with the utmost exactness; as, that fits me to a t.

TABANIDÆ, the horsefly family, comprising large dipterous insects, which in the female have a proboscis inclosing six sharp lancets, and in the male four; the eyes are very large and cover nearly the whole head; thorax oblong, and abdomen triangular. They are notorious for their attacks on horses and cattle, piercing them, sucking their blood, and causing them great pain.

TABASCO, a gulf state of Mexico, named from a river running into Campeche Bay; area 10,374 square miles; pop. about 194,000. The surface is generally flat except in the S. part, and the soil is fertile, producing a fine variety of coffee. Capital, San Juan Bautista.

TABERNACLE, a slightly constructed temporary building or habitation; a tent, a pavilion. Figuratively, a temple; a place of worship; a sacred place; specifically, the sacred tent built by Moses and maintained as the central place of worship for Israel till Solomon built the temple. Also, the human frame as the temporary abode of the soul.

In Jewish antiquities, more fully denominated Tabernacle of the Congregation, and Tabernacle of Witness, a tent constructed by direction of Moses, under divine authority, to be a local habitation for Jehovah while His people moved from place to place in the wilderness—a temple being obviously unsuitable to the period of the wandering. To obtain materials for the construction of this sacred tent free-will offerings were solicited, and the Jews, in response, brought gold, silver, "brass" (copper), cloths, rams' skins dyed red, oil, spices, precious stones, etc. (Exod. xxv: 1-9; xxxvi: 1-5). Bezaleel and Aholiab, men divinely endowed with genius for the purpose, were the actual builders (xxxv: 30-34; xxxvi: 4). The tabernacle was 30 cubits (i. e., 45 feet) long, 10 cubits (15 feet) wide, and 10 cubits (15 feet) high. The material was shittim (acacia) wood. The interior was divided into an outer room 20 cubits long by 10 broad, called the Holy Place, or Sanctuary, and an inner apartment 10 cubits (15 feet) long by 10 broad, named the Most Holy Place, or Holy of Holies. At the E. or open end, were five pillars of acacia wood, overlaid with gold, supporting a veil or curtain of fine linen with needlework of blue, crimson, and scarlet. Each pillar stood on a brass socket and was furnished with golden hooks. Between the Holy Place and the Place Most Holy was another veil or curtain of the same material as the first, but the pillars supporting it rested on silver sockets. Four different kinds of curtains or coverings supplied the place of a roof.

Within the Holy Place on the N. side, was the golden table with the shew-bread on it, and on the S. side the golden candle-stick, and the golden altar of incense. In the Holy of Holies were the Ark of the Covenant and the mercy-seat (Exod. xxvi: 1-37; xxxvi: 1-38; Heb. ix: 1-5). Around the tabernacle was the court of the tabernacle, 100 cubits (150 feet) long, by 50 cubits (75 feet) broad, surrounded by 60 pillars, each five cubits (7½ feet) high, with silver capitals and hooks, and brass sockets. The four pillars in the E. side supported a veil or curtain constituting the gate of the court. The brazen altar and the laver were in the courtyard. Around the latter were the tents of the Levites, and beyond these those of the other tribes, three on each side of the tabernacle. Only the priests entered the Holy Place. This they did twice daily, in the morning to extinguish the lights, in the evening to light them anew. None but the high priest could enter the Holy of Holies, and he only once a year, on the great day of Atonement. The Gershonites, the Merarites, and the Kohathites took charge of the tabernacle and its furniture when these

were removed from place to place. The tabernacle was first set up by Moses on the first day of the second year after the Israelites had left Egypt. After they had reached Canaan it was located at Shiloh (I Sam. iv: 3-22). In Saul's time it was at Nob (I Sam. xxi: 1, and Mark ii: 26). When Solomon became king it was at Gibeon (I Kings iii: 4). Afterward Solomon laid it up in the Temple, of which in all its leading features it had been the model (I Kings viii: 4, II Chron. v: 5). See TEMPLE.

In the Roman Church a receptacle for the consecrated Host for benediction and the ciborium containing the smaller Hosts which the laity receive. In its present form—a small structure of marble, metal, or wood, placed in the center of the E. side of the altar—the tabernacle dates from the 16th century. Its original form was that of a dove; about the middle of the 14th century it was sometimes placed in an aumbry above the altar. A lamp constantly burns before the tabernacle, which is kept locked, the key never passing out of the charge of the clergy. The name tabernacle is also given to (1) a niche for an image, (2) a reliquary, (3) the aumbry near the high altar when used to contain the reserved sacrament, and (4) the abbot's stall in choir.

As a nautical term, an elevated socket for a boat's mast, or a projecting post to which a mast may be hinged when it is fitted for lowering to pass beneath bridges.

TABERNACLES, FEAST OF, in Jewish antiquities, *Chhag hassukkoth*, one of the three leading Jewish feasts, on the recurrence of which all the males were required to present themselves at Jerusalem. During this feast the people dwelt on their housetops or elsewhere in booths made of the branches of trees, in commemoration of their tent life in the wilderness. Called also the Feast of Ingathering, because it was a feast of thanksgiving for the completion of the harvest and the vintage. It lasted for 8 days, from the 15th to the 23d of Tisri, corresponding to October. The first and eighth days were holy convocations.

TABLATURE, in anatomy, a division or parting of the skull into two tables. In art, a painting on a wall or ceiling. In music, a general name for all the signs and characters used in music; those who were well acquainted with these signs were said to sing by tablature.

Also, a peculiar system of notation employed for instruments of the lute class, for viols, and certain wind instruments. The earliest systems of notation, like the music of Asiatic nations to this day, were different sorts of tablature. That which may be called the modern tablature was invented not earlier than the 16th century. In England tablature was employed for all stringed instruments, the number of lines employed being regulated by the number of strings the instrument possessed. Tablature for wind instruments was expressed by dots on a stave of 6, 7, or 8 lines, according to the number of holes in the instrument, the number of dots signifying the number of holes to be stopped by the fingers. Organ tablature was a system of writing the notes without the stave by means of letters. Thus, the several octaves were called great, little, 1 and 2-line octaves, according to the style of letter employed to indicate them. The name has also been applied to figured bass.

TABLE-LAND, in physical geography, a plateau; a plain existing at some considerable elevation above the sea. Volcanic rocks often make such table-lands, as in central India; so do limestones. Or a sea bed or a lake bed, or a great stretch of country, may be upheaved. The chief table-lands are in the Old World, extensive, low-lying plains rather than table-lands characterizing the New. One occupies about half the surface of Asia, being 5,500 miles from E. to W., and from 700 to 2,000 miles from N. to S. In Europe there are table-lands in parts of Switzerland, France, Spain, and Bavaria. African table-lands exist in Morocco, Abyssinia, the region of the Victoria Nyanza, etc. In North America there are plateaux along the Pacific, Labrador, etc., and in South America, in Brazil and the adjacent countries.

TABLE MOUNTAIN, a mountain in Pickens co., S. C.; height, 4,000 feet. Also a mountain of South Africa, S. of Table Bay, its highest point being right over Cape Town. It is about 3,500 feet high and level on the top. It joins the Devil's Mount on the E., and the Sugar Loaf or Lion's Head on the W.

TABOO, or **TABU**, from *tapu*, a Polynesian word, denoting an institution which was formerly in existence throughout Polynesia and New Zealand, but has now to a large extent disappeared before the spread of Christianity and civilization. The word signifies something set apart, either as consecrated or accursed, the idea of prohibition being conveyed in either case, whence the English word, tabooed, *i. e.*, forbidden. For example, in New Zealand the person of a chief was strictly taboo, and hence might not be touched; while the volcano Tongariro

was taboo as being the supposed residence of demons, and even to look on it was at one time forbidden. The system seems to have had its origin in a superstitious dread of the unseen powers of evil, and the chiefs, quick to perceive the power which it would place in their hands, appear to have adopted it from remote times as a political engine, the priests readily co-operating with them for the sake of the influence which it gave them likewise. The chiefs were themselves amenable to the regulations of the taboo, but in a much less degree than their subjects, and possessed a wide discretionary power, which was limited only by precedent, of declaring objects to be taboo. The taboo could be removed only by the person by whom it was imposed, or by one greatly his superior in rank, but courtesy usually kept the latter power in abeyance. So potent was the superstition, that Scherzer states that among the Maoris even hostile tribes were in the habit of leaving unharmed all persons and things protected by the taboo. The idols, temples, persons, and names of the king were taboo (or sacred), and almost everything offered in sacrifice was taboo to the use of the gods. The prohibitions and requisitions of the taboo were strictly enforced, and every breach of them punished with death, unless the delinquent had powerful friends who were either priests or chiefs.

TABOR, a small shallow drum used to accompany the pipe and beaten by the fingers. The old English tabor was hung round the neck, and beaten with a stick held in the right hand, while the left hand was occupied in fingering a pipe. The pipe and tabor were the ordinary accompaniment of the morris dance.

TABOR, MOUNT, a solitary elevation on the N. E. border of the plain of Esdrælon. It is remarkable for the symmetry of its form, which resembles a truncated cone, from certain points appearing almost hemispherical. The top measures about half a mile across, and is about 1,300 feet above the level of the plain. Now crowned by a confused mass of broken walls, towers, etc., it has a history extending from the invasion of Canaan by the Israelites (Josh. xix: 12, 22; Judg. iv.) down to the present time. It is not mentioned in the New Testament.

TABORITES, a section of Calixtines, who received their name from a great encampment organized by them on a mountain near Prague in 1419, for the purpose of receiving the Communion in both kinds. On the same spot they founded the city of Tabor, and, assembling an insurrectionary force, marched on Prague under the lead of Ziska (July 30, 1419), and committed great atrocities under the pretence of avenging insults offered to the Calixtine custom of communicating under both kinds. On the death of King Wenceslaus (Aug. 16, 1419) they began to destroy churches and monasteries, to persecute the clergy, and to appropriate church property on the ground that Christ was shortly to appear and establish His personal reign among them. They were eventually conquered and dispersed in 1453 by George Podiebrada (afterward King of Bohemia).

TABRIZ, or TABREEZ (the ancient Tauris), a city of Persia, capital of the province of Azerbijan, on the Aigi, 36 miles above its entrance into Lake Urumia. It lies at the inner extremity of an amphitheater, about 4,000 feet above sea-level, with hills on three sides, and an extensive plain on the fourth. It is surrounded with a wall of sun-dried brick, with bastions, and entered by 7 or 8 gates. There are numerous mosques, bazaars, baths, and caravanserais. The citadel, originally a mosque, and 600 years old, was converted by Abbas Mirza into an arsenal. The blue mosque dates from the 15th century. Tabriz has manufactures of silks, cottons, carpets, leather and leather goods, etc. It is the great emporium for the trade of Persia on the W., and has an extensive commerce. Exports and imports annually over $100,000,000. In the World War it was occupied first by the Turks and then by the Russians. It has frequently suffered from earthquakes. Pop. about 200,000.

TABULATA, in zoölogy, a group of Madreporaria Perforata. Tabulate corals, having the visceral chamber divided into stories by tabulæ, and with the septa rudimentary or absent. The group is of doubtful stability, some recent genera, as *Millepora, Heliopora,* etc., having been removed from it, and various fossil genera *Favosites, Chætetes, Syringopora, Halysites,* etc., being placed in it provisionally. Families, *Favositidæ, Chætetidæ, Thecidæ, and Halysitidæ.* From the Silurian onward.

TACAHOUT, or TACOUT, the name of small, irregularly-rounded, tuberculate galls produced by a species of cynips on the twigs of a tamarix (probably *T. articulata*) in Algeria and Morocco. They contain a large quantity of gallic acid, and are used in photographic prep-

arations. The above-named species of tamarix, as also *T. gallica* and *T. dioica,* supply a similar gall in India—the mahi of the Punjab and sakun of Sindh; used as a mordant in dyeing and in tanning.

TACAMAHAC, the name given to a bitter balsamic resin, the produce of several kinds of trees belonging to Mexico and the West Indies, the East Indies, South America, and North America. The balsam poplar or tacamahac is one of these.

TACCA, a tropical genus of monocotyledonous herbs, some of whose species have a large tuberous root; *e. g.,* the *T. pinnatifida,* a plant of the shores of the South Sea Islands. Its tubers, which resemble new potatoes, contain a large proportion of starch, and this being separated by rasping and maceration, is largely used as an article of food. It bears the name of South Sea, Tahiti, and Fiji arrowroot, and Otaheiti salep, and is also esteemed as a medicinal agent in dysentery and diarrhœa.

TACHINIDÆ, a family of *Brachelytra,* now merged in *Staphylinidæ;* small, excessively agile beetles of convex tapering form, with pentamerous tarsi. They frequent flowers.

TACITUS, the historian, is known to us chiefly from autobiographical touches in his own writings and from allusions in Pliny's letters. His full name is matter of doubt—CORNELIUS TACITUS being his nomen and cognomen; but whether

TACITUS

his prænomen was PUBLIUS or GAIUS can only be conjectured. Born perhaps in Rome (less probably in Terni), under the Emperor Claudius between A. D. 52 and 54, it is inferred that his family was respectable from his education, his profession, and his marriage. He studied rhetoric in Rome under M. Aper, Julius Secundus, and, likely enough, Quintilian; rose to eminence as a pleader at the Roman bar; and in 77 or 78 married the daughter of Agricola, the conqueror and governor of Britain. He filled a quæstorship under Vespasian, who made him prætor and member of a priestly college. In 89 A. D. he left Rome, probably for Germany, where, doubtless as governor, he must have acquired his knowledge of the features, natural and social, of the country; and he did not return till 93, when he found his father-in-law had recently died. He was an eye-witness of Domitian's reign of terror. We have his own testimony as to the blessed change wrought by the accession of Nerva and Trajan.

Under the former emperor he became consul suffectus, succeeding the great and good Virginius Rufus, on whom he delivered in the Senate a splendid *oraison funèbre*. In A. D. 99, conjointly with the younger Pliny, he prosecuted the political malefactor, Marius Priscus, which won him the thanks of the Senate. After this we lose sight of him, but may assume it as certain that he saw the close of Trajan's reign, if not the opening of Hadrian's. The high reputation he enjoyed in life is attested by the eulogistic mention of him repeatedly made in Pliny's letters, and in the 3d century the Emperor Tacitus, proud to claim kinship with him, built in his honor a tomb which was still standing in the later decades of the 16th century, when it was destroyed by Pope Pius V. The same emperor also issued an edict by which the works of his namesake were to be copied out 10 times yearly for presentation to as many public libraries.

In spite of this multiplication of copies we possess but a moiety of what he wrote. His earliest work, the "Dialogues de Oratoribus," treats, in conversational form, of the decline of eloquence following on the change for the worse in the education of the Roman youth under the empire. It has reached us entire. Next comes the "Agricola," the literary character of which it is difficult to define. Quite a library has accumulated on the question whether it is a "laudatio funebris," or an "apologia" written to shield the memory of Agricola, or a historical panegyric framed for political ends. But it will always be read for its elevation of style, its dramatic force, its invective and its pathos. For English readers its interest is unique. The third work, the "Germania," or "De situ, moribus, et populis Germaniæ," is a monograph of the greatest value on the ethnography of Germany. Fourth in order are the

"Historiæ," or the history of the empire from the accession of Galba in A. D. 69 to the assassination of Domitian in 97. of the 12 books originally composing it only the first 4 and a fragment of the 5th are extant.

Tacitus is at his strongest in this narrative. His material was drawn from contemporary experience; and though the imperial archives were closed to him, he had at command the personal information open to a man of his position, to say nothing of correspondence (as of Pliny). He yearned for the return of an aristocratic oligarchy—the Rome of the Scipios and the Fabii. He is, on this account, a partisan, but is able to justify the most trenchant contrasts between the greatness of Republican and the deterioration of Imperial Rome, which latter he contrasts disadvantageously with the freedom and simplicity of even barbarian Germany. To his peculiar satirical gift which often makes him a "Juvenal in prose" he gives free rein from time to time. He had no appreciation of the higher qualities of the Jews, and his attitude to the growth of Christianity is that of a prejudiced, if cultured Roman.

The qualities conspicuous in the "Historiæ" are maintained in his last work, the so-called "Annales," a history of the Julian line from Tiberius to Nero (A. D. 14 to 68). Of their 16 books only 8 have come down to us entire, 4 are fragmentary, and the others lost. In these, as in all his writings, his avowed aim was a noble one, to perpetuate virtue, and to stigmatize baseness in word or deed. Among the more obvious defects which lower his value as a historian are his weakness in geography and his carelessness as to strategic details.

TACTITUS, MARCUS CLAUDIUS, a Roman emperor; born in Terni, Umbria, about A. D. 200; was elected on the death of Aurelian, A. D. 275, when in his 75th year. He was descended from the great historian, and had been twice consul; but he reigned only six months, in which short space he displayed singular wisdom, vigor, and moderation. He was assassinated at Tyana, in Cappadocia, in 276.

TACK, in nautical language: (1) The lower forward corner of a fore-and-aft sail. (2) The lower, weather corner of a course, or lower square sail. (3) The rope by which the forward lower corner of a course or staysail is drawn forward and confined. (4) A rope by which the lower corner of a studding-sail is drawn outward and held to the boom. (5) Hence, the course of a ship in regard to the position of her sails; as, the starboard tack or port tack; the former when she is close-hauled with the wind on her starboard, the latter when close-hauled with the wind on her port side. To tack is to change the course of a ship by shifting the tacks and position of the sails from one side to the other; to alter the course of a ship through the shifting of the tacks and sails. Tacking is an operation by which, when a ship is proceeding in a course making any acute angle with the direction of the wind on one of her bows, her head is turned toward the wind, so that she may sail in a course making nearly the same angle on the other bow. This is effected by means of the rudder and sails. A small sharp-pointed nail.

TACOMA, a city and county-seat of Pierce co., Wash.; on the Puyallup river and Commencement Bay; at the S. extremity of Puget Sound, and on the Northern Pacific railroad; 25 miles N. E. of Olympia. It is built on rising ground which reaches an altitude of 300 feet above the river. Here are Puget Sound University (M. E.), Pacific University (Luth.), Annie Wright Seminary (P. E.), Tacoma Academy, the Academy of the Visitation (R. C.), Masonic and public libraries, Ferry Museum of Art, city hall, court house, St. Joseph's, Fannie Paddock and County Hospitals, Seaman's Friend Society, Children's Home, etc. Near the city is the State Asylum for the Insane. The city contains waterworks, street railroad and electric light plants, a number of parks, numerous churches, National and State banks, and several daily, weekly, and monthly newspapers. There are many thriving industries. The city has an extensive jobbing and wholesale trade, and large interests in coal, lumber, grain, and flour. Tacoma was settled in 1868, made the terminus of the Northern Pacific railroad in 1873, selected for the county-seat in 1880, and by the union of Old Tacoma and New Tacoma became a city in 1883. Pop. (1910) 83,743; (1920) 96,965.

TACONIC MOUNTAINS, a range of mountains connecting the Green mountains of western Massachusetts with the highlands of the Hudson. The Taconic system, in geology, was named from the characteristic strata of this range, a metamorphic rock, now known to be of the Lower Silurian system.

TACTICS, MILITARY, the science which enables one of two opposing bodies of troops to be stronger than the other at every crisis of an engagement. STRATEGY (*q. v.*), which has precisely the same objects, merges into tactics as the

enemy comes within striking distance, and the latter science is therefore sometimes defined as the strategy of the battlefield. Modern writers use different terms for the various branches of tactical science; grand tactics and manœuvre tactics, for the marshaling of large masses (30,000 and upward) of men on the battlefield; minor tactics, for the conduct of small bodies, such as advanced and rear guards, outposts, patrols, etc.; fighting tactics, for the combat whatever the numbers of the force; fire tactics, for the best use of guns and rifles, the massing of their fire, and the selection of the target; and the special tactics of cavalry, artillery, or infantry, combined tactics, siege tactics, and mining tactics.

In Judges xx. we read of a favorite and dangerous manœuvre, the Israelites feigning to retreat before the Benjamites, so as to draw them on till their flanks and rear were exposed to the "liers in wait." Hannibal at Cannæ and William the Conqueror at Hastings were among the many successful imitators of these tactics. Others, like the Duke of Burgundy in 1476 at Granson, lost their armies through attempting it with unsteady troops. Frederick the Great owed his victory at Mollwitz to the rapid fire and steady discipline of his men, and the former was chiefly due to the introduction of iron ramrods. His later battles give us good examples of manœuvre tactics. At Leuthen he engaged the Austrians, immovable in their chosen position, with his advanced guard, while his main body under cover of some hills and foggy weather marched in open column of companies round their flank, wheeled into line and rolled up their army. At Waterloo Napoleon showed an example of combined tactics on a large scale. By cavalry charges he obliged the British infantry to form squares, which then became targets for his massed artillery. When under stress of this "hard pounding" they opened out into line, a renewed charge of cavalry obliged them to take the denser formation again. At Gravelotte the German armies (some 240,000 men) showed an unparalleled instance of grand tactics by marching to their positions across country in seven large masses, each consisting of one complete army corps. Fighting tactics must depend chiefly on the arms in use. The mail-clad horsemen of the 15th century never succeeded in defeating the solid phalanx of pikemen opposed to them by the Swiss Confederation till the employment of artillery prevented the latter retaining such a massive formation. The English archer, protected in front by palisades and on the flanks by spearmen, destroyed the chivalry of France at

Cressy and Poitiers, but at Bannockburn was ridden down by the Scotch cavalry, because the flanking spearmen had been omitted. Gustavus Adolphus, by employing cartridges, enabled his infantry to fire more quickly than his opponent and so to form on a wider front. The invention of the bayonet, doing away with the necessity for pikemen to protect the musketeers, still further increased the firepower of infantry. The British two-deep line overthrew, by its enveloping fire and charge, the column formation of the French in the Peninsula and of the Russians at the Alma, though in this battle its defects are shown in the confusion caused by moving to the attack over broken ground. In the battles of the Franco-German War of 1870-1871 it was found impossible to advance against the fire of modern breech-loading rifles except by rushes of comparatively thin lines of skirmishers, constantly re-enforced by supports and reserves in rear. The magazine rifle and smokeless powder of to-day still further complicate the problem, presented to the assailant, of how to get to within 500 yards of the enemy without being destroyed.

In warfare against savages large numbers, fanatical courage, and rapid movements have to be met by special tactics. Thus the crescent-shaped enveloping attack of the Zulus and the rapid attacks of the Sudanese Arabs were received by the British in the impenetrable-square formation or by forming "laagers"; opposing a material obstacle to the onslaught of an enemy unprovided with artillery. Thus, too, the Indians of the Western plains were met by a style of fighting resembling their own, and which the American troops also found serviceable in encounters with the Filipinos.

Cavalry tactics, apart from the exceptional use of dismounted men, are much the same as in the time of the Byzantine empire. Cavalry fight by shock action only, and the power of man and horse has not altered. Artillery tactics consist in massing the fire of every gun as soon as possible on important points, and overwhelming the enemy's guns and infantry with projectiles at ranges of 2 miles or more, not shunning closer quarters if the necessity arises.

Siege tactics belong to fortification, but follow the same general course as other combined tactics. Thus in defense the guns oblige early deployment and co-operate with the infantry in repelling the advance, while in the attack they destroy the material defenses and keep down the fire of the place so as to enable the assault to be delivered. During the siege mining tactics will be made use of on both sides. The functions of the

I—17

cavalry are first to try to drive off the enemy's cavalry and effect reconnoissances on both sides; then on the attacker's side to complete the investment, and afterward secure the besieging troops against surprise. For instruction of tactics in the World War, see WAR, and related articles.

TACTICS, NAVAL, the art of manoeuvring ships and fleets for the purpose of battle. Naval strategy, on the other hand, is the science of combining and employing fleets or single ships in order to carry out defined operations at sea or against an enemy's coast, for obtaining command of the sea or certain portions of it. Though fleets had existed and battles at sea been fought from the earliest periods, it was not till toward the close of the 16th century, in the reign of Queen Elizabeth, that naval war began to assume definite form. War at sea at this time does not appear to have been carried on on any definite plan, and consisted principally, if we except the attempt of the Great Armada, of raids on the enemy's commerce and coast towns. Perhaps the first organized attempt to obtain command of the sea as a distinct aim of the operations carried on are to be found in the three wars between the Dutch and English of 1652, 1665, and 1672. Both parties made desperate attempts to destroy the trade of the other, but in the second war Holland, considering the command of the sea the more important object, temporarily gave up her commerce, Dutch merchant ships being forbidden to put to sea. The net result of the three wars was to leave the honors pretty evenly divided between the two combatants. Several efforts were made by the French, between 1690 and their crushing defeat at Trafalgar, to obtain the command of the sea in order to effect the invasion of England. The first of these attempts, affording one of the best examples of the value of a thorough grasp of strategical principles, was foiled by the Earl of Torrington. An experienced seaman and profound strategist, the earl was forced against his better judgment, by direct orders from the queen and council, to attack the vastly superior forces under Tourville, and accordingly he gave battle (June 30, 1690) off Beachy Head. He was defeated, but skillfully drew off and fell back under the shelter of the Gunfleet Shoals at the mouth of the Thames. Here, though "beaten, inferior, and shut up behind sandbanks," yet from the strategic position it now held this fleet still remained such a "power in observation" as to paralyze the action of the victorious and superior force; and the French admiral, after some ineffective attempts at landing, returned to Brest. During the Napoleonic wars, the English fleets having more or less complete command of the sea, the strategy of the commanders seems to have resolved itself into blockade of the enemy where possible, or a close observation of his movements with a view to prevent any junction of his scattered forces; and if he ventured to put to sea, into efforts to bring him to action as soon as possible.

The line of battle consisted in a fleet of ships being extended in a straight line either ahead or abreast one ship of another, keeping as close together as weather permitted, so that at all times every ship should be ready to sustain and relieve one another. It was directed that each ship in the line should keep within half a cable's length (about 50 fathoms) of one another. It was introduced into the English navy by Sir William Penn. At the battle of the Nile (1798) Nelson doubled on the van of the French line and attacked it on both sides, while the other ships of the line, the whole fleet being at anchor, could afford no assistance; but at Trafalgar, where his brilliant career terminated with a decisive victory, he broke the enemy's line in two places, bearing down on it in two columns.

Steam may be said to have revolutionized naval strategy and tactics; whereas the best-laid schemes were often frustrated by foul winds and gales, now the great steam power of battleships and cruisers renders them independent of wind and to a great extent of bad weather. As a set-off, however, to this, the coal endurance of ships and the replenishing of their supplies of fuel become important factors in deciding on their movements. The value of a blockade was demonstrated in the World War (1914-1918). The British were unable to effect a complete blockade of Germany, but it was effective to the extent of so reducing the amount of supplies entering the Empire that the German masses suffered great hardships, and thus were sown the seeds of the subsequent revolution.

The first real test of the ironclad as developed by modern naval science was given during the war between Japan and China, in 1894. Each of the contending nations had navies, which, while small, included a couple of the best battleships and cruisers of the world. The only fault with such a test is that the Japanese were so much superior to the Chinese in the skill with which they manœuvred their ships that the battle cannot be taken as a wholly fair test. One thing sufficiently established was the effectiveness of the modern vessel of war and its death-dealing power. The battle lasted six hours. The Japanese lost no ships, while they destroyed seven of the Chinese fleet of 10 and put others to flight. The Japanese loss was 200 men and that of the Chinese six times as great. See CHINA: JAPAN.

The Japanese-Chinese War, however, did not settle many of the great problems of marine warfare, and really proved nothing but the superior skill and prowess of the Mikado's subjects. Since then have been fought the most remarkable naval battles in history. See MANILA BAY: SANTIAGO DE CUBA: JUTLAND BANK, BATTLE OF: FALKLAND ISLANDS, BATTLE OF: SUBMARINES: NAVY: NAVY, UNITED STATES.

TADPOLE, the larva of the anurous amphibia, sometimes so far extended as to include larvæ of the urodela, which undergo a much less complete metamorphosis. At first the young have no respiratory organs or limbs. They are all head and tail with simple entire gills which soon disappear, to be followed by

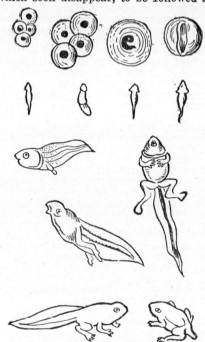

METAMORPHOSIS OF A FROG

others of more complicated structure, situated within the cavity of the body as in fishes. After a certain length of time the hind legs begin to appear, the head becomes more developed, and the body assumes a more compact form. Still later the forelegs are found to exist fully formed beneath the skin and ready ultimately to burst forth. The tadpole at first seems to derive its subsistence from the fluid absorbed within its body and on the surface, but soon begins to seek its food amidst softened or decomposing vegetable matter. From that period the tadpole begins to assume more and more the appearance of a frog. Toes appear on its hind legs, the tail very rapidly disappears by absorption, and finally the forelegs become fully developed and the metamorphosis of the tadpole is completed.

TAEL, a money of account in China, the value of which varies considerably according to locality and the rate of exchange. It is worth from 0.724 to 0.806 to the American dollar. The tael is also a definite weight, equal to 1.208 ounces troy.

TAFFRAIL, originally the upper flat part of a ship's stern, so called because frequently ornamented with carving or pictures; now a transverse rail which constitutes the uppermost member of a ship's stern.

TAFT, WILLIAM HOWARD, 27th President of the United States; born in Cincinnati, O., Sept. 15, 1857; was graduated at Yale College in 1878, at the Law School of Cincinnati College in 1880; and was admitted to the bar in 1881. He was collector of internal revenue in the 1st District of Ohio in 1882; practiced law in 1883-1887; was judge of the Superior Court of Ohio in 1887-1890; subsequently judge of the U. S. Circuit Court; and Professor of Law at the University of Cincinnati in 1896-1900. He became (1900) president of the Philippine Commission, and on June 5, 1901, the first civil governor of the Philippine Islands. In August, 1903, President Roosevelt nominated Governor Taft to be secretary of war to succeed Secretary Root, when the latter should resign in January, 1904. The selection was frankly made in order that he might continue to direct the administration of Philippine affairs, although residing in the United States. This constituted a recognition of his work in the Philippines.

He at once took up a new line of service for the department—the pacification of trouble in various lands where the United States had the right to attempt adjustments. From 1900 to 1907 he traveled fully 100,000 miles and spent 360 days at sea in his diplomatic missionary work. In 1906 he was sent to Cuba by

the President to reconcile the warring factions, and for a short time served as provisional governor of that island. Early in 1907 he visited Cuba, Porto

WILLIAM HOWARD TAFT

Rico, and Panama, investigating disturbed conditions; then going to the Philippine Islands, where, on October 16, he opened the first Philippine Assembly at Manila. Continuing his journey around the world, Mr. Taft was welcomed in several Asiatic and European capitals with most cordial expressions of friendship for America. His visit to Japan especially helped to cement the bonds of amity and good-will, which short-sighted agitators, particularly on the Pacific Coast, had been striving for several years to strain, if not to break. In St. Petersburg Mr. Taft delivered a noteworthy address on the subject of universal peace. On his return he was frequently mentioned as the "logical" candidate of the Republicans for the Presidency in 1908, and was indorsed for that office by many Republican State conventions. He was nominated in June, and, resigning the war portfolio at once, made a vigorous personal campaign. In November he was elected, receiving a popular vote of 7,811,143, as against 6,-328,601 for William J. Bryan, the Democratic candidate. The vote in the Electoral College was: Taft, 321; Bryan, 162. In January, 1909, at the request of President Roosevelt, Mr. Taft made a visit of inspection to the Panama Canal with a party of engineers. Immediately after his inauguration, March 4, 1909, he convened Congress in extraordinary session to revise the tariff, and the bill enacted became effective on August 5. In 1910 he secured from a none-too-friendly Congress the enactment of much beneficial legislation, including laws authorizing postal-savings banks, requiring publicity for campaign funds, creating a Bureau of Mines and Mining, and several important measures dealing with railroads, conservation, reclamation, the tariff, and the Lighthouse Service. During 1911 he was particularly active in his efforts to secure arbitration treaties with England and trade reciprocity with Canada. The treaty with England was duly signed by Secretary Knox and Ambasador Bryce on August 3. The reciprocity treaty with Canada failed of ratification by the Canadian Parliament. Among other beneficial acts passed during his administration were the establishment of the Parcels Post, Children's Bureau (1912); direct election of senators. In 1912 he ran a second time for President, though opposed by Roosevelt, who ran on a third ticket, and both were defeated by Woodrow Wilson. Later he filled the chair of Kent Professor of Law at Yale; participated in movements to establish international peace. During the World War he was joint chairman of the National Labor Conference Board. He took oath as Chief Justice of the United States Supreme Court on July 11, 1921.

TAGAL, a small seaport town on the island of Java, capital of the province of the same name. The Dutch province is in northern Java, and has a population of 819,509.

TAGANROG, a seaport of Russia, in the province of the Don Cossacks, on the N. shore of the Sea of Azov; 15 miles W. of the mouth of the Don. Pop. 71,000.

TAGORE, RABINDRANATH, a Hindu poet, born in 1860. He was long well known in India and gained a worldwide reputation in 1913, when he was awarded the Nobel prize for literature. At the age of 17 he went to Europe, where he completed his education. On returning to India, he became known as an educator and philosopher and was the founder of a university in Bengal. His poetry, which was contributed to magazines in India, possessed extraordinary merit and charm. Much of it was trans-

lated into English. He made many visits in the United States, where he lectured and read from his books. He was made a knight by King George, in 1915. His best known writings are: "The Crescent Moon" (1913); "The Gar-

TAGORE, RABINDRANATH

dener" (1913); "Poems"; "The Realization of Life" (1913); "Essays"; "Chitray" (1913); "The King of the Dark Chamber" (1914); "Short Stories" (1915); "Fruit-gathering: Nationalism" (1917); "Lover's Gift" (1918).

TAGUS, the largest river in the Spanish peninsula, which, rising between the Sierra de Albarracin and the Sierra Molina, on the frontier of Aragon and New Castile, flows S.; then, holding a W. course through the rest of Spain, enters Portugal, when, pursuing a more S. direction, it passes Lisbon, forming the magnificent harbor of that city, and, spreading into a splendid estuary, finally mingles its waters with the Atlantic after a course of 625 miles. Above the capital of Portugal it has a width of 5 miles; at the city a breadth of 2 miles; but, in consequence of its deep banks and impetuous current, the Tagus is but little adapted to mercantile purposes and is at present only navigable to Abrantes.

TAHITI, an island giving name to a small archipelago, also called SOCIETY ISLANDS (*q. v.*), in the middle of the Pacific; a French possession. Pop. about

12,000. Chief town Papeete, pop. 3,600. Exports consist of copra, mother-of-pearl, vanilla, cocoanuts, and oranges. Value, $2,000,000 annually.

TAHOE, LAKE, a beautiful body of water at the base of the Sierra Nevada mountains, on the boundary line between Placer co., Cal., and Douglas and Ormsby cos., Nev. It is about 20 miles long and 12 miles wide, and about 6,250 feet above sea-level. The scenery about it is strikingly picturesque. Its outlet is the Truckee river.

TAILOR BIRD, the *Orthotomus sutorius,* a small bird about 6 inches long; general color olive - greenish; wings brown, edged with green; crown of the head rufous, inclining to gray on the nape; tail light brown; outer feathers narrowly tipped with white; under surface of the body white; legs flesh-colored. The male has the two center tail-feathers lengthened. A native of India, the Eastern Peninsula, China, etc. It is found in gardens, hedgerows, orchards, jungles, etc., sometimes in pairs, sometimes in small flocks, feeding on ants, cicadellas, and other small insects. Its name of tailor bird is derived from its nest, which is enclosed in leaves sewn with cobwebs, silk from cocoons, thread, wool, and vegetable fiber. The nest itself is formed of cotton-wool with fine loose hairs, etc. Eggs 3 or 4; in different nests they are of different colors, some being white, spotted with rufous or reddish-brown, others bluish-green.

TAIMYR (tī'mēr), a peninsula of Northern Siberia, extending into the Arctic Ocean, between the mouth of the Yenisei and Khatang Gulf, and containing Cape Chelyuskin, the most N. land in Asia.

TAINE (tān), **HIPPOLYTE ADOLPHE,** a French writer; born in Vouziers, Ardennes, France, April 21, 1828; was educated at the College Bourbon and the Ecole Normale. In 1854 his first work, an "Essay on Livy," was crowned by the Academy; in 1864 he was appointed professor in the School of Fine Arts in Paris; and in 1878 he was elected to a seat in the Academy. His "History of English Literature," one of the best and most philosophical works on the subject, appeared in 1864 (4 vols.); his "Philosophy of Art" in 1865; his "Notes on England" in 1872; and his "Origins of Contemporary France" in 1875-1884. He died in Paris March 5, 1893.

TAIPINGS, the name given by foreigners to the followers of Hung Hsiüch'wan (S'eiw-tseuen), who raised the standard of rebellion in China in 1851, and whose enterprise was finally suppressed in 1865.

The leader Hung was born in 1813 in a poor agricultural village of the district of Hwâ, in Canton province. His only chance of rising in the world being by literary distinction, he became a diligent student, but he never succeeded in taking the first degree at the provincial capital. Returning home from another disappointing competition in 1837, he fell into a long illness in which he saw visions, and conceived the idea of changing the religion of the empire and subverting the ruling Manchâu dynasty.

In 1844 in company with the elder of the two converts, Hung went into the adjacent province of Kwang-hsî, where they made many converts, and gathered them into communities which they called "Churches of God." Hung began also to give forth arrangements and decrees as revelations communicated to him by "the Heavenly Father," and the "Heavenly Elder Brother."

After some years of uncertain struggle with the official authorities, the insurgents (for such they were now) took possession of the district city of Yung-an. There they hailed their leader as emperor of the dynasty of Taiping (Grand Peace), and adopted T'ien Kwo (Kingdom of Heaven) as the name of his reign. After being kept for some time in a state of siege in the city by their opponents, on the night of April 7, 1852, they burst forth, scattered their besiegers, and commenced their march to the N. They passed from Kwang-hsî into Hû-nan, got command of the Hsiang river, and before the end of the year had reached the great Yang-tsze river. Launching forth on it, and taking on the way the capitals of Hû-pei and An-hûi, they encamped before Nanking on March 8, 1853. Within 10 days it had fallen into their power, and every man of the Manchâu garrison been put to the sword.

Their host, grown in the 12 months from under 10,000 probably to more than 100,000, proclaimed the Taiping dynasty anew, and swore fealty to the heavenly king. In a few months a large force was dispatched N. to terminate the contest by the capture of Peking. This expedition did wonders, traversed the two provinces of An-hûi and Honan, then marched W. to Shan-shî, from which, turning E. again, it penetrated into Chih-lî and finally occupied an entrenched position only about 20 miles from Tientsin. But the rebellion had there reached the limit of its advance. Though the expedition met with no great defeat, sufficient re-enforcements did not reach them and the leaders were obliged to retreat toward Nanking in 1855.

From this time the rebel cause began to decay. The moral enthusiasm which had distinguished it in Kwang-hsî disappeared. The imperial government, moreover, rallied its forces, and a desperate struggle ensued between them and the rebels.

How the struggle would have ended was still uncertain, when the imperialists began to call in the assistance of foreigners. A body of men of different nationalties entered their service under an American, Frederick T. Ward. He was a very capable man, and did the imperialists good service till he was killed in 1862. Then the British authorities at Shanghâi were prevailed on to organize a more effective force, and to put the whole auxiliary movement under the direction of Col. Charles ("Chinese") Gordon. The Taipings fought with the courage of despair. Nanking was invested by the imperialists and taken at last on July 19, 1864. Hung, the leader of the rebels, was not found. It is supposed that he killed himself by poison a few weeks before rather than become a captive. See GORDON, CHARLES.

TAIT, ARCHIBALD CAMPBELL, Archbishop of Canterbury; born in Edinburgh, Scotland, Dec. 22, 1811; was educated at the Edinburgh Academy and Glasgow University, whence he passed as a Snell exhibitioner to Balliol College, Oxford. In due time he became fellow and tutor, and was one of the four tutors who in 1841 protested against Newman's "Tract 90." In 1842 he was appointed successor to Dr. Arnold as head master of Rugby, in 1849 became Dean of Carlisle, and in 1856 Bishop of London, as successor to Blomfield. Here he did much to bring the teaching of the Church home to the people. A friend of compromise, though a foe to needless innovations, he promoted moderate measures; and though strongly hostile to Colenso's views, intervened to secure him fair play. The same love of the *via media*, he manifested when (having declined the archbishopric of York in 1862) he was in 1868 made primate of all England by Mr. Disraeli. He assisted in composing the strifes raised by the question of Irish disestablishment, but was less successful with the Public Worship Regulation Act and the Burials Bill. He took a keen interest in missions, and greatly helped to extend and improve the organization of the Church in the colonies. The Lambeth Conference of 1878 took place under his auspices. He died Dec. 3, 1882. Among his many publications were: "The Dangers and Safeguards of Modern Theology" (1861), and "The Word of God and the Ground of Faith" (1863).

TAIWAN, the native name for the island of FORMOSA (*q. v.*).

TAI-YUEN, a town of China, capital of Shan-si; on the Fuen-Ho, an affluent of the Hoangho, 250 miles S. W. of Peking. For many years the residence of the emperors, it is noted for its magnificent mausoleums. The chief manufactures are sword blades and knives.

TAJ MAHAL, or **MEHAL** ("Gem of Buildings"), a famous mausoleum, erected at Agra, India, by Shah Jehan for his favorite wife. It is 186 feet square with the corners cut off, and consists of two tiers of arches, with a single-arched porch in the middle of each side, the whole surmounted by a dome 58 feet in diameter and about 210 feet in height, flanked by 4 octagonal kiosks. The interior is divided into four domed chambers in the corners, and a large central arcaded octagon, all connecting by corridors. The central octagon contains two cenotaphs surrounded by a very noticeable openwork marble rail. The only light admitted enters through the delicately pierced marble screens of the windows. The decoration is especially noticeable for the stone mosaics of flower themes and arabesques, much of them in agate, jasper, and bloodstone. The entire structure stands on a white marble platform 18 feet high and 313 feet square, with tapering cylindrical minarets 133 feet high at the corners.

TAKAHIRA, KOGORO, a Japanese diplomat; born in Iwate, in 1854. After holding several minor positions in the diplomatic service, he became consul-general in New York, in 1891. He afterwards served as minister at The Hague, Rome, and Vienna. In 1899 he was assistant foreign minister of Japan. In the following year he was appointed minister at Washington, serving until 1905. In that year he was one of the Japanese representatives at the Peace Conference. He was made a member of the House of Peers, in 1906. In 1907 he was appointed ambassador to Italy, and was ambassador to the United States in 1908-1909.

TAKAMINE, JOKISHI, a Japanese-American chemist; born at Takaoka, Japan, in 1854. He was educated at the Engineering College of the Imperial University of Tokio and at the University of Glasgow, and the Andersonian University, Glasgow. From 1881 to 1884 he was head chemist of the Imperial Department of Agriculture and Commerce, Tokio, and from 1884 to 1885 imperial Japanese commissioner to the Cotton Centennial Exposition at New Orleans. In 1887 he organized and erected the first super-phosphate works at Tokio. After coming to America in 1890, he applied new processes to fermentation, resulting in the production of diastatic enzyme (Takadiastase), now used largely as a starch digestant, established a research laboratory in New York, originated a process for isolating the active principles of the suprarenal glands, the product being known as ADRENALIN (*q. v.*), and became consulting chemist of Parke, Davis & Co., Detroit. He was a member of the Royal Japanese Academy of Science. Died July 22, 1922.

TALAVERA DE LA REINA (täl-ä-vä'rä dä lä rä-ē'nü), a picturesque town of Spain in the province of Toledo, beautifully situated on the Tagus, 75 miles S. E. of Madrid. It still manufactures pottery, and keeps up its famous fair in August. Here, on July 27-28, 1809, Sir Arthur Wellesley, with 19,000 British and 34,000 Spaniards, defeated 50,000 French troops under Joseph Bonaparte and Marshals Jourdan and Victor.

TALBOT, ETHELBERT, an American Protestant Episcopal clergyman, born at Fayette, Mo., in 1848. He was educated at Dartmouth College and at the General Theological Seminary, and received honorary degrees from both these institutions and from the University of Missouri. He became a deacon and priest in 1873; was rector of St. James' Church and St. James Military Academy, Macon, Mo., from 1873 to 1887; was consecrated missionary bishop of Wyoming and Idaho in 1887, and was transferred to the see of Central Pennsylvania (now Bethlehem) in 1898. He wrote, besides many magazine articles, pamphlets and sermons: "My People of the Plains"; "A Bishop Among His Flock"; "Tim—Autobiography of a Dog"; "A Bishop's Message."

TALBOT, MARION, an American educator, born at Thun, Switzerland, of American parents, in 1858. He was educated at Boston University and at the Massachusetts Institute of Technology. From 1890 to 1892 he was instructor of domestic science at Wellesley College. In 1892 he went to the University of Chicago, serving there as assistant professor of sanitary science from 1892 to 1895 and an associate professor of household administration since 1905. After 1892 he was also dean of women. He was a member of various educational and scientific societies and one of the founders and for many years an officer of the Association of the Collegiate Alumnæ. He wrote "Home Sanitation" (with E. H. Richards, 1887); "Education of Women" (1910); "A Modern Household" (with S. P. Breckinridge (1912); and "House Sanitation") 1912.

TALC, an orthorhombic mineral occurring in short hexagonal prisms and plates, also in globular and stellated groups, compact, massive. Cleavage, basal; luster, pearly; color, apple-green, white, shades of gray; sectile; feel, greasy. Composition, varying with the amount of water present, but essentially a hydrated silicate of magnesia which, when pure, would contain: Silica, 62.0; magnesia, 33.1; water $4.9=100$, the formula being $6MgO5SiO_2+2HO$. Dana divides as follows: (1) Foliated; (2) massive (steatite or soapstone); (*a*) Coarse granular, including potstone; (*b*) Crypto-crystalline (French chalk); (*c*) Rensselæriate, cryptocrystalline, but more often pseudomorphous; (*d*) Indurated, a very abundant mineral. Being thoroughly incombustible it is of great value in the manufacture of fireproof wall paper, paper window curtains, etc. Even in its crude state it is found to yield one of the best lubricants known. Mixed with common grades of soap, it makes them as pleasant to the touch as the choicest brands. It is also largely used in the manufacture of patent wall plaster, in which its addition gives a smooth, glossy finish to walls and ceilings that no other substance lends. Talc powder, duly refined, is exquisitely soft and fine grained. So, too, it makes an unsurpassed molding sand for casting metals in, both its fireproof and fire-grained qualities being very valuable in fine work. Mixed with rubber, it renders it more elastic and less liable to crack. From it is also made the "French chalk" used by tailors, and shoe dealers use it in powdered form to enable one to pull on a tight-fitting shoe. The principal talc mines in the U. S. are in St. Lawrence co., N. Y. Virginia and the western part of North Carolina produces the purest soapstone. Also a commercial name for mica (*q. v.*).

Oil of talc: A cosmetic common in the 17th century, consisting of talc calcined. See SOAPSTONE.

TALCA, a town of Chile, capital of the province of Talca, on the Claro, connected by rail with Santiago; has manufactures of ponchos; area of province, 3,864 square miles; pop. (1918) 131,071. Pop. of capital, 42,563.

TALENT, figuratively: (1) A gift, endowment, or faculty; some peculiar faculty, ability, power, or accomplishment, natural or acquired (a metaphor borrowed from the parable in Matt. xxv: 14-30). (2) Mental endowments or capacities of a superior kind; general mental power (used in either the singular or the plural). (3) Hence, used for talented persons collectively; men of ability or talent. (4) Habitual backers of horses, or takers of odds, as opposed to the bookmakers, or layers of odds.

In Greek antiquity, the name of a weight and also of a denomination of money among the ancient Greeks, and also applied by Greek writers and their translators to various standard weights and denominations of money among different nations; the weight and value differing in the various nations and at various times. As a weight, those in general use were the Euboïc or Attic talent = 56 pounds 11 ounces troy, and the Æginetan = about 82¼ pounds. The Attic talent contained 60 Attic minæ. As a denomination of money, it was a talent's weight of silver, or a sum of money equivalent to this; so that in our current coin the Attic talent would be worth $1,185.84. The great talent of the Romans was equal to $483.25, and the little talent to $364.87½. The Hebrew talent (II Sam. xii: 30) was equal to 93 pounds 12 ounces avoirdupois; and as a denomination of money it has been variously estimated at from $1,520.31 to $1,926.54. The marginal note in the authorized version to Matt. xviii: 24, says that "a talent is 750 ounces of silver, which, at 5s. ($1.20) the ounce, is £187, 10s. ($900)."

Ministry of all the Talents, a ministry of which Lord Grenville was the head, and Fox his colleague and supporter. It was formed on Jan. 26, 1806, three days after the death of Pitt, and, after undergoing some changes was dissolved on March 25, 1807. Its nickname was given from the boast of Mr. Canning and others that it contained all the talent of the country—*i. e.*, of both political parties in the State.

TA-LIEN-WAN, a bay on the east coast of the Liaotung Peninsula, Manchuria. It is ice-free throughout the year, and as a result of its depth and roominess it is of considerable importance. The port of Dalny is situated at its head. The bay, with the surrounding territory, was leased by Russia from China in 1898, and in 1905 was surrendered to Japan.

TALIPOT, TALIPAT, or TALIPUT, the *Corypha umbraculifera*, a palm tree,

native of Ceylon and the Malabar coast, and cultivated in Bengal and Burma. It has a tall, cylindrical stem, with a soft rind and soft pink internal pith, both formed of vascular bundles. The leaves are in a cluster at the top of the stem, and are fan-shaped. A tree at Peradeniya, in Ceylon, was described in the "Indian Agriculturist" for November, 1873, as having a stem 84 feet high, terminated by a flower panicle of 20 feet, making 104 feet in all, the girth of the stem 3 feet from the ground round the persistent bases of the leaves was 13 feet 4 inches; at 21 feet from the ground 8 feet 3 inches; the leaves were about 10 feet in diameter, and the age of the tree about 40 years. The pith is made into a kind of sago, the leaves are written upon by the natives with a steel stylus; they are, moreover, made into fans, mats, and umbrellas.

TALISMAN, a species of charm, consisting of a figure engraved on metal or stone when two planets are in conjunction, or when a star is at its culminating point, and supposed to exert some protective influence over the wearer of it. The terms talisman and amulet are often considered nearly synonymous, but the proper distinctive peculiarity of the former is its astrological character. A species of talisman which has acquired considerable celebrity is the abraxas. A species of talisman at present in use in Asia is a piece of paper on which the names of the Seven Sleepers and their dog Kitmer are inscribed. Pasted on the walls of houses, it is believed to be a protection against ghosts and demons. Phylacteries were used as talismans; and in Christian Byzantium phylacteries were made bearing the figure of Solomon, the compeller of demons. See ASTROLOGY: DIVINATION: INCANTATION: MAGIC.

TALKING MACHINE. See GRAMOPHONE.

TALLADEGA, a city of Alabama, the county-seat of Talladega co. It is on the Southern, the Birmingham and Atlantic, and the Louisville and Nashville railroads. It is an important educational center and the seat of the State schools for the deaf, dumb, and blind, Talladega College, and the Alabama Synodical College for Young Ladies. Its industries include cotton and cottonseed oil mills, chemical plants, hosiery factories, fertilizer factories. Pop. (1910) 5,854; (1920) 6,546.

TALLAHASSEE, a city, capital of the State of Florida, and county-seat of

Leon co.; on the Carrabelle, Tallahassee, and Georgia, and the Florida Central and Peninsula railroads; 194 miles E. of Mobile, Ala. Here are the State Normal, Agricultural and Industrial Institute for Colored Pupils, State Seminary, several libraries, artesian water plants, a street railroad, National and State banks, and a number of weekly newspapers. Tallahassee is in a fruit-growing and farming section. It has cotton, cigar and ice factories, and railroad construction and repair shops, and an assessed property valuation of nearly $1,000,000. Pop. (1910) 5,018; (1920) 5,637.

TALLAHATCHIE, a river in northern Mississippi which unites at Greenwood with the Yallobusha to form the Yazoo river. It is about 240 miles long and is navigable for 100 miles.

TALLAPOOSA, a river r u n n i n g through Georgia and Alabama. It unites with the Coosa about 10 miles N. E. of Montgomery, in the latter State, and forms the Alabama river. It is nearly 250 miles long and is navigable for about 40 miles.

TALLEMANT DES REAUX, GÉD-ÉON (tä-luh-mo*ng*' dā rä-ō'), a French chronicler; born in La Rochelle, France, about 1619. At 19 he visited Italy in company with the future Cardinal de Retz, and at an early age married his cousin Elizabeth Rambouillet, whose ample fortune enabled him to give himself to letters and to society. About 1650 he bought for 115,000 livres the seignorial estate of Plessis-Rideau in Touraine, and was permitted to change its name to that of Des Réaux. His famous work, the "Historiettes," was written from 1657 to 1659, and is invaluable as a complete picture of the society of his time. He was still living in 1691, but was certainly dead by 1701. His brother, the ABBÉ TALLEMANT (1620-1693), was a man of wit and an academician, but his "Plutarch's Lives" (1663) brought him little credit. His cousin PAUL TALLEMANT (1642-1712), early began to scribble verses, at 18 wrote his "Trip to the Isle of Love," an ingenious commentary on Mlle. de Scudèry's famous "Carte de Tendre" (Map of Tenderness), and entered the Academy in 1666.

TALLEYRAND - P É R I G O R D, **CHARLES MAURICE DE** (tä-lā-ro*ng*-pā-rē-gor'), **PRINCE OF BENEVENTO**, a French diplomatist; born in Paris, France, Feb. 13, 1754. Though the eldest of three brothers he was, in consequence of lameness caused by an accident, deprived of his rights of primogeniture, and devoted, against his will, to the priesthood. His high birth and great ability procured him rapid advancement, and in 1788 he was consecrated Bishop of Autun. On the meeting of the States-General he was elected deputy for Autun. He sided with the popular leaders in the revolutionary movements; and his advocacy of the abolition of tithes and the transference of Church lands to the State gained him great popularity. In 1790 he was elected president of the National Assembly. When the civil constitution of the clergy was adopted he gave his adhesion to it. For this he was excommunicated by a papal brief, and thereupon renounced his episcopal

TALLEYRAND-PERIGORD

functions (1791). In 1792 he was sent to London charged with diplomatic functions, and during his stay there was proscribed for alleged royalist intrigues. Forced to leave England by the provisions of the Alien Act, in 1794 he sailed for the United States, but returned to France in 1796. The following year he was appointed minister of foreign affairs; but being suspected of keeping up an understanding with the agents of Louis XVIII. he was obliged to resign in July, 1799.

He now devoted himself entirely to Bonaparte, and after the latter's return from Egypt contributed greatly to the events of the 18th Brumaire (Nov. 10, 1799), when the directory fell and the consulate began. He was then reappointed minister of foreign affairs, and for the next few years was the executant of all Bonaparte's diplomatic schemes. After the establishment of the empire in

1804 he was appointed to the office of grand-chamberlain, and in 1806 was created Prince of Benevento. After the peace of Tilsit in 1807 a coolness took place between him and Napoleon, and became more and more marked. In 1808 he secretly joined a royalist committee. In 1814 he procured Napoleon's abdication, and afterward exerted himself very effectually in re-establishing Louis XVIII. on the throne of his ancestors. He took part in the Congress of Vienna, and in 1815, when the allies again entered Paris, he became president of the council with the portfolio of foreign affairs; but as he objected to sign the second peace of Paris he gave in his resignation. After this he retired into private life, in which he remained for 15 years. When the revolution of July, 1830, broke out, he advised Louis Philippe to place himself at its head and to accept the throne. Declining the office of minister of foreign affairs he proceeded to London as ambassador, and crowned his career by the formation of the Quadruple Alliance. He resigned in November, 1834, and quitted public life forever. He died in Paris May 17, 1838. His "Memoirs" were published in 1891.

TALLIEN, JEAN LAMBERT, a French revolutionist; born in Paris in 1769. His talent for writing and speaking soon brought him to the front at the Revolution. After being for some time connected with the "Moniteur," he became editor of the "Ami des Citoyens," a journal after the fashion of Marat's "Ami du Peuple." A prominent Jacobin, he became after Aug. 10 secretary of the Insurrectionary Commune, was one of the leading "Septembrists," and afterward eloquently defended the massacres he had promoted. His services on this occasion gained him a seat in the Convention, where he of course joined the Mountain, and was an earnest defender of Marat, and a savage advocate for the execution of the king. Sent by the Convention to Bordeaux and the W. departments in 1794, he at first distinguished himself by a cruelty and profligacy worthy of the most infamous of the Terrorists. In the prison of Bordeaux, however, he met the beautiful Madame de Fontenay, née Senhorita Tereza de Cabarrus, for whom he conceived a violent passion, and liberated from prison.

Recalled to Paris, he managed by an assumption of revolutionary fervor to avoid an immediate downfall, but the hatred and suspicion of Robespierre were not allayed. Madame de Fontenay was imprisoned. Tallien placed himself at the head of the party afterward known as the Thermidorians, vigorously attacked the triumvirate of terror, and ultimately brought about its downfall. From this point his political influence declined. Madame de Fontenay, on the other hand, whom he now married, became the most prominent personage in Parisian society. Tallien continued in the legislature till 1798, when he accompanied Bonaparte to Egypt in the character of a *savant*. The ship in which he was returning was captured by an English cruiser, and he was *fêted* by the Whig party in London in 1801. In 1802 he was divorced from his wife, who afterward married the Prince de Chimay, and died Nov. 16, 1831. Tallien, after holding for some years the post of French consul at Alicante, died in Paris Nov. 16, 1820, in poverty and obscurity.

TALLMAN, CLAY, an American public official, born in Ionia co., Mich., in 1874. He was educated at Michigan Agricultural College, the University of Colorado, and the University of Michigan. From 1895 to 1902 he taught in the public schools. Beginning the practice of law in 1905 at Rhyolite, Nev., he became interested in politics, and from 1908 to 1912 was a member of the Nevada Senate, from 1910 to 1911 chairman of the Democratic State Central Committee of Nevada and in 1912 an unsuccessful candidate for Congress. In April, 1913, he was appointed chief law officer of the reclamation service, and in June of the same year commissioner of the general land office.

TALLOW, in chemistry, a name applied to the harder and less fusible fats occurring chiefly in the animal kingdom, the most common being beef and mutton tallow. When pure it is white and almost tasteless, and consists of stearin, palmitin, and olein in varying proportions.

Tallow is of two kinds, viz., white and yellow candle tallow, and common soap tallow. The white candle tallow, when good, is brittle, dry and clean. Yellow candle tallow, when good, should be clean, dry, hard when broken, and of a fine yellow color throughout. Soap tallow is used for making soap, and for greasing machinery. A great deal of tallow is also used for the dressing of leather.

TALLOW TREE, the *Stillingia sebifera,* a native of China. The leaves are rhomboidal, tapering at the tip, with two glands at the top of the petiole. The fruits are about half an inch in diameter, and have three seeds, which are covered by a kind of wax used in China, for making candles, whence the name tallow tree. They are boiled in large cauldrons, then sufficiently bruised to enable the fat to be removed without breaking the seeds, and pressed. The candles made from this wax are coated with bees' wax to prevent them from melting in hot weather. The wood is hard, and used for printing blocks, and the leaves for dyeing black. Also *Vateria indica*, a native of the Malabar coast, which yields white dammar.

TALLY, a notched stick employed as a means of keeping accounts. In buying or selling it was customary for the parties to the transaction to have two sticks, or one stick cleft longitudinally into two parts, on each of which was marked with notches or cuts the number or quality of goods delivered, or the amount due between debtor and creditor, the seller keeping one stick and the buyer the other. The mode of keeping accounts by tallies was introduced into England by the Normans, 1066. Besides accounts, other records were formerly kept on notched sticks, as almanacs, in which redletter days were signified by a large notch, ordinary days by small notches, etc. Such were formerly very common in most European countries. In England tallies were long issued in lieu of certificates of indebtedness to creditors of the state.

The system of issuing exchequer tallies was abolished by an act of George III., and by acts of William IV., the accumulated tallies were ordered to be destroyed. They were accordingly burned in a stove in the House of Lords, but the stove being over-heated, unfortunately set fire to the paneling of the room, and the Houses of Parliament were destroyed. In general, a tally is anything made to correspond with or mark another. A label or ticket of wood or metal used in gardens for the purpose of bearing either the name of the plant to which it is attached, or a number referring to a catalogue. Also, a certain number of cabbages.

TALMA (täl-mä'), **JOSEPH FRANÇOIS**, a French actor; born in Paris, France, Jan. 15, 1763. He was educated at Mazarin College, and afterward went to London with his father, a dentist; studied in the hospitals there, and on returning to Paris, was apprenticed to a dentist. He had been on the stage, however, both in London and Paris, and made his professional début Nov. 21, 1787, at the Comédie Française. He founded, with a few others, the theater afterward known as the Théatre de la République. He won his fame as a tragedian, but made many improvements in the naturalness of stage productions. He wrote "Memoirs of Lekain, and Reflections on that Actor and the Theatric Art" (1825), which was republished in 1856 under a slightly different title. His own "Memoirs" were edited by Alexandre Dumas (1856). He died in Paris Oct. 19, 1826.

TALMADGE, JAMES EDWARD, an American geologist, born at Hungerford, Berkshire, England, in 1862. He came to the United States in 1876 and became a member of the Mormon Church. He was educated at Brigham Young Academy, Lehigh University and Johns Hopkins University. From 1884 to 1888 he was professor of chemistry and geology at Brigham Young Academy; from 1888 to 1893 president of Latter Day Saints College; and from 1894 to 1897 president of the University of Utah. After his resignation from the presidency he retained the chair of geology until 1907, since which time he has been a consulting and mining geologist. He was also director of the Deseret Museum, Salt Lake City, from 1891 to 1919, and was ordained one of the twelve apostles of the Church of Jesus Christ of Latter Day Saints in 1911. He traveled extensively in Europe and frequently lectured in the British Isles on geology and other features of life in the western United States. He was a member of various British and American geographical and geological societies and wrote, besides many articles on geological and microscopical subjects in technical journals: "First Book of Nature" (1888); "Domestic Science" (1891); "The Articles of Faith" (1899); "The Book of Mormon, an Account of Its Origin, Etc." (1899); "Tables for Blowpipe Determination of Minerals" (1899); "The Great Salt Lake, Present and Past" (1900); "The Story of Mormonism" (1907); "The Great Apostasy" (1909); "The House of the Lord" (1912); "The Philosophy of Mormonism" (1914); "Jesus the Christ" (1915); "The Vitality of Mormonism" (1919).

TALMAGE, THOMAS DE WITT, an American clergyman; born in Bound Brook, N. J., Jan. 7, 1832; was graduated at the New Brunswick Theological Seminary in 1856; and ordained pastor of the Reformed Dutch Church in Belleville, N. J., in the same year. He was pastor of the Central Presbyterian Church in Brooklyn, N. Y., in 1869-1894, during which time this well-known place of worship was three times destroyed by fire. Feeling himself unable to build another church edifice, he resigned his charge and spent some time in Europe; becoming on his return associate and later full pastor of the First Presbyterian Church in Washington, D. C. He held this charge till 1899, when he resigned in order to apply himself wholly to literary work. He was for many years the editor of the "Christian Herald" and was the author of "Crumbs Swept Up," "Woman: Her Powers and Privileges"; "From Manger to Throne"; "Every-Day Religion"; etc. He died in Washington, D. C.. April 12, 1902.

TALMUD, the name of the fundamental code of the Jewish civil and canonical law, comprising the "Mishna" and the "Gemara," the former as the text, the later as the commentary and complement. The oldest codification of Halachoth, or single ordinances, is due to the school of Hillel. Simon, son of Gamaliel II., and great-grandson of Gamaliel I., mentioned in the New Testament, and his school carefully sifted the material thus brought together. He died A. D. 166. His son Jehudah Hannasi, commonly called Rabbi, who died 219, and his disciples brought the work to its close in six portions (Sedarim), 63 treatises (Mesichtoth), and 524 chapters (Perakim), which contain the single "Mishnas." But besides this authoritatively compiled code there were a number of other law collections, partly anterior to it, and not fully embodied in it, partly arising out of it—as supplements, complements, bylaws, and the like—partly portions of the ancient Midrash, partly either private text-books composed by the masters of the academies for their lectures or enlargements of the existing "Mishna." All this additional material was collected, not rarely together with the dissensions which begot it, under the name of "Baraitoth," "foreign," "external," by Chaiya and his school, in the succeeding generation.

Not to be confounded with them, however, are the collections of "Toseftas," "supplements," or "Great Mishnas," which, commenced at the time of Jehudah Hannasi himself, and continued after his death by his scholar Chaiya and Hoshaiya, embody much of what has been purposely left out in the concise "Mishna," which only embraced the final dicta and decisions. Such "additions" we possess now to 52 treatises, forming together 383 Perakim or chapters. All these different sources of the "Oral Law" —finally redacted before the end of the 3d century, though probably not committed to writing till A. D. 550—belong to the period of from about 30 B. C. to about A. D. 250.

The further development of this supplementary, oral, or second law—in fact rather an exegesis thereof—together with the discussions raised by apparent contradictions found in the individual enactments of the Mishnic doctors, is called "Gemara"—i. e. discussion, complement, or, according to another explanation, doctrine. This "Gemara" contains, apart from the Halacha, which is generally written in Aramaic, also a vast number of non-legal, chiefly Hebrew, fragments —homiletic matter, tales, legends, and the like—called Haggada.

There are two "Talmuds," the one called the "Talmud of the Occidentals," or the "Jerusalem (Palestine) Talmud," which was closed at Tiberias, and the other the "Babylonian Talmud." The first of these now extends over 39 treatises of the "Mishna" only, though it once existed to the whole of the first 5 Sedarim or portions. It originated in Tiberias in the school of Johanan, who died A. D. 179. There is less discussion and more precision of expression in this than in the second or "Babylonian Talmud," emphatically styled "our Talmud," which was not completed until the end of the 5th century, and which makes use of the former. As the real editor of the "Babylonian Talmud" is to be considered Rabbis Ashe, president of the Academy of Sora in Babylonia (A. D. 375-427).

Both the "Mishna" and the Palestine "Gemara" had, notwithstanding the brief period that had elapsed since their redaction, suffered greatly, partly by corruptions that had crept into their (unwritten) text through faulty traditions, partly through the new decisions arrived at independently in the different younger schools—of which there flourished many in different parts of the Dispersion— and which were at times contradictory to those arrived at under different circumstances in former academies. To put an end to these disputes and the general confusion arising out of them, which threatened to end in sheer chaos, Rabbi Ashe, aided by his disciple and friend Abina or Rabina I. (abbreviated from Rab Abina), commenced the cyclopean task of collecting anew the enormous mass of Halachistic material which by that time had grown up.

This took him, with the assistance of 10 secretaries, no less than 30 years; and many years were spent by him in the revision of the work. The final close of the work, however, is greatly due to Rab Abina II., head of the Sora Academy (473-499). He was the last of the Amoraim expounders who used merely oral tradition. After them came the Saboraim, the reflecting, examining, critical, the real completers of the Babylonian Talmud, and by many in ancient and modern times declared to have first re-

STREET IN ALEPPO, SYRIA, CROWDED WITH REFUGEES WHO CAME FROM TURKEY IN 1923

See Syria, p. 216

AUTOMOBILE BRIDGE ACROSS TAMPA BAY

From International Newsreel Corp.

See Tampa, p. 241

duced "Mishna" and "Talmud" to writing.

The "Babylonian Talmud," as now extant, comprises the "Gemara" to almost the whole of the 2d, 3d, and 4th Sedarim (portions), further to the first treatise of the first, and to the first of the last order. The rest, if it ever existed, seems now lost. The whole work is about four times as large as the Jerusalem one, and its 36 treatises, with the commentaries generally added to them in our editions (Rachi and Tosafoth), fill 2,947 folio leaves. The language of the Talmud is, as we said, Aramaic (western and eastern), closely approaching to Syriac. The additional matter—quotations and fragments from older Midrash and Gemara collections, Haggada, etc.—is principally written in Hebrew.

The masters of the "Mishna" (Tannaim) and of the "Gemara" (Amoriam) were followed by the Saboraim. The code of the oral law had come to a close with the second named; and not its development, but rather its proper study, elucidation, and carrying into practice was the task of the generations of the learned that followed.

The Saboraim no longer dared to contradict, but only opined on the meaning and practicability of certain enactments, and undertook the task of inculcating and popularizing the teachings laid down by their sires; apart from bestowing proper care upon the purity of the text, and adding some indispensable glosses.

The best comentaries of the "Mishna" are by Maimonides and Bartenora; of the "Babylonian Talmud" by Rashi and the Tosafists of France and Germany. An abstract of the Talmud for practical legal purposes by Maimonides is called "Mishne Thorah." The "Mishna" was first printed at Naples, 1492; the "Talmud of Jerusalem" at Venice, by D. Bomberg, 1523. The "Babylonian Talmud" was first published at Venice by him in 1520. It is generally printed in 12 folios, the text on the single pages being kept uniform with the previous editions to facilitate the references. No translation of the "Gemara" has ever been carried further than a few single treatises. The complete "Mishna," on the other hand, has been translated repeatedly into Latin, German, Spanish, etc., by Surenhus, Rabe, Jost, and others. We must refrain here from attempting a general characterization of the Talmud, a work completely *sui generis*, which is assuredly one of the most important records of humanity.

TALUS, in geology, a sloping heap of rocky fragments broken off from the face of a steep rock by the action of the weather, and accumulating at its base. So called from its resemblance to a talus in fortification. In surgery, a variety of club-foot, in which the heel rests on the ground, and the toes are drawn toward the leg.

TAMAQUA, a borough in Schuylkill co., Pa.; on the Little Schuylkill river, and on the Philadelphia and Reading, and the Central of New Jersey railroads; 40 miles N. of Reading. Here are a high school, waterworks, electric lights, National and State banks, and several daily and weekly newspapers. It has large coal interests, flour, powder, and planing mills, machine shops, and several foundries. Pop. (1910) 9,462; (1920) 12,363.

TAMAR, a small river in England, flowing between the counties of Cornwall and Devonshire; empties into Plymouth Sound, 2 miles above Plymouth; length about 60 miles. Also a river of Tasmania, formed by the union of the North and South Esk, and flowing into Bass's Straits at Fort Dalrymple.

TAMARACK, the American or black larch, *Larix pendula* or *americana*, called also *Abies pendula*. It has weak and drooping branches, which sometimes take root, forming a natural arch. The leaves are clustered and deciduous, the cones oblong with numerous spreading scales. It constitutes a feature of the forests in Canada and the northern United States. Its timber is valuable, but less so than the larch. It is cultivated in Europe, being more graceful and greener than the common larch.

TAMARIN, the name of certain South American monkeys. The tamarins are active, restless, and irritable little creatures, two of the smallest being the silky tamarin (*Midas rosalia*) and the little lion monkey (*M. leonina*), the latter of which, though only a few inches in length, presents a wonderful resemblance to the lion.

TAMARIND, the *Tamarindus indica*. Leaves abruptly pinnate, with many pairs of small leaflets; flowers in racemes; calyx straw-colored; petals yellow, streaked with red, filaments purple, anthers brown. It is an evergreen tree, 80 feet high by 25 in circumference, cultivated in India as far N. as the Jhelum. The wood, which is yellowish-white, sometimes with red streaks, is hard and close-grained. It is very difficult to work, and is used in India for turning wheels, mallets, oil and sugar mills, etc.

It furnishes excellent charcoal for the manufacture of gunpowder. The pulp of the legumes pressed in syrup is a delicious confection. The flowers and fruit are used in India as an astringent or as a mordant in dyeing, especially with safflower; the leaves furnish a yellow dye. The seeds yield a clear, bright, fluid oil, with an odor like that of the linseed; their powder mixed with thin

SEED

POD

TAMARIND: BRANCH IN FLOWER

SEED-POD SECTION

glue makes a strong cement for wood. The West Indian and South American variety of *T. indica* (variety *occidentalis*) has legumes only 3 times as long as broad, whereas the Indian tree has them 6 times as long.

The tamarinds sold in the United States are chiefly West Indian tamarinds. They differ from the Black or East Indian tamarinds, of which the preserved pulp is black. In pharmacy tamarinds are used as gentle laxatives; they are refrigerant from the acids which they contain, and, when infused, constitute a cooling drink in fevers. They enter into the *Confectio sennæ*. In India the seeds are given in dysentery, etc.; in the Mauritius a decoction of the bark is given in asthma.

TAMATAVE, a seaport on the coast of Madagascar and the chief commercial center of the island; pop. about 15,000.

TAMAULIPAS, (tä-mou-lē'päs). a State of Mexico, bordering on Texas and the Gulf of Mexico; is about 400 miles long and 130 miles broad; area,

30,831 square miles; pop. about 257,000. The surface is diversified and the soil generally fertile. It produces most of the grains, fruits and woods of the temperate zone. Iron, silver, and salt are the chief mineral products. Stock of all kinds is raised and a considerable trade in them and other articles is carried on. The principal ports are Tampici and Matamoras.

TAMBELAN ISLANDS, a group in the China Sea, between Borneo and Singapore. They are under Dutch control.

TAMBOURINE, or TAMBOURIN, an ancient pulsatile musical instrument of the drum class, popular among all European people, but particularly those of the S. The Biscayan and Italian peasantry employ it on every festal occasion. It is formed of a hoop of wood, sometimes of metal, over which is stretched a piece of parchment or skin; the sides of the hoop are pierced with holes, in which are inserted pieces of metal in pairs, called jingles. Small bells are sometimes fastened on to the outer edge of the hoop. It is sounded by being struck with the knuckles, or by drawing the fingers or thumb over the skin, which produces what is called "the roll," a peculiar drone. Also a stage dance formerly popular in France. It was of a lively measure, and accompanied with a pedal bass in imitation of "the roll."

TAMBOUR WORK (French, *tambour,* a drum), a species of embroidery on muslin or other thin material, worked on circular frames which resemble drum heads. The practice of tambouring is rapidly being replaced by pattern weaving. See EMBROIDERY.

TAMBOV, a province of Russia, S. of Nijni-Novgorod and Vladimir, between the basins of the Oka and the Don; area, 25,710 square miles; pop. about 3,555,000. It is one of the largest, most fertile, and most densely peopled provinces of central Russia. More than two-thirds of the surface is arable. The principal crops are corn and hemp. Before the World War vast numbers of excellent horses, cattle, and sheep were reared. The chief industrial establishments are distilleries, tallow-melting works, sugar works, and woolen mills. TAMBOV, the capital, 263 miles S. E. of Moscow, is built mostly of wood. It has a great trade in corn and cattle. Pop. about 71,500.

TAMILS, the name of a race which inhabits South India and Ceylon. The Tamils belong to the Dravidian stock of the inhabitants of India, and are therefore to be regarded as among the original inhabitants who occupied the country before the Aryan invasion from the N., but they adopted the higher civilization of the Aryans. The Tamil language is spoken not only in south India and Ceylon, but also by a majority of the Indian settlers in places further E., as Pegu and Penang. There is an extensive literature, the greater part of it in verse. Among the chief works are the "Kural" of Tiruvalluvar, an ethical poem, and the Tamil adaptation of the Sanskrit "Ramayana."

TAMMANY, SOCIETY OF, or CO-LUMBIAN ORDER, formed in New York City in 1789, as a counterweight to the so-called "aristocratic" Society of the Cincinnati; deriving its name from a noted friendly Delaware chief named Tammany, who had been canonized by the soldiers of the Revolution as the patron saint of America. The grand sachem and 13 sachems were intended to typify the President and the governors of the 13 original States.

The society was at first a social organization, but about 1800 the majority of its members were in sympathy with Aaron Burr, and the society entered politics under his standard. From the first the qualities that have always been most prominent in it prevailed, thorough organization and a thorough canvass. Tammany was for a short time allied with DeWitt Clinton, but they separated and Tammany came to be recognized as the regular Democratic faction. It had thus gained a position in New York politics. Tweed was its "boss" in the days of his success, and his overthrow dealt it a severe blow, though it has always recovered its position. He was followed by John Kelly; he in turn by Richard Croker, who directed the society's course in National and State campaigns till 1902. In January, 1902, Croker brought about the appointment of Lewis Nixon as chairman of the Finance Committee, the office in which the control of the organization resides. In 1903 Charles F. Murphy became leader, a position held until his death. Tammany elected George B. McClellan and the entire ticket. Mr. McClellan was reelected. In 1910 W. J. Gaynor was Tammany's successful candidate for mayor. John P. Mitchel won on a fusion ticket in 1913, but was defeated by the Tammany nominee, John F. Hylan, in 1917.

Tammany's organization and traditions both tend to make it subject to the control of a small clique, and its large following in a State which is always

I—18

doubtful gives it an influence in National politics otherwise out of proportion to its numerical strength.

TAMMERFORS, the chief manufacturing city of Finland; 50 miles N. W. of Tavastehus. It is situated on a rapid which connects two lakes and affords motive power to cotton, linen, paper, and woolen mills. Pop. (1917) 46,353.

TAMMUZ, a Syrian deity for whom the Jewish women held an annual lamentation (Ezek. viii: 14), doubtless borrowing the practice from the Phœnicians. Tammuz has generally been identified with the Phœnician sun god Adonis, or the Egyptian god Osiris. The Adonia, or feast in honor of Adonis, commenced with the new moon of July, when on a certain night an image of the god was laid out on a bed by women, and bewailed in woful ditties. After a time spent in this way, lights were brought in and the mouths of the mourners anointed by the priest, who whispered, "Trust ye, communicants, the god having been saved, there shall be to us, out of pains, salvation."

TAMPA, a city and county-seat of Hillsboro co., Fla.; on Hillsboro river, Tampa Bay, and the Atlantic Coast Line, Seaboard Air Line, and Tampa Northern railroads; 30 miles E. of the Gulf of Mexico. It is in a lemon and orange-growing region, and is one of the favorite health resorts of Florida. It contains many hotels, the Convent of Holy Names, Female Seminary, waterworks, street railroad and electric-light plants, National banks, and several daily, weekly, and monthly periodicals. Its chief industry is the manufacture of cigars. During the Spanish-American War, Tampa was one of the great mobilization camps. Pop. (1910) 37,782; (1920) 51,608.

TAMPA BAY, the largest inlet of the Gulf of Mexico, on the W. coast of Florida. It affords excellent anchorage, and at its entrance are many islands.

TAMPICO (täm-pē′kō), a seaport town in the State of Tamaulipas, Mexico, on Lake Tampico, near the Gulf of Mexico. It has some good dwellings in the Spanish style, military and naval monuments, and an important trade with the United States and Great Britain, amounting to $100,000,000 annually. The principal exports are specie, hides, tallow, bones, and jerked beef. Pop. about 36,000.

TAMSUI, a town on the N. coast of Formosa, one of the treaty ports, with a trade in tea. Pop. 95,000.

TAMWORTH, a town on the border of Stafford and Warwick shires, England; at the confluence of the Tame and Anker; 110 miles N. W. of London. Burned by the Danes in 911, and rebuilt by the Princess Ethelfleda, it was the seat of a castle of the Saxon kings, which was afterward held by the Marmion, Ferrars, and other families, and now belongs to the Marquis of Townshend. That castle, which ranges in date between Saxon and Jacobean times, crowns a knoll 130 feet high; in its noble round keep is a room where Mary, Queen of Scots, was a prisoner. The Church of St. Edith, restored since 1870, at a cost of £10,000, has some interesting monuments and a curious double tower staircase. There are also a bronze statue of Peel, the new Jubilee municipal buildings and assembly rooms, a town hall (1701), a grammar school (1858; rebuilt 1868), almshouses founded by Thomas Guy, a cottage hospital, recreation grounds, etc. The manufactures include elastic tape, small wares, paper, etc.; and in the vicinity are market gardens and coal pits. A municipal borough, chartered by Elizabeth, Tamworth, returned two members to Parliament till 1885. Pop. (1917) 8,000.

TANA, a river in the extreme N. of Norway; forming part of the boundary between it and Russia. Also a river of East Africa, within the British sphere of influence; rising in Mount Kenia, navigable for about 100 miles in the rainy season.

TANAGERS (*Tanagridæ*), a family of the Passeriformes, or perching birds, containing nearly 400 species; the bill is usually conical (sometimes depressed or attenuated), more or less triangular at the base, with the cutting edges not

SCARLET TANAGER

much inflected, and frequently notched near the tip of the upper mandible. This last character will generally serve to distinguish the tanagers from the finches,

to which they are very closely allied; while on the other hand they have strong affinities to the American warblers (*Mniotiltidæ*). They are mostly birds of small size, some of the genus *Euphonia*, being hardly four inches in length. This genus, with its ally *Chlorophonia*, is remarkable in having no gizzard; the birds belonging thereto feed chiefly on ripe fruits, which, with insects, form the principal food; some, however, feed on seeds and grain, like the finches. With the exception of a few species which visit North America in summer, the tanagers are confined to Central and South America and the West Indies. Some genera of tanagers are remarkable for their beauty of plumage. Many are also pleasant songsters, such as the organist tanager (*Euphonia musica*) of San Domingo; the male of this species has the upper parts purplish-black, the cap blue, and the forehead, rump, and under parts yellow; the female being olive-green, with a blue cap, and lighter and yellowish below. The scarlet tanager (*Pyranga rubra*), visiting the E. parts of North America in summer, and ranging S. in winter to Ecuador, Peru, and Bolivia, is also a songster; it is larger than the preceding species, and the male is scarlet, with black wings and tail, while the female is olive, with the wings and tail brown. Tanagers do well in captivity.

TANAGRA, the type genus of the family *Tanagridæ*, with 12 species, ranging from Mexico to Bolivia and La Plata.

TANANA VALLEY, a district, watered by the River Tanana and its tributaries, belonging to the Yukon watershed, Alaska. Area, 25,000 square miles. Pop. (white) about 7,000, the natives, Tananas, decreasing in number. During twelve months ending in 1915 gold valued at $66,000,000 was mined. Gold is the chief mineral, though coal beds extend from Upper Nenana to the Delta river, and in the Bonnefield district there is an area of 600 square miles with lignite coal. On the whole the abundant grass, rich soil and extensive woodland make the Tanana valley a favorable region for settlement, and it is estimated that there will soon be at least 50,000 acres under homestead.

TANCRED, a hero of the first crusade; son of the Marquis Odo the Good and of Emma, Robert Guiscard's sister; born in Sicily in 1078; in 1098 assumed the cross, and with his cousin Bohemond set out on the crusade. Through the Byzantine empire they marched to Constantinople, whence Tancred crossed the Bosporus disguised as a common soldier, that so he might escape from swearing allegiance to the emperor. Alexios followed the Crusaders, and Tancred reluctantly, yielding to Bohemond's counsel, took the required oath. At Dorylaion (July 4, 1097) his bravery saved the camp of priests and women; his banner was the first to float from the towers of Tarsus, though Baldwin's jealousy dislodged it thence. In the siege of Antioch he slew, say chroniclers, 700 infidels; with Robert of Normandy he first set foot in the Holy City, July 15, 1099. Appointed by Godfrey de Bouillon prince of Galilee, he founded churches in Nazareth, in Tiberias, and on Mount Tabor, and helped at Ascalon to guard the new Christian kingdom against the Fatimite caliph. His efforts on Godfrey's death (1100) to secure the crown of Jerusalem to Bohemond only roused Baldwin's jealousy again; but his own principality he held successfully against both Turks and Greeks, even Edessa owning his supremacy. He was busy with plans for bringing the Syrian chieftains under his sway, when he died in Antioch of a wound received in battle (1112).

TANDAH, a town in the district of Fyzabad, Oude, British India; 3 miles from the Ghogra river; 100 miles S. E. of Lucknow. It is the seat of the largest weaving colony in the province, and manufactures both coarse cloth and fine muslin.

TANEY, ROGER BROOKE, an American statesman; born in Calvert co., Md., March 17, 1777; was graduated at Dickenson College in 1795; admitted to the bar in 1799, and elected to the house of delegates in the autumn of the same year. During the war with Great Britain he led the wing of the Federal party that upheld the policy of the government. In 1816 he was sent to the State Senate; in 1827 became attorney-general of Maryland and in December, 1831, succeeded John M. Berrien as attorney-general of the United States. He was appointed Secretary of the Treasury under President Jackson on Sept. 24, 1833, but was forced to resign the next year, owing to his action with regard to the removal of the treasury deposits. On Dec. 26, 1835, however, he was nominated chief-justice of the United States and confirmed by the United States Senate on March 15, 1836. While in this office he rendered decisions on many important cases, notably those of Dred Scott, and Sherman M. Booth, both bearing on the Fugitive Slave Law. He died in Washington, D. C., Oct. 12, 1864.

TANGANYIKA (-yē'kä), a lake of Central Africa, to the S. of Lake Albert Nyanza. It extends from about lat. 3° 25' to 8° 40' S., and from lon. 29° 20' to 32° 20' E. It is 420 miles long, has an average breadth of about 30 miles, and is 2,700 feet above the level of the sea. The basin in which it lies is inclosed by an almost continuous series of hills and mountains. It is fed by numerous rivers and streamlets, and discharges by the river Lukuga into the Kongo. There are several London Missionary Society stations on Tanganyika, and on the E. shore is the Arab town of Ujiji. A carriage road, 210 miles, runs to Nyassa. Tanganyika was discovered by Speke and Burton in 1858.

TANGANYIKA TERRITORY is the former German East Africa; administered by a British governor, under League of Nations mandate. Capital, Dar-es-Salaam.

TANGENT, in geometry, a straight line which meets or touches a circle or curve in one point, and which, being produced, will not cut it. In Euclid (III. 16, Cor.) it is proved that any line drawn at right angles to the diameter of a circle at its extremity is a tangent to the circle. In trigonometry, the tangent of an arc or angle is a straight line, touching circle of which the arc is a part at one extremity of the arc, and meeting the diameter passing through the other extremity; or it is that portion of a tangent drawn at the first extremity of an arc, and limited by a secant drawn through the second extremity. The tangent is always drawn through the initial extremity of the arc, and is reckoned positive upward, and consequently, negative downward. The tangent of an arc or angle is also the tangent of its supplement. The arc and its tangent have always a certain relation to each other, and when the one is given in parts of the radius, the other can always be computed by means of an infinite series. Tables of tangents for every arc from 0° to 99°, as well as of sines, cosines, etc., are computed and formed into tables for trigonometrical purposes. Two curves are tangent to each other at a common point, when they have a common rectilinear tangent at this point. A tangent plane to a curved surface is the limit of all secant planes to the surface through the point. The point is called the point of contact. Two surfaces are tangent to each other when they have, at least, one point in common; through which, if any number of planes be passed, the sections cut out by each plane will be tangent to each other at the point. This point is called the point of contact. Another definition is this: Two surfaces are tangent to each other when they have a common tangent plane at a common point. This point is the point of contact.

Artificial tangents, tangents expressed by logarithms. Methods of tangents, the name given to the calculus in its early period. When the equation of a curve is given, and it is required to determine the tangent at any point, this is called the direct method of tangents, and when the subtangent to a curve at any point is given, and it is required to determine the equation of the curve, this is termed the inverse method of tangents. These terms are synonymous with the differential and integral calculus. Natural tangents, tangents expressed by natural numbers. To go (or fly) off at a tangent, to break off suddenly from one course of action, line of thought, or the like, and go on to something else.

TANGHIN (*Tanghinia venenifera*), a tree of Madagascar, natural order *Apocynaceæ*, bearing a fruit the kernel of which, about the size of an almond, is highly poisonous. Trial by tanghin was formerly used in Madagascar as a test of the guilt or innocence of a suspected criminal. The person undergoing the ordeal was required to swallow a small portion of the kernel. If his stomach rejected it he was deemed innocent, but if he died, as happened in most cases, he was deemed to have deserved his fate and suffered the punishment of his crime.

TANGIER (tän-jēr'), **TANGIERS** (tän-jērz'), **TANJA**, a seaport and the diplomatic capital of Morocco; near the entrance of the Strait of Gibraltar. It stands on a height near a spacious bay and presents a very striking appearance from the sea. It is the principal center of commerce in Morocco, has considerable trade with Europe and is the residence of the foreign consuls and diplomatic corps. Tangier is said to have been founded by the Carthaginians, from whom it passed successively to the Goths and Arabs. It was taken from them by the Portuguese in 1471, by whom it was ceded to the British in 1662 as a part of the dowry of Catharine of Braganza; abandoned to the Moors in 1684, bombarded by the Spaniards in 1790, and by the French in 1844. Pop. (1918) 46,000; European 11,000. Made a neutral area under the Tangier Statute of 1925.

TANGIER ISLAND, an island of Virginia, in Chesapeake Bay, nearly opposite the mouth of the Potomac river. N. of this island extends a range of islands mostly in Somerset co., Md., dividing Tangier Sound from the rest of the bay. This sound is noted for its oysters.

TANJORE (native, Tanjúr, or Tanjávúr), a town of India, capital of a district in the Madras province; 180 miles S. S. W. of Madras city, in the midst of an extensive plain, on one of the branches of the lower Kaveri. The principal edifices of Tanjore are the palace of the old rajahs, a dismantled fort and the Great Pagoda. This last has a perpendicular part 2 stories in height, 82 feet square, and above that 13 stories, forming an elongated pyramid about 100 feet high. The basement section is simple in outlines, but adorned by niches and pilasters; the pyramidal portion is somewhat elaborately sculptured; and the whole is crowned by a dome (said to consist of a single stone), which brings the total height to 190 feet. The temple stands in one of two great courtyards, and in the same court stand several small shrines, one of which is so beautifully carved as to rival in interest the great temple. The date of the latter is not certainly known, but is with much probability referred to the beginning of the 14th century. Silks, jewelry, carpets, copper vessels, and artistic models in clay, etc., are manufactured. Pop. about 60,500.

TANKS, engines of war first employed by the British in their attack on the Somme (France) on Sept. 15, 1916. The application of the invention to war purposes is credited partly to Major-General E. D. Swinton of the Royal Engineers and later of the British War Cabinet, who was the well-known "Eye-witness" of the early part of the war, and to Sir William Tritton, who had it built and first used in action. But the propelling principle was the caterpillar farm tractor, invented about 1900 by Benjamin Holt of Stockton, Cal., which was used by the British army for towing huge guns over difficult fields. The development to a self-propelled fort heavy enough to withstand all but the heaviest calibred enemy fire and yet mobile under unfavorable conditions was a simple one. As a motor-driven armored vehicle, carrying machine guns and similar pieces, it served principally both for purposes of defense and attack. The muddy ground, shell craters, trenches, trees, and barbed wire were traversed where an advance would have been impossible to infantry not so provided for. In essentials it acted as a sort of land battleship for the protection of attacking troops. The success of the tank was due in the first place to its internal combustion engine, and in the second place to the traction device developed by Holt. The mechanism had tracks on the sides, composed of a series of steel shoes linked

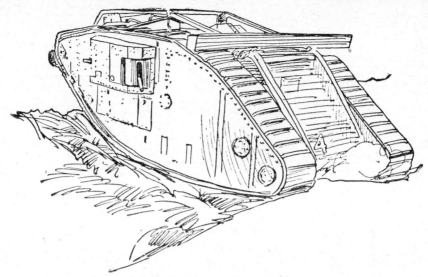

BRITISH TANK—HEAVY TYPE

together, with joints shielded from dirt and mud, with idler pulleys for laying the shoes down in front and driving sprockets for picking them up in the rear. The uprights on the inner surface of the shoes formed continuous rail-like bands upon which the truck wheels rolled carrying the weight of the machine. The mode of locomotion in the tractor and the tank is the same, each lays down its own rails and rolls over them. The track belts run lengthwise clear around the body, the shape bringing the additional track surface into contact with the ground, and so distributing it that the pressure of a twelve-ton tractor per square inch is actually less than that of an ordinary man's shoe. The first experimental tank weighed about 40 tons. Its noise and cumbersomeness greatly hindered its effectiveness, but the idea proved to be sound and mechanical experts worked hard to improve it. As time went on and the improvements were effected the personnel so engaged began to be very numerous and a separate tank corps was formed under a general officer.

Later on in the war it was seen that the tank was to prove a decisive weapon. In the last phase of the war there was no other instrument that played a greater part in bringing victory to the side of the Allies. In 1916 a total of only 50 were shipped to France from the British

FRENCH TANK—HEAVY TYPE

AMERICAN TANK—HEAVY TYPE

shops. Before the end of the war the total number reached immense proportions, and the improvements effected in them enabled General Foch to attack without preliminary bombardment in the summer of 1918, in the great counter-offensive which proved the final turning-point of the war.

The Germans on their side began to build tanks as a measure of defense, but the Allies in this one particular had got greatly ahead of them and the German tank never played any great part in the war. The secret had been well kept from the beginning and it was indeed from the fact that it was presented to have no other purpose but to serve as a drinking water container for Mesopotamia that the machine received the name that stuck to it. As the weight and mobility of the tanks were improved they began to give real service to the Allied ranks. The light tanks, which appeared in great numbers in 1918, proved the most effective of any. The French Renault tank was known as the "Baby Tank." The light British tank was known as the "Whippet." Each of these carried two men and a machine gun, one man directing the tank and the other operating the gun. These tanks were easy to operate. They could go at a rate of 12 miles an hour, could climb a hill well, cut barbed wire, and turn with ease in muddy and swampy ground. In weight they did not exceed 7 tons. Some of the other types of tanks went up to nearly 50 tons. Of this heavy type was the American tank, which aimed at uniting all the best characteristics that had proved effective in the war and ended by being exceedingly cumbersome. These big tanks carried two six-pounder rapid-fire Hotchkiss guns and 4 Lewis machine guns. Some of them were armored with quarter-inch chrome steel and the engines were 105 horse-power of the Knight salient type. Some of the tanks were armed with a short-barrelled 75 mm. gun. The armor of most of the tanks was made strong enough to turn anything less powerful than a shell from a big gun, and when the Germans placed field guns in the first line this armor had

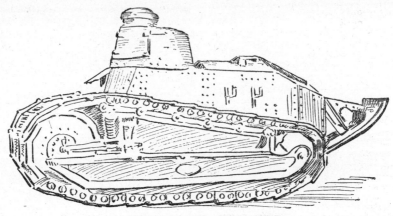

FRENCH TANK—SMALL TYPE

to be increased in strength. What came to be called the "male" tank was distinguished from the "female" tank by its offensive weapons. The "male" tank was equipped with quick-firing guns capable of firing shells effective in putting machine guns out of action. The "female" tank carried machine guns only

his favor he had behind him an admirable system of strategic railroads.

Rennenkampf himself, with a large army, was in the neighborhood, but his subordinate in command, Samsonov, with about 200,000 men was advancing through the lake region, defeating a German force near Frankenau. Flushed by

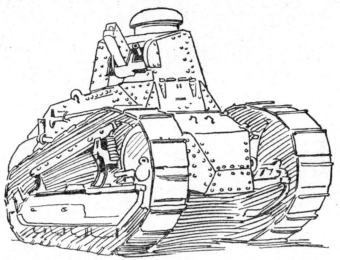

AMERICAN WHIPPET TANK

effective merely in meeting an infantry charge. All available wall space in the tanks was used for storing ammunition, and the vehicle was made as self-sustaining as possible, although it was recognized from the beginning that its most effective use was as a co-operative and auxiliary arm, to attacking infantry.

TANNENBERG, BATTLE OF, a great battle which takes its name from a village in East Prussia, in the Mazurian Lakes region, was one of the first important general engagements between German and Russian forces in the World War. In the early weeks the Russians, under Rennenkampf, had invaded East Prussia and defeated the German retaining forces, under von François, who were forced back on Konigsberg. The German General Staff, alarmed by this serious situation, immediately made heroic efforts to retrieve their disaster and heavy reinforcements were sent to East Prussia under the command of General von Hindenburg, already retired, but recognized as one of the best informed German officers regarding the topography of the difficult lake region in East Prussia. In all he had about 150,000 men, with which to drive back the much superior forces of the Russians, but in

his victory, he decided to advance to Allenstein, through a country of small lakes, bogs and marshes. The nature of the country made it impossible for any large army to march in a compact mass, and Samsonov was obliged to divide his army into two main columns.

On Aug. 26 he encountered a strong German force. This was von Hindenburg's newly organized army, who had taken a position across the railroad from Allenstein to Soldau. With his intimate knowledge of the country, Hindenburg had arranged his position in such a way that he had a large area of lakes and swamp, utterly impassable, immediately in front of him. Thus only his flanks were open to attack, and he could re-enforce either wing without danger from attack against his front. The Russians attacked, and until the last day of the month it seemed that they were to win another victory here. Then Hindenburg counter-attacked with such skill that he deceived Samsonov regarding his intentions, and caught the right flank of the Russians unexpectedly, at the same time getting possession of the only road by which they could have retreated. The Russians were driven deeper and deeper into the bogs and marshes. They found their guns sinking into the soft mire.

Whole regiments were thrown into the lakes and drowned, and panic took possession of the rest. On Aug. 31 Samsonov himself was killed, and what remained of his army then was nothing more than a panic stricken mob. The Germans took 50,000 prisoners and hundreds of guns and large quantities of munitions and other supplies.

It was this striking victory which sent the name of Hindenburg sweeping over Germany as that of a great hero who had saved the country from threatening humiliation. He was at once made a field marshal and given full command of the Eastern Front.

TANNER, BENJAMIN TUCKER, an American clergyman of the A. M. E. Church, born at Pittsburgh, Pa., in 1835. Educated at Avery College and Western Theological Seminary, he was ordained in the A. M. E. ministry and elected bishop in 1888, serving as editor of the "Christian Recorder," the organ of the A. M. E. Church, for 16 years. He was the founder and for four years the editor of the "A. M. E. Church Review" and a member of the Negro-American Academy. He wrote: "The Origin of the Negro"; "Is the Negro Cursed?"; "Apology for African Methodism"; "Outlines of African Methodist Episcopal Church History"; "The Dispensations in the History of the Church"; "The Negro in Holy Writ"; "A Hint to Ministers, Especially of the African Methodist Episcopal Church"; "The Color of Solomon— What?" Died Jan. 15, 1923.

TANNER, THOMAS, an English clergyman; born in Market Lavington, Wiltshire, England, Jan. 25, 1674; after graduating from Queen's College, Oxford, was in 1696 elected a Fellow of All Souls. He had already a high reputation as an antiquary, and Wood at his death in 1695 left him the care of his papers. He took orders, and became in succession chaplain to his father-in-law, Bishop Moore of Norwich, chancellor of Norwich, prebendary of Ely, rector of Thorpe near Norwich, archdeacon of Norwich (1710), canon of Christ Church, Oxford (1723), and Bishop of St. Asaph (1732). An improved and enlarged edition of his "Notitia Monastica" (on Monasteries, 1695), appeared in folio under the care of his brother in 1744. But Bishop Tanner's fame rests hardly less securely on his great posthumous biographical and bibliographical work—the labor of 40 years, "Bibliotheca Britannico-Hibernica" (British Hibernian Library, ed. by Dr. D. Wilkins, 1748). His edition of Wood's "Athenæ Oxonienses" (The Oxonian Atheno), he had published in two volumes, folio, in 1721. He

died in Oxford Dec. 14, 1735. See WOOD, ANTHONY.

TANNHÄUSER, or **TANHÄUSER** (tän-hoi'-zer), in old German legend, a knight who gains admission into a hill called the Venusberg, in the interior of which Venus holds her court, and who for a long time remains buried in sensual pleasures, but at last listens to the voice of the Virgin Mary, whom he hears calling on him to return. The goddess allows him to depart, when he hastens to Rome to seek from the Pope (Pope Urban) absolution for his sins. The Pope, however, when he knows the extent of the knight's guilt, declares to him that it is as impossible for him to obtain pardon as it is for the wand which he holds in his hand to bud and bring forth green leaves. Despairing, the knight retires from the presence of the pontiff, and enters the Venusberg once more. Meanwhile the Pope's wand actually begins to sprout, and the Pope, taking this as a sign from God that there was still an opportunity of salvation for the knight, hastily sends messengers into all lands to seek for him. But Tannhäuser is never seen again. The Tannhäuser legend has been treated poetically by Tieck, and Richard Wagner has adopted it (with modifications) as the subject of one of his operas.

TANNIC ACID, tannin, a term applied to certain astringent substances occurring in the bark and other parts of plants, and widely distributed, in one form or another, throughout the vegetable kingdom. They are mostly amorphous, have a rough but not sour taste, a slight acid reaction, and color ferric salts dark blue or green. Their most characteristic reaction is that of forming insoluble compounds with gelatin, solid muscular fiber, skin, etc., which then acquires the property of resisting putrefaction, as in the tanning of leather.

TANSY (*Tanacetum*), a genus of *Compositæ*, numbering about 50 species of strong scented herbs, often shrubby below, with alternate, usually much-divided, leaves, and solitary or corymbose heads of rayless yellow flowers. The genus is represented in Europe, North and South Africa, temperate and cold Asia, and North America. Common tansy (*T. vulgaris*) has long had a reputation as a medicinal herb, causing it to be much grown in gardens in the past. It possesses bitter, tonic, vermifuge, and febrifuge properties. The plant is a native of northern Europe, Siberia, and northwest America, and occurs in a wild state in Great Britain, but as met with along the sides of streams, etc., is often of garden origin. It now holds a place in gardens mainly for the young leaves, which are shredded down and employed to fla-

TANSY

vor puddings, omelets and cakes. A variety with leaves doubly curled is generally preferred.

TANTAH, a town of lower Egypt; on the railway about 50 miles N. of Cairo. It has many large public buildings, besides a palace of the Khedive, and is celebrated in connection with the Great Moslem saint Seyyidel-Bedawi, to whom a mosque is here erected. Tantah has three great annual fairs, which are held in January, April, and August, and at the latter 500,000 persons are said to congregate from the surrounding countries. Pop. about 74,000.

TANTALEM ISLAND, an island in the Gulf of Siam, on the E. coast of the main peninsula, from which it is separated by a narrow strait; 65 miles long by 20 wide.

TANTALITE, an orthorhombic mineral of rare occurrence, found in granite rocks rich in albite or oligoclase; luster, metallic; color, black; streak, reddish brown to black; opaque, brittle. Composition: A tantalate of the protoxides of iron and manganese, part of the tantalic acid being sometimes replaced by oxide of tin, forming a stanno-tantalate. Formula $(FeOMnO)$, TaO_5.

TANTALUM, a pentad metallic element, symbol, Ta., at. wt. 182, discovered in 1803 by Ekeberg in the minerals tantalite and yttrotantalite. The metal is obtained by heating the fluotantalate of potassium or sodium with metallic sodium in a covered iron crucible, cooling, and washing out the soluble salts with water. It is a black powder, insoluble in sulphuric, hydrochloric, nitric, or even in nitrohydrochloric acid, but is slowly dissolved in warm aqueous hydrofluoric acid, very rapidly when nitric acid is present.

TANTALUS, in Greek mythology, a King of Lydia, son of Zeus. He was father of Niobe and Pelops, by Dione, one of the Atlantides, and is represented by the poets as punished in Hades with an insatiable thirst, and placed up to the chin in the midst of a pool of water, which flowed away as soon as he attempted to taste it. There hung also above his head a bough, richly loaded with delicious fruit, which, as soon as he attempted to seize it, was carried away from his reach by a sudden blast of wind. He was thus punished either for theft, cruelty, and impiety, or lasciviousness; for the causes are variously stated.

TANTIA TOPI ("the weaver who became an artilleryman"); the most energetic of the rebel ringleaders during the Sepoy Mutiny of 1857. He commenced as a lieutenant of Nana Sahib, of whom he is said to have been a relation; but after the latter had fled into Nepal, he continued the war for several months, retreating with great rapidity through Bundelcund and central India, but was finally captured, tried, and hanged in April, 1859. He was the last armed rebel in the field.

TANTRA, in Hindu sacred literature, one of the compositions, great in number and in some cases extensive, always assuming the form of a dialogue between Siva and his bride in one of her many forms, but chiefly as Uma and Parvati, in which the goddess asks her consort for directions how to perform certain ceremonies. In giving her the necessary prayers and incantations he warns her that it must on no account be divulged to the profane. The Tantrikas, or followers of the Tantras, consider them a fifth Veda, and attribute to them equal antiquity and superior authority. They were composed chiefly in Bengal and eastern India. The Saktas are great supporters of the Tantras.

TAOISM, or TAONISM, one of the three religions of China. Its founder, Laotse, lived, according to tradition, in the 6th century B. C. Tao is a word meaning "way." The whole teaching was vague and unsatisfactory; but its followers made a great advance on those that had preceded them, by believing firmly that ultimately good would gain the victory over evil, and by insisting that good should be returned for evil, as the sure way to overcome it. The head of the body was a sort of patriarch, who had the power of transmitting his dignity and office to a member of his own family, and the descendants of the first are said to have held the office for centuries. Tao was afterward personified, and regarded as the first being of the universe. The Taoists attributed to him eternity and invisibility; but they do not seem to have regarded him as being in any way able to assist or comfort his followers. All they had to do was to contemplate him and his virtues, and to strive to keep in the "way." When Taoism appears as a definite factor in the history of China, in the 3d century B. C., it appears as a congeries of superstitions. Taoism was largely modified by Buddhism, some of the doctrines and practices of which it adopted; but it still adheres to its old superstitions, though in its treatises it enjoins much of the Confucian and the Buddhistic morality.

TAORMINA, a town on the E. coast of Sicily; on a lofty rock 900 feet above the sea; 35 miles S. W. of Messina. It has numerous relics of antiquity, as an aqueduct, tesselated pavements, and the remains of a theater, reckoned one of the most splendid ruins in Sicily, and commanding a view of almost unparalleled magnificence. Taormina (ancient Tauromenium), founded by the Siculi in the 4th century B. C., was long a Roman possession. It was taken by the Saracens in 902 and 962, by the Normans in 1078, by the French in 1676, and in 1849 by the Neapolitans under Filangleri.

TAOS, the most N. of the Pueblo tribes of North American Indians. They live in New Mexico, in a village of the same name, on the Rio de Taos, 50 miles N. of Santa Fé, and number about 400.

TAPAJOS, a river of Brazil, rises in the Serra Diamantina, 20 miles from the headwaters of the Paraguay, and after a N. course of 1,100 miles, joins the Amazon in lon. 35° W. The Tapajos is a dark, wide stream, and is navigable throughout most of its length. Steamers ply on its lower course for several hundred miles.

TAPESTRY, an ornamental textile used for the covering of walls and furniture, and for curtains and hangings. In its method of manufacture it is intimately related to Oriental carpets, which are made in precisely the same way as certain kinds of tapestry, the only distinction being that carpets are meant for floor-covering alone. Fine storied tapestries are, however, much more elaborate and costly than any carpets, and they have altogether different artistic pretensions. Tapestries are divided into two classes, according as they are made in high warp or low warp looms. The former in manufacture have their warp threads stretched in a vertical manner with a roller at the top around which the warps are wound, and another at the bottom for receiving the finished tapestry. On the low warp looms the warp is extended horizontally, there being an arrangement in both for shedding or separating the warp into two leaves, front and back, as in ordinary weaving. It is in high warp looms that the most elaborate storied or pictorial tapestries are made, low warp looms being more largely devoted to the production of still life and non-pictorial decorative compositions. Notwithstanding these differences, it is difficult to distinguish between tapestries which have been made on high and low warp looms respectively, though the latter are more rapidly and consequently less expensively woven.

The art of tapestry-working is of high antiquity, and it may be that the curtains of the tabernacle "of blue and purple and scarlet, with cherubim of cunning work" (Exod. xxvi: 1), were a kind of tapestry, though more probably they were of needle work. The so-called Bayeaux Tapestry is really embroidered work of the period of William the Conqueror. The art of tapestry working, and indeed all fine weaving, came to Europe from the East, and so well was this recognized that during the Middle Ages the fabric was generally known as *Sarrazinois*. So far as is known the art of high warp tapestry weaving was first practiced in Flanders toward the end of the 12th century, and it flourished in the rich and prosperous towns of Arras, Valenciennes, Lille, Brussels, etc., and from the predominant importance of the first of these towns storied tapestries came to be generally known as "Arras." The disasters which overwhelmed the land during the contest with the Spanish power led many of the most skillful of the tapestry weavers to seek an asylum in foreign lands, and thus the art spread to various European centers. Repeated attempts had been made in France from the middle of the 16th century onward to establish the industry, but it was not till two Flemish workers, Comans and De la Planche, were engaged for an establishment formerly occupied by a family of wool dyers called Gobelin, that the industry was successfully founded and the famous Gobelins factory begun.

The manufactures of the Savonnerie, an establishment founded by Henri IV. for velvet-pile carpets and hangings, was in 1826 combined with the Gobelins, and the two industries are now carried on together by the state. There is also a state factory for low warp tapestries at Beauvais; and at Aubusson and Felletin commercial tapestries are very largely made for furniture covering, etc., in establishments which in earlier times were celebrated for their tapestries *de luxe*. Tapestries were also made at an early period in England. In 1619 an establishment was founded at Mortlake by Sir Francis Crane, and under his guidance works of the highest merit were produced.

Tapestries—especially the high warp storied varieties—are the textiles of kings. In earlier times the monarchs of Europe resorted to the Netherlands for pieces for the decoration of their palaces; and when the manufacture came to be more disseminated it was almost entirely under state supervision and control that the work was carried on.

It was for tapestry that Raphael produced the immortal series of cartoons illustrating the acts of Christ and the Apostles which were executed in Brussels for the Sistine Chapel. Seven of these cartoons, purchased by Charles I. under the advice of Rubens, are now in South Kensington Museum.

TAPEWORM, an intestinal worm, *Tænia solium*, in form somewhat resembling tape. Its length is from 5 to 15 yards, and its breadth from two lines at the narrowest part to four or five at the other or broader extremity. At the narrow end is the head, which is terminated

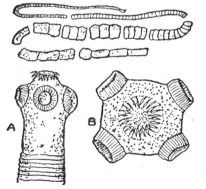

TAPEWORM. A AND B—HEAD ENLARGED

anteriorly by a central rostellum, surrounded by a crown of small recurved hooks, and behind them four suctorial depressions; then follow an immense number of segments, each full of micro-

scopic ova. The segments are capable of being detached when mature, and reproducing the parasite. There is no mouth; but nutrition appears to take place through the tissues of the animal, as algæ derive nourishment from the sea water in which they float. The digestive system consists of two tubes or lateral canals, extending from the anterior to the posterior end of the body, and a transverse canal at the summit of each joint.

The tapeworm lives in the small intestines of man, affixing itself by its double circle of hooks. When the reproductive joints or proglottides become mature, they break off and are voided with the stools. They may get into water, or may be blown about with the wind, till some of them are at length swallowed by the pig, and produce a parasite called *Cysticercus cellulosæ*, which causes measles in the pig. When the measly pork is eaten by man, a tapeworm, the ordinary *T. solium,* appears in his intestines. This species mainly affects the poor, who are the chief pork-eaters. Called more fully the pork tapeworm. The beef tapeworm, *T. mediocanellata,* has no coronet of hooks on the head. The segments are somewhat larger than in the ordinary tapeworm. It is 15 to 23 feet long. The cysticercus of this species forms measles in the ox, and is swallowed by man in eating beef. It chiefly affects the rich. The broad tapeworm, *Bothriocephalus latus,* is 25 feet long by nearly an inch broad, and chiefly affects the inhabitants of Switzerland, Russia and Poland.

The adult sexual *Tæniadæ* live for the most part in birds and mammals, the larval "bladder worms" or *Cysticerci* occur in both higher and lower animals.

Two *Tæniadæ* are in the adult sexual state parasitic in man: *Tænia solium,* with the bladder worm stage in the pig; *T. saginate* or *mediocanellata,* with bladder worm in the ox; and some others, *T. cucumerina, T. nana, T. flavomaculata,* and *T. madagascariensis,* occasionally occur. They infest the small intestine, and there also *Bothriocephalus latus* (larval in pike and burbot) may be found. Moreover tænioid bladder worms also occur in man, the most important being that of *T. echinococcus,* which lives as an adult tapeworm in the dog.

The presence of tapeworm in the small intestine need not be dangerous, but it is usually troublesome, giving rise to disturbances of digestion, colic-like pains, diarrhœa, or, on the contrary, constipation, besides less local effects, such as anæmic and neurotic states. Of anthelmintics—which are intended to expel the parasite from the intestine—there is no lack in the pharmacopœia.

TAPIOCA, the powdered root or rhizome of *Manihot utilissima* (*Jatropha manihot*). The root, which is about 30 pounds in weight, and is full of poisonous juice, is washed, rasped, or rasped and grated, to a pulp. This, being well bruised and thoroughly washed, is heated on iron plates, by which process the poison is drawn off. The powder, when dry, consists of pure starch, and is baked into bread by the natives of Central America. In the United States and Europe it is generally made into puddings, and forms a light and nutritious diet. Pearl tapioca is made from prepared grain.

TAPIR, any individual of the genus *Tapirus*. The South American tapir (*T. americanus*) is about the size of a small

HEAD OF MALAYAN TAPIR

ass, but more stoutly built, legs short, snout prolonged into a proboscis, but destitute of the finger-like process which is present in the elephant's trunk. The skin of the neck forms a thick rounded crest on the nape, with a short, stiff mane. It is plentiful throughout South America, ranging from the Isthmus of Darien to the Straits of Magellan. The color is a uniform deep brown, but the young are marked with yellow stripes and spots. There is another American species inhabiting the Cordilleras; the

SOUTH AMERICAN TAPIR

back is covered with hair, and the nasal bones are more elongated, on which account Gill has given it generic rank. The Malayan tapir (*T. malayanus*) is rather larger than the American species, and has a somewhat longer proboscis; it is maneless. The color is glossy black, with the back, rump, and sides white, the

two colors being distinctly marked off from each other without any graduation. Tapirs inhabit deep recesses of forests, delighting in water, and feeding on young shoots of trees, fruits, and other vegetable substances. They are inoffensive, never attacking man, and are easily tamed. Their flesh is eaten, but is somewhat dry, and their hides are made into leather.

TAPPAN, EVA MARCH, an American author, born at Blackstone, Mass., 1854. She was the daughter of the Rev. Edmund March Tappan, and was educated at Vassar College and the University of Pennsylvania. Her works include: "Charles Lamb, the Man and the Author"; "In the Days of Alfred the Great"; "In the Days of William the Conqueror"; "In the Days of Queen Elizabeth"; "Our Country's Story"; "Robin Hood, His Book"; "American Hero Stories"; "When Knights Were Bold"; "The House with the Silver Door"; "The Farmer and His Friends"; "Diggers in the Earth"; "Food Saving and Sharing"; "The Little Book of Our Country".

TAPTI, a river of Bombay, India; rising in the Betus district of the Central Provinces, and flowing 450 miles W. through the Sátpura uplands and the districts of Candeish and Surat to the Gulf of Cambay; 17 miles below the town of Surat. Even small vessels of 40 to 50 tons burden cannot ascend higher than Surat. The port of Suwali at the mouth is now deserted, and the lower channels of the river are being silted up.

TAR, a product of the destructive distillation of various organic substances; but the tars of commerce are obtained 1st from the distillation of coal, etc., for gas (gas tar or coal tar), and 2d from the distillation of wood (wood tar). Gas or coal tar, which was formerly regarded as a troublesome and almost useless by-product of the gas manufacture, is now a substance of so much value that it is second only in importance to the gas itself. Its value has arisen almost entirely from the fact that it is the source of the wide range of important dyeing substances, which, derived from aniline, phenol (carbolic acid), and anthracene respectively, may all be classed as tar colors. Coal naphtha obtained by distillation from coal tar is a mixture of several hydrocarbons of different degrees of volatility, the lightest being benzol and toluol, and the earlier part of the distillate is composed of a mixture of these two, and that part is utilized for the preparation of aniline as the basis of the aniline colors. The material remaining in the retort after the light oils are distilled over constitutes artificial asphalt, but this on further distillation at a higher heat gives off "heavy oils," leaving in the retort pitch a substance which when cold is hard, black, and shining, and breaks with a glassy fracture. The principal constituents of the heavy oil are carbolic acid (phenol), cresylic acid (cresol), and in the later stages of the distillatory process anthracene is obtained. All these substances are industrially important.

Wood tar is obtained as a by-product in the destructive distillation of wood for the manufacture of pyroligneous acid (wood vinegar) and methyl alcohol (wood spirit). Wood tar has several constituents in common with coal tar; its most characteristic fluid ingredients being hydrocarbons with methylic acetate, acetone, eupione, and creosote, with solid resinous matters, paraffin, anthracene, chrysene, etc. It possesses valuable antiseptic properties, chiefly owing to the creosote it contains, from which substance its principal value for most purposes is derived. In addition to its various uses in the arts of coating and preserving timber and iron in exposed situations, and for impregnating ships' ropes and cordage, it has various applications for external use in medicine owing to its antiseptic properties.

TARA, a parish in Meath co., Ireland, 21 miles N. W. of Dublin. It was a royal residence in the early days of Ireland, and from the hill of Tara was brought the famous stone long used in the coronation of the Scotch kings at Scone. It is now in the chair of Edward the Confessor at Westminster. A sort of Parliament used to be held at Tara, in which all the nobles and principal scholars of Ireland met to institute new laws or to extend and renew old ones, and to examine and correct the national annals and history of the country.

TARAI. See TERAI.

TARA FERN *Pteridium aquilina esculenta*), a species of bracken, the rhizome of which was used as food by the Maoris before the British settlement of New Zealand. It is found in Australia, Japan, and the Hawaiian Islands.

TARANTISM (tăr'an-tĭzm), a dancing mania attributed to the bite of the tarantula spider. It was especially prevalent at Taranto, in Apulia, Italy.

TARANTELLA, or **TARANTELLE,** in music, a rapid Neapolitan dance in triplets; so called because it was popularly thought to be a remedy against the

supposed poisonous bite of the tarantula spider, which was said to set people dancing. Older specimens of the dance are not in triplets. The dance was in vogue in the 16th century.

TARANTO (ancient Tarentum), a seaport of southern Italy, in the province of Lecce; on a rocky islet between the Mare Grande, or Gulf of Taranto, and the Mare Piccolo, an extensive natural harbor on the E. side of the town; 72 miles S. S. E. of Bari. The harbor is sheltered by two small islands, San Paolo and San Pietro, the Chœrades of antiquity, and is closed by Cape San Vito on the S. E. The town is joined to the mainland by a six-arched bridge on the E. side, and on the W. by an ancient Byzantine aqueduct. The principal buildings are a modernized cathedral dedicated to St. Cataldo, a reputed 6th-century Irish missionary, by tradition the first bishop of Tarentum, and a castle erected by Charles V. The Mare Piccolo is still famous for its shellfish. The honey and fruit are still famous also, and among the manufactures are textiles, soap, and olive oil.

The ancient Tarentum, founded by a body of Spartan emigrants about 708 B. C., grew to be the sovereign city of Magna Græcia. Here flourished about 400 B. C. the philosopher and geometer Archytas, under whom it became the center of the Pythagorean sect. At the height of its greatness it insolently provoked a quarrel with Rome (281), was saved for a while by Pyrrhus, King of Epirus, but taken in 272, and retaken and punished severely in 207 for revolting to the side of Hannibal five years before. Later it belonged to Byzantine, Saracen, and Norman, and shared the fortunes of the kingdom of Naples. Pop. about 56,000.

TARANTULA (-ran'tu-lä), the *Lycosa tarantula*, a large spider with a body about an inch in length; its bite

TARANTULA

was formerly supposed to produce tarantism, and it doubtless, in some cases, produces disagreeable symptoms.

It is a native of Italy, but varieties, or closely allied species, are found throughout the S. of Europe. The tarantulas of Texas and adjacent countries are large species of Mygale. Also, a dance, or the music to which it is performed. See TARANTELLA.

TARAPACÁ, till 1883 the extreme S. province of Peru, but annexed by Chile after the war; area, 18,125 square miles; pop. (1895) 89,751. The country contains vast fields of nitrate of soda, as well as silver mines, deposits of guano, and flocks of sheep, alpacas, etc. Capital, IQUIQUE (q. v.). See CHILE.

TARARE, a town of France, department of the Rhone, on the Tardine, among the Beaujolais Mountains; 21 miles N. W. of Lyon. It has two fine churches of the Madeleine and St. André, and manufactures fine muslins, tarlatans, plush, velvets, and other textures, to the value of 7,000,000 francs yearly. Pop. (1906) 12,016.

TARASCON, a walled town of France, in the Provençal department of Bouches-du-Rhône; 14 miles S. W. of Avignon and 8 N. of Arles. King René's castle, dating from 1400, is picturesque and well preserved; and a Gothic church (1187-14th century) is dedicated to St. Martha, who here is said to have subdued a dragon. But Tarascon is chiefly famous through associations with the immortal Tartarin. It has manufactures of woolen and silk fabrics, "saucissons d'Arles," etc. Pop. about 8,500.

TARBAGATAI (-tī'), a range of mountains, 10,000 feet high, in Russian central Asia, on the frontier between Semipalatinsk on the N. and Chinese Zungaria.

TARBELL, EDMUND C., an American landscape and figure painter, born at West Groton, Mass., in 1862. He was educated at the Boston Museum School, and studied with Boulanger and Lefebvre in Paris. He then went to Boston and soon developed a reputation by his Impressionist representations of New England interiors. His better known works include: "Josephine and Mercie" (Corcoran Art Gallery, Washington); "Woman in Pink and Green" and "Girl Reading" (Cincinnati Museum); "The Venetian Blind" (Worcester Museum); "The Golden Screen" (Pennsylvania Academy, Philadelphia); "Afternoon Tea" (Wilstach Collection, Philadelphia). He is a member of the National Academy, of the "Ten American Painters," and of the National Institute of Arts and Letters.

TARBELL, IDA MINERVA, an American writer; born in Erie co., Pa., Nov. 5, 1857; was graduated at Allegheny College; studied in Paris 1891-1894; was associate editor of "The Chautauquan" (1883-1891), of "McClure's Magazine" (1894-1906), and of "The American Magazine" (1906-1915). She

IDA MINERVA TARBELL

wrote: "Life of Napoleon Bonaparte" (1895); "Life of Madame Roland" (1896); "Life of Abraham Lincoln" (1900); "History of the Standard Oil" (1904); "Father Abraham" (1909); "The Tariff of Our Times" (1911); "The Ways of Woman" (1915); "New Ideals in Business" (1916); etc.

TARBES (tärb), a town in the S. of France, capital of department of Hautes-Pyrenées; on the left bank of the Adour; 30 miles E. S. E. of Pau. The cathedral is the principal building. There is a government cannon foundry in the place which is the seat of an active general trade. Pop. about 28,600. Tarbes dates from the time of the Romans, and its bishopric was founded in the year 420. It was in the hands of the English in the 13th and 14th centuries.

TARDIEU, ANDRÉ PIERRE GABRIEL AMÉDÉE, a French administrator and journalist, born in 1876. After graduating from the École Normale, he entered the diplomatic service and was, during 1897, attached to the French embassy in Berlin. For a longer period he was employed in the Foreign Office, then, in 1899, became secretary in the presidency of the Council of Ministers, a position he held for three years. Then followed a period in which he devoted himself to journalism and was editor of the "Revue des Deux Mondes," and foreign editor of the "Temps." In 1908 he made a brief visit to the United States, gathering material for a book. During the beginning of the World War he was chief censor, a position he later abandoned to take his place in the trenches. In 1917 he came to the United States as head of the French mission. He was

ANDRE PIERRE G. TARDIEU

the youngest delegate to the Peace Conference, in 1918, and was a member of the Supreme Council. Among his various works is "The Mystery of Agadir."

TARE, the common name of different species of *Vicia*, a genus of leguminous plants, known also by the name of vetch. There are numerous species and varieties of tares or vetches, but that which is found best adapted for agricultural purposes is the common tare (*V. sativa*), of which there are two principal varieties, the summer and winter tare. They afford excellent food for horses and cattle, and hence are extensively cultivated throughout Europe. The tare mentioned in Scripture (Mat. xiii: 36) is supposed to be the DARNEL (*q. v.*). *V. sativa* is found in fields in the United States.

TARENTUM, a borough of Pennsylvania, in Allegheny co. It is on the Allegheny river, and on the Pennsylvania railroad. It is an important industrial center and has manufactures of plate glass, bottles, lumber, steel and iron novelties, steel billets, etc. Pop. (1910) 7,-414; (1920) 8,925.

TARGET, a shield or buckler of a small size, circular in form, cut out of ox-hide, mounted on light but strong wood, and strengthened by bosses, spikes, etc.; often covered externally with a considerable amount of ornamental work. Also, the mark set up to be fired at in archery, musketry, or artillery practice, or the like. Rifle targets are generally square or oblong metal plates, and are divided into three or more sections—the bull's-eye, inner (or center), and outer, counting from the center of the target to the outside. In some targets there is a fourth division commonly called MAGPIE (*q. v.*).

TARGET PRACTICE. The use of stationary targets for practice in the United States Army has given place to that of appearing and disappearing targets, which stimulate activity and increase the skill of the gunners. American soldiers, and particularly those of the regular service, have the reputation of being the best shots in the world.

For recruits who have not seen such service, the "surprise" targets prove excellent schooling in quick aim and rapid firing. Of these moving targets there are several varieties. In infantry firing at appearing targets, a section, or company, is marched forward to some marked point, when nearing it a target suddenly comes into view. It represents a body of cavalry crossing the plains ahead. The infantry forms in the direction as quickly as possible and opens fire. The target remains in sight only 15 or 20 seconds, after which it is replaced by other targets appearing and disappearing in turn and representing the successive positions of the cavalry. One form of target alternately folds and opens up. It simulates an enemy advancing and kneeling to fire.

The appearing and disappearing targets are worked from a pit position. Light lines leading along the ground and reeving through pulleys enable the operator in his safety cellar to flash a target into view at any desired time. For artillery firing there are frames mounted parallel to the line of fire, and which can be thrown into view by merely turning them so that they will show at right angles to the line of fire. To catch aim quickly, and fire rapidly and with accuracy is the object striven for in this system of target practice.

The proficiency of American gunners in the naval engagements of 1898 attracted much attention. It has been attributed, very correctly, to the pains taken in target practice. Once a month, every ship in the United States Navy, no matter whether she is in a home or a foreign port, is compelled to go to sea for target practice. A float containing a canvas target is turned adrift on the sea while the vessel manœuvres around it for position exactly as if she were entering an engagement. Most of the floating navy targets average about 15 feet in height. The ranges for target practice vary with the size of gun used from 1,000 to 5,000 yards. The auxiliary cruiser "Gloucester," firing at a 6-foot triangular target with her small rapid-fire guns, literally peppered the canvas at a range of 2,000 yards. During the regular gun practice every rifle on the ship is brought into action.

TARGOWITZ, a small town in the province of Kieve, Russia; noted for the Targowitz Confederation or plot formed here (May 14, 1702) by five Polish nobles, who were instigated by Catherine II. Its object was the overthrow of the new constitution, and it led to the second partition of POLAND (*q. v.*).

TARGUM, the general term for the Aramaic versions—often paraphrases—of the Old Testament, which became necessary when, after and perhaps during the Babylonian Exile, Hebrew began to die out as the popular language, and was supplanted by Aramais.

The origin of the Targum itself is shrouded in mystery. The first signs of it—as an already fixed institution—have been found by some in Neh. viii: 8, and according to tradition Ezra and his coadjutors were its original founders. At first, and indeed for many centuries, the Targum was not committed to writing, for the same reason that the "Oral Law" or Halakhah itself was not at first intended ever to become fixed as a code for all times. In the course of time, however, both had to yield to circumstances, and their being written down was considered preferable to their being utterly forgotten, of which there was no small danger. Yet a small portion only of the immense mass of oral Targums that must have been produced has survived.

All that is now extant are three distinct Targums on the Pentateuch, a Targum on the Prophets, Targums on the Hagiographa—viz. on Psalms, Job, Proverbs, the five "Megilloth" (Song of Songs, Ruth, Lamentations, Esther, Ecclesiastes), another Targum on Esther, one on Chronicles, one on Daniel, and one on the apocryphal pieces of Esther. The most important of the three Pentateuch Targums is the one named after Onkelos, probably a corruption of Akylas (Aquila, a proselyte, one of Gamaliel's pupils), whose Greek version had become so popular

that this Aramaic version was honored with being called after it. This Targum seems to have been originally produced among the scholars of R. Akiba between A. D. 150 and 200 in Palestine, and sent to Babylonia, where it was more needed; wherefore it is called Babli. Here it was probably edited about 300, and afterward voweled in the Babylonian method. Subsequently voweled in the Palestinian method, it spread from Palestine over the world. It is an excellent translation for the people, and adheres more closely to the Masoretic text than any other ancient translation. It is useful for the exegete, the linguist, and the antiquary.

Two other Targums on the Pentateuch have hitherto been known as Targum Jonathan ben Uzziel and Targum Jerushalmi. They are of the Palestinian or Syrian growth. Jerushalmi is fragmentary, and appears to be a Haggadic supplement to Ônkelos. The Pseudo-Jonathan, by its maturer angelology, its abbreviations, and other signs, appears to be a later recension of the Jerushalmi. It cannot well have been composed before 750. As a version this Targum is of small importance; but it is valuable as a storehouse of allegories, parables, sagas, and the like popular poetry of its time. Its general use lies more in the direction of Jewish literature itself, as well as of archæology and antiquities of the early Christian centuries, than in that of a mere direct interpretation of the Bible text.

The Targum on the Prophets is ascribed to one R. Joseph, president of the Babylonian academy of Sora about 322. This Targum, while tolerably literal in the first—the historical—books, gradually becomes a frame for Haggada, which it introduces at every turn and at great lengths.

Joseph the Blind, to whom the foregoing Targum is ascribed, is the reputed author of Targums on the Hagiographa. Several centuries lie between him and them, their date being approximately 800 and 1,000. Certain distinctions between the different books must further be made. The Targums on Psalms, Job, and Proverbs were probably contemporaneous compositions due to private enterprise in Syria. The two former are made more paraphrastic than the last, which resembles closely the Syriac version. The paraphrase on the five "Megilloth" mentions the Mohammedans, and is of later date, probably one man's work. It is principally a collection of more or less poetical fancies, traditions, and legends to which the single verse in hand merely seems to furnish the keynote. Its dialect lies somewhat between the East and West Aramaic.

The Targum on the Book of Chronicles
—almost unknown till it was printed in
the 17th century—also belongs to a late
period, and was probably composed in
Palestine. A Persian version of a Targum on Daniel (unedited) is all that has
been discovered on that book as yet. It
was probably composed in the 12th century, the influence of the early Crusades
being plainly visible in it. By 900 in
Africa and Spain the Targum had begun
to be disused in public, Arabic, or the
national language being substituted. In
Yemen the Aramaic Targum is still used
in the ancient manner, the meturgeman
standing beside the reader and rendering
verse by verse.

TARIFA (-rē'fä), the most S. town of
Europe; a seaport of Spain, in the province of Cadiz in Andalusia; 21 miles S.
W. of Gibraltar. The town is still quite
Moorish in aspect, and retains its alcazar
and battlemented Arab walls. A causeway connects it with a small island, on
which are some powerful fortifications
and a lighthouse, 135 feet above the sea-
level. Tunny and anchovy fishing is and
has been since Roman times the principal
occupation of the inhabitants, but the
preparation of leather is also carried on,
and there is a trade in sweet oranges.
Tarifa, called Julia Joza by Strabo, was
occupied in A. D. 710 by the pioneers of
the Moorish invasion, under Tarif Abû-
Zor'a, whence it obtained its Arabic
name of Jezîret-Tarîf (Tarîf's island).
It was taken from the Moslems, after an
obstinate siege, in 1292, by Sancho IV.
of Castile, and its first Spanish governor
was Alonzo Perez de Guzman, celebrated
in the Romancero for his valiant defense
of the town against the besieging Moors
in 1294. During the Peninsular War
Tarifa was successfully defended by
Gough with 1,800 British troops and 700
Spaniards against a besieging army of
10,000 French (December, 1811, to January, 1812). Pop. about 12,500.

TARIFF, a list or table of goods with
the duties or customs to which they are
liable, either on exportation or importation; a list or table of duties or customs
to be paid on goods imported or exported,
whether such duties are imposed by the
the government of a country or are
agreed on between the governments of
two countries having commerce with each
other. The scale of duties depends on
the supply and demand of goods, the interests and wants of the community, etc.,
and is therefore constantly changing.
The tariff legislation of the United
States has been constantly fluctuating,
and has grown yearly in importance as
a question of foreign policy. The most
noted tariff bill ever passed by Congress

I—19

was that taking its name from the then
chairman of the Committee on Ways and
Means, the late President McKinley.
This tariff imposed high duties on imports, some specific and others ad va-
lorem. It was repealed in 1894 by the
passage of the Wilson bill, which became
a law by the refusal of President Cleveland to sign or veto it. On the tariff
question the nation has generally been
pretty evenly divided, or with but a
slight preponderance in favor of a high
protective duty. Of former tariff measures that proposed in 1833 by Henry
Clay, of Kentucky, and known as the
compromise tariff, occupies the most
prominent place in American history.
Though Great Britain is now regarded
as a free-trade country, yet on her tariff
are listed 19 articles of import, from
which she derives an average of about
20 per cent. of her total revenue. The
British tariff is based not on an ad va-
lorem tax, but depends entirely on a
specific import, in some cases modified
by a range of price between the highest
and lowest figures, which it sets for an
article. Thus for spirits worth a certain
amount per gallon, the tax is so much
per barrel, while for spirits of the next
higher grade (according to price per gallon) a higher duty per barrel is collected.

BOOTH TARKINGTON

TARKINGTON, (NEWTON) BOOTH,
an American author and playwright;
born in Indianapolis, 1869; graduate of
Princeton University. In 1902-1903 he
was a member of the State House of
Representatives of Indiana. His chief
vocation, however, has been that of a
novelist and a writer of short stories.
His first book, "The Gentleman from Indiana," appeared in 1899, but it was his

"Monsieur Beaucaire," published in 1900, which first gained him his wide popularity. Among his short stories the "Penrod Stories" have been most popular, on account of their quality of rich humor. Among his many works are: "The Two Vanrevels" (1901); "Seventeen" (1916); "Ramsey Milholland" (1919). Among his plays are: "The Man from Home" (1906); "Getting a Polish" (1909); "The Country Cousin" (1917); "Up from Nowhere" (1919); and "Clarence" (1919).

TARN, a river of southern France, which rises on the S. slope of Mount Lozère, near Florac, in the department of Lozère; flows through the departments of Aveyron, Tarn, Haute-Garonne, and Tarn-et-Garonne; and finally joins the Garonne. Its whole course is 230 miles, of which about 100 miles beginning at Alby are navigable.

TARN, a department of France, in Languedoc, named from the above river; area, 2,231 square miles; pop. about 324,-000. The surface is intersected by hills, which generally terminate in flat summits, on which, as well as their sides, cereals and vines are cultivated. The minerals include iron and coal, both of which are partially worked. Woolens, linens, hosiery, etc., are manufactured; capital, Alby.

TARN-ET-GARONNE, a department of France, named after its two chief rivers; area, 1,441 square miles; pop. about 182,500. This department belongs to the basin of the Garonne which traverses it S. to N. W., and receives within it the accumulated waters of the Tarn and Aveyron which are both navigable. The arable land raises heavy crops of wheat, maize, hemp, tobacco, grapes, and fruit of all kinds. The most important manufactures consist of common woolen cloth and serge, linen goods, silk hosiery, cutlery, leather, etc.; capital, Montauban.

TARNOPOL, a town of Galicia, Poland; on the Sered river; 80 miles S. E. of Lemberg. It has a Roman Catholic and a Greek church, a Jesuit college, upper gymnasium, etc. Before the World War there was considerable trade in corn and other agricultural products. A great horse market with horse races was held annually. Pop. about 35,000.

TARNOW, a town of Galicia, Poland, 47¾ miles E. of Cracow, on the navigable Dunjec river, not far from the mouth of the Vistula. It is the seat of a bishop, and has a town house and cathedral with curious statues of the princes of Ostrog and Tarnow. The chief trade before the World War was in corn, linen, leather, and timber. Pop. about 37,000. See WORLD WAR.

TARO (Colocasia macrorhiza, or Arum esculentum), a plant of the natural order Araceæ, of the same genus with the Cocco (q. v.) or Eddoes, and cultivated for its roots, which are a principal article of food in the South Sea Islands. A pleasant flour is made of taro. The plant has no stalk; broad, heart-shaped leaves spring from the root; and the flower is produced in a spathe. The leaves are used as spinach.

TARPEIA (-pē'yä), one of the vestal virgins of Rome, the daughter of Spurius Tarpeius, governor of the citadel on the Capitoline Hill. She agreed to open the gates to the Sabines if they would give her "what they wore on their arms" (meaning their bracelets). The Sabines, "keeping their promise to the ear," crushed her to death with their shields, and she was buried in that part of the hill called the TARPEIAN ROCK (q. v.).

TARPEIAN ROCK, a rock on the Capitoline Hill at Rome, named from the maid Tarpeia. Traitors were cast down this rock and so killed.

TARQUINIUS, LUCIUS, surnamed PRISCUS (the first or the elder), in Roman tradition the 5th King of Rome. The family of Tarquinius was said to have been of Greek extraction, his father Demaratus being a Corinthian who settled in Tarquinii, one of the chief cities of Etruria. Having removed with a large following to Rome, Tarquinius became the favorite and confidant of the Roman king, Ancus Martius, and at his death was unanimously elected his successor. According to Livy he made war with success on the Latins and Sabines, from whom he took numerous towns. Tarquinius also distinguished his reign by the erection of the Cloaca Maxima, the Forum, the wall round the city, and, as is supposed, he commenced the Capitoline Temple. After a reign of about 36 years he was killed by assassins employed by the sons of Ancus Martius in 578 B. C.

TARQUINIUS, LUCIUS, surnamed SUPERBUS ("the proud"), the last of the legendary kings of Rome, was the son of Lucius Tarquinius Priscus. Tarquin, on reaching man's estate, murdered his father-in-law, King Servius Tullius (the date usually given for this event is 534 B. C.), and assumed the regal dignity. He abolished the privileges conferred on the plebeians; banished or put to death the senators whom he suspected, never filled up the vacancies in the senate, and rarely consulted that body. He continued the great works of his father, and advanced the power of Rome abroad both by wars and alliances. By the marriage of his daughter with Octavius Mamilius of Tusculum, the most powerful of the Latin chiefs, and other political measures, he caused himself to be recognized as the head of the Latin confederacy. After a reign of nearly 25 years a conspiracy broke out by which he and his family were exiled from Rome (510 B. C.), an infamous action of his son Sextus being part of the cause of the outbreak (see LUCRETIA). He tried repeatedly, without success, to regain his power, and at length died in Cumæ in 495 B. C.

TARR, RALPH STOCKMAN, an American scientist; born in Gloucester, Mass., Jan. 15, 1864; was graduated at the Lawrence Scientific School, Harvard University, in 1891. He was an assistant on the United States Fish Commission and in the Smithsonian Institution in 1882-1883, and assistant in the United States Geological Survey in 1888-1891; assistant Professor of Geology at Cornell University in 1892-1897; and in the latter year became Professor of Dynamic Geology which position he held until his death in 1912. His publications include: "Economic Geology of the United States" (1893); "Elementary Physical Geography" (1895); "Elementary Geology" (1897); "First Book of Physical Geography" (1897); "Physical Geography of New York" (1902); "Geography of Science" (1902); "Alaskan Glacier Studies" (1914); "College Physiography" (1914).

TARRAGONA, a seaport in Spain; capital of a province of the same name; on the Francoli, at its mouth in the Mediterranean on a limestone rock. The chief building is the large cathedral, a fine Gothic building partly of the 11th century. The town was founded by the Phœnicians, and became of great importance under the Romans. In its environs are an ancient amphitheater, a circus, an aqueduct, etc. It was taken and sacked by the French under Suchet in 1811. It has a trade in corn, oil, wine, fruit, etc. Pop. about 24,500.

TAR RIVER, a river in North Carolina, which rises in Granville co., flows S. E., and enters Pamlico Sound by a wide estuary. The lower part of it is called Pamlico river. It is about 200 miles long.

TARRYTOWN, a village in Westchester co., N. Y.; on the Hudson river, and on the New York and Hudson river railroad; 27 miles N. of New York. Its precincts include Sleepy Hollow. The Hudson here has an expansion called Tappan Zee, and the village is built on rising ground, commanding an extensive view. It contains a Revolutionary Soldiers' Monument and other objects of interest, Irving Institute, a number of libraries, a National bank, and weekly newspapers. It has manufactories of plumbers' tools, tile, automobiles, and shoes. It is celebrated as the place where Major André was captured, and also as the place where the remains of Washington Irving were interred. Pop. (1910) 5,600; (1920) 5,807.

TARSHISH, a place frequently mentioned in the Old Testament. It is now generally identified by Biblical critics with the Tartessus of the Greek and Roman writers, a district of Southern Spain, near the mouth of the Guadalquivir, settled by the Phœnicians.

TARSUS, the ancient capital of Cilicia, and one of the most important cities in Asia Minor; on the Cydnus river; 12 miles from the sea in the midst of a productive plain. It was a great emporium for the traffic carried on between Syria, Egypt, and the central region of Asia Minor. In the time of the Romans two great roads led from Tarsus, one N. across the Taurus by the "Cilician Gates," and the other E. to Antioch by the "Amanian" and "Syrian Gates." Tarsus, which was sacred to Baal Tars, and is thought by some to have been founded by Sennacherib, 690 B. C., was probably of Assyrian origin, but the first historical mention of it occurs in the "Anabasis" of Xenophon, where it figures as a wealthy and populous city, ruled by a prince tributary to Persia. In the time of Alexander the Great it was governed by a Persian satrap; it next passed under the dominion of Seleucidæ, and finally became the capital of the Roman province of Cilicia (66 B. C.). At Tarsus Antony received Cleopatra, when as Aphrodite she sailed up the Cydnus, with magnificent luxury. Under the early Roman emperors Tarsus was as renowned for its culture as for its commerce, Strabo placing it, in respect to its zeal for learning, above even Athens and Alexandria. The natives were vain and luxurious; a Moslem general estimated their number at 100,000. Weaving goats' hair was the staple manufacture. It was the birthplace of the apostle PAUL (q. v.), who received the greater part of his education here; the Stoic Antipater and the philosopher Athenodorus were also natives, and here the Emperor Julian was buried. Gradually, during the confusions that accompanied the decline of the Roman and Byzantine power, it came into the hands of the Turks, and fell into comparative decay; but even yet this modern, squalid, and ruinous city, under the name of Tarso or Tersus, has a population of about 25,000, and exports corn, cotton, wool, gall nuts, wax, goats' hair, skins, hides, etc.

TARTAR, the substance called also argal, or argol, deposited from wines incompletely fermented, and adhering to the sides of the casks in the form of a hard crust. What is called tartar emetic is a double tartrate of potassium and antimony, an important compound used in medicine as an emetic, purgative, diaphoretic, sedative, febrifuge, and counter-irritant. Tartar of the teeth is an earthy-like substance which occasionally concretes on the teeth and is deposited from the saliva. It consists of salivary mucus, animal matter, and phosphate of lime.

TARTARIC ACID, $C_4H_6O_6$, the most important of vegetable acids, occurs in many fruits, especially the grape. During fermentation the juice of the grape deposits the substance known in commerce as tartar or argol. This substance, essentially the bitartrate of potash, is hardly soluble in cold water, but may be crystallized by cooling from its solution in boiling water. Thus purified it is known as cream of tartar, having the composition $KHC_4H_4O_3$.

TARTARS, or **TATARS**, originally certain Tungusic tribes in Chinese Tartary, but extended to the Mongol, Turkish and other warriors, who under Genghis Khan and other chiefs were the terror of the European Middle Ages. The name, originally Turkish and Persian *Tatar*, was doubtless changed to Tartar, either consciously or unconsciously, because they were supposed to be like fiends from hell (Greek *tartaros*, "hell"). The term is used loosely for tribes of mixed origin in Tartary, Siberia, and the Russian steppes, including Kazan Tartars, Crim Tartars, Kipchaks, Kalmucks, etc., and has no definite ethnological meaning. In the classification of languages Tartaric is used of the Turkish group. See MONGOLIAN: TURANIAN; TURKS.

TARTARUS, according to Hesiod, the the son of Æther and Gæa, and father of the giants Typhœus and Echidna. In the Iliad, Tartarus is a place as far beneath Hades as heaven is above the earth —a dark desolate region into which Zeus hurled the rebel Titans. Afterward the name was sometimes used as a synonym of Hades, but more frequently to denote a place of punishment.

TARTARY, properly **TATARY**, the name under which, in the Middle Ages, was comprised the whole central belt of central Asia and eastern Europe, from the Sea of Japan to the Dnieper, including Manchuria, Mongolia, Chinese Turkestan, Independent Turkestan, the Kalmuck and Kirghiz steppes, and the old khanates of Kazan, Astrakhan, and the Crimea, and even the Cossack countries; and hence arose a distinction of Tartary into European and Asiatic. But latterly the name Tartary had a much more limited signification, including only Chinese Turkestan and Western Turkestan. It took its name from the Tatars or TARTARS (*q. v.*).

TASHKEND, or **TASHKENT**, the capital of Russian Turkestan; 300 miles N. E. of Samarcand; on a small river which empties itself into the Syr-Daria or Jaxartes. It consists of an ancient walled city and a new European quarter with broad streets bordered by canals and avenues of trees. The Russian citadel lies a little to the S. There are extensive military stores, official buildings, Russian schools of all grades, an observatory and geographical society, Russian and Kirghiz newspapers, and a brisk trade with Russia and other parts of Central Asia. It is connected with the European system of telegraphs, and has manufactures of silk, leather, felt goods, and coarse porcelain. Once capital of a separate khanate, Tashkend was in 1810 conquered by Khokand, and since 1865 has been Russian. Pop. about 272,000. See TURKESTAN.

TASMAN, ABEL JANSZOON, a Dutch navigator; born probably in Hoorn, about 1600. Commissioned by Van Diemen, the governor of the Dutch Indies, to explore the S. coast of the Australian continent, he left Batavia with two ships, Aug. 14, 1642; passed Mauritius Oct. 8, and on Nov. 24 discovered a coast which he called Van Diemen's Land, but which is now known as Tasmania. He sailed along its S. and E. coasts without being aware of its insular character, and proceeding further E. discovered (Dec. 13) the S. island of New Zealand (Jan. 6), the Fiji Islands, returning to Batavia June 15, 1643. His account of this voyage was reprinted at Amsterdam in 1722. On Jan. 29, 1644, he set out on a second voyage to explore the coasts of New Guinea and Australia, from which he never returned.

TASMANIA, formerly Van Diemen's Land, an island in the Southern Ocean, 100 miles S. of Australia, from which it is separated by Bass Strait; greatest length, 186 miles; mean breadth, **165**

miles; area, 26,215 square miles; pop. (est. 1919), 270,881. The capital is Hobart on the S. coast; pop. with suburbs (1919), 40,352.

Topography. — The island may be roughly described as heart-shaped. The coasts, which are all much broken and indented, have some excellent harbors. The islands belonging to Tasmania are numerous, the principal being the Furneaux group, on the N. E. extremity. Tasmania is traversed by numerous mountain ranges, the chief summits of which are Mount Humboldt, 5,520 feet; Mount Wellington, 4,195 feet; and Ben Lomond, 5,002 feet. The prevailing rocks are crystalline, consisting of basalt, granite, gneiss, quartz, etc. The chief rivers are the Derwent the Huon, the Arthur, and the Tamar. The chief lake is Lake Westmoreland, which covers an area of 28,000 acres; Lake Sorell, 17,000 acres; Lake St. Clair, 10,000 acres.

Climate. — The climate is very mild. Mount Wellington is frequently covered with snow in the summer months; but at Hobart, in its immediate vicinity, snow never falls. In December, January and February, the summer months, during which there is little rain, the average temperature is 62°, extreme 100° to 110°. The mean temperature throughout the year is about 55°.4. The average rainfall is about 24.05 inches.

Agriculture. — Much of the soil of Tasmania is well adapted for cultivation. Wheat, oats, barley, potatoes, peas, beans and hops are largely cultivated, and the fruit includes grapes, cherries, plums, quinces, mulberries, peaches, apricots, walnuts, filberts, almonds, etc. Fruit-preserving forms an important industry.

Zoölogy. — Kangaroos and other herbivorous animals of the pouched kind are numerous. There are two marsupial carnivorous animals called the Tasmanian wolf and the Tasmanian devil, both of which are destructive to sheep. The natural forests are chiefly of the eucalyptus or gum tree, pine, and acacia tribe.

Mineralogy. — Among the minerals are gold, silver, copper, iron, tin, coal, freestone, limestone, and roofing slate. Smelting works have been erected at Hobart for the iron which abounds in that district.

Commerce. — The staple export from Tasmania is wool, and the other articles include gold, tin, timber, grain, fruit, hides and bark. In jam, hops, hides and skins, 1917-1918 the exports were valued at £1,459,748. Principal minerals produced in 1918: Gold, 10,529 ounces; silver-lead, 7,241 tons; copper, about 6,000 tons; coal, 60,163 tons. Revenue, 1917-1918, £1,503,047; expenditures, £1,-459,748.

Government. — The colony is divided into 18 counties, which are again subdivided into parishes. Another division is into electoral districts for returning members to the legislative council and house of assembly. The constitution is settled by the Act 18 Victoria (1854), supplemented by acts passed in 1871 and 1885, by which are constituted a legislative council and house of assembly, called the Parliament of Tasmania. The legislative council is composed of 18 members, and the house of assembly of 36 members, the latter being elected for five years. The governor is appointed by the crown, and he has a responsible cabinet of four official members, the colonial secretary, treasurer, attorney-general, and minister of land and works.

Religion. — The majority of the colonists belong to the Church of England, Roman Catholics, Methodists and Presbyterians ranking next in the order named. Education is compulsory, and the higher education is under a council, who hold examinations and grant degrees. In 1918 there were 486 elementary and 16 high schools.

History. — Tasmania was discovered in 1642 by Abel Janszoon Tasman, who named it after Van Diemen, the governor of the Dutch East Indies. It was visited by Cook in 1769, and during the next 20 years by various navigators. In 1797 Bass discovered the strait which has been called after him. The first settlement was made in 1803 by a guard with a body of convicts, who settled at Restdown, but afterward removed to the site now occupied by Hobart. The development of the country made slow progress till the land was divided into small allotments and farming stock and government pensions reckoned as capital. Convict labor was supplied, and at a very moderate expense farms were cleared for cultivation. Sheep, cattle, and horses were introduced, and the raising of stock has always been carried on with great success. Till 1824 Tasmania was a dependency of New South Wales, but in that year it was made an independent colony. For a series of years the prosperity of the colony was retarded by the hostility of the natives and the depredations of escaped convicts, known by the name of bush-rangers. The aborigines have ceased to exist, in 1853 transportation was abolished, and about the same time the name of Tasmania was officially adopted on the petition of the colonists. When gold was discovered in Australia in 1851, a rapid emigration from Tasmania to Australia began to take place.

This naturally gave a great check to its prosperity, but for years it has now been fairly prosperous and progressing with moderate rapidity.

TASMAN SEA, a name given to that part of the Pacific inclosed by Australia and Tasmania on the one side, and New Zealand and smaller islands on the other.

TASSO, TORQUATO, an Italian epic poet; born in Sorrento, Italy, March 11, 1544. He was early sent to the school of the Jesuits at Naples, and subsequently pursued his studies under his father's superintendence at Rome, Bergamo, Urbino, Pessaro, and Venice. At the age of 16 he was sent to the University of Padua to study law, but at this time, to the surprise of his friends, he produced the "Rinaldo," an epic poem in 12 cantos. The reputation of this poem procured for Torquato an invita-

TORQUATO TASSO

tion to the University of Bologna, which he accepted. Here he displayed an aptitude for philosophy, and began to write his great poem of "Gierusalemme Liberata" (Jerusalem Delivered). While engaged on it he secured a patron in Cardinal Louis d'Este, to whom he had dedicated his "Rinaldo." He was introduced by the cardinal to the court of Alfonso II. of Ferrara. Here he remained from 1565 to 1571, when he accompanied the cardinal on an embassy from the Pope to Charles IX. of France. Having quarreled with his patron, Tasso returned to Ferrara, and in 1573 brought out the "Aminta," a pastoral, which was represented at the court. In 1575 he completed his epic of "Gierusalemme Liberata" (Jerusalem Delivered).

About this time he became a prey to morbid fancies, believed that he was persistently calumniated at court, and systematically misrepresented to the Inquisition. In 1577 he stabbed a domestic of the Duchess of Urbino, was imprisoned, but soon released. For some time afterward he acted in an irresponsible manner, and was finally by the duke's orders confined as a madman in the hospital of St. Anne, Ferrara. Here he remained from 1579 to 1586, till he was released at the solicitation of Vincent di Gonzaga. Broken in health and spirit, he retired to Mantua, and then to Naples. Finally, in 1595 he proceeded to Rome at the request of the Pope, who desired him to be crowned with laurel at the capitol, but the poet died on April 25, while the preparations for the ceremony were being made. Tasso wrote numerous poems, but his fame rests chiefly on his "Rime," or lyrical poems, his "Aminta," and his "Jerusalem Delivered."

TASSONI, ALESSANDRO, an Italian poet; born in Modena in 1565; studied law in Bologna and Ferrara; became secretary of Cardinal Colonna in 1597; and accompanied him to Spain in 1600. In 1612 he entered the service of Carlo Emanuele of Savoy, for whom he had a high regard, but he was soon forced by the intrigues of his political enemies to give up his post. In 1626 he obtained the office of secretary to Cardinal Lodovisio, and after the cardinal's death was appointed in 1632 chamberlain to Francis I. of Modena. By his hostile "Considerazioni sopra le Rime del Petrarca" (Modena, 1609) he acquired the name of "Petrarchomastix"; in his "Pensieri Diversi" (Rome, 1612) he made a similar attack on Homer and Aristotle, and maintained that in everything—in literature as well as in science—the moderns had the pre-eminence; and in the "Secchia Rapita" (Paris, 1622), a mock-heroic poem ostensibly describing the contest that arose from the rape of a Bolognese bucket by the people of Modena, he treats everything ancient as old-fashioned, and indulges in hilarious but cynical mockery of the general round of human life. His patriotism was severely wounded by the encroachments of the Spanish power, and in his "Filippiche" (Lat. ed. 1878), and his "Manifesto" (1855), he laments the decay of Italian independence. He died in Modena in 1635. The "Secchia Rapita" is his most popular work; it is regularly reprinted from time to time.

TASTE, one of the special senses. The parts of the mouth affected by sapid substances are the surface and sides of the tongue, the roof of the mouth, and the entrance to the pharynx. The mucous membrane is invested by stratified squamous epithelium, which, over the surface of the tongue, covers little vascular projections termed papillæ. One can see the papillæ of the sides and upper part of the tongue with the naked eye, as little sharp or rounded projections; the latter, thickly clustered at the tip and sides, may appear, if the system is out of order, as little red points like those of a strawberry. In the cat tribe the papillæ are hard and curved backward into the mouth, so that the animal can use the tongue as a scraper to remove the flesh from the bones of its prey. The pointed papillæ are termed "filiform." They are essentially the same in structure, differing alone in shape and size. At the back of the tongue are some 8 or 10 papillæ of quite a different nature, called "circumvallate." They are arranged to form a V with its angle pointing backward. These are hardly papillæ at all, but may be looked on rather as tiny patches of mucous membrane trenched out from the surrounding parts.

Into these trenches Ebner's glands secrete a watery albuminous fluid, keeping them perpetually moist and free from foreign particles. In the epithelium lining these trenches curious little bodies called taste bulbs are lodged; and, as these are the parts which are probably more especially concerned in taste, they must be carefully described. Each taste bulb looks like a flask-shaped barrel or box, the walls of which are composed of flat elongated epithelial cells fitted side by side like the staves of a cask. The taste bulbs open each by a little pore into the trench, and into the deeper part a nerve enters. The cask is probably for the protection of the sensory cells which it contains. These cells are much elongated, and end each in a tiny bristle which projects with those of their companion cells from the little pore into the trench, and is here moistened by the juice of Ebner's gland and whatever sapid substance may be present. The impressions which these sensory cells receive from the bristles, say by the action of a bitter like "hops," is carried by the delicate nerve which starts from the opposite end of the cell out of the taste bulb directly to the brain. Within each taste bulb are other cells, which separate and support the sensitive cells, and are similar to analogous structures seen in the sensory epithelium of the eye, and nose, and ear.

While it is almost certain that these taste bulbs are organs of taste, it is not equally certain that other parts are not involved. It may be remarked that substances capable of dissolving in the juices of the mouth are alone tasted. Marble, wood, flint, are devoid of taste, and so is pure starch; these are all of them quite insoluble in water. By the aid of various means we can convert the last-named substance into a very soluble "dextrine," yet this is tasteless. Another chemical product of the starch is a soluble substance termed "dextrose," which has a sweet taste and is commonly termed "grape sugar." These examples will serve to illustrate the general fact that substances to be tasted must be in solution, though not all soluble substances are capable of giving rise to this sensation.

The various taste sensations are not equally produced on stimulating the whole of the gustatory area, and indeed each taste seems to have some special locality at which it is most acutely felt. If we take a piece of quassia or a hop leaf and chew it, we shall at first be unconscious of taste, and it is only when the juice of the mouth laden with these bitter principles passes to the back of the mouth that the taste is felt at all.

Our knowledge of what really takes place when an external agency affects the senses, sets up a nerve motion which travels to the brain and there induces a sensation, is very limited.

When Newlands, Lothar Meyer, and Mendelèef discovered what is termed the Periodic Law in chemistry, it occurred to an English scientist to see if this law holds good for taste and smell; this was found to be the case (see "Proceedings" of the Royal Society of Edinburgh, 1885-1886; and "Brain," 1886). Newlands found that if we arrange the elements in a series, beginning with that one which has the lowest and passing to that which has the highest atomic weight, a periodic recurrence of function or property is found.

There is a general resemblance in physical properties between the 1st, 8th, 15th, etc., and between the 2d, 9th, 16th, etc. Those elements picked out of the series from their resemblance and periodic recurrence Mendelèef arranged in groups (see ATOMIC THEORY), and found that similar compounds of these elements have similar tastes. To take as an example (group 1), the chlorides of lithium, sodium, potassium, rubidium, cæsium are all salt, while the sulphates of these elements are all saline bitters. It is evident that this group of elements, similar in their physical properties, can also produce similar tastes, and we can correlate taste a physiological effect with some common physical quality.

Like smell, the sense of taste is placed at the entrance of the alimentary canal, and affords us knowledge of the nature of the food about to be eaten. We have so far adapted ourselves to our environments that, as a rule, those substances which please these senses are salutary foods, and the converse is equally true. This is however, a rule with many exceptions.

TATE, NATHUM, an English poet; born in Dublin, Ireland, about 1652; received his education in Trinity College; and went to London, where he engaged in literary pursuits, and was appointed poet laureate. He was the author of several dramatic pieces; assisted Dryden in the second part of "Absalom and Achitophel"; altered and arranged Shakespeare's "King Lear" for the stage; and wrote, in conjunction with Dr. Nicholas Brady, the metrical version of the Psalms which used to be appended to the English Book of Common Prayer. He died in London, England, Aug. 12, 1715.

TATIAN, a Christian apologist; born early in the 2d century (110, Zahn); was an Assyrian by birth; studied Greek philosophy; and wandered about as a sophist round the Roman world; but about 150 at Rome was won to Christianity by the simple charm of the Old Testament Scriptures and the example of the purity and courage of the Christians. He became a disciple of Justin, in whose lifetime he wrote his "Oratio ad Græcos," a glowing and uncompromising exposure of the faults of heathenism as compared with the new "barbarian philosophy." After Justin's death (166) Tatian fell into evil repute for heresies, and he retired to Mesopotamia, probably Edessa, writing with characteristic fearlessness and vigor, treatise after treatise, all of which have perished. He was certainly infected with gnostic notions of the universe, the supreme God, the demiurge, and the world of æons; but the notions of his which gave most offense were his excessive asceticism, his rejection of marriage and animal food, and adoption of the practices of the Encratites. Neither the place nor date of his death is known, but it took place perhaps at Edessa, and probably about 180.

Of his writings one maintained a place of importance in the Syrian Church for 200 years, and supplies one of the most interesting chapters in the history of sacred literature. This was the "Diatessaron," a gospel freely constructed out of the four gospels known to us, not a harmony in the modern sense, but a kind of patchwork gospel. This Harnack thinks was written in Greek; but Zahn and most other scholars, among them

Lagarde, Bäthgen, Lightfoot, and Hilgenfeld, in Syriac. There is no mention of the "Diatessaron" in any Latin writer before the middle of the 6th century. In the 5th century this work was used in the Syrian churches as the form in which the gospel was read, and further back still we find evidence of its use in the 3d century "Doctrines of Addài." The Syriac text of the "Homilies" of the former was edited by Professor Wright in 1869, and Zahn has proved that the key to the difficulty of his gospel citations is the fact that he used the "Diatessaron." Bar-Salibi, a Syrian bishop (12th century), distinctly states that Ephraem wrote an exposition of Tatian's "Diatessaron." Lightfoot printed his famous article on Tatian (May, 1877), ignorant of the fact that a year before Dr. Moesinger of Salzburg had published at Venice a Latin translation of the same commentary, made as early as 1841 by Father Aucher of the Mechitarist monastery of San Lazzaro from the Armenian edition of Ephraem's works. published in 1836 (4 vols.). The first scholar to make this remarkable discovery widely known was Ezra Abbot in his "Authorship of the Fourth Gospel" (1880).

In 1881 Zahn published his masterly monograph on Tatian's "Diatessaron," containing a reconstruction of the text from the Latin, based on Mœsinger's Latin version of Ephraem's Commentary, on the quotations in Aphraates, and occasional parallels with the "Codex Fuldensis." He showed that Tatian's original Syrian text agreed in great part with the Curetonian Syriac, and evidently preceded the Peshito or reformed Syriac text. The fresh interest thereby aroused in the question led Ciasca of the Vatican Library to examine anew the Arabic MSS. there. The existence of one was already known, it having been partially described by Assemani, Rosenmüller, and Akerblad. In 1886 Antonios Morcos, vicar-apostolic of the Catholic Copts, forwarded to Rome a 9th-century MS., which Agnostino Ciasca edited for the jubilee of Pope Leo XIII., and this was found both in contents and arrangement to correspond with the work edited by Mœsinger.

Harnack thus sums up the conclusions that may be drawn from what may be considered as proved: (1) In Tatian's time there was still no recognized New Testament Canon, and the texts of the gospels were not regarded as inspired. (2) About 160 three of our four gospels were already in existence and authoritative, and the fourth on equality with the three synoptics. (3) The text of the gospels in 160 was substantially the same as it is now, save that intentional changes and interpolations were made later, as the passage about the church being built on Peter the rock.

TATTOOING, the custom of marking the skin with figures of various kinds by means of slight incisions or punctures and a coloring matter. The word itself is Tahitian (*ta*, "a mark"), but the practice is very widely spread, being universal in the South Sea Islands, and also found among the North and South American Indians, the Dyaks, the Burmese, Chinese, and Japanese, and common enough still among civilized sailors. It is expressly forbidden in Scripture (Lev. xix: 28), from which it is to be concluded that it was common among the neighboring nations. Undoubtedly the main cause of its origin was the desire to attract the admiration of the opposite sex, but this fundamental human desire does not of course exclude motives for tattooing for religious or other ceremonial purposes, or for mere ornament apart from sexual considerations. Among the Polynesians the operation is attended with circumstances of ceremony, and the figures represented are often religious in signification or symbolic of rank, not seldom the totem or special tribal badge. The New Zealanders were distinguished by elaborate tattooing of the face, and many of their heads are preserved in European museums.

Whatever may be the case elsewhere, its origin in Japan, where it reached its greatest perfection, is neither ceremonial nor symbolical, but merely cosmetic. Its end is to take the part of a garment or decoration, those parts of the body only being tattooed which are usually covered, and only in the cases of such workmen as runners, grooms, bearers, who work in a half-nude state. The head, neck, hands, and feet are never tattooed, and it is found among the lower classes alone, and very seldom among women, and these only the dissolute. The usual objects illustrated are large dragons, lions, battle scenes, beautiful women, historical incidents, flowers—never obscene pictures. The colors employed are black, which appears blue, derived from Indian ink, and various shades of red, derived from cinnabar. The artist uses in his work exceedingly fine sharp sewing needles, fixed firmly 4, 8, 12, 20, or 40 together, and, arranged in rows in a piece of wood. A skilful artist can cover the whole back or breast and belly of a grown man in a day. Among the Ainos again the tattooing is done on the exposed parts of the body, and largely practiced by women. The Igorrotos in

the mountainous region above Luzon tattoo elaborately, but in series of lines and curves. Tattooing has often been employed as a badge of brotherhood in some cause, and more often still as a means of identification for slaves and criminals. The so-called branding of the letters D. and B. C. on military deserters and incorrigible characters, only given up in 1879, was merely tattooing with needles and India ink. The war paint of the ancient Briton and Red Indian braves still survives in the paint-striped face of the circus clown. Among the lower-class criminal population of Europe the practice of tattooing is still common, but almost exclusively among males.

TAUCHNITZ, KARL CHRISTOPH TRAUGOTT (touh'nits), a German printer and bookseller; born in Grosspardau, near Leipsic, Oct. 29, 1761. Bred a printer, he set up in 1796 a small printing business of his own in Leipsic, with which he shortly after conjoined publishing and typefounding, and all his enterprise only added to his prosperity. In 1809 he began to issue editions of the Greek and Latin classics, the elegance and cheapness of which carried them over the learned world. He was the first to introduce (1816) stereotyping into Germany, and he also applied it to music. On his death Jan. 14, 1836, the business was continued by his son, KARL CHRISTIAN PHILIPP TAUCHNITZ (1798-1884). A nephew of the elder Tauchnitz, CHRISTIAN BERNHARD, BARON VON TAUCHNITZ, born in Schleinitz Aug. 25, 1816, also founded in 1837 a printing and publishing house in Leipsic. In 1841 he began his well-known collection of "British Authors," of which 2,600 volumes appeared within the first 50 years. The enterprising publisher was ennobled in 1860, and made one of the few Saxon life-peers in 1877. He died Aug. 14, 1895.

TAUNTON, a city and county-seat of Bristol co., Mass.; on the Taunton river, and on the New York, New Haven and Hartford railroad; 36 miles S. of Boston. It contains a public library, court house, United States government building, State Hospital for the Insane, waterworks, electric lights, electric street railroads, National and savings banks, and several daily, weekly, and monthly periodicals. Taunton is a noted manufacturing city, having numerous cotton mills, machine and printing-press works, foundries, nail and tack mills, brick and tile works, stove and furnace works, an extensive britannia-ware plant, a jewelry factory, copper works, shoe-button factories, and locomotive works. It was incorporated as a town in 1639, and chartered as a city in 1864. Pop. (1910) 34,259; (1920) 37,137.

TAUNTON, a town in Somersetshire, England; in the valley of the Tone; 45 miles S. W. of Bristol. Here about 710, Ina, the West Saxon king, built a fortress, which, passing with the manor to the bishops of Winchester, was rebuilt by Bishop William in the first quarter of the 12th century. Added to in the 13th and 15th centuries, this castle received Perkin Warbeck (1497), and was held by Blake during his famous defense of the town (1644-1645). In its great hall, fitted up now as a museum, Judge Jeffreys opened the "Bloody Assize," hanging 134 and transporting 400 of the inhabitants of Taunton and the neighborhood who had accorded Monmouth an enthusiastic welcome (1685); and here too Sydney Smith made his "Mrs. Partington" speech (1831). The church of St. Mary Magdalene has a noble perpendicular tower 153 feet high (about 1500; rebuilt 1858-1862); and other buildings are the Elizabethan shire hall (1858), the municipal buildings (formerly the grammar school founded by Bishop Fox in 1522), King's College school (1880), Independent college (1847-1870), Wesleyan Institution (1843), Huish schools (1874), Bishop Fox's girls' school, hospital (1809-1873), barracks, etc. Formerly one of the great "clothier towns" of Somerset, Taunton now has shirt, collar, glove, and silk manufactures, with a large agricultural trade. Pop. about 22,500.

TAUNTON, RIVER, a small river in Massachusetts, which rises in Plymouth county, flows S. W. through Bristol county, and empties into Mount Hope Bay (Narragansett Bay) at the city of Fall River. It is navigable to Taunton and affords extensive water power.

TAUNUS (tou'nös), a mountain range of Western Germany, mainly in the Prussian province of Hesse-Nassau, extending E. from the Rhine, N. of the Main; highest summit, Great Feldberg, 2,886 feet. It is well wooded, and exhibits much picturesque scenery.

TAURIDA, a province of southern Russia, which includes the peninsula of the Crimea; bounded on the E., S., and S. E. by the Sea of Azov and the Black Sea; area 23,312 square miles; pop. about 2,133,000. The greater part of it belongs to the Nogai Steppe, only 9-11 being under cultivation, and at least a half unenclosed pasture land. From the steppe there is a gradual rise through the Isthmus of Perekop to the Crimea, some of whose ranges attain an elevation of 5,000 feet. The only river of importance is the Dneiper, which forms the N. W. boundary. Salt lakes abound on the treeless steppes. Vines and orchard trees are cultivated to a certain extent, but cattle-breeding is the main employment of the inhabitants. The population is mixed, about one-third of the whole being Little Russians, and rest Nogal Tartars, German colonists, Bulgarians, Greeks, and Armenians. The chief towns are Simferopol the capital, Sebastopol, Feodorsia, and Kertch.

TAURIDS, meteors which appear about Nov. 20, and which have their radiant in Taurus. Fire balls are occasionally seen among them.

TAURUS, in astronomy, the Bull. The second of the zodiacal constellations. It is bounded on the E. by Gemini, on the W. by Aries, on the N. by Perseus and Auriga, and on the S. by Orion and Eridan-

THE CONSTELLATION TAURUS

us. It is composed of many small stars, but has a large one (Aldebaran) situated in the midst of a group called the Hyades. They constitute the Bull's forehead and eye. Another group falling within the limits of Taurus is that of the PLEIADES (*q. v.*). It is situated on the shoulder of the Bull. Taurus contains also the Crab cluster. Also the second sign of the zodiac (8). The sun enters it about April 22.

TAURUS, a mountain chain in Asiatic Turkey, stretching for about 500 miles from the Euphrates to the Ægean Sea, latterly running N. of the Gulf of Adalia. In the E. it takes the name of Alma Dagh, in the W. that of Bulghar Dagh. It descends steeply to the sea on the S.; N. it merges gradually into the plateau of Asia Minor. It is connected by the Alma-Dagh with the chain of Lebanon:

and by Anti-Taurus, with **Ararat, El-burz**, and the Caucasus.

TAUSSIG, EDWARD DAVID, a rear-admiral of the United States navy, born in St. Louis in 1847. He graduated from the United States Naval Academy in 1867 and became an ensign in 1868, going through the grades till he became a rear-admiral in 1908. He was commended to the department in 1868 for services dur-ing the earthquake at Africa. He served on the European and Pacific stations in the coast survey and commanded the Bennington in 1898-9. He served in the Philippines in 1900 and commanded the battleship Massachusetts, in 1904. He was commandant at the Navy Yard, Norfolk, Va.; retired in 1909. Died 1921.

TAUSSIG, FRANK WILLIAM, an American economist; born in St. Louis in 1859. He studied at Harvard and taught there for ten years, becoming in 1892 professor of economics. In 1904-1905 he was president of the American Economic Association. His works in-clude: "The Tariff History of the United States"; "Protection to Young Industries as Applied in the United States"; "His-tory of the Present Tariff, 1860-83"; "The Silver Situation in the United States"; "Wages and Capital"; "Princi-ples of Economics"; "Some Aspects of the Tariff Question"; "Inventors and Money Makers". He was for some years editor of the "Quarterly Journal of Economics."

TAUTPHŒUS, B A R O N E S S VON (tout'fē-ös), an Irish novelist; born (Jemima Montgomery) in Ireland in 1807. She wrote the popular novels: "Cyrilla"; "Quits"; "At Odds"; "The In-itials." She died in Munich Nov. 12, 1893.

TAVISTOCK, a market town of Devon, England, 11 miles N. of Plymouth and 31 S. W. of Exeter; in a trough of the hills on the Tavy's left bank, with Dartmoor stretching away from it to the E. An old stannary town, till 1885 governed by a portreeve, it is the center of what not many years ago was a great mining district. Two gateways, a porch, and the refectory are the chief remains of its once magnificent Benedictine ab-bey, founded in 961 by Ordgar, ealdor-man of Devon, the father of the infa-mous Elfrida. It was rebuilt between 1285 and 1458; was the seat of a very early printing press; and had a rev-enue of $4,510 at the dissolution in 1539; when it was conferred on the first Lord Russell, remaining still with his descen-dant, the Duke of Bedford. The parish church (1318) is a fine structure, with a west tower (106 feet) resting on arches. Tavistock has also a guildhall (1848), corn market (1839), covered markets (1863), statues of the 7th Duke of Bedford by Stephens (1864) and Drake by Boehm (1883, a very fine one presented by the 9th Duke), and the Kelly College (1877), founded by Ad-miral B. M. Kelly. Drake and William Browne were natives, Pym and William Lord Russell members; and the Right Hon. W. H. Smith was educated at the grammar school. Pop. about 4,500.

TAVOY, a district in the Tenasserim division of British Burma; area, 5,308 square miles; pop. about 110,000. The country is mountainous with thick for-ests and jungle, and the chief rivers are the Tavoy and the Tenasserim. The chief town and the headquarters of the deputy-commissioner is Tavoy, about 30 miles from the mouth of the river of the same name; pop. 25,000. There is also an Island of Tavoy, the largest and most N. of the extensive chain which fronts the Tenasserim coast. It is about 18 miles long and 2 broad, and on the E. side there is a well-sheltered harbor called Port Owen.

TAX, a contribution imposed by au-thority on people to meet the expenses of government or other public services. (1) A government imposition, or charge made by the State on the income or property of individuals, or on products consumed by them. A tax is said to be direct when it is demanded from the very persons who it is intended or de-sired should pay it, as a poll tax, income tax, property tax, taxes for keeping dogs, etc. An indirect tax is one demanded from one person, who is expected and intended to recoup or indemnify himself at the expense of another, as customs and excise duties. (2) Any rate or sum imposed on individuals for municipal, county, or other local purposes, as police taxes, taxes for the repairs of roads, bridges, etc., poor tax, drainage tax, etc.

Tax applies to or implies whatever is paid by the people to the government, according to a certain estimate; the cus-toms are a species of tax which are less specific than other taxes being regulated by custom rather than any definite law; the customs apply particularly to what was customarily given by merchants for the goods which they imported from abroad. The predominant idea in con-tribution is that of common consent; it supposes a degree of freedom in the agent which is incompatible with the ex-ercise of authority expressed by the other terms, hence the term is with more propriety applied to those cases in which men voluntarily unite in giving toward any particular object; as charitable contributions, or contributions in support of a war; but it may be taken in the general sense of a forced payment, as in speaking of military contribution.

Also a disagreeable or burdensome duty or charge; an oppressive demand or exaction; a requisition; as, this is a heavy tax on his time and strength. See SINGLE TAX; INCOME TAX.

TAXIDERMY, the name given to the art of putting up natural history specimens in the dried state. It includes the skinning and stuffing of fishes, reptiles, amphibians, birds, and mammals; insects and other invertebrata. But it does not properly comprise the making of wet zoological preparations which are to be preserved in spirits; nor, strictly speaking, does it include the articulating of skeletons, though this is usually treated of in books on taxidermy.

For the skinning of animals a few tools, such as scalpels, scissors, and forceps, are required. Incisions must be made in certain directions. Care has to be taken not to stretch the skin in detaching it from the body, and it is necessary to avoid soiling the plumage of birds or the hair and fur of mammals with blood or grease. The skull and certain wing and leg bones are left in their place to preserve as perfectly as possible the form of these parts in case of the skin being afterward mounted. Arsenical soap is largely used for preserving skin. To preserve bird skins some prefer powdered white arsenic (arsenious acid) either alone or mixed with powdered alum. But sometimes powdered oak bark and a little camphor are added, the proportions being arsenic 1 part, alum, 1 part, bark 2 parts, camphor ½ part. These dry powders should be well rubbed, and the soapy mixtures carefully brushed into the wet surface of skins. For cleaning feathers, and especially those that are light colored, powdered plaster of Paris is very effective. Wherever bird skins or the fur-covered skins of mammals are kept, camphor or naphthaline should be present. Benzene is also very useful. Butterflies, moths, and other insects require to be kept in drawers or boxes of a peculiar construction to prevent the escape of the vapor of camphor or other preservative.

Before the taxidermist can stuff or mount well he requires some training in anatomy and modeling, and a knowledge of the external forms of animals, as well as some acquaintance with their habits.

TAXUS, in botany, the yew, the typical genus of the order *Taxaceæ. T. Caccata,* the common yew, is an ever-green tree which often attains a great size. Specimens of remarkable antiquity are commonly seen in old churchyards. The timber is extremely durable and valuable, and was formerly much used for making bows. Its leaves and young branches act as narcotic-acrid poisons when eaten by man or the lower animals. *T. Canadensis,* the dwarf yew, or ground hemlock, is a small, evergreen shrub, with the general aspect of a dwarf hemlock spruce (*Pinus Canadensis*).

TAY, a river of Scotland, draining nearly the whole of Perthshire, and pouring into the German Ocean a greater bulk of water than any other British river; rises on Benloy, on the Argyllshire border, at an altitude of 2,980 feet. Thence it winds 118 miles E. N. E., S., S. S. E., and E.—for the last 25 miles as a tidal estuary, ½ mile to 3¼ miles broad, which separates Perth and Forfar shires from Fife. In the first 25 miles of its course it bears the names of Fillan and Dorchart; it then traverses Loch Tay, and it afterward passes Aberfeldy, Dunkeld, Stanley, Perth, Dundee, and Broughty-Ferry. Its principal affluents are the Tunnel (58 miles long, and sometimes regarded as a N. head stream), Isla, Almond, and Earn. The Tay, as it is the most beautiful of Scottish rivers, so it is unrivaled for its salmon fisheries. Vessels of 100 tons can ascend as high as Perth, but even to Dundee the navigation of the firth is much impeded by shifting sandbanks.

TAY, LOCH, a lake in Perthshire, Scotland, 355 feet above sea-level, and extending 14½ miles N. E. from Killin to Kenmore, ½ to 1½ miles broad, 15 to 100 fathoms deep, and covering 6,550 acres. It is a magnificent Highland lake, flanked on the N. W. by Ben Lawers (4,004 feet), and containing near its foot a wooded islet, with a fragment of an Augustinian priory, founded in 1122 by Alexander I., who here buried his queen, Sibylla. In September, 1842, Queen Victoria was rowed up Loch Tay, on which a steamer was first launched in 1883, and a railway to which, at Killin, was opened in 1886.

TAYGETUS, a part of a lofty ridge of mountains in Greece, which, traversing the whole of Laconia from the Achæsn frontier, terminates in the sea at the promontory of Tænarus. Its outline, particularly as seen from the N., is of a more serrated form than the other Grecian mountains. In winter it is covered with snow, which renders the vicinity extremely cold. In summer it reflects a powerful heat upon the Spartan plain, from which it keeps the salubrious visits of the W. winds, and thus makes it one of the hottest places in Greece.

TAYLOR, ALONZO ENGLEBERT, an American university professor, born at Alden, Ia., in 1871. He studied at Cornell College, Ia., at De Pauw University, at the University of Berlin, and the University of Pennsylvania, becoming an M.D. in 1894. In 1899-1910 he was professor of pathology in the University of California, and has been Rush professor of physiology and chemistry in the University of Pennsylvania since 1910. He was appointed as secretary on the War Trade Board in 1917. He is a member of the Association of American Physicians and of the American Association of Pathologists.

TAYLOR, ALBERT REYNOLDS, an American university president, born at Magnolia, Ill., in 1846. He studied at Illinois State Normal University and was professor of natural science at Lincoln University, 1872-1882. He was president of the State Naval School of Kansas, 1882-1901; and president of the James Milliken University, Decatur, Ill., 1901-1913; acting president of the same, 1915-1919; and president emeritus after 1919. He has lectured before Chautauquas. His works include: "The Church at Work in the Sunday School"; "Civil Government in Kansas"; "The Study of the Child"; "The Government of the State and Nation."

TAYLOR, a borough of Pennsylvania in Lackawanna co. It is on the Lackawanna River and on the Central of New Jersey, the Delaware and Hudson, and the Delaware, Lackawanna, and Western railroads. It is the center of an important coal mining region and has manufactories of silk. Pop. (1910) 9,060; (1920) 9,876.

TAYLOR, a city of Texas, in Williamson co. It is on the Missouri, Kansas and Texas, and the International and Great Northern railroads. It is the center of an important cotton region, and its industries include live stock, wool, and the manufacture of machine-shop products, flour, cottonseed oil. The repair shops of the International and Great Northern Railroad are here. It is watered largely by artesian wells. Pop. (1910) 5,314; (1920) 5,965.

TAYLOR, BERT LESTON, an American writer, born at Goshen, Mass., in 1866. He was educated at the College of the City of New York and later entered journalism. He became known in connection with a humorous column in the Chicago Tribune, headed "A Line-o'-Type or Two." His works include: "Line-o'-Type Lyrics"; "The Well in the Wood"; "The Log of the Water Wagon"; "The Charlatans"; "Extra Dry"; "A Line-o'-Verse or Two"; "The Pipesmoke Carry"; "Motley Measures." He died in 1921.

TAYLOR, BAYARD, an American writer and traveler; born in Kennett Square, Chester co., Pa., Jan. 11, 1825. He learned the trade of a printer; contributed to various magazines; made a journey through Europe on foot in 1844-1845; on his return published "Views Afoot in Europe," and in this way gained a position on the staff of the New York "Tribune." He afterward traveled extensively, giving his experiences in "Eldorado" (1850); "Central Africa" (1854); "The Lands of the Saracens" (1854); "Visit to India, China, and Japan" (1855); "Northern Travel" (1858); "Crete and Russia" (1859); "Byways of Europe" (1869); and "Egypt and Iceland" (1874). He also published several novels; various volumes of verse, such as "Rhymes of Travel" (1848); "A Book of Romances, Lyrics, and Songs" (1851); "Poems and Ballads" (1854); "Poems of the Orient" (1855); "The Masque of the Gods" (1872); and a translation of Goethe's "Faust" in the original meters. He resided in Germany for lengthened periods, was for some time United States secretary of legation at Petrograd, and latterly was United States minister to Germany. **He died** in Berlin Dec. 19, 1878.

TAYLOR, BENJAMIN FRANKLIN, an American author; born in Lowville, N. Y., July 19, 1819. He was for several years connected with the Chicago "Evening Journal." He wrote: "Pictures of Life in Camp and Field" (1871); "The World on Wheels, etc." (1874); "Song of Yesterday" (1877); "Between the Gates" (1878); "Summer Savory, etc." (1879); "Dulce Domum" (1884); "Theophilus Trent," a novel (1887); etc. Among his best-known poems are "Isle of the Long Ago," "Rhymes of the River," and "The Old Village Choir." He died in Cleveland, O., Feb. 24, 1887.

TAYLOR, FREDERICK WINSLOW, an American efficiency engineer, born at Germantown, Pa., in 1856. He studied at the Stevens Institute of Technology and later employed at the Midvale Steel Company, Philadelphia, as foreman, master mechanic, chief draftsman, and chief engineer. Afterward he organized the management of several manufacturing concerns, such as the Bethlehem Steel, Cramp's Shipbuilding and the Midvale Steel companies. He has had success as an inventor, patenting

100, and developed the Taylor-White process for treating high-speed tools, for which he received a gold medal in Paris. His works include: "Concrete, Plain and Re-enforced"; "Art of Cutting Metals"; "Concrete Costs"; "Principles of Scientific Management"; "Shop Management."

TAYLOR, GRAHAM, an American social worker, born at Schenectady, N. Y., in 1851. He was educated at Rutgers College, and from there in 1870 went to the Reformed Theological Seminary at New Brunswick, N. J. In 1880 he became pastor of the Fourth Congregational Church at Hartford, Conn., acting also for four years ending in 1892 as professor of practical theology at Hartford Seminary. He then became professor of social economics at the Chicago Theological Seminary and from 1894 resident warden of the Chicago Commons Social Settlement, which he founded. He was president of the Chicago School of Civics and Philanthropy, and associate editor of "The Survey." He wrote "Religion in Social Action."

TAYLOR, HANNIS, an American lawyer, born at Newbern, N. C., in 1851. He studied at the University of North Carolina, and during 1893-1897 was United States Minister to Spain. He then practiced law in Washington, D. C., and began writing literature dealing with the law. He is recognized as one of the leading authorities in the United States on international law. His works include: "The Origin and Growth of the English Constitution" (2 vols.); "International Public Law"; "The Science of Jurisprudence"; "The Origin and Growth of the American Constitution"; "Life of Cicero."

TAYLOR, ISAAC, known as TAYLOR OF ONGAR; an English minister and author; born in London, England, in 1759. He was originally an engraver. Besides sermons, he published many volumes, chiefly for the young; among which are: "Advice to the Teens"; "Beginnings of British Biography"; "Beginnings of European Biography"; "Biography of a Brown Loaf"; "Book of Martyrs for the Young"; "Bunyan Explained to a Child"; "Child's Life of Christ"; "Mirabilia; or, The Wonders of Nature and Art"; "Scenes in America, in Asia, in Europe, in Foreign Lands." He died in Ongar, Dec. 11, 1829.

TAYLOR, JEREMY, "the modern Chrysostom"; born in Cambridge, England (baptized Aug. 15, 1613). He studied as a sizar at Caius College, and took his degree of M. A. in 1633. Shortly after he was admitted to holy orders, and his fine appearance and vivid eloquence soon attracted admiration. He won Laud's favor, and through the influence of that prelate was made a fellow of All Souls' College, Oxford. In 1638 he was appointed rector of Uppingham in Rutlandshire. In the civil war, Taylor, whose intellect was impregnably entrenched in reverence for ecclesiastical antiquity, naturally took the royal side, and so lost all his preferments. For many years he lived in retirement in Wales, busily engaged in writing books. In 1658 he went, on the invitation of the Earl of Conway, to Ireland. Immediately after the Restoration he was made Bishop of Down and Connor, which see, as also that of Dromore, he held till his death at Lisburne Aug. 13, 1667. Taylor's writings may be classified as practical, theological, casuistic, and devotional. Under the first head we have a "Life of Christ" (1649), which deals with the main incidents of the gospel narrative, and steers clear of theological discussions: "Holy Living" (1650) and "Holy Dying" (1651), and "Sermons" (1651-1653). To the second class belong his "Episcopacy Asserted" (1642), a temperate and reasoned defense of the principles of his Church, with which may be classed his "Apology for Authorized and Set Forms of Liturgy," "The Liberty of Prophesying" (1648), "The Doctrine of Repentance, or Unum Necessarium" (1655), a work condemned by his brethren for its arguments as to the nature of sin, and "Dissuasion from Popery" (1647). His chief casuistic work is his "Ductor Dubitantium" (1660), while his best devotional work is his "Golden Grove" (1655).

His writings are distinguished in their best parts by a sweet, rich, and solemn eloquence and an artless grace of style. Emerson calls him the "Shakespeare of divines." Personally he was a man of a truly Christian disposition and of such a noble charity that he stands out in gracious contrast to most of his contemporaries.

TAYLOR, (JOSEPH) DEEMS. American composer; born in New York, December 22, 1885. He was educated at New York University. He worked successively on the editorial staffs of the Encyclopedia Britannica, the New York Tribune and Collier's Weekly, serving the Tribune (1916-1917) as correspondent in France. In 1921 he became music critic of the New York World. Earliest among his published musical compositions was "The Echo" (1910), a musical comedy; his symphonic poem "The Siren Song" (1912) gained the orchestral prize of the National Federation of Musical

Clubs. This was followed by the orchestral pieces "Through the Looking Glass" (1918) and "Portrait of a Lady" (1919). Coöperating with Edna St. Vincent Millay, he wrote to her book the score of "The King's Henchman," an opera which the Metropolitan Opera Company of New York produced in 1927.

TAYLOR, LAURETTE (*née* Cooney), an American actress born in New York City in 1887. She married (1) Charles A. Taylor, (2) J. Hartley Manners. She began as a child actress, and for some years toured the country, played in stock at Seattle, Washington, and in 1909 appeared in "The Devil" in New York City. Her first conspicuous success was as Luana in "The Bird of Paradise," but former rôles were eclipsed by her appearance in the title rôle in her husband's comedy, "Peg o' My Heart," which ran through over 600 performances in New York in 1912-14 and over 500 in London. She starred at the same time in "Happiness," also composed by her husband.

TAYLOR, MARY IMLAY, an American author, born at Washington, D. C. She was educated by private tutors, and started writing early. Her first work, "The Rebellion of the Princess," was brought out in 1903. Her other works include: "On the Red Staircase"; "The Impersonator"; "My Lady Clancarty"; "The Reaping"; "Caleb Trench"; "The Long Way"; "The Man in the Street"; "Children of Passion"; "Who Pays?"; "A Candle in the Wind"; "The Wild Fawn."

TAYLOR, THOMAS, styled THE PLATONIST, an English author; born in London, England, May 15, 1758. His works comprise 63 volumes, of which 23 are large quartos. Among them are treatises on arithmetic and geometry; on the Eleusinian and Bacchic mysteries; an essay on the "Rights of Brutes," in ridicule of Thomas Paine's "Rights of Man"; a "History of the Restoration of the Platonic Theology"; and a volume of "Miscellanies in Prose and Verse." His main labor was the translating of great classical Greek and Latin works. His translation of Plato was in five volumes, and was printed at the expense of the Duke of Norfolk. Of his translation of Aristotle only 50 complete copies were struck off, the expense being defrayed by W. Meredith, a retired tradesman. He died in London, Nov. 1, 1835.

TAYLOR, TOM, an English dramatist; born in Sunderland, in 1817. He received his education at Glasgow University and Trinity College, Cambridge; became professor for two years in University College, London; was called to the bar (1845), and went to the N. circuit; appointed, in 1854, secretary to the Board of Health; wrote and adapted for the stage a great number of plays; and succeeded Shirley Brooks (1873) as editor of "Punch." The most popular of his plays are: "New Men and Old Acres"; "Masks and Faces" (in collaboration with Charles Reade); "Still Water Runs Deep"; "The Overland Route"; and "The Ticket of Leave Man." His historical dramas include: "The Fool's Revenge"; "Joan of Arc"; " 'Twixt Axe and Crown"; "Lady Clancarty"; "Anne Boleyn"; etc. He also published biographies of B. R. Haydon (1853), C. R. Leslie (1859), and Sir Joshua Reynolds (1865). He died in Wandsworth, England, July 12, 1880.

ZACHARY TAYLOR

TAYLOR, ZACHARY, an American statesman, 12th President of the United States; born in Orange co., Va., Sept. 24, 1784. He was the son of a Virginia colonel, who served in the Revolutionary War. The family removed to Kentucky in 1785. In 1808 he was appointed a lieutenant of infantry, and in 1810 promoted to captain. In 1812 he was appointed to the command of Fort Harrison, near the present city of Terre Haute, Ind., which he defended with his troops from the attack of a large force of Indians, for which he was brevetted major. He served in the Black Hawk War of 1832, and in 1837 was given full command in Florida, where he defeated the Indians in the battle of Okechobee, thereby putting an end to the Indian War. In 1840 he was given command in the southwest. When Texas was annexed, he marched to Corpus Christi. In 1846 he was ordered to the Rio Grande, the Mexican invasion having been already planned. He established a camp opposite Matamoras. The Mexicans claimed that the Neuces was the actual Texas boundary, and the Mexican commander ordered Taylor to withdraw. Acting under orders from his government, he refused. Fearing his base of supplies at Point Isabel would be cut off, Taylor marched for that place. On the way he was attacked, and won the two victories of Palo Alto and Resaca de la Palma, on two successive days. Having been ordered to send his best troops to re-enforce General Scott, he won the victory of Buena Vista, nevertheless, in 1847, with a force much inferior to the enemy's. In 1848 he was nominated by the Whig Convention for the presidency, and was elected. Inaugurated on March 4, 1849, he died in Washington, D. C., July 9, 1850. On account of his promptness and abrupt manner he was called "Old Rough and Ready."

TAYLORVILLE, a city of Illinois, the county-seat of Christian co. It is on the Wabash, the Chicago and Illinois Midland, and the Baltimore and Ohio Southwestern railroads. It is the center of an important agricultural and stock raising, and coal mining region. Its industries include the manufacture of paper, chemicals, brick, tile, and agricultural implements. It has the St. Vincent Hospital, a public library, and a handsome courthouse. Pop. (1910) 5,446; (1920) 5,806.

TCHAD, CHAD, or TSAD, LAKE, a large fresh-water lake of central Africa, in the Sudan, having the territories of Bornu, Kanem, and Bagirmi surrounding it; length, about 150 miles; breadth, about 100 miles; area, about 30,000 square miles, in the rainy season and about 7,000 in the dry season. Its principal feeder is the Shari from the S., and its shores are low and marshy. The lake (which has no outlet) swarms with turtles, fish, crocodiles, and hippopotami. It contains a number of small islands, which are densely peopled, as are also great part of its shores, especially in the W., where is the large town Kuka, capital of Bornu.

TCHERNAYA (cher'nĭ-ä), a river in the Crimea. On Aug. 16, 1855, the lines of the allied army at this place were attacked by 50,000 Russians under Prince Gortchakoff, who was repulsed with the loss of 3,329 slain, 1,658 wounded, and 600 prisoners. The brunt of the attack was borne by two French regiments under General D'Herbillon. The loss of the allies was about 1,200; 200 of these were from the Sardinian contingent, which behaved with great gallantry, under the command of General La Marmora. The Russian General Read, and the Sardinian General Montevecchio, were killed. The object of the attack was the relief of Sebastopol, then closely besieged by the English and French.

TCHUDI, a name given by the Russians to the Finnic races in the N. W. of Russia. It is now more generally applied to designate the group of peoples of which the Finns, the Esthonians, the Livonians, and the Laplanders are members.

TEA, the dried leaf of an evergreen shrub of the natural order *Ternstrœmiaceæ*, for which the Linnæan botanical name of *Thea Chinensis* is generally current, though the genus *Thea* is by recent systematists merged in *Camellia*, and the plant is now called *C. Thea* of Link. It includes *C. Bohea*, the China plant, and *C. Theifera*, the indigenous Assam plant. Whether the tea shrub is indigenous in China and Japan is a doubtful question. It appears to have been imported thither from Assam and Cachar,

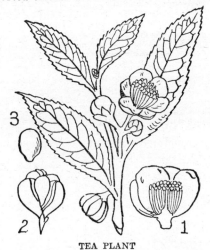

TEA PLANT

1—Flower   2—Fruit   3—Seed

and possibly also from Siam and Cochin. The fact has been historically established that the culture of tea existed in China in the 4th century, and in Japan in the 9th century, and from these countries it was exclusively obtained for any other part of the globe till the time of the present generation. The import appears to have reached Europe during the early part of the 17th century, but we do not hear of any substantial arrival in England till 1657, and for a long time the high price kept its use limited to the wealthy class. At the present day it is estimated that half the human race uses tea habitually or occasionally.

The discovery of the indigenous plant in the forest country of Upper Assam was made in 1834, and since 1840 its cultivation there has taken very firm root, as also in Cachar, Sikkim, the northwestern Himalaya, and other parts of India. The spread of tea field cultivation in northwestern India is mainly due to the late Dr. W. Jameson, who established government plantations in Dhera Dhoon, Kumaon, Gurwal, and Kangra. Since then private individuals and companies have taken part in extending its cultivation in these districts. Tea was introduced into Java as an agricultural plant about 1835; into Carolina about 1845; into Brazil in 1860.

A damp, warm climate, with rains to the extent of 70 or even 100 inches, well spread over the year, and copious in spring, is above all adapted for tea culture. Rich forest land in its virgin state is preferable to any other. The plants must be kept in vigorous growth by the suppression of weeds, periodical turning of the soil, judicious pruning, and adequate manuring. The number of tea plants per acre varies from 1,860 to 2,700 according as they are placed five feet or four feet apart. The yield per acre after the fourth or fifth year is approximately 240 pounds in India and 320 pounds in Assam. Picking and manufacture extend from April to October, during which period 20 pickings are calculated on. The Indian plan for black tea may be briefly described.

The operation of plucking is simply the removal from the bush by the finger and thumb of the young shoots with three or four leaves. The produce, after being weighed, is laid in a cool place, and the following day is spread out thinly on mats in the sun, whereby the leaf becomes sufficiently flaccid for rolling without much breakage. The rolling is slow and laborious handwork, performed on a common deal table. The fermentation is effected by thoroughly shaking up the leaf, throwing it loosely into a heap, and covering closely with mats or carpets—the length of time required depending on the quality and state of the weather. Then succeeds firing in metal pans at a temperature of 240° or 250°. After a few minutes of this treatment it is brushed out, thrown on a table, and
I—20

again quickly rolled while hot. The same process of firing and rolling is repeated, and finally the leaf is exposed to the sun, or placed over charcoal fires to dry. For making green tea the series of operations are somewhat different to the above, the firing being for a longer period and at a higher temperature, and instead of fermentation a little sweating only is permitted.

The youngest and therefore smallest leaves produce the most delicate flavored tea. In ordinary commerce four kinds of black and six of green tea are recognized, but the difference between them consists chiefly in size. In the first, Congou forms the bulk of the British import, Pekoe and Souchong being finer and dearer kinds, and Bohea coarser; and in the green the various Hysons and Gunpowder are most famous. The Ceylon teas include Pekoes, Pekoe, Souchong, Congou, etc. The so-called "English Breakfast" is Souchong. In normal times the world crop of tea is about 800,000,000 pounds. In 1918 the United States imported 151,314,132 pounds, a third coming from Japan. In 1880 the U. S. Agricultural Dept. established a tea plantation at Summerville, S. C., and later at Pierce, Texas. Hlassa brick tea is pressed in the form of a brick, and is prepared when used with butter and salt. It is preferred to all other teas by the natives of central Asia and Tibet.

An infusion of tea as a beverage has trifling actual nutritive value, but it increases respiratory action and stimulates greater activity of the brain; its effect on the nervous system being due to the essential oil and the theine, while the 14 per cent. of tannin it contains is an astringent.

Substitutes for tea have been found in a number of plants, some of which contain the same stimulating property, such as maté, guarana, cola nut, and coffee leaves. Others have been selected by our early colonists, etc., for infusion, and the cognomen tea has in consequence been given to the plants. Thus we have Australian tea for several species of *Leptospermum* and *Melaleuca*, Labrador tea is *Ledum latifolium*, Mountain tea is *Gaultheria procumbens*, New Jersey tea is *Ceanothus Americanus*, New Zealand tea is *Leptospermum scoparium*, Oswego tea is *Monarda didyma*, Botany Bay tea is *Smilax glycyphylla*, and West Indian tea is *Capraria biflora*.

TEACHERS COLLEGE, an institution for the training of teachers and school administrators, and for research in the field of education. It was founded in New York City in 1888 and in 1898 became a part of the educational system of

Columbia University. There were, in 1924, 4,773 students in college, including the educational department, and the practical arts department. The faculty numbered 267. The library contains about 60,000 volumes.

TEACHERS' PENSIONS, the granting of pensions to teachers after superannuation by the state, municipality or by a combination of either of these two and a professional organization of the teachers themselves. Teachers may be divided into two classes: contributory and non-contributory. Contributory pensions are granted from a fund partly made up of donations or subscriptions, by the teachers and in part by the state or municipality. Non-contributory pensions are granted outright by the state or municipality. The latter system is practiced in Germany, while the former is practiced in England and France. Germany and France also provide for the widows, orphans and other dependents of teachers as well.

It was not till about 1895 that the duty of providing pensions for teachers was taken up in the United States. Previous to that pensions had been granted through the medium of mutual aid associations, all the funds being contributed by the teachers themselves. Since then state aid has been granted in Arizona, California, Illinois, Indiana, Maine, Maryland, Michigan, Massachusetts, Minnesota, Montana, Nebraska, Nevada, New Hampshire, New Jersey, New York, North Dakota, Rhode Island, Utah, Vermont, Virginia and Wisconsin. Of these the non-contributory system is practiced only in Arizona, Maine, Maryland, New Hampshire, Rhode Island and Virginia. Of the contributory system that in Massachusetts is most typical.

There the teachers are required to contribute from three to seven per cent. of their salaries toward the pension fund, to which the state adds an equal amount. Thirty years service, or a minimum age of sixty years entitles the recipient to retirement on a pension in proportion to his contributions. Of the municipalities in this country which have been foremost in providing retirement pensions are New York, Detroit, Mich., and St. Louis, Mo. In Brooklyn, N. Y., a contributory system was adopted by which only a cent a year was deducted from the salaries of the teachers. In 1905 the state legislatures amended the city charter which enabled both Brooklyn and New York to adopt a contributory system, which was at the time supposed to be the most advanced of its kind. In 1915 the pension fund was declared to be bankrupt, since which time a new system has been adopted.

TEAK, *Tectona grandis,* one of the most valuable timbers known; the wood of a large deciduous tree (natural order *Verbenaceæ*) with leaves from 10 to 20 inches in length, and from 8 to 15 inches in breadth. The tree, which has small white flowers in panicles, is found in central and southern India, where however, it is now scarce in some localities in which it was formerly plentiful. There are extensive forests of it in Burma and Siam, and it extends into Java and some neighboring islands. In India growing teak is placed under the management of a conservator of forests, and very little is now exported from that country. The wood is of a quiet yellow color, tending to brown, and like many other kinds of timber has a characteristic odor. It is classed as a hardwood, though it is only of medium hardness, taking, however, a good polish; and it is straight grained and strong.

Teak does not shrink much in seasoning, and it is believed to expand and contract less by differences of temperature than most woods.

A sticky elastic extract, to some extent resembling india-rubber, is obtained from teak by treating the wood with naphtha or ether. It is probably this which prevents iron in contact with it from rusting; hence its use for backing the armor plates of warships.

The pores of the wood are sometimes filled with a white substance, which has been ascertained to be phosphate of lime (calcium phosphate). There is a high percentage both of this substance and of silica in the ash of teak, and this no doubt explains why carpenters and other tradesmen consider it gritty. White ants rarely attack the wood if it is sound, but nevertheless logs of it are often badly worm-eaten.

In India teak is used for all kinds of work where strength and durability are required, such as for building ships, houses and bridges, also for the construction of railway carriages and furniture. In England it is largely employed in ship-building. The leaves of the tree yield a red dye. Being of large size they are used in India for plates and for thatching.

African teak (*Oldfieldia Africana*) is imported from the W. coast of Africa; it is also a valuable timber, but less so than true teak.

TEAL, a popular name for any individual of the genus *Querquedula*. They are the smallest of the ducks, and widely distributed over the world, generally frequenting rivers and lakes, and feeding, principally at night, on aquatic insects, worms, small mollusks and vegetable mat-

TEA PICKING IN JAPAN

See Tea, p. 272

THE MASSACHUSETTS INSTITUTE OF TECHNOLOGY

See Technical Education, p. opposite

ter. The common teal, *Q. crecca,* is plentiful in most parts of Europe; length is about 14 inches, head of male brownish-red, the body transversely undulated with dusky lines, white line above and another below the eye, speculum black and green. It nests on the margins of lakes or rivers, collecting a mass of vegetable matter, lining it with down, and laying 8 or 10 eggs. The flesh is extremely delicate, and the bird might be advantageously introduced into the poultry yard. *Q. circia* is the garganey, or summer teal; *Q. carolinensis,* the green-winged teal of the United States, closely resembles the common teal, but has a white crescent in front of the bend of the wings; *Q. discors,* with the same habitat, is the blue-winged teal. *Aix gatericulata* the Mandarin duck, is sometimes called the Chinese teal.

TEASDALE, SARA (MRS. ERNST B. FILSINGER), an American author, born at St. Louis, Mo., 1884. She was educated at private schools in St. Louis, and is a member of the Poetry Society of America and the St. Louis Artists' Guild. Her works include: "Sonnets to Duse, and Other Poems"; "Helen of Troy, and Other Poems"; "Rivers to the Sea"; "Love Songs." She has also been editor of "The Answering Voice" and "One Hundred Love Lyrics by Women." She received the Columbia University Poetry Society of America prize, awarded in 1917 to "Love Songs."

TEASEL, in botany, the genus *Dipsacus.* About 150 species are known, natives of the temperate parts of the Old World and of America. This order consists of herbaceous and half-scrubby exogenous plants with opposite or whorled leaves, and flowers in heads. The only valuable species of the order, *D. fullonum,* fuller's teasel, is four feet high, the bracts hooked, the flowers oval, pale purple or whitish. It is probably only a variety of *D. sylvestris.* It grows best in a stiff loam. The crooked awns or chaffs are fixed around the circumference of large broad wheels or cylinders, and woolen cloth is held against them. They raise a nap on it which is afterward cut level. A piece of fine broadcloth requires 1,500 or 2,000 of them to bring out the nap, after which the teasels are broken and useless. Steel substitutes for teasels have been tried, but ineffectually; they are not sufficiently pliant, and tear the fine fibers of the cloth. Also in mechanics and cloth manufacture, any contrivance used as a substitute for teasels in the dressing of woolen cloth.

TECHNOLOGY, the science which treats of the arts, more particularly the mechanical. It is properly the science of the arts. Its object is not itself, *i. e.,* the practice of art, but the principles which guide or underlie art, and by conscious or unconscious obedience to which the artist secures his ends. In its ordinary acceptation, however, it includes only the utilitarian arts, and in fact only some of these. Painting, sculpture, music, poetry, do not come within its sphere.

TECHNICAL EDUCATION. Technical education as the term is now used is a branch of professional education. The name itself might properly include military education, agricultural education, or industrial education. But these branches have their own specific designations, and it is only with the last named that technical education is likely to be confused. And yet there is a difference. Industrial education looks to increasing the efficiency of human effort in producing material goods. It develops skill of hand without rising to the dignity of a profession. It teaches trades, it establishes manual training schools, it takes the workman from his task and patiently shows him a better way of working. It is fostered by the Federal Government, by the states, by cities, and by private corporations.

Technical education looks to the higher training of the individual. It is based on scientific study. It begins with fundamental branches, as Mathematics, Physics and Chemistry, and proceeds to apply these to the problems of daily life. It stimulates the discovery of new truth, but more constantly the new application of old truth. It is engineering education in the widest possible use of that term. In its beginnings it was elementary, but there was a constant effort to elevate the study into the rank of the learned professions. This effort was furthered by the intimate relation existing between the mechanic arts and the fundamental sciences. This made the engineer a student. There was and is no easy road into the profession of engineering.

The first engineering school, afterward called the Rensselaer Polytechnic Institute, was opened in 1825 at Troy, N. Y., through the generous aid of Stephen van Rensselaer. Mr. van Rensselaer was a Harvard graduate and keenly alive to industrial development. He was familiar with the Fellenberg School at Hofwyl, Switzerland, a kind of manual training school for the poor. He stated the aim of his new school to be the instruction of persons "in the application of science to the common purposes of life." Prior to this time there seems to have been no conception of engineering as a profession in any part of the United States. Such engineering work as was done fell to men trained at West Point, or in foreign schools, or in the school of personal experience. It is probable, too, that van Rensselaer had no definite purpose of establishing a new professional class. However, after the death of Amos Eaton, the first senior professor, the Rensselaer Polytechnic Institute became more definitely a school of civil engineering.

In spite of growing industrial development no further schools of this nature were established until 1847. In that year a school of applied science was started at Yale, which afterward grew into the Sheffield Scientific School, and the Lawrence Scientific School was established at Harvard. The University of Michigan also made preparations at the same time for a course in civil engineering. These were the only engineering schools opened before the Civil War. The Rensselaer Institute graduated 318 men before 1860, and the Lawrence Scientific School at Harvard 49, as has been said in spite of "an unconcealed disdain on the part of the regular faculty."

The next impulse to technical education came from the Federal Government with the passage of the famous Morrill Act in 1862. The starting point of this legislation was a desire to promote agricultural education, but the mechanic arts were included in the plan and seem to have reaped in some quarters a more profitable harvest than agriculture. When the states received their land script some turned over the funds to existing institutions, some established agricultural schools, some colleges of agriculture and the mechanic arts, and some made the land grant the basis for a full university development. At present there are 46 institutions operating as land grant colleges under the Morrill Act and including engineering education in their program.

Following the history of engineering education one step further we note the continued establishment of private institutions, as the Worcester Polytechnic in 1868, the Stevens Institute in 1871, the Case School of Applied Science in 1881, and the Rose Polytechnic in 1883. The Massachusetts Institute of Technology was chartered in 1861, but not opened until 1865. It received assistance from the Morrill Act, but rapidly grew beyond the limits of a state institution. At the same time colleges and universities developed engineering work as a legitimate branch of professional education. Prof. C. R. Mann in his valuable monograph (Bulletin No. 11 Carnegie

Foundation, 1918) sums up the record as follows: "The four schools of 1860 increased to 17 by 1870, to 41 by 1871, to 70 by 1872, and to 85 by 1880. Now there are 126 engineering schools of college grade, of which 46 are land grant colleges operating under the Morrill Act, 44 are professional schools in universities, 20 are attached to colleges, and 16 are independent. The number of students has increased from 1,400 in 1870 to 33,000 in 1917, and the annual number of graduates in engineering from 100 in 1870 to 4,300."

The first engineering course offered was in civil engineering. In 1828 Professor Eaton lectured on this subject—so designated—at the Rensselaer Polytechnic. In 1839 an unsuccessful effort was made to establish a national society of civil engineers. The American Society of Civil Engineers was established in 1852, and held its first national convention in 1869. Next to civil engineering comes mechanical engineering in extent of popularity. Electrical engineering and mining engineering follow next in order. Some institutions offer only one or two courses, others like Columbia University or the Massachusetts Institute of Technology offer the greatest possible variety. The term engineering has been widened to include every possible phase of scientific work, as chemical, metallurgical, electrochemical, sanitary, textile, automotive, highway, hydraulic, marine, etc.

Engineering schools are in the main co-ordinate with colleges, requiring for admission the completion of a high school course, and giving four years of instruction before conferring the first degree, which corresponds to the degree of B.A. or B.S. in college. Later come special courses widely differentiated leading to higher degrees. The curriculum is divided between general subjects, as English, mathematics, and modern languages, the fundamental sciences, especially chemistry and physics, and technical engineering subjects. The proportion assigned to each group varies with each institution, but the percentage given to technical work has steadily increased. This has necessitated the early differentiation of the various courses. Often this appears before the end of the first year. It reflects the specialization of modern industry. Another result deplored but not yet corrected is the congestion of the course. This is one of the pressing problems of engineering education. The first degree given engineering students has many varied names, but bachelor of science, bachelor of science in engineering, and bachelor of engineering seem to be the most popular. Subsequent courses of study are provided covering two or three years and leading to higher specialized degrees as C.E., M.E., E.E., etc.

An interesting experiment in technical education is the co-operative plan of work introduced in the University of Cincinnati in 1906. By this plan practical work is united with theoretical throughout the whole course. This plan is described in a Bulletin of the U. S. Bureau of Education (1916), No. 37, "The Co-operative System of Education," by C. W. Park. A thorough study of engineering education was made by Prof. C. R. Mann and published in 1918 by the Carnegie Foundation as a special bulletin under the auspices not only of the Carnegie Foundation but of a joint committee on engineering education of the National Engineering Societies.

Technical education is a new form of professional training. It is the direct outgrowth of the deeper and more general knowledge of the forces of nature—a knowledge which has come forth largely within the last seventy years. Technical education is most directly studied in, and functions through, the schools of engineering, although there have developed many schools whose teaching is limited to special subjects.

The schools of engineering have grown up co-ordinate with the college of liberal learning. Students enter them directly from the high school. They have not yet become co-ordinate with the professional schools of medicine or of law or of theology. The present movement, however, is toward making the engineering co-ordinate with the other professional schools—its course being subsequent to the college of liberal learning.

Such an advancement in technical education is the special purpose of many of its supporters.

Engineering schools include several types. Among them are civil, sanitary, mechanical, electrical, and mining engineering. The tendency of recent years has been to split up these different courses into finer differentiations.

The teaching given in schools of engineering is largely through laboratories which are, as a rule, well equipped and well administered. Each department usually is organized with a head and several subordinates. These departments are in most schools co-ordinate with each other—their relationships heading up in a general faculty and a president.

Although the teaching in schools of engineering is largely technical, yet it is commonly recognized that success in the vocation of the engineer depends quite as largely upon general qualities as upon professional. Answers made by some several thousand engineers in response to a circular sent out by the Carnegie Foundation for the Advancement of Teaching, of New York, respecting the comparative worth of personal attributes and of technical abilities, showed that three-fourths of all those who replied, believe that the general qualities were of higher value than the special. Character, a sense of responsibility, integrity, common sense, judgment, initiative, efficiency, thoroughness, industry and understanding of men, were declared to have a weight of seventy-five per cent. in any determination of vocational success. Personal character was, in a word, the most comprehensive value.

The course of study usually covers four years and is quite as arduous as the study of medicine or of law. The student begins his day in the laboratory early in the morning and continues until late afternoon. The year usually covers thirty-six weeks, and a summer school also invites his attendance. In certain cases, through attendance of the summer sessions, he is able to abbreviate somewhat his period of residence.

The expense of the student in the engineering schools is perhaps the heaviest, with the possible exception of the medical, of any professional college. The laboratory fees are many. Little time is allowed for his self-support, in case he should desire to earn his way. In certain schools is found a co-operative method by which the student spends one-half of his time in receiving instruction and the other half in practicing or working in industrial plants. The University of Cincinnati is the most outstanding example of such co-operation. Two groups of students are made, which alternate with each other in bi-weekly periods. The University is thus able to use its full equipment with a full quota of students, and also to take advantage of the shop. The course at Cincinnati is finished in five years of eleven months each. This method is regarded by some as the best. It is also regarded by others as at the present time, of doubtful value.

Students of engineering schools on graduation enter factories and offices of a type for which their preceding studies have fitted them. The stipend which they receive in their first year is usually small—about $125.00 per month would perhaps be the average; but for the abler men the progress is rapid toward large incomes.

Schools of engineering have played a large part in the development of the civilization of the United States. They are of special worth in a country whose material resources are yet to be developed. In the development of such resources, however, the engineering school finds that it is not to neglect the human factor. For the best schools recognize that the student is a man before he is an engineer. A large philosophy of life is looked upon as of value in itself, as well as of value in promoting the worth and the efficiency of the application of technical training.

Among the chief schools are the Rensselaer Polytechnic Institute, founded in 1824; the Lawrence Scientific School of Harvard University, founded in 1847; the Sheffield Scientific School of Yale University, founded also in 1847; both these schools waiting some thirteen years for development. The Massachusetts Institute of Technology in Boston, founded in 1861; Worcester Polytechnic Institute, founded in 1865; Lehigh University, South Bethlehem, Pa., founded in 1866; the Stevens Institute of Technology, at Hoboken, N. J., founded in 1870; Case School of Applied Science at Cleveland, founded in 1880; and Rose Polytechnic Institute of Indiana, founded in 1883. The schools more recently established have been, usually, parts of a university.

TECK, an ancient German principality, named from a castle on "the Teck," a limestone peak in the Swabian Alb, 20 miles S. E. of Stuttgart. Held by various families from the 11th century on, it passed in 1498 to the Dukes of Würtemberg. In 1863 the King of Würtemberg conferred the principality on Duke Albert of Würtemberg's son (born 1837) who in 1866 married the Princess Mary of Cambridge. Their daughter, Princess Victoria Mary married July 6, 1893, Prince George, afterwards George V of England.

TECUMSEH, an American Indian; born near Springfield, O., about 1768; first appeared in a fight with Kentucky troops on Mad river in 1788. In 1805, with his brother, Ellskwatawa, he projected the union of all the western Indians against the whites, His defeat in the battle of Tippecanoe ruined these plans, but he continued his efforts among the southern tribes, and ultimately succeeded in inciting the Creek Nation to insurrection. He then joined the English, and commanded the Indian allies in the campaigns of 1812-1813. He was in the action of Raisin river, and after being wounded at Maguaga was made a Brigadier-General in the royal army. He led 2,000 warriors in the siege of Fort Meigs, where he saved the American prisoners from massacre; and commanded the right wing under General Proctor in the battle of the Thames, Canada, where his Indians were driven back and he himself killed, Oct. 5, 1813.

TE DEUM ("*Te Deum laudamus,*" "We praise thee, O God"), a well-known Latin hymn of the Western Church—so called from its first words—sung at the end of matins on all feasts except Innocents' Day, and on all Sundays except during penitential seasons. The hymn is one of the most simple, and at the same time most solemn and majestic, in the whole range of Latin hymnology. Its authorship is uncertain. The chronicle of Bishop Datius of Milan (died about 552), which is both unauthentic and worthless, describes the "Te Deum" as the joint production of St. Ambrose and St. Augustine, into which they both burst forth by a common inspiration on occasion of the baptism of Augustine. Hence the "Te Deum" is commonly called the "Ambrosian Hymn." The first actual reference to it is in the rule of Cæsarius of Arles, who was made a bishop in 502, and it is at any rate certain that it arose as early as the 5th century, and in its modern form was used by Hincmar of Rheims in the 9th century. It is ascribed by some authorities to Hilary of Arles, by others to some disciple of Cassian of Marseilles, but in no case is the evidence at all satisfactory. The hymn in its current form consists of 29 verses; the first 21 verses are uniform in the four oldest versions current, and it seems probable that verses 1-10 were a Greek hymn dating back to the 2d century, though Bishop John Wordsworth in Julian's "Dictionary" thinks verses 7-9 are a reminiscence of Cyprian, not vice versa, and that the Greek form of verses 1-10 is a translation from the Latin, not an original composition. In the Anglican morning prayer it follows the first Lesson, except when the Benedicite is preferred as its alternative. It is frequently used also in the services of both Presbyterian and Congregational Churches, and there are more than 20 metrical renderings of it in English hymnology.

TEEL, or **TEEL-SEED,** an Indian name for *Sesamum indicum* and its seed.

TEES, a river in the N. of England, rising on Cross Fell, in Cumberland, and flowing 70 miles E., mainly along the boundary between Durham and Yorkshire, till it falls into the North Sea, 4 miles below Stockton. Owing to works carried out since 1853 it is now navigable to that town for vessels of large burden, those works including the construction of two breakwaters at the mouth.

TEFFT, LYMAN BELCHER, an American college president, born at Exeter, R. I., in 1833. He was educated at

Brown University and Rochester Theological Seminary, graduating in 1860. He was ordained to the Baptist ministry in 1862, and was pastor at Prescott, Wis., 1862-1863; Winona, Minn., 1863-1866; Norwich, Conn., 1866-1869; Mankato, Minn., 1869-1871, and Colchester, Conn., 1871-1874. He was instructor and acting principal at Nashville Normal and Theological Institute, 1874-1893, and president of Hartshorn Memorial College, Richmond, Va., 1893-1912. He wrote "Curiosities of Heat" and "Institutes of Moral Philosophy." Died Nov. 29, 1926.

TEGEA (tej'ē-ä), a city of Arcadia, in ancient Greece. It took part in the battle of Platæa in 479 B. C.; was on the side of Sparta in the Peloponnesian and Corinthian wars, but opposed her at the battle of Mantinea in 362 B. C.; and joined the Arcadian Confederacy and the Ætolian and Archæan Leagues. Tegea contained a famous temple to Athena Alea, which was burned about 394 B. C., but restored by Scopas. It was a peripteros of Doric architecture, 154 feet long by 72 feet wide, with respectively 13 and 6 columns. The E. pediment bore sculptures representing the slaying of the Calydonian boar; the W. pediment, the combat of Achilles and Telephus. The columns of the cells were Corinthian and Ionic.

TEGNER, ESAIAS, a Swedish poet; born in Kyrerud, Värmland, Nov. 13, 1782. In 1799 he entered the University of Lund, where he studied theology and philosophy, and became "Adjunkt" of Æsthetics in 1805, and Professor of Greek in 1812. After he had been elected to the Swedish Academy (1818), and graduated in theology, he was appointed Bishop of Wexiö, where he remained till his death. His first great works were his "Svea" (1811), crowned by the Academy; the idyl "Nattvardsbarnen" (1821), and "Axel" (1822), whose subject is drawn from the age of Karl XII. It was by his "Frithjofs Saga" (1825) that Tegner won his highest fame. This poem has been translated into almost every European language. Its German translations number 19, of which the best are by Simrock (1875), Zoller (1875), Von Kleinburg (1875), and Möhnike (1877). Two works left incomplete at his death are "Helgönabacken" and "Gerda," the latter an epos placed in the time of Valdemar the Great. Tegner's "Samlade Skrifter" have been published by his son-in-law, Böttiger (7 vols. 1847-1850), and his posthumous works by El Tegnér (3 vols. 1873-1874). His rich humor and lively fancy, his warm and manly feeling, and his wealth of high thoughts

expressed in noble forms, entitle him to rank among the greatest poets of his time. He died in Wexiö, Sweden, Nov. 2, 1846.

TEGUCIGALPA, the capital of a department of the same name in Honduras; situated in a fertile valley 3,400 feet above the sea; on both sides of the Rio Grande, with mountains rising round about. It has an active trade and gold and silver mines. Pop. about 30,000.

TEHERAN, or TEHRAN, the capital of Persia; 70 miles S. of the shore of the Caspian Sea; on a wide plain, dotted here and there with mud-built villages, and pierced with many circular pits, which reach down to the great subterranean watercourses, on which, in this region, the life of animal and plant is altogether dependent. To the N. runs in a general E. and W. direction the lofty range of the Elburz mountains, rising in Demavend to the height of nearly 20,000 feet above sea-level. The old wall and ditch (4 miles long) were leveled in 1868, and the space thus gained made into a much needed circular road or boulevard. Fortifications, consisting of a bastioned rampart and ditch, were at the same time commenced on a much more extended scale. This enceinte, with its 12 gates and inclosing an area about 10 miles in circumference, was completed in 1873. The town rapidly extended beyond its old limits, more especially on the N. side, where many fine streets, gardens, and buildings soon made their appearance, among which may be specially mentioned the handsome buildings and grounds of the British Legation. The Shah's palace, entirely reconstructed since 1866, occupies the citadel, and is both spacious and cheerful, its large courtyards being laid out with gardens and numerous fountains. Besides his town palace, the Shah has five others in the immediate neighborhood, which he occupies at different seasons of the year. The foreign legations and rich natives are also in the habit of resorting in summer to the cool slopes at the foot of the Elburz, where many of them have commodious houses and fine gardens.

The bazaars, some of which are very handsome structures, are filled with every kind of native and foreign merchandise. From Teheran lines of telegraph radiate in almost every direction to the extremities of the kingdom, by far the most important being the lines of the Indian Government Indo-European Telegraph Department and those of the English Indo-European Telegraph Company. In 1886 a short line of rail way was constructed from Teheran to Shah Abdul Azim, a shrine and place of pilgrimage about 6 miles S. of the town. Tramways were also laid down in different parts of the city; and gas was introduced (by a Belgian company) in March, 1892. In the vicinity of Teheran are the ruins of Rei, the "Rhages" of the Book of Tobit, known in the time of Alexander the Great under the name of "Ragæ" and the birthplace of Harûn-al-Raschid. In 1913 the police were placed under the direction of Swedish officers. Swedes are chiefly in command of the Persian troops. Pop. about 220,000.

TEHUACAN, a town in the State of Puebla, Mexico. It has a mineral spring and there are the ruins of magnificent temples. It is 125 miles S. E. of the City of Mexico. Pop. about 9,000.

TEHUANTEPEC, a town of Mexico; in the State of Oaxaca; 14 miles above the mouth of a river of the same name, falling into the Pacific Ocean. On account of a dangerous bar the river is little used for navigation. The town is near the S. side of the Isthmus of Tehuantepec, the narrowest part of North America, having the Gulf of Tehuantepec on the Pacific side, the Bay of Campeachy on the Atlantic side; width, about 115 miles. A ship railway across the isthmus was projected by James B. Eads, and after his death it was built by an English firm for the Mexican Government at a cost of $20,-000,000, and opened for 150 miles in 1907.

TEIGNMOUTH, a seaport and watering place of South Devon, England; 15 miles S. of Exeter; on the N. bank of the mouth of the Teign, here spanned by a bridge (1827) 557 yards long. Numerous villas have sprung up on the hills to the N. and along the "Den," a public lawn stretching three-fourths of a mile above the beach, and a promenade pier was constructed (1866). The two Anglican churches, St. Michael (with a good chancel, 1872) and St. James, are poor edifices of the early part of the 19th century; but a fine Roman Catholic church, in Geometrical Decorated style, has been built (1878) in connection with St. Scholastica's Abbey (1865). Other buildings are the public assembly rooms (1826), theater (1849), market house, public baths, etc. Beyond shipbuilding and fishing Teignmouth has no special industries, but there is a considerable trade. The exports are principally pipe and potter's clay and granite, and the imports, coal, culm, timber, etc. Teignmouth was burnt by the Danes

(930) and French (1338 and 1690), on the last occasion losing 116 houses. Pop. about 9,000.

TEIXEIRA E MATTOS, ALEXANDER LOUIS, a British writer, born at Amsterdam, Holland, in 1865. He was brought to England when nine years old and later acted as London correspondent for Dutch papers. He was editor of "Dramatic Opinions" in 1891, and editor of "Candid Friend" in 1901-1902. He has translated the works of several well known European writers from Dutch, Danish, French, German, and Flemish, among them Carl Ewald, Maurice Mæterlinck, J. H. C. Fabre, and Maurice Leblanc.

TELAUTOGRAPH, an instrument which will at any distance transmit accurately and to the smallest detail in exact facsimile anything that may be written or drawn on the transmitting device. Two instruments are used, one to transmit and one to record. Both are nearly identical in form, size, and general arrangement, and each carries a wide strip of paper controlled by a synchronizing device which causes the one to follow the movements of the other. On the transmitter anything can be written or drawn and the recording stylus of the receiving instrument follows the movements of the transmitting stylus or pencil and thus produces an exact facsimile of the writing or drawing.

The Telechirograph invented by Gruhn is a modification of the Telautograph.

TEJUS, the type-genus of *Tejidæ*, with three species, from Brazil and Mendoza.

TELEGRAPH, an apparatus or process for the rapid communication of intelligence between distant points, especially by means of electro-magnetism. The invention of the electric telegraph, as now used in all parts of the world, is due to Samuel F. B. Morse, who, in 1832, during a homeward voyage from France to New York, conceived the idea of writing on a distant strip of moving paper by means of a pencil worked by an electromagnet and a single conducting circuit, and who in 1844 completed the first line between Washington and Baltimore, and transmitted the first message May 27 of that year. The invention of the Leyden jar, and the discovery of the fact that the earth and intervening bodies of water may be employed as part of an electric circuit, were among the most important steps which gradually led to the completion of the present system of telegraphy. There are now about 500,000 miles of line in operation in the world, using over 1,000,000 miles of wire.

The leading principle in the Morse and other allied instruments is that by the depression of a key or other method, an electric circuit is "closed" or completed, and a signal is transmitted along the wire to the distant station, where, on its arrival, it reproduces the signal by the action of an electro-magnet or otherwise. Electrically the Morse consists of a transmitting key and an electro-magnet and armature; while mechanically it consists of a lever, with circular wheel or disk attached to the armature, and a clockwork arrangement, by which the paper tape to be printed on is carried forward under the disk. In the first Morse instruments the marks were made on the paper with a pointed style (the instrument being thus known as the "embosser"), but by the invention of the ink writer, a form of register now much used in Europe and Asia, the legibility and permanence of the record are secured, besides the advantage that a very light current will serve to make the marks.

The instrument most in use in the United States and Canada, as well as in India and to some extent in Europe, is the "sounder," which is simply a Morse register stripped of all its parts except the electro-magnet, the lever, and the spring, the operator reading by the clicking sounds caused by the opening and breaking of the circuit. By this method the message is read and copied simultaneously, the speed of transmission is greatly increased, and the experience has proven that the proportion of errors is much diminished. The American Morse alphabet, used in the United States and Canada, is as follows:

A	.—	W	.— —
B	—...	X	.—.. —
C	.. .	Y	.. ..
D	—..	Z	... .
E	.	&	. ...
F	.—.	1	.— —.
G	— —.	2	..—..
H	....	3	...—.
I	..	4	....—
J	—.—.	5	— — —
K	—.—	6	......
L	— —	7	— —..
M	— —	8	—....
N	—.	9	—..—
O	. .	0	— — — —
P	.....	(.)	..— —..
Q	..—.	(,)	.—.—
R	. ..	(;)	—.—.
S	...	(?)	—..—.
T	—	(!)	— —..
U	..—	(" ")	.—..—.—
V	...—		

The International Morse alphabet is used in all other parts of the world. The signals, as given below, are arranged in the groups, and accompanied by the mnemonic phrases adopted by the British Postoffice when, in 1870, the transfer of the telegraphs to the government rendered necessary the rapid training of thousands of operators throughout the kingdom:

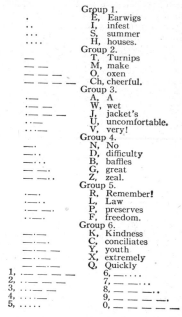

Group 1.		
.	E,	Earwigs
..	I,	infest
...	S,	summer
....	H,	houses.

Group 2.		
—	T,	Turnips
— —	M,	make
— — —	O,	oxen
— — — —	Ch,	cheerful.

Group 3.		
.—	A,	A
.— —	W,	wet
.— — —	J,	jacket's
.—.	U,	uncomfortable.
..—.	V,	very!

Group 4.		
—.	N,	No
—..	D,	difficulty
—...	B,	baffles
— —.	G,	great
—.. .	Z,	zeal.

Group 5.		
.—..	R,	Remember!
.—..	L,	Law
.— —.	P,	preserves
..—.	F,	freedom.

Group 6.		
—.—.	K,	Kindness
—.—.	C,	conciliates
—.— —	Y,	youth
—..—	X,	extremely
— —.—	Q,	Quickly

1,	.— — — —	6,	—.....
2,	..— — —	7,	— —...
3,	...— —	8,	— — —..
4,	....—	9,	— — — —.
5,	.....	0,	— — — — —

Each figure is represented by five signals, but on busy circuits expert clerks adopt the practice of "sending short," omitting all after the first dash in the figures 1, 2, 3, and 4, and all before the last dash in 7, 8, 9, and 0. It is stated that Professor Morse founded his alphabet upon information given him by his brother, a journalist, as to the numerical relation of the letters in the English alphabet, the simplest signal (a dot) being given to E, and the next simplest (a dash) to T, those letters occurring most frequently in our language. The international alphabet is considered preferable, as it contains no spaced letters, which sometimes gives rise to errors in reading.

The process of transmitting more than one communication at the same time over the same line, known as the "duplex" method, was first introduced in the United States, and afterward in Europe, by J. B. Stearns, of Massachusetts, who made his first successful experiment in 1852. The "quadruplex" method was invented by Thomas A. Edison in 1874. Subsequent improvements have been made, and the multiple process, in one form and another, is now extensively used, by means of which the working capacity of the lines is increased at least 25 per cent. An automatic telegraph, in which the message was transmitted from a strip of paper punched with holes representing the letters, was invented in 1846 by Alexander Bain, of Scotland, and afterward improved by Siemens, of Berlin; Humaston, of Connecticut; and Wheatstone, of England. The autographic process, transmitting a facsimile of the original dispatch, was first brought out in 1848 by F. C. Bakewell, of London, and improved by Abbé Casselli, of Florence; Lenoir and Meyer, of France; and Sawyer, of Washington, D. C. (see TELAUTOGRAPH). The printing telegraph for recording messages in Roman characters was first suggested by Alfred Vail, of New Jersey, in 1837. The first model of this telegraph was made by Wheatstone in 1841. Various modifications of this instrument by different inventors are now in use for transmitting private dispatches and for the reporting of commercial and financial fluctuations. In 1918 there were 238,000 miles of pole lines in the United States and 35,000 in Canada, not including the railroad companies' special lines. There are over 435,000 miles of lines in other countries, and over 200,000 miles of submarine cables.

See SUBMARINE TELEGRAPHY: WIRELESS TELEGRAPHY.

TEL-EL-AMARNA, or **TELL-EL-AMARINA,** the modern name of a mass of ruins a little to the N. of Assiout, on the E. bank of the Nile, representing the capital of the heretic Egyptian king AMENHOTEP IV. (*q. v.*). Here was found in 1887 a collection of tablets in Babylonian cuneiform, at that period—some time before the exodus of the Israelites out of Egypt—used as a kind of *lingua franca* for all western Asia. These tablets were mainly reports from the Egyptian governors of Palestine, Syria, Mesopotamia, and Babylonia, some of which implored help against the HITTITES (*q. v.*), then pressing S. Of about 230 tablets 160 went to Berlin Museum and 82 to the British Museum.

TEL-EL-KEBIR (the great mound), a locality midway on the railway between Ismailia and Cairo; the scene on the morning of Sept. 13, 1882, of the capture by Gen. Sir Garnet Wolseley of Arabi Pasha's entrenched camp, defended by 26,000 men. The British loss was about 430 killed and wounded, the Egyptians' 1,500.

TELEMACHUS, in mythology, the son of Ulysses and Penelope; was an infant when his father left home to join in the war against Troy; but during his 20 years' absence grew into manhood. Under the guidance of Athene, who had assumed the appearance of Mentor, Telemachus set out in search of his long-lost sire, after having vainly endeavored to eject his mother's troublesome suitors from the house. Having visited Pylos and Sparta, Telemachus returned home to Ithaca, where he found his father in the guise of a beggar, and with him proceeded to slay the suitors. In modern times Telemachus is known chiefly as the hero of Fénelon's romance, which was once very popular as a school book.

TELEMETER, an instrument for determining the distance of an object whose linear dimensions are known, from its apparent length or height, when viewed between two parallel wires of a telescope.

TELEOLOGY, in philosophy, a branch of metaphysics; the doctrine of final causes and of the uses which every part of nature was designed to subserve; the argument from design in proof of the existence of God. The expression "final causes" was introduced by Aristotle, and the extension which he gave to the idea of causation drew his followers away from studying the proper object of physical science. Bacon said on the subject: "Inquiry into final causes is fruitless, and like a virgin dedicated to God, produces nothing." The context shows that his objection was not to the investigation of final causes in themselves, but to the supposition that this study was a branch of physics. Descartes objected to the study of final causes, believing that to do so successfully was beyond the faculties of man; and most of the French philosophers of the 18th century for various reasons ignored teleology. Modern physical science confines itself rigorously as its name suggests, to the investigation of physical causes. Also, the doctrine of ends in morality, prudence or policy, and æsthetics.

TELEOSAURUS, a genus of fossil crocodiles, the remains of which occur in the lower Jurassic rocks. They are found associated with marine fossils, and the peculiar modification of their skeleton seems to have specially fitted them for an aquatic life.

TELEPATHY, the power of communication between one mind and another by means unknown to the ordinary sense organs, and usually called thought transference. Members of the Society for Psychical Research believe that they have established the fact that such power exists in the material universe and have attempted to turn the assumption to account in the explanation of certain unexplained natural phenomena. Telepathy is not clairvoyance, for it has been demonstrated by many experiments care-

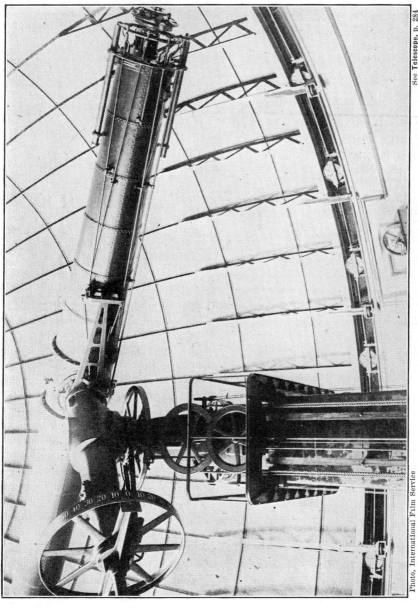

Photo, International Film Service

See Telescope, p. 284

THE 26-INCH EQUATORIAL TELESCOPE AT THE UNITED STATES NAVAL OBSERVATORY, WASHINGTON

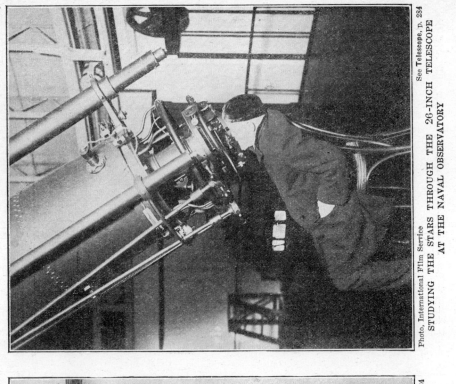

Photo, International Film Service

See Telescope, p. 284

STUDYING THE STARS THROUGH THE 26-INCH TELESCOPE
AT THE NAVAL OBSERVATORY

See Telescope, p. 284

THE FAMOUS BRUCE TELESCOPE AT THE YERKES OBSERVA-
TORY, MUCH USED FOR PHOTOGRAPHS OF THE SKY

fully made by competent persons that sensations, ideas, information and mental pictures can be transferred from one mind to the other without the aid of speech, sight, hearing, touch or any of the ordinary methods by communicating such impressions or information. Some persons can voluntarily project the mind or some independent mental activity a distance of 100 or 1,000 miles so that it can make itself known and recognized, perform acts and even carry on a conversation with the person to whom it is sent.

Scientific work on thought transference began systematically in England in 1882, when the Society for Psychical Research was founded under the presidency of Professor Sidgwick of Cambridge.

Professor Crookes has outlined a theory according to which thought transference is effected by inconceivably minute and rapid ether waves. After pointing out that vibrations of ether of a certain rapidity produce light, he says that there are higher rates of vibrations which are utterly imperceptible to our senses and it is not inconceivable that intense thought, concentrated toward a sensitive being with whom the thinker is in close sympathy, may induce a telepathic chain along which brain waves can go straight to their goal without loss of energy due to distance.

TELEPHONE, an instrument for transmitting sounds or speech to distances where such would be inaudible through aërial sound waves. This definition excludes speaking tubes, which act simply by preserving and concentrating sound waves. Telephonic action depends on the fact that sound waves in air are capable of communicating vibrations to a stretched membrane, and if by any means such vibrations can be transmitted with true resemblance to another membrane at any distance, such receiving membrane will reproduce the sound. This capacity of a single vibrating membrane to reproduce the most complicated sounds, as of speech, is in reality the greatest mystery connected with the matter; all else relates to the mechanism of transmission only. The essential nature of the operation is well shown in the common toy telephone sold in the streets, in which the floors of two small tin cups consist of stretched membranes, or even of paper. The two membranes are connected by a long piece of twine. If now one cup be held to the mouth and spoken into, the voice communicates vibrations to the membrane. The stretched twine communicates similar vibrations to the membrane of the other cup, and if its cavity be held to the ear the sounds will be heard. This is the true mechanical telephone. The term is more commonly applied to the electrical telephonic apparatus so much used in modern life, but the principle is precisely similar. Such apparatus generally belongs to one of two main classes.

The true inventor of the first telephone was undoubtedly Philip Reis, who showed, in 1861, that variations in an electric current caused by a vibrating membrane could reproduce the necessary vibrations. Reis in this way transmitted musical sounds and even words; but his apparatus was imperfect, and it was reserved for Alexander Graham Bell to perfect that which is still commonly used and known as the Bell telephone, though it is the nearly unanimous opinion of electricians that Bell's patent has been held by courts of law to cover far more ground than is really due to him, much to the public detriment and to the hindrance of progress. In Bell's telephone there is a cylindrical steel magnet, surrounded at one end by a coil of wire, whose ends are connected by wire with the circuit or line wire. It will now be understood that any change in the power of the magnet will cause currents in this wire. Near, but not touching, the magnet's end is stretched a very thin sheet of iron, as a membrane, which is spoken to through the mouthpiece. Thus made to vibrate, the iron membrane approaches to and recedes from the magnet; and as it acts toward this as an armature, tending to close the magnetic circuit, the effect is to produce fluctuating degrees of free magnetism, which again produce fluctuating or undulating currents in the line wire. But if these fluctuating currents are received in a precisely similar instrument, they in its coil produce variable magnetic force in the magnet, and this reproduces vibrations in the second iron membrane, which reproduce the sound. The second class of instruments are based on the microphone. If part of a galvanic current is composed of two or three pieces of matter (preferably charcoal) in loose contact, variations in the current produce variations in the contact pressure of the loose pieces, and the converse. Hence, instead of a vibrating membrane causing undulating currents by means of a magnet as in the Bell method, it may abut against such a series of mere contacts, and thus cause an undulating or variable current, which again is capable of converse action. A microphone is thus capable, with more or less modification, of being used as a telephone, and the employment of either method is a question of practical conditions. The Bell telephone is independent of any battery, being self-acting;

but its feeble currents are incapable of transmitting speech to a distance; hence most of the modifications in magnetic telephones have had the design of increasing the power, as by using both poles of the magnet, and in other ways. The microphone, on the other hand, uses the power of a battery in its circuit, but in some respects appears less delicately sensitive than the free membrane. In practice it is very general to employ some form of microphone as the transmitting or speaking instrument, and the Bell telephone, or one of its modifications, as the receiving or hearing instrument.

There are now many forms of telephone in use, the principal varieties being the bi-telephone, in which there are two receivers, one for each ear; the capillary telephone, in which electro-capillarity is used to produce telephonic effects; the chemical telephone, in which chemical or electrolytic action is utilized; the electrostatic telephone, which utilizes electrostatic disturbances in the reproduction of sound; the reaction telephone, in which two mutually reacting coils are used; and the thermo-electric telephone, in which a thermo-electric battery is used. The last-named telephone has never been used in practice. In 1892 a long-distance telephone was erected between Chicago and the larger E. cities.

Telephony at distances of thousands of miles came only after the invention of devices to restore the electric current as it diminished with distance. Boston was connected with Omaha in 1909, New York with Denver, 1911, with San Francisco, 1914. Five vacuum tube repeaters are used between New York and Los Angeles. Radiotelephony, the transmission of telephone conversation carried by radio, was established across the Atlantic on a commercial basis in 1927, the first connection being between New York and London Jan. 7.

TELESCOPE, an optical instrument to assist the naked eye in examining distant objects. It does this in two ways—by magnifying the apparent angular dimensions of the object, and by collecting more light than the pupil of the eye could alone do to form the image on the retina. One point should be noted that is often misunderstood. If any object is large enough to be seen distinctly as a surface by the naked eye, it cannot be made to appear any brighter in a telescope; in fact, it will always be fainter on account of the loss of light by reflection, and absorption in the object glass and eye piece. If, however, the object is faint and rather small to the naked eye, like a distant clock face in the twilight, it can be read more easily in a telescope. If the person should approach the clock face till it subtended the same angular dimensions as its image in the telescope, he could read it more distinctly, and it would appear more brightly illuminated than in the telescope at the first distance, provided he shielded his eyes from surrounding stray light, which is another way in which the telescope sometimes helps in seeing faint objects. If, however, the sources of light examined are from points, like the apparent images of a star, which remain practically points under all magnifying powers, then these images will appear more and more bright the larger the aperture of the telescope, provided the whole of the emergent pencil of rays from the object glass enters the pupil of the eye. With large telescopes and low magnifying powers the emergent pencils are generally too large for this.

Essential Parts.—The essential parts of a telescope are: (1) Either a concave mirror or a system of lenses, called the objective, for bringing to a point in the focal plane the cone of rays which proceeds from each point of the luminous object and falls upon the objective (for objects at a very great—practically infinite—distance these cones of rays that fall upon the objective may be regarded as cylinders). (2) An eye piece consisting of one or more lenses for examining and magnifying the image formed in the focal plane of the objective. (3) A tube or framework of some kind to hold the objective and the eye piece in their proper relative positions. These are all the essential parts of the simple telescope itself, regarded as an optical instrument only. But for the purposes of convenient use many other accessories of mounting and conveniences of handling are required. Moreover, a telescope fitted only as an optical instrument, for looking at objects simply, is of very little scientific value in these modern days of exact measurement and quantitative determination of everything examined, so that in many forms of astronomical, geodetic, and laboratory instruments the optical telescope or microscope is only one of the important parts of the whole, the accessory apparatus attached to it, or to which it is attached, constituting in some instruments the more important feature of the whole. Moreover, for purposes of greater convenience in handling and pointing or of comfort to the observer, many considerable modifications of the optical part itself are introduced, as in the "broken back" transit, where the cone of rays from the objective of the eye piece is reflected at right angles in its course and brought out at one end of the axis, where the observer works in one position without having to follow the revolutions of the eye piece, as in the ordinary form. Also in the equatorial-coudé, or elbow-equatorial, first equatorial telescope introduced at the Paris Observatory by Loewy, the observer sits in one position at the upper end of the equatorial axis, which is itself a part of the telescope tube, the rest of it branching off at right angles from the lower end with the objective at the outer end of this branch, with a large mirror in front of this objective turning on an axis which enables the instrument to be pointed to any polar distance, and the motion of the whole round the polar axis tube reaching any hour angle from the meridian. Another mirror at the lower end of this axis reflects the rays up to the focal plane at the upper end, where the observer at the eye piece has the whole instrument under his control, and works as he would at a microscope, having, moreover, this end inclosed in a warmed room built round the eye piece end if he so desires.

Reflectors and Refractors.—Two principal forms of astronomical telescopes are in use today, reflectors and refractors. In the first the rays are brought to a focus by falling on a concave mirror; in the second by passing through a system of lenses. In this connection it is worth noting that in French the word *telescope* generally refers to reflectors, *lunette* denoting refractors. Though refractors were first invented, no very important astronomical discoveries were made, as we look at telescopic discoveries today, till the invention and use of reflectors by Herschel. There are several forms of reflectors, the Herschelian, in which the mirror is tipped a little in the tube, so that the rays are brought to a focus at the upper end near one side, the observer looking down the tube; the Newtonian, in which a small plane mirror is introduced at an angle of 45°, and reflects the beam out at the side of this tube; and the Gregorian, or Cassegranian, in which the large mirror is pierced in the center and the rays are reflected back through it from a second flat, concave, or convex mirror part way up the tube. In the first two forms the observer must work in an awkward position at the top of the telescope; in the latter he works at the bottom, as in a refractor, and the telescope is much shorter. Reflectors are cheaper, easier to construct, and can be rendered perfectly achromatic, so that they are equally good for optical, photographic, and spectroscopic work. Here, however, their superiority ends. They are awkward to handle and use, their reflecting power constantly diminishes by tarnish

I—21

so that they must be frequently repolished or resilvered, they require more accurate figuring at first, they do not give so much light for the same aperture, even in their best reflecting condition, and, most important of all, any distortion through flexure—they are very heavy— or through local effects of temperature, causes almost infinitely more distortion in the images than the same degree of flexure or distortion of a lens; for when a lens bends, one side becomes more convex and the other more concave, and these nearly counterbalance each other, while the effect of bending or distorting a mirror is to deflect the rays just twice the whole amount. This is why a reflector has to be humored and handled in the most careful manner, and special precautions taken in the mounting and support of the mirror; while a refractor, once finished, can be roughly used, and still it will give better definition than the average reflector. A refractor corrected for optical work cannot be used with good results for photography unless a third lens is attached in front of the objective, or one of the lenses of the objective turned over and their distance changed; and, with any construction whatever in a refractor, the spectroscope must be adjusted to a different focal length for different wave lengths of the spectrum. With respect to the distortions produced by flexure, etc., in reflectors, it should be noted that any form of refractor which uses a mirror as a part of its construction is open to the same objection. It is for this reason that telescopes of the form of the equatorial-coudé, in which there are two reflections from mirrors, are not likely to be in demand where the best definition is a point to be sought after. This form of telescope makes an excellent form for a rapid and convenient comet-seeker.

With the growth in size of telescopes their use and management becomes more difficult, and the mounting has become as important a party as any in the construction of large modern telescopes.

In 1918 the second largest telescope (72 inch) was mounted on Little Saanich Mountain, Vancouver Island, B. C. There are three 60-inch telescopes in the Western Hemisphere; one is at the National Observatory, Argentina, another was constructed for Harvard University, at Ealing, England, and another was erected at Mt. Wilson, U. S. A., in 1908.

See LENS: OBSERVATORY: LICK OBSERVATORY: YERKES OBSERVATORY.

TELESCOPE FISH, or TELESCOPE CARP, in ichthyology, the most highly-prized of the many varieties of *Cyprinus* (*Carassius*) *auratus*, the goldfish. The dorsal fin is absent, the tail is much enlarged, sub-triangular or tri-lobate, and the protruding eyes are set in pedicels.

TELEVISION, the instantaneous transmission by electric or radio impulse of images of actual and moving objects. Two systems of such transmission were demonstrated in 1927. That of Dr. Herbert Ives, developed in the American Bell Telephone laboratories, converted the component spots of light coming from the object into a succession of impulses, transmitted and received through identical perforated revolving screens. At the receiving end the impulsions acted on an image field composed of 2,500 patches of tin foil, each illuminated more or less brightly eighteen times a second by the passage of current through neon gas. A synchronous moving picture of a distant object was thus produced.

TELL, WILLIAM, the champion of Swiss liberty; was a native of Burglen, in the canton of Uri. He was distinguished by his skill in archery, his strength and courage. He joined the league of the Three Forest cantons formed to free the country from Austrian tyranny. The Austrian governor of Switzerland, Herman Gessler, required the Swiss to uncover their heads before his hat and is said to have condemned Tell, for refusing, to shoot an apple from the head of his own son. Tell was successful, but confessed that a second arrow, which he bore about his person, was intended, in case he had failed, for the punishment of the tyrant, and he was therefore retained prisoner. While crossing the Lake of the Four Cantons, or Lake of Lucerne, in the same boat with Gessler, a violent storm arose. Tell was set free, and he conducted the boat to the shore, but springing on a rock, pushed off the boat. He had fortunately taken his bow with him; the governor finally escaped the storm, and Tell shot him dead on the road to Küssnacht. This event was the signal for a general rising, and a protracted war between the Swiss and Austrians. The uprising is said to have happened on Nov. 7, 1307; the citizens agreed to surprise and demolish the castles in which the imperial governors resided. This compact being effected, the cantons joined in a league which gave birth to the Helvetian Confederacy. The story of Tell's shooting the apple is not recorded by contemporary writers.

TELLER, HENRY MOORE, an American statesman; born in Granger, N. Y., May 23, 1830; was admitted to the bar in 1856; practiced law in Illinois in 1858-1860; went to Colorado in 1861; was major-general of the Colorado militia in 1862-1864; United States Senator in 1876-1882, and 1885-1897; Secretary of the Interior in President Arthur's cabinet in 1882-1885; and was a delegate to the National Republican Convention in St. Louis in 1896, from which he withdrew because of a financial plank in the platform. He was again elected to the United States Senate in 1897, which office he held until 1909. He died in 1914.

TELLICHERRI, a seaport town and military station of British India, in the district of Malabar, Madras presidency. The site of the town is very beautiful, and the neighboring country highly productive. There is a natural breakwater abreast of the fort, formed by a reef of rocks running parallel to the shore. The town, with suburbs, occupies about 5 square miles. Coffee, cardamons, and sandalwood are the chief exports. The East India Company founded a factory here in 1683, which was reduced to a residency in 1766. Pop. about 28,000.

TELLURIUM, in chemistry, symbol Te, at. wt. 128, an element of rare occurrence, found in few minerals, in association with gold, silver, and bismuth. It possesses many of the characters of a metal, but bears so close a resemblance to selenium in its chemical properties that it is generally placed in the sulphur group. It has the color and luster of silver, is very brittle, a bad conductor of heat and electricity; sp. gr. 6.26; melts below a red heat, and volatilizes at a higher temperature. Like sulphur, it forms both oxides and acids. It occurs in six-sided prisms with basal edges replaced; crystallization hexagonal; has lately been found in more complex forms; more often massive and granular; hardness, 2-2.5; sp. gr. 6.1-6.3; luster, metallic; color, tin-white; brittle. A telluride mineral containing tellurium and gold, with occasionally some iron was originally found at the Maria Loretto mine, Transylvania, where it was mined for the gold it contained. Gold has been found associated with various tellurides, in several of the United States.

TEMBULAND, a district of the Transkeian Territories in eastern South Africa; bounded by Cape Colony, Basutoland, and Natal. Tembuland has an excellent climate and a fertile soil, which is well suited for pastoral and agricultural purposes. The coast regions are adapted to the growth of sugar, cotton, and coffee. The minerals include coal and copper. Area, 3,339 square miles; pop. about 236,086. Europeans (1918), 4,204.

TEMESVAR, a royal free city of Hungary; consisting of the fortified city or "citadel," with four suburbs; on the Bega canal; 160 miles S. E. of Budapest. It has a fine cathedral, an ancient castle, a magnificent Episcopal residence, manufactures of flour, tobacco, cloth, silk, paper, leather, wool, and oil, and a brisk transit trade in grain, wax, honey, and brandy with Transylvania, Servia, and Rumania. Temesvar has endured a great number of sieges—the latest being that of 1849, when it was besieged and bombarded for 107 days by the Hungarian insurgents, but was relieved by Haynau. Pop. about 72,500.

TEMPERANCE MOVEMENT, a movement designed (1) to minimize or (2) to abolish the use of alcoholic liquors as beverages. In the first sense the word "temperance" is used strictly, i. e., the aim at moderation in the use of liquors; in the second sense it is equivalent to total abstinence. The Jewish Nazarites and Rechabites acted on total abstinence principles (Num. vi: 1-21, Jer. xxxv: 1-6), as did the Encratites of the 2d Christian century. Most of the higher Hindu castes and all the Mohammedans nominally abstain from intoxicating liquor. The earliest modern temperance order was that of St. Christopher, founded in Germany in 1517, the members of which were pledged not to drink more than seven goblets of liquor at a meal, "except in cases where this measure was not sufficient to quench thirst." In 1600 the Landgrave of Hesse established another temperance order. The United States was earlier than England in the modern temperance movement. In 1651 the people of East Hampton, Long Island, endeavored to limit the sale of intoxicating drinks. In 1760 the religious societies began to protest against drinking at funerals; in 1789 a resolution was passed by farmers to abstain from liquor during that year; and in 1790 medical men, led by Dr. Rush, protested against the use of spirits, and four year later he recommended total abstinence.

The first total abstinence pledge was drafted by Micaiah Pendleton of Virginia. In 1812 the Rev. H. Humphrey recommended total abstinence, as did Dr. Lyman Beecher, and various temperance societies arose. Not, however, till 1836 was the American Temperance Union formed on the basis of total abstinence. In 1840 the Washingtonians were founded in the city of Baltimore, and in 1842 the Sons of Temperance were instituted in New York City. From 1845 commenced the various orders with ritual and insignia, which have gradually been extended to or imitated in Europe. As early as 1818 a total abstinence society, believed to have been the first in date throughout the world, had been founded at Skibbereen, in Ireland. In England the movement began at Bradford, in February, 1830. The British and Foreign Temperance Society was formed in London early in 1831. On Aug. 23, 1832, Joseph Livesey, then a member of the Preston Temperance Society, drew up the teetotal pledge, the first signers of which are known as the "seven men of Preston." This inaugurated the modern teetotal movement. In 1838 Father Theobald Mathew, a Capuchin friar, became the apostle of temperance for Ireland, and by the end of 1839 obtained 1,800,000 recruits to the cause. The United Kingdom Band of Hope Union was founded in May, 1855. In 1868 the Independent Order of Good Templars, probably the most widespread of all temperance organizations, was planted in England by Joseph Malins. In 1873 Cardinal Manning and Father Nugent commenced a vigorous temperance movement among the Roman Catholics. The feeling in favor of temperance is steadily growing, and the numerous societies with their large membership constitute a very potent social and political force.

The National Woman's Christian Temperance Union, with its auxiliary state and territorial unions, besides that of the District of Columbia, is the largest society ever composed exclusively of women and conducted entirely by them. It has been organized in every State and Territory of the nation, and locally in about 10,000 towns and cities. Great Britain, Canada and Australia, Hawaiian Islands, New Zealand, India and Japan, Madagascar and South Africa, have also organized, and there are local unions in almost every civilized nation. This society is the lineal descendant of the great temperance crusade of 1873-1874, and is a union of Christian women for the purpose of educating the young; forming a better public sentiment; reforming the drinking classes; and securing the entire abolition of the liquor traffic. In Maine, under the earlier efforts of the apostles of total abstinence, prohibition was carried as a measure of State policy, and the Maine liquor law formed the basis of subsequent similar enactments in other States. By 1911, local option had been adopted by 33 States. Under the Act of Nov. 21, 1918, the manufacture and sale of liquors was prohibited from May 1, 1919. (Wartime Prohibition Act.) On Jan. 29, 1919, Acting Secretary of State Polk issued a proclamation (36 States having confirmed) prohibiting the manufacture and sale of liquor after Jan. 16, 1920.

TEMPERATURE, the thermal condition of a body which determines the interchange of heat between it and other bodies. Our first ideas of temperature are derived from our sensations of hot and cold. The effect of adding heat to a body is to make it hotter, unless it is at its melting or boiling point. This rise of temperature is accompanied by volume changes, on which all our practical methods of measuring temperature depends. Now, though the idea of temperature is familiar enough, its true significance is difficult to understand. So-called thermometric measurements of temperature are not measurements in the strict scientific sense of the term. They are simply the comparison of certain other effects which accompany change of temperature in special bodies. A scientific measure of temperature should be independent of any particular substance, and should depend solely on the fundamental properties of heat itself. This absolute measure of temperature was first given by Lord Kelvin (Sir W. Thomson), who based his system on Carnot's thermodynamic cycle. The kinetic theory of gases has given us a definition of temperature in terms of the kinetic energies of the molecules. The assumption is that the molecules are free from molecular forces; the conclusion is in agreement with Boyle's, Gay-Lussac's, and Charles's laws. As no gas obeys these laws rigorously, the inference is that intermolecular actions come into play, so that only part of the temperature can be expressed in terms of the kinetic energies of the molecules. The same is true, but in a much greater degree, for liquids and solids, for which as yet no kinetic theory has been formulated.

From experiments made by Kelvin and Joule, the absolute zero of temperature was found to be 274 centigrade degrees below the freezing point of water, or— 461° F. This agrees almost exactly with the value deduced from the kinetic theory of gases. From our present standpoint, therefore, we cannot expect to get a colder temperature. The coldest natural temperature hitherto registered on the earth's surface is—88.8° F., which was observed in January, 1886, at Verkhoyansk in Siberia (lat. 67° 34' N. and lon. 133° 51' E.). Olszewski has, in his experiments on the liquefaction of the gases, measured temperatures as low as—373° F. by means of a hydrogen thermometer. Guesses have been made from time to time as to the temperature of space,

Pouillet, for example, putting it at—238° F. and Fourier at—58°. From our present physical outlook, however, the phrase "temperature of space" is meaningless. Only where matter is can a true temperature exist.

In meteorology the distribution of atmospheric temperature is one of the most important problems calling for discussion. The mean annual temperature over the whole surface of land and sea is perhaps about 45° F. At Verkhoyansk the lowest monthly mean averages—61.2° F. The highest monthly mean averaged over several years may be set down at fully 110° F., and is experienced in the N. W. parts of India, where the thermometer in free shaded air not unfrequently touches 125° F. Loomis in his "Meteorology" gives 133° F. as the highest authentic reading, made in the Great Desert of Africa. To facilitate the study of the distribution of temperature at the earth's surface, it is usual to construct charts of isotherms. These are lines, each of which is drawn through all places having the same mean monthly, mean seasonal or mean annual temperature.

The periodic changes of atmospheric temperature are due to the sun. The earth itself has, however, a distinct temperature, which increases at the rate of 1° F. for every 50 or 60 feet of descent through the few miles of crust accessible to us. On this real earth temperature the mean annual temperature of the air must to a large extent depend.

TEMPERATURE OF THE BODY. The terms cold-blooded and warm-blooded animals serve roughly to indicate, the former, those animals which possess a temperature little raised above that of the surrounding medium; the latter, those with one considerably higher. Fishes, frogs, and reptiles are cold-blooded animals, while birds and quadrupeds are warm-blooded. Heat is produced through the combination of the oxygen of the atmosphere with the carbon and hydrogen of the blood and tissues. A much larger quantity of carbon and hydrogen is added to the blood from the food than the ordinary nutrition of the body demands; and the oxygen inhaled from the atmosphere, uniting with these elements, produces heat, carbonic acid, and water—the latter products representing the ashes of the bodily fire. Thus the temperature of the living body depends on chemical change. It is produced by the oxidation of combustible materials derived from the tissues and from the blood. The quantity of carbon and hydrogen which in any given period unite with oxygen in the body, may be accounted for by the quantity of heat generated in the same period. The temperature of an animal must thus be proportionate to its respiration, and to the activity and frequency of its breathing movements.

The circumstances which influence the temperature of the human body in health are very varied. The normal temperature of the internal parts varies from 98.5 to 99.5. The average temperature of the armpit is 98.6. In infant life the temperature is about 1° F. above that of the adult; and the temperature of old age resembles that of infancy. The temperature of the female slightly exceeds that of the male; and the temperature of the human body falls to its lowest level in the early morning. The influence of disease on temperature is very marked. In typhus fever and pneumonia the temperature may rise to 106° F. On the side of lowness of temperature may be mentioned cases of *morbus cæruleus*, in which the blood is imperfectly ærated, when the temperature may sink to 77.5° F.

TEMPERING, in metal work, the process of producing in a metal, particularly steel, that peculiar degree of hardness and elasticity which adapts it for any of the purposes to which it is to be applied. The malleable metals generally increase in hardness by being hammered or rolled, and hammer-hardening—that is, hammering without the application of heat, is frequently employed for hardening some kinds of steel springs. Steel is for most purposes hardened by plunging it while hot into water, oil, or other liquid to cool it slowly. Nearly every kind of steel requires a particular degree of heat to impart to it the greatest hardness of which it is susceptible. If heated, and suddenly cooled below that degree, it becomes as soft as iron; if heated beyond that degree, it becomes very hard, though brittle. Bronze is tempered by a process reverse to that adopted with steel. Cooling bronze slowly hardens it. The sudden cooling makes it less frangible, and is adopted with gongs. A method of tempering much practiced is by the use of electricity, by means of which the article to be tempered is heated.

TEMPEST, MARIE SUSAN, an English actress, born in London in 1866, her father's name being Etherington. She went to a convent in Belgium and studied music in Paris and London. She began playing at the Comedy Theater in London in 1885, her first role being in "Boccaccio." Her impersonations of Nell Gwyn and Becky Sharp brought her into prominence as a leading comedienne, and her later parts of Polly Eccles in "Caste," Peggy O'Mara in "All-of-a-Sudden Peggy," Becky Warder in "The Truth," and Kitty in "The Marriage of Kitty" established her position on the English stage. In 1915 she revived "The Duke of Killiecrankie." Miss Tempest in 1898 married Cosmo Gordon-Lennox.

TEMPLARS, a famous military order, which, like the Hospitallers and the Teutonic Knights, owed its origin to the Crusades. In the year 1119 two comrades of Godfrey de Bouillon, Hugues de Payen and Geoffroi de Saint-Adhémar, bound themselves and seven other French knights to guard pilgrims to the holy places from the attacks of the Saracens, taking before the patriarch of Jerusalem solemn vows of chastity, poverty, and obedience. King Baldwin II. gave them for quarters part of his palace, which was built on the site of the Temple of Solomon close to the Church of the Holy Sepulcher. Hence they took their name as Templars, and the houses of the order, as at Paris and London, that of the Temple. At the Council of Troyes (1128) Bernard of Clairvaux drew up its rule in 72 statutes, substantially the groundwork of the statutes as finally revised in the middle of the 13th century. The order at first consisted of knights alone, but later its members were grouped as knights, all of noble birth, chaplains, and men-at-arms (*fratres servientes*), besides mercenaries, retainers, and craftsmen affiliated and enjoying its protection. The knights took the vows for life or for a certain period, and they alone wore the white linen mantle, with the eight-pointed red cross on the left shoulder (granted by Pope Eugenius III.), and white linen girdle; black or brown garments were worn by all others. The seal of the order showed the Temple, later two riders—a Templar and a helpless pilgrim—on one horse.

The discipline of the order was austere, excluding all needless luxury or display in food, dress, or armor, and all worldly pleasures were forbidden. At the head of the whole order stood the Grand-master; under him Masters, Grand Priors, Commanders, or Preceptors ruled the various provinces of Jerusalem, Tripoli, Antioch and Cyprus, Portugal, Castile and Leon, Aragon, France and Auvergne, Aquitaine and Poitou, Provence, England, Germany, Italy (Middle and Upper), Apulia and Sicily. Second in command to the Grand-master stood the Seneschal, his deputy; next the Marshal, whose business, moreover, was to provide arms, horses, and all the material of war. The Templars were by a papal bull in 1172 rendered independent of the authority of the bishops, owning allegiance to the Pope alone. Their houses enjoyed right of sanctuary, and they often preserved the treasure of kings and nobles.

The Templars, at once knights and monks, realized the two dearest of mediæval ideals, and men of the highest courage and purest devotion flocked into their ranks, bringing with them their wealth to fill their coffers. Already by 1260 the order is said to have numbered 20,000 knights, and these perhaps the finest fighting men the world has seen. Charges of pride, of immorality and impieties, of secret heresies, and even of betraying Frederic II. to the infidel (1229) and St. Louis to the Soltan of Egypt (1250) were yet to be hurled against the order; never, from the beginning to the end of their two centuries of history, was a Templar charged with cowardice before the enemy. The most famous successors of Hugues de Payen (died 1136) were Bernard de Tremelai, who fell at Ascalon in 1153; Eudes de Saint-Amand (died 1179), who won a glorious victory over Saladin at Ascalon (1177), only to fall next year into the Sultan's hands after a disastrous battle; Gerard de Riderfort, who suffered a terrible defeat near Nazareth in 1187, a second at Hittin two months later, and died in battle under the walls of Acre in 1189; Robert de Sable, who aided Richard Cœur de Lion to gain a glorious victory in the plain of Arsouf (1191), and bought from him the island of Cyprus, which was soon transferred to Guy de Lusignan, whereupon Acre became the seat of the order, the famous stronghold of Pilgrim's Castle being built, whose stupendous ruins exist to this day; Peter de Montaigu, whose courage helped to take Damietta in 1219; Hermann de Perigord, who rebuilt the fortress of Safed; Guillaume de Sonnac, slain beside St. Louis at the Nile in 1250; Thomas Berard, an Englishman, under whom Safed was lost in 1266, Jaffa and Antioch in 1268; and Guillaume de Beaujeu, who lost Tripoli in 1290, and fell in the bloody capture of Acre in 1291. The remnant of the Templars sailed to Cyprus, and the latest dying gleams of the order's vigor in the East were the rash attempts to capture Alexandria (1300), and to establish a settlement at Tortosa (1300-1302) under the last and most ill-fated of its grandmasters.

The Templars had failed in their work; their usefulness was past; the order had now only to sink into extinction in one of the darkest tragedies of history. Their wealth and pride had sowed a har-vest of fear and hatred; their loyalty to the Pope and their exceptional privileges had long since aroused the jealousy of the bishops; their bitter quarrels with the Hospitallers, which blazed into open warfare in Palestine in 1243, had shocked the moral sense of Christendom; and the exclusiveness and secrecy with which all their affairs were conducted opened a door for all manner of sinister suspicions among the populace. Philip the Fair of France was a king who covered with a thin veneer of piety a character of complete unscrupulousness; he had succeeded in placing Clement V., a miserable creature of his own, on the papal throne (1305), and in his minister Guillaume de Nogaret and the officers of the Inquisition he found servants of character unscrupulous as his own. In the wealth of the Templars he saw a tempting prize, and the train of treachery was soon complete.

The Grand-master Jacques de Molay was summoned from Cyprus by the Pope in 1306; he went taking with him the treasure of the order, and awaited his fate in France. On Oct. 13, 1307, the Grand-master and 140 Templars were seized at the Temple and flung into prison. Two degraded Templars supplied some of the charges the king required; tortures, infamous beyond the infamies of the Inquisition, provided the remainder. In August, 1308, Clement sent throughout Christendom the 127 articles of interrogation for the accused, and evidence in detail self-contradictory beyond all parallel was quickly accumulated. In the 225 witnesses sent to the papal commission (1310-1311) from various parts of France the depositions, as Mr. Lea points out, occur most suspiciously in groups of identity according to the bishops from whose preliminary tribunals they had come.

Philip held a so-called national assembly at Tours (May, 1308) which obsequiously expressed its approval of the condemnation. The Pope now took the formal responsibility upon himself by personally examining 72 Templars brought before him, when those who had already confessed under torture confirmed their confessions, knowing well that the penalty of retraction was burning forthwith as a relapsed heretic. The Pope contended that the fate of the order as an institution must be submitted to a general council. Meantime, to the public commission appointed to examine into the charges at Paris, there came (March, 1310), as many as 546 Templars who offered to defend the order against all the charges. Four of these were at length commissioned to be present at the investigation on behalf of the order, when suddenly the commission was startled by the news that the provincial council of Sens was about to sentence without further hearing those Templars who had offered to defend the order. On May 12, 1310, 54 knights were slowly burned to death.

The commission at once suspended its sittings, but at length, after many delays, on June 5, 1311, transmitted its report to Clement to help the General Council in its deliberations. The closing act in this drama of papal duplicity was Clement's failure to gain over the Council at Vienne, and the suppression of the order without formal condemnation, by the bull "Vox in excelso" (March 22, 1312). The bull "Ad Providam" (May 2) laid it under perpetual inhibition, and transferred its property to the Hospital of St. John of Jerusalem. The persons of the Templars were handed over to the provincial councils, with the exception of the chiefs of the order, who were reserved to the jurisdiction of the Holy See. On March 19, 1314, Jacques de Molay and the gray-haired Geoffrey de Charney, Master of Normandy, were brought from prison to receive judgment, when, to the dismay of the churchmen and the astonishment of all, they rose and solemnly declared their innocence and the blamelessness of the order. That same day, on the Isle des Juifs in the Seine, they were slowly roasted to death, declaring with their last breath that the confession formerly wrung from them by torture was untrue.

In England the trials were conducted with much less inhumanity. The charges for the most part failed to be established, and most of the prisoners were granted penances and permitted to escape with a formal abjuration, while a fair provision was made for their support. The last Master of the Temple in England, William de la More, died a prisoner in the Tower, to the last maintaining the innocence of the order. The memory of the various preceptories and possessions in England, Scotland, and Ireland survives in place names; the round Temple Church in London, consecrated in 1185, was restored by the Benchers of the Inner and Middle Temple (1839-1842). In Spain, Portugal and Germany the order was found innocent; almost everywhere in Italy, save in the case of six at Florence, the charges broke down.

TEMPLE, a city of Texas, in Bell co. It is on the Gulf, Colorado, and Santa Fe and the Missouri, Kansas and Texas railroads. Its industries include cottonseed oil mills, cotton gins, foundries, flour mills, candy factories, and a cold-storage plant. It has a sanitarium, two hospitals, and a public library. Pop. (1910) 10,993; (1920) 11,033.

TEMPLE, an edifice erected and dedicated to the service of some deity or deities, and connected with some pagan system of worship. The term is generally applied to such structures among the Greeks, Romans, Egyptians, and other ancient nations, as well as to structures serving the same purpose among modern heathen nations. Among all ancient nations the usual plan of a temple was rectangular, seldom circular. Among the Greeks rectangular temples were classed in forms, according to their architectural peculiarities.

The circular temples, which are far from common, and in which Corinthian columns are usually employed, were, for the most part, intended for the worship of Vesta. Among the Etruscans the form of the temples differed from the Grecian, the ground plan more nearly approaching a square, the sides being in the proportion of five to six. The interior of these temples was divided into two parts, the front portion being an open portico resting on pillars, while the back part contained the sanctuary itself, and consisted of three cellæ placed alongside one another. The inter-columniation was considerably greater than in Grecian temples. Among the Romans a temple, in the restricted sense of an edifice set apart for the worship of the gods, consisted essentially of two parts only—a small apartment or sanctuary, the cella, sometimes only a niche for receiving the image of the god, and an altar standing in front of it, upon which were placed the offerings of the suppliant. The most celebrated temples of the ancients were those of Jupiter Olympus in Athens, of Diana (or Artemis) at Ephesus, of Apollo at Delphi, and of Vesta at Tivoli and Rome.

It is also an edifice erected among Christians as a place of public worship; a church; and the name of two semi-monastic establishments of the Middle Ages —one in London, the other in Paris—inhabited by the Knights Templar. The Temple Church in London is the only portion of either now existing.

TEMPLE, SOLOMON'S, the building reared by Solomon as a habitation for Jehovah, though the king was aware that God could not be confined to an earthly edifice, or even to the heaven of heavens. It was built on Mount Moriah (II Chron. iii: 1), chiefly by Tyrian workmen, and had massive foundations. Its dimensions were 60 cubits (90 feet) long; 20 cubits (30 feet) wide, and 30 cubits (45 feet) high. The stone for its erection was dressed before its arrival, so that the edifice arose noiselessly (I Kings vi: 7); the floor was of cedar, boarded over with planks of fir; the wainscoting was of cedar, covered with gold, as was the whole interior. The Temple was surrounded by an inner court for the priest. here was also a Great or Outward Court, called specially the Court of the Lord's House. This temple was destroyed by the Babylonians during siege of Jerusalem under Nebuchadnezzar. On the return from Babylon, a temple, far inferior to Solomon's, was commenced under Zerubbabel, B. C. 534, and, after a long intermission, was resumed B. C. 520, and completed B. C. 516, under Darius Hystaspes. The second temple was gradually removed by Herod, as he proceeded with the building or rebuilding of a temple, designed to rival the first rather than the second. The work was commenced B. C. 21 or 20. In the courts of this temple Jesus preached and healed the sick. It caught fire during the siege of Jerusalem under Titus, and notwithstanding his efforts to save it, was burned to the ground.

TEMPLE UNIVERSITY, an institution for higher education, in Philadelphia, founded in 1888. In 1907 the name was changed from Temple College to Temple University. It has a law school, a theological school, a medical school, and a department of elementary education. In 1919 there were 4,602 students and 305 members of the faculty. President, R. H. Conwell, D.D.

TEMPLE, SIR WILLIAM, an English statesman; born in London, in 1628; was educated at Emanuel College, Cambridge. He afterward passed six years in France, Holland, Flanders, and Germany. On his return (1654), not choosing to accept office under Cromwell, he occupied himself in the study of history and philosophy. After the Restoration (1660) he was nominated one of the commissioners from the Irish Parliament to the king. On the breaking out of the Dutch War (1665) he was employed in a mission to the Bishop of Münster, who offered to attack the Dutch, and in the following year was appointed resident at Brussels, and received the honor of a baronetcy. In conjunction with DeWitt he concluded the treaty between England, Holland, and Sweden (Triple Alliance, 1668), the result being to oblige France to restore her conquests in the Netherlands. He also attended, as ambassador extraordinary, when peace was

concluded between France and Spain at Aix-la-Chapelle (1668), and subsequently residing at The Hague as ambassador, became familiar with the Prince of Orange, afterward William III. Recalled in 1669, Sir William remained in retirement at Sheen till 1674, when he was again ambassador to the States-General, and engaged in the Congress of Nimeguen, by which a general pacification was latterly effected, 1679. He was instrumental in promoting the marriage of the Prince of Orange with Mary, eldest daughter of the Duke of York (James II., 1677). Shortly after his return he was elected to represent the University of Cambridge in Parliament. In 1681 he retired from public life altogether. Swift was an inmate of his house for some time. His Memoirs and Letters are especially interesting to the student of history. His Miscellanies consist of essays on various subjects: "Gardening," "The Cure of the Gout," "Ancient and Modern Learning," "Health and Long Life," "Poems and Translations," etc. He died in Moor Park, Surrey, Jan. 27, 1699.

TEMPLIN, OLIN, an American college dean, born at Camden, Ind., in 1861. He studied at the University of Kansas, of Gottingen, and of Berlin, leaving this last in 1889. He was assistant professor of mathematics, 1884-1890; associate professor of philosophy, 1890-1893, and professor and head of the department from 1893 of the University of Kansas. He has been dean of the College of the Liberal Arts and Sciences from 1903. He was director of the school and college activities in connection with the United States Food Administration, 1917-1919.

TEMPO, in music, a word used to express the rate of movement or degree of quickness with which a piece of music is to be executed. The degrees of time are indicated by certain words such as *lento* (slow), *adagio* or *largo* (leisurely), *andante* (walking pace), *allegro* (gay or quick), *presto* (rapid), *prestissimo* (very rapid), etc.

TEMPORAL BONE, in anatomy, a bone articulating posteriorly and internally with the occipital bone, superiorly with the parietal, anteriorly with the sphenoid, the malar, and the inferior maxillary bone. It constitutes part of the side and base of the skull, and contains in its interior the organ of hearing.

TEMPORAL POWER, the power which the Pope exercised as sovereign of the States of the Church. Pius VII. was partially deprived of his dominions by Napoleon I. in 1797, and entirely in 1808. The Pope replied by a bull of excommunication; he was then arrested and kept a close prisoner in France till the fall of Napoleon in 1814, when he was reinstated in the government of an undiminished territory. The temporal power was again attacked in 1848, when Pius IX. was driven from Rome, and a republic was established by Mazzini and Garibaldi. In 1849 General Oudinot was sent by Louis Napoleon, president of the French Republic, to Rome, and his army drove out the revolutionists and brought the Pope back. For 10 years the Pope's power was not attacked, but Cavour (1810-1861) was working steadily for a "United Italy," and in 1870 Victor Emmanuel, King of Italy, took possession of the papal territory, leaving the Pope only the Vatican. An annual donation of 2,000,000 lire was guaranteed to him by the Italian Parliament, but he never accepted it. Also, the power exercised by the Popes in the Middle Ages of excommunicating, and after excommunication deposing or procuring the deposition of a sovereign who had fallen into heresy.

TEMRYUK, a fortified town of south Russia, in the Kuban district of the Caucasus; on a peninsula on the S. side of the Sea of Azov, in the bay of Temryuk.

TENAFLY, a borough of New Jersey, in Bergen co. It is essentially a residential town. It has manufactures of cloth and window shades. It has a hospital, a home for the aged, and several other institutions. Pop. (1910) 2,756; (1920) 3,585.

TENANT, in law, one who occupies, or has temporary possession of lands or tenements, the titles of which are in another, the landlord. A "tenant at will" is one who occupies lands or tenements for no fixed term other than the will of the landlord. A "tenant in common" is one who holds lands or tenements along with another or other persons. Each share in the estate is distinct in title, and on the death of a tenant his share goes to his heirs or executors. A "tenant for life" (in Scotland, a "life-renter") is one who has possession of a freehold estate or interest, the duration of which is determined by the life of the tenant or another. An estate for life is generally created by deed, but it may originate by the operation of law, as the widow's estate in dower, and the husband's estate by courtesy on the death of his wife.

TENANT RIGHT, a term specifically applied to an Irish custom, long prevalent in Ulster, either ensuring a permanence of tenure in the same occupant without liability to any other increase of rent than may be sanctioned by the general sentiments of the community, or entitling the tenant of a farm to receive purchase money amounting to so many years' rent on its being transferred to another tenant; the tenant having also a claim to the value of permanent improvements effected by him. In course of time the advantages of tenant right granted to the Ulster farmers were claimed by the farmers in the other provinces of Ireland, and the custom spread to a considerable extent. At last, under the management of Gladstone and Bright, the Landlord and Tenant Act of 1870 was passed. By it the Ulster tenant right and other corresponding customs received the force of law, and the outgoing tenant became entitled to compensation from the proprietor to an amount varying according to circumstances. The act contained other provisions giving compensation for improvements, but as it did not succeed in doing away with all grievances a fresh bill was prepared and passed under the name of the Land Law Act, 1881, which established a land commission to revise rents, and to fix them for 15 years. This measure has been amended by subsequent acts.

TENASSERIM, a territory in India, acquired by Great Britain after the war in 1825; the S. division of Burma; is a long narrow strip between the sea and the mountains of the Siamese frontier; area, 46,590 square miles; pop. 980,000. There are seven districts—the town of Maulmain, Taungngu, Schwe-gyin, Salwen, Amherst, Tavoy, and Mergui; the chief towns being Maulmain Taung-ngu, and Tavoy. The town of Tenasserim, which has, through wars and other misfortunes, sunk to be a village of only 577 inhabitants, is 33 miles from the seat at the junction of the Great and Little Tenasserim rivers, the former of which has a total course of about 400 miles.

TENCIN, MADAME DE (Claudine Alexandrine Guérin), a French author; born in Grenoble in 1681; entered the religious life; but soon found its restraints intolerable. Finally, in 1714, she went to Paris, where her wit and beauty soon attracted to her a crowd of lovers, among them personages as great as the Regent and Cardinal Dubois. She had much political influence. But her importance died with the regent and the cardinal in 1723. In 1726 she lay a short time in the Bastille, after the tragic scandal caused by one of her lovers shooting himself in her house. Her later life was most decorous, and her salon became one of the most popular in Paris. One of her oldest lovers was Fontenelle; D'Alembert was one of her children. Her romances,

"Memoirs of the Courte de Comminges" (1735), "The Siege of Calais" (1739), and "The Misfortunes of Love" (1747), show taste, passion, and style. Madame de Tencin's "Correspondence" with her brother appeared at Paris in 1790; the "Letters to the Duc de Richelieu" in 1806. She died in Paris, Dec. 4, 1749.

TENDER, in law, an offer of money or other thing in satisfaction of a debt or liability. Legal tender, coin or paper money, which so far as regards the nature and quality thereof, a creditor may be compelled to accept in satisfaction of his debt. In this country gold and silver coin are a legal tender to any amount, so far as a debt admits of being paid in gold or silver; and national treasury notes or greenbacks are also legal tender. Plea of tender, in law a plea by defendant that he has been always ready to satisfy the plaintiff's claim, and now brings the sum demanded into court. Tender of amends, in law, an offer by a person who has been guilty of any wrong or breach of contract to pay a sum of money by way of amends.

TENDON, the white fibrous tissue reaching from the end of a muscle to bone or some other structure which is to serve as a fixed attachment for it, or which it is intended to move. Tendons have been divided into (1) Funicular, or rope-like, as the long tendon of the biceps muscle of the arm. (2) Fasicular, as the short tendon of that muscle and as the great majority of tendons generally. (3) Aponeurotic or tendinous expansions, sometimes of considerable extent, and serviceable in strengthening the walls of cavities, as, for example, the tendons of the abdominal muscles. The tendons commence by separate fasicles from the end of each muscular fiber, and they similarly terminate by separate fasicles in distinct depressions in the bones, besides being closely incorporated with the periosteum. In some birds whose tendons are black the periosteum is black also. If a tendon is ruptured by an accident, or divided by the surgeon (tenotomy), the two ends, if not too far separated, unite with extreme readiness, by the formation of intervening plastic material, which soon acquires great firmness. The tendons most frequently ruptured are the ACHILLES TENDON (*q. v.*), and tendons of the rectus femoris and the triceps humeri.

Among the diseases of tendons are inflammation and one of the forms of whitlow known as *paronychia gravis*, or tendinous whitlow. Fibrous tumors and small cartilaginous enlargements are often found in tendons.

TENDRIL, in botany, a curling and twining thread-like process by which one plant clings to another body for the purpose of support. It may be a modification of the midrib, as in the pea; a prolongation of a leaf, as in Nepenthes; or a modification of the inflorescence, as in the vine. They have been divided into stem tendrils and leaf tendrils. Called also cirrhus, and by the old authors capreolus and clavicula.

TENEDOS, an island of Greece, on the W. coast of Asia Minor; 15 miles S. W. of the Dardanelles, about 6 miles long and 3 miles broad. The channel which separates it from the mainland is 3 miles broad. The interior of the island is very fertile, and is remarkable for the excellence of its wines. Corn, cotton, and fruits are also produced. On the E. side of the island, near the sea, is the town of Tenedos. It was occupied by Greece during the Balkan War and by the treaty with Turkey in 1920 became a Greek possession. Pop. about 5,000.

TENEMENT HOUSE, a house divided into tenements occupied by separate families. In tenement houses the landlord does not usually reside on the premises. Apartments are let in suites and single rooms. Owing to their crowded condition these houses present problems of sanitation impossible of solution, and are breeding places of disease and nurseries of plagues in times of epidemics. In some cities tenement houses are under police surveillance, and stringent laws have been enacted to secure sanitary conditions and to prevent over-crowding, but their existence is still a problem that sociologists have vainly tried to solve.

TENERIFE, PEAK OF, or **PICO DE TEIDE,** a famous dormant volcano, the highest summit in the CANARY ISLANDS (*q. v.*), in the S. W. of the island of Tenerife, 12,200 feet above sea-level. The lower slopes of the mountain are covered with forests, or laid out in extensive meadows, yielding rich grass; but the upper ridges and peak, properly so called, are wild, barren, and rugged in appearance. The Peak El Piton and its two inferior neighbors, the Montana Blanco and Chahorra (9,880 feet), rise from a rugged circular plain of lava debris and pumice, 7,000 feet above sea-level, about 8 miles in diameter, and fenced in by an almost perpendicular wall of rock. From the crevices sulphurous vapors are constantly exhaling. The wall of the crater at the top is formed of broken and jagged porphyritic lava rocks, is elliptical, 300 feet in diameter, and 70 deep. The color of the whole is white. There is an ice cave at an altitude of 11,000 feet. The peak can be seen more than 100 miles off. In 1795 and 1798 there was volcanic activity here.

TENIERS, DAVID, the name of two celebrated Dutch artists of the Flemish school, father and son, both natives of Antwerp, Holland, in which city the elder was born in 1582. Having studied under Rubens, he spent six years in Rome. On his return he occupied himself principally in the delineation of fairs, rustic sports, and drinking parties, which he exhibited with such truth, humor, and originality, that he may be considered the founder of a style of painting which his son afterward brought to perfection. His pictures are mostly small. He died in

DAVID TENIERS

Antwerp, July 29, 1649. His son, born in Antwerp, Dec. 15, 1610, was taught painting by his father, whom he excelled in correctness and finish. He became highly popular, was appointed court painter to the Archduke Leopold William, governor of the Netherlands, and gave lessons in painting to Don John of Austria. He specially excelled in outdoor scenes, though many of his interiors are masterpieces of color and composition. His general subjects were fairs, markets, merry-makings, guard rooms, taverns, etc., and his pictures, which number over 700, are found in all the important public and private galleries of Europe. His etchings are also highly esteemed. He died in Brussels, Belgium, April 25, 1690.

TENISON, THOMAS, an English clergyman; born in Cottenham, Cambridgeshire, Sept. 29, 1636, studied at Corpus Christi in Cambridge, and after holding several cures was made Bishop of Lincoln by William III. in 1691, and primate of all England three years later. He was a favorite at court, held many important state offices, and attended Mary and William on their death beds. He crowned Queen Anne and George I., being a strong supporter of the Hanoverian succession, and died Dec. 14, 1715.

TENNANT, WILLIAM, a Scotch poet; born in Anstruther, Fifeshire, May 15, 1784, studied for some time at the University of St. Andrews, was for several years a clerk, devoted himself then to teaching, and, being a good Oriental linguist, was in 1835 appointed to the chair of Oriental languages in St. Mary's College, St. Andrews. His chief production is "Anster Fair," a humorous poem of Scottish life in the same stanza as Byron's "Don Juan," which it preceded, being published in 1812. Besides "Anster Fair," Tennant was the author of several other poems and some dramas. None of them, however, attained any success. Grammars of the Syriac and Chaldee tongues were also published by him. He died near Dollar, Scotland, Feb. 15, 1848.

TENNESSEE, a State in the South Atlantic Division of the North American Union; bounded by Kentucky, Virginia, North Carolina, Georgia, Alabama, Mississippi, Arkansas, and Missouri; admitted to the Union, June 1, 1796; capital, Nashville; number of counties, 95; area, 42,050 square miles; pop. (1890) 1,767,-518; (1900) 2,020,616; (1910) 2,184,789; (1920) 2,337,885.

Topography.—Topographically, Tennessee is divided into three sections: East Tennessee, an extensive valley, and agriculturally one of the most important sections of the State, stretches from the E. boundary to the middle of the Cumberland tableland, which has an average elevation of 2,000 feet above the sea, and abounds in coal, iron, and other minerals. Middle Tennessee extends from the dividing line on the tableland to the lower Tennessee river; and west Tennessee from the Tennessee river to the Mississippi. The Unaka mountains, a part of the Appalachian chain, run along the E. boundary, and have an average elevation of 5,000 feet above the sea. The Mississippi, with the Tennessee and the Cumberland, drains three-fourths of the State. The two latter are navigable for a considerable distance, and other rivers with numerous tributaries supply valuable water power.

Geology.—The geological formations are varied. The Unaka range, the valley of east Tennessee and the Central basin are almost entirely occupied by Lower Silurian deposits, and the tableland of the Cumberland by the Carboniferous. The W. portion of the State is mostly

Upper Silurian and Devonian, and the plateau W. of the Tennessee, Cretaceous and Tertiary. The Mississippi river bottoms are of recent alluvial deposit.

Mineralogy.—The State is rich in its mineral resources, asbestos, kaolin, granite, copper, iron, manganese, barytes, clay, building stones, lead, and zinc being among the leading products. The most important mineral product is coal. The coal fields have an area of about 4,400 square miles. In 1922 the production was 4,877,000 tons, compared with 5,904,-593 tons in 1918. The State is also an important producer of copper. The production in 1922 was 14,226,000 pounds, compared with 15,053,598 pounds in 1918. Pig iron production is about 200,000 tons annually, valued at about $2,500,000. Other mineral products of considerable importance are zinc, sandstone, marble, limestone, and clay products. The total value of the mineral products is about $25,000,000 annually. Limestone caves are found in many places, few having been explored.

Agriculture.—The soil is exceedingly fertile, nearly every agricultural product thriving well, according to locality. The principal grain crops are Indian corn, wheat, and oats; and cotton, tobacco, flax, and hemp are extensively cultivated. The rearing and fattening of live stock are carried on under peculiar advantages, and immense numbers of hogs grow up on the mast of the forests, which cover a very large area. The acreage, production, and value of the principal crops in 1922 were as follows: corn, 3,280,000 acres, production 75,440,000 bushels, value $59,598,000; oats, 229,000 acres, production 4,122,000 bushels, value $2,-185,000; wheat, 472,000 acres, production 4,484,000 bushels, value $5,515,000; tobacco, 130,000 acres, production 94,250,-000 pounds, value $20,735,000; hay, 1,-434,000 acres, production 1,923,000 tons, including wild hay; potatoes, 32,000 acres, production 2,560,000 bushels, valuue $2,816,000; cotton, 985,000 acres, 391,000 bales, value $47,897,000.

Manufactures.—In 1921 there were 2,245 manufacturing establishments in the State, employing 75,446 wage earners. The capital invested was (1919) $410,203,000; wages (1921) totaled $65,741,000; cost of materials, $225,-951,000; value of the finished products, $374,038,000.

Banking.—On Sept. 14, 1923, there were reported National banks in operation having $17,164,000 capital, and resources of $267,588,000, including outstanding loans of $139,394,000. There were (1919) 416 State banks, with $17,-

349,000 capital, and $9,148,000 surplus. The exchanges at the United States clearing houses at Memphis for the year 1923 aggregated $1,145,000,000; those at Nashville, $982,600,000.

Transportation.—Railway line mileage in the State in 1922 totaled 4,022. The lines having the longest mileage are the Illinois Central, Louisville and Nashville, Nashville, Chattanooga and St. Louis, the Southern Railway, and the Tennessee Central.

Education.—School attendance is compulsory throughout the State, and the employment of children under 14 years of age in workshops, factories, or mines is prohibited. Separate schools are maintained for white and colored children. There were in 1922 elementary and secondary schools with 642,126 pupils enrolled, and with 15,220 teachers. There were also 229 public high schools, with 23,571 pupils. The expenditure for elementary and secondary schools was $15,-155,000. There are 4 public normal schools, and 26 universities and colleges, the most important of which are the University of Chattanooga, the University of Tennessee at Knoxville, Fisk University (colored) at Nashville, Vanderbilt University at Nashville, Cumberland University at Nashville, and University of the South at Sewanee. There are seven colleges for women, eight commercial schools, a manual training school, and three universities for colored students.

Finance.—The receipts of State revenue for the year 1922 amounted to $15,-465,000, and the disbursements to defray all government costs totaled $15,130,000, including capital outlays of $3,968,000. The bonded debt of the State was $17,-942.000, and the total value of taxable wealth in the State was $3,975,000,000.

Charities and Corrections.—The charitable and correctional institutions are under the State board of control. The most important institutions are the State Penitentiary at Nashville, training and agricultural school for boys, industrial school and school for the blind, all at Nashville, school for deaf and dumb at Knoxville, and a vocational reformatory for girls at Tullahoma. There are three hospitals for the insane.

Churches.—The strongest denominations in the State are the Methodist Episcopal, South; African Methodist; Regular Baptist, Colored; Cumberland Presbyterian; Methodist Episcopal; Disciples of Christ; Roman Catholic; Presbyterian, South; Primitive Baptist; Protestant Episcopal; and Presbyterian, North.

State Government.—The governor is

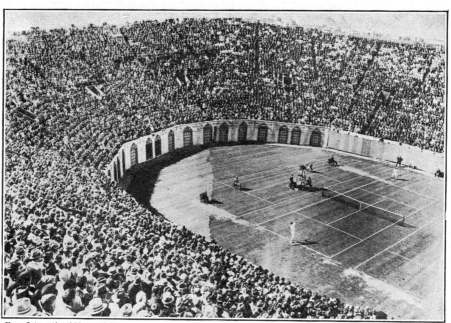

From International Newsreel Corp. See **Tennis, Lawn**, p. 297

TENNIS WATCHED BY THOUSANDS: THE 1925 TILDEN-JOHNSON SINGLES
CHAMPIONSHIP AT FOREST HILLS, LONG ISLAND

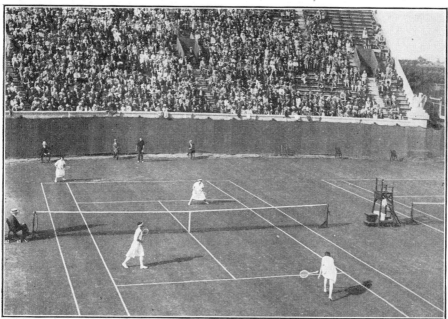

From International Newsreel Corp. See **Tennis**, p. 297

WOMEN'S CHAMPIONSHIP TENNIS, 1925: HELEN WILLS IN
FARTHER COURT, NEAR NET

Photo, Western Newspaper Union

A TENT ENCAMPMENT OF AMERICAN TROOPS

See **Tent**, p. 299

elected for a term of two years. Legislative sessions are held biennially and are limited in length to 75 days each. The Legislature has 33 members in the Senate and 99 in the House. There are 10 Representatives in Congress.

History.—In 1756 a settlement was formed near Knoxville, then a part of North Carolina; Nashville was settled near the close of the Revolution; in 1790 Tennessee was organized as a territory with Kentucky; and admitted in 1796 to the Union as a separate State. In January, 1861, a proposition to secede from the Union was defeated, but in June carried by a majority of 57,567. In 10 months the State raised 50 regiments for the Southern Confederacy, while 5 or 6 were also recruited for the Union. The State was the scene, at Knoxville and Chattanooga, of some of the most important operations of the war. In 1870, after adoption of the 15th amendment to the Constitution of the U. S. and of a new State constitution, Tennessee was readmitted to representation in Congress. The State attracted attention by a statute, passed in 1925, forbidding the teaching in public schools of doctrines such as evolution, and by the conviction of John T. Scopes, a teacher of Dayton, Tenn., under this law.

TENNESSEE, a river of the United States, formed by the union of two streams in the E. part of the State of Tennessee, flows S. W., passes through the N. part of Alabama, then flows N. through the W. part of Tennessee and Kentucky, and enters the Ohio, of which it is the largest tributary, about 10 miles below the confluence of the Cumberland. Length, about 1,200 miles. It is navigable 259 miles for steamers to Florence, at the foot of the Mussel-shoal rapids, which are passed by a canal 36 miles long; and above these there is navigation for boats for 250 miles.

TENNESSEE, SOCIETY OF THE ARMY OF THE, the second society composed of soldiers organized during the Civil War. The preliminary meeting for the formation of the society was held in the Senate Chamber at the State capitol, Raleigh, N. C., April 14, 1865. Membership in the society was restricted to officers who had served with the Old Army of the Tennessee. The society erected in Washington, at a cost of $50,000, a handsome bronze statue of Maj.-Gen. John A. Rawlins, and has also placed an appropriate memorial, costing $23,000, over the grave of Maj.-Gen. James B. McPherson, at Clyde, O., and equestrian statue of General McPherson in Washington, and a monument in memory of Gen. John A. Logan in Washington.

TENNESSEE, UNIVERSITY OF, a coeducational non-sectarian institution in Knoxville, Tenn.; founded in 1794; reported at the close of 1901: Professors and instructors, 85; students, 721; volumes in the library, 17,100; productive funds, $425,000; grounds and buildings valued at $611,000; benefactions, $86,386; president, Harcourt A. Morgan, LL.D.

TENNIEL, JOHN, an English artist; born in London in 1820. He was almost entirely self-taught, and his first picture was exhibited while he was little more than a boy. He painted one of the frescoes in the Houses of Parliament in 1845, and produced but few pictures afterward. In 1851 he became connected as an illustrator with "Punch," and contributed illustrations to that paper, in particular the weekly political cartoon. He also illustrated many Christmas and other books, including "Æsop's Fables," "Ingoldsby Legends," "Alice's Adventures in Wonderland," etc. He was knighted in 1893. He died in 1914.

TENNIS, LAWN, an out-door game played with balls, which are of hollow rubber, covered with smooth white cloth, cemented to the ball, on a piece of smooth, level sward. It remotely resembles tennis. The players are separated from each other by a low net, stretching across the ground, over which they strike a tennis ball with rackets resembling tennis bats. The net should be 42 inches high at the sides of the court and 36 inches high in the middle. Each ball is two and a half inches in diameter and weighs two ounces. The weight of the racket may vary from 10 to 20 ounces. The modern game of lawn tennis was originated by Major Wingfield in Wales in 1874, and introduced into the United States the same year by F. R. Sears and James Dwight.

TENNYSON, ALFRED, LORD, an English poet; born in Somersby, England, Aug. 6, 1809. He received his early education from his father, attended Louth Grammar School, and in due course proceeded to Trinity College, Cambridge, where in 1829 he won the chancellor's medal by a poem in blank verse, entitled "Timbuctoo." As early as 1827 he had published in conjunction with his brother Charles "Poems by Two Brothers," but his literary career may be said to date from 1830, when he published a volume entitled "Poems, Chiefly Lyrical." Its success was sufficient to encourage the poet to prepare a second collection, which appeared in 1833, and contained such poems as "A Dream of Fair Women," "The Palace of Art," "Œnone," "The Lady of Shalott," and others. At this time he sustained a great loss in the death of his friend Arthur Hallam. It was not till 1842 that he again appealed to the public with a selection of his poems in two volumes, and it is from this time that we find his work beginning to receive wide recognition. The collection then issued included "Morte d'Arthur," "Locksley Hall," "The May

ALFRED LORD TENNYSON

Queen," and "The Two Voices," all of which, it was almost at once acknowledged, entitled him to rank high among poets. His reputation was more than sustained by the works that immediately followed. These were: "The Princess, a Medley" (1847); "In Memoriam" (1850), written in memory of his friend Arthur Hallam; and the "Ode on the Death of the Duke of Wellington" (1852). The latter was his first great poem after receiving the laureateship (1850) upon the death of Wordsworth. Thereafter hardly a year passed without his adding some gem to our language. "Maud and Other Poems" was published in 1855; "Idylls of the King" followed in 1858; "Enoch Arden and Other Poems," in 1864; "The Holy Grail and Other Poems," in 1869;

"The Window, or the Songs of the Wrens," in 1870; and "Gareth and Lynette," in 1872, the latter volume, which included the "Last Tournament," completing the series of poems known as the "Idylls of the King." In 1855 the University of Oxford conferred on Tennyson the honorary degree of D.C.L., and in 1869 the fellows of Trinity College, Cambridge, elected him an honorary fellow. So long ago as 1833 he had had printed for private circulation a poem entitled "The Lover's Tale"; in 1879 this was republished, together with a sequel entitled "The Golden Supper." In the following year appeared "Ballads and Other Poems." Among his later compositions are the dramas "Queen Mary" (1875); "Harold" (1876); and "The Cup." The latter was successfully produced by Mr. Irving at the Lyceum Theater in 1881, as had also been "Queen Mary." "The Falcon," another drama, was produced by Mr. and Mrs. Kendal in 1882, and "The Promise of May" was brought out at the Globe Theater the same year. "The Cup" and "The Falcon" were published as a single volume in 1884, and in the same year appeared the historical drama of "Becket." In 1885 appeared "Tiresias and Other Poems"; in 1886 "Locksley Hall: Sixty Years After," which also included "The Promise of May"; in 1889 "Demeter and Other Poems," and in 1892 his last book, "The Death of Œnone: Akbar's Dream and Other Poems." Tennyson was raised to the peerage in 1884 as Baron Tennyson of Aldworth, Sussex, and Freshwater, Isle of Wight. He died in Aldworth, England, Oct. 6, 1892, and was buried in Westminster Abbey.

TENNYSON, FREDERICK, an English poet, brother of Alfred; born in Louth, Lincolnshire, June 5, 1807. He was educated at Trinity College, Cambridge, and in 1828 took the medal for a Greek poem. He published various volumes of verse, including "Days and Hours" (1854); "The Isles of Greece" (1890); "Daphne, and Other Poems" (1891). He died in London Feb. 26, 1898.

TENNYSON, HALLAM, LORD, an English biographer, son of Alfred; born Aug. 11, 1852; was educated at Marlborough College, and Trinity College, Cambridge. He wrote "The Life of Alfred, Lord Tennyson" (2 vols. 1897), contained a complete bibliography of his father's works; various magazine articles; and edited Charles Turner's "Collected Sonnets." He was appointed governor of South Australia (1899-1902); edited the Eversley edition of his father's works, and published "Tennyson and His Friends." Died December 2, 1928.

TENT, a portable pavilion or lodge, consisting of some flexible material, such as skins, matting, canvas, or other strong textile fabric, stretched over and supported on poles. Among uncivilized and wandering tribes tents have been the ordinary dwelling places from the earliest times, but among civilized nations they are principally used as temporary lodgings for soldiers when engaged in the field, for travelers on an expedition, or for providing accommodation, refreshment, etc., for large bodies of people collected together out of doors on some special occasion, as at horse races, fairs, cricket matches, or the like. Military tents are made of canvas, supported by one or more poles, and distended by means of ropes fastened to pegs driven into the ground. Tents of a large size, such as are used for out-of-door fêtes, are known as marquees.

Also an apparatus used in field photography; a substitute for the usual dark room. It consists of a box provided with a yellow glass window in front, and furnished with drapery at the back, so as to cover the operator and prevent access of light to the interior. It is usually provided with shelves and racks inside, developing tray, and a vessel of water overhead, having an elastic tube passing to the inside, to convey water for washing the plate.

In Scotland, a kind of pulpit of wood erected out-of-doors, in which clergymen used to preach when the people were too numerous to be accommodated within doors.

TENTERDEN, CHARLES ABBOT, BARON, an English jurist; born a barber's son in Canterbury, Oct. 7, 1762. A foundationer at King's School, Canterbury, of which he was captain at 17, he gained an exhibition which enabled him to proceed to Corpus Christi College, Oxford. Here he obtained a scholarship; in 1784 the chancellor's medal for Latin verse, in 1786 for an English essay; graduated in 1785, and soon after became fellow and tutor of his college. Entered at the Middle Temple, he was called to the bar by the Inner Temple in 1796. He joined the Oxford circuit and obtained a large practice. In 1801 he became recorder of Oxford, and next year published his clear and learned treatise on the "Law Relative to Merchant Ships and Seamen." In 1816 he accepted a puisne judgeship in the Court of Common Pleas; and in 1818 he was knighted, and chosen to succeed Lord Ellenborough as Chief-Justice of the King's Bench. He was raised to the peerage in 1827. In the House of Lords he strongly opposed the
I—22

Catholic Relief Bill, and in his last speech he made a vow that if the Reform Bill, that "appalling bill," passed, he would never again take his seat as a peer. He fell ill at Bristol, while presiding at the trial of the mayor for misconduct during the Reform riots, and died suddenly, Nov. 4, 1832.

TENURE, the act, manner, or right of holding property, especially real estate. Land may be held according to two main principles, feudal or allodial (see these words). The former is the principle universal in England. In the United States the title to land is essentially allodial, and every tenant in fee-simple has an absolute and perfect title. Yet in technical language his estate is called an estate in fee-simple, and the tenure free and common socage. Also the consideration, condition, or service, which the occupier of land gives to his landlord for the use of his land; and the manner of holding in general; the terms or conditions on which anything is held or retained.

TENURE-OF-OFFICE ACT, in the United States, a bill passed by Congress in February, 1867, limiting the powers of the President in removals from office. Among other things it took from the President the power to remove members of his cabinet excepting by permission of the Senate, declaring that they should hold office "for and during the term of the President by whom they may have been appointed, and for one month thereafter, subject to removal by and with the consent of the Senate." President Johnson vetoed this bill (March 2) when it was passed over his veto and became a law.

TENURES OF LAND. Nearly all the real property of England is supposed to have been granted by a superior lord, and to be held from him in consideration of certain services to be rendered to him by the tenant. By an act of Parliament, military tenures were changed into socage.

TEPLITZ, a watering place in Bohemia; situated in a beautiful valley near the Erzgebirge; 20 miles N. W. of Leitmeritz. The baths are supplied from about a dozen hot alkalo-saline springs, are taken exceedingly hot, and have great virtue in restoring persons afflicted with gout, rheumatism, etc. One of the springs is used also for drinking. Pop. about 27,000.

TERAI, or TURRYE, the name of the narrow strip of swampy jungle which uniformly underlies the lowest ridge of the Himalaya mountains in the N. of India, continuously from Kumaon to Assam. This is about 15 miles wide, and is kept perpetually moist by rivulets. It is overgrown with jungle and enormous grasses, the home of tigers and other wild beasts. Proceeding from the W., the first portion lies in the Rohilcund division of the northwest provinces, forming the district of Terai, with an area of 920 square miles; the chief town Kashipur. The next portion, bordering Oudh and Behar, lies chiefly within Nepal territory. The third piece was annexed from Bhutan after the War of 1864, and is known as the East and West Duars.

TERAPHIM, in Jewish antiquities, household gods, like the Roman penates. The "images" which Rachel stole from her father Laban are called in Hebrew teraphim (Gen. xxxi: 19, 34, 35). Perhaps they were the "strange gods" given up by Jacob's household, and by him hid under the "oak" at Shechem (xxxv: 2, 4). Again, the "image" which Michael put in David's bed, and which was intended to be mistaken for him, is called in Hebrew teraphim, a plural form, though apparently only with a sigular meaning. It was probably of the human form and size (I Sam. xix: 13). Samuel denounced them (I Sam. xv: 23), and Josiah put them away, with wizards, idols, etc. (II Kings xxiii: 24). The English reader must have recourse to the Revised Version to find where the word teraphim occurs in the Old Testament, as in all but one passage (Hosea iii: 4) the Authorized Version translates it by other words.

TERATOLOGY, the study of malformations or abnormal growths, animal or vegetable. Deformities of the animal kingdom may involve the whole body, as shown by the dwarf; may involve shape, as clubfoot or hairlip; may involve color, as in the albinos. Those of the vegetable world deal with abnormal forms, like the four-leaved clover; production of double-flowering plants; bulbous modification of the roots; the metamorphosis of the organs, etc., as well as changes in the form of plants brought about by the skill of gardeners and agriculturists.

TERAUCHI, FIELD MARSHAL, COUNT SEIKI, a Japanese statesman; born in Choshu, in 1852, and a member of the famous Choshu clan, of which Prince Ito and Prince Yamagata were also members. He died in Tokio, in 1919, his death being reported a month before its actual occurrence, on account of the state of unconsciousness which preceded it. He entered the army in

1871, and rose rapidly in rank, becoming a major in 1879. For a short period he went abroad and studied the military systems of France and Germany. In 1882 he became secretary to the Minister of War. In 1897 he was made Inspector-General of military education. During the war against Russia, in 1904-1905, he was Minister of War, and the remarkable efficiency shown by the Japanese armies in the field and their systems of supply was largely due to the administrative skill of General Terauchi. After the war, he was sent to Korea to administer that country as a Japanese dependency. In 1916 he became Premier, which post he held until 1918, when he and his whole cabinet were compelled to resign on account of their reactionary policies.

TERBIUM, in chemistry, a metal, supposed by Mosander in 1843 to exist, together with erbium and yttrium, in gadolinite. Subsequent investigations have thrown considerable doubt on its existence, and it is now believed to be yttria contaminated with the oxides of the cerium metals.

TERBURG, or TERBORCH, GERARD, a Dutch genre painter; born in Zwolle, Holland, about 1617. His father, a historical painter, gave him his first lessons in painting. He continued his studies at Haarlem, and afterward visited Germany, Italy, Spain, England, and France. On the meeting of the Peace Congress, at Münster in 1646, he painted the assembled plenipotentiaries, which is now in the National Gallery, London. He subsequently visited Madrid, London, and Paris, whence he returned to Overyssel, married, and became burgomaster of Deventer. His portraits and pictures of social life are remarkable for elegance. He excelled in painting textile fabrics, particularly satin and velvet. He died in Deventer Dec. 8, 1681.

TERCENTENNIAL EXPOSITION AT JAMESTOWN, an historic, military, naval and marine exhibition, commemorating the first permanent settlement of immigrants from the British Isles in America, on Hampton Roads, near Norfolk, Va., lasting from April 26 to Nov. 30, 1907. Buildings in colonial style were raised at Sewall's Point, covering an area of 400 acres, with three miles of waterfront. Exhibits of food products, machinery, manufactures of every kind, medicinal products, minerals and metals, and pertaining to the army, navy, liberal and fine arts, were housed in the buildings. There were scenic representations of life in early Virginia and an effort was made to reproduce conditions among which the first Virginian immigrants had to live. An Arts and Crafts Village showed colonial articles in fabrics, woods, and metals. American history from the date of the Jamestown settlement was portrayed. A large convention hall was erected in a central position, and an auditorium where meetings and musical festivals were held and attended by great numbers. Over $1,500,000 was contributed by the Government, $50,000 of the sum being devoted to the erection of a monument commemorating the settlement.

TERCE, one of the two legal life rents in the law of Scotland, being a real right constituted without covenant or sasine. By it a widow who has not accepted any special provision is entitled to the life rent of one-third of her husband's heritable (real) estate, provided the marriage has lasted for a year and a day, or has produced a living child. If special provision is granted by a husband to his wife by any antenuptial or postnuptial contract or other deed, the wife shall be thereby excluded from her terce unless the contrary be provided in the same deed. The life rent bears its proportion of burdens affecting the estate. The mansion house is not subject to the right of terce.

TERCEIRA, an island of the Atlantic, one of the Azores; greatest length, 20 miles; average breadth, 13 miles; area, 223 square miles. The soil possesses great natural fertility, and heavy crops of grain, pulse, etc., and abundance of oranges, lemons, and other fruits are produced; capital, Angra. Pop. about 50,000.

TERCINE, in botany, Mirbel's name for what he considered a third coating of some seeds, internal to the secundine and primine. It is really only a layer of the primine or secundine, or the secundine itself. Called by Malpighi the chorion.

TERCY, FRANÇOIS, a French poet; born in Lons-le-Saulnier, Jura, about 1774. He wrote: "Epithalamium of Napoleon and Marie Louise" (1810); "Birth of the King of Rome" (1811); "Death of Louis XVI.," an idyl in the ancient style (1816); "Death and Apotheosis of Marie Antoinette" (1817); "Death of Louis XVIII." (1818). He died in Le Mans, Oct. 1, 1841.

TEREBAMIC ACID, in chemistry, formula, $C_7H_{11}NO_3 = (C_7H_8O_2)'' \begin{Bmatrix} H_2 \\ H \end{Bmatrix} \begin{Bmatrix} N \\ O \end{Bmatrix}$; terebamide prepared by heating terebic acid ($C_7H_{10}O_4$) in ammonia gas to 140-160°.

It is slightly soluble in cold, very soluble in hot water and in alcohol.

TEREBELLA, in surgery, a trepan or trephine. In zoölogy, the typical genus of *Terebellidæ*.

TEREBINTACEÆ, or **TEREBINTHACEÆ**, in botany, an order distinguished by Jussieu in 1789, and including all the turpentine-bearing plants. These are now distributed among the orders *Amyridaceæ, Anacardiaceæ, Connaraceæ, Xanthoxylaceæ*, etc.

TEREBINTH TREE, in botany, the *Pistacia terebinthus*, the Chio or Cyprus turpentine tree. Leaves unequally pinnate, generally three pairs with a terminal one; flowers small; fruit small, dark, purple, rounded, and furrowed. The turpentine flows from incisions in the stem and is left to harden. A gall produced on the tree by the puncture of insects is used in dyeing and for tanning one kind of morocco leather.

TEREBRA, in zoölogy, the auger shell; a genus of *Buccinidæ*. Shell long, pointed, many-whorled; aperture small; canal short; operculum pointed, nucleus apical. Animal blind, or with eyes near the summit of minute tentacles. All the shells are smooth and ornamented with variegated spots, generally red, brown, and orange. Recent species 110, mostly tropical. Fossil 24, from the Eocene of Great Britain, France, and Chile.

TEREBRALIA, in zoölogy, a subgenus of *Potamides*. Shell pyramidal, columella with a prominent fold toward its apex, and a second less distinct one on the basal fronts of the whorls. From India and North Australia. *T. telescopium* is so abundant near Calcutta that the shells are burned for lime.

TEREBRANTIA, a section of hymenopterous insects, characterized by the possession of an anal instrument organized for the perforation of the bodies of animals, or the substance of plants. The borer (*terebra*) is peculiar to the female, and is composed of three long and slender pieces, of which two serve as a sheath for the third.

TEREBRATELLA, in zoölogy, a genus of *Terebratulidæ*, with 25 species distributed among several sub-genera. Shell smooth or radiately plaited; dorsal valve longitudinally impressed; hinge-line approximately straight; beak with a flattened area on each side of the deltidium, which is incomplete, foramen large; loop attached to the septum. The genus appears first in the chalk formation.

TEREBRATULA, in zoölogy and palæontology, the type genus of *Terebratulidæ.* Shell smooth, convex; beak truncated and perforated; foramen circular; deltidium of two pieces frequently blended; loop very short, simple, attached by its crura to the hingeplate. Animal attached by a pedicle; brachial disk trilobed, center lobe elongated and spirally convoluted. *Terebratula* proper has three recent species, from the Mediterranean, Vigo Bay, and the Falkland Islands; fossil, 120, from the Devonian onward. Subgenera: *Terebratulina, Waldheimia, Meganteris,* and *Rensselæria,* the latter from the Silurian to the Devonian.

TEREBRATULIDÆ, in zoölogy, a family of *Brachiopoda.* Woodward enumerates five genera, to which Tate adds two others. Shell minutely punctate; usually round or oval, smooth or striated; ventral valve with a prominent beak and two curved hinge-teeth; dorsal valve with depressed umbo, a prominent cardinal process between the dental sockets, and a slender shelly loop. Animal attached by a pedicle, or by the ventral valves; oral arms united by a membrane, variously folded, sometimes spiral at their extremities. The family is numerous and widely distributed in time and space. The generic and sub-generic forms are usually classified according to the modifications of the loop or calcified support for the respiratory and alimentary organs, the simplest and highest type of this loop being found in *Terebratula.* The family was represented in Silurian seas, and reached its maximum about the dawn of the Tertiary epoch, since when many of its representatives have become extinct.

TEREBRATULINA, in zoölogy, a subgenus of *Terebratula.* Loop short, rendered annular in the adult by the union of the oral processes. Recent species six, from the United States, Norway, Cape, and Japan; fossil 22, from the Oxford Clay.

TERECAMPHENE, in chemistry, a solid crystallizable body, somewhat resembling camphor, produced by heating to 220° the solid hydro-chloride prepared from French turpentine, with potassium stearate or dry soap. It melts at 45° and boils at 160°.

TERECHRYSIC ACID, $C_6H_8O_5$; an acid, said to be obtained, together with oxalic, terephthalic, and terebic acids, in the watery liquid obtained by oxidizing oil of turpentine with nitric acid diluted with an equal bulk of water.

TEREDINA, in zoölogy, a sub-genus of *Teredo.* The valves have an accessory valve in front of the umbones; the aperture of the tube is sometimes shaped like an hour glass, or six-lobed.

TEREDO, in botany, any disease in plants produced by the boring of insects.

In zoölogy and palæontology, a genus of *Pholadidæ,* worm-like mollusks, having a sucker-like foot with a foliaceous border, and long, cord-like gills; shell globular, open in front and behind, lodged at the inner extremity of a burrow, in whole or in part lined with shell; valves three-lobed, concentrically s t r i a t e d. Known species; recent, 21, from Great Britain, Norway, the Black Sea, and the tropics, to 119 fathoms deep. *T. navalis,* the ship worm, is a soft, cylindrical, somewhat vermiform mollusk, two or two and a half feet long, with two small shells at its anterior extremity. It bores into timber, and is exceedingly destructive to ships. In 1731 and 1732 it created alarm in Holland by boring into the piles constituting part of the defense of the country against the inroads of the sea. Though teak is not so easily attacked as many other kinds of timber, yet it does not wholly escape. The best protection against the teredo is metal sheathing and broad-headed iron nails hammered into the wood. Fossil species 24, from the Lias onward. Used also of any individual of the genus.

TEREK, a river in Russian Caucasia, rises near Mount Kasbec, flows in an E. direction, and enters the Caspian by many branches after a course of 350 miles. It has a descent, after reaching the plain (Mosdok), of 40 centimeters to the kilometer, and is utilized for irrigation in the district to which it gives name, and which is specially noted for its warm springs and petroleum wells. The district lying between the province of Stavropol and the highlands of Daghestan, has an area of 34,637 square miles.

TERENTIUS AFER, PUBLIUS (more commonly TERENCE), a Roman poet; born in Carthage, whence his surname Afer, 185 B. C. Some authorities place him 10 years earlier. He was the last of the comic dramatists of Rome of whom we have anything remaining. The extant records of the life of Terence are more than apocryphal. He was either taken prisoner in war or sold in the slave market. His purchaser, or at all events the Roman into whose hands he fell, was a senator, Lucanus Terentius. On obtaining his freedom he took his patron's name. A liberal education followed, and we soon find him the friend and associate of the great and noble. He was gifted with dramatic genius. Terence was beyond question the chief dramatist of his time. He used, moreover, the Latin tongue with singular grace and elegance. Critics have denied to him the possession of lively humor. Terence was the interpreter of Menander; but he was more than a mere translator. His six comedies that remain belong to the "Fabula Palliata." It is said that Terence went to Greece and translated 108 of Menander's plays. Whether he was lost on his homeward voyage, as some say, or lost his transcripts and died of grief in consequence, we have no means of deciding. He died in his 26th year, 159 B. C. The following are his comedies, with the years of their production: (1) "Andria" (The Woman of Andros), 166 B. C.; (2) "Hecyra" (The Stepmother), 165 B. C.; (3) "Hauton-timoroumenos" (The Self-Tormentor), 163 B. C.; (4) "Eunuchus" (The Eunuch) 162 B. C.; (5) "Phormio," 162 B. C.; (6) "Adelphi" (The Brothers), 160 B. C.

The *edito princeps* of Terence was published at Strassburg in 1470. The works of Terence have been translated into almost every European tongue.

TERESA, or **THERESA, ST.**, one of the most remarkable of the women saints of the modern Roman calendar; born in Avila, Old Castile, Spain, March 28, 1515, of the noble house of Cepeda. Even as a child she was remarkable for piety of a most enthusiastic kind; and, educated in a convent in her native city, she entered a convent of the Carmelite order there in 1534. In this convent she continued to reside for nearly 30 years, but it was not till about the year 1539 that her constitution became strong enough to permit her to follow, even in an imperfect way, the observances of conventual life. After a time her religious exercises reached a most extraordinary degree of asceticism. Her prayers were almost continual, and she was reported to be favored with visions, ecstasies, and other supernatural visitations. The fame of her sanctity spread not only throughout Spain, but into almost every part of the Church.

The most notable and permanent fruit of the enthusiastic spirituality of Teresa is the reform of the Carmelite order, of which she became the instrument. After a time she obtained permission from the Holy See to remove with her little community to a humble house in Avila, where she re-established in its full rigor the ancient Carmelite rule, as approved by Innocent IV. in 1247, with some additional observances introduced by herself.

This new convent of St. Joseph's was established in 1562, in which year she assumed the name of Teresa de Jesus; and in 1565 she obtained from the Pope, Pius IV., a formal approval for the rule as modified by her. In 1567 the general of the Carmelite order, F. Rubeo, was so struck, during his visitation of the convents at Avila, with the condition of that over which Teresa presided that he urged on her the duty of extending throughout the order the reforms thus successfully initiated. Teresa entered on the work with great energy, and though she met with much opposition, nevertheless succeeded in carrying out her reforms.

In 1579 the Carmelites of the stricter observance established by Teresa were released from the jurisdiction of the old superiors, and united into a distinct association, with a separate head and a distinct organization which was approved in 1580 by Pope Gregory XIII. Under this new constitution the association flourished and extended; and within her own lifetime no fewer than 17 convents of women and 16 of men accepted the reforms which she had originated. Teresa died at Alba, Oct. 4, 1582, and was canonized by Gregory XV. in 1622, her feast being fixed on Oct. 15. She left a number of works, which have at all times maintained a high reputation among a large section of her own Church; their merits are also acknowledged by non-Catholic writers. The best-known treatises are her autobiography, "The Way of Perfection," "The Book of the Foundations," and "The Interior Castle." Her works in the original Spanish fill two folio volumes (Salamanca, 1587). Biographies have been written in Spanish, French, Italian, German and English.

TERHUNE, ALBERT PAYSON, an American author, born at Newark, N. J., in 1872. He was educated at Columbia and traveled on horseback through Syria and Egypt investigating leper settlements, and living among the Bedouins of the desert. He has been on the staff of the New York "World" since 1894. His works include "Syria from the Saddle"; "Columbia Stories"; "Dr. Dale—A Story Without a Moral"; "The Secret of the Blue House"; "The Shadow of the Prophet"; libretto of "Nero" (a comic opera); "Caleb Conover"; "Railroader"; "Dad"; "Dollars and Cents"; "The Locust Years"; "Bruce"; "The Pest."

TERHUNE, MARY VIRGINIA, ("Marion Harland"), an American author; born in Amelia co., Va., Dec. 21, 1831; received an academic education, and early began to write for

ALBERT PAYSON TERHUNE

the press. She contributed extensively to numerous magazines, was for several years the editor of "Babyhood" and "The Home Maker"; conducted departments in "Wide Awake" and "St. Nicholas"; and served on the editorial staff of the Chicago "Daily News." Her publications include: "The Story of Mary Washington"; "A Gallant Fight"; "A Story Without a Moral"; "Where Ghosts Walk"; "The Long Lane." Died June 3, 1922.

TERM, a limit; a boundary; a bound; a confine; the extremity of anything; that which limits its extent. The limitation of an estate; or, rather, the whole time or duration of the holding of an estate. The time in which a court is held or open for the trial of causes. The time during which instruction is regularly given to students in universities and colleges. A word or expression; the word by which a thing is expressed; that which fixes or determines ideas; a word or expression that denotes something peculiar to an art. The subject or predicate of a proposition in logic. In algebra, a member of a compound quantity. In the plural, conditions; propositions stated or promises made, which, when assented to or accepted by another, settle the contract and bind the parties.

TERMES. See TERMITES.

TERMINALIA, in Roman antiquities, a festival celebrated annually on Feb. 23, in honor of Terminus, the god of boundaries. It was then usual for peasants to assemble near the principal landmarks which separated their fields, and, after they had crowned them with garlands and flowers, to·make libations of milk and wine, and to sacrifice a lamb or a young pig. The public festival was celebrated at the sixth milestone on the road to Laurentum, because at one time that was the limit of Roman territory.

In botany (as a pseudo-singular), the typical genus of *Terminaleæ*. Trees and shrubs with alternate leaves, usually crowded at the end of the branches. From the tropics of Asia and America. *T. chebula* is a large and valuable tree, 80 to 100 feet high, growing in India and Burma. The fruit is ellipsoid or obovoid and five-ribbed, from three-quarters of an inch to an inch and a quarter in length. The pounded rind gives the black myrobalan. The bark of the tree is used for tanning and dyeing. There are often galls on it, which are also used for dyeing. Another of the myrobalans is *T. belerica*, 60 or 80 feet high. It grows in India. The leaves and the fruit are used for tanning and dyeing. Other Indian species said to be used for tanning and dyeing are *T. arjuna*, *T. catappa*, *T. citrina*, *T. paniculata*, and *T. tomentosa*. The fruits of *T. catappa*, sometimes called the almond, are eaten; so are the kernels of *T. chebula*, which, however, if taken in large quantities, produce intoxication. A gum like gum arabic is exuded from its bark. *T. chebula* was believed by the old Hindus to be alterative and tonic. The fruits of *T. belerica* are astringent and laxative; the other Indian species are also medicinal. The milky juice of *T. benzoin* becomes fragrant on being dried. It is burnt in churches in Mauritius as a kind of incense. A drastic resin flows from *T. argentea*, a Brailian species. The root of *T. latifolia* is given in Jamaica in diarrhœa. The bark of *T. alata* is astringent and antifebrile. The wood of *T. tomentosa*, when polished, resembles walnut, and has been used in India for making stethoscopes.

TERMINI, a seaport on the N. coast of Sicily; 23 miles E. S. E. of Palermo. The industries are tunny and sardine fishing. The ancient Thermæ Himerenses here was founded by the Carthaginians in 408 B. C., after the destruction of the Greek city of Himera. Under the Roman rule it flourished through its baths. Of these some fragments still exist, as well as of a theater, an aqueduct, etc. Pop. about 21,000.

TERMINUS, in mythology, a divinity among the Romans supposed to preside over boundaries, frontiers, and landmarks. He was represented with a human head and neck, placed on a plinth, or column, and being destitute of legs or arms, was thus supposed to testify his immovable and steadfast character.

of wood, especially in a state of incipient decay, they help many trees to their fall, and they are destructive pests in human dwellings. The termite society consists for the most part of wingless, sexually immature individuals, children, potentially of both sexes, which do not grow up. Besides these workers there is a

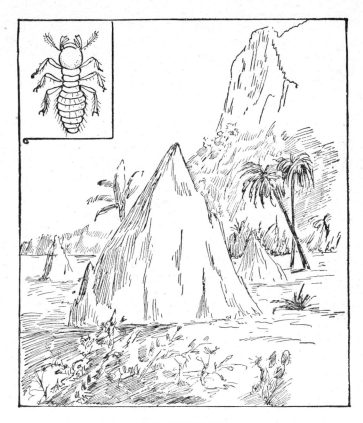

NEST OF TERMITES
In the upper left corner, one of the workers

TERMITES (*Termitidæ*), a family of insects in the order *Corrodentia*, or, according to some systems, *Pseudo-Neuroptera*. They are often called "white ants," but ants are hymenopterous insects, and do not occur before Tertiary times, whereas the termites seem to have lived from Carboniferous ages onward. Yet, like the ants, the termites are social insects living in colonies and building "nests," or "hills." They are widely distributed in tropical countries but they also occur in the temperate parts of North and South America, and a few have established themselves in Europe. As their food consists for the most part

less numerous caste of large-headed, strong-jawed soldiers. The workers collect food, form burrows and tunnels, build "hills," and care for the males, females, eggs, and larvæ. The males and females have wings, which the latter lose after the impregnation. Then, indeed, the female or queen undergoes a remarkable change, becoming enormously distended with eggs and sometimes attaining a length of two to five inches or more. The queen is extremely prolific, having been known to lay 60 eggs in a minute, or about 80,000 eggs in a day. In the royal chamber a male is also kept. It is hardly necessary to say that the queen could not leave if she would. But to understand this imprisonment we must notice that in spring the young winged males and females leave the nest in a swarm, after which pairing takes place; the survivors becoming the imprisoned "rulers" and parents of new colonies.

But Fritz Muller has shown that besides the winged males and females there are (in at least many cases) wingless males and females which never leave the termitary in which they are born, being kept as complementary or reserve reproductive members, useful should not a winged royal pair be forthcoming. Sometimes this casualty occurs, and then the wingless pairs become parents. The complementary kings die before winter; their mates live on, widowed, but still maternal, till at least another summer. The workers are diligent in tending the king and queen, in removing the laid eggs, and in feeding the larvæ.

In general appearance and size a wingless termite is ant-like, but the winged forms are much larger and flatter, and their wings are quite different. The workers have large broad heads and strong jaws adapted for gnawing; the soldiers have still larger heads and longer jaws.

The most remarkable termitaries are those of *Termes bellicosus*, abundant on the W. coast of Africa. They are sugarloaf-like in shape, 10 to 20 feet in height, and, though built of cemented particles of earth, are strong enough to bear a man's weight. Internally, as the figure shows, there are several stories and many chambers, some for the workers, one for the king and queen, others for the eggs and young, others for storing supplies of compacted minced wood. But the termites do not all build such gigantic nests; for some build their homes on the branches of trees and apparently out of masticated woody material.

In Africa *T. bellicosus* and *T. arborum* are common species; in North America *T. flavipes* is very common. A few species— *T. lucifugus*, *T. flavicollis*, and *T. flavipes*—all probably introduced—occur in Europe. Besides *Termes* there are other genera, such as *Eutermes*, *Calotermes*, and *Anoplotermes*.

The termines seem to be of use in destroying decaying wood and in loosening the soil. They also afford food for ant eaters and other insectivorous mammals and for birds. But to dwellers in warm countries they are pests, destroying the timbers of houses and all sorts of wooden furniture. Effecting entrance from underground, they hollow out the interior, leaving only a deceptive shell, which at length collapses. Even in Europe *T. lucifugus* has proved very destructive in some parts of France, notably in the navy yard of Rochefort. Yet to the naturalist their social life, their reproductive relations, and their architectural instincts are most interesting marvels demanding further research.

TERN, in ornithology the popular name of any species of the genus *Sterna*. They are slenderly built birds, with long, narrow, sharp-pointed wings, and forked tail, from which, as well as from their swift and circling manner of flight, they are often called sea swallows. The thick, soft, close plumage is colored light blue, black, and white, varying but little with sex, age, or season of the year. They are extensively distributed, inhabiting every zone, but prefer warm and temperate climates to the colder regions, which they only visit for a short period during the year. All are exceedingly active, and from sunrise to sunset on the wing. They walk badly and are not good swimmers, so that they are tossed about like corks. They feed on small fish and marine animals.

TERNATE, one of the M o l u c c a Islands, area, about 25 square miles; contains a remarkable volcano (5,600 feet), and produces tobacco, cotton, sago, sulphur, saltpeter, etc. The town Ternate is the seat of a native sultan and of the Dutch resident.

TERNI, a cathedral town in central Italy; between the two arms of the Nera; 70 miles N. N. E. of Rome. About 2 miles off is the famous cataract of Velino, 500 feet high, celebrated by Byron in his "Childe Harold." Terni is the ancient Interamna Umbrica, perhaps the birthplace of Tacitus. Pop., about 33,000.

TERNINA MILKA, a German dramatic soprano; born in Vezisce, Croatia, in 1863. After studying under Dr. Josef Gansbacher, of Vienna, she acquired experience in Leipsic, Graz, and Bremen. In 1890 she became prima donna in Munich, where her success was great. Her talents were recognized throughout Germany, and she was a favorite in Russia and America. She first appeared in England at Covent Garden Opera House as Isolde in 1898, and further attracted attention by exceptionally fine impersonations of Brünnhilde and Fidelio, appearing in the former rôle with great success in New York City during the season of 1896. Owing to poor health she made few public appearances after 1906.

TERNSTRŒMIACEÆ, a natural order of polypetalous dicotyledonous plants, consisting of trees or shrubs, with alternate simple usually coriaceous leaves without stipules. The flowers are generally white, arranged in axillary or terminal peduncles, articulated at the base. This order is one of great economical importance, as it includes the genus *Thea*, from which the teas of commerce are obtained. The favorite garden camellia also belongs to it. The plants belonging to the order are principally inhabitants of Asia and America.

TERPENES, in chemistry, a term applied to a series of hydrocarbons having the generic formula CnH_2n-4. They may be all classed under two heads, those produced by synthetical means, as valylene, C_5H_6, and carpene, C_9H_{14}; and those formed in plants, as the turpentines, $C_{10}H_{16}$. With the exception of the last, the terpenes have been very incompletely investigated. They are colorless or yellowish liquids, are insoluble in water, but soluble in alcohol, ether, chloroform, benzine, and in the fixed and volatile oils.

TERPILENE, an inactive hydrocarbon, produced by the action of weak reagents on the solid dihydrochloride, $C_{10}H_{16}\cdot2HCl$.

TERPINE, formula, $C_{10}H_{20}O_2H_2O$, a crystalline body, obtained by shaking for some time a mixture of eight parts oil of turpentine, two parts dilute nitric acid and one part alcohol. It forms large, brilliant, colorless, short, rhombic prisms, soluble in boiling water, alcohol, and ether, melts at 103°, and sublimes at a higher temperature in long needles.

TERPINOL, formula, $C_{20}H_{34}O$; a liquid of hyacinth-like odor, produced by heating an aqueous solution of terpine with hydrochloric and sulphuric acids. It boils at 168°, and has a sp. gr. .852.

TERPODION, in music, a keyed instrument invented by John David Buschmann, of Hamburg, about 1816, resembling a pianoforte in appearance, but producing notes from blocks of wood struck with hammers. The sound could be increased or diminished at pleasure.

TERPSICHORE, in classical antiquities, one of the muses, daughter of Jupiter and Mnemosyne. She presided over dancing, of which she was reckoned the inventress, and in which, as her name intimates, she took delight. To her was sometimes ascribed the invention of the cithara, rather than to Mercury. She is represented as a young virgin crowned with laurel and holding in her hands a musical instrument.

TERRACE, a raised level space or platform of earth, supported on one or more sides by masonry, a bank or platform of turf or the like, such as may be seen in gardens, where they are used for ornament, cultivation, or promenade. In physical geography and geology, a platform, often of soft material, flat above and more or less steep on the sides. They often mark where the bed of the ocean or of a lake was successively situated during the intervals between elevatory movements.

TERRA-COTTA, an Italian term for pottery or earthenware. The name is not ordinarily applied to pottery vessels with thin walls, but is confined to statues, statuettes, bas-reliefs, and architectural members such as columns, cornices, friezes, consoles, and the like made of burnt clay. But the term is not necessarily confined to articles of a decorative character. The color of terra-cotta is either buff, yellow, or red, the former being the more common. Many masterpieces of ancient Greek and Roman sculpture are executed in this material, and a considerable number of works in burnt clay, by Italian artists who lived in the Middle Age and early Renaissance periods, are also exquisite productions. Architectural ornaments of a very effective kind were also executed in this material in ancient times.

Distinguished modern sculptors sometimes produce works in terra-cotta, and in recent years it has been increasingly employed, either partly or wholly, for the fronts and other portions of important buildings.

TERRA DI SIENNA, a ferruginous, ocherous earth, used as a pigment in both oil and water-color painting in its raw state and when burnt. In the latter instance it becomes of a deep orange tint, and dries more rapidly. It is transparent and durable; mixed with various blues, it yields many useful tints of green.

TERRAPIN, the popular name of several species of fresh-water or tide-water tortoises forming the family *Emydidæ*, distinguished by a horny beak, a shield covered with epidermic plates, and feet partly webbed. They are active in their habits, swimming well and moving with greater agility on land than the land tortoises. They are natives of tropical and warmer temperate countries, many being natives of North America. They feed on vegetables, fish, reptiles, and other aquatic animals. Their flesh is much esteemed. One species, called the salt-water terrapin (*Malaclemys concentrica*), is abundant in the salt-water marshes around Charlestown. The chicken tortoise (*Emys reticularia*), so

DIAMOND-BACK TERRAPIN

named from its flavor, is also an esteemed American species.

In the United States terrapin have become so scarce that "farms" have been started for their culture. One of these farms is at Beaulieu, Ga. P. M. Strong, the manager of this farm, in speaking of his farm and its inhabitants, says: "The terrapin is gradually disappearing. The Chesapeake Bay terrapin, that is so highly vaunted, has practically left us. There are very few of them now obtainable, and the greater portion of the terrapin now eaten in Maryland are the black stocks from South Carolina. Our black stock are fast reaching this point, though we certainly hope to postpone the ultimate extinction for many a day yet.

"Our terrapin 'crawls' at Beaulieu produce more terrapin probably than any other crawl in the country. I think, by the way, that there is but one other, and that is on the Eastern Shore, near Crisfield. Our crawls are right on the river. The larger is 310 by 60 feet and is divided into three compartments for three sizes. The smaller crawl is for the baby terrapin and is 100 by 8 feet. Through both crawls there is a 'trunk,' or ditch, running, connected with the

river, making a circuit of the farm and returning to the river again. The bottom of the crawls is on a level with the low tide and is covered with a layer of mud about six inches deep. Into this the terrapin burrow in winter and remain the best part of the time. Floodgates are at the opening of both crawls, so we can let in or out the water at will. Our average population of terrapin is about 40,000, one-half bulls and the other half heifers.

"The feeding of the terrapin is a puzzling thing. I have not yet found whether it is necessary for a terrapin to eat at all. Once I made an experiment and put a number of terrapin in a separate crawl, kept them there for a year and gave them absolutely nothing to eat.

"One way of catching them, used in the salt marshes, is for the darkies to go tramping through the mud and water, sometimes up to their waists. If they pass any terrapin these will rise out of the mud to see what the disturbance is. I have agents all along the coast who collect from the darkies and fishermen in their territory all the terrapin that are caught. Then I make periodical trips in a boat and bring them all in to the crawl. There they are fattened and kept till sold. Terrapin certainly

RED-BELLIED TERRAPIN

have as much sense as chickens, though no one would choose one for a pet. When the men go in to feed them they whistle, and terrapin from all over the crawl, thousands of them, come swimming through the water, piling over each other in their efforts to get close to the man with the shrimp and crabs."

TERRASSON, JEAN, a French author; born in Lyons in 1670. He wrote "Sethos," a sort of philosophical novel, which contains some curious details regarding the customs of ancient Egypt, and the initations into the religious mysteries (3 vols. 1731); "Dissertation on Homer's Iliad" (1715); "Justification of the India Company" (1720). He died in Paris, 1750.

TERRAVERDE, a name given to two kinds of native green earth used as pigments in painting; one obtained from Monte Baldo, near Verona, the other from the island of Cyprus. The former has much more body than the latter and is very useful in landscape painting in oil colors. It is a siliceous earth colored by the protoxide of iron, of which it contains about 20 per cent. It is not affected by exposure to strong light or impure air.

TERRE HAUTE, a city and county-seat of Vigo co., Ind.; on the Wabash river, and on the Vandalia, the Chicago and Eastern Illinois, the Terre Haute and Southeastern, the Cleveland, Cincinnati, Chicago, and St. Louis, and other railroads; 73 miles W. of Indianapolis. The city is built in a farming section, near the extensive block coal mines of Clay co. It contains the Rose Polytechnic Institute, the State Normal School, St. Mary's Institute (R. C.), Old Ladies' Home, St. Ann's Orphan Asylum, St. Anthony's Hospital (R. C.), Union Home for Invalids, court house, United States Government building, several libraries, National, State, and savings banks, and several daily, weekly and monthly periodicals. The city has waterworks, a sewer system, well paved streets, and street railroad and electric light plants. Terre Haute is an important manufacturing city, having flour and hominy mills, rolling mills, blast furnaces, tool factories, meat-packing establishments, casting works, nail works, paving brick, and other clay works, railroad car shops, and a number of large grain elevators. Pop. (1910) 58,157; (1920) 65,914.

TERRELL, a city of Texas, in Kaufman co. It is on the Texas and Pacific and the Texas Midland railroad. It is the center of an important truck farming, cotton raising, and agricultural region. Its industries include cotton gins, flour mills, canning factory, cotton mills, etc. It is the seat of the North Texas Hospital for the Insane, and a public library, Elks' Home, and a military school for boys. Pop. (1910), 7,050; (1920), 8,349.

TERRELL, EDWIN HOLLAND, an American diplomatist; born in Brookville, Ind., Nov. 21, 1848; was graduated at De Pauw University in 1871; studied in Europe in 1873-1874; and practiced law in Indianapolis in 1874-1877. He was a delegate to the Republican National Conventions from Texas in 1880 and 1888; United States minister to Belgium in 1889-1893; conducted the negotiations for the United States with the six powers holding possessions in the Kongo basin and secured from them the "Protocol" of Dec. 22, 1890, granting the United States and its citizens full commercial privileges, etc. He was minister plenipotentiary to negotiate a commercial treaty with the Kongo Free State in 1891; commissioner to and vice-president of the International Monetary Conference at Brussels in 1892; and was one of the Republican State Committee in 1894-1900. He died July 3, 1900.

TERRIER, a name originally applied to any breed of dog used to burrow underground, but now applied to any small dog. Terriers may be divided into three classes: those able to follow their game into its earth, those kept for hunting above-ground, and those kept merely as companions. Among terriers proper the fox terrier holds the position of greatest popularity. The Scotch terrier, though long familiar in Scotland, only became generally known about 1870. The Scotch terrier is identical with the breed often erroneously alluded to as the old or working Skye terrier. He is a small, compact dog, short in the leg; coat short, hard, and dense; ears erect; and with a keen, bright expression. In character he is generally alert and active, and makes a splendid companion. The third variety used for going to ground is the Dandie Dinmont, called after the character in Scott's novel of "Guy Mannering," a character founded on Mr. Davison, a well-known Border farmer, who was one of the founders of the breed. The Dandie is a low and powerful dog, very courageous, a quality probably gained by an admixture of bulldog blood, but headstrong and difficult to keep under control. Dandies are divided into "peppers" and "mustards"—i. e., those colored slate-blue and those of a light yellow. The coat is rather longer than the Scotch terrier, but not so hard.

Among terriers kept for hunting above ground the most popular is the Irish terrier, a dog larger and considerably leggier than the fox terrier, but built on the same lines. The coat is like the Scotch terrier's, but a light red in color. The ears used always to be cut to a fine point, standing erect, but are now allowed to fall over in their natural shape. The Bedlington is popular in the N. of England; the bull terrier also makes a good sporting dog, but is kept mainly as a companion. The Airedale is growing in popularity, but its large size unfits it for any proper terrier work. It somewhat resembles an overgrown blue Bedlington, but lacks the same courage. Among terriers kept as companions the Skye is probably the most common. The black-and-tan, though an ancient breed, has been supplanted by the white English terrier. Japan gives us the shan-shong, resembling the Skye, and malta, a tiny terrier with long silky hair like a Blenheim spaniel. The toy terrier is a cross from the black-and-tan, as is the Yorkshire terrier. Both varieties are fit only to be used as house dogs and are not true terriers.

TERRITORY, a term applied in the United States to an area similar to a State of the Union, but not having the independent position of one. The unorganized Territories are under the direct control of Congress. Each organized Territory has a governor, appointed by the President for four years, and ratified by the Senate. The Legislature, officially known as the Legislative Assembly, is composed of a council and a house of representatives, chosen every two years by the people. A delegate to Congress is elected for the same term. He has the right of debate, but not a vote in the House. Territorial legislation is subject to Congressional control. Territorial courts are provided for, the judges of which are appointed by the President for four years, and confirmed by the Senate, and over which the Supreme Court of the United States has appellate jurisdiction. Territories are usually admitted as States on attaining a sufficient population. Territories are now administered according to their special requirements, especially in the case of those of recent acquisition, viz. the Panama Canal Zone (1904) and the Virgin Islands (1917).

TERROR, REIGN OF, the term usually applied to the period of the French revolutionary government from the appointment of the revolutionary tribunal and the committee of public safety (April 6, 1793) to the fall of Robespierre (July 27, 1794).

TERRY, ALFRED HOWE, an American military officer; born in Hartford, Conn., Nov. 10, 1827; studied law at Yale College and began its practice in 1848. From 1854 to 1860 he was clerk of the Superior and Supreme Courts of Connecticut. At the outbreak of the Civil War he was colonel of a regiment of militia, which was mustered for the United States service in the first call for volunteers with Terry still at its head. In April, 1862, he was made a Brigadier-General of volunteers, and served in the operations about Charleston, and in the siege operations at Forts Wagner

and Sumter. He commanded a division in the Virginia campaign of 1864, having command of a corps from May to July. He was in charge of the expedition which captured Fort Fisher in January, 1865, for which he was made a Major-General of volunteers, and Brigadier-General in the regular army, receiving also the thanks of Congress. In March, 1865, he was placed in command of the 10th Corps, and in June, of the Department of Virginia. From 1869 to 1872 he was at the head of the Department of the South, and after 1872 had charge of various divisions and departments of the army. In March, 1886, he was promoted to the major-generalship, made vacant by the death of General Hancock, and in the following April took command of the Department of the Missouri. He retired in 1888, and died in New Haven, Conn., Dec. 16, 1890.

TERRY, ELLEN ALICE, an English actress; born in Coventry, England, Feb. 27, 1848, and made her first appearance on the stage during Charles Kean's Shakespearian revivals in 1858, playing the parts of Mamillius in "The Winter's Tale" and Prince Arthur in "King John." When only 14 she was a member of Mr. Chute's Bristol Company. She reappeared in London, March, 1863, as Gertrude in "The Little Treasure," and till January, 1864, played Hero in "Much Ado About Nothing," Mary Meredith in "Our American Cousin," and other secondary parts. In that year she married Watts, the painter, and left the stage, but reappeared again in October, 1867, in "The Double Marriage" at the New Queen's Theater, London. She afterward joined Mr. and Mrs. Bancroft at the Prince of Wales' Theater, where she acted the part of Portia. On Dec. 30, 1878, she made her first appearance at the Lyceum, and, in conjunction with Mr. Irving, played in the longest runs ever known of "Hamlet," "The Merchant of Venice," "Romeo and Juliet," and "Much Ado About Nothing." She also appeared as Viola in "Twelfth Night," Henrietta Maria in "Charles I.," Camma in Tennyson's tragedy of "The Cup," Ruth Meadows in "Eugene Aram," as Marguerite in W. G. Wills' "Faust" (revived in 1849), as Lady Macbeth in "Macbeth," as Lucy Ashton in "Ravenswood," as Queen Catherine in "Henry VIII.," as Cordelia in "King Lear," as Rosamonde in "Becket" (1893), as Imogen in "Cymbeline" (1896); as Madame Sans-Gêne (1897); and in "Peter the Great" (1898). She accompanied Mr. Irving on his numerous American tours, playing with unprecedented success all over the United States. Her jubilee was celebrated at the Drury Lane Theatre, London, in 1906. She published "The Story of My Life" (1908), and "The Russian Ballet." Died July 21, 1928.

TERRY, HENRY TAYLOR, an American lawyer; born in Hartford, Conn., Sept. 19, 1847; was graduated at Yale College in 1869, and admitted to the Connecticut bar in 1872. In 1878 he became Professor of Law at the Imperial University of Tokyo, Japan, but returned to the United States in 1884, and began the practice of his profession in New York city. In 1894 he resumed his chair in the Imperial University. His publications include: "First Principles of Law," "Leading Principles of American Law," "The Common Law," etc.

TERRY, MILTON SPENSER, an American educator; born in Coeymans, N. Y., Feb. 22, 1840; was graduated at Troy University and the Yale Divinity School; held pastorates in various Methodist Episcopal churches in New York city in 1863-1884; and in 1885 was made Professor of Christian Doctrines in the Garret Biblical Institute, Northwestern University. He was the author of "Commentary on the Old Testament," "Biblical Hermeneutics," "The Sibylline Oracles," "Rambles in the Old World," "Biblical Apocalyptics," etc.

TERRY, SILAS, WRIGHT, an American naval officer; born in Kentucky, Dec. 28, 1842; was appointed to the navy in 1858. At the outbreak of the Civil War he was assigned to the "Dale" in the Atlantic Coast Blockading Squadron, in which he served till 1863, when he was transferred to the "Black Hawk," of the Mississippi Squadron. Soon afterward he was placed in command of the transport "Benefit" to carry dispatches and supplies to Admiral Porter; and for gallant service in the execution of this commission he was advanced five numbers and appointed to the staff of Admiral Porter, under whom he served till the close of the war. Afterward he cruised on the "Ticonderoga" in European waters; was executive officer on the flagships "Severn" and "Worcester"; inspector of the Maryland Lighthouse District; and commanded the "Marion," attached to the South Atlantic Squadron. In 1887 he went to Washington, D. C., where he was engaged on board duty till 1892. He was promoted captain in 1893, and during the American-Spanish War commanded the receiving ship "Franklin" at Norfolk. He was made commander of the navy yard at Washington, D.

C., March 24, 1900; and on March 29, following, was promoted rear-admiral.

TERSCHELLING, an island of the Netherlands; 10 miles off the coast of Friesland, between the islands of Vlieland and Ameland. It is about 15 miles long by 3 broad, is flat and sandy, and exposed in some parts to inundation. The inhabitants are chiefly pilots and fishermen.

TERSTEEGEN, GERHARD, a German poet; born in Mörs, Germany, Nov. 25, 1697. Among his works are: "The Spiritual Garden" (1729); "Crumbs" (1773). Among his religious songs and hymns the more notable are: "Shout, ye Heavens, for Joy," and "Now the Day is Ended." He died in Mühlheim, on the Ruhr, April 3, 1769.

TERTIARIES, a name given by Church writers to a class in the Roman Catholic Church who, without entering into the seclusion of a monastery, aspire to practise in ordinary life all the substantial obligations of the scheme of virtue laid down in the Gospel. It was under St. Francis and the mendicant orders generally that the institute of Tertiaries reached its full development. Similar lay associations were organized in connection with the Dominican, Carmelite, and Augustinian, as well as with certain of the more modern orders; and a brotherhood of the same character had already been formed by the Templars. The institute of Tertiaries, properly so called, is quite distinct from that of the lay "confraternities" which exist in connection with the several orders, and the objects of which are very similar.

TERTIARY, a color, as citrine, russet, or olive, produced by the mixture of the two secondary colors. More correctly speaking, they are grays, and are either red-gray, or yellow-gray, when these primaries are in excess, or they are violet-gray, orange-gray, or green-gray, when these secondaries are in excess. In ecclesiastical affairs, a member of a Third Order, whether living in the world or in community.

In geology, the third leading division of fossiliferous sedimentary rocks; called also the Cainozoic or Kainozoic. The succession and importance of the Primary (Palæozoic) and the Secondary (Mesozoic) rocks were understood before the nature and extent of the Tertiary were recognized, these last strata being confounded with the superficial alluviums. They were observed to occur in patches (some of fresh-water and others of marine origin) in small areas or basins in the Secondary rocks. The first properly understood strata of Tertiary age were those in the vicinity of Paris, described by Cuvier and Brongniart in 1810. Other Tertiary strata were shortly afterward discriminated in England, in London, in Hampshire, in Suffolk, in the Subapennine hills in Italy, near Bordeaux and Dax in the S. of France, and elsewhere. As early as 1828, Mr. (afterward Sir Charles) Lyell had conceived the idea that the Tertiary strata might be classified by the percentage of extinct species of shells which they contained. He found in 1829 that Deshayes of Paris had independently come to the same conclusion, and the latter geologist, after comparing 3,000 fossil with 5,000 living shells, intimated that in the Lower Tertiary strata about 3½ per cent. of the species were identical with recent ones; in the Middle Tertiary about 17 per cent.; in the Upper Tertiary, in the oldest beds 35-50, and in the more modern ones 90-95 per cent. To these three Lyell gave the names Eocene, Miocene, and Pliocene respectively, words which have since gained universal currency. The foregoing percentages are now known to be only approximately accurate. Next the newer Pliocene beds were called by Lyell Pleistocene, a name afterward transferred to the Post Tertiary, and Oligocene was proposed by Beyrich for beds intercalated between the Eocene and the Miocene. A gap, as yet only partially filled, occurs between the Chalk and the Eocene. This gap has been utilized to draw a natural line between the Secondary and the Tertiary beds. It probably arose from an upheaval of the sea bed. Thus, with the Eocene, as the name imports, the dawn of the present system of things began, and the percentage of shell species shows that the transition has gone on without stoppage or hiatus till now. Other classes present evidence of the same kind; but, as Lyell was the first to point out, which he did in 1830, Shell species have a longevity far exceeding that of the Mammalia. No recent mammal appears in the Eocene, though in Eocene strata various mammalian families which have well-known living representatives appear for the first time. Among the animals the Tertiary is the age of Mammals; among plants it is the age of Dicotyledons, the Cycads and Conifers of the Upper Secondary rocks having given place to plants belonging to many orders and a vegetation only less varied than now. For the most part evidences of gold are lacking in rocks of the Tertiary period.

Also in geology the period of time during which the Tertiary strata were deposited. It cannot yet be measured even approximately. When it commenced, England, as proved by the fruits in the London clay at Sheppey, was a tropical or sub-tropical country. The temperature fell till the Newer Pliocene, by which time the climate was semi-Arctic. During the deposition of the Tertiary, there was a great increase of land both in Europe and America.

In the plural, in ornithology the tertials; wing feathers having their origin from the humerus. They are a portion of the quills. They are not scapulars, though Cuvier calls them by this name; nor do they cover the scapulars. Their use is to fill up the interval between the body and the expanded wing, and to oppose a broader surface of resistance to the air.

TERTULLIANUS, QUINTUS SEPTIMIUS FLORENS (more commonly TERTULLIAN), a theologian of the Western Church; born of heathen parents in Carthage about 160. His father was a Roman centurion under the proconsul of Africa. The details of his life are little known, but the strongly marked character of the man comes out in every page of his numerous writings. He had a liberal education, and shows extensive acquaintance with poetry, history, and law, and considerable knowledge of philosophy and science. Though he calls the philosophers "the patriarchs of heretics" and the learning of secular literature "folly with God," he speaks of the delight he once had in the indecent profanities of the public plays, and confesses that he had fallen into the greatest sins. He nowhere says much about his personal religion, but calls himself "a sinner of all brands, and fit only for penitence, and asks his readers to remember in their prayers Tertullian the sinner." He had sufficient command of Greek to write in that language his earliest treatises, all of which are lost. Jerome mentions that he was a presbyter of the Catholic Church, whether at Rome or Carthage is unknown. Tertullian himself speaks of his having lived at Rome. Eusebius says "he was accurately acquainted with the Roman laws and one of the most distinguished men in Rome." It is possible that before his conversion he had practised there as an advocate or rhetorician. He did not become a Christian till about 190, and he has not recorded the history of his conversion.

That he was married is shown by his two books "To the Wife," in which he argues against second marriages. Some time between 199 and 203 his opposition to the spirit of worldliness in the church culminated in his becoming a leader of the Montanist sect. According to Jerome, this was owing to "the envy and insults of the clergy of the Roman Church," but the chief causes were doubtless the uncompromising character of his natural disposition, and his repugnance to the laxity of the Roman clergy in their reception of the *Lapsi*, and very probably the favor shown to the Patripassian heresy by the Roman bishops Zephyrinus and Callistus. He died between 220 and 240, "in decrepit old age" (Jerome). Augustine says that he at last withdrew from the Montanists, and "propagated conventicles of his own," which is rendered less likely by the fact that the Montanist sect survived in Africa till the 5th century, under the name of "Tertullianists."

Tertullian was a man "of an eager and vehement disposition" (Jerome), who threw all his great gifts of learning, imagination, eloquence, and wit into the religious controversies of his time for 30 years (190-220). Along with the Roman love for substantiality and strength, he had the "bitter, stern, and harsh temper" which Plutarch ascribes to the Carthaginians. He wanted the sweet reasonableness and calmness, the feeling for harmonious form, and the instinct for speculative thought that distinguish the greatest Greek fathers of the Church. He had the heart of a Christian with the adroit intellect of an advocate. His aim is always to make his adversaries appear ridiculous and contemptible. He pours unsparingly on them a fiery stream of strong argument and satire, mixed with the sophisms, insinuations, and hyperboles of a special pleader. His style is most vivid, vigorous, and concise, abounding in harsh and obscure expressions, abrupt turns, and impetuous transitions, with here and there bursts of glowing eloquence, reminding the reader at the time of Carlyle, at another of Lamennais. What appear to be African provincialisms Niebuhr contends are only words and expressions taken from the ancient Latin writers.

He was the first to give such words as *persona, liberum, arbitrium, trinitas, satisfacio, sacramentum, substantia*, etc., the place they hold in Christian theology. Many sentences of Tertullian's, as, for example, "the blood of the martyrs is the seed of the Church"; "Christ is truth, not custom"; "It is absolutely credible because absurd—it is certain because impossible"; "the human race has always deserved ill of God"; "the unity of heretics is schism"; "it is contrary to religion to compel religion"; "how wise an arguer does ignorance seem to herself to be," have become proverbial. "Who

can sufficiently extol the eloquence of Tertullian!" exclaims Vincentius of Lerinum; "almost every word conveys a thought, every sentence is a victory. He is among the Latins what Origen is among the Greeks—the greatest of all." Like Origen, Tertullian was a man of great genius, sincerity, and zeal, a vigorous ascetic, and an indefatigable worker, and, though wielding great influence over his contemporaries, was never more than a presbyter. Like him, too, this champion of the Christian faith against all opponents, Jews, heathens, and heretics, was himself a heretic to the majority of the Christians of his time. Both show the same contempt of the world and enthusiasm for martyrdom. But in the tendency of their views the contrast between them is as striking as in their natural temper and their literary style. Tertullian is an intense realist, with leanings toward materialism, Origen a pure idealist. Origen, like Justin, holds that Greek philosophy was "a preparation for the Gospel," "a fragment of eternal truth from the theology of the ever-living Word." Tertullian thinks that "philosophers are blockheads when they knock at the gates of truth," and that "they have contributed nothing whatever that a Christian can accept." "The eloquence of the one," says Pressensé, "is broad and transparent like his genius: it is a noble, full, majestic river; that of the other is a turbid mountain torrent. Origen speaks to philosophers as a Christian philosopher: Tertullian is a tribune of the people passionately haranguing the crowd in the forum or at the cross roads; he is the ancient orator, with his vehement gestures, his vivid images, his grandiose pathos."

His writings have been called "Tracts for the Times." Most of them are short. They are a rich mine of information as to the relations between Christians and heathens in his time. Though perhaps not the first of the Latin Christian writers, Tertullian was the creator of ecclesiastical Latinity, and impressed upon the language a new character, as he bent it to the service of Christian ideas. His works are divided into three classes:

(1) Controversial writings against heathens and Jews. His "Apologetic" (ed. by Woodham, 1843; by Bindley, 1891), addressed to the Roman authorities, is an attempt to establish the Christian's right to toleration. A popular edition of this work is presented in his two books, "To the Nations," as Uhlhorn and Hauck believe, of earlier date. In his "Concerning the Testimony of the Soul" he acutely develops the thought that Christianity responds to the religious necessi-

ties and postulates of human nature.
The treatise "Against the Jews" is to
prove that prophecy is fulfilled in Christ.

(2) Against heretics. He formulates
this position juristically in his "Against
the Proscription of Heretics." Against
the gnostic attempts to volatilize Christianity in gnostic spiritualism he maintained its reality as a practical form
of life in his "Concerning Baptism,"
"Against Hermogenes," "Against Val-
entinians," "Concerning the Soul" (in
which he contends that even the soul is
material), "Concerning the Body of
Christ" (against Docetism), "Concerning
the Resurrection of the Body," and the
five books "Against Marcio." Against
the Patripassian heresy he wrote the
book "Against Praxeas."

(3) Practical and ascetic treatises. It
is especially in these writings relating to
Christian life and discipline that we can
trace Tertullian's increasing hostility to
the Church and adoption of the Montanist views, which had great influence
among African Christians. He hailed the
testimony of "free prophecy" as God's
witness against the laxity which the
Catholic Church had shown in dealing
with the sensual weaknesses of the great
multitude within her pale. Hence the
division of these treatises into "Pre-Mon-
tanist" and "Montanist." To the former class belong "Concerning Baptism,"
"Concerning Penitence," "To Martyrs,"
"De Spectaculis," "Concerning Idolatry,"
"Concerning Discourse," "Concerning Patience," and "To a Wife"; to the latter,
"Concerning the Chaplet," "Concerning
Fugitives Under Persecution," "Scorpi-
ace," "An Exhortation on Chastity,"
"Concerning Monogamy," "Concerning
Jejunius," "Against Fasting," and "Concerning Pallius"; while "Concerning Vir-
gin's Veils" marks the transition stage.

Tertullian had a greater influence on
the Latin Church than any theologian
between Paul and Augustine. His Mon-
tanism indeed prevented it from being
exercised directly, but Cyprian, who
called Tertullian "his master," was the
interpreter who gave currency to his
views. The following is a summary of
Harnack's estimate of Tertullian, whom
he calls "the founder of Western Christianity." Tertullian's Christianity was
molded by the enthusiastic and strict
faith of the early Christians on the one
hand, and by the anti-gnostic *regula fidei*
on the other. A trained jurist, he sought
to express all religion in legal formulas,
and conceived the relation between God
and man as one of civil law. "God appears always as the powerful partner,
who watches jealously over his rights."
Further, his theology shows a syllogistic-

dialectic stamp; it does not philosophize;
it reasons, using now the argument, *ex
auctoritate*, now the argument *e ratione*.
He shows striking power of psychological
observation. Finally, his writings have
a strong practical evangelic tendency;
with their vivid appeal to the reader's
will, and their simple concrete expression of the Gospel, they appealed not to
theologians only, but to all. In virtue
of these characteristics Tertullian became the type of the Christianity of the
Western Church.

TERUTERO, in ornithology, *Vanellus cayennensis*; the Cayenne sandpiper
of Latham, described by Azara. It is
very common in parts of South America.
It approaches the European lapwing in
its size, its tuft, and in the general tone
of its colors; but it stands higher, and
is armed with a spur at the folds of
the wing. Its eggs, which are often deposited on the bare ground in October
or November, are four or fewer, of a
clear olive color marbled with black, and
are esteemed a delicacy, like those of the
plover in England.

TESCHEMACHERITE (after E. F.
Teschemacher, who first announced it),
a native carbonate of ammonia, occurring both in crystals and massive in
guano deposits. Crystal system not ascertained; hardness, 1.5; sp. gr. 1.45;
color, yellowish to white. Composition:
Ammonia, 32.9; carbonic acid, 55.7;
water, 11.4=100, yielding the formula
$(\frac{1}{2}NH_4O + \frac{1}{2}HO) CO_2$.

TESHO LAMA, the abbot of the great
monastery at Krashis Lunpo; one of the
great Lamas, the other being the Dalai
Lama, who has the political supremacy.
When either dies it is necessary for the
other to ascertain in whose body the celestial being whose outward form has
been dissolved has been pleased again
to incarnate himself. For that purpose
the names of all the male children born
just after the death of the deceased
Grand Lama are laid before his survivor, who chooses three out of the
whole number. Their names are inscribed on tablets and put into a casket,
whence one is selected by the abbots
of the great monasteries to fill the place
of the dead Lama. The Tesho Lama
is often called Pantshen Rinpotshe (the
Glorious Teacher).

TESCHEN, a city in Poland sixty-
three miles west-southwest of Cracow, situated on the Olsa, and formerly
capital of the duchy of the same name.
Its industries consist largely of carriage
works, clock factories, breweries and distilleries, textile mills and bookbinderies.

It is notable in history as the place in which was signed the treaty terminating the war of the Bavarian Succession, on May 13, 1799. Pop. about 25,000.

TESLA, NIKOLA, an American electrical inventor; born in Smiljan, Austria-Hungary, in 1857; studied engineering in the Ecole Polytechnique, Paris; and in 1884 came to the United States, and for several years was employed at Edison's laboratory, near Orange, N. J. He then opened a laboratory of his own. In 1888 he completed his discovery of the rotating magnetic fluid by the invention of the rotary field-motor, the multiphase system of which is used in the 80,000 horse power plant built to transmit the water power of Niagara Falls to Buffalo and other cities. He invented many methods and appliances for the use of electricity, among them the production of efficient light from lamps without filaments, and the production and transmission of power and intelligence without wires. Among his wonderful inventions is that of the electrical oscillator, by which he claimed the electric current can be received from its source and given an intensity which will enable a copper wire to carry 50,000 horse-power across the ocean. In November, 1898, Tesla announced the discovery of, and on May 1, 1900, patented, a method of transmitting electrical energy without wires. Working along the same line Guglielmo Marconi invented his wireless-telegraphy. In 1901 Tesla discovered that the capacity of the electrical conductor is variable, thus opening up a new field for scientific research. In 1906 he was forced into litigation concerning some of his patents, but won his case.

TESSELLATED PAVEMENT, a pavement of rich mosaic work, made of squares of marbles, bricks, or tiles, in shape and disposition resembling dice, and known as tesseræ.

TESSERA, a small cubical or other geometrical form of marble, earthenware, ivory, glass, etc., used for tessellated pavements, ornamenting walls, etc., colored tiles or bricks, usually cubical, laid in patterns, as a mosaic pavement. In antiquity, a small piece of wood, bone, or metal, used as a ticket of admission to the theaters in ancient Rome, or as a certificate given to gladiators, containing their names, that of the consul, and the day on which they had won their distinction in the circus.

TESTACELLA, in zoölogy and palæontology, a genus of *Limacidæ*, with three recent species, from the S. of Europe, the Canary Isles, and Great Britain. Shell small and ear-shaped, placed at hinder extremity of the body which is elongated, broadest behind, tapering toward the head. The species are subterranean in habit, feeding on earthworms, and visiting the surface only at night. During the winter and in long periods of drought they form a sort of cocoon in the ground by the exudation of mucous; if this be broken away the animal may be seen in its thin, opaque, white mantle, which rapidly contracts till it extends but a little way beyond the margin of the shell. Fossil species two, from Tertiary strata.

TEST ACT, in English history, an act passed in 1563 by which an oath of allegiance to Queen Elizabeth, and of abjuration of the temporal authority of the Pope, was exacted of all holders of office, lay or spiritual, within the realm, except peers. Also, an act passed in 1678, by which it was enacted that all persons holding any important office, civil or military, under the crown or receiving money therefrom, should take the oaths of allegiance and supremacy, subscribe a declaration against transubstantiation, and receive the sacrament of the Lord's Supper according to the usage of the Established Church. It was repealed in 1828.

TESTI, FULVIO, COUNT, an Italian poet; born in Ferrara, Italy, Aug. 23, 1593. He was one of the most notable lyric poets of Italy in his time. Besides songs and ballads, he wrote: "Arsinda; or, the Line of the Princes d'Este," a drama; "The Isle of Alcina," a tragedy; an uncompleted epic, "Constantine"; "Italy," a poem in 43 stanzas in which he portrays the situation of Italy under the Spanish yoke. He died in Modena, Italy, Aug. 28, 1646.

TESTING, the process of examining various substances by means of chemical reagents, with the view of discovering their composition. The term testing is usually confined to such examinations as seek to determine what chemical elements or groups of elements are contained in any substance, without inquiring as to the quantity of these elements. Testing is carried out either by the application of chemical reactions to solid substances, or by the application of reagents in solution to a solution of the substance under examination.

TESTING CLAUSE, in Scotch law, the clause in a formal written deed or instrument by which it is authenticated according to the form of law. It consists essentially of the name and designation of the writer, the number of pages of which the deed consists, the names and dsignations of the witnesses, the name and designation of the person who penned the deed, and the date and place of signing.

TESTING MACHINES, machines used for the accurate testing of iron, steel and other materials used in constructive work. The problem which these machines are intended to solve is the adjustment with certainty of a safe margin of strength with a minimum of weight, which can be determined only by experimental tests on full sized sections of the materials used in the construction. One method is to use machines designed to test small sample pieces under such conditions that the breaking strength of the test-piece is measured by the machine, and from the figures thus obtained is calculated the strength per square inch of the full-sized constructive material. A common feature of such machines is the common steelyard balance, supported by knife edges. There are several machines of this class, some of them built up to 100,000 pounds capacity and over. The hydraulic testing machine, invented by A. H. Emery, was originally used at the United States arsenal at Watertown, Mass. The greatest peculiarity of the Emery testing machine is the method by which the stress produced on the piece tested is conveyed to the scale and accurately weighed by mechanism that is entirely without friction, and hence responds to the same increment of load regardless of the amount of strain on the specimen. This result is accomplished by receiving the load against a flat closed cylinder called the hydraulic weighing head. One of the government experiments with this machine was the breaking by tension of a forged iron link 5 inches in diameter between the eyes, at a strain of 722,800 pounds, and immediately after a horse-hair $\frac{7}{1000}$ of an inch in diameter was slowly strained, and, after stretching 30 per cent, snapped under the recorded strain of 16 ounces.

TEST OATH, an oath prescribed by the United States Congress, July 2, 1862, to be taken by persons in the former Confederate States appointed to office under the National government. The text was as follows:

"I, A. B., do solemnly swear (or affirm) that I have never voluntarily borne arms against the United States since I have been a citizen thereof; that I have voluntarily given no aid, countenence, counsel, or encouragement to persons engaged in armed hostility thereto; that I have neither sought, nor accepted, nor attempted to exercise the functions of any office whatever, under any authority or pretended authority in hostility to the United States; that I have not yielded a voluntary support to any pretended government, authority, power, or constitution within the United States, hostile or inimical thereto. And I do further swear (or affirm) that, to the best of my knowledge and ability, I will support and defend the Constitution of the United States against all enemies, foreign and domestic; that I will bear true faith and allegiance to the same; that I take this obligation freely, without any mental reservation or purpose of evasion, and that I will well and faithfully discharge the duties of the office on which I am about to enter, so help me God."

TEST PAPERS, in chemistry, are made by dipping unsized paper into an alcoholic solution of a vegetable coloring matter which changes color when exposed to the action of an acid or alkaline solution. The paper, after being gently dried, is cut into slips of a suitable size. Hence, by dipping the appropriate test papers into any solution, one can ascertain whether it is acid, alkaline, or neutral. Litmus and turmeric are most commonly used as the coloring matters; litmus for the detection of acids, and turmeric for that of alkalies. Test papers are also employed for detecting sulphuretted hydrogen, etc., and for such a purpose the paper must be dipped in the solution of an appropriate substance. Thus acetate of lead paper becomes black in presence of sulphuretted hydrogen, while starch paper becomes blue when touched with iodine.

TESTUDINARIA (so named from the resemblance which the great, rugged, cracked root of the plant bears to the shell of a tortoise), in botany, the elephant's foot or Hottentot's bread; a genus of *Dioscoreæ*, akin to *Dioscorea,* but with the seeds winged only at the tip, instead of all round. Rootstock above ground sometimes four feet in diameter. Stems occasionally 40 feet long; flowers small, greenish-yellow. *T. elephantipes* is the common elephant's foot or Hottentot's bread. The rootstock is a large, fleshy mass, covered with a thick bark, cracked deeply in every direction. The Hottentots in time of scarcity made use of the fleshy inside of the root as a kind of yam.

TESTUDINIDÆ, the land tortoises; a family of *Chelonia,* very widely distributed in both hemispheres, but absent from Australia. The carapace is very convex; claws blunt; feet club-shaped, adapted for progression on land only; neck retractile. They are vegetable feeders, and the greater part of the species belong to the type genus *Testudo.* In some classifications the family includes the freshwater tortoises, now generally made a separate family of *Emydidæ.* The family appears in the Miocene of Europe and the Eocene of North America.

TESTUDO, in Roman antiquity, a cover or screen used in assaults on fortified towns. In cases where the town was of small size and accessible on every side, while the force at the disposal of the besiegers was large, a ring of soldiers was drawn round the walls, a portion of whom kept up a constant discharge of missiles on those who manned the battlements, while the rest, advancing on every side simultaneously, with their shields joined above their heads so as to form a continuous covering like a shell of a tortoise (*testudine facta*), planted scaling ladders against a number of different points, and, at the same time, endeavored to burst open the gates. Also applied to a movable structure, on wheels or rollers, used to protect sappers.

In mining, a shelter similar in shape and design employed as a defense for miners, etc., when working in ground or rock which is liable to cave in.

In medicine, an encysted tumor, from a supposed resemblance to the shell of a tortoise.

In music, a name applied to a species of lyre, because, according to the legend recounted at full length in the Homeric hymn, the frame of the first lyre was formed by Hermes out of the shell of a tortoise.

In zoölogy, the tortoise; the type genus of *Testudinidæ*, with 25 species. Most abundant in the Ethiopian region, but also extending over the Oriental region, into the S. of Europe and the Eastern States of North America. Thorax convex, rather globular, and solid; breast-bone solid, with 12 shields, those of the throat separated; five toes on fore feet, four on the hinder pair.

TETANUS, stiffness or spasm of the neck; a disease common to mankind and animals. It is characterized by the contraction of a greater or less number of muscles by paroxysmal spasms, which aggravate the contractions and by troubles more or less accentuated in the calorification of the circulation and respiration. It is most commonly located in the jaw and begins with painful stiffness at the maxillary muscles and the muscles at the nape of the neck or by difficulty in swallowing. The progress of tetanus is either acute or chronic. The acute form develops in from one to four days; the chronic form may last a fortnight. In acute tetanus the average number of deaths ranges from 65 to 80 per cent. The disease is caused by a bacillus which secretes a very active poison, and that earth from the street or garden and especially from stables or manured land is swarming with these bacilli. It is the contact of the earth with any kind of wound, especially wounds in the hands or feet, which is the most important factor in the development of tetanus. No certain remedy for tetanus has as yet been discovered though antitetanic serum has been successfully used as a preventive. A very simple preventive of lockjaw is here given. As soon as possible after the wound is received hold the part affected for 20 minutes in the smoke of woolen or flannel. This is easily procured by placing butts or pieces of woolen or flannel cloth on a shovelful of hot coals.

TETARD, JEAN (tuh-tä'), a French philosophical and polemical writer; born in Longvic, Burgundy, in 1770. Among his writings are: "Moral Essay on Man in His Relation to God" (1818); "Against Obscurantism and Jesuitism" (1826); "Indelible and Historic Character of Jesuitism and Doctrinism" (1832). He died in Paris in 1841.

TÊTE-DU-PONT, in fortifications, a redan or lunette resting its flanks on the bank of a river and inclosing the end of a bridge for the purpose of protecting it from an assault.

TETHYS, in Greek mythology, the greatest of the sea deities, wife of Oceanus, daughter of Uranus and Terra, and mother of the chief rivers of the universe, Nile, Peneus, Simois, Scamander, etc., and about 3,000 daughters called Oceanides. The name Tethys is said to signify nurse. In astronomy, a Satellite of Saturn. Its mean distance from the center of Saturn is 188,000 miles; its periodic time, 1 day, 21 hours, 18 minutes, 25.7 seconds. In zoölogy a genus of *Tritoniadæ*, with one species, from the Mediterranean, animal elliptical, depressed; head covered by a broadly expanded fringed disk with two conical tentacles; stomach simple. It attains a foot in length, and feeds on other mollusks and on small crustacea.

TETRABRANCHIATA, in zoölogy, an order of *Cephalopoda*, comprising three families; *Nautildæ*, *Orthoceratidæ*, and *Ammonitidæ*, though in some recent classifications the second family is merged in the first. Animal creeping, protected by an external shell; head retractile within the mantle; eyes pedunculated; mandibles calcareous; arms very numerous; body attached to shell by adductor muscles and by a continuous horny girdle; branchiæ four; funnel formed by the union of two lobes which do not constitute a distinct tube. Shell external, in the form of an extremely elongated cone, either straight or variously folded or coiled, many-chambered, siphuncled; the inner layers and septa nacreous, the outer layers porcellanous.

In palæontology, they attained their maximum in the Palæozoic period, decreasing from that time onward, and being represented at the present by the single genus *Nautilus.* The *Nautilidæ* proper and *Orthoceratidæ* are pre-eminently Palæozoic, while the *Ammonitidæ* are almost exclusively Mesozoic.

TETRACERA, in botany, a genus of *Delimeæ,* owing its scientific name to the fact that its four capsules are recurved like horns. Shrubs or small trees, often climbing, with alternate, stalked, feather-nerved, naked leaves, often rough above, and panicled or racemose inflorescence. A decoction of *T. breyniana* and *T. oblongata* is given in Brazil in swelling of the legs. *T. tigarea* is diaphoretic, diuretic, and antisyphilitic.

TETRACHORDON. in music, an instrument similar in appearance to a cottage pianoforte, and like it played by finger-board, but the tone, instead of being produced by striking, is obtained by means of a cylinder of india-rubber charged with resin, kept in motion by a pedal, variety of tone being gained by the depth of pressure on the keys by the fingers. It is called the tetrachordon from an idea that its sounds are similar to those produced by a string quartet. The instrument is constructed also with self-acting machinery. Milton used the word as the title of one of his treatises on marriage, occasioned by his disagreement with his wife, Mary Powell. He explained the word in the sub-title: "Expositions upon the Four Chief Places of Scripture which treat of Marriage."

TETRADYMITE, a rhombohedral mineral found sometimes in crystals, but more frequently granular, massive, or foliated, often with auriferous ores; luster, bright metallic; color, pale steel-gray; in thin laminæ, flexible. Composition: Somewhat variable, but consists principally of bismuth and tellurium. Dana divides as follows: (*a*) Free from sulphur, with formula Bi_2Te_3; (*b*) Sulphurous, with formula, $Bi_2(\frac{2}{3}Te+\frac{1}{3}S)_3$, and (*c*) Seleniferous Also the same as joseite and wehrlite.

TETRAGONIACEÆ, a small order of plants, alliance Ficiodales. No petals, and several consolidated carpels. They are succulent, leaved, herbaceous plants, or small shrubs, chiefly natives of New Zealand.

TETRAGONURUS, in ichthyology, a genus of *Atherinidæ,* with a single species. Body sub-elongate, scales strongly keeled and striated; first dorsal of numerous feeble spines, and continuous with the second. It is a rare fish, more frequently met with in the Mediterranean than in the Atlantic. Nothing is known of its habits, but as, when young, it accompanies the Medusæ, it must be regarded as a pelagic form. At a later period of its existence it probably descends to greater depths, coming to the surface only at night. It attains a length of about 18 inches.

TETRAGRAPTUS, in palæontology, a genus of *Graptolitidæ* from the Skiddaw and Quebec groups (Lower Silurian). The polypary consists of four simple mono-prionidian branches, springing from a central non-celluliferous connecting process, which bifurcates at each end. The celluliferous branches do not subdivide, and the base may be enveloped in a peculiar horny disk.

TETRAGYNIA, an order of plants in Linnæus' artificial system. It consisted of plants having four pistils. The classes Tetrandria, Pentandria, Hexandria, Heptandria, Octandria, and Polyandria, have each an order *Tetragynia.*

TETRAHEDRITE, a name given to a group of minerals having considerable diversity in composition, but presenting the same general formula. Named from the prevailing tetrahedral habit of its crystals. Crystallization isometric, frequently twinned; luster, metallic; color and streak, steel-gray to iron-black; opaque; fracture, sub-conchoidal, uneven; brittle. Composition, essentially a sulphantimonite of copper, with the formula $4CuS+Sb_2S_3$; but in consequence of part of the copper being frequently replaced by iron, zinc, silver, mercury, and occasionally cobalt, and part of the antimony by arsenic or bismuth, the general formula is usually written as $4(Cu, Fe, Zn, Ag, Hg)+(Sb, As, Bi)_2S_3$. Dana divides tetrahedrites as follows: (1) An antimonial series. (2) An arsenio-antimonial series. (3) A bismuthic-arsenio-antimonial and an arsenical series, in which the antimony is entirely replaced by arsenic. The varieties are: (1) Ordinary, containing very little or no silver. (2) Argentiferous = freibergite. (3) Mercuriferous = schwatzite, spaniolite, and hermesite. (4) Platiniferous. Fieldite, aphthonite and polytelite are subspecies. An abundant ore in many parts of the world, sometimes, where rich in silver, mined for that metal only.

TETRAHEDRON, or **TETRAE-DRON,** in geometry, a polyhedron bounded by four triangles. If the middle points of the faces be properly joined, two and two, the lines joining them are the edges of a second tetrahedron. A regular tetrahedron is one in which the faces are equal and equilateral triangles. If the middle points of the faces be joined two and two, the lines joining them form the edges of a regular tetrahedron. All regular tetrahedrons are similar solids.

TETRALOGY, in Greek drama, the name given to a collection of four dramatic compositions—a trilogy and a satyric piece—exhibited together on the Athenian stage for the prize given at the festival of Bacchus. The expression tetralogy is sometimes applied by modern authors to a series of four connected plays.

TETRAMERA, in zoölogy, in Latreille's classification, a section of the Coleoptera. They are distinguished by the atrophy of the fourth tarsal joint in all the feet, so that they have only four freely articulating joints. The atrophied joint is generally extremely minute, and concealed in the deep notch of the third joint, which, in the majority of the species, is bilobed and clothed beneath with a brush of minute hairs. The section includes more than a third of the whole order, and all the species are vegetable feeders.

TETRAONINÆ, a typical sub-family of the *Tetraonidæ*, chiefly from the N. parts of the Palæarctic and Nearctic regions, with the following genera: *Tetrao, Bonasa, Centrocercus, Dendragopus, Canace, Falcipennis, Pediocætes, Cupidonia,* and *Lagopus.* They are rather large in size, heavy in body, with small heads, the nasal fossæ filled with feathers concealing the nostrils; neck moderately long; wings short, rounded, and concave beneath; stout legs and feet; toes with pectinations of scales along the edges, hind toe elevated above the plane of the rest; tarsi covered with feathers, in *Bonasa* partially, in *Lagopus*, to the claws.

TETRAONYX, in zoölogy, an Asiatic genus of *Emydæ*, having five toes, but one on each foot without a nail. Twenty-five marginal scales. Species, *T. lessonii* and *T. baska.*

TETRAOPHASIS, in ornithology, the *Lophophorus obscurus;* often made a separate genus of the sub-family *Lophophorinæ,* connecting the *Phasianinæ* with *Tetraogallus,* and so with the *Perdicinæ.* This bird was discovered by Pére David in Tibet and described by him. General color brown, marked with darker shades; bare skin of face red, tarsi and feet horncolor. The sexes are alike in plumage; female destitute of spurs.

TETRARCH ("governor of the fourth part," *i. e.,* of a country), a title originally designating what is signified by its etymology, the governor of one of four divisions of a kingdom or country; but in the usage of the later Roman empire given undistinguishingly to all minor rulers, especially in the E., possessing sovereign right within their territory, but dependent on the emperor, and in many cases removable at his pleasure. This was especially the case in Syria, where the princes of the family of Herod are called indiscriminately by this title (Luke iii: 1) and by that of king (Matt. xiv: 9).

TETRASTYLE, in architecture, having or consisting of four columns; having a portico consisting of four columns; as the Temple of Fortuna Virilis at Rome; a portico, etc., consisting of four columns. A cavædium was called tetrastyle when the beams of the compluvium were supported by columns placed over against the four angles of a court.

TETRODON, or **TETRAODON**, in ichthyology, the type genus of *Tetrodontina,* having the upper and lower jaws divided by a mesial suture, so as to separate the dentition into four distinct portions. More than 60 species are known, from tropical and sub-tropical seas. In some the dermal spines are extremely small, and may be absent altogether, and many of them are highly ornamented with spots or bands. A few live in large rivers; as, *T. psittacus,* from Brazil; *T. fahaka,* from the Nile and West African rivers, and *T. fluviatilis,* from brackish waters and rivers of the East Indies.

TETROLIC ACID, $C_4H_4O_2$; a monobasic acid prepared by heating chlor *alpha* crotonic acid with alcoholic potassic hydrate on the water-bath, decomposing the potassium salt formed with sulphuric acid, and extracting with ether. It crystallizes in rhombic tables, soluble in alcohol and ether, melts at 76.5°, and boils at 203°.

TETUAN, a seaport town of Morocco, Africa, in the province of El Garb; on the Mediterranean, immediately within the Straits of Gibraltar, 22 miles from Ceuta. The environs are carefully planted with vineyards and gardens; the grapes are exquisite, and the oranges reckoned, by some, superior to any in the world. In 1861 the Spanish government, having determined to abandon its claims against Morocco, declared Tetuan the property of Spain, rendered it impregnable, and colonized its territory. The exports are wool, silk, cotton, leather, etc. Pop. about 25,000.

TETRAZZINI, LUISA, an Italian soprano, born at Florence, in 1874. When quite young she sang operas which she had heard from her elder sister, Eva, practice, and after three months' study under Cecherini at the Liceo Musicale of Florence made her debut as Inez in L'Africaine, and sang in Rome and other cities. Later she toured Russia and Spain, and was acclaimed at Buenos Aires. After visiting Mexico and California she sang at Covent Garden, Lon-

LUISA TETRAZZINI

don, in 1907, and in New York, in 1908. These tours established her reputation and she was acclaimed a successor to Patti. In recent years she has sung in the chief cities of Europe and America.

TETZEL, JOHANN, a German preacher; born in Leipsic, Germany, about 1455. He entered the order of the Dominicans, and in 1502 was appointed by the Roman see a preacher of indulgences, and carried on for 15 years a very lucrative trade in them. His life was so corrupt that at Innsbruck he was sentenced to be drowned for adultery, but got off through powerful intercession. Having traveled to Rome, he was absolved by Pope Leo X., and now carried on the sale of indulgences with still greater effrontery. Luther came out with his theses against this crying abuse in 1517, and the popular indignation aroused, brought on the REFORMATION. (*q. v.*). A great part of the money acquired by his traffic in indulgences was used for the erection of St. Peter's church at Rome. Tetzel died in Liepsic July 14, 1519.

TEUCRIUM, a genus of plants, order *Lamiaceæ*, consisting of herbs and shrubs widely dispersed throughout the world, but abounding chiefly in the northern temperate and subtropical regions of the Eastern Hemisphere. They are called germanders. Several species were formerly reputed to possess medicinal virtues, but are now discarded. The genus is represented in North America by *T. Canadense*, the wild germander, about two feet high, found in fields and roadsides throughout the United States.

TEUDPOSIS, in palæontology, a genus of *Teuthidæ*, or a sub-genus of *Loligo*, with five species, from the Upper Lias and Oölite of France and Württemberg. Pen like the *Loligo*, but dilated and spatulate behind.

TEUFFEL, WILHELM, a German philologist; born in Ludwigsburg, Germany, Sept. 27, 1820. His greatest work is the "History of Roman Literature" (1870). He wrote also: "Exercises in Latin Style" (1887); "Studies in Greek and Roman, and also in German Literary History" (1871); and edited with notes several Greek and Roman classics. He died in Tübingen, where he was professor in the university, March 8, 1878.

TEUTATES, in mythology, a deity mentioned by Lucan as being worshipped with sacrifices not unlike those of Moloch.

TEUTHIDÆ, in zoölogy, calamaries, or squids; a family of dibranchiate Cephalopods, section Octopoda. Body elongated; fins short, broad, and mostly terminal; shell horny, consisting of a shaft and two lateral expansions or wings. There are 18 genera, very widely distributed, which D'Orbigny divided into two sub-families: *Myopsidæ* (having the eyes covered with skin) and *Oigopsidæ* (having the eyes naked, fins terminal and united, forming a rhomb).

TEUTHIDIDÆ, in ichthyology, a family of *Acanthopterygii Perciformes*, with a single genus. Body oblong, strongly compressed, covered with small scales; lateral line continuous; one dorsal, the spinous portion being the more developed; anal with seven spines; ventrals thoracic, with an outer and an inner spine, with three soft rays between.

TEUTHIS, the sole genus of the family *Teuthididæ*, with about 30 species from the Indo-Pacific. They are small herbivorous fishes rather more than a foot long.

TEUTOBURG FOREST, or TEUTO-BURGER WALD, a hilly district of Germany, in Westphalia, where Arminius defeated the Roman general Varus, 9 A. D. See ARMINIUS.

TEUTONES, or **TEUTONS,** in antiquity, a powerful German tribe, which, in alliance with the Cimbri, advanced into Illyria, and defeated the consul Cn. Papirius Carbo, at Noreia 113, B. C. They afterward forced their way into Roman Gaul, and defeated Manlius and Scipio 105 B. C.; and they invaded Spain 104 B. C. On their retreat from Spain, they were met by the Romans, under Marius, at Aquæ Sextiæ, the modern Aix, and totally defeated, 102 B. C.

TEUTONIC CROSS, in heraldry, a name sometimes given to a cross potent, from its having been the original badge assigned by the Emperor Henry VI., to TEUTONIC KNIGHTS (*q. v.*).

TEUTONIC KNIGHTS, one of the three military-religious orders of knighthood founded during the period of the Crusades. Certain merchants of Bremen and Lübeck, witnessing the sufferings of the wounded Christians before Acre in 1190 were so moved with compassion that they erected tent hospitals for them. There had been a German hospital in Jerusalem from 1128 to 1187; and the new arrangement at Acre was in some sort a continuance of this, being called the Hospital St. Mary of the Germans in Jerusalem. The new hospital, the attendants and founders of which formed themselves into a monastic order with the same rules as the Knights Hospitallers of St. John, found a patron in Duke Frederick of Swabia and through him secured the countenance of his brother the Emperor Henry VI., and the confirmation of the Pope (1191). Seven years later it was converted into a knightly or military order; and the change was stamped with the papal approval in 1199. The knights, in addition to the usual monastic vows, bound themselves to tend the sick and wounded, and wage incessant war on the heathen. Their distinguishing habiliment was a white mantle with a black cross.

About the year 1225 the Duke of Masovia (in Poland) invited the Teutonic Knights to help him against the heathen Prussians. The grand-master, Hermann von Salza, sent a body of knights, who experienced little difficulty in establishing themselves in the territories of the heathen. Twelve years later they were strengthened by the absorption into their order of the Brethren of the Sword, a military order which had been formed to convert to Christianity with the sword the Livonians, Esthonians, and Courlanders. At length the successive encroachments of the knights roused the Prussians to bitter opposition. A fierce warfare was then carried on for nearly a quarter of a century; but by 1283 the knights were masters of the territory lying between the Vistula and the Memel, and as heirs of the extinct Brethren of the Sword they had also extensive possessions in Livonia and Courland. After subduing the Prussians, the order entered on a hundred years' contest against the Lithuanians. But a most serious blow was struck at the knights by the conversion of the Lithuanians to Christianity and the accession (1386) of their prince to the throne of Poland.

From this time, having lost their main raison d'être—fighting against the heathen—the order began to decline. During the period of its prosperity, however, it had acted as the principal force in the politics of Baltic countries; and both by its own exertions and by the encouragement it gave to the Hanseatic traders it was the means of spreading German civilization and manners throughout what are now the Baltic states. The order suffered an incalculable loss of prestige through the terrible defeat inflicted on them by the Poles and Lithuanians at Tannenberg in 1410. A desperate attempt to recover their power resulted (1466) in he loss of West Prussia and the alienation of the esteem and affection of their subjects in East Prussia, which they could only retain as a fief of Poland. In 1525 the order was secularized; its grand-master, Albert of Brandenburg-Anspach, being created hereditary Duke of Prussia under the suzerainty of Poland. The headquarters of the order—for it still possessed several estates scattered throughout the German empire and in one or two other countries—was fixed at Mergentheim in Swabia, and its possessions were reorganized in 12 bailiwicks. Thus it existed till 1801, when the estates W. of the Rhine were annexed by France; in 1909 the order was entirely suppressed by Napoleon in all the German states. This left only a couple of bailiwicks in Austria and one at Utrecht; and these still exist, severely aristocratic in both countries. The Austrian branch, reorganized in 1840, justifies its existence by maintaining an organization for the care of the wounded in war.

TEUTONIC PEOPLES, a term now applied: (1) to the High Germans, including the German inhabitants of Upper and Middle Germany and those of Switzerland and Austria. (2) The Low Germans, including the Frisians, the Plattdeutsch, the Dutch, the Flemings, and the English descended from the Saxons, Angles, etc., who settled in Britain. (3) The Scandinavians, including the Norwegians, Swedes, Danes and Icelanders.

TEUTSCH, GEORG DANIEL, a Transylvanian historian; born in Schässburg, Transylvania. He was bishop of the Saxons of Transylvania, and wrote: "History of the Transylvania Saxons" (2d ed. 1874); "Compend of the History of Transylvania"; "Documents for the History of Transylvania" (1857); "The Reformation in the Transylvanian Saxonland" (6th ed. 1886); "Documentary History of the Evangelical Church in Transylvania" (2 vols. 1862-1863). He died in Hermannstadt, Transylvania, July 2, 1893.

TEWFIK PASHA, Khedive of Egypt; born Nov. 15, 1852; eldest son of Ismail Pasha; succeeded on his father's abdication in 1879, in virtue of the arrangement of 1866 between Ismail and the Sultan. The chief events of his reign were the insurrection of Arabi, the war with the Mahdi, the pacification of the Sudan frontiers, and the steady improvement of the condition of Egypt under English administration. Tewfik, a pious Moslem, utterly alien to his father's love of luxury and extravagance, was throughout loyal to his engagements with Great Britin. He died Jan. 7, 1892, and was succeeded by his eldest son Abbas.

TEWKESBURY, an old market town of Gloucestershire, England; on the Avon at its confluence with the Severn; 9 miles N. N. W. of Cheltenham, and 15 S. by E. of Worcester. On the site of the cell of the hermit Theoc, from whom the place got its name, was founded in 715 a monastery, refounded in 1102 by Robert Fitzhamon as a great Benedictine abbey. Its noble church, consecrated in November, 1123, measures 317 feet by 124 feet across the transepts, and remains essentially Norman, in spite of later additions—Early English, Decorated, and Perpendicular. It was restored by Scott in 1875-1879. Special features are the W. front and the massive central tower, 132 feet high. Many of the Clares, Despencers, Beauchamps, and other lords of Tewkesbury are buried here, as also the murdered Prince Edward and (possibly) Clarence; and in 1890 a tablet was erected to Mrs. Craik, the scene of whose "John Halifax" is laid in Tewkesbury. The place has also a town hall (1788), a corn exchange (1856), Telford's iron bridge over the Severn (1824) with span of 176 feet, a free grammar school, etc. Manufacture of mustard was previously the chief industry. It has now been replaced by the shoe trade. Within half a mile was fought (May 4, 1471), the battles of Tewkesbury, in which the Yorkists under Edward IV. gained a crowning victory over the Lancastrians.

The town was incorporated by Elizabeth in 1574.

TEXARKANA, a city partly in Miller co., Ark., and partly in Bowie co., Tex.; on the Texas and Pacific, the St. Louis Southwestern, and the St. Louis, Iron Mountain and Southern railroads; 145 miles S. W. of Little Rock. Though a unit each part of the city has a separate municipal government, the part in Arkansas being the county seat of Miller county. It contains street railroad and electric light plants, numerous churches, business colleges, United States government building, a National and other banks, and several daily and weekly newspapers. It has machine and boiler works, a cotton compress, a cottonseed oil mill, ice factories, car shops, etc. Pop. of part in Miller co., Ark., (1910) 5,655; (1920) 8,257; in Bowie co., Tex. (1910) 9,790; (1920) 11,480; total (1910) 15,545; (1920) 19,737.

TEXAS, a State in the South Central Division of the North American Union; bounded by Oklahoma, Arkansas, Louisiana, New Mexico, the States of Chihuahua, Coahuila, Tamaulipas in Mexico, and the Gulf of Mexico; admitted to the Union Dec. 29, 1845; capital, Austin; number of counties, 253; area, 265,780 square miles; pop. (1890) 2,235,527; (1900) 3,048,710; (1910) 3,896,542; (1920) 4,663,228.

Topography—The surface in the N.W. is covered with mountains, which, in proceeding S. E., subside into hills and undulating plateaus, succeeded on approaching the Gulf of Mexico, by low alluvial plains. These extend inland from 20 to 80 miles, are furrowed with deep ravines, and consist for the most part of rich prairie or forest land. The hilly region behind this is formed chiefly of sandstone and limestone ridges, separated by valleys of considerable fertility. In the mountainous region many of the summits are lofty, and covered with snow several months of the year. The general slope of the country gives all the rivers a more or less southerly direction. The Rio Grande, rising in Colorado, forms the W. and S. W. boundary of the state, from the 32d parallel to the sea. The Red river, which has its source in the Staked Plain, forms the greater part of the N. boundary. The other important rivers are the Colorado, the Brazos, the San Jacinto and Trinity, and the Sabine, which, during the greater part of its course, is the boundary between Texas and Louisiana. A long chain of lagoons stretches along the Gulf of Mexico.

Geology—The Alluvial, Tertiary, Cretaceous, and Carboniferous periods are

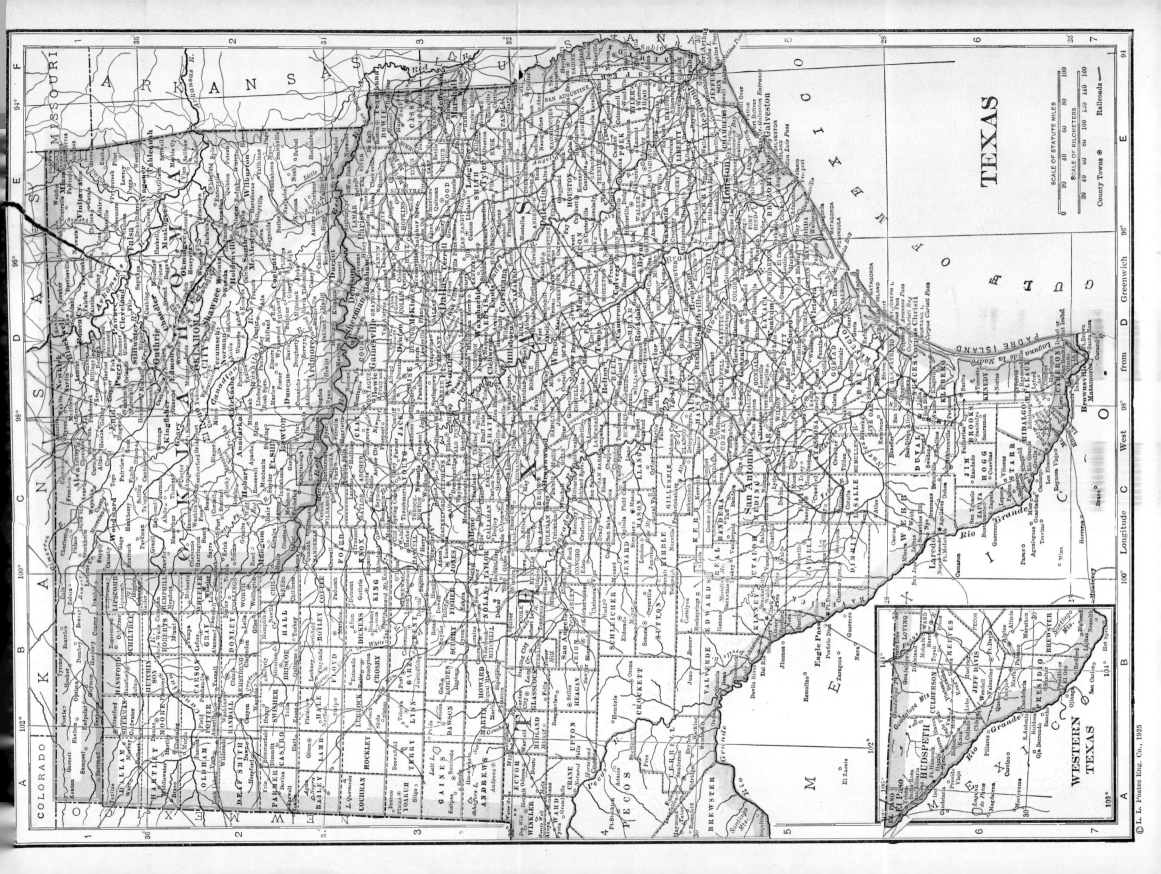

TEXAS

SCALE OF STATUTE MILES

SCALE OF KILOMETERS

County Towns ⊙   Railroads

WESTERN TEXAS

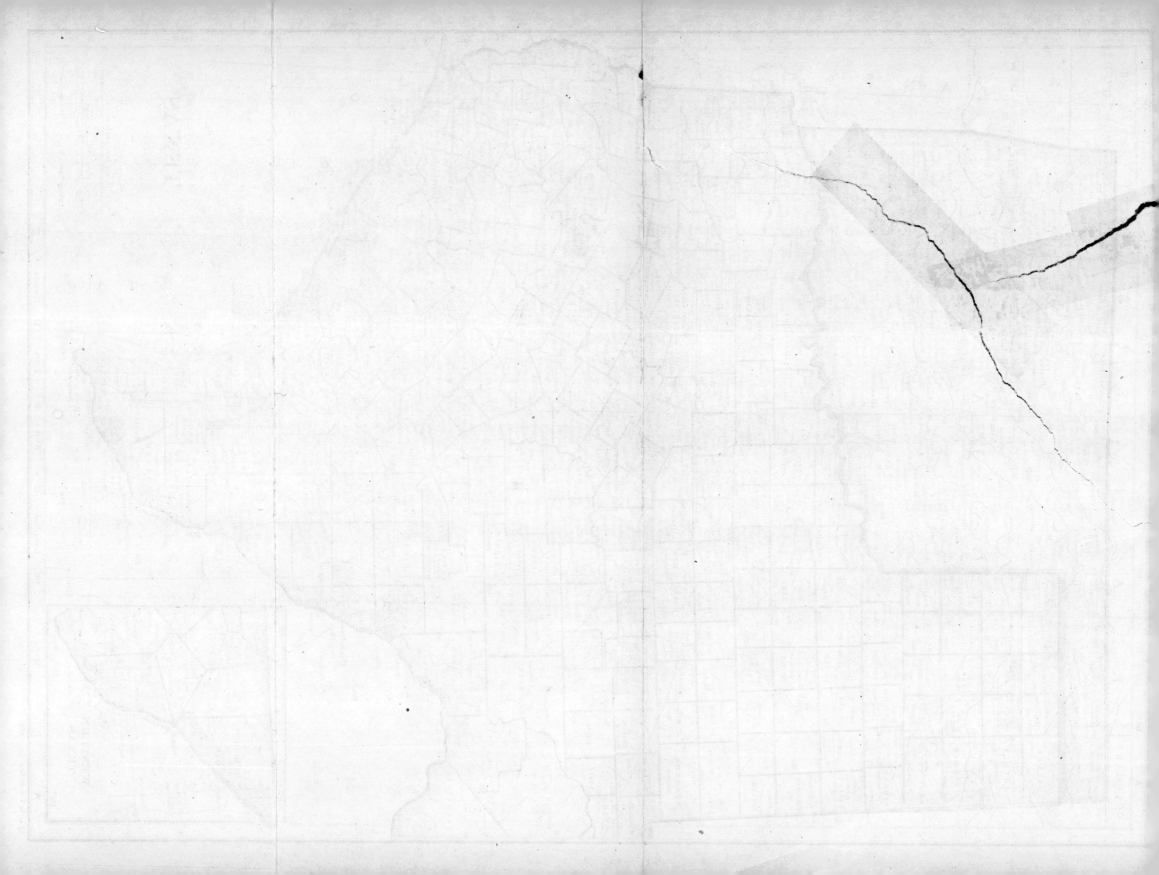

well represented in Texas. The Alluvial extends along the coast, and is bordered by the Tertiary, with wide expansion in the E. N. W. of the Tertiary are extensive tracts of Cretaceous formations, extending W. along the Red river and S. to San Antonio. The W. portion of the state is principally of Carboniferous formations with extensive coal measures.

Mineralogy.—Coal is the most valuable mineral product, but extensive beds of iron, lead, silver, bismuth, and gold are also found. Salt, building stones, clay, arsenic, antimony, mineral oils, and fertilizers are among smaller productions. There are numerous mineral springs and oil wells. In the latter part of 1900 extensive oil fields were discovered near Beaumont, and produced a great boom in the Texas oil industry. The mineral production is of great importance. Its value has been increased in recent years by the enormous development of the petroleum fields. This was especially notable in the years after 1917. The production in 1922 was 118,684,000 barrels of 42 gallons each. The production of coal is of great importance. There were mined in 1922 about 1,106,000 tons, compared with 2,204,266 tons in 1918. The production of natural gas in 1922 was 47,945,000,000 cubic feet. Other important mineral products are quicksilver, salt, gypsum, granite, clay products, asphalt, and zinc.

Agriculture.—The soil of Texas is, as a whole, extremely fertile. The two staple products are cotton and maize, both of which are largely cultivated in the lower or coast region, where sugar cane and tobacco also grow luxuriantly. Wheat, rye, oats, and barley are chief crops in the northern plains; cotton in the black lands; there and at lower levels fruits in almost endless variety are abundant. The forests contain large tracts of oak. The pastures are often covered with the richest natural grasses, and the rearing of cattle is carried on to the greatest advantage. Texas is one of the most important agricultural States. It has over 420,000 farms, with about 120,000,000 acres of farm land, of which about 30,-000,000 acres is improved land. In the arid region a large area has been reclaimed under the Federal Reclamation Act. The acreage, value, and production of the principal crops in 1922 were as follows: Corn, 5,729,000 acres, production 114,580,000 bushels, value $95,101,000; oats, 1,455,000 acres, production 33,465,-000 bushels, value $18,406,000; wheat, 1,249,000 cres, production 9,992,000 bushels, value $10,991,000; hay, 871,-000 acres, production 1,295,000 tons, including wild hay; potatoes, 39,000

acres, production 2,418,000 bushels, value $3,869,000; peanuts, 172,000 acres, production 96,320,000 lbs., value $3,853,000; sorghums, 1,970,000 acres, production 39,400,000 bushels, value $39,400,000; cotton, 11,874,000 acres, production 3,-222,000 bales, value $378,572,000; rice, 191,000 acres, production 5,959,000 bushels, value $5,363,000.

Manufactures.—In 1921 there were 3,566 manufacturing establishments employing 88,707 wage earners. Capital invested totaled (1919) $585,776,000. The amount paid in wages was (1921) $103,946,000; cost of materials used $570,042,000; and the value of the product $842,438,000.

Banking.—On Sept. 14, 1923, there were reported National banks in operation having $72,765,000 in capital, and resources of $860,173,000, including loans to a total of $488,713,000. There were, in 1919, 834 State banks, with $25,080,000 in capital, and $8,577,000 surplus. The exchanges at the United States clearing houses at Dallas and Houston for 1923 were $2,932,000,000.

Transportation.—The railway line mileage in the State in 1922 was 16,151.

Education.—There were (1922) 1,166,-512 pupils enrolled in the public elementary schools, and 76,395 in the public high schools. Elementary and secondary teachers numbered 32,137. There are separate schools for white and colored children, and the employment of illiterate children under 14 years of age in factories, etc., is prohibited. There are six normal schools. The most important universities and colleges are the University of Texas at Austin, Agricultural and Mechanical College at College Station, College of Industrial Arts at Denton, Baylor University at Waco, Baylor College at Belton (Texas), Christian College at Fort Worth, Southern Methodist University at Dallas, Howard Payne College at Brownwood, Southwestern University at Georgetown, Austin College at Sherman, and Rice Institute at Houston.

Finance.—The receipts for the year 1922 amounted to $41,859,000, and the disbursements to $45,843,000, including $1,469,000 expended in capital outlays. Expenditures were at the rate of $9.48 per capita. The bonded debt amounted, net of sinking fund assets, to $6,145,000; estimated taxable wealth totaled $9,453,-000,000.

Churches.—The strongest denominations in the State are the Methodist Episcopal, South; Regular Baptist, South; Regular Baptist, Colored; Roman Catholic; African Methodist; Disciples of Christ; Methodist Episcopal; Cumberland

Presbyterian; Presbyterian, South; Lutheran, General Council; Protestant Episcopal; and Primitive Baptist.

State Goverment.—The Governor is elected for a term of two years. Legislative sessions are held biennially and are unlimited in length. The Legislature consists of two houses, the Senate composed of 31 members and the House of 142 members. There are 18 Representatives in Congress.

History.—The first settlement in Texas was made at Taleta by the Spanish in 1682, 12 miles north of the present El Paso. It afterward in conjunction with Coahuila became one of the States of the Mexican Confederation. Several colonies of American citizens, invited by the Mexicans, settled in the central and E. section, and gradually increased in numbers. When Santa Ana overthrew the federal system Zacatecas rebelled but was soon subdued. Texas then revolted from the Mexican government, and in 1836 declared itself independent. Santa Ana attempted to reduce it, but failed, being himself beaten and taken prisoner at the battle of San Jacinto by General Houston. Texas now was an independent republic, till 1845. It then became one of the United States, which claimed as Texan territory all the land as far as the Rio Grande, enforcing this claim by the successful war with Mexico. Texas joined the Confederacy in February, 1861, was overcome in 1865, and was under military control till 1870, when it was restored to Statehood.

TEXAS, UNIVERSITY OF, a coeducational non-sectarian institution in Austin, Tex.; founded in 1883; it had in the year 1924: Professors and instructors, 358; students, 8,762; volumes in the library number over 35,000; president, W. M. W. Splawn.

TEXEL, an island belonging to the province of North Holland, at the entrance to the Zuider Zee. It is separated from the mainland by a narrow strait, called the Marsdiep, contains about 35,000 acres of arable and pasture lands, and has a population of about 6,500 inhabitants, who keep some 35,000 sheep, famous both for their wool and their cheese. The Marsdiep channel or part of it is also often called the Texel; and here or hereabouts many important naval battles have been fought. Blake defeated Tromp and De Ruyter in 1653; Prince Rupert fought De Ruyter in 1673; Duncan blockaded the Texel (for a time with a single ship) in 1797; and a Dutch fleet of 12 ships of war and 13 Indiamen surrendered to Admiral Mitchell in 1794.

TEXTILE MANUFACTURING. Those manufactures in the industrial field comprise the production from raw materials of silk, cotton, wool, flax, jute and hemp, as well as knit goods, including hosiery, with laces, embroideries and braids, with their accessories. The industry has grown in recent times to enormous dimensions. The Census Reports of 1910 showed increase of 74.4 per cent in the capital invested in the first decade of the present century, over the last decade of the last century; and 79.2 per cent increase in the annual value of the products manufactured. It is shown moreover that despite the increased quantitative production by improved machinery the increase in the number of workers in the textile industries in each decade has exceeded the growth in population since 1860. An idea of the growth of the several industries forming parts of the group is also conveyed by the statistics relating to the consumption of raw materials. Except during the decade in the southern states in which the Civil War was fought there has been a steady increase in the amount of cotton used. The amount of wool used during the two decades preceding 1880 showed an increase of 300 per cent. A like increase would probably have had to be recorded in respect to cotton during the same period had the conditions been unsettled. But no sooner had the effects of the Civil War begun to be overcome than cotton took an upward trend. During the three decades preceding 1910 the consumption of cotton steadily increased and the figures point to a striking development in the cotton manufacturing industry of the South. The United States Department of Agriculture reported the cotton crop of the United States for 1919 at 11,421,000 bales of 500 pounds each. This estimate indicated a small crop, representing a reduction of about 8 per cent from the five-year average of 1914-18. The area planted was 33,566,000 acres, a reduction of 1,100,000 acres below the average of 1914-18. The farm value of the crop and lint was nevertheless $2,034,658,000, based on the prices prevailing on Dec. 1, 1919, which made it the most valuable cotton crop produced in the United States up to and including the year 1924. The world's production of cotton exclusive of linters in 1918 was, according to the Bureau of Census, 17,769,000 bales of 500 pounds net, and the consumption for the year ending July 31, 1919, was approximately 15,970,000 bales. In 1919 the resources of the textile industries were called upon to meet unprecedented demands owing to the shortage produced

TEXAS HORSE RANCH

See Texas, p. 322

PORTLAND CEMENT WORKS NEAR HOUSTON. TEXAS

See Texas, p. 322

by the war. In 1919 about 75 new cotton mills or large additions were built in the United States, the yarn industry in the division making the greatest gain, 22 new mills being listed under hosiery and five under coarse yarns. In 1919 there were 289 new textile mills erected in the United States.

In cotton manufacturing the mills of Lancashire have long held the lead, though the development of the textile industries in the United States is likely before long to carry supremacy to this side of the Atlantic. The United States for a number of years has spun more pounds of raw material, but the spindles have run mostly on the coarse or medium-sized yarns. Wool is grown and manufactured in various countries, and Great Britain, Ireland, France, Germany, Austria Hungary, with one or two adjacent countries produce all except about one-sixth of the wool produced in Europe. England, Ireland and Scotland between them have perhaps the most important woolen industries. France produces a finer quality of woolen cloth than the United States, which is gradually assuming, on the other hand, a leading position in the carpet industry, which consumes large quantities of wool.

In no line in this group of industries, perhaps, is the United States progressing more rapidly than in the manufacture of silk, in which it now surpasses all other countries. Already in the early years of the present century it surpassed France in the value of the product, in spite of the fact that the industry in this country dates back little further than the year 1870. The only serious competitors of the United States in this field that remain are China and Japan, whose exact status cannot be determined as reliable statistics are not available in regard to either. Japan in 1919 was reported as acquiring high-power looms and modern equipment for her silk factories, and was estimated to be manufacturing over 100 per cent more silk than she manufactured in previous years. Raw silk comes to the United States mainly from China, Japan and Italy, and from these and other countries were imported in 1918 an estimated total of 32,865,453 pounds. In the 10 months ending October, 1919, Japan alone provided the United States with $194,000,000 worth of raw silk out of the $251,000,000 worth imported in the 10 months ending October. China sent $45,000,000 worth; Italy $11,000,000; while the imports from other countries were less than $1,000,000 worth. In 1919 manufacturers of silk in the United States had to pay higher prices for raw silk from other countries than in the previous years. In spite of the fact the value of imports of raw silk was the largest on record, exceeding $300,000,000 as against $180,000,000 in 1918, $156,000,000 in 1917, and $120,000,000 in 1916. The amount, despite the higher cost, was greater than in all the preceding years. The price of raw silk imported was the highest recorded averaging $8.42 per pound in October, as against an average of $3 per pound in 1915. In the United States in 1920 the demand for silk goods continued as strong as ever, and the volume of business recorded was greater than in any previous year.

TEYTE, MAGGIE, an English soprano, born in Wolverhampton in 1890. She studied music under Jean de Reszke at Paris, and made her first appearance at Monte Carlo in 1908 as Zerlina in Mozart's "Don Giovanni." She then became a member of the Opéra Comique, whence she went to London and sang during the season of 1910. From 1910 to 1915 she was attached to the Chicago Opera Company and toured all over the United States, establishing her reputation particularly by her rendering of the roles of Mimi in "La Bohème" and Mélisande in "Pelléas et Mélisande."

TEZCUCO, or **TEZCOCO,** a lake of Mexico, about 2½ miles E. of the city of Mexico, 15 miles long and 9 miles in its greatest width. It was formerly much more extensive and contained numerous islands, on which the old city of Mexico was built. Its waters are strongly impregnated with salt. Also a town on the above lake, 16 miles E. N. E. of Mexico, anciently of considerable importance, of which only the ruins of its palaces and temples remain. It contains numerous handsome modern edifices. Pop. about 6,000. District 60,000.

THAARUP, THOMAS, a Danish poet; born in Copenhagen, Denmark, in 1749. Some of his dramatic compositions, among them "The Birthday" and "Peter's Wedding," are regarded as equal to the best in Danish literature. His "Song of Love and Fatherland" ranks as a lyrical classic. He died in 1821.

THACHER, JOHN BOYD, an American reformer; born in Ballston, N. Y., Sept. 11, 1847; was graduated at Williams College in 1869; member of the New York Senate in 1884-1885, when he introduced the measures which resulted in the tenement house reforms; mayor of Albany, N. Y., in 1886-1887, 1896-1897; and chairman of the Bureau of Awards at the World's Columbian Exposition in Chicago in 1893. He was the author of several books, including: "The Continent of America, Its Discovery and Its Baptism"; "The Cabotian Discovery"; etc. He died Feb. 25, 1909.

THACKERAY, WILLIAM MAKEPEACE, an English novelist; born in Calcutta, India, July 18, 1811. At the age of seven Thackeray was sent to England for his education, and was placed at the Charterhouse School, London, afterward continuing his studies at Cambridge. He left the university without taking a degree; and being well provided for he chose the profession of artist. He spent several years in France, Germany, and Italy, staying at Weimar, Rome, and Paris, but gradually became convinced that art was not his vocation, and having meanwhile lost his fortune, he resolved to turn his attention to literature. His first appearance in this sphere was as a journalist. Under the names of George Fitz-Boodle, Esq., or of Michael Angelo Titmarsh, he contributed to "Frazer's Magazine" tales, criticisms, verses, etc., which were marked by great knowledge of the world, keen irony, or playful humor. It was in this magazine that "The Great Hoggarty Diamond," "Yellowplush Papers," and "Barry Lyndon" appeared. In 1840 he published separately the "Paris Sketch-book," in 1841 the "Second Funeral of Napoleon" and the "Chronicle of the Drum," and in 1843 the "Irish Sketch-book." None of these writings, however, attained to any great popularity. In 1841 "Punch" was started, and his contributions to that periodical, among others, "Jeame's Diary" and the "Snob Papers," were very successful. In 1846-1848 his novel of "Vanity Fair" was published in monthly parts, with illustrations by himself; and long before its completion its author was unanimously placed in the first rank of British novelists. His next novel was the "History of Pendennis," completed in 1850. In 1851 he delivered a course of lectures in London on the "English Humorists of the 18th Century," which were repeated in Scotland and America, and published in 1853. Another novel, "The History of Henry Esmond," appeared in 1852, and was followed by "The Newcomes" (1855), "The Virginians" (1859), a sort of sequel to Esmond; "Lovel the Widower," "The Adventures of Philip," and "Denis Duval," which was left unfinished at his death. In 1855-56 he delivered a series of lectures in the United States— "The Four Georges," and afterward in England and Scotland. In 1859 he became editor of the "Cornhill Magazine," in which his later novels and the remarkable "Roundabout Papers" appeared, but he retired from that post in 1862. He wrote a good deal of verse, half-humorous, half-pathetic, and often wholly extravagant, but all characterized by grace and spontaneity. He undoubtedly ranks as the classical English humorist and satirist of the Victorian reign, and one of the greatest novelists, essayists, and critics in the literature. A collection of letters by Thackeray was published in 1887. He died in Kensington Palace Gardens, London, Dec. 24, 1863.

THAER, WILHELM ALBRECHT, a German agriculturist; born in Lüdersdorf, near Wriezen, on the Oder, Aug. 6, 1828. He was appointed professor in the University of Giessen, 1871. He is author of a "System of Agriculture" (1877); "Ancient Egyptian Husbandry" (1881); "Weeds in Rural Economy" (1881); "Researches in Tenant-Farming" 1890). He died Dec. 14, 1906.

THAÏS, a famous Athenian courtesan, She accompanied Alexander, who, during an orgy, was persuaded by her to destroy the city of Persepolis. After the death of the Macedonian conqueror, she became the wife of Ptolemy, King of Egypt.

THALAMEPHORUS, or THALAMEPHOROS, in Egyptian antiquities, a kneeling figure supporting a shrine or inscribed tablet. These statues probably represent priests and initiated women who carried about in processions the statues of the gods. It was usual for such processions to stand still from time to time, when the priests, kneeling probably, presented to the people the images of the deities, either to be worshipped or kissed.

THALAMIFLORÆ, a class of exogenous or dicotyledonous plants in which the petals are distinct and inserted with the stamens on the thalamus or receptacle.

THALASSICOLLIDA, in zoölogy, a family of Radiolaria. The animals consist of structureless cysts containing cellular elements and protoplasm, surrounded by a layer of protoplasm giving off pseudopodia, which commonly stand out like rays, but sometimes run into another, and so form networks. The best known genera are Thalassicolla, Sphœrozoüm, and Collosphæra. They are all marine, being found floating passively on the surface of most seas, and vary in size from an inch in diameter downward.

THALASSICOLLINA, an approximate synonym of THALASSICOLLIDA (q. v.).

THALASSINIDÆ, in zoölogy, a widely distributed family of macrurous Decapoda. Abdomen long, not very solid, carapace small and compressed; first pair of legs large; sternal plate long and narrow.

THALASSIOPHYLLUM, in botany, a genus of algals, akin to *Laminaria,* but having the frond spirally wound around the stem. Found on the N. W. shores of Arctic America.

THALASSOCHELYS, in zoölogy, the loggerhead turtle; a genus of Chelonidæ, equivalent to the genus Caouana of older authors, with two or three species from tropical seas. Plates of the carapace not imbricated; 15 plates on the disk; jaws slightly curved toward each other at their extremity.

THALASSOPHRYNE, in ichthyology, a genus of Batrachidæ, with two species, from the Atlantic and Pacific coasts of Central America. The spinous dorsal is formed by two spines only, each of which is hollow, like the opercular spine, and conveys the contents of a poison bag situated at the base. The poison bags have no external muscular layer, and are situated immediately below the thick, loose skin which envelops the spines; the ejection of the poison can therefore only be effected by the pressure to which the poison bag is subjected the moment the spine enters another body.

THALBERG, SIGISMOND, a Swiss pianist; born in Geneva in 1812, where he received his early education under the supervision of his mother, the Baroness Wetzlar. At the age of 10 he was removed to Vienna, where he continued his studies under the best masters, in preparation for a diplomatic career. Thalberg's first appearance as a pianist was at the age of 14, when he played at an evening party at Prince Metternich's. This success was followed up by numerous appearances in Paris, till, overcoming his father's scruples, he was allowed to abandon diplomacy for music. He made tours in 1839 through Belgium, Holland, England, and Russia, and afterward through Spain, Brazil, and North America, finally settling down at Naples in 1858. Thalberg married Madame Boucher, daughter of the celebrated Lablache. His musical compositions comprise more than 90 numbers, principally fantasies and variations. His operas "Cristina" and "Florinda"—the latter played before the queen in London in 1851—were absolute failures. As a pianist, in graceful and brilliant execution and in manual dexterity, he had scarcely a rival. He died in Naples April 27, 1871.

THALER, a silver coin formerly in use in Germany, of the value of about 75 cents.

THALES, the earliest of the Greek philosophers, called the father of philosophy; born in Miletus 640 B. C. He was the founder of the Ionic school, one of the chief sources of Grecian philosophy. He visited Egypt for instruction in the sciences professed by the priesthood. Besides abstract philosophy, he studied geometry and astronomy, and tradition credits him with predicting a solar eclipse. His ancient biographers mention among his services to astronomy a calculation of the length of the year, and of the interval between solstices and equinoxes. He left nothing in writing. He died about 550.

THALIA, one of the nine Muses. She was the patron of comedy, and is usually represented with the comic mask and the shepherd's crook in her hand. One of the Graces was also called Thalia.

THALICTRUM, in botany, meadow-rue; a genus of *Ranunculaceæ,* tribe Anemoneæ. Known species 50, from the temperate and colder parts of the Northern Hemisphere. Three familiar species are *T. alpinum,* the Alpine; *T. minus,* the lesser; and *T. flavum,* the common meadow-rue. The most common is *T. minus.* It has three or four pinnate leaves, with roundish or wedge-shaped leaflets, trifid and toothed, and diffuse panicles of generally drooping flowers. It is found in stony pastures, especially in limestone or chalky districts. There are four sub-species. The root of *T. foliolosum,* from the temperate parts of the Himalayas, is given in India as a tonic and aperient in convalescence after fever, in chronic dyspepsia, etc.

THALITE, in mineralogy, a variety of saponite occurring in amygdaloidal rocks on the N. shore of Lake Superior.

THALIUM, in mineralogy, a name given to a supposed new element which apparently has no existence.

THALLEIOCHIN, in chemistry, dalleiochin; a green substance produced by the action of chlorine and then ammonia on a solution of quinine. In dilute solutions it remains dissolved as a bright emerald green color, and forms a highly delicate test for the presence of small quantities of quinine.

THALLENE, a solid hydrocarbon isomeric with anthracene obtained from the last products which pass over in the distillation of American petroleum. **It**

is distinguished by a green fluorescence, and, when illuminated by violet and ultra-violet light, exhibits a fluorescent spectrum containing light-green bands.

THALLIUM, in chemistry, a triad metallic element discovered by Crookes in 1861, and widely distributed as a constituent in iron and copper pyrites in blende, native sulphur, and in many kinds of ores; symbol Tl., at. wt. 203.64. It can be distilled with the sulphur by heating pyrites to a bright-red heat, then dissolving out the excess of sulphur by boiling with caustic soda, collecting and washing the sulphide of thallium, converting it into sulphate, and precipitating the thallium in the metallic state by the action of pure metallic zinc. The spongy metal is compressed, dried, and fused into a bright metallic button by heating under cyanide of potassium. It is a perfect metal, with high luster, not quite so white as silver, but free from the blue tinge of lead. It has a sp. gr. of 11.80-11.91, melts at 293°, is a very soft metal with less tenacity than lead, and almost devoid of elasticity. It communicates an intense green hue to a colorless flame, and its spectrum consists of one intensely brilliant and sharp green line, coinciding with the number 1442.6 on Kirchhoff's chart.

THAMES, the most important river of Great Britain; usually said to rise about 3 miles S. W. of Cirencester in Gloucestershire, near a bridge over the Thames and Severn canal, called Thameshead Bridge, but is more properly formed by the Isis, Churn, Colne, and Leach, which have their sources on the E. side of the Cotswold Hills, and unite near Lechlade, where the counties of Gloucester, Wilts, Berks, and Oxford border on each other. Proceeding from Lechlade, where it becomes navigable for barges, it flows first E. N. E., then S. S. E., past Oxford and Abingdon to Reading, then N. W. past Great Marlow, and S. E. past Windsor to Staines. From Staines it pursues a circuitous course E., passing the towns of Chertsey, Kingston, Richmond and Brentford, separating the counties of Middlesex and Surrey, and passing through London. Below London its course E. to the Nore, between Kent and Essex, is 47 miles. Its total course is estimated at 250 miles. Its tributaries include the Windrush, Cherwell, Thame, Colne, Brent, Lea, and Roding, on the left; the Kennet, Loddon, Wey, and Mole, on the right. Thameshead Bridge is 376 feet above sea-level; the junction of the Colne above Lechlade is 243 feet. At London Bridge the width of the river is 266

yards, at Woolwich 490 yards, at Gravesend 800 yards, and 3 miles below, 1,290 yards. The basin of the Thames has an area of 5,400 square miles, and belongs entirely to the upper part of the Secondary and to the Tertiary formations. The depth of the river in the fair way above Greenwich to London Bridge is 12 to 13 feet, while its tides have a mean range of 17 feet and an extreme rise of 22 feet. By means of numerous canals immediate access is given from its basin to those of all the great rivers of England.

THAMUGAS, "the Numidian Pompeii," near the Aures Mountains, in Algeria; 22 miles from Batna, which is half-way by rail from Constantine to Biskra. Here are in the solitude extensive remains of colonnades, temples, a forum, a triumphal arch in honor of the Emperor Trajan (founder of the city), and numerous statues and inscriptions coming down to the 5th century, when the Roman city was destroyed by the barbarians.

THANE, a title of honor or dignity among the Anglo-Saxons. In England a freeman not noble was raised to the dignity of a thane by acquiring a certain amount of land (five hides in the case of a lesser thane), by making three sea voyages, or by receiving holy orders. The thanes had the right of voting in the Witenagemot, not only of their own shires, but also of the whole kingdom, on important questions. There were two orders of thanes: The king's thanes, or those who attended at his court and held lands immediately from him, and ordinary thanes, or lords of the manor, and who had a particular jurisdiction within their limits. On the cessation of his actual personal service about the king, the thane received a grant of land. After the Norman conquest, thanes and barons were classed together, and the title fell into disuse in the reign of Henry II. In Scotland, thane signified originally a count or earl, one who ruled a county, or even in some cases a province. Afterward the title was applied to a class of non-military tenants of the crown, and continued in use till the end of the 15th century.

THANET, OCTAVE, pseudonym of ALICE FRENCH, an American novelist; born in Andover, Mass., March 19, 1850. She published: "Knitters in the Sun"; "Otto the Knight"; "Stories of a Western Town"; "An Adventure in Photography"; "Expiation"; "The Heart of Toil"; "A Slave to Duty."

THANET, ISLE OF, a district of England, in the county of Kent, at the mouth of the Thames; separated from the mainland by the Stour river on the S. and the Nethergong on the W., with an area of 26,500 acres. On its shores are the well-known watering places Ramsgate, Margate, and Broadstairs; and on the North Foreland, in the N. E., is a lighthouse, 85 feet high, visible 19 miles. Pop. about 72,500.

THANKSGIVING DAY, in the United States, an annual festival of thanksgiving for the mercies of the closing year. Practically it is a National harvest festival, fixed by proclamation of the President and the governors of States, and ranks as a legal holiday. In 1789 the Episcopal church formally recognized the civil government's authority to appoint such a feast, and in 1888 the Roman Catholic church also decided to honor a festival which had long been nearly universally observed—though nowhere with such zest as in the New England States, where it ranks as the great annual family festival, taking the place which in England is accorded to Christmas. The earliest harvest thanksgiving in America was kept by the Pilgrim Fathers at Plymouth in 1621, and was repeated often during that and the ensuing century; Congress recommended days of thanksgiving annually during the Revolution, and in 1784 for the return of peace—as did President Madison in 1815. Washington appointed such a day in 1789 after the adoption of the Constitution, and in 1795 for the general benefits and welfare of the nation. Since 1817 the festival has been observed annually in New York, and since 1863 the Presidents have always issued proclamations appointing the last Thursday in November as Thanksgiving Day.

THANN (tän), a town of Upper Alsace, Germany; on the Thur river; 23 miles S. W. of Kolmar. It dates back to 995 and in 1325 became the property of the House of Hapsburg. In 1632 it was captured by the Swedes (during the Thirty Years' War) and in 1675 the French under Turenne blew up the castle of Engelburg, the ruins of which overlook the town. Thann has manufactures of silk, cotton, chemicals, and machinery, and contains the beautiful church of St. Theobald (Roman Catholic) with a spire of delicate openwork 325 feet high.

THAPSIA, the deadly carrot; the typical genus of *Thapsidæ*. Perennial herbs with doubly or trebly pinnate leaves, and large compound umbels of yellow flowers without involucres or involucels. *T. garganica* is found in the S. of Europe and Northern Africa; *T. silphion* is a
I—24

variety of it rather than a distinct species. *Thapsia* is a powerful rubefácient, and is used in medicine in the form of a sparadrap.

THASO, the ancient Thasos, an island in the Ægean sea, a few miles S. of the Macedonian coast, belonging to Turkey. It is of a circular form, about 16 miles in diameter, and is traversed by high woody hills which yield large quantities of timber.

THATCH, straw, or any other dry vegetable substance, laid on the top of a building, rick, etc., to keep out the wet. There are many different materials for thatching, but the straw of wheat and rye when well laid form the neatest and most secure covering for general purposes. The reed though expensive, is a highly valuable article for the purpose of thatch, where a lasting roof is required.

THAUMASTURA, in ornithology, the sheartail; a genus of *Trochilidæ*, with two species, from the humid districts of Peru. The genus is distinguished by the peculiarly shaped tail, the feathers of which are pointed, the middle ones being greatly elongate. Several pairs are generally met with together. The males are extremely pugnacious, driving off every other kind of humming bird which ventures to enter their territory. The plumage of the sexes is different, the female being much duller in color.

THAUSING, MORITZ (tou'sing), an Austrian art critic; born in Leitmeritz, in Bohemia, June 3, 1838. He became professor of the science of æsthetics in the University of Vienna, 1873. He wrote: "Dürer: History of His Life and His Art" (1876); "J. J. Callot's Sketch-Book" (1881); "Art Letters from Vienna" (1884). He died in Leitmeritz, Aug. 14, 1884.

THAXTER, MRS. CELIA (LEIGHTON), an American poet; born in Portsmouth, N. H., June 29, 1836. She spent her childhood and most of her later life at the Isles of Shoals. Her works are: "Poems" (1872); "Among the Isles of Shoals" (1873); "Poems" (1874); "Drift Weed" (1879); "Poems for Children" (1884); "The Cruise of the Mystery," etc. (1886); "Idyls and Pastorals" (1886); "The Yule Log" (1889); "An Island Garden" (1894); "Letters" (1895); "Stories and Poems for Children" (1895). She died on the island of Appledore, Isles of Shoals, Aug. 26, 1894.

THAYER, ALEXANDER WHEELOCK, an American writer on music and musicians; born in 1817. He contributed to the "Dictionary of Music"; was musical critic of the New York "Tribune"; afterward was consul at Trieste, 1859-1897. He published: "Signor Masoni," etc. (1862); "The Hebrews and the Red Sea" (1893); and three volumes of "Life of Beethoven" (1866-1887). He died in Trieste, July 15, 1897.

THAYER, ABBOT HANDERSON, an American figure, landscape, and portrait painter; born at Boston, Mass., in 1849. He studied at the Beaux Arts, Paris, under Gerome and Lehmann, being much influenced by Bastien-Lepage, and, on return to the United States, first painted portraits and landscapes, but later gave his energy to the production of idea figures. The most notable of his works are: "Young Woman" (Metropolitan Museum, New York); "Caritas" (Boston Museum); "Winged Figure" (Albright Art Gallery, Buffalo); "A Virgin" (Freer Collection, National Gallery, Washington); and "Virgin Enthroned." He was for two years president of the Society of American Artists. Died May 29, 1921.

THAYER, CHARLES SNOW, an American librarian; born at Westfield, Mass., in 1865. He was educated at Amherst, Yale, and Göttingen, leaving the latter university in 1901. In 1886-92 he was a bank clerk at Minneapolis, and became assistant pastor of the Union Congregational Church at Providence, R. I., in 1900. Since August, 1902, he has been librarian of the Case Memorial Library and associate professor of bibliology at the Hartford Theological Seminary. He was ordained to the Congregational ministry in 1902 and is a member of the Society of Biblical Literature and Exegesis.

THAYER, ELI, an American educator; born in Mendon, Mass., June 11, 1819; was graduated at Brown University in 1845, and soon afterward became principal of the Worcester Academy. He founded the Oread Institute, a school for girls, in Worcester, Mass., in 1848; served for several years as a member of the Worcester school board; became alderman of that city in 1853, and was a member of the State Legislature in 1853-54. While there he originated and organized the "Emigrant Aid Company," and labored till 1857 to obtain the support of the Northern States for his plan to send anti-slavery settlers to Kansas. He was a member of Congress in 1856-1861, when he made his famous speeches on "Central American Colonization," "Suicide of Slavery," and the admission of Oregon. While the Civil War was in progress he proposed a plan for the military colonization of Florida as a war measure. Subquently he urged his colonization scheme as a remedy for polygamy in Utah; wrote and published several books; and invented a hydraulic elevator, a safety steam boiler, and an automatic boiler cleaner. He died in Worcester, Mass., April 15, 1899.

THAYER, EMMA HOMAN, an American author; born in New York city, Feb. 13, 1842; was educated at Rutgers College and took a course in art at the National Academy of Design, New York city, where she exhibited numerous figure paintings; settled in Colorado in 1882, and made sketches of the flora of that vicinity. Her publications include: "Wild Flowers of Colorado" (1885); "Wild Flowers of the Pacific Coast" (1887); "The English American" (1889); "Petronilla, the Sister" (1898); "A Legend of Glenwood Springs" (1900); and "Dorothy Scudder's Science" (1901). She died in 1908.

THAYER, JAMES BRADLEY, an American educator; born in Haverhill, Mass., Jan. 15, 1831; was graduated at Harvard College in 1852 and at its law school in 1856; admitted to the bar in Boston the same year and practiced there till 1873, when he became Royall professor of law at Harvard University. Professor Thayer was the author of many well-known law books. He died in Cambridge, Mass., Feb. 14, 1902.

THAYER, JOSEPH HENRY, an American educator; born in Boston, Mass., Nov. 7, 1828; was graduated at Harvard University in 1850 and at the Andover Theological Seminary in 1857; preached in Salem, Mass., in 1859-1864; was professor of sacred literature at Andover Theological Seminary in 1864-1884; and in the latter year became professor of New Testament criticism and interpretation in the Harvard Divinity School. His publications include: "Books and Their Use"; "The Change of Attitude Toward the Bible"; "A Greek-English Lexicon of the New Testament"; "A Biographic Sketch of Elzra Abbott," etc. He died in 1901.

THAYER, MARTIN RUSSELL, an American jurist; born in Petersburg, Va., Jan. 27, 1819; was graduated at the University of Pennsylvania in 1840, and admitted to the Pennsylvania bar in 1842. He was appointed by the governor to revise the revenue laws of Pennsylvania in 1862; was a member of Congress in 1863-1867; judge of the district court of Philadelphia in 1867, and presiding judge of the Court of Common Pleas in 1874-

1896. His publications include: "The Duties of Citizenship"; "The Battle of Germantown"; "The Philippines"; "What Is Demanded of the United States by the Obligations of Duty and National Honor"; and many essays, speeches, reviews, etc. He died in 1906.

THAYER, SYLVANUS, an American military officer; born in Braintree, Mass., June 9, 1785; was graduated at Dartmouth College in 1807; and the United States Military Academy in 1808; and assigned to the Engineer Corps. He was employed on engineer duty on the E. coast, and as an instructor of mathematics at the Military Academy; was promoted to 1st lieutenant, July 1, 1812; took part in the War of 1812-1815; was chief engineer on the Niagara frontier, at Lake Champlain, and in the defense of Norfolk, Va.; was promoted captain of engineers in 1813, and brevetted major in 1815 for distinguished services. In 1815 he was sent to Europe to examine military works and schools, and to study the operations of the allied armies before Paris; was recalled in 1817 on being appointed superintendent of the United States Military Academy, which post he held till 1833, when he resigned. During his administration he organized the institution on its present basis. He was brevetted major in 1823, lieutenant-colonel in 1828, and colonel in 1833. In 1838-1863 he was engaged in the construction of defenses in and about Boston harbor. He was promoted lieutenant-colonel of engineers in 1838, colonel in 1863, and brevet brigadier-general May 31, 1863, and was retired the following day. He was a member of various scientific associations; gave $70,000 to found the Thayer School of Civil Engineering at Dartmouth College; $10,000 to Braintree for a public library; and bequeathed $300,000 for the endowment of an academy in Braintree. He was the author of "Papers on Practical Engineering" (1844). He died in South Braintree, Mass., Sept. 7, 1872. His body was reinterred in West Point, Nov. 8, 1877, where a statue was raised to his honor, which bears the inscription, "Colonel Thayer, Father of the United States Military Academy."

THAYER, WILLIAM MAKEPEACE, an American clergyman; born in Franklin, Mass., Feb. 23, 1820. His books attained great popularity, several being reprinted abroad in German, French, Italian, Greek, Swedish, etc. Among his works are: "The Bobbin Boy" (1859); "The Pioneer Boy" (1863); a Series of Biographers (10 vols. 1859-1863); "Youth's History of the Rebellion"

(1863-1865); "White House Stories" (1880-1885); "Marvels of the New West" (1887); "Life of Garfield"; "Men Who Win"; "Women Who Win"; "From the Tannery to the White House"; "In the Meshes"; "Ethics of Success"; etc. He died in Franklin, Mass., April 7, 1898.

THAYER, WILLIAM ROSCOE, an American author; born in Boston, Mass., Jan. 16, 1859; studied in Europe, and was graduated at Harvard University in 1881; became editor of the "Harvard Graduates' Magazine" (1892-1915). His publications include "Confessions of Hermes" (1884); "The Best Elizabethan Plays" (1890); "The Dawn of Italian Independence" (1893); "Poems, New and Old" (1894); "History and Customs of Harvard University" (1898); "Throne-Makers" (1899); "Short History of Venice" (1903); "Life and Times of Cavour" (1911); "Life and Letters of John Hay" (1915); "Germany Against Civilization" (1916); "Letters of John Holmes"; "Theodore Roosevelt." He was an overseer of Harvard, vice-president American Historical Association, member of Academy of Arts and Letters. Died 1923.

THEATER, or THEATRE, a building devoted to the representation of dramatic spectacles; a playhouse. Among the Greeks and Romans theaters were the chief public edifices next to the temples. The theater of Marcellus at Rome, the external walls of which are still in existence, contained seats for 30,000 spectators. The Greek theaters were semicircular; that part in which the chorus danced and sang was called the orchestra; behind this, and facing the audience, was the stage for the performers who took part in the drama; the back of the stage being filled in by a permanent architecturally decorated scene. Roman theaters also formed semi-circles, with seats rising in the form of an amphitheater for the spectators, at the chord of which was the stage (*scena*), with its permanent decorations. The orchestra, which was the space between the stage and the lowest tier of spectators, was employed by the Greeks for theatrical purposes, whereas the Romans turned it into seats for the senators. The topmost tier was generally crowned with a covered portico. The theaters were either open or were protected against the sun and rain by an awning stretched over them. The *scena* consisted of the *scena* in a restricted sense, answering to the modern scene, and the *pulpitum* or stage. The scene itself, in accordance with a critical canon observed with much solitude by the Grecian dramatists, was very rarely changed during the course of the same play, though the *scena versatilis*, the turning scene, and the *scena ductilis*, the shifting scene, were not altogether unknown. The *pulpitum* again was divided into *proscenium*, or space in front of the scene, where the actors stood while actually engaged in the business of the play, and the *postscenium*, or space behind the scene, to which they retired when they made their exits. Modern theaters are generally constructed on a semi-circular or horse-shoe plan, with galleries running round the walls.

Also, a room, hall, or other place, generally with a platform at one end, and ranks of seats, rising as they recede, or otherwise arranged so as to afford the spectators a full and unobstructed view of the platform. Such rooms are used for public lectures, anatomical demonstrations, surgical operations, etc.

THEATINE, in Church history, any member of a congregation of Regular Clerks, which derived its name from Theate (now Chieti), a fortified city of the Abruzzo, of which John Peter Caraffa, one of the founders of the Congregation, was bishop. Associated with Caraffa were St. Cajetan, Paul Consiglieri, and Boniface de Colle; the first steps toward the formation of the new congregation were taken in 1524, and in the following year it was approved by Pope Clement VII. The object of the founders was the promotion of spiritual life among Christians and the removal of irregularities among the secular clergy. The members took the three vows, and practiced rigid poverty, for they even abstained from asking alms. In the popedom of Caraffa, who was elected in 1555, and took the title of Paul IV., the congregation spread over the continent, but is at present confined to Italy.

THÉÂTRE FRANÇAIS, or **COMÉDIE FRANÇAISE**, the theater in the Palais Royal, Paris, in which the classical drama of France receives its most perfect and artistic representation, dates from 1680, when Louis XIV. combined the actors of the Hotel Bourgogne and Molière's company, and gave them a special organization and a yearly subvention of $2,400. In 1770 the theater was established in the Tuileries, in 1782 was removed to a new building where the Odéon now is, and after the troublous times of the revolution was finally established in the Palais Royal. The present constitution dates from 1803. The committee of six, presided over by government officials, names the *sociétaires* (the actors and actresses who belonged to the staff) and the less permanent *pensionnaires*, superintends all financial arrange-

ments, makes a point of reproducing from time to time the really great French plays, and sits in judgment on new plays submitted. The subvention is now $48,000. The Théâtre Français is remarkable for perfect study, artistic dignity, and harmonious ensemble.

THEBAINE (named from Thebes, in Egypt, from the vicinity of which comes some of the opium of commerce), $C_{19}H_{21}NO_3$; thebaia; one of the less important bases existing in opium; obtained by treating the extract of opium with milk of lime, washing the precipitate with water, and, after drying, exhausting it with boiling alcohol. On evaporation a residue is obtained, from which ether dissolves out the thebaine. It crystallizes from alcohol in quadratic tablets, having a silvery luster, tastes acrid, and is extremely poisonous. It melts at 12.5°, is insoluble in water, very soluble in alcohol and ether, and is colored deep red with sulphuric acid.

THEBAN LEGION, according to tradition, a body composed of Christians, who submitted to martyrdom rather than attack their brethren during the persecution of the Emperor Maximin, or sacrifice to the gods, about A. D. 286. Their leader, Maurice, was canonized.

THEBES, the name of a celebrated Egyptian city, formerly the capital of southern or upper Egypt; called by the Egyptians Tuabu, by the Hebrews No-Amon, by the Greeks Thebæ, and at a later period Diospolis Magna. It lies in the broadest section of the valley of the Nile, in about latitude 26° N., at a spot where the desert on the W. sheers away to the girdling range of the Libyan mountains, leaving a broad plain, partly cultivated, on which stand the famous twin statues, one of which is known as the "vocal Memnon," and behind them the temples grouped about the modern district of Kurna and Medînet-Habû. The Nile divides this W. part or Necropolis of Thebes, anciently called "Libyan suburb," from the extensive ruins now known by the names of the villages Luxor (el-Uksur, "the palaces") and Karnak which stand on the E. bank, with the low range of the Arabian hills for a background.

The traditional foundation of Thebes goes back to the 1st dynasty, but no buildings have hitherto been found earlier than some slight constructions of the 11th dynasty, 2500 B. C., who appear to have founded the original temple of Amen-Ra, the special god of the city. Its most flourishing period was under the 18th, 19th and 20th dynasties, or from about 1600 to 1100, when it had supplanted Memphis, the ancient capital of the Pharaohs. The central situation of Thebes secured it from the attacks of the N. enemies of Egypt, and contributed to its prosperity; and here the worship of Amen-Ra arose in all its splendor; magnificent palaces and temples were built in its different quarters by the great monarchs of the Theban dynasties, and were added to by later kings, down to the time of the Ptolemies and Antonines, to the 2d century A. D.

In the plenitude of its power it sent forth an army of 20,000 war chariots; but about 1100 B. C. the Bubastite and Tanite dynasties removed the capital again to the N., to Sais and Memphis, and thenceforth Thebes declined in importance. At the Persian conquest in the 6th century B. C. Cambyses obtained a spoil of nearly $10,000,000 from the city, and destroyed many of its noblest monuments. The foundation of Alexandria still further injured it; and at the time of Strabo Thebes was only a cluster of small villages. Its temples, tombs, and ruins were frequently visited by Greek and Roman travelers, including the Emperor Hadrian. At a later period a considerable Christian population lived there under the empire; but at the Arab invasion the inhabitants fled to Esné. Thebes is now inhabited only by Fellahîn, by a few officials, and by the migratory visitors to the three hotels at Luxor.

Of the monuments on the W. or Libyan side the principal are the three temples of Seti I. and Rameses II. and III., known respectively as El-Kurna, the Rameseum (or Memnonium), and Medî-net-Habû. Close to the Rameseum is the fallen and broken colossus of the founder, the largest statue in Egypt, originally nearly 60 feet high. Near by are also some remains of two temples of Amenoph III. and two colossal statues. Some way behind the Rameseum, on a spur of the hills, is a terraced temple of Queen Hatasu (18th dynasty), known as Deyr-el-Bahri, near which a remarkable series of 39 royal and priestly mummies, papyri, etc., were found by Emil Brugsch in 1881. At Medînet-Habû is a pile of buildings, of which the chief is the great temple of Rameses III. (the Rhampsinitus of Herodotus), with sculptures representing his victories over the Philistines, and a calendar with inscriptions dated in the 12th year of his reign. Near here, to the N. W., are the cemeteries of the sacred apes, and further on the valley of the Tombs of the Queens, consisting of 17 sepulchres, supposed to be the tombs of the Pallacides of Amen, mentioned by Diodorus and Strabo. Near them, among the hills, are the Bibân-el-Mulûk, or Tombs of the Kings of the 19th and 20th dynasties, 16 in number.

On the E. bank the chief monuments are at Luxor, the beautiful temple of Amenoph III. (18th dynasty), added to by Rameses II., with its well-known obelisk, the fellow of which was removed to the Place de la Concorde at Paris; and the still more magnificent temple or, rather, group of temples, at Karnak, the sanctuary of which, built by Osirtasen I. of the 12th dynasty, was added to by the monarchs of the 18th. The most remarkable part of this wonderful mass of pylons, courts, and obelisks is the great hall, 170 feet by 329 feet, built by Seti I. and Rameses II., with its central avenue of 12 massive columns, 62 feet high and 12 feet in diameter, and its 122 other columns, and two obelisks (originally four), one of which is the tallest in Egypt, 108 feet high. On the walls the sculptures tell the glorious history of those two warrior kings. Here, too, is the so-called Portico of the Bubastites, built by Shishak, I., recording his expedition against Jerusalem, 971 B. C. Thebes of to-day (*Thevæ*) has a population of about 3,500.

The Thebaid, the territory of Thebes, was a term applied to various areas at various times, but generally to one of the three main divisions of Egypt. It is specially familiar to us as being a favorite place of retreat for Christian hermits.

THEBES, or THIVA, the capital of Bœotia in ancient Greece; founded, according to tradition, by a colony of Phœnicians, under Cadmus, 1550 B. C., or 1400 B. C. They were driven out by the Bœotians, 1124 B. C. Platæa, one of the Bœotian cities, revolted from Thebes 510 B. C., and applied for help to Athens. A war ensued between Thebes and Athens, in which the latter was victorious. This caused much animosity between Thebes and Athens, and in the Persian War, 480 B. C., the Thebans deserted the cause of Greece and fought against the Athenians at Platæa, 479 B. C. The Athenians invaded Bœotia, and established a democratic government in Thebes, 456 B. C. The Thebans were allies of the Spartans in the Peloponnesian War, 431 B. C.-404 B. C. Sparta having claimed supremacy over the whole of Greece, the Thebans joined the Athenians, 395 B. C. The peace of Antalcidas put an end to the war, 387 B. C., and deprived Thebes of her supremacy over Bœotia. The Spartans, who treacherously seized the citadel of Thebes, 382 B. C., were defeated at Leuctra in July, 371 B. C.; and the Thebans regained their power in Greece. Thebes was razed to the ground by Alexander III., 335 B. C., after which it never again formed an independent state. Cassander restored the city, 315 B. C., and it was taken by Demetrius, 293 B. C., and again 290 B. C. The Thebans were defeated in an attempt to expel the Bulgarians from Greece in 1040, and their city was plundered by the Normans of Sicily in 1146. It was one of the most flourishing cities of Greece during the 10th and 11th centuries. It was almost wholly destroyed by an earthquake in 1893.

THECLA, a virgin saint of the early Church; a member of a noble family of Iconium in Lycaonia, where she was converted by the preaching of St. Paul, and having devoted herself to a life of virginity, suffered a series of persecutions from her intended bridegroom, as well as from her parents. She is said to have died at the age of 90 in Seleucia. The apocryphal "Acts of Paul and Thecla" were edited by Tischendorf.

THECLA, in entomology, the hairstreak; a genus of *Lycænidæ*. Fore wings wholly dark brown, or with a large blotch of some other color, or with pale markings near the hinder margin; hind wings with a transverse pale line below, which is entire, interrupted, or nearly obsolete. Larvæ feeding on trees, shrubs, or papilionaceous plants. Common in all temperate regions. *T. rubi*, the green hairstreak, has the under side of the wings green; the rest have not this character. *T. belulæ*, the brown hairstreak, has the under side of the hind wings with two slender white streaks. *T pruni*, the dark hairstreak, has an orange band with a row of black spots; *T. album*, the black hairstreak, a black line; and *T. quercus*, the purple hairstreak, has two small orange spots instead of the band. The first of the five is the most common.

THECODONTIA, in palæontology, an order of *Reptilia* founded by Owen. Vertebral bodies biconcave; ribs of trunk long and bent, the anterior ones with a bifurcate head; limbs ambulatory, femur with a third trochanter; teeth with the crown more or less compressed, pointed, with trenchant and finely-serrate margins, implanted in distinct sockets. Two genera, *Thecodontosaurus* and *Palæosaurus*, from the Trias, near Bristol. Huxley regards them as Dinosaurian.

THECOSMILIA, in palæontology, a genus of Actinozoa. One species from the Rhætic or Lower Lias; from the Jurassic rocks of Great Britain, and others from the Cretaceous and Tertiary.

THECOSOMATA, in zoölogy, a section of *Pteropoda*. Animal with external shell; head indistinct; foot and tentacles rudimentary, combined with the fins; mouth situated in a cavity formed by the union of the locomotive organs; respiratory organ contained within a mantle cavity. There are two families: *Hyaleidæ* and *Limacinidæ*.

THEINE, in chemistry, formula $C_8H_{10}N_4O_2$, an organic base, occurring in tea leaves, in Paraguay tea, guarana, and in small quantities in cocoa seeds. It is also formed synthetically from theobromine by union with methyl, yielding methyl-theobromine, or theine. To prepare it from tea the leaves are extracted with hot water, the solution precipitated with lead acetate, and the filtrate freed from lead by sulphydric acid. On evaporation of the solution and allowing it to stand for some time, the theine crystallizes out. Purified by animal charcoal, it forms tufts of white silky needles, slightly soluble in cold water and alcohol, melting at 225°, and subliming unchanged at a higher temperature. Tea leaves contain from 2 to 4 per cent. of theine, to which the stimulating effect of tea is partly ascribed. At the present day caffeine is the preferred term.

THEINER, AUGUSTIN, a German canonist; born in Breslau, Silesia, April 11, 1804; was appointed prefect of the Vatican archives, 1855; but was deprived of that office during the Vatican Council on the charge of giving to certain oppositionist bishops secret documents of the curia. His first notable work was a tractate in opposition to the rule of clerical celibacy, "The Introduction of Obligatory Celibacy" (2 vols. 1828). His other principal works are: "History of the Return of the Reigning Houses of Brunswick and Saxony to the Bosom of the Catholic Church" (1843); an edition of Balonius's "Church Annals," with a continuation (1856-1857); "Diplomatic Code of the Temporal Dominion of the Holy See" (1863); "Temporal Sovereignty of the Holy See Judged by the General Councils of Lyons and Constance" (1867). He died in Civita Vecchia, Italy, Aug. 10, 1874.

THEIPVAL, a village and district near the River Somme, France, which was the scene of much fighting in the recent World War. It began to figure conspicuously in the news during the battle of the Somme in the summer of 1916, when on July 19 a British attack on

Guillemont was bloodily repulsed by the Germans though an advance was made near Theipval. On August 18, 1916, the British again attacked along a front of 11 miles between Theipval and Guillemont and captured important positions on Theipval ridge, the Germans unsuccessfully counter-attacking on the following day. It continued the scene of fighting during the autumn, and on Sept. 26, 1916, was captured by the British.

THEISM, etymologically equivalent to belief in a god or gods, and as such opposed to ATHEISM (*q. v.*), is now usually understood to mean the doctrine of the one, supreme, personal God, "in whom we live, and move, and have our being"—as distinguished from POLYTHEISM (*q. v.*), which recognizes more gods than one; from PANTHEISM (*q. v.*), which denies the divine personality; from AGNOSTICISM (*q. v.*), which denies that we can know anything of God; and from DEISM (*q. v.*), which, etymologically equivalent to Theism, is generally defined as recognizing the personality of God, but denying His providence and active presence in the life of the world. Deism further explicitly rejects revelation and trinitarian conceptions of the godhead, while Theism may or may not accept these doctrines.

Theism as the doctrine of the nature and attributes of God covers a large part of the field of theology and speculative philosophy. But in practice it is usually restricted to the maintenance of the thesis that God may be known; the history of the origin and development of the idea of God; and the statement, criticism, and defense of the arguments for the existence of God. The main part of its work is apologetic, in opposition to the hostile systems and theories, rather than a scheme of systematic THEOLOGY (*q. v.*).

No competent apologist now stakes the existence of God on any one argument, or exhibits the proof as a series of syllogisms. It is rather maintained that the study of human history, of human nature, especially on its moral and spiritual side, and of the world as far as science reveals it to us make for the existence of a God, demand such a postulate as the key to the universe, and render the belief in a personal God greatly more probable than any other thesis. But it is necessary to name what are often referred to us the four great arguments for the existence of God. (1) The ontological argument first formulated by St. Anselm proceeds from the notion of a most perfect being to infer his existence; without actual existence the idea would fall short of perfection.

The argument was restated in a different shape by DESCARTES (*q. v.*) and by Samuel Clarke, and, though very contemptuously treated by Kant, is still an element of the argument that without a God the world is a chaos.

(2) The cosmological argument, employed by Aristotle, Aquinas, and a host of Christian authors, is an application of what is called the principle of Casuality. We cannot conceive an infinite regression of finite causes; therefore beyond the last or first of the finite causes is the Infinite. From motion the argument is to a mover.

(3) The theological argument, or argument from design, proceeds from the order and arrangement of the universe, the reign of law and beauty and adaptation, to the intelligent and supreme fountain of order. This is the most familiar of the arguments, especially on the lines laid down by Paley.

(4) The moral argument was that relied on by Kant when he destructively criticized the other three, and forms a part of the most theistic arguments. God is a postulate of our moral nature; and the moral law in us implies a lawgiver without us.

THEISS, a river of Hungary, formed in the E. of the kingdom by the junction of the Black and the White Theiss, both descending from the Carpathians and flowing into the Danube about 20 miles above Belgrade; length, about 800 miles. It is the second river in Hungary, being inferior only to the Danube, with which, for about 100 miles, the lower part of its course is almost parallel. Its principal tributary is the Maros from the E.

THEMIS, in Greek mythology, one of the Titanides, the daughter of Uranus and Ge, was after Metis married to Zeus, and bore him the Horæ—Eunomia ("Equity"), Dike ("Justice"), and Eirene ("Peace"); also the Moirai or Fates. She was regarded as the personification of order and justice, or of whatever is established by use and wont; and as such was charged by Zeus to convoke the gods and preside over them when assembled, being likewise represented as reigning in the assemblies of men. In art Themis holds a cornucopia and a pair of scales.

THEMISTOCLES, an Athenian general and statesman; born about 520 B. C. His father, Neocles, belonged to an undistinguished family of the middle class; his mother was a Carian. Ambitious, he used his archonship of 493 for the promotion of his political plans. He saw what was best for Athens when he convinced his countrymen that a powerful fleet was absolutely necessary for their welfare. During the war with Persia which followed, Themistocles, commander of the Athenian squadron, which numbered 200 of the 324 vessels engaged, to avoid dissension was content to serve under the Spartan Eurybiadas, a man of narrow mind and hopeless obstinacy. On

THEMISTOCLES

the eve of Salamis it required all the influence of Themistocles' vehement personality and threats to induce his timid superior and colleagues to await the attack of the enemy. In his eagerness to precipitate a collision, he sent by night a messenger to urge the Persian generals to make an immediate attack, as the Greeks had resolved on retreat.

Intimation of the Persian advance was brought at nightfall by his rival Aristides, who had been ostracized in 483 B. C. The Peloponnesians refused to continue the pursuit of the Persians beyond Andros. From that place Themistocles sent a second message to Xerxes urging him to hasten back before the Greeks carried out their project of breaking down the bridges. The victor of Salamis was now the foremost name in the minds and mouths of men. The rebuilding of the walls of Athens by his advice on a scale far larger than anything in existence aroused great uneasiness among the allies of Sparta, but, by a series of adroit stratagems, Themistocles succeeded in cajoling the ephors till the walls had reached a height sufficient for defense. But his popularity was now waning, and the Spartan faction in Athens was plot-

ting his ruin. Plutarch tells us that he provoked the anger and resentment of the citizens by his insufferable arrogance. In 471 B. C. ostracism was demanded, and he was banished from Athens. Argos was his first retreat, but so long as he remained there Sparta could have no security or peace. His condemnation on the false charge of implication in the treason of Pausanias drove him from Argos. He fled to Corcyra, and after a series of hairbreadth escapes was compelled to seek shelter in Asia. Artaxerxes received his suppliant with the greatest favor, and listened with attention to his schemes for the subjugation of Greece. He resided at Magnesia till about 453 B. C.

It is said that the young king was so affected with joy that he was heard at night to cry thrice in his dreams, "Themistocles, the Athenian, is mine." After the Persian fashion, the town of Lampsacus was appointed to supply him with wine, Magnesia with bread, and Myus with other provisions. At Magnesia he lived securely till about 453 B. C.

"In a word," says Thucydides, "Themistocles, by natural force of mind, and with the least preparation, was of all men the best able to extemporize the right thing to be done." Of his moral character the great historian says nothing. But if his patriotism seems at times to have been but a larger kind of selfishness, it must be remembered that Themistocles was possessed of the conviction that no one could realize the dream of a great Athenian empire but himself. The sentence passed on him was a bitter return for the unparalleled services he had rendered his country, and, due as it was to Spartan influence and jealousy, proved all the harder for a man of spirit to bear.

THENARD, LOUIS JACQUES, a French chemist; born in La Louptière (Aube), May 4, 1777; studied chemistry in Paris under Vauquelin; was appointed (1810) professor at the Collège de France, and later at the Polytechnic School and in the philosophical faculty of the university; in 1825 was created baron, and in 1852 peer of France. In 1837 he resigned his professorship at the Polytechnic School, and in 1840 that at the university. In 1842, however, he became grand officer of the Legion of Honor, and in 1850 member of the Council of Public Instruction. His chief work is "Treatise on Elementary Chemistry" (5 vols., Paris, 1813-17; 6th ed., 1833-36). Along with Gay-Lussac he published in 1816 "Physico-Chemical Researches," and for several years was coeditor of the "Annals of Chemistry" and "Annals of Physics and Chemistry." He died in Paris, June 21, 1857.

THEOBALD, LEWIS, an English writer; born in Sittingbourne, England, about 1690; was brought up to the profession of the law, but early turned his attention to literature. Pope was meanly jealous of him, and ridiculed him in his "Dunciad." Theobald, however, had his revenge, his edition of Shakespeare (1733) completely supplanting Pope's. He did great service to literature by this painstaking work, many of his emendations having been adopted by subsequent editors. He died in September, 1744.

THEOCRACY, that government of which the chief is, or is believed to be, God himself, the priests being the promulgators and expounders of the divine commands. The most notable theocratic government of all times is that established by Moses among the Israelites.

THEOCRITUS, a Greek poet; a native of Syracuse and son of Praxagoras and Philina. Suidas, however, says that some made him the son of Simichus or Simachidas, and that he was a native of Cos and only a metoikos at Syracuse. This statement vanishes on investigation. Theocritus seems to have been intimately associated with the poet Aratus, author of the "Phænomena." The court of the Ptolemies was the mart of intellect then; and it is known that Theocritus at least once in his life visited that great center of poetry and philosophy. More than one of his idylls may have been written there. His 10th "Idyll" was unquestionably written at Syracuse, after the accession of Hiero (270 B. C.). The inference from all that can be gleaned from the poet himself, as to his period, is that he flourished 284-262 B. C. It is at least certain that Theocritus was in Syracuse during the reign of Hiero II., and it is extremely probable that his 16th "Idyll" was written after that monarch's alliance with the Romans, 263 B. C.

How he spent his later years is wholly unknown. The genuineness of some of the idylls is disputed. This could hardly be otherwise. But the chief glory of Theocritus lies in his being the founder of a fresh and fertile school of poetry. Bion and Moschus, a little later, achieved distinction in the same walk. Vergil drawing from the same sweet well enriched Roman literature with poems of marvelous beauty, however inferior to those of his prototype. His idylls might have been written yesterday. In character they are mimetic and dramatic. In-

nocence, simplicity, fidelity—the characteristics of the early Sicilian race—constitute his objective theme. The "Adoniazusæ," a masterpiece of depiction of female character, is characterized throughout by genuine dramatic force and spirit.

THEOCRITUS

It may be mentioned that the pieces, the genuineness of which is disputed, are the 12th, 17th, 18th, 19th, 20th, 26th, 27th, 29th, 30th. For full information on the integrity of the poems, the reader is referred to the works of Eichstädt (1794); E. Rheinhold (1819), and A. Wissova (1828), with the prefaces of Wharton, Meineke, and Wüstemann in their editions of Theocritus. The editio princeps of the idylls without place or date is supposed to have been printed at Venice in 1481. The next is the Aldine (1495). More recent editions are those of Wharton (1770); Brunck (1772); Gaisford (1816, 1820-1823); Meineke (1825); Wüstermann (1830); Wordsworth (1844), and Paley (1863). One of the best versions in verse is C. S. Calverly's (1869). Andrew Lang's prose version (1889) may be commended.

THEODICY, a philosophy, a vindication of the Deity in respect of the organization of the world and the freedom of the human will. The term is specially applied to a defense of theism against atheism, which Leibnitz undertook by publishing, in 1710, his "Essay on Theodicy," respecting the goodness of God, the liberty of man, and the origin of the Bible.

THEODOLITE, a most important instrument for measuring horizontal and vertical angles, but particularly adapted for accurately measuring the former. Its principle is identical with that of the altitude and azimuth instrument; the construction and purpose of the two, however, differ, the latter being employed for astronomical purposes, while the theodolite is used for land surveying; but the better instruments of this class may be employed for observing the altitude of celestial bodies. The vertical circle is not generally, however, of sufficient size, nor so graduated as to be available for very accurate astronomical observations.

When a point is to be viewed with the telescope, the telescope is moved so that the image of the point coincides with the intersection of the cross wires. The vertical limb is divided into degrees, and is capable of being read by means of the vernier and the microscope to thirds of a minute. A pair of plates, constituting

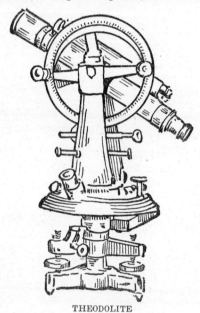

THEODOLITE

at their edge the horizontal limb of the instrument are free, when unclamped, to move independently of each other. The plate carries a magnetic compass and two spirit levels at right angles to each other, by means of which the circle may be brought accurately into the horizontal plane by raising or depressing it by means of the screws. The plate is furnished with two verniers, diametrically opposite to each other, the degrees marked on which are read off by the microscope. By the motion of the telescope, on the horizontal axis of the vertical limb, altitudes and vertical angles can be measured, while, by its motion on the vertical axis, the angular dis-

tances between two objects can be ascertained by the readings on the horizontal circle.

Before using a theodolite, it should be properly adjusted; that is, the different parts should be brought to their proper relative positions. The theodolite is in proper adjustment only under the following conditions: (1) When the intersection of the cross wires is in the axis of the telescope. (2) When the axis of the attached level is parallel to the axis of the telescope. (3) When the axes of the levels on the horizontal limb are perpendicular to the axis of the horizontal limb. (4) When the axis of the vertical limb is perpendicular to the axis of the horizontal limb.

THEODORA, the famous consort of the Byzantine emperor, Justinian I.; was, according to the dubious evidence of Procopius, the daughter of Acacius, a bearward at Constantinople; and had already been by turns actress, dancer and harlot, when she won the heart of the austere and ambitious Justinian, to become in succession, his mistress, his wife, and the sharer of his throne (527). There was a law which forbade a member of the senate to marry an actress, but Justinian cleared the way by repealing it. She displayed force and dignity on the Imperial throne; she became Justinian's trustiest counsellor, bore a chief share in the work of government, and saved the throne by her high courage at the crisis of the Nika riots (532). She lavished her bounty on the poor, and especially on the unfortunate of her own sex, and died at 40 (548), her slender and graceful frame worn out by the anxieties of State. Her character descended to history unspotted till the appearance (1623) of the "Secret History" of Procopius, the work of a man who had enjoyed the full favor and confidence of the court, and had in his other writings openly extolled the triumphs and the wisdom of Justinian and Theodora, whose reputation he was the while laboring in secret to destroy. His stories satisfied his first editor, Nicholas Alemannus, and later Gibbon and Dahn, but other writers have very properly questioned the testimony of Procopius regarding Theodora's profligacy after she became a queen.

THEODORE OF MOPSUESTIA, an exegete of the early Church; born in Antioch about the middle of the 4th century. He was the friend of Chrysostom and the pupil of Libanius, but it was Diodorus of Tarsus from whom he imbibed his zeal for Biblical studies. About the year 383 he became a presbyter in Antioch, and about 392 he was chosen Bishop of Mopsuestia in Cilicia. Theodore wrote commentaries on almost all the books of Scripture, of which only remain, in the Greek, that on the Minor Prophets; in Latin translations, those on the lesser epistles of Paul, besides many fragments, especially on the epistle to the Romans. When the Nestorian controversy broke out his polemical writings were attacked, and after a century of fanatical agitation were formally condemned by Justinian in the "Tria Capitula" (544). The fifth œcumenical council —that of Constantinople in 553—confirmed the emperor's condemnation, and Theodore's name vanished from the list of orthodox writers. He died at peace with all men in 428 or 429.

THEODORE, "King of Corsica," otherwise Baron Theodore de Neuhoff, son of a Westphalian noble in the French service; born in Metz in 1686; was successively in the French, Swedish, and Spanish service; was ruined in Law's speculations (see LAW, JOHN); and after leading an adventurer's life settled at Florence in 1732. As a representative of the Emperor Charles VI., he was induced by Corsican acquaintances to head a Corsican rising against the Genoese; and with the support of Turkey and a ship and munitions from the Bey of Tunis landed in Corsica in March, 1736, and was crowned Theodore I. He was in a few months driven to flight, as he was again on a second attempt in 1738, and on a third in 1743. After many wanderings he settled in London in 1749. Imprisoned by his creditors, he was liberated by a subscription supported by Walpole, but died soon after, Dec. 11, 1756. In Spain he had married an Irish lady, daughter of the Earl of Kilmallock. His only son by her, known as Colonel Frederick, wrote a book on "Corsica," and at the age of about 72 shot himself in the porch of Westminster Abbey, Feb. 1, 1797.

THEODORE II., King of Abyssinia; born in the province of Kwara in 1818; for many years a rebel; finally fought his way to the throne in 1855. He was a man of great parts, an inveterate foe of Islamism, a born ruler, and an intelligent reformer. But intolerance of any power save his own finally made a tyrant of him; and in consequence of the imprisonment of Consul Cameron and other British subjects he brought on himself a war with England, which ended, April 13, 1868, in the storming of Magdala and the death (supposedly by suicide) of Theodore. See ABYSSINIA.

THEODORET, a church historian; born in Antioch about 390; early entered a monastery; and in 423 became Bishop of Cyrus, a city of Syria. Here he labored with the utmost zeal, and he himself claims to have converted over 1,000 Marcionites. As a foremost representative of the school of Antioch he became deeply involved in the great Nestorian and Eutychian controversies, and was finally deposed by the celebrated Robber Council of Ephesus in 449. This was reversed by the general council of Chalcedon in 451, but Theodoret did not long survive his restoration, dying about the year 457.

His works were edited by Shulze and Nösselt (1769-1774), and consist of commentaries on Canticles, the Prophets, Psalms, and the whole of St. Paul's Epistles; a "History of the Church," from A. D. 325 to 429, in five books (ed. by T. Gaisford, 1854); "Religious History," being the lives of the so-called Fathers of the Desert; the "Eranistes," a dialogue against Eutychianism; "A Concise History of Heresies," together with orations and letters.

THEODORIC, King of the Ostrogoths; born in Pannonia in 455; son of Theodemir, King of the Ostrogoths of Pannonia. From his eighth to his 18th year he lived as a hostage with the Emperor Leo at Constantinople. Two years after his return he succeeded to the throne. In 493, after several bloody engagements, Theodoric induced Odoacer, who had assumed the title of King of Italy, to grant him equal authority. The murder of Odoacer at a banquet soon after opened the way for Theodoric to have himself proclaimed sole ruler. Theodoric ruled with great vigor and ability. Though, like his ancestors, he was an Arian, he never violated the peace or privileges of the Catholic Church. He died in Ravenna, Italy, Aug. 30, 526.

THEODORIC I., King of the Visigoths, succeeded Wallia in 420. During the interval, 426-436, he made war on the Romans three times and attempted to take the city of Narbonne. He obtained territory both in Spain and Gaul, and subsequently became the ally of the Romans against Attila, whom he defeated at Châlons-sur-Marne in 451, but lost his life in the battle. His son Thorismund succeeded him.

THEODORIC II., son of Theodoric I., acquired the throne by the murder of his brother Thorismund in 452, but was himself killed by Euric, another of the sons of Theodoric I. During his short reign he increased the empire of the

Visigoths, and advanced almost as far as the Loire. He was killed in 466.

THEODORUS. See THEODORE OF MOPSUESTIA.

THEODORUS STUDITA (THEODORE OF STUDIUM: SAINT), a Greek theological writer, abbot of Studium, was born A. D. 759 at Constantinople. He became head of the monastery of Saccudium in Bithynia, was banished to Thessalonica soon afterward for having excommunicated Constantine VI, but was recalled after the emperor's death in 797. At the monastery of Studium in Constantinople, he then became the leader of a campaign in favor of asceticism and monastic reforms. He opposed the iconoclasts (see ICONOCLAST), was involved in many ecclesiastical controversies and was banished and recalled several times during the years 809-824. He finally left Constantinople and lived at various monasteries in Bithynia, on Chalcitis and on 'the peninsula of Tryphon near Acrita, where he died, Nov. 11, 826. His Letters, Catecheses, and various discourses are among his most important works. He was famous for his industry in copying manuscripts.

THEODORUS, I., Pope, succeeded John IV. in 642. He excommunicated Paulus, patriarch of Constantinople, and condemned the heresy of the Monothelites. His successor was Martin I. He died in 649.

THEODORUS II., succeeded John IX. in 897, but died in less than a month after his election.

THEODOSIUS THE ELDER, a Spaniard by birth and a skillful Roman general; was sent to Britain in A. D. 367 to repel the inroads of the Caledonians and restore order to the diocese. He made London his headquarters, and was so successful in his undertakings that he formed the country between Hadrian's Wall and the Forth and Clyde into a new province of the empire, called Valentia in honor of the reigning emperors. After a victorious campaign on the Upper Danube against the Alemanni he quelled a formidable revolt in Africa under Firmus the Moor, and was executed at Carthage in 376 on some unknown and probably groundless charge.

THEODOSIUS I., THE GREAT, son of Theodosius the Elder; one of the most notable and most capable of the later Roman emperors; born in Cauca, Spain, about 346; served under his father in Britain, Germany, and Africa, and won fame as a general by his exploits in Mœsia. On his father's death he retired

to his native farm, whence he was summoned by Gratian to become his colleague in the purple and emperor in the East (379). It was a critical time. The Goths, too numerous and formidable to be attacked en masse, flushed, too, with their recent Cannæ like victory at Adrianople and the total defeat of his predecessor Valens, were roaming the country at will. His military reputation was equal to the strain. He made Thessalonica his headquarters, and within four years broke up the vast Gothic army, attached many of its members to the empire as faithful soldiers and allies, and restored tranquility to the troubled country S. of the Danube.

A serious illness in 380 led to his baptism as a Trinitarian, and, as a consequence, to the restoration of the religious unity of the empire and the promulgation of various edicts against Arianism and other heresies. He appointed Gregory Nazianzen Archbishop of Constantinople, and summoned the second general council, which met there (381) to supplement the labors of Nicæa. The murder of Gratian at Lyons, the advance toward Italy of the upstart Maximus proclaimed emperor in Britain, and the arrival of Valentinian II. (with his mother Justina and his sister Galla) begging for help led to Theodosius' marriage with Galla, to his victory at Aquileia (388), and to the restoration of his youthful colleague. Hereafter for some years Theodosius lived at Milan enjoying the friendship and respect of its bishop St. Ambrose.

Theodosius was able, just, even generous, virtuous, and religious, but inclined to indolence and of a passionate temper. He had canceled, on the entreaties of its bishop and the penitence and humiliation of its leading citizens, the severe measures meted out to Antioch after a riot (387) in which the imperial statues had been contemptuously overthrown; but in 390, when the governor of Thessalonica was lynched by a circus mob for his punishment of a brutal but favorite charioteer, Theodosius, in spite of expostulations, ordered the people of the city to be invited into the circus and there massacred. At least 7,000 were thus put to death. Thereupon Ambrose wrote to Theodosius upbraiding him for the deed, and later withstood his attempt to enter the church at Milan. The bishop only readmitted the emperor to the sacrament after eight months' retirement and public penance performed in the face of the whole congregation. In 392 Valentinian II. was murdered and in 394 Theodosius, then at Constantinople, again marched W., this time against the Frankish general Arbogast and his puppet, Emperor

Eugenius. After a stubborn fight at the Fridigus river, lasting two days, Theodosius gained a complete victory, and for four months ruled as sole Roman emperor. He expired in the arms of Ambrose on Jan. 17, 395. Almost immediately thereafter followed the barbarian invasions of Greece and Italy, which led directly to the subsequent Teutonic settlements in the S. and indirectly to the formation of the kingdoms of modern Europe.

THEODOSIUS II., son of Arcadius, and grandson of Theodosius I.; succeeded his father in 408, in the Empire of the East. The government was carried on, during the greater part of his reign, by his sister Pulcheria. In his reign was compiled and published the celebrated code of laws, styled after him the "Theodosian Code." He died in 450.

THEODOSIUS III., Emperor of Constantinople; nominated in succession to Anastasius II., 716. After a reign of two years he abdicated in favor of Leo III.

THEOGNIS OF MEGARA (thē-og'nis), a Greek elegiac poet; flourished in the latter half of the 6th century B. C. There are 1,389 verses preserved under his name, of importance in enabling us to understand the state of parties and the problems of society in the Greece of that time.

THEOLOGY, a term applied by the classic authors to treatises on the nature and worship of the gods, such as the "Works and Days" of Hesiod, and the "On the Nature of the Gods" of Cicero. Augustine quotes Eusebius and Varro as dividing theology into three kinds: the fabulous, that of the poets; the natural, that of the philosophers; and the political, that of the priests and the common people. The first and second kinds could be changed according to the will of the investigators; but the last could not be altered without national consent.

In Christianity, theology is the science which treats of divine things, especially of the relations of man to God. Theology is primarily divided into natural and supernatural, or revealed; the former deduced by reason from a survey of the universe, the latter founded on revelation. Natural religion is recognized in Scripture (Ps. xix: 1-6, Rom. i: 19, 20), and is held to establish the being, power, wisdom, and goodness of God, the obligation of His moral law and the folly and danger of transgressing it, and the immortality of the soul. Revealed religion is considered to superadd to these doctrines those of the Trinity, the creation and fall of man, the penalty of sin, the mission, work, and atoning death of Christ, His resurrection, ascension, and second advent, with many other doctrines. Before a theology embracing the teaching of the Bible on these subjects can be constructed, the following sciences are required: Biblical criticism, to ascertain the exact text of certain works claiming to be inspired, and, if possible, their time, place, and human authorship; apologetics, to establish and defend their claim to inspiration; hermeneutics, to investigate the principles of interpretation; exegesis, to carry those principles into practice by actual interpretation. Dogmatic theology follows; its province being to bring together and classify the doctrines scattered through the Bible; polemic theology defends these against adversaries; practical theology reduces them to practice, and pastoral theology investigates the most approved methods of presenting them to the people.

The New Testament theology constitutes the chief basis of the theologies of all churches. It was followed by that of the Apostolic Fathers, and then by that of the Fathers in general. It varied according to the idosyncrasy of the several writers. The application of the commandants of the moral law to individual conduct gave rise to moral theology. The Protestant theology, which commenced with Luther and Zwingli, was professedly founded on Scripture, interpreted by private judgment, the right of exercising which was boldly asserted; that of the Roman Catholics was founded on the consensus of the Fathers, the decisions of councils, and of the Holy See, and not on the results of individual investigation. Fearless and resolute exercise of private judgment in Germany, Holland, the Protestant cantons of Switzerland, etc., has resulted in rationalism, which has also arisen in most continental countries in union with Rome, by a reaction against authority. In the Methodist, Baptist, Reformed Episcopal, Presbyterian and English dissenting churches, evangelical theology is generally accepted, though here and there more or less latent rationalism prevails.

THEOPHANY, specially the appearance of God to the patriarchs in the form of an angel or in human form; also the incarnation and second coming of Christ.

THEOPHILANTHROPY, in comparative religions, the name given to a system of natural religion which arose in the time of the first French Republic, and which had for its cardinal doctrines the adoration of God and love of man. In 1796 five heads of families—Chémin, Mareau, Janes, Haüy, and Mandar—associated themselves, and in December held their first meeting at a house in the Rue St. Denis for the purpose of divine worship and moral instruction, according to the dictates of natural religion. Their services consisted of moral discourses, singing, and prayer. One of their adherents was Revellière-Lépaux, a member of the Directory, who allowed them the use of the 10 parish churches of Paris, which they fitted up and adorned with religious and moral inscriptions, an ancient altar, a basket of flowers as an offering to the Supreme Being, a pulpit, and allegorical paintings and banners. In 1802 Napoleon I. forbade them to hold their meetings in the churches, and after this time they no longer appear as a body.

THEOPHILUS, a legendary coadjutor-bishop at Adana in Cilicia, who, when deposed from his office through slanders, gave his soul in bond to the devil, and consequently was reinstated the next morning. But he was soon overtaken with remorse, and through 40 days' fasting and prayers prevailed on the Virgin to make intercession for him. She tore the bond from the devil, and laid it upon the breast of the repentant sinner as he lay asleep in the church. Theophilus then made a public confession of his crime and of the mercy of the Virgin, and died three days after. This forerunner of the Faust legend must have reached the West during the 10th century.

THEOPHRASTA (named after Theophrastus, the philosopher), the typical genus of *Theophrasteæ*. Only known species, *T. jusieui*. It is a small tree with an unbranched stem, and a tuft of long, evergreen leaves at the top, giving it a superficial resemblance to a palm tree. Calyx and corolla campanulate, the former cartilaginous, the latter with a short tube, having a dilated throat with an angularly-lobed, fleshy ring, and a spreading limb; stamens five. Fruit, a spherical berry with the seeds half immersed in the placenta. *T. jussieui* is a native of San Domingo and is cultivated for its fine leaves.

THEOPHRASTUS, a Greek philosopher; often called the "father of botany"; a native of Eresus, in Lesbos; flourished in the 4th century B. C. He became a pupil of Plato at Athens, and made, at the academy, the acquaintance of Aristotle; but he quitted the academy after Plato's death, and was absent from Athens for some years. On his return he gladly studied philosophy under his friend Aristotle, who had so high a regard for him as to bequeath to him his library, and to name him his successor. Theophrastus had extraordinary success as head of the Lyceum, and was attended, it is said, by 2,000 disciples. Among them were Demetrius, Phalereus, and Menander. A charge of impiety was brought against him, but he successfully defended himself, and generously interposed to save his adversary from the popular vengeance. He was, however, compelled to leave Athens in 305 B. C., under the law which banished all philosophers. The law was soon repealed and he returned to his post and peacefully taught and commented on the system of his master, Aristotle, till his death. His writings were very numerous, but have perished with the following exceptions: His work entitled "Characters," a set of his lively sketches of vicious and ridiculous characters; treatises on the "History of Plants," on the "Causes of Plants," and on "Stones"; a work on the "Senses," and several fragments. The "Characters" served as the model for La Bruyère's work with the same title; it has been several times translated into English, French, and German.

THEOPHYLACTUS, surnamed SIMOCATTA (thē-ō-fil-ak′tus), a Byzantine historian; born in Locri about 570. Three of his works are extant: "History of the Emperor Maurice"; "Problems of Physics"; "Letters, Moral, Rural, and Amorous,"—of these there are 85, in which are imitated the letters of Aristænetus. He died in Locri about 629.

THEOPOMPUS OF CHIOS, a Greek historian; born about 378 B. C. His principal historical works were "The Hellenics," in 12 books, and "The Philippics," in 58 books; the former being a continuation of Thucydides, and the latter a general history of his own times, with the reign of Philip of Macedon as central point.

THEORBO, in music, an old stringed instrument resembling the lute in form or tone. It had two necks, to the longest of which the bass strings were attached. It was employed for accompanying voices, and was in great favor during the 17th century. It differed from the lute in the possession of its two necks, whence it is sometimes called cithara bijuga. The strings were usually single in the theorbo, and when double, or tuned in octaves or in unison with the bass or treble notes, the instrument was called the arch lute or chittarone.

THEOREM, in geometry, a proposition to be proved; a statement of a principle to be demonstrated; that is, the truth of which is required to be made evident by a course of reasoning called a demonstration. In the synthetical method of investigation, which is that for the most part employed in geometry, it is usual to state the principle to be proved before commencing the demonstration, which proceeds by a regular course of argumentation to the final conclusion, confirmatory of the principle enunciated. The principle being proved, it may properly be employed as a premise in the deduction of new truths. The principle, as enunciated before the demonstration, is the theorem; its statement after demonstration constitutes a rule or formula, according as the statement is made in ordinary or in algebraic language. A theorem differs from a problem in this, that the latter is a statement of something to be done, the former of something to be proved.

THEORIA MOTUS, or THEORIA MOTUS CORPORUM CŒLESTIUM, the names by which is usually quoted the work of Gauss, in which he first showed the method of computing an orbit from three determinations of a planet's or comet's position, and thus rescued astronomers from the danger of losing the newly discovered asteroid Ceres after it had disappeared in the region of the sun. The full title of the work is "Theoria Motus Corporum Cœlestium in Sectionibus Conicis Solum Ambientium." It was first published at Hamburg in 1809. An English translation by Rear-Admiral C. H. Davis, U. S. N., then superintendent of the Nautical Almanac Office, was published in Boston in 1857, at the joint expense of the "Nautical Almanac" Office and the Smithsonian Institution. A French translation by Dubois was published at Paris in 1864, and a German one by Hasse at Hanover in 1865. The work also contains an exposition of the theory of the method of Least Squares, and is one of the most important astronomical works extant.

THEOSOPHY, a name which since the time of Ammonius Saccas, in the 3d century after Christ, has been used in the West to cover various schools of religious philosophy, which all unite in the fundamental conception that man, in his innermost nature, is a spiritual being, one in his essence with the Universal Spirit manifested in and through the universe. In this general sense it includes mystics differing from one another in details. In the East the system now called Theosophy has been known for ages under the titles of Atma Vidya ("spirit science"), Brahma Vidyâ ("science of Brahma"), Gupta Vidyâ ("secret science"), and other similar names. All

alike, in East and West, draw inspiration and their methods from the "Wisdom Religion," the ancient esoteric philosophy. This claims among its initiates the men who have given to the world fragments of the teaching as basis for world-religions, men like Buddha, Confucius, Zarathustra, Pythagoras, Plato, Jesus, and more ancient sages such as Manu, Nârada, and other great Rishis. In the 16th century Paracelsus and Giordano Bruno are among its grandest exponents, and in our own day its messenger was a woman of Russian birth, Helena Petrovna Blavatsky (1831-1891).

The Esoteric Philosophy, or Wisdom Religion, is a body of teaching, philosophical, scientific, and religious, which is believed to be preserved from generation to generation by a brotherhood of initiates scattered over the world, but preserving close and intimate relations with one another. To a group of these stationed in Tibet the founding of the Theosophical Society in 1878 is ascribed, and they are constantly referred to in theosophical literature as Mahâtmas, Arhats, Masters, Brothers, or Adepts. They are men who have evolved the spiritual nature till the physical body and brain consciousness have become ductile instruments for the spiritual intelligence. By virtue of this evolution they are said to have gained control over natural forces which enables them to bring about results that appear to be miraculous.

This philosophy teaches as basic principles an eternal existence beyond human cognition, existence *per se*, absoluteness or "beness." A periodical aspect of this is life, consciousness, manifesting itself in and as the universe, primarily emanating as the dual root substance, matter on its negative, and spirit, or energy, on its positive side. This duality is the note of the manifested universe, manifestation being held to be impossible without the "pairs of opposites," positive-negative, active-passive, light-darkness, and the like, ultimating at one part of the chain of evolution in sex difference, male-female. Spirit and matter are therefore not separable, but are merely the opposed poles of the one root substance, and are present in every particle, as the poles in each fragment of a broken magnet. Evolution consists in the gradual densifying of the root substance through seven stages or planes of differentiated existence, the matter aspect becoming more and more prominent as the evolution proceeds, and the spirit aspect becoming more and more hidden; thus matter reaches its fullest differentiation, evolving the whole of its capacities as a vehicle. From this point of completest materiality begins the running curve, during which matter becomes translucent to spirit, and spirit becomes self-conscious on all planes. It manifests itself as brain intellect on the most material plane, and recovers all its super-intellectual powers on the ascending arc, but always with the addition of self-consciousness and individuality, till, at the completion of the cycle, matter has become a perfect objective presentment of spirit, a perfect vehicle of spiritual activity.

The seven stages of cosmical evolution, aspects of the universâl Divine consciousness, correspond with seven stages of human evolution, apects of the human consciousness, by each of which man can cognize directly the correspondingly cosmic state.

These in man are distinguished as: (1) Atmâ, pure spirit, one with the universal spirit. (2) Buddhi, the vehicle of Atmâ and inseparable from it, sometimes spoken of as the spiritual soul. (3) Manas, the mind, the ego or individualizing principle, called the rational or human soul. These three are the immortal part of man, Manas striving for union with Buddhi, such union making the spiritual ego, the spiritual man perfected. The remaining principles form the quaternay, the perishable part of man. These are: (4) Kâma, the emotions, passions, and appetites. (5) Prâna, the vitality. (6) Linga Sharîra, the astral double. (7) Sthûla Sharîra, the physical body. (These principles are generally numbered in reversed order, starting from the physical, Sthûla Sharîra being taken as 1 and Atmâ as 7.) At death, it is taught, the physical body and the astral double disintegrate together; the vitality returns to the universal life; the passional nature, in its own ethereal envelope, exists for a longer or shorter period, according as it dominated, or was subservient to, the higher nature, but ultimately fades away. The higher triad has, during earth life, been joined to the lower nature of Manas, the mind; this Manas is divided into higher and lower, the higher striving upward, the lower entangled with Kâma, and held by the desire for material life which is at the root of all manifestation. At death the higher triad gradually separates itself from the lower nature, the lower mind which is but a ray of the higher returning to its source, carrying with it the experiences gained during incarnation; the triad, with this added experience, the harvest of life, enters on a period of repose, the state of Devachan, a state of consciousness apart from the physical body, in which the intelligence is free from physical limitations. Devachan is a state of consciousness in which the experiences of the lately concluded earth life are assimilated, its best aspirations have their fruition, and the communion of the consciousness with other consciousnesses is freed from physical limitations, and is more complete and satisfying. This stage endures for a period proportionate to the stage of evolution reached on earth, and is concluded by the re-entry of the consciousness into the embodied condition.

The method of evolution, according to theosophy, is reincarnation. The reincarnating ego, the agent in progress, is the Manas. In the past, when physical evolution, guided by the indwelling spirit, had produced man's physical form, Manas first became incarnate therein, and has since reincarnated after each devachnic interlude. Throughout each incarnation it labors to evolve in the body it inhabits the capacity to respond to its impulses, but it is through the molding of successive bodies that it accomplishes its task of human elevation. The thoughts produced by its activity are real things on the mental plane, made of subtle matter, "thought stuff," a form of ether. The thoughts of each life ultimate in a thought body, that expresses the result of that incarnation, and this thought body serves as a mold into which is built the physical body which forms the next dwelling to the ego.

The "innate character" which the child brings into the world is the result of its own past and is physically expressed in its brain and nervous organization. The reincarnating ego is drawn by affinity to the nation and family fitted to supply the most suitable physical, material, and physical environment. The physical particles thence supplied are stamped with the racial and family characteristics, bodily and mental, but this arrangement is dominated by the thought body resulting as above stated.

Mental and moral capacities gained by struggle in one of many incarnations become innate qualities, exercised "naturally," without effort, in a later incarnation, and thus progress is secured. This law, by which all causes work out their due effects, is called Karma (the Sanskrit word for action), and according to this all thoughts, good and bad, leave their traces on the thought body and reappear as tendencies in future lives. No escape from this sequence of cause and effect is possible; all our past must work itself out, but as the same agent that made the past is making the present it sets up fresh cause in meeting the effects of the past. Thus, a trouble generated by past action is inevitable; it is in our Karma. But met badly, it sets up fresh cause for bad Karma in the future; or met well it generates good Karma. We made our present destiny in our past, and we are making our future destiny in our present. Reincarnation crushes out all differences of race, sex, class; Karma so interweaves human lives that each can only find happiness and perfection as all find it. It is claimed by theosophy that these facts in nature yield a scientific basis for ethics, and make the practical recognition of human brotherhood a necessary condition of accelerated evolution.

The chief agent in founding the Theosophical Society was Madame H. P. Blavatsky, who, with Col. H. E. Olcott, W. O. Judge, and others, established it in New York in 1875. In 1879 the headquarters were transferred to Madras. In 1887 Madame Blavatsky visited London, from which epoch dates the great literary activity that has recently characterized it. There are now over 300 branches in Europe, India, American, and the colonies, and a large literature. The society has three declared objects, viz.: (1) To form a nucleus of the universal brotherhood of humanity, without distinction of race, creed, sex, caste, or color. (2) To encourage the study of comparative religion, philosophy, and science. (3) To investigate unexplained laws of nature and the powers latent in man. The society is unsectarian. No articles of faith need be subscribed to by an adherent, the only condition of membership being an assent to the first object.

No dogmas are forced on members, as is the case with religions, and the teachings which are promulgated are merely propositions which can be verified by the student in the course of his progress in the study of occultism. Any individual member has a right to make any declaration of personal belief he pleases, on the understanding that the Society is not implicated.

THERA, an island in the Grecian archipelago, the most S. of the Cyclades; 41 square miles. It possess extraordinary geological interest on account of the volcanic transformations of which it has been the theater. The whole island is simply one side of a vast crater, the other side of which has sunk into the sea. From the site of the ancient center of volcanic energy small islands have at different times been raised, the last in 1866. Many volcanic convulsions have been witnessed and recorded in Thera during historic time; e. g., 198 B. C., A. D.
I—25

1573, A. D. 1710, besides the occurrences of 1866, when two small islands emerged. The soil is exceedingly fertile.

THERAPEUTÆ, an ascetic sect, supposed to have lived on Lake Mareotis, near Alexandria. Their discipline resembled that of the Essenes, but was more severe in food and in the preference for the solitary life to the common fellowship. Throughout the week each lived in his lonely dwelling, but on the Sabbath they assembled for worship. The sole authority for their existence, "The Contemplative Life," is not now attributed to Philo but to an early Christian writing about 300 A. D.

THERAPEUTICS, the science which treats of the healing of diseases. It deals with the form, manner, and time in which drugs should be administered, if needful to administer them at all; it instructs how to avoid incompatible combinations, and classifies remedial agents. Therapeutics also investigates the laws of health, and how it can be preserved. Another branch of it is dietetics.

THERAPON, in ichthyology, a genus of *Percidæ*, with about 20 species, some of which are more or less marine, spread over the Indo-Pacific. Body oblong, compressed, with scales of moderate size; teeth villiform; branchiostegals six. They are all of small size, and may be readily recognized by the blackish longitudinal bands with which the body is ornamented.

THERIACA, originally a compound prepared by Andromachus of Crete, physician to the Emperor Nero, which continued in high repute till recent times. In Venice, Holland, France, and other places it had to be prepared with certain solemnities in the presence of the magistrates. It received its name from the belief that it was an antidote to the poison of venomous creatures. The word treacle is a corruption of theriaca, and was first applied to a syrup, medicine, or electuary, and then, from similarity of appearance, to the uncrystallized residue obtained in the preparation of sugar, and known as molasses.

THERIDIIDÆ, in zoölogy, a very extensive family of *Dipneumoneæ*. Small or moderate-sized spiders, with the abdomen generally large, as compared with the cephalothorax, and broadly ovate. Fore legs usually the longest; eyes in two transverse rows. These spiders are found among foliage, and sometimes construct irregular webs. The species are most numerous in temperate climates, and the greater number belong to the Eastern Hemisphere.

THERIODONTIA, in palæontology, an order of *Reptilia*, founded by Owen for the reception of a number of remains from deposits in South Africa of Triassic or Permian age. The dentition is of the carnivorous type, consisting of incisors, canines, and molars.

THERIOMORPHA, in zoölogy, Owen's name for the tailless amphibians (frogs and toads), more generally called *Anoura*, or *Batrachia Salientia*. It is a synonym of Huxley's *Batrachia*, a name used by Owen to designate the class *Amphibia*.

THERMÆ. In the Roman thermæ, the baths were of secondary importance. They were a Roman adaptation of the Greek gymnasium, contained exedræ for the philosophers and rhetoricians to lecture in, porticoes for the idle, and libraries for the learned, and were adorned with marbles, fountains, and shaded walks and plantations.

THERMIDOR, *i. e.*, the "Hot Month," formed, in the calendar of the first French Republic, the 11th month, and lasted from July 19 to Aug. 18. The 9th Termidor of the Republican year 2 (July 27, 1794) is historically memorable as the date of Robespierre's fall, and the termination of the Reign of Terror. The name Thermidorians was given to all those who took part in this fortunate coup d'état, but more particularly to those who were desirous of restoring the monarchy.

THERMO BAROMETER, an instrument for measuring altitudes by means of determining the boiling point of water. They consist essentially of a small metallic vessel for boiling water, fitted with very delicate thermometers, which are only graduated from 80° to 100°; so that each degree occupying a considerable space on the scale, the tenths, and even the hundredths of a dgree, may be estimated, and thus it is possible to determine the height of a place by means of the boiling point to within about 10 feet.

THERMO CHEMISTRY All chemical reactions are accompanied by changes in temperature. Exactly when this fact was first observed, it is impossible to say, but it must have been in the very early years of chemical investigation, for the phenomenon is so marked that

it could not long escape notice. In the majority of cases, there is a rise in temperature, or, in other words, heat is evolved, but in some cases, the temperature falls, or heat is absorbed. Reactions of the former type are known as *exothermic*, those of the latter as *endothermic*. The first law governing these thermal changes was formulated by Lavoisier and Laplace, who stated, as the result of their investigations, that: *The amount of heat which is required to decompose a compound into its constituents is exactly equal to that which was evolved when the compound was formed from these constituents.* A second law of even greater importance was discovered by Hess, who demonstrated that: *The heat evolved in a chemical reaction is the same whether it takes place in one or in several stages.* For instance, carbon may be burned either to carbon monoxide or carbon dioxide, according to conditions. Carbon monoxide may be burned to carbon dioxide, so that in either case the final chemical change is from carbon to carbon dioxide. The above law (known as the "Constancy of the heat sum") is, as a matter of fact, a direct consequence of a wider law—the principle of the conservation of energy—but it was worked out by Hess experimentally. Of recent years important progress has been made in this branch of science as the result of researches carried out by Julius Thomson, of Copenhagen, and Berthelot, the famous French chemist. Thomsen devised new apparatus for making thermo-chemical determinations, and collected a mass of thermo-chemical data whose value can scarcely be over-estimated. Berthelot also made improvements in apparatus, and his discoveries have resulted in a great advance in elucidating the theories underlying thermo-chemical phenomena. Three of the fundamental principles which he laid down are:

(1) The thermal change due to a chemical reaction depends (providing no external work is done) only on the condition of the system at the beginning and end of the reaction, and not on the intermediate conditions.

(2) The heat evolved in a chemical reaction is a measure of the corresponding physical and chemical work.

(3) Every chemical change which occurs without the addition of external energy tends to produce that substance or system of substances the formation of which is accompanied by the evolution of the maximum amount of heat. This generalization is found to be not true in every case, but it applies to so many instances that it is generally held

to indicate some natural law which is not, at present, fully understood.

The *Heat of Formation* of a substance is the amount of heat liberated or absorbed when the substance is produced by a direct combination of the elements of which it is composed. It is customary to determine the heat of formation on gram-molecular weights; so that, quantitatively, the heat of formation of any substance is expressed as the amount of heat liberated or absorbed when a gram-molecular weight of the substance is formed by combination of its elements. In those cases where compounds cannot be formed from direct combination of elements, it is necessary to determine the heat of formation indirectly. This is commonly done by first burning the elements in oxygen, then burning the compound in oxygen, and determining in each case the heat liberated. The products of combustion will, in each case, be the same, so that the difference in the heat liberated in the two cases will give the heat of formation of the compound.

THERMOCROSIS, in physics, heat coloration. A red flame, looked at through a red glass appears quite bright, but through a green glass it appears dim or scarcely visible. So in like manner heat which has traversed a red glass passes through another red glass with little diminution, but is almost completely stopped by a green glass. To these different obscure calorific rays Melloni gave the name of thermocrosis.

THERMODYNAMIC ENGINE, any form of heat engine (as gas or steam engines) by means of which a percentage of the heat lost by one body called the source, on account of its connection with another body called the refrigerator, is converted into kinetic energy or mechanical effect, and made available for the performance of work. The efficiency of a heat engine is the ratio of the heat available for mechanical effect to the total heat taken from the source. A reversible engine is called a perfect engine, because it is the most efficient engine between the temperatures of its source and refrigerator.

THERMODYNAMICS, the branch of theoretical physics which treats of heat as a mechanical agent, and is the basis on which the modern doctrine of energy is built. The second interpretation given by Newton of his third law of motion all but enumerates the principle of the conservation of energy. Ignorant, however, of the true nature of heat, he was unable to trace the mechanical loss caused by friction to its final issue. Not till more than a century after the publication of the "Principia" was any attempt made to fill the gap, and then the valuable experimental results of Rumford (1798) and Davy (1799), though conclusively disproving the accepted caloric theory, were given to an unappreciative world, and failed to excite any real interest till 40 years later, when their discoveries were rediscovered. In 1812 Davy wrote, "The immediate cause of the phenomenon of heat then is motion, and the laws of its communications are precisely the same as the laws of the communication of motion." Here then the dynamical theory of heat was enunciated, but it was carried no further, and not till the experiments of Colding and Joule, executed independently about 1840, were published, can thermodynamics be regarded as established.

About the same time Séguin and Mayer approached the same object, and deduced from experiment values of the mechanical equivalent of heat. They, however, went to work on hypotheses or rather different forms of the same hypothesis which are now known to be false; so that their claims as the founders of the doctrine of energy cannot be maintained against those of Colding and Joule, who went to work in a legitimate way. Mayer, however, deserves great merit for the manner in which he developed and applied the conservation principle. In the more restricted sphere of thermodynamics, Clausius, Rankine, and Thomson have been the great developers; and to the last-mentioned is due the modification of Carnot's forgotten cycle of operations to suit the true theory, and the deduction therefrom of the doctrine of the dissipation of energy.

Thermodynamics is based on two laws. The first law enunciates heat to be a form of energy and subject to the conservation principle—an experimental truth rigorously established by Joule. Clerk Maxwell gives it in the form: When heat is transformed into work or work into heat, the quantity of work is mechanically equivalent to the quantity of heat. A given quantity of work can always be transformed into an equivalent quantity of heat; but in transforming heat into work a certain limitation exists which is expressed in the second law of thermodynamics. This law asserts that it is impossible, by physical processes, to transform any part of the heat of a body into mechanical work except by allowing heat to pass from that body to another at a lower temperature; or in Thomson's words, it is impossible by means of inanimate material agency to derive mechanical effect from any portion of matter by cooling it below the temperature of the coldest of the surrounding objects. This is the law on which Carnot's principle is based—a principle which has led to results of the highest conseuence. The principle is that the efficiency of a reversible engine is the greatest that can be obtained from a given range of temperature. Now a reversible engine in Carnot's sense is an altogether unrealizable heat engine, which can be made to go through a complete cycle of operations, either forward or backward. In other words, not merely is the engine able to do work while it transforms a given quantity of heat from the boiler to the condenser, but, by an expenditure of an equivalent quantity of work upon it, may be made to take back the same quantity of heat from the condenser to the boiler. In subjecting such an engine to a cycle of operations, the engine must be brought back to its original condition before any conclusion can be drawn regarding the relation between the heat which has disappeared and the work which has been done.

Séguin, when he assumed that the work done by an expanding heated body was the equivalent of the heat which it loses, and Mayer, when he went to work on the hypothesis that the amount of heat produced in compressing a gas is equivalent to the work done in compression, violated this principle, so that their conclusions were logically untrustworthy. It is easily demonstrable on the conversation principle that Carnot's reversible engine is the most perfect possible engine, and that consequently all reversible engines working between the same temperatures have the same efficiency. For a small difference of temperature the efficiency is a function only of the temperature, and this efficiency, divided by the difference of temperatures, is called Carnot's function. Thomson, defining temperature as the reciprocal of Carnot's function, has constructed a scale of temperature absolutely independent of the nature of the thermometric substance. Hence, if t is the temperature measured according to this absolute scale of the source of heat, and t that of the refrigerator or condenser, the efficiency may be expressed by the fraction $\dfrac{t-t'}{t}$. Now the efficiency is defined as the ratio of the work done to the heat supplied expressed in dynamical measure. Hence, if W is the work done, H the heat supplied to the engine, and h the heat given out to the condenser,

all expressed in dynamical measure, we have

$$\frac{W}{H} = \frac{t-t'}{t}$$

$$W = H - h$$

whence $\dfrac{h}{H} = \dfrac{t'}{t}$

or, in a reversible engine, the heat rejected is to the heat received as the absolute temperature of the refrigerator is to the absolute temperature of the boiler. From the first of these equations it is evident that the heat supplied cannot be wholly transformed into work unless the refrigerator is at absolute zero of temperature, a practical impossibility. Consequently, in a material system only a part of the intrinsic energy is available for work, and this available portion or entropy is continually diminishing because of the universal tendency of heat to diffuse itself, and reduce the system to a uniform temperature, when of course no work can be produced. This is Thomson's principle of the dissipation of energy.

THERMOELECTRICITY, electricity produced at the junction of two metals, or at a point where a molecular change occurs in a bar of the same metal, when the junction or point is heated above or cooled below the general temperature of the conductor. Thus when wires or bars of metal or different kinds, as bismuth and antimony, are placed in close contact, end to end, and disposed so as to form a periphery or continuous circuit, and heat then applied to the ends or junctions of the bars, electric currents are produced. The thermoelectric battery, or pile, an apparatus much used in delicate experiments with radiant heat, consists of a series of little bars of antimony and bismuth (or any other two metals of different heat-conducting power), having their ends soldered together and arranged in a compact form; the opposite end of the pile being connected with a galvanometer, which is very sensibly affected by the electric current induced in the system of bars when exposed to the slightest variations of temperature. To the combined arrangement of pile and galvanometer the name of thermomultiplier is given. Two metal bars of different heat conducting power having their ends soldered together, and the combined bar then usually bent into a more or less horseshoe or magnet form for the purpose of bringing their free ends within a conveniently short distance, designated a thermoelectric pair, are much used in thermoelectric experiments. But as the electric current developed in a single pair is very weak, a considerable number are usually combined to form a thermoelectric pile or battery. Bismuth and antimony are the metals usually employed, the difference in electromotive forces being greater between any other two metals conveniently obtainable.

THERMOGRAPH, a thermometer provided with a recording device. The form generally used has a crescent shaped bulb, filled with alcohol and hermetically sealed. A change in the temperature affects the curve of the bulb, and the alteration of form is communicated to a series of multiplying levers, which in turn exaggerate the motion, and give impetus to a recording pen. This pen makes a tracing on the ruled paper of a moving cylinder. Bartlett's thermograph is especially designed for greenhouses, having a register for indicating in the office the temperatures prevailing in the different houses. This apparatus is sometimes arranged so that a rise in temperature to 100° will ring a gong. Thus arranged it serves as a warning of fire.

THERMOMETER, in physics, an instrument for measuring intensity of heat or temperature, by means of expansion of a liquid or gas. Mercury is generally employed, and an ordinary thermometer consists of a spherical or cylindrical glass bulb at the end of a very fine tube, the bulb being completely filled and the tube partly filled, with mercury, while the space above the mercury contains only a small quantity of mercury vapor, which offers no resistance to the expansion of the mercury. A rise of temperature is indicated by a rise of the mercury in the tube, owing to expansion and, conversely, a fall of temperature is indicated by a fall of the mercury in the tube. A graduated scale is attached with two fixed points: the lower, or freezing point, and the upper, or boiling point, of water. The distance between the two fixed points is then divided into a certain number of equal parts, or degrees, which are continued above and below the two fixed points. On the Centigrade or Celsius thermometer (used by scientific men all over the world and in general use on the continent of Europe), the distance between the two points is divided into 100 degrees, the freezing point being 0°, and the boiling point being 100°; on the Réaumur thermometer (used only in N. W. Europe), the distance is divided into 80 degrees, the freezing point being 0° and the boiling point 80°; on the Fahrenheit thermometer (in general use in the United States and England), the distance is divided into 180 degrees, but, since zero is 32 degrees below the freezing point, the freezing point is 32°, and the boiling point is 212°. Degrees above 0° are termed + degrees, while those below 0° are termed — degrees.

$$C. \div 5 \times 9 + 32 = F. \qquad F. - 32 \div 9 \times 4 = R.$$
$$R. \div 4 \times 9 + 32 = F. \qquad C. \qquad \div 5 \times 4 = R.$$
$$F. - 32 \div 9 \times 5 = C. \qquad R. \qquad \div 4 \times 5 = C.$$

Mercury can only be used for temperatures between — 40° and + 675°, since it freezes at 40° and boils at 675°. For lower temperatures alcohol is used; and for high temperatures air thermometers are employed, in which changes of temperature are measured by the expansion or contraction of a known volume of air. In deep-sea thermometers, used for ascertaining the temperature of the sea, the bulb is specially protected against the pressure of the water.

THERMOPYLÆ, a famous pass leading from Thessaly into Locris, and the only road by which an invading army can penetrate from Northern into Southern Greece. It lies S. of the present course of the river Spercheius, between Mount Œta and what was anciently an impassable morass bordering on the Maliac Gulf. In the pass are several hot springs, from which Thermopylæ probably received the first part of its name. Thermopylæ has won an eternal celebrity as the scene of the heroic death of LEONIDAS (q. v.) and his 300 Spartans in their attempt to stem the tide of Persian invasion (480 B. C.). Again in 279 B. C. Brennus, at the head of a Gallic host, succeeded, through the same treachery that had secured a victory to Xerxes, in forcing the united Greeks to withdraw from the pass.

THERMOPYLÆ OF AMERICA, a phrase applied to Fort Alamo, Tex.; in allusion to the heroic defense of it, made in 1836, by a small body of Texans against a force of Mexicans 10 times their number. During the subsequent struggle for independence the Texan war cry was "Remember the Alamo!" the Mexicans having murdered the six defenders of the fort whom they found alive on its surrender.

THERMOSCOPE, an instrument for indicating relative differences of temperature. The term was applied by Count Rumford to an instrument invented by him, and similar in principle to the differential thermometer of Professor Leslie.

THEROID, animal; having animal propensities or characteristics; specifically applied to idiots, who in habits or appearance resemble any of the lower animals.

The word is of recent introduction, but the extraordinary resemblances presented by some of the weak-minded to certain birds and mammals have attracted attention for a very long period. Pinel speaks of "a young female idiot * * * who, in the form of her head, her tastes, her mode of living, seemed to approach to the instincts of a sheep."

THEROPODA, in palæontology, an order of Cope's sub-class *Dinosauria*, consisting of carnivorous forms, which are believed to have preyed on the weaker herbivorous members of the class. Feet digitigrade, digits with prehensile claws; vertebræ, more or less cavernous; fore limbs very small, limb bones hollow. The order comprises four families (*Megalosauridæ, Zanclodontidæ, Amphisauridæ,* and *Labrosauridæ*) and two groups, or sub-orders (*Cœluria* and *Compognatha*).

THERSITES, in mythology, son of Agrius, whom Homer, in the "Iliad," makes the ugliest and most impudent of the Greeks before Troy. His name became a synonym for dastardly impudence. Later poets say he was slain by Achilles for calumniating him.

THESEUS, in heroic history, a King of Athens, and the son of Ægeus by Æthra, the daughter of Pittheus, was educated at the house of his father-in-law at Trœzen. On arriving at years of maturity he was sent by his mother to Athens, a sword being given him by which he might make himself known to Ægeus. On his way from Trœzen he destroyed Corynetes, Sigomis, Sciron, Cercyon, Procrustes, and the celebrated Phæa. He was not well received at Athens, and Medea attempted to poison him before his arrival was publicly known. The Palatides, who attempted to assassinate him, he put to death by his own hand. He next destroyed the bull of Marathon; and at Crete, by means of Ariadne who was enamored of him, he killed the Minotaur, and thereby redeemed the Athenians from the annual tribute of seven chosen youths and as many virgins to be devoured by the monster. On ascending his father's throne he ruled the Athenians with mildness, made new laws and regulations, and by his policy won the friendship of the King of the Lapithæ. Theseus, in conjunction with Pirithous, carried off Helen, the daughter of Leda, but whom he was compelled to restore. While he was in captivity, Mnestheus obtained the crown, and Theseus on his return attempted to eject the usurper, but, failing, he retired to the court of Lycomedes, a king of the island of Scyros, who, jealous of his fame, carried him to a high rock and threw him down a precipice. The children of Theseus, after the death of Mnestheus, recovered the Athenian throne.

THESMOPHORIA, an ancient festival held exclusively by women in several districts of Hellas, especially Athens and Arcadia, in honor of Demeter Thesmophoros ("the lawgiver") as the foundress of agriculture, and thereby of ordered civil life, with the institution of marriage. At Athens the festival extended to three days, beginning with Oct. 24. On the first day there was a procession to the temple of Demeter at Halimos, S. E. of the city; on the second a strict fast; and on the third day, called Kalligeneia ("the bearer of a fair offspring") a joyous and unrestrained carousal. The licentiousness of the Thesmophoria is caricatured in the "Thesmophoriazouzai" of Aristophanes.

THESIUM, in botany, the bastard toadflax, a genus of *Santalaceæ*. Flowers small, green; perianth four or five-cleft, persistent; stamens with a small fascicle of hair at their base; drupe ribbed, crowned with the persistent perianth. Known species about 60, all from the Eastern Hemisphere. *T. linophyllum* is a perennial parasite on roots, with diffuse stems, minute flowers, green outside, white inside, with green ovoid fruit.

THESMOTHETE, in Greek antiquity, a lawgiver; a legislator; one of the six inferior archons at Athens who presided at the election of the lower magistrates, received criminal informations in various matters, decided civil causes on arbitration, took the votes at elections, and performed a variety of other offices.

THESPESIA, in botany, a tribe of *Hibisceæ*. Trees with large entire leaves; involucre three-leaved, deciduous; calyx truncate; style simple; stigmas five; fruit almost woody; capsule with five cells, each with about four seeds. *T. populnea* is a tree 40 or 50 feet high, with the foliage so dense at the top that it has been called the umbrella tree. It has roundish, cordate, pointed, five to seven-veined leaves; the flowers, which are large, are yellow, with a dark-red center. The tree is very common along the seacoast of South America, the West Indies, the Pacific Islands, part of Africa, India and Burma. It has been planted along roadsides throughout India, and especially in Madras city. It yields a gum, a deep-red, somewhat thick oil, used in cutaneous affections. The capsule and flowers furnish a yellow dye, and the bark a good fiber. *T. lampas* is a small bush, common in the tropical jungles of India, with a good fiber, as has *T. populnea*.

THESPIAN (from the name of Thespis, the reputed founder of the Greek drama, who was born in Xarca, Attica, and flourished about 550 B. C.), pertaining or relating to the representation of dramatic tragedy, or to the Tragic Muse; as the Thespian art.

THESPIUS, in mythology, a king of the Thespiades, and father of 50 daughters, all of whom bore children to Hercules. The Thespiades were conducted to Sardinia by Iolus.

THESSALONIANS, EPISTLES TO THE, the Pauline epistles. The first epistle to the Thessalonians, the earliest extant epistle of the Apostle Paul, was written at Corinth probably about the beginning of the year A. D. 53, or, at latest, in A. D. 54, within a year and a half of the founding of the Church at Thessalonica under the circumstances related in Acts, xvii: 1-10. Some time after leaving Thessalonica, the apostle had heard of "sufferings" to which his converts there had been subjected by their unbelieving fellow-countrymen (I Thess. ii: 14; iii: 2-4), and there was some cause for fear lest "the tempter" had "tempted" them from their faith (iii: 5). He accordingly sent Timothy from Athens to learn further about their state, and to "establish" and "comfort" them (iii: 2, 5). Timothy brought back to the apostle, then in Corinth, a fairly satisfactory account of their faith and loyalty, but mentioned some matters of Christian doctrine and life in which they were deficient; hence the epistle.

Of the two parts of which it is composed the first is mainly personal and explanatory (i.-iii.), and the second ethical and doctrinal (iv., v.), warning in particular against sins of impurity, perhaps also of commercial greed (iv: 6), and still more specially against a tendency of the Thessalonians toward pious idleness in view of Christ's imminent second coming and toward a hopeless sorrow on account of those of their number who had already died. With regard to the second coming, the apostle's own doctrine is that it may be expected at any time.

The second epistle consists of three parts. The first part is introductory, and mainly an expression of the writer's thankfulness for the steadfastness the Thessalonians have displayed under continued persecution (i. 1-12). The second part (ii. 1-12) is eschatological and warns the readers against supposing "that the day of the Lord is now present" (so revised version; authorized version has "at hand"). On the contrary, it will not be except the falling away ("the apostasy") come first, and the man of sin be revealed, the son of perdition, he that opposeth and exalteth himself against all that is called God or that is worshipped; so that he sitteth in the temple of God, setting himself forth as God. The third and concluding part of the epistle (ii. 13-iii. 18) is of a practical nature, and substantially repeats the exhortations of I Thessalonians.

The genuineness of this epistle was first doubted by J. E. Ch. Schmidt (1801); the volume of opinion in this sense has steadily increased since then, and is now very great. The argument turns chiefly on ii. 1-12. The difficulty about the eschatological passage in question is, in a word, that no traces of such a view occur in any other writing of the Apostle Paul, whether prior or subsequent to the supposed date of II Thessalonians. It is impossible to fix with any accuracy the date of the verses in question. They are conceived in the spirit of a great deal of the apocalyptic that was current in Jewish (and in a less degree in Christian) circles during the last two centuries of Judaism. On the hypothesis of its genuineness, in whole or in part, II Thessalonians must have been written shortly after I Thessalonians and before the apostle's sojourn of 18 months in Corinth had come to an end. Apart indeed from ii. 1-12, II Thessalonians may conceivably have been written before I Thessalonians, a view which has been argued for by Grotius among others.

THESSALY, the largest division of ancient Greece; lay S. of Macedonia and E. of Epirus; being separated from the latter by Mount Pindus, and from the former by the Cambunian Mountains; the Maliac Gulf and Mount Œta bounding it on the S. It is a vast plain shut in on every side by mountains; on the N. and W. by those already named, on the S. by Mount Othrys, and on the E. by Mounts Pelion and Ossa, the only opening being the Vale of Tempe in the N. E., between Ossa and Olympus. This plain is drained chiefly by the Peneus river (now Salambria) and its tributaries, and is the most fertile in all Greece. Thessaly was originally inhabited by so-called Pelasgians, who, however, were either expelled or reduced to slavery by Dorian immigrants from the more rugged region of Epirus about 1000 B. C. The Penestæ, descendants of the old inhabitants, held a position analogous to that of the Helots in Sparta. There were four districts—Hestiæotis, Pelasgiotis, Thessaliotis, and Phthiotis; Magnesia on the coast being a minor division. The government appears to have been oligarchial in the separate cities—of which Pharsalus, Larissa, Heracleum, and Pheræ were chief power—being in the hands of the Alenads and Scopads. About 374 B. C. Jason, tyrant of Pheræ, was elected Tagus (chief-magistrate) of all Thessaly. The rule of Jason's successors became so unbearable that aid was sought from Philip of Macedon, who in 344 subjected the country to Macedonia. Thessaly remained subject to the Macedonian kings till the victory of Cynoscephalæ, in 197 B. C., brought it under the protection of Rome. Under the emperors Thessaly was united with Macedonia, but after Constantine it was a separate province. In A. D. 1204 with other portions of the Eastern Empire, it came under the dominion of the Venetians, and in 1355 was taken by the Turks. The restoration to Greece of Thessaly S. of the Salambria was recommended by the Berlin Congress in 1878; and subsequently various modifications of the Greco-Turkish frontiers were proposed, the Greeks endeavoring to secure the cession of the whole of Thessaly. War between Greece and Turkey seemed imminent; but in 1881 Turkey agreed to cede, and Greece to accept, Thessaly S. of the ridge of mountains forming the watershed of the Salambria (the ancient Peneus), by much the largest and most fertile section of the province. The Greek portion constitutes the three monarchies of Larissa, Trikhala, and Phthiotis with Phocis.

THETIS, in mythology, one of the sea deities, who was courted by Neptune and Jupiter. But when the gods were informed that the son she would bring forth must become greater than his father they ceased their solicitations; and Peleus, the son of Æacus, was permitted to gain her hand. Thetis became mother of several children, among them Achilles whom she rendered invulnerable by plunging him in the waters of the Styx, except that part of the heel by which she held him.

THETIS, in zoölogy, a genus of *Myacidæ*. Shell sub-orbicular, ventricose, thin, translucent, granulated on the surface, and with a slightly nacreous interior. Hinge teeth one or two. Known species: Recent five from Great Britain, France, India, etc.; fossil 17, from the Neocomian of Great Britain, Belgium, France, and Southern India onward.

THEURGY, the working of some divine or supernatural agency in human affairs; a working or producing effect by supernatural means; effect of phenomena brought about among men by spiritual agency; specifically: (1) Divine agency or direct interference of the gods in human affairs, or the government of the world. (2) The act or art of invoking deities or spirits, or by their intervention conjuring up visions, interpreting dreams, receiving or explaining oracles, etc.; the power of obtaining from the gods, by means of certain observances, words, symbols, or the like a knowledge of the secrets which surpass the power of reason, to lay open the future, etc. (3) That species of magic which more modern professors of the art allege to produce its effects by supernatural agency, as contradistinguished from natural magic. (4) A system of supernatural knowledge or power believed by the Egyptian Platonists to have been divinely communicated to a hierarchy, and by them handed down from generation to generation.

THEURIET, ANDRÉ, a French author; born in Marly le Roi, near Paris, Oct. 8, 1833; studied law in Paris, and received in 1857 a place in the office of the minister of finance. He published in 1867 "The Woodland Road," a volume of poems. Later poems were "The Peasants of Argonne, 1792" (1871), and "Blue and Black" (1872). But Theuriet is best known by his novels, which include: "Mlle. Guignon" (1874); "The Marriage of Gerard" (1875); "The Fortune of Angeli" (1876); "Our Children" (1892); etc. He died April 23, 1907.

THEVETIA (named by Linnæus after its describer, Thevet, a French Franciscan, of the 16th century), in botany, a genus of *Carisseæ*. Inflorescence consisting of terminal or lateral cymes. Calyx five-parted, with many glands inside at its base; corolla salver-shaped, closed by four scales; fruits slightly fleshy, with a hard stone inside. *T. neriifolia* is cultivated in tropical America, whence it has been introduced into India. The milky juice is very poisonous, the bitter and cathartic bark is a febrifuge, and an oil extracted from the kernels is emetic and purgative.

THIEF, in ordinary language, one who steals or is guilty of theft; one who takes the goods or personal property of another without his knowledge or consent, and without any intention of returning it; one who deprives another of property secretly or without open force, as opposed to a robber, who uses open force or violence. In the times of Queen Elizabeth and James I. no such sharp distinction was made as we now draw between a robber and a thief. The word is also used as a term of reproach, and applied especially to a person guilty of cunning, deceitful, or secret actions.

THIERRY, AMÉDÉE SIMON DOMINIQUE, a French historian; born in Blois, France, Aug. 2, 1797; was made a member of the Institute, 1841, and senator, 1860. He assisted his brother Augustin in several of the great works produced by the latter, and himself wrote "History of the Gauls" (1828); "History of Gaul under the Normans" (1840); "Stories and Tales of Roman History" (1860); "History of Attila and his Successors"; etc. He died in Paris March 27, 1873.

THIERRY, JACQUES NICOLAS AUGUSTIN, a French historian; born in Blois, France, May 10, 1795. He was for some time associated as secretary and coadjutor with St. Simon, whose socialistic views he embraced. In 1816 he published a treatise entitled "The Nations and Their Mutual Relations." His celebrated work on the Norman conquest of England was published at Paris in 1825, and attained great success both in France and in England. "Letters on French History" appeared in 1827, and "Ten Years of Study" (essays) in 1834. He was summoned by Guizot, then minister of public instruction, to Paris, and intrusted with the editing of the "Account of the Unedited Historical Works on the Third Estate," for the collection of documents relative to the history of France. In 1840 he published "Account of the Times of the Merovingians." He died in Paris May 22, 1856.

THIERS, JEAN BAPTISTE (tē-ār′), a French theological writer; born in Chartres, France, in 1636. His treatises on theological and ecclesiastical subjects are very numerous; but he owes whatever celebrity he has to his "History of Wigs, wherein is Shown their Origin, their Use, their Form, the Abuse and Irregularity of Ecclesiastics' Wigs" (1690). He died in Vibraye, France, in 1703.

THIERS (tē-ār′), LOUIS ADOLPHE, a French statesman; born in Marseilles, France, April 16, 1797. He studied law and at the age of 22 was admitted advocate. He soon relinquished law, however, for literature and politics (1821). After a long struggle with poverty in Paris, he won a high reputation as a political writer for the "Constitutionalist" and other journals. He took part with Armand Carrel and Mignet in the foundation of the "National" (1830) which aided in the downfall of the Bourbons; and during the July revolution of 1830, the office of the "National" was the headquarters of the revolutionary party. In the government of Louis Philippe, Thiers held several offices, till (1840) he found himself at the head of the ministry for a few months, and then retired into private life. After the revolution of 1848 he was elected deputy to the Assembly, and voted for the presidency of Louis Napoleon, but was ever after one of his fiercest opponents; and at the coup d'état (Dec.

LOUIS ADOLPHE THIERS

2, 1851) he was arrested and banished. Returning to France in the following year, he remained in comparative retirement till 1863, when he was elected one of the deputies for Paris.

During the terrible crisis of 1870-1871 he came to the front as the one supreme man in France. After the fall of Paris he was returned to the National Assembly, and on Feb. 17, 1871, he was declared chief of the executive power. The first duty imposed on him as such was to assist in drawing up the treaty of peace, whereby France lost Alsace and Lorraine and agreed to pay an enormous indemnity; his second was to suppress the Communist insurrection. This done, his next task was to free the soil of the invaders by the payment of the ransom, which was effected in an incredibly short space of time. The Assembly in August, 1871, prolonged his tenure of office and changed his title to that of President. In November, 1872, Thiers declared himself in favor of the republic as a definitive form of government for France, and thus to some extent brought about the crisis which resulted in his being deprived of the presidency. He accepted his deposition with dignity, and went quietly into retirement. M. Thiers' chief works are: "History of the French Revolution" (6 vols. 1823-1827); and "History of the Consulate and the Empire" (20 vols. 1845-1862). The latter obtained for him the academic prize of $4,000. He died near Paris, Sept. 3, 1877.

THIERSCH, FRIEDRICH WILHELM, a German classical scholar; born in Kirchscheidungen, Prussian Saxony, June 17, 1784; studied theology and philology at Leipsic and Göttingen, and in 1809, following a call to the newly-founded Munich Lyceum, there founded a Philological Institute. The enthusiasm he had shown in the German War of Liberation he presently directed to Hellenic regeneration, and in 1831 visited Greece, where on the murder of Capo d'Istria he coöperated toward the election of Otto of Bavaria to the throne. Returning to Munich, he was elected president of the Academy in 1848. His most important work was his "Greek Grammar." He died in Munich Feb. 25, 1860.

THIERSCHITE (after F. von Thiersch, the discoverer), a mineral substance occurring as an incrustation on the marbles of the Parthenon, at Athens. Stated to be an oxalate of lime originating from the action of vegetation on the marble.

THIETHALDINE, $C_6H_{12}(C_2H_5)NS_2$; prepared from ethylamine in the same way as thiamethaldine. Has not been obtained pure.

THIETSIE, a resinous substance used as a varnish by the Burmese. It exudes from *Melanorrhœa usitatissima* in the form of a very viscid, light-brown liquid. The main portion is soluble in alcohol, and is very tenacious. The remaining portion is insoluble in ether, and changes, on exposure to the air, to a deep black and nearly solid substance.

THIGH BONE, the femur, the largest bone in the skeleton, situated between the os innominatum and the tibia. In the erect position of the body it inclines inward, and slightly backward as it descends. At its superior extremity is its neck; its shaft terminates beneath in two condyles, united anteriorly, but separated posteriorly by a deep intercondylar fossa or notch.

THILLY, FRANK, an American educator; born in Cincinnati, O., Aug. 18, 1865; was graduated at the University of Cincinnati in 1887, and studied at the Universities of Berlin and Heidelberg in 1887-1891; was instructor in logic and history of philosophy at the Sage School of Philosophy, Cornell University, in 1892-1893; Professor of Philosophy at the University of Missouri (1893-1904), of Psychology (1904-1906); Professor of Philosophy, Cornell, from 1906 on. Dean of the College of Arts, Editor International Journal of Ethics, President American Philosophical Society (1912). Author "A History of Philosophy" (1914); Translation of Weber's "History of Philosophy" (1896), etc.

THIMBLE, a metallic cap or sheath used to protect the end of the finger in sewing. Seamstresses use a thimble having a rounded end with numerous small pits or indentations. Those used by tailors are open at the end. The manufacture of thimbles is very simple. Coin silver is mostly used, generally silver dollars, which are melted, and cast into solid ingots. These are rolled into the required thickness, and cut by a stamp into disks of any required size. A solid metal bar the size of the inside of the intended thimble, moved by powerful machinery up and down in a bottomless mold of the size of the outside of the thimble, bends the circular disks into the thimble shape as fast as they can be placed under the descending bar. The work of brightening, polishing, and decorating is done on a lathe. First the blank form is fitted with a rapidly revolving rod. A slight touch of a sharp chisel takes thin shavings from the end, another does the same on the side, and the third rounds off the rim. A round steel rod, dipped in oil and pressed on the surface, gives it a lustrous polish.

THIRD INTERNATIONAL or COMMUNIST INTERNATIONAL, a permanent body representing the Communist parties of all nations. It was founded in 1919, but had as its precursor the organization supporting the Bolshevik revolution in Russia. Previously the Second International, a Socialist rather than Communist body, had broken up after 1914 owing to the war in Europe. The present body, also known by its abbreviation as the Komintern, has its headquarters in Moscow, and was directed until 1926 by Gregory Zinovieff. It stimulates Communist propaganda in divers countries and undertakes to regulate the organization of Communists in the various nations.

THIRLAGE, an old servitude, or rather service, enjoyed by the proprietor of a mill over the neighboring lands "thirled" to it, whereby the possessors (and tenants) of the land were bound to have their grain ground at that mill, and to pay as "multure" or duty a certain proportion of the grain ground, varying from $\frac{1}{30}$ to $\frac{1}{12}$ of the corn ground. The possessors of the astricted lands were called suckeners; the multure paid by those who were not bound, but used the mill, was out-sucken multure. Since 1799 this class of local burdens has almost entirely disappeared by commutation, voluntary renunciation, or private agreement. Such a servitude or easement was rare in England.

THIRLMERE, a narrow sheet of water in Cumberland co., England, in the heart of the Lake district, lying 533 feet above sea-level, and 3 miles long by ¼ mile wide, between Derwentwater and Grasmere. It was acquired as a water supply by Manchester. The work was begun in 1886, and the entire system was completed in 1894.

THIRST, a sensation resulting from a peculiar state of the system, but especially of the mucous membrane of the fauces, usually caused by an insufficient supply of liquid. In cases of extreme thirst there is a peculiar sense of clamminess in the mouth and pharynx, which, with the other disagreeable feelings, is almost immediately relieved by the introduction of liquid into the stomach, where it is absorbed by the veins. That the thirst is relieved by the absorption of the fluid, and not by its action as it passes over the mucous membrane, which seems to suffer most, is proved by the facts (1) that injection of liquids into the stomach through a tube (in cases of wounded œsophagus), and (2) the injection of thin fluids, as water, into the blood, remove the sensation of thirst.

An excessive thirst is often an important morbid symptom. It may arise from two very opposite conditions—one a condition of excitement, and the other of depression. Whenever the blood is in a state requiring dilution, and is too stimulating, as in fevers and inflammations, there is thirst; and, again, in cases of excessive secretion and exhaustion, as for example in cholera and in the two forms of diabetes, there is great thirst, which sometimes also attends the lowest stages of prostration in malignant diseases.

THIRTY TYRANTS, a body of men of the higher classes who usurped the government of Athens 404-403 B. C. Of these, Critias was the most noted. They were expelled by the democratic party led by Thrasybulus. Also a name given to a number of pretenders to the Roman empire during the reigns of Gallienus and Aurelian, A. D. 259-274.

THIRTY YEARS' WAR (1618 to 1648), a war in Germany, at first a struggle between Roman Catholics and Protestants. Subsequently it lost its religious character and became a struggle for political ascendancy in Europe. On the one side were Austria, nearly all the Roman Catholic princes of Germany, and Spain; on the other side were, at different times, the Protestant powers and France. The occasion of this war was found in the fact that Germany had been distracted ever since the Reformation by the mutual jealousy of Catholics, Lutherans, and Calvinists. Certain concessions had been made to the Protestants of Bohemia by Rudolph II. (1609), but these were withdrawn by his successor Matthias in 1614, and four years afterward the Bohemian Protestants were in rebellion. Count Thurn at the head of the insurgents repeatedly routed the imperial troops, compelling them to retire from Bohemia, and (1619) invaded the archduchy of Austria. Matthias having died in 1619, he was succeeded by Ferdinand II., who was a rigid Catholic, but the Protestants elected as their king Frederick, Elector Palatine, who was a Protestant. Efforts at mediation having failed, the Catholic forces of Germany marched against Frederick, who, with an army of Bohemians, Moravians, and Hungarians, kept the field till Nov. 8, 1620, when he was totally routed at Weissenberg, near Prague, by Duke Maximilian of Bavaria. The Protestant cause was now crushed in Bohemia, and the people of that province suffered cruel persecution. The dominions of Frederick, the Palatinate of the Rhine included, were now conquered, the latter being occupied by Count Tilly, assisted by the Spaniards under Spinola. At the Diet of Ratisbon (March, 1623) Frederick was deprived of his territories, Duke Maximilian receiving the Palatinate.

Ferdinand, whose succession to the throne of Bohemia was thus secured, had now a favorable opportunity of concluding a peace, but his continued intolerance toward the Protestants caused them to seek foreign assistance, and a new period of war began. Christian IV. of Denmark, induced partly by religious zeal and partly by the hope of an acquisition of territory, came to the aid of his German coreligionists (1624), and being joined by Mansfeld and Christian of Brunswick, advanced into Lower Saxony. There they were met by Wallenstein, Duke of Friedland, who in 1626 defeated Mansfeld at Dessau, while Tilly was also successful in driving Christian back to Denmark. In the peace of Lübeck which followed (May, 1629)

Christian of Denmark received back all his occupied territory, and undertook not to meddle again in German affairs. After this second success, Ferdinand again roused his people by an edict which required restitution to the Roman Catholic Church of all church lands and property acquired by them since 1552.

To the assistance of the Protestants of Germany, in these circumstances, came Gustavus Adolphus, King of Sweden, who landed (1630) with a small army on the coast of Pomerania. Joined by numerous volunteers, and aided by French money, he advanced, and routed Tilly at Breitenfeld (or the battle of Leipsic, September, 1631), victoriously traversed the Main and the Rhine valleys, defeated Tilly again near the confluence of the Lech and the Danube (April, 1632), and entered Munich. Meanwhile the emperor sought the aid of Wallenstein, by whose ability and energy Gustavus was obliged to retire to Saxony, where he gained the great victory of Lützen (November, 1632), but was himself mortally wounded in the battle. The war was now carried on by the Swedes under the chancellor Oxenstierna, till the rout of the Swedish forces at Nördlingen (September, 1634) again gave to the emperor the preponderating power in Germany. The Elector of Saxony, who had been an ally of Gustavus, now made peace at Prague (May, 1635), and within a few months the treaty was accepted by many of the German princes.

The Swedes, however, thought it to their interest to continue the war, while France resolved to take a more active part in the conflict. Thus the last stage of the war was a contest of France and Sweden against Austria, in which the Swedish generals gained various successes over the imperial forces, while the French armies fought with varied fortunes in West Germany and on the Rhine. Meanwhile the emperor had died (1637), and had been succeeded by his son, Ferdinand III. The struggle still continued till in 1646, the united armies of the French under the great generals Turenne and Condé, and the Swedes advanced through Suabia and Bavaria. The combined forces of Sweden, Bavaria, and France were then about to advance on Austria, when the news reached the armies that the peace of Westphalia (1648) was concluded, and that the long struggle was ended.

THIRLWALL, CONNOP, an English bishop and historian; born in Stepney, Middlesex, England, Jan. 11, 1797; was a child of almost unexampled precocity,

learned Latin at three, read Greek at four, and at 11 published "Primitæ" (1809), a volume of poems and sermons. He next went to Charterhouse; entered Trinity College, Cambridge, in October, 1814, and in February following carried off the Craven and Belle scholarship and the highest honors. In October he was elected to a Trinity fellowship, and next spent about a year on the Continent, making fast friendship with Bunsen at Rome. He entered as a law student at Lincoln's Inn in February, 1820. He was called to the bar in 1825, but the natural bent of his mind prevailed, and in 1827 he took orders. Already in 1825 he had translated Schleiermacher's "Essay on St. Luke" and written an introduction—a remarkable performance for a barrister. His return to Cambridge was marked by the commencement, in conjunction with his dear friend Julius Hare, of a translation of Niebuhr's "History of Rome" (vol. i. 1828; ii. 1832). Their famous "Philological Museum" (1831-1833) saw only six numbers, but contained some remarkable papers, among them Thirlwall's "On the Irony of Sophocles." In 1834 he signed the petition in favor of the admission of dissenters to academical degrees, and in May put forth a weighty pamphlet in defense of the measure. The master of the college, Dr. Christopher Wordsworth, called on him to resign the assistant-tutorship, which he did at once, though under protest. Almost immediately he was presented by Lord Brougham to the quiet Yorkshire living of Kirby-Underdale. Here he wrote for "Lardner's Cyclopædia" his "History of Greece" (8 vols. 1835-1847; improved ed. 1847-1852).

In 1840 Lord Melbourne raised Thirlwall to the see of St. David's, and within six months thereafter he preached in perfect Welsh. For 34 years he labored with the utmost diligence in his diocese, building churches, parsonages, and schools, and augmenting poor livings (to the extent of $150,000 from his own pocket). His "Primary Charge" (1840) was a catholic-spirited apology for the Tractarian party. Thirlwall joined in the encyclical letter censuring "Essays and Reviews," but was one of the four bishops who refused to inhibit Bishop Colenso. He supported the Maynooth grant, the admission of Jews to Parliament, and alone among the bishops voted for the disestablishment of the Irish Church. He was appointed chairman of the Old Testament Revision Committee, and resigned his see in May, 1874, retiring to Bath, where he died July 27, 1875. The nobilty of his character is revealed in "Letters to a Friend," edited by Dean Stanley, in 1881.

THISBE, in classical legend, a Babylonish maiden beloved by Pyramus. They lived in contiguous houses, and as their parents would not let them marry, they contrived to converse together through a hole in the garden wall. On one occasion they agreed to meet at Ninus's tomb, and Thisbe, who was first at the spot, hearing a lion roar, ran away in a fright, dropping her garment on the way. The lion seized the garment and tore it. When Pyramus arrived, and saw the garment, he concluded that a lion had eaten Thisbe, and he stabbed himself. Thisbe, returning to the tomb, saw Pyramus dead, and killed herself also. The story is travestied in "The Midsummer's Night's Dream," by Shakespeare.

THISTLE, the common name of prickly plants of the tribe *Cynaraceæ*, natural order *Compositæ*. There are numerous species, most of which are inhabitants of Europe, as the musk thistle (*Carduus nutans*), milk thistle (*C. marianus*), welted thistle (*C. acanthoides*), slender-flowered thistle (*C. tenuiflorus*), the spear thistle (*Cnicus lanceolatus*), and field thistle (*Cnicus arvensis*), a well-known plant very troublesome to the farmer. The blessed thistle, *Carduus benedictus* of the pharmacopœias, *Cnicus benedictus* or *Cirsium benedictum* of modern botanists, is a native of the Levant, and is a laxative and tonic medicine. The cotton thistle belongs to the genus *Onopordon*. The common cotton thistle (*O. acanthium*) attains a height of from four to six feet. It is often regarded as the Scotch thistle, but it is doubtful whether the thistle which constitutes the Scotch national badge has any existing type, though the stemless thistle (*Cnicus acaulis* or *Cirsium acaule*) is in many districts of Scotland looked on as the true Scotch thistle. Some dozen species of thistle are common in the United States, spreading from New England to Florida; Canada thistle is one of the severest pests of the farmer, W. and S.

THISTLE, ORDER OF THE, a Scotch order of knighthood, sometimes called the Order of St. Andrew. It was instituted by James VII. (James II. of England) in 1687, when eight knights were nominated. It fell into abeyance during the reign of William and Mary, and was revived by Queen Anne in 1703. As at present constituted, the order consists of the British sovereign and knights to the number of sixteen. The insignia consist of a collar, badge, jewel, star, and ribbon. The collar is composed of golden thistles and leaves connected by crossed sprigs of rue, enameled. The badge is a golden eight-pointed star, whereon is an enameled figure of St. Andrew, bearing in front of him his cross in silver; it is worn attached to the collar. The jewel is worn round the neck with the ribbon. The star is of four points, with a St. Andrew's Cross embroidered in silver upon it. In the center is a green and gold thistle within a circle of green, bearing the motto in golden letters; ribbon, dark green; motto: *Nemo me impune lacessit* (No one provokes me with impunity). Besides the knights ordinary, there are extra knights (Princes), and a dean, a secretary, the lyon king of arms, and the gentleman usher of the green rod.

THOBURN, JAMES MILLS, an American clergyman; born in St. Clairsville, Ohio, March 7, 1836; was graduated at Allegheny College in 1857; joined the Pittsburgh Conference of the Methodist Episcopal Church in 1858, and engaged in missionary work in India in 1859. He was presiding elder at the India Conference in the United States in 1886-1888, and in the latter year was elected missionary bishop of India and Malaysia, and devoted himself to mission work until 1908. He was author of "My Missionary Apprenticeship in New York," "Missionary Sermons," "India and Malaysia," "Light in the East," "The Deaconess and Her Vocation," "Christless Nations," "The Church of the Pentecost," "The Christian Conquest of India." Died 1922.

THOLEN, an island of the Netherlands, in the province of Zeeland, N. of the Ooster Schelde; area, 51 square miles. It has a rich soil, and is protected by dykes. Wheat, rye, barley, oats, flax, madder, beans, and potatoes are its products. The chief town has the same name.

THOMAS, ARTHUR LLOYD, an ex-governor of the State of Utah, born in 1851; educated in the public schools of Pittsburgh, Pa. From 1879 to 1887 he was secretary of Utah Territory, being a member of the commission to collect and codify the laws of Utah in 1884. In 1889 he was elected governor of the State for four years. During his term, and largely through his influence, the practice of plural marriages was formally renounced by the Mormon Church. He called the first National Irrigation Congress in Salt Lake City in 1890, and the First International Irrigation Congress in Los Angeles, Cal., in 1891. From 1898 until 1914 he was postmaster in Salt Lake City.

THOMAS, AUGUSTUS, an American playwright, born in St. Louis, Mo., 1859, and educated in the public schools of his native city. For two years after leaving school he studied law, then became page boy in the 41st United States Congress. Next he spent six years in practical railroading in the freight department, after which he became a writer and illustrator on St. Louis, Kansas City and New York newspapers, becoming editor and proprietor of the Kansas City Mirror. He also became interested in politics and was a Democratic candidate for the state legislature. Gradually he took up the writing of plays, the first of which were for publication only. Later his dramatic works were produced and immediately attained a wide popularity. Among his productions are: "The Burglar"; "Colorado"; "The Man of the World"; "New Blood"; "The Earl of Pawtucket"; "The Witching Hour"; "The Harvest Moon"; and "Kentuck."

THOMAS (to-mä'), CHARLES LOUIS AMBROISE, a French musical composer; born in Metz, the capital of Lorraine, Aug. 5, 1811. He entered the Paris Conservatory in 1828, where he carried off the first prize for piano playing in 1829, for harmony in 1830, following up these two successes by gaining the Grand Prix for musical composition in 1832. Before he had reached the age of 26 Thomas had produced a cantata, a requiem mass for orchestra, and numerous pieces for pianoforte, violin, and orchestra. His first success in opera was with "The Double Ladder" in 1837; followed by "Mina" (1843); "Betty" (1846); "Midsummer Night's Dream" (1850); "The Carnival of Venice" (1853); "The Romance of Elvire" (1860); "Mignon" (1866); "Hamlet" (1868); "Francesca of Rimini" (1882); with innumerable other operas, cantatas, part songs, and choral scenas. Thomas was appointed a member of the Institute in 1851, Professor of Composition in 1852, and succeeded Auber as director of the Conservatory in 1871. He received the Grand Cross of the Legion of Honor in 1880. He died Feb. 12, 1896.

THOMAS, CHARLES SPAULDING, a United States Senator, born in Darien, Ga., 1849. Early in his boyhood he went out to Michigan, then to Denver, where he practiced law from 1871 to 1879. Afterward he removed to Leadville, Colo., where he took up his law practice, but returned to Denver in 1885. From 1884 to 1896 he was a member of the Democratic National Committee. In 1899 he was elected governor of Colorado for a term of two years. In 1900 he was temporary chairman of the Democratic National Convention, held in Kansas City. In 1913 he was elected to the United States Senate for the unexpired term (1913-15) of Charles J. Hughes. In 1915 he was re-elected, but was defeated for renomination in 1920.

THOMAS, CALVIN, an American educator; born in 1854; was graduated at the University of Michigan, where he became Professor of Germanic Languages and Literatures; in 1896, he became professor of German at Columbia University. His publications include "Goethe and the Conduct of Life"; "Poetry and Science"; "What is Republicanism?"; "Have We Still Need of Poetry?" He died in 1919.

THOMAS, EARL DENISON, an American soldier, born in McHenry, Ill., 1847, and graduate of the United States Military Academy. During the Civil War he served in the Eighth Illinois Cavalry, though still a boy less than twenty. In 1869 he was commissioned a first lieutenant in the Fifth United States Cavalry. During the Spanish-American War he was appointed inspector general of volunteers. In 1907 he had attained the rank of brigadier-general. In 1890 he was brevetted first lieutenant "for gallant services in action against Indians near Fort McPherson." During 1906-7 he was in charge of the Province of Pinar del Rio, in Cuba, and in 1910 he was in charge of operations on the border of Arizona and New Mexico during the Mexican troubles; retired in 1911.

THOMAS, EDITH MATILDA, an American poet; born in Chatham, O., Aug. 12, 1854. She contributed to many periodicals, and published in book form: "A New Year's Masque," etc. (1885); "The Round Year" (1886); "Lyrics and Sonnets" (1887); "Children of the Seasons" Series (1888); "Babes of the Year" (1888); "Babes of the Nations" (1889); "Heaven and Earth" (1889); "The Inverted Torch" (1890); "Fair Shadow Land" (1893); "In Sunshine Land" (1895); "In the Young World" (1895); "A Winter Swallow With Other Verse" (1896); "The Guest at the Gate" (1909); "The White Messenger." Died, 1925.

THOMAS, ELMER. U. S. Senator from Oklahoma; born in Indiana, 1876. He completed his education at De Pauw University. Studying law, he was admitted to the Bar, and moved to Oklahoma, in 1900. He was elected to the first State Senate of Oklahoma and retained his seat until 1920. In 1922 he won a seat in the House of Representatives, where he continued to serve until 1927. In 1926 he was elected Senator.

THOMAS, GEORGE HENRY, an American military officer; born in Southampton co., Va., July 31, 1816; was graduated at the United States Military Academy in 1840; took part in the Florida War in 1840-1842, and the war with Mexico in 1846-1848; participated in the Seminole campaign in 1849-1850; and served on frontier duty in California and Texas in 1850-1860. At the outbreak of the Civil War he was made a colonel of Cavalry and took part in the operations in the Shenandoah valley in the summer of 1861, and later as commander of a division in the Army of the Ohio was actively engaged in the operations in Tennessee and Mississippi. Afterward, under General Rosecrans, as commander of a corps of the Army of the Cumberland, he engaged in the battles of Murfreesboro and Chickamauga, and in 1863, as commander of the Army of the Cumberland, he bore an important part in the battle of Missionary Ridge and in the Atlanta campaign under Sherman. In October, 1864, he was sent to Nashville to oppose the Confederates under Hood, whom he finally defeated before Nashville, Dec. 15, 1864. For his services in these operations he was promoted Major-General; received the thanks of Congress, and was presented with a gold medal by the State of Tennessee. After the war he commanded the Department of the Tennessee; was chief of the 3d Military District, comprising Georgia, Florida, and Alabama, and in 1868 was placed in command of the 4th Military Division, comprising the territory of the Pacific and Alaska, and continued in this capacity till his death, in San Francisco, Cal., March 28, 1870.

THOMAS, JESSE BURGESS, an American clergyman; born in Edwardsville, Ill., July 29, 1832; was graduated at Kenyon College in 1850; practised law in Chicago, Ill., in 1857-1862; was ordained in the Baptist Church; pastor of the First Baptist Church, Brooklyn, N. Y., in 1864-1869 and 1874-1888 and of the Michigan Avenue Baptist Church, Chicago, 1869-1874. He accepted the chair of Church History at Newton Theological Institution in 1888. He was the author of "The Old Bible and the New Science"; "The Mould of Doctrine"; and "Significance of the Historical Element in Scripture." He died in 1915.

THOMAS, JOHN, an American military officer; born in Marshfield, Mass., in 1725; was appointed a surgeon in the army in 1746; served on the medical staff of General Shirley's regiment in 1747; became colonel of provincials in 1759, and in 1760, in command of a regiment under General Amherst, was engaged in operations against the French at Lake Champlain and at Montreal. During the Revolutionary War he raised a regiment of volunteers and was appointed Brigadier-General; took part in the siege of Boston; forced the British to evacuate Dorchester; and participated in the Canadian campaign. He died in Chambly, Canada, June 2, 1776.

THOMAS, JOHN LLOYD, an American humanitarian; born at Witton Park, England, 1857. As a boy he came to this country and finished his education in Utica, N. Y. In 1888 he removed to New York City and became a newspaper writer and editor. In 1896 he became manager of the Mills Hotels and Model Dwellings Corporation, which position he has held ever since. He has lectured on social questions in Canada and Great Britain and throughout this country. For several years he was secretary of the National Prohibition Party. He has made a special study of housing for the working classes in European countries, on which subject he has lectured and written extensively.

THOMAS, JOHN MARTIN, an American college president; born in Fort Covington, N. Y., 1869. He graduated from the Union Theological Seminary in 1893, after which he was ordained a Presbyterian minister, becoming pastor in East Orange, N. J., where he remained until 1908. In that year he was appointed president of Middlebury College in Vermont. From 1910 until 1914 he was chairman of the Vermont State Board of Education. He is the author of "The Christian Faith and the Old Testament" (1908). During the world war he served as chaplain in the United States Army, with the rank of first lieutenant.

THOMAS, JOSEPH, an American lexicographer; born in Cayuga co., N. Y., Sept. 23, 1811. He was with Thomas Baldwin, author of "Baldwin's Pronouncing Gazetteer." In 1851-1852 appeared his first book of "Etymology," followed by an edition of Oswald's "Etymological Dictionary." In 1854 he prepared "A New and Complete Gazetteer of the United States"; and in 1855 "A Complete Geographical Dictionary of the World" (popularly known as "Lippincott's Gazetteer of the World"). In 1864 appeared his comprehensive "Medical Dictionary"; and in 1870 his "Universal Pronouncing Dictionary of Biography and Mythology." He died in Philadelphia, Pa., Dec. 24, 1891.

THOMAS, M. CAREY, an American educator; born in Baltimore, Md., Jan. 2, 1857; was graduated at Cornell University in 1877; studied at Johns Hopkins University in 1877-1878, and in Germany in 1879-1883; and in 1885 became Professor of English at Bryn Mawr College. In 1894 she was made president of the institution, and in 1895-1899 was also a member of the board of trustees of Cornell University. Her publications include "Sir Gawayne and the Green Knight"; "Education for Women" (1900). Mrs. Mary Garret, a benefactress of Bryn Mawr, left her $15,000,000 for educational purposes.

THOMAS, NATHANIEL SEYMOUR, an American bishop; born in Faribault, Minn., 1867. Having finished his schooling in this country he studied at Cambridge, in England. In 1891 he was ordained deacon, and priest in 1893. From 1891 to 1892 he was rector of Grace Church, in Ottawa, Kan., then became professor of ethics at Bethany College, Topeka, Kan. A year later he became professor of theology at the Kansas Theological School, where he remained until 1895, when he received an appointment as chaplain at the Unitel States penitentiary at Leavenworth, Kan. In 1902 he was elected to the bishopric of Salina, Kan., which he declined. In 1909 he was consecrated Bishop of Wyoming.

THOMAS, THEODORE, a German-American musician; born in Esens, Hanover, Germany, Oct. 11, 1835. He first played in public at the age of six. In 1845 his family removed to the United States and for two years he played violin solos at concerts in New York. He then traveled for a time in the South, and returning to New York in 1851, he played at concerts and at the opera; at first as one of the principal violinists, and afterward an orchestral leader, till 1861. In connection with others he began a series of chamber concerts in 1855, which were continued till 1869. His first symphony concerts were given in 1864-1865, and extended (excepting from 1869 to 1872) till he left New York, in 1878, to take the direction of the College of Music at Cincinnati. He remained in Cincinnati till 1880, when he resigned this position and returned to New York. With brief intervals he was conductor of the Brooklyn Philharmonic Society from 1862-1891, and of the New York Philharmonic Society from 1877-1891. From 1866 to 1878 he gave a series of summer concerts nightly in various cities; and in 1869 he made his first concert tour in the Eastern and Western States, which he repeated from time to time afterward. He conducted five music festivals in Cincinnati (1873, 1875, 1878, 1880, and 1882), one in Chicago (1882), and one in New York (1882). In the winter of 1885-1886 he organized a series of popular concerts in New York, and in the same season he became the conductor of the newly-established American Opera, holding that position for two years. In 1891 established his orchestra permanently at the Auditorium in Chicago. In 1893 he was musical director at the World's Fair, till Aug. 10, when he resigned. He died in Chicago, Ill., Jan. 4, 1905.

THOMAS, WILLIAM WIDGERY, an American diplomat, born in Portland, Me., 1839, graduated from Bowdoin, 1860, then studied law. He began his diplomatic career in 1862 as United States bearer of dispatches during which service he carried a treaty to Turkey. He became vice-consul-general at Constantinople, later acting consul at Galatz, then was consul at Gothenburg, Sweden, where he remained till 1865. He then resigned and completed his law studies at Harvard. In 1866 he was admitted to the bar and began practice in Portland, Me. In 1883 he again entered the diplomatic service as Minister-resident to Sweden and Norway, where he remained till 1905.

THOMAS À KEMPIS. See KEMPIS.

THOMAS AQUINAS. See AQUINAS, THOMAS.

THOMAS OF LONDON. See BECKET, THOMAS À.

THOMAS, ST., called Didymus, or the twin (this being the meaning of both forms of his name), one of the 12 apostles of Jesus Christ. He is presumed to have been a native of Galilee. He is distinguished in sacred history by his disbelief of the resurrection of his Master; on which Jesus vouchsafed to permit him to put his fingers into His wounds, and Thomas exclaimed, "My Lord and my God!" He is supposed to have suffered martyrdom in Coromandel, India, where there are still Christian churches which are called by his name. Efforts have been made by the Roman Catholic theologians of Spanish America to prove that the apostle visited the Western Continent and that St. Thomas was the person who was afterward worshipped as Quetzalcoatl.

THOMASIUS, CHRISTIAN, a German author; born in Leipsic, Germany, Jan. 1, 1655, studied at Frankfort-on-the-Oder (1675-1679); returned to his native town and lectured on law. In 1687 he adopted the German language in place of the Latin, as the vehicle of his expositions, and commenced an unconventional monthly journal. But this work and his advanced views on theological subjects excited so much opposition that he was forced to leave Leipsic, and went first to Berlin, and afterward (1690) to Halle, where his lectures were the means of establishing a university, since famous. In this university Thomasius became Professor of Jurisprudence. He broke away completely from traditional pedantry and mediæval terminology, and was a courageous opponent of trial for witchcraft and the use of torture. His specialty was international law (*jus naturale*) and ethics. He wrote "Thoughts and Reminiscences" (1723-1726); and "History of Wisdom and Folly" (1693). He died in Halle, Sept. 23, 1728.

THOMASVILLE, a city and countyseat of Thomas co., Ga.; on the Atlantic Coast Line, Atlanta, Birmingham and Atlantic, and the Florida Central railroad; 32 miles N. E. of Tallahassee, Fla. Here are a court house, South Georgia College, Young's College, the School for Colored Pupils, waterworks, electric lights, National and State banks, and several newspapers. It is a noted winter health resort. The city has iron foundries and machine shops. Pop. (1910), 6,727; (1920), 8,196.

THOMASVILLE, a city of North Carolina, in Davidson co. It is on the Southern and the Carolina and Yadkin railroads. Its industries include machine shops, a woodworking plant, cotton mills, chair factories, etc. It is the seat of the Thomasville Baptist Orphanage. Pop. (1910), 3,877; (1920), 5,676.

THOMPSON, AUGUSTUS CHARLES, an American clergyman; born in Goshen, Conn., April 30, 1812; was educated at Yale University and graduated at the Hartford Theological Seminary in 1838; studied abroad in 1838-1839; was ordained in the Congregational Church, became pastor of the Eliot Congregational Church, Roxbury, Mass., in 1842. He was a delegate to the Mildmay Missionary Conference in 1878 and the London Missionary Conference in 1888. His publications include "Better Land" (1855); "Morning Hours in Patmos" (1860); "The Mercy Seat" (1863); "Seeds and Sheaves" (1869); "Moravian Missions" (1882); "Foreign Missions" (1889); "Protestant Missions" (1894); "Eliot Memorial" (1900); etc. He died in 1901.

THOMPSON, DANIEL GREENLEAF, an American author; born in Montpelier, Vt., Feb. 9, 1850; was graduated at Amherst College in 1869; taught for three years, and was admitted to the New York bar in 1872. Thereafter he practiced his profession in New York, while his leisure hours were devoted to literary pursuits, lecturing, etc. He

I—26

made notable contributions to many periodicals; was the author of several books; and an active member of many literary and social clubs and societies. He died in New York city, July 10, 1897.

THOMPSON, DENMAN, an American actor; born in Girard, Pa., in 1833; began his professional career as a dancer, Irish character and general utility man. Later he starred in the comedy "Joshua Whitcomb," a play of his own, which was afterward remodeled as "The Old Homestead." He died April 14, 1911.

THOMPSON, ERWIN W., an American diplomatic official; born in Colquitt co., Ga., 1859, and graduated from Cornell University in 1881. His earlier years were spent in journalism and investigations of cotton and markets in Europe for the Department of Commerce. In 1914 he was appointed commercial attaché of the Department of Commerce and assigned to duty at Berlin and the Scandinavian capitals. Later he became manager of the district office of the United States Department of Commerce in New Orleans, La.

THOMPSON, FRANCIS, an English poet; son of a Lancashire physician; born about 1863. He was educated at Ushaw College, near Durham, and studied medicine at Owens College, Manchester. He determined to take up literature, however, and went to London. His first appearance in print was in the columns of "Merrie England." Collected volumes appeared as follows: "Poems" (1893); "Sister Songs" (1896); "New Poems" (1897); "A Renegade Poet" (1910), and several religious books. He died in 1907.

THOMPSON, FRANK ERNEST, an American educator; born in Duquoin, Ill., 1871. In 1901 he became an assistant instructor of education at Leland Stanford University; then, a year later, instructor in the State Normal School in San Francisco. He became professor and director of the College of Education of the University of Colorado in 1907.

THOMPSON, HELEN BISHOP, an American educator; born in Chillicothe, Ohio. From 1903 till 1907 she was an assistant instructor at the Kansas State Agricultural College, then became professor of household economics at Lincoln College, in Lincoln, Ill. (1909-12). Was professor of home economics at New Hampshire College (1913-15), then professor of dietetics (1915-18) at the Connecticut College for Women, at New London. In 1918 she became dean of the division of home economics and professor of nutrition and dietetics at the Kansas State Agricultural College.

THOMPSON, SIR HENRY, an English surgeon; born in Framlingham, England, Aug. 6, 1820; was educated at University College, London; appointed surgeon of the University College Hospital (1863); Professor of Clinical Surgery (1866), consulting surgeon (1874). In 1884 he was made Professor of Surgery and Pathology in the Royal College of Surgeons, London. He was surgeon extraordinary to Leopold I., King of Belgium (1864) and to Leopold II. (1866); and was knighted in 1867. He was the first medical man in England to bring the subject of cremation before the public, and was president of the Cremation Society of London from its organization in 1874. He wrote many medical works, several of which have been translated into the chief languages of Europe. He is also known as a painter, having exhibited at the Royal Academy, London, and the Salon, Paris. Among his works are "Pathology and Treatment of Stricture of the Urethra" (1886); "Practical Lithotrity and Lithotomy" (1863); "Tumors of the Bladder" (1884); "Calculus Disease" (1888); "Modern Cremation, Its History and Practice" (1889); two novels, "Charley Kingston's Aunt" (1885), and "All But" (1886). He died in London, April 18, 1904.

THOMPSON, HOLLAND, an American educator and editor; born in Randolph co., N. C., 1873 and graduate of the University of North Carolina. He began his career as principal of the high school at Concord, N. C. (1895-9), became a fellow of Columbia in 1899 and was tutor of history there, later instructor (1902-6) and assistant professor (1906). He finally became associate professor at the College of the City of New York. He has been editor-in-chief of "The Book of Knowledge" and editor of "The People and the Trusts" (1912) and "The World War" (1920).

THOMPSON, HUGH MILLER, an American clergyman; born in County Londonderry, Ireland, June 5, 1830; was graduated at the Nashotah Theological Seminary, Wis., in 1852; was ordained in the Protestant Episcopal Church in 1856, and was Professor of Church History at the Nashotah Theological Seminary and editor of the "American Churchman," Chicago, in 1860-1870. He held the rectorship of Christ Church, New York City, in 1871-1875, and that of Trinity, New Orleans, in 1876-1883. He was consecrated Bishop of Mississippi in 1887. Dr. Thompson was the author of "Unity and Its Restoration" (1859); "Sin and

Penalty" (1862); "Kingdom of God" (1872); "The World and the Kingdom" (1888); "The World and the Wrestlers" (1895); "More Copy" (1897). He died at Jackson, Miss., Nov. 17, 1902.

THOMPSON, HUSTON, United States Federal Trade Commissioner; born in Lewisburg, Pa., 1875; graduated from Princeton in 1897, then studied law at the New York Law School. He began his law practice in 1899 in Denver, Colo., became lecturer on law at the University of Denver Law School (1903-6), then assistant attorney-general of Colorado 1907-9). In 1913 he became an assistant attorney-general of the United States. In 1918 he was appointed Commissioner of the Federal Trade Commission to fill an unexpired term and was re-appointed in 1919.

THOMPSON, JAMES WESTFALL, an American university professor; born in Pella, Ia., 1869; graduated from Rutgers College and studied in the Sorbonne in Par's. In 1895 he became assistant professor of history in the University of Chicago, being finally professor of medical history in 1913. He has written a number of works, among which are: "Development of French Monarchy Under Louis VI" (1895); "The Last Pagan" (1916); and a number of contributions to various magazines.

THOMPSON, JOSEPH ADDISON, an American college president; born at Ross Grove, De Kalb co., Ill., 1860, graduated from Monmouth College, 1882, and studied at Princeton Theological Seminary. He was ordained to the ministry in 1886, and became president of Tarkio College, in 1887. He was a member of the 9th General Council of the Alliance of Reformed Churches and a member of the State Executive Committee of the Y. M. C. A. in Missouri since 1908.

THOMPSON, (JAMES) MAURICE, an American author; born in Fairfield, Ind., Sept. 9, 1844. He was a Confederate soldier in the Civil War; afterward State geologist of Indiana, 1885-1889. He wrote nature studies. He published in book form: "Hoosier Mosaics" (1875); "The Witchery of Archery" (1878); "A Tallahassee Girl" (1882); "Songs of Fair Weather" (1883); "At Love's Extremes" (1885); "Byways and Bird Notes" (1885); "Sylvan Secrets" (1887); "A Fortnight of Folly" (1888); "The Story of Louisiana" (1888); "Poems" (1892); "King of Honey Island" (1892); "The Ethics of Literary Art" (1893); "The Ocala Boy" (1895); "Alice of Old Vincennes" (1900). He died Feb. 15. 1901.

THOMPSON, JOHN POLK, an American inventor; born in Glasgow, Scotland, in 1838; came to the United States in 1848, and assumed charge of the Sprague Cotton Mill in Baltic, Conn., in 1864. Subsequently he was president of the Voluntown, Robeson and other cotton mills, and invented 14 distinct mechanical devices, each of which produced a radical improvement in methods of carding, stop and let-off motions, and self-threading shuttles. He died in Olneyville, R. I., Sept. 16, 1899.

THOMPSON, SIR JOHN SPARROW DAVID, a Canadian jurist; born in Halifax, Nova Scotia, Nov. 10, 1844; was called to the bar in 1865; elected to the executive council and to the office of attorney-general of Nova Scotia in 1878; appointed queen's counsellor in 1879 and judge of the Supreme Court in 1882; and in 1895 became minister of justice and attorney-general of Canada. He was a member of the Provincial Assembly of Nova Scotia in 1877-1882; was elected to the Dominion Parliament in 1885, 1887, and 1891; was attached to the British Fishery Commission at Washington, D. C., in 1887; represented Great Britain before the Bering Sea Arbitration Tribunal, in Paris in 1893, and in 1894 was made a member of the Queen's Privy Council. He died in Windsor, England, Dec. 12, 1894.

THOMPSON, LAUNT, an American sculptor; born in Abbeyleix, Ireland, Feb. 8, 1833; went to Albany, N. Y., in 1847, and there entered the office of a professor of anatomy. Later he studied sculpture under Erastus D. Palmer, produced several portrait busts and ideal heads of merit, and in 1850 removed to New York City, where he became an associate of the Academy of Design in 1859; an academician in 1862; and vice-president in 1874. After traveling in Italy for several years he returned to New York and thereafter devoted himself to his art work. His productions include a bust entitled "Elaine"; "Morning Glory," a medallion; statues of Abraham Pierson at New Haven, Conn., and of Winfield Scott, at Washington, D. C.; portrait busts of William C. Bryant in the Metropolitan Museum, New York City, Edwin Booth as Hamlet, S. F. B. Morse, etc. He died in 1894.

THOMPSON, MORTIMER M., pseudonym "Q. K. PHILANDER DOESTICKS, P. B.," an American humorist; born in Riga, N. Y., Sept. 2, 1830. He contributed at first to the daily an1 in later years regularly to the weekly newspapers, and published in book form in 1855-1857: "Doesticks:

What He Says"; "Plu-Ri-Bus-Tah," a travesty of "Hiawatha"; "The Witches of New York"; "Nothing to Say"; "The Elephant Club." He died in New York city, June 25, 1875.

THOMPSON, RICHARD WIGGINSON, an American lawyer; born in Culpeper co., Va., June 9, 1809; removed to Indiana, and was admitted to the bar there in 1834. The same year he was elected to the legislature, serving two terms; was a presidential elector on the Harrison and Tyler ticket; and in 1841 was elected to Congress. In 1843 he began to practice law in Terre Haute, was reelected to Congress in 1847; and during the Civil War had charge of a recruiting post near Terre Haute and was provost marshal of the district. In 1877 he became Secretary of the Navy, but retired in 1881 to become chairman of the American Committee of the Panama Canal Company. His publications include: "The Papacy and the Civil Power"; "The History of the Protective Tariff"; "Footprints of the Jesuits"; "Recollections of Sixteen Presidents, From Washington to Lincoln," etc. He died in Terre Haute, Ind., Feb. 9, 1900.

THOMPSON, ROBERT ELLIS, an American educator; born near Lurgan, Ireland, April 5, 1844; was graduated at the University of Pennsylvania in 1865 and ordained to the Presbyterian ministry in 1874. He was Professor of Latin and Mathematics in the University of Pennsylvania in 1868-1871, of Social Science there in 1871-1881, and of History and English in 1881-1892. He lectured on protective tariff at Harvard University in 1885, at Yale in 1886-1887, and on theology at the Princeton Theological Seminary in 1891. He was editor of the "Pennsylvania Monthly" in 1870-1881, and of the "American Weekly" in 1881-1892; was on the staff of the "Sunday-School Times," and in 1894 was chosen president of the Central High School of Philadelphia. His publications include "Social Science and National Economy"; "Protection to Home Industry"; "History of the Presbyterian Churches of America"; "De Civitate Dei," etc.

THOMPSON, SLASON, an American journalist and playwright, born in Frederickton, N. B., 1849, studied law and was admitted to the bar in 1870. He entered journalism by becoming a member of the staff of the San Francisco Call, in 1876, then, two years later, came to New York and joined the New York Tribune. He was one of the founders of the Chicago Herald in 1881, and has held editorial positions with the Chicago Record and a number of other large dailies. He is the author of a biography of Eugene Field (1902), and has written some plays, among which are "M'liss" (1878) and "Sharps and Flats" 1900).

THOMPSON, VANCE, an American author; born in Cincinnati, O., April 17, 1863; was graduated at Princeton University in 1883; studied at the University of Jena, Germany, and was a dramatic critic in New York City in 1890-1897. He wrote "Berwyn Kennedy"; "The City of Torches"; "A Flash of Honor"; "Writers of Young France"; "Killing the Mandarin"; "The Carnival of Destiny"; "The Night Watchman" (1914) ; "Ego Book"; "Eat and Grown Thin" (1914) ; "Drink and Be Sober" (1911) ; "Woman" (1917).

THOMPSON, WILL L., an American song-writer; born in Beaver co., Pa., Nov. 7, 1847; was educated at the Boston Musical School and the Boston Conservatory of Music in 1870-1875 and later studied in Germany, where he was graduated at the Leipsic Conservatory of Music. His works include "Thompson's Class and Concert"; "Thompson's Popular Anthems"; about 100 popular songs, such as "Gathering Shells on the Sea Shore"; "Drifting with the Tide"; "Come Where the Lilies Bloom"; and contributions to almost every hymnal and gospel song collection published in the United States. His "Softly and Tenderly Jesus is Calling" has had a world-wide publication. He died Sept. 20, 1909.

THOMPSON, WILLIAM BOYCE, an American banker; born in Virginia City, Mont., 1869, and finished his education at the School of Mines of Columbia University. He has been a director of the Federal Reserve Bank of New York since its organization. He was a delegate to the Republican Convention in 1916; and was head of the American Red Cross Mission to Russia for four months during 1917, his reports of Russian conditions at that time attracting general public interest.

THOMPSON, WILLIAM HALE, mayor of Chicago, Ill.; born in Boston, Mass., 1869. In early infancy he was taken to Chicago by his parents, where he received a common school education. For five years he worked on various cattle ranches in Colorado, Wyoming and Montana, and was then manager of a cattle ranch in Nebraska for three years. He then took up the management of his father's real estate interests and, later, of his own. In 1900 he was elected alderman from the Second Ward. In 1915 he was elected Mayor of the city for a term of four years, and again in 1919. Since 1916 he has been a member of the Republican National Committee.

THOMPSON, WILLIAM HEPWORTH, an English classical scholar; born in York, England, March 27, 1810; studied at Trinity College, Cambridge; became Regius Professor of Greek in 1853; and in 1866 succeeded Whewell as master of his college. He projected a great edition of Plato, but accomplished only the "Phædrus" and "Gorgias." He died Oct. 1, 1886.

THOMPSON, WILLIAM OXLEY, an American educator; born in Cambridge, O., Nov. 5, 1855; was graduated at Muskingum College in 1878, and at the Western Theological Seminary in Allegheny City, Pa., in 1882. He was ordained to the Presbyterian ministry in the latter year; held pastorates in Odebolt, Ia., in 1882-1885; and in Longmont, Col., in 1885-1891; was president of Miami University in Oxford, O., in 1891-1899; and on July 13, 1899, was chosen president of the Ohio State University.

THOMPSON, WILLIAM HOWARD, United States Senator; born in Crawfordsville, Ind., 1871. As a small child he went to Kansas with his parents. In 1886 he graduated from the Seneca Normal School, then for two years studied law under his father, being admitted to the bar of Kansas in 1894. In 1906 he was elected judge of the 32d Judicial District. In 1913 he was elected to the United States Senate for the term 1913-1919. In 1916 he was a delegate-at-large to the Democratic National Convention and was there a member of the platform committee.

THOMPSON, WORDSWORTH, an American artist; born in Baltimore, Md., May 26, 1840; began the study of art in Paris in 1861, and in the following year became a pupil of Charles Gleyre. In 1868 he came to the United States; settled in New York City, and in 1873 sent to the National Academy a picture entitled "Desolation," which secured his election as academician in 1875. In 1878 he became a member of the Society of American Artists, sending to the first exhibition a picture entitled "The Road to the Sawmill." He was a constant exhibitor at the National Academy. His pictures are chiefly Oriental and American historical scenes. He died in Summit, N. J., Aug. 28, 1896.

THOMPSON-SETON, ERNEST, an American author and artist; born in South Shields, England, Aug. 14, 1860; lived in the backwoods of Canada in 1866-1870, and on the Western plains in 1882-1887; was educated at the Toronto Collegiate Institute and Royal Academy, London; became official naturalist to the government of Manitoba; studied art in Paris in 1890-1896; was one of the chief illustrators of the "Century Dictionary" and author and illustrator of "Wild Animals I have Known," "The Biography of a Grizzly," "The Trail of the Sandhill Stag," "Wild Animal Play for Children," "Lives of the Hunted," etc., and became a popular lecturer on wild animal life. In December, 1901, his name was legally changed from Seton-Thompson to Thompson-Seton.

THOMS, WILLIAM JOHN, an English author; born in Westminster, England, Nov. 16, 1803. He began life as a clerk in the Chelsea Hospital; later was clerk to the House of Lords, and its deputy-librarian in 1863-1882; was secretary of the Camden Society from 1838 till 1873; founder of "Notes and Queries" (1849), and its editor down to 1872. He gave the name ("Athenæum," August, 1846) to the new subject of study, "folklore." His books include: "A Collection of Early Prose Romances" (3 vols., 1828; enlarged ed. 1858); "Lays and Legends of Various Nations" (4 vols., 1834); "Anecdotes and Traditions Illustrative of Early English History and Literature" (Camden Soc., 1838); "Hannah Lightfoot, Queen Charlotte, and Chevalier D'Eon" (1867); "Human Longevity" (1873); besides a translation of Worsaae's "Primeval Antiquities of Denmark" (1849); and an edition of Stow's "Survey of London" (1875). He died in London, Aug. 15, 1885.

THOMSEN, VILHELM LUDVIG PEDER, a Danish philologist; born in Copenhagen, Denmark, Jan. 25, 1842. His principal works are: "The Magyar Language" (1866); "Influence of the Germanic Languages on the Finno-Lappish" (1870); "Relations between Ancient Russia and Scandinavia" (1879); "Relations between the Finnish and the Baltic Languages" (1890).

THOMSENOLITE (after Dr. Julius Thomsen, of Copenhagen), a mineral resulting from the alteration of cryolite. Crystallization monoclinic, occurring in prisms with horizontal striæ, and also massive resembling chalcedony; hardness, 2.5-4; sp. gr. 2.74-2.76; luster, vitreous, on some faces pearly; color, white; transparent to translucent. Composition: Fluorine 52.2; aluminum, 15.0; calcium, 15.4; sodium, 7.6; water, 9.8=100, which is equivalent to the hitherto accepted formula, $2(CaNa)F+Al_2F_3+2H2O$; but Brandl has shown that the formula should be written $[NaCa]$ $F_2+Al_2F_6+H_2O$.

THOMSON, ARTHUR CONOVER, an American bishop of the Protestant Episcopal Church; born in Fredericksburg, Va., in 1871. He graduated from the Theological Seminary of Virginia in 1893; was ordained deacon in the same year, and priest in 1895. In 1893 he was rector of South Farnham Parish, Rappahannock, Va., then went, in 1895, to the Church of the Resurrection in Cincinnati, Ohio, and finally was rector of Trinity Church, in Portsmouth, Va., from 1899 until 1917. In the latter year he was consecrated suffragan bishop of the diocese of south Virginia, and bishop coadjutor two years later.

THOMSON, SIR CHARLES WYVILLE, a Scotch biologist; born in Bonsyde, Scotland, March 5, 1830; was educated at the University of Edinburgh; and became professor of mineralogy and geology in Queen's College, Belfast, in 1854. In the dredging expeditions of the "Lightning" and "Porcupine" (1868-1869) he took part, afterward publishing in "The Depths of the Sea" (1869) the substance of his discoveries in regard to the fauna of the Atlantic. In 1869 he became fellow of the Royal Society; in 1870 professor of natural history in the University of Edinburgh. In 1872 he was appointed scientific chief of the "Challenger" expedition, which was absent from England over three years, during which time 68,800 miles were surveyed. On his return he was knighted and drew up for the government a report on the natural history specimens collected on the expedition. But he only lived to publish a preliminary account of the expedition. "The Voyage of the 'Challenger'" (1877). He died in Edinburgh, March 10, 1882.

THOMSON, EDWARD WILLIAM, an American author; born in Toronto, Canada, Feb. 12, 1849. He served in the Union army during the Civil War; returned to Canada; became an engineer and then a journalist. He wrote: "Old Man Savarin, and Other Stories"; "Walter Gibbs," a book for boys; "Between Earth and Sky"; also the metrical portions of M. S. Henry's version of "Aucassin and Nicolette."

THOMSON, ELIHU, an American electrician; born in Manchester, England, March 29, 1853; came to the United States; was graduated at the Central High School of Philadelphia in 1870, and taught there as professor of chemistry and mechanics in 1870-1880. In the latter year he resigned to enter the Thomas-Houston and General Electric Companies. Subsequently he secured more than 500 patents for inventions which included the Thomson method of electric welding. He was awarded the Grand Prix, in Paris, in 1899 and 1900, for electrical inventions, received the decoration of Chevalier of the Legion of Honor, for electrical research, etc.; was a trustee of the Peabody Academy of Science in Salem, Mass., a member of the Corporation of the Massachusetts Institute of Technology in Boston, Mass.; and a member of many American and foreign electrical engineering and scientific societies. President International Electrical Congress, St. Louis, 1904. President Electro-technical Commission, succeeding Lord Kelvin in 1909. First winner of the Edwin Gold Medal, etc.

THOMSON, FRANK, an American engineer; born in Chambersburg, Pa., July 5, 1841; spent four years in the Altoona shops of the Pennsylvania railroad, where he became an expert mechanical engineer, and during the Civil War rendered valuable assistance as 2d assistant secretary of war, in the construction of bridges and railroads and the transportation of troops. Appointed superintendent of the eastern division of the Philadelphia and Erie railroad in June, 1864; general manager of the department of motive power of the Pennsylvania railroad in 1873; and a year later (July 1, 1874) became general manager of the Pennsylvania railroad system, E. of Pittsburgh and Erie. On Oct. 1, 1882, he became 2d vice-president; in 1888 1st vice-president, and on Feb. 3, 1897, elected president of the Pennsylvania Railroad Company. He died in Merion, Pa., June 5, 1899.

THOMSON, GEORGE, a Scotch song collector; born in Limekilns, Scotland, March 4, 1757; was educated at Banff; removed to Edinburgh, where he was secretary to the "Board of Trustees for the Encouragement of Arts and Manufactures" (1780-1830). In 1792 he formed the idea of collecting every existing Scotch melody, and of giving to the world "all the fine airs both of the plaintive and lively kind." The result appeared in six volumes of Scotch songs, followed by two of Irish songs, and three of Welsh melodies. A large number of well-known authors were engaged to supply words to the melodies—among them Thomas Campbell, Professor Smyth, Sir Walter Scott, and Joanna Baillie—but the most prolific writer was the poet Burns, who contributed over 120 songs to the collection. Besides the pianoforte accompaniment, according to Thomson's arrangement, each song was to have a prelude and coda, with accompaniments for violin, flute, and violon-

cello. For this portion of the work, Thomson secured the services of Pleyel, Kozeluch, Haydn, Beethoven (who received $2,750 for his share of the work), Mozart, Weber, Hummel, Hogarth, and Bishop. The first volume was published three years after the death of Burns. He died in Leith, Scotland, Feb. 18, 1851.

THOMSON, JAMES, a Scotch poet, born in Ednam, Scotland, Sept. 11, 1700. He was educated at Jedburgh School and Edinburgh University and studied for the ministry. In 1725 he went to London and became a tutor. In 1733 he held a position in the Court of Chancery, and on losing this position was given a pension. In 1744 he was appointed surveyor-general of the Leeward Islands. His most famous poem is "The Seasons" (1726-1730), and next to this "The Castle of Indolence" (1748). He wrote some plays, among them being "Sophonisba" (1730) and "Tancred and Sigismunda" (1745). He died near Richmond, England, Aug. 27, 1748.

THOMSON, JAMES, a Scotch poet and journalist; born in Port Glasgow, Scotland, Nov. 23, 1834. He was brought up in an orphan asylum, and became an army tutor. Most of his life was spent in journalism, and at one time he was special correspondent in Spain for "The World," New York. He suffered much from insomnia, which he made the subject of a powerful poem by that name; and died a victim to the drugs and alcoholic stimulants he used to relieve it. His best-known work is "The City of Dreadful Night" (1870-1874). Others of high quality are: "The Doom of a City" (1857) and "Our Ladies of Death" (1861). He died in London, England, June 3, 1882.

THOMSON, SIR JOSEPH (JOHN), British scientist; born December 18, 1856, near Manchester. He attended Owens College, Manchester, and later Trinity College, Cambridge. Becoming Cavendish Professor of Experimental Physics at Cambridge University, he carried out a series of researches that enlarged the knowledge of the phenomena of electricity. Among the matters that he elucidated were the passage of electricity through gases, the structure of light, and the mass and charge of the electron. He created at Cambridge an extensive and elaborately equipped research laboratory, which became the working place of physical investigators from many parts of the world. His scientific achievements gained him the Nobel Prize for physics in 1906, knighthood in 1908, the Order of Merit in 1912 and a great number of medals and other high scientific honors. In 1918 he became Master of Trinity College, Cambridge. His writings, apart from the numerous and important works summarizing his researches, include treatises, notably "Elements of the Mathematical Theory of Electricity and Magnetism" (1895 and later editions).

THOMSON, JOSEPH, an English explorer; born in Penpont, Scotland, Feb. 2, 1858; was educated at Edinburgh. When 20 years of age he accompanied Keith Johnston to Central Africa, assuming full charge of the expedition on the death of Mr. Johnston. In 1882 he explored the Royuma river in East Africa, and in 1884 made an important journey through Masai Land, in East Equatorial Africa. Among his other achievements are an expedition to the Atlas Mountains and one to the river Niger. He published: "Through Masai Land," "To the Central African Lakes and Back," "Travels in the Atlas and Southern Morocco," "Life of Mungo Park," etc. He died in London, Aug. 2, 1895.

THOMSON, T. KENNARD, an American consulting engineer, born in Buffalo, N. Y., in 1864. He graduated from the University of Toronto in 1886, then began an extensive experience in bridge, railroad, and foundation work. He was retained for the foundation work in the Commercial Cable Building, the Life, United States Express, the Singer, and the Municipal buildings in New York City. He was consulting engineer of the Barge Canal and has designed bridges to be built over the Niagara to commemorate the victory of the World War.

THOMSON, THOMAS, a Scotch chemist; born in Crieff, Scotland, April 12, 1773. He adopted the medical profession, specializing on chemistry. In 1802 he published "System of Chemistry," which obtained rapid success both in Great Britain and on the Continent. It was followed in 1810 by his "Elements of Chemistry," and in 1812 by his "History of the Royal Society." In 1813 he went to London and commenced there a scientific journal, the "Annals of Philosophy." The lectureship (afterward the regius professorship) in chemistry in Glasgow University was conferred on him in 1817. His great work on the atomic theory was published in 1825 under the title of "Attempt to Establish the First Principles of Chemistry by Experiment." In 1830-1831 he published his "History of Chemistry" in two volumes, and in 1836 appeared his "Outlines of Mineralogy." He died in Kilmun, July 2, 1852.

THOMSON, THOMAS, a Scotch antiquary; brother of John Thomson; born in Dailly, Scotland, in 1768. He was called to the Scotch bar in 1793, appointed deputy clerk register in 1806 and principal clerk of session in 1828. He was one of the founders of the "Edinburgh Review" and president of the Bannatyne Club, for which and for the Maitland Club he edited numerous valuable works. He died near Edinburgh, Oct. 2, 1852.

THOMSON, WILLIAM, an English clergyman; born in Whitehaven, England, Feb. 11, 1819; was educated at Shrewsbury School and Queen's College, Oxford, of which he was successively fellow, tutor, and head. In 1858 he was chosen preacher of Lincoln's Inn, and in 1859 was appointed one of her majesty's chaplains in ordinary. Two years later (1861) he was raised to the Episcopal bench as Bishop of Gloucester and Bristol, but before he had held the appointment a year he was transferred to the archbishopric of York. Dr. Thomson was the author of a number of works, including: "An Outline of the Necessary Laws of Thought"; "The Atoning Work of Christ, Viewed in Relation to Some Current Theories"; "Crime and Its Excuses"; "Life in Light of God's Word" (sermons); "Limits of Philosophical Inquiry"; "Design in Nature," and a series of essays entitled "Word, Work, and Will." He died in York, England, Dec. 25, 1890.

THOMSON, SIR WILLIAM (LORD KELVIN), a British scientist; born in Belfast, Ireland, June 26, 1824; was educated at Glasgow University and Cambridge University, and was Professor of Natural Philosophy in the University of Glasgow after 1846. He was electrician for the Atlantic cables of 1857-1858 and 1865-1866, being knighted on the successful completion of the latter; was electrical engineer for the French cable (1869), the Brazilian and River Plata cable (1873), the West Indian cables (1875), and the Mackay-Bennett Atlantic cable (1879). He invented the mirror galvanometer and siphon recorder for submarine telegraphy, and various kinds of apparatus for navigation and deep-sea exploration. His scientific papers have been published under the titles "Reprints of Papers on Electrostatics and Magnetism" (1872); "Mathematical and Physical Papers" (1882-1890); "Popular Lectures and Addresses"; "On Heat"; "On Elasticity." In 1867, in collaboration with Professor Tait of Edinburgh, he issued his first volume of "A Treatise on Natural Philosophy" (2d ed. in 2 parts, 1879). From 1846 to 1853 he was editor of the "Cambridge and Dublin Mathematical Journal," and also connected with the "Philosophical Magazine." He was president of the British Association for the Advancement of Science, and of the Royal Society of London. He was made an officer of the Legion of Honor (1889) and a peer (1892) and received various degrees, decorations, etc., both at home and from foreign countries. In June, 1895, the Glasgow University celebrated the 50th anniversary of his election to the chair of natural philosophy, one feature being a cable dispatch sent around the world and back in four minutes. He died Dec. 17, 1907.

THOMSON, WILLIAM McCLURE, an American clergyman; born in Springfield (now Spring Dale), O., Dec. 31, 1806. In 1833 he went as missionary to Syria and Palestine, remaining till 1876. His chief work, "The Land and the Book" (2 vols. 1859-1860; 3 vols. 1880 1886), is an accepted authority on Palestine and Syria. He has also published: "The Land of Promise"; "Travels in Palestine" (1865). He died in Denver, Col., April 8, 1894.

THOMSONITE (after R. D. Thomson), a member of the group of Zeolites. Crystallization, orthorhombic, occurring as individual crystals, but more often in radiated groups, also compact; hardness, 5-5.5; sp. gr. 2.3-2.4; luster, vitreous to pearly; color when pure, snow-white, brittle; pyro-electric. Composition: Silica, 38.9; alumina, 31.6; lime, 12.9; soda, 4.8; water, 13.8 = 100. Formula, $2SiO_2AL_2O_3$ (¾ CaO + ¼ NaO) 2½ HO. Prof. James D. Dana divides as follows: 1. Ordinary: (1) in regular crystals; (2) in slender prisms, sometimes radiated; (3) radiated fibrous; (4) spherical aggregations of radiated fibers or crystals; (5) massive. 2. Mesole: including scoulerite. 3. Chalilite. Occurs in cavities in old amygdaloidal lavas, and metamorphic rocks.

THONISEN, JEAN JOSEPH (ton'issen), a Belgian jurist; born in Hasselt, Belgium, Jan. 21, 1817. He was Professor of Jurisprudence at the University of Louvain. Among his writings are: "Socialism and Its Promises" (1850); "Socialism in the Past" (1851); "Belgium in the Reign of Leopold I." (4 vols. 1855); "The Pretended Necessity of the Death Penalty" (1864); "The Penal Laws of the Athenian Republic" (1876). He died in Louvain, Belgium, Aug. 17, 1891.

THOR, the son of Odin and Jörd; in northern mythology, the highest of the Æsir after Odin. He is the strongest of all the gods, and defends Asgard and Midgard against the Jotuns. His king-dom is called Thrudvangar; his palace, Bilskirnir, has 540 rooms, and is the largest in the world. He rides in a car driven by two he-goats amid thunder and lightning. His mailed hands grasp the hammer Mjölnir, well known of the Jotuns, for many of their skulls has it crushed. When he girds on his Belt of Strength his power is doubled. His wife is called Sif, and his sons are named Modi and Magni.

THORACIC DUCT, the name applied to the tubular structure in which the absorbent system of vessels may be said to terminate, and into which the lacteals of the intestine ultimately pour their contained fluid. It thus receives (1) the products of digestion or chyle from the lacteal vessels of the intestine, and (2) the lymph or fluid, brought as the elaborated waste-matters of the body from the tissues by the absorbent system of vessels or lymphatics. Being poured into the thoracic duct, these products, which are destined to replenish the blood, and thus renovate the tissues, are in due course poured into the circulation. The thoracic duct of man exists as a tubular structure attaining a length of about 18 or 20 inches. It extends from the second lumbar vertebra to the root of the neck, where it ends in the angle formed by the junction of the left internal jugular and subclavian veins, into which vessels its contents are therefore poured. At its commencement in the abdomen it exhibits a dilatation, termed the receptaculum chyli, which receives the lymphatics of the lower extremities. The thoracic duct has a flexuous course, and exhibits an irregular or contracted appearance. It is provided internally with valves, preventing the backflow of its contained fluid. Occasionally it divides above into two branches; and a right thoracic duct is normally found as a short trunk attaining about an inch in length, and devoted to the reception of the lymph from the right side of the head and neck, from the right side of the chest and heart, and from other regions on that side of the body. In birds, the right thoracic duct may be equally developed with the left.

THORAX, the breast, and specially the bones inclosing it. It is somewhat conical, with convex walls. Its upper opening is contracted, and bounded by the first dorsal vertebra, the first pair of ribs, and the manubrium of the sternum. Its inferior margin slopes downward on each side to the 12th rib; its longitudinal axis is directed upward and somewhat backward; its transverse diameter at the widest part greatly exceeds the distance from the breast to the back. It consists of the dorsal vertebræ, the sternum, the ribs, and the costal cartilages, and contains the lungs, the heart, etc. The muscles of the thorax are: The intercostals, levatores costarum, the sub-costals, triangularis sterni, with which may be included the diaphragm. In comparative anatomy, the part of the trunk above or anterior to the diaphragm. In entomology, the central diversion of the body of insects. It is formed of three consolidated somites or segments; the prothorax, the mesothorax, and the metathorax. Also, a breastplate, cuirass, or corselet.

THORBECKE, HEINRICH (tŏr-bek'e), a German Orientalist; born in Meiningen, Germany, March 14, 1837. He was appointed professor in the University of Halle, 1887. His studies were directed mainly to the poetry of the Bedawin and the history of Arabic. He was author of: "Life of Antarah, the Pre-Islamite Poet" (1868); "Al Ashâ's Song of Praise to Mohammed" (1875); "M. Sabbâg's Grammar of Conversational Arabic in Syria and Egypt" (1886). He died in Mannheim, Germany, Jan. 3, 1890.

THORBURN, GRANT, pseudonym LAWRIE TODD, an American author; born in Dalkeith, Scotland, Feb. 18, 1773; emigrated to America in 1794. As the hero of Galt's novel, "Lawrie Todd," he was a well-known figure in New York, where he followed the business of seedsman. He was noted for his charity. His publications in book form include: "Forty Years' Residence in America" (1834); "Men and Manners in Great Britain" (1834); "Fifty Years' Reminiscences of New York" (1845); "Hints to Merchants," etc. (1847); "Notes on Virginia" (1848); "Life and Writings of Grant Thorburn" (1852-1853). He died in New Haven, Conn., Jan. 21, 1863.

THOREAU, HENRY DAVID (thō'-rō), an American author; born in Concord, Mass., July 12, 1817, and educated at Harvard University, where he graduated in 1837. From that time till 1840 he was a schoolmaster. He engaged also in land surveying, carpentering and other handicrafts, but devoting a great part of his time to study and the contemplation of nature. In 1845 he built for himself a hut in a wood near Walden pond, Concord, Mass., and there for two years lived. After quitting his solitude, Thoreau pursued his father's calling of pencil maker at Concord. Besides contributing to the "Dial" and other periodicals, he published "A Week on the Concord and Merrimac Rivers" (1849), and "Walden, or Life in the Woods" (1854). After his death appeared "Excursions in Field and Forest," "The

HENRY DAVID THOREAU

Maine Woods," "Cape Cod," and "A Yankee in Canada." Thoreau was a friend of Emerson. He died in Concord, May 6, 1862.

THORN, a sharp conical projection constituting the growing point of a branch which has proved abortive. That this is its origin is shown by the fact that sometimes trees, which are thorny in their wild state, have their spines converted into branches when long cultivated in a garden, as is the case with the apple and the pear. A thorn differs from a prickle, which is so superficial that it comes away when the bark is peeled off, while in similar circumstances a thorn, being deep seated, remains. Sometimes thorns bear leaves, as in the whitethorn.

THORN, a strongly fortified town in the province of West Prussia, on the right bank of the Vistula (here spanned by a viaduct 1,100 yards long), 31 miles E. S. E. of Bromberg. Founded by the Teutonic order in 1231, and a member of the Hanseatic League, Thorn contains a town hall and a number of other buildings remarkable for their beautiful gables and interiors; became a Polish town in 1454; and was annexed to Prussia in 1793, and again finally in 1815. It became an important fortified stronghold in the 17th century: was five times besieged between 1629 and 1813; and since 1878 has been made a fortress of the first rank by Prussia, the old fortifications being removed, and a series of detached forts built. Copernicus was a native; and a colossal bronze statute of him was erected in 1853. An active trade in corn and timber is carried on. Pop. about 46,000.

THORN APPLE, *Datura*, a genus of plants of the natural order *Solanaceæ*, having a tubular five-cleft calyx, a large funnel-shaped five-lobed corolla, and an imperfectly four-celled, prickly, or unarmed capsule. The species of this genus are annual herbaceous plants, rarely shrubs or trees; they are in general narcotic, and productive of wild excitement or delirium. The common thornapple, or stramonium (*D. stramonium*), is an annual plant, with smooth stem and leaves, white flowers, and erect prickly capsules, a native of the East Indies, but now often met with in Europe, as also in Asia, the N. of Africa, and North America. It contains a peculiar alkaloid, daturine, which is practically identical in its action with atropine. The leaves and seeds are employed in medicine. A variety with pale violet flowers and purplish violet stem is frequently cultivated in gardens as an ornamental plant.

THORN APPLE

Still more narcotic is the soft-haired thorn apple (*D. metel*), a native of the S. of Asia and of Africa. The Thugs of India employed it in order to stupefy their victims, or, in other cases, to poison them outright. From its seeds, along with opium, hemp, and certain spices, a strong intoxicating substance is prepared, which the Mohammedans of India use in order to produce in themselves a state of exhilaration. The use of it destroys the constitution. *D. tatula*, another Indian species, has similar properties. *D. sanguinea*, the red thorn apple of Peru, is used by the Indians to prepare a very powerful narcotic drink called tonga, which stupefies when very diluted, and when strong brings on ma-

niacal excitement. The beautiful *D. fastuosa* has flowers externally of a violet color, and white within, and is cultivated as an ornamental plant, especially a variety with what are called double flowers, which consist rather of two corollas, one within the other. *D. arborea*, a native of Peru and Colombia, is cultivated in flower gardens in Europe. It has pendulous white flowers, 9 to 12 inches long, which diffuse a sweet smell at night.

THORNBACK, the name of a species of ray (*Raia clavata*), distinguished by the short and strong recurved spines, rising from a broad osseous tubercular base, which are scattered over the back and tail. Two of these broad-based spines occupy the central ridge of the nose.

THORNBURY, GEORGE WALTER, an English author; born in London in 1828. Beginning his literary career in Bristol at the age of 17, he soon after settled in London, where for 30 years he was almost continuously at work writing for "Household Words," "Once a Week," and "Athenæum," etc. Among his numerous works are "Shakespeare's England," "Songs of the Cavaliers and Roundheads," "Haunted London," "Legendary and Historic Ballads," and a "Life of Turner," under the supervision of Ruskin. He died in London, June 11, 1876.

THORNDIKE, EDWARD LEE, an educator; born in Williamsburg, Mass., Aug. 31, 1874; was graduated at Wesleyan University in 1895; pursued postgraduate studies at Harvard and Columbia Universities in 1895-1898; was instructor of genetic psychology at the Teachers' College of Columbia University in 1899-1901, and in the latter year was made adjunct professor. He was the author of "The Human Nature Club" (1900); "Educational Psychology" (1903); "The Origin and Nature of Man" (1913); "The Psychology of Learning" (1914).

THORNE, JOSEPH, an American inventor; born in Marlboro, N. Y., Feb. 17, 1826; was of Quaker parentage; served through the Mexican War; became an engineer and was associated with Elias Howe while he was perfecting his sewing machine. Afterward he was connected with the Singer Company; established and operated a factory in Scotland; invented a typewriter, a sewing machine, a typesetting and distributing machine, etc. He died in Sing Sing, N. Y., May 4, 1897.

THORNHILL, SIR JAMES, an English painter; born in Melcombe, Regis, England, in 1676. He was much engaged in the decoration of palaces and public buildings. Among his best efforts may be mentioned the dome of St. Paul's, the saloon and refectory at Greenwich Hospital, and some rooms at Hampton Court. His forte was in the treatment of allegorical subjects. He was court painter to George I., by whom he was knighted in 1715. He was the teacher of Hogarth, who became his son-in-law. He died near Weymouth, England, May 13, 1734.

THORNTAIL, in ornithology, a popular name for all the species of two genera of humming birds—*Gouldia* (four species) and *Discura* (one). The tail feathers in the first genus are much elongated and sharply pointed, and the tarsi are covered with a tuft of feathers. Discura has a racket at the end of the tail.

THORNTON, MATHEW, an American statesman; born in Ireland about 1714; came to America in 1717; engaged in the expedition against Louisburg as surgeon in the New Hampshire troops; took an active part in the overthrow of the royal government in New Hampshire; was president of the provincial convention of 1775 and speaker of the assembly in 1776; and served as judge of the Superior Court in 1776-1782. He was a delegate to the Continental Congress in 1776; and a signer of the Declaration of Independence; a member of the General Court of Massachusetts; and in 1785 was appointed a member of the General Council. He died in Newburyport, Mass., June 24, 1803.

THORNYCROFT, WILLIAM HAMO, an English sculptor; born in London, March 9, 1850; studied at the Royal Academy schools. "Artemis" (1880) was his first success; others were: "Teucer" (1881); "The Mower" (1884); and the portrait statues of General Gordon in Trafalgar Square (1885); and of John Bright at Rochdale (1892); Queen Victoria in the Royal Exchange; and a bust of Coleridge for Westminster Abbey (1885); a statue of Gladstone, etc. He was made a member of the Royal Academy in 1888. Medal of Honor, Paris, 1900. Died Dec. 19, 1925.

THORNYCROFT, SIR JOHN ISAAC, an English engineer; born in Rome, Italy, Feb. 1, 1843; studied practical engineering; designed the "Ariel," a fast steamboat; drew the plans for the "Miranda," the forerunner of the modern torpedo boat; went through the engineering course at Glasgow University; studied shipbuilding at Govan on the Clyde, and finally settled in Chiswick, England, as a designer and builder of torpedo boats and there constructed several such vessels for the British navy. He also invented a turbine-engine for low-draft vessels.

THOROUGH WAX, THOROW-WAX, or **THROW-WAX,** in botany, the *Bupleurum rotundifolium.* The stem is branched; the leaves ovate, perfoliate; the flowers greenish-yellow, with large bracts; fruit with striate interstices. The name was given by Turner because, as he says, "the stalke waxeth thro the leaves." It was formerly used as a vulnerary. It is a native of Europe and Western Asia; rare in Great Britain.

THOROUGHWORT, in botany, the *Eupatorium perfoliatum.* The stem is round, erect, and hairy; the leaves subsessile, opposite, wrinkled, pale underneath and hairy; the 12 to 15 florets tubular. It grows in bogs in North America. The whole plant is intensely bitter. A decoction of the leaves has been given as a febrifuge. In larger quantities it is emetic, sudorific, and aperient. Called also boneset and crosswort.

THORP, the Scandinavian equivalent of the German *dorf,* "a village," in local nomenclature sometimes stands by itself, *e. g.,* Le Torp, in Normandy; but oftener appears as a suffix, as in English Althorpe, Wilstrop, and Norwegian Clitourps. Being Danish rather than Norwegian, this suffix often helps us to determine whence Scandinavian settlers arrived in England; and while it is very common in East Anglia, it occurs very seldom in Westmorland, but once in Cumberland, and never in Lancashire.

THORPE, BENJAMIN, an English scholar; born about 1782. Among his numerous publications are an English edition of "Rask's Anglo-Saxon Grammar," "Ancient Laws and Institutes of the Anglo-Saxon Kings," "The Gospels in Anglo-Saxon," an edition of "Beowulf," "The Anglo-Saxon Chronicle," "Northern Mythology," etc. He died in London, July 19, 1870.

THORPE, FRANCIS NEWTON, an American author; born in Swampscott, Mass., April 16, 1857; was educated at Syracuse University and at the Law School of the University of Pennsylvania; was admitted to the bar; fellow professor of constitutional history at the latter institution in 1885-1898. He was the author of "The Government of the People of the United States" (1889); "Franklin and the University of Pennsylvania"

(1893); "The Story of the Constitution" (1891); "The Government of the State of Pennsylvania" (1894); "The Constitution of the United States with Bibliography" (1894); "A Constitutional History of the American People, 1776-1850" (1898); "A History of the United States for Junior Classes" (1901); "The Civil War" (1906); "History; the Career of Man on Earth" (1909); "The House and Household" (1910); "An American Fruit Farm" (1915); "Essentials of American Constitutional Law" (1917).

THORPE, ROSE HARTWICK, an American author; born in Mishawaka, Ind., July 18, 1850; received a high school education. She became widely known because of her poem "Curfew Must Not Ring Tonight." Her other publications include "Fred's Dark Days" (1881); "Nina Bruce" (1886); "The Chester Girls" (1887); "The Year's Best Days" (1889); "Temperance Poems" (1887); "Sweet Song Stories" (1898); etc.

THORWALDSEN, ALBERT BARTHOLOMEW (BERTEL) (tor'valdsĕn), a Danish sculptor; born in Copenhagen, Denmark, Nov. 19, 1770. At first he helped his father to cut figure heads in the royal dockyard, then, after some years' study at the Academy of Arts,

THORWALDSEN

he won the privilege of studying three years abroad. Going to Rome (1797) he studied the works of Canova the sculptor, and Carstens the painter. In 1803, he received a commission from Sir Thomas Hope to execute in marble a statue of Jason. Commissions flowed in and his unsurpassed abilities as a sculptor became everywhere recognized. In 1819 he returned to Denmark, and his journey through Germany and his reception at Copenhagen resembled a triumph. After a year in Copenhagen he returned to Rome, visiting on his way Berlin, Dres-

den, Warsaw, and Vienna. He remained at Rome till 1838, when he undertook another journey to Copenhagen, purposing to establish there a museum of his works and art treasures. His return was a sort of national festival. The remainder of his life was spent chiefly in the Danish capital. Thorwaldsen was eminently successful in his subjects chosen from Greek mythology, such as his Mars, Mercury, Venus, etc. His religious works, among which are a colossal group of Christ and the Twelve Apostles, St. John Preaching in the Wilderness, and statues of the four great prophets, display grandeur of conception. Chief among his other works are his statues of Galileo and Copernicus, and the colossal lion near Lucerne, in memory of the Swiss guards who fell in defense of the Tuileries. He died in Copenhagen, March 24, 1844. The Thorwaldsen Museum, opened in 1846, contains about 300 of the works of the sculptor.

THOTH, or TAUT, an Egyptian deity identified by the Greeks with Hermes (Mercury), to whom was attributed the invention of letters, arts, and sciences. The name is equivalent in significance to the Greek Logos, and Thoth is a mythical personification of the divine intelligence.

THOTHMES III. (Tehuti-mes), an Egyptian king of the 18th dynasty; lived about 1600 B. C. and reigned for 54 years. He was famous for his conquests and carved upon the temple walls of Karnak the names of 625 vanquished cities and nations.

THOU, JACQUES AUGUSTE DE (tö), a French statesman and historian; born in Paris, Oct. 8, 1553. Henry IV. employed him in several important negotiations, and in 1593 made him his principal librarian. In 1595 he succeeded his uncle as chief-justice, and during the regency of Mary de Medici he was one of the directors-general of finance. His greatest literary labor was the composition in Latin of a voluminous "History of his own Times" (Historian sui Temporis), comprising the events from 1545 to 1607, of which the first part was made public in 1604. To this work, which is remarkable for its impartiality, he subjoined interesting "Memoirs" of his own life. He died May 7, 1617.

THOUGHT TRANSFERENCE. See TELEPATHY.

THOUS, in zo-ology, according to Hamilton Smith, a section of *Cadidœ,* having the form of wolves on a small scale; not more than 18 inches high; structure very light; tail rather short,

                                        See **Timber**, p. 398

ON THE WAY TO THE SAWMILL: THE DYNAMITING OF A LOG JAM
IN THE COURSE OF A RIVER DRIVE

See Thrace, p. opposite

TEMPORARY CITY NEAR DEDEAGATCH, WESTERN THRACE, OF GREEKS DEPORTED FROM TURKISH THRACE

forming a scanty brush, tip black; fur close, hard; livery mostly chequered, or penciled with black and white, extremities buff; they are not gregarious and do not burrow. From Africa and Southwestern Asia. Some of the species are now classed with *Canis* and others with *Vulpes.*

THOUSAND ISLANDS, a group of small islands numbering about 1,800 in the St. Lawrence, immediately below Lake Ontario. They belong partly to Canada and partly to the State of New York, and have become a popular summer resort.

THRACE, the ancient name of the Turkish province of Rumeli. It is said to have been peopled by a tribe of Pelasgians. The authentic history of the country commences with the formation of the Greek settlements in the 6th century B. C. Of these, the principal were Byzantium (675 B. C.), Selymbria, Abdera (560 B. C.), Mesembria, Dicæa, Maronea, Ænus, Cardia, Sestus, Amphipolis, etc.; but their want of union enabled the Thracian chiefs of the interior to preserve their independence. In 513 B. C., Darius, King of Persia, marched through Thrace on his way to punish the European Scythians, and on his return, left Megabazus, with 80,000 men, to subdue the country. In this he partially succeeded, but new disturbances and complications arose between the Persians and Greeks, which resulted (480 B. C.) in the famous expedition of Xerxes. The rise of the Macedonian kingdom, under Philip II. (359 B. C.), destroyed the independence of a great part of Thrace. Under the Government of Lysimachus, Thracia was incorporated with Macedonia, and became complete. On the fall of the Macedonian kingdom (168 B. C.), it passed into the hands of the Romans, and subsequently shared the vicissitudes of the Roman empire. In 305, it was overrun by Alaric, and in 447, by Attila. In 1353, Amurath obtained possession of all its fortresses, except Constantinople. By the treaty of Neuilly in 1919 Bulgaria agreed to give Thrace to Greece, which ceded Eastern Thrace to Turkey in 1922.

THRACIA, in zo-ology, a genus of *Anatinidœ.* Shell oblong, nearly equivalve, slightly compressed, attenuated and gaping behind; cartilage processes thick; pallial sinus shallow. Animal with the mantle closed; foot linguiform; siphon rather long, with fringed orifices. They live in water from 4 to 120 fathoms deep. Recent species 17, from the United States, Greenland, Great Britain, Norway, the Mediterranean, the Canaries, China, etc.; fossil 36, from the Lower Oölite, if not the Trias, onward.

THRASYBULUS, an Athenian general, who in the time of the Thirty Tyrants, took refuge at Thebes. Having gained some followers, he marched against the usurpers and expelled them. In commemoration of this triumph, a yearly festival was instituted at Athens. Thrasybulus wisely procured the passing of a general amnesty, which decreed that no one but the principals should be punished. He subsequently displayed great valor in Thrace, and slew the Lacedæmonian general with his own hand. Trasybulus fell in a battle with the Aspendians, who were the allies of Sparta, 394 B. C.

THREAD, a compound cord consisting of two or more single yarns, doubled and twisted. In the trade it is divided into lace, stocking, and sewing thread. Any fibrous substance, such as cotton or flax, when it is to be woven, is first spun into yarn, which is sometimes called thread. Sewing thread, however, always consists of at least two or more yarns twisted together. In the spinning of yarn the process is the same whether it is to be woven into cloth or twisted into thread. Beginning with the spun yarn, the stages in the process of manufacturing a six-cord cotton thread (a very common kind) are: (1) The yarn is doubled and wound on bobbins; (2) the double yarn is then twisted into a two-ply thread; (3) the thread is next rewound on bobbins for the second twist; (4) the thread is twisted a second time on the twisting frame, three two-ply threads being thus formed into a six-cord thread; (5) the thread is rewound on large bobbins, from which it is reeled into hanks for bleaching or dyeing; (6) the bleached or dyed thread is next rewound on bobbins for spooling; (7) spooling—*i. e.,* winding the thread on small bobbins called spools or pirns for use. The spindles of the spooling machine run at a speed of 7,000 revolutions per minute.

Paisley is, however, the principal seat of the manufacture in Great Britain. The making of thread on an industrial scale was begun in that town in 1722 by Christian Shaw of Bargarran. She had obtained information from Holland about the process of making linen thread, and what she and her friends manufactured was sold at the time under the name of "Balgarran thread." The industry did not become of great importance so long as flax was the material used. But in the early part of the 19th century, when the spinning machines of Hargreaves, Arkwright, and others came largely into use, the manufacture of cotton thread was begun in Paisley, and its progress has been on the whole rapid. This has been especially the case since 1860 through the constantly increasing use of sewing machines for both domestic and factory purposes. The mills of Messrs. J. & P. Coats, Limited, are spread over 40 acres of ground, and give employment to fully 5,000 persons; and this firm has also established works at Pawtucket, R. I., and at Petrograd. Next in importance are the works of the Messrs. Clark. In the United States thread is made in several States. The Clarks have large thread mills in Newark and Harrison, N. J.

Linen thread is made at Johnstone, near Paisley, Belfast, Nottingham, and other places. Although a much less quantity of it is manufactured, it is perhaps used for a greater variety of purposes than cotton thread. Silk thread, the stronger kinds of which are called twist, is now used to a very large extent for sewing dyed articles of dress.

Cotton was first used in the manufacture of sewing thread at Pawtucket, R. I., by Samuel Salter in 1794.

THREAD CELLS, the name given to certain. peculiar cells or cysts, found chiefly in the tissues of *Cœlenterate* animals. They contain fluid, and are provided with an internal thread-like filament. Under pressure the cell ruptures, the thread is everted, and the fluid escapes. These cells form a poison apparatus for paralyzing prey.

THREAD WORMS, the name for thread-like intestinal worms of the order *Nematoda.* The *Oxyuris vernicularis* occurs in great numbers in the rectum of children particularly.

THREATENING, menacing, especially with ulterior designs. By the common law of England to threaten bodily hurt is a civil injury against the person, and pecuniary damages can be recovered for interruption of a man's business through fear of such threats. Any person accusing or threatening to accuse any other person of infamous or other crimes, with the view to extort gain, is guilty of felony. Similar provisions are made against sending or delivering any letter threatening any house, ship, etc., or to wound or maim cattle; sending or delivering any threatening letter demanding any property or valuable. Any person who maliciously sends or delivers, knowing the contents, any letter threatening to kill or murder any person, or to burn or destroy any coal breaker, house, barn, or other building, or any rick or stack of grain or other agricultural produce, in most States is considered guilty

of a misdemeanor, and on conviction is liable to fine and imprisonment. The English statutes on this subject have been adopted in the United States generally.

THREE-HORN CHAMELEON, the *Chamœleon oweni* from Fernando Po. The male has a long horn over each eye, and another at the end of the muzzle, whence the popular name.

THREE HOURS' AGONY, or THREE HOURS' SERVICE, a devotion practised on Good Friday, from noon till three o'clock, in commemoration of the Passion. It was introduced by Father Messia, S. J., of Lima, about 1730, and reached Rome in 1738. It was introduced into the English Church about 1865, and was rendered legal by the Act of Uniformity Amendment Act (1872), which permits additional services, consisting of any prayers from the Liturgy or Bible, with address or sermon, and hymns. The service consists, in all cases, of hymns, collects, or litanies, and addresses, generally on "the seven words from the cross," though this last feature is sometimes varied by meditations on other details of the Passion. The editor of the "Dictionary of Religion" notes that the name of the devotion may possibly occasion a mistake as to the length of our Lord's sufferings. (Mark xv: 25, 34.)

THREE KINGS, the name given in the Roman Church to the Magi, who came from the East to adore the Infant Jesus (Matt. ii: 1-12). They are probably called kings from Psalm lxxii: 10, which verse is used as an antiphon in the office for Epiphany. According to tradition, their names were Gaspar, Melchoir, and Balthazar, and on their return to the East they received baptism. The Empress Helena is said to have brought their bones to Constantinople, whence they were removed to Milan, and afterward to Cologne. The Chapel of the Three Kings, built by the Emperor Maximilian (1459-1519), in Cologne Cathedral, is supposed to contain their relics.

THREE RIVERS, a city of Michigan, in St. Joseph co. It is on the Michigan Central and the New York Central railroads, and is at the junction of the St. Joseph, Portage, and Rocky rivers. Its industries include the manufacture of cars, railroad supplies, marine engines, leather, knit goods, paper, brass goods, and machine-shop products. It has a public library. Pop. (1910) 5,072; (1920) 5,209.

THREE RIVERS, a city and port of entry in St. Maurice co., Quebec, Canada;

at the confluence of the St. Maurice and St. Lawrence rivers, and on the Canadian Pacific railroad; 95 miles N. E. of Montreal. Here are a bishop's residence, a cathedral, college, convents, and many handsome residences. The city has an extensive trade in lumber, and manufactures boots, shoes, stoves, car-wheels, and ironware. Three Rivers was founded by Laviolette under orders from Champlain in 1634. A battle which proved disastrous to the Americans was fought here on June 16, 1776. Pop. about 10,000.

THRESHER SHARK, also called the Fox Shark, a genus of sharks containing but one known species, *Alopias vulpes*, with a short conical snout, and less formidable jaws than the white shark. The upper lobe of the tail fin is very elongated, being nearly equal in length to the rest of the body, and is used as a weapon to strike with. Tail included, the thresher attains a length of 13 feet. It inhabits the Atlantic and the Mediterranean, and is sometimes met with on the coasts of Great Britain.

THRESHING MACHINE. See Tools and Machinery.

THRIFT, in botany, the genus *Armeria*, called also seapink, specifically *Armeria vulgaris* or *maritima* (*Statice Armeria*, Linn.): leaves densely fascicled, linear, usually one-nerved, pubescent or ciliate, with impressed points both above and below; inflorescence a scape, bearing a head of rose-colored, pink, or white flowers, surrounded by a brown membranous, three-leaved involucre, and intermixed with scales. It is found on seacoasts and on mountains, and is well adapted for edging in gardens.

THRINAX, in botany, the thatch palm, a genus of *Sabalidæ*. Calyx six-cleft, corolla none; stamens 6, 9, or 12, united at the base; ovary one-celled, with a single, erect ovule; fruit round. *T. argentea* is the silver thatch palm, the leaves of which are used in Jamaica for thatch. In Panama it is made into brooms.

THRINCIA, in botany, a genus of *Scorzonereæ*, now reduced to a sub-genus of *Leontodon*. The pappus of the outer flowers consists of toothed scales, that of the inner is formed of feathery hairs. The buds are drooping. Common in all temperate regions, and popularly known as dandelion and lion's tooth. It has lanceolate, almost sinuo-dentate, leaves, somewhat hispid, and single flower scapes of yellow flowers. It grows in gravelly pastures, flowering in July and August.

I—27

THRING, EDWARD, an English educator; born in Alford Rectory, Somersetshire, Nov. 29, 1821; was educated at Eton and King's College, Cambridge, of which he was elected fellow. He took orders, and served in curacies at Gloucester and elsewhere, but in September, 1853, found the work of his life in the appointment to be head master of Uppingham school. He found it insignificant, but made it one of the healthiest and best equipped among the public schools of England. He finally limited the number of boys to 330, 30 to each boarding house, and he gave himself for 34 years with restless energy to the task of educating these in the highest sense of the word. No man ever estimated more highly the worth of life: no schoolmaster since Arnold was more successful in imprinting on the characters of his pupils a high ideal of duty as the great end of life. The manly fiber of his own nature, his earnestness and honesty, his firm discipline, and his stern denunciation of cowardice and wrong gave a distinctive character to the school. His publications include volumes of school songs and lyrics, an English grammar, a Latin gradual and a construing book: "Thoughts on Life Science," anonymously (1869); "The Theory and Practice of Teaching" (1883); "Uppingham Sermons" (2 vols. 1886); "Addresses" (1887); "Poems and Translations" (1887); and "Uppingham School Songs and Borth Lyrics" (1887). He died Oct. 22, 1887.

THRIPS, a genus of minute insects, order *Hemiptera*, sub-order *Homoptera*, closely allied to the *Aphides*. They are extremely agile and seem to leap rather than fly. They live on flowers, plants, and under the bark of trees. *T. cerealium* is a common species, scarcely a line in length or in extent of wing, residing in the spathes and husks of cereals, especially wheat, to which it is most injurious.

THROAT, the anterior part of the neck of an animal, in which are the œsophagus and windpipe, or the passages for the food and breath.

THROAT, DISEASES OF THE. The diseases of the throat met with in the practice of medicine do not differ materially from the diseases of other parts of the body The most frequent form of sore throat is that of a simple erythematous inflammation. The mucous membrane of the pharynx, palate, and tonsils is congested and swollen, and the sub-mucous connective tissue may be greatly relaxed. The treatment of this form of sore throat is very simple. The patient should be confined to bed in order to secure rest and an equable temperature. A gentle but efficient laxative should be given, and if the pain is severe and the pulse accelerated, a small quantity of morphia and aconite may be added to the aperient. The diet should be light and easily digestible, and the free use of demulcent drinks may be encouraged. The inhalation of steam will be of service in the acute stage, and if the membrane be very much relaxed, astringent solutions of alum, nitrate of silver, carbolic acid, or chlorate of potash, may be topically applied in the form of a spray. In phlegmonous sore throat there is a higher grade of inflammatory action, the disease being designated amygdalitis, quinsy, or tonsilitis. Ulcerated sore throat is often described under the name of angina maligna, or tonsilitis maligna, and is usually attended with typhoid symptoms. It is occasionally attendant on diphtheria, and sometimes follows scarlatina, measles, smallpox, dysentery, and enteric fever. The pain is not so severe as in ordinary sore throat, but soon after the commencement of the affection the tonsils and the surrounding structures are seen to be studded with dark ash-colored ulcers. The disease is apt to extend to the upper part of the pharynx and to the nasal passages, but the larynx is seldom involved. In severe cases death may occur from syncope, coma, or from gradual exhaustion of the vital forces. Membranous sore throat is characterized by the exudation of a fibrinous material, which coagulates into a false membrane. This form of sore throat is often met with during the prevalence of diphtheria and is by many physicians considered a mild form of that disease.

THROATWORT, in botany: **(1)** *Campanula trachelium*, the nettle-leaved bellflower; a tall, hispid plant, with an angled stem, ovate-lanceolate leaves, and bluish-purple flowers; found in England, the European continent, etc. (2) *C. cervicaria*, which has light-blue flowers, and is a native of Germany. (3) *Digitalis purpurea*.

THROMBOLITE, an amorphous mineral of uncertain composition, occurring with malachite on a fine-grained limeston at Rezbanya, Hungary; hardness, 3.4; sp. gr., 3.38-3.67; luster, vitreous; color, shades of green; opaque. Composition stated to be a hydrated phosphate of copper, but the result of the latest analysis by Schrauf points to its analogy with stetefeldite, partzite, etc.

THROMBOSIS, in pathology, local formation of clot, called a thrombus,

either in the heart or a blood-vessel during life. When it occurs in the systemic veins it is called *Phlegmasia dolens*.

THROMBUS, in pathology, a tumor formed by blood effused from a vein and coagulated in the adjacent tissue; the coagulum or clot, usually fibrinous in texture, which partially or totally closes a vessel in a thrombosis.

THROOP, a borough of Pennsylvania, in Lackawanna co. It is on the New York, Ontario and Western and the Delaware, Lackawanna and Western railroads. It adjoins Scranton. Its chief industries are coal mining and the manufacture of silk. Pop. (1910) 5,133; (1920) 6,672.

THRONE, the chair used on occasions of state by a king, emperor, or Pope. It is usually raised, and often surmounted with a canopy. The term is also applied to the seat of a bishop in his cathedral church, and is a common metaphor to express sovereign power.

THRONE OF JAMSHEED, THE, Persepolis, so named by its Persian founders. Jamsheed removed the seat of government from Balkh thither.

THRUSH, in ornithology, the name for any of the *Turdidœ*. They are universally distributed except in New Zealand, and are very highly organized birds, and it is for this reason, perhaps, as well as on account of their omnivorous diet, that they have been able to establish themselves on a number of remote islands. They differ widely in their

THRUSH

habits and in their habitat; some are gregarious, others live solitarily or in pairs. The wood thrush (*Turdus mustelinus*) is abundant in North America in summer, as far N. as Hudson Bay, retiring to tropical and sub-tropical regions in winter. It is rather smaller than the song thrush, and very similar to it. Several other species are found in North America. The type genus *Turdus* has several European species, but to only three of these is the name thrush applied. The song thrush, throstle, or mavis (*Turdus musicus*), the missel thrush (*T. viscivorus*), and white thrush (*T. varius*). The song thrush, common, is not quite nine inches long; back and upper surface brown of slightly different shades, chin white, abdomen and tail coverts grayish-white; throat, breast, and flanks, together with the sides of the neck, yellow, thickly spotted with dark-brown. It is one of the best-known European song birds, and in captivity is easily taught simple airs. It is found all over Europe, but leaves some of the N. parts in winter, being thus practically a bird of passage. It feeds on insects, worms, slugs, snails, and in the summer greedily devours cherries and smaller fruit. It usually builds a cup-shaped nest in a thick bush or shrub, and lines the interior with mud, clay, or dung. The eggs are four to six in number, bright bluish-green, with brownish spots. They usually produce two broods in the season.

THRUSH, sometimes called INFANTILE SORE MOUTH, or DIPHTHERIA OF THE MOUTH, essentially a disease of early infancy. It is very frequently met with in connection with the artificial feeding of young children, and is evidently connected with impaired nutrition. It may also be the result of inflammation of the mucous membrane of the mouth, or it may depend on the development of cryptogamic vegetation on the mucous membrane. The symptoms are numerous small white spots on the mucous membrane of the mouth, the inner surface of the lips, and especially near the angles of the mouth, the inside of the cheeks, the tongue, and sometimes on the gums. The spots are generally of a circular form, about the size of a pin's head, and are firmly adherent. Sometimes the spots coalesce, and the mouth may be extensively coated with a false membrane, a condition sometimes called aphtha.

THRUSH, in veterinary surgery, an affection of the horse's frog, appearing as a severe and acute inflammation, which usually proceeds to ulceration, and which is accompanied by a fetid discharge. The best application for it is mineral tar. Calomel dressing is to be substituted for the tar in severe and intractable cases, and ulcerated and loose parts of the frog are to be carefully removed.

THUCYDIDES, historian of the Peloponnesian War; born in the deme Halimus most probably in 471 B. C.; was the son of Olorus and Hegesipyle, and was related to Miltiades and Cimon. An Athenian of good family, he must have known Sophocles, Euripides, Aristophanes, Phidias, Protagoras, Gorgias, and possibly Herodotus and Æschylus. He was further possessed, either by inheritance or by acquisition through marriage, of gold mines in that part of Thrace lying opposite the island of Thasos. We know from himself that he was one of the sufferers from the terrible plague of Athens, and also one of the few who recovered. He held military command, and he had under him an Athenian squadron of seven ships at Thasos, 424 B. C., when he failed to relieve Amphipolis, which fell into the hands of Brasidas. Condemned to death as a traitor, he took refuge in exile and retired to his Thracian estates. His exile enabled him to associate with Peloponnesians quite as much as with the Athenians; and he probably spent some time also in Sicily. According to his own account, he lived in exile 20 years, and probably returned to Athens after the destruction of its walls, in 404. How or when he died is unknown.

But he did not live long enough to revise Book VIII. or to bring his history down to the end of the war.

If Herodotus was "the father of history," Thucydides was the first of critical historians, and no better account of his methods can be given than is contained in his own words: "Of the events of the war I have not ventured to speak from any chance information, nor according to any notion of my own; I have described nothing but what I either saw myself or learned from others, of whom I made the most careful and particular inquiry. The task was a laborious one, because eye witnesses of the same occurrences gave different accounts of them, as they remembered or were interested in the actions of one side or the other." There is hardly a literary production of which posterity has entertained a more uniformly favorable estimate than the history of Thucydides. This high distinction he owes to his undeviating fidelity and impartiality as a narrator; to the masterly concentration of his work, in which he is content to give in a few simple yet vivid expressions the facts which it must have often taken him weeks or even months to collect, sift, and decide upon; to the sagacity of his political and moral observations, in which he shows the keenest insight into the springs of human action and the mental nature of man; and to the unrivaled descriptive power exemplified in his account of the plague of Athens, and of the Athenian expedition to Sicily. Often, indeed, does the modern student of Greek history share the wish of Grote, that the great writer had been a little more communicative on collateral topics, and that some of his sentences had been expanded into paragraphs, and some of his paragraphs into chapters. But this want cannot have been felt by the contemporaries of Thucydides, while the fate of other ancient historians warns us that had his work, like theirs, been looser in texture, or less severely perfect, it would not have survived, as it has done, the wearing influence of time, or remained, in its own language, the *ktema es aei*—the "possession for ever"—and it has proved to the world.

THUCYDIDES

It has been reserved for the 19th century to impeach the credibility, depreciate the matter, and to condemn the style of Thucydides. As these indictments, however, usually conclude with the statement that Thucydides remains nevertheless the greatest of historians, they might here be passed over in silence were it not in the first place that they serve to show that Thucydides' fame is proof against the solvents of modern criticism, and next that they help us to a more complete understanding of the qualities which have given to Thucydides' work such a wonderful hold over the intellects and imaginations of all his readers and critics. The attacks on Thucydides' credibility have proceeded from Germany, but have met with little acceptance there, and have found only one English-speaking follower, Professor Mahaffy. The most serious outcome of the discussion seems to be that Thucydides' knowledge of the topography of the Platæa was defective, and that his account of the siege is consequently in accordance with the situation rather as he conceived it than as it actually was. But, even if we accept this application of the methods of modern criticism, it must not be imagined that those methods have all the same tendency. On the contrary, the actual treaty which Thucydides quotes in v. 47 has been discovered of late years, and confirms the accuracy and truth of the historian in a most unexpected and startling manner. The exact amount of accuracy or inaccuracy in Thucydides' account of the siege of Platæa is matter of opinion; his accuracy in the matter of the treaty is not—it is beyond dispute. But, after all, it is not by tests such as these, welcome as they are, that we can form all adequate opinion on the credibility of Thucydides.

As an Athenian comedian remarks, we do not believe a man because he takes an oath—we trust the oath because we believe in the man. And so we believe in Thucydides, not because we have external tests to apply (for we have not enough), but because the universal experience of all who read him is a feeling of conviction that his intention was to speak the truth, so far as he could ascertain it. This conviction is ultimately due to the fact that in the man's work we are brought directly into touch with the man, and we judge his character as we judge that of any acquaintance whom we know in the flesh.

No man can devote himself for 27 years to composing a work without putting a good deal of himself into the work, or without writing his character down in it—unconsciously, but none the less legibly. What, then, are the qualities of character which impress the reader of Thucydides? In the first place, his impartiality. This is a quality unknown to Latin historians for instance. Tacitus will not admit that the Romans were ever defeated—the result was, at most, indecisive—even though the subsequent movements of the troops, as described by himself, clearly show that the Romans lost. Thucydides, on the other hand, though an Athenian, never extenuates even the mistakes of the Athenians; and though himself banished by them, sets down naught in malice against them. Next, the reader feels that Thucydides strove—and that always—to ascertain facts, and to put down as facts nothing but facts. This conviction is forced on one in many ways, some of which are palpable enough to admit of being clearly indicated.

To begin with, there is the fact that, when in search of a subject, Thucydides did not, like all other historians before him, choose a period of ancient history, which, being ancient, must be based on vague hearsay or dim tradition. He preferred contemporary history and events which he himself witnessed in part, while he could obtain the evidence of eye witnesses for the remainder. Nor did he wait till the conclusion of the war before setting about his task; from the very beginning he began collecting his facts. Next, his history is not designed to prove or illustrate any theory. He himself, in the passage quoted above, disclaims all attempt to adapt facts "to any notion of his own"; and it is evident that beginning to write, as he began, at the commencement of the war, when its course and its issue were yet in the future, he could not have designed to bring its history into conformity with any preconceived or *a priori* theory.

Herodotus, writing the history of the past, was in a position to trace the finger of destiny in what had happened, and to explain history by means of final causes. But Thucydides, when he undertook to record the present, thereby deliberately elected to confine himself to efficient causes. This preference for efficient causes and for "scientific" history, in the best sense of the term, is intimately connected with the "positive" nature of his history—that is to say, with his perpetual endeavor to record facts and to distinguish them from inferences drawn from facts. A clear consciousness of this difference is involved in one of the most characteristic features of his history—that is, the marked difference between his narrative and the speeches which he introduced into it. The former contains facts, and facts only, facts stated with a precision and objectivity which— *e. g.*, in his description of the symptoms of fever in sufferers from the great plague—have been the marvel of all subsequent generations, and the greatest marvel to those who by special professional knowledge are competent to judge. The speeches, on the other hand, are not what the speakers actually said—but of this Thucydides warns the reader at the beginning, showing clearly at once the ddistinction he drew between facts and inference, and his anxiety that the reader should realize the distinction. In fine, most of the untruth in this world is due not to deliberate perversion, but to the simple fact that so many people are quite unconscious what truth is. When, then, we find that Thucydides had a conception of historic truth and fact such as 2,000 subsequent years have been unable to improve, and that he strove strenuously all his life to live up to that conception and write up to it, we can well understand that even 19th-century criticism acknowledges itself incapable of shaking his credibility.

As for the subject of Thucydides' history, if the Peloponnesian War was not a matter of importance in universal history, it was at least not Thucydides' fault that he was not a contemporary with some more important war. But we may beg leave to doubt whether the Peloponnesian War was of inferior interest for the fortunes of mankind. Had it not been for the exhaustion it induced, Greece would not have succumbed to the Macedonian, and consequently Alexander's conquests would never have spread Greek culture over the ancient world. But, apart from this, Thucydides' history is the history of the effects of empire on an imperial state; and, as such, will always be of enthralling interest to citizens of sovereign communities. Finally, Thucydides' style, criticized by Dionysius and condemned by Mure, is (in the speeches) difficult beyond all possibility of dispute. To throw the blame of this obscurity on the unformed condition of Attic Greek at the time when Thucydides wrote is warrantable indeed, but is no adequate defense. To point, on the other hand, to the tract "On the Athenian Polity" as proof that Attic prose could be translucent in Thucydides' time is beside the point, for Attic, as is well known, could only be written well by those who lived continuously in Athens, and Thucydides was exiled for many a year. But, in truth, the question whether it is Thucydides or the literary age in which he lived that is to be blamed for his obscurity is a wholly irrelevant question. Obscurity, whatever be its cause, is a crime in a writer. But it is a crime which carries its own punishment, for it diminishes the number of an author's readers. The exact amount of criminality is not to be determined on any abstract principles or by the exercise of any mysterious "taste"; it admits of one simple practical test—viz., has the obscurity of his style (in so far as it exists), as a matter of fact, prevented him from attaining fame? In the case of Thucydides it has had no such effect, as all testify. People will not read a difficult author if there is an easier one out of whom they can get as much. That Thucydides has, in spite of his difficulty, always been read is in itself sufficient testimony that there is no other historian to rank with him.

THUG, or THAG, the name given in the N. provinces of India to a member of a fraternity who looked on murder as the sole means of staying the wrath of the goddess Kali, and derived their principal means of support from the plunder of their victims. In old times, according to Hindu mythology, Kali made war on a race of giants, from every drop of whose blood sprang a demon. These demons multiplied, and at last the goddess created two men to whom she gave handkerchiefs, with which they strangled their infernal beings. When the men had finished their task the goddess gave them the privilege of using the handkerchief against their fellows, and so the class of Thugs is said to have arisen. Though worshipping a Hindu goddess, the majority of the Thugs were Mohammedans. They usually traveled in gangs, the members of which had ostensibly some honest calling in their own community, and in selecting their victims always endeavored to pitch on persons of property in order that while propitiating the goddess they might enrich her worshipers. Various steps were taken to suppress the Thugs, both by the native and the English governments, and in 1829 Lord William Bentinck adopted such stringent measures that in six years (1830-1835) 2,000 of them were arrested; and of these, 1,500 were convicted and sentenced to death, transportation, or imprisonment, according to the gravity of the charges proved against them. In 1836 a law was passed making the fact of belonging to a gang of Thugs punishable by imprisonment for life with hard labor, and though some gangs continued to operate sporadically for many years, the system is now powerless.

THULSTRUP, THURE DE, an American artist and illustrator; born in Sweden in 1848. He graduated from the National Military Academy in Stockholm, and was for a while minister of war in the Swedish Cabinet. He later served as an officer in the French army in Algeria, then studied art in Paris. Later he went to Canada as topographical engineer. Coming to New York, he began his career as illustrator, and for many years was a regular contributor to the "New York Graphic," "Leslie's Weekly," "Harper's Weekly," and a number of other similar publications.

THUMB FLINT, in anthropology, a popular name for a short form of scrapers, the long varieties of which are sometimes known as "finger flints." Evans thinks that these names, "though colloquially convenient, are not sufficiently definite to be worthy of being retained."

THUMB-SCREW, a former instrument of torture for compressing the thumbs. It was employed in various countries, Scotland in particular; called also thumbikins or thumbkins.

THUN, LAKE OF, a body of water 11 miles long and 2 miles wide, in the canton of Berne, Switzerland. It lies about 1,800 feet above sea-level, in a beautiful region annually visited by great numbers of tourists. On its E. shore is the town of Interlaken, and on its W., Thun, the latter being the starting point of tourists to the Bernese Oberland. There are steamers on the lake and the two towns are joined by a railroad.

THUNBERGIA (named after Carl Petter Thunberg, 1743-1828), a Swedish traveler, botanist, and professor of natural history at Upsal, in botany a genus of *Gardenidœ,* sometimes made a synonym of *Gardenia.* Involucre two-leaved; calyx about 12-toothed; corolla campanulate; capsule beaked, two-celled. Handsome and fragrant climbers, cultivated in gardens for the beauty of their flowers. *T. fragrans* has cordate, acuminate leaves; *T. grandiflora* angular, cordate leaves, larger flowers with no inner calyx, and the anthers bearded and spurred. Both are natives of the East Indies.

THUNDER, the violent report which follows a flash of lightning. It commences the same moment as the flash; but, as the sound travels only at the rate of about 1,100 feet a second, while light does so at the rate of 190,000 miles, the flash of the lightning is the first to be perceived, and thus a means is afforded of calculating the distance of the lightning. The noise of the thunder arises from the disturbance produced in the air by the electric discharge, but why the sound should be so prolonged has been differently explained. The old hypothesis was that the sound was echoed from every precipice, from every building, and from every cloud in the sky. Another is that the lightning itself is a series of discharges, each producing a particular sound according to the distance at which it commences, and the varying densities of the portions of air which it traverses before reaching the ear. A third conjecture is that the noise arises from the zig-zag movement of the electric fluid, the air at each salient angle being at its maximum compression.

THUNDER BIRD, an imaginary bird occurring in the mythology of races of low culture, and personifying thunder or its cause. Among the Caribs, Brazilians, Harvey Islanders, and Karens, Bechuanas, and Basutos, there are legends of a flapping or flashing thunder bird, which seem to translate into myth the thought of thunder and lightning descending from the upper regions of the air, the home of the eagle and the vulture.

THUNDERBOLT, in heraldry, the thunderbolt is represented as a twisted bar in pale, inflamed at each end, surmounting two jagged darts in saltire, between two wings expanded, with streams of fire issuing from the center.

THUNDER FISH, a species of fish of the family *Siluridæ*, found in the Nile, which, like the torpedo, can give an electric shock. It is the *Malapterurus electricus* of the naturalists.

THUNDERING LEGION, a Roman legion containing some Christians, which (A. D. 174) fought under Marcus Antoninus against the Marcomanni. The Roman army was shut up in a defile and ready to perish with thirst, when a thunderstorm with heavy rain relieved them of their distress, and so terrified the enemy that a complete victory was gained. The Christians attributed the deliverance to the prayer. The heathen also considered the interposition supernatural, but ascribed it to Jupiter, Mercury, or to magic. Also a legion composed of Christian soldiers raised in the Thebaïs, and led by St. Maurice. The name existed long before it was applied to either of these two legions.

THURGAU, a canton N. E. of Switzerland; bounded mainly by the Lake of Constance and the cantons of Zürich and St. Gall; area, 381 square miles; capital, Frauenfeld. It differs much in physical conformation from most other Swiss cantons, in having no high mountains, though the surface is sufficiently diversified. The whole canton belongs to the basin of the Rhine, to which its waters are conveyed chiefly by the Thur and its affluents, and partly also by the Lake of Constance, including the Untersee. The principal crops are grain and potatoes; large quantities of fruit are also grown. In many places the vine is successfully cultivated. The manufactures consist chiefly of cottons, hosiery, ribbons, lace, etc. Pop. about 135,000.

THURIBLE, in ecclesiastical usage, a censer, a vessel for burning incense. Their present form, according to Martigny, dates only from the 12th century. The modern thurible consists of a metallic vessel or cup, sometimes of gold or silver, but more commonly of brass or lateen, in which burning charcoal is placed, with a movable perforated cover. Chains are attached, so that the thurible may be waved to and fro.

THURIFER, in ecclesiastical usage, the attendant at high mass, solemn vespers, and benediction, who uses the thurible, either by simply waving it to and fro or for incensing the clergy, choir, and congregation, and at certain times pre-sents it to the officiating priest that he may incense the altar or the Host.

THÜRINGERWALD (tü′rĭng - er - valt), or Forest of Thuringia, a mountain chain in the center of Germany, stretching S. E. to N. W. for about 60 miles. Its culminating points are the Beerberg and the Schneekopf, which have each a height of about 3,220 feet. The mountains are well covered with wood, chiefly pine. The minerals include iron, copper, lead, nickel, cobalt, etc.

THURINGIA (German, Thüringen), the name still borne by that part of the ancient Saxon area which is generally bounded by the Werra, the Saale, and the Harz mountains; the Thuringian states being the minor Saxon duchies, the two Schwarzburgs, the two Reuss principalities, and small parts of Prussia, Saxony, and Bavaria. The district got its name from the Thuringian tribe of Germans, who were found inhabiting it in the 5th century. The Thuringian forest is a series of wooded mountain ridges occupying a great part of this area. It is about 70 miles long, and belongs to the Sudetic system.

THURINGITE, a hydrated silicate of alumina, and the protoxide and peroxide of iron, which occurs in the form of an aggregation of minute olive-green scales in Thuringia.

THURLOW, EDWARD, LORD, an English jurist; born in Bracon-Ash, Norfolk, England, in 1732. He was called to the bar in 1754, made king's counsel in 1761, and won great reputation by his speech in the Douglas case. In 1768 he entered Parliament. In 1771 he became solicitor-general and zealously supported the policy of the government toward the American colonies. In 1778 he was made lord-chancellor, being raised to the peerage as Baron Thurlow. Pitt suspected Thurlow of intriguing with the Prince of Wales, and from this time an open disagreement took place between them. Pitt demanded his dismissal, to which the king at once agreed, and he was deprived of the great seal, June, 1792. He died in Brighton, England, Sept. 12, 1806.

THURMAN, ALLEN, GRANBERY, an American jurist; born in Lynchburg, Va., Nov. 13, 1913; was admitted to the bar in 1835; elected as a Democrat to Congress in 1844; chosen judge of the Supreme Court of Ohio in 1851; and was elected United States senator in 1869 and 1874. While in Congress he drafted and secured the adoption of the "Thurman Act"; supported the "Bland-Allison Act";

took part in framing the bill providing for the Electoral Commission; and was a member of the commission and a warm defender of its constitutional authority. He served also on the International Monetary Commission in Paris in 1881; was an unsuccessful candidate for the nomination for the vice-presidency in 1876, 1880, and 1884; and in 1888 when again presented for that office was nominated by acclamation, but not elected. He died in Columbus, O., Dec. 12, 1895.

THURN AND TAXIS, PRINCES OF, formerly a princely house with high rank, hereditary dignities, and vast possessions in Austria, Bavaria, Württemberg, Prussia, and Belgium, the heads of the two main lines being resident at Ratisbon and at Laucin in Bohemia. Descended from the Della Torre of Milan (whence the first part of their name), with a castle of Tasso or De Tassis (whence the second), members of this house have been distinguished in connection with posts. One established posts in Tyrol in 1460; another, ennobled in 1512, established the first post between Vienna and Brussels in 1576. His descendant became in 1595 grand-master of the posts of the Holy Roman empire, and secured the right of carrying on the posts of the empire which extended from Hamburg to Rome, and from Paris to Vienna, for himself and his heirs as a hereditary privilege. In 1681 the principality of Thurn and Taxis in the Netherlands was conferred on the head of the house; and in 1698 the princely rank and title were made hereditary, and passed to all members of the house. The postal privileges were gradually limited by the governments of the various countries; but it was not till 1867 that Prussia secured by treaty with the family the abolition of the monopoly.

THURSDAY, the fifth day of the week. The word was originally Thor's day, i. e., the day of Thor, the god of thunder. The Romans similarly called the day *dies Jovis*=the day of Jove or Jupiter, the god corresponding to the Scandinavian Thor.

THURSDAY ISLAND, a small island of Queensland, Australia, in Normanby Sound, Torres Straits. It is a government station, and the harbor—Port Kennedy—is one of the finest in this quarter. It is in the direct track of all vessels reaching Australia by Torres Straits; is the center of a large and important pearl and trepang fishery; and is a depot of trade with New Guinea.

THURSTON, E. TEMPLE, an English novelist; born in 1879. He published two books of poems in 1895, and wrote "The Apple of Eden" in 1897, ultimately published in re-written form in 1905. He had a first four-act play, "Red and White Earth," produced in 1902, and dramatized "John Chilcote, M. P.," by his first wife, K. C. Thurston, in 1905. His works include: "Traffic"; "The Evolution of Katherine"; "The Realist"; "Sally Bishop"; "Mirage"; "The City of Beautiful Nonsense"; "The Greatest Wish in the World"; "The Patchwork Papers"; "Tars"; "Driven"; "The Cost."

THURSTON, KATHERINE CECIL, a British novelist; born in Cork, Ireland, in 1864. In 1901 she was married to E. Temple Thurston, an English novelist, from whom she is separated. Her first book was "The Circle," published in 1903, but her name was established mainly by her second novel, "John Chilcote, M. P.," which achieved great popularity, and was republished in the United States under the name of "The Masquerader." Her other works include: "The Gambler"; "Mystics"; "The Fly on the Wheel"; and "Max."

THURSTON, JOHN MELLEN, an American lawyer; born in Montpelier, Vt., Aug. 21, 1847; was admitted to the bar in 1869; was a delegate to the National Republican Conventions in 1884, 1888, 1892, and 1896; was United States senator from Nebraska in 1895-1901, and in 1897 rose to special prominence because of his speeches in the Senate advocating prompt intervention on behalf of Cuba. He was also a United States commissioner at the St. Louis Exposition in 1901. He died in 1916.

THURSTON, ROBERT HENRY, an American educator; born in Providence, R. I., Oct. 25, 1839; was graduated at Brown University in 1859; worked in his father's shops in 1859-1861; was an assistant engineer in the navy in 1861-1865; assistant professor of natural philosophy at the United States Naval Academy in 1865-1871; professor of mechanical engineering at Stevens Institute of Technology in 1875-1885; and in 1885 was made director of Sibley College at Cornell University. He was also president of the American Society of Mechanical Engineers; vice-president of the American Institute of Mining Engineers, and of the American Association for the Advancement of Science; United States commissioner to the Vienna Exposition in 1873; a member of numerous United States and State commissions; and the inventor of several testing machines, engine governors and other devices. His publications include "Friction and Lubrication," "Materials of Engineering," "History of the Steam Engine," "Manual of the Steam Boiler," about 300 monographs. He died Oct. 25, 1903.

THWAITES, REUBEN GOLD, an American historian; born in Dorchester, Mass., May 15, 1853. After a high-school training he pursued by self-instruction a collegiate course and took the postgraduate studies at Yale University in 1874-1875; was managing editor of the "Wisconsin State Journal," Madison, in 1876-1886. In the latter year he became secretary of the State Historical Society of Wisconsin. His publications include "Historic Waterways" (1888); "The Story of Wisconsin" (1890); "The Colonies, 1492-1750" (1891); "Stories of the Badger State" (1900). He also edited "The Wisconsin Historical Collections" (Vols. IX.-XV., 1888-1900); "Chronicles of Border Warfare" (1895); "History of the University of Wisconsin" (1900); and "The Jesuit Relations" (73 vols., 1896-1901); "School History of the United States" (1912), etc. He died in 1913.

THWING, CHARLES FRANKLIN, an American educator; born in New Sharon, Me., Nov. 9, 1853; was graduated at Harvard University in 1876, and at Andover Theological Seminary in 1879; president (1890) of Western Reserve University. He is the author of "American Colleges: Their Students and Work"; "Within College Walls"; "The College Woman"; "The American College in American Life"; "College Administration"; "God in His World"; "Letters From a Father to His Son on Entering College" (1912); "Letters From a Father to His Daughter on Entering College" (1913), etc.

THWING, EDWARD WAITE, an American missionary; born in Boston in 1868. He graduated from the Princeton Theological Seminary in 1892. He was immediately ordained a Presbyterian minister and sent as a missionary to China. In 1895 he became professor of theology and natural philosophy in the Christian College at Canton. In 1901 he was appointed superintendent of Chinese missionary work in Hawaii; in 1909 Chinese secretary of the International Reform Bureau. He acted as legislative agent for the bureau at the World Conference of Nations on Opium, held in Shanghai in 1909.

THYESTES. See ATREUS.

THYMUS GLAND, a reddish-brown body found in higher animals; in man, next the wind pipe and extending to the base of the heart. It contains microscopic groups of white blood cells and interspersed whorls of dark cells (Hamall's corpuscles). Normally the thymus atrophies at puberty. Its absence in many child idiots has been reported. Its persistence in adult years is associated with the condition known as status lymphaticus, involving physical and psychological abnormalities. The thymus is supposed to have for its function the regulation of physical processes of childhood.

THYROID BODY, or **GLAND,** in anatomy, a soft, reddish, and highly vascular organ, consisting of two lateral lobes united by their lower ends by a transverse portion called the isthmus. It forms a rounded projection upon the trachea and larynx. It is one of the vascular glands, or glands without ducts. It has an important relation with the functions of the brain. The removal of the gland causes loss of mental vigor. Goiter is a disease of this gland, and in extreme cases extirpation is resorted to.

THYROID CARTILAGES, in anatomy, two flat lateral plates, continuous in front, forming a narrow V-like angle. In the male it is called Adam's apple.

THYROPTERA, in zoölogy, a genus of *Vespertilionidæ*, forming a separate group of that family. Muzzle elongated, slender; crown cone considerably elevated above the forehead; nasal apertures circular; ears funnel shaped; bases of the thumbs and soles of the feet with highly specialized organs in the shape of hollow suctorial disks. There is but one species, *T. tricolor*, from Brazil.

THYRSACANTHUS, in botany, a genus of *Gendarusseæ;* tropical American shrubs or herbs, leaves large, and a long raceme of fascicled or cymose flowers.

THYRSITES, in ichthyology, a genus of *Trichiuridæ*, with several species from tropical and sub-tropical seas. Body rather elongate, for the most part naked; first dorsal continuous, the spines are of moderate length, and extend on to the second; from two to six finlets behind the dorsal and anal; several strong teeth in jaws, and teeth on palatine bones. The species attains a length of from four to five feet, and is esteemed as food.

THYRSUS, in classical antiquities, one of the most common attributes or emblems of Bacchus and his followers. It consisted often of a spear or staff wrapped with ivy and vine branches or of a lance having the iron part thrust into a pine cone. In botany, a kind of inflorescence consisting of a panicle, the principal diameter of which is in the middle between the base and the apex; a compact panicle, the lower branches of which are shorter than those in the middle; example, the lilac.

TIARA, the head covering of the ancient Persians; the crown of the ancient Persian kings. These alone had the privilege of wearing the tiara erect; the nobility and priests wore it depressed or turned down on the fore side. Its form is described variously by different authors, so that it must have varied at different periods. According to Xenophon it was encompassed with the diadem, at least on ceremonial occasions. Also the triple crown worn by the Pope on certain occasions as a sign of his temporal power, of which it is a badge, as the keys are of his spiritual jurisdiction. Nicholas I. (858-867) is said to have been the first to unite the princely crown with the miter, though the Bollandists think this was done before his time. The common statement that Boniface VIII. (about 1300) added the second is incorrect, for Hefele shows that Innocent III. is represented wearing the second crown, in a painting older than the time of Boniface. Urban V. (1362-1370) is supposed to have added the third crown. In its present form the tiara consists of a high cap of cloth of gold, encircled by three coronets, and surmounted by a mound and cross of gold; on each side is a pendant, embroidered and fringed at the end, and powdered with crosses of gold. The tiara is placed on the Pope's head at his coronation by the second cardinal deacon in the loggia of St. Peter's, with the words: "Receive the tiara adorned with three crowns, and know that thou art father of princes and kings, ruler of the world and vicar of our Saviour, Jesus Christ. Also a crown, a diadem.

TIBBALLS, WILLIAM HUNTINGTON, an American educator; born in Union, N. J., Dec. 22, 1848; was graduated at Oberlin College in 1875; had charge of city schools in Ohio, Michigan and Wisconsin for many years; Professor of Philosophy and Literature in Parks College for six years; held the same chair at Salt Lake College for three years; and was president of the Utah State Christian Endeavor Union in 1897-1898. He conducted extensive mining operations, and contributed to literary and educational magazines.

TIBER (Italian, Tevere; Latin, Tiberis), the chief river of central Italy, and the most famous in the peninsula. It rises in a dell of the Tuscan Apennines (province Arezzo), about 11 miles N. of the village of Pieve Santo Stefano. Its course till it reaches Perugia is S. S. E.; thence, as far as Rome, it pursues, along an irregular zigzag line, a S. direction; but when it enters the plain of the Campagna it curves S. S. W., and enters the Mediterranean by two branches, which inclose the Isola Sacra, or Sacred Isle. Of these the N., the Fiumicino, alone is navigable; the Fiumara is silted up with sand. The entire course of the river is about 260 miles—only 145 direct from source to sea. The most celebrated towns on or near its banks are Perugia, Orvieto, Rome, and Ostia; and its chief affluents are the Nera and the Velino and Teverone or Aniene (Anio) from the left, and the Paglia with the Chiana from the right. In its upper course it is rapid and turbid, and of difficult navigation. It is navigable for boats of 50 tons to the confluence of the Nera, 100 miles from its mouth, and small steamers ascend to within 7 miles of that point. The Tiber is supplied mainly by turbid mountain torrents, whence its liability to sudden overflowing of its banks; even the oldest Roman myth, that of Romulus, being inseparably associated with an inundation. Its waters, too, are still discolored with yellow mud, as when Vergil described it.

TIBERIAS. See GALILEE.

TIBERIUS, CLAUDIUS NERO CÆSAR, a Roman emperor; born Nov. 16, 42 B. C.; was the son of Tiberius Claudius Nero and Livia Drusilla, who became the wife of Octavianus Cæsar in 38 B. C. Tiberius and his brother Drusus were brought up in the household of their stepfather, who from the year 27 B. C. was the Emperor Augustus. They were early initiated into public affairs, and in 16-15 B. C., at the head of a Roman army, subdued the Rhæti and Vindelici. Tiberius now returned to Rome to celebrate his first triumph, and in 13 B. C. was appointed consul together with P. Quintilius Varus. Meanwhile, Drusus carried on the war in Germany with great success, but died in 9 B. C., in consequence of a fall from his horse. Tiberius hastened to Germany, and, after having carried his brother's body to Rome, returned and prosecuted the war with great vigor. In 7 B. C., having led his army across the Rhine into the country already half conquered by Drusus, he returned to Rome, becoming consul for the second time, and celebrating his triumph in the same year. In 12 B. C. he had been compelled by Augustus to divorce his wife, Vipsania Agrippina, and become the third husband of his infamous daughter Julia; but, disgusted by her profligacy, and by Augustus having appointed as his successors Caius and Lucius Cæsar, her two sons by her second husband, Marcus Vispanius Agrippa, he voluntarily retired to Rhodes in 6 B. C., where he passed seven years in seclusion.

He returned to Rome A. D. 2, in which year Lucius Cæsar died in Massilia, on his way to Spain, while his brother Caius died a year and a half later in the East from a wound which he had received in the Parthian war. Tiberius was accordingly adopted by Augustus as his successor in A. D. 4. In the same year he led an army into Germany, marched to the Elbe, and defeated the Sigambri, Bructeri, and Cherusci. The suppression of a revolt in Pannonia and Dalmatia procured for him the honor of a third triumph. He was now sent once more against the Germans, who, under their great chief Arminius, had cut off Quintilius Varus, with three legions. Accompanied by the young Germanicus, he crossed the Rhine, and during the years A. D. 11 and 12 traversed the countries E. of that river. On the death of Augustus, in 14, Tiberius became emperor. He was much respected for the dignity of his demeanor and reputed virtue. For some years he affected to take no active part in public affairs, while he gradually destroyed the last remnants of the ancient republic, abolishing the "comitia," and transferring the election of public officers to the subservient senate. After the death of Germanicus in 19, not without suspicion of poisoning, Tiberius was much plotted against, which caused him to become gloomy and depressed in mind.

In his 67th year he retired to the Island of Capreæ to enjoy seclusion, leaving to Ælius Sejanus, commander of the Prætorian guards, the direction of public affairs, and a long and uniform series of cruelties followed. Awakened at last to the ambitious schemes of his favorite, Tiberius ordered the senate to condemn Sejanus, and the latter, with his family and friends, was put to death in 31. Some time after this, Tiberius took up his residence at Misenum, where, as at Capreæ, he plunged himself into the most disgusting debauchery. On March 16, A. D. 37, he fell into a lethargy, and being believed to be dead, Caligula was proclaimed emperor. Tiberius, however, recovered, but he was suffocated in his bed by Macro, to save himself and the young emperor. The elaborate picture of the emperor given in the first six books of the "Annals of Tacitus" can hardly be considered a fair representation of his character. That Tiberius was a brave and skillful soldier and a careful financier cannot be doubted; while, however, unpopular at Rome, he was regarded by the provincials as a wise and beneficent ruler. Perhaps a taint of the insanity which was characteristic of the Claudian house, and a vein of superstition and fatalism, go far to explain the disgraceful acts of his later years.

TIBERIUS CONSTANTINE, called TIBERIUS II., one of the most virtuous emperors of Constantinople, was a native of Thrace, and was brought up at the court of Justinian. He succeeded to the throne in 578, and having suppressed the conspiracy of Sophia, widow of his predecessor, reigned unchallenged till his death in 582.

TIBET, a dependency of the Chinese Empire, in central Asia, between China and India; area about 463,200 square miles; pop. about 2,000,000. The native name is Bod of Bodyul. Tibet is enclosed by the Kuenlun and the Himalaya Mountains. These claims run E. from a mountain knot at the S. extremity of the Pamir highland, and continue to diverge from each other till they reach the meridian of Lhassa, when they draw slightly nearer to the E. and S. E., where Tibet is bounded by ranges which separate it from China and Indo-China.

Topography.—Tibet is the loftiest region of such extent on the globe. Its table-lands vary in height from 17,000 to 10,000 feet. It has been estimated that their average height is that of the summit of Mont Blanc. The table-lands are loftiest in the W. and N., whence they slope gradually to the S. and E. Bonvalot certified to the existence of volcanoes. The lowest lands in Tibet are the grooves in which the Indus runs W. and the Sanpo E. to the bends where they turn to the S., cross the Himalayas, and descend into India. The mountain girdle which surrounds Tibet has made it an obstacle across which conquerors from Mongolia could not enter India without making a long detour. Another consequence of these barriers has been that Tibet has remained to the present day the region of the globe least known to geographers.

Provinces.—Tibet is divided into provinces equal in extent to European states. There are (1) Chaidam (Tsaidam), a name sometimes given to the country between the Nanling and Altentagh chains and the Kuenlun. It includes the Koko-Nur lake and the Chaidan marsh, and its cold and scanty pastures are frequented by nomads, among whom is the Tibetan race known as the Tanguts. (2) Katchi, also described as the great N. plain, a lofty region of steppes very little known, but crossed by a road from Kiria, in Turkestan, and leading to the gold fields of Thok-Jalung, one of the highest inhabited spots on the globe. (3) East Nari, including Khorsum and Dokthol, an elevated Himalyan country in which the Indus and Sanpo take their rise. It is a country of pastures with a few cultivated tracts. In it is the Lake Manasarowar, surface 15,000 feet high, a sheet of water sacred alike to Tibetans and Hindus (4) West Nari, or Little Tibet, consisting of Ladakh and Balti, now dependencies of Kashmir (Indian empire). (5) Yu-tsang, composed of the provinces of Yu and Tsang. It includes the valley of the Sanpo, or Brahmaputra, between the meridians of 87° and 92°, the most populous part of Tibet. The Sanpo becomes navigable at Janglache—elevation 13,600 feet. Yu-tsang is traversed by a well-frequented road from E. to W. The capital of Yu is Lhassa; that of Tsang, Shigatze. (6) Kham, the province drained by the upper courses of the great rivers of China and Indo-China, which run in deep valleys, making it difficult to cross the country. Two great roads traverse Kham, connecting Lhassa with Darchiendo (Ta-chien-lu), emporium of Chinese trade with Tibet.

Climate and Agriculture.—Tibet lies in the latitudes of Delhi, Cairo, Algiers, and Naples, but its inland position and elevation give it a cold, dry, and extreme climate. On the tablelands, at an elevation of 14,000 feet, the thermometer in May sinks to 7° F. below zero, and over the whole country an arctic winter prevails for five or six months. Owing to the dryness of the air, it loses its conductivity, and the inhabitants, dressed in sheepskins, give out long electric sparks on approaching conducting substances. Flesh exposed to the air does not putrefy, but dries and can be reduced to powder. There is a very short but excessively hot summer, more especially in the valleys of the Indus and Sanpo, where the high temperature is more oppressive to Europeans than that of the Indian plains. The N. and W. tablelands are without trees. They abound in steppes, in which pasture herds of wild animals — yaks, horses, asses, goats, antelopes, etc. The pastures of the S.

POTALA PALACE AT LHASSA, TIBET

The shortest and official road passes through Litang (13,400 feet) and Batang (8,150 feet) on the Yangtze river, and Chiamdo, the capital of Kham, on the Mekhong, and over lofty passes into Lhassa. The commercial road crosses the rivers higher up, where the water courses are less difficult and there is an abundance of pasture. Near Darchiendo the country seems to be independent alike of China and Tibet, and farther W. is Darge, a district described as rich and flourishing. Chiamdo and other parts of Kham are under the direct rule of China.

tablelands supply food to the flocks and herds of a large nomad population. Agriculture is confined chiefly to the valleys of the Indus and Sanpo, the grain chiefly grown being barley; the kitchen herbs and fruits of Europe are also cultivated. Irrigation and terrace cultivation are necessary to secure even scanty crops.

Minerals.—The mineral products of Tibet are of high value, and include gold, silver, iron, copper, zinc, mercury, cobalt, borax, salt, sulphur, etc., but few mines are yet developed.

Industries and Commerce.—The Tibetans are good blacksmiths and cutlers; their chief industrial occupation, however, is the preparation of woolen cloth. They are active traders, and large caravans, in which yaks and sheep are the beasts of burden, are constantly traversing the country on their way to the great fairs in Tibet and the entrepôts of the surrounding countries. Lhassa is the chief mart, and here are found silk, carpets, tea, and hardware from China; leather goods and live stock from Mongolia; rice, tobacco, sugar, pearls, coral, etc., from the S. At one time there was a busy commerce with India, but since Tibet became a Chinese dependency the passes have been closed. In 1894 Yatung, on the frontier of India, was opened by treaty as a trade mart, and the Chinese and Indian Governments each stationed an official at that post. The most important commerce is in the hands of rich Tibetan and Chinese traders, who jealously watch anything likely to interfere with the existing great routes. Of the distribution of population in Tibet little is known. The most densely peopled part of the country is certainly the basin of the Sanpo, in which are the towns of Shigatze and Lhassa.

Ethnology, etc.—The Tibetans are a Mongolic race, much more closely allied to the Burmese than to the Chinese or Mongols proper. They are broad-shouldered and muscular, and have Mongol features, but not in an exaggerated form. They are said to be intelligent, but without initiative. The Tibetans by race people nearly the whole of Tibet. A few nomads, Mongols and Turkish tribes, have penetrated into the N. steppes, and Chinese in large numbers have colonized the S. E. In Tibet polyandry is practiced, the husbands of one wife being generally brothers. This form of marriage is almost universal among the poor. The rich are polygamists. Both systems check population. In Little Tibet, where monogamy has penetrated from the W., population increases rapidly.

Religion and Literature.—There exist in Tibet two religions: (1) The Bon or Bon-Pacreed, which is a development of Mongol Shamanism, and is the native religion; and (2) Lamaism, a form of the Buddhism introduced from India. The Tibetan clergy are very numerous, there being, it is estimated, one monk for every family. The Tibetan language as spoken differs much from the old written language; it has been losing its monosyllabic character. Books abound in Tibet, and every monastery has its library. The literature consists chiefly of translations from the Sanskrit and of religious works.

The art of engraving by wooden blocks has for centuries been used by the Tibetans.

Government.—Since 1720 Tibet has been a dependency of China, which, however, interferes only with foreign and military affairs. There are two imperial Chinese residents or Ambans at Lhassa. Civil and religious government are left to the Tibetan clergy. In theory, supreme rule is in the hands of the Dalai Lama, the sovereign pontiff, who resides at Lhassa. The Tesho, or Bogdo Lama, who has an inferior spiritual power, resides at Shigatze. The Dalai Lama hands over the active duties of government to the de-sri, or king, who rules with the assistance of four ministers.

History.—The earliest date in Tibetan history which can be relied on as historical is A.D. 639, when the King Sbrongtsan-Sgam-po introduced Buddhism from India and founded Lhassa. His dominions extended from the Himalayas, N. to the Koko-Nur lake. In the Middle Ages, down to the 10th century, the Tibetan country is said in the Chinese annals to have extended to the Gulf of Bengal, then described as the Tibetan sea. In the 9th century a war broke out with China, which terminated in 821, when bilingual tablets still existing were erected at Lhassa. In 1071 eastern Tibet was broken up into small states, opening the country to Chinese and Mongol invasion. Kublai Khan, who annexed Tibet to his vast empire, called to his court a Tibetan monk, Phagspa. The latter converted his patron and the Mongols to Buddhism, and the sovereignty of Tibet was conferred on the Dalai Lamas. In 1720 the Chinese, after many struggles, finally conquered Tibet. Seven years later Batang and other parts of Kham were detached from Tibet and incorporated with the Chinese province of Szechuen. Early in the 18th century Lamas, under the guidance and instruction of Jesuit missionaries, carried out a survey of the Tibetan part of the Chinese empire. From the information supplied, D'Anville in 1733 prepared a map of Tibet. In 1840 Ladakh was conquered by the Maharajah of Kashmir, and now is a British dependency. In 1854 there was a struggle between Tibet and Nepal, which ended in a treaty by which both countries recognized the suzerainty of China.

Eleven years later, in consequence of the refusal of the Tibetan authorities to allow Europeans to enter their country, a system was organized by Major Montgomerie of the Indian Government, in the interest of science, by which pundits or educated Indians were sent as explorers into Tibet. By this means the old maps were corrected and much valuable geographical knowledge was obtained. Prejevalski and other Russian explorers have done for northern Tibet what the pundits have done for the south. Among other explorers and travelers may be mentioned Marco Polo, who made Tibet known to Europe in the 13th century; Bogle and Turner sent out by Warren Hastings in the 18th century; and in the 19th, Manning, Captain Strachey, the Jesuits Huc and Gabet, Bower, the brothers Schlagintweit, Miss Taylor, Dr. Sven Hedin and A. H. Savage Landor.

Sikkim, a frontier State through which passes an important route from India into Tibet, became a British dependency in 1850. In 1888 it was attacked by a Tibetan force, and, as the Chinese government declined and probably was unable to interfere, the invaders were punished by the Anglo-Indian troops. The question was finally settled in March, 1890. The Chinese disavowed the war and recalled their Ambah from Lhassa. Britain retained her possessions. In 1889-1890 the journey of M. Bonvalot and Prince Henri d'Orleans across central Asia from Kuldja to Tonking attracted the attention of French politicians and English merchants; but the practical efforts of the French to open a route to the Mekong river signally failed. In 1899 a Russian envoy paid a visit to the Dalai Lama in Lhassa, and the latter in turn sent a mission to St. Petersburg in 1900. In 1904-1905 Lhassa was reached by a small English armed force by fighting, and this force was withdrawn after British terms were complied with. A protest made by China led to an Anglo-Chinese conference in 1906, which resulted in China's suzerainty over Tibet. In 1911, during the Chinese Revolution, the Tibetans expelled the Chinese government. In 1912 the Anglo-Indian government protested against China's assumed sovereignty over Tibet, which led to a tripartite conference at Suila in 1913, but nothing satisfactory resulted and the question involved is still unsettled.

TIBET DOG, or **TIBET MASTIFF,** a variety of *Canis familiaris*, about the size of a Newfoundland dog, but with a head resembling that of the mastiff, and having the flews large and pendent. The color is usually deep black, with a bright brown spot over each eye; the hair is long, and the tail bushy and well curled. This variety is extremely savage, and has been known from classic times, when it was employed by the Romans, especially under the emperors, in the games of the circus.

TIBIA, the shin bone, with the exception of the femur, the longest bone in the skeleton. It is the anterior and inner of the two bones of the leg, and alone communicates the weight of the trunk to the foot. It is slightly twisted, and articulates with the femur, fibula, and astragalus. Its superior extremity is thick and expanded, with two condylar surfaces supporting the femur, and an external and an internal tuberosity; the shaft is three-sided, the inner surface convex and subcutaneous; the inferior is smaller than the superior extremity, and forms a thick process called the internal malleolus. The tibia corresponds with the radius of the arm. In entomology, the fourth joint of the leg. In music, a kind of pipe, a common musical instrument among the Greeks and Romans. It had holes at proper intervals, and was furnished with a mouthpiece.

TIBULLUS, ALBIUS, a Roman elegiac poet; born presumably in Gabii, about 54 B. C. His prænomen and parentage are unknown, though he was certainly born to a considerable estate. His father seems to have died early, but his

ALBIUS TIBULLUS

mother and sister survived him. While still a youth he acquired the friendship of the orator, poet, and statesman, M. Valerius Messala, on whose staff he was commissioned by Augustus, 30 B. C., to crush a revolt in Aquitania. In this campaign the poet displayed capacity enough to win him distinction and decorations, but he disliked a soldier's life and spent his time after the war in Roman society and in retirement at Pedium. He fell in love with Plania, whose husband was on service in Cilicia. Under the sobriquet of Delia she is the heroine of his first book of elegies, but his devotion did not survive the discovery that he was not her only lover. In his second book of elegies Delia is replaced by Nemesis — this inamorata being a fashionable courtesan, with many other admirers besides Tibullus.

Tibullus died in 19 B. C., immediately after Vergil, universally deplored in Rome, and years afterward the subject of a magnificent elegy by Ovid. Doubt has been thrown on his identity with the Albius of Horace, but we are loath to part with the picture that poet gives of him, pacing pensively his woodland walks at Pedum, blessed with fortune, with personal beauty, and with all the capacities of refined enjoyment. His character, amiable, generous, loyal to his friends, is reflected in his poems, which, "most musical, most melancholy," by their limpid clearness and their unaffected finish still justify Quintillian in placing him at the head of Roman elegy properly so called. The third book can hardly, even in part, be considered as his, while the fourth, also by another hand, is yet memorable for the 11 poems on the loves of Sulpicia and Cerinthus—Sulpicia's being unique as specimens of a Roman lady's passionate outburst in verse.

TIBY, PAUL ALEXANDRE (tib-ē') a French miscellaneous writer; born in Paris in 1800. He wrote: "Memoirs of a Young Priest, Collected and Published by a Layman" (1824); "Statistical Accounts of the French Colonies" (1837); "Two Convents in Mediæval Times: The Abbey of St. Gildas and the Paraclete in the Time of Abelard and Heloise" (1851). He died in Paris, May 10, 1871.

TIC DOULOUREUX, a painful affection of a facial nerve, a species of neuralgia. It is characterized by acute pain, attended with convulsive twitchings of the muscles, and continuing from a few minutes to several hours. It occurs on one side of the face, and may be caused by a diseased tooth, by inflammation in the ear passage, by exposure to cold, by dyspepsia, etc. The removal of a tooth, warm applications, the employment of electric currents over the nerve, or morphia administered subcutaneously, are sometimes efficient.

TICHBORNE TRIAL, a famous conspiracy case in the legal records of England, in which Arthur Orton, generally known as Thomas Castro, an Australian butcher, claimed to be heir to the Tichborne estates. Of the three sons of Sir Thomas Tichborne, the eldest, Roger Charles, died at sea in 1854; the second succeeded his father and died in 1866,

and the youngest was acknowledged heir. Lady Tichborne, doubting her eldest son's death, advertised for him, and Castro succeeded in convincing her of his identity with Roger Charles. She died before the trial to recover property had begun. This occurred in 1871, and Castro was nonsuited. He was charged with perjury, proved guilty, and sentenced (Feb. 28, 1874) to 14 years of penal servitude. The first trial lasted 103 days, and the second 188.

TICHODROMA, in ornithology, the wallcreeper; a genus of *Certhiidæ*, with one species, ranging from Southern Europe to Abyssinia, Nepal, and the N. of China. Bill slightly curved, nostrils with membranous scale. Wings long and rounded, tip of feathers soft.

TICHORHINE, in palæonthology, the English translation of the specific name of the woolly rhinoceros (*R. tichorinus*), which has reference to the fact that the nostrils are completely separated by a bony septum.

TICINO (tē-chē'no; German and French, Tessin), a river of Switzerland and north Italy, which rises in Mount St. Gothard, and after a course of about 120 miles joins the Po on the left. It traverses Lake Maggiore and separates Piedmont from Lombardy.

TICINO, a canton in the S. of Switzerland; area, 1,088 square miles. The N. and greater part of this canton is an elevated and mountainous region, the Splügen, St. Bernardin, and Mount St. Gothard forming its N. boundary. The chief river is the Ticino, and there are numerous small lakes. Lake Maggiore is partly within the canton. In the N. the principal occupations are cattle rearing and the preparation of dairy produce. In the S. the olive, vine, figs, citrons, and pomegranates are grown. Manufactures and trade are unimportant. The chief towns are Bellinzona, Locarno, and Lugano. Pop. about 160,000.

TICKNOR, CAROLINE, an American author; born in Boston, Mass. She wrote stories and articles published in various magazines; was author of "A Hypocritical Romance and Other Stories" (1896); "Miss Belladonna, a Child of To-day" (1897); and was one of the editors of "The International Library of Famous Literature"; "Masterpieces of the World's Literature"; and "The World's Greatest Orations."

TICKNOR, GEORGE, an American historian; born in Boston, Mass., Aug. 1, 1791. He was graduated at Dartmouth College in 1807, and was admitted to the bar in 1813. In 1815 he embarked for Europe, and visited the chief capitals for the purpose of pursuing his studies. On his return in 1820 he was appointed Professor of Modern Languages and Literature in Harvard University. In 1835 he resigned his professorship, and for the next three years traveled in Europe with his family. In 1849 he published a "History of Spanish Literature" (3 vols. 8vo, New York), corrected and enlarged editions being subsequently published. It was at once recognized by scholars as a work of value, and has been translated into Spanish and German. He produced in 1863 "The Life of William Hickling Prescott," the historian, with whom he had maintained a close friendship. He died in Boston, Jan. 26, 1871.

TICONDEROGA, a village in Essex co., N. Y.; on Lake Champlain, and on the Rutland and the Delaware and Hudson River railroads; 90 miles N. of Albany. Here is the outlet of Lake George, which falls 150 feet in 1½ miles and affords excellent water power. It has manufactories of machinery, paint, air engines, graphite, blank books, pulp, paper, etc., and an assessed property valuation of about $800,000. Ticonderoga figured prominently during the Colonial and Revolutionary periods. In 1755 the French erected a fort here and named it Carrillon. Two years later Montcalm started from this place with 9,000 men and captured Fort William Henry on Lake George. In 1758 General Abercrombie endeavored to take the French fort, and was repulsed after losing 2,000 men; but in 1759 it fell into the hands of General Amherst together with Crown Point. Both were then enlarged and strengthened at a heavy expense. In 1775 the works were taken by Ethan Allen while weakly garrisoned. Two years later the fort surrendered to General Burgoyne, and after being dismantled was abandoned. Pop. (1910) 2,475; (1920) 2,102.

TIDE, a regular periodic oscillation to which the surface of the sea at any place is subject. The oscillation takes place about twice a day, the periodic time being, on an average, about 12 hours and 26 minutes. Consequently, if high tide occurs at noon one day, it will occur next day some 50 minutes later. This is precisely the interval of time which elapses between two successive meridian passages of the moon; and that there must be some connection between the tides and our satellite was early recognized by astronomers. The explanation, however, was lacking till Newton proved them to be a necessary consequence of the law of gravitation. The phenomenon of the tide is, indeed, a case of perturbations, of exactly the same nature as the irregularities which the action of the sun produces on the motions of the moon. If we compare the attraction of the moon on a particle of the earth's surface with the attraction exerted on the earth as a whole, we readily see that, according as the particle is on the nearer or further side of the earth, the former attraction is greater or less than the latter; and it is to this difference of attraction, to which the waters yield, that the whole phenomenon of tide is due. The nearer waters are driven toward the moon, the further waters away from it. If the earth were spherical and uniformly covered with water, the tendency would be to make the water arrange itself in the form of a spheroid with the longer axis pointing toward the moon; and did the earth always present the same face to the moon, this would be rigorously the case.

Such is the equilibrium theory of tides, as originally given by Newton. It accounts so far for the phenomena, such as the simultaneous existence of high water at places diametrically opposite, but does not even approximately correspond to the true state of affairs. Newton was fully aware of this, and indeed has given the solution of the problem on other and truer assumptions. If the hypothetical earth covered uniformly with water is rotating, so as to present each point of its surface successively to the moon, each particle of water will be moving with a certain momentum which will be suffering retardation or acceleration according to its position relatively to the moon. The longer diameter of the water ellipsoid will consequently not point in the direction of the moon; and the result will be the formation of two diametrically opposite waves, flowing round the earth in a direction contrary to its rotation. This is the kinetic theory, which forms the basis of Laplace's theory of tides. It also fails in practical application, since the continuity of the surface waters on the earth is very much broken by the distribution of land.

More recently Young and Airy have approached the question as one of wave motion, basing their theory on the motion of waves in canals. Until comparatively recent times we have been regarding the moon as the sole tide-producing agent, but it is evident that the sun must have a similar action, though not so marked because of its much greater distance. It was proved by Newton that the disturbing forces exerted by two bodies on the same particle are directly as their masses, and inversely as the cubes of their distances; hence the ratio of the disturbing force exerted by the sun to that exerted by the moon 7 : 16. The principal tidal wave is that caused by the moon, but on it must be superposed that due to the sun. When the sun and moon are in syzygy, at times of new and full moon, their tidal waves will be superposed crest on crest, and the effect will be what is called a spring tide. When they are in quadrature, trough will coincide with crest, the lunar tide will be partially neutralized by the solar tide, and the result will be the so-called neap tide. The average spring tide will be to the average neap tide as $16 + 7 : 16 - 7 = 23 : 9$.

Besides this effect in amplitude, another effect is caused by this combination of tides, namely the priming and lagging of the tides. For when the two vertices do not coincide, the maximum of the resultant tidal wave will be at a point intermediate to the vertices, so that the time of high water will be now in advance now behind the time it would have been had the moon been the sole agent. Not only, then, are the waters of the ocean subject to diurnal and semi-diurnal oscillations, but these are subject to a monthly, semi-monthly, and even annual variation, besides being more or less affected by prevailing winds and coast configuration. The height of the tidal wave which circulates round the earth is not great—at most some 7 feet, a very small quantity compared to the size of our globe. In estuaries, bays, creeks, straits, etc., however, the difference between high and low water is much greater than this—as much as 50 feet in the Bay of Fundy, Nova Scotia. The explanation of such phenomena is to be found in the momentum with which the water is pushed forward by the advancing wave. In such a sea as the Mediterranean, which is all but cut off from communication with the great oceans, and which is itself not sufficiently extensive to be very perceptibly acted on by the sun and moon, the tides are very small, not exceeding a few inches.

The attempt to establish a complete theory from abstract principles has proved a failure; and the only true method by which to get an insight into the particular laws which govern tidal action at any given place is continued observation. By means of Lord Kelvin's tide gauge a graphical representation of the tidal oscillation at any place can be easily obtained; and by harmonic analysis of the curve, the constituent factors may be easily discovered, and the comparative effects of their several causes estimated.
I—28

One efficient cause in retarding tides has not been mentioned, namely, fluid friction, which, as first noticed by Kant, must act as a continual brake to the earth in its rotation; and this gradual slackening in the earth's speed of rotation must go on till the day is of the same length as the lunar month, when matters will be as required in the equilibrium theory given above.

TIDE GAUGE, an instrument in harbors to measure the rise and fall of the tides. A common form consists of a graduated spar, 24 feet long, and having boxes at the side, in which is a float with an elevated stem. The spar is secured to a pier or quay, or is anchored in a frame and secured by guys. The rod is ¾ inch in diameter, and is supported by a cork of three inches cube. The stem is guided by staples in the spar.

TIECK, LUDWIG (tek), a German writer; born in Berlin, Prussia, May 31, 1773. He was educated at the University of Halle, and at Göttingen and Erlangen. He published the tale of "Abdailah," and a novel entitled "William Lovell" (three vols. Berlin, 1795-1796). His "Peter Lebrecht, a History Without Adventures," and "Peter Lebrecht's Popular Tales." At Jena in 1799-1800, associating with Schlegele, Brentano and others gave rise to the Romantic School of Germany, so called. In 1799 he published "Romantic Poems" (2 vols. 1799-1800), and in 1804 appeared his comedy "The Emperor Octavian." His "Phantasus" (3 vols. Berlin, 1812-1815), however, gave the first sign of his having freed himself from the mysticism and extravagances of his earlier works. In 1817 he visited England, where he collected material for his Shakespeare. He resided at Ziebingen till 1918, when he removed to Dresden. From this period date his famous tales ultimately published complete in 12 volumes (Berlin, 1853), the principal being "Dichterleben" (A Poet's Life —Shakespeare); "Der Tod des Poeten" (The Poet's Death — Camoens); the "Witches' Sabbath," etc. In 1826 he published his "Dramaturgic Leaves." His study of Shakespeare resulted in "Shakespeare's Vorschule" (2 vols. Leipsic, 1823-1829); and the continuation of the German translation of Shakespeare commenced by Schlegel. Tieck was invited to the Prussian court in 1841, awarded a pension, the rank of a privy councillor and supervised the Prussian stage. He died in Berlin, April 28, 1853. His brother, CHRISTIAN FRIEDRICH (1776-1851), was celebrated as a sculptor.

TIEDEMAN, CHRISTOPHER GUS-TAVUS, an American writer on law;

born in Charleston, S. C., July 16, 1857; was graduated at the College of Charleston in 1876 and at the Columbia Law School in 1879; was Professor of Law in the University of Missouri for ten years and held the same chair in New York University for six years. He was the author of "The Law of Real Property" (1883); "Limitations of Police Powers" (1886); "Commercial Paper" (1889); "Unwritten Constitution of the United States" (1890); "Sales of Personal Property" (1891); "State and Federal Control of Persons and Property" (1900), etc. He died in New York, Aug. 25, 1903.

TIEDEMANN (tē'de-män), **DIEDRICH**, a German philosopher; born in Bremerwörde, near Bremen, April 3, 1748. He was Professor of Philosophy in the University of Marburg. He wrote: "Researches on the Origin of Languages" (1772); "System of the Stoic Philosophy" (1777); "The First Philosophers of Greece" (1780); "Origin of the Magic Arts" (1787); "Spirit of Speculative Philosophy from Thales to Berkeley" (6 vols., 1790-1797); "Theætetus: or Human Knowledge" (1794). He died in Marburg, Sept. 24, 1803.

TIEDGE (tēd'ge), **CHRISTOPH AUGUST**, a German poet; born in Gardelegen, Prussia, Dec. 14, 1752. He enjoys distinction as the author of "Urania" and "Mirror for Women." He also wrote "Wanderings Through Life's Market" and "Elegies." His admirers are many, and his poetry has been compared with that of Cowper. He died in Dresden, March 8, 1841.

TIELE, CORNELIUS PETRUS, a Dutch theologian; born in Leyden, Netherlands, Dec. 16, 1830. He studied at the university there and at the Remonstrants' Seminary at Amsterdam, and became Remonstrant pastor at Rotterdam (1856), professor in the seminary translated to Leyden (1873), and Professor of the History of Religions in the University of Leyden in 1877. From its foundation in 1867 he collaborated with Kuenen, Loman, and Rauwenhoff in editing the well-known "Theologisch Tijdschrift," and he published a long series of important theological works. Of his writings there have been translated into English the "Comparative History of the Egyptian and Mesopotamian Religions" (1869-1872); "Outlines of the History of Religion to the Spread of the Universal Religions" (1876); English translation by J. E. Carpenter, 1878. Other works discuss the Gospel of St. John (1855), the Religion of Zarathustra (1864),

"Babylonian-Assyrian History" (1886-1887), etc. He died in 1902.

TIEMANNITE, a massive granular mineral, first found at several localities in the Harz Mountains, but since at several places in the United States; hardness, 2.5; sp. gr., 7.1-7.37; luster, metallic; color, steel to blackish lead gray. Composition: A selenide of mercury. Dana suggests the formula HgSe, but points out that the analyses mostly correspond with Hg_6Se_5, which requires selenium, 24.8, mercury, $75.2 = 100$.

TIENTSIN (tē-ent-sēn'), a large city and river port of China, in the province of Chihlî, on the right bank of the Peiho; 34 miles from the mouth of the river. It is the port of the city of Peking, from which it is distant 80 miles S. E. The river is generally frozen over from about December 15 to March 15, and the business at other times carried on by means of boats and junks is taken up by sledges, which swarm on the river. By the treaty of Tientsin, signed here in 1858, the port was declared open. Settlement concessions are held by the British, French, Japanese, Belgian, and Italian Governments. In 1881 Tientsin was connected by telegraph with Shanghai (the line extending to Peking), and there is a railway from Tientsin to the mouth of the Peiho and southward to Pukow on the Yangtze. The city does an export business of about $35,000,000. There is also a large though recently disturbed trade with Russia via Siberia. Pop. about 800,000. See BOXERS.

TIEPOLO (tē-ā'pō-lō), **GIOVANNI BATTISTA**, an Italian painter, the last of the great Venetian school; born in Venice, Italy, March 5, 1692; modeled himself on Paul Veronese. His first works were in the adornment of churches and palaces in and about Venice; in 1750-1753 he executed a great series of frescoes in the archiepiscopal palace at Würzburg, and in 1760 was engaged on the palace of Madrid. He was a most productive painter, rich in color (especially in the easel pictures) and clear (though incorrect) in drawing. His chief works were the Old Testament histories—the palace of Udine and the frescoes at Madrid. He died in Madrid, Spain, March 27, 1769. His two sons were also painters, and, like their father, etchers also.

TIERNAN, FRANCES FISHER (pseudonym, CHRISTIAN REID), an American novelist; born in Salisbury, N. C. Her many works include: "Valerie Aylmer" (1870); "Mabel Lee" (1871); "Morton House" (1871); "Ebb Tide" (1872);

"Nina's Atonement'" (1873); "Carmen's Inheritance" (1873); "A Daughter of Bohemia" (1873); "A Gentle Belle" (1875); "Hearts and Hands" (1875); "A Question of Honor" (1875); "The Land of the Sky" (1875); "After Many Days" (1877); "Bonny Kate" (1878); "A Summer Idyl" (1878); "Hearts of Steel" (1882); "Armine" (1884); "Roslyn's Fortune" (1885); "Miss Churchill" (1887); "A Child of Mary" (1887); "Philip's Restitution" (1888); "The Land of the Sun"; "A Woman of Fortune"; "Chase of an Heiress"; etc.

TIERRA DEL FUEGO, an achipelago consisting of a group of several large and numerous small islands, lying off the S. extremity of South America; in lat. 54° S., lon. 70° W.; separated from the continent by the Strait of Magellan. Its extreme S. point is formed by Cape Horn. The principal island, Tierra del Fuego, sometimes known as King Charles South Land, is divided between Chile and Argentine Republic, to the latter of which Staten Island also belongs. All the other islands and islets are included in Chile. The shores of the archipelago are generally much broken by and indented with bays and arms of the sea, with mountains rising abruptly from the water. These fjords, as a rule, contain deep water at their shoreward extremities, with bars, or, more properly, banks at the sea entrances; in this feature, as well as in their scenery, resembling many of the salt water lochs on the W. coast of Scotland.

The whole group is mountainous, the high hills of the mainland (Tierra del Fuego) attaining a height of 7,000 feet, the snow line being at an altitude of 4,000 feet above sea-level. There are some dreary plains and a few fertile river valleys, with areas of marshy ground between Useless and St. Sebastian Bays. None of the rivers are important, unless it be the Juarez Celman, which is believed to be navigable for a considerable distance above its mouth. Toward the N. the plains produce good pasturage and sheep farming is carried on. Forests of beech, winter's bark, magnolia, and cypress cover large areas. Few island groups situated so close, to continental land exhibit a poorer fauna than is here presented, the guanaco, tucu-tucu (a small rodent), dog, fox, and rat being the only quadrupeds, with the exception of the lately introduced farm stock. The dog is semi-domesticated, and is kept by the natives in immense numbers. Birds, however, are abundant and various, including *Vanellus cayanus, Surnia funerea,* owls, gulls, falcons, and a great variety of sea birds. Seals and sea-lions, once almost innumerable along the shores, have grown scarce and wild, especially in the N. portion.

The land of Tierra del Fuego is rapidly rising, and the coast line has advanced 3 kilometers since the date of the surveys of Captain King (1826-1828) and Fitzroy (1831-1836). The rocks are principally volcanic, but sedimentary strata are not uncommon on the principal island, and probably on some others. Granite, syenite, porphyry, quartz, serpentine, trachite, diorite, and sandstone comprise the principal rocks. Some coal, of a poor description, and a little gold have been found. Settled weather never lasts for more than a fortnight at a time. December, January and February are the warmest months. March is exceedingly boisterous always, and during its course occur the most destructive gales.

The people are savages of a low type, divided into three tribes, the Onas (or Aonas), the Yaghans, and the Alkaluts, the Yaghans being now supposed to be the aborigines. In the eastern part, under the Argentine Government, the population is about 3,000, of whom one-third are whites.

TIFFANY, CHARLES COMFORT, an American clergyman; born in Baltimore in 1829; was educated at Dickinson College, Andover Theological Seminary, and the Universities of Halle, Heidelberg and Berlin; ordained in the Protestant Episcopal Church in 1866; held charges in Boston and New York in 1867-1890; and became archdeacon of New York in 1893. He wrote "Expressions in Church Architecture"; "Modern Atheism"; "History of the Protestant Episcopal Church"; "The Prayer Book and the Christian Life." He died Aug. 20, 1907.

TIFFANY LOUIS COMFORT, an American artist; born in New York City, Feb. 18, 1848; studied art in New York and Paris; has done considerable decorative work; discovered the "Tiffany Favrile Glass," and some of his designs for stained glass windows have become famous. He was president and art director of the Tiffany Glass & Decorating Co., and a member of many American and foreign art associations. Mr. Tiffany received a gold medal and was made a Chevalier of the Legion of Honor by the French Government in 1900; gold medal, Dresden, 1901; and gold medal, Turin, 1902; A. M., Yale, 1903.

TIFFIN, a city and county-seat of Seneca co., O., on the Sandusky river, and on the Pennsylvania, the Cleveland, Cincinnati, Chicago and St. Louis, and the Baltimore and Ohio railroads; 42 miles S. E. of Toledo. Here are Heidelberg University, Ursuline Academy, public library, hospital, St. Francis's Orphans' Home, street railroads, electric lights, National and 'State banks, and a number of daily, weekly and monthly periodicals. It has manufactories of machinery, wire nails, bent wood, lanterns, agricultural implements, glass, emery wheels, pottery, etc. Pop. (1900), 10,989; (1910), 11,-894; (1920), 14,375.

TIFLIS, a province of the republic of Georgia, extending on both sides of the Kur river from the central chain of the Caucasus Mountains on the N. to the Armenian plateau on the S.; area 15,777 square miles. Steppes and fertile plains are found in the center, but much of the surface is mountainous, covered with off-shoots from the Caucasus and Mount Ararat, reaching in some peaks to 12,000 feet. The soil is fertile and yields abundant tobacco, cotton, indigo, wheat and fruit. Numerous rich petroleum springs and mineral wells exist, and excellent timber is produced from the extensive forests of oak, elm, maple, and chestnut. Pop. about 1,400,000.

TIFLIS, the capital of the republic of Georgia, and chief city in the territory of the Caucasus, lies in a narrow valley on both sides of the Kur, 184 miles E. S. E. of Poti by rail. In its architecture and in the manners of its inhabitants the city presents a singular mixture of Asiatic and European features. The city is the seat of the civil and military authorities of Transcausia, and has 42 churches (23 Armenian), 2 mosques, a gymnasium, and several upper schools, a library, a botanic garden, a hospital, and a theater. It has active manufactures of woolens, silks, cottons, armor, and leather, and is the emporium for the important Russian trade with Persia. It is connected with Teheran by telegraph. Tiflis was the scene of active military operations during the World War, and 1919-1920. See GEORGIA. Pop. about 300,000.

TIGER, in zoölogy, the *Felis tigris* (*Tigris regalis,* Gray), the largest and most dangerous of the *Felidæ,* exceeding the lion slightly in size and far surpassing him in destructiveness. It is purely Asiatic in its habitat, but is not by any means confined to the hot plains of India, though there it reaches its highest development both of size and coloration. It is found in the Himalayas at certain seasons, at a high altitude. It is met with to the E. throughout Chinese Tartary, and as far N., it is said,

as the island of Saghalien, where the winter is very severe. The full-grown male Indian tiger is from 9 to 12 and the tigress from 8 to 10 feet from the nose to the tip of the tail, and from 36 to 42 inches high at the shoulder. It is the only member of the family ornamented with cross stripes on the body—a scarce type of coloration among mammals. The ground color of the skin is rufous or tawny yellow, shaded with white on the ventral surface. This is varied with vertical black stripes or elongated ovals and brindlings. On the face and posterior surface of the ears the white markings are peculiarly well developed. The depth of the ground color and the intensity of the black markings vary, according to the age and condition of the animal. In old tigers the ground becomes more tawny, of a lighter shade, and the black markings better defined. The ground coloring is more dusky in young animals.

TIGER

Though possessed of immense strength and ferocity, the tiger rarely attacks an armed man, unless provoked, though often carrying off women and children. When pressed by hunger or enfeebled by age and incapable of dealing with larger prey, like buffaloes, the tiger prowls around villages, and, having once tasted human flesh, becomes a confirmed man eater. When taken young the tiger is capable of being tamed. The tiger was known to the ancients; frequent mention of it occurs in both Greek and Latin writers, and, like the lion, it was habitually seen in the games of the circus. No reference is made to it, however, in the Bible. The jaguar (*Felis onca*) is sometimes called the American tiger, and *Felis macrocelis,* from the Malayan Peninsula, the clouded tiger.

In sugar making, a tank having a perforated bottom, through which the molasses escapes. Also, a boy in livery whose special duty is to attend on his master while driving out; a young male servant or groom. Colloquially, a kind of growl or screech after cheering; as, three cheers and a tiger.

To buck (or fight) the tiger: to gamble (slang).

TIGHE, MARY (BLACHFORD), an Irish poet; born in Dublin, Ireland, in 1773; married her cousin, Henry Tighe, of Woodstock, M. P., in 1793. Though her poem "Psyche, or the Legend of Love," was privately printed (1805), it was only after her death, March 24, 1810, that her writings were given to the world. The first edition was in 1811, and they have been frequently reprinted. The "Psyche" is written in the Spenserian stanza; and at least, by Leigh Hunt's admission, occasionally, contains a fancy not unworthy of a pupil of Spenser. Her other poems are short occasional pieces, frequently of a religious cast. It is probably as the subject of Moore's lyric, "I saw thy form in youthful pride," and of Mrs. Hemans's "Grave of a Poetess," that Mrs. Tighe is destined to be longest remembered.

TIGRIDIA, the tiger flower, a genus of plants, order *Iridaceæ*, containing only one species, *T. Pavonia*, distinguished by the three outer segments of the perianth being larger, and by the filaments being united into a long cylinder. It is a native of Mexico, and much cultivated in flower gardens for the singularity and great beauty of its flowers, which are, however, evanescent. The root is a scaly bulb.

TIGRIS, next to the Euphrates, the greatest river of former Asiatic Turkey; rises on the S. slope of the Armenian Taurus range in Kurdistan to the S. of Lake Goljik. It has a sinuous course in a S. E. direction, almost parallel to that of the Euphrates, which river it joins at Kurna, after a course of 1,060 miles. The joint stream, called the Shat-el-Arab, after a further course of 90 miles, enters the head of the Persian Gulf. In its upper course the Tigris flows through fine pasture land, frequented by nomad Kurds and Arabs, and from Diarbekir, where it becomes navigable for small craft, to Mosul, a distance of 200 miles, its banks are highly cultivated in some places. Below this point, again, as far as Bagdad (250 miles), it traverses unpeopled wastes, while from Bagdad to its mouth the steep banks are overgrown with high reeds and brushwood, and are haunted by lions and other beast of prey. Its affluents, the Bitlis, Great and Little Zab, the Dyala, all flow from the highlands to the N., the country separating it from the

Euphrates being a streamless waste. The chief places on the Tigris are Diarbekir, Mosul, and Bagdad, and the ruins of Nineveh, Selucia, Ctesiphon, and Opis. Like the Euphrates, the Tigris rises in spring with the melting of the snow on the Armenian Mountains; and during the latter half of May, when the flood is at its height, the whole country between and beyond these rivers, for over 100 miles between Bagdad and Bussorah, is converted into a lake. The arrowy stream either loses less water by irrigation or receives more from its affluents than the Euphrates, for it is the larger of the two at the point of confluence. In the World War the Tigris was the scene of heavy fighting between the Turkish and Anglo-Indian armies in 1915, 1916 and 1917.

TIGRISOMA, in orinthology, a genus of *Ardeidæ*, with four species from tropical America and Western Africa. Bill as in *Ardea*; face and sometimes chin, naked; legs feathered almost to the knees; innner toe rather shorter than outer; claws short, stout, regularly curved; anterior scales reticulate or hexagonal.

TIKOOR, or **TIKUL,** in botany, the *Garcinia pedunculata*, a tall tree, a native of Rungpur, Goalpara and Sylhet in India. The fruit is large, round, smooth and, when ripe, yellow. The fleshy part is of a very sharp, pleasant taste, and is used by the natives for curries, and for acidulating water; if cut into slices it will keep for years, and might be used in lieu of limes, on board ship on long voyages.

TIKUS, in zoölogy, a small insectivorous mammal, from Malacca and Sumatra, described by Sir Stamford Raffles as *Viverra gymnura*, but now known as *Gymnurus rafflesii*. Externally, it is not unlike an opossum with a lengthened muzzle; greater portion of the body, upper part of legs, root of tail, and stripe over the eye black, the other parts white. It possesses glands which secrete a substance with a strong musky smell.

TILDEN, DOUGLAS, an American sculptor; born in Chico, Butte co., Cal., May 1, 1860; lost his hearing as a result of scarlet fever and in consequence was educated at the State Institution for the Deaf in Berkeley, Cal., where he was graduated in 1879. Later he took up the study of sculpture and in 1893 was appointed a member of the jury on sculpture at the World's Columbian Exposition in Chicago. He was a member of the National Sculpture Society, the New York Art Club, the San Francisco Art

Association, etc., and Professor of Sculpture at the Mark Hopkins Art Institute. His works include "Baseball Player"; "Tired Boxer"; "Indian Bear Hunt"; "Football Players," etc.

TILDEN, SAMUEL JONES, an American statesman; born in New Lebanon, N. Y., Feb. 9, 1814; was educated at the University of New York; studied law with Benjamin F. Butler, and was admitted to the bar in 1841; began practice in New York City, and became actively interested in politics; was elected to the State Assembly in 1845; and was a delegate to the Constitutional Convention of 1846. His most celebrated cases as a practising lawyer were the contest of the election of Azariah C. Flagg to the comptrollership of New York City; the opposition of the heirs of the murdered Dr. Burdell to a demand by Mrs. Cunningham for a power of administration over his estate, and the defense of the Pennsylvania Coal Company against a demand for the payment of extra tolls to the Delaware and Hudson Canal Company. During the Civil War he maintained that the struggle with the South could be terminated without resorting to acts not warranted by the Federal Constitution. Mr. Tilden became leader of the Democratic party in New York State in 1868, and in that capacity strenuously opposed the corrupt administration of the Tweed faction. In 1874 he was elected governor of New York, and during his term of office broke up the notorious "canal ring." In 1876 he was nominated for the presidency of the National Democratic Convention. In the election Hayes received 4,033,295 popular votes, and Tilden, 4,284,265. In 1877, on the finding of the Electoral Commission, the presidency was awarded to the Republican candidate by an electoral vote of 185 to 184. Mr. Tilden died in "Greystone," his country-seat, near Yonkers, N. Y., Aug. 4, 1886. The bulk of his fortune, which consisted of several million dollars, was bequeathed to trustees to be used for establishing a great public library in New York City, but his will was contested successfully. An heir relinquished her share of the estate and this became the nucleus and the beginning of the Tilden Foundation and the New York Public Library. See HAYES, RUTHERFORD BIRCHARD; NEW YORK PUBLIC LIBRARY.

TILE, a kind of thin slab of baked clay, used for covering roofs, paving floors, lining furnaces or ovens, constructing drains, etc. Tiles, both flat and curved, were in great demand in Roman architecture. Roofs were covered with the flat and curved tiles alternating. Tiles are manufactured by a similar process to bricks. Roofing tiles are of two sorts, plain tiles and pantiles; the former are flat, and are usually made ⅝ inch in thickness, 10½ inches long, 6¼ wide. They weigh from 2 to 2½ pounds each, and expose about one-half to the weather; 740 tiles cover 100 superficial feet. They are hung on the lath by two oak pins, inserted into holes made by the molder. Pantiles, first used in Flanders, have a wavy surface, lapping under and being overlapped by adjacent tiles of the same rank. Crown, ridge, hip, and valley tiles are semicylindrical, or segments of cylinders, used for the purposes indicated. Siding tiles are used as a substitute for weatherboarding. Holes are made in them when molding, and they are secured to the lath by flat-headed nails. The gauge or exposed face is sometimes indented, to represent courses of brick. Fine mortar is introduced between them when they rest on each other. Siding tiles are sometimes called weather tiles and mathematical tiles; these names are derived from their exposure or markings. They are variously formed, having curved or crenated edges, and various ornaments either raised or encaustic. Dutch tiles, for chimneys, are made of a whitish earth, glazed and painted with various figures. Draintiles are usually made in the form of an arch, and laid on flat tiles called soles. Paving tiles are usually square and thicker than those used for roofing. Galvanized iron tiles have been introduced in France. They are shaped like pantiles. In brass founding, the cover of a brass furnace, now made of iron, but formerly a flat tile. In metallurgy, a clay cover for a melting pot. As a slang term, a tall stiff hat; a tall silk hat, or one of that shape.

TILEFISH, a fish discovered accidentally by fishermen trawling for cod near Nantucket. It is a brilliantly colored fish, weighing from 10 to 30 pounds.

TILESTON, MARY WILDER, an American author, born in Salem, Mass., Aug. 20, 1843. She was the daughter of Caleb and Mary Wilder (White) Foote, and was married to John Boies Tileston in 1865. Among her many works are: "Quiet Hours," a book of poems (1874); "Selections from Marcus Aurelius Antoninus" (1876); "Selections from the Imitation of Christ" (1876); "The Blessed Life" (1878); "Selections from Fénelon" (1879); "Selections from Dr. John Tauler" (1882); "Heroic Ballads" (1883); "Daily Strength for Daily

Needs" (1883); "Sugar and Spice" (1885); "Tender and True" (1892); "Selections from Isaac Penington" (1892); "Prayers, Ancient and Modern" (1902); "Joy and Strength for the Pilgrim's Day" (1902); "Memorials of Mary Wilder White" (1903); "Children's Treasure Trove of Pearls" (1908); "The Child's Harvest of Verse" (1910); "Caleb and Mary Wilder Foote" (1918).

TILLMAN, BENJAMIN RYAN, an American legislator; born in Edgefield co., S. C., Aug. 11, 1847; was educated at Bethany Academy. He became prominent in a discussion for industrial and technical education and other reforms in 1886; founded Clemson Agricultural and Mechanical College, at Fort Hill, for boys, and Winthrop Normal and Industriaal College at Rock Hill, for girls; was elected Democratic governor of South Carolina in 1890 and 1892; was conspicuous in the Constitutional Convention of South Carolina in 1895; and was elected United States Senator in 1895 and 1900. Re-elected 1906 and 1912. He died in 1918.

TILLMAN, SAMUEL ESCUE, an American military officer; born near Shelbyville, Tenn., Oct. 2, 1847; was graduated at the United States Military Academy and commissioned 2d lieutenant of artillery in 1869; transferred to the Engineer Corps in 1872 as 1st lieutenant; served on frontier duty in Kansas in 1869-1870; was assistant Professor of Chemistry, Mineralogy, and Geology in the Military Academy in 1870-1873 and 1979-1880; assistant Professor of Philosophy in 1875-1876; and Professor of Chemistry, Mineralogy, and Geology after 1880. He was assistant astronomer in the United States expedition to Tasmania to observe the transit of Venus in 1874-1875; and author of "Essential Principles of Chemistry" (1884); "Elementary Mineralogy" (1894); "Descriptive General Chemistry" (1899); "Important Minerals and Rocks" (1900); etc.

TILLOTSON, JOHN ROBERT, Archbishop of Canterbury; born in Sowerby, Yorkshire, England, in October, 1630. He studied at Claire Hall, Cambridge, graduated B.A. in 1650, and became a fellow the year after. In 1650 he became tutor in the house of Edmund Prideaux, attorney-general under the Protector. He is said to have received his orders from Sydserf, Bishop of Galloway, and at any rate he was a preacher by 1661, when we find him ranged among the Presbyterians at the Savoy Conference. He submitted at once to the Act of Uniformity (1662); in 1663 became rector of Keddington, in

Suffolk, the year after preached at Lincoln's Inn, where his mild, evangelical, but undoctrinal morality was at first little relished. He married a niece of Oliver Cromwell, and became lecturer at St. Lawrence's Church, in the Jewry. In 1670 he became a prebendary, in 1672 dean of Canterbury. Along with Burnet he attended Lord Russell on the scaffold (1683).

In 1689 he was appointed clerk of the closet to King William and dean of St. Paul's, and in April, 1691, was raised to the see of Canterbury, vacant by the deposition of the Nonjuror Sancroft. His "Posthumous Sermons," edited by his chaplain, Dr. Ralph Barker, filled 14 volumes (1694). A complete edition of his whole works, including 254 sermons, appeared in three volumes folio, 1707-1712; with a good "Life" by Dr. Thomas Birch, 1752; and an annotated selection of his sermons by G. W. Weldon (1886). Burnet said he was the best preacher of his age. He died Nov. 22, 1694.

TILLY, JOHANN TSERKLÆS, COUNT VON, one of the most notable generals of the Thirty Years' War; born in the castle of Tilly, Brabant, Belgium, in February, 1559. He was at first educated under Jesuit supervision for the priesthood, but a strong bias toward a military career soon showed itself, and he abandoned the Church for the army.

COUNT VON TILLY

He served under Alva during the revolt in the Netherlands, and afterward with distinction in Hungary. Maximilian, Duke of Bavaria, appointed him commander of his forces, and in 1620, two years after the beginning of the Thirty Years' War, he utterly routed the Bohemians. During the next period of the contest he defeated in turn the two Protestant leaders. In 1622 he drove from the Palatinate Christian, Duke of Brandenburg, and in August next year defeated him in a three days' engagement at Stadtlohn in Münsterchen. In 1625 he led the army of the Catholic League against Christian IV., of Denmark, who commanded the army of Lower Saxony, and defeated him in the battle of Lutter. Along with Wallenstein he forced the Danish king to agree to the disgraceful peace of Lübeck (1629). Next year Wallenstein was forced to resign the command of the imperial forces, and Tilly succeeded him. In May, 1631, Tilly sacked with ferocious cruelty the town of Madgeburg. As he himself complacently wrote, since the destruction of Troy and Jerusalem nothing had equalled it. Gustavus Adolphus was too late to save, but not to avenge Madgeburg. In September, 1631, he defeated Tilly at Breitenfeld, and again at Rain on the Lech. In both battles Tilly was wounded. He died in Ingolstadt, April 30, 1632, a few days after his second defeat. Tilly was an able general, but a man of narrow intellect. Not personally ambitious, nor caring for money, he was a fanatical Roman Catholic, ready to sacrifice everything for his Church.

TILMATURA, in ornithology, sparkling tails; a genus of *Trochilidæ*, with one species, *T. duponti*, from Guatemala. Wings rather short and somewhat sickle-shaped; tail feathers pointed, the outermost narrow toward the tip, which is curved inward.

TILMUS, in pathology, a picking of the bedclothes, through cerebral excitement, toward the conclusion of any serious disease. It is a very unfavorable symptom.

TILSIT, a town of Prussia, province of East Prussia; at the junction of the Tilse with the Memel or Niemen, which is crossed by a fine railway bridge (1875), 53 miles S. E. of Memel. It has a schloss (built 1537, partially burnt 1876), a fine rathhaus, four churches, two hospitals, a gymnasium (since 1586), a realschule of the first class (1839), and a large barrack. Tilsit manufactures paper, leather, linens, woolens, and beer, has iron founding and sugar refining, and considerable commerce in horses, timber, corn, and produce. The town is historically interesting as the place where, on a raft in the river, the peace of 1807 was concluded between Napoleon, Alexander, and Friedrich Wilhelm III., by which the last was deprived of one-half of his dominions. In the World War the Russians captured the city in

1914, but were unable to hold it. Pop. about 40,000.

TILTON, THEODORE, an American journalist; born in New York City, Oct. 2, 1835; was graduated at the College of the City of New York; editor of the "Independent" in 1856-1871; founded the "Golden Age," but withdrew from it after two years. He caused a wide sensation in 1874 by charging Henry Ward Beecher with criminal intimacy with his wife, and by suing him for $100,000 damages. The trial resulted in the disagreement of the jury. In 1883 Mr. Tilton settled in Paris, France. His publications include: "The Sexton's Tale, and other Poems" (1867); "Proof-Sheets from an Editor's Table" (1869); "Tempest-Tossed" (1875); "Suabian Stories" (1882); etc. He died May 25, 1907.

TIMBER, trees cut down, squared, or capable of being squared, into beams, rafters, boards, planks, etc., to be employed in the construction of houses, ships, etc., or in carpentry, joinery, etc. Timber is usually sold by the load. A load of rough or unhewn timber is 40 cubic feet, and a load of squared timber 50 cubic feet, estimated to weigh 2,000 pounds. In the case of planks, deals, etc., the load consists of so many square feet. Thus, a load of one-inch plank is 600 square feet, a load of planks thicker than one inch equals 600 square feet divided by the thickness in inches. The term is often used for all kinds of felled and seasoned wood. It is also a general term for growing trees yielding wood suitable for constructive purposes. The chief are fir, pine, oak, ash, elm, beech, sycamore, walnut, chestnut, mahogany, teak, etc.

In the United States there are 300 species of trees, the smallest of which grows to a height of 30 feet. In South America the number is much greater, and India possesses about 900 species of timber trees. The species in England do not exceed 30, and in France or Germany there are only a few more. Yet, though the kinds of wood are so much more limited in European countries, there are almost as few in general use in the United States as in Europe. The smallness of the number of species of timber known to commerce is at first glance very remarkable, but it is accounted for in this way. The great consumption of timber is for architectural and other constructive works which are usually carried out on a scale of some magnitude, and for such purposes large quantities of the kind or kinds chosen are required. It is very desirable, therefore, that the wood selected should be plentiful, durable, more or less easily worked, fairly uniform in quality, and moderate in price.

As yet the very useful timbers have been obtained from gregarious species of trees growing in the forests of the N. temperate regions of the globe, and the most important of these are a few kinds of fir and pine. From the tropics, where the social species are fewer, come the harder, heavier, and more richly colored or figured kinds, some of which are used in Europe and North America only for furniture and decorative purposes. Some of these tropical woods are, however, of extraordinary strength, and possess other valuable properties which will bring them sooner or later into use for building purposes. This is all the more certain to be the case as both in North America and in Europe the forest-covered land is being stripped of its best timber at a rapidly increasing rate. Trees are of such slow growth that it takes many years before they are large enough to yield useful timber; so that when the primitive forests of a country are once cut down the keeping up of a supply by planted trees is a very difficult matter.

Chief Commercial Timbers.—The following are the best known and most used timbers in Great Britain. Baltic redwood (*Pinus sylvestris*), perhaps the most generally useful of all, is employed for roofing and flooring, and often for all other internal and external wood work of better-class houses and other buildings. It is also used for paving streets and many other purposes. This wood in the cut state is called "yellow deal" in England. American yellow pine (*Pinus strobus*), called white pine in its native country, is also very largely imported for the internal joiner work of buildings, parts of furniture, etc., but it is not suited for external work. Like the last, it is an excellent and easily worked timber. Baltic white wood (*Abies excelsa*) has for a considerable number of years taken the place of redwood for joists, flooring boards, roof timbers, etc. It is a distinctly inferior wood. American pitch pine (*Pinus rigida*), found over a large extent of country in the Eastern States, is an important timber. It has been much used in England for open roofs and for the whole of the wood-fittings of churches, halls, and the like. The annual rings of this wood are strongly marked, so that its planed surface looks striped. It is a heavy and highly resinous, but not very easily worked wood. The Douglas or Oregon pine (*A. Douglasii or Pseudotsuga Douglasii*) of northwestern America, between 200 and 300 feet in height, yields a timber of great length without knots,

suitable for masts, spars, and many other purposes.

Under the name of Californian redwood, the timber of *Sequoia sempervirens* has of late years been to some extent imported into Great Britain. Like the last, the tree is of great size, and the wood is easily got free of knots. It is of a pleasing red color (most of the so-called red pine woods are nearly white), and easily worked in the longitudinal direction, but difficult to cut clean across the grain. Another recently imported wood is the Kauri pine of New Zealand. The Kauri (*Dammara australis*) is also a majestic tree, and the wood is highly prized for all general purposes in its native country. It seems to have some tendency to warp, but this may be owing to defective seasoning. We may mention among coniferous woods that of the deodar (*Cedrus Deodara*), which, though not used in Great Britain, is extremely durable, and of great importance in northern India.

Among the more important American coniferous timbers, some of which have been already referred to, are the white pine (*Pinus strobus*), called in England yellow pine; the yellow pine of the Eastern States (*Pinus mitis*); the hemlock; the black spruce; the Douglas pine; Californian redwood; the white cedar (*Chamœcyparis thyoides*); the red cedar (*Juniperus virginiana*); as well as the larch or tamarack (*Larix americana*).

Of timbers from dicotyledonous or, as they are sometimes called, foliaceous trees oak is the most important. The oak timber grown in the N. of Europe is obtained from two or three varieties of one species of Quercus, or from distinct but closely allied species. The timber possesses in a high degree the useful properties of a hardwood. It is strong, tough, elastic, and not too heavy. Its sp. gr. averages about .800. Few woods are more durable or less affected in exposed situations by alternations of wet and dry weather. It is still used largely in shipbuilding and for many purposes in civil architecture, but for the latter it is much more expensive than pine wood. Oak has the defect of rusting iron which pierces it or which is in contact with it. One or two American oaks also yield valuable timber. Teak, from an Indian tree, is next in importance to oak as a constructive timber. It has just the opposite effect on iron, as it protects the metal from rust, a property which gives it great value as a backing for the armor plating of ships. Teak is neither quite so hard nor so strong as oak, but it is as difficult to cut with tools, and it is rather lighter when thoroughly seasoned.

Besides its extensive use in shipbuilding, it has been of late years used for external architectural work. Elm, though of much less consequence than oak as building timber, is nevertheless a good deal employed for engineering purposes; it is also used in shipbuilding for keels and other parts under water. Elm is only of great durability if kept either quite dry or constantly wet. For other timbers belonging to the same great class of trees, such as ash, beech, hornbeam, sycamore, lime, and birch, which have more restricted applications, see their respective heads. In the S. of Europe the timbers of the chestnut (*Castanea vesca*) and the walnut are extensively used.

There are a few exceptionally remarkable timbers which may just be named. Greenheart, which is of extraordinary strength, is believed to contain some principle which resists the attacks of boring worms when used for piles. Sabicu (*Lysiloma sabicu*), which is plentiful in Cuba, is another immensely strong wood. Both these timbers are heavier than water, and are used in shipbuilding. The Jarrah wood (*Eucalyptus marginata*) of Western Australia is believed to be extremely durable for sleepers and paving blocks. Recently a few of the streets of London have been paved with it. Lignum vitæ (*Guaiacum officinale*) is of all woods the one which comes nearest to a strong metal in resistance to tear and wear.

Furniture and Ornamental Woods.—Mahogany is by far the most important of furniture woods, and it has many minor applications as well. Perhaps no other timber has such valuable properties for the construction of cabinets, sideboards, tables, or casing of any sort. For a hardwood it is easily worked; it is close-grained, takes a fine polish, and is very durable; if well seasoned it is not apt to warp, shrink, or crack, and its color improves with age. Some pieces of finely "curled" or figured mahogany bring a very high price. Oak, though also an excellent wood for furniture, is more difficult to season, more laborious to work, and less easy to obtain free of defects. The black walnut (*Juglans nigra*) of Canada and the United States is much used for furniture. It is of a pleasing dark color, and comes nearer Spanish mahogany in suitability for cabinet work, but is not so hard. Italian or Circassian walnut (*Juglans regia*) is harder, and as a rule much more richly figured. It has been used for centuries for carving and furniture in Italy and other European countries. Much old walnut furniture is badly "worm eaten." Brazilian rosewood, the product of a much smaller tree

than any of the above, is a strong, hard, heavy material, but fairly easily worked. It is of a dark, rich brown color, with beautiful streaks and cloud-like markings of a still darker tint, which more nearly resembles those of a colored marble than any other known wood. It has been long used in Europe for costly furniture. Satinwood, of which there are two kinds much the same in appearance, is something like rosewood in hardness and fineness of grain. Owing to their closeness of grain neither holds glue well. Except that it is of a different and much lighter color, the figure of satinwood much resembles the "curl" of mahogany.

Ebony is another of the costly cabinet woods which is also hard and heavy. It is particularly close in the grain, so that it is suitable for drawing instruments as well as for cabinets, caskets, and the like. Ebony is black or nearly black in color, and has been prized for making furniture with ivory and other "inlays" from ancient Egyptian times. Beautiful work of this kind is still made in Paris. The strikingly mottled Calamander wood of Ceylon and the fine marble wood of the Andaman Islands are both from ebenaceous trees. Among the very beautiful and for the most part costly woods used only for veneering and inlaying furniture and small ornamental articles are tulip wood (*Physocalymma florida*), snake or letter wood (*Brosinum aubletii*), purple heart (*Copaifera Martii*), and zebra wood (*Connarus guianensis*) from the tropical parts of America; to which may be added Amboyna wood from Singapore. Bird's-eye maple, a beautifully spotted or "eyed" light wood, is used in its native country (North America) for furniture, and was formerly much in favor for this purpose in England. In the S. of Europe the wood of the olive and of the orange are used for cabinet work. In Australia some species of acacia, such as black wood (*A. melanoxylon*) and myallwood (*A. homalophylla*), which are dark woods, the former, especially, often beautifully figured, are used for furniture; so also are several other woods, including forest oak (*Casuarina torulosa*), muskwood (*Olearia argophylla*), and cypress pine (*Frenela robusta*), Queensland tree. Of late years, under the name of African mahogany, the botanical source of which is still uncertain, a wood somewhat resembling ordinary mahogany has been imported in some quantity into England from the coast of Guinea, and seems to be coming into favor for some kinds of cabinet work.

Nature of Wood.—The stem or trunk of an ordinary exogenous tree consists of a central pith and rings or zones of fibro-vascular bundles (composed of numerous cell forms) through which medullary rays radiate. In a growing tree of this class the new wood forms next the bark, and is called sap-wood (alburnum). Gradual changes occur in these annual rings or layers of new wood as they become older, and in time, which varies from one to many years, they get hardened or solidified into ripe wood or heart wood (duramen), of which all useful timber consists. These changes are of a chemical and physical character, and, although it is the hardening of the wood of a growing tree with age that gives it its technical value, yet the change is, physiologically, an incipient process of degradation which ends in decomposition. It is only in a few kinds of trees, however, that the decay of the wood is rapid. This duramen or heartwood, when properly treated after felling, is generally of a lasting nature, and in the hardwoods especially is usually of a darker color than the sapwood; but in some pine woods the sapwood, soon after the tree is cut down, gets darker than the heart wood, and is of a bluish or greenish color.

The properties of wood depend partly on the mode of union of the fibers, and partly on the constituents, such as gum, resin, tannic acid, etc., which occur in the cellular and intercellular spaces. But there is also a small proportion of nitrogenous constituents which set up a kind of fermentation in damp wood, and especially in young spongy wood, exposed to the air, and are the cause of its decay. In other circumstances, however, even in the presence of moisture, but where the access of oxygen is prevented, some kinds of wood will keep for an enormous length of time. Pieces of wood have been taken out of the lignite beds of the newer geological formations which are scarcely distinguishable from sound timber recently cut. The timber used in the construction of a house or other building should be thoroughly dried before being put in, and air allowed to circulate about it. This is especially necessary with regard to joists and flooring near the surface of the ground, otherwise damp and want of ventilation will render them peculiarly liable to be attacked by dry rot.

The apparent sp. gr. of wood varies from 0.383 (poplar wood) to 1.333 (lignum vitæ), and perhaps some kinds are even denser. But the sawdust of nearly all woods is heavier than water, and the actual specific gravity (*i. e.*, of the wood apart from enclosed air) is much the same in all. The quality and the apparent specific gravity of timber from the same species of tree often widely vary. Soil, climate, whether they grow in close proximity, and other conditions determine to a large extent the value of wood from trees of a like kind. For example, the timber of the Scotch fir (*Pinus sylvestris*) brought from the Baltic varies so much that the Swedish wood is only two-thirds the price of that which comes from Danzig, while the wood of the same tree grown in Scotland is of less value than either. With mahogany the qualities differ far more. Spanish or Cuban mahogany is of much greater value than, and sometimes twice as heavy as, Honduras or Bay mahogany from the same species of tree. Each of these varieties again is found to differ greatly in quality in different samples of the wood.

Seasoning of Timber.—Trees, and especially deciduous trees, should always be felled in winter, as in that season they contain the least amount of natural sap. They should not be allowed to remain long on the ground where they are cut down, but, as soon as possible, the logs ought to be stacked with packing pieces between them, to allow the sap freely to evaporate. They should also be covered in from the weather. When the logs are cut up into planks or boards, these are usually in the first place laid horizontally, with lathes or fillets between them, and allowed to remain in this position for six months completely protected from rain. Afterward they are placed for the same length of time in a vertical position on racks and kept a little apart. Most ordinary woods require this length of time to season them properly in a natural way, though some are ready for use sooner than others. The seasoning of timber can be hastened by steaming or boiling it, or, in the case of planks and thin cut wood, by placing it in hot air chambers. Natural seasoning is, however, by far the best. For cabinet work and the better kinds of joinery the naturally seasoned wood is, just before being used, usually put for a week or 10 days in a stove heated to about 120° F. The thorough seasoning of wood is of great importance, but too frequently is only partially effected.

Preservation of Timber.—For the external woodwork of buildings oil paint is usually employed, and the painting should be renewed every four or five years. Wooden ships and boats are coated with tar or pitch. But for such purposes as pavement, sleepers, piles, etc., treatment with certain chemicals which penetrate the wood more deeply has been proposed. Three methods of doing this have been chiefly tried, and of these the impregnation with bichloride of mercury is called kyanising; when sulphate of zinc is used the process is termed burnettising; and the third method—the only one extensively practiced in Great Britain—is creosoting. The latter consists in steeping the wood in creasote oil, from 8 to 12 pounds being required for every cubic foot of timber. Since 1882 a new process introduced by H. Aitken, of Falkirk, has been under trial—namely, the soaking of timber, according to its bulk, from 2 to 12 hours in melted napthaline. This is a volatile substance, which must so far be against its efficiency, but the results of the experiments are said to give good promise of success.

TIMBUKTU, a city of the Sudan, Central Africa, in lat. 17° 37′ N. and lon. 3° 5′ W.; 6 miles N. of the Niger at the extreme N. point of its course. The town is triangular in shape, and at present is less than three miles in circumference, though formerly it was much larger. The wall or rampart which surrounded it was destroyed by invaders in 1826, and has not been rebuilt. The streets are for the most part straight and unpaved, with a gutter in the center. Most of the houses are of clay, and some are two stories high, a very unusual thing in Negroland. On the outskirts there are a good many conical huts of matting. Of the mosques, two are especially noteworthy from their great size and imposing appearance, viz., that of Sankoré in the N., and the great mosque in the W. angle of the town. The latter is 286 feet long and 212 feet wide. Timbuktu has also two markets. The climate is unhealthy, and the surrounding country being desert, or nearly so, all supplies of food are brought by the Niger from Sandsanding to Kábara, the port of Timbuktu. The manufactures are confined to a little iron work, and to leather bags, pouches, cushions, etc., made by the Tuarick women. The place owes its importance entirely to its commercial situation, which makes it the entrepôt for the trade between the N. and S. of the Sahara. In addition to the Niger there are two main channels by which commerce flows to Timbuktu, viz., the caravan routes from Morocco on the N., and Ghadames on the N. E. The principal articles of trade are gold in rings, salt, English calico, red cloth, cutlery, looking-glasses, rice, negro corn, kola nuts (a substitute for coffee), ginger, tobacco, dates, and tea. Timbuktu was founded toward the end of the 11th century, and became known to Europeans in 1373. Pop. (1917), about 16,000.

TIME. Time and space are the two great elements with which the astronomer in the observatory has to deal; consequently a great part of astronomical work, and a great part of the equipment of every observatory, is devoted to the determination of time in various ways and for various purposes.

Measurement of Time.—This is accomplished by the joint work of the clock and watchmakers, and of the astronomer who makes observations of the transits of the heavenly bodies across the meridian to determine the necessary daily corrections to these instruments. For no piece of chronometric apparatus, even the best constructed astronomical clock, can begin to approach in regularity of running the motions of the heavenly bodies, especially the rotation time of the earth on its axis, on which most time determinations depend. The principal pieces of apparatus used for keeping time are various forms of clocks and watches. Before the invention of these instruments the measurement of time was very rough, the most accurate being the method of the sundial; but as this was only good in the day time and when the sun was shining, various rougher devices were employed, such as running sand in the hour glass, the water clocks, or clepsydræ, or even a burning candle. The senseless division of the day into two periods (of 12 hours each), which was probably originally brought about by the use of the sun's shadow in the day time and something or nothing else in the night, is one of the relics of barbarism which seems to be the hardest to get rid of. Even the division into 24 hours (instead of decimals of the whole day, as it ought to be) is bad enough, but, on account of the radical change necessary in the construction of all clocks and watches in order to bring this about, it will probably be a long time in coming. But the small changes necessary in the dials in order that they may read up to 24 hours instead of 12 makes it surprising that there is so much opposition to the proposal of the railroad managers simply to print their time tables with the day divided in that way.

Different Kinds of Time.—Two different kinds of time, with different actual lengths of the unit, are in common use— mean solar and sidereal. The mean solar day marks the average interval of the return of the sun to the sme meridian. The time marked by the return of the actual sun is not uniform, and is called apparent time. The difference between mean and apparent time is called the equation of time. Mean solar time is that in common use, but the mean solar day is used in two different ways; the one called the civil day, or civil time, begins the day at midnight, and is the one used by the people at large. The other, used by astronomers, begins the day at mean noon, reckoning it from 0 to 23 + hours. The day begins 12 hours later than the civil day, or 12 hours earlier, according to how the matter is viewed. Thus at 6 P. M., Jan. 23, the astronomer calls it Jan. 23 days 6 hours, or Jan. 23.25 days, if he expresses it decimally. Likewise he calls Jan. 24 at 6 A. M. Jan. 23 days 18 hours, or Jan. 23.75 days. If we consider that 23.25 days and 23.75 days are still parts of the 23d day, then the astronomical day is half a day behind; but if they are to be regarded as parts of the 24th day, as they should be just as much as 1850 is regarded as the middle of the 19th and not the 18th century, then the astronomical day is 12 hours ahead of the civil. It is simply a question of interpretation. The astronomical time as above defined is generally called simply "mean time," to distinguish it from either civil time or sidereal time.

Sidereal time is of an entirely distinct length from mean solar, the sidereal day marking the successive transits of the vernal equinox over the meridian, and being very nearly equal to the rotation time of the earth on its axis. The sidereal day equals 23 hours 56 minutes 4.090 seconds of mean solar time, and there is one more sidereal day in the year than solar days. The sidereal day is not of absolute uniform length, as the precession of the equinoxes is not absolutely uniform, but the variations in its length are out in decimal places of seconds beyond those given above. Sidereal time is only used in observations by astronomers. All observations with transit instruments for the determination of the right ascensions of the heavenly bodies are recorded by sidereal clocks, and the observation made simply for the purpose of getting the corrections to a mean time clock for the purpose of time distribution are generally made on the stars, using a sidereal clock or chronometer, and then the mean time clock is compared with the sidereal afterward to determine its correction.

Time Signal.—Many observatories send out time signals either daily, hourly, or sometimes continuously every second, or every other second, to various parts of the country for the purpose of giving accurate time to all sorts of industries. They are sent over the telegraph lines, the wires being permanently run into the observatories for the purpose, and the signals are generally sent automatically by a distributing clock which is kept as near the exact times as possible. An electric current passes through the clock and is broken or closed regularly by a toothed wheel on the second hand arbor of the clock. Perhaps the best known set of time signals is that sent out by the Naval Observatory at Washington. It is as follows: three or four minutes before noon, whenever the telegraph companies switch in the loops to the observatory, the clock begins to send out make-circuit signals every second over the various lines, the minutes being indicated by leaving out the seconds 55, 56, 57, 58, and 59 in each, and the half minutes by leaving out the 29th second of each. The click following such a one-second gap then always indicates the beginning of a half-minute, and the first following a gap of five seconds indicates the beginning of a minute, except at the exact noon. Just before this there is a gap of 10 seconds, and then exactly at noon the circuit closes and remains closed for just a whole second, the beginning of the mark indicating exact noon. The closing for a whole second is in order to make sure that that particular mark goes through all the telegraph lines, for the particular signal is made to do a great many things at different places, such as the dropping of time balls and it is more important that this particular second be distinctly sent than any of the others. After the break at the close of the noon signal the telegraph companies quickly switch out the loops to the observatory, and the lines immediately resume their normal work. In the city of Washington this particular noon signal drops a time ball on the top of the State, War, and Navy Department building, and it also automatically corrects, by setting forward or back exactly to 0 hours 0 minutes 0 seconds, all the clocks in the department buildings of the government, no matter how much they may have gained or lost since the preceding noon.

Local, Universal and Standard Time.— Local mean time is that indicated by the transits of the sun at any particular meridian, and of course this differs for places of different longitudes on the surface of the earth. In fact, the difference of longitude between two places is simply the difference of their local times, and the accurate determination of this difference is one of the most common kinds of astronomical work, especially in the principal observatory of any country. The operation consists simply in making the most accurate determination possible of the clock-corrections at each observatory and then comparing the clocks by telegraphic time signals with each other. But if this local time is used as the standard time at every place it causes the greatest confusion to people traveling from one place to another and to the railroads connecting them. England early adopted the time of the Greenwich meridian for the whole country, and likewise France that of Paris. In the United States uniformity was more difficult on account of the great difference of longitude of its different parts. San Francisco time being nearly four hours slower than the local time in the E. part of Maine. But an excellent compromise was brought about in 1883, principally through the influence of the railroads, pushed on by a few scientific men, and it resulted in the present system of standard time throughouut the country. This is based on Greenwich time, and differs from it at any place by some whole number of hours, the minutes and seconds being the same over the whole country, and exactly the same as those of Greenwich. The E. part of the country uses time five hours slower than that of Greenwich, or Greenwich five-hour time; i. e., when it is standard noon in the E. part of the United States it is 5 P. M. at Greenwich. In the Mississippi valley they use Greenwich six-hour time. The dividing line is not an arbitrary one, but is settled by the railroads, generally where they find it most convenient to change at the end of divisions of the roads. The Pennsylvania roads change at Pittsburgh. The cities and towns along the roads adopt the time of the nearest railroad, and no inconvenience results even where the difference of standard from local time is something more than half an hour. The only inconvenience is in cities like Pittsburgh, where two different hours are used by different railroad systems centering there. But the trouble is infinitely less than it was when there were more than 70 different standards of railroad time in the country. Out on the plains they use Greenwich seven-hour time, and on the Pacific slope Greenwich eight-hour time. These four standards are commonly called the Eastern, Central, Mountain, and Pacific time, respectively. See DAYLIGHT SAVING.

While the above is not an ideal system, it is about the best that can be used at the present time. If the people at large can ever be educated up to the standard of dissociating entirely 12 o'clock from noon, then we can adopt a universal time for all parts of the earth. This is already done by many scientific men, especially astronomers, meteorologists, and those having any thing to do with terrestrial magnetism, it being necessary in all these matters to have a common universal time for use, and Greenwich time, either mean or civil, as defined above, is almost universally adopted for these purposes. Such a time is also a necessity in international telegraphic communication, and, once adopted, would be found of universal convenience. Its introduction would come about much easier if at the same time the 12 or 24-hour division of the day could be abandoned, and the decimal division of a universal day come into general use. This, however, involves the abandonment of all existing time pieces and the purchase of new ones showing the decimal division of the day, and as this involves a large financial outlay it will be very difficult of introduction.

TIMOLEON, a Greek general; born of a noble family at Corinth in the beginning of the 4th century B. C. He saved the life of his brother Timophanes in a battle with the Argeians; but his patriotism was stronger than his personal affections, and when that brother sought to establish a "tyranny," Timoleon procured his assassination, 366 B. C. This act, though publicly approved, preyed on his mind, and he lived retired for 20 years. In 344, when Timoleon was 50 years old, ambassadors from Syracuse arrived at Corinth imploring aid against Dionysius the younger, who was seeking to recover his authority over the city. Timoleon was made leader of the Corinthian expeditionary force, and ultimately made himself master of Syracuse, repelling the efforts of the Carthaginian allies in a great battle at Crimissus (399 B. C.). In six years he succeeded in clearing Sicily of tyrants and in establishing free democratic constitutions. His work now done, he resigned his power and lived a private citizen profoundly respected, till his death in 337-336. Plutarch and Cornelius Nepos have written his life.

TIMON, an Athenian misanthrope; born near Athens, and lived in the last part of the 5th century B. C. The faithfulness of his friends and successive disappointments soured his nature, and drove him into solitude, where he is said, however, to have welcomed Alcibiades. His name has become proverbial, and his story is familiar through the tragedy of Shakespeare.

TIMOR (tē-mōr'), the most important of the chain of islands which stretch E. from Java; length 300 miles; area 17,698 square miles; pop. approximately, 119,239. A chain of wood-clad mountains runs throughout its entire length; one peak, Allas, near the S. coast, being

11,500 feet in height. It is less volcanic than its smaller neighbors of the Sunda group, but it contains some quiescent or extinct volcanoes. Magnetic iron, porphyry, gold, copper, and sulphur are found. Otherwise the natural wealth of the island is not great, the comparatively dry climate producing a much less luxuriant vegetation than in Java. The exports are mainly maize, sandalwood, wax, tortoiseshell, and trepang. Separated from the Australian region by the Arafura sea, the island shows few Australian types among its fauna and flora, which resemble those of Java, Celebes, and the Moluccas. The population is mainly Papuan, mixed with Malay and other elements. The smaller W. portion belongs to the Dutch, with its capital at Kupang; the E. part is Portuguese, capital Delhi; but native chiefs really govern the island.

TIMORLAUT (tē-mōr'lout) ("Timor lying to seaward"), a small group of islands in lat. 6° 40'-8° 23' S., lon. 130° 26'-132° E, 260 miles E. of Timor. It consists of eight considerable islands of volcanic formation and a great number of coral islets. The chief islands are Yamdena, Larat, and Selaru; the first, by far the largest has an area of 1,100 square miles. All three are very mountainous. The group lying within the range of the damp S. E. winds which blow through Torres Strait has a much more humid climate than Timor, and luxuriant forests ascend to the very summits of the mountains. The natural wealth of the islands is as yet undeveloped, and tortoise-shell and bêche-de-mer are the chief articles of trade. The natives resemble those of Northwestern New Guinea in appearance, and are fierce and treacherous.

TIMOTHEUS, a famous Greek musician and dithyrambic poet. He died about 357 B. C.

TIMOTHY ("one who honors God"), one of the companions of St. Paul on his missionary travels. Timothy was born either at Lystra or Derbe; his father was a Greek, his mother a Jewess (Acts xvi: 1-2). Both his mother, Eunice, and his grandmother, Lois, were Christians (II Tim. i:5), having probably been converted by St. Paul on his first missionary tour through Lycaonia (Acts xiv: 6). Hence Timothy early knew the [Jewish] scriptures, probably with Christian interpretations (II Tim. iii: 15); but his actual conversion seems to have been effected through the instrumentality of St. Paul, if, indeed, this be the meaning of the phrase "my own son in the faith"

(I Tim. i: 2). His constitution was feeble, sensitive, with a certain tendency to asceticism, yet not free from temptation to "youthful lusts" (II Tim. ii: 22). He was strongly recommended to St. Paul by the Christians at Lystra and Iconium. The apostle therefore chose him as missionary colleague, and had him circumcised for the sake of facilitating his work among the Jews (Acts xvi: 3). He thoroughly gained the confidence and affection of St. Paul, and was with him in Macedonia and Corinth (A. D. 52-53; Acts xvii; 14, xviii: 5; I Thess. i: 1), and at Ephesus, from which he was dispatched for special duty to Corinth (A. D. 55-56; I Cor. iv: 17, xvi: 10). Returning, he was with St. Paul when the second epistle to the Corinthians and that to the Romans were penned (II Cor. i: 1; Rom. xvi: 21), as also when he passed through Asia Minor prior to his arrest (A. D. 57-58; Acts xx: 4), and during his imprisonment at Rome (A. D. 61-63; Cal. i:1; Philem. 1; Phil. i:1). Probably about A. D. 64 he was left in charge of the Ephesian church. In Heb. xiii: 23 his own imprisonment and liberation are recorded. Tradition makes him ultimately suffer martyrdom, either in A. D. 96 or in A. D. 109.

The First Epistle of Paul the Apostle to Timothy.—An epistle addressed by St. Paul to Timothy. Some persons in the Ephesian church had taught, or appeared disposed to teach, a doctrine different from that of the apostle. Paul therefore, on departing from Macedonia, left Timothy behind to restrain these false teachers (I Tim. i: 3-7), pretentious men too much given to profitless "fables and endless genealogies" (verse 4). Paul charged Timothy to preach the Gospel, defining it as a "faithful saying, and worthy of all acceptation, that Christ Jesus came into the world to save sinners" i: 5-20). Paul then commends prayer (ii: 1-8), defines the position of women in the Christian church (9-15), explains the duties of a bishop (iii: 1-7), and of a deacon and his wife (iii: 8-13), and, expressing the hope that he soon may see Timothy (iii: 14), he gives him personal counsel (15), presents as beyond controversy the mystery (hidden thing) of godliness (16), predicts by the Spirit perilous times (iv: 1-4), adds fresh injunction to his younger colleague (v-vi), explaining what his action should be toward elderly and younger men, and elder and younger women (v: 1-16), the Christian functionaries called elders (17), slaves (vi: 1-2), the rich (17-19), and what should be his conduct in the office which he held in trust (20-21). Eusebius summed up the verdict of Christian antiquity in placing the first epistle to Timothy among the Homologoumena. Modern rationalistic critics, from Schmidt and Schleiermacher to Renan, have denied its authenticity, of which, however, there have been powerful defenders. Various dates have been assigned it; one of the most probable is A. D. 56.

The Second Epistle of Paul the Apostle to Timothy.—An epistle written by St. Paul after he had become a prisoner (i: 8) in Rome (17), in bonds (ii: 9), who had been at least once judicially examined and been required to make his "answer" (iv: 16), a crisis which, however, ended in his being "delivered out of the mouth of the lion" [Nero (?)] (iv: 17). Commencing by expressing his love for Timothy, and his earnest desire to see him (i: 1-5), he exhorts him to steadfastness in the faith (6-18), to hardiness and unworldliness (ii: 1-7), to the avoidance of frivolous and entangling questions, to purity (ii: 8-23), and to meekness under provocation (24-26). His counsels are all the more fervent that many have deserted him for heresy or the world (i: 15, ii: 17, iv: 10), and he foresaw that a general impatience of sound doctrine was destined to appear (iii: 1-17, iv: 1-4). A certain air of sadness pervades the epistle, but the writer looks forward to his probably near martyrdom in tranquil trust in his Redeemer whom he had served so long and so well (iv: 6-8). He closes with sundry greetings and with the benediction. The evidence for the authenticity of the epistle is the same as that for the previous letter. Two dates assigned it are A. D. 63, and July or August A. D. 65. It seems to have been the last of St. Paul's epistles.

TIMOTHY GRASS (*Phleum pratense*), hard coarse grass with cylindrical spikes from 2 to 6 inches long. It is used mixed with other grasses for permanent pasture, and grows best in tenacious soils. It is extensively cultivated throughout Great Britain, and also in North America. Timothy Hanson first recommended it, hence its name. Swine refuse it.

TIMROD, HENRY, an American poet; born in Charleston, S. C., Dec. 8, 1829. His only volume of "Poems" was published in 1860; reprinted and edited with memoir by Paul H. Hayne, 1873. He died in Columbia, S. C., Oct. 6, 1867.

TIMUR (tē-mör'), called also TIMUR BEG and TIMUR LENK (that is, Timur the Lame), and, by corruption, TAMERLANE,

a celebrated Oriental conqueror, of Mongol or Tartar race; born in the territory of Kesh, near Samarcand, in 1336. His ancestors were chiefs of the district, and Timur by his energy and abilities raised himself to be ruler of all Turkestan (1370). By degrees he conquered Persia and the whole of Central Asia, and extended his power from the great wall of China to Moscow. He invaded India (1398), which he conquered from the Indus to the mouths of the Ganges, massacring, it is said, on one occasion 100,-000 prisoners. On his way from India to meet the forces of Bajazet, the Turkish sultan, he subjugated Bagdad, plundered Aleppo, burned down the greater part of Damascus, and wrested Syria from the Mamelukes, after which he overran Asia Minor with an immense army. Bajazet's army was completely defeated on the plain of Ancyra (Angora), in 1402, and the Sultan was taken prisoner. The conquests of the Tartar now extended from the Irtish and Volga to the Persian Gulf, and from the Ganges to the Grecian Archipelago. He was making mighty preparations for an invasion of China when death arrested his progress at his camp at Otrar, beyond the Sir-Daria, in 1405, and his empire immediately fell to pieces. He is the reputed author of the "Institutions of Timur" and the "Autobiography of Timur," both translated into English. He is the hero of Marlowe's "Tamburlaine."

TIN, in chemistry, a white, metallic, easily fusible metal, not much affected by exposure to dry or moist air at ordinary temperatures, but becoming oxidized superficially when heated, burning with a brilliant flame if the temperature be raised sufficiently high. It dissolves in hydrochloric acid, with the evolution of hydrogen, forming hydrated chloride of tin. Strong nitric acid acts on it violently, producing an insoluble hydrated binoxide of the metal, a considerable amount of ammonia being formed at the same time by the decomposition of the water and nitric acid present. Cold dilute sulphuric acid has no action on it, but if the concentrated acid be used the metal is converted into the sulphate, while sulphurous acid escapes. Hot dilute sulphuric acid also converts it into sulphate of tin, hydrogen being evolved. The tin which is imported from Banca is nearly pure; that made in England generally contains small quantities of arsenic, copper, iron, and lead. In its chemical characteristics, tin has but few alliances. In some of its properties, however, it seems related to tantalum and titanium. Its chemical combinations are numerous and important, and its resistance to oxidation and to the action of vegetable acid renders it extremely useful for domestic purposes. Symbol St. Prof. Forrest Shepherd, of Missouri, advanced an assertion that tin is not a simple, but a compound metal. His opinion, nevertheless, so far as we know, is not the result of analyses, but of speculation and inconclusive analogies.

In metallurgy, tin is a white metal, with a slight yellowish tinge, and a brilliant metallic luster. It is wanting in tenacity, but is extremely malleable at a temperature of 212°. It has a great tendency to crystallize, and its crystalline form may be easily shown by rubbing a piece with a little nitric or hydrochloric acid, when it assumes the appearance known as *moire métallique*. By slow cooling it may be procured in octohedral crystals, and on bending a piece of tin backward and forward, a peculiar crackling or grating sound is heard, from the friction of the internal crystals. It fuses at 442° F., but it is not sensibly volatilized at that or any higher temperature. If it is stirred while melted till it cools, it may be obtained in a state of powder. Its brilliancy and power of resisting atmospheric changes render it exceedingly useful in the arts as a covering for other metals. What is ordinarily called tin in domestic language, is sheet-iron covered with a layer of tin, a process which is explained further on. Copper is also very well fitted for being coated with this metal. In India, it is applied instead of steel and iron to articles by way of ornament, and there is no reason why our artisans should not take pattern from their more artistic Eastern brethren.

For the manufacture of tin plates, the best soft charcoal iron is obliged to be used. After it has been rolled and cut to the requisite size, its surface is made chemically clean by immersion for a few minutes in dilute sulphuric acid. The sheets are then heated to a red heat in a reverberatory furnace, withdrawn, allowed to cool, hammered flat, and passed between polished rollers, and then washed in dilute acid. This preparation is needed to free the surface of the iron from the slightest portion of oxide, to which the tin would not adhere. In order to tin them, they are plunged one by one into a vessel of tallow, from which they are transferred to a bath of tin. From this they are taken after a certain time, allowed to drain, and dipped again. The superfluous tin at the edge of the plate is removed by dipping it in the melted tin once more, and detaching it by giving the plate a sharp blow. The tin and iron form a perfect alloy with each other.

I—29

The appearance known as *moire métallique* is given by sponging the surface of the tin with dilute nitro-hydrochloric acid, washed with water, and afterward varnished with plain or colored varnish. Copper is tinned in the same way, but with greater ease, it being so much less difficult to clean the surface of that metal than iron. Tinfoil is made by beating pure tin to the requisite thinness. The alloys of tin are numerous and important. The principal of these are Britannia metal, consisting of equal parts of brass, tin, antimony, and bismuth; pewter, 4 tin, and 1 lead; Queen's metal, 9 tin, and 1 each of antimony, bismuth, and lead; the various solders; bell-metal, 78 copper, 22 tin; bronze, copper, with 4 to 6 per cent. of tin; gun metal, 78 copper and 22 tin; and several others. Speculum metal, used for the mirrors of reflecting telescopes, is a steel-white, hard, brittle alloy, of 1 part of tin and 2 of copper. An amalgam of tin and mercury is used for silvering looking glasses. A sheet of tinfoil is laid on an edged slab of stone carefully levelled, and mercury is poured on it till it forms a layer ⅛ inch thick. Glass is laid down on this, and the table is tilted to let the superfluous mercury run off, weights being gradually placed on the glass to facilitate the operation. Tin ores are met with but in few localities.

Cornwall, Banca, Mexico, and above all of late years the Straits Settlements are the chief tin sources. The most celebrated tin mines are those of Cornwall, England, which have been worked uninterruptedly from the earliest historic periods. In the United States, crystals of the oxide of tin have been found in localities of Massachusetts, New Hampshire, New York, New Jersey, Virginia, California, Missouri, and perhaps in other States. Some of the mines, as those of Missouri and California, seem promising. Our product in 1916 was 140 short tons, most of which came from Alaska. In 1919, the world produced 125,760 metric tons of tin, of which the United States imported about 50 per cent. The only ore of importance is tin stone, a hard dark-brown crystalline body consisting of the binoxide in a crystalline condition. To extract the metal, the ore is first stamped and washed, to get rid of the lighter particles of sand or earth adhering to it. It is then roasted, to free it from arsenic and sulphur, and again washed to carry off the sulphate of copper and oxide of iron. The washed ore is mixed with from one-fifth to one-eighth its weight of powdered anthracite or charcoal, and with a small portion of lime to form a fusible slag with any of the remaining gangue. The charge is placed on the hearth of a low-crowned reverberatory furnace, and the doors are closed up. Heat is applied very gradually for five or six hours, care being taken to raise the temperature high enough to cause the carbon to reduce the tin without melting the siliceous gangue, which would form with the binoxide an enamel troublesome to remove. When nearly all the tin is reduced, the heat is raised considerably, the slags being thus rendered fluid and capable of floating on the top of the melted metal. The tin is then run off into cast iron pans, from which it is ladled off into molds to form ingots. The tin thus procured is far from being pure; it is therefore submitted to the process of lignation, which consists in heating the ingots to incipient fusion. By this means the purer tin which fuses at a comparatively low heat separates, running down, and leaving the impure portions behind. The less fusible portion, when remelted, forms block tin and the part which has run out is again melted and agitated with wet stakes. The steam thus formed bubbles up to the surface, carrying with it all other mechanical impurities contained in the tin. The mass is then skimmed and allowed to cool. When just about to set, the upper half is ladled out, the other metals and impurities having sunk into the bottom half, from the tendency that this metal has to separate from its alloys. The finest quality of tin is frequently heated to a temperature just short of its melting point. At this heat it becomes brittle, and is broken up into masses, showing the crystals of the metal, and forming what is known as grain tin. The formation of crystals is to some extent a guarantee of its purity, since impure tin does not become brittle in this way. English tin generally contains small quantities of arsenic, copper, iron and lead.

Chlorides of Tin.—There are two chlorides of tin, the protochloride and the per or bichloride. The protochloride, $SnCl$, may be prepared in the anhydrous state by the action of dry hydrochloric acid on tin at a gentle heat. The hydrated chloride is obtained by dissolving the metal in hydrochloric acid diluted with an equal bulk of water. It crystallizes in transparent needles, containing two equivalents of water. It is a powerful reducing agent, and is much used by dyers for altering reducible coloring matters, such as sesquoixide of iron and peroxide of manganese. It is also used as an antichlore. It forms crystallizable double salts with the alkaline chlorides. The bichloride, perchloride, or fuming liquor of Libavius, $SnCl_2$, is made by passing chlorine over an inclined tube, fitted to a receiver, and containing pieces of tin-foil rolled up. It is used to a considerable extent in solution in dyeing. It absorbs sulphuretted and phosphuretted hydrogen, and forms a compound of ammonia. In some respects it plays the part of an acid—chlorostannic acid.

Oxides of Tin.—There are two oxides of tin—the protoxide and the binoxide. The protoxide is prepared in a variety of ways, too prolix for description here, and is only interesting in a chemical point of view. When heated in air, it burns like tinder, and is converted into the binoxide. The only ore of tin, tin-stone, is a form of the binoxide.

Sulphides of Tin.—There are two sulphides of tin—the protosulphide, formed by fusing together metallic tin and sulphur. The bisulphide, when prepared in the dry way, is known by the name of "aurum musivum," or mosaic gold, and is used as bronze powder in coarse decorative works. It is prepared by fusing together seven parts of flowers of sulphur and six of salammoniac with an amalgam of 12 parts of tin and 6 of mercury.

TINCTURE, in chemistry, the finer and more volatile parts of a substance, separated by a menstruum; an extract of a part of the substance of a body communicated to the menstrumm. In heraldry, the name given to the colors, metals, or tints used for the field or ground of an emblazoned shield, including the two metals *or* and *argent* or gold and silver, the several colors, and the furs. In pharmacy, a colored solution of some animal or vegetable principle. Tinctures are very numerous, commencing with the tincture of aconite and the tincture of aloes. Different menstrua are employed; chiefly rectified spirit, proof spirit, compound spirit of ammonia, and spirit of ether.

TINDAL, MATTHEW, an English deist; born in Devonshire, England, in 1657; studied at Lincoln and Exeter Colleges, Oxford; graduated B.A. in 1676; and was elected Fellow of All Souls in 1678. In opinions he was first High Church, then Roman Catholic (1685); next Low Church, and finally Rationalist. His chief work, "Christianity as Old as the Creation, or the Gospel a Republication of the Religion of Nature," was published anonymously in 1730. The argument of the book is that Christianity, as far as it is true, must be the religion of nature; for as God is unchangeable, so is human nature. He attacks many of the statements in Scripture, especially those bearing on Jewish history in the ordinary rationalistic manner; but he does not explicitly deny the truth of the Christian revelation. Of Tindal's other works the following are the most important: "Four Discourses of Obedience to the Supreme Powers" (1694); "Rights of the Christian Church Asserted" (1706); "New High Church Turned Old Presbyterian" (1709); "A High Church Catechism" (1710). He died in Oxford, Aug. 16, 1733.

TINDALE, WILLIAM. See TYNDALE.

TINDER, any substance artificially rendered readily ignitable but not inflammable. Before the invention of chemical matches it was the chief means of procuring fire. The tinder, ignited by a spark from a flint, was brought into contact with matches dipped in sulphur. Tinder may be made of half-burnt linen, and of various other substances, such as amadeu, touchwood, or German tinder.

TINGLEY, KATHERINE (nee Westcott), an American theosophist; born at Newburyport, Mass., in 1852. She founded the Universal Brotherhood, a theosophical organiation, and as head of it gained recognition of the successor of Madame Blavatsky. She toured many countries preaching theosophy in 1897 and 1904. The headquarters of the Brotherhood, formerly at New York, were removed to Point Loma, Cal., where she established an orphanage, a Raja Yoga Academy, and a School of Antiquity. She edited the "Century Path" and wrote: "The Mysteries of the Heart Doctrine"; "A Nosegay of Everlastings"; "Theosophy and Some of the Vital Problems of the Day."

TINKER, CHAUNCEY BREWSTER, an American college professor; born in Auburn, Me., 1876. He graduated from Yale in 1899 and became associate instructor in English at Bryn Mawr in 1902; instructor in English in 1903; assistant professor in 1908; then professor of English literature at Yale in 1913. Among his works are: "A Critical Bibliography of the Translations of Beowulf" (1903); "Selections from Ruskin" (1908); "Dr. Johnson and Fanny Burney" (1911); "The Salon and English Letters" (1915). During 1918-1919 he was captain in the Military Intelligence Division of the general staff, United States Army.

TINO, or **TENOS,** an island of Greece, in the nomarchy of the Cyclades; immediately S. E. of Andros; area, 81 square miles. It is 18 miles long by 8 broad, and is traversed by high mountains, the terraced slopes of which yield wine, wheat, melons, figs, etc. Marble, in block or wrought into various kinds of vessels and ornaments, and silk, raw or made into gloves and stockings, are the chief exports. The chief town, Tino, on the S. coast, is the seat of a Roman Catholic bishop, has two Roman churches, and a small harbor. To the N. of it is the white marble church of Penagia Evangelistria, a famous resort of pilgrims.

TINTAGEL (-tä′jel) **HEAD,** a cliff 300 feet high on the W. coast of Cornwall, about 22 miles W. of Launceston, and but 6 miles from Camelford—the Camelot of Arthurian legend. Partly on the mainland and partly on the so-called island, almost cut off by a deep chasm from the rest of the promontory, stand the imposing ruins of the castle where King Arthur held his court. His spirit still hovers around the scene of his splendor in the form of the red-legged chough, a beautiful Cornish bird already rare in Leland's time. The oldest part of the existing ruins is the keep, apparently of a Norman construction, but there need hardly be a doubt that a Saxon, and perhaps earlier a British stronghold, occupied the same site. The castle was still habitable in 1360, when we read of its being provisioned.

TINTERN ABBEY, a famous abbey in Monmouthshire, England, on the right bank of the Wye river; 5 miles to the N. of Chepstow; was founded for Cistercian monks in 1131 by Walter, second son of Richard Fitz-Gilbert de Clare. Rebuilt by Roger de Bigod (1269-1288), it is an excellent example of the Transition style from Early English to Decorated, the most striking features of its cruciform church (228 by 150 feet) being the central belfry arches, and four great windows with their lace-like tracery. The dismantling of the abbey followed close on the dissolution (1337), when the ruins were granted to the ancestor of the Dukes of Beaufort.

TINTORETTO IL, a V e n e t i a n painter; real name JACOPO ROBUSTI; received his well-known surname from the fact of his father being a dyer (*Tintore*); born in Venice in 1512. He studied for a few days under Titian, but soon deserted the studio of the master for some unknown reason, and subsequently became a devoted student of antique sculpture, of anatomy, and of the works of Michael Angelo. On the walls of his studio he inscribed the ambitious motto, "*Il disegno di Michelangelo ed il colori di Tiziano,*" and such was the ardor and rapidity of his labor, reflected in the intensity of his style, that he acquired the nickname of Il Furioso. It was admitted by Sebastian del Piombo that Tintoretto could paint as much in two days as he could in as many years. The palaces and churches of Venice were rapidly adorned by him with vivid representations of historical, mythological, and scriptural subjects, but only a few of his frescoes survive. The only works said to bear his name are: "The Crucifixion," in the Scula di San Rocco (engraved by Agostino Caracci), the "Miracle of the Slave" in the Academy, and the "Marriage of Cana" in the Church of Santa Maria della Salute. His largest work, "Paradise," on the ceiling of the library in the Doges' palace, is 84½ feet by 34, and contains upward of 100 figures. Other famous works are "Belshazzer's Feast," the "Tiburtine Sibyl," "Last Supper," "Worship of the Golden Calf," "Last Judgment," and "Slaughter of the Innocents." About a third of his works are symbolical, and he frequently makes ingenious use of the winged lion of St. Mark. He certainly belongs to the greatest class of painters. Daring and passionate in imagination, Tintoretto sought to vary by dramatic movement the romantic motives of the Venetian school, and brought to perfection the poetry of chiaroscuro with something of Angelo's sublimity. Tintoretto died in Venice, May 31, 1594. His favorite daughter, MARIETTA, who was an excellent portrait painter, died in 1590, but his son, DOMENICO, also a painter, lived till 1637.

TINWORTH, GEORGE, an English artist in terra-cotta; born in London, England, Nov. 5, 1843. He was the son of a poor wheelwright, and while working in his father's shop took to wood carving of his own accord. In 1861 he found opportunity to get lessons in an art school at Lambeth, and in 1864 entered the Royal Academy schools. He soon began exhibiting figures and groups of figures at the Royal Academy, and in 1867 obtained a permanent appointment in the great Doulton art pottery. The works by which he became famous were mainly terra-cotta panels with groups of figures in high relief illustrating scenes from sacred history, which happily combine grace, strength, and divinity with originality of design, dramatic effectiveness, and devout feeling. An important example is the reredos in York Minster, with 28 terra-cotta panels.

TIPPECANOE, a river of Indiana, which rises in the N. part of the State, flows W. S. W. and S. 200 miles, and empties into the Wabash 10 miles above Lafayette. It is famous for the battle fought near its mouth, Nov. 7, 1811, in which the Indians, under Tecumseh's brother, the prophet, were defeated by General Harrison.

TIPPERARY, a county of Ireland, province of Munster, surrounded by King's County, Queen's County, Kilkenny, Waterford, Cork, Limerick, Clare, and Galway; area, 1,659 square miles. It lies in the basin of the Suir, which rises in the N. of the county and forms part of the S. boundary before passing through Waterford to the sea. The surface, for the most part level, is diversified by hill ranges, of which the chief are the Galtees (3,015 feet), Knockmeledown (2,150 feet), Slievenaman (2,364 feet), the Devil's Bit (1,600 feet), the Keeper (2,278 feet), and Slievenamuck (1,215 feet). The Shannon and Lough Derg form part of the W. boundary, separating Tipperary from Galway and Clare; and other streams which water it are the Brosna, Nenagh, and Mulkear. There are many small lakes, and among the more fertile districts are the plain of Ormond and Golden Vale. The prevailing rocks are clay, slate, greywacke, sandstone, and limestone; and among the minerals are anthracite, coal, copper, zinc, and lead mixed with silver. The soil, calcareous loam, is in parts singularly productive. The crops include potatoes, oats, wheat, turnips, and mangel-wurzel. Clonmel is the chief town. There are numerous antiquities, including the Holy Cross Abbey at Cashel, and Cahir Castle. The Mitchellstown caves, on the border of Cork, are of great extent and contain fine stalactite deposits. Pop. about 152,000.

TIPPERARY (Irish Gaelic, Tiobrad Arann, "the well of the district of Ara"), a market town in the county of the same name; on the Arra, an affluent of the Suir; 24½ miles N. W. of Clonmel and 110 S. W. of Dublin. Lying at the base of the Slievenamuck mountains, near the center of the Golden Vale, on the direct road from Clonmel to Limerick, it carries on a considerable trade in butter, corn, flour, etc. The daily butter market is said to be next in importance to that of Cork. Tipperary is the headquarters of the Union Agricultural Society, and it has a spacious corn and provision market, in which markets are held on Thursdays and Saturdays. There is a fine parish church, a Gothic Roman Catholic church with a spire 156 feet high, a Presbyterian church, a Methodist chapel, a town hall, etc. Pop. about 6,000.

TIPPOO SAHIB, more correctly TIPU SULTAN, Sultan of Mysore, and son of

Hyder Ali; born in 1749. From the French officers in his father's service he acquired a considerable acquaintance with European military tactics. This knowledge he put to effective use during his father's various wars by completely routing Colonel Bailey (1780 and 1782), and Colonel Braithwaite on the banks of the Coleroon (1782). On the death of his father he was crowned with little ceremony, returning at once to the head of his army, which was then engaged with the British near Arcot. In 1783 he captured and put to death most of the garrison of Bednur; but news of the peace between France and England having reached his French allies, they retired from active service, and Tippoo ultimately agreed to a treaty (1784) stipulating for the *status quo* before the war. He allowed his inveterate hatred of the English to overcome his judgment as to invade (1789) the protected state of Travancore. In the ensuing war (1790-1792) the British, under Colonel Stuart and Lord Cornwallis, were aided by the Mahrattas and the Nizam. He was ultimately compelled (1792) to resign one-half of his dominions, pay an indemnity of 3,030 lakhs of rupees, restore all prisoners, and give his two sons as hostages for his fidelity. Nevertheless, his secret intrigues in India against the British were almost immediately resumed; another embassy was sent to the French; and the invasion of Egypt by the latter in 1798 and Tippoo's machinations having become known to the governor-general almost simultaneously, it was resolved to punish the perfidious Sultan. Hostilities commenced in March, 1799, and two months after, Tippoo was driven from the open field, attacked in his capital of Seringapatam, and after a month's siege slain in the breach at the storming of the fort (May 4).

TIPULA, the crane fly, the typical genus of *Tipulidæ*. The antennæ have all the articulations, but the first almost cylindrical; the second globular. About 50 species are known from Europe. *T. oleracea* is the very common species called by children daddy long-legs. It is about an inch long, hoary brown, with four brown streaks on the thorax; the legs brownish-yellow, the thighs, tibiæ, and tarsi blackish toward their ends. It deposits about 300 shining black eggs in or on the ground. The larvæ, called grubs and leather-jackets, are dingy gray or brownish worms destitute of feet; they feed on the roots of grasses and other plants, and are often very destructive. When full grown they are an inch or an inch and a half long. The change to the pupa state takes place underground; the pupa itself has respiratory tubes. A smaller species, *T. hortulana*, is common in gardens. The largest species in Europe is the great crane fly, *T. gigantea*, an inch and a quarter in length.

TIPULIDÆ, crane flies, a family of *Nemocera*. Antennæ longer than the head, with 13 or more joints, rarely pectinated. Compound eyes, rounded or oval; ocelli none. Front of the head beaked, proboscis short, fleshy; palpi four-jointed; abdomen and legs long and slender; wings with numerous veins, some of them cross veins. The larvæ of most species live in rotton wood; a few are aquatic. Distribution world-wide.

TIRABOSCHI, GIROLAMO (tē-rä-bos'kē), an Italian historian of literature; born in Bergamo, Italy, Dec. 28, 1731. He wrote a celebrated "History of Italian Literature" (14 vols., 1770-1782), a work of wonderful erudition, accuracy, and completeness, extending from the first beginnings of modern culture in Italy down to the 18th century, and dealing with every branch of literature. Among his other writings are: "Historical Memoirs of Modena" (4 vols., 1793-1794). He died in Modena, June 3, 1794.

TIRAILLEUR (ti-rä-yur'), a name originally applied in France during the Revolution of 1792 to light-armed bodies, who were thrown out from the main body to bring on an action, cover an attack, or generally to annoy or deceive the enemy; a skirmisher, a sharpshooter.

TIRE, an iron band around the fellies of a wheel. The circular continuous tire is of American origin. In Europe tires were till lately generally made in sections arranged to break joints with the fellies. The rim tire is expanded by heating, and then shrunk on so as to tightly compress the wheel, and bolted; in the sectional tire, bolts only are relied on to hold the parts together. Steel railway tires are always of the former kind. India-rubber wheel tires, solid and pneumatic, are used on bicycles, automobiles, ambulances, light vehicles, and steam fire engines, for the purpose of decreasing the jar on the vehicle, and as a means of increasing the tractive adherence.

TIREE, or TYREE, an island of the Hebrides, belonging to Argyleshire. It is about 14 miles long, and reaches 6 in breadth, is generally low, flat, and fertile, but has several heights of 400 feet. Agriculture and fishing are the leading industries.

TIREBUCK, WILLIAM EDWARDS, an English writer; born in Liverpool, England, in 1854. For some years connected with the Liverpool "Mail" and "Yorkshire Post," he afterward devoted himself to writing novels; the most popular are: "Saint Margaret" (1888); "Dorrie" (1891); "Sweetheart Gwen" (1893); "Miss Grace of All Souls" (1895); "Meg of the Scarlet Foot" (1898); "The White Woman" (1899). His other writings include "Dante Gabriel Rossetti" (1882), and "Great Minds in Art" (1888). He belonged to the "Liverpool group" of English authors, including Hall Caine, William Watson, and Richard Le Gallienne.

TIRESIAS (ti-rē′shius), in Greek mythology, a famous prophet, who, according to one legend, was struck blind by the goddess Athene because he had seen her bathing. Another legend represents Hera as depriving him of his sight because, being made arbiter in a dispute between her and Zeus, he had decided in favor of the latter; when Zeus as a compensation granted him the inner vision of prophecy, and prolonged his life for several generations. He is consequently prominent in many of the mythical stories of Greece, but at last found death after drinking from the well of Tilphossa. Tiresias is the theme for a fine poem by Lord Tennyson (1885).

TIRLEMONT (ter-le-mông′), a town of Belgium; in South Brabant, on the Great Geete, 30 miles E. S. E. of Brussels. It has two fine churches of the 12th and 13th centuries, and manufactures of machinery, hosiery, flannel, leather, sugar, etc. Once a large and prosperous city, Tirlemont was ravaged by Marlborough in 1705; and here the French, under Dumouriez, defeated the Austrians in 1793. It was captured by the Germans in the first year of the World War and held by them until the armistice. Pop. about 17,500.

TIRNOVA, a town of Bulgaria, on the Jantra; 35 miles S. S. E. of Sistova; amid strange limestone rocks. It became in 1235 the seat of the Bulgarian patriarch, and has more than once served as the capital. Dyeing is carried on, silk and coarse cloth are manufactured. Pop. about 15,000.

TIRPITZ, ALFRED VON, a German admiral, notorious as the dominating figure behind the German submarine warfare policy during the World War. He was born in Kustrin, 1849, and educated in the Marine Academy, from which he graduated at the age of 17. After his period of sea service he entered

the Office of Marine; then, in 1898, became minister of state of Prussia. In 1911 he was made lord high admiral, and it was as such that he had the power to

ALFRED VON TIRPITZ

develop the submarine branch of the German navy. After the failure of his submarine policy, in 1917, he was compelled to resign and retired into the obscurity of private life.

TIRYNS (tī′rinz), or **TIRYNTHUS,** one of the oldest cities of ancient Greece, in Argolis, 2 miles from Nauplia. It was celebrated for its massive walls, which were popularly attributed to the Cyclops, and are the finest existing specimens of the military architecture of the heroic age of Greece. The ruins at present occupy the lowest hill of several which rise out of the plain, the S. E. part of the wall having a remarkable covered gallery 36 feet in length and 5 in breadth. The origin of Tiryns belongs to the mythical period, and in 468 B. C. it was entirely destroyed by the Argives.

TISCHENDORF, LOBEGOTT FRIEDRICH KONSTANTIN (tish′en dorf), a German Biblical critic; born in Lengenfeld, Saxony, Jan. 18, 1815; studied at Leipsic; and in 1845 became professor extraordinary there, becoming Professor Ordinary of Theology in 1859. He made several visits to the East, and brought back valuable MSS., the most remarkable being (in 1859) the very famous Sinaitic Codex. Tischendorf was continually engaged in editorial labors, and was broken down by overwork in 1873. He died in Leipsic, Dec. 7, 1874.

TISDALL, FITZGERALD, an American educator; born in New York city, March 15, 1840; was graduated at the College of the City of New York in 1859; tutor in the Free Academy, New York, in 1860; director of Cooper Union Schools of Science and Art in 1870; and Professor of Greek Language and Literature in the College of the City of New York after 1879. He lectured extensively; visited Europe several times; and was a member and councillor of the American Institute of Archæology and a member of the American Philological Association.

TISRI, in the Jewish calendar, the first month of the civil, and the seventh of the ecclesiastical year. It corresponded to part of our September and October. The Great Day of Atonement and the Feast of Tabernacles fell within its limits. Called in I Kings viii; 2, Ethanim (=streaming rivers), because the rivers, swelled by the autumnal rains, were then in flood. The name tisri occurs in the Palmyrene inscriptions and was probably not confined to the Jews.

TISSANDIER (tē-song-dyā'), GASTON, a French aeronaut and chemist; born in Paris, France, Nov. 21, 1843. Besides textbooks of chemistry, he wrote for the "Library of Wonders," volumes on "Water," "Coal," "Fossils," "Photography"; in collaboration with Glaisher and Flammarion, "Aerial Voyages." He died Nov. 21, 1899.

TISSOT (tē-sō'), CLAUDE JOSEPH, a French philosopher; born in Fourgs Doubs, Nov. 26, 1801. He translated most of Kant's writings into French. Among his original works are: "Of the Beautiful, Especially in Literature" (1830); "Short History of Philosophy" (1840); "The Mania of Suicide and of Revolt" (1840): "Parceling of the Land and Division of Property" (1842); "Principles of Morality" (1866); "Catholicism and Public Instruction" (1874); "Insanity Considered Especially in its Relations to Normal Psychology" (1876). He died in Dijon, Oct. 7, 1876.

TISSOT, PIERRE FRANÇOIS, a French historian and miscellaneous writer; born in Versailles, France, in 1768. Among his works are: "Reminiscences of Prairial 1st to 3d" (1799), an interesting page of French history; "Vergil's Bucolics," in French verse (1800); "The Three Irish Conspirators; or, Emmet's Shade" (1804); "The Wars of the Revolution to 1815" (1820); "Vergil Compared with Ancient and Modern Poets" (4 vols. 1825-1830); "Complete History of the French Revolution" (6 vols. 1833-1836). He died in 1854.

TISSUE, a very fine transparent silk stuff used for veils; white or colored. It was formerly interwoven with gold or silver threads and embossed with figures. Also a very thin kind of paper and cloth interwoven with gold. In entomology, a European geometer moth, *Scotosia dubitata*. The fore wings have numerous transverse wavy lines; the larva feeds on buckthorn.

In histology, a set of cells modified for the performance of a special function; the fabric of which the organs of plants and animals are composed. The structure of tissues, with very few exceptions, is imperceptible to the unassisted eye, and requires the aid of the microscope for its resolution. Tissues which are absent from plants occur in animals; these are called animal tissues, and have a relation to movement or to sensation, as the muscles and nerves. But plants preserve, protect, and sustain themselves, and the corresponding tissues in animals are spoken of as the vegetable tissues; of this kind are epithelium and bone. Tissues always present the same general arrangement in the same organism, but are combined in different ways in different organisms. In the lower forms of life, whether animal or vegetable, the distinctions between tissues become less and less obvious, and there are organisms so extremely simple that the tissue of their bodies is of a uniform cellular character.

Animal Tissues.—The term tissue is used in dealing with (*a*) the structure of organs, which are composed of various tissues; and (*b*) specially of the component parts of organs. In the first and wider sense, the anatomical individual is made up of osseous tissue, or bone; muscular tissue, or flesh; adipose tissue, or fat; cartilaginous tissue, or gristle; connective tissue, serving to bind the whole together; and pigmentary tissue, or coloring matter. In dealing with animal tissues in the strict sense, histological analysis shows them to be much more differentiated and elaborate in structure than those of plants. They may be divided into (*a*) Epithelium, consisting of nucleated protoplasmic cells, forming continuous masses, either arranged in a single layer, or stratified and forming several superimposed layers. The lining of the tubes and alveoli of secreting and excreting glands and the sensory or terminal parts of the organs of sense consist of epithelium. (*b*) Connective tissue, a name applied to a variety of tissues developed from the same embryonal element, serving more or less as framework or connecting substance for nervous, muscular, glandular, and vascular tissues. In the embryo and in the growing condition one may be changed into the other, and in the adult they gradually shade off one into the other. These tissues are divided into three groups: The epidermal, which covers the exterior of the plant, and usually consists of a single layer of cells; (2) the fibro-vascular, which traverses the body of the plant in the form of bundles, and is characterized by the presence of tubes and vessels, and of long, pointed, prosenchymatous cells—the wood fibers; (3) the fundamental tissue, which fills up the rest of the space, and consists principally of parenchyma.

TISZA, KOLOMAN BOROSJENO VON, a Hungarian statesman; born in Geszt, Hungary, Dec. 16, 1830; was educated for the civil service; devoted much time to travel; was elected to the Hungarian Parliament in 1860; and later became leader of the Moderate Radicals, which party he united with the Liberals in 1875. He was appointed Minister of the Interior in the same year and prime minister in 1876. In 1876-1878 he opposed the policy of Russia and Pan-Slavism, and resigned with his cabinet when the financial condition of the Austrian government was found to be insufficient to meet the expense of the Bosnian occupation. Subsequently, however, he resumed this office and held it till 1890, when he resigned. He died in Budapest, Hungary, March 23, 1902.

TISZA, STEPHAN, COUNT, Hungarian statesman, born in Budapest, in

COUNT STEPHAN TISZA

1861; died in 1918, at the hand of an assassin. After finishing his studies in Berlin and Heidelberg and Vienna he was given a post in the Ministry of the Interior, in 1882. He was a strong supporter of the union with Austria and on the strength of this policy became Premier and Minister of the Interior in 1903-1906. In 1913 he again became Premier, and was believed to be one of the most influential figures in precipitating the World War. His Cabinet was compelled to resign in 1917, its war policies having by that time become discredited.

TITANIUM, a very rare metallic element, discovered by Gregor in 1789. Symbol Ti; at. wt. 50. It is never found in the metallic state, but may be obtained by heating the double fluoride of potassium and titanium with potassium in a covered crucible, or by mixing titanic oxide with one-sixth of its weight of charcoal and exposing to the strongest heat of an air furnace. It is a dark-green, heavy, amorphous powder, having under the microscope the color and luster of iron. It dissolves in warm hydrochloric acid, with evolution of hydrogen, and, when heated in the air, burns with great splendor. Like tin, it forms two classes of compounds—the titanic, in which it is quadrivalent, and the titanous, in which it is trivalent. The spectroscope shows that there is titanium in the sun.

TITANS, in Greek mythology, were six sons and six daughters of Uranos and Gaia, named Okeanos, Koios, Kreios, Hyperion, Iapetos, and Kronos; Theia, Rhea, Themis, Mnēmosynē, Phoibē, and Tethys. Uranos having banished to Tartarus the Hekatoncheires ("the hundred-handed") and the Cyclōpes, Gaia called the Titans to avenge their brothers. They rose and freed them, deposed Uranos, and set Kronos in his place. Kronos and the Titans were in their turns put down by the sons of Kronos and Rhea, named the Olympioi, with Zeus at their head, but not till after a long struggle, in which Zeus brought to his aid the Cyclōpes and Heckatoncheires, whom Kronos had again imprisoned in Tartarus. Zeus quelled the Titans with the lightning given him by the Cyclōpes, hurled them to Tartarus, placing them under the care of the Hekatoncheires. This struggle, called the Titanomachia, was regarded as symbolic of the conflict of reason and order with the rude forces of nature.

TITHE, etymologically a 10th, historically a 10th part of the titheable produce of the land paid to the clergy.

The payment of tithe to the clergy originated in the recognition of a moral and religious duty. The discharge of this acknowledged obligation acquired the force of custom, then received the sanction of ecclesiastical law, and finally passed into the national jurisprudence of England and other Christian countries.

The first recorded instance of the payment of tithe is the offering of Abraham to Melchisedec (Gen. xiv: 20) ; the second precedent is the vow of Jacob at Bethel (Gen. xxviii: 22). The consecration of a fractional portion of the produce of the land to the uses of the ministers of religion formed part of the Mosaic law. The tribe of Levi were maintained from this source, not having lands assigned to them like the other tribes. Neither patriarchal usage, nor precedents of Mosaic law, nor the Levitical economy were binding on Christians; but they doubtless suggested to the clergy the precept and to the people the practice of paying tithes to the ministers of religion. The system is not specially enjoined in the New Testament, and no claim to tithes is urged by the Christian clergy as representatives of the Levitical priesthood. In the enthusiastic bounty of early Christianity voluntary offerings sufficed.

Some evidence does exist in the ante-Nicene Fathers that tithes were held to be due under the Gospel as well as under the Mosaic law; on the other hand, Selden is possibly right in maintaining that the custom of paying tithe cannot be traced before the 4th century. Whether this be so or not is immaterial. At the end of the 4th century the evidence is overwhelming (Hilary, Ambrose, Chrysostom, Jerome, Augustine) that the moral and religious duty of paying tithes was recognized, and had acquired the force of custom. As a moral and religious custom the payment of tithes was enjoined by the public acts of councils and churches, and enforced by moral and religious sanctions (e. g., Councils of Tours, 567; Macon, 589; Rouen, 650; etc.). The last stage was reached when the state added the civil sanction to the ecclesiastical sanction. In doing so the state recognized the already accepted customary duty, and the corresponding customary rights. It created no new burden; it appropriated no part of what had hitherto been a public fund or public revenue. On the Continent the attachment of legal sanctions to ecclesiastical customs dates from Charlemagne's legislation in 779 and 787. Henceforward tithes were enforced by temporal penalties.

Before Augustine landed in Kent (597) the custom of paying tithes had been enjoined by the public acts of continental councils. As a duty the payment of tithes was preached by the first missionaries; as a custom it was speedily established by their successors. But it was not till 785 that the custom was enjoined by ecclesiastical legislation. In 785 two Italian bishops were sent by Pope Adrian I. to recommend 29 Latin injunctions to the observance of the Anglo-Saxon church. Among them was one injunction which urged the payment of tithes as a means of securing to the payer the blessing of God. Thus the customary discharge of a recognized religious duty was for the first time enforced in England by the public act of an ecclesiastical council.

This ecclesiastical injunction was subsequently confirmed and extended by royal orders in Episcopal councils, in national synods, and in proclamations of peace. But it was not till 970 that the state recognized the customary duty and its corresponding customary right by adding the civil to the ecclesiastical sanction. It is now agreed that the so-called grant of King Offa is an idle story relating to Peter's pence, and that the so-called grant of King Ethelwulf rests on a misconstruction of a document which has no reference to tithes. No law, no charter, no authentic public document exists by which the state professes to confer the rights to tithes upon the Church. But the laws of King Edgar (970) attached a legal punishment to neglect of the customary and religious duty of paying tithes, and provided means of enforcing the corresponding customary right by temporal penalties. These laws were subsequently confirmed by successive sovereigns, though it was not till after the Conquest that the payment became general. The process by which tithes grew from a moral into a legal duty does not explain their special allocation as the local endowments of parishes. In their appropriation as part of the parochial system three stages may be distinguished: (1) before 970; (2) from 970 to the end of the 12th century; (3) from 1200 onward.

(1) *Before 970.*—During the first three centuries of the Anglo-Saxon church there was in each diocese one common treasury, into which were paid the tithes and other offerings of the faithful. As to the distribution of these funds by the bishop, different usages prevailed in different parts of Western Christendom. In the Roman dioceses the customary division was fourfold: (1) the clergy, (2) the poor, (3) the fabrics of churches,

(4) the bishop. In some of the French and Spanish dioceses the division was threefold, the bishop being omitted. What usage prevailed in the Anglo-Saxon church is unknown. No division, quadripartite or tripartite, was ever enjoined by law or canon in England.

(2) *From 970 to End of 12th Century.* —In this transition period the parochial system grew up, and local appropriations were made to particular churches out of the common fund. Edgar's legislation (970) shows that the parochial system was already growing. His legislation points to the fact that landowners were building churches on their estates for their own and their tenants' benefit, and were endowing them with some portion of the tithe, which they otherwise paid to the diocesan treasury or to the nearest monastic or conventual establishment. It distinguishes three kinds of churches: (1) the mother church, general monastic or conventual; (2) churches with burial grounds attached, in private patronage on the estates of private landowners; (3) churches similarly situated, but without burial grounds. It recognizes the general presumption in favor of paying to the mother church the tithe of the district which it served, but if there was a church of the second class within the district it was entitled to a portion of the local tithe. In these churches we have the future appropriations of local tithes to parish churches.

Rectories together with tithes might be "appropriated" to monastic or non-parochial corporations. The appropriators performed their duties by vicars. At the dissolution of the monasteries the rectorial tithes which had belonged to the dissolved communities passed to the crown, and were from time to time granted out to subjects, who became lay rectors or "impropriators" as they were called to distinguish them from the original "appropriators," who must of necessity have been spiritual. The Tithe Commutation Act of 1836 provided for the commutation of tithes in England and Wales into a money payment or rent charge. Though the annual payment varies with the septennial average price of corn, it is fixed in the sense that the amount payable in each year is calculated on a rent charge or fixed valuation. The effect of this act is to render the old distinctions between great and small tithes, prædial, mixed, and general tithes, and between the various modes of payment by "moduses" matters of antiquarian knowledge. The value of the tithes commuted in 1836 to tithe rent charge was at par value £4,053,985, 6s. 8½d. Of this sum £962,289, 15s. 7¼d.

is payable to lay impropriators, leaving £3,091,695, 11s. 1¼d. for ecclesiastical owners. Of this latter sum £678,897, 1s. 1¾d. is payable to Ecclesiastical Commissioners. The remainder, £2,412,708, 9s. 11½d., is payable to parochial incumbents. At the present values this sum is worth about in round numbers £1,800,-000. To this sum may be added about £8,000 for extraordinary tithe in Kent and Cornwall. In Ireland the settlement was effected by a general commutation of tithe into a money rent charge, regulated by a valuation of the tithes (one-fourth being deducted for the cost of collection), and payable by the proprietors, who should receive it from the occupiers of the land. By the Irish Church Act, 1869, this rent charge became vested in the commissioners of church temporalities, with power to sell such rent charge to the owner of the land charged therewith at 22½ years' purchase. Power is also given to such purchaser to pay by instalments for 52 years, at the rate of 4½ per cent. on the purchase money, deducting the estimated charge for poor rate; the rent charge being extinguished at the expiration of the 52 years. The Extraordinary Tithe Act, 1886, frees lands not at present cultivated as hop ground, orchard, fruit, plantation, or market garden, from liability to the separate tithe which, under the Act of 1836, could be claimed as extraordinary. It also provides for the redemption of the extraordinary tithe in existence upon the land actually under cultivation. The Tithe Rent Charge Recovery Act of 1891 has not materially affected the principle of the act of 1836. But instead of the old remedy of distress by the tithe-owner, it substitutes a process through the county court; instead of permitting the tenant to be the conduit pipe of the land-owner's payment, it makes the landowner alone liable; instead of the corn averages absolutely determining the amount of tithe rent charge which is payable, provision is made in certain cases for the reduction or the suspension of payment.

In 1891 a Royal Commission reported in favor of the compulsory redemption of tithes up to the value of 40s., of the abolition of the existing minimum of 25 years' purchase of the principle of allowing the parties to make their own bargains subject to the approval of the Board of Agriculture.

TITHING, an ancient subdivision of England, forming part of 100, and consisting of 10 householders and their families held together in a society, all being bound for the peaceable behavior of each other, the chief of whom was the tithing man.

TITHONUS (-thō'nus), in Greek mythology, a son, or nephew, of Laomedon, King of Troy. He was beloved by Eos (Aurora, Morning), who importuned Zeus to make him immortal. Her prayer was granted, but she had neglected to ask for continual youth, and in time her lover took on all the signs of extreme age. Tithonus's prayer to the gods to be relieved of the burden of old age was answered by his being metamorphosed into a grasshopper.

TITIAN (tish'un), or **TIZIANO, VECELLIO,** (tēt-se-ä'nō va-chel'lē-o), one of the most distinguished of the great Italian painters, and head of the Venetian school; born in Pieve di Cadore, in the Carnic Alps, in 1477. He studied under Giovanni Bellini of Venice, and in 1507 was associated with the painter Giorgione in executing certain frescoes. In 1511 he was invited to Padua, where he executed three remarkable frescoes still to be seen. In 1512 he completed the unfinished pictures of Giovanni Bellini in the Sala del Gran Consiglio at Venice, and the senate were so pleased that they gave him an important office. To this period are attributed his pictures of the "Tribute Money" and "Sacred and Profane Love." In 1514 he painted a portrait of Ariosto at Ferrara, and after his return to Venice he painted an "Assumption of the Virgin" (1516), considered one of the finest pictures in the world; it is now in the Academy of the Fine Arts in Venice. About 1528 he produced his magnificent picture, "The Death of St. Peter the Martyr"—"a picture," says Algarotti, "in which the great masters admitted they could not find a fault," unfortunately destroyed by fire in 1867.

In 1530 the Emperor Charles V. invited him to Bologna to paint his portrait and execute various other commissions. In 1532 he again painted the emperor's portrait, and he is said to have accompanied Charles to Madrid, where he received several honors. He remained, it is said, three years in Spain, in which country many of his masterpieces, such as "The Sleeping Venus," "Christ in the Garden," "St. Margaret and the Dragon," are still to be found. In 1537 he painted an "Annunciation," and in 1541 he produced "The Descent of the Holy Ghost on the Apostles," "The Sacrifice of Abraham," and "David and Goliath." In 1543 he painted his picture of "The Virgin and San Tiziano"; and in 1545 he visited Rome, where he painted the famous group of Pope Paul III.,

the Cardinal Farnese, and Duke Ottavio Farnese. He was patronized as warmly by Philip II. as by his father Charles V.

Of Titian's private life but little is known. Titian excelled as much in landscape as in figure painting, was equally great in sacred and profane subjects, in ideal heads and in portraits, in frescoes

VECELLIO TITIAN

and in oils; and though others may have surpassed him in single points, none equalled him in general mastery. As a colorist he is almost unrivalled, and his pictures often reach the perfection of sensuous beauty. He died of the plague in 1576 aged 99, having painted to the last with almost undiminished powers.

TITICACA, a remarkable lake, slightly saline, in the heart of the Andes; partly in Peru and partly in Bolivia; 12,545 feet above the sea-level. It lies N. W. and S. E., and is 120 miles in length, with an average width of from 50 to 60 miles. The S. portion, measuring 24 by 21 miles, is almost severed from the main body of the lake by a projecting peninsula. The lake discharges at its S. W. extremity by the Desaguadero into the salt Lake Aullagas, which has no known outlet. The E. shore of Lake Titicaca is abrupt and mountainous, but the W. and S. W. shores are low and level, and are skirted by thick beds of tall rushes swarming with waterfowl, and of floating weed, which affords food to cattle when the scanty land pastures are exhausted. The lake is deep and stormy, so that ice forms near the shores only. It contains a number of strange fishes, and eight species of marine crustaceans, which seem to indicate that it was once at the sea-level. There are eight habitable islands, the largest being Titicaca, which gave its name to the lake, and has an area of 20 square miles. It was the sacred island of the Incas, who laid it out in terraces planted with consecrated maize and flowers, and irrigated by channels supplied from the royal bath at the top. According to Squier, the name Titicaca probably signifies "Tiger Rock," and is due to a fancied resemblance of the rugged crest of the island to a wildcat. The lake is now navigated by steamers, and may be reached by railway from the seaport of Mollendo, 346 miles distant.

TITIENS, or TEIEJENS, TERESA, a German operatic singer; born in Hamburg, Germany July 18, 1831. She appeared as Lucrezia in her native town in her 16th year, and soon established her position as the chief lyric artist in Germany before her début in London, on April 13, 1858, as Valentine in "The Huguenots." Her success here was so decided that she made that country her future home. She followed Mr. Mapleson's fortunes at the Opera House in the Haymarket and at Drury Lane, and was the chief attraction of his management. Nature not only gifted her with a voice of marvelous strength and brilliant quality, but with a dramatic force illumined by the fire of genius. As Norma, Donna Anna, Semiramide, Medea, and Leonora, she was unequalled by any of her contemporaries. In the concert room and in oratorio her success was unequivocal. She died in the full maturity of her powers on Oct. 3, 1877. A monument was erected to her memory in All-Souls' Cemetery, Kensal Green, London, in November, 1878.

TITLE, an appellation; a name. Also, an appellation of dignity, distinction, or pre-eminence given to persons; as, titles of honor, which are words or phrases belonging to certain persons as their right in consequence of certain dignities being inherent in them or conferred on them; as, emperor, king, czar, prince, etc. In the United States there are no titles of distinction save those of professional men, which are conferred by authorized institutions as rewards for distinguished merit. Titles of nobility, conferred by any foreign power on any officer or employee of the United States government, are prohibited by the Constitution, and any foreigner who may hold a title of nobility must, on becoming a citizen of the United States, renounce formally all pretensions to such distinction. The President, governors of States, and ministers of foreign nations are addressed, and spoken of, as your or his "Excellency," save in the case of speaking to the President, who should be addressed as "Mr. President." The Vice-President, members of the Cabinet and members of Congress, heads of departments, assistant secretaries, comptrollers and auditors of Treasury, clerks of the Senate and House of Representatives, State Senators, law judges, mayors of cities, etc., are entitled "Honorable" and formally addressed as "Your Honor."

The five orders of nobility in England are distinguished by the titles of duke, marquis, earl, viscount, and baron. The dignity of baronet is distinguished by that word placed after the name and surname of the holder of the dignity, and also by the title of Sir prefixed to the name. This title, like that of the peers, is hereditary. The dignity of knighthood, which is not hereditary, is distinguished by the title of Sir prefixed to the name and surname of the holder. An archbishop is styled His Grace the Lord Archbishop of ——; a bishop, the Right Reverend the Lord Bishop of ——. Members of the Privy Council are entitled to be styled Right Honorable. Certain municipal offices have also titles attached to them; as, The Right Honorable the Lord Mayor of London, The Right Honorable the Lord Provost of Edinburgh, etc. Also the inscription in the beginning of a book, containing the subject of the work, and usually the names of the author, and publisher, date, etc.; a title page. Or a particular section or division of a subject, as of a law, a book, or the like; especially a section or chapter of a law book.

Ecclesiology and Church history: (1) A condition precedent to, or a claim in favor of, ordination, such as a sphere of parochial or other spiritual work, always required by a bishop, except in certain specified cases, which are specified in Canon 33 of the Anglican Church. In the Roman Church the title formerly required from every ordinand was that of a benefice (*titulus beneficii*), i. e., he was bound to show that he had been nominated to a benefice whose revenues were sufficient for his decent maintenance. The Council of Trent (1545-1563) added two other titles (1) of patrimony (*titulus patrimonii*), where the ordinand had sufficient private property to maintain him respectably, and (2) of pension (*titulus pensionis*), where some solvent person or persons bound themselves to provide for the cleric about to be or-

TOBACCO CROP READY FOR CUTTING, IN THE REGION NEAR LEXINGTON, KY.

See **Tobacco**, p. 422

See **Tobacco,** p. 422

TOBACCO DRYING IN THE ISLAND OF JAMAICA

dained. The vow of evangelical poverty (*titulus paupertatis*) in a religious order is a valid title; and the students of Propaganda and certain other colleges, and candidates for holy orders in missionary countries, have a title from the mission from which they are ordained or the seminary in which they were educated (*titulus missionis vel seminarii*). The acceptance of this last title imposes on the bishop the responsibility of providing for the support of the ordained, should he become incapable of discharging his functions. (2) A titular church, or the district or parish assigned to it among English and Roman Catholic Churches.

TITMOUSE (plural, **TITMICE**), in ornithology, a popular name for any individual of the sub-family *Parinæ*. They are remarkable for the boldly defined color of their plumage and their quick, irregular movements, running rapidly along branches in quest of insects, and often clinging thereto with their back downward. They feed not only on insects, but on grain and seeds, and not infrequently kill young and sickly birds with strokes of their stout, strong bill. They are very pugnacious, and the hens show great courage in defense of their nests. The young are fed chiefly on caterpillars, and a pair of blue tits have been observed to carry a caterpillar to their nest, on an average, every two minutes, during the greater part of the day, so that these birds must be extremely serviceable in preventing the increase of noxious insects. The chickadee, so named from its note, is the blackcap titmouse (*Parus atricapillus*), found chiefly in the North American continent. Seven species are well known in Europe; but one, the crested titmouse (*Parus cristatus*), is only an accidental visitor. The great titmouse (*P. major*) is about six inches long; head and throat black; cheeks white; back, breast, and sides yellowish; wings and tail grayish. The blue titmouse (*P. cœruleus*), which is so called from the bluish tinge in its plumage, and the coal titmouse (*P. ater*), named from its black head and neck, are the commonest British species; the others are the long-tailed titmouse (*Acredula caudula, Parus caudatus*), the marsh titmouse (*P. palustris*), and the bearded titmouse (*Panurus biarmicus*), or reedling.

TITTMAN, OTTO HILGARD, an American geodesist, born in Belleville, Ill., in 1850. After a common school training he entered the service of the United States Coast and Geodetic Survey. In 1874 he went to Japan as an assistant astronomer in the Transit of Venus expedition. In 1895 he was appointed assistant in charge of the United States Coast and Geodetic Survey office, becoming superintendent in 1909, which position he resigned in 1915. He has at various times represented the United States in demarking the boundaries with Canada and was Commissioner of Northern Boundaries under the Treaty of 1908.

TITTONI, TOMMASO, an Italian statesman and diplomat, born in Rome in 1854. He received his education at the universities of Rome and Oxford and entered politics. He was elected to the Chamber of Deputies in 1886, and in 1897 was appointed prefect of Naples, and a year later became a Senator. In 1903-1906 he was Minister of Foreign Affairs, and, after a brief interval, returned

TOMMASO TITTONI

to the position which he held till 1910. In that year he went to Paris as ambassador. He has been a member of the Permanent Court of Arbitration of The Hague since 1912. He continued as Italian ambassador in France during the great war till 1916, playing no small part in the negotiations which brought Italy into the war on the side of the Allies. In 1916 he became Minister of State, and at the conclusion of the war in 1918 took part in the peace negotiations. His works include: "Sei anni di Politica Estera" (published in 1912 and later translated as "Italy's Foreign and Colonial Policy") (mostly discourses); "The Responsibility of the War."

TITRATION, in chemistry, the process of estimating the amount of an element or compound contained in a solution, by the addition to it of a known quantity of another chemical capable of reacting on it. The end of the process is determined by the complete precipitation of the compound, or by the discharge and production of some definite color in the mixed solutions. See ANALYSIS.

TITULAR BISHOP, a title substituted by Pope Leo XIII, for the older one of bishop *in partibus infidelium.*

TITULAR CHURCH, a name given to the parish churches of Rome, as distinct from the patriarchal churches, which belonged to the Pope, and from the oratories. Each titular church was under a cardinal priest, had a district assigned to it, and a font for baptism in case of necessity.

TITTMAN (tit'män), **FRIEDRICH WILHELM**, a German historian; born in Wittenberg in 1784. His "Study on the Amphictyonic League" (1812) was crowned by the Berlin Academy. His principal work is a "History of Henry the Illustrious" (2 vols. 1845-1846). Among his other writings are: "A View of the Civilization of our Times" (1835); "On Life and Matter" (1855); "Aphorisms of Philosophy" (1850); "Nationality and the State" (1861). He died in 1864.

TITUS, the Roman prænomen but the usual name for the 11th of the 12 Cæsars, Titus Flavius Sabinus Vespasianus, the eldest son of Vespasian and Flavia Domitilla; born in Rome, Dec. 30, A. D. 40. He was brought up at the court of Nero along with Britannicus, and early served with credit as tribune in Germany and Britain, and in Judæa under his father. On Vespasian's elevation to the throne Titus was left to prosecute the Jewish war, which he brought to a close by the capture of Jerusalem after a long siege (70). Both father and son enjoyed a joint triumph in 71. About this time Titus received the title of Cæsar, and took a share in the work of government. He gave himself up to pleasure, and his attachment to Berenice, the daughter of

Herod Agrippa I., grievously offended the Romans. But no sooner had Titus assumed the weight of undivided power (79) than his whole character became changed. He assumed the office of Pontifex Maximus in order to keep his hands free from blood. He completed the Colosseum and built the baths which bear his name, and lavished his beneficence on the sufferers from the great eruptions of Vesuvius, which overwhelmed Herculaneum and Pompeii (79), and the great three days' fire at Rome, followed by pestilence the year after. Titus was now the idol of his subjects. He loved to give. But unhappily he died suddenly at his patrimonial villa in the Sabine country, Sept. 13, 81, not without the suspicion that he had been poisoned by his younger brother Domitian.

TITUS, a companion of St. Paul, though not mentioned in the Acts of the Apostles. He seems to have been converted by the apostle (Tit. i: 4), probably at Antioch A. D. 50 or 51, and in the same year accompanied him to Jerusalem, and was present at that first council which recognized Gentile converts as part of the Church, and exempted them from the burden of the Mosaic ritual (cf. Acts xv. 1-35 with Gal. ii: 1-3). Paul soon afterward practically carried out the liberty thus accorded by refusing to require Titus, who by birth was a Greek, to be circumcised (Gal. ii: 3-5). Titus was subsequently with Paul at Ephesus (A. D. 56), whence the former was sent on a special mission to the Corinthians, perhaps carrying with him Paul's second epistle to that Church (II Cor. viii: 6, 22, 23, xii: 18). When Titus returned (A. D. 57) he found the apostle in Macedonia (II Cor. vii: 5-6, 13-15). Subsequently (probably A. D. 65 or 66) he was left in Crete to arrange the affairs of the Church and "ordain elders in every city" (Tit. i: 5). Returning thence to Rome he was dispatched by Paul (A. D. 66 or 67) to Dalmatia (II Tim. iv: 10). According to tradition Titus returned to his work in Crete, and died a natural death at an advanced age,

The Epistle of Paul to Titus, the third of St. Paul's pastoral epistles. It was written to give Titus directions respecting the organization of the Cretan Church. There is a considerable resemblance between some passages in Titus and others in the Epistles to Timothy. The external evidence in favor of the epistle to Titus is somewhat stronger than for those to Timothy. The three together are called the pastoral epistles.

TITUSVILLE, a city in Crawford co., Pa.; on Oil creek and the New York

Central and Pennsylvania railroads; 18 miles N. of Oil City. Here are a public library, high school, waterworks, electric lights, churches, National and State banks, and several daily and weekly newspapers. The first petroleum well in the United States was opened in the suburbs of the city in 1859, and since then the principal industry has been the production of oil. The city also has manufactures of soap, silk goods, radiators, chairs and furniture, engines, boilers, steel and iron forgings, oil-well drilling tools, etc. Pop. (1910), 8,533; (1920), 8,432.

TIUMEN, a town in western Siberia; at the confluence of the Tjumenka with the Tura, a tributary of the Tobol; 138 miles S. W. of Tobolsk. It is regularly built (chiefly of wood), has 10 stone churches, a mosque, etc. There are manufactures of soap, tallow candles, and textile fabrics, bell and iron foundries, potteries, and shoemaking. Tiumen is also a great center of transit traffic—boats coming here from the Obi, Irtish, Tobol, and Tura, and unshipping goods for the W. and S. A great market is held here in January. Pop. about 35,000.

TIVERTON, a town in N. Devon, England; 18 miles N. of Exeter; on the slope of a hill above the confluence of the Exe and Loman, from whose two fords it derives its Old English name of Twy-ford-ton. The chief of its three churches, St. Peter's (136 feet long by 82 feet wide, with a tower 110 feet high), dates from 1073, but was partly rebuilt in the 16th and was thoroughly restored in the 19th century. Other edifices are the town hall (1864), in late Venetian style, with a tower of 80 feet, a market house (1830), and the grammar school ("free" in name but not in fact), which, founded by Peter Blundel in 1604, and familiar to every reader of Blackmore's "Lorna Doone," has given place to a modern structure. The historic building, however, will remain intact. The cloth trade has declined since the 17th century, and lace making is now the leading industry. Pop. (1901) 10,382.

TIVOLI, an old Roman town in Italy, in the province of Rome; beautifully situated on the left bank of the Teverone; 17 miles E. N. E. of Rome. It is interesting from the number of antiquities it contains, the most remarkable of which are the remains of the temples of Vesta and the Sibyl, and the villas of Mæcenas and Hadrian. Near the town is the Villa d'Este, erected in 1549. In 1826 a serious inundation destroyed many houses, and in consequence a new chan-

I—30

nel was formed for a part of the waters of the river, by the construction of two shafts through the limestone rock of Monte Catillo, 870 feet and 990 feet long respectively. In 1834 this new channel was opened by Folchi in the presence of Pope Gregory XVI., and a new waterfall was thus formed 330 feet high. Pop. about 15,000.

TLAXCALA (tläs-kä'lä), the smallest State of Mexico; on the plateau of Anahuac; nearly surrounded by Puebla, and touching Mexico State on the W.; area 1,534 square miles. Pop. 1919, 192,000. In Aztec days Tlaxcala was the seat of an independent republic, which survived for a time under the protection of the Spaniards. The capital, Tlaxcala, stands 7,300 feet above the sea, and has some manufactures of woolens.

TLEMCEN, a town in the province of Oran, Algeria; 88 miles S. W. of Oran, with which it is connected by railway. It occupies the site of the Roman city of Pomaria, and under the Moors, in the 12th and 13th centuries, was a place of great importance, with a pop. of nearly 150,000. It stands on the N. slope of a steep mountain, at a height of 2,500 feet, in the midst of a well-irrigated and richly cultivated country, which especially abounds in fruit trees. The chief exports are olive oil, dried fruit, corn, wool, sheep and cattle, dressed alfa cloths, carpets, and leather goods. It has 23 mosques, two of which are fine specimens of Moorish architecture. Pop. about 28,000.

TOAD, in zoölogy, the popular name of any species of the family *Bufonidæ,* which is almost universally distributed,

TOAD

but is rare in the Australian region, one species being found in Celebes and one in Australia. Three species are European; the common toad (*B. vulgaris*) and the natterjack (*B. calamita*), and *B. variabilis.* The common American species is *B. lentiginosus,* and is more active than the European species, moving principally by leaping. The first is the type of the family. The body is swollen and heavy-looking, covered with a warty skin, head large, flat, and toothless, with a rounded, blunt muzzle. There is a swelling above the eyes covered with pores, and the parotids are large, thick, and prominent, and secrete an acrid fluid, which probably gave rise to the popular stories about the venom of the toad, or they may owe their origin to the fact that when handled or irritated these animals can eject a watery fluid from the vent. The toad has four fingers and five partially webbed toes. The general color above is a brownish-gray, the tubercules more or less brown; under surface yellowish white, sometimes spotted with black. Toads are terrestrial, hiding in damp, dark places during the day, and crawling with the head near the ground, for their short limbs are badly adapted for leaping. They are extremely tenacious of life, and can exist a long time without food.

TOBACCO, a very important plant, belonging to the natural order *Atropaceæ,* or night-shade order. The introduction of the use of tobacco forms a singu-

TOBACCO PLANT

lar chapter in the history of mankind. According to some authorities smoking was practised by the Chinese at a very early date. At the time of the discovery of America, tobacco was in frequent use among the Indians, and the practice of smoking, which had with them a religious character, was common to almost all the tribes (see CALUMET). The name of tobacco was either derived from the term used in Haiti to designate the

pipe, or from Tabaca in Santo Domingo, whence it was introduced into Spain and Portugal in 1559 by a Spaniard. It soon found its way to Paris and Rome, and was first used in the shape of snuff. Smoking is generally supposed to have been introduced into England by Sir Walter Raleigh, but Camden says the practice was introduced by Drake and his companions on their return from Virginia in 1585. It was strongly opposed by both priests and rulers. Pope Urban VIII. and Innocent IX. issued bulls excommunicating such as used snuff in church, and in Turkey smoking was made a capital offense. In the canton of Bern the prohibition of the use of tobacco was put among the 10 commandments immediately after that forbidding adultery. The "Counterblast" or denunciation written by James I. of England is a matter of history. All prohibitions, however, regal or priestly, were of no avail, and tobacco is now the most extensively used luxury on the face of the earth.

The most commonly cultivated tobacco plant (*Nicotiana tabacum*) is glutinous, and covered with a very short down; the stem upright, four or five feet high, and branching; the leaves are lanceolate, from 6 to 18 inches long; the flowers are terminal and rose-colored. A less esteemed species is *N. rustica*, distinguished by a short yellowish-green corolla. The best Havana cigars are made from the leaves of *N. repanda*. All the tobacco plants are natives of America, and that continent has continued the principal producer, the chief tobacco-growing country being the United States, and, above all, Kentucky, North Carolina, and Virginia. It was first cultivated in Holland early in the 17th century, and soon extended to other countries, including Austria, Germany, Russia, the Balkan Peninsula, Asiatic Turkey, France, British India, Cuba, Brazil, the Philippine Islands, Japan, and Australia. The cultivation in Great Britain was forbidden from an early date till 1866, when it was permitted under certain conditions.

Tobacco owes its principal properties to the presence of a most poisonous alkaloid named NICOTINE (*q. v.*). In the manufacture of tobacco the leaves are first thoroughly cleansed with salt and water. The midrib of the leaf is then removed; the leaves are again sorted, and the large ones set apart for making cigars. The leaves may either be cut finely for use in pipes, as is the case with "shag" tobacco, or they are moistened and pressed into cakes, which are designated cavendish; or they are pressed into sticks, as negrohead; or again the leaves may be spun in the form of a rope of greater or less thickness; the smallest twist is called pigtail. The midribs, separated in the first process of manufacture, are preserved to be converted into SNUFF (*q. v.*). Cigars, cigarettes, and cheroots are favorite forms of manufactured tobacco. As the best leaf is grown in Cuba, so also are the best cigars made there. The leaf used for the manufacture of Manila cheroots is grown chiefly on the island of Luzon. The production of tobacco in the United States in 1923 was estimated at 1,474,786,000 pounds.

TOBAGO, the most S. of the Windward Islands; belonging to Great Britain; 75 miles S. E. of Grenada and 18½ miles N. E. of Trinidad; 24 miles long and 7 miles wide; pop. about 21,000. The island was discovered by Columbus in 1498, and named by him Assumption; the name of Tobago is supposed to have arisen from the free use of tobacco by the Caribs when first visited by Europeans. It has been frequently contested between Dutch, Spaniards, and French, but came into British possession in 1763. The island is volcanic, its surface being irregular and picturesque, and abounding in conical hills and spurs, all connected by a ridge running through the interior, the greatest elevation of which is 1,800 feet above the level of the sea. From the high ridge descend deep and narrow ravines, which terminate in small alluvial plains. Scarborough is its chief town, pleasantly situated on the S. side, and at the base of a conical hill rising 425 feet in altitude, crowned by Fort King George, now without garrison. The chief exports are rum, molasses, cocoanuts and livestock to the amount of from $100,000 to $200,000. The imports run from $100,000 to $150,-000. The island was united with the colony of Trinidad in 1889, and has a commissioner appointed by the governor.

TOBIT, in the Apocrypha, a book generally placed between II Esdras and Judith, and containing 14 chapters. A pious man, Tobit by name, resident in Thisbe in Naphthali, was taken captive by Enemessar (Schlmaneser), King of Assyria, and located in Nineveh.

TOBOL, a river of Siberia, which rises in the W. slope of the Ural Mountains, in the province of Orenburg, and joins the Irtish at the town of Tobolsk, after a course of about 550 miles.

TOBOLSK, a town of Western Siberia, capital of a province, at the confluence of the Irtish and the Tobol, nearly 2,000 miles E. of St. Petersburg. It is well built, with timber houses and wide and regular streets, and its position on the two great rivers is picturesque; but its situation, considerably N. of the great commercial highway between Russia and Siberia, and at a distance from the more productive regions of the country is unfavorable for the development of commerce. Pop. about 25,000.

TOCQUEVILLE, ALEXIS CHARLES HENRI MAURICE CLÉREL DE, a French politician; born in Verneuil, July 29, 1805. His father was Hervé Louis François Joseph Bonaventure Clérel, Comte de Tocqueville (1772-1856), peer of France, politician and historian, and a writer of some merit. The son studied philology at Metz and at Paris (1823-1826). In 1827 he was appointed *juge auditeur* of the tribunal of Versailles. In 1831-1832 he was sent by the French government, along with his friend M. de Beaumont, to the United States to inspect and report on the American prison system. They published a joint work on their return, entitled "Of the Penitentiary System in the United States and its Application in France" (Par. 1832; 3d er. 1845). This treatise, which was crowned by the Academy, recommends the solitary confinement of prisoners. In 1832 Tocqueville resigned his office under government, and, after a brief visit to England, gave himself up to the composition of the first of his two great works, "Democracy in America" (1835-1840, 15th ed. 1868). This work is in reality a treatise on the general principles which ought to be taken as the rule of action by all democratic governments. These are, in brief: (1) full extent of individual liberty with all its concomitants (as freedom of the press, etc.); (2) careful avoidance of centralization. The bearing of this on French politics is obvious. This work was received with the favor it deserved; the Academy awarded to it a special prize of 8,000 francs, and a quick succession of honors was bestowed on the author. In 1837 he was appointed chevalier of the Legion of Honor; in 1839 he was chosen by the electors of Valagnes as their representative; and in 1841 he was elected member of the Academy. For some years practical politics occupied all his attention. In 1849 he entered the Odilon Barrot Cabinet as minister of foreign affairs, but the coup d'état of Dec. 2—to which, as may be imagined, he was strongly opposed—drove him from office. He then occupied himself with "The Old Government and the Revolution" (1856, 7th ed. 1866). This is his greatest work. It was meant to be an exposition of the manner in which the post-revolution France grew out of the pre-revolution France. Tocqueville intended to follow it up by others dealing with the great events in the later history of France. He was engaged at these when he died in Cannes, April 16, 1859. Besides the works mentioned above, he wrote "Etat Social et Politique de la France" (1834); "Le Droit au Travail" (1848). His "Complete Works" (9 vols. 1860-1865) were edited by his friend M. de Beaumont, who also edited his "Correspondance" (1860).

TODD, EDWARD HOWARD, an American college president, born at Council Bluffs, Ia., in 1863. Graduating from the Simpson College of Indianola, Ia., in 1886, he became Methodist-Episcopal pastor of the Valisca (Iowa) Circuit. In 1888 he was ordained deacon, and in 1890 went to the West Church of Boston as student pastor. After that he was successively pastor in Vancouver, B. C., Tacoma, Seattle and a number of other cities. In 1910 he became vice-president of the Willamette University, in Washington. Since 1913 he has been president of the College of Puget Sound.

TODD, HENRY DAVIS, JR., American army officer, born in Claverack, N. Y., 1866. After graduating from the United States Military Academy, he entered the artillery of the United States Army. During 1908-12 he served on the General Staff, and had reached the rank of colonel in 1913. He was in command of the artillery which supported the First American Division during the St. Mihiel offensive, in France, in 1918, and commanded the 58th Brigade during the Meuse-Argonne offensive. After the armistice he was stationed in Luxemburg with the Army of Occupation. On demobilization of the 33rd Division he was assigned to the General Staff College at Washington, D. C.

TODLEBEN, FRANZ EDWARD, a Russian military engineer; son of one of the Kaufmanns; born in Mitau, Kurland, May 8, 1818; educated at Riga, and at the College of Engineers in St. Petersburg. He served in the Caucasus against Schamyl, 1848-1851, and under General Schilders in the Danubian campaign of 1853-1854, and on the outbreak of the Crimean War was ordered to the defense of Sebastopol against the Allies. By cumulating the fire of the garrison on the works of the Allies, and pushing forward with prodigous energy the construction of the fortifications of defense, Todleben rapidly turned the tables on his enemy and prolonged the siege 349 days. Todleben was raised to the rank of general of engineers, and received the order of St. George in 1858. The "Journal of the Defense" was subsequently expanded into the "Defense of Sevastopol" (1863-1870). Todleben was intrusted with the defense of Nicolaiev and Cronstadt, and as "adjoint" to the inspector-general of engineering (the Grand-Duke Nicholas), he exercized *de facto* the functions of that office from 1860. In September, 1877, after the failure of the great attack on Plevna, he was summoned to the direction, and completely changing the Russian tactics completed the investment by the construction of works on the W. side, and so, by intercepting all reinforcements and supplies, ultimately starved Osman Pasha into surrender on Dec. 11, with 20,000 men and 60 guns. On March 28, 1878, Todleben succeeded the Grand-Duke Nicholas as Commander-in-Chief of the army in Turkey, and in December following was appointed general of the 7th Grenadiers, and by special ukase the regiment received his name. He died in Soden, Germany, July 1, 1884.

TOGA, the principal outer garment and characteristic national dress of the ancient Romans, who were hence designated as emphatically the *Gens Togata*

TOGA

("the toga-wearing nation"), while the Greek pallium distinguished foreigners. The right of wearing it was the exclusive privilege of citizens, its use being forbidden to Peregrini and slaves. It was, moreover, the garb of peace, in contradistinction to the sagum of the soldier. When the young Roman was regarded as fit to enter on the business of life (at what age this was is uncertain, probably it depended on circumstances), he threw off the *toga prætexta*, and assumed the *toga virilis*. The *toga prætexta* was also the official dress of the higher magistrates. The *toga picta*, an embroidered robe, was worn by a general in his triumphal procession. Candidates for any office wore a *toga candida*—that is a toga which had been artificially whitened by the application of chalk or other similar substance; so arrayed they were styled *candidati* (whence our word candidate). Mourners wore a *toga pulla* of naturally black wool.

TOGO, HEIHACHIRO, COUNT, Japanese admiral; born at Kagoshima in December, 1847. He entered the navy in 1863 and participated in the civil war of 1868. From 1871 to 1878 he studied in England at the Royal Naval College, Greenwich, and on board British warships. In 1894 when in command of the cruiser "Naniwa" he fired on and sank the Chinese transport "Kowshing," which led to the war between China and Japan. In 1900 he became vice-admiral. In the war with Russia he was appointed naval commander-in-chief and on Feb. 8, 1904, made a successful attack with torpedoes on the Russian fleet at Port Arthur, though war had not actually been declared. On May 27, 1905, he gave battle to the Russian Baltic fleet under Admirals Rojestvensky and Nebogatoff on its way to Vladivostok off Tsu Island, in Korea Strait, and practically annihilated it. In 1912 he was made Admiral of the fleet, and Chief of the General Naval Staff.

TOKAY (to'koi), a town of Hungary, at the confluence of the Bodrog, with the Theiss; 113 miles N. E. by E. of Budapest. It derives its celebrity from its being the entrepôt for the sale of the famous sweet wine of the same name, made in the hilly tract called the Heyaltya, extending 25 or 30 miles N. W. from the town. When new, Tokay wines are of a brownish-yellow muddy color, which, when very old, changes to a greenish tint. The best qualities are extremely rich and luscious, but cloying. The finest and oldest varieties of Tokay bring large prices. Inferior Hungarian wines are frequently sold under this name, and many French and German imitations are also in the market. Pop. about 5,500.

TOKYO, formerly called YEDDO, the capital of Japan, and chief residence of the mikado; on a bay of the same name; on the S. E. coast of Hondo, the largest of the Japanese islands, and connected by rail with Yokohama and Kanagawa. The bulk of the houses are of wood, but there are many new buildings of brick and stone. The greater part of the town is flat, and intersected by numerous canals crossed by bridges. The streets are generally narrow and irregular. Education is well organized, and there are 700 private and elementary schools. Tokyo contains the imperial university, and it may be considered the center of the political, commercial, and literary activity of Japan. The total area of the city is about 30 square miles. It is composed of a number of towns rather than forming a single city. The Sumida River divides the city in two equal parts. The eastern portions along the river border and fronting the bay, are level and low. The western portions rise into hills of considerable height, with a dense population in the valleys separating them. The chief architectural feature of the city is the palace enclosure within the grounds of the ancient castle. The palace of the Emperor is constructed in mixed Japanese-European architecture. It stands in the midst of a beautiful park called Fukiage. East of the capital is the commercial portion of the city, with many important banks, shops, hotels and dwellings. A long street passes from northeast to southwest, through the city, and forms the main thoroughfare. It is a broad street with rows of trees and has electric cars and electric lights. A series of earthquakes, Sept. 1-3, 1923, in great part destroyed the city, which was later laid out anew and rebuilt largely in more substantial fashion.

In the northern part of the city is the arsenal, to which is attached a beautiful garden. Other notable buildings are he Imperial University, the Imperial Museum, and several great temples. On the west bank of the Sumida is the Imperial Park. In the southern part of the city is Shiba Park. Beyond this is the temple of Sankakuji. The city has many delightful suburbs. It has few industrial interests, although there are numerous factories in the neighborhood. Pop., about 2,300,000.

TOLEDO, a city of Ohio, the county seat of Lucas co. It is on the Maumee river, on both sides. The river is crossed by many bridges. Toledo is the third railroad center in America, and is the terminus of many important railway lines, including the Pennsylvania, the Hocking Valley, the Clover Leaf, the Pere Marquette, and the Grand Trunk. There are in all 17 railroads, operating 22 divisions. In addition there are 10 interurban lines. A belt line, 22 miles long, connects all railroads. The city is the most important shipping point of cargo coal on the Great Lakes, situated as it is at the west end of Lake Erie and at the foot of the upper chain of the Great Lakes. It is also the natural receiving point for the iron traffic from the Lake Superior region and of grain and lumber from the northwest. The city has an area of 31.51 square miles, and is most attractively laid out. It has about 245 miles of streets, of which about 250 are paved. There are 8 parks, well distributed, comprising a total of 1,533 acres, and including municipal golf courses and wading and swimming pools. Among the important public buildings are the Jessup W. Scott High School, the Morrison R. Waite High School, St. Patrick's Cathedral, a court house, post office, Newsboys' Building, Toledo Club, and the Chapel State Hospital for the Insane. The Museum of Art is one of the most beautiful buildings devoted to art in the United States. The school system is unusually effective. It includes open air schools, and other modern developments in educational lines. Over 45,000 pupils are enrolled in the public schools and nearly $2,000,000 are spent annually for educational purposes. Its two high schools rank among the finest educational institutions in the United States. In addition there are many parochial and private schools. There are over 140 churches. The industries of the city are diversified, and include the manufacture of automobiles, automobile parts and accessories, plate glass, cut glass, machinery, refined oil, sugar, elevators, women's clothing, children's vehicles, etc. There were in 1920 four national and fourteen State banks, with deposits of $82,632,236 and a surplus of $7,047,279. There were also ten building loan associations with deposits aggregating $8,800,546. Many conventions and annual meetings are held in the city. The Terminal Auditorium has a seating capacity of over 5,000. The Farmers' Exposition alone brings 150,000 people to the city each year.

Toledo is the outgrowth of two townships, Port Lawrence, settled in 1817, and Vistula, settled in 1832. It was a famous battle ground in Indian wars. The village was incorporated in 1836 and with the opening of the Wabash and Erie Canal in 1843 and the Miami and Erie Canal in 1845 it grew rapidly. Pop.

(1900), 131,822; (1910), 168,497; (1920), 243,109.

TOLEDO (tō-la'tho), a famous city of Spain; capital of a province, and long the capital of the whole country; on the N. bank of the Tagus, by which it is encompassed on three sides, 40 miles S. S. W. of Madrid. It is situated on a number of hills, 2,400 feet above sea-level; and the climate, excessively hot in summer, is bitterly cold in winter. The Tagus, surrounding the city on the E., S. and W., and flowing between high and rocky banks, leaves only one approach on the land side, which is defended by an inner and an outer wall, the former built by the Gothic King Wamba in the 7th century, the latter by Alfonso VI. in 1109, and both remarkable for the number and beauty of their towers and gates. Seen from a distance the city has a most imposing appearance; within it is gloomy, silent, inert, and its narrow streets are irregular, ill-paved, and steep. In the middle of the city rises the lofty, massive cathedral, surrounded by numerous churches and convents, mostly deserted. The cathedral, built in 1227-1493, on the site of a former mosque (consecrated to Christian uses in 1086, but pulled down to make way for the new church), is a large oblong edifice with semi-circular apse, and belongs to the simplest, noblest style of Spanish-Gothic, with a few touches of the florid Gothic, classical, and Saracenic styles. The interior is more impressive than the exterior, which is blocked by other buildings on all sides save one. It was ransacked and plundered in 1808, but it still contains some admirable stained glass, and pieces of sculpture. The cathedral is 404 feet long and 204 feet wide, and has five naves; the tower is 329 feet high. Connected with the cathedral are an extraordinary number of chapels, of great interest, alike from their architectural beauty, their decorations, and their historical associations. The great square or Zocodover, thoroughly Moorish in its architectural character, is a fashionable promenade, and was long the site on which heretics were burned and bull-fights took place. Moorish architecture is conspicuous in some churches, and in two gateways. The Alcazar, or old palace, the fortress commanded by the Cid, rebuilt as a palace in the time of Charles V. and subsequently, occupied the highest part of the city, but was burned down in 1887. The buildings of the town include a theological seminary, one or two old palaces, hospitals, what was once a great monastery, town hall, etc. There are manufactures of church ornaments and vestments in gold, silver, and silk, and confections. The best Spanish is said to be spoken here. Toledan sword blades, famous since old Roman times, are still made. Pop. about 22,000. Province, area 5,919 square miles; pop. 440,000.

Toledo, the Toletum of the Romans, is of very early origin. It was the capital of the Goths during their dominion; in 714 it fell into the possession of the Moors, who retained it till 1085, when it was permanently annexed to the crown of Castile as capital. In the days of its highest prosperity it is said to have contained 200,000 inhabitants. It was the headquarters of the Inquisition. The university, founded in 1498, is long since extinct. The whole place has now a dilapidated and broken-down appearance.

TOLENTINO (tō-len-te'nō), a small town of Central Italy, in the province of Macerata, with a fine cathedral. Here Pope Pius VI., in 1797, concluded a humiliating peace with Bonaparte, and in the neighborhood, in 1815, Murat, at the head of the Neapolitans, was defeated by the Austrians under Bianchi. Pop. (1901) 12,875.

TOLSTOY, COUNT LYOF (or LEV, English **LEO) NIKOLAIEVITCH,** a Russian novelist; born on the family estate of Yasnaya Polyana in the province of Tula, Russia, Sept. 9, 1828. He served in the Crimean War, and after-

COUNT LYOF TOLSTOY

ward traveled extensively. In 1861 he took up permanent residence on his country estate. Among his earliest works are: "Detsvo" (Childhood), "Otrchestvo" (Boyhood), and "Iunost" (Youth); also "Cossacks," "Sevastopol,"

and a number of military sketches. "War and Peace" was published in 1865-1868; "Anna Karénina" in 1875-1878. His peculiar doctrines are promulgated in "My Confession," "In What My Faith Consists," etc.; many of them are forbidden in Russia. His later works are: "The Kreutzer Sonata" (1888), "Death of Ivan Ilyitch" (1884-1886); "Master and Man" (1895). Nearly all have been translated into English and most other languages. He died Nov. 19, 1910.

TOLTECS, a Mexican race who are supposed to have been supreme in Central America from the 7th to the 11th centuries. They were completely obliterated by the AZTECS (q. v.) and Tezcucans, who held the country when the Spaniards first landed. The latter races were of a martial spirit, but they were indebted to their arts, their civilization, and their religion to their milder predecessors. See Prescott's "History of the Conquest of Mexico," book i.

TOLU BALSAM, a resin or balsam obtained from a tree of tropical South America, the *Myrospermum* (*Myroxylon*) *toluiferum* or *Peruiferum*. Tolu balsam has a brownish-yellow color, becomes quite hard and may be formed into a powder, has a pleasant aromatic flavor, and is used in certain medicinal preparations, though having little or no virtue of its own.

TOLUCA (-lö'kä), a town of Mexico, capital of Mexico State; 45 miles W. S. W. of Mexico City, in a valley nearly 8,800 feet above the sea. It contains a fine cathedral, manufactures paints, soap, and candles, and has a thriving trade in pork, sausages, etc. Near the town is the extinct volcano, Nevado de Tolúca. Pop. about 33,000.

TOM, a river in Siberia, which unites with the Obi near Tomsk; length about 450 miles.

TOM, MOUNT, a mountain in Hampshire co., Mass., near Northampton, on the Connecticut river, opposite Mount Holyoke; is about 1,335 feet high.

TOMAHAWK, an Indian hatchet or ax used in war and in the chase, not only in hand-to-hand combats, but also by being thrown to a considerable distance so as to strike the object with the sharp edge. The native tomahawks have heads of stone attached by thongs, etc., but steel tomahawks are supplied to the Indians by the governments and traders with whom they deal, and a pipe is usually attached to the poll. A hole is drilled through the bottom of the bowl and the poll of the ax, to meet one passing through the length of the handle. As a nautical term, a poleax. To bury the tomahawk means to make peace; it being the custom of the Indians to bury the tomahawk during the time of peace; so to dig up the tomahawk means to go to war, to fall into dispute.

TOMALES (-mä′les) **BAY,** an arm of the Pacific, on the coast of California, 35 miles N. W. of San Francisco.

TOMATO, or **LOVE APPLE** (*Lycopersicum esculentum*), a plant of the natural order *Solanaceæ,* so named by Tournefort, but subsequently combined by Linnæus with the genus *Solanum,* now, however, recognized as a distinct genus under the name of the earlier botanist. It is distinguished from *Solanum* by the stamens having the anthers connected by a thin membrance, and by their cells opening in longitudinal slits on the sides, not in pores at the apex as in that genus. The fruit is fleshy, usually red or yellow. The tomato is one of a genus of several species, all natives of South America, chiefly on the Peruvian side. It is the only species in cultivation in Europe, into which it was brought by the Spaniards in 1583. In the warmer countries of Europe, the United States and other countries in which the summer is warm and prolonged, it has long been cultivated for the excellent qualities of the fruit as an article of diet.

Though it was introduced into Great Britain as early as 1596, the consumption of its fruit there is still small as compared with some other European countries and America. Like its near relative the potato, the tomato is subject to attacks of phytophthora—the potato-disease fungus, and the fruit is liable to a disease also of fungus origin, which causes considerable loss to inexperienced growers, but rarely attack the plants of those who understand their treatment under glass. Its use in any way as food is considered beneficial in affections of the liver, indigestion, and diarrhœa. The word tomato is derived from the Spanish-American name *tamate,* and the English name love apple has arisen from its supposed aphrodisiac properties.

TOMB, a monument erected over a grave, in order to mark the resting place, and preserve the memory, of the deceased. In early ages, and among the Eastern nations, it sometimes became the practice to place the remains of the dead in excavated sepulchers, whose interior was often decorated with painting or otherwise. Where the usage was to burn the dead their bones and ashes were placed in urns in these receptacles. Some of the most remarkable rock tombs were those of Egypt. The rock tombs of Persia and Lycia have imposing architectural façades.

In the earlier centuries of Christianity the burial of the dead in churches was prohibited. The first step which led to its adoption was the custom of erecting churches over the graves of martyrs; then followed the permission of kings and emperors to be buried in the church porch. The most important tombs of the Middle Ages are generally within churches or cloisters. The earlier examples consist of a simple stone coffin, or sarcophagus, often with a low gabled lid and a sculptured cross. An altar tomb, or tomb in the form of a table, followed; and in the 13th century a species of tomb was introduced, consisting of a sarcophagus, on which rests a recumbent figure of the deceased, the whole being surmounted by a canopy, often of exquisite symmetry and richness.

TOMBIGBEE, a river which rises in Tishomingo co., Miss., and after an irregular course of 450 miles, joins the Alabama river 45 miles above Mobile; the united stream is called Mobile river below the junction. It is navigable for 410 miles from Mobile Bay.

TOM COD, or **FROST FISH,** a species of cod (*Morrhua pruinosa*) of the North Atlantic, usually abundant in the mouths of the rivers after the first frosts of autumn. It is from 4 to 12 inches long, olive-green above, and silvery below.

TOME, JACOB, an American philanthropist; born in Manheim township, York co., Pa., Aug. 13, 1810; went to Port Deposit, Md., in 1833, and there began operations in lumber and grain which yielded him vast wealth. In 1864, as chairman of the Finance Committee of the Maryland Senate, he relieved the seemingly hopeless financial condition of the State and reduced its indebtedness to less than $1,000,000. In 1884 he presented to Dickinson College, of which he was a trustee, a valuable building for scientific uses. His largest gift was for the foundation of the Jacob Tome Institute, at Port Deposit, $1,600,000, a sum that was increased by his will to more than $3,500,000. He died in Port Deposit, Md., March 16, 1898.

TOMLINSON, EVERETT TITS-WORTH, an American author, born in Shiloh, N. J., in 1859. He entered Williams College in the class of 1879, and after graduating became principal of the high school of Auburn, N. Y., then, in 1883, became headmaster of the preparatory department of Rutgers College.

TOMB OF GEORGE WASHINGTON AT MOUNT VERNON

TOMB OF THE UNKNOWN SOLDIER IN ARLINGTON NATIONAL CEMETERY

In 1888 he devoted himself entirely to his literary work. Among his books are: "The Search for Andrew Field" (1894); "The Boy Soldiers of 1812" (1895); "Under Colonial Colors" (1902); "The Camp Fire of Mad Anthony" (1907); and "The Story of General Pershing" (1917).

TOMMY ATKINS, a name given to privates of the British army. It is said to have originated in the custom of making out blanks for military accounts with the name, "I, Tommy Atkins," etc. Kipling has immortalized it in verse.

TOMPKINS, DANIEL D., an American statesman; born in Fox Meadows, Westchester co., N. Y., June 21, 1774; was graduated at Columbia College in 1795 and admitted to the New York bar in 1796. He was a member of the legislature and the State Constitutional Convention in 1801; member of Congress in 1804, but soon he resigned to become Judge of the Supreme Court of New York. He was Governor in 1807-1817, and Vice-President of the United States in 1817-1825. He was a delegate to the State Constitutional Convention of 1821, contributed money and troops to the national government in the War of 1812, during which he commanded the 3d Military District; and in a message to the New York legislature in 1817, recommended the total abolition of slavery in that State, an act which brought about the passage of the bill against slavery which took effect on July 4, 1827. He died in Staten Island, N. Y., June 11, 1825.

TOMSK, a town in Western Siberia, on the Tom; 2,809 miles E. of St. Petersburg. Situated on the great trade route from Tiumen to Irkutsk, and near the main line of the Siberian railway, it has long been the seat of an important transit trade. Leather and carriages are manufactured; and a university was established in 1888. Great part of the town was burned in 1890. Pop. about 117,000. The province of TOMSK, extending to the Chinese frontier, has an area of 331,159 square miles, more than 2½ times the size of Great Britain and Ireland, and a population about 4,000,000.

TON, a denomination of weight equivalent to 20 hundredweights, or 2,240 pounds. In the United States goods are sometimes weighed by the short ton, of 2,000 pounds, the hundredweight being reckoned at 100 pounds, but it is decided by Act of Congress that, unless otherwise specified, a ton weight is to be understood as 2,240 pounds avoirdupois.

TONAWANDA, a city of New York, in Erie co. It is on the Niagara river, the Erie canal, and on the New York Central and the International railroads. It is an important lumber market and its industries include the manufacture of steel, lumber, paper boards, etc. It has an armory, a high school, a public library, and a park. Pop. (1910) 8,290; (1920) 10,068.

TONAWANDA CREEK, a stream in Western New York which flows into the Niagara river 10 miles N. of Buffalo; length 75 miles.

TONE, THEOBALD WOLFE, an Irish revolutionist; born in Dublin, Ireland, June 20, 1763; was educated at Trinity College; studied law in London, and was called to the bar at the Middle Temple (1789). He was an ardent sympathizer with the doctrines of the French Revolution, and, having promoted the combination of the Irish Catholics and Dissenters, founded the Society of United Irishmen in 1791. The discovery of his secret negotiations with France drove him to the United States (1795). He sailed for France in 1796, and became Brigadier-General in Hoche's projected expedition to Ireland. He served in the Bavarian army in 1797, and in 1798 was captured on board a French squadron bound for Ireland. He was taken to Dublin, and sentenced to death by a court-martial, but committed suicide in prison, Nov. 19, 1798.

TONE-GAWA, the longest river in Japan; navigable for nearly 100 miles for flat-bottomed junks, but the coast is treacherous at its mouth, which is often closed by an impassable bar. It empties into the Pacific E. of Toyko; length, about 240 miles.

TONGA, or FRIENDLY ISLANDS, a group in the S. Pacific Ocean, forming an archipelago of very considerable extent, and consisting of more than 150 islands, the greater part of which are either mere rocks or shoals, or desert spots. Most of them are of coral formation; but some of them are volcanic in their origin, and in Tofoa there is an active volcano. The principal member of the group is Tongatuba or Sacred Tonga. The Tonga Islands were discovered by Tasman in 1643, but were named by Captain Cook, from the firm alliance that seemed to subsist among the natives, and from their courteous behavior to strangers. Among the products of the islands are yams, plantains, cocoanuts, hogs, fowls, fish, and all sorts of shell fish. The islands were first visited by missionaries in 1797. In 1827 the

Wesleyan Methodists succeeded in the work of evangelization, and their labors were finally crowned with such success that most of the inhabitants are now Christians. Nearly all the islands are under the rule of one Christian chief; but by an agreement made between England, Germany, and the United States in 1899 the islands are under the protectorate of Great Britain. Total area 385 square miles. Pop. (1917) 23,766, Europeans 347.

TONGUE, in human anatomy, a muscular organ in the mouth, covered with mucous membrane, the muscular structure rendering it of use in mastication, deglutition, and the articulation of speech, while the mucous membrane, which is endowed with common and tactile sensibility, constitutes it the seat of the sense of taste. The tongue occupies the concavity of the arch of the lower jaw; its basal or hinder part is connected with the hyoid bone, while beneath it is attached by means of the genio-glossus muscle to the lower jaw. The tongue is marked along the middle for nearly its whole length by a slight furrow called the raphe, often terminating behind in a depression called the foramen cœcum, within which mucous glands open. The upper surface of the tongue in front of the foramen is covered with small eminences called papillæ, some circumvallate, others fungiform, and the rest filiform, the last being the most numerous. Behind these are numerous small racemose glands, called lingual glands.

TONIC, in medicine, any remedy which improves the tone or vigor of the fibers of the stomach and bowels, or of the muscular fibers generally. Tonics may be said to be of two kinds, medical and non-medical. Medical tonics act chiefly in two ways: (1) Indirectly, by first influencing the stomach and increasing its digestive powers; such being the effect of the vegetable bitters, the most important of which are calumba, chamomile, cinchona bark, gentian, taraxacum, etc. (2) Directly, by passing into and exerting their influence through the blood; such being the case with the various preparations of iron, certain mineral acids, and salts. The non-medical tonics are open-air exercise, friction, cold in its various forms and applications, as the shower bath, sea bathing, etc.

TONKING, or **TONQUIN,** since 1884 a French possession, is the N. E. portion of the Indo-Chinese peninsula, bordering on China. Area, 119,660 square miles; pop. 6,200,000. Europeans, 6,000. Capital Hanoi, also of all French and Indo-China. The name has been used for various areas in this region. The main feature of the country is the Sang-koi or Red river (variously spelt Sang-koi, Sang-coi, etc), coming from Yunnan, and traversing the whole of Tonking lengthwise, with a large delta. The chief produce is rice, silk, sugar, pepper, oil, cotton, tobacco, and fruits, with some copper and iron; and companies are now working coal and antimony mines at one or two places on the coast, especially near the chief port of Haiphong. Products valued at $10,000,000 annually. The French scheme of tapping the resources of Yunnan by means of the Song-koi has proved impracticable, the navigation of the upper course being very difficult.

TONNAGE, in regard to ships, a measure both of cubical capacity and of dead-weight carrying capability. The term, used by itself, may have reference severally to "builders' old measurement" tonnage (B. O. M.), "register" tonnage, "displacement" tonnage, "freight" tonnage, etc., each of which expressions is more or less current in shipping circles. From very early times in the history of shipping a scale of one sort or other must have been employed to determine the relative capacity or carrying power of different vessels, and in point of fact the term "tonnage" in this connection can be traced back for at least 500 years. In Great Britain the first Act of Parliament dealing with the subject was passed in 1422, a second was introduced in 1694, and a third in 1720, but the application of these was limited to particular classes of ships, or those employed in particular trades.

"Displacement" tonnage is by general consent regarded as the fairest measure for the tonnage of naval ships since they are designed to carry certain maximum weights and to float at certain load lines which are fixed with reference to the character of service. It has for many years been the official tonnage for the warships of France and other European nations, and since 1872—prior to which date the B. O. M. rule was the only one employed—the tonnage of British naval ships has been based on the displacement principle. The United States navy has also adopted displacement tonnage; in fact, it is all but universally employed.

"Freight" tonnage, a system of measurement commonly employed in connection with stowage by merchants and shipowners, although it has no legal capacity, is simply a measure of cubical capacity. A freight ton, or "unit of measurement cargo," simply means 40 cubic feet of space available for cargo, and is therefore two-fifths of a register ton.

In connection with yachts tonnage is measured by special rules for the purpose of regulating time allowances in racing. These rules are numerous and varied almost as the yacht clubs and associations employing them, but the rule which has hitherto been most generally adopted in Great Britain is known as the "Thames Rule," and is simply a slight modification from the B. O. M. tonnage.

TONNAGE, AND POUNDAGE, certain duties on wine and other mercnan-dise, which began to be levied in England in the reign of Edward II. They were at first granted to the crown by the vote of Parliament for a limited number of years, and renewed on their expiry. The object of these imposts was said to be that the king might have ready money in case of a sudden emergency demanding it for the defense of the realm and the guarding of the sea. Charles II. and James II. obtained grants of tonnage and poundage for life, but William III. only for limited periods; and by three statutes of Anne and George I. these imposts were made perpetual, and mortgaged for the public debt. The Customs Consolidation Act of 1787 swept away tonnage and poundage and similar charges, and substituted a new and single duty on each article.

TONSILITIS, inflammation of one or both of the tonsils, generally extending also to the palate and uvula. It brings with it dryness, pain, and heat of the throat, with difficulty of swallowing, and often ends in abscesses, one at least of which suppurates. It is a common disease in moist variable weather.

TONSILS, in anatomy, two glands, one on each side of the palate between its pillars. They consist of a number of deep mucous follicles or cryptæ, surrounded by and deposited in cellular tissue arranged in a somewhat circular form. They are sometimes called amygdalæ. See TONSILITIS.

TONSON, JACOB, an English publisher; born in London, England, in 1656. He commenced business in Chancery Lane in 1677, removed to Gray's Inn in 1697, and thence in 1712 to the Shakespeare's Head, opposite Catherine Street in the Strand. He retired from business in 1720, and died March 18, 1736. He is worthy of remembrance as Dryden's regular publisher, as the originator of the miscellanies which bear his name, as having brought out the first good editions of Milton and the first complete octavo edition of Shakespeare, and as the secretary of the Kit Cat Club, which used to meet in his villa at Barn Elms, on the Thames.

TONSURE, in ecclesiology and Church history, the shaving of the crown in a circle, which is a distinguishing mark of clerks in the Roman Church. Most of the mendicant and cloistered orders allow only a narrow strip of hair to grow round the head, all above and below being shaved; the tonsure of secular clerics is small. The tonsure is a necessary preliminary to entering the clerical state, whether secular or religious; in the former case it is conferred by the bishop of the diocese, in the latter by the head of the religious house, if a mitered abbot. It invests the receiver with all the privileges of a cleric, and furnishes a means to distinguish the higher from the lower clergy, as the extent of the tonsure increases with the rank till the priesthood is reached. Also, the act of admission to the clerical state. At first it was never given without some minor order being conferred at the same time, but this practice ceased in the 7th century.

TONTINE, a term derived from the name of Lorenzo Tonti, a Neapolitan, who settled in Paris in Cardinal Mazarin's time, and proposed in 1653 to raise a fund of $125,000,000 for the relief of the national exchequer by means of a financial association, of which the great prize should ultimately accrue to the longest liver. There were to be shares of $1,500. The subscribers were to be divided into 10 classes according to age; and for each class a fixed sum was annually to be divided equally among the members of the class. In this way, while each member should get fair interest from the first on his capital, the profit falling to survivors would increase as years went on, and the last survivor would receive the whole of the interest due to the class he belonged to. The tontine is a lottery of annuities—or compounded of lottery and annuity—and was frequently had recourse to in France in the 18th century, with government sanction.

TOOKE, JOHN HORNE, an English political writer; born in Westminster, England, June 25, 1736; was educated at Westminster and Eton; afterward going to St. John's College, Cambridge. In 1760 he entered the Church, and obtained the living of New Brentford. The year 1771 witnessed his contest with Junius, in which, in the general opinion, he came off victor. In 1773 he resigned his benefice to study for the bar (to which from being in orders he was not admitted); and by his legal advice to Mr. Tooke of Purley he became that gentleman's heir and assumed his name. In 1777 he was prosecuted for a seditious libel condemning the American war, and his trial resulted in a year's imprisonment and a fine of $1,000. He was a short time member of Parliament for Old Sarum. He wrote several political pamphlets and an ingenious linguistic work entitled "Epea Pteroenta, or the Diversions of Purley." He died in Wimbledon, England, March 18, 1812.

TOOLE, JOHN LAURENCE, an English comedian; born in London, March 12, 1831. His father was well known in the city as civic toastmaster. While a clerk in a wine merchant's office, he devoted his leisure to private theatricals with a success which induced him to take to the stage as a profession. Toole made his first public appearance at the Haymarket Theater on July 22, 1852, on the occasion of a benefit to Mr. Webster. After a thorough training in the provinces he was engaged at St. James' Theater in 1854. Thence he passed to the Lyceum, and an engagement of several years as leading comedian at the New Adelphi followed. He made a professional tour in the United States in 1875, and in Australia in 1891, and with these exceptions he appeared regularly in every season in London for many years, latterly in a theater under his own management. His strength lay in broad and even farcical humor. Many farces, such as the "Area Belle," "Ici On Parle Français," "The Spitalfield Weavers," "The Pretty Horsebreaker," and "The Steeplechase," owe their popularity almost entirely to his versatility; and among his most prominent and successful impersonations are Paul Pry, Caleb Plummer in "The Cricket on the Hearth," Joe Bright in "Through Fire and Water," Uncle Dick in "Uncle Dick's Darling," and Chawles in "A Fool and His Money." He died July 30, 1906.

TOOLS AND MACHINERY. The history of tools goes back to the very beginning of human life. First, of course, tools were used exclusively for agricultural purposes, and for a long period were of the most primitive nature. As human activities became more complex, the use of tools spread rapidly. Their development, however, for a long time, was very slow. This did not change until steam, electricity, and water power became available for general use. Not until then were many tools developed into machinery.

The most remarkable and diversified improvements in tools and machinery took place beginning with the latter half of the nineteenth century. Gradually in many industries, and somewhat later, in agriculture, a change took place from hand work to machine work, not, of course, resulting in the total exclusion of the former by the latter.

Almost with the beginning of the more general use of machines, an extended controversy arose regarding its effect on industry. There is no doubt that the substitution of machinery for hand tools and of machine work for hand work has far-reaching and deep effects on employment, the individual laborer, output, and quality. Just what the ultimate effects are is still a matter of controversy. Undoubtedly, whenever hand work is changed to machine work in a given field of endeavor, there occurs at first a serious displacement of existing employment conditions. As a rule the use of machinery involves the employment of fewer persons, and in many instances it also does away with the need for highly skilled labor. On the other hand, as machinery becomes gradually adopted in a given field, the result frequently, if not always, is a widening of this field, and, therefore, eventually need for larger numbers of workmen. Then, too, as machinery is gradually developed and becomes more complicated, there again arises a need for more skilled labor.

In the same manner, the individual workman is affected. The use of machinery undoubtedly tends, in many instances, towards mere routine labor. One and the same process frequently is repeated over and over again. Naturally, this requires a lower grade of mentality in the laborer than was needed when a large number of diversified processes had to be performed by one and the same individual. On the other hand, the laborer frequently is enabled by the use of machinery to increase his earnings. It may, therefore, be said that while the use of machinery is at times apt to have a disadvantageous influence on the laborers' mentality, it is just as apt to greatly improve his material comforts.

There is no doubt that the use of machinery instead of hand work has resulted in vastly increased output. Indeed, in many instances, the invention of a given piece of machinery was more or less forced by the absolute necessity to increase output, either in order to meet increased demand, or else in order to reduce costs.

It is claimed by many that the quality of machine products is much lower than that of similar products produced by hand work. While this is without doubt true in many instances, it is, to a certain extent, offset by the greater uniformity. Then, too, it must be remembered that many products which now supply some of the most important needs of our daily life were not available until machines had been invented by means of which they could be produced.

The various kinds of machinery which are used today in civilized countries are so numerous that even a condensed list is impossible. Hardly any human endeavor today is carried on without the use of some kind of machinery. Most machinery is driven by power other than human. Animal, steam, electric and water power all are employed in connection with the use of machinery.

Agricultural Implements.—This term is commonly used to designate all tools, machinery, and other implements employed in the manifold processes connected with farming. The most ancient agricultural implements were, without doubt, restricted to those which required human strength only. All agricultural work for many centuries used to be done by the use of flails, hoes, rakes, scythes, sickles, and spades. All of these were worked by hand. When animal power became available to do some of the work which human beings had formerly done, there appeared primitive harrows and plows. Not until more comparatively modern times were other forms of farming implements and machinery invented and developed. During the nineteenth century especially, this development made vast progress. Indeed, many of the most useful pieces of farming machinery were not invented until then. Today, practically every operation required in farming is performed by means of some machine or implement. Just as is the case with machinery used in fields of human endeavor other than farming, electric, steam, water, wind, and other artificial forms of power are gradually supplanting hand and animal power. The soil now is prepared for planting by specially constructed plows, harrows, fertilizing machines, and other cultivators. Planting is done by means of mechanical planters and seeders. Crops are harvested by means of mechanical hay rakes, hay forks, mowers, reapers, and a large variety of other harvesting implements, each adapted for its special use. After the crops have been gathered, mechanical threshing machines, fanning mills, hullers, huskers, shellers, and other seed separators are employed. That branch of agriculture devoted to the production and utilization of milk, dairying, has also vastly progressed as a result of the invention and introduction of numerous forms of dairy machinery. Included in these are creaming imple-

ments, the most important of which is the separator. This implement has proven a great saver of labor and in various other ways has wrought such changes in the daily industry that it has become revolutionized. Other dairy machinery of importance include butter workers, cheese presses, cheese vats, hand and power churns, etc.

The plow is one of the most important agricultural implements, being used for breaking up the soil and for inverting the upper strata. The two principal types are soil plows and stubble plows. The latter is generally represented in American plows. The first American patent was granted to Charles Newbold, in 1797. Nowbold's plow was made of cast iron. The modern American plow, however, is based on a plow patented in 1819 by Jethro Wood. This, too, was made of cast iron. John Lane in 1836, and John Deere in 1837, substituted steel for cast iron. There are many special kinds of plows, such as sub-soil plows, hillside or swivel plows, double mold-bord plows, trench or ditching plows, double-furrow or gang plows, sulky plows, disc plows, etc. Steam and electricity is frequently used in connection with plows. The most recent development has been the gasoline tractor. The use of power other than horse power is especially advantageous on large farms and in places where fuel is cheaper than horses and feed, and where land is level.

The harrow is an implement used for covering seeds, for destroying weeds, for producing dust mulch for the purpose of conserving moisture, and for smoothing and pulverizing plowed land. There are four principal modern types of harrows, the curved knife and pulverizing, the disc, the smoothing, and the spring tooth harrow.

Cultivators are agricultural implements used for destroying weeds, for loosening the soil between rows of plants, for preparing the soil for planting, and for other similar purposes. Cultivators provided with a seat for the operator and with various levers for the control of the implement, are called rider cultivators. Simpler forms are designated as walker cultivators.

Reaping and mowing machines are of comparatively modern development. Several machines were invented in England in the latter part of the eighteenth and the early part of the nineteenth century. In 1822 Henry Ogle patented a side-draft machine which included some of the essential features of modern reapers, such as reels, a reciprocating knife over stationary finger, dividers, and platform. The first American patent for a reaping machine was granted in 1803 to Richard French and T. J. Hawkins, of New Jersey. Peter Gaillard, of Pennsylvania, in 1812, patented the first grass cutting machine. This was superseded in 1822 by another grass cutter, patented by Jeremiah Bailey, also of Pennsylvania. The latter machine was built on the revolving-cutter plan, with side draft, arranged so as to keep the cutter at a uniform distance from the ground. Of various other machines invented during this period, that of William Manning, of New Jersey (1831), possessed a cutting device which resembled very closely that used later by Hussey and McCormick. It was these two later inventors who, the former in 1833, and the latter in 1834, took out patents for improved reaping machines which combined the best features of all the various machines which up to that time had been brought out in England and in America. There was comparatively little difference between the Hussey and the McCormick reaper. The latter had a serrated edge knife which, instead of the pointed sections of Hussey's machine, possessed a wavy outline. It also had a divider and reels, but no seat for the attendant. It was a side-draft machine and could be either drawn or pushed. These two machines formed the basis of later reapers which have now been brought to a high state of perfection.

Self-acting rakes date back to 1848, when Nelson Platt patented such an implement. Great improvements have been made since then, some of the most important appearing in a machine built by McCormick in 1861.

Binding of grain by machinery was first attempted by John E. Heath, of Ohio, in 1850. His binder used twine or cord. Later machines used also straw and wire. The modern binder is based chiefly on a machine patented in 1858, and known as the Marsh harvester.

The combined header and thresher is most likely the most complicated and at the same time the most advanced type of harvester. It heads, threshes, cleans, and sacks the grain at one operation. It is used extensively in certain parts of the western United States and Australia. Such machines are usually pushed through the grain either by a traction engine or by horses, a large number of the latter being necessary for each machine, the capacity of which ranges from 60 to 125 acres per day.

Mowing machines have kept step with the development of reaping machines, and, indeed, many mowers are designed so as to be used as reapers also.

Threshing machines are implements used to separate the grain or seed of plants from the straw or haulm. Not until the end of the eighteenth century did various attempts to supersede the primitive flail by mechanical implements succeed. In 1786 a Scotch mechanic, Andrew Meikle, designed a threshing machine which, in spite of the fact that many inventors have tried to improve it, remains today essentially the same. Practically all modern threshing machines are based on the principles first developed by Meikle. In America greatly improved threshing machines are now in use, most of the improvements having been made since 1840. The most up-to-date threshing machine performs mechanically practically all operations involving the cutting of the bands of the sheaves, automatic feeding, thorough separation of grain from straw, winnowing and weighing the grain, depositing it in sacks or loading it into wagons, and removing and stacking the straw. Although there are in existence special threshing machines adapted to different kinds of grain and to a large variety of conditions, the parts of the most modern thresher are so adjustible that one and the same machine can be used for all kinds of grain and under all kinds of conditions.

Amongst the more important special threshing machines should be mentioned those for threshing beans, clover, peanuts, peas and rice, and others for husking maize, and shredding fodder. As a rule, bean and pea threshers are equipped with two cylinders which run at different rates of speed. Still another additional cylinder for hulling is usually to be found in clover hullers. Many important and useful accessory devices have been invented which are used in connection with threshing machines. The most important of these are automatic band cutters and feeders, loaders, stackers, and grain measurers. In the early days of the threshing machine, horse power was used most frequently and it is still used to a considerable extent. However, portable steam engines and internal combustion engines are gradually superseding horse power. In those parts of the United States where rice is cultivated engines with straw-burning furnaces have been used and have given satisfaction.

Nowhere else has more progress been made in the use of farming machinery than in the United States, and the remarkable productivity and prosperity which agriculture enjoys in this country are to no slight degree due to this fact. The last United States census of the manufacturers (1914) shows 601 establishments devoted to the manufacture of agricultural implements of all kinds. These employed 58,118 persons; had a capital of $338,531,673; paid salaries and wages amounting to $47,603,790; and produced goods valued at $164,068,835. The export of agricultural implements from this country to foreign countries is of importance and is steadily growing. In 1890 the value of agricultural implements from the United States was $3,-859,184. By 1900 it had increased to $16,099,149. It then remained stationary for the next two years, increasing slowly until 1905, when it amounted to $20,721,-741. In 1910 it had reached $28,124,033. In the last year previous to the World War (1913) it reached the large sum of $40,572,352. The effect of the World War was especially noticeable in the agricultural implement industry. In 1914 the exports had fallen to about $32,000,000, and in 1915 to $10,300,000, a figure lower than any since 1898. A slight improvement was shown in 1916, with total exports of over $17,600,000; these rose, in 1917, to over $26,500,000; in 1918 to over $35,000,000; and in 1919 to $41,195,494, the highest total yet achieved. This, however, was exceeded in 1920, when the exports of agricultural implements were valued at $46,277,269.

TOOMBS, ROBERT, an American statesman; born in Wilkes co., Ga., July 2, 1810; was graduated at Union College, Ky., studied law at the University of Virginia; was a Whig member of Congress from Georgia in 1845-1853; and a United States Senator in 1853-1861. He was expelled from the Senate in 1861, and in the same year was elected to the Confederate Congress and also became Confederate Secretary of State. He resigned to become a Brigadier-General in the Confederate army. After the war he resided abroad till 1867. He refused to take the oath of allegiance to the United States Government, being to the end of his life bitterly opposed to the reconstruction policy of the government. He died in Washington, Ga., Dec. 15, 1885.

TOOTH, one of the hard bodies in the mouth, attached to the skeleton, but not forming part of it, and developed from the dermis or true skin.

True teeth consist of one, two, or more tissues, differing in their chemical composition and in their microscopical appearances. Dentine, which forms the body of the tooth, and "cement," which forms its outer crust, are always present, the third tissue, the "enamel," when present, being situated between the dentine and cement. The dentine, which is
I—31

divided by Owen into hard or true dentine, vaso-dentine, and osteo-dentine, consists of an organized animal basis, disposed in the form of extremely minute tubes and cells, and of earthy particles. The tubes and cells contain, besides the calcareous particles, a colorless fluid, which is probably transuded blood plasma, or liquor sanguinis, and contributes to the nutrition of the dentine. In hard

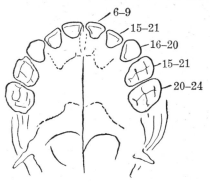

FIRST TEETH
The figures refer to months after birth

or true dentine the dentinal tubes proceed from the hollow of the tooth known as the pulp cavity, in a slightly wavy course, nearly at right angles to the outer surface. When a part of the primitive vascular pulp from which the dentine is developed remains permanently uncalcified, red blood is carried by "vascular canals" into the substance of the tissue. Such dentine is called vaso-dentine, and is often combined with true dentine in the same tooth, as, for example, in the large incisors of certain rodents, the tusks of the elephant, and the molars of the extinct megatherium. When the cellular basis is arranged in concentric layers around the vascular canals and contains "radiated cells," like those of bone, this is termed osteo-dentine, resembles true bone very closely. The cement always corresponds in texture with the osseous tissue of the same animal, and wherever it occurs in sufficient thickness, as on the teeth of the horse or ox, it is traversed like bone by vascular canals. The enamel is the hardest of all the animal tissues, and contains no less than 96.4 per cent. of earthy matter (mainly phosphate of lime), while dentine contains only 72 per cent. and cement and ordinary bone only 69 per cent. of earthy matter.

In a few fishes the teeth consist of a single tissue—a very hard kind of non-vascular dentine. Teeth consisting of dentine and vaso-dentine are very common in fishes. In all fishes the teeth are shed and renewed, not once only, as in mammals, but frequently during the whole course of their lives. Tortoises and turtles, toads, and certain extinct saurians are toothless. Frogs have teeth in the upper, but not in the lower jaw. Newts and salamanders have teeth in both jaws and upon the palate; and teeth are found on the palate as well as on the jaws of most serpents. In reptiles, as a general rule, the base of the tooth is anchylosed to the bone which supports it. The completion of a tooth is soon followed by preparation for its removal and succession, the faculty of developing new tooth germs being apparently unlimited in this class. The extinct *Odontornithes* are the only birds with teeth. Of mammals there are a few genera and species devoid of teeth. The

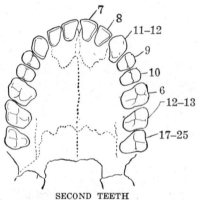

SECOND TEETH
The figures refer to years after birth

true ant-eaters, the pangolins, and the echidna are strictly toothless. It is only in the mammals that we have a well-marked division of the teeth into the four kinds of incisors, canines, premolars, and molars.

The teeth are so admirably adapted for the special purposes which they are called on to fulfill that it is generally easy, from a careful examination of them, to say to what class of animals they belong, and to draw various conclusions regarding the habits and structure of the class generally. Thus, in carnivorous animals the molars are not grinding teeth, but present sharp cutting edges, and those of the upper and lower jaw overlap each other, resembling a pair of scissors in their action. In insectivorous animals the molars have a tuberculate surface, with conical points and depressions, so arranged as to lock into each other. In frugivorous animals, living on soft fruits, these teeth are provided with rounded

tubercles, while in herbivorous animals they have a broad, rough surface, resembling a millstone.

Diseases of the Teeth.—Decay (caries) is by far the most common of the diseases which affect the teeth, and consists in a gradual and progressive disintegration of the tooth substance. The exciting cause of caries has been proved to be due to the action of micro-organisms producing lactic acid.

Decay is rarely met with on smooth surfaces exposed to the friction of food and the direct washings of the saliva. It usually begins in some pit or groove in the enamel or between the teeth, such points forming a lodgment for the development of the organisms. Once the enamel has been penetrated the decay proceeds more rapidly, spreading laterally beneath the as yet healthy enamel and toward the pulp. Caries is most common in early life, by far the greater number of cavities making their appearance between the ages of 6 and 18. Pain may be felt soon after the enamel has been penetrated, or may be delayed until the nerve (pulp) has become almost or quite exposed. Ultimately the pulp becomes exposed when the pain increases and may become very violent, especially if the nerve be pressed on by food forced into the cavity by mastication. Should this take place the pulp becomes acutely inflamed and soon dies, when the pain may either cease or go on till an alveolar abscess is formed.

Periostitis and Alveolar Abscess.—Periostitis is an inflammation of the membrane (periosteum) which covers the roots of the teeth and lines their sockets. It may be either general or local. When general the majority of all of the teeth are commonly involved. When the disease is local—confined to one or two teeth—it may result from a blow or some such injury, or it may proceed from an inflamed pulp; but by far the most common cause is the presence of a dead nerve, the poisonous products of which are liable at any time to cause violent inflammation at the end of the root.

Alveolar abscess may be defined as a suppuration around the root or roots of a tooth. It is of two varieties, acute and chronic. Its causes are those of periostitis, which precedes it, the continuous and throbbing nature of the pain indicating the formation of matter (pus) within the surrounding bone.

Exostosis is characterized by an increase in the thickness of the cementum, the external of the two hard tissues forming the roots of the teeth. Its forms vary from a small nodule or patch to a quantity sufficient to invest the entire root or roots of the same or adjoining teeth. Exostosis may often cause neuralgic pains about the jaws.

Impaction and Difficult Eruption of the Wisdom and other Teeth.—It is not uncommon to find certain of the temporary teeth firmly set in the adult jaw, and occupying the place of the permanent ones. In such cases the permanent tooth is usually present in the body of the jaw, but it has been retarded in eruption by being too deeply imbedded in the bone. Impaction may also be due to an abnormal direction of growth. Such teeth may appear late in life after all the others are lost, and the bone overlying them has been absorbed and so exposed them. When these cases do occur they are responsible for the popular but incorrect idea of a third set of teeth. An impacted tooth seldom gives rise to any trouble, unless it be an upper or lower wisdom, particularly the latter. The cutting of these teeth is sometimes accompanied by distressing symptoms which may be protracted for months or years, unless they are removed by extraction of the tooth.

Absorption of the Alveoli.—The gradual wasting of the bone which surrounds and supports the roots of the teeth, accompanied by a simultaneous recession of the gums, is one of the changes which mark the approach of old age. This wasting may, however, occur in middle life without any visible cause, though the majority of such cases are due to chronic inflammation of the gums, with or without the deposition of tartar. Heredity, or the use of too hard a tooth brush, may likewise be accountable. The teeth most affected are the front ones; but the reverse of this is not unusual. The gums, especially in front, gradually recede and lay bare the roots; the teeth now become loosened and finally drop out.

Toothache is not so much a disease as a symptom. Its chief causes are mentioned under caries and alveolar abscess. When toothache is due to caries with or without simple exposure of the pulp, the attack is brought on by taking hot or cold, sweet or acid fluids, and is seldom of long duration. To afford relief in such cases as these, gently wash out the cavity with a solution of carbonate of soda; then, drying it carefully with a piece of cotton-wool, take a very small pellet of wool dipped in eucalyptus oil and place it in the bottom of the cavity; over this place a piece of cotton wool large enough to fill the cavity and saturated with the following solution: 1 drachm of mastic in 1½ ounce of eau de cologne. This should be changed daily. When the pain is caused by the forming of an alveolar abscess the tooth will be found insensitive to change of temperature but very susceptible to pressure. The patient now becomes feverish, and the pain, which is at first of a dull heavy character, becomes more intense, throbbing, and continuous, till pus has been formed and discharged through the gum. Provided the tooth is likely to prove useful and the patient cannot consult a dentist, the gum should be carefully painted with tincture of iodine, or the old-fashioned plan of placing a roasted fig over the root may be resorted to; at the same time it is well to give an aperient such as epsom salts, followed by a full dose of quinine—6 to 8 grains for an adult. Great reliief follows this treatment, wihch is, of course, only temporary.

Hygienic Care of the Teeth.—Many of the diseases of the teeth and gums might be prevented or greatly retarded by proper attention to the cleansing of these organs. The implements best fitted for this purpose comprise the quill toothpick, waxed silk thread and brushes, with suitable powders. An excellent tooth powder is composed of precipitated chalk, 2 ounces; light magnesia, 2 ounces; oil of cinnamon, 8 drops; thymol crystals, 4 grains; otto of roses, 10 drops. The teeth should be brushed twice daily, in the morning and in the evening. The brush, used properly, should be pressed against the teeth and the handle rotated so as to make the bristles sweep vertically between and over them; this, coupled with an up-and-down motion, will thoroughly cleanse the interspaces; the inner surfaces of the back teeth are best cleaned in a like manner, while the corresponding parts of the upper and lower incisors are effectually reached by a vertical drawing movement. The brush should be of medium texture, and the bristles of unequal length, and not too closely placed.

TOPAZ, a mineral, ranked by mineralogists among gems, characterized by having the luster vitreous, transparent to translucent; the color yellow, white, green, blue; fracture subconchoidal, uneven; sp. gr. 3,499. It is harder than quartz. It is a silicate of aluminum, in which the oxygen is partly replaced by flourine. It occurs massive and in crystals. The primary form of its crystal is a right rhombic prism. Topazes occur generally in igneous and metamorphic rocks, and in many parts of the world, as Cornwall, Scotland, Saxony, Siberia, Brazil, etc. The finest varieties are obtained from Brazil and the Ural Mountains. Those from Brazil have deep yellow tints; those from Siberia have a bluish tinge; the Saxon topazes are of a pale wine-yellow, and those found in the Scotch Highlands are of a sky-blue color. The purest from Brazil, when cut in facets, closely resemble the diamond in luster and brilliance.

TOPEKA, a city of Kansas, the county seat of Shawnee co. It is on the Kansas river and the Missouri Pacific, the Union Pacific, the Atchison, Topeka and Sante Fe, the Leavenworth and Topeka, and the Chicago, Rock Island, and Pacific railroads. It has an area of about 16 square miles. The city is laid out in unusually attractive lines and the streets are adorned with beautiful shade trees. The notable buildings include the State Capitol, the Kansas Memorial Building, public library, United States Government building, State Museum, county court house, city hill and an auditorium. It is the seat of Washington College, and also has a State insane asylum and a State reform school, as well as many important local and charitable institutions. The industries are chiefly those connected with the Santa Fe Railroad shops. There are also manufactures of machinery, lumber, boilers, woolen goods, etc. There is a considerable wholesale jobbing business. Topeкa was founded in 1854 by eastern anti-slavery men following the passage of the Kansas-Nebraska Bill. In 1856 an antislavery convention adopted the Topeka Constitution and the Topeka Government was established. This, however, was soon broken up by United States troops. In 1857 it was chartered as a city and in 1861 became the capital of the State. Pop. (1910), 43,684; (1920), 50,022.

TOPHET, in Scripture, a place in the immediate vicinity of Jerusalem, considered by Milton to be identical with the valley of Hinnom, but described in Scripture as in that valley (II Kings xxiii: 10; Jer. vii: 31). It was S. E. of Jerusalem (Jer. xix: 2), and has been prepared of old for some king of Israel, or for Moloch (Isa. xxx: 33). Whatever its primary design, "high places" were erected there, and it became the chief seat of the worship of Moloch in Palestine (II Kings xxiii: 10; Jer. vii: 31); Josiah not merely stopped that cruel form of idolatry, but defiled the place (II Kings xxiii: 10; Jer. xix: 13), apparently by making it the receptacle of the filth of the capital. It became a burial ground ultimately overcrowded with bodies (Jer. vii: 31, 32; xix: 6, 11).

TOPLADY, AUGUSTUS MONTAGUE, an English theologian and hymnologist; born in Farnham, Surrey, England, Nov. 4, 1740; was educated at Westminster and Trinity College, Dublin. After holding a curacy for some years in Somersetshire, he was presented in 1768 to the vicarage of Broadhembury, Devonshire. His works were published in six volumes in 1825; new edition in one volume, 1837, with a memoir. Though a voluminous writer — and a strenuous defender of Calvinism against John Wesley—Toplady is now hardly known except as the author of the hymn "Rock of Ages," one of the most exquisite expressions of evangelical faith and fervor to be found within the compass of the English tongue. A Latin version by Mr. Gladstone "Translations by Lord Lyttleton and the Right Hon. W. E. Gladstone," 1861) has added fresh beauty to the original. He died in London, Aug. 11, 1778.

TORBERT, ALFRED THOMAS ARCHIMEDES, an American military officer; born in Georgetown, Del., July 1, 1833; was graduated at the United States Military Academy in 1855; spent five years on frontier duty in Texas, Florida, New Mexico and Utah. In the latter half of 1862 he won distinction in the battles of Manassas and Crampton's Gap; was made Brigadier-General of volunteers on Nov. 29, of that year. He afterward took part at Gettysburg, Rappahannock Station, Matadequin Creek, etc. He captured Cold Harbor on May 31, 1864. He particularly distinguished himself on Sept. 19, 1864, routing the enemy at Winchester, and on Oct. 9 won the cavalry battle at Tom's river. On Dec. 22 and 23 he had command at Liberty Mills and Gordonsville. In March, 1865, he was brevetted Major-General, U. S. A., for gallantry during the war. He served as consul-general to Paris in 1873-1878. He was drowned Sept. 30, 1880, while a passenger on the steamer "Vera Cruz."

TORCELLO, a small island in the Lagoon of Venice, 6 miles above that city. It was a place of some importance in the 10th and 11th centuries. It contains an ancient Byzantine cathedral of Santa Maria, and a church of Santa Fosca, both of which are beautiful specimens of architecture and are rich in interior decorations.

TORCH LAKE, a lake lying chiefly in Antrim co., Mich.; and separated from the E. side of Grand Traverse Bay by a narrow strip of land. It communicates with Lake Michigan. Length 14 miles.

TORGAU, a fortified town in Saxony, Prussia; on the Elbe; 31 miles N. E. of

Leipsic. It is inclosed by a wall and has manufactures of woolen goods, hosiery and leather. Its chief building is the castle, Hartenfels. It was fortified by Napoleon in 1810; was besieged by the Allies in 1813 and surrendered Jan. 14, 1814. Pop about 11,000.

TORMENTIL, in botany, *Potentilla tormentilla, formerly Tormentilla officinalis.* The stem is slender, the leaves three-foliolate, more rarely five-foliolate; the petals usually four in place of the normal five of other Potentillas. Abundant on heaths, copses, and dry pastures, flowering from June to September. The rootstock, which is very astringent, is used for tanning.

TORNADO, a whirlwind, continuing but a brief period, and covering only a small area. It is distinct from the hurricane and the cyclone, is more local, and at the center of its vortex is extremely violent, lifting houses and animals into the air. It is most prevalent in the Mississippi Valley, and in the Spring of the year. Its center moves usually in a north-easterly direction at a rate of thirty miles or more an hour, and covers a track from a few rods to a mile or more in width. The severe tornado of Mar. 18, 1925, caused over 800 deaths, chiefly in Illinois.

TORONTO, a city of Canada, the capital of the Province of Ontario. It is on the north shore of Lake Ontario, on an inlet called the Bay of Toronto. The city has a water front of about 10 miles, and extends inland about 6 miles. The harbor has accommodations for the largest vessels passing the Welland canal. All three trans-continental railroads of Canada traverse the city. It has a total area of about 32 square miles. Here is held the annual Canadian National Exhibition, lasting 2 weeks each year, attended by about 1,000,000 visitors and noted for agricultural, industrial and art exhibits. The business section contains many handsome office buildings, ranging from 12 to 20 stories in height. The notable buildings include the Provincial Legislative Building, the University of Toronto, City Hall and the governor's house. There are over 100,000 buildings in the city limits. The street system includes 531 miles of streets and 140 miles of lanes. In 1920 there were 88,254 registered pupils in public and private schools, and 15,034 in attendance at the high, technical, and commercial schools. There are 32 colleges, 13 libraries, and 8 public hospitals.

In industrial importance Toronto ranks second among the cities of Canada. The value of the products of the 125 industries in 1918 was $456,250,198. The assessed valuation in 1919 was $642,816,690. The bank clearings in the same year amounted to $4,251,644,303. The customs receipts in 1919 amounted to $32,956,819. The net debt of the city was $77,836,811, while the revenue was $25,502,586. Toronto is the greatest live-stock market of Canada. The city was founded in 1749 as a French trading post, and was chosen as the provincial capital in 1792. It was incorporated as a city in 1834. Pop. (1919) 325,302; (1921) 521,893.

TORONTO, UNIVERSITY OF, an institution for higher education, at Toronto, Canada; founded as King's College in 1827. It assumed its present title in 1849. It has a medical school, an agricultural college, a college of dentistry, pharmacy, music, practical science, veterinary science, etc. There are about 5,000 students and about 400 instructors.

TORPEDO, in ichthyology, the type genus of *Torpedinidpæ*, with the characters of the family. There are six species distributed over the Atlantic and Indian oceans; three of these occur in the Mediterranean, and two, *T. marmorata* and *T. hebetans*, are sometimes found on the British coast. The electric organs consist of many perpendicular prisms, mostly hexagonal, the whole forming a kidney-shaped mass. Each column in the living fish appears like a clear trembling jelly. Hunter counted 470 of these columns in a specimen of *T. marmorata,* and says that the partitions between them are full of arteries, which bring the blood direct from the gills. These organs convert nervous energy into electricity. Each organ receives one branch of the trigeminal and four branches of the vagus, the former and the three anterior branches of the latter being each as thick as the spinal cord. The fish gives the electric shock voluntarily, to stun or kill its prey or in self-defense); but to receive the shock the object must complete the circuit by communicating with the fish at two distinct points, either directly or through the medium of some conducting body. The force of the discharge varies with the size and vigor of the fish; large and healthy specimens can inflict severe shocks sufficient to disable a man. The electric currents generated in these fish possess all the other known powers of electricity; they render the needle magnetic, decompose chemical compounds, and emit sparks. Also the common name of any individual of the genus. In southern European waters the best known species is *T. marmorata.* It is dark brown in color, lighter round the eyes. Specimens have been taken weighing 100 pounds, but they usually average about half that weight, with the disk about 30 inches broad. *T. hebetans*, more rarely met with, is dark chocolate-brown above, white beneath. They are also called cramp fish and numb fish. A well-known American species is *T. occidentalis*.

TORPEDO BOATS, small vessels built for speed and fitted with tubes for firing torpedoes by either compressed air or gunpowder. They are of two classes: those with powerful engines designed to steal on an enemy under cover of darkness, and those which can be used on the surface or submerged to do their work unseen beneath the water. The first torpedo boat was built about 1873, by Thornycraft, of England, for the Norwegian Government. This had a speed of 15 knots an hour, which has been raised in subsequent vessels of the kind to over 30 knots. The first of the present class of torpedo boats was built by Thornycraft in 1887 for the Spanish Government. The torpedo boat destroyer does not differ essentially from the torpedo boat, except in its greater speed and its power, owing to its greater weight, to maintain that speed in the face of a considerable sea. Its armament is also heavier and its guns of longer range. In the American-Spanish War, Admiral Cervera had three torpedo boat destroyers in his ill-fated squadron and all were destroyed by the American ships, two of them, the "Pluton" and "Furor," at Santiago, by the converted yacht "Gloucester." They form a useful protection to larger ships in battle, and in the World War were employed in great numbers by the combatants. The torpedo boat destroyer developed from the torpedo boat. See SUBMARINE MINES AND NAVIGATION.

TORPEDO-BOAT DESTROYER, a torpedo boat of a most formidable kind, designed for the destruction of ordinary torpedo boats. The destroyers are usually armed with one 12-pounder gun and from three to five 6-pounder guns, besides their equipment of torpedoes, and carry a crew of four officers and about 40 men. They are capable of 30 knots an hour, and, as they carry from 70 to 100 tons of coal, can make a voyage of 1,300 to 1,500 miles without recoaling. The World War introduced many improvements in destroyers. They performed invaluable services in naval operations. In the battle of Jutland the German destroyers raised a smoke-screen before the German fleet, which enabled the German admiral to withdraw his ships from immediate danger from British guns. See TORPEDO BOATS.

TORPEDOES. The torpedoes known to modern warfare are all automobile; that is to say, they run by their own power, differing in this respect from projectiles fired from guns, which otherwise they rather closely resemble. And not only do they run by their own power, but they carry a complicated mechanism by which they steer themselves, regulate the depth at which they run, and render themselves harmless after a certain length of time if they fail to hit their mark.

Torpedoes of various forms have been known and used for several centuries, but the automobile torpedo of today is essentially a development of the last fifty years, having been invented about 1870 by an Englishman, Whitehead, who, failing to secure recognition from the British naval authorities, took his invention to Austria, where it was at once adopted. It was slow in making its way in other countries, and even as late as the beginning of the World War, in 1914, was regarded in many quarters as of no great practical value. It accomplished nothing in the Spanish-American War of 1898 and little or nothing in the Russo-Japanese War of 1904; and even those who had most faith in its possibilities were unprepared for the manifestation of its efficiency given by the Germans in the first months of the World War and thereafter. A large part of this efficiency was due, of course, to the remarkable development of the submarine, a development which at that time had been carried much farther in Germany than elsewhere. But the outstanding feature of the submarine campaign was the thoroughness with which the two factors—the torpedo and submarine—had been adapted to each other. Both the British and the American navies took the lessons of the war to heart and both have now, a little late, carried both the torpedo and the submarine far beyond the point attained by the German navy at its best.

Figure 1 shows the principal features of the torpedo. At the forward end is the *war-head*, A, carrying the explosive charge, 600 pounds of gun-cotton or trinitro-toluol. The fuse by which the charge is exploded on striking projects from the nose of the war-head but is rendered inactive until the torpedo is fired by a safety device which is released by pressure of the water. For purposes of drill the war-head is replaced by an *exercise-head* made of soft metal which collapses when it strikes a hard surface, thus indicating that the target—often the side of a friendly battleship—has been hit.

Immediately abaft the head is the *air-flask*, B, a large compartment charged with air under high pressure and furnishing the motive power for the engine, D. In a pipe leading from the air-flask to the engine is the starting-valve, connected with a small lever on the outside of the torpedo which is tripped automatically when the torpedo is fired.

The engine in the latest American torpedo is a turbine, but reciprocating engines are still used abroad. The shaft runs through the *after-body*, E, to the *propellers*, of which there are two, RR, in tandem, one being keyed to the shaft and the other to a sleeve around the shaft and connected with it by a beveled gear. The propellers turn in opposite directions, one right, the other left, and must be balanced perfectly, as the slightest difference in their action would cause the torpedo to diverge from its initial course and might make it run in a circle and, in an extreme case, strike the ship from which it had been fired.

The *rudder*, R, abaft the propellers, is placed horizontally, not vertically, its

pedo. The essential feature of this device is the utilization of the pressure of the water, which varies with every variation in the depth, to actuate the horizontal rudder already described and so steer the torpedo up or down, as may be necessary. The figure shows the immersion-chamber (water-tight), and the engine compartment (open to the sea), separated by a water-tight bulkhead. In the immersion-chamber is a sleeve carrying the *hydrostatic-piston*, which is held by a spring in contact with a flexible diaphragm forming a part of the water-tight bulkhead. The tension of the spring can be varied to correspond with the pressure of the water for any desired depth. If we suppose the spring to be given a tension equal to that of the water at a depth of 15 feet, the piston will remain at rest when the torpedo is running at that depth. If the torpedo rises, the pressure of the water on the flexible diaphragm will be less than the tension of the spring and the piston will move to the right, carrying with it a rod which is attached to the rudder, and steering

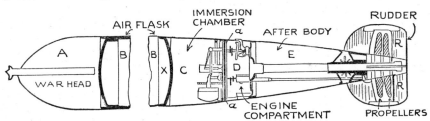

DIAGRAM OF TORPEDO—FIG. 1

purpose being to steer the torpedo up and down, not to right and left. Very small vertical rudders are used in connection with the Gyro gear, described later, but these are not shown in the drawing.

The *brains* of the torpedo are in the *immersion-chamber*, C, between the air-flask and the engine compartment. Here is placed the mechanism by which the torpedo is governed in many ways. A gyroscopic device opposes any tendency to deviate from the initial course. A depth-regulator insures running at a prescribed depth, usually from 15 to 20 feet. A soluble plug opens a valve after a certain time and causes the torpedo to sink if it has missed its mark. An automatic throttle-valve keeps the air pressure constant during the discharge of the air-flask, insuring a uniform speed throughout the run. Of these devices, only the depth-regulator, Figure 2, will be described, this being, perhaps, the most characteristic feature of the tor-

the torpedo down. If it dives too deep, the balance of pressure is disturbed in the opposite direction and the torpedo is steered up. And so on, until the torpedo becomes steady at the depth for which the spring is adjusted.

The range of the most powerful torpedoes in use in 1921 is approximately 12,000 yards (six miles) and at this range a stationary target of the length of a dreadnaught can be struck three times out of four. Naturally the conditions are greatly modified and the accuracy enormously reduced when both the firing ship and the target ship are moving at considerable speed. The ships sunk by German torpedoes during the war were all attacked at short range, usually less than a thousand yards.

While torpedoes may be launched from battleships, all of which are fitted with elaborate arrangements for the purpose, they are more effectively fired from smaller craft—destroyers and submarines—the high speed of the destroyer and the invisibility of the submarine giving such a craft a great advantage in the use of a weapon like the torpedo, which is essentially a weapon of surprise. One of the developments promised for the future is a torpedo airplane, which shall carry a torpedo, with arrangements for launching it from a height of several thousand feet while flying at full speed. There is promise also of a torpedo which can be controlled from the firing ship or from a shore station, by radio. Lastly may be mentioned a possible combination of these two plans, the torpedo being

called from its having housed some survivors from the Armada); and St. Michael's Chapel, on a hilltop, is thought to have been connected with the abbey. St. John's Church, by Street, is a striking early English edifice; and other buildings are the town hall, museum, and theater. Torquay is a great yachting station; its chief industries are the working up of Devonshire marbles and the manufacture of terra-cotta. Pop. about 39,000.

TORQUE, in archæology, a twisted collar of gold, or other metal, worn

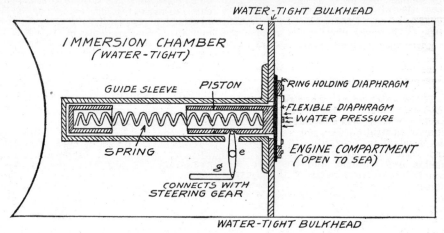

DIAGRAM OF DEPTH REGULATOR—FIG. 2

launched from an airplane at a great distance from the target, and controlled by radio from the airplane and so guided directly to the mark.

TORQUAY, a watering place of South Devon, England; occupying a cove on the N. side of Tor Bay, 23 miles S. of Exeter and 220 W. S. W. of London. Tor Abbey was founded here for Premonstratensian monks in 1196; and Tor Bay is famous in history as the place where in 1688 William of Orange landed at Brixham, and during the war with France was often used as a naval rendezvous. But till the beginning of the 19th century Torquay itself was little more than an assemblage of fishermen's huts. About that time the advantages of its climate—which are a peculiarly sheltered position, an equable temperature (mean 44° in winter, 55° in summer), and freedom from fogs—caused it to be resorted to by consumptive patients, and it soon acquired a European celebrity, which still is almost unrivaled. The remains of the abbey include some crypts and the 13th-century "Spanish barn" (so-

around the neck in ancient times by the people of Asia and the N. of Europe, and apparently forming a great part of the wealth of the wearer. Among the ancient Gauls gold torques appear to have been so abundant that about 223 B. C. Flaminius Nepos erected to Jupiter a golden trophy made from the torques of the conquered Gauls. The name of the Torquati, a family of the Manlian Gens, was derived from their ancestor, T. Manlius, having in 361 B. C. slain a gigantic Gaul in single combat, whose torque he took from the dead body and placed on his own neck. The commonest form is that known as funicular, in which the metal is twisted, with a plain, nearly cylindrical portion at both ends, which are turned back in opposite directions, so that each end terminates in a kind of hook by which the torque was fastened. Bronze torques are, as a rule, thicker and bulkier.

TORQUEMADA, THOMAS DE, the first inquisitor-general of Spain; born in Valladolid, Spain, in 1420. He became prior of a Dominican monastery at Segovia, and succeeded in persuading Ferdinand and Isabella to crave from the Pope the appointment of the "Holy Office" of the Inquisition. Torquemada was appointed its head, and began in 1483 that infamous work which has left his name a byword for pitiless cruelty. He has given a subject to Longfellow and to Hugo. He died in Avila, Spain, Sept. 16, 1498.

TORRE DEL GRECO, a town in Italy, situated on the Bay of Naples, 7 miles S. E. of Naples. Its industries are fishing and coral working. It has been several times destroyed by earthquakes and eruptions from Mount Vesuvius. Pop. about 36,000.

TORRENS LAKE, a large shallow salt lake of South Australia, about 40 miles N. of Spencer's Gulf. In the dry season it is merely a salt marsh.

TORRENS' LAND SYSTEM, a plan of land transfer drawn up by Sir Robert Torrens, and by him put in operation in Australia. It is now used in all the Australian provinces, in Tasmania and New Zealand, and in British Columbia and Ontario, and has been attempted in various parts of the United States (Minnesota, Colorado, Washington, New York, North Carolina, Mississippi, etc.). Its object is to make the transfer of land as simple as that of bank stock, and render the title of the holder thereof as free from danger or difficulty as ordinarily the title of the holder of bank stock is to the shares he holds. A land registry is established under the control of an officer known as the master of titles, by whom all land transactions are registered. A title may be registered as absolute or possessory; if absolute, the title must be approved by the master of titles before the ownership can be registered in fee simple. The first registration of a person as owner with absolute title will vest in that person an estate in fee simple in the land, subject to any incumbrances that may be entered on the register. If a possessory title is required, the applicant is registered as owner on giving such evidence of title as may be prescribed. The registration of any person as first owner, with a possessory title only, will not interfere with the enforcement of any estate, right, or interest adverse to the title that may then exist or arise at a later date. Should it appear to the master of titles that an absolute title to any land can only be held for a limited period or subject to reservations, he may except from the effect of registration any estate, right, or interest arising before a specified date, or arising under a special instrument or otherwise particularly described in the register. A title granted under such conditions is to be called a qualified title. The master of titles must give to the first registered owner a "land certificate," and this certificate must say whether the title of the owner is "absolute," "qualified," or "possessory." An insurance fund is created to indemnify persons who may suffer loss through misdescription, omission, or other error in any certificate of title, or in any entry on the register. This fund is provided by laying a tax of one-fourth of one per cent. on the value of the land on the first certificate of title being granted, in addition to registration fees. The master of titles settles all questions as to the liability of the fund for compensation.

TORRES STRAIT, the strait which separates Australia from New Guinea, being about 80 miles across. It is crowded with islands, shoals, and reefs, rendering its navigation difficult.

TORRES VEDRAS, a town of Portugal in the province of Estremadura; on the Sizandro, 30 miles N. of Lisbon; celebrated in connection with the famous lines of defense behind which Wellington retired after the vain effort to hold the Portuguese frontier against the French. The outermost of the line stretched 29 miles from Alhambra on the Tagus to the sea at the mouth of the Sizandro; the second, from 6 to 10 miles behind, from Quintella on the Tagus to the mouth of the St. Lorenza, a distance of 24 miles. The third, much shorter, lay S. W. of Lisbon, at the very mouth of the Tagus, and was meant as a cover if embarkation were necessary. The whole lines consisted of 152 redoubts, with 534 pieces of ordnance and 34,125 men. The "great work at Monte Agraca" had a perimeter of 2,435 feet, an armament of 25 guns, and a garrison of 1,590 infantry. The allies entered the retreat which the foresight of Wellington had provided in October, 1810, and held the French at Bay till March, 1811. The enemy then retired, and Wellington issued on his career as the liberator of the peninsula.

TORREY, BRADFORD, an American author; born in Weymouth, Mass., Oct. 9, 1843. He was educated in the public schools, taught two years, then entered business in Boston. In 1886 he became assistant editor of the "Youth's Companion." He was a close student of birds, and wrote largely on this subject for the magazines. His essays have been collected into the following volumes:

"Birds in the Bush" (1885); "The Foot-path Way"; "A Rambler's Lease"; "A Florida Sketch-Book"; "Spring Notes from Tennessee" (1896); "A World of Green Hills" (1898); "Friends on the Shelf" (1906); "Field Days in California" (1913). He died in 1913.

TORRINGTON, a city in Litchfield co., Conn.; on the Naugatuck river; about 28 miles W. by N. of Hartford. It contains many churches, a high school, waterworks, electric lights, banks, and daily and weekly newspapers. Torrington has manufactories of woolen goods, hardware, plated goods, machinery, needles, etc., and an assessed valuation of nearly $6,000,000. It was the birthplace of John Brown. Pop. (1910) 15,483; (1920) 20,623.

TORSION, in mechanics, the force with which a body, as a thread, wire, or slender rod, resists a twist, or the force with which it tends to return to its original state on being twisted. Such machines as capstans and windlasses, also axles, which revolve with their wheels, are, when in action, subjected to be twisted, or undergo the strain or torsion. If a slender rod of metal be suspended vertically, so as to be rigidly fixed at the point of suspension, and then twisted, through a certain angle, it will, when the twisting force ceases to act, untwist itself or return in the opposite direction with a greater or less force or velocity, till it comes to rest in its original position. The limits of torsion within which the body will return to its original state depend on its elasticity, and the force with which it tends to recover its natural state is termed elasticity of torsion. This force is always proportional to the angle through which the body has been twisted. If a body is twisted so as to exceed the limit of its elasticity, its particles will either be wrenched asunder or it will take a set, and will not return to its original position on the withdrawal of the twisting force.

In surgery, the twisting of the cut end of a small artery in a wound or after an operation, for the purpose of checking hemorrhage. The bleeding vessel is seized by an instrument called a torsion forceps, drawn out for about a quarter of an inch, and then twisted round several times, till it cannot untwist itself.

TORSTENSSON, LENNART, a Swedish general in the Thirty Years' War; born in Torstena, Sweden, Aug. 17, 1603; became in his 15th year page to Gustavus Adolphus; and in 1630, as captain of the bodyguard, accompanied the king to Germany, where he highly dis-tinguished himself in the battle on the Lech, April 5, 1632. He was taken prisoner before Nuremberg, Aug. 12, 1632, and six months in a subterranean dungeon shattered his health and obliged him to return to Sweden. In 1641 he became commander-in-chief of the Swedish army. He entered Schlesien through Sachsen, took Glogau and Schweidnitz, turned into Moravia and captured Olmütz. Obliged to retreat into Sachsen before the Archduke Leopold and Piccolominin, he turned on his pursuers and inflicted a severe defeat at Breitenfeld, Nov. 2, 1642. In consequence of Denmark's declaration of war against Sweden, in December he burst into Denmark, and in six weeks subjugated the whole peninsula, with the exception of the fortresses Rendsburg and Glückstadt. After defeating the Austrian general Gallas at Jüterbok, Nov. 23, 1644, he returned into Bohemia, defeated Katzfield at Jankau, March 6, 1645, overran Moravia, and demolished the fortifications before Vienna. He then laid siege to Brünn, but was forced to retreat into Bohemia. He was made Count of Ort. a by Christina in 1647, and died in Stockholm, April 7, 1651.

TORT, in law, denotes injustice or injury. Actions on torts or wrongs are all personal actions for trespasses, nuisances, assaults, defamatory words, and the like.

TORTOISE, in zoölogy, a name formerly taken to include all the *Chelonians,* but now, unless qualified by an adjective, confined to the individuals of the family

GIANT TORTOISE

Testudinidæ. Tortoises, in the wider sense, are sluggish reptiles, long-lived, and extremely tenacious of life under adverse surroundings, and have survived from remote antiquity, while higher animal types, formerly contemporaneous with them, have become extinct, and have been succeeded by very different forms. They have an osseous exoskeleton, which is combined with the endoskeleton to form a kind of bony case or box in which the body of the animal is inclosed, and which is covered by a coriaceous skin, or, more usually, by horny epidermic plates. The exoskeleton consists essentially of two pieces: a dorsal piece, generally convex (the carapace), and a ventral piece, usually flat or concave (the plastron), by some regarded as an abnormally developed sternum, while others consider the bones of which it is composed as integumentary ossifications. All the bones of the skull, except the lower jaw and the hyoid bone, are anchylosed. There are no teeth, and the jaws are cased in horn, so as to form a kind of beak. Tongue, thick and fleshy; heart three-chambered, ventricular septum imperfect. The lungs are voluminous, and respiration is effected by swallowing air. All will pass prolonged periods without food, and will live and move for months after the removal of the entire brain.

The most familiar example of true or land tortoises is the dry land terrapin of the Southern States (see TERRAPIN). It is found in the countries bordering on the Mediterranean, and is said to range as far N. as Switzerland and the S. of France. It is about 12 inches long; the scales are granulated in the center, streaked on the margins, and spotted or marbled with black and yellow. A suc-

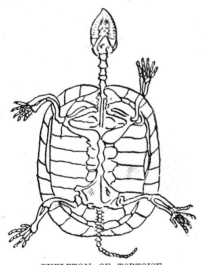

SKELETON OF TORTOISE

culent vegetable diet is common to the whole family, and all but the tropical species hibernate. The Greek tortoise is an article of food in the S. of Europe, and the flesh of all the species appears to be good, while their eggs are regarded as delicacies. But the most interesting forms are gigantic tortoises formerly found in great numbers in the Mascarene and Galapagos Islands. Five species of

this group are known, and two of them, *Testudo elephantina*, the gigantic land tortoise of Aldabra, and *T. abingdonii*, the Abingdon Island tortoise, grow to enormous size.

In military terms, a method of defense, used by the ancients, formed by the troops arranging themselves in close order and placing their bucklers over their heads, making a cover resembling a tortoise shell; a TESTUDO (*q. v.*).

TORTOISE-SHELL, a popular name for the partial or entire outside covering of the carapace and plastron present in many of the *Chelonia*. It is in the form of thin plates, united together at their edges, and corresponding, to a certain extent, with the underlying bones of the shell. The number, size, position, coloring, and ornamentation of these plates differ greatly even in genera and species. Also, the name given to the horny epidermic plates of *C. imbricata*, the hawk's-bill turtle. The largest of these plates are about 18 inches long by 6 broad, and rarely exceed one-eighth of an inch in thickness. Tortoise-shell is semi-transparent, and mottled with various shades of yellow and brownish-red. Its value depends on the brightness and form of the markings. Tortoise-shell is used for making combs, snuff boxes, and many fancy articles. The Indian Islands furnish the largest supply for the European and Chinese markets, the chief seats of the trade being Singapore, Manila, and Batavia, from which are exported yearly about 26,000 pounds, of which Singapore sends about a half.

TORTOISE-SHELL BUTTERFLY, the name given to two butterflies. The small tortoise-shell, *Vanessa urticæ*, one of the commonest of butterflies, is of a bright red brown, and has on its costal margin three large black spots, beyond the third of which is a white one. The space between the first and third spots is yellow. The large tortoise-shell, the larva of which feeds on the elm, is much rarer. It is deep fulvous, with a broad, dark border.

TORTOLA, a British West Indian island, chief of the Virgin Islands; area, 26 square miles. It is bare and rugged, rising to a height of 1,600 feet. It contains Roadtown, the capital of the group.

TORTURE, the infliction of pain. It has been largely used in many countries as a judicial instrument for extracting evidence from unwilling witnesses, or confessions from accused persons, and in the despotisms of the East is still so used; the callousness of torturers and tortured being almost equally remarkable. In ancient Athens slaves were regularly examined by torture. Under the Roman republic only slaves could be tortured; under the empire torture, besides being much used in examining slaves, was occasionally inflicted even on freemen, to extract evidence of the crime of *læsa majestas*. At a later period torture came to be largely employed by the Inquisition, and it was only in 1816 that it was prohibited by a papal bull.

TORY, a political party name of Irish origin, first used in England about 1679, applied originally to Irish Revolutionary Catholic outlaws, and then generally to those who refused to concur in the scheme to exclude James II. from the throne. The nickname, like its contemporaneous opposite Whig, in coming into popular use became much less strict in its application, till at last it came simply to signify an adherent of that political party in the State who disapproved of change in the ancient constitution, and who supported the claims and authority of the king, church, and aristocracy, while their opponents, the Whigs, were in favor of more or less radical changes, and supported the claims of the democracy. In modern times the term has to some extent been supplanted by Conservative.

TOSCANINI, ARTURO, an Italian orchestral conductor, born at Parma, in 1867. He studied at the Conservatory of Parma, and first conducted at Turin, being later engaged for the Dal Verme in Milan, where Gatt-Casazza secured his services for La Scala. There he had opportunities of exhibiting his ability as an operatic and symphonic conductor, and, as a result, became, in 1908, principal conductor at the Metropolitan Opera House, New York. His musical memory is remarkable and he directed without score more than a hundred operas of all nationalities and schools.

TOSTI, SIR FRANCESCO PAOLO, an Italian composer; born in Ortona, Italy, April 9, 1846. He was famous as a composer of songs in Italian, French, and English; among his best-known ballads being "For Ever and For Ever" and "Beauty's Eyes." In 1875 he went to London and in 1880 was appointed singing teacher to the royal family. He wrote the operas, "The Grand Duke"; "The Prima Donna"; etc. He was Knighted in 1908. He died in 1916.

TOTEM, a natural object, one of a class taken by a tribe, a family, or a single person, and treated with superstitious respect as an outward symbol of an existing intimate unseen relation. The totem is considered as helpful to the man, who in his turn abstains from killing it if an animal, or eating it if a plant, and who often assimilates himself to it by wearing its skin or the like, or tattooing its picture on his body. The whole members of the clan who have a totem in common count themselves of one blood, and claim the totem as their common ancestor. The restriction on killing and eating it is absolute, and sometimes men are tabooed from touching or even looking at it under pain of death or expulsion from the tribe. Elaborate ceremonies connected with birth, marriage, and death point more closely to the identification of the man and the totem, and such ceremonies as those of the Australians at puberty are intended to initiate the youth into the restrictions that must be observed in sexual commerce.

TOTNES, a municipal borough and market town of Devonshire, England, pleasantly situated on the slope of a steep hill on the right bank of the Dart; 29 miles S. S. W. of Exeter and 24 E. N. E. of Plymouth. The Dart is navigable to this point for vessels of 200 tons, and Brut the Tojan is fabled to have landed here; the "Brutus Stone," on which he first set foot, may be seen in the main street. At least, Totnes is a place of great antiquity, and retains two gateways, remains of the walls, a quaint guildhall, a good many antique houses, and an interesting **Perpendicular**

TOUCAN

church (1432; restored by Scott, 1874), with a noble red sandstone tower and a fine stone screen. The Norman castle of Judhael de Totnes, that crowns the hilltop, is represented by the circular shell keep. There is a grammar school (1568); and on the "Plains," near the river, stands a granite obelisk to the Australian explorer Wills, who was a native, as also was the Hebraist Kennicott. The borough was incorporated by King John. Pop. about 4,000.

TOUCAN, in ornithology, the popular name of any bird of the genus *Rhamphastus*, often applied to the whole family *Rhamphastidæ*. They are all natives of tropical America, and are easily distinguished by their enormous bill, irregularly toothed along the margin of the mandibles. All the species live in pairs in the shade of the forests, occasionally congregating in small parties, but never approaching the human habitations. In the true toucans the ground color of the plumage is generally black; the throat, breast, and rump adorned with white, yellow and red; the body is short and thick; tail rounded or even, varying in length in the different species, and capable of being turned up over the back when the bird goes to roost. Toucans have been described as carnivorous; in captivity they will readily devour small birds, but probably in a state of nature their diet consists almost exclusively of fruit. They are remarkable among birds for a regurgitation of food, which, after being swallowed, is brought up to undergo mastication, an operation somewhat analogous to the chewing of the cud among ruminants. They are easily tamed, and bear confinement well, even in cold climates.

TOUCH, in fine arts, the peculiar handling usual to an artist, and by which his work may be known. In music, the resistance made to the fingers by the keys of a pianoforte or organ. Also, the peculiar manner in which a player presses the keyboard, whether light, pearly, heavy, clumsy, firm, etc. In obstetrics, the examination of the mouth of the womb by actual contact of the hand or fingers.

In physiology, the sense through which man takes cognizance of the palpable properties of bodies. In a wide application, it is sometimes called the general sense, because by it we become conscious of all sensory impressions which are not the objects of smell, sight, taste, or hearing, which are called the special senses; even these, however, are held by modern biologists to be highly specialized forms of touch, which is often called the "mother of all the senses." In a more limited application, touch is applied to that modification of general sensibility which is restricted to the tegumentary surface or to some special portion of it, and which serves to convey definite ideas as to the form, size, number, weight, temperature, hardness, softness, etc., of objects brought within its

cognizance. These sensations are received by the terminations of the cutaneous nerves and thence conveyed to the brain. The sense of touch is distributed over the surface of the body, but is much more acute in some parts than in others, e. g., in the hand. It is also capable of great improvement and development; and the blind, who have to depend largely on the sense of touch for guidance, acquire extraordinarily delicate and accurate powers of perception with the fingers; difference of form, size, consistence, and other characters, being readily recognized that are quite inappreciable to those who possess good vision, without special education.

In comparative physiology, the lower anthropidæ have both the hands and feet thickly set with tactile papillæ, and the surface of the prehensile tail which some possess is furnished with them in abundance. Other organs of touch exist in the vibrissæ, or whiskers, of the cat, and of certain rodents. In the Ungulata, the lips and nostrils are probably the chief seat of tactile sensibility, and this is especially so with the Proboscidea. In birds, tactile papillæ have been discovered in the feet, and they are also present in some lizards. Organs of touch are found in the tentacles of the Cephalopoda and Gasteropoda, the palpi and antennæ of insects, and the palpi of the Arachnida.

TOUL, a town of France, department of Meurthe-et-Moselle, on the Moselle, 12 miles W. of Nancy. It is strongly fortified, and has a fine Gothic cathedral, completed in the 15th century. Toul was taken in the Franco-German War after a siege of five weeks, Sept. 23, 1870. Pop. (1906), 13,345.

TOULON, a French naval arsenal of the first class, in the department of Var; beautifully situated on a deep inlet of the Mediterranean, forme dby the peninsula of Sépet; 40 miles S. E. of Marseilles. It is built at the foot of the Pharon Hills, which protect the city on the N., and are partly covered with fine forests. Defended by a strong citadel, girt with a double-bastioned wall, and surrounded by some 15 forts and redoubts, it is, next to Brest and Cherbourg, the principal naval station of France. The town is divided into old and new parts, the former quaint and dingy, the latter containing the public buildings erected by Louis XIV. and several spacious squares, as the Champs de Battaile, Puget, and St. Pierre. Among the chief buildings are the Hôtel de Ville with cariatides by Puget, the Hôtel de l'Intendance, the cathedral of St. Marie

Majeure, dating from the 11th century, but greatly altered, a naval hospital erected by Louis XIV., the hospital of St. Mandrier, on the Sépet, a public library, and a handsome theater. The Mourillon tower, built 1848, in six *étages*, commands a magnificent view. The Bagne for convicts, established by Colbert in 1682, was removed in 1872. The *port militaire*, one of the largest in Europe, comprises the old Darsa, formed under Henri IV., the new under Louis XIV., and the Darsa of Castigneau; three repairing docks and three arsenals: (1) The *arsenal maritime*, built by Vauban, with a general magazine, a cordage factory, a foundry, a naval museum, a park of artillery, and an armory. (2) That of Castigneau (area 17 hectares), with bakeries, copper works, forges, etc. (3) That of Mourillon, with steam sawmills, covered slips, and large fosses for the conservation of timber. The naval port, the equipment of which is singularly complete, and the cost of which amounted to upward of 160,000,000 francs, is separated from the roadstead by hollow bomb-proof moles, lined with batteries. A great number of the inhabitants (some 10,000) are employed in the arsenal works, and of recent years there has sprung up a considerable trade with Algeria. Toulon has an agreeable climate; at its Jardin des Plantes palms grow in the open air. Toulon is said to have been founded by a Roman soldier, Telo Martius, and was known as Telo in the 4th century. It was destroyed by the Arabs in 889, and again in the 12th century, but in the 16th century it had become a stronghold of some importance. On Aug. 27, 1793, it was taken by the English, who were forced on Dec. 19 following to surrender it to the Republicans after firing the shipping. Napoleon, a simple officer, then first evinced his genius for war. Pop. about 107,000.

TOULOUSE, a city of France, the capital anciently of Languedoc, and now of the department of Haute-Garonne; 160 miles S. E. of Bordeaux and 466 S. by W. of Paris. It is situated in a broad and pleasant plain, on the right bank of the Garonne river, with the Canal du Midi sweeping round its E. and N sides. The Garonne is crossed here by a beautiful bridge (1543-1626), nearly 300 yards long, which connects Toulouse with the suburb of St. Cyprien. The city, with the exception of the S. faubourg, is not particularly handsome (though the broad quays have rather an imposing appearance), nor has it many fine public buildings. One may note, however, the cathedral, containing the tombs of the Counts of Toulouse; the *Capitole*, or town hall (1769); the church of St. Sernin (11th to 15th century); and the Musée, with its interesting collection of antiquities, forming an almost uninterrupted chain in the history of art, from the Gallo-Roman to the Renaissance period. Toulouse is the seat of an archbishop, has a university academy, an academy of "flor-la games" (Sociéte des Jeux Floraux), claiming to date from a troubadours' contest in 1323, academies of arts, sciences, antiquities, etc., schools of law, medicine, and artillery, an observatory, botanic garden, and a public library of 200,000 volumes. Toulouse manufactures woolens, silks, leather, cannon, steam engines, tobacco, brandy, etc., and carries on a great trade with Spain. Its liver and truffle pies are celebrated throughout the S. of France. Pop. about 150,000.

Tolosa was, in Cæsar's time, a city within the limits of the Roman *provincia*, and had been originally the capital of the Volcæ Tectosages, a Gallic tribe noted for its wealth and consequence. In A. D. 412 the Visigoths made it the capital of their kingdom; and after the time of Charlemagne it was under the sway of counts, who made themselves independent about 920, but in 1271 the "county of Toulouse" was reunited to the crown of France by Philippe le Hardi. Its literary celebrity reaches as far back as the Roman empire. Early in the Middle Ages, under the Counts of Toulouse, it became a seat of Provençal poetry, and it suffered terribly in Simon de Montfort's crusade against the Albigenses. The Parliament of Toulouse had a great reputation, but unhappily it is likely to be remembered by one of its most iniquitous decisions, that delivered in the case of the Calas family. In the battle of Toulouse (April 10, 1814) the French under Soult were defeated by Wellington. Cujacius was born, and Fermat died, in Toulouse.

TOURAINE, an ancient province of France; bounded N. by Maine, E. by Orléanais and Berry, S. by Berry and Poitou, and W. by Anjou and Poitou. It now forms the department of Indre-et-Loire.

TOURCOING, a town of France, department of Nord; 9 miles N. N. E. of Lille; is a well-built thriving manufacturing town, the staple manufactures being woolen, cotton, linen, and silk stuffs, besides dye works, soap works, sugar refineries, machine works, etc. It was captured and almost destroyed by the Germans in 1914. Pop. about 82,000.

TOURGEE, ALBION WINEGAR, an American jurist and author; born in Williamsfield, O., May 2, 1838; was graduated at Rochester University, N. Y., in 1862; admitted to the bar, 1864, served in the Civil War in the Union army, and was wounded on two occasions; at the close of the war commenced the practice of law at Greensboro, N. C., and at the Southern loyalist convention at Philadelphia, 1866, drew up the report on the condition of the States lately in revolt. In 1868 he became judge of the Superior Court of North Carolina. Besides compiling "A Code of Civil Procedure for North Carolina" he wrote "A Fool's Errand"; "An Appeal to Cæsar"; "Bricks Without Straw"; "The Story of a Thousand"; "The Man Who Outlived Himself"; "Letters to a King"; etc. In 1897 he was appointed United States consul at Bordeaux, France. He died there May 21, 1905.

TOURMALINE, a widely-distributed mineral, the transparent colored varieties being used as gem-stones. Its crystallization, is rhombohedral, hemimorphic; prisms often triangular. Hardness, 7-7.5; sp. gr. 2.94-3.3; luster, vitreous; color, shades of black the most frequent, but also blue, green, red, often of rich shades, sometimes red internally and shades of green externally. Composition: Very variable, the oxygen ratio for the protoxide and sesquioxide, and also for the boric acid, varying considerably. Dana distinguishes the following varieties: (1) Rubellite; shades of red, frequently transparent. (2) Indicolite; of an indigo-blue color. (3) Brazilian sapphire of jewelers; Berlin blue. (4) Brazilian emerald (Chrysolite or Peridot); green and transparent. (5) Peridot of Ceylon; honey-yellow. (6) Achroite; colorless. (7) Aphrizite; black. (8) Columnar and black, without cleavage or trace of fibrous texture. A series of analyses and sp. gr. determinations, made by Rammelsberg, has suggested the following subdivisions: (1) Magnesia tourmaline, mean sp. gr. 3-3.07; (2) Iron-magnesia tourmaline, mean sp. gr. 3.11; (3) Iron-tourmaline, sp. gr. 3.13-3.25; (4) Iron-manganese-lithia tourmaline, mean sp. gr. 3.083; (5) Lithia tourmaline, mean sp. gr. 3.041. The blowpipe reactions vary with the composition, which is essentially a boro-silicate of protoxide and sesquioxide. Occurs in granites, notably the albitic varieties, schists, and dolomite.

TOURNAMENT, an encounter between armed knights on horseback in time of peace, as an exercise of skill (which was rewarded by honorary distinctions), and usually an adjunct of some great event, as a royal marriage, etc. The tournament was one of the most cherished institutions of the Middle Ages, furnishing, as it did, an exciting show, and giving the combatants an opportunity of exhibiting their skill, courage and prowess before their friends. The arms employed were usually lances without heads, and with round braces of wood at the extremity, and swords without points and with blunted edges. Occasionally, however, the ordinary arms of warfare were used, and it not infrequently happened that the tournament ended in a hostile encounter. Certain qualifications of birth were required for admission to the tournaments. The place of combat was the lists, a large open space surrounded by a rope or railing, and having galleries erected around for the spectators, the heralds, and the judges. The tilting armor was of light fabric, and generally adorned with some device of a lady's favor. The prizes were delivered to the successful knights by the queen of beauty, who had been chosen by the ladies or appointed by the king.

In modern usage, a competition or contest of skill, in which a number of individuals take part; as, military tournament; cycling tournament; billiard tournament, etc.

TOURNAY, a town in the Belgian province of Hainault; on the Scheldt; near the French frontier; 35 miles W. S. W. of Brussels. Its splendid Romanesque cathedral, 400 feet long, has five towers and pictures by Jordaens, Rubens, and Gallait; and there are also the churches of St. Quentin and St. Brice (with the grave of King Childeric), the belfry (1190), and a bronze statue (1863) of the Princess d'Epinoy, who in 1581 valiantly defended Tournay against Parma. Though one of the oldest towns in Belgium, it has quite a modern appearance, with fine suburbs and beautiful broad streets. The chief manufactures are hosiery, linen, Brussels carpets, and porcelain; but there are few large workshops, most of the fabrics being executed by the people in their own houses. Tournay, the ancient Tornacum, or Turris Nerviorum, was in the 5th and the beginning of the 6th century the seat of the Merovingian kings, subsequently belonged to France, but in 1526 was included in the Spanish Netherlands. During May, 1794, it was the scene of several hotly contested fights between the French and Austro-English armies, the most important of which was that of May 19, in which Pichegru beat the Duke of York. The town was devastated during the German invasion of 1914. Pop. about 37,000.

TOURNIQUET, an instrument for compressing the main artery of the thigh or arm, either for the purpose of preventing too great a loss of blood in amputation, or to check dangerous hemorrhage from accidental wounds or to stop the circulation through an aneurism. For the last purpose special forms of tourniquet are required, which do not compress the whole limb.

The common tourniquet consists of three parts—viz. (1) a pad to compress the artery; (2) a strong band which is buckled round the limb; and (3) a bridge-like contrivance over which the band passes, with a screw whose action raises the bridge and consequently tightens the band.

The credit of the invention of this most useful instrument is usually ascribed to the French surgeon Morel, who, in 1674, used a stick passed beneath a bandage, and turned round so as to twist it up to the requisite degree of tightness, as a means of preventing the undue loss of arterial blood in amputations of the limbs. A much improved screw tourniquet was invented by Petit in 1718, the same in principle as that described above. Many surgeons now use in preference a strong elastic band, wound two or three times round the limb—a method first introduced by Esmarch.

TOURS, a town in France, capital of the department of Indre-et-Loire; on the Loire; 145 miles S. W. of Paris. The Loire is here crossed by two suspension bridges, a railway bridge, and a fine stone bridge 1,423 feet long. Many of the streets are spacious, and there are several historic chateaus in the neighborhood. The principal edifice is the cathedral (Tours being an archbishopric), flanked by two towers, 205 feet high, a fine building begun in the 12th, completed in the 16th centry. Of the old abbey church of St. Martin of Tours only two towers remain. The modern buildings include the church of St. Joseph, the theatre, and the musuem. Manufactures include silk, cloth, carpets, chemicals, etc., and there is a large printing and publishing establishment. Tours was known to the Romans by the name of Cæsarodunum. In later times it became famous for its silk manufactures, and had a population of 80,000, when the revocation of the edict of Nantes deprived it of nearly half its inhabitants, a blow from which it has never recovered. In 1870 Tours was the seat of the government of national defense. Pop. about 73,-000.

TOUSSAINT L'OVERTURE, DOMINIQUE FRANCOIS (surname added for his bravery in once making a breach in the ranks of the enemy), one of the liberators of Haiti; born a slave in 1743; joined the negro insurgents in 1791; and in 1795, for his services against the Spaniards, was made by the French Convention general of brigade, in 1797 general of division, and a little later chief of the army of Santo Domingo. Soon after he cleared the British and Spaniards entirely out of the island, quickly restored order and prosperity, and about 1800 began to aim at independence of France. Bonaparte having, after the peace of Amiens, proclaimed the re-establishment of slavery in Santo Domingo, Toussaint declined to obey, whereupon General Le Clerc was sent with a strong fleet to compel him. The liberator soon submitted, but was treacherously arrested, sent to France, and flung into a damp, dark dungeon at Fort de Joux, near Besançon, where he died after 10 months, April 27, 1803.

TOWER, CHARLEMAGNE, an American diplomatist; born in Philadelphia, Pa., April 17, 1848; was graduated at Harvard University in 1872, and admitted to the bar in 1878. He acquired large business interests and became an officer and director in several corporations; and was identified with the Academy of Natural Sciences and other similar organizations. In 1897 he was appointed United States minister to Austria-Hungary, and in January, 1899, was made ambassador to Russia. Ambassador to Germany, 1902-1908. He is the author of 'The Marquis de La Fayette in the American Revolution" (2 vols. 1895). Died Feb. 24, 1923.

TOWER, RALPH WINFRED, an American curator, born in Amherst, Mass., in 1870. He studied at Colby and Brown, and later at Leipzig. He then became demonstrator of anatomy in the medical department of Harvard University, then instructor in chemical physiology (1895-1898); assistant professor (1898-1901); and assistant professor at Brown University (1901-03). For nine years he was curator of physiology, then, in 1912 he became curator of physiology and anatomy in the Museum of Natural History in New York. He wrote a "Laboratory Course in Chemical Physiology" (1897), and many papers and pamphlets. Died Jan. 26, 1926.

TOWER HILL, a hill in London, **near** the famous Tower of London, and the place where many political prisoners were executed.

TOWER OF LONDON, the most ancient and historically the most interesting pile in the English metropolis; a mass of buildings on the N. side of the Thames, immediately to the E. of the ancient city walls, its ramparts and gates surrounded by a dry ditch in pentagonal shape; in outer circuit measuring 1,050 yards. Within this the whole of the buildings are encircled by a double line of walls and bulwarks, in some places 40 feet high and 12 feet thick; the space between the walls being known as the outer ward, and the interior as the inner ward. The inner ward was formerly the royal quarter. The outer ward was the folks' quarter. The inner ward is defended by 12 massive and conspicuous towers, stationed at unequal dis-

also tragedy succeeded tragedy, and the innocent blood of many of England's bravest and most beautiful poured forth in a cruel stream.

The first State prisoner was Flambard, Bishop of Durham, who effected his escape in 1100 and fled to Normandy. The noble Wallace suffered a cruel imprisonment and terrible death here in 1305. Richard, Duke of Gloucester, haunts the pile like a specter. He murdered Henry VI. in the Hall Tower. The infant princes, his nephews, were smothered in the Bloody Tower; their supposed remains, found in the reign of Charles II., now lie in Westminster Abbey. Clarence, according to tradition, was drowned by Richard in wine in the Bowyer Tower, and Hastings condemned to death in the Council Chamber. The remains of King Henry VIII.'s beheaded queens, Anne Boleyn and Katherine Howard, lie in St.

TOWER OF LONDON AND BRIDGE

tances, and possessing distinctive names and formations. In the center, rearing its head proudly above them all, stands the main quadrangular building and great Norman keep known as the White Tower. To the N. are the barracks, and to the N. W. the Church of St. Peter and Vincula. The entrance to the buildings is on the W. side by the Lion's Gate.

Tradition ascribes the origin of the Tower to Julius Cæsar. The White Tower was reared by William the Conqueror, probably as a secure place of shelter for himself and a menace to the turbulent citizens. It was designed by Gundulph, Bishop of Rochester, and bears a sister likeness to Rochester Castle.

For centuries the Tower was a palace, a prison, a fortress, and a court of law. Here the Plantagenet kings held their gay tournaments, magnificent revels, and pompous religious ceremonials. Here

Peter's Church. A group of ghastly executions are associated with the reign of Mary, prominent among which are those of Lady Jane Grey, the wise, fair, and pious "Twelfth Day queen," her consort Dudley, and her father-in-law, Northumberland. Imprisoned together in the Garden Tower, Cranmer, Ridley, and Latimer searched the New Testament together. Sir Walter Raleigh was thrice confined in the Tower which bears his name in many places. Here he wrote his "History of the World," and beguiled his solitude with chemical experiments. Sir T. Overbury was poisoned in the Tower in 1613, and Strafford was beheaded in 1641, Laud in 1645. The last of the numerous executions in the Tower, but a few of which have been mentioned, was that of Lord Lovat in 1747. The government of the Tower is vested in the Constable, usually an officer of high military rank. In the White Tower is the Chapel of St. John, which formerly held the records, one of the finest specimens of Early Norman style. The banqueting Hall and Council Chamber adjoining is used as an armory, and is filled with 60,-000 stand of arms, kept in perfect order and beautifully arranged. Beauchamp Tower, which was restored in 1853 by Mr. Salvin, is to the W., and the Horse Armory to the S. The latter, built in 1826, contains a gallery 150 feet long by 33 feet wide, in which are 22 equestrian figures clothed in the distinctive armor of the reigns from Edward I. to James II. A staircase from the Horse Armory leads to an ante-chamber filled with weapons and trophies taken in British struggles in the East. Queen Elizabeth's Armory in the White Tower contains arms and armor of her reign, various instruments of torture, and the block on which Lord Lovat was beheaded. The Jewel House contains several crowns, including that for the coronation of Queen Victoria (valued at £111,900), the Kohinoor diamond, and the diadems, scepters, and jewels constituting the Regalia. To the N. W. of the Tower is Tower Hill, where, till within about 150 years, stood the scaffold for the execution of traitors.

TOWLE, GEORGE MAKEPEACE, an American author; born in Washington, D. C., Aug. 27, 1841; was graduated at Yale University in 1861, and at Harvard Law School in 1863. He was United States consul at Nantes, France, in 1866-1868; and at Bradford, England, in 1868-1870. His works include: "Glimpses of History" (1865); "Henry the Fifth" (1866); "American Society" (1870); "The Eastern Question" (1877); "Servia and Rumania" (1877); 'Beaconsfield" (1878); "Young Folks' Heroes of History" (1878-1880); "Modern France" (1879); "Men of Mark" (1880); "England and Russia in Asia" (1885); "England in Egypt" (1885); "Literature of the English Language." He died in Brookline, Mass., Aug. 10, 1893.

TOWNE, CHARLES HANSON, an American editor and author, born in Louisville, Ky., in 1877. He studied one year at the New York City College, but soon after devoted himself to his literary work. Among his works are: "Youth and Other Poems"; "Jolly Jaunts with Jim"; and "Shaking Hands with England." In 1919 he wrote the English lyrics for Offenbach's opera "La Belle Helene." He is the editor of "For France" (1917); "The Balfour Visit" (1917); and has composed a number of songs, one of which is "The Magic Casement." For a while he was editor of "The Smart Set" Magazine, but in 1920 became editor of McClure's Magazine.

TOWNSEND, CHARLES ELROY, a United States senator, born in Concord, Jackson co., Mich., in 1856. Graduating from the University of Michigan, in 1878, he studied law and was admitted to the bar in 1895. For a while he was Register of Deeds of Jackson co. In 1888 he was a delegate to the Republican National Convention, and in 1903 he was elected to Congress from the Second Michigan District, then reelected for a second term. In 1910 he was nominated at the primaries, then, a year later, elected by the legislature to the United States Senate for the term 1911-1917 and again for 1917-1923.

TOWNSEND, CHARLES HENRY TYLER, an American entomologist and biologist, born in Oberlin, Ohio, in 1863. He studied at the Columbian (now George Washington) University in Washington, D. C., at the School of Medicine, then became assistant entomologist in the United States Department of Agriculture. In 1891 he became professor of entomology and zoölogy at the Agricultural College of New Mexico and the state experiment station. In 1909 he became permanent director of the entomological stations of the United States, and, in 1914, entomological assistant in the Bureau of Entomology of the United States Department of Agriculture. Since 1919 he has been chief entomologist of the State of Sao Paulo, Brazil.

TOWNSEND, EDWARD WATERMAN, an American author; born in Cleveland, O., Feb. 10, 1855. His stories and sketches, first printed in the daily journals, were collected under the titles: "Chimmie Fadden, Major Max, and Other Stories"; "Chimmie Fadden Explains, Major Max Expounds"; "A Daughter of the Tenements"; "Near a Whole City Full." In collaboration he wrote several plays: "Chimmie Fadden"; "Daughter of the Tenements"; "The Marquis of Michigan," "Beaver Creek Farm" (1907); "The Climbing Courvatell's" (1909).

TOWNSEND, GEORGE ALFRED, pseudonym GATH, an American war correspondent; born in Georgetown, Del., Jan. 30, 1841. He became a journalist in 1860; was special correspondent for the New York "Herald" and New York "World" in 1860-1864; afterward public lecturer, and war correspondent in the Austro-Prussian War (1866). His publications in book form are: "Campaigns of a Non-Combatant" (1865); "Life of Garibaldi" (1867); "Life of Abraham Lincoln" (1867); "The New World and the Old"; "Poems" (1870); "Washington Outside and Inside" (1871); "Bohemian Days" (1881); "The Entailed Hat" (1884), and "Katy ᶜf Catoctin; or, The Chain-Breakers" (1886), novels; "Life of Levi P. Morton" (1888); "Tales of Gapland"; etc.

TOWNSHEND, CHARLES, SECOND VISCOUNT, an English statesman; born in Rainham, Norfolk, March 10, 1674; succeeded to the peerage December, 1687, and took his seat as a Whig in the House of Peers, 1695. After acting as a commissioner for arranging the Scotch Union (1706), he was joint plenipotentiary with Marlborough in the conference at Gertruydenburg (1709), and then, as ambassador to the States-General, signed the Barrier Treaty. For this he was censured by the House of Commons, and declared an enemy to the queen and kingdom. He thereupon entered into communication with the Elector of Hanover, who, on his accessison as George I., appointed Townshend secretary of state, 1714. In 1717 he became lord-lieutenant of Ireland; and he was again secretary of state from February, 1721, to May, 1730, when he retired on account of differences with his brother-in-law and colleague, Sir Robert Walpole. He died in Rainham, June 21, 1738.

TOWNSHEND, CHARLES, an English statesman; grandson of the 2d Viscount; born in 1725; entered the House

SIR CHARLES VERE FERRERS TOWNSHEND

of Commons in 1747; and became a commissioner of trade and plantations in 1749. He was a lord of the admiralty in 1754, member of the privy-council in 1756, secretary of war in 1761-1763;

chancellor of the exchequer in 1766. He supported Granville's stamp act (1765), and introduced the celebrated resolutions for taxing the American colonies (June 2, 1767). From so often changing his political opinions he was known as the "weathercock," but he had a great reputation for oratory and wit. He died in Oxfordshire, Sept. 4, 1767.

TOWNSHEND, SIR CHARLES VERE FERRERS, a British general, born in 1861. He entered the Royal Marines in 1881, but preferring the army to the navy, became a soldier in 1886 and was promoted through the ordinary grades, becoming major general in 1911. He was included in the Sudan and Nile expeditions of 1884 and 1885, and in the Hunza Nagar expeditions of 1891 and 1892. He was in command at Chitral Fort, and served in the Dongola expedition in 1898 and in the South African War in 1899-1900. Afterward he did service in India and was assistant adjutant general of the Ninth Division Army there in 1907-1909. In 1912-1913 he was in command of a division of the Territorial Force. When the European war broke out in 1914 he became commander-in-chief of the British forces in Mesopotamia and was shut up by the Turks for five months in Kut el Amara, at the end of which in April, 1916, he surrendered with his army and was taken prisoner.

TOWNSHIP, the corporation of a town; the district or territory of a town. Also, a territorial district, subordinate to a county, into which many of the States are divided, and comprising an area of 5, 6, 7, or perhaps 10 miles square, the inhabitants of which are invested with certain powers for regulating their own affairs, such as repairing roads, providing for the poor, etc.

TOWNSLEY, CLARENCE PAGE, an American army officer, born in De Kalb, St. Lawrence co., N. Y., 1855. After graduating from the State Normal School at Potsdam, N. Y., he entered the United States Military Academy, then studied at the artillery school at Fort Monroe, Va. In 1916 he reached the rank of brigadier-general, and that of major-general in 1917. During 1912-1916 he was superintendent of the United States Military Academy.

TOXICOLOGY, that branch of medicine which treats of poisons and their antidotes, or of the morbid and deleterious effects of excessive and inordinate doses and quantities of medicine.

TOYNBEE, ARNOLD, an English reformer; born in London, England, Aug. 23, 1852. His early acquirements were mostly in the direction of modern literature and philosophy. He spent two years at a military college, but left on finding that he had mistaken his profession. During the four years he spent at Oxford he became a prominent figure. Endowed with the gift of fluent speech, he began to address audiences of working men; and to help them, took up residence in Commercial Road, Whitechapel, in 1875, and associated himself with the religious work carried on there by the Rev. S. A. Barnett. From the inspiration of his example and teaching during this period sprang the idea of Toynbee Hall. He died in 1883, owing to overstrain following on two lectures directed against Henry George's "Progress and Poverty." A course of lectures delivered at Oxford between 1881-1882 on the economic history of England, along with other popular addresses, was published in 1884 under the title of "The Industrial Revolution," with Memoir by Jowett.

TOYNBEE, PAGET, an English educator and writer; born in 1855, at Wembledon, near London. He was educated at Haileybury College, Hertfordshire, and Balliol College, Oxford, and worked as private tutor from 1878 to 1892. He has made himself particularly noted by his studies of Dante. His works include: "Specimens of Old French"; "Historical French Grammar"; "Ricerche e Note Dantesche"; "Critical Text of the Divine Commedia"; "Life of Dante"; "Dante Studies and Researches"; "Dante in English Literature, from Chaucer to Cary"; "A Concise Dictionary of People, Names and Notable Matters in the Works of Dante"; "The Correspondence of Gray, Walpole, West, and Aston."

TOYNBEE HALL, a settlement organized in Commercial street, Whitechapel, London, as a memorial to Arnold Toynbee, (q. v.), in January, 1885, under the direction of the Rev. S. A. Barnett. It partakes somewhat of the nature of both a college and a club, the idea being to connect the memorial of Toynbee with the study of "political economy in its social aspects, to which he devoted the scholar half of himself, and with his work among the artisan population of our great cities, to which he gave the other, the missionary half." This is carried out by the members of the universities of Oxford and Cambridge who find residence there. The idea of college settlements suggested by this work was enthusiastically carried out in the United States.

TRACERY, in architecture, the species of pattern work formed or traced in the head of a Gothic window by the mullions being continued, but diverging into arches, curves, and flowing lines enriched with foliations. The styles varied in different ages and countries, and are known as geometrical, flowing, flamboyant, etc. Also the subdivisions of groined vaults, or any ornamental design of the same character for doors, paneling, ceilings, etc.

TRACHEA, or WINDPIPE, the tube extending from the larynx, or organ of the voice, and from the level of the fifth cervical vertebra to the third dorsal vertebra, at which latter point the trachea bifurcates or divides into two main bronchi or divisions, one supplying each lung with air tubes. The average length of the trachea is $4\frac{1}{2}$ inches and its diameter about three-fourths of an inch. the latter measurement being greater in males than in females. The trachea consists of fibrous membranes united by elastic cartilaginous rings, rendering the tube flexible and patent. The cartilages are circular but imperfect rings, each being joined posteriorly by fibrous membrane. They vary from 16 to 20 in number. The muscular fibres of the trachea are of longitudinal and transverse arrangement. The trachea is lined with mucous membrane, the epithelium of which is ciliated. The trachea receives blood from the inferior thyroid arteries, and nerves from the pneumogastric and recurrent trunks, and also from the sympathetic system. The right bronchus, or one of the main divisions of the trachea, is wider and shorter than the left. It enters the lung opposite the fourth dorsal vertebra. The left bronchus is smaller and more oblique than the right and enters the left lung at the level of the fifth dorsal vertebra.

Diseases and Injuries of the Trachea.— The trachea is liable to inflammation and its products, and frequently suffers from extension of disease from the larynx. Acute inflammation may occur as an idiopathic affection, or a symptom of other disease, as smallpox, measles, typhus, tuberculosis, croup, etc. The symptoms are pain in the windpipe from the top of the sternum, expectoration of mucus, sometimes in regular rings, and a peculiar brazen-like cough. When confined to the larynx there is no hoarseness. Chronic inflammation usually accompanies follicular pharyngo-laryngitis, tuberculosis, and syphilis. Constriction of the trachea may be produced by aneurismal or other tumors pressing externally on the trachea; or the symptoms may be produced by pressure on the nervous trunk, or the inferior laryngeal fibers. Constriction may also depend on undue muscular contraction, the seat thereof being immediately above the bifurcation of the trachea. Foreign bodies occasionally pass through the larnyx into the trachea, and the accident is a formidable one, which not infrequently proves fatal.

TRACHEOTOMY, the opening of the trachea or windpipe. It may be done in three different positions, viz., between the cricoid and thyroid cartilages, above the thyroid isthmus, and below it, and all three operations are often termed tracheotomy. The operation is performed as follows: An incision is made in the middle line, from an inch and a half to two inches, downward from the cricoid cartilage through the skin and deep fascia. Any arteries wounded in this incision being secured, the subcutaneous connective tissue is divided, fold after fold, the large vessels being pressed aside or ligatured when required. The sterno-hyoid and sterno-thyroid muscles are then separated by the handle of the knife, exposing the upper portion of the trachea, which is usually covered by the isthmus of the thyroid gland, which may be drawn up with a hook if it is unusually broad. The trachea should be carefully dissected till three rings are exposed. A sharp tenaculum is then thrust into it, and it is raised somewhat upward and steadied, and then divided from below upward by a sharp-pointed bistoury inserted into one of the interspaces. The completion of the operation is confirmed by the peculiar hissing sound with which the air rushes out of the open wound. The next step is the introduction of the canula, which soon becomes obstructed with mucus, and the inner tube must often be withdrawn for the purpose of cleansing it. The canula must be secured by a piece of tape round the neck, and the edges of the wound above and below the canula may be brought together by stiches or by adhesive plaster.

TRACTARIANISM, in Church history the name given to the Catholic revival in the Church of England which commenced at Oxford in 1833, whence it is sometimes called the Oxford Movement. The leaders of the movement were two celebrated Fellows of Oriel—John Keble and John Henry (afterward Cardinal) Newman, with whom were joined Richard Hurrell Froude, Arthur Philip Perceval, Frederick William Faber, William Palmer of Magdalen, and William Palmer of Worcester, Edward Bouverie Pusey, and Isaac Williams; and one cele-brated Cambridgeman, Hugh James Rose. On July 14, 1833, Keble preached an Assize Sermon, entitled the "National Apostasy," at Oxford, which so moved Newman that he arranged a meeting of the clergy named above at Rose's rectory at Hadleigh. Faber, Pusey, and Williams were not present; but Newman broached the idea of "Tracts for the Times," which was adopted, and urged that they should be supported and supplemented by higher pulpit teaching. In 1843 Newman resigned the incumbency of St. Mary's, Oxford, and the chaplaincy of Littlemore, and in September, 1845, was received into the Roman Church, as were others of the tract writers about the same time. With Newman's secession, Tractarianism came to an end, or, more properly speaking, developed into a Catholic section of the Anglican Establishment. The general teaching of the Tractarians included Apostolic Succession, Baptismal Regeneration, Confession, the Real Presence, the Authority of the Church, and the value of Tradition.

TRACTORS, the name applied to motor vehicles employed as drawing power and is thus to be distinguished from vehicles used for carrying. The "tanks" that played such a notable part in the World War were developed by adapting to them a principle already in use on the larger farm tractors—the caterpillar wheel tread. This enabled them to drive over obstacles, rough ground and trenches and gave great drawing power. Of necessity, the engine employed in tractors must be more than ordinarily powerful.

The perfection of a comparatively cheap tractor by Henry Ford, and its manufacture on a large scale, has placed it in wide use. It is employed largely in agricultural work where tractors perform all the heavy drawing tasks from plowing the ground to reaping the product. It is widely used also in industrial plants where the transportation of heavy loads is necessary. Indeed, the application of the tractor is practically limitless, and its use adds infinitely to the efficiency of industry of all kinds where the drawing of heavy loads is a necessity.

TRACT SOCIETY. In the 17th century several traces are found of associations for printing and promoting the sale of religious works, but none of them seems to have existed long. The Society for Promoting Christian Knowledge, founded in 1701, had for one of its objects "the dispersion, both at home and abroad, of Bibles and tracts of religion." In 1750 was formed the Society for Promoting Religious Knowledge Among the

Poor, not, like the former, confined to the Church of England, but embracing Christians of all denominations. The Religious Tract Society (1799) originated with the Rev. George Burder. Its beginnings were humble, but it soon expanded, translating the Bible and tracts into over 200 languages. In 1825 the American Tract Society was founded and since then it has been publishing books, tracts, and periodicals, representing the best Christian literature approved by all Evangelical Christians, and is the almoner of their gifts to the destitute. Its total issues at home, in 20 languages, number 479,400,000 copies. It has helped foreign missions, in 100 languages, to many millions of copies. Its colporteurs have visited 14,985,116 families.

TRACY, BENJAMIN FRANKLIN, an American lawyer; born in Owego, N. Y., April 26, 1830; was admitted to the bar in 1851; served as district attorney of Tioga co. in 1853-1854; and was a member of the New York Legislature in 1861-1862. He raised the 109th and 137th Regiments of New York volunteers in July and August, 1862; took a distinguished part in the operations at the front in 1862-1865, and in the latter year was promoted Brigadier-General of volunteers for gallantry in battle. He was United States district attorney for the Eastern District of New York in 1866-1873; judge of the Court of Appeals in 1881-1882; Secretary of the Navy in the cabinet of President Harrison in 1889-1893; president of the commission which drafted the charter for Greater New York in 1895-1896; and unsuccessful candidate for mayor under the new charter in 1897. He died in 1915.

TRACY, LOUIS, an English author, born at Liverpool, in 1863. He was educated privately in Yorkshire and in France, and began journalism on the Northern Echo, Darlington, and then at Cardiff. He went to Allahabad, India, in 1889, returned to England in 1893, and helped T. P. O'Connor to start "The Sun" newspaper in London. He then traveled in the United States and India, and when the war broke out became Commandant of the Whitby District Volunteers. He came to the United States in 1917, and had charge of a British propaganda bureau in New York. His works include: "The Final War"; "The Postmaster's Daughter"; "The Revellers." Died August 4, 1928.

TRADE, BOARD OF, in the United States a body of men selected from among the business men of a city, and appointed to represent and act for the whole business community in advancing and protecting their interests.

TRADE MARK, the name or mark under which any one trades. It is a mode of connecting certain goods in the mind of the public with a particular manufacturer or seller; and its function is to give a purchaser a satisfactory assurance of the make and quality of the article he is buying. A trade mark is the property of the person legally adopting it, and he has a right—antecedent to and independent of the various trade mark acts—to prevent any one else from using it to his prejudice.

Water marks on paper, dating from the 14th century, are among the oldest trade marks. Trade marks appear to have become a prominent feature in the industrial life of England in the early part of the 18th century. The law relating to them has pursued the following course of development: (1) At first no right of property in a trade mark was recognized, and only the actual, fraudulent, and injurious use by one person of the mark of another was restrained and punished. (2) In 1838, however, in the case of Millington *versus* Fox, Lord Chancellor Cottenham granted a perpetual injunction against the defendant, though no intentional fraud was established. Since that time the English Court of Chancery has uniformly interfered to prevent the infringement of trade marks on the principle of protecting property alone, and it was unnecessary for the plaintiff to prove that his rights had been intentionally invaded. (3) The Courts of Common Law did not imitate the wise liberality of the Court of Chancery, and down to 1873 proof of fraud on the part of an infringer was of the essence of a common-law action for damages. The Judicature Act of 1873 provided, however, that in any conflict between the rules of law and of equity the latter should thenceforth prevail.

The Registration of Trade Marks.— At common law a trade mark could be acquired only by actual user; it must have been "so applied in the market as to indicate to purchasers that the goods to which it was attached were the manufacture of a particular firm." By the English Trade-marks Registration Act, 1875, a Register of Trade Marks was established at the Office of the Commissioner of Patents (now the Patent Office), and it was provided that the registration of a trade mark should thenceforth be equivalent to public user. This provision is in substance repeated in the Patents Acts, 1883-1888, by which the registration of trade marks is now regulated. The registration of a person as proprietor of a trade mark is *primâ facie*, and after five years is conclusive evidence of his right to the exclusive use of the said mark (subject to the provisions of the acts); and no person can institute proceedings for infringement unless the mark alleged to be infringed has been registered, or—in the case of marks in use prior to the Act of 1875—has been declared by the certificate of the comptroller-general to be non-registrable.

Under the provisions of the International Convention for the Protection of Industrial Property an applicant for registration of a trade mark in any one of the contracting States may obtain protection in any of the other contracting States by application there within three or, in the case of countries beyond the seas, four months from the date of the first application. The subsequent application is antedated to the date of the first, and is consequently not defeated as otherwise it might have been by prior user in the protected interval. In the United States there is a good deal of difference between the laws of the various States on this subject.

Registration in the United States.— The following are the regulations for registration for foreign countries: Owners of trade marks used in commerce with foreign nations or with Indian tribes, if such owners be domiciled in the United States or located in any foreign country or tribe which by treaty, convention, or law affords similar privileges to citizens of the United States, may obtain registration of their trade marks by filing in the Patent Office a statement specifying name, domicile, location, and citizenship of the party applying, the class of merchandise, and the particular description of goods comprised in said class to which the trade mark has been appropriated, a description of the trade mark itself, a drawing illustrating it, which drawing must be of a standard size, and a statement of the mode in which the trade mark is applied or affixed to the goods, and of the length of time during which the trade mark has been used. This statement must be signed by the owner of the trade mark and must be accompanied by a written declaration, verified by the person or by a member of the firm or by an officer of the company applying, to the effect that such party has at the time a right to the use of the trade mark sought to be registered and that no other person, firm, or corporation has the right to such use.

The fee for examining and registering a trade mark is $25, which includes the certificate. This fee should accompany the application. The certificate of registration is issued in the name of the United States of America, under the seal of the Department of the Interior, and signed by the Commissioner of Patents. It remains in force for 30 years from its date, except in a case where the trade mark is claimed for and applied to an article not manufactured in this country, but receives protection under the laws of a foreign country for a shorter period. In that case it ceases to have any force in this country at the time the trade mark ceases to be protected in the foreign country.

At any time during the six months previous to the expiration of the 30 years the mark may be re-registered for the same term. The right to the use of a trade mark is assignable by an instrument in writing, which instrument may be recorded in the Patent Office, but said instrument will not be recorded prior to the filing of an application, and it must identify the application by serial number and date of filing, or, where the mark has been registered, by the certificate number and the date thereof. Consult Elfretti's "Patents, Copyrights, and Trade Marks." See COPYRIGHT: PATENTS.

TRADE SCHOOLS. See TECHNICAL EDUCATION.

TRADES UNION, or **TRADE UNION,** an organized body of workmen in any trade, manufacture, or industrial occupation associated together for the promotion of their common interests, such as wages and hours of labor.

Previous to 1824 combinations of workmen were illegal in England, as they still are in most European continental countries. The Trade Union Act (1871) provided for the registration of trade societies, and accorded a certain measure of protection for their funds; but this Act was accompanied and practically nullified by the Criminal Law Amendment Act. An agitation took place which resulted in the passing of Mr. Mundella's Trade Union Act Amendment Act, in 1876. By this Act every legal grievance of which the unions complained was redressed, and now nearly every trade society in the kingdom is duly registered and stands in much the same position as any other trade corporation. In the early days of trades unions, one of their most important functions was that of organizing strikes; but of late years there has been a reluctance to resort to such extreme measures. In 1860 a Board of Arbitration was established at the request of the lace workers in Nottingham, and since then similar boards have been formed by the trades in Staffordshire, Middlesborough, Cleveland, Bradford, Sheffield, and other places.

TRADE WIND, in meteorology, in the plural, certain ocean winds, blowing constantly in one direction or very nearly so, can be calculated on beforehand by the mariner and are therefore beneficial to trade. They exist on all open oceans to a distance of about 30° N. and S. of the equator, blowing from about the N. E. in the Northern and from the S. E. in the Southern Hemisphere. Where they meet they neutralize each other, creating a region of calm N., and the same distance S. of the equator. Atmospheric air expands by heat, and, expanding, naturally ascends, its place being supplied by a rush of colder and consequently of denser air beneath. The process is continually in progress, to a great extent, everywhere throughout the tropics, but especially above the land. If the globe consisted solely of land, or solely of water, and had no rotation, the cold currents would travel directly from the N. and S. poles to the equator; but the rotation of the earth deflects them from their course. The atmosphere lags behind the moving planet, especially at the equator, where the rotation is about 1,000 miles an hour. Neither the direction nor the area of the trade winds remains fixed. Since they supply the place of rarefied air, which is ascending, they must follow the movement of the sun, blowing to the point of greatest rarefaction, as a cold current coming through a keyhole goes to the fire. Hence, the area of the trade winds extends from two to four degrees farther N. than usual when the sun is at the Tropic of Cancer, and the same number of degrees farther S. than usual when he is at the Tropic of Capricorn. In the former case the S. E. trade wind declines further from the E. from its N. limit, sometimes passing the equator, while the N. E. trade wind approaches an E. direction more than at other times. The region of calms also changes its position. As the difference of pressure is not great, the trade wind is generally moderate in strength, especially in the opposite hemisphere from that in which the sun is at the time. The trade winds were not known till Columbus' first voyage. They are most marked on the Atlantic and Pacific Oceans, where they occur between 9° and 30° N., and between 4° and 22° S. in the former, and between 9° and 26° N., and between 4° and 23° S. in the latter ocean, but become modified in the vicinity of land, so as to lose their distinctive character. In the Indian Ocean and in Southeastern Asia they become altered into monsoons.

TRADING WITH THE ENEMY ACT, a Federal law passed on October 5, 1917, restricting exportations for the purpose of preventing goods exported from this country reaching Germany. Under the authority granted him by the Espionage Act, passed June 15, 1917, President Wilson issued a proclamation on July 9, 1917, forbidding the exportation of food stuffs, grains and steel, except by special license of the Government. One section of this act authorized the President to restrict exports, even to the point of declaring an embargo. On August 27, 1917, a second proclamation was published, placing the exportation of all goods under the control of the Exports Administrative Board, especially in the case of those exports destined for the Scandinavian countries. On September 7 an embargo on gold was declared. In its natural sequence followed the Trading with the Enemy Act, forbidding trade with enemies of the United States, and also giving the Government authority over imports. On October 15 the President placed the control of exportation and importation under the jurisdiction of the War Trade Board and the Secretary of the Treasury. The effect of these various measures was to cause a tremendous shrinkage in our foreign trade, not only with European countries, but with South America. A blacklisting system was also adopted, similar to the British blacklist, which practically excluded the trade of some 1,600 South American firms from the United States.

TRADUCIANISM, the doctrine that the human soul, as well as the body, is produced by natural generation. St. Augustine seems to have inclined to this belief without committiing himself to it or, on the other hand, pronouncing in favor of the opinion that the soul was immediately created by God and infused into the embryo when sufficiently organized.

TRAFALGAR, a low and sandy cape on the S. W. coast of Spain, at the N. W. entrance of the Strait of Gibraltar. The famous naval battle in which Nelson lost his life, after defeating a larger French and Spanish fleet under the command of Villeneuve and Gravina, was fought off this cape, Oct. 21, 1805. The Franco-Spanish fleet lost 19 ships out of 33.

TRAGEDY, a dramatic poem representing an important event, or a series of events, in the life of some person or persons, in which the diction is elevated, and which has generally a tragic or fatal catastrophe; that species of drama which represents a tragical situation or a tragical character. Tragedy originated among the Greeks in the worship of Dionysus. Thespis first introduced dialogue in the choral odes, and made one entire story occupy the pauses in the chorus. His first representation was in 535 B. C. He was succeeded by Phrynichus and Chœrilus, and is said to have written 150 pieces, none of which has come down to us. Æschylus (525-456 B. C.) added a second actor, diminished the parts of the chorus, and made the dialogue the principal part of the action. He also introduced scenery, and masks for actors, and is also said to have introduced the custom of contending with trilogies, or three plays at a time. In his later years he added a third actor.

ARTHUR TRAIN

Sophocles (495-405 B. C.) further improved the scenery and costume. In the hands of Euripides (480-405 B. C.) tragedy deteriorated in dignity; one of his peculiarities was the prologue, or introductory monologue, in which some god or hero opens the play, telling who he is, what has already happened, and what is the present state of affairs. He also invented tragi-comedy. The first Roman tragic poet was Livius Andronicus, a Greek by birth, who began to exhibit in 240 B. C. He was succeeded by Nævius (died 204 B. C.), and Ennius (239-169 B. C.) The only complete Roman tragedies that have come down to us are the 10 attributed to Seneca (A. D. 2-65). The first English tragedy is "Gorboduc, or Ferrex and Porrex," acted in 1562. See DRAMA.

TRAGOPAN, a name of certain beautiful birds of the genus *Ceriornis,* and of the family *Phasianidæ,* closely allied to the common fowl. *C. satyra,* a common species, is a native of the Himalayas. The plumage is spotted, and two fleshy protuberances hang from behind the eyes. When the bird is excited it can erect these protuberances till they look like a pair of horns. A large wattle hangs at either side of the lower mandible.

TRAILL, HENRY DUFF, an English author; born in Blackmeath, England, Aug. 14, 1842; graduated at St. John's, Oxford, in 1864. He was called to the bar in 1868, but soon took to literature. He wrote: "Lives" of Strafford, "William III.," "Sterne," "Coleridge," and others; also "Central Government" (1881); "Recaptured Rhymes" (1882); "The New Lucian" (1884); "Two Proper Prides"; "From Cairo to the Sudan Frontier"; "Lord Cromer"; "The New Fiction"; etc. He edited "Social England: A Record of the Progress of the People," in six large volumes, and in 1897 was made editor of the weekly review, "Literature." He died in 1900.

TRAIN, ARTHUR (CHENEY), an American author and lawyer; born in Boston, 1875. After studying law he was admitted to the bar of Massachusetts and New York. In 1901 he became assistant district attorney for New York co. In 1910 he was appointed special deputy attorney-general of the State of New York to investigate and prosecute political offenders in Queens co. Among his works are: "McAllister and His Double" (1905); "The Prisoner at the Bar" (1906); "True Stories of Crime" (1908); "The Goldfish" (1914); "The World and Thomas Kelly" (1917); and "The Earthquake" (1918).

TRAJAN, in full, **MARCUS ULPIUS TRAJANUS,** Roman emperor; born in Spain, A. D. 52; the son of Trajanus, a distinguished Roman commander under Vespasian. He served against the Parthians and on the Rhine, where he acquired so high a character that Nerva adopted him and created him Cæsar in 97. Nerva died in 98, and Trajan, who was then in Germany, peaceably succeeded to the throne. One of his greatest military achievements was his defeat of the Dacians, and the reduction of Dacia to a Roman province. It is supposed that it was in commemoration of this war that he erected at Rome the column which still remains under his name. In 103 he wrote the famous epistle to Pliny, governor of Pontus and Bithynia, directing him not to search for Christians, but

TRAJAN

to punish them if brought before him. For some years Trajan occupied himself with the work of administration, but in 114 he set out on an expedition against the Parthians which resulted in the reduction of Armenia to a Roman province. He is said to have been sensual in his private life, but his good qualities as a ruler were such that even 250 years after his death senators greeted a new emperor with the wish that he might be more fortunate than Augustus and better than Trajan. He died in Cilicia in A. D. 117, after having nominated Hadrian as his successor.

TRAJAN'S COLUMN, a celebrated monument in Rome, Italy, and the *chef-*

d'œuvre of Apollodorus; erected by the Roman senate and people in honor of the emperor in A. D. 114. It still stands in the Forum of Trajan, and is constructed entirely of marble. The shaft is 87 feet high, and whole, including pedestal and statue, 147 feet. Around the column runs a spiral band 3 feet wide and 660 feet long, covered with well-preserved reliefs from Trajan's war with the Dacians, comprising, besides animals, etc., 2,500 human figures. Beneath the column Trajan was interred, and on it was placed his statue, for which that of St. Peter has been substituted. A staircase in the interior, of 184 steps, leads to an open platform at the top.

TRAJAN'S WALL, a line of fortifications in the S. of the Dobrudscha; extends from the Danube, at Czernavoda, to a point on the Black Sea, near Kustendji, a distance of 37 miles. It consists of a double (in some parts a triple) line of earth ramparts about 10 feet high, bounded on its N. side by a natural fosse formed by a marshy valley, which was long erroneously regarded as an old course of the Danube. The wall was an important defense in the Russo-Turkish War of 1854, and the invaders were twice repelled in attempts to pass it—at Kostelli (April 10), and Czernavoda (April 20-22). A railway was constructed along the route in 1860, and the great cost has been the main obstacle to a project of carrying a ship canal across the valley for the purpose of avoiding the long and difficult passage by the Sulina mouth of the Danube. Another wall of the same name, constructed by a Roman legion A. D. 105-155, stretches from the Pruth E. to the Black Sea, and is included in the territory "restored" to Russia by the treaty of Berlin, July 13, 1878.

TRAMMEL, PARK, a United States senator; born in Macon co., Alabama, in 1876. As a child he was taken to Florida by his parents, where he attended the public schools until 15, when he became, first, clerk, then bookkeeper, in a store in Tampa, Fla. He studied law at Cumberland University, in Tennessee, and was admitted to the bar in 1899. In 1900 he was elected Democratic mayor of Lakewood, Fla., and in 1903 he was elected to the Florida House of Representatives, then to the State Senate two years later. During 1909-1913 he was attorney-general of Florida. In 1913 he was elected governor for a term of four years. In 1917 he was sent to the United States Senate for the term 1917-1923.

TRANCE, a condition closely allied to sleep, but differs from it as regards duration and profound insensibility to external impressions. Death trance is, according to Dr. Mayo, a positive status; a period of repose, the duration of which is sometimes definite and predetermined, though unknown. "The basis of death trance is suspension of the action of the heart, of breathing, and of voluntary motion; generally, likewise, of feeling and intelligence; and the vegetative changes in the body are suspended. With these phenomena is joined loss of external warmth, so that the usual evidence of life is gone." There are no well-authenticated cases on record in which trance has simulated death for any length of time. See CATALEPSY: HYSTERIA.

TRANI, a town of South Italy, in the province of Bari; on the Adriatic; 95 miles W. N. W. of Brindisi. It is an archbishop's see, has a cathedral, built about 1100, with a Romanesque portal and bronze doors of 1175, the fine church Sta. Maria Immaculata, several convents, a castle, a theater, an orphanage, a high school, a technical school, and a priests' college. Trani has important fisheries, and considerable trade in oil, corn, almonds, figs, and excellent wine. Trani is the ancient Turenum of the Peucetii, and was in the Middle Ages an important seaport. It was taken and burnt by the French in 1779. Pop. about 35,000.

TRANSCAUCASIA, the tract of territory formerly belonging to Russia, and extending between the Caucasus on the N. and Turkey in Asia and Persia on the S. The provinces on both sides of the Caucasus, with the added Armenian districts, constitute Caucasus or Caucasia in the widest sense, and are under one central authority, with 10 minor provinces; but the territory is sometimes divided into North Caucasus, Transcaucasia, and Armenia. Transcaucasia comprises several provinces; total area, 94,405 square miles; pop. 7,500,000. In February, 1918, the Republic of Transcaucasia was formed, but lasted only five weeks. The Tartans, Georgians and Armenians comprising the population were unable to agree, and the two latter peoples set up republics of their own.

TRANSCENDENTALISM, in philosophy, a term applied to the Kantian philosophy from the frequent use of the term transcendental by Kant, who gave it a meaning quite distinct from that which it till then bore. The Transcendentalism of Kant inquires into, and then denies, the possibility of knowledge respecting what lies beyond the range of experience. Kant distinguished knowledge into *a priori* (not originating from experience) and *a posteriori* (derived from experience), thus giving to the phrase, *a priori* knowledge, a meaning different from that which it had borne in philosophy since the days of Aristotle; and he applied the epithet transcendental to the knowledge that certain intuitions (such as time and space) and conceptions, to which he gave the Aristotelian name of categories, were independent of experience. Necessity and strict universality are for Kant the sure signs of non-empirical cognition. Transcendental philosphy is a philosophy of the merely speculative pure reason; for all moral practice, so far as it involves motive, refers to the feeling, and feeling is always empirical.

The word is applied also to the philosophy of Schelling and Hegel, who assert the identity of the subject and object.

In theology, the name given to a religious movement in New England in 1839, in which Emerson and Channing took a prominent part.

TRANSEPT, in architecture, that part of a church which is placed between the nave and the choir, extending transversely on each side, so as to give to the building the form of a cross. The transept was not originally symbolical, but was derived from the transverse hall or gallery in the ancient basilicas, at the upper end of the nave, its length being equal to the united breadth of the nave and aisles. This accidental approximation to the form of a cross was perceived by later architects, who accordingly lengthened the transept on each side so as to make the ground plan of the church completely cruciform.

TRANSFIGURATION, FEAST OF THE, a festival instituted in honor of the Transfiguration of Christ (Matt. xvii: 2); is one of the 12 great feasts which come next after Easter in dignity. In the Anglican church it is only a black-letter feast. It is commonly said to have been instituted in the West by Pope Calixtus III. (1455-1458), but is mentioned in the 9th century. Both Greeks and Westerns keep it on Aug. 6.

TRANSFORMATION MYTH, a myth which represents a human being as changed into an animal, a tree or plant, or some inanimate being.

TRANSFORMISM, in biology, the hypothesis that all existing species are the product of the metamorphosis of others forms of living beings; and that the biological phenomena which they exhibit are the results of the interaction, through past time, of two series of factors: (1) a process of morphological and concomitant physiological modification; (2) a process of change in the condition of the earth's surface.

TRANSFUSION OF BLOOD, a surgical operation by which blood is conveyed directly from the body of one person to that of another. The earliest case of transfusion of blood on record is that of Pope Innocent VIII., who was unsuccessfully operated on in April, 1492. Various experiments were afterward made by Wren and Lower in the transfusion of blood from one animal to another, and by Denys of Montpellier in injecting the blood of calves into human subjects; but the experiments were not attended with any great success, so that the operation fell into desuetude. It was not till about the year 1824, when Dr. Blundell published his work on "Physiological and Pathological Researches," that the transfusion of blood was regarded as a legitimate operation in obstetric surgery; its use was long restricted to cases of profuse hemorrhage in connection with labor and rare cases of sudden and profuse hemorrhage from other causes. The operation was performed by taking blood, instantly before injection, from the arm of a healthy person; but Dr. Brown-Sequard held that the blood of various animals could be used indiscriminately, provided only certain precautions be taken. Blood transfusion became common in surgical practice after 1910, owing to Carrel's improvements in vein suture and the development of a system for direct passage of blood from blood donor to subject.

TRANSIT, in astronomy, the passage of a heavenly body over the meridian. Also the passage of one of the inferior planets, Mercury or Venus, over the sun's disk, Mercury being so near the sun, and so difficult to observe with accuracy, its transits are not nearly so important to astronomers as those of Venus. In 1716 Dr. Halley published a paper in the "Philosophical Transactions," advising that the transits of Venus over the sun's disk which would occur in A. D. 1761 and 1769 should be taken advantage of for the purpose of ascertaining the sun's distance from the earth. Though he was dead long before these dates arrived, the government of the day acted on his suggestion. In 1769 the celebrated Captain Cook was sent to Otaheite for the purpose of noting the transit, another observer being dispatched to Lapland. The observations of the latter being erroneous, the distance of the sun was exaggerated by about three millions of miles. In 1874, when the next transit occurred, all civilized nations sent out scientific men to observe it. It was known that it would be invisible at Greenwich, but expeditions were sent out by the British Government to the Sandwich Islands, to New Zealand, Egypt, Rodriguez, and Kerguelen Island. Other nations occupied other stations, and the weather proved suitable at most places for accurate observation.

Transits of Venus come, after long intervals, in pairs, eight years apart; and another transit took place on the afternoon of Dec. 6, 1882. In the British Isles the weather was generally unfavorable, clouds with occasional snowflakes obscuring the sky at Greenwich, and through nearly all Great Britain, except on the W. coast. At Dublin partial observations were obtained; and of various British expeditions sent abroad complete success was obtained in Madagascar and at the Cape of Good Hope. Observers from the United States and other countries were also successful. The observation of the distance the planet moves to the right and left of the sun, in describing its orbit, enables an astronomer to ascertain the relative distance of the two luminaries. The relative breadth of the sun's diameter as compared with his distance from the earth is also easily ascertained. If, then, two observers on the surface of our sphere take their stations at judiciously selected points, as widely apart as possible, and note a transit of Venus, the planet will have a lesser line to traverse at the one place than the other, and will do it in a shorter time. From accurate notation of the difference in time taken in connection with the difference in length it is possible to calculate, first, the breadth of the sun and, secondly, his distance from the earth. When the materials obtained in connection with the two transits were worked out, it was found, as Hansen had suspected, that the sun's distance had been over-estimated, and it was reduced from 95,300,000 to 92,700,000 miles.

In engineering, a portable instrument resembling a theodolite, designed for measuring both horizontal and vertical angles. It is provided with horizontal and vertical graduated circles, one or two levels, and a compass, and is mounted upon a tripod stand.

TRANSIT INSTRUMENT, an instrument designed accurately to denote the time when a heavenly body passes the meridian. It consists of a telescope supported on a horizontal axis, or pivots, the extremities of which terminate in cylindrical trunnions resting in metallic supports shaped like the upper part of the letter Y, and hence termed the "Y's," and imbedded in two stone pillars. In

See Tree, p. 492

TREE FERNS IN TASMANIA

See Transport, p 465

TRANSPORT "LEVIATHAN," PREVIOUSLY THE GERMAN LINER "VATERLAND," WHICH CARRIED MANY THOUSAND
AMERICAN SOLDIERS ACROSS THE ATLANTIC

order to relieve the pivots from friction and facilitate the turning of the telescope, counterpoises are provided operated through levers, carrying friction rollers, on which the axis turns. When the instrument is in proper adjustment, the telescope should continue in the plane of the meridian when revolved entirely round on its axis, and for this purpose the axis must lie in a line directly E. and W. To effect this adjustment its ends are provided with screws by which a motion, both in azimuth and altitude, may be imparted. The telescope has a series of parallel wires crossing its object glass in a vertical direction. When a star, designed to be the subject of observation, is seen approaching the meridian, the observer looks at the hour and minutes on a clock placed at hand for the purpose. He then notes the passage of the star across such wire, listening at the same time to the clock beating seconds. The exact time at which the star passes each wire is then noted and the mean between the time of passing each two wires equidistant from the center being taken gives a very close ap-

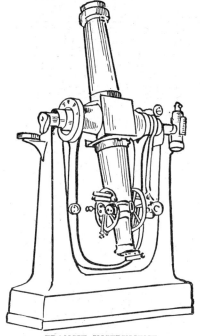

TRANSIT INSTRUMENT

proximation to the truth. The transit instrument is the most important of what may be called the technical astronomical instruments. The smaller and portable kinds are used to ascertain the local time by the passage of the sun or other object over the meridian, while the larger and more perfect kinds, in first-class observatories, are used for measuring the positions of stars, for forming catalogues, its special duty being to determine with the greatest accuracy the right ascension of heavenly bodies.

TRANSMIGRATION, in comparative religions, metempsychosis; the doctrine of the passage of the soul from one body into another. It appears among many savage races in the form of the belief that ancestral souls return, imparting their own likeness to their descendants and kindred, and Tylor thinks that this notion may have been extended so as to take in the idea of rebirth in bodies of animals. In this form the belief has no ethical value. Transmigration first appears as a factor in the gradual purification of the spiritual part of man, and its return to God, the source and origin of all things, in the religion of the ancient people of India, whence it passed to the Egyptians, and, according to Herodotus, from them to the Greeks. It was one of the characteristic doctrines of Pythagoras, and Pindar the Pythagorean lets the soul return to bliss after passing three unblemished lives on earth. Plato in the dream of Er deals with the condition and treatment of departed souls; and extends the period of the return of souls to God to 10,000 years, during which time they inhabit the bodies of men and animals. Vergil, Persius and Horace allude to it, and Ovid sets forth the philosophy and pre-existences of Pythagoras. Traces of it appear in the "Apocrypha," and that at least some Jews held it in the time of Jesus seems indicated in the disciples' question (John ix: 2). St. Jerome alludes to the existence of a belief in transmigration among the Gnostics, and Origen adopted this belief as the only means of explaining some Scriptural difficulties, such as the struggle of Jacob and Esau before birth (Gen. xxv: 22), and the selection of Jeremiah (Jer. i: 5). In modern times Lessing held it and taught it, and it formed part of the system of Swedenborg.

TRANSMISSION OF ELECTRIC POWER. Under this heading are considered methods of conveying electrical energy from one locality to another. The need for such transmission arises chiefly from economic causes. In the center of a city, electricity can seldom be generated except at high cost. It is a common practice to produce the electricity at some point where there is a cheap source of power (such, for instance, as water power, or a readily available and abundant supply of coal) and then to convey it to the city in the manner outlined below. It is obvious that the site of the central supply station will depend not only on the cost of generating the electricity, but also on the cost of transmitting it to the point where it is to be used. Before considering the methods of transmitting, therefore, it will be advisable to examine, briefly, the different factors determining its cost.

The first factor will clearly be the distance which has to be covered. The greater the distance, the more metal will have to be used for conveying the current, and the greater will be the expenditure on constructing and maintaining the service lines. The second factor is the voltage at which the current is supplied. Electric power is the product of the voltage and the current, and the greater the voltage, the smaller may be the current, and, consequently, the smaller the cross-section of the cable carrying the current. In other words, by using a high voltage and a low current, the amount of copper required will be much smaller than when the current is greater and the voltage power lower, while the amount of power supplies will be no less. Assuming that the efficiency remains constant, the amount of copper required will be proportional to the square of the distance and inversely proportional to the square of the voltage. It is, therefore, economical to have the sources of supply located at a great distance from the point of consumption only when the permissible voltage is very high. It is for this reason that alternating current is always used when supplied over long distances. Large direct current generators cannot supply current at a higher voltage than 1,500 volts, and so alternating current generators are used. (See DYNAMO-ELECTRIC.) A typical high-voltage transmission system consists of the power station in which are located the generators and the "step-up transformers," and the cables to transmit the current to the terminal station, at which are located the "step-down transformers," from which the current is supplied to various sub-stations. The transformer is a piece of apparatus which receives electricity at one voltage and delivers it at another, the "step-up transformers" raising the voltage, while the "step-down transformers" lower it. For many purposes, alternating current is unsuitable or undesirable, and it is frequently necessary to transform the current from alternating to direct. This is done by means of a motor generator set. The motor is driven by the alternating current, and in turn drives a direct-current dynamo.

The cable for conveying the current is nearly always of copper, but aluminum is occasionally used. The wires are bare and in overhead systems are supported on wooden poles fitted with cross-arms cr on steel towers. The former are used for lower voltage systems, the wires being supported on glass or porcelain insulators fixed on to the cross-arms. For higher voltages, however, the steel tower is now commonly used, a suspension type of insulator replacing the so-called pin insulators. Occasionally the cable is laid underground, especially in parts of Europe, where the overhead system is comparatively uncommon. The cable in this case is insulated with paper impregnated with rosin oil, or some similar substance, and is then frequently sheathed in lead.

From what has been said regarding the economy of high voltages, it would seem that the logical procedure would be to generate electricity at the higest possible voltage. There are certain practical considerations, however, which limit the permissible voltage. Insulating supports are bulky, costly and liable, under some atmospheric conditions, to flashover, at higher voltage than 60,000. Moreover, when two parallel wires carrying a current are suspended in air, it is found that there is a considerable loss of energy between them, and this loss increases rapidly with voltages above 50,000. The only way to overcome this loss is to keep the wires widely separated, but it is obvious that there is a limit to the possible separation. To obtain satisfactory separation entails increase in cost of construction. To meet exceptional conditions, 150,000-volt transmission was first installed, after many years of hesitation, in 1913; and in 1923 the Southern California Edison Co. first used 220,000 volts, transmitting 275 miles. Voltage in general practice remained lower.

Considerable stress is laid on the economical aspect of transmission because this is very often the determining factor in choosing a site for a central station. One site may be preferable to another as far as amount of available power is concerned, and there may be no insurmountable difficulties in the way of constructing the service lines to the terminal station, but the second site may be chosen on the grounds that cost of transmission will be so much less. To indicate how large a figure this cost reaches in some cases, it may be stated that the cost of transmission equipment for a 150-mile line will amount to at least 20 per cent. and may be as high as 38 per cent. of the total cost of the generating and transmission system. Under present conditions, the greatest distance it has been found profitable to transmit power for regular consumption does not greatly exceed 220 miles. Connections for exchange of power have been made between stations more than twice this distance apart. They serve for emergency use in cases of abnormal demand or deficiency of output in the field of either generating station. A widespread linking of transmission systems in the U. S. for emergency coöperation took place in the present decade, tending to make power transmission increasingly an interstate activity.

Some of the details of the transmission equipment may now be briefly described. A device of some importance is the *Lightning Arrester*. This is used to protect the system against lightning discharges and other abnormally high voltages. The aluminum arrester is commonly used, which consists of a nest of aluminum cones immersed in an electrolyte, the cones being covered with a film of hydroxide. At a low voltage, only a very low current can flow through this contrivance, but when the voltage rises the possible current that it can carry is very high. As soon as the voltage drops below a certain critical point, the high resistance is restored and the current falls correspondingly. The arrester acts, so to speak, as a safety valve, releasing high voltages just as the safety valve on a steam line will release high steam pressure. The actual service line itself is protected from lightning by running a steel wire parallel to the upper wires, this steel wire being grounded at every support. The lightning passes to the ground through this wire rather than through the copper wires and glass or porcelain insulators. *Switches* are another important detail in high voltage systems. Oil switches are most commonly used, in which the contacts are immersed in insulating oil, thus preventing the formation of an arc when a current is broken. They are generally operated at a distance by a system of levers, or by means of a small motor, and important switches are frequently arranged with each pole in a separate chamber of brick or concrete. On the *switchboard* are assembled ammeters, voltmeters, wattmeters, rheostats, and all the levers for controlling the generating and transmitting system, so that the man in charge can tell almost at a glance the condition of any part of the circuit.

In cases where the area of distribution is small, direct instead of alternating current is used. In order to take care of variation in pressure in the supply line, caused by fluctuation in consumption, a storage battery is connected in parallel with the dynamo. When consumption is small, excess current from

I—33

the dynamo flows to the batteries and charges them. When consumption is high, current from the dynamo is supplemented with that from the batteries.

TRANSMISSION OF POWER, the doing of useful work at a distance from the engine or whatever other source supplies the energy. The revolving shaft of a screw steamer transmits rotary motion through a considerable distance; but for long-distance transmission ordinary mechanical devices, if they do not altogether fail, lose greatly in efficiency. Cable cars also form a good illustration. It is in electricity, however, that we find the most promising agent for indefinite transmission of power. Thus a dynamo-electric machine may be worked by a waterfall; its voltage or potential may be transmitted along wires to distant stations, and there transformed into currents capable of driving an electric motor and keeping a whole factory in operation.

Over 60,000 horse power of electric current generated by Niagara Falls is in use in the many factories established at Niagara Falls and in Buffalo, N. Y., 26 miles away. In the latter city street railways, grain elevators and manufacturing plants are run by this current, which is brought to the outskirts of the city over bare copper wires, and then distributed through the city in underground conduits.

TRANSPORT, a ship or vessel employed by a government for carrying soldiers, warlike stores, or provisions from one place to another. At the beginning of the Spanish-American War the United States had no ships of this class. A number of coastwise crafts were purchased and hastily transformed into transports, on which troops were shipped to Manila and other points. Although so hastily fitted up, they proved adequate. When the war closed, the United States Government fitted up a number of these vessels as model transports. They have every convenience and comfort, including gymnasiums, bath-rooms, hospitals and electric lights, etc. When the United States entered the World War in 1917 all the transports were in use as ocean freighters, but by remodeling the seized German ships and by borrowing transports from England the millions of American soldiers were carried across the sea with a minimum loss of life.

TRANSPORTATION, a punishment till recent times in general practice in Great Britain for crimes of the more serious description, but falling short of the penalty of death. It varied in duration from seven years to the termination of the criminal's life, according to the magnitude of the offense. Australia, Tasmania, and Norfolk Islands were the stations to which convicts from England were conveyed. Transportation was abolished by an act passed in 1857, and superseded by penal servitude. This act, however, reserved to the privy-council the right of ordering convicts to be transported, and it was only in 1868 that transportation to Western Austraila actually ceased.

TRANS-SIBERIAN RAILWAY, a railway system of Russia, extending from St. Petersburg to Port Arthur. The entire distance from St. Petersburg to Vladivostok is 6,677 miles. The original cost was $172,525,000. The first sod was cut at Vladivostok on May 24, 1891. To facilitate the work of construction, the line was divided into three parts. The first started from the European frontier in the Ural, and ran E.; the second from Vladivostok, on the Pacific, ran W.; while the third, the middle section, near Lake Baikal, joined the other two. The whole line was opened for passenger traffic in December, 1901. In 1905 a line was laid around the southern end of Lake Baikal which obviated a boat trip on the lake which passengers were formerly forced to take.

TRANSUBSTANTIATION. The meaning of the theological term transubstantiation is made apparent in the following canon of the Council of Trent: "If any one shall say that, in the most holy sacrament of the Eucharist, there remains the substance of bread and wine together with the body and blood of our Lord Jesus Christ, and shall deny that wonderful and singular conversion of the whole substance of the bread into the body, and of the whole substance of the wine into the blood, the species of bread and wine alone remaining—*which conversion the Catholic church most fittingly calls transubstantiation*—let him be anathema." The canon quoted was intended as a condemnation of the theories of impanation and consubstantiation. According to the theory of impanation, which was advocated chiefly by Osiander in the sacrament of the Eucharist, the bread and wine were hypostatically or personally assumed by the Divine Word. According to the theory of consubstantiation, which was favored by the large majority of the Lutherans, the substance of the bread and wine remains together with the body and blood of Jesus Christ, but without being hypostatically assumed.

The doctrine of transubstantiation is then an article of Roman Catholic faith.

Furthermore, the Council of Trent in the same Session xiii. declares that this doctrine "has always been the conviction in the Church of God." Protestant divines call in question the truth of this declaration, and assert that the doctrine was unknown before the Middle Ages. Roman Catholic theologians, on the other hand, while admitting that the term transubstantiation is comparatively new, profess their ability to prove by a catena of witnesses, commencing with the earliest ages of the church, that the doctrine conveyed by the term has been believed from the first. That the term is comparatively new is unquestionable. Cardinal Franzelin, indeed ("De Eucharistia," p. 177), gives instances of its use by Catholic writers in the 11th and 12th centuries. Nevertheless it was not formally adopted into the doctrinal phraseology of the Church before 1215, when it was employed in a profession of faith drawn up by the fourth Lateran Council. After this period we find the term again employed in a "confession of faith," which was presented for subscription to Michael Palæologus, the Greek emperor, by Pope Clement IV. (1267), and was professed by the emperor in the second Ecumenical Council of Lyons held in 1274 under Pope Gregory X.

TRANSVAAL COLONY, formerly the South African Republic; since 1910 a State of the Union of South Africa; area, 110,450 square miles; lying between the Vaal and the Limpopo rivers; bounded N. by British South African territory, E. by Portuguese East Africa and Zululand, S. by Natal and the Orange River Colony, and W. by Bechuanaland. The population numbers over 300,000 whites and over 1,000,000 natives. Johannesburg, the principal city, had in 1918 a population of 137,166 whites and about the same number of natives. Prior to its annexation to Great Britain the republic was ruled by a president elected for five years, only native Boers having the franchise; and a legislature of two houses, each of 27 members, elected for four years. The president had a council of four official members. One-third of the population is estimated to be engaged in agriculture, the lands of the colony generally, outside the mining districts, being extremely productive, and the demand for farm products in the mining regions very great, even in excess of the local products at the present time. From the establishment of the republic, troubles arose with the natives around them, and during one of these disturbances the British intervened in 1877 and annexed the territory. The Boers, however, rose in rebellion in 1880, and after a short war, in which the British were worsted, the independence of the country, subject to the "suzerainty" of the British crown, was again recognized. In 1884 a new convention was signed giving the Transvaal independence in the management of its internal affairs, but placing certain restrictions on its authority to make treaties with foreign powers. In 1886 gold was discovered in the RAND (*q. v.*). About 23,000 whites and 250,000 natives are employed in the mines. The gold output of 1916 was valued at £38,110,000.

In 1899 trouble again arose between the Transvaal Government and the Uitlanders. The latter sent numerous petitions to the Queen of England to help them in their contentions against the Boers. A conference was arranged between President Krüger and Sir Alfred Milner, the British high commissioner at Cape Town, which was held May 31, 1899, at the capital of the Orange Free State; but it failed to yield any benefits, as Krüger declined to make the so-called "reforms" that Milner demanded, and Milner declined to submit disputes to international arbitration in the way Krüger suggested. The chronic source of trouble in the Transvaal was the fact that the Englishmen who went there for gold-mining purposes were determined on obtaining the right to vote as citizens of the Transvaal republic, while still keeping their status as British subjects.

On Oct. 10, 1899, the Transvaal Government sent an ultimatum to Great Britain demanding the withdrawal of all her troops in the Transvaal. The reply to this being unsatisfactory, the Transvaal declared war Oct. 11, 1899, the Orange Free State supported its sister republic, and the next day a Transvaal force invaded Natal. The first months of the war were marked by Boer aggressions and successes. At the close of 1899 three British forces were being besieged, respectively at Ladysmith, Kimberley, and Mafeking, and three British armies had been checked and were inactive, awaiting the arrival of reinforcements. The British losses had been 7,630 in killed, wounded and missing. These unexpected reverses awoke Great Britain to the magnitude of the task before her. Lord Roberts and Lord Kitchener and 100,000 men were dispatched to South Africa and by the end of January there were 250,000 British troops in the field. Before the arrival of these troops, however, the Boers continued to gain victories. At the Tugela river and at Spion Kop (a small hill N. of the river) the British were defeated and compelled to relinquish their plan of relieving **Ladysmith**.

With the arrival of Lord Roberts at the front, Feb. 9, the aspect of the war changed. Lord Kitchener reorganized the army and departments; Lord Roberts began the invasion of the Orange Free State; and in rapid succession followed the relief of Kimberley (Feb. 15); the surrender of General Cronje with 4,600 men (Feb. 27); the relief of Ladysmith (Feb. 28); the surrender of Bloemfontein, the capital of the Orange Free State; the relief of Mafeking (May 16); and the surrender of Pretoria (June 5). On Sept. 8, at Spitzkop, General Buller defeated a large force of Boers under General Botha, and with this battle organized resistance came to an end. President Krüger fled to Europe, and the only opposition offered the British was by isolated bands of Boers, who carried on a guerrilla warfare. On Sept. 3 the South African (Transvaal) republic was officially annexed by Great Britain under the name of the Transvaal Colony, and on Dec. 14 Sir Alfred Milner was appointed its administrator. In January, 1902, the government of the Netherlands made official overtures to Great Britain to act as a peace intermediary between her and the Boers. Great Britain refused the offer on the ground that any conditions of peace must be made in South Africa, and not by the Boer representatives in Holland. The British Liberal Government of 1906 offered the Transvaal a new constitution, and in 1907 an election was held at Pretoria, where General Louis Botha was appointed the first Premier. In 1910 the Transvaal was joined to the UNION OF SOUTH AFRICA (*q. v.*).

TRANSVAAL WAR, a war between the (then) South African Republic and Great Britain in 1880-1881. The Boer victory at Majuba Hill, Feb. 27, 1881, was soon followed by peace.

TRANSYLVANIA, a former grandduchy and crown-land of the Austro-Hungarian monarchy; joined to Rumania in December, 1918; surrounded by Hungary, the Bukovina, Moldavia, and Wallachia; area, 22,312 square miles; pop. (1919) 2,678,867. Transylvania is so called from its position beyond the wooded Carpathians; its interior is a table-land intersected by spurs from the Carpathian ranges, rising in the S. (in Negoi) to 8,060 feet, in the N. to 7,000, in the W. to 5,840, and in the E. to 5,700, while its average elevation is about 1,500 feet above the sea, its lowest point being where the river Maros enters Hungary (566 feet). The chief rivers, all belonging to the Danube system, are the Aluta, falling into the Danube, Samos, and Maros (tributaries of the Theiss), and the Bistritz, an affluent of the Sereth. Of the whole area, 23 per cent. is arable, 25 per cent. meadowland, and 38 per cent. forest. The best wine is produced in the valleys of the Samos, Kotel, and Maros. The mining industries of Transylvania include the production of iron ores and pig iron. Other mineral products are gold, silver, quicksilver, copper, coal, and salt. Tanning and the manufacture of linens, woolens, and glass are also important. Originally a part of Dacia, Transylvania was conquered by King Stephan I. in 1004, and united to Hungary. About this period the country was invaded by Germans, probably from the Rhine districts, who named it Siebenbürgen, after the seven fortified towns built by them. Ever since, this little Saxon colony has retained, unchanged, its peculiar laws and language; here we find cities with names like Kronstadt, Hermanstadt, Klausenburg, Elizabethstadt, and Mühlenbach, in a district surrounded by places with Slavonic, Magyar and Wallachian names. From 1526 to 1699 Transylvania was an independent kingdom under the Zapolya princes. Completely subdued by Leopold I. in 1687, and united to Hungary in 1713, it became a grand-duchy in 1765. In 1848 it was the theater of a bloody struggle between Bem and the Russians, and was for a time united to Hungary. In 1849 it become an independent crown-land of Austria, and in 1867 an integral part of the kingdom of Hungary.

TRAP, a term rather loosely and vaguely applied by the earlier geologists to some or all of the multifarious igneous rocks that belong to the palæozoic and secondary epochs, as distinct from granite on the one hand and the recent volcanic rocks on the other. Trap rocks often assume a terraced appearance, whence their name from trappa, the Swedish for stair. Their composition may be described as consisting chiefly of felspar and hornblende. Trap rocks of crystalline structure are distinguished as greenstones, basalts, clink stones, compact feldspar, and feldspar porphyries, while the softer and more earthy varieties are known as claystones, claystone porphyries amygdaloids, trap tuffs, and mackes. BASALT (*q. v.*) is the most compact, the hardest, and the heaviest of the trap rocks. The hill scenery of trappean districts is often picturesque.

TRAPANI, a coast town in the W. of Sicily; 23 miles W. of Palermo. The cathedral of St. Lorenzo, a town house,

a lyceum and a library are the chief public buildings. The town is well built, strongly fortified, and has a good natural harbor. The manufacture of sea salt is the chief industry, but corn, wine, fish and coral are also exported. Tripani is the ancient Drepanum or Drepana. It was fortified by Hamilcar in 260 B. C., and here in 249 Adherbal defeated the Roman fleet. Near it is Mount Eryx, now Monte S. Giuliano. Important discoveries of human and other bones in caves were made in 1869. Pop. (1901) commune, 61,000.

TRAPEZIUM, as defined by Euclid, any quadrilateral except a square, an oblong, a rhombus, and a rhomboid. Later Greek geometers seem to have used the word in the more restricted sense of a quadrilateral with one pair of parallel sides; and the word trapezoid was introduced to describe a quadrilateral which had no two sides parallel. On the Continent the words are so distinguished to this day. By English geometers and writers on mensuration the words got interchanged as regards their significance, so that with us a trapezoid is generally defined as a quadrilateral with two parallel sides. Thus English writers have retained trapezium in the broader sense, and have used trapezoid in the restricted sense of a Euclidean trapezium with two sides parallel. The continental custom is historically and etymologically the better. There is, however, hardly a necessity for both words, since the word quadrilateral is now invariably used by modern geometers for a four-sided figure which is not a parallelogram.

TRAPEZOID BONE, in anatomy, a bone of the wrist of which the superior surface articulates with the scaphoid bone, the external with the trapezium, the internal with the os magnum, and the inferior with the second metacarpal bone. It is smaller than the trapezium, has its largest diameter from before backward, and its posterior surface, which is much larger than the anterior one, pentagonal.

TRAPHAGEN, FRANK WEISS, an American chemist; born in Eaton, O., July 20, 1861; was graduated at the School of Mines, Columbia University, in 1882. He then pursued special studies in analytical and applied chemistry. He was Professor of Chemistry in the College of Montana in 1887-1893. In the latter year he accepted the chair of chemistry at the Montana State College and became chemist of the Montana Agricultural Experiment Station, and in 1917 was appointed professor of metallurgy in the South Dakota School of Mines. He was the author of bulletins on "Drinking Water"; "The Alkali Soils of Montana"; "The Sugar Beet in Montana"; etc.; and of "A New Departure in Cyanide Treatment" (1899); "Some Notes on the Estimation of Carbohydrates" (1899); "Notes on Alkali Soil in Montana" (1899); "Food Adulteration in Montana"; "Labor and Industry" (1900); etc.

TRAPPIST, a religious order, celebrated for its extraordinary austerities, is so called from an abbey of the Cistercian order, founded in the middle of the 12th century, in the narrow valley of La Trappe, near Mortagne, in the Norman department of Orne—called "the trap" because of its inaccessibility. In the first half of the 17th century the abbey of La Trappe fell, with other ecclesiastical preferments, to Dominique Armand-Jean le Bouthillier de Rancé (1626-1700), originally an accomplished but worldly courtier, who suddenly turned his back on the vanities of the world. It was in 1662 that he commenced his reforms. At first he encountered violent opposition from the brethren; but his firmness overcame it all. He himself entered on a fresh novitiate in 1663, made anew the solemn profession, and was reinstalled as abbot. The monks were forbidden the use of meat, fish, wine, and eggs. All intercourse with externs was cut off.

The reform of De Rancé is founded on the principle of perpetual prayer and entire self-abnegation. By the Trappist rule the monks are obliged to rise at two o'clock A. M. for matins in the church, which lasted till half-past three; and after an interval occupied in private devotion they go at half-past five to the office of prime, which is followed by a lecture. At seven they engage in their several daily tasks, indoors or out, according to the weather. At half-past nine they return to the choir for successive offices of terce, sext, and none; at the close of which they dine on vegetables dressed without butter or oil, or on vegetable soup, and a little fruit. Milk and cheese are used save in time of fast; the sick are allowed eggs. The dietary is not the same in all the houses of the order. In some, light beer or wine is sparingly allowed. The principal meal is succeeded by manual labor for two hours, after which each monk occupies an hour in private prayer or reading in his own cell till four o'clock, when they again assemble in the choir for vespers. The supper consists of bread and water, and after a short interval of repose is followed by a lecture.

At six o'clock they recite compline in choir, and at the end spend half an hour in meditation, retiring to rest at eight o'clock. The bed is a hard straw mattress, with a coarse coverlet; and the Trappist never lays aside his habit, even in case of sickness, unless it should prove extreme. Perpetual silence is prescribed, save in cases of necessity, and at certain stated times; only the abbot and the guest-master are allowed to speak to strangers. But conversation by means of manual and other signs are practiced. The minor practices and observances are devised so as to remind the monk at every turn of the shortness of life and the rigor of judgment; and the last scene of life is made signal in its austerity by the dying man being laid during his death-agony on a few handfuls of straw, that he may, as it were, lay aside on the very brink of the grave even the last fragment of earthly comfort to which the necessities of natural had till then compelled him to cling.

The reformed order of La Trappe scarcely extended beyond France in the first period of its institution. The inmates of La Trappe shared, at the Revolution, the common fate of all the religious houses of France; they were compelled to quit their monastery. But a considerable number of them found a shelter at Valsainte, in the canton of Fribourg, in Switzerland. In the vicissitudes of the Revolutionary War they were driven from this house; and a community numbering about 250, together with a large number of nuns who had been established for purposes of education, found refuge at Constance, at Augsburg, at Munich, and even in Russia. During the Revolutionary War small communities obtained a certain footing in Italy, Spain, America, England, and, notwithstanding the prohibitory law, even in France, at Mont Genèvre. After the Restoration they resumed, by purchase (1817), possessions of their old home at La Trappe, which continued to be the head monastery of the order. During the course of the next 50 years they formed many establishments in France, the house of La Meilleraye being one of the famous abbeys. When, in 1880, 1,450 brethren of the order were expelled from France, only a comparatively small number were left. In England the Cistercian house of St. Bernard, in Leicestershire, is Trappist; so is the convent at Stapehill, in Dorset. In Ireland the order has houses at Mount Melleray, near Cappoquin; in Waterford, and at Roscrea, in Tipperary. America has houses at Gethsemane, in Kentucky; at New Melleray, near Dubuque, Ia.; at Tracadie, in Nova Scotia, and at Oka, on the Ottawa river, 36 miles from Montreal; there are houses in Germany, Algiers, Italy, and Belgium. In 1908 it was claimed that the Trappists numbered 4,000 monks, occupying 71 monasteries.

TRASIMENUS, LAKE, a shallow Italian lake lying between the towns of Cortona and Perugia. Surrounded on all sides by hills, it is about 10 miles in length by 8 in breadth; area, 50 square miles; elevation above the sea about 850 feet; depth about 25 feet. There is no outlet, and the margins are flat and overgrown with reeds, but of late largely planted with eucalyptus trees. The lake is memorable for the great victory obtained there by Hannibal in 217 B. C. over the Romans, when 15,000 Romans, including the commander, the Consul Caius Flaminius Nepos, were slain, and 10,000 captured, Hannibal losing only 1,500 men. The lake was partly drained in 1898, uncovering 5,500 acres.

TRASK, JOHN WILLIAM, an American sanitarian, born in Bug City, Mich., in 1877. Graduating from the University of Michigan, he was appointed assistant surgeon in the United States Public Health Service. In 1907 he passed as assistant surgeon, becoming assistant surgeon general in 1909. He served in Detroit, Mich.; Fort Stanton, N. M.; Chicago and Washington, D. C. In 1909 he was given charge of the division of Sanitary Reports and Statistics, which position he held till 1918, when he became medical director of the United States Employees' Compensation Commission. He is the author of "Vital Statistics" (1914), and a great number of contributions to technical magazines.

TRASK, KATE NICHOLS (KATRINA TRASK), an American author, born in Brooklyn, N. Y. She has written a great number of short stories for the general magazines, besides which she has written "Sonnets and Lyrics" (1894-1903); "Lessons in Love" (1900); "Not Bound" (1903); "Night and Morning" (1906); and "Without the Walls" (1919).

TRASK, WILLIAM BLAKE, an American author; born in Dorchester, Mass., Nov. 25, 1812; received a common school education and learned the trade of cabinet making. Later he devoted himself to historical and antiquarian researches. He wrote "Memoir of Andrew H. Ward" (1863) and was the editor of "The Journal of Joseph Ware" (1852); "Baylie's Remarks on General Cobb" (1864); "The Bird Family" (1871); and "The Seaver Family" (1872). He also aided in compiling "History of Dorchester." He died in 1906.

TRAUB, PETER EDWARD, an American army officer, born in New York, N. Y., in 1864. He graduated from the United States Military Academy in 1886, and then entered the cavalry arm of the service. In 1914 he took charge of the Philippine Constabulary Service, with the rank of colonel. He was made brigadier-general in 1917. In 1907 he was assistant professor of modern languages in the United States Military Academy. From 1917 to 1919 he served with the American Expeditionary forces in France and participated in the battles of Seicheprey, St. Mihiel and many others. In 1918 he became a major-general.

TRAUN, LAKE OF, a small but beautiful lake in Upper Austria, near the town of Gmunden. The river Traun passes through the lake and enters the Danube.

TRAUTWINITE, a microcrystalline mineral, occurring in crystals, the system of which has not yet been determined; hardness, 1-2; color, green; luster, dull; streak, light-gray. Analysis yielded: Silica, 21.78; sesquioxide of chromium, 38.39; sesquioxide of iron, 13.29; alumina, 0.81; lime, 18.58; magnesia, 7.88; loss on ignition, 0.11=100.84. Occurs on chromite in Monterey co., Cal.

TRAVANCORE, native Tiruvánkod, a protected State in the extreme S. of British India; bounded on the N. by Cochin, on the E. by British territory and on the W. by the Indian Ocean. The State pays a yearly tribute of $80,000 to Great Britain, and is politically connected with the province of Madras; area 7,294 square miles; pop. about 3,500,000, mainly Hindus, belonging to 420 castes, from Brahmans to Negroid hillmen. Nairs are over a fourth of the total, Mohammedans only 7 per cent. There are many native Christians of the Syrian rite and some black Jews. At the S. extremity of the State is Cape Comorin; the Western Ghats run along the E. side. W. of the foothills is a level belt, 10 miles wide, covered with cocoanut and areca palms. On the elevations the soil is light and gravelly; in the valleys it is in general a deep black mold. Travancore shares with Cochin the lagoons or backwaters along the coast. The chief produce is copra, coir, tobacco, nut oil, areca nut, ginger, pepper, cardamoms, beeswax, coffee and timber. The rajahs are intelligent, have been faithful to the English alliance, cherish education, and govern well. The capital is Trivandrum;

other principal places are Aulapolai and Quilon.

TRAVERSE CITY, a city of Michigan, the county-seat of Grand Traverse co. It is at the mouth of the Boardman river, on Grand Traverse Bay, and on the Pere Marquette, the Grand Rapids and Indiana, the Traverse City, and other railroads. It is an attractive and popular summer resort. It is also the center of an important fruit-growing region, and its industries include the manufacture of baskets, lumber, farm implements, shoes, machine-shop products, etc. It contains the Northern Michigan Insane Asylum. Pop. (1910) 12,115; (1920) 10,925.

TRAVERSE TABLE, in navigation, a table by means of which the difference of latitude and departure corresponding to any given course and distance may be found by inspection. It contains the lengths of the two sides of a right-angled triangle, usually for every quarter of a degree of angle, and for all lengths of the hypotenuse from 1 to 100. In railroading, a platform on which cars are shunted from one track to another of a switch table.

TRAWLING, a mode of fishing in which a net in the form of a large bag, with a strong framework keeping the mouth properly distended, is dragged along the bottom of the sea. It is the mode chiefly adopted in deep-sea fishing, and has largely developed in recent years, being much prosecuted by small steam vessels specially built for the purpose, but it is not ordinarily allowed within three miles of the shore. In Scotland the term trawling is often improperly applied to fishing for herring with the seine.

TREADMILL, a wheel driven by the weight of persons treading on the steps of the periphery; originally an invention of the Chinese to raise water for the irrigation of the fields. It is employed in some prisons, where it forms part of the "hard labor" of persons convicted. The usual form is a wheel 16 feet long and 5 in diameter, several such wheels being coupled together when necessary for the accommodation of the prisoners. The circumference of each has 24 equidistant steps. Each prisoner works in a separate compartment, and has the benefit of a hand rail. The wheel makes two revolutions per minute, which is equivalent to a vertical ascent of 32 feet. The power may be utilized in grinding grain or turning machinery. Its use, as part of the machinery of "hard labor" in prisons, is now greatly restricted, as the weak and strong are by it compelled to equal exertion.

TREASON, HIGH, that crime which is directly committed against the supreme authority of the State, considered to be the greatest crime that can be committed. Formerly in England certain offenses against private superiors were ranked as petit or petty treason, and it was in opposition to such offenses that treason against the sovereign was called high treason; but by an act of George IV. high treason was made the only treason. The present law of treason in England comprehends the following descriptions, namely: (1) Compassing or imagining the king's death. (2) Violation of the king's companion (meaning the queen), his eldest daughter, unmarried, or the wife of the eldest son and heir. (3) Levying war against the king in his realm. (4) Adhering to his enemies in his realm, and giving them aid and comfort in the realm or elsewhere. (5) Counterfeiting the great or privy seal. (6) Slaying the chancellor, treasurer, etc. The third of the offenses detailed in this statute is now treason felony and has a milder punishment than treason annexed to it. Clause 5 is now repealed. The English law condemns the person convicted of treason to be drawn in a hurdle to the place of execution, there to be hanged, and then beheaded and quartered; and a conviction was followed by forfeiture of land and goods and attainder of blood; but this is now restricted to hanging, forfeiture and attainder being abolished. The concealment of treason is called misprison of treason.

In the United States treason consists in levying war by a citizen against the country, or adhering to its enemies. In the session of Congress (1901-1902) several measures were introduced making any attack on the life of the President, Vice-President, or certain other government officials an act of treason, and punishable by death. The provision was also introduced that the offender should be tried by the Federal Courts, thus removing such cares from the jurisdiction of State courts at the place of the occurrence.

TREASURY DEPARTMENT, one of the executive branches of the United States Government; the fiscal branch of the Government. It controls the collection, custody, and disbursement of the public revenue. It is presided over by a secretary, who directs the collection, safe-keeping, and disbursement of the revenue, submits to Congress the estimates of annual expenditures, and of the probable revenue; prepares plans for the improvement and management of the revenue, and for the support of public credit; prescribes the forms of keeping and rendering all public accounts; collects and registers statistics of commercial and manufacturing operations, and in general directs the business of the department, in all of which he has the aid and advice of three assistant secretaries and the assistance of a corps of bureau officers who attend to matters of administrative detail in their respective services. Payments are made on warrants issued by the secretary or an assistant secretary, countersigned by either the first or second comptroller, and registered by the register of the treasury. The office of the Treasurer of the United States is a bureau of the Treasury Department, and is specially charged with the custody of the public money. Other important branches of the Treasury Department are the Bureau of Engraving and Printing, Bureau of the Mint, Office of the Comptroller of the Currency, and the Secret Service Division engaged in the detection and prevention of counterfeiting.

TREATY, specifically, an agreement, contract, or league between two or more nations or sovereigns, formally signed by commissioners, duly accredited, and solemnly ratified by the several sovereigns or supreme authorities of each state. Treaties include all the various transactions into which States enter between themselves, such as treaties of peace, or of alliance, offensive or defensive, truces, conventions, etc. Treaties may be entered into for political or commercial purposes, in which latter form they are usually temporary. The power of entering into and ratifying treaties is vested in monarchies in the sovereign; in republics it is vested in the chief magistrate, senate, or executive council; in the United States it is vested in the President, by and with the consent of the Senate. Treaties may be entered into and signed by the duly authorized diplomatic agents of different States, but such treaties are subject to the approval and ratification of the supreme authorities.

TREATIES OF VERSAILLES AND ST. GERMAIN, SUMMARY. The preamble names as parties of the one part the United States, the British Empire, France, Italy, and Japan, described as the Five Allied and Associated Powers, and Belgium, Bolivia, Brazil, China, Cuba, Ecuador, Greece, Guatemala, Haiti, the Hedjaz, Honduras, Liberia, Nicara-

gua, Panama, Peru, Poland, Portugal, Roumania, Serbia, Siam, Czecho-Slovakia, and Uruguay, who with the five above are described as the allied and associated powers, and on the other part, Germany.

It states that bearing in mind that on the request of the then Imperial German Government an armistice was granted on November 11, 1918, by the principal allied and associated powers in order that a treaty of peace might be concluded with her, and whereas the allied and associated powers, being equally desirous that the war in which they were successively involved directly or indirectly and which originated in the declaration of war by Austria-Hungary on July 28, 1914, against Serbia, the declaration of war by Germany against Russia on Aug. 1, 1914, and against France on Aug. 3, 1914, and in the invasion of Belgium should be replaced by a firm, just, and durable peace, the plenipotentiaries (having communicated their full powers found in good and due form) have agreed as follows:

From the coming into force of the present treaty the state of war will terminate. From the moment and subject to the provisions of this treaty, official relations with Germany, and with each of the German States, will be resumed by the allied and associated Powers.

SECTION I
LEAGUE OF NATIONS

The covenant of the League of Nations constitutes Section I of the peace treaty, which places upon the League many specific, in addition to its general, duties. It may question Germany at any time for a violation of a neutralized zone east of the Rhine as a threat against the world's peace. It will appoint three of the five members of the Sarre Commission, oversee its régime, and carry out the plebiscite. It will appoint the High Commissioner of Danzig, guarantee the independence of the free city, and arrange for treaties between Danzig and Germany and Poland. It will work out the mandatory system to be applied to the former German colonies, and act as a final court in part of the plebiscites of the Belgian-German frontier, and in disputes as to the Kiel Canal, and decide certain of the economic and financial problems. An International Conference on Labor is to be held in October under its direction, and another on the international control of ports, waterways, and railways is foreshadowed.

MEMBERSHIP

The members of the League will be the signatories of the covenant and other

States invited to accede who must lodge a declaration of accession without reservation within two months. A new State, dominion, or colony may be admitted, provided its admission is agreed to by two-thirds of the assembly. A State may withdraw upon giving two years' notice, if it has fulfilled all its international obligations.

SECRETARIAT

A permanent secretariat will be established at the seat of the League, which will be at Geneva.

ASSEMBLY

The Assembly will consist of representatives of the members of the League and will meet at stated intervals. Voting will be by States. Each member will have one vote and not more than three representatives.

COUNCIL

The Council will consist of representatives of the Five Great Allied Powers, together with representatives of four members selected by the Assembly from time to time; it may co-opt additional States and will meet at least once a year.

Members not represented will be invited to send a representative when questions affecting their interests are discussed. Voting will be by States. Each State will have one vote and not more than one representative. A decision taken by the Assembly and Council must be unanimous except in regard to procedure, and in certain cases specified in the covenant and in the treaty, where decisions will be by a majority.

ARMAMENTS

The Council will formulate plans for a reduction of armaments for consideration and adoption. These plans will be revised every ten years. Once they are adopted, no member must exceed the armaments fixed without the concurrence of the Council. All members will exchange full information as to armaments and programs, and a permanent commission will advise the Council on military and naval questions.

PREVENTING OF WAR

Upon any war, or threat of war, the Council will meet to consider what common action shall be taken. Members are pledged to submit matters of dispute to arbitration or inquiry and not to resort to war until three months after the award. Members agree to carry out in arbitral award and not to go to war with any party to the dispute which complies with it. If a member fails to carry out the award, the Council will propose the necessary measures. The Council will formulate plans for the es-

tablishment of a permanent court of international justice to determine international disputes or to give advisory opinions. Members who do not submit their case to arbitration must accept the jurisdiction of the Assembly. If the Council, less the parties to the dispute, is unanimously agreed upon the rights of it, the members agree that they will not go to war with any party to the dispute which complies with its recommendations. In this case, a recommendation, by the Assembly, concurred in by all its members represented on the Council and a simple majority of the rest, less the parties to the dispute, will have the force of a unanimous recommendation by the Council. In either case, if the necessary agreement cannot be secured, the members reserve the right to take such action as may be necessary for the maintenance of right and justice. Members resorting to war in disregard of the covenant will immediately be debarred from all intercourse with other members. The Council will in such cases consider what military or naval action can be taken by the League collectively for the protection of the covenants and will afford facilities to members co-operating in this enterprise.

VALIDITY OF TREATIES

All treaties or international engagements concluded after the institution of the League will be registered with the secretariat and published. The Assembly may from time to time advise members to reconsider treaties which have become inapplicable to involve danger to peace.

The covenant abrogates all obligations between members inconsistent with its terms, but nothing in it shall affect the validity of international engagements such as treaties of arbitration or regional understandngs like the Monroe Doctrine for securing the maintenance of peace.

THE MANDATORY SYSTEM

The tutelage of nations not yet able to stand by themselves will be intrusted to advanced nations who are best fitted to undertake it. The covenant recognizes three different stages of development requiring different kinds of mandatories:

(a) Communities like those belonging to the Turkish Empire, which can be provisionally recognized as independent, subject to advice and assistance from mandatory in whose selection they would be allowed a voice.

(b) Communities like those of Central Africa, to be administered by the mandatary under conditions generally approved by the members of the League, where equal opportunities for trade will be allowed to all members; certain abuses, such as trade in slaves, arms, and liquor will be prohibited, and the construction of military and naval bases and the introduction of compulsory military training will be disallowed.

(c) Other communities, such as Southwest Africa and the South Pacific Islands, but administered under the laws of the mandatary as integral portions of its territory. In every case the mandatary will render an annual report, and the degree of its authority will be defined.

GENERAL INTERNATIONAL PROVISIONS

Subject to and in accordance with the provisions of international convention, existing or hereafter to be agreed upon, the members of the League will in general endeavor, through the international organization established by the Labor Convention, to secure and maintain fair conditions of labor for men, women and children in their own countries and other countries, and undertake to secure just treatment of the native inhabitants of territories under their control; they will entrust the League with the general supervision over the execution of agreements for the suppression of traffic in women and children, &c.; and the control of the trade in arms and ammuntion with countries in which control is necessary; they will make provision for freedom of communication and transit and equitable treatment for commerce of all members of the League, with special reference to the necessities of regions devastated during the war; and they will endeavor to take steps for international prevention and control of disease. International bureaus and commissions already established will be placed under the League, as well as those to be established in the future.

AMENDMENTS TO THE COVENANT

Amendments to the covenant will take effect when ratified by the Council and by a majority of the Assembly.

SECTION II
BOUNDARIES OF GERMANY

Germany cedes to France Alsace-Lorraine, 5,600 square miles to the southwest, and to Belgium two small districts between Luxemburg and Holland, totaling 382 square miles. She also cedes to Poland the southeastern tip of Silesia beyond and including Oppeln, most of Posen, and West Prussia, 27,686 square miles, East Prussia being isolated from the main body by a part of Poland. She loses sovereignty over the northeastern tip of East Prussia, 40 square miles

north of the river Memel, and the internationalized areas about Danzig, 729 square miles, and the Basin of the Sarre, 738 square miles, between the western border of the Rhenish Palatinate of Bavaria and the southeast corner of Luxemburg. The Danzig area consists of the V between the Nogat and Vistula Rivers made a W by the addition of a similar V on the west, including the city of Danzig. The southeastern third of East Prussia and the area between East Prussia and the Vistula north of latitude 53 degrees 3 minutes is to have its nationality determined by popular vote, 5,785 square miles, as is to be the case in part of Schleswig, 2,787 square miles.

SECTION III
BELGIUM

Germany is to consent to the abrogation of the treaties of 1839, by which Belgium was established as a neutral State, and to agree in advance to any convention with which the allied and associated Powers may determine to replace them. She is to recognize the full sovereignty of Belgium over the contested territory of Moresnet and over part of Prussian Moresnet, and to renounce in favor of Belgium all rights over the circles of Eupen and Malmedy, the inhabitants of which are to be entitled within six months to protest against this change of sovereignty either in whole or in part, the final decision to be reserved to the League of Nations. A commission is to settle the details of the frontier, and various regulations for change of nationality are laid down.

LUXEMBURG

Germany renounces her various treaties and conventions with the Grand Duchy of Luxemburg, recognizes that it ceased to be a part of the German Zollverein from January first, last, renounces all right of exploitation of the railroads, adheres to the abrogation of its neutrality, and accepts in advance any international agreement as to it reached by the allied and associated powers.

LEFT BANK OF THE RHINE

As provided in the military clauses, Germany will not maintain any fortifications or armed forces less than fifty kilometers to the east of the Rhine, hold any manœuvres, nor maintain any works to facilitate mobilization. In case of violation, "she shall be regarded as committing a hostile act against the Powers who sign the present treaty and as intending to disturb the peace of the world." "By virtue of the present treaty, Germany shall be bound to respond to any request for an explanation which the

Council of the League of Nations may think it necessary to address to her."

ALSACE-LORRAINE

After recognition of the moral obligation to repair the wrong done in 1871 by Germany to France and the people of Alsace-Lorraine, the territories ceded to Germany by the Treaty of Frankfort are restored to France with their frontiers as before 1871, to date from the signing of the armistice, and to be free of all public debts.

Citizenship is regulated by detailed provisions distinguishing those who are immediately restored to full French citizenship, those who have to make formal applications therefor, and those for whom naturalization is open after three years. The last-named class includes German residents in Alsace-Lorraine, as distinguished from those who acquired the position of Alsace-Lorrainers as defined in the treaty. All public property and all private property of German ex-sovereigns passes to France without payment or credit. France is substituted for Germany as regards ownership of the railroads and rights over concessions of tramways. The Rhine bridges pass to France with the obligation for their upkeep.

For five years manufactured products of Alsace-Lorraine will be admitted to Germany free of duty to a total amount not exceeding in any year the average of the three years preceding the war, and textile materials may be imported from Germany to Alsace-Lorraine and re-exported free of duty. Contracts for electric power from the right bank must be continued for ten years. For seven years, with possible extension to ten, the ports of Kehl and Strassbourg shall be administered as a single unit by a French administrator appointed and supervised by the Central Rhine Commission. Property rights will be safeguarded in both ports and equality of treatment as respects traffic assured the nationals, vessels, and goods of every country.

Contracts between Alsace-Lorraine and Germany are maintained save for France's right to annul on grounds of public interest. Judgments of courts hold in certain classes of cases, while in others a judicial exequatur is first required. Political condemnations during the war are null and void and the obligation to repay war fines is established as in other parts of allied territory.

Various clauses adjust the general provisions of the treaty to the special conditions of Alsace-Lorraine, certain matters of execution being left to conventions to be made between France and Germany.

THE SARRE

In compensation for the destruction of coal mines in northern France and as payment on account of reparation, Germany cedes to France full ownership of the coal mines of the Sarre Basin with their subsidiaries, accessories and facilities. Their value will be estimated by the Reparations Commission and credited against that account. The French rights will be governed by German law in force at the armistice, excepting war legislation, France replacing the present owners, whom Germany undertakes to indemnify. France will continue to furnish present proportion of coal for local needs and contribute in just proportion to local taxes. The basin extends from the frontier of Lorraine as re-annexed to France N. as far as St. Wendel, including on the W. the valley of the Sarre as far as Sarre Holzbach, and on the E. the town of Homburg.

In order to secure the rights and welfare of the population and guarantee to France entire freedom in working the mines, the territory will be governed by a commission appointed by the League of Nations and consisting of five members, one French, one a native inhabitant of the Sarre, and three representing three different countries other than France and Germany. The League will appoint a member of the Commission as Chairman to act as executive of the Commission. The Commission will have all powers of government formerly belonging to the German empire, Prussia, and Bavaria, will administer the railroads and other public services, and have full power to interpret the treaty clauses. The local courts will continue, but subject to the Commission. Existing German legislation will remain the basis of the law, but the Commission may make modification after consulting a local representative assembly which it will organize. It will have the taxing power but for local purposes only. New taxes must be approved by this assembly. Labor legislation will consider the wishes of the local labor organizations and the labor program of the League. French and other labor may be freely utilized, the former being free to belong to French unions. All rights acquired as to pensions and social insurance will be maintained by Germany and the Sarre Commission.

There will be no military service, but only a local gendarmerie to preserve order. The people will preserve their local assemblies, religious liberties, schools, and language, but may vote only for local assemblies. They will keep their present nationality except so far as individuals may change it. Those wishing to leave will have every facility with respect to their property. The territory will form part of the French customs system, with no export tax on coal and metallurgical products going to Germany, nor on German products entering the basin and for five years no import duties on products of the basin going to Germany or German products coming into the basin. For local consumption French money may circulate without restriction.

After fifteen years a plebiscite will be held by communes to ascertain the desires of the population as to continuance of the existing régime under the League of Nations, union with France or union with Germany. The right to vote will belong to all inhabitants over twenty resident therein at the signature. Taking into account the opinions thus expressed, the League will decide the ultimate sovereignty. In any portion restored to Germany the German Government must buy out the French mines at an appraised valuation. If the price is not paid within six months thereafter, this portion passes finally to France. If Germany buys back the mines the League will determine how much of the coal shall be annually sold to France.

SECTION IV.

GERMAN AUSTRIA

Germany recognizes the total independence of German Austria in the boundaries traced.

CZECHO-SLOVAKIA

Germany recognizes the entire independence of the Czecho-Slovak state, including the autonomous territory of the Ruthenians S. of the Carpathians, and accepts the frontiers of this state as to be determined, which in the case of the German frontier shall follow the frontier of Bohemia in 1914. The usual stipulations as to acquisitions and change of nationality follow.

POLAND

Germany cedes to Poland the greater part of Upper Silesia, Posen and the province of West Prussia on the left bank of the Vistula. A Field Boundary Commission of seven, five representing the allied and associated powers and one each representing Poland and Germany, shall be constituted within fifteen days of the peace to delimit this boundary. Such special provisions as are necessary to protect racial, linguistic or religious minorities and to protect freedom of transit and equitable treatment of commerce of other nations shall be laid down in a subsequent treaty between the principal allied and associated powers and Poland.

EAST PRUSSIA

The southern and eastern frontier of East Prussia as touching Poland is to be fixed by plebiscites, the first in the regency of Allenstein between the southern frontier of East Prussia and the northern frontier, or Regierungsbezirk Allenstein, from where it meets the boundary between East and West Prussia to its junction with the boundary between the circles of Oletsko and Angersburg, thence the northern boundary of Oletsko to its junction with the present frontier, and the second in the area comprising the circles of Stuhm and Rosenberg and the parts of the circles of Marienburg and Marienwerder E. of the Vistula.

In each case German troops and authorities will move out within fifteen days of the peace, and the territories be placed under an international commission of five members appointed by the principal allied and associated powers, with the particular duty of arranging for a free, fair and secret vote. The commission will report the results of the plebiscites to the powers with a recommendation for the boundary, and will terminate its work as soon as the boundary has been laid down and the new authorities set up.

The principal allied and associated powers will draw up regulations assuring East Prussia full and equitable access to and use of the Vistula. A subsequent convention, of which the terms will be fixed by the principal allied and associated powers, will be entered into between Poland, Germany and Danzig, to assure suitable railroad communication across German territory on the right bank of the Vistula between Poland and Danzig, while Poland shall grant free passage from East Prussia to Germany.

The northeastern corner of East Prussia about Memel is to be ceded by Germany to the associated powers, the former agreeing to accept the settlement made, especially as regards the nationality of the inhabitants.

DANZIG

Danzig and the district immediately about it is to be constituted into the "free city of Danzig" under the guarantee of the League of Nations. A high commissioner appointed by the League and President of Danzig shall draw up a constitution in agreement with the duly appointed representatives of the city, and shall deal in the first instance with all differences arising between the city and Poland. The actual boundaries of the city shall be delimited by a commission appointed within six months from the peace and to include three representatives chosen by the allied and associated powers, and one each by Germany and Poland.

A convention, the terms of which shall be fixed by the principal allied and associated powers, shall be concluded between Poland and Danzig, which shall include Danzig within the Polish customs frontiers, though a free area in the port; insure to Poland the free use of all the city's waterways, docks and other port facilities, the control and administration of the Vistula and the whole through railway system within the city, and postal, telegraphic and telephonic communication between Poland and Danzig; provide against discrimination against Poles within the city, and place its foreign relations and the diplomatic protection of its citizens abroad in charge of Poland.

DENMARK

The frontier between Germany and Denmark will be fixed by the self-determination of the population. Ten days from the peace German troops and authorities shall evacuate the region N. of the line running from the mouth of the Schlei, S. of Kappel, Schleswig, and Friedrichstadt along the Eider to the North Sea S. of Tonning; the Workmen's and Soldiers' Councils shall be dissolved, and the territory administered by an international commission of five, of whom Norway and Sweden shall be invited to name two.

The commission shall insure a free and secret vote in three zones. That between the German-Danish frontier and a line running S. of the Island of Alsen, N. of Flensburg, and S. of Tondern to the North Sea, N. of the Island of Sylt, will vote as a unit within three weeks after the evacuation. Within five weeks after this vote the second zone, whose boundary runs from the North sea S. of the Island of Fehr to the Baltic S. of Sygum, will vote by communes. Two weeks after that vote the third zone, running to the limit of evacuation, will also vote by communes. The international commission will then draw a new frontier on the basis of these plebiscites and with due regard for geographical and economic conditions. Germany will renounce all sovereignty over territories N. of this line in favor of the associated governments, who will hand them over to Denmark.

HELIGOLAND

The fortifications, military establishments, and harbors of the Islands of Heligoland and Dune are to be destroyed under the supervision of the Allies by German labor and at Germany's expense. They may not be reconstructed, nor any similar fortifications built in the future.

RUSSIA

Germany agrees to respect as permanent and inalienable the independency of all territories which were part of the former Russian empire, to accept the abrogation of the Brest-Litovsk and other treaties entered into with the Maximalist government of Russia, to recognize the full force of all treaties entered into by the allied and associated powers with states which were a part of the former Russian empire, and to recognize the frontiers as determined thereon. The allied and associated powers formally reserve the right of Russia to obtain restitution and reparation on the principles of the present treaty.

SECTION V.

GERMAN RIGHTS OUTSIDE EUROPE

Outside Europe, Germany renounces all rights, titles, and privileges as to her own or her allies' territories to all the allied and associated powers, and undertakes to accept whatever measures are taken by the five allied powers in relation thereto.

COLONIES AND OVERSEAS POSSESSIONS

Germany renounces in favor of the allied and associated powers her overseas possessions with all rights and titles therein. All movable and immovable property belonging to the German empire, or to any German state, shall pass to the government exercising authority therein. These governments may make whatever provisions seem suitable for the repatriation of German nationals and as to the conditions on which German subjects of European origin shall reside, hold property, or carry on business. Germany undertakes to pay reparation for damage suffered by French nationals in the Cameroons or its frontier zone through the acts of German civil and military authorities and of individual Germans from the 1st of Jan., 1900, to the 1st of August, 1914. Germany renounces all rights under the convention of the 4th of Nov., 1911, and the 29th of Sept., 1912, and undertakes to pay to France in accordance with an estimate presented and approved by the Repatriation Commission all deposits, credits, advances, etc., thereby secured. Germany undertakes to accept and observe any provisions by the allied and associated powers as to the trade in arms and spirits in Africa as well as to the General Act of Berlin of 1885 and the General Act of Brussels of 1890. Diplomatic protection to inhabitants of former German colonies is to be given by the governments exercising authority.

CHINA

Germany renounces in favor of China all privileges and indemnities resulting from the Boxer Protocol of 1901, and all buildings, wharves, barracks for munitions of warships, wireless plants, and other public property except diplomatic or consular establishments in the German concessions of Tientsin and Hankow and in other Chinese territory except Kiao-Chau, and agrees to return to China at her own expense all the astronomical instruments seized in 1900 and 1901. China will, however, take no measures for disposal of German property in the legation quarter at Peking without the consent of the Powers signatory to the Boxer Protocol.

Germany accepts the abrogation of the concessions at Hankow and Tientsin, China agreeing to open them to international use. Germany renounces all claims against China or any allied and associated government or the internment or repatriation of her citizens in China and for the seizure or liquidation of German interests there since Aug. 14, 1917. She renounces in favor of Great Britain her state property in the British concession at Canton, and of France and China jointly of the property of the German school in the French concession at Shanghai.

SIAM

Germany recognizes that all agreements between herself and Siam, including the right of extraterritoriality, ceased July 22, 1917. All German public property, except consular and diplomatic premises, passes without compensation to Siam, German private property to be dealt with in accordance with the economic clauses. Germany waives all claims against Siam for the seizure and condemnation of her ships, liquidation of her property, or internment of her nationals.

LIBERIA

Germany renounces all rights under the international arrangements of 1911 and 1912 regarding Liberia, more particularly the right to nominate a receiver of the customs, and disinterests herself in any further negotiations for the rehabilitation of Liberia. She regards as abrogated all commercial treaties and agreements between herself and Liberia and recognizes Liberia's right to determine the status and condition of the re-establishment of Germans in Liberia.

MOROCCO

Germany renounces all her rights, titles, and privileges under the Act of Algeciras and the Franco-German agreements of 1909 and 1911, and under all treaties and arrangements with the Sherifian empire. She undertakes not to intervene in any negotiations as to Morocco between France and other powers, accepts all the consequences of the French protectorate, and renounces the capitulations; the Sherifian government shall have complete liberty of action in regard to German nationals, and all German protected persons shall be subject to the common law. All movable and immovable German property, including mining rights, may be sold at public auction, the proceeds to be paid to the Sherifian government and deducted from the reparation account. Germany is also required to relinquish her interests in the State Bank of Morocco. All Moroccan goods entering Germany shall have the same privilege as French goods.

EGYPT

Germany recognizes the British Protectorate over Egypt declared on Dec. 18, 1914, and renounces as from Aug. 4, 1914, the capitulation and all the treaties, agreements, &c., concluded by her with Egypt. She undertakes not to intervene in any negotiations about Egypt between Great Britain and other powers. There are provisions for jurisdiction over German nationals and property and for German consent to any changes which may be made in relation to the Commission of Public Debt. Germany consents to the transfer to Great Britain of the powers given to the late Sultan of Turkey for securing the free navigation of the Suez Canal. Arrangements for property belonging to German nationals in Egypt are made similar to those in the case of Morocco and other countries. Anglo-Egyptian goods entering Germany shall enjoy the same treatment as British goods.

TURKEY AND BULGARIA

Germany accepts all arrangements which the allied and associated powers made with Turkey and Bulgaria with reference to any rights, privileges or interests claimed in those countries by Germany or her nationals and not dealt with elsewhere.

SHANTUNG

Germany cedes to Japan all rights, titles, and privileges, notably as to Kiao-Chau, and the railroads, mines and cables acquired by her treaty with China of March 6, 1897, by and other agreements as to Shantung. All German rights to the railroad from Tsing-tao to Tsinanfu, including all facilities and mining rights and rights of exploitation, pass equally to Japan, and the cables from Tsing-tao to Shanghai and Che-foo, the cables free of all charges. All German state property, movable and immovable, in Kiao-Chau is acquired by Japan free of all charges.

SECTION VI.

MILITARY, NAVAL AND AIR

In order to render possible the initiation of a general limitation of the armaments of all nations, Germany undertakes directly to observe the military, naval, and air clauses which follow.

MILITARY FORCES

The demobilization of the German army must take place within two months of the peace. Its strength may not exceed 100,000, including 4,000 officers, with not over seven divisions of infantry and three of cavalry, and to be devoted exclusively to maintenance of internal order and control of frontiers. Divisions may not be grouped under more than two army corps headquarters staffs. The great German General Staff is abolished. The army administrative service, consisting of civilian personnel not included in the number of effectives, is reduced to one-tenth the total in the 1913 budget. Employees of the German states, such as customs officers, first guards, and coast guards, may not exceed the number in 1913. Gendarmes and local police may be increased only in accordance with the growth of population. None of these may be assembled for military training.

ARMAMENTS

All establishments for the manufacturing, preparation, storage, or design of arms and munitions of war, except those specifically excepted, must be closed within three months of the peace, and their personnel dismissed. The exact amount of armament and munitions allowed Germany is laid down in detail tables, all in excess to be surrendered or rendered useless. The manufacture or importation of asphyxiating, poisonous, or other gases and all analogous liquids is forbidden, as well as the importation of arms, munitions, and war materials. Germany may not manufacture such materials for foreign governments.

CONSCRIPTION

Conscription is abolished in Germany. The enlisted personnel must be maintained by voluntary enlistments for terms of twelve consecutive years, the number of discharges before the expiration of that term not in any year to exceed 5 per cent. of the total effectives. Officers remaining in the service must agree to serve to the age of 45 years, and newly appointed officers must agree to serve actively for 25 years.

No military schools except those absolutely indispensable for the units allowed shall exist in Germany two months after the peace. No associations such as societies of discharged soldiers, shooting or touring clubs, educational establishments or universities may occupy themselves with military matters. All measures of mobilization are forbidden.

FORTRESSES

All fortified works, fortresses, and field works situated in German territory within a zone of fifty kilometers E. of the Rhine will be dismantled within three months. The construction of any new fortifications there is forbidden. The fortified works on the southern and eastern frontiers, however, may remain.

CONTROL

Interallied commissions of control will see to the execution of the provisions for which a time limit is set, the maximum named being three months. They may establish headquarters at the German seat of government and go to any part of Germany desired. Germany must give them complete facilities, pay their expenses, and also the expenses of execution of the treaty, including the labor and material necessary in demolition, destruction, or surrender of war equipment.

NAVAL

The German navy must be demobilized within a period of two months after the peace. She will be allowed 6 small battleships, 6 light cruisers, 12 destroyers, 12 torpedo boats, and no submarines, either military or commercial, with a personnel of 15,000 men, including officers, and no reserve force of any character. Conscription is abolished, only voluntary service being permitted, with a minimum period of 25 years' service for officers and 12 for men. No member of the German mercantile marine will be permitted any naval training.

All German vessels of war in foreign ports and the German high sea fleet interned at Scapa Flow will be surrendered, the final disposition of these ships to be decided upon by the allied and associated powers. Germany must surrender 42 modern destroyers, 50 modern torpedo boats, and all submarines, with their salvage vessels. All war vessels under construction, including submarines, must be broken up. War vessels not otherwise provided for are to be placed in reserve or used for commercial purposes. Replacement of ships, except those lost, can take place only at the end of 20 years for battleships and 15 years for destroyers. The largest armored ship Germany will be permitted will be 10,000 tons.

Germany is required to sweep up the mines in the North Sea and the Baltic Sea, as decided upon by the allies. All

German fortifications in the Baltic, defending the passages through the belts, must be demolished. Other coast defenses are permitted, but the number and caliber of the guns must not be increased.

WIRELESS

During a period of three months after the peace German high power wireless stations at Nauen, Hanover, and Berlin will not be permitted to send any messages except for commercial purposes, and under supervision of the allied and associated governments, nor may any more be constructed.

CABLES

Germany renounces all title to specified cables, the value of such as were privately owned being credited to her against reparation indebtedness.

Germany will be allowed to repair German submarine cables which have been cut but are not being utilized by the allied powers, and also portions of cables which, after having been cut, have been removed, or are at any rate not being utilized by any one of the allied and associated powers. In such cases the cables, or portions of cables, removed or utilized, remain the property of the allied and associated powers, and accordingly fourteen cables or parts of cables are specified which will not be restored to Germany.

AIR

The armed forces of Germany must not include any military or naval air forces, except for not over 100 unarmed seaplanes to be retained till Oct. 1 to search for submarine mines. No dirigible shall be kept. The entire air personnel is to be demobilized within two months, except for 1,000 officers and men retained till October. No aviation grounds or dirigible sheds are to be allowed within 150 kilometers of the Rhine, or the eastern or southern frontiers, existing installations within these limits to be destroyed. The manufacture of aircraft and parts of aircraft is forbidden for six months. All military and naval aeronautical material under a most exhaustive definition must be surrendered within three months, except for the 100 seaplanes already specified.

PRISONERS OF WAR

The repatriation of German prisoners and interned civilians is to be carried out without delay and at Germany's expense by a commission composed of representatives of the allies and Germany. Those under sentence for offenses against discipline are to be repatriated without regard to the completion of their sentences. Until Germany has surrendered persons guilty of offenses against the laws and customs of war, the allies have the right to retain selected German officers. The allies may deal at their own discretion with German nationals who do not desire to be repatriated, all repatriation being conditional on the immediate release of any allied subjects still in Germany. Germany is to accord facilities to commissions of inquiry in collecting information in regard to missing prisoners of war and of imposing penalties on German officials who have concealed allied nationals. Germany is to restore all property belonging to allied prisoners. There is to be a reciprocal exchange of information as to dead prisoners and their graves.

GRAVES

Both parties will respect and maintain the graves of soldiers and sailors buried on their territories, agree to recognize and assist any commission charged by any allied or associate government with identifying, registering, maintaining or erecting suitable monuments over the graves, and to afford to each other all facilities for the repatriation of the remains of their soldiers.

SECTION VII.

RESPONSIBILITIES

The allied and associated powers publicly arraign William II. of Hohenzollern, formerly German emperor, not for an offense against criminal law, but for a supreme offense against international morality and the sanctity of treaties.

The ex-emperor's surrender is to be requested of Holland and a special tribunal set up, composed of one judge from each of the five great powers, with full guarantees of the right of defense. It is to be guided "by the highest motives of international policy with a view of vindicating the solemn obligations of international undertakings and the validity of international morality," and will fix the punishment it feels should be imposed.

Persons accused of having committed acts in violation of the laws and customs of war are to be tried and punished by military tribunals under military law. If the charges affect nationals of only one state, they will be tried before a tribunal of that state; if they affect nationals of several states, they will be tried before joint tribunals of the states concerned. Germany shall hand over to the associated governments, either jointly or severally, all persons so accused and all documents and information necessary to insure full knowledge of the incriminating acts, the discovery of the offenders, and the just appreciation of the responsibility.

In every case the accused will be entitled to name his own counsel.

SECTION VIII.

REPARATION AND RESTITUTION

"The allied and associated governments affirm, and Germany accepts, the responsibility of herself and her allies for causing all the loss and damage to which the allied and associated governments and their nationals have been subjected as a consequence of the war imposed upon them by the aggression of Germany and her allies."

The total obligation of Germany to pay as defined in the category of damages is to be determined and notified to her after a fair hearing, and not later than May 1, 1921, by an interallied Reparation Commission.

At the same time a schedule of payments to discharge the obligations within thirty years shall be presented. These payments are subject to postponement in certain contingencies. Germany irrevocably recognizes the full authority of this commission, agrees to supply it with all the necessary information and to pass legislation to effectuate its findings. She further agrees to restore to the allies cash and certain articles which can be identified.

As an immediate step toward restoration Germany shall pay within two years one thousand million pounds sterling in either gold, goods, ships, or other specific forms of payment.

This sum being included in, and not additional to, the first thousand million bond issue referred to below, with the understanding that certain expenses, such as those of the armies of occupation and payments for food and raw materials, may be deducted at the discretion of the allies.

Germany further binds herself to repay all sums borrowed by Belgium from her allies as a result of Germany's violation of the treaty of 1839 up to Nov. 11, 1918, and for this purpose will issue at once and hand over to the Reparations Commission 5 per cent. gold bonds falling due in 1926.

While the allied and associated governments recognize that the resources of Germany are not adequate, after taking into account permanent diminution of such resources which will result from other treaty claims, to make complete reparation for all such loss and damage, they require her to make compensation for all damage caused to civilians under seven main categories:

(a) Damages by personal injury to civilians caused by acts of war, directly

or indirectly, including bombardments from the air.

(b) Damages caused to civilians, including exposure at sea, resulting from acts of cruelty ordered by the enemy, and to civilians in the occupied territories.

(c) Damages caused by maltreatment of prisoners.

(d) Damages to the allied peoples represented by pensions and separation allowances, capitalized at the signature of this treaty.

(e) Damages to property other than naval or military materials.

(f) Damages to civilians by being forced to labor.

(g) Damages in the form of levies or fines imposed by the enemy.

In periodically estimating Germany's capacity to pay, the Reparations Commission shall examine the German system of taxation, first to the end that the sums for reparation which Germany is required to pay shall become a charge upon all her revenues prior to that for the service or discharge of any domestic loan; and, secondly, so as to satisfy itself that in general the German scheme of taxation is fully as heavy proportionately as that of any of the powers represented on the commission.

The measures which the allied and associated powers shall have the right to take, in case of voluntary default by Germany, and which Germany agrees not to regard as acts of war, may include economic and financial prohibitions and reprisals and in general such other measures as the respective governments may determine to be necessary in the circumstances.

The commission shall consist of one representative each of the United States, Great Britain, France, Italy, and Belgium, a representative of Serbia or Japan taking the place of the Belgian representative when the interests of either country are particularly affected, with all other allied powers entitled, when their claims are under consideration, to the right of representation without voting power. It shall permit Germany to give evidence regarding her capacity to pay, and shall assure her a just opportunity to be heard. It shall make its permanent headquarters at Paris, establish its own procedure and personnel; have general control of the whole reparation problem; and become the exclusive agency of the allies for receiving, holding, selling, and distributing reparation payments. Majority vote shall prevail, except that unanimity is required on questions involving the sovereignty of any of the allies, the cancellation of all or part of Germany's obligations, the time and manner of selling, distributing, and negotiating bonds issued by Germany, any postponement between 1921 and 1926 of annual payments beyond 1930, and any postponement after 1926 for a period of more than three years of the application of a different method of measuring damage than in a similar former case, and the interpretation of provisions. Withdrawal from representation is permitted on twelve months' notice.

The commission may require Germany to give from time to time, by way of guarantee, issues of bonds or other obligations to cover such claims as are not otherwise satisfied. In this connection and on account of the total amount of claims bond issues are presently to be required of Germany in acknowledgment of its debt as follows: 20,000,000,000 marks gold, payable not later than May 1, 1921, without interest; 40,000,000,000 marks gold bearing 2½ per cent. interest between 1921 and 1926, and thereafter 5 per cent., with a 1 per cent. sinking fund payment beginning 1926; and an undertaking to deliver 40,000,000,000 marks gold bonds bearing interest at 5 per cent., under terms to be fixed by the commission.

Interest on Germany's debt will be 5 per cent. unless otherwise determined by the commission in the future, and payments that are not made in gold may "be accepted by the commission in the form of properties, commodities, businesses, rights, concessions, &c." Certificates of beneficial interest, representing either bonds or goods delivered by Germany, may be issued by the commission to the interested powers, no power being entitled, however, to have its certificates divided into more than five pieces. As bonds are distributed and pass from the control of the commission, an amount of Germany's debt equivalent to their par value is to be considered as liquidated.

SHIPPING

The German government recognizes the right of the allies to the replacement, ton for ton and class for class, of all merchant ships and fishing boats lost or damaged owing to the war, and agrees to cede to the allies all German merchant ships of 1,600 tons gross and upward; one-half of her ships between 1,600 and 1,000 tons gross, and one-quarter of her steam trawlers and other fishing boats. These ships are to be delivered within two months to the Reparations Committee, together with documents of title evidencing the transfer of the ships free from encumbrance.

"As an additional part of reparation," the German government further agrees to build merchant ships for the account of the allies to the amount of not exceeding 200,000 tons gross annually during the next five years.

All ships used for inland navigation taken by Germany from the allies are to be restored within two months, the amount of loss not covered by such restitution to be made up by the cession of the German river fleet up to 20 per cent. thereof.

DYESTUFFS AND CHEMICAL DRUGS

In order to effect payment by deliveries in kind, Germany is required, for a limited number of years, varying in the case of each, to deliver coal, coal-tar products, dyestuffs and chemical drugs, in specific amounts, to the Reparations Commission. The commission may so modify the conditions of delivery as not to interfere unduly with Germany's industrial requirements. The deliveries of coal are based largely upon the principle of making good diminutions in the production of the allied countries resulting from the war.

Germany accords option to the commission on dyestuffs and chemical drugs, including quinine, up to 50 per cent. of the total stock in Germany at the time the treaty comes into force, and similar option during each six months to the end of 1924 up to 25 per cent. of the previous six months' output.

DEVASTATED AREAS

Germany undertakes to devote her economic resources directly to the physical restoration of the invaded areas. The Reparations Commission is authorized to require Germany to replace the destroyed articles by the delivery of animals, machinery, etc., existing in Germany, and to manufacture materials required for reconstruction purposes; all with due consideration for Germany's essential domestic requirements.

Germany is to deliver annually for ten years to France coal equivalent to the difference between the annual pre-war output of Nord and Pas de Calais mines and the annual production during the above ten-year period. Germany further gives options over ten years for delivery of 7,000,000 tons of coal per year to France, in addition to the above; of 8,000,000 tons to Belgium, and of an amount rising from 4,500,000 tons in 1919 to 1920 to 8,500,000 in 1923 to 1924 to Italy at prices to be fixed as prescribed in the treaty. Coke may be taken in place of coal in the ratio of three tons to four. Provision is also made for delivery to France over three years of benzol, coal tar, and of ammonia. The commission has powers to postpone or annul the above deliveries, should they interfere unduly with the industrial requirements of Germany.

Germany is to restore within six months the Koran of the Caliph Othman, formerly at Medina, to the king of the Hedjaz, and the skull of the Sultan Okwawa, formerly in German East Africa, to his Britannic Majesty's government.

The German government is also to restore to the French government certain papers taken by the German authorities in 1870, belonging then to M. Reuher, and to restore the French flags taken during the war of 1870 and 1871.

As reparation for the destruction of the Library of Louvain, Germany is to hand over manuscripts, early printed books, prints, &c., to the equivalent of those destroyed.

In addition to the above, Germany is to hand over to Belgium wings, now in Berlin, belonging to the altar piece of "The Adoration of the Lamb," by Hubert and Jan van Eyck, the center of which is now in the Church of St. Bavon at Ghent, and the wings, now in Berlin and Munich, of the altar piece of "The Last Supper," by Dirk Bouts, the center of which belongs to the Church of St. Peter at Louvain.

FINANCE

Powers to which German territory is ceded will assume a certain portion of the German pre-war debt, the amount to be fixed by the Reparations Commission on the basis of the ratio between the revenue and of the ceded territory and Germany's total revenues for the three years preceding the war. In view, however, of the special circumstances under which Alsace-Lorraine was separated from France in 1871, when Germany refused to accept any part of the French public debt, France will not assume any part of Germany's pre-war debt there, nor will Poland share in certain German debts incurred for the oppression of Poland. If the value of the German public property in ceded territory exceeds the amount of debt assumed, the states to which property is ceded will give credit on reparation for the excess, with the exception of Alsace-Lorraine. Mandatory powers will not assume any German debts or give any credit for German government property. Germany renounces all right of representation on, or control of, state banks, commissions, or other similar international financial and economic organizations.

Germany is required to pay the total cost of the armies of occupation from the date of the armistice as long as they are maintained in German territory, this cost to be a first charge on her resources. The cost of reparation is the next charge, after making such provisions for payments for imports as the allies may deem necessary.

Germany is to deliver to the allied and associated powers all sums deposited in Germany by Turkey and Austria-Hungary in connection with the financial support extended by her to them during the war, and to transfer to the allies all claims against Austria-Hungary, Bulgaria, or Turkey in connection with agreements made during the war. Germany confirms the renunciation of the treaties of Bucharest and Brest-Litovsk.

On the request of the Reparations Commission, Germany will expropriate any rights or interests of her nationals in public utilities in ceded territories or those administered by mandataries, and in Turkey, China, Russia, Austria-Hungary, and Bulgaria, and transfer them to the Reparations Commission, which will credit her with their value. Germany guarantees to repay to Brazil the fund arising from the sale of Sao Paulo coffee which she refused to allow Brazil to withdraw from Germany.

SECTION IX.

OPIUM

The contracting powers agree, whether or not they have signed and ratified the opium convention of Jan. 23, 1912, or signed the special protocol opened at The Hague in accordance with resolutions adopted by the third opium conference in 1914, to bring the said convention into force by enacting within twelve months of the peace the necessary legislation.

RELIGIOUS MISSIONS

The allied and associated powers agree that the properties of religious missions in territories belonging or ceded to them shall continue in their work under the control of the powers, Germany renouncing all claims in their behalf.

SECTION X.

ECONOMIC CLAUSES

CUSTOMS

For a period of six months Germany shall impose no tariff duties higher than the lowest in force in 1914, and for certain agricultural products, wines, vegetable oils, artificial silk, and washed or scoured wool this restriction obtains for two and a half years more. For five years, unless further extended by the League of Nations, Germany must give most favored nation treatment to the allied and associated powers. She shall impose no customs tariff for five years on goods originating in Alsace-Lorraine, and for three years on goods originating in former German territory ceded to Poland with the right of observation of a similar exception for Luxemburg.

SHIPPING

Ships of the allied and associated powers shall for five years and thereafter under condition of reciprocity, unless the League of Nations otherwise decides, enjoy the same rights in German ports as German vessels, and have most favored nation treatment in fishing, coasting trade, and towage even in territorial waters. Ships of a country having no seacoast may be registered at some one place within its territory.

UNFAIR COMPETITION

Germany undertakes to give the trade of the allied and associated powers adequate safeguards against unfair competition, and in particular to suppress the use of false wrappings and markings, and on condition of reciprocity to respect the laws and judicial decisions of allied and associated states in respect of regional appellations of wines and spirits.

TREATMENT OF NATIONALS

Germany shall impose no exceptional taxes or restriction upon the nationals of allied and associated states for a period of five years, and, unless the League of Nations acts, for an additional five years German nationality shall not continue to attach to a person who has become a national of an allied or associated state.

MULTILATERAL CONVENTIONS

Some forty multilateral conventions are renewed between Germany and the allied and associated powers, but special conditions are attached to Germany's readmission to several. As to postal and telegraphic conventions Germany must not refuse to make reciprocal agreements with the new states. She must agree as respects the radio-telegraphic convention to provisional rules to be communicated to her, and adhere to the new convention when formulated. In the North Sea fisheries and North Sea liquor traffic convention, rights of inspection and police over associated fishing boats shall be exercised for at least five years only by vessels of these powers. As to the international railway union she shall adhere to the new convention when formulated. China, as to the Chinese customs tariff arrangement of 1905 regarding Whangpoo, and the Boxer indemnity of 1901; France, Portugal, and Rumania, as to The Hague Convention of 1903, relating to civil procedure, and Great Britain and the United States as to Article III. or the Samoan Treaty of 1899, are relieved of all obligations toward Germany.

BILATERAL TREATIES

Each allied and associated state may renew any treaty with Germany in so far as consistent with the peace treaty by giving notice within six months. Treaties entered into by Germany since Aug. 1, 1914, with other enemy states, and before or since that date with Rumania, Russia, and governments representing parts of Russia, are abrogated, and concessions granted under pressure by Russia to German subjects are annulled. The allied and associated states are to enjoy most favored nation treatment under treaties entered into by Germany and other enemy states before Aug. 1, 1914, and under treaties entered into by Germany and neutral states during the war.

PRE-WAR DEBTS

A system of clearing houses is to be created within three months, one in Germany and one in each allied and associated state, which adopts the plan for the payment of pre-war debts, including those arising from contracts suspended by the war. For the adjustment of the proceeds of the liquidation of enemy property and the settlement of other obligations, each participating state assumes responsibility for the payment of all debts owing by its nationals to nationals of the enemy states, except in case of pre-war insolvency of the debtor. The proceeds of the sale of private enemy property in each participating state may be used to pay the debts owed to the nationals of that state, direct payment from debtor to creditor and all communications relating thereto being prohibited. Disputes may be settled by arbitration by the courts of the debtor country, or by the mixed arbitral tribunal. Any ally or associated power may, however, decline to participate in this system by giving six months' notice.

ENEMY PROPERTY

Germany shall restore or pay for all private enemy property seized or damaged by her, the amount of damages to be fixed by the mixed arbitral tribunal. The allied and associated states may liquidate German private property within their territories as compensation for property of their nationals not restored or paid for by Germany. For debts owed to their nationals by German nationals and for other claims against Germany, Germany is to compensate its nationals for such losses and to deliver within six months all documents relating to property held by its nationals in allied and associated states. All war legislation as to enemy property rights and interest is confirmed and all claims by Germany against the allied or associated governments for acts under exceptional war measures abandoned.

Pre-war contracts between allied and associated nationals, excepting the United States, Japan, and Brazil, and German nationals are cancelled except for debts for accounts already performed.

AGREEMENTS

For the transfer of property where the property had already passed, leases of land and houses, contracts of mortgages, pledge or lien, mining concessions, contracts with governments and insurance contracts, mixed arbitral tribunals shall be established of three members, one cl.osen by Germany, one by the associated states and the third by agreement, or, failing which, by the President of Switzerland. They shall have jurisdiction over all disputes as to contracts concluded before the present peace treaty.

Fire insurance contracts are not considered dissolved by the war, even if premiums have not been paid, but lapse at the date of the first annual premium falling due three months after the peace. Life insurance contracts may be restored by payments of accumulated premiums with interest, sums falling due on such contracts during the war to be recoverable with interest. Marine insurance contracts are dissolved by the outbreak of war except where the risk insured against had already been incurred. Where the risk had not attached, premiums paid are recoverable, otherwise premiums due and sums due on losses are recoverable. Reinsurance treaties are abrogated unless invasion has made it impossible for the reinsured to find another reinsurer. Any allied or associated power, however, may cancel all the contracts running between its nationals and a German life insurance company, the latter being obligated to hand over the proportion of its assets attributable to such policies.

INDUSTRIAL PROPERTY

Rights as to industrial, literary, and artistic property are re-established. The special war measures of the allied and associated powers are ratified and the right reserved to impose conditions on the use of German patents and copyrights when in the public interest. Except as between the United States and Germany, pre-war licenses and rights to sue for infringements committed during the war are cancelled.

SECTION XI.
AERIAL NAVIGATION

Aircraft of the allied and associated powers shall have full liberty of passage and landing over and in Germany territory, equal treatment with German planes as to use of German airdromes, and with most favored nation planes as to internal commercial traffic in Germany. Germany agrees to accept allied certificates of nationality, airworthiness, or competency or licenses and to apply the convention relative to aerial navigation concluded between the allied and associated powers to her own aircraft over her own territory. These rules apply until 1923, unless Germany has since been admitted to the League of Nations or to the above convention.

SECTION XII.
FREEDOM OF TRANSIT

Germany must grant freedom of transit through her territories by rail or water to persons, goods, ships, carriages, and mails from or to any of the allied or associated powers, without customs or transit duties, undue delays, restrictions, or discriminations based on nationality, means of transport, or place of entry or departure. Goods in transit shall be assured all possible speed of journey, especially perishable goods. Germany may not divert traffic from its normal course in favor of her own transport routes or maintain "control stations" in connection with transmigration traffic. She may not establish any tax discrimination against the ports of allied or associated powers; must grant the latter's seaports all factors and reduced tariffs granted her own or other nationals, and afford the allied and associated powers equal rights with those of her own nationals in her ports and waterways, save that she is free to open or close her maritime coasting trade.

FREE ZONES IN PORTS

Free zones existing in German ports on Aug. 1, 1914, must be maintained with due facilities as to warehouses, packing, and shipping, without discrimination, and without charges except for expenses of administration and use. Goods leaving the free zones for consumption in Germany and goods brought into the free zones from Germany shall be subject to the ordinary import and export taxes.

INTERNATIONAL RIVERS

The Elbe from the junction of the Ultava, the Ultava from Prague, the Oder from Oppa, the Niemen from Grodno, and the Danube from Ulm are declared international, together with their connections.

The riparian states must ensure good conditions of navigation within their territories unless a special organization exists therefor. Otherwise appeal may be had to a special tribunal of the League of Nations, which also may arrange for a general international waterways convention.

The Elbe and the Oder are to be placed under international commissions to meet within three months, that for the Elbe composed of four representatives of Germany, two from Czecho-Slovakia, and one each from Great Britain, France, Italy, and Belgium; and that for the Oder composed of one each from Poland, Russia, Czecho-Slovakia, Great Britain, France, Denmark, and Sweden. If any riparian state on the Niemen should so request of the League of Nations, a similar commission shall be established there. These commissions shall, upon request of any riparian state, meet within three months to revise existing international agreement.

THE DANUBE

The European Danube Commission reassumes its pre-war powers, but for the time being with representatives of only Great Britain, France, Italy, and Rumania. The upper Danube is to be administered by a new international commission until a definitive statute be drawn up at a conference of the powers nominated by the allied and associated governments within one year after the peace.

The enemy governments shall make full reparations for all war damages caused to the European Commission; shall cede their river facilities in surrendered territory, and give Czecho-Slovakia, Serbia, and Rumania any rights necessary on their shores for carrying on improvements in navigation.

THE RHINE AND THE MOSELLE

The Rhine is placed under the Central Commission to meet at Strassbourg within six months after the peace, and to be composed of four representatives of France, which shall in addition select the President, four of Germany, and two each of Great Britain, Italy, Belgium, Switzerland, and the Netherlands. Germany must give France on the course of the Rhine included between the two extreme points of her frontiers all rights to take water to feed canals, while herself agreeing not to make canals on the right bank opposite France. She must also hand over to France all her drafts and designs for this part of the river.

RHINE-MEUSE CANAL

Belgium is to be permitted to build a deep draft Rhine-Meuse canal if she so desires within twenty-five years, in which case Germany must construct the part within her territory on plans drawn by Belgium; similarly the interested allied governments may construct a Rhine-Meuse canal, both, if constructed, to come under the competent international commission. Germany may not object if the Central Rhine Commission desires to extend its jurisdiction over the lower Moselle, the upper Rhine, or lateral canals.

Germany must cede to the allied and associated governments certain tugs, vessels, and facilities for navigation on all these rivers, the specific details to be established by an arbiter named by the United States. Decision will be based on the legitimate needs of the parties concerned and on the shipping traffic during the five years before the war. The value will be included in the regular reparation account. In the case of the Rhine shares in the German navigation companies and property such as wharves and warehouses held by Germany in Rotterdam at the outbreak of the war must be handed over.

RAILWAYS

Germany, in addition to most favored nation treatment on her railways, agrees to cooperate in the establishment of through ticket services for passengers and baggage; to ensure communication by rail between the allied, associated, and other States; to allow the construction or improvement within twenty-five years of such lines as necessary; and to conform her rolling stock to enable its incorporation in trains of the allied or associated powers. She also agrees to accept the denunciation of the St. Gothard convention if Switzerland and Italy so request, and temporarily to execute instructions as to the transport of troops and supplies and the establishment of postal and telegraphic service, as provided.

CZECHO-SLOVAKIA

To assure Czecho-Slovakia access to the sea, special rights are given her both north and south. Toward the Adriatic she is permitted to run her own through trains to Fiume and Trieste. To the north, Germany is to lease her for ninety-nine years spaces in Hamburg and Stettin, the details to be worked out by a commission of three representing Czecho-Slovakia, Germany, and Great Britain.

THE KIEL CANAL

The Kiel Canal is to remain free and open to war and merchant ships of all nations at peace with Germany; subjects, goods and ships of all States are to be treated on terms of absolute equality, and no taxes to be imposed beyond those necessary for upkeep and improvement for which Germany is to be responsible. In case of violation of or disagreement as to those provisions, any State may appeal to the League of Nations, and may demand the appointment of an international commission. For preliminary hearing of complaints Germany shall establish a local authority at Kiel.

SECTION XIII.

INTERNATIONAL LABOR ORGANIZATION

Members of the League of Nations agree to establish a permanent organization to promote international adjustment of labor conditions, to consist of an annual international labor conference and an international labor office.

The former is composed of four represetatives of each State, two from the Government, and one each from the employers and the employed; each of them may vote individually. It will be a deliberative legislative body, its measures taking the form of draft conventions or recommendations for legislation, which, if passed by two-thirds vote, must be submitted to the lawmaking authority in every State participating. Each Government may either enact the terms into law; approve the principles, but modify them to local needs; leave the actual legislation in case of a Federal State to local legislatures; or reject the convention altogether without further obligation.

The international labor office is established at the seat of the League of Nations as part of its organization. It is to collect and distribute information on labor throughout the world and prepare agenda for the conference. It will publish a periodical in French and English and possibly other languages. Each State agrees to make to it for presentation to the conference an annual report of measures taken to execute accepted conventions. The governing body, in its Executive, consists of twenty-four members, twelve representing the Governments, six the employers, and six the employees, to serve for three years.

On complaint that any Government has failed to carry out a convention to which it is a party, the governing body may make inquiries directly to that Government, and in case the reply is unsatisfactory may publish the complaint with comment. A complaint by one Government against another may be referred by the governing body to a commission of inquiry nominated by the Secretary General of the League. If the commission report fails to bring satisfactory ac-

tion the matter may be taken to a permanent court of international justice for final decision. The chief reliance for securing enforcement of the law will be publicity with a possibility of economic action in the background.

The first meeting of the conference will take place in October, 1919, at Washington, to discuss the eight-hour day or forty-eight-hour week; prevention of unemployment; extension and application of the international conventions adopted at Berne in 1906, prohibiting night work for women, and the use of white phosphorus in the manufacture of matches; and employment of women and children at night or in unhealthy work, of women before and after childbirth, including maternity benefit, and of children as regards minimum age.

LABOR CLAUSES

Nine principles of labor conditions were recognized on the ground that "the well-being, physical and moral, of the industrial wage earners is of supreme international importance." With exceptions necessitated by differences of climate, habits and economic development. They include the guiding principle that labor should not be regarded merely as a commodity or article of commerce; the right of association of employers and employees; a wage adequate to maintain a reasonable standard of life; the eight-hour day or forty-eight-hour week; a weekly rest of at least twenty-four hours; which should include Sunday wherever practicable; abolition of child labor and assurance of the continuation of the education and proper physical development of children; equal pay for equal work as between men and women; equitable treatment of all workers lawfully resident therein, including foreigners; and a system of inspection in which women should take part.

SECTION XIV—GUARANTEES

As a guarantee for the execution of the treaty German territory to the west of the Rhine, together with the bridgeheads, will be occupied by allied and associated troops for a fifteen years' period. If the conditions are faithfully carried out by Germany, certain districts, including the bridgehead of Cologne, will be evacuated at the expiration of five years; certain other districts including the bridgehead of Coblenz, and the territories nearest the Belgian frontier will be evacuated after ten years, and the remainder, including the bridgehead of Mainz, will be evacuated after fifteen years. In case the Interallied Reparations Commission finds that Germany has failed to observe the whole or part of her obligations, either during the occupation or after the fifteen years have expired, the whole or part of the areas specified will be reoccupied immediately. If before the expiration of the fifteen years Germany complies with all the treaty undertakings, the occupying forces will be withdrawn.

All German troops at present in territories to the east of the new frontier shall return as soon as the allied and associated governments deem wise. They are to abstain from all requisitions and are in no way to interfere with measures for national defense taken by the Government concerned.

All questions regarding occupation not provided for by the treaty will be regulated by a subsequent convention or conventions which will have similar force and effect.

SECTION XV.

MISCELLANEOUS

Germany agrees to recognize the full validity of the treaties of peace and additional conventions to be concluded by the allied and associated powers with the powers allied with Germany, to agree to the decisions to be taken as to the territories of Austria-Hungary, Bulgaria, and Turkey, and to recognize the new States in the frontiers to be fixed.

Germany agrees not to put forward any pecuniary claims against any allied or associated power signing the present treaty based on events previous to the coming into force of the treaty.

Germany accepts all decrees as to German ships and goods made by any allied or associateed prize court. The Allies reserve the right to examine all decisions of German prize courts. The present treaty, of which the French and British texts are both authentic, shall be ratified and the depositions of ratifications made in Paris as soon as possible. The treaty is to become effective in all respects for each power on the date of deposition of its ratification.

TREATY OF ST. GERMAIN, SUMMARY

On June 2 there had been handed to the Austrian delegates a preliminary treaty which covered certain points, but left others to be dealt with later.

Austria must accept the covenant of the league of nations and the labor charter.

She must renounce all her extra European rights.

She must demobilize all her naval and aerial forces.

Austria must recognize the complete independence of Hungary.

Austrian nationals, guilty of violating international laws of war, to be tried by the Allies.

Austria must accept economic conditions and freedom of transit similar to those in German treaty.

Sections dealing with war prisoners and graves are identical with German treaty.

Guarantees of execution of treaty corresponds to those in German pact.

Boundaries of Bohemia and Moravia to form boundary between Austria and Czecho-Slovakia, with minor rectifications.

Allies later to fix southern boundary (referring to Jugoslavia).

Eastern boundary Marburg and Radkersburg to Jugoslavia.

Western and northwestern frontiers (facing Bavaria and Switzerland) unchanged.

Austria must recognize independence of Czecho-Slovakia and Jugoslavia.

Austria is recognized as an independent republic under the name "Republic of Austria."

Austria must recognize frontiers of Bulgaria, Greece, Hungary, Poland, Rumania, Czecho-Slovakia and Jugoslavia as at present or ultimately determined.

Boundaries of Austria, Czecho-Slovakia and Jugoslavia to be finally fixed by mixed commission.

Czecho-Slovakia and Jugoslavia must agree to protect racial, religious and linguistic minorities.

Both new Slav nations and Rumania must assure freedom of transit and equitable treatment of foreign commerce.

Austria must recognize full independence of all territories formerly a part of Russia.

Brest-Litovsk treaty is annulled.

All treaties with Russian elements concluded since revolution annulled.

Allies reserve right of restitution for Russia from Austria.

Austria must consent to abrogation of treaties of 1839 establishing Belgian neutrality.

Austria must agree to new Belgian boundaries as fixed by Allies.

Similar provisions with respect to neutrality and boundaries of Luxemburg.

Austria must accept allied disposition of any Austrian rights in Turkey and Bulgaria.

She must accept allied arrangements with Germany regarding Schleswig-Holstein.

Austrian nations of all races, languages and religions equal before the law.

Clauses affecting Egypt, Morocco, Siam, and China identical with German treaty.

Entire Austro-Hungarian navy to be surrendered to Allies.

Twenty-one specified auxiliary cruisers to be disarmed and treated as merchantmen.

All warships, including submarines, under construction shall be broken up and may be used only for industrial purposes.

All naval arms and material must be surrendered.

Future use of submarines prohibited.

Austrian wireless station at Vienna not to be used for military or political messages to Austria's late allies without Allies' consent for three months.

Austria may not have naval or air forces.

She must demobilize existing air forces within two months and surrender aviation material.

Austrian nationals cannot serve in military, naval or aerial forces of foreign powers.

She may send no military, naval or aerial mission to any foreign country.

Penalties section identical with German treaty excepting reference to German kaiser. New states required to aid in prosecution and punishment of their nationals guilty of offenses against international law.

Economic clauses in general similar to those in German treaty. Austria given access to Adriatic.

Austria must abandon all financial claims against signatories.

Treaty to become operative when signed by Austria and three of the principal powers.

On July 21 an amplified treaty with Austria-Hungary taking up matters omitted from the first paper was given to the delegates from that country. A summary of the articles follows:

In addition to the published summary of the terms of June 2, the new clauses provide for reparation arrangements very similar to those in the treaty with Germany, including the establishment of an Austrian subsection of the Reparations Commission, the payment of a reasonable sum in cash, the issuing of bonds, and the delivery of livestock and certain historical and art documents.

The financial terms provide that the Austrian pre-war debt shall be apportioned among the former parts of Austria, and that the Austrian coinage and war bonds, circulating in the separated territory, shall be taken up by the new governments and redeemed as they see fit.

Under the military terms the Austrian army is henceforth reduced to 30,000 men on a purely voluntary basis.

Paragraph 5, relating to the military situation, says that the Austrian army shall not exceed 30,000 men, including officers and depot troops. Within three months the Austrian military forces shall be reduced to this number, universal military service abolished and voluntary enlistment substituted as part of the plan "to render possible the initiation of a general limitation of armaments of all nations."

The army shall be used exclusively for the maintenance of internal order and control of frontiers. All officers must be regulars, those of the present army to be retained being under obligation to serve until 40 years old, those newly appointed agreeing to at least twenty consecutive years of active service. Non-commissioned officers and privates must enlist for not less than twelve consecutive years, including at least six years with the colors.

Within three months the armament of the Austrian army must be reduced according to detailed schedules and all surplus surrendered. The manufacture of all war material shall be confined to one single factory under the control of the States, and other such establishments shall be closed or converted. Importation and exportation of arms, munitions and war materials of all kinds are forbidden.

Paragraph 8 (on reparation) reads, in substance: The allied and associated Governments affirm, and Austria accepts, the responsibility of Austria and her allies for causing loss and damage to which the allied and associated Governments and their nationals have been subjected as a consequence of the war imposed upon them by the aggression of Austria and her allies. While recognizing that Austria's resources will not be adequate to make complete reparation, the allied and associated Government request, and Austria undertakes, that she will make compensation for damage done to civilians and their property, in accordance with categories of damages similar to those provided in the treaty with Germany.

The amount of damage is to be determined by the Reparations Commission provided for in the treaty with Germany, which is to have a special section to handle the Austrian situation. The commission will notify Austria before May 1, 1921, of the extent of her liabilities and of the schedule of payments for the discharge thereof during a period of thirty years. It will bear in mind the diminutions of Austria's resources and capacity of payment resulting from the treaty.

As immediate reparation, Austria shall pay during 1919, 1920, and the first four months of 1921, in such manner as provided by the Reparations Commission, "a reasonable sum which shall be determined by the commission."

Three bond issues shall be made—the first before May 1, 1921, without interest; the second at 2½ per cent. interest between 1921 and 1926, and thereafter at 5 per cent. with an additional 1 per cent. for amortization beginning in 1926, and a third at 5 per cent. when the commission is satisfied that Austria can meet the interest and sinking fund obligations. The amount shall be divided by the allied and associated Governments in proportions determined upon in advance on a basis of general equity.

The Austrian section of the Reparations Commission shall include representatives of the United States, Great Britain, France, Italy, Greece, Poland, Rumania, the Serbo-Slovene State, and Czecho-Slovakia. The first four shall each appoint a delegate with two votes and the other five shall choose one delegate each year to represent them all. Withdrawal from the commission is permitted on twelve months' notice.

Paragraph 9 (Financial).—The first charge upon all the assets and revenues of Austria shall be the costs arising under the present treaty, including, in order of priority, the costs of the armies of occupation, reparations, and other charges specifically agreed to and, with certain exceptions, as granted by the Reparations Commission for payments for imports. Austria must pay the total cost of the armies of occupation from the armistice of Nov. 3, 1918, so long as maintained, and may export no gold before May 1, 1921, without consent of the Reparations Commission.

Each of the States to which Austrian territory is transferred and each of the States arising out of the dismemberment of Austria, including the Republic of Austria, shall assume part of the Austrian pre-war debt specifically secured on railways, salt mines, and other property, the amount to be fixed by the Reparations Commission on the basis of the value of the property so transferred.

Similarly, the unsecured bonded pre-war debt of the former empire shall be distributed by the Reparations Commission in the proportion that the revenues for the three years before the war of the separated territory bore to those of the empire, excluding Bosnia and Herzegovina.

No territory formerly part of the empire, except the Republic of Austria, shall carry with it any obligation in respect of the war debt of the former Austrian Government, but neither the Governments of those territories nor their nationals shall have recourse against any other State, including Austria, in respect of war debt bonds held within their respective territories by themselves or their nationals.

Austria, recognizing the right of the Allies to ton-for-ton replacement of all ships lost or damaged in the war, cedes all merchant ships and fishing boats belonging to nationals of the former empire, agreeing to deliver them within two months to the Reparations Commission. With a view to making good the losses in river tonnage, she agrees to deliver up 20 per cent. of her river fleet.

The allied and associated powers require, and Austria undertakes, that in part reparation she will devote her economic resources to the physical restoration of the invaded areas. Within sixty days of the coming into force of the treaty the governments concerned shall file with the Reparations Commission lists of animals, machinery, equipment, and the like destroyed by Austria which the government desire replaced in kind, and lists of the materials which they desire produced in Austria for the work of reconstruction, which shall be reviewed in the light of Austria's ability to meet them.

As an immediate advance as to animals, Austria agrees to deliver within three months after ratification of the treaty 4,000 milch cows to Italy and 1,000 each to Serbia and Rumania; 1,000 heifers to Italy, 300 to Serbia, and 500 to Rumania; 50 bulls to Italy, and 25 each to Serbia and Rumania; 1,000 calves to each of the three nations; 1,000 bullocks to Italy and 500 each to Serbia and Rumania; 2,000 sows to Italy, and 1,000 draft horses and 1,000 sheep to both Serbia and Rumania.

Austria also agrees to give an option for five years as to timber, iron, and magnesite in amounts as nearly equal to the pre-war importations as Austria's resources make possible. She renounces in favor of Italy all cables touching territories assigned to Italy, and in favor of the allied and associated powers the others.

Austria agrees to restore all records, documents, objects of antiquity and art, and all scientific and bibliographic material taken away from the invaded or ceded territories. She will also hand over without delay all official records of the ceded territories and all records, documents and historical material possessed by public institutions and having a direct bearing on the history of the ceded territories which have been removed during the past ten years, except that for Italy the period shall be from 1861.

As to artistic archæological, scientific or historic objects formerly belonging to the Austro-Hungarian Government or Crown, Austria agrees to negotiate with the State concerned for an amicable arrangement for the return to the districts of origin on terms of reciprocity of any object which ought to form part of the intellectual patrimony of the ceded districts, and for twenty years to safeguard all other such objects for the free use of students.

The war debt held outside the former empire shall be a charge on the Republic of Austria alone. All war securities shall be stamped within two months with the stamp of the State taking them up, replaced by certificates, and settlement made to the Reparations Commission.

The currency notes of the former Austro-Hungarian Bank circulating in the separated territory shall be stamped within two months by the new governments of the various territories with their own stamp, replaced within twelve months by a new currency, and turned over within twelve months to the Reparations Commission. The bank itself shall be liquidated as from the day after the signature of the treaty by the Reparations Commission.

States to which Austrian territory was transferred and States arising from the dismemberment of Austria shall acquire all property within their territories of the old or new Austrian Government, including that of the former royal family. The value is to be assessed by the Reparations Commission and credited to Austria on the reparation account.

Property of predominant historic interest to the former kingdoms of Poland, Bohemia, Croatia, Slavonia, Dalmatia, Bosnia, Herzegovina, the Republic of Ragusa, the Venetian Republic or the episcopal principalities of Trent and Bressanone may be transferred without payment.

Austria renounces all rights as to all international financial or commercial organizations in allied countries, Germany, Hungary, Bulgaria, Turkey, or the former Russian Empire. She agrees to expropriate, on demand of the Reparations Commission, any rights of her nationals in any public utility or concession in these territories, in separated districts, and in mandatary territories, to transfer them to the commission within six

months, and to hold herself responsible for indemnifying her nationals so dispossessed.

She also agrees to deliver within one month the gold deposited as security for the Ottoman debt, renounce any benefits accruing from the treaties of Bucharest and Brest-Litovsk, and transfer to the allied and asscciated Governments all claims against her former Allies.

Any financial adjustments, such as those relating to banking and insurance companies, savings banks, postal savings banks, land banks or mortgage companies in the former monarchy, necessitated by the dismemberment of the monarchy, and the resettlement of public debts and currency, shall be regulated by agreements between the various governments, failing which the Reparations Commission shall appoint an arbitrator or arbitrators, whose decision shall be final.

Austria shall not be responsible for pensions of nationals of the former empire who have become nationals of other States.

As for special objects carried off by the House of Hapsburg and other dynasties from Italy, Belgium, Poland, and Czecho-Slovakia, a committee of three jurists appointed by the Reparations Commission is to examine within a year the conditions under which the objects were removed and to order restoration if the removal were illegal. The list of articles includes among others:

For Tuscany, the Crown Jewels and part of the Medici heirlooms; for Modena a Virgin by Andrea del Sarto and manuscripts; for Palermo, twelfth century objects made for the Norman Kings; for Naples, ninety-eight manuscripts carried off in 1718; for Belgium, various objects and documents removed in 1794; for Poland, a gold cup of King Ladislas IV., removed in 1772; and for Czecho-Slovakia various documents and historical manuscripts removed from the Royal Castle of Prague.

TREBIZOND, the principal Turkish port on the Black Sea; on the N. E. coast of Asia Minor, and the second commercial city of the empire; 110 miles N. W. of Erzerum. It is finely situated on the steep slope of the Kolat Dagh (800 feet high) facing the sea, and is partly surrounded by walls, and further defended by a Genoese citadel on an adjoining hill, and by forts at the mouth of the harbor. The gorge-like course of a mountain stream traverses Trebizond, and is crossed by several bridges. The coast is high and crested with pine woods, and from the sea the irregularly-built town, with its minarets and gardens, has a striking appearance. There are 18 mosques, 15 Christian churches, and many elegant baths and spacious bazaars. The industries, chiefly weaving and dyeing, are unimportant; but the products of the surrounding country, which form part of the exports of Trebizond, comprise considerable quantities of boxwood, loupes or walnut-tree knobs, valued in France for veneers, beans, wheat and Indian corn, fruits and provisions, nuts and walnuts, skins, wool, tiftick and fillick, and tobacco. Trebizond is an emporium for the Persian trade, but has suffered greatly from the opening of the railway from Tiflis to Poti, and the diversion of trade to Batoum. It is a terminus for caravans from Erzerum, Armenia, Kurdistan, Tabriz, etc., and has regular communication by steam line with Constantinople, the Danube, and French ports. The harbor is only an open roadstead, and during the autumn equinoxes vessels have to shelter either at Batoum or at Platina, 6 miles W. Besides the opening of the Poti railway, the want of good roads in the interior, the neglect of the larger crown forests, and the imposition of heavy custom dues, have checked Trebizond's prosperity. Trebizond, founded by a colony from Sinope, 756 B. C., was a great trading town in Xenophon's time, and continued to flourish as an emporium for the Indian trade under the Roman empire. Its period of greatest prosperity as capital of the Comnenian empire of Trebizond began in 1204 and lasted till 1461, when David, last of the Comnenes, was captured by Mohammed II. Since then Trebizond has belonged to the Porte. Pop. about 55,000. The city was captured by the Russians in 1916, but disorganization had already begun in the army and they made only a weak attempt to hold it.

TREBLE, in music, of or pertaining to the highest vocal or instrumental part, sung by boys, or played by violins, oboes, clarinets, or other instruments of acute tone.

TREE, in botany, any woody plant rising from the ground, with a trunk, and perennial in duration; an arborescent plant as distinguished from a shrub, an under-shrub, and an herb. The classification of plants which at first suggests itself as the most natural one is into trees, shrubs, and herbs. This is still the popular classification as it was that of the oldest observers (I Kings iv: 33); but it violates all natural affinities, and has long since been abandoned by botanists. Trees occur in many orders, their stems varying in structure according to the sub-kingdoms to which they belong. They may be exogenous, or of that modification of the exogenous stem which exists in gymnogens, or may be endogenous or acrogenous. The age of certain trees, especially of exogens, is often great, and, when cut down, the number of years they have existed can be ascertained by counting the annual zones. Some of the giant cedars of California are more than 100 feet in circumference, 400 feet high, and certainly 3,000 years old. Von Martius describes the trunks of certain locust trees in Brazil as being 84 feet in circumference and 60 feet where the boles become cylindrical. From counting the annual rings of one, he formed the opinion that it was of about the age of Homer; another estimate increased the age to 4,104 years, but a third one made the tree first grow up 2,052 years from the publication of Martius' book (1820). A baobab tree (*Adansonia digitata*) in Senegal was computed by Adanson, A. D. 1794, to be 5,150 years old; but he made his calculations from the measurement of only a fragment of the cross section, and, as zones differ much in breadth, this method of computation involves considerable risk of error. Sir Joseph Hooker rejects the conclusion. Most trees are deciduous, *i. e.*, have deciduous leaves, a few are evergreen. To the latter kind belong those coniferous trees which form so conspicuous a feature in the higher temperate latitudes, while deciduous trees prevail in lower latitudes. The planting of trees is now more attended to than formerly, especially in cities and on the prairie lands of the United States. See FORESTRY.

TREE FROG, in zoölogy, any individual of the family *Hylidæ.* They are of small size, more elegant in form than the true frogs, of brighter colors, and more active habits. They feed on insects, which they pursue on the branches of shrubs and trees. The European tree frog (*Hyla arborea*) is common in the middle and S. of the Continent, and ranges into Asia and the N. of Africa. It becomes very noisy on the approach of rain, and is often kept in confinement as a kind of barometer. The common tree frog of North America is *Hyla versicolor*, replaced in the S. by the green tree frog, *H. viridis.*

TREE TOAD, in zoölogy, a popular name for several of the *Hylidæ.* Used without a qualifying epithet, it is equivalent to tree frog. With a qualifying epithet, it is limited to particular species. *Hyla versicolor* is the changeable tree toad, *Trachycephalus lichenatus* is the

See Tree, p. opposite

A TRAVELER'S TREE. THE THIRSTY TRAVELER WHO FINDS SUCH A
TREE CAN OBTAIN FROM ONE TO TWO QUARTS OF WATER
BY CUTTING ONE OF THE BRANCHES

AMERICAN SOLDIERS RESTING IN A SHALLOW TRENCH IN THE ARGONNE FOREST

See Trench Warfare, p. 494

lichened, and *T. marmoratus* the marbled tree toad.

TREE, SIR HERBERT BEERBOHM, an English actor-manager; born in London, in 1853. He made his first appearance as an actor in 1877 as Grimaldi at the Globe, and attracted attention in 1884 in "The Private Secretary." In 1887 he produced as manager of the Comedy Theatre "The Red Lamp" and from 1887 to 1896 was manager at the Haymarket. He opened in 1897 Her Majesty's (later His Majesty's) Theatre with "Seats of the Mighty" and there produced many notable successes. Later he elaborately produced the plays of Shakespeare, himself taking leading parts. He died in 1917.

TREILLE, in heraldry, a lattice; it differs from fretty in that the pieces do not interlace under and over, but cross athwart each other, and are nailed at the joint. Called also trellis.

TREITSCHKE, HEINRICH VON, a German historian; born in Dresden, Germany, Sept. 15, 1834; was educated at Heidelberg, Tübingen, Bonn and Leipsic. He devoted himself to the study of history and became Professor of History at Freiburg in 1863, and held the same chair at Heidelburg in 1867-1874. In the latter year he accepted the similar chair at the University of Berlin. He was the author of "Ten Years of German Struggles"; "Socialism and its Patrons"; "Two Emperors"; and the "History of Germany in the Nineteenth Century," which was his principal work, but was left unfinished. He died in Berlin, April 28, 1896.

TRELAWNY, SIR JONATHAN, an English clergyman; from Westminster passed in 1663 to Christ Church, Oxford, and became bishop in turn of Bristol (1685), Exeter (1688), and Winchester (1707); he was one of the Seven Bishops tried under James II., and is the hero of R. S. Hawker's well-known ballad, "And shall Trelawny die?" This was based on a contemporary refrain, the strong feeling aroused among the Cornishmen due rather to Trelawny's being head of an ancient Cornish house than to his being a bishop or even a martyr in a good cause. Trelawny died in 1721.

TRELAWNY, EDWARD JOHN, an English author; born in London, Nov. 13, 1792. He is remembered as a picturesque and somewhat theatrical adventurer (supposed to be drawn by Byron in "The Corsair"), the friend of Byron, Shelley, etc., and Byron's companion (1823) in the Greek war of liberation. He wrote a novel called "Adventures of a Younger Son" (1830); but his best-known work is "Recollections of the Last Days of Shelley and Byron" (1858), re-issued in 1878 as "Records of Byron, Shelley, and the Author." His body was cremated, and the ashes interred near Shelley's at Rome. His portrait is preserved in Millais's painting "The North-west Passage." He died in Sompting, Sussex, Aug. 13, 1881.

TREMELLINI, an order or sub-order of hymenomycetous Fungals, the species of which are of a gelatinous texture, sometimes, though rarely, with a cretaceous nucleus, their hymenium in the more typical genera covering the whole surface without any definite upper or under side; sporophores scattered, often lobed or quadripartite; spores often producing secondary spores of spermatia. They grow upon branches or stumps of trees, in crevices of the bark, or on the dead wood, rarely on the ground. Found chiefly in temperate climates, though some are tropical. A widely distributed representative is the jew's-ear.

TREMOLITE, a mineral, a variety of hornblende. It is a silicate of calcium and magnesium, is white or colorless, and usually occurs in long, prismatic crystals.

TREMOCTOPUS, in zoölogy, a subgenus of *Octopus*, with three species, from the Atlantic and Mediterranean. Some or all of the arms are webbed half-way up, and there are two large aquiferous pores on the back of the head.

TREMOLANT, an organ and harmonium stop which causes the air as it proceeds to the pipes or reeds to pass through a valve having a movable top, to which a spring and weight are attached. The up-and-down movement of the top of the valve gives a vibratory movement to the air, which similarly affects the sound produced. On American organs, a fan-wheel by rotating in front of the wind chest causes a tremolo.

TREMONT, the early name by which Boston, Mass., was known. It arose from the three hills on which the city is built. It has also been called Trimount, or Trimountain.

TRENCH, RICHARD CHENEVIX, an English clergyman; born in Dublin, Ireland, Sept. 9, 1807; was graduated at Trinity College, Cambridge, in 1829. He entered the Church, and became curate at Hadleigh (1833-1835), incumbent at Curdridge (1835-1840), curate to Archdeacon Wilberforce at Alverstoke (1840-

1844), rector of Itchenstoke (1844-1845), was Hulsean lecturer 1845-1846, Professor of Theology at King's College, London (1846-1858), dean of Westminster (1856-1863), and was finally consecrated archbishop of Dublin, Jan. 1, 1864. He was the author of a collection of poems, and a popular writer on philological and theological subjects. His works include: "Notes on the Parables" (1841); "Notes on the Miracles" (1846); "On the Study of Words" (1851); "Proverbs and Their Lessons" (1853); "Synonyms of the New Testament" (1854); "English, Past and Present" (1855); "On Plutarch" (1874); "Lectures on Mediæval Church History" (1878); and many others. He died March 28, 1886.

TRENCHARD, STEPHEN DECATUR, an American naval officer; born in Brooklyn, N. Y., July 10, 1818; was appointed to the navy in 1834; took part in the Seminole War in Florida; served on board the "Saratoga" in the war with Mexico; was in the "Powhatan" on her diplomatic cruise to China and Japan in 1857-1860; and commanded the "Rhode Island" in both attacks on Fort Fisher. He was promoted captain in 1866; commodore in 1871; served on the examining board in 1871-1872, and as lighthouse inspector and on headquarters duty in 1873-1875; became rear-admiral in 1875; commanded the North Atlantic squadron in 1876-1878, and was retired in 1880. He died in New York City, Nov. 15, 1883.

TRENCHARD, SIR HUGH MONTAGUE, a British officer, born in 1873. He entered the army in 1893, and became a captain in 1900, going through the grade to major-general, to which he was promoted in 1916. He served with the Imperial Yeomanry, Bushmen Corps, South Africa, 1899-1902, and afterward with the Canadian Scouts, being dangerously wounded. He was with the West African Frontier Force in 1906. In the European war he became commandant of the Central Flying School, and finally in 1918 Chief of the Air Staff with the title of Air-Marshal.

TRENCH FEVER, a disease supposed to develop in troops who have been in the trenches, but apparently liable to attack individuals temporarily in training camps or convalescent hospitals. Efforts were made during the war to find the specific germ responsible for the disease, and organisms from a number of patients were cultivated on artifical mediums. The germ was found in the periosteum around with blood vessels of the tibialis anticus muscle, and occa-

sionally in the blood. It showed itself in the form of a disk, about one-fortieth the size of a red blood corpuscle. Significance attaches to the fact that the micro-organism is likewise located in the stomach walls of the body louse, and the inference is that the vermin plays a part in the spread of the malady. Dr. M. Mandel, medical director of the United States Army Base Hospital No. 12, describes the disease as a distinct clinical entity, and defines it as an acute infectious disease of unknown etiology and self-limited course, characterized clinically by cyclic febrile attacks, intense headache and backache, and pains over the tibial which are particularly severe at night. The rise in temperature is from 101° to 104° F., preceded by chilly sensations. The febrile attacks may be repeated, but convalescence usually follows the third.

TRENCH WARFARE. Like everything else in military affairs, the use of the trench received a great development during the recent great war. Under the old conditions the trench was simply an excavation in the ground long or short, broad or narrow, the earth from which was thrown directly in front to form a barricade. The trench might be a temporary affair or it might be an element in a permanent and extensive fortification. They could play a part both in attack and defense. The dimensions of a trench, and its intricacy or simplicity, would naturally be determined largely by the length of time it was intended to use it. Troops kneeling would require a depth that would leave them space to see over the parapet. Men standing would require greater depth that parapets might be cut at the sides to stand on if greater depth was needed for protection. In the hastily dug trenches proper for soldiers engaged in attacking a depth of a couple of feet would be ample. The soldier lying prone would necessarily only hold the trench till he was enabled to advance still further.

In the development of military service that preceded the great war military engineers had long spoken of the value of the trench and the part it was likely to play in future warfare. In every European army, the troops, apart from the engineering unts, had been taught to construct trenches of established types. It was foreseen that in modern warfare large armies would confront each other for long periods with their ends resting on the mountains and the sea and that opposing lines would be parallel to each other long distances and for indefinite periods. The idea then was to maintain the front line at a depth suitable for standing, with room for the coming and going of a single file of soldiers. Arrangements on the top of the trench would help the soldier to find shelter and at the same time watch the enemy and hit him if possible. The faces of the trench were held firmly in a perpendicular position by planks, or sacks of earth. The spaces in front of the trenches were cleared so as to leave an obstructed view, and obstructive barriers, such as barbed wire, were placed in positions where it was expected that the enemy might attack. All these methods received great development during the World War.

As the war progressed, and it was seen that the troops might continue to confront each other in almost the same positions for months and even for years, trench warfare naturally assumed proportions not before conceived of. The simple parallel lines of no great depth that had been the rule and theory hitherto were transformed into complicated designs that increased in depth, in variety, and in intricacy according to the conditions in a particular district. The line sank into subterranean passages and broadened into large covered areas with divisions for resting, eating, diversion, and sleeping. Attention had to be paid to the draining in swampy districts, and where the danger was great fortifications built of concrete and of great strength were built up. The simple straight or curving line was in many places transformed into a zigzag or labyrinth pattern, and communicating trenches connected the front trenches with those behind and these again with the forces at the rear. The war took on the character of mutual siege conditions, and this was largely due to the grip on the ground deevloped by trench work. The single trench line that proved so hard to capture in the Civil War of the United States grew into an elaborate network of trenches deep below the surface and forming part of great plans covering large areas in the rear. A trench defended by barbed wire proved a difficult position to attack, and the great multiplication of machine guns, which the Germans provided as one of the great surprises of the war, made a position thus doubly protected almost impenetrable. An enormous expenditure of projectiles was found necessary to prepare the way for an attack that might result in the capture of two or three front lines. This it was calculated that preceding one such attack a French battery, near Arras, sent into the German lines more projectiles than the entire German artillery in the war of 1870-

I—35

1871. Yet this tremendous fire was a necessary preliminary, if the barbed wire was to be cut, the machine guns destroyed and the trenches leveled. The arrival of the tank, which was in effect an armored motor car and military tractor, able to cross trenches and shell craters, proof against machine gun and rifle fire, and itself armed with machine guns, solved a problem that had hitherto been baffling. Nevertheless the trench showed itself capable of developments that are sure to affect all future warfare. Trenches, under the development of warfare, may be dug to any depth, may be expanded to any breadth, may be divided and designed on any pattern, and may be re-enforced to any extent conditions may warrant. In view of the great part aeronautics are likely to play in the future warfare, the roof of the trench is likely to be a matter of immense importance, and trenches that lead to underground cities are not an impossible conception. Under the circumstances it was only in the nature of things that the mining of trenches was one of the great occupations of the war and approaches were made in that manner which would have been impossible overground.

TRENCK, FRIEDRICH VON DER, BARON, a Prussian officer, celebrated for his adventures and misfortunes; born in Königsberg in 1726, and at the age of 17 he was presented to the king, Frederick II., as a student who was well worthy the royal patronage. Frederick rapidly advanced him in the army, and manifested much regard for him; but Trenck having won the heart of Princess Amelia, the king's sister, his enemies had him accused and arrested. He was imprisoned in the fortress of Glatz, but contrived to effect his escape. He then visited the N. of Europe, Austria, and Italy. In 1758 he was seized at Danzic and was conveyed to Magdeburg, where, loaded with irons, he was for years incarcerated. On procuring his liberation, in 1763, he withdrew to Vienna, after which he went to Aix-la-Chapelle, where literature, politics, and commerce alternately occupied his attention. At his castle of Zwerbeck, in Hungary, he wrote his "Memoirs," a book read all over Europe. In 1791 he settled in France, joined the Jacobins, and in 1794 was charged with being a secret emissary of the King of Prussia, and died by the guillotine.

TRENDELENBURG, FRIEDRICH ADOLF, a German philosopher; born in Eutin, Germany, Nov. 30, 1802. He set forth the ethical aspect of his philosophy in the treatise "The Ethical Idea of Right and Law," and the æsthetic aspect in "Niobe" (1846) and "The Cathedral of Cologne" (1853). He wrote also "Natural Justice on the Ground of Ethics" (2d ed. 1860). His principal claim to distinction as a thinker rests on his acute criticism of the systems of Kant and Hegel. He died in Berlin, Jan. 24, 1872.

TRENT, or **TRIENT**, an old town of Italy in the Tyrol; on the left bank of the Adige; 54 miles N. N. E. of Verona. It has two suburbs, San Martino and Santa Croce, and in its environs villages rise beautifully above one another on the mountain slopes. Of the town, which is quite Italian in its character, the finest squares are the Piazza d'Armi and the Piazzi del Duomo, the latter adorned with a fountain, and containing the courts of justice. Among the 15 churches the finest are the Cathedral, a Romanesque basilica, with two domes, founded in 1048, begun in its present form in 1212, and completed in the 15th century; Santa Maria Maggiore, where the celebrated Council of Trent sat from 1545-1563, containing an admirable organ, and adorned with portraits of the members of the council; and the Church dell' Annunziata, with a high cupola resting on four pillars. Other buildings are the town hall, the Palace of Justice, the theatre, and the Palazzo Buon Consiglio, formerly the residence of the prince-bishops, now a barrack. The town has two monasteries, a theological institute, an upper gymnasium, and a public library and museum. The industries are silk spinning and weaving, dyeing, iron founding, and the manufacture of cloth, pottery, and cards. In the vicinity are great marble quarries. Trent was a Roman colony, became in the 4th century the seat of a bishop, and in 574 of a Lombard duke. In 1027 Konrad II. granted to its bishops princely rank and the fief of the town. The bishropic was secularized in 1803, and added to the Austrian crown-lands. It is in the territory awarded to Italy by the treaty of St. Germain. Pop. about 30,000.

TRENT, COUNCIL OF, the 18th in order and the first in importance of the "Œcumenical" councils recognized by the Roman Catholic Church; was called forth by the Reformation in the 16th century, and demanded by both parties in the contest, for the reform of church discipline and the settlement of the points of controversy. After being repeatedly postponed, it was convened at Trent as an exclusively Roman council by Pope Paul III., Dec. 13, 1545. In March, 1547, it was transferred to Bologna, but was reopened at Trent, by Pope Julius III., May 1, 1551. It was broken up, Jan. 18, 1562, in consequence of the victorious advance of the Elector Moritz, but was recalled by Pope Pius IV., Dec. 4, 1563, and reached its close, at its 25th session, Dec. 4, 1563. Its decrees and canons, which were confirmed by a bull of Pius IV., Jan. 26, 1564, are drawn up with much clearness and precision, though the doctrines of the Protestants are often exaggerated or falsified. They were immediately acknowledged in Spain, Portugal, Italy, Poland, and Catholic Germany, and, in their doctrinal part, in France.

TRENTINO, THE, the name of that part of Tyrol which adjoined Italy before the World War.

This territory constituted one of the claims for which Italy entered the World War on the side of the Allies, in 1915, and was immediately occupied by the Italian army on beginning operations against the Austrians.

The territory in question is in the southern part of the Tyrol, covers the Adige Valley, being watered by the Adige river, and its chief center of population is the city of Trent, whence the name of the Trentino is derived. This southern valley is bounded on the E. by the Trent (or Trentino) Alps, on the W. by the Ortler Alps, which project down into the fields of Lombardy. The main chain is cleft toward the center of the Trentino by a deep depression, in which lies the Brenner Pass. Included with the Adige Valley, in the Italian claims, were the Roveredo Valley and the Valley of the Sarca, or district of Riva, on Lake Garda. The claims of Italy rested not only on the nationality of the population of the Trentino, but on a historical basis as well. In early times this whole country had been in possession of the Romans. Later it fell to the Germanic barbarians who invaded Lombardy. During the Napoleonic Wars the southern Tyrol, or the Trentino, was annexed to Italy, in 1814, but was given back to Austria in the year following. During the Austrian administration, however, the Italian inhabitants made continuous efforts to be separated from the German Tyrol, as a separate administrative unit, at least. Economically, too, the interests of the people were Italian, as their entire trade was with the S., their wood and cattle being exchanged for the grains grown in the plains of Lombardy. Italy's lack of national unity, till the middle of last century, and, later, her interests in Africa, compelling her to seek an alliance with Germany and Austria, prevented her for this long period from supporting the ambitions of the Italians of the Trentino to become a part of the Italian nation.

TRENT, WILLIAM PETERFIELD, an American author; born in Richmond, Va., Nov. 10, 1862; was graduated at the University of Virginia in 1884; and in 1888 became Professor of English and of History in the University of the South. In July, 1900, he was appointed Professor of English Literature at Columbia University, New York city. He made a special study of southern men and times, and published: "Life of William Gilmore Simms"; "English Culture in Virginia"; "Southern Statesmen of the Old Régime"; "Balzac's Comédie Humaine"; "John Milton"; "Authority of Criticism"; etc.

TRENT AFFAIR. In October, 1861, Capt. Charles Wilkes, U. S. N., intercepted at sea the British mail steamer "Trent," bound from Havana to St. Thomas, and took off two Confederate commissioners, accredited to France, Messrs. Mason and Slidell, who were among her passengers. They were taken to Boston and imprisoned in Fort Warren, but were released on Jan. 1, 1862, on the demand of the British Government, and permitted to proceed to Europe. The affair created intense excitement at the time, but Secretary Seward accepted England's demand as an adoption of the American doctrine which denied the right of search, and on that ground replied that the prisoners would be cheerfully given up.

TRENTON, a city and county-seat of Grundy co., Mo.; on the Crooked Fork of Grand river, and on the Chicago, Rock Island and Pacific railroad; 102 miles N. E. of Leavenworth, Kan. It contains Avalon College (United Brethren), a court house, churches, National and other banks, and several newspapers. It has flour and woolen mills and an assessed property valuation exceeding $1,200,000. Pop. (1910) 5,656; (1920) 6,951.

TRENTON, a city of New Jersey, the capital of the State, and the county-seat of Mercer co. It is on the Delaware river, the Delaware and Raritan canal, and on the main line of the Pennsylvania and of the Philadelphia and Reading railroads. The city is connected by electric lines with Philadelphia, northern New Jersey, and New York, while there is a large traffic on the canal and by steamship and barges on the Delaware river to the south. The city is connected with Morrisville in Pennsylvania by bridges over the river. Trenton is an important industrial city and is noted for the wide variety and extent of its manufactures. The industrial zone had, in 1920, 200 manufacturing plants with $120,000,000 invested and 40,000 employees. The value of the finished product was nearly $175,000,000. The leading industries are the manufacture of pottery, rubber, wire, machinery, structural steel and linoleum, automobiles, bedding and spring mattresses, bricks, candy, cigars, clothing, furniture, hosiery, silk and woolen yarns, steam turbines, watches, etc. Trenton has a total area of 19 square miles. The assessed property valuation in 1919 was $76,177,195 in real estate and $16,030,800 in personal property. The net public debt was $6,110,437. The annual cost of maintaining the city government was $1,665,169. There were enrolled in the public schools 15,336 pupils and the cost of maintaining the schools was $734,606. It is the seat of the State Normal and Model School, School of Industrial Arts, and several private schools. It contains three hospitals, State home for girls, a reformatory, State hospital for the insane, and a State prison. The notable public buildings include the State Capitol, Masonic Temple, and the State Armory. The city has two parks. The spot where Washington planted his cannon during the Battle of Trenton is marked by a statue.

History.—The site of Trenton was settled as early as 1679 by Mahlon Stacy and other Quakers. Judge Trent purchased a large plantation here about 1715, and the place became known as Trent Town, subsequently shortened to Trenton. It became the State capital in 1790, but prior to that year the Legislature often met here. The town was incorporated in 1792. After the Revolutionary War the Continental Congress once met here and discussed the feasibility of making Trenton the National capital, but State jealousies defeated the movement. On Dec. 25, 1776, the town was the scene of night attack by Washington on the British troops, whom he surprised by crossing the Delaware, when the floating ice was supposed to have rendered it impassable. A monument erected by the National and State governments commemorates this event. Pop. (1910) 96,815; (1920) 119,289.

TREPANNING, the operation of cutting a circular opening into the skull by means of a surgical instrument called a trepan or trephine. This consists of a handle, to which is fixed a small hollow steel cylinder, of about $\frac{1}{2}$ to 1 inch in diameter, having teeth cut on its lower edge so as to form a circular saw. The operation of trepanning is resorted to for the purpose of relieving the brain from pressure; such pressure may be caused by the depression of a portion of the cranium, or it may be produced by an extravasation of blood, or by the lodgment of matter betwixt the skull and the dura mater, occasioned by a blow upon the head, or the inflammation of the membranes of the brain.

TREPOMONADIDÆ, in zoölogy, a family of pantostomatous *Flagellata*, with a single genus, *Trepomonas*. Animalcules naked, free-swimming, asymmetrical; two flagella separately inserted; no distinct oral aperature.

TREPOMONAS, the type genus of *Trepomonadidæ*, with a single species, *T. agilis*, from marsh water with decaying vegetable substances.

TRERON, in ornithology, tree pigeons; a genus of *Columbidæ* (the Vinago of Cuvier), with 37 species, ranging over the whole Oriental region, and E. to Celebes, Amboyna and Flores, and the whole Ethiopian region to Madagascar. Formerly made the type genus of the lapsed family *Treronidæ*.

TRERONIDÆ, in ornithology, a family of *Columbacei*, approximately equivalent to the genus *Treron*. Bill large, strong, compressed at sides, tip very hard, hooked; nostrils exposed; tarsi short, partly clothed with feathers below tarsal joint; the whole foot formed for perching and grasping; claws strong, sharp, and semicircular.

TRESCOTT, WILLIAM HENRY, an American diplomatist; born in Charleston, S. C., Nov. 10, 1822; was graduated at Charleston College in 1840; admitted to the bar in 1843; assistant Secretary of State from June, 1860, till South Carolina seceded; represented that State in Washington after the war till the differences arising from the reconstruction acts were adjusted. He settled permanently in Washington in 1875, and there resumed the practice of law; was counsel for the United States before the Fishery Commission at Halifax in June, 1877; was a commissioner with General Grant to arrange a commercial treaty with Mexico in 1882; and served in other important diplomatic capacities. His publications include: "A Few Thoughts on the Foreign Policy of the United States" (1849); "Diplomatic System of the United States" (1853); "The Diplomatic-History of the Administrations of Washington and Adams" (1857); etc. He died in Pendleton, S. C., May 4, 1898.

TRESPASS, in law, a physical interference with the person or property of another. However innocent the act, if it be voluntary, a legal wrong is done. Thus, if pursued by a wild beast you deliberately take refuge in another man's house, you commit a trespass; but if you rush there in mere blind fear you do not. Again, if you drive in so careless a manner as to hurt any one, though unintentionally, this is a trespass. If animals or, indeed, any chattels are on a man's land doing damage, they may be seized and impounded till compensation be made. This remedy is called distress damage feasant. It is similar to distress at common law—*e. g.*, there is no power of sale. If a dog worry cattle or sheep, the owner is liable. Formerly it was necessary to prove scienter —*i. e.*, knowledge by the master of the animal's vicious disposition. *Scienter* must still be proved in other cases, and generally when animals, not savage by nature, do hurt—a legal doctrine quaintly parodied in the vulgar saying that the dog is entitled to his first bite. Even in complete absence of real injury an action for trespass will lie, for, says Lord Denman, those rights are an extension of that protection which the law throws round the person. A verdict of a farthing damages is, however, the frequent and appropriate compensation for injury without damage (*injuria sine damno*).

As will be seen, there are various kinds of trespass: (1) trespass to goods, which consist in damaging them physically, as asportation—*i. e.*, carrying them away; (2) trepass to the person, which is either battery, assault, or false imprisonment. Battery is an active attack on any one. Assault is an attempted battery; both are criminal offenses as well as civil wrongs. False imprisonment is usually classed among the latter. It consists in depriving a man of his liberty without lawful excuse. Compelling any one to submit by the exhibition of superior force, though no actual violence be used, is a wrong of this nature. If a constable intervene, the question is, did he do so of his own initiative, or at the prompting of a third party? In the second case only, even if the arrest be illegal, can the third party be held liable for the false imprisonment? Trespass to the person may be justified on the ground that a man was acting in self-defense, that it was necessary to stop a breach of the peace, to apprehend a felon, or to assist police officers in the execution of their duty, and that the person arrested was dangerous to himself and others.

As regards trespass to land, since a plaintiff must succeed by the strength of his own, not by the weakness of his adversary's case, bare possession is a good title as against a wrong doer; so the occupier may turn out an intruder, using, on his refusal to depart peaceably, as much force as is necessary. If the possessor be forcibly turned out, he may forcibly re-enter, even though outer doors be broken open to effect the purpose. But this must be done immediately, otherwise the owner, though entitled to possession, will, if he use violence, render himself criminally liable under the statutes of forcible entry. In making a distraint for rent or in levying an execution, but not executing criminal legal process, it is a trespass to break open the outer door. Though the general rule is that an entry on another land is a trespass, yet in certain cases of necessity an entry is excused— e. g., to abate a nuisance or to prevent the spread of fire. A customary right of recreation or right of way will excuse what would otherwise be a trespass. Cut glass or spikes on a wall are allowable as a defense against intruders; but not man traps or spring guns (except inside a dwelling house), at least since 1827. Even before that a trespasser could recover for damages so done to him, unless he had notice of the existence of the engines in question. The mere act of trespassing on another's land is not a criminal offense, but by statute it is when in pursuit of game, on railways, on places where explosives are stored or animals afflicted with contagious disease are confined. Besides the remedies for trespass—viz., forcible expulsion and an action for damages—an injunction may be granted, even for a bare trespass, since the Judicature Act of 1873. The law of the United States is based on the English law.

The term trespass, in Scotch law, is borrowed from that of England. It is restricted to trespass to land.

TREVELYAN, SIR CHARLES EDWARD, a British statesman; son of Archdeacon Trevelyan of Taunton; born April 2, 1807; was educated at the Charterhouse and Haileybury College; and entering the East India Company's Civil Service held important posts under Lords Auckland and Bentinck. His vigorous action promoted the abolition of Indian transit and town dues, and the introduction of educational institutions on a European model. In 1840 he was appointed assistant secretary to the treasury, and in 1848 was made K. C. B. for his attempts to relieve the distress caused by the Irish famine. With Sir Stafford Northcote and others he was long engaged in the revision of the civil establishments which led to the Civil Service being thrown open to public competition. He was governor of Madras from 1859 to 1860, when he was recalled for protesting against the new taxes then imposed by the government of India. In 1862 he became financial minister in India, a post in which he inaugurated important fiscal reform and a vast extension of public works, and which he resigned on account of ill health in 1865. He was created a baronet in 1874. Trevelyan married Miss Hannah More Macaulay in 1834 and was the author of "Education of the Irish People" (1838); "The Irish Crisis" (1848); "Purchase System in the British Army" (2d ed. 1867); "The British Army in 1868" (1869); etc. He died in London, June 19, 1880.

TREVELYAN, GEORGE MACAULAY, an English historian, born in 1876. He was educated at Harrow and Trinity College, Cambridge. His works include: "England in the Age of Wycliffe"; "England Under the Stuarts"; "The Poetry and Philosophy of George Meredith"; "Garibaldi's Defence of the Roman Republic"; "Garibaldi and the Thousand"; "Garibaldi and the Making of Italy"; "The Life of John Bright"; "Clio, a Muse, and Other Essays."

TREVELYAN, SIR GEORGE OTTO, a British statesman; son of Sir Charles E. T.; born in Rothley Temple, Leicestershire, July 20, 1838, and passing from Harrow to Trinity College, Cambridge, graduated as second classic. He entered the East India service by competition, but soon returned from India and was elected Liberal representative of Tynemouth in 1865, and of the Scottish Border Burghs in 1868. In the second Gladstone administration he was appointed Civil Lord of the Admiralty (December, 1868), but resigned office in July, 1870, being opposed to the Educational Bill of the ministry. He strongly advocated, in and out of Parliament, a sweeping army reform, including the abolition of purchase, effected in 1871. The Volunteer movement had his active support, and he opposed the Regimental Exchanges Bill of 1875. With impetuous rhetoric and fiery invective he has severely criticized the Conservative foreign policy, declaring that war with Russia was only avoided by the resignation of "the two brave peers" (Carnarvon and Derby), and that apart from the question of justice the Afghan War was opposed to the interests of the Indian empire. In Feb. 22,

1878, he moved the resolution on the extension of the County Franchise, which was lost by 52 votes. Trevelyan's literary works comprise: "Letters from a Competition Wallah" (1864); "Cawnpore" (1865); "Ladies in Parliament and other Poems" (1869); "Life and Letters of Lord Macaulay" (2 vols. 1876; 2d ed. 1877); "The Early History of Charles James Fox" (1880; "American Revolution" (1909); "George III. and Charles Fox" (1914).

TREVENA, JOHN, pseudonym of an English novelist, Ernest George Henham, born in 1873. Delicate in health he sought health in wandering and finally settled at Dartmoor, the scene of several of his novels. The works under his own name include: "Menotah: A Tale of the Canadian North West"; "God, Man and the Devil"; "Trenbrae"; "Bonanza: A Story of the Outside"; "Scud: The Story of a Feud"; "The Plowshare and the Sword"; "Krum: A Study of Consciousness." Works under his pseudonym include: "A Pixy in Petticoats"; "Furze the Cruel"; "Arminel of the West"; "Heather"; "The Dartmoor House that Jack Built"; "Matrimony"; "Moyle Church Town."

TREVES, a city of Rhenish Prussia; on the Moselle; in a valley between low vine-covered hills of ruddy sandstone; 69 miles S. W. of Coblenz and 111 S. S. W. of Cologne. The river is crossed here by an eight-arch bridge, 623 feet long, whose Roman piers date from 25 B. C. "A quiet, old-fashioned town, Treves," Freeman says, "has a body of Roman remains far more numerous and varied, if not individually more striking, than any other place north of the Alps can show." These include the "Porta Nigra," 118 feet long, and 95 high, one probably of the five gates by which Trèves was entered in Constantine's time; the so-called Roman baths (more probably part of an imperial palace); and a basilica built of Roman brick by Constantine for a court of justice, but demolished in great measure to make room for an electoral palace in 1614. This, however, was removed, and the basilica fitted up for a Protestant church in 1856. Beyond the walls are the ruins of an amphitheater that could seat 30,000 spectators; and 6 miles off is the "Igelsäule" or "Heidenthurm," a monumental column, 71 feet high, sculptured with bas-reliefs of the 2d century. The cathedral of SS. Peter and Helena is an interesting structure of various antiquity, but chiefly in the early German Romanesque style of the 11th century. The most famous of its relics is the seamless or "Holy Coat,"

which consists of "connected fragmentary particles of material." Said to have been brought to Treves by the Empress Helena, it is first referred to in 1106 by an anonymous monk, and was not a source of revenue till 1512. It was visited by nearly 2,000,000 pilgrims in 1891, the first time of exhibition since 1844. A "Holy Coat" is also shown at Argenteuil and in 19 other places. Connected with the cathedral by a cloister is the beautiful Liebfrauenkirche (1243); and there is a library of over 100,000 volumes and many MSS., among them the "Codex Aureus" of the Gospels, presented to the abbey of St. Maximin by Charlemagne's sister, Ada. A university, founded in 1472, was suppressed in 1798. The industries comprise manufactures of woolens, cottons, and linens, besides a brisk trade in corn, timber, and Moselle wine. Pop. about 47,000.

Treves, which claims to be 1,300 years older than Rome, derives its name from the Treviri, a Gallic or, more probably, a Belgic people, who in Cæsar's time inhabited a large district between the Meuse and the Rhine. Their capital, Augusta Trevirorum, seems to have become a Roman colony in the reign of Augustus, and ultimately was the headquarters of the Roman commanders on the Rhine, and a frequent residence of the emperors, especially Constantine. Sacked by Attila in 451, it passed to the Franks in 463, to Lorraine in 843, to Germany in 870, and back to Lorraine in 895, and was finally united to Germany by the Emperor Henry I. The Archbishop of Treves was, as chancellor of Burgundy, one of the electors of the empire, a right which originated in the 12th or 13th century, and which continued till the French Revolution. The last elector removed to Coblenz in 1786; and Treves was the capital of the French department of Sarre from 1794 till 1814, since which time it has belonged to Prussia.

TREVES, SIR FREDERICK, a British surgeon, born in Dorchester, in 1853. He was educated at the Merchant Taylors' School and became Hunterian professor of anatomy and Wilson professor of pathology at the Royal College of Surgeons in 1881-1886 and examiner in surgery at Cambridge in 1891-1896. He was lord rector of Aberdeen University from 1905 to 1908. He acted as consulting surgeon in the South African War, was surgeon-extraordinary to Queen Victoria, and in 1902 operated on Edward VII. for perilyphilitis. He wrote "System of Surgery," and published other works on medicine, war experience, and travel. Died Dec. 7, 1923.

TREWIA, in botany, the typical genus of *Trewiaceæ*. Leaves opposite, entire, without stipules; flowers diœcious, males in long, racemes, females axillary, solitary; males, sepals three to four, stamens many; females, calyx three to four-cleft, style four-cleft; drupe five-celled, each cell with a single seed. Known species one, *T. nudi-flora*, an Indian deciduous tree, growing in the sub-Himalayas. The wood is used for drums and agricultural implements.

TRIACANTHINA, in ichthyology, a group of *Sclerodermi*, with three genera, having the range of the family. The skin is covered with small, rough, scalelike scutes; dorsal, with from four to six spines; a pair of strong movable ventral spines joined to the pelvic bone.

TRIACANTHUS, in ichthyology, a genus of *Triacanthina*, with five species ranging from the Australian seas to the N. of China. *T. brevirostris*, from the Indian Ocean, is the most common.

TRIÆNOPS, in zoölogy, a genus of *Phyllorhininæ*, with one species from Persia and another from East Africa. Noseleaf, horse-shoe-shaped in front, tridentate behind; ears without a distinct antitragus, the outer margin of the ear conch arising from the posteriors of the eyelids.

TRIANGLE, in building, a gin formed by three spars; a staging of three spars. In draughting, a three-cornered straight-edge, used in conjunction with the T-square for drawing parallel, perpendicular, or diagonal lines. It has one right angle, the two others being each of 45°, or one of 30° and the other of 60°. In ecclesiology, a symbol of the Holy Trinity represented by an equilateral triangle.

In geometry, a portion of a surface bounded by three lines, and consequently having three angles. Triangles are either plane, spherical, or curvilinear. A plane triangle is a portion of a plane bounded by three straight lines called sides, and their points of intersection are the vertices of the triangle. Plane triangles may be classified either with reference to their sides or their angles. When classified with reference to their sides, there are two classes: (1) Scalene triangles, which have no two sides equal. (2) Isosceles triangles, which have two sides equal. The isosceles triangle has a particular case, called the equilateral triangle, all of whose sides are equal. When classified with reference to their angles, there are two classes: (1) Right-angled triangles, which have one right angle.

(2) Oblique-angled triangles, all of whose angles are oblique; subdivided into (a) acute-angled triangles, which have all their angles acute; and (b) obtuse-angled triangles, which have one obtuse angle. The sides and angles of a triangle are called its elements; the side on which it is supposed to stand is called the base, and the vertex of the opposite angle is called the vertex of the triangle; the distance from the vertex to the base is the altitude. Any side of a triangle may be regarded as a base, though in the right-angled triangle one of the sides about the right angle is usually taken. The three angles of a plane triangle are together equal to two right angles, or 180°; its area is equal to half that of a rectangle or parallelogram having the same base and altitude; in a right-angled plane triangle the square of the side opposite the right angle is equal to the sum of the squares of the other two sides.

In music, a bar of steel bent into the form of a triangle. It is suspended by one angle and struck with a small rod. In pottery, a small piece of pottery placed between pieces of biscuit ware in the seggar to prevent the adherence of the pieces when fired. In surveying, since every plane figure may be regarded as composed of a certain number of triangles, and as the area of a triangle is easily computed, the whole practice of land surveying is nothing more than the measurement of a series of plane triangles. Arithmetical triangle, a name given to a table of numbers arranged in a triangular manner, and formerly employed in arithmetical computation. It is equivalent to a multiplication table.

```
1
1  1
1  2  1
1  3  3  1
1  4  6  4  1
1  5 10 10  5  1
1  6 15 20 15  6  1
```

Curvilinear triangle, a triangle whose sides are curved lines of any kind whatever; as, a spheroidal triangle, lying on the surface of an ellipsoid, etc.

Mixtilinear triangle, a triangle in which some of the lines are straight and others curved.

Spherical triangles take the names, right-angled, obtuse-angled, acute-angled, scalene, isosceles, and equilateral, in the same cases as plane triangles. Two spherical triangles are polar, when the angles of the one are supplements of the sides of the other, taken in the same order. A spherical triangle is quadrantal, when one of its sides is equal to 90°.

TRIANGLE OF FORCES, in mechanics, a term applied to that proposition which asserts that if three forces, represented in magnitude and direction by the sides of a triangle taken in order, act on a point, they will be in equilibrium; and conversely, if three forces acting on a point, and in equilibrium, be represented in direction by the sides of a triangle taken in order, they will also be represented in magnitude by the sides of that triangle.

TRIANGLE OF HESSELBACH, in anatomy, a triangular interval at the part of the abdominal wall through which the direct inguinal hernia passes.

TRIANGLE OF SCARPA, in anatomy, a triangular depression between the muscles covering the outer side of the femur and the adductor muscles on the inner side. It affords a passage for the femoral artery.

TRIANGULUM, in astronomy, the triangle; one of the 48 ancient constellations. It is of small size, and is situated S. E. of Andromeda, N. of Aries, and W. of Perseus. The largest star, Alpha Trianguli, is only of the third magnitude.

TRIANGULUM AUSTRALE, in astronomy, the Southern Triangle; a S. constellation of small size, but having the three stars which define it so prominent that they are sometimes called the triangle stars. The constellation is between Pavo and Centaurus.

TRIANGULUM MINUS, in astronomy, the Lesser Triangle; an obsolete constellation of small size between Triangulum and Aries. It was established by Hevelius.

TRIANOSPERMA, in botany, a genus of *Cucurbiteæ*, akin to *Bryonia*, but having only three seeds. They are climbing plants, with tendrils and monœcious flowers. Stamens three, ovary three-celled. Fruit globular, fleshy. Natives of the West Indies and Brazil. *T. ficifolia*, called also *B. ficifolia*, is an active purgative, and said to be a purifier of the blood. *T. tayuya* is given in Brazil in small doses as an emetic and in large ones as a purgative.

TRIANTHEMA, in botany, a genus of *Sesuveæ*. Sepals oblong, colored on the inside; stamens 5 to 12; styles one or two, filiform; capsule, oblong, truncate, circumscissile. Weeds from the tropical parts of both hemispheres and the sub-tropics of Africa. *T. crystallina*, *T. monogyna* (*T. obcordata* of Roxburgh), *T. pentandra*, and *T. decandra*, are natives of India. The tender leaves and the tops of the second and third species are eaten by the natives; the seeds of the first also serve as food during famine. *T. pentandra* is used as an astringent in abdominal diseases, and is said to produce abortion. The roots of *T. decandra* and *T. monogyna*, the latter combined with ginger, are given as cathartics.

TRIASSIC SYSTEM. This forms the basement group of the Mesozoic or Secondary strata, and was formerly associated with the Permian system under the name of the New Red Sandstone. The term trias has reference to the threefold grouping of the system in Germany, where the strata are more fully developed than in Great Britain. In our area the system rests unconformably on the upturned and denuded edges of the Permian and older Palæozoic strata. It is well developed in the central plains of England, whence a long belt extends N. from Nottingham to the valley of the Tees, while another band stretches down the Severn valley into Devonshire. Small areas likewise occur in Dumfriesshire and near Elgin, and also in the N. of Ireland. The system, however, assumes more importance in Central Europe, where it occurs at the surface over a wide tract between the Thüringerwald in the E. and the Vosges Mountains in the W., and between Basel in the S. and Hanover in the N. N. of that region it continues underneath overlying formations, but appears again and again at the surface where these latter are wanting. Trias is also met with in Heligoland and the S. of Sweden. In all the regions now noted the strata appear to have been deposited in inland seas.

In the Alpine regions the Trias differs much from that of England and Germany. It attains a thickness of many thousand feet, and forms ranges of mountains. The lower division consists chiefly of fossiliferous limestones, the middle of shales, marls, limestones, and dolomites, while the Rhætic is built up mainly of limestones and dolomites. Thus in Northwestern and Central Europe we have one well-defined type consisting of strata which have accumulated for the most part in inland seas, while in the Alpine regions the character of the beds betokens more open water. In France isolated areas of Trias occur, some of which approximate in appearance to those of England, while others resemble those of Germany. In Spain and Portugal both the German and Alpine types are represented.

In North America the Trias is well developed, as in Nova Scotia, Prince Edward Island, the Connecticut valley; the W. side of the Hudson river, and S. W. through Pennsylvania into Virginia; North Carolina. Strata believed to be of the same age cover wide areas in the W. territories, extending from the E. borders of the Rocky Mountains into Alaska, British Columbia, and California. Brick-red sandstones and marls are a prominent feature in all those areas. Like the similar rocks of Europe they contain few fossils, but animal tracks and footprints are of frequent occurrence. On the whole the American strata above referred to resemble the English type of the Trias. But on the Pacific slope, in Northern California and Mexico, the strata yield a plentiful marine fauna and resemble the type of the Alpine Trias.

Life of the Period.—The predominant plants were cycads (Pterophyllum, Zamites, etc.), horsetails (Equiseta), ferns, and conifers, especially the cypress-like Voltzia. In the red beds of the Trias few fossils occur, our knowledge of the life of the period (more especially the invertebrate life) being derived from the Rhætic, the Muschelkalk, and the marine strata of the Alpine Trias. Foraminifera, sponges, star corals, and echinoderms were tolerably numerous. One of the most beautiful fossils is the lily encrinite (*Encrinus liliiformis*) of the muschelkalk. Among lamellibranchs myophoria, avicula, pecten, cardium were common forms. A number of palæozoic genera of gasteropods (*Loxonema, Murchisonia,* etc.) appear, commingled with newer forms. The same is the case with the cephalopods, such old genera as *Orthoceras, Cyrtoceras,* and *Gonialtites* occurring along with *Ceratites* and other species of the great tribe of Ammonites. This remarkable association of palæozoic and mesozoic genera is most notable in the Alpine Trias. In the same strata occur the earliest traces of dibranchiate cephalopods, represented by the internal bone or shell (belemnites). The triassic fishes are ganoids and placoids—the latter represented by spines and palate teeth (*Ceratodus*), Labyrinthodonts abounded. Lizard-like reptiles (*telerpeton, hyperodapedon*) were numerous, while crocodiles (*stagonolepis*) made their first appearance. The same is the case of the extinct group of dinosaurs —terrestrial reptiles, some of which could walk on their hind feet, which were often only three-toed—their front feet being four-toed. Swimming reptiles (*Nothosaurus*) have also been recorded from the Trias. Another remarkable group of reptiles were represented by dicynodon, which had a horny beak and

carried two large tusk-like teeth in the upper jaw. The Trias is further remarkable for having yielded the earliest relics of mammalia.

Physical Conditions.—The British Triassic strata afford evidence of having, for the most part, been deposited in a great inland sea or salt lake, from the waters of which sodium chloride (rock salt), gypsum, and other chemically-formed materials were precipitated. This inland sea covered a large part of England, and extended N. into Southern Scotland and across what is now the area of the Irish Sea into the N. E. of Ireland. It is possible also that the same sea stretched into Northern France. Another but smaller lake is indicated by the red sandstones of Elgin.

On the Continent during a large part of the Triassic period an inland sea extended W. from the Thüringerwald across the Vosges country into France, and stretched N. from the confines of Switzerland over what are now the low grounds of Holland and North Germany. In this ancient sea the Harz Mountains formed an island. In the earlier stages of the period the conditions resembled those that obtained in Great Britain, but the thick muschelkalk with its numerous marine forms seems to indicate an influx of water from the open sea. Afterward, however, this connection was closed, and the subsequent accumulations point to increasing salinity, during which chemical formations (gypsum, rock salt, etc.,) took place, while the marine fauna disappeared. Toward the close of the period, after the great inland lake had been largely silted up, a partial influx of the sea introduced a fauna comparable to that of the English Rhætic. It seems highly probable that the lands surrounding the inland lakes of Central and Northwestern Europe were more or less dry and sandy regions, like the great wastes of Central Asia. Many of the sandstones in the Bunter series of England are made up of grains so completely worn and rounded that they exactly recall the appearance presented by the wind-blown sands of desert regions. Some geologists therefore infer that in the earlier stages of the Triassic period large tracts of Great Britain were sandy deserts before the inland sea attained its greatest development. The Alpine Trias, which is mostly marine, shows that, while continental and lacustrine conditions obtained in central and N. W. Europe, an open sea existed toward the S.— a Mediterranean of much greater extent than the present. From the fact that Triassic rocks with characteristic fossils occur within the Arctic regions it may be inferred that the climate of the period was generally genial or warm.

TRIBE, an aggregate of stocks—a stock being an aggregate of persons considered to be kindred—or an aggregate of families, forming a community usually under the government of a chief. The chief is possessed of despotic power over the members of the tribe, which is one of the earliest forms of the community among all the races of men.

TRIBONIANUS, a Roman jurist of the 6th century, of Macedonian parentage, but born in Paphlagonia. He held under the Emperor Justinian the offices of quæstor, master of the imperial household, and consul. He is famous chiefly through his labors in connection with the Code of Justinian and the Pandects. He died in 545.

TRIBUNE, in Roman antiquities, properly the chief-magistrate of a tribe. There were several kinds of officers in the Roman state that bore the title. (1) The plebeian tribunes, who were first created after the secession of the commonalty to the Mons Sacer (A. U. C. 260), as one of the conditions of its return to the city. They were especially the magistrates and protectors of the commonalty, and no patrician could be elected to the office. At their first appointment the power of the tribunes was very small, being confined to the assembling of the plebeians and the protection of any individual from patrician aggression; but their persons were sacred and inviolable, and this privilege consolidated their other powers, which, in the later ages of the republic, grew to an enormous height, and were finally incorporated with the functions of the other chief magistracies in the person of the emperor. The number of the tribunes varied from 2 to 10, and each of these might annul the proceedings of the rest by putting in his veto. (2) Military tribunes were first elected in the year A. U. C. 310, in the place of the consuls, in consequence of the demands of the commonalty to be admitted to a share of the supreme power. The number of the military tribunes was sometimes six and sometimes three. For above 70 years sometimes consuls were elected and sometimes military tribunes; at last the old order was permanently restored, but the plebeians were admitted to a share of it. (3) Legionary tribunes, or tribunes of the soldiers, were the chief officers of a legion, six in number, who commanded under the consul, each in his turn, usually about a month; in battle each led a cohort Also, a bench or elevated place; a raised seat or stand.

Specifically, the throne of a bishop, and a sort of pulpit or rostrum where a speaker stands to address an audience.

TRICHIA, in botany, a genus of Myxogastres or gasteromycetous Fungi, having a stalked or sessile, simple, membranous peridium bursting at the summit; spiral threads, which carry with them the spores. The threads and spores are often bright colored. Species numerous, occurring on rotten wood, etc.

TRICHIASIS, in pathology, the growth of one or more of the eyelashes in a wrong direction, ultimately bringing it in contact with the anterior portion of the eyeball. Sometimes this is the natural mode of growth, but more frequently it is produced by a disease of the eyelid, or its inversion. The cure is slowly and steadily to remove each eyelash with a broad-pointed and well-grooved forceps, and then repeatedly apply spirits of wine to the place to destroy the follicles.

TRICHIDIUM, in botany, a tender, simple, or sometimes branched hair, which bears the spores of certain fungals, as in the genus Geastrum

TRICHILIA, in botany, the typical genus of Trichilieæ. Trees of shrubs with unequally pinnate, rarely trifoliolate leaves; flowers in axillary panicles; calyx four or five cleft; petals four or five overlapping; stamens 8 or 10, united into a tube; fruit capsular, three-celled; seeds, two in each cell. Known species about 20, the majority from America, the remainder from Africa. The bark of Trichilia emetica, called by the Arabs roka and elcaija, is a violent purgative and emetic. The Arab women mix the fruits with the perfumes used for washing their hair; the seeds are made into an ointment with sesamum oil, and used as a remedy for the itch. T. cathartica is also a purgative. T. moschata, a Jamaica plant, has an odor of musk wood. T. catigoa, now Moschoxylon catigoa, the catigua of Brazil, stains leather a bright yellow.

TRICHINA, in zoölogy, a genus of Nematoidæ, established by Owen for the reception of the minute spiral flesh worm, T. spiralis, discovered in human muscle by Sir James Paget, in 1835, when a student at St. Bartholomew's Hospital, London. Mr. Hilton, of Guy's, had previously noticed gritty particles in human muscles, and recognized them as the results of parasites, afterward shown (by Owen) to be young trichinæ. The trichinæ met with in human muscle are minute immature worms, spirally coiled in small oval cysts, scarcely visible to the naked eye, measuring 1/78 inch in length and 1/136 inch in breadth. Sometimes the worms are not encysted, and measure 1/25 inch in length and 1/360 inch in breadth. The mature and reproductive trichinæ inhabit the intestinal canal of mammals, including man, and live for four or five weeks, attaining ability to reproduce on the second day of their introduction. The male is about 1/18 and the female 1/8 inch long. The eggs are hatched within the female, and as soon as the embryos are expelled they bore their way into the muscles, and there in about 14 days assume the form known as T. spiralis, often setting up trichiniasis. Thus the only way in which trichinæ can get into the human system is by being swallowed alive with pieces of imperfectly-cooked muscle in which they are encysted. The pig is the great source of infection to man, as it is peculiarly liable to the presence of encysted trichinæ.

TRICHINIASIS, a disease produced by the presence of trichinæ within the human system, and within the bodies of other animals liable to infestation. The first well-marked case occurred at Dresden in 1860, the patient being a servant girl, who was admitted to hospital, having taken ill on Jan. 12. The patient died after a short illness characterized by symptoms of lung inflammation, rheumatic pains, spasmodic contractions of the limbs, and other abnormal conditions, indicating some obscure lesion the nature of which was imperfectly understood. It was discovered at the post-mortem examination that in the muscles of this patient numerous larval trichinæ were encysted, while mature trichinæ were found in the intestines. Previously to her illness the patient had assisted in making pork sausages, and had eaten some of the meat in a raw state, this fact accounting for the trichinose infestation. Zenker, who records the case, recognized in the symptoms those of a new lesion caused by the presence and development of trichinæ, within the tissues of man.

The preliminary symptoms are loss of appetite, prostration, and general debility, which continue for about a week. Pains of a rheumatic character, œdema, or dropsy and swelling of the limbs, along with fever, next occur, indicating the progress of the trichinæ brood from the digestive system to the muscles. This stage of trichiniasis is unquestionably the most dangerous. It is during the migration of the trichinæ from the alimentary canal, and as they force their way through to the muscular system,

that the patient experiences the most severe symptoms and stands in greatest danger. Severe pains are experienced at this period in a typical case of trichiniasis, and even breathing may be executed with difficulty owing to the lesions of the muscles. Diarrhœa is also prevalent, the symptoms on the whole bearing a resemblance to those of gastric fever. In about four weeks after the commencement of the symptoms the disease begins to abate. In severe cases the diarrhœa may continue, and often aids a fatal issue, arising from the prostration, together with the total derangement of the secretions. In an acute case of trichiniasis death has been known to occur as early as the fifth day of the disease, while a fatal issue has been allayed as late as the 42d day. Epidemics of trichiniasis have chiefly occurred on the Continent, where the habit of eating smoked and uncooked sausages is widespread. At Hattstädt, in October, 1863, an epidemic of this disorder affected 158 persons, a fatal result occurring in 28 cases

An examination of pig's flesh shows that trichinæ are frequently found in the muscles. No external signs in the pig afford evidence of the presenec of trichinæ, and the microscopic examination of the flesh is the only true test of infestation. A temperature of 167° F. is sufficient to kill trichinæ larvæ, and the prohibition against uncooked or imperfectly cooked animal food of all kinds, is to be rigorously insisted on in the rules of hygiene. The treatment of trichiniasis appears to consist in active purgation in the early stages of the disease, with the view of removing the worms from the intestine, calomel being the purgative usually given.

TRICHINOPOLI, the chief town of the district of the same name, Madras presidency, British India; on the Cauvery river; 320 miles S. S. W. of Madras. It is celebrated for its fort, which was built (circa 1570) by a native prince of Madura, and formed the object of all the wars between the English and the French in Southern India between 1749 and 1763, when Clive first rose to fame. The fort occupies a granite cliff rising 500 feet above the plain, crowned with a small pagoda, with a cave temple hewn out of its S. face. The walls have been leveled and the moat filled up, and the whole is now being laid out as a boulevard. Trichinopoli is the headquarters of the brigadier commanding the Southern Division of the Madras army. There are barracks for European troops and artillery. In the church is the tomb of Bishop

Heber, who died here in 1826. The manufactures include jewelry, paintings on talc, paper and pith ornaments. Pop. about 124,000. The district of Trichinopoli, which lies on both banks of the Cauvery, landward of Tranjore, has an area of 3,515 square miles. It abounds with gneiss, granite, iron ore and limestone. The products are rice, cotton, sugar, oil seeds, and tobacco. The exports include saltpeter, hewn stone for building, and grindstones. The imports are English piece goods. Besides the manufactures of the town, basket boats are made of wicker work covered with hides.

TRICKETT, WILLIAM, an American lawyer; born in England, in 1840; was graduated at Dickinson College in 1868 and was admitted to the bar in 1876. He was made dean of Dickinson School of Law in 1890; was candidate for the Superior Court of Pennsylvania on the Democratic ticket in 1898. He was the author of "Law of Liens in Pennsylvania" (3 vols. 1882); "Law of Limitations in Pennsylvania" (1884); "Law of Assignments in Pennsylvania" (1884); "Law of Boroughs in Pennsylvania" (2 vols. 1893 and 1898); "Law of Streets and Roads in Pennsylvania" (1894); "Law of Guardians in Pennsylvania" (1900); and "Law of Partition in Pennsylvania" (1900).

TRICLINIUM, in Roman antiquities, in early times, the whole family sat together in the atrium, or public room; but when mansions were built upon a large scale, one or more spacious banqueting halls commonly formed part of the plan, such apartments being classed under the general title of triclinia. The word triclinium, however, in its strict signification, denotes not the apartment, but a set of low divans or couches grouped round a table; these couches, according to the usual arrangement, being three in number, and arranged round three sides of the table, the fourth side being left open for the ingress and egress of the attendants, to set down and remove the dishes. Each couch was calculated to hold three persons, though four might be squeezed in. Men always reclined at table, resting on the left elbow, their bodies slightly elevated by cushions, and their limbs stretched out at full length their right arm free.

TRICOLOR, a flag or banner having three colors; specifically, a flag having three colors arranged in equal stripes or masses. The present European tricolor designs are: For Belgium, black, yellow, red, divided vertically; France, blue, white, red, divided vertically; Holland, red, white, blue, divided horizontally; Italy, green, white, red, divided vertically. During the revolution of 1789 in France the revolutionists adopted as their colors the three colors of the city of Paris for their symbol. The three colors were first devised by Mary Stuart, wife of Francis II. The white represented the royal house of France; the blue, Scotland; and the red, Switzerland, in compliment to the Swiss guards, whose livery it was. In botany, *Amaranthus tricolor*, a species from China, with bright foliage, but insignificant flowers.

TRIESTE, a city of Italy and most considerable trading town on the Adriatic; at the head of the Gulf of Trieste, an arm of the Gulf of Venice; 370 miles S. S. W. of Vienna. In 1849 it was constituted an imperial free city, and attached and belonging to it is a territory 36 square miles in extent. The city of Trieste, in which the population of the district is almost wholly amassed, consists of the old town, the new town, or Theresienstadt, and two suburbs, Josefstadt and Franzenstadt. The old town, built on the slope of a steep hill, crowned by a castle (1508-1680), is distinguished by its narrow streets and black walls. It contains the cathedral, a Byzantine edifice built between the 5th and 14th centuries, into the walls of which stones bearing Roman inscriptions and carving have been built, and the tower of which is said to rest on the foundation of a temple of Jupiter. The new town, with broad streets built in regular parallelograms and handsome houses, occupies the plain that fronts the sea. Between these two divisions runs the Corso, the chief thoroughfare. The Tergesteo (1840), in the new town, is a splendid modern edifice, containing an exchange and reading rooms, and the offices of the Austrian Lloyd's. Trieste, which from 1719 till July 1, 1891, was a free port, has a very fine new harbor (1868-1883). The manufactures are very extensive, including ship-building, rope-making, and the manufacture of soap, rosoglio, white lead, leather, etc. A great agricultural exhibition was held at Trieste in 1882. Pop. (1910) 157,765, nearly all Catholics, and mostly Italian-speaking.

Trieste, the ancient Tergeste or Tergestum, was of importance under the Romans, and first receives historical mention 51 B. C., when it was overrun and plundered by neighboring tribes. In 1382 it passed finally into the hands of Austria. It owes its prosperity chiefly to the Emperor Charles VI., who constituted it a free port, and to Maria

THE CITY OF TRENT, CAPITAL OF THE TRENTINO, WON BY ITALY AS A RESULT OF THE WAR

See **Trent**, p. 496

TOBLINO CASTLE IN THE TRENTINO

See **Trentino**, p. 496

Theresa. Since 1816 Trieste has borne the title of the "Most Loyal of Towns." Charles Lever and Sir Richard Burton were consuls there. The city suffered heavily in the World War from bombardment. In 1918 it was united to Italy.

TRIGGS, OSCAR LOVELL, an American author; born in Greenwood, Ill., Oct. 2, 1865; was graduated at the University of Minnesota in 1889, and then studied in the Universities of Oxford and Berlin. In 1892 he became connected with the English Department of the University of Chicago. He was the author of "Browning and Whitman: a Study in Democracy" (1893); "The Changing Order" (1901); and many review articles. He also edited Lydgate's "Assembly of Gods" (1895); and "Selections from Prose and Poetry of Walter Whitman" (1898).

TRIGONOMETRY, o r i g i n a l l y the branch of geometry which had to do with the measurement of plain triangles. This gradually resolved itself into the investigation of the relations between the angles of the triangle, for the simple reason that all triangles having the same set of angles are similar, so that if, in addition, one side is given the other two at once follow. It is easy to show from the Sixth Book of Euclid that, if we fix the values of the angles of a triangle, the ratio of the sides containing any one of these angles is the same whatever be the size of the triangle. This ratio is a definite function of the angles; and it is with the properties of such ratios that trigonometry has now to deal. The fundamental ratios are obtained from a

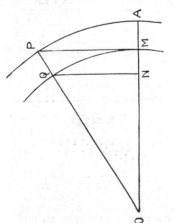

right-angled triangle, of which one angle is the angle under consideration. It will suffice to show what these ratios are and how they have received their names. Let POM be the angle considered, PM being drawn perpendicular to OM. With center O describe the two circles PA and MQ. The appropriate measure of the angle at O is the ratio of the subtended arc to the radius—*i. e.*, either AP/OP or MQ/OM (see CIRCLE). This measure we shall adopt throughout, and shall represent it by the symbol θ. If QN is drawn perpendicular to OM, then the ratio of any pair of sides of the triangle OQN is equal to the ratio of the corresponding sides of triangle OPM. All the possible ratios which can be formed are the so-called trigonometrical or circular functions of the angle θ. Thus the ratio PM/OP or QN/OQ is the sine of θ. It is evidently half the chord of the angle $2/\theta$; and its value is numerically less than 0, because PM being less than the chord PA is less than the arc PA. Again, the ratio PM/OM is the tangent of θ. MP is, in fact, the geometrical tangent drawn from the one extremity of the arc MQ till it meets the radius through the other extremity. For a similar reason the ratio OP/OM or OQ/ON is called the secant of the angle θ. In the same way the ratios OM/OP, OM/PM, OP/PM are respectively the sine, tangent, and secant of the angle OPM, which is the complement of the angle POM. Hence these ratios, regarded as functions of θ, are called the cosine, cotangent, and cosecant of θ. For any given angle there are, then, six trigonometrical functions. It is obvious that these functions are mutually dependent. Indeed, if any one is given the other five can be at once calculated. For instance, the well-known relation $OM^2+MP^2=OP^2$ gives at once by dividing by OP^2

$$(\sin. \theta)^2 + (\cos. \theta)^2 = 1,$$

or, as it is usually written,

$$\sin.^2 \theta + \cos.^2 \theta = 1.$$

Then, again, the cosecant is the reciprocal of the sine, and the secant of the cosine. The tangent is the ratio of the sine to the cosine; and the cotangent is the reciprocal of the tangent. The sine and cosine are never greater than unity, and the secant and cosecant are never less than unity. The tangent is less or greater than unity according as the angle POM is less or greater than half a right angle.

Suppose OP to rotate counter-clockwise. Then as the angle AOP increases from zero to a right angle the sine evidently grows from zero to unity; while at the same time the cosine diminishes from unity to zero. Continuing the increase so that AOP becomes an obtuse angle, we find that the sine begins to diminish, and that the cosine begins to increase numerically but toward the left of O. In other words, the cosine becomes negative, and continues so till OP has completed three right angles. In the same way, as AOP passes through the value of two right angles and becomes re-entrant, the sine becomes negative, being thenceforward measured downward till OP has made one complete revolution. After one complete revolution both sine and cosine, and also secant and cosecant, begin to go through exactly the same cycle of changes in magnitude and sign as at first. There are, therefore, periodic functions, and their period is $2n$ or four right angles. The tangent and cotangent, however, go through their cycle of changes in half this period or two right angles. All possible numerical values of the functions are obtained in the first quadrant. It is therefore sufficient in constructing tables of the trigonometrical functions to tabulate for angles from 0° to 90° inclusive. For example, the angle 130° (90°+40°) has the same sine as the angle of 50 (90°-40°); and its cosine differs only by being negative. Of greater practical importance than the tables of the functions themselves are the table of their logarithms. These are generally tabulated for every degree and minute of angle from 0° to 90°; and proportional parts are added by which is readily calculated the number corresponding to an angle involving seconds of arc.

The calculation of the functions and their logarithms is a sufficiently laborious task. It is generally effected by means of series, though the values for certain particular angles can be found by the simplest of arithmetical operations. Thus, the cosine of 60° is evidently $\frac{1}{2}$; sine 60° is therefore $\frac{1}{2}\sqrt{3}$; tangent 60° is $\sqrt{3}$; and so on. What might be called the fundamental series for the sine and cosine in terms of the arc are:

$$\sin.\ \theta = \theta - \frac{\theta^3}{1.2.3} + \frac{\theta^5}{1.2.3.4.5} - \frac{\theta^7}{1.2.3.4.5.6.7} + \cdots$$

$$\cos.\ \theta = 1 - \frac{\theta^2}{1.2} + \frac{\theta^4}{1.2.3.4} - \frac{\theta^5}{1.2.3.4.5.6} + \cdots$$

If we make all the signs in these two series positive we get two other functions of θ, which are called the hyperbolic sine and cosine of θ, and are written sinh. θ and cosh, θ respectively. Related to these functions are the hyperbolic tangent, cotangent, secant, and cosecant; and they are connected by relations similar to, though not quite identical with, the ordinary circular functions. We may see, by adding the series with signs all positive, that the sum of the hyperbolic sine and cosine is the exponential of θ. Demoivre's theorem gives the corresponding equation for the circular sine and cosine.

The reason for the names circular and hyperbolic may be partially indicated thus: The relation $\cos.^2 \theta + \sin.^2 \theta = 1$ may be put in the form $x^2 + y^2 = a^2$, which is the equation of a circle of radius a, referred to rectangular axes. The equation of the rectangular hyperbola is $x_2 - y^2 = a^2$, to which there corresponds the relation $\cosh._2 \theta - \sinh.^2 \theta = 1$. The hyperbolic sines and cosines are really exponential functions, and are not periodic. They are of constant occurrence both in the higher analysis and in mathematical physics. To facilitate their use in calculation, tables have recently been constructed.

Besides the series given above, there are many others, some of which are particularly serviceable for calculating the values of the functions or the values of their logarithms. There are also the converse series, by which an angle is found in terms of one of its circular functions. One of the simplest, and at the same time most historically famous of these is Gregory's series, which expresses an angle in ascending powers of its tangent. It is as follows:

$$\theta = \tan.\ \theta - \tfrac{1}{3}\tan.^3 \theta + \tfrac{1}{5}\tan.^5 \theta - \tan.^7 \tfrac{1}{7} \theta + \cdot$$

Of great importance are the addition formulæ which express any required function of the sum or difference of two given angles in terms of the trigonometrical functions of these angles. They are readily established for the circular functions by application of the elementary theorems of orthogonal projection. Similar formulæ hold for the hyperbolic functions. As plane trigonometry has to do chiefly with the solution of plane triangles, so spherical trigonometry is devoted to the discussion of spherical triangles. In navigation, geodesy, and astronomy the formulæ of spherical trigonometry are in constant use. The ordinary text-books on trigonometry do little more than present the subject in its practical bearings. It is impossible to make any progress in the higher mathematics without a thorough knowledge of the properties of the trigonometrical functions.

TRILOGY, a series of three dramas, which, though complete each in itself, bear a certain relation to each other, and form one historical and poetical picture. The term belongs more particularly to the Greek drama. In Athens it was customary to exhibit on the same occasion three serious dramas, or a trilogy, at first connected by a sequence of subject, but afterward unconnected, and on distinct subjects, a fourth or satyric drama being also added, the characters of which were satyrs. Shakespeare's "Henry VI." may be called a trilogy.